THE OXFORD HANDBOOK OF

EARLY CHINA

THE OXFORD HANDBOOK OF

EARLY CHINA

Edited by
ELIZABETH CHILDS-JOHNSON

OXFORD
UNIVERSITY PRESS

OXFORD
UNIVERSITY PRESS

Oxford University Press is a department of the University of Oxford. It furthers
the University's objective of excellence in research, scholarship, and education
by publishing worldwide. Oxford is a registered trade mark of Oxford University
Press in the UK and certain other countries.

Published in the United States of America by Oxford University Press
198 Madison Avenue, New York, NY 10016, United States of America.

Library of Congress Cataloging-in-Publication Data
Names: Childs-Johnson, Elizabeth, editor.
Title: The Oxford handbook of early China / edited by Elizabeth Childs-Johnson.
Description: New York, NY: Oxford University Press, 2020. |
Includes bibliographical references and index.
Identifiers: LCCN 2020025136 (print) | LCCN 2020025137 (ebook) |
ISBN 9780199328369 (hardback) | ISBN 9780197523247 (epub)
Subjects: LCSH: China—History—To 221 B.C.—Handbooks, manuals, etc.
Classification: LCC DS741.62 .O94 2020 (print) |
LCC DS741.62 (ebook) | DDC 931—dc23
LC record available at https://lccn.loc.gov/2020025136
LC ebook record available at https://lccn.loc.gov/2020025137

1 3 5 7 9 8 6 4 2

Printed by Sheridan Books, Inc., United States of America

CONTENTS

SECTION III FIRST DYNASTY OF THE BRONZE AGE: XIA PERIOD

SECTION IV THE FIRST HEIGHT OF THE BRONZE AGE: THE SHANG PERIOD

SECTION V THE SECOND HEIGHT OF THE BRONZE AGE: THE WESTERN ZHOU PERIOD

SECTION VI THE THIRD HEIGHT OF THE BRONZE AGE: SPRINGS AND AUTUMNS PERIOD

SECTION VII THE IRON AGE–WARRING STATES PERIOD

LIST OF CONTRIBUTORS

Dingyun Cao Institute of Archaeology, CASS

Elizabeth Childs-Johnson Old Dominion University

Constance A. Cook Lehigh University

Scott Cook Yale-NUS College

Carine Defoort University of Leuven

Yuzhou Fan Nanjing University

Xiangming Fang Zhejiang Provincial Institute of Cultural Relics Archaeology

Albert Galvany The University of the Basque Country UPV/EHU

Nu He Institute of Archaeology, CASS

Maria Khayutina Institute of Sinology, Ludwig-Maximilians University of Munich

Wengcheong Lam Chinese University of Hong Kong

Vincent S. Leung Lingnan University

Xiang Li University of Pittsburgh

Bin Liu Zhejiang Provincial Institute of Cultural Relics and Archaeology

Guoxiang Liu Institute of Archaeology, CASS

Yu Liu Institute of Archaeology, CASS

John S. Major Independent Scholar

Andrew Meyer Brooklyn College

Yuri Pines Hebrew University of Jerusalem

Moss Roberts New York University

Charles Sanft University of Arizona

Jie Shi Bryn Mawr College

Jonathan Smith Christopher Newport University

Guoding Song Beijing Normal University

Yan Sun Gettysburg College

Chung Tang Shandong University

Mana Hayashi Tang Washington University in St. Louis

Paul Nicholas Vogt Indiana University

Fang Wang Jinsha Site Museum

Yadi Wen Southern University of Science and Technology

Andrew Womack Yale University

Xiaolong Wu Hanover College

Hong Xu Institute of Archaeology, CASS

Changping Zhang Wuhan University

SECTION I

INTRODUCTION AND BACKGROUND

INTRODUCTION AND BACKGROUND

BY ELIZABETH CHILDS-JOHNSON, OLD DOMINION UNIVERSITY

I am glad to have the opportunity to bring 34 authors together for a joint project to put early China on the map of ancient world cultures from an interdisciplinary perspective. Too often, surveys of early China have been narrowly focused on anthropological/ archaeological, historical, or literary/paleographical subjects, without the benefit of a broader cultural perspective. Many recent books on early China in English have tended to take a strictly anthropological/archaeological point of view; examples include Campbell 2014 (appeared 2016), Shelach-Lavi 2015, Underhill 2013, and Liu and Chen 2012. Others take a specialized approach to regional studies (e.g., Flad 2011; Flad and Chen 2013; Liu 2004; Liu and Chen 2003; Shelach-Lavy 1999, 2009; Underhill 2002). There have been fewer general histories (including social and cultural history) of the whole time span of early China; see Major and Cook 2017 and Feng Li 2013. Others are comprehensive in outlook but more restricted in time, such as Feng Li on the Western Zhou (2006, 2008) and Xiaolong Wu on the Warring States–period site of Zhongshan (2017).

Anthropological and archaeological studies usually are limited to questions concerning the beginning and rise of civilization, or hierarchies of settlements with a particular culture. Historical studies often concern specific events at the expense of broader context. What has been lacking, to date, is a coordinated, multidisciplinary approach focused on the period before the establishment of imperial rule, encompassing the whole span of time from the Neolithic through Eastern Zhou eras, ca. 5000–250 BCE. This long era was the nursery of Sinitic culture, laying the groundwork for practices, beliefs, and traditions that extended into later periods. Thus, to fill this void in publications about early China we have gathered together various specialists from different disciplines to produce both introductory essays and essays that focus on specific issues in each one of the six chronologically successive eras covered (Neolithic, Xia/Erlitou,

Shang, Western Zhou, Springs and Autumns, and Warring States). Thus, for example, introductions to the Neolithic include one covering the north and one covering the south. One author takes a chronological approach (Early, Middle, and Late phases of the Northern Neolithic) and another analyzes the Southern Neolithic from the point of view of advances in the arts, agriculture, and settlement patterns.

Our goal is to present up-to-date material in a multivarious universe that casts new light on our understanding of early China. Due to archaeological discoveries of the past 30 to 40 years, increasingly rich data in terms of new texts and new material finds from tombs and settlement sites have profoundly enhanced our picture of early China and its cultural achievements in multiple directions. We need to emphasize that this early theater is mainstream China, the major pacesetter for modern China and its belief systems and cultural markers.

Our approach is multidisciplinary in covering fields of archaeology, anthropology, art history, architecture, metallurgy, literature, religion, paleography, cosmology, prehistory, and history. The material covered is analyzed chronologically, beginning with the Neolithic and ending with the Warring States era of the Eastern Zhou period. The northern Neolithic in chapter 1 by Andrew Womack is analyzed in terms of Early, Middle, and Late phases, whereas the southern Neolithic from the same time period (7/6000–2000 BCE) is analyzed according to new and major cultural issues, such as the appearance of rice agriculture and plows, patterns of increasingly formalized settlements, and advanced handicrafts. This approach is exemplified in chapter 2 by Xianming Fang, who describes the artistic style of Songze as "open and liberated" due to the evident humor of, for example, wild boar sculptures that are both naturalistic and symbolic.

What is completely new to the late phase of the Neolithic is what I, in earlier publications, have termed the Jade Age, a period from ca. 3500–2000 BCE during which jade was exploited as a material possessing particular religious and socio-political power. Reinforcing this concept of the Jade Age in the present volume are three analytical essays. Chung Tang and colleagues focus on the earliest (5000 BCE) production of slit jade earrings in the Xinglongwa culture in the northeast (chapter 3). The creation of jade earrings gave rise to a cultural trait that was to characterize China both past and present—a reverence not only for the beauty and quality of jade but a belief in jade's intrinsic spiritual power and related properties. In chapter 4, I continue the focus on jade by analyzing why three major overlapping cultures exploiting jade (Hongshan, Liangzhu, and Longshan/Erlitou) are responsible for catalyzing civilization in the East Asian Heartland. Two regional studies follow, the first by Bin Liu in chapter 5 on the site of Mojiaoshan in Yuhang, Zhejiang—the richest culture in the evolution of the Jade Age; and the second by Nu He in chapter 6 on the site of Taosi in Shanxi, on the outskirts of the Sinitic world in this era but pivotal to novel advances within the Jade Age time frame. Bin Liu explains why Mojiaoshan may be a "capital" of the Liangzhu civilization—a concept with which many scholars may not agree—but also why the same site may be described as a "water city." Bin Liu, the leader of excavations at the site, describes the most advanced early system of water control in its time and a feat of hydraulic engineering, designed with 51 inner and outer city rivers and streams, most of them man-made but others natural, either tunneled or dammed, surrounding a palatial enclosure encompassing some 3 million square meters.

The Neolithic site of Taosi in Linfen, Shanxi, is equally dramatic due to what has been excavated and examined in detail as an outdoor center for astronomical observations. Nu He, the primary archaeologist directing excavations at Taosi, conjures up a cosmological system of Taiji dualism at Taosi as revealed by excavations of the rammed-earth solar observatory along with later textual data. He illuminates a solar-lunar calendar and Four Directions cosmology based on other unique discoveries, including a lacquered gnomon shadow template and a copper disk with 29 teeth he identifies as a small "moon wheel."

The Erlitou culture or Xia dynasty remains a historical enigma. The site of Erlitou was discovered as early as 1959 but, as of today, there has still been no resolution about the culture's historicity other than abundant archaeological data without any discovery of writing. The debate about whether or not the site is the Xia-dynasty capital of Yu the Great or a late Xia king cannot be resolved by presently available information in the complete absence of inscriptional evidence citing Xia or its alleged rulers. These matters are reviewed in the introduction to the historiography of "Xia" in chapter 7 by Hong Xu. Yet innovative advances in archaeology, as amplified by Xu, show that by the end of the Longshan period, independent walled cities began to lose their turbulent independence in favor of what Xu calls "breaking away" in forming stable settlement complexes, incorporating and integrating other surrounding settlements, as represented at the site of Xinzhai, transitional between Longshan and Erlitou. Erlitou emerged as the most stable city-state, bringing a full stop to warring factions and developing a core government and culture ca. 1750 BCE that is equivalent to "Earliest China" and the first state and civilization.

The other chapters in the Erlitou/Xia section focus on finds identifying new and stunning cultural achievements. Hong Xu and Xiang Li clarify in chapter 8 why Erlitou is the earliest territorial state and capital settlement in Chinese history by describing major archaeologically revealed features and the reach of the Erlitou culture. The metallurgist Yu Liu analyzes the bronze-casting revolution together with Hong Xu in chapter 9, which led to the beginning of the Bronze Age in China. He also presents documentation of the variations in chemical composition of bronze and how the singular technology of piece-mold casting worked during the Erlitou period. The chapter on the Erlitou *yazhang* [*zhang*] jade blade with dentated handle, although first published in 2015 in Chinese by Chung Tang and Fang Wang, is considerably updated and revised in chapter 10. Citing the extensive presence of *zhang* not only throughout the East Asian Heartland but also beyond its frontiers, Tang and Wang show why the Erlitou *yazhang* was a material symbol of political order and why this jade blade may be used to define primary states such as Erlitou and Erlitou's influence on competitive states in south China.

The fourth section is devoted to Shang-period topics and new data that help to characterize the period culturally. Jonathan Smith with Yuzhou Fan introduce the culture and history of Shang and oracle bone inscriptions in chapter 11, commenting on their origin and historical significance and offering new interpretations for their periodization, an issue that has plagued the field for years. Guoding Song provides in chapter 12 the latest archaeological data for identifying early Shang finds at the Shang cities of Zhengzhou and Yanshi, in addition to neighboring early Shang city sites, such as Dongxiafeng, Fucheng, and Wangjinglou, and middle Shang cities at Huanbei, Xiaoshuangqiao, and Xingtai in Hebei. Changping Zhang introduces in chapter 14 new data for understanding bronze-casting technology during the late Erligang through Yinxu periods (ca. 1600–1056 BCE), which during the Erligang period were mainly adjustments in balancing bronze vessel attachments and positioning blind cores. The growing complexity of mold divisions by the Late Shang period leads to new casting in the form of a composite mold set and the introduction of casting-on and pre-casting techniques. One of the most important sources of archaeological and inscriptional data of the Late Shang period came with the discovery of the intact tomb of Fu Zi (Fu Hao). Dingyun Cao presents in chapter 16 a detailed analysis of inscriptions on burial objects found in her tomb, M5 at Xiaotun, and her divinatory texts mentioning her and her relations. She was the first queen of King Wu Ding and produced his first heir, Small King Fu Ji. In my own chapter 13 I provide new interpretations for certain architectural structures, such as *she* altars and pyramidal mounds, leading to a new periodization of those structures at the late Shang capital, Yinxu at Anyang in Henan. Separately, in Chapter 15, I expound on new data for Shang belief systems, characterized by a common belief in spirit metamorphosis, exorcism, and royal ancestor worship. "Yi 異" is the Shang oracle bone term for this system of belief. Metamorphosis is a concept directly reflecting the ritual image of the metamorphic power mask—an ancestral spirit power characterized by human and wild animal attributes and standardized conventions of representation.

Strides in ironing out the grooves and ridges in Western Zhou historiography are presented in the introductory chapter of this next phase in China's Bronze Age. In chapter 17 Maria Khayutina introduces primary sources; legendary origins; surnames and marital relations; proto-Zhou ceramic chronologies; relations with Shang before, during, and after the conquest; and various accounts defining "Western" Zhou history, the chronology of kings, and political doctrine. She is careful to point out what is known and what is not known about the Western Zhou historical period of ca. 1046–771 BCE. She also makes a point of differentiating Chinese titles and kinship terms from names by italicizing the former throughout her chapters (e.g., Zhou *Bo*: Zhou is a name and *bo* is a title/kinship term).

Nicholas Vogt follows this historical introduction in chapter 18 by analyzing the major characteristics of government and social organization of the Western Zhou period. In developing his analysis, he employs representative transcriptions and translations of inscriptions on ritual bronze vessels. Among these complex and difficult-to-translate inscriptions (e.g., He *zun*, Mai *fangzun*, Xiao Yu *ding*) several noteworthy trends in ritual and political control are identified: rites as concepts of "ritual assemblies," "nexus ancestors," "persuasive royal strategies," and the "relaying of royal rites through bronze [inscriptions]." Although scholars may not agree entirely with his conclusions that early Zhou ritual contrasts with the character of Shang ritual, that hypothesis may only be justified by a close comparison of the two. In turn, Constance A. Cook addresses rites and mortuary practices in chapter 19 by considering data from both archaeological excavations and texts and bronze vessel inscriptions. She observes the gradually increasing emphasis in Zhou vessel inscriptions on *de* 德 (translated as "virtue" or "morality" when referring to Confucian texts of the late Warring States and subsequent imperial times) as something originating from Shangdi 上帝 and Tian 天, bestowed on the first Zhou king as a form of lineage authority and cosmological power. *De* may be understood as a "source of life energy and political authority," complemented by ostentatious rites and coercive displays that recognized Zhou power.

Yan Sun's chapter, 20, is devoted to another aspect of ritual bronze evolution, focused less on inscriptional data and more on stylistic change and changes in ritual bronze assemblages during the Western Zhou period. Although she employs mainland Chinese views of inscriptions as historic documentation for a chronological sequence—an approach that many scholars outside of China find unhelpful—she incorporates the latest archaeological data to bring this field of art up to date. Scott Cook presents a superb survey of the many aspects of music and instruments present during the Western and Eastern Zhou eras in chapter 21. He introduces not only archaeological data, instrumental types, and assemblages (various types of bells, chime stones, drums, winds, and strings) but also musical theory, musical practice, musical philosophy, and musical institutions.

Scholars contributing articles to the next phase of Zhou history, the Springs and Autumns period, include Yuri Pines covering not only history but historiography and intellectual developments as well and Wu writing on art and its achievements in chapter 24. Pines in chapter 22 assesses the very convoluted and complex history of the multi-state system during the Springs and Autumns period, ca. 770–453. He presents a nuanced and accurate portrayal of what he describes as one of China's "deepest systemic crises," covering the rise and fall of a multi-state order, an account of ethnocultural identities (e.g., peoples known as Chu, Rong, or Di), the rise of hereditary ministerial lineages, capital dwellers as political activists, and finally "cultural unity at the age of fragmentation." In a following chapter 25 Pines treats the study of history as represented by two primary Springs and Autumns texts, the *Springs and Autumns Annals* (of the Lu state) and one of its commentaries, the *Zuozhuan*. Although Pines states that the former "may well compete for the designation as the most boring and the least inspiring of Chinese classics," he explicates why the two historical texts are so different: one is based on flavorless, ritually correct "Zhou-based hierarchal rankings" and the other is "the fountainhead of traditional Chinese historiography." A distinctly aristocratic outlook and a multistate order with a ministerial-lord rulership replaces monarchic rule. Xiaolong Wu tackles the overwhelming excavated data for the numerous states of the Springs and Autumns era in chapter 24, producing in some cases exquisite works of art and in others more mundane works. He divides his study into five geographical sections, describing and tabulating the five areas and their chronologies.

A team of 10 distinguished scholars address Warring States issues (ca. 453–221 BCE) with fresh and invigorating approaches. Topics range from historical background, reform, and individual philosophers (e.g., Mozi and Confucius) to the rise of iron-working, novel architecture and art, and military arts; and from the position of "*shi* 士," urbanization, capitals, and population records to Chu religion. Wencheong Lam introduces this era in chapter 26 by sorting out what we know and do not know about how iron-working (iron technology, bloomery iron, and iron-casting) flourished during the Warring States period. His major points revolve around the three most powerful states of Jin (Han, Wei, Chao), Qin, and Chu and their differing contributions based primarily on archaeological evidence along with textual evidence about iron technology during this revolutionary era of change and reform. He is able to reach a preliminary conclusion that iron-working was probably more advanced in the Chu state despite the lack of discovery of any iron foundry in capital areas of Chu. Yuri Pines follows this introduction in chapter 25 by highlighting the historical and related events of competing "hero-states," providing textual and paleographic sources (or lack thereof) and employing the year 453 BCE as the starting point of Warring States history, since it was then that the state of Jin dissolved into Wei, Han, and Zhao. As background to the history of the multi-state system he analyzes, for example, the decline of the Wei state and the "ephemeral alliances" between Qin and other rival states. His account of peripatetic persuaders (*youshui* 遊說) who could find themselves "serving Qin in the morning and Chu in the evening (朝秦幕楚)" helps document the unprecedented geographic and social mobility of the era. His second contribution to this section of the book, chapter 27, relates to institutional reform and reformers, especially as seen in the career of the Warring States Qin diplomat, Shang Yang. Pines takes Qin as exemplary of the new socially mobile yet heavily bureaucratic direction the state and later imperial Qin would take. Aided by the reforms of his adviser Shang Yang, Pines outlines how the lord—later king—of Qin eliminated the hereditary aristocracy, created military conscription for all, and created an "agro-managerial state."

In addition, other scholars document new aspects of political, military, and economic reforms of the Warring States period. Charles Sanft presents archaeological evidence in chapter 28 for the multiplicity of many state capitals and their need for double, fortified walls. He follows this with new data from written texts about population registries—something that appears unique to this era; he provides concrete examples of new administrative controls, translations of Chu governmental "ledgers" (*dian* 典), and registries of households (*hu* 戶) from Liye, Hunan. Next he documents ritual oaths (*shi* 誓); the swearing of covenants (*meng* 盟); and tallies (*fujie* 符節), "a class of objects that served as official symbols of authority and authorization over a long period in premodern China, typically in contexts of military command, diplomacy, resource control, and movement through passes and gates." Albert Galvany analyzes a different aspect of Warring States history in chapter 29—the army, military arts, treatises on military affairs (including of course the most famous military text in Asia, Sunzi's *Art of War*), and warfare itself. Galvany outlines major features of innovative change expressed by: (1) "the rise of instrumental rationality" and a "new total warfare"; (2) "the decline of the warrior and emergence of the commander (the demise of the aristocratic warrior and his traditional values coincides with the emergence of the figure of the strategist or commander)"; (3) "the essential of discipline," explaining that "[w]ith the introduction of armies consisting of peasant masses, the art of warfare confronted one of its most delicate and decisive tasks: transforming a shapeless and anarchic mass of peasants lacking any trace of a military tradition into an orderly and compliant organism ready to execute"; (4) "the art of deception," metaphorically represented by water; and (5) "from economic awareness to the idea of deterrence: the art of non-war."

The next part of the Warring States section features "[s]ocial, intellectual and religious transformations." Andrew Meyer opens this section on "the *shi* class, diplomats, and urban expansion" in chapter 30. With engaging anecdotal description, Meyer documents the rollercoaster ride of the so-called *shi* class of "knights," the rise of diplomats, and the rapidity of commercialism and urbanization that took place during this disruptive but peripatetic age. Particularly insightful is his contextualization of the literary *shi* figure, Su Qin, "who is said to have brokered his own rise to the prime ministerial seat of six states simultaneously...and stopped the advance of Qin and brought down the throne of Qi in the third century BCE." Moss Roberts, a senior scholar of classical Chinese literature, profiles and reviews six thinkers of this age in chapter 31: Confucius along with his later disciple Mencius, Mozi, Laozi, Zhuangzi, and Han Feizi. Casting Confucius as one who organized a graduate school of political management focusing on the *junzi* (ideal man) who espouses virtue and intellect, Roberts contrasts this with his disciple Mencius, who re-envisions his ideals in emphasizing the significance of human nature (*xing*), the seedbed of *renyi* (benevolence and righteousness). Xunzi was "an institutionalist and a structuralist" hovering between Confucianism and Legalism. Han Feizi was Mencius's opposite, an anti-Confucianist in favor of Legalism and the concept that "Dao is what gave birth to Law." As Roberts points out, the Dao for Laozi negates ancestral authority in subjecting it to the authority of ten thousand things (*wanwu* 万物), which embodies a "law" that the Dao must follow. Zhuangzi totally rebels in favoring a oneness with nature, negating the hierarchical social identity so critical to Confucius.

Vincent Leung (chapter 32) and Carinne Defoort (chapter 33) both address the philosopher Mozi or Master Mo, famous in his day but relatively little-known today. Defoort identifies three historic steps (Warring States, imperial periods, and twentieth century) for understanding Mozi and his association with *jian ai* 兼愛, variously translated as "universal love" or "impartial caring." The idea of "inclusive care" gradually evolved with the writing of the book *Mozi*. In the second phase, Han classicists used the works of Mencius to support Confucius's values of humaneness and righteousness and relegate Moism to the status of a heterodox theory. That view lasted through the early imperial period until the Tang dynasty, as reflected in "Reading Mozi" 讀墨子 by Han Yu 韓愈 (768–824). The rise of *jian ai* in the post-imperial era is primarily tied to Sun Yirang's *magnum opus* on Mozi in 1893, along with translations by James Legge, and to the developing modern ideology of Sun Yatsen (1966–1925), a Christian Democrat who elevated Mozi to one of the sages of the world. Vincent Leung, on the other hand, introduces us to new values of Mozi, hidden in what Leung describes as his "etiological method" of writing—his toolbox for analysis of the "etiology of disorder." Mozi says there are "three criteria" to test truth—a forerunner of inductive and deductive reasoning involving invocation of past leaders and sages (good doctors who knew what needed to be done and did it). Yet for Mozi moral principles were not human constructs but a fact of the cosmos: the source of all moral principles is Tian (Heaven). Mozi, as pacifist and anti-war hero and promoter of meritocracy, impartiality, and universal love, perhaps provides instruction for today's world in such matters as universal healthcare, preservation of the natural world, and the cessation of war.

Two chapters, one by John Major and myself (chapter 34), the other by Jie Shi (chapter 35), round out this section on the Warring States with an analysis of Chu religion and art, and of the revolution that characterized all arts of this period, respectively. Major and Childs-Johnson categorize Chu religion as one probably based on a Sinified version of shamanism, probably linked with Shang belief and practice. Jie Shi divides his chapter according to artistic, macro, and micro categories, beginning with cities, palaces, funerary parks, and tombs, followed by the arts of bronze, jade, lacquer, and textiles, and ultimately an analysis of figurative and pictorial art. Everything created seemed to be new and huge, such as the palatial complex of Fangying Terrace No. 1 (*Fangying tai* 放鷹臺), which featured a multi-terraced structure, surrounded by endless courtyards and galleries, rising to 23 meters; another example is the palatial palace at Xianyang (Palace Complex No. 1) where another new type of building called *guan* 觀 (literally "building for overlooking") is preserved alongside a novel suspended bridge that once connected two large-scale terraces. The micro arts are equally novel and revolutionary, exploiting new secular interests and new artistic techniques as represented by the lost-wax and welded bronze set of *zun* and *pan* shapes from the tomb of Marquis Yi of Zeng, splendid and sculpturally exquisite in their décor of numerous tiny S-shaped dragons densely packed into an intricate composition of openwork on vessel rims.

It is with great pleasure that I offer this rich collection of cutting-edge research on pre-imperial China in one volume, the *Oxford Handbook on Early China*.

Elizabeth Childs-Johnson, July 20, 2017

ACKNOWLEDGEMENTS

Overwhelming support from colleagues and family made the production of this interdisciplinary study of early China possible. I would like to extend my sincere thanks to every scholar who prepared chapters for this volume and tolerated requests that may have seemed superfluous or exigent. The editorial staff has been tremendous. Thanks go to Chief Editor, Stefan Vranka, Assistant Editor, Isabelle Prince, and Project Manager, Dharuman Bheeman I am especially tremendously indebted to John N. Major for his unstinting editorial help in reviewing many of the chapters and of my own contributions. I also owe profound thanks to Yuri Pines for his patience and editorial advice on preparing chapters and subtitle divisions for the Springs and Autumns and Warring States periods. This has been a long-time project in the making and I thank all authors, particularly Albert Galvany, Xiang Li, Jonathan Smith, Hong Xu, Guoding Song, Dingyun Cao, Chung Tang, Xiangming Fang, Changping Zhang, Wencheong Lam, Carine Defoort, Moss Roberts, and Jie Shi for their liberal help in getting out what we appreciate will be a major contribution to the study of early China in all its cultural manifestations from the Neolithic through pre-imperial periods.

I also acknowledge with warm thanks to my husband, Edward M. Johnson and son, Nathaniel for their encouragement and perserverance in making the volume final. To them this volume is dedicated.

BIBLIOGRAPHY

Anne P. Underhill, *Craft Production and Social Change in Northern China,* Wiley-Blackwell, 2002.

Anne P. Underhill, ed. *A Companion to Chinese Archaeology.* Wiley/Blackwell 2013.

Feng Li, *Bureaucracy and the State in Early China: Governing the Western Zhou,* Cambridge University Press, 2008.

Feng Li, *Early China: A Social And Cultural History (New Approaches to Asian History),* Cambridge University Press, 2013.

Gideon Shelach-Lavy, *Prehistoric Societies on the Northern Frontiers of China: Archaeological Perspectives on Identity Formation and Economic Change during the First Millennium BCE.* London, Approaches to Anthropological Archaeology Series, Equinox, 2009.

Gideon Shelach-Lavy. *Leadership Strategies, Economic Activity, and Interregional Interaction: Social Complexity in Northeast China.* New York: KluwerAcademic/Plenum Press, 1999.

Gideon Shelach-Lavi, *The Archaeology of Early China.* Cambridge University Press, 2015.

John S. Major and Constance S, Cook, *Ancient China.* New York: Routledge Major and Cook 2017.

Li Liu, *The Chinese Neolithic: Trajectories to Early States (New Studies in Archaeology),* Cambridge University Press, 2004.

Li Liu and Xingcan Chen, *State Formation in Early China (Debates in Archaeology),* London: Gerald Duckworth & Co., 2003.

Li Liu and Xingcan Chen, *The Archaeology of China from the late Paleolithic to the Early Bronze Age,* Cambridge University Press, 2012.

Roderick B. Campbell, *The Archaeology of the Chinese Bronze Age.* (Cotsen Institute, University of California, LA.), 2014 (appeared 2016).

Rowan K. Flad. *Salt Production and Social Hierarchy in Ancient China: An Archaeological Investigation of Specialization in China's Three Gorges,* Cambridge University Press, 2011.

Rowan K Flad and Pochan Chen, *Ancient Central China: Centers and peripheries along the Yangzi river,* Cambridge University Press, 2013.

Xiaolong Wu, *Material Culture, Power, and Identity in Ancient China.* Cambridge University Press, 2017.

SECTION II

NEOLITHIC FARMERS, CERAMICS, AND JADE

CHAPTER 1

THE NEOLITHIC REVOLUTION IN THE NORTH CA. 7/6000–2000 BCE: XINGLONGWA, XINLEI, YANGSHAO, HONGSHAN, AND RELATED CULTURES(INEQUALITY/ SOCIAL COMPLEXITY) IN NEOLITHIC NORTHERN CHINA

BY ANDREW WOMACK, YALE UNIVERSITY

IT has now been nearly 100 years since pioneering researchers Ding Wenjiang, Johan Gunnar Andersson, and their colleagues at the China Geological Survey (Figure 1) first unearthed the remains of a number of major Neolithic sites across northern China (Fiskesjö and Chen 2004). In the intervening century our knowledge of this time period has been transformed from legends beyond the edge of the earliest historical texts to a view of Neolithic China as a period awash with a multitude of cultural traditions (Figure 2). While this century of research focused heavily on defining these traditions through typology and later pushing back and refining dates for early social and techno-logical developments, recent trends have moved toward detailed scientific analysis of finds and increasing collaboration across the field. This in turn is leading to a better understanding of everything from subsistence practices to social organization and is redefining many of our views of the Neolithic period in northern China.

FIGURE 1 J. G. Andersson and colleagues examine Neolithic Chinese vessels (photograph by Johan Gunnar Andersson, ca. 1925, in Lanzhou, Gansu, China). Source: National Museums of World Culture, Sweden, Museum of Far Eastern Antiquities.

This chapter seeks to summarize the results of the last century of research on the Neolithic period in northern China (Figure 3), while at the same time addressing the latest major developments and debates in this field. Although several books have in recent years been devoted to this time period (Liu and Chen 2012; Shelach 2015; Underhill 2013), or even to individual subregions, this chapter will serve as a general introduction to the period with references provided for those who wish to explore individual topics in more detail. Information will be provided on each major cultural tradition, defined as groups who shared similar artifact types and social practices over a specific geographic range and time period. These groups will be approached in a comparative manner, breaking down traditions along broad geographic regions and comparing material cultural across these regions during the early, middle, and late Neolithic. While major developments and breaks in cultural traditions of course took place at different time periods in different regions, the division here of the Neolithic into three parts is based around broad changes that in many cases transcended localized developments. However, it is not meant to indicate that all traditions changed in the same way at any given point. In the same way the geographic breakdown of cultural traditions does not mean that a specific group of people was always confined to a specific geographic region; it is just that the core area of archaeological finds that have defined that tradition are located in that general area.

In the same way, the focus of this chapter on northern China is not meant to disconnect it from other regions. As will become readily apparent, interregional interaction was occurring throughout the Neolithic and early historic period and was critical to major cultural developments in virtually every region. Influences ranging from technological innovations such as bronze-casting to agricultural methods such as paddy

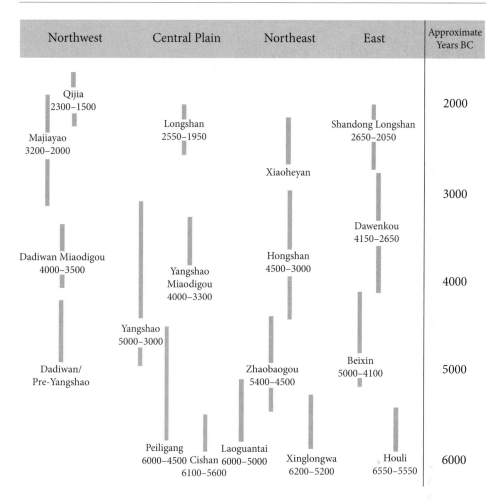

FIGURE 2 A timeline of cultural traditions discussed in this chapter along with approximate dates (BCE).

farming were flowing between north and south, likely accompanying individuals or groups who were moving or trading between these regions. The focus on the north here, however, serves two purposes. The first is practical, in that more than a single chapter is needed to even briefly cover the expanse of Neolithic China. The second reflects, to some extent, the trajectory of Chinese archaeology. Up to the 1990s, central control of archaeological work, and a close alignment with history, meant that the majority of archaeological research was focused on the northern Central Plain and surrounding regions (Chang 1999; von Falkenhausen 1995). While this did not preclude archaeological work, especially rescue excavations around major construction projects, in other regions it did mean that the majority of research-focused archaeology was occurring in the north. It was also occurring with a particular goal: to connect prehistoric cultural traditions with the earliest dynasties known from later written sources, the Xia, Shang, and Zhou (see Hong Xu, Chapter 7; von Falkenhausen 1993). Overall it was quite successful in identifying early dynasties, including the later Shang and Zhou through

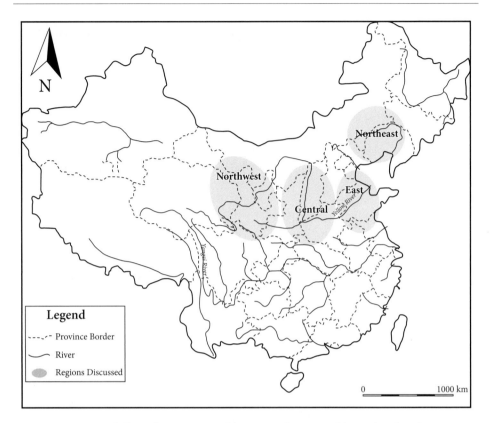

FIGURE 3 A map of China showing general location of regions addressed in this chapter.

written records including oracle bones and bronze inscriptions. Drawing connections with earlier traditions has met with mixed results. Many early motifs and object forms from the late Neolithic and early Bronze Age, such as ritual bronze vessels that reflect earlier ceramic items, have allowed scholars to trace the origins of dynastic Chinese culture back beyond the earliest written texts. Other cases, such as the identification of the Xia dynasty with Erlitou or other early Bronze Age traditions, have been highly debated, if less conclusive.

While this chapter will not specifically focus on building connections with later historic materials, it will approach the cultural traditions of northern China as related groups that in some ways can be seen as part of a larger northern Chinese Neolithic tradition. Although independent developments or adaptations of external technology or culture took place, there are nevertheless many aspects of material culture, and potentially social organization and ritual practice, that are shared among multiple cultural traditions, particularly in the middle to late Neolithic. By discussing each cultural group individually, but within the context of wider chronological and geographic scales, this chapter seeks to highlight both the individual innovations and the larger shared traditions that define the Neolithic period in northern China.

Introduction to the Early Neolithic Period, 7/6000–4000 BCE

The transition from a gathering and hunting subsistence base to one that also incorporates various levels of horticulture, agriculture, and animal husbandry has, just as the title of this chapter suggests, often been termed a revolution in human history (Childe 1936). However, developments in China, as elsewhere, were a much slower and more varied set of changes than those typically associated with the term revolution (Underhill 1997:105). Transitions in stone tool technology beginning in the late Pleistocene (18,000–10,000 BCE), including an increase in grinding stones, suggests early movement toward a more diverse diet than that of preceding periods, which likely included an increasing reliance on nuts and grains (see Liu et al. 2010 for a study of a slightly later site). However, exactly what happened between this period and the appearance of the earliest domesticated millet in northern China around 6500 BCE remains unclear due to a lack of excavated sites (Shelach 2015). While some researchers acknowledge that climatic changes likely influenced decisions to cultivate certain crops such as broomcorn millet (Lu et al. 2009), it is likely that a number of social and environmental factors played a role in changing subsistence practices. For example, other scholars view the move toward settled agriculture as a social and economic strategy that reduced risks in variable environments (Shelach 2015:65). Whatever the cause, by the seventh to sixth millennia BCE a true transformation was underway across northern China, with settled villages, another development related to agricultural production, dotting the landscape. This section will outline what these communities looked like across northern China including pottery styles, common tools and objects, housing, village layout, settlement patterns, subsistence strategies, and burial practices. Information about social organization will also be discussed so that readers can track changes and developments in each area through time. As this chapter will show, there was more than just an agricultural revolution underway during this time period.

The early Neolithic in northwest China: Pre-Yangshao and Dadiwan

The first remains of Neolithic cultures in northwest China were uncovered by Swedish geologist and archaeologist Johan Gunnar Andersson and his Chinese colleagues in southern Gansu Province in the 1920s (Andersson 1923, 1943). A hiatus in excavation in the 1930s and 1940s was broken with the resumption of archaeological activities, first general surveys of known sites and then rescue excavations, in the late 1940s and 1950s. Although many site locations have been recorded from chance finds, no large-scale, systematic survey of the Gansu-Qinghai region has taken place (An 1981; Chen 2013;

Hung 2011; Xie 2002). While significant information is available about burial practices and to some extent site distributions for these cultures (Li et al. 1993), so far only a small number of habitation sites in this region have been excavated (Chen 2013; Xie 2002).

The earliest known Neolithic cultures in this region appeared around 6000 BCE, with the majority of sites situated in eastern Gansu in the Tianshui and upper Wei River regions as well as the Hanshui Valley region. These pre-Yangshao finds are typically assigned to the Laoguantai, Baijia, and Dadiwan cultures and date between 6000–5000 BCE. Since fewer than 10 sites have been discovered to date, however, they are not as well understood as later cultures in the region (Wang 2012:213).

The most thoroughly explored and complete site from this period in northwestern China is undoubtedly Dadiwan. Located in eastern Gansu's Qinan County, this site was occupied from approximately 5800–2900 BCE, a time period encompassing the Dadiwan (or alternatively Laoguantai) and early, middle, and late Yangshao cultural traditions. Dadiwan is of particular importance due to the early agricultural remains that have been discovered there, including some of the earliest domesticated broomcorn millet in China. Excavators of the site have hypothesized that the earliest pre-Yangshao levels represent a period where the occupants were experimenting with low levels of agriculture while still relying on gathering and hunting for the majority of their subsistence. Later phases with more abundant remains of both foxtail and broomcorn millet reflect the increasing importance of agriculture (Barton et al. 2009; Zhang et al. 2010:1,639–1,640). Large numbers of microliths in the lower levels of the site reflect a technological tradition that was largely unchanged from the late Paleolithic. Over time these microliths decreased alongside an increase in pottery (Zhang et al. 2010:1,641). The pottery itself is generally fine brown sandyware with vessel types including jars, bowls, and urns, some of which have three miniature feet forming a tripod. These were found along with graves; storage pits; and three small, semi-subterranean houses dating to the earliest phase of the site (5800–5300 BCE) (Qi et al. 2006:942). In the early stages of occupation hunting was still clearly an important aspect of subsistence, with wild deer making up nearly half of the recovered faunal remains. Pigs, both wild and domesticated, however, were also playing an important role, making up 21% of remains (Liu and Chen 2012:151), with their mandibles also being included in some burials (Qi et al. 2006:68). This practice is a precursor of what would become a widespread burial offering across northern China in subsequent periods.

The early Neolithic in the Central Plain: Laoguantai, Cishan, and Peiligang

As is the case in many other areas of East Asia, there are few known remains from the transitional period between the Upper Paleolithic and early Neolithic in the Central Yellow River Valley of northern China. While this might lend itself to the idea that the move toward agriculture, the production and use of ground stone tools and pottery, and increased sedentism was a true revolution, this may also reflect a lack of attention to these early and often difficult to detect sites (Zhu 2013; Shelach 2015:50). In fact, new discoveries, such as those at the Lijiagou site in Henan Province (Beijing and Zhengzhou 2011) provide evidence that technologies such as pottery and ground stone tool production came about in northern China slowly over hundreds or thousands of years instead of as the quick "revolutions" that we might imagine (Underhill 1997:105).

Better understood are the cultural traditions of the early to early middle Neolithic that have been uncovered in this region, including the Laoguantai (6000–5000 BCE) (Zhang and Wei 2004:60), Peiligang (6000–4500 BCE), and Cishan (6100–5600 BCE) (Zhang and Wei 2004:54). Critical questions for this early period relate to the transition from gathering and hunting to agriculture, beginning with the role that human intervention in the growth and propagation of wild species played in this transition. The sites representing the Laoguantai cultural tradition were first excavated in the 1950s along the Weishui and Hanshui rivers (Zhu 2013:172); more recently additional sites have been discovered throughout the Guanzhong and upper Hanshui River areas as well as in eastern Gansu Province (Zhang and Wei 2004:56). The Laoguantai cultural tradition is defined by ceramics with predominately sandy paste including bowls, jars, and cups, some of which were decorated with cord marks or, more rarely, red painting. Even during this relatively early time period ceramic production involved careful preparation, as the clay used for certain vessels was clearly prepared either by adding temper or removing natural inclusions before being used for potting. Based on spiral finishing marks on some vessels it has also been posited that an early form of the slow wheel such as a turntable was used during this period to finish some vessel forms; however, no wheel remains have yet been recovered (Zhu 2013:178).

Aside from pottery, numerous ground and flaked stone tools, as well as bone, tooth, and shell tools, have been found at Laoguantai sites (Zhang and Wei 2004:58).

While more information on Laoguantai subsistence is needed, it seems that cultivated broomcorn millet did contribute to subsistence. At the same time rice was beginning to be cultivated in areas south of those occupied by the Laoguantai tradition; however, there is no direct evidence for rice cultivation at Laoguantai sites. Although hunting and fishing likely contributed the majority of meat and animal products used by the Laoguantai peoples, there is some evidence for the presence of domesticated animals at some sites, potentially including dogs, pigs, cattle, sheep, chicken, and water buffalo. Many of these remains are disputed, and further evidence is needed to clarify which animals actually show signs of domestication (Zhu 2013:176–177).

The few Laoguantai settlements that have been excavated are generally located on river terraces and range in size from 1,000–20,000 m^2. Most sites contain many pits, with only a few houses and graves. The houses that have been uncovered are generally round, semi-subterranean structures. Graves are shaft tombs and primarily contain one individual in the extended supine position; however, flexed side burials and multiple burials have also been uncovered. Child urn burials have also been found (Zhang and Wei 2004:58).

Sites of the Cishan and Peiligang cultural traditions were first excavated in the 1970s in Henan and Hebei Provinces, respectively. While these cultures have in some cases been viewed as a single tradition, they now are typically seen as two separate but related traditions. The Peiligang cultural tradition is characterized by coarse red and yellow-brown vessels and fine red vessels that include flat-bottomed jars, tripods, two-handled jars, and bowls (Figure 4). While most Peiligang ceramics are plain, some have incised designs carved into them (Zhu 2013:172). Kilns discovered at Peiligang sites also show the relatively sophisticated nature of pottery production during that period (Li Jiazhi et al. 1996:472–474).

Peiligang sites have generally not provided significant evidence of agricultural production, although millet remains have been discovered (Henan 1983:1,065). Other evidence of subsistence practices comes from the discovery of significant numbers of ground stone tools including spades, sickles, axes, and grinding stones. It has been hypothesized that these are indicative of the harvesting and processing of wild or domesticated grains. These tools were carefully made and ground on all sides, marking an increase in sharpness and durability over previous periods. Harder stones, such as turquoise, were also first fashioned into ornaments during this period; however, production levels were very low (Zhu 2013:179).

Unlike the preceding Laoguantai period, several Peiligang settlements and cemeteries, primarily along the middle Yellow River, have been excavated. Sites are similar in size to the few known Peiligang sites and are located in hills or on floodplains. One of the best

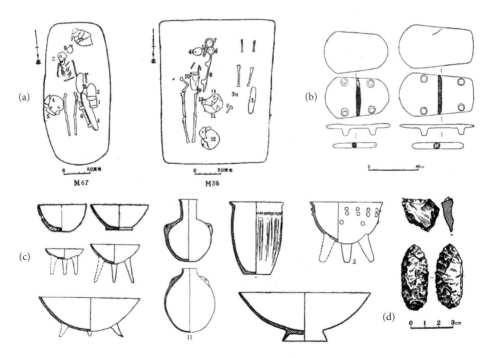

FIGURE 4 A Graves, B grinding stones, C pottery, and D chipped stone tools from the Peiligang cultural tradition (after Henan 1983).

known Peiligang sites is Jiahu, where dozens of houses and hundreds of graves and pits were excavated. Based on remains from this and other sites, structures ranged in size from 2–40 m² and contained many artifacts including stone, bone, tooth, shell, and antler tools (Henan 1999:34–37). Most Peiligang graves are simple rectangular pits with single, supine, extended remains. The majority of burials contain only a few stone or ceramic items that often appear in sets including a bowl and two types of jars. Occasionally a single burial will contain 10 or more vessels, although the reason for these increased numbers of grave goods remains unclear (Henan Working Team 1984:28–29).

Distributed primarily to the east of Peiligang sites, the Cishan cultural tradition is characterized by its sandy gray-yellow flat-bottomed pottery cups, jars, and bowls that are often tempered with mica. People in this area also produced fine-paste reddish three-legged bowls and shallow dishes. Similar to Peiligang pottery, the majority of Cishan pieces are undecorated, while some have incised geometric decorations consisting of short lines (Zhu 2013:173).

Cishan sites have provided significant information on early agriculture in this region, including being the source of the earliest known broomcorn millet, which dates between 8300 and 6700 BCE (Lu et al. 2009). At the Cishan type-site foxtail millet remains were found in nearly one-third of all storage pits, which, if full, would have contained an astounding 50 metric tons of grain (Tong 1984:201). However, it seems unlikely that all of these pits were ever in use simultaneously or were typically filled to capacity. They also could have had roles other than grain storage. Remains of domesticated and wild animal bones have also been uncovered at Cishan sites. While remains of domesticated dogs, pigs (Yuan and Flad 2002) and, controversially, sheep or goat have been discovered, it is likely that hunting, gathering, and gardening were still important subsistence strategies alongside early agriculture (Zhu 2013:177). Unlike the Peiligang tradition, few Cishan settlement or cemetery sites have been fully excavated, leaving a gap in our knowledge of social organization and settlement layout.

Significant changes clearly were taking place during the early and early middle Neolithic period in and around the Central Plain. While these cultural traditions each revealed distinct features and distinct approaches to subsistence and craft production, together they paint a picture of societies that were experimenting with new ways to live. From relying increasingly on the cultivation of domesticated grains or tending of wild crops; to evidence of domestication of a wider variety of animals; to new methods of pottery production using kilns, tempers, and well-prepared clay, these cultural traditions helped set the stage for later technological and social change in this region.

THE EARLY NEOLITHIC ON THE EAST COAST: HOULI AND BEIXIN

The earliest known Neolithic cultural tradition in eastern China, the Houli, dates to approximately 6550–5550 BCE. Like other areas of China, archaeological remains from the preceding several millennia are scarce, in this case consisting of only a few cave sites. Despite this dearth of material, pottery from these early cave sites appears to show some continuity of form with Houli vessels, indicating some form of cultural continuum dating back at least to 8000 BCE (Wang Fen 2013:399). Objects from the Houli cultural tradition were first identified in the 1970s and 1980s, although it was not until the early 1990s that full excavations of Houli sites took place. What they revealed was a tradition marked by sandy red pottery occasionally with folded lips, nipple-shaped feet, pricked designs, and decorative clay strips that increased vessel strength. The majority of vessels are cauldron cooking pots, although ovoid water vessels, two-handled jars, and several other jar and cup shapes have been uncovered. Houli pottery production was at a relatively early stage of development with simple molding and coiling used to produce vessels that were then fired in small vertical pit kilns (Wang Fen 2013:392).

While Houli subsistence practices centered on gathering, hunting, and fishing, there is evidence that low levels of agricultural production were taking place and that experiments in domestication were also occurring. Remains of both broomcorn and foxtail millet have been uncovered at Houli sites (Jin 2007). Rice remains have also been discovered, but whether or not they are from domesticated or wild varieties remains debated (Crawford et al. 2006). Similar debates also occur around the level of domestication shown in the numerous pig remains that have been recovered at Houli sites, with some scholars arguing that these remains represent early stages of the domestication process (Kong 1996, 2000).

Stone tools also provide some information on Houli subsistence practices. Large numbers of pecked and polished stone axes, grinding slabs, and other tools including hypothesized sickle blades have been recovered at Houli sites. Generally tools associated with food processing are more numerous than tools associated with preparing fields, leading some scholars to believe that gathering and processing wild plants made a more significant contribution to subsistence than agriculture did at this time. Three nephrite jade chisels have also been recovered from Houli sites, but these were likely utilitarian items. Numerous antler, shell, and bone tools have also been recovered from Houli sites (Wang Fen 2013:390–391).

Only a few Houli sites have been excavated, and many of these have been badly damaged by modern activities; however, these investigations have shed light on Houli settlement organization. Settlements were generally located near rivers, and in at least one case, had a surrounding moat. Sites, up to 14 ha in size, have houses placed together in small groups that some scholars believe may have been divided along kinship lines. Much like structures in other parts of Neolithic China, Houli houses were semi-subterranean, single-roomed, rectangular or square structures approximately 30–50 m² in size with baked earthen clay walls and floors (Shandong 2000a:24). Artifacts found inside the structures indicate that different areas were used for living, production, and cooking. Some other, smaller structures contain no hearths but larger numbers of tools and production debris, perhaps indicating that they were used primarily for production or storage (Wang Fen 2013:395).

Relatively few Houli burials have been uncovered. Cemeteries were generally placed outside of settlement areas, and many have been badly damaged by modern activities. Most excavated graves were simple vertical pit graves, or in some cases vertical pit graves with a niche containing a single supine corpse. There are generally very few grave goods; oyster shells and a few pieces of pottery are the most common objects (Shandong and Zhangqiu 2003:9–11). Based on the egalitarian nature of burials and settlement organization it appears that there were no significant differences in status or wealth among Houli peoples (Wang Fen 2013:407).

The Beixin (5000–4100 BCE) cultural tradition falls chronologically after the Houli period and appears to contain a mixture of traits from both the Houli tradition as well as the Peiligang tradition to the west (Luan 1997:37, 46–51). Currently more research and particularly more ^{14}C dates are needed to clarify the transitional periods between these cultures. Over 100 sites with Beixin remains have been discovered, primarily in Shandong Province and just to the south in northern Jiangsu Province. The Beixin cultural tradition is recognized by its relatively refined pottery, including both fine and coarse wares often tempered with shell, talc, or mica. Typical vessel forms include tripods, cauldrons, and tall-necked jars as well as lids for these vessels (Figure 5) (Luan 1998:268). For the first time in this region some vessels are painted (Zhongguo Shandong 1984:175–175). Overall the level of technical skill in pottery production increased significantly as clay was carefully prepared and tempered according to use and then fired at a relatively high temperature (Wang Fen 2013:403).

Agriculture played a significant role in the subsistence practices of Beixin peoples. Remains of broomcorn and foxtail millet have been recovered at Beixin sites (Jining 1996:290) as well as large numbers of stone tools associated not just with plant and grain harvesting and processing but especially with field preparation. At the site of

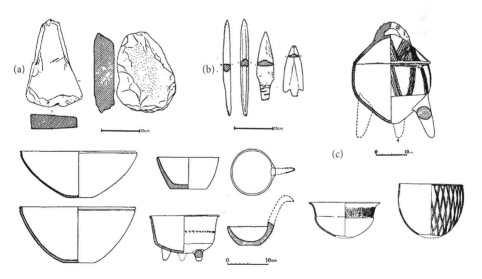

FIGURE 5 A Stone and B bone tools and C ceramic vessels of the Beixin cultural tradition (after Zhongguo and Shandong 1984).

Beixin alone more than 1,000 stone shovels have been recovered; axes are also much more common than in the preceding period. Rice remains have also been discovered, especially at sites in northern Jiangsu. It appears that by this point pigs had become fully domesticated and, along with cattle and chicken, were playing a larger role in the Beixin diet (Wang Fen 2013:402–403). At the same time, however, it seems that gathering plants, hunting, and gathering aquatic resources such as shellfish also contributed heavily to subsistence (Zhongguo Kaogu 1999). In addition to stone tools, numerous finely crafted shell, bone, tooth, and antler tools have been found. These materials were also used to make decorative ornaments that were attached to clothing or placed in hair. The finest ornaments are bone hairpins with round tops (Wang Fen 2013:403).

Especially during the latter part of the Beixin period, the number of settlements and site size increased significantly. A typical site was surrounded by a moat that separated the settlement area from the cemetery area. Much like the preceding Houli, houses were constructed in groups of three to four, which scholars think reflect kinship ties. The houses, around 10 m², are significantly smaller than Houli-period houses and are semi-subterranean and round or oval in form. Most houses had a single room with a sloped entryway and a single hearth in the center. The small size of the houses may mean that each one was inhabited by a nuclear family, with several houses together representing production and consumption groups (Wang Fen 2013:404).

Beixin-period burials are typically simple vertical pit graves, although a small number of multiple burial graves also have been uncovered. Additionally, in northern Jiangsu, stone cist burials have been discovered, where a pit is dug and then lined on the sides and roof with flat stones. Most burials still only contain a few burial goods, such as tools and ornaments. Burials are grouped together in cemeteries located outside settlements. Some scholars suggest that the arrangement of graves in cemeteries reflects the arrangement of houses in settlements, indicating that people were buried near to other members of their kin group. Overall it appears that there were no major differences in wealth or status among Beixin peoples, as during the Houli period (Wang Fen 2013:405–407).

THE EARLY NEOLITHIC IN THE NORTHEAST: XINGLONGWA, ZHAOBAOGOU, AND XINLE

While investigations into the Neolithic cultures of northeastern China have been undertaken since the early 1900s, acknowledgment of pre-Hongshan-period cultures did not occur until relatively recently with the official recognition of the Xinglongwa (6200–5200 BCE) and Zhaobaogou (5400–4500 BCE) cultural traditions (Shelach and Teng 2013:40; Suo and Li 2011). Sites belonging to the Xinglongwa tradition have been discovered in eastern Inner Mongolia, western Liaoning, northern Hebei, and northern Shanxi Province (Suo and Li 2013:52) and are typically identified by scatters of coarse, sand-tempered pottery. Xinglongwa pottery is the earliest identified in the northeast and is typically quite soft and multicolored, an indication of low and uneven firing temperature (Figure 6). Vessels are all handmade and most forms are simple flat-based jars with wide mouths; occasionally they are decorated with simple incised or impressed designs (Shelach and Teng2013:42). Aside from vessels, clay was also used to make small anthropomorphic figurines, the use of which is still unclear (Shelach-Lavi 2000:394–395).

Aside from pottery, Xinglongwa peoples also produced a variety of stone tools, including hoes, axes, grinding stones, and microlith blades (Suo and Li 2013:54). Stone figurine heads, as well as larger stone anthropomorphic statues also have been dated to this period. Much like the pottery figurines, the use of these stone objects is still debated (Shelach and Teng 2013:50); however, these objects may mark the genesis of a tradition that continued into the later Hongshan period in spectacular fashion with the so-called "Goddess Temple" and its larger-than-life clay statues. Aside from basic stone, jade was also occasionally worked, typically to produce personal ornaments such as pendants and earrings. Bone was also used to produce finer tools such as needles, blade handles, and harpoons. Bone and other animal products such as tooth, horn, and shell were all used to produce ornaments (Zhongguo 1985:870–871).

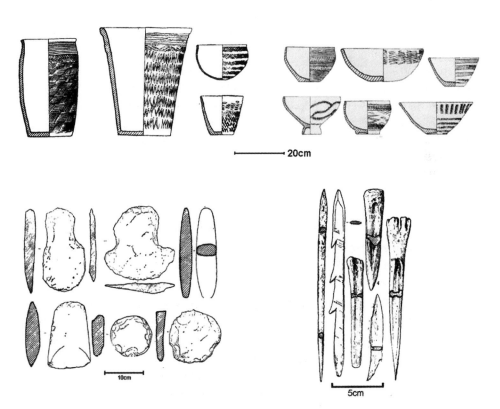

FIGURE 6 Stone and bone tools and pottery vessels of the Xinglongwa cultural tradition (after Neimenggu 1985).

In addition to tools pointing to the cultivation and processing of plants beginning in the Xinglongwa period, carbonized grains of domesticated millet also have been discovered. However, at the one Xinglongwa site where systematic floatation took place, foxtail and broomcorn millet only made up a small percentage of the total recovered plant remains. Aside from millet cultivation, hunting and gathering were also major contributors to the Xinglongwa diet. This is represented by finds of numerous remains of bones from wild animals, especially deer, and by use-wear on grinding stones. It appears that the process of pig domestication had also begun, with reports of fully or partially domesticated pig bones coming from some sites (Liu and Chen 2012:130–132).

Xinglongwa settlements contained rows of 50–80 m² rectangular, semi-subterranean houses that were occasionally surrounded by ditch enclosures. Numerous storage pits have also been discovered both within and outside of the houses. Burials have also been found beneath house floors (Liu and Chen 2012:130), although at some sites they have more commonly been found just outside the settlements. Burials are typically single interments in simple pit graves, which were sometimes topped with stones (Suo and Li 2013:56). These graves generally contained few objects, often simple ornaments that may have been attached to the clothing of the deceased. The richest known burial was placed not in an external cemetery but directly under a house. It contained jade, bone, shell, and ceramic artifacts and two complete pigs (Yang and Liu 1997:34). While there was clearly some special status associated with this individual, the exact meaning of these offerings remains unknown.

Zhaobaogou sites occupy a similar geographic range to those of the Xinglongwa tradition. Zhaobaogou pottery is generally similar to that produced during the Xinglongwa period, although some finer, darker vessels were also produced during this period. A wider range of vessel types was produced with shapes expanding to include jars, beakers, and bowls (Zhongguo Neimenggu 1988:2–4). Techniques of vessel decoration also expanded, with incising and stamping now also being used to create more complex geometric patterns as well as animal motifs (Zhu 1990). Zhaobaogou settlements and houses are similar to those of Xinglongwa, with the exception that Zhaobaogou sites have not been found with surrounding ditches (Shelach and Teng 2013:41).

The Xinle cultural tradition, first discovered in the early 1970s near Shenyang, slightly postdates the Zhaobaogou. While few Xinle sites have been investigated, excavations at the type-site revealed numerous artifacts including pottery, bone, and stone tools, house remains, and some of the earliest known carved jade objects in China (see chapter 2 on Xinle jade by Tang Chung). The site itself contained numerous remains of square or rectangular semi-subterranean houses with fire-hardened walls and floors and central hearths. Ceramics were largely limited to coarseware deep-bellied jars and bowls. Vessels were produced using coiling and some were occasionally red slipped. Carved jade objects include axes, chisels, and several beads. Several jet objects were also uncovered (Yu 2002). Such finds attest to the advanced nature of stone carving during this early period in northeastern China, thus setting the stage for the later jade carving for which this region is so well known during the Middle Neolithic period.

Introduction to the middle Neolithic, 4000–3000/2500BCE

While there was significant variability in the many cultural traditions that were flourishing across China during the Early Neolithic period, there were also many similarities including the adoption of various levels of agriculture and animal husbandry, the production of ground stone tools, the development of sedentary villages with semi-subterranean houses, and the creation of pottery using increasingly sophisticated production facilities and techniques. During this early period we also see only limited evidence of specialized production and social stratification. While objects such as jade ornaments or painted pottery may have taken some specialized knowledge to produce, production levels probably were not so great as to require full-time specialization in a specific task. Residential buildings also show little differentiation in size or construction, and burials, while in many cases containing a few grave goods, rarely show significant differences in quantity or quality.

During the Middle Neolithic period, however, significant social changes began to take place. While growing cultural interaction resulted in more widely shared kinds of objects and ideas, it also appears that there were increasing differences in levels of specialization and stratification among varying cultural traditions. These are often expressed in the production of presumably highly specialized items such as jades and beautiful ceramics; the construction of large houses and public structures; the use of large and richly furnished tombs; and increases in site sizes, with some bigger sites being surrounded by smaller outlying villages (Shelach 2015:95–96). While virtually every cultural tradition can be characterized in one or more of these ways, there was also a great deal of variation. Our increasingly detailed knowledge of this period is now allowing us to understand at a much finer level the changes that were taking place across northern China. This includes the differences that exist within the burial practices of the Yangshao and the varied subsistence practices within the Dawenkou cultural tradition. In addition to providing a general introduction to the main characteristics of each cultural tradition, this section highlights both the significant variability within traditions and shared characteristics that transcended cultural and geographic divides.

The middle Neolithic in the Northwest: Gansu Yangshao/Miaodigou/Dadiwan

Following the pre-Yangshao period there was a major expansion of early Yangshao -sites in eastern Gansu. These early Yangshao sites in Gansu are often referred to as belonging to the Miaodigou type (ca. 4000–3500 BCE) of the Yangshao culture or as Dadiwan Miaodigou (Wang 2012:214). These sites are located primarily in the eastern portion of the province. Excavations at Dadiwan have revealed the presence of a well-organized village that included dozens of small to medium houses fanning out from an open square, with the entire area surrounded by a ditch (Figure 7). The houses were square or rectangular semi-subterranean structures with small entranceways facing toward the central square (Gansu 2003:22–23). Similar house structures have been found at other Yangshao Miaodigou sites in the region (Gansu 2012:17–18). Next to the square at Dadiwan was a larger structure of about 130 m², inside which numerous stone and bone tools and ceramic vessels were found. This was perhaps some sort of communal structure. The central square held several dozen simple pit burials that were accompanied by a few ceramic vessels and in some cases stone or bone tools. Urn burial for infants was also practiced (Gansu 2003:28–31). Pottery from these sites is similar to that of the Yangshao period in northern central China and included several types of painted fineware vessels as well as coarser jars and urns (Gansu 2012:19–28). The similarity in form and designs to vessels produced in adjacent areas to the east shows the close connections between these two regions during this period.

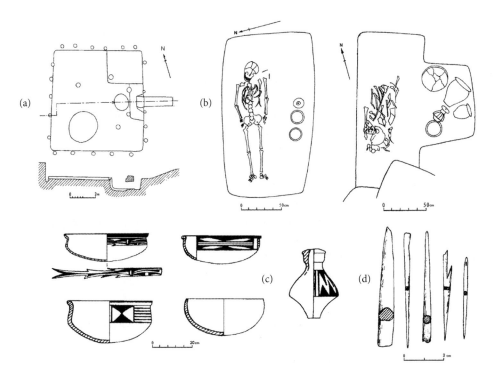

FIGURE 7 A Typical house, B graves, C pottery, and D bone tools from the Yangshao phase of the Dadiwan site (after Gansu 2003).

The middle Neolithic in the Central Plains: Yangshao (5000–3000 BCE) and Miaodigou (4000–3300 BCE)

The Yangshao cultural tradition consists of a number of regional groups that inhabited the areas in and around the central Yellow River Valley from approximately 5000 to 3000 BCE (Liu and Chen 2012:189). First unearthed by local farmers at Yangshao Village in Henan Province around the turn of the twentieth century, and then brought to a larger audience by Andersson, the Yangshao tradition is characterized by their distinct red pottery and use of polished stone tools (Chang 1999:49). Today thousands of sites have been uncovered and the culture has been divided into four large subgroups: the core area along the Wei River Basin; Central Henan Province; Northern Henan and Southern Hebei Province; and Eastern Gansu and Qinghai Provinces.

Most Yangshao villages were located on loess terraces above rivers or local tributaries. Subsistence was based around millet farming, hunting, gathering, fishing, and limited animal husbandry. This has been evident from the archaeological record through abundant finds of stone and ceramic farming implements such as hoes and axes, grain preparation and storage implements such as grinding stones and ceramic storage pots, and botanical remains. Hunting and fishing are evidenced by finds of stone spear and arrow points; bone fishhooks, harpoons; and stone sinkers for nets, as well as by finds of bones of a wide variety of animals and fish. Additionally, many fish and net motifs appear on painted pots and jars such as those found at the Yangshao Banpo type-site in modern day Xi'an. There is also evidence of domesticated dogs and pigs at some Yangshao sites. Finally, it appears that hemp and silkworms may have also been cultivated and that sewing and basket-weaving were well known (Chang 1986:112–113).

The pottery of the Yangshao culture was handmade using the coiling technique. The characteristic red or grey-brown pottery was decorated either using dark red or black ocher-based pigments or with impressed designs such as cords or mats. A number of different shapes and sizes were produced, the most common being tall, wide-mouthed storage jars, bowls, basins, cups, flasks, pointed-bottom jars, and cooking tripods (Fitzgerald-Huber 1999:54–67) along with ceramic spindle whorls, knives, net sinkers, and sling balls (Chang 1983:122). At some sites symbols regarded as proto-characters have been found incised into finished pieces (Guo 1972:5–7). The kilns themselves were generally located outside of villages. In the case of Banpo they were the only aspect of the village aside from the cemetery to be located outside of the ditch enclosing the village (Chang 1983:116).

Yangshao villages generally ranged in size from 50,000–60,000 m^2 and were composed of a number of waddle and daub semi-subterranean houses arranged in groups around a central plaza. It has been hypothesized that these house groupings were based along lineage lines. Animal pens and numerous storage pits were located among the houses. In the case of the Banpo site a ditch 5–6 m wide and deep surrounded the entire area (Chang 1983:116, 119). Chang (1983:114) proposed that the inhabitants of these villages periodically shifted location, often returning to an abandoned site after a number of years had passed, however this hypothesis has been rejected by other scholars (Peterson and Shelach 2010:252).

The cemeteries used by Yangshao peoples show a wide variety of burial practices. Typically the deceased were buried in a cemetery located outside of the main settlement, although the specific location of the cemetery varies from site to site. In some sites infants were buried among village houses in urns, while at others they were placed in a cemetery without urns (Fitzgerald-Huber 1999:54–67). At some cemeteries all of the burials are individual with a few dual burials, while at others the majority of burials are group burials. It has been suggested that such group burials reflect collective ancestor veneration (Liu 2004:135). Some cemeteries show only primary interment while others have mostly secondary interments. Body layout is often in rows, which has been hypothesized at some cemeteries, such as Yuanjunmiao, to indicate burial along lineage lines (Zhang 1985:21–23). The bodies were typically placed in an extended supine position with their heads pointing to the west; however, at some cemeteries orientation varies, as does the position of the body. In some secondary burials the bones are placed in piles under the skull while at others they are arranged in the original position of burial. Burial goods generally consist of no more than a few dozen objects; often only a few ceramics along with personal items such as tools, necklaces, and pendants were included. In some instances it is adult males who receive the most goods, while in other cases children have the richest burials (Liu 2004:131). It is apparent that the burial practices of the Yangshao peoples as a whole were extremely varied with no clear indication of why certain methods were preferred by certain groups and little indication of significant social stratification being present in these communities.

MIAODIGOU

For many years the Miaodigou cultural tradition was considered as part of the Yangshao culture, but more recently it has been recognized as a unique tradition in its own right (Li 2013:213). Part of the reason for this previous connection is the similarity of Miaodigou and Yangshao pottery. Miaodigou pottery is typically red fineware with vessel types including jars, bowls, cauldrons, and ring foot jars. The fineware is frequently painted with black geometric designs that often take the form of animals. Some pieces were also slipped white before paint was applied. Coarseware vessels were produced and often finished with cord marking (Li 2013:215). In addition, Miaodigou potters produced ceramic bracelets and knives. Stone was used for making knives and other tools, while bone was used for making tools, ornaments, and hairpins. Initially known primarily from settlement sites, more recent excavations, particularly those at the site of Xipo (Zhongguo and Henan 2010), have shed light on the mortuary practices of this group.

During the Miaodigou period there was a significant increase in settlement size and density across the landscape in the northern plain region of southern Shanxi, western Henan, and Shaanxi Provinces. Settlements such as Xipo included both large and small semi-subterranean structures. Circular, inward-facing settlement layouts with surrounding moats continued from the previous Yangshao tradition, but on a significantly larger scale (Li 2013:219). Buildings included small pit houses as well as a few much larger semi-subterranean structures up to 240 m^2 in size, which had painted rammed-earth walls that were supported by dozens of posts.

Miaodigou cemeteries show clear differentiation in the size and layout of burials (Zhongguo and Henan 2010:293–297). While many burials are rectangular shaft tombs around 2 m^2 in size with a few basic pottery vessels or tools, others range up to 17 m^2 and contain dozens of grave goods such as large ceramic vessels, jade axes, bone hairpins, and ivory and jade bracelets. In these elaborate burials there is evidence of the body having been wrapped in cloth, special mud having been used to fill the pit, and wooden planks being placed over the burial (Zhongguo and Henan 2010:83–91). Some scholars have interpreted these large graves as belonging to early elites who sought to attract followers using elaborate funerary rituals and feasting, which may have been carried out in the large building previously discussed (Li 2013:224). This increasing level of stratification and complexity is also seen further to the east around the same time period.

The middle Neolithic on the east coast: Dawenkou

The Dawenkou cultural tradition (4150–2650 BCE) follows immediately after the Beixin tradition and exhibits many Beixin characteristics. First discovered in the 1950s, to date more than 600 sites belonging to the Dawenkou cultural tradition have been discovered in Shandong Province and adjacent regions of Jiangsu, Anhui, and Henan Provinces. The Dawenkou tradition, like others across China, is identified by its pottery, which is much more diverse than that of previous periods and includes finely made black, red, and white wares with typical shapes including tripods, stemmed dishes, bowls, pitchers, jars, and cups (Figure 8). During this period significant advances were made in pottery production, including the use of the fast wheel, development of kilns that could fire at higher and more stable temperatures and atmospheres, and the use of kaolin clay–based slips. While painted pottery is common in the Early Dawenkou period, by the later part of the period it nearly disappears completely (Luan 2013:416–417). Significant changes in pottery production mirror the many other technological and social changes that were occurring during this period in eastern China.

While Dawenkou peoples continued to follow a mixture of subsistence practices, millet seems to have made up a significant portion of the diet at many sites, with rice playing a larger role at more southern sites. There is also some indication that in the later

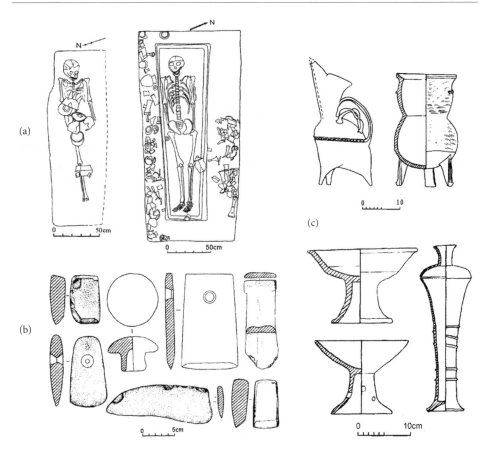

FIGURE 8 A Dawenkou graves, B stone tools, and C pottery (after Shandong 2000).

Dawenkou period higher-ranking individuals ate more rice than millet; however, as of 2015 only a single study on this topic has been undertaken (Qi et al. 2004:46–47). In addition to agriculture, gathering, hunting, fishing, and animal husbandry were also important subsistence practices. Domesticated animals included pigs, cattle, chickens, and dogs, with pig remains being by far the most abundant at most sites. Portions and in some cases entire pigs were included in some Dawenkou burials, indicating the importance of this animal and the importance of burial for displaying or sharing wealth (Underhill 2000:111–121; 2002:140–141). Large finds of wild animal remains, especially in eastern coastal sites, show the continuing importance of hunting. Additionally, shell mounds provide evidence of the role that the gathering of aquatic resources played at these sites in the Dawenkou period (Zhongguo 1988:17).

During the middle and late Dawenkou there was a significant increase in numbers of settlements, however, there is currently no clear evidence of the emergence of a settlement hierarchy during this period (Luan, personal communication 2015). Settlements contained houses that are 10–20 m², semi-subterranean, square structures that likely housed 5–7 people. Houses were arranged in groups that are thought to reflect kinship ties, with each house representing an independent unit of consumption. In some late Dawenkou sites a new housing structure, row houses, are seen, which consist of 2–13 attached rooms of 11–18 m² in size. These are thought to have encompassed individual kinship groups, with larger rooms used for living and cooking and smaller rooms serving as storage spaces. Many sites at this time are surrounded by moats, with some larger sites also having rammed-earth walls surrounding part or all of the residential area (Luan 2013:422–426; Shandong 2000b).

The majority of Dawenkou burials are single interments, although some sites also have secondary, multiple burials, usually of two individuals, either two males or a male and female. Typical Dawenkou burial practices include the placement of one or more river deer teeth in the hand or hands of the deceased. Burials often contained pottery vessels, including some specialized vessels, such as high-stemmed cups, that seem to have been produced only for use in the burial ceremony or for placement in the graves. Numbers of vessels varied more widely than in earlier periods, with most graves having a few vessels; however, by the Late Dawenkou period some individual graves had over one hundred vessels. These richer graves also typically had large grave pits, inner and outer wooden coffins, and in some cases pig mandibles or entire pigs. Based on this evidence it seems clear that social differentiation was increasing during the Dawenkou period (Luan 2013:429; Underhill 2000:121–122; 2002).

THE MIDDLE NEOLITHIC IN THE NORTHEAST: HONGSHAN

Significant changes were taking place in northwestern China around 4500–3000 BCE with the emergence of the Hongshan cultural tradition. Based on the results of archaeological survey projects that have taken place in the region (Chifeng 2011:108–116; Peterson et al. 2010; Shelach 1998) it seems that there was significant population growth between the Zhaobaogou and Middle Hongshan period, with increasing numbers of settlements appearing across the landscape before a rapid decline at the end of this period. While there is clear evidence that many Zhaobaogou traditions, such as pottery production and some ritual beliefs, continued during the Hongshan, changes, particularly in subsistence strategies, external contacts, and social organization and stratification were also underway.

Hongshan pottery shows some continuity with earlier traditions, however, alongside local forms many new types of pottery and decorative techniques emerged, often similar to forms and styles from the Central Plain. New tools were also beginning to be used alongside earlier types. Of particular importance are spades and knives, made of both stone and ceramic, which were likely used for harvesting cereals. These objects along with the discovery of domesticated millet at some sites point to the adoption of cereal cultivation alongside earlier hunting and gathering practices. Remains of domesticated pigs also point to limited animal husbandry. Interestingly, different numbers of certain tool types such as knives (associated with agriculture) and grinding stones (associated with earlier reliance on nuts and tubers) have been discovered at different sites, leading some scholars to hypothesize that agriculture was relied on to a greater or lesser extent at different sites (Liu and Chen 2012:177). Hongshan settlement sites themselves are generally small villages made up of rows of semi-subterranean houses. While more data is needed to better understand village layout and daily life, significant efforts have been spent investigating Hongshan ritual and ceremonial sites (Liu and Chen 2012:178).

Hongshan is perhaps best known for the discovery of the so-called "Goddess Temple" at the site cluster of Niuheliang (Barnes and Guo 1996). Survey and excavation in and around this area has led to the idea of the "temple" as being part of a much larger ritual landscape nearly 50 km² in area. The landscape includes numerous late Hongshan ritual structures such as stone-faced platforms surrounded with pottery cylinders (Guo 1995) as well as stone cairns, placed in and around the platforms, many of which contain a few extremely richly furnished burials (Figure 9). Burial goods include numerous carved jade objects such as animal and human figures, ornaments, *bi* discs, axes, adzes, and beads. The focus of the burials is currently thought to have been ritual experts who perhaps conducted ceremonies at these platforms and temples. The Goddess Temple itself is made up of two large, semi-subterranean structures in which numerous parts of unfired clay statues of animal and female human figures have been found. The statues range in size from life-size to three times life-size and have been the subject of considerable debate. The fact that all of the human figures are female has given the structure the name Goddess Temple, however, the exact nature of this structure remains unclear (Barnes and Guo 1996). A regional survey has revealed that there are several smaller groups of ritual structures in other parts of the Hongshan landscape that also contain artifacts similar to those at

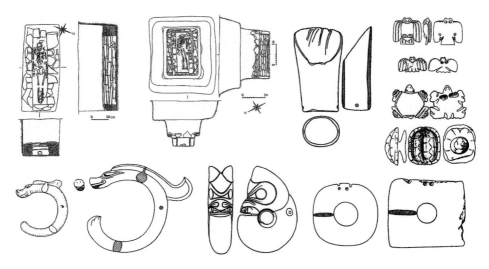

FIGURE 9 Elaborate Hongshan cultural tradition burials and carved jade items (after Childs-Johnson 2009).

Niuheliang; however, the area around Niuheliang, with its multitude of ritual structures, tombs, and artifacts, is still viewed as the core zone of Hongshan ritual life.

Based on these finds, some scholars envision these smaller groups of ritual structures as being at the core of localized Hongshan polities, with each area having its own ritual structures and specialists that served the local community. These specialists would have gained prestige from the important role they played in ritual life, while outside of this sphere there may have been less social differentiation among the population based on economic production (Drennan and Peterson 2006:3,962–3,964; Peterson 2006:201–202). Additionally, differentiation may have occurred between those who lived in or around the core zone and participated in ritual life there and those who lived in more peripheral areas. Further investigation is needed to clarify differences between these groups and to better understand the role of both ritual and day-to-day life throughout the Hongshan cultural tradition.

INTRODUCTION TO THE LATE NEOLITHIC / EARLY BRONZE AGE (3000–2000/1500BCE)

During the Late Neolithic period many of the trends that had begun during the Middle period, including increasing social stratification, specialization, interregional interaction, and technological advances, reached new heights, particularly in the Central Plain and on the east coast. In these regions the construction of massive platform buildings and tombs containing hundreds of grave goods that were difficult to produce or acquire marked the emergence of new levels of leadership and social inequality. The production of these grave goods also attests to higher degrees of specialization that likely involved full-time, specialized production by larger groups of individuals. Increasing levels of elite-sanctioned violence, both through warfare and sacrifice, shows not only the power of these early leaders but also the competition that went along with increasing or holding one's control over land, resources, and people. However, the move toward increasing specialization and inequality was not universal.

In some areas it has been proposed that a mixture of climatic and social change led some groups to largely abandon the elaborate burials and ritual structures that marked the middle or early late Neolithic and to instead revert to seemingly more egalitarian social structures or less specialized production (Jin Guiyun 2004:494–500). For example, in the northeast the elaborate ritual structures and artifacts of the Hongshan cultural tradition largely disappear during this period. Around the same time in the west evidence of interactions with groups originating further north and west resulted in the introduction of a number of new technologies, crops, and ideas. While crops such as wheat and barley and technology including metal working were slowly adopted and adapted, these would eventually go on to have a major impact across the region. When eventually combined with traditions further east, these new introductions would set the stage for many of the later traditions and stylistic motifs that mark the emergence of a distinctly "Chinese" civilization during the early dynastic period.

THE LATE NEOLITHIC IN THE NORTHWEST: MAJIAYAO AND QIJIA

Shifts in the ceramic record, significant increases in site numbers, and geographic expansion of sites, as well as changes in burial practices around 3000 BCE have led archaeologists to view a transition from the Yangshao or Dadiwan cultural tradition to the Majiayao tradition (3200–2000 BCE). Based again on ceramic typology and seriation, the Majiayao tradition can be divided into three distinctive subphases: the Majiayao (3200–2650 BCE), Banshan (2650–2300 BCE), and Machang (2300–2000 BCE). While each subphase saw shifts in settlement patterns and minor changes in ceramic types, overall the material culture of these subphases shows general continuity (Hung 2011:17).

Majiayao peoples practiced millet-based agriculture, raised domesticated pigs and dogs, and also relied on hunting and gathering for subsistence, although rice and later wheat and barley were also cultivated in small quantities. Sites are generally under 12 ha {1 ha = 2.47 acres} in size and dwellings were small, semi-subterranean structures. Majiayao's most characteristic feature is their elaborately painted ceramic vessels (Figure 10), which are part of a material culture that also includes polished stone tools, microliths, bone items, and China's earliest bronze artifacts. These vessels include finewares painted in black, red, and occasionally white geometric designs including whirlpools, nets, saw-tooth patterns, and occasionally human and anthropomorphic figures. Coarsewares were also produced, and these often are covered with cord and

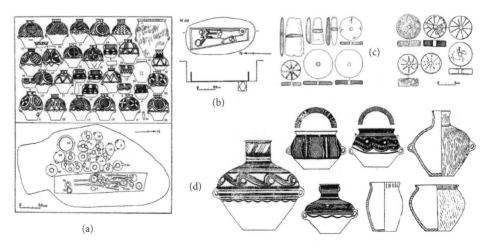

FIGURE 10   **A** Richly furnished Machang grave, **B** typical Banshan grave, **C** Banshan stone tools, and **D** Banshan pots (after Qinghai and Zhongguo 1984 [**A, C, D**] and Gansu 1978 [**B, C**]).

applique (Qinghai and Beijing 1976:31–51). Recent studies have shown that in at least some instances painted fineware vessels were exchanged over long distances and perhaps acted as prestige goods, especially in funerary contexts (Hung 2011:69–74). Coarsewares also appear to have been exchanged at the local level (Womack et al. 2019).

The middle and late Majiayao period subphases, termed Banshan and Machang, saw increasingly large numbers of painted storage jars placed in pit burials at some sites, to the point that during the Machang phase some burials were expanded horizontally or included ramps to accommodate large numbers of vessels. This is particularly apparent at the site of Liuwan in eastern Qinghai Province (Qinghai and Zhongguo 1984). While not all burials received such large numbers of grave goods, during all periods most received at least a few vessels. It has been hypothesized that large numbers of grave goods indicated the ability of some individuals to achieve higher status through their ability to redistribute grain to followers (Allard 2002:19). However, the exact roles that these individuals played, as well as their status and the overall levels of inequality and complexity during this period, remain difficult to assess due to a lack of excavated habitation sites.

QIJIA

Following the Majiayao cultural tradition, the Qijia cultural tradition, typically assigned to the early Bronze Age, displays similar lifeways including a focus on millet cultivation, but the transition between the two periods has not been closely investigated. Based on ceramic typology it seems that the Qijia tradition has characteristics of both the Machang subphase of the Majiayao tradition as well as aspects of the more easterly Changshan and Keshengzhuang II traditions (Chen Pin 2013:9–10; Wang 2012:221–222). Although the geographic range of the Qijia tradition extended somewhat further to the north and west, many sites were occupied during both periods, and some cemeteries show an overlap with material from both Late Majiayao and Qijia periods. In contrast to Majiayao, Qijia pottery is largely plain or cord marked and rarely painted, although slips are common on certain vessel types (Figure 11). The vessels themselves are typically orange or grey and shapes include jars, bowls, cauldrons, and tripods. It should be noted, however, that there is significant regional variation in ceramic types. During this period the range of domesticated animals expanded to include sheep or goats and cattle. Significantly more bronze artifacts, including tools and small ornaments, were produced or acquired. Other aspects of material culture, such as housing and tools, remained largely unchanged (Chen Honghai 2013:108–109).

Little is currently known about Qijia habitation sites due to a lack of excavation, although this is beginning to change in recent years (Womack et al. 2017). Based on the few Qijia houses that have been uncovered we know that they were generally small, semi-subterranean structures that often had lime plastered floors and a central hearth. The limited number of structures, as well as some unusual "stone rings" found at some

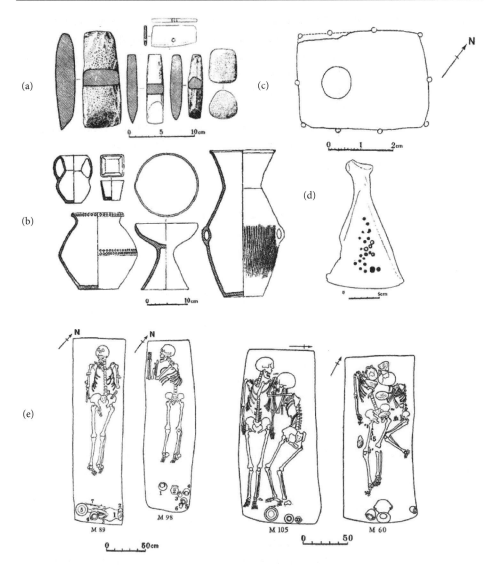

FIGURE 11 A Qijia cultural tradition stone tools, B ceramics, C house foundations, D a scapula used for pyromancy, and E graves (after Zhongguo 1974).

Qijia sites, has led some scholars to hypothesize that Qijia peoples were in the process of transitioning to a pastoral lifestyle and lived at least part of the time in tents instead of houses (Zhongguo 1974:31–38). Currently a lack of excavated material makes such hypotheses difficult to test. Qijia cemeteries were typically placed near settlements. During the Qijia period graves were largely similar in construction to some types of Majiayao burials. However, they contain a wider variety and reduced number of primarily plain vessels (Chen Pin 2013:14–41). Some graves also contain carved jade items or other exotic goods rarely seen during the Majiayao period. Debates continue about the presence of human and animal sacrifices (Chen Honghai 2013:110–112). Despite these extraordinary items being placed in some graves, it does not appear that these graves or the individuals they contained were otherwise set apart from the general population, since grave construction and size remained the same even in graves with these unusual items. There also does not seem to be any indication of unusually large buildings in habitation sites such as those identified for the Hongshan, Longshan, and other societies with evidence for social ranking. While more information is needed, it currently appears that the Qijia peoples were not as socially stratified as their neighbors on the Central Plain and eastern coast.

The late Neolithic in the Central Plains: Longshan

Artifacts from the Longshan cultural tradition were first identified in northern China's Central Plains in the 1930s. Excavations at Hougang, Anyang, Henan Province in 1931 resulted in the chronological placement of Longshan after Yangshao but before the Shang dynasty. In the following decades characteristic Longshan black pottery was discovered at sites across northern China including in Shanxi, Shaanxi, Hebei, and Shandong. Over time it was decided that there were significant regional variations within Longshan cultural traditions, which in turn led to the naming of regional Longshan cultural traditions such as Shandong Longshan (Zhao 2013:237), discussed in the next section. This section will focus on the core Longshan area in north China's Central Plain and will use Longshan to encompass the larger cultural tradition in this region from 2550–1950 BCE. Individual treatment of various subcultures will be left to more specialized works on this period.

The earlier part of the Longshan period, also known as the Miaodigou II culture in Henan and Shaanxi, marks the transition between Miaodigou and Longshan. Many traditions continue from earlier periods, such as semi-subterranean, round houses grouped together within moated settlements, and the reliance on a mixture of agriculture, hunting, raising livestock, and gathering for subsistence. However, changes that would fully develop in the later Longshan also have their origins in this period. These changes include closer relations, indicated by similar pottery forms, with other cultural groups to the east and south (Zhao 2013:238–239); more technologically sophisticated pottery production as well as production of specialized religious or ceremonial items such as large stone discs; and increasing social stratification, as indicated by a clear division of small, medium, and large graves, with the largest containing the most numerous and elaborate burial goods (Liu 1996).

The Middle and Late Longshan period, coinciding in Henan with Wangwan III, in southern Shanxi with Taosi, and in Shaanxi with Keshengzhuang, saw the continuation and elaboration of these trends along with diverse regional developments. Here general traits that largely transcend regional boundaries will be discussed in order to provide an overview of the major social and technological changes that were taking place in this period.

Overall there was a significant change in settlement patterns between the Yangshao and Longshan periods, with there being nearly 2.5 times as many settlements during the latter. This likely reflects significant population growth throughout the Central Plain region. Settlements also increased in size compared to those of earlier periods, with the largest ranging from 40–100 ha (Zhao 2013:242–243). Although there are many issues with creating arbitrary classes or tiers of settlements based on size, it does seem that there were also distinct medium- and small-sized settlements that were clustered around the largest centers. Some scholars interpret this as reflecting the development of regional social hierarchies that were both in competition, as exhibited by large settlement walls and deep moats, and in exchange relationships, exhibited by exotic trade goods in some burials, with one another (Zhao 2013:243).

The large settlements themselves (Henan 1992, 2002, 2008) often had an area that was surrounded by rammed-earth walls that are typically rectangular in shape with outer moats and gaps where gates likely stood. The rammed-earth method was also used at some sites to construct platform mounds atop which, based on remaining post holes, large structures were constructed. Scholars have suggested these served as elite houses, communal meeting areas, or ceremonial or religious structures (Zhao 2013:245–246). Outside of the walls the settlements continued with house structures, storage pits, graves, and production areas. At some sites the Beixin tradition of row houses continued, while at others the majority of houses were single or double roomed, semi-subterranean structures of varying shapes. A new, entirely subterranean type of house has also been discovered at some Longshan sites (Zhao 2013:248). Another new development, using lime to plaster house floors and walls, also began during this period (Henan Gongzuodui 1959:42).

Remains of millet, rice, and some wheat have all been discovered at Longshan sites, along with remains of domesticated animals including pig, dog, sheep or goat, and cattle. Overall millet remained the most important grain; however, these other grains, along with gathered plants and domestic and wild animals, all contributed to the middle and late Longshan diet. Stone tools suitable for clearing fields and harvesting grain are abundant, however, significant numbers of tools possibly used for warfare or hunting, such as projectile points and sling balls have also been recovered. Needles and spindle whorls attest to the importance of cloth production, while complex kilns show advances made in pottery production (Zhao 2013:249–250). Finally, there have been some signs that experiments with metal production, specifically copper and bronze, were taking place at some Longshan sites (Henan Gongzuodui 1982:453–454).

A relatively small number of later Longshan graves have been excavated in Henan Province, with most being urn burials of infants and a few single adult interments. At the site of Taosi (Figure 12), however, many more graves have been excavated with spectacular and informative results. The massive Taosi cemetery covers an area nearly 1.5 × 2 km in area and is thought to contain thousands of graves. While the cemetery has only been

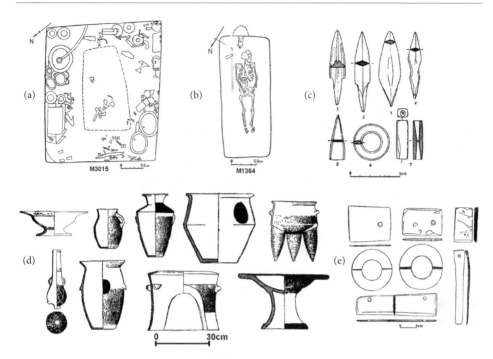

FIGURE 12   A Large and B medium graves, C stone and bone tools, D ceramic vessels, and E jade ornaments from the Taosi cemetery (after Zhongguo and Shanxi 1983).

partially excavated, more than 1,000 rectangular pit graves of varying depths and sizes have been uncovered (Liu and Chen 2012:222). The excavators have placed these into three categories based on size: small (<2 × 0.6 m), medium (<2.5 × 1 m), and large (up to 3.2 × 2.7 m) (Zhongguo and Linfen 1983:32).

While over 600 small graves have been excavated, these simple pit graves typically contain only a single interment and few if any grave goods. In medium graves, more than 80 of which have been excavated, the deceased were provided with numerous grave goods including painted wooden coffins; pottery vessels; ornaments made of stone, wood, and jade; jade ritual objects; and pig mandibles. While the medium-sized graves perhaps correspond with the richest graves of the Middle Neolithic period in this region, the largest graves pushed elaborate burials to new heights. The six large tombs contained painted wooden coffins that were placed in finely prepared burial chambers. Among the hundreds of grave goods were entire sets of pottery vessels, musical instruments including copper bells and alligator-skin drums, and dozens of stone and jade ritual objects and ornaments (Linfenshi 2008; Zhongguo and Linfen 1983:35). According to Chang (1999:60) the hierarchical clustering seen at Taosi likely reflects lineage grouping, a tradition seen in many earlier Neolithic cemeteries. However, the hierarchical nature of the burials at Taosi seems to point to social inequality reaching new extremes in at least some parts of the Longshan cultural tradition.

THE LATE NEOLITHIC ON THE EAST COAST: SHANDONG LONGSHAN

The Shandong Longshan cultural tradition (ca. 2650–2050 BCE), which actually encompasses sites in Shandong as well as in adjacent regions of Henan, Jiangsu, and Anhui, shares many traits with its Longshan neighbors on the Central Plains (Sun 2013:436). However, this regional tradition is distinct enough in its own right to warrant individual treatment here. Although the first Longshan-period sites were discovered in Shandong in the 1930s, it was not until the 1950s that it became recognized as its own distinct regional subtype (Liang 1954). Since then over 2,000 Longshan-period sites have been discovered throughout Shandong, and significant regional variation has been noted.

The Shandong Longshan subsistence base involved raising foxtail and broomcorn millet as well as rice and wheat (Jin 2007:18), although foxtail millet makes up the majority of grain remains. Pigs, dogs, sheep or goat, chicken, and cattle were also raised for meat. Hunting and fishing also contributed to the diet, although seemingly to a lesser extent than in previous periods. Evidence for these activities comes not only from plant and animal remains but also from numerous remains of stone and bone tools for clearing fields and harvesting, as well as for hunting and fishing (Sun 2013:448).

By the Longshan period pottery production was highly developed, with most pots being constructed on a fast wheel and fired in well-controlled kilns, likely indicating production by highly skilled, specialized potters. Of particular note are the eggshell-thin blackware goblets that have been discovered at numerous sites (Sun 2013:445; Underhill 2002:148–156). Other major products being produced during this period include stone and carved jade tools and ornaments, and textiles. McGovern and colleagues (2005:262–266) have also found evidence of fermented beverage production. Some finds of copper and brass also have been reported (An 2000:33–34), but these were very small and were likely the result of early experimentation. A number of these goods were seemingly produced for consumption outside of their production area, leading some scholars to suggest that there were early forms of market exchange taking place during this period (Sun 2013:451). In the coastal regions salt production was also a major specialized activity during this period (Liu and Chen 2012:218).

Due to the piecemeal nature of systematic survey in this region it is difficult to generalize about settlement patterns during this time period (Underhill, personal communication 2015). Nevertheless, the large number of Longshan sites discovered throughout Shandong indicates that significant population growth did occur. Based on the location of known sites it also appears that there is some variability in settlement placement across the landscape. For example, settlements in some regions cluster around rivers, while in others they are focused around large centers that are spread more or less evenly across the landscape (Sun 2013:439). Regional centers during this period were much larger than during previous periods, with some sites expanding to more than 200 ha.

A typical large center would have a core area surrounded by a wall made of rammed earth as well as a moat. Inside the core area were houses, pits, and a few larger buildings, perhaps ceremonial structures or elite housing, which often were constructed on pounded-earth platforms. Beyond this would be additional housing and production areas.

Mortuary practices during the Early Longshan period in Shandong were in many ways similar to those of the preceding Dawenkou period as well as those of adjacent Longshan groups. Small numbers of elite graves contained extensive assemblages of elaborate grave goods, including sets of difficult-to-produce ceramic goblets and other vessels, jade objects, musical instruments, and pig skulls and mandibles (Liu and Chen 2012:218). By the Middle Longshan period, however, these mortuary practices began to change. Fewer graves contained ceramic vessels of any kind, and those that did generally had fewer than during the preceding period. This may reflect that social inequality was increasing and becoming more entrenched. While exactly how this inequality was achieved and maintained varied by region and over time, it is clear that mortuary rituals likely both reflected and helped reinforce these inequalities (Underhill 2002:248–253). Equally unclear is the cause of the relatively sudden population decline that occurred in some regions beginning around 2000 BCE (Liu and Chen 2012:220). More research will be necessary to understand these complex social changes in this region.

The late Neolithic decline in the Northeast: Xiaoheyan

While sites were growing larger and societies were becoming more complex in the Central Plain region, the successors to the Hongshan cultural tradition in northeastern China, the Xiaoheyan, followed a different trajectory. While data for the post-Hongshan occupation of this region are scarce, it currently appears that there was a steep decline in population and numbers of settlement beginning around the start of the third millennium BCE. This coincides with a shift in tool sets away from harvesting knives and toward microblades and projectile points, likely indicating a decline in agricultural production and a rise in hunting and gathering (Li Xinwei 2008:117–131). While a lack of excavated sites makes it difficult to draw conclusions about the nature of the Hongshan-Xiaoheyan transition, as well as Xiaoheyan social organization, some scholars have argued that climatic change and specifically a number of droughts during the Late Hongshan period (An Zhisheng et al. 2000:758–760) precipitated the collapse of Hongshan's agriculturally based complexity (Jin Guiyun 2004:494–500). In fact, at least one scholar (Song 2002) has hypothesized that elaborate late Hongshan religious practices were undertaken by elites in an attempt to seek divine intervention to save crops in a quickly drying world. While this idea clearly resonates in today's society, like so many aspects of this chapter, more data and research are needed on this topic.

CONCLUDING REMARKS

In many ways this chapter is a snapshot of our understanding of the northern Chinese Neolithic period at a point in time when our knowledge of this subject is rapidly changing. In the past decade a host of new scientific research methods, collaborative projects and, to a lesser extent, theoretical approaches have been adopted and applied to archaeology in China. This is quickly increasing the resolution at which we can understand the past, with new site-specific research, such as on local diets, production practices, and migration patterns, feeding into the established narratives of Neolithic cultures that have been summarized here. This material has also helped scholars begin to address larger questions relating to topics including the transition to agriculture, early animal domestication, the transition to settled village life, the move toward increased specialization in production, increases in trade and interregional interaction, and the development of social hierarchies. Whether this abundance of new data will fundamentally change our view of the Neolithic period established over the past century is yet to be seen; however, new discoveries and approaches will undoubtedly provide increased clarity on our views of this period in northern China.

BIBLIOGRAPHY

Allard, Francis 2002. "Mortuary Ceramics and Social Organization in the Dawenkou and Majiayao Cultures." *Journal of East Asian Archaeology* 3(3–4):1–22.

An, Zhimin 安志敏 1981. "The Neolithic of Early China 中国的新石器时代." *Kaogu* 3:252–260.

An, Zhimin 安志敏 2000. "On Early Copper and Bronze Objects in Ancient China." In *The Beginnings of Metallurgy in China*. Edited by H. R. Katheryn Linduff and Sun Shuyun. Lewiston: Edwin Mellen Press.

An, Zhisheng, S. Porter, J. E. Kutzbach, X. Wu, S. Wang, X. Liu, X. Li, and W. Zhou 2000. "Asynchronous Holocene Optimum of the East Asian Monsoon." *Quaternary Science Reviews* 19(8):743–762.

Andersson, Johan Gunnar 1923. "An Early Chinese Culture." *Bulletin of the Geological Survey of China* 5(1):1–58.

Andersson, Johan Gunnar 1943. *Researches into the Prehistory of the Chinese*. Stockholm: Museum of Far Eastern Antiquities.

Barnes, Gina, and D. S. Guo 1996. "The Ritual Landscape of 'Boar Mountain' Basin: The Niuheliang Site Complex of North-Eastern China." *World Archaeology* 28(2):209–219.

Barton, Loukas, S. D. Newsome, F. H. Chen, H. Wang, T. P. Guilderson, and R. L. Bettinger 2009. "Agricultural Origins and the Isotopic Identity of Domestication in Northern China." *Proceedings of the National Academy of Sciences* 106(14):5,523–5,528.

Beijing Daxue Kaogu Wenbo Xueyuan 北京大学考古文博学院, and Zhengzhoushi Wenwu Kaogu Yanjiuyuan 2011. "The Excavation of the Lijiagou Site in Xinmi City, Henan 河南新密市李家沟遗址发掘 简报." *Kaogu* 4:291–297.

Chang, Kwang-chih 1983. *Art, Myth, and Ritual: The Path to Political Authority in Ancient China*. Cambridge, MA: Harvard University Press.

Chang, Kwang-chih 1986. *The Archaeology of Ancient China*. New Haven, CT: Yale University Press.

Chang, Kwang-chih 1999. "China on the Eve of the Historical Period." In *The Cambridge History of Ancient China: From the Origins of Civilization to 221 BCE*. Edited by M. Loewe and Edward L. Shaughnessy, 37–73. Cambridge, UK: Cambridge University Press.

Chen, Honghai 陈洪海 2013. "The Qijia Culture of the Upper Yellow River Valley." In *A Companion to Chinese Archaeology*. Edited by A. P. Underhill, 105–124. West Sussex: Wiley-Blackwell.

Chen, Pin 陈玭 2013. "The Origins and Chronology of the Qijia Culture: The Type-Site of Qijiaping 齐家文化的 分期与源流:以齐家坪遗址为中心." PhD diss., Beijing: Beijing University.

Chifeng International Collaborative Archaeological Research Project 2011. *Settlement Patterns in the Chifeng Region*. Pittsburgh: Center for Comparative Archaeology, University of Pittsburgh.

Childe, George V. 1936. *Man Makes Himself*. London: Rationalist Press Association.

Childs-Johnson, Elizabeth 2009. "The Art of Working Jade and the Rise of Civilization in China." In *The Jade Age and Early Chinese Jades in American Museums*. Edited by Elizabeth Childs-Johnson and Fang Gu, 291–393. Beijing: Kexue chubanshe.

Crawford, Gary, X. Chen 陈雪香, and J. Wang 王建华 2006. "Houli Culture Rice from the Yuezhuang site, Jinan 山东济南长清月庄遗址发现后李 文化时期的碳化稻." *Dongfang kaogu* 3:247–251.

Drennan, Robert D., and C. Peterson 2006. "Patterned Variation in Prehistoric Chiefdoms." *Proceedings of the National Academy of Sciences of the United States of America* 103(11):3,960–3,967.

Falkenhausen, Lother von 1993. "On the Historiographical Orientation of Chinese Archaeology." *Antiquity* 67(257):839–849.

Falkenhausen, Lother von 1995. "The Regionalist Paradigm in Chinese archaeology." In *Nationalism, Politics, and the Practice of Archaeology*. Edited by P. Kohl and C. Fawcett, 198–217. Cambridge, UK: Cambridge University Press.

Fen, Wang 2013. "The Houli and Beixin Cultures." In *A Companion to Chinese Archaeology*. Edited by A. P. Underhill, 387–410. West Sussex: Wiley-Blackwell.

Fiskesjö, Magnus, and X. Chen 2004. *China before China: Johan Gunnar Andersson, Ding Wenjiang, and the Discovery of China's Prehistory; A Companion Guide for the New Exhibit at the Museum of Far Eastern Antiquities*, bilingual edition (English and Chinese). Stockholm: Östasiatiska museet.

Fitzgerald-Huber, Louisa G. 1999. "The Yangshao Culture: Banpo." In *The Golden Age of Chinese Archaeology: Celebrated Discoveries from the People's Republic of China*. Edited by Xiao Yang, 54–67. London: Yale University Press.

Gansusheng Bowuguan Wenwu Gongzuodui 甘肃省博物馆文物工作队. 1978. Guanghe Dibaping Banshan Leixing Mudi 广河地巴坪"半山类型"墓地. *Kaogu Xuebao* 2:193–210.

Gansusheng Wenwu Kaogu Yanjiusuo 甘肃省文物考古研究所. 2003. "Excavation of the Settlement of Early Yangshao Culture on the Dadiwan Site in Gansu 甘肃秦安县大地湾遗址仰韶文化早期聚落发掘简报." *Kaogu* 6:19–31.

Gansusheng Wenwu Kaogu Yanjiusuo 甘肃省文物考古研究所. 2012 "A Report on the Excavation at the Neolithic Site of Gaositou in Lixian County, Gansu Province 甘肃礼县高寺头新石器时代遗址发掘报告." *Kaogu yu Wenwu* 4:14–34.

Guo, Dashun 1995. "Hongshan anxxd Related Cultures." In *The Archaeology of Northeast China: Beyond the Great Wall*. Edited by S. M. Nelson, 21–64. London, Routledge.

Guo, Moruo 郭沫若 1972. *The Dialectal Development of Ancient Writing: On Script and Writing in Ancient China.* Stockholm: Publications for the Association of Oriental Studies.

Henan Wenwu Kaogu Yanjiusuo 河南省文物考古研究 1999. *Wuyang Jiahu* 舞阳贾湖. Beijing: Kexue chubanshe.

Henan Wenwu Kaogu Yanjiusuo 河南省文物考古研究 2002. "Excavation of the Longshan Culture City-Site at Guchengzhai in Xinmi City, Henan 河南新密市古城寨龙山文化城址发掘简报." *Huaxia Kaogu* 2:53–82.

Henan Wenwu Kaogu Yanjiusuo 河南省文物考古研究 2008. "Excavation of Puchengdian Site in Pingdingshan City, Henan 河南平顶山蒲城店遗址 发掘简报." *Wenwu* 5:32–49.

Henan Wenwu Yanjiusuo 河南省文物研究所 1992. "Excavation of the Site at Haojiatai, Yancheng 郾城郝家台遗址的发掘." *Huaxia Kaogu* 3:62–91.

Henansheng Wenwuju Gongzuodui 河南省文化局文物工作队 1959. "Preliminary Report of the Huizui Site, Yanshi, Henan`河南偃师灰嘴遗址发掘简报." *Wenwu* 12:41–42.

Henan Yihaodui, Zhongguo Shehui Kexueyuan Kaogu Yanjiusuo IA, CASS 中国社会科学院考古研究所河南一队 1982. "Excavation of the Meishan Site in Linru, Henan Province 河南临汝煤山遗址发掘报 告." *Kaogu Xuebao* 4:427–476.

Henan Gongzuodui 1 of IA, CASS 中国社会科学院考古研究所河南一队 1983. "Henan Xinzheng City, Shawoli Neolithic Site 河南新郑沙窝李新石器时代遗址." *Kaogu* 12:1,057–1,065.

Henan Gongzuodui 1 of IA, CASS 中国社会科学院考古研究所河南一队 1984. "The 1979 Peiligang Excavation Report 1979 年裴李岗遗址发掘报告." *Kaogu Xuebao* 1:23–52.

Hung, Ling-yu 2011. *Pottery Production, Mortuary Practice, and Social Complexity in the Majiayao Culture, NW China (ca. 5300–4000 BP).* Washington University.

Jin, Guiyun 靳桂云 2004 "Climate and Environmental Changes of the Mid-Holocene Epoch in North China 燕山 南北长城地带中全新世气候环境的演化及影响." *Kaogu Xuebao* 4:485–505.

Jin, Guiyun 靳桂云 2007. "Excavation and Research on Ancient Chinese Wheat 中国早期小的考古发现与研 究." *Nongye Kaogu* 4:11–20.

Jing, Yuan, and R. K. Flad 2002. "Pig Domestication in Ancient China." *Antiquity* 76(293):724–372.

Jiningshi Wenwu Kaogu Yanjiushi 济宁市文物考古研究室 1996. "Excavation at the Site of Zhangshan in Jining City, Shandong Province 山东济宁市张 山遗址的发掘." *Kaogu* 4:289–295, 316.

Kong, Qingsheng 孔庆生 1996. "The Faunal Remains from the Site of Xiaojingshan 小荆山遗址中的动物遗骸." *Huaxia Kaogu* 2:23–24.

Kong, Qingsheng 孔庆生 2000. *Faunal Remains from the Neolithic Site of Qianbuxia: Collections of Archaeological Reports on the Shandong Highway Project* 山东省高速公路考古报告集. Beijing: Kexue chubanshe.

Li, Fei 李非, S. Li 李水城, and T. Shui 水涛 1993. "Ancient Culture and Environment in the Hulu River Valley 葫芦河流域的古文化与古 环境." *Kaogu* 9:822–842.

Li, Jiazhi 李家治, Z. Zhang 张志刚, Z. Deng 邓泽群, and B. Liang 梁宝鎏 1996. "Research on Early Neolithic Pottery: Discussions of Pottery Origins 新石器时代早期陶 器的研究——兼论中国陶器起源." *Kaogu* 5:83–91.

Li, Xinwei 李 新 伟 2008. *Development of Social Complexity in the Liaoxi Area, Northeast China.* Oxford: British Archaeological Reports.

Li, Xinwei 李 新 伟 2013. "The Later Neolithic Period in the Central Yellow River Valley Area, c. 4000–3000 BCE." In *A Companion to Chinese Archaeology.* Edited by A. Underhill, 213–235. West Sussex: Wiley-Blackwell.

Liang, Siyong 梁思永 1954. "Longshan Culture: One of the Chinese Prehistoric Cultures 龙山文化-中国文明的史 前期之一." *Kaogu xuebao* 7:5–14.

Linfenshi Wenwuju 临汾市文物局 2008. "山西襄汾县陶寺城址发现陶寺文化中期大型夯土建筑基址." *Kaogu* 3:195–198.

Liu, Li 1996. "Mortuary Ritual and Social Hierarchy in the Longshan Culture." *Early China* 21:1–46.

Liu, Li 2004. *The Chinese Neolithic: Trajectories to Early States*. Cambridge, UK: Cambridge University Press.

Liu, Li, and X. Chen 2012. *The Archaeology of China: From the Late Paleolithic to the Early Bronze Age*. Cambridge: Cambridge University Press.

Liu, Li, J. Field, R. Fullagar, C. Zhao, X. Chen, and J. Yu 2010. "A Functional Analysis of Grinding Stones from an Early Holocene Site at Donghulin, North China." *Journal of Archaeological Science* 37(10):2,630–2,639.

Lu, Houyuan, J. Zhang, K. Liu, N. Wu, Y. Li, K. Zhou, M. Ye, T. Zhang, H. Zhang, and X. Yang 2009. "Earliest Domestication of Common Millet (Panicum miliaceum) in East Asia Extended to 10,000 Years Ago." *Proceedings of the National Academy of Sciences* 106(18):7,367–7,372.

Luan, Fengshi 栾丰实 1997. *Archaeological Studies on the Haidai Region* 海岱地区考古研究. Jinan: Shandong Daxue chubanshe.

Luan, Fengshi 栾丰实 1998. "A Study of the Beixin Culture." *Acta Archaeologica Sinica* 3:265–288.

Luan, Fengshi 栾丰实 2013. "The Dawenkou Culture in the Lower Yellow River and Huai River Basin Areas." In *A Companion to Chinese Archaeology*. Edited by A. Underhill, 411–434. West Sussex: Wiley-Blackwell.

McGovern, Patrick, A. P. Underhill, H. Fang, F. Luan, G. R. Hall, H. Yu, C. Wang, F. Cai, Z. Zhao, and G. M. Feinman 2005. "Chemical Identification and Cultural Implications of a Mixed Fermented Beverage from Late Prehistoric China." *Asian Perspectives* 44(2):249–275.

Peterson, Christian 2006. "Crafting" Hongshan Communities? Household Archaeology in the Chifeng Region of Eastern Inner Mongolia, PRC. PhD Diss., Anthropology, University of Pittsburgh.

Peterson, Christian, X. Lu, R. D. Drennan, and D. Zhu 2010. "Hongshan Chiefly Communities in Neolithic Northeastern China." *Proceedings of the National Academy of Sciences* 107(13):5,756–5,761.

Peterson, Christian, and G. Shelach 2010. "The Evolution of Early Yangshao Period Village Organization in the Middle Reaches of Northern China's Yellow River Valley." In *Becoming Villagers: Comparing Early Village Societies*. Edited by M. S. B. J. R. Fox, 246–276. Tucson: Amerind Foundation and University of Arizona Press.

Qi, Guoqin, Z. Lin, and J. An 2006. "Dadiwan yizhi dongwu yicun jianding baogao." In *Qin'an Dadiwan*. Edited by Gansusheng Wenwu Kaogu Yanjiusuo. Beijing: Wenwu Chubanshe.

Qi, Wuyun 齐乌云, J. Wang 王金霞, Z. Liang 梁中合, X. Jia 贾笑冰, J. Wang 王吉怀, Z. Su 苏兆庆, and Y. Liu 刘云涛 2004. "On the Diet of the People Represented by the Human Bones Unearthed from the Upper Shuhe River Valley in Shandong 山东沭河上游出土人骨的食性分析研究." *Huaxia Kaogu* 2:41–47.

Qinghaisheng Wenwu Guanli Chu Kaogudui 青海省文物管理处考古队, and Beijing Daxue Lishixi Kaogu Zhuanye 北京大学历史系考古专业 1976. "Preliminary Results from the First Excavation of Liuwan Primitive Society Graves at Ledu, Qinghai 青海乐都柳湾原始社会墓葬第一次发掘的初步收获." *Wenwu* 1:67–78.

Qinghaisheng Wenwu Guanlichu Kaogudui 青海省文物管理處考古隊, and Zhongguo Shehuikexueyuan Kaogu Yanjiusuo 中國社會科學院考古研究所 1984. *Qinghai Liuwan: The Cemetery of an Early Society at Liuwan in Ledu* 青海柳灣 - 樂都 柳灣原始社會墓地. Beijing, Wenwu chubanshe.

Shandongsheng Wenwu Kaogu Yanjiusuo 山东省文物考古研究所 2000a. "Report on the 1997 Excavation at the Neolithic Site of Xihe in Zhangqiu County, Shandong Province 山东章丘市西河新石器时代遗址 1997 年的发掘." *Kaogu* 10:15–28.

Shandongsheng Wenwu Kaogu Yanjiusuo 山东省文物考古研究所 2000b. "Report on the Excavation of the Xigongqiao Dawenkou Site 山东滕州市西公桥大汶口文化遗址发掘简报." *Kaogu* 10:29–45.

Shandongsheng Wenwu Kaogu Yanjiusuo 山东省文物考古研究所, and Zhangqiushi Bowuguan 章丘市博物馆 2003. "Report on Excavation at the Site of Qianbuxia in Weifang City, Shandong Province 山 东章丘市小荆山后李文化环壕聚落勘探报告." *Huaxia Kaogu* 33:3–11.

Shelach-Lavi, Gideon 1998. "A Settlement Pattern Study in Northeast China: Results and Potential Contributions of Western Theory and Methods to Chinese Archaeology." *Antiquity* 72(275):114–127.

Shelach-Lavi, Gideon 2000. "The Earliest Neolithic Cultures of Northeast China: Recent Discoveries and New Perspectives on the Beginning of Agriculture." *Journal of World Prehistory* 14(4):363–413.

Shelach, Gideon, and M. Y. Teng 2013. "Earlier Neolithic Economic and Social Systems of the Liao River Region, Northeast China." In *A Companion to Chinese Archaeology*. Edited by Anne Underhill, 35–54. West Sussex: Wiley-Blackwell.

Shelach, Gideon 2015. *The Archaeology of Early China*. Cambridge: Cambridge University Press.

Song, Yuqin 2002. *Zhongguo Wenming Qiyuan de Rendi Guanxi Jianlun* 中国文明起源的人地关系简论. Beijing: Kexue Chubanshe.

Sun, Bo 孙 波 2013. "The Longshan Culture of Shandong." In *A Companion to Chinese Archaeology*. Edited by A. Underhill, 435–458. West Sussex: Wiley-Blackwell.

Suo, Xiufen 索秀芬, and S. Li 李少兵 2011. "Xinglongwa Periodization and Dating 兴隆洼文化分期与年代." *Wenwu* 8:47–54.

Suo, Xiufen 索秀芬, and S. Li 李少兵 2013. "Typological Research into the Xinglongwa Culture 兴隆洼文化的类型研究." *Kaogu* 11:52–61.

Tong, Weihua 佟伟华 1984. "Origins of Agriculture and Related Questions at the Cishan Site 磁山遗址的原始农业 及其相关问题." *Nongye Kaogu* 1:194–207.

Underhill, Anne P. 1997. "Current Issues in Chinese Neolithic Archaeology." *Journal of World Prehistory* 11(2):103–160.

Underhill, Anne P. 2000. "An Analysis of Mortuary Ritual at the Dawenkou Site, Shandong, China." *Journal of East Asian Archaeology* 2(1) 93–127.

Underhill, Anne P. 2002. *Craft Production and Social Change in Northern China*. New York: Springer.

Underhill, Anne P. 2013. *A Companion to Chinese Archaeology*. West Sussex: Wiley-Blackwell.

Wang, Fen 王 芬 2013. "The Houli and Beixin Cultures." In *A Companion to Chinese Archaeology*. Edited by A. P. Underhill, 389–410. West Sussex: Wiley-Blackwell.

Wang, Hui 王辉 2012. "Variants and Patterns in the Neolithic and Bronze Age Cultures of the Gansu-Qinghai Region 甘青地区新石器-青铜时代考古学文化的谱系与格局." *Kaoguxue yanjiu* 9:210–243.

Womack, Andrew, Y. Jaffe, J. Zhou, L. Hung, H. Wang, S. Li, P. Chen, and R. Flad 2017. "Mapping Qijiaping: New Work on the Type-Site of the Qijia Culture (2300–1500 BCE) in Gansu Province, China." *Journal of Field Archaeology* 42(6):488–502.

Womack, Andrew, H. Wang, J. Zhou, and R. Flad 2019. "A Petrographic Analysis of clay Recipes in Late Neolithic North-Western China: Continuity and Change." *Antiquity* 93(371):1161–1177.

Xie, Duanjie 謝端琚 2002. *Prehistoric Archaeology of the Gansu and Qinghai Region* 甘青地區史前考古. Beijing, Wenwu chubanshe.

Yang, Hu 杨虎, and G. Liu 刘国祥 1997. "Inquiry into the Graves within Houses of the Xinglongwa Culture and Related Questions 兴隆洼文化居室葬俗及相关问题探讨." *Kaogu* 1:27–36.

Yu, Chongyuan 于崇源 2002. "Analysis of the Xinle Culture 新乐文化浅析." *Shiqian Yanjiu* :297–300.

Zhang, Dongju, F. Chen, R. L. Bettinger, L. Barton, D. Ji, C. Morgan, H. Wang, X. Cheng, G. Dong, T. P. Guilderson, and H. Zhao 2010. "Archaeological Records of Dadiwan in the Past 60 ka and the Origin of Millet Agriculture." *Chinese Science Bulletin* 55(16):1, 636–1,642.

Zhang, Jiangkai 张江凯, and J. Wei 魏峻著 2004. *Neolithic Archaeology, Xin shi qi shi dai kao gu* 新石器时代考古. Beijing, Wenwu chubanshe.

Zhang, Zhongpei 张忠培 1985. "The Social Structure Reflected in the Yuanjunmiao Cemetery." *Journal of Anthropological Archaeology* 4(1):19–33.

Zhao, Chunqing 赵春青 2013. "The Longshan Culture in Central Henan Province, c. 2600–1900 BC." In *A Companion to Chinese Archaeology*. Edited by A. Underhill, 236–254. West Sussex: Wiley-Blackwell.

Zhongguo Kexueyuan Kaogu Yanjiusuo Gansu Gongzuodui 中国科学院考古研究所甘肃工作队 1974. "Excavation Report for the Site of Dahezhuang in Yongjing County, Gansu 甘肃永靖大 何庄遗址发掘报告." *Kaogu Xuebao* 2:29–62.

Zhongguo Shehui Kexueyuan Kaogu Yanjiusuo 中国社会科学院考古研究所 1988. *Report of Sanlihe Site in Jiaoxian* 胶县三里河. Beijing: Cultural Relics Publishing House.

Zhongguo Shehui Kexueyuan Kaogu Yanjiusuo 中国社会科学院考古研究所 1999. *Environmental Archaeology of Shell Midden Sites in East Shandong Peninsula* 胶东半岛贝丘遗址环境考古. Beijing: Sheke wenxian.

Zhongguo Shehui Kexueyuan Kaogu Yanjiusuo 中国社会科学院考古研究所, and Shanxi Gongzuodui Linfen Diqu Wenhuaju 山西工作队临汾地区文化局. 1983. "Excavation of Taofen Temple Cemetery, Xiangfen, Shanxi, 1978-1980, 1978—1980 年山西襄汾陶寺墓地发掘简报." *Kaogu* 1:30–42.

Zhongguo Shehui Kexueyuan Kaogu Yanjiusuo 中国社会科学院考古研究所, and Henan Wenwu Kaogu Yanjiusuo 河南省文物考古研究 2010. *Xipo Cemetery in Lingbao* 灵宝西坡墓地. Beijing: Wenwu chubanshe.

Zhongguo Shehui Kexueyuan Kaogu Yanjiusuo Shanxi Gongzuodui 中国社会科学院考古研究所山西工作队, and Linfen Diqu Wenhuaju 临汾地区文化局 1983. "Excavation Report of the 1978-1980 Season at the Taosi Site, Linfen, Shanxi 1978-1980 年山西襄汾陶寺墓地发掘简报." *Kaogu* 1:30–42.

Zhongguo Shehui Kexueyuan Kaogu Yanjiusuo Neimenggu Gongzuodui 中国社会科学院考古研究所内蒙古工作队 1985. "A Report on the Excavation of the Xinglongwa Site, Aohan Banner, Inner Mongolia 内蒙古敖汉旗兴隆洼遗址发掘简报." *Kaogu* 10:865–874.

Zhongguo Shehui Kexueyuan Kaogu Yanjiusuo Neimenggu Gongzuodui 中国社会科学院考古研究所内蒙古工作队 1988. "Preliminary Report on the Excavation of Zhaobaogou Site Number One, Aohan Banner, Inner Mongolia 内蒙古敖汉旗赵宝沟一号遗址发掘简报." *Kaogu* 1:1–6.

Zhongguo Shehui Kexueyuan Kaogu Yanjiusuo Shandongdui 中国社会科学院考古研究所山东队 1984. "Report on Beixin Culture Remains in Tengxian County, Shandong Province 山东滕县北辛遗址发掘报告." *Kaogu Xuebao* 2:159–191.

Zhu, Yanping 朱延平 1990. "Analysis of the 'Birds and Beast Drawing' on the Zun Vessel from Xiaoshan 小山尊形器"鸟兽图"试析." *Kaogu* 4:360–365.

Zhu, Yanping 朱延平 2013. "The Early Neolithic in the Central Yellow River Valley, c. 7000, BCE." In *A Companion to Chinese Archaeology*. Edited by A. Underhill, 169–193. West Sussex: Wiley-Blackwell.

CHAPTER 2

···

THE NEOLITHIC REVOLUTION IN THE SOUTH CA. 7/6000–2000 BCE: MAJIABANG, HEMUDU, DAXI, AND SONGZE CULTURES

···

BY XIANGMING FANG, ZHEJIANG INSTITUTE
OF ARCHAEOLOGY

THE evolution of the Neolithic Age in southern China can be traced back as early as one to two million years ago to the sites of Yuchanyai in Hunan and to Rentong and Diaotonghuan sites in Wannianxian, Jiangxi province. We concentrate here on the last phase from 7000 to 2000 bce as the era representing the Neolithic revolution in south China. The middle and lower reaches of the Yangzi River are the main areas for these archaeological cultures. The middle reaches include chronologically Pengtoushan-Chengbei and Tangjia → Daxi → Qujialing → Shijiahe → Late Shijiahe (see Figure 1), and the lower reaches include Shanshang–Xiao Huangshan → Kuahuqiao → Majiabang-Hemudu → Lingjiatan-Songze → Liangzhu → Qianshanyang-Guangfulin (Figure 2). As analyzed in this chapter, specialized features of this Neolithic phase in the south include rice farming and agriculture, dug-out circumscribing trench settlements, platform altars, and precocious arts.

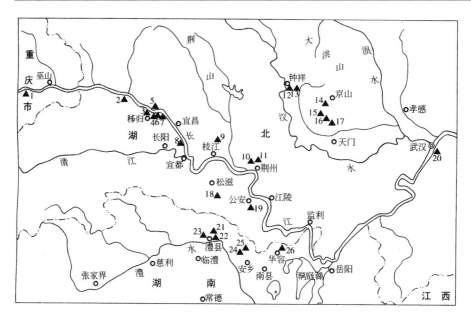

FIGURE 1 Distribution of major sites of the Daxi Culture. 1. Wushan Daxi 2. Zigui Gongjia Dagou 3. Zigui Chaotianzui 4. Yichang Zhongbaodao 5. Yichang Wuxiangmiao 6. Yichang Yangjiawang 7. Yichang Qingshuinan 8. Yichang Honghuatao 9. Zhijiang Guanmiaoshan 10. Jiangling Zhujiatai 11. Jiangling Maojiashan 12. Zhongxiang Liuhe 13. Zhongxiang Bianfan 14. Jingshan Zhujiazui 15. Jingshan Chujialing 16. Jingshan Youziling 17. Tianmen Tanjialing 18. Songze Guihuashu 19. Gongan Wangjiagang 20. Wuchang Fangyingtai 21. Fengxian Sanyuangong 22. Fengxian Dingjiagang 23. Fengxian Chengtoushaan 24. Anxiang Huachenggang 25. Anxiang Yangjiagang 26. Haurong Chengushan.

BEGINNING OF RICE FARMING AND AGRICULTURAL ADVANCES

The middle and lower reaches of the Yangzi River are the main source of rice farming during the Neolithic, as represented at the sites of Shanshang, Pujiang in Zhejiang, and Pengtoushan in Lixian, Hunan (Zhejiang 2016b:253; Hunan 2006:182). Rice remains at these sites can be traced back to 8000 to 6500 bce. In the lower strata of the Shangshan site, common rice husk, rice leaf, and rice stem remain as carboniferous material in pottery. This condition indicates that the food resource of rice had become an important part of the economic life of the local mountain people. On the basis of remains in ceramics, it is evident that the practice of rice farming had already begun. Analytical results showed that the rice husk had the same characteristics as the cultivated rice, and the rice hull shape had the short and wide, non-wild types. During the Hemudu cultural period, although fishing and hunting economies occupied a considerable proportion of their livelihood, a mature rice agriculture was also in evidence. A large mass of rice accumulation is represented within the first phase of the Hemudu culture at Yuyao site (Figure 3). Just 7 km southwest

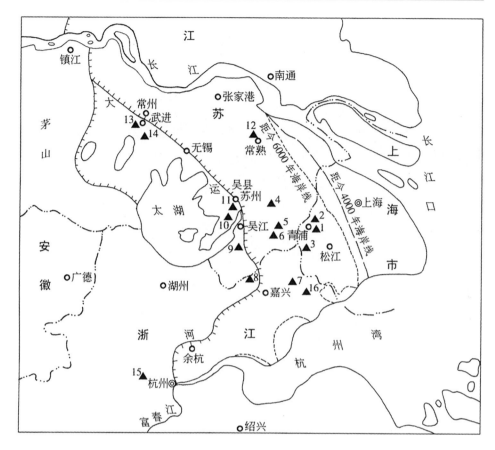

FIGURE 2 Distribution of major remains of the Songze Culture. 1. Qingpu, Songze; 2. Qingpu, Fuquanshan; 3. Songjiang, Tangmiao; 4. Wuxian, Caoxieshan; 5. Wuxian, Zhanglingshan; 6. Wuxian, Denghu; 7. Jiaxing, Dawen; 8. Jiaxing, Shuangqiao; 9. Wujiang, Longnan; 10. Suzhou, Yuecheng; 11. Zhangjiagang, Xujiawan; 12. Changxu Qiandigang; 13. Wujing, Sidun; 14. Changzhou, Yudun; 15. Yuhang, Wujiabu; 16. Jiaxing, Nanhebang (Shiqian Dili Yanjiu 1984).

of Yuyao at Tianluoshan site, two layers of cultural settlement provided two layers of ancient paddy fields (Beijing Daxue 2011:16).

The lower strata currently is the earliest known from any prehistoric site in China. These paddy fields also show a direct association with the village layout. More than one ridge of a paddy field and field paths along with external channels were also unearthed. In the southern part of Majiabang site in Jiaxing, Zhejiang Province, soil samples were deeply drilled by scale probe rods, thus providing further evidence of the rice-farming areas. These were confirmed by phytolithic and seed analysis (Zhonggong Zhejiang 2016:37). Hemudu and Majiabang rice cultural remains from subsequent Songze and Liangzhu cultural eras continue to serve as pioneers of highly developed rice agriculture (also see Fuller et al. 2015).

The plow is the representative tool for rice farming of the Hemudu and Majiabang cultures. Bone and wooden plows have been unearthed at Zhejiang's Yuyao Hemudu,

FIGURE 3 First phase rice paddy accumulation within the Hemudu ruins (Zhejiang 2003: colorplate 41.2).

Yuyao Tianluoshan, Tongxiang Luojiajiao, and at Changxing Jiang Jiashan sites (see for example Zhejiang 2003:colorplate 1). Up to 154 examples of plows were excavated from the earliest layer of cultural remains at Hemudu sites. Most were bone plows, primarily created from deer scapula. Other plow materials included rhinoceros iliac bones, bones from other large-scale animals, and some bones larger than the tiger's shoulder blade (Zhejiang 2007:12; Luojiajiao 1981:28; Zhejiang 2009a:67). The example, Hemudu T224 (4):175 bone plow (Figure 4) is constructed out of a Sika deer scapula, and its shallow groove still retains the residual handle that would have been tied to a pole, measuring a length of 18 cm, with a blade width of 9.8 cm (Zhejiang 2003:85). Based on experimental use of the bone plow in a marsh wetland environment, it is evident that bone plows could easily be used to open drainage channels and promote production efficiency.

Stone plows appeared during the Songze cultural period alongside other new agricultural production tools. The largest number of unearthed stone plows come from a late-Songze-culture cemetery in Pashan, Huzhou, Zhejiang (Zhejiang 2006:452–455). Out of 61 tombs, 21 stone plows were unearthed. The stone plows formed isosceles triangles with double-waisted blades and a concave posterior edge. Holes for binding averaged over 1.3 cm wide. The stone plow unearthed from the Songze-culture site at Jiangjiashan, Changxing in Zhejiang has a triangular plowshare, side wings, and a

FIGURE 4 Hemudu site T224 (4):175 bone plow (Zhejiang 2003: colorplate 26.1).

combined length of 35 cm (Figure 5). During the Liangzhu cultural period, the stone plow shape was enlarged and its use expanded to extend over a larger geographical range, incorporating the Taihu Basin to Qiantang River to the southeast of Zhejiang Province and Zhoushan Islands. The split stone plow from the Liangzhu cultural site at Zhuangqiao, Pinghu, Zhejiang measured a total length of 51 cm, and the head part showed use and traces of wood measuring 106 cm long (Zhejiang 2005:13) This agricultural tool is consistent functionally with the *li* 犁 plow used in later historical contexts.

Rice farming requires the formation of paddy fields, complex water irrigation systems, and timely sunshine. The development and maturation of rice farming is thus naturally bound to promote the process of social complexity and changes in settlement patterns.

SETTLEMENT STRATEGIES

With the expansion of settlement and community size, construction technology made rapid progress, especially in wood and wood technology. For example, mortise and tenon components were complex in including various formations, such as a stump tenon, beam head tenon, pin hole tenon, dovetail and flat body column eyes, corner

FIGURE 5 In situ context of stone plow blades from the Jiangjiashan Songze cultural site (Zhejiang and Liangzhu Bowuguan 2014:230).

column insert eyes, straight railings with insert eyes, cutting boards, as well as cutting and digging tenons (see Figure 6). Other highly skilled aspects of processing technology were unearthed at Hemudu, Tianluoshan, and other Hemudu cultural sites (Zhejiang 2003:14–27, 2007:6). Regarding wood structures and the history of wood construction, the Hemudu culture maintains a pivotal position. According to the direction and combination of rows of piles, it is presumed that at least six aboveground column-type buildings (including the longest, No. 10) were constructed. The wall of one building, No. 10, has a breadth of at least 23 m and a depth of about 7 m. Another 1.3 m-long front porch aligned a long hall. The discovery of these long houses shows that the basic unit of the internal organization of the settlement was dominated by the extended family. Common wells served these settlements and accommodated a village's living requirements.

A multi-level wooden wall representing architecture with columns, a wooden bridge, a food storage pit, sporadic tombs, and a wooden fence of a wooden bridge with external road were uncovered at the Tianluoshan site. The bridge was a single-plank bridge (Figure 7).

The development of column architecture was relatively advanced in the lower reaches of the Yangzi River during this period. Building No. 22 at the Daxi-culture site in Hubei at Zhijian, Guanmiaoshan revealed a wall base of nearly 6 m, with a door

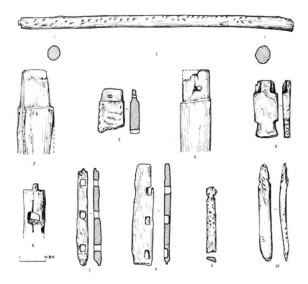

FIGURE 6 Wood remains showing various mortise and tenon components used in building at Hemudu, Yaoshan, Zhejiang (Zhejiang 2003:23, figure 110).

FIGURE 7 Edge of the village with wooden fence and single-plank style bridge thoroughfare at Tianluoshan (Zhejiang 2007:29).

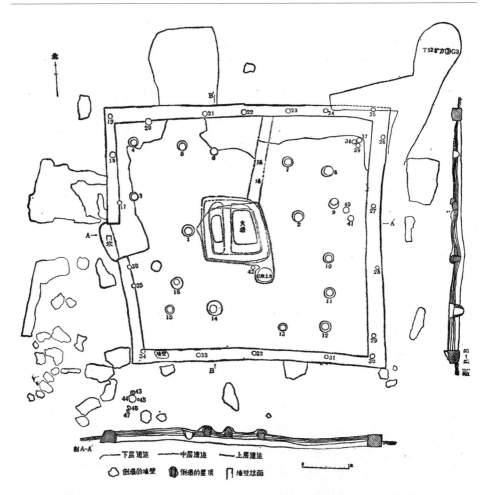

FIGURE 8 Ground plan of F22 at Guanmiaoshan site (Hubei 1983:22, figure 6).

opening to the west and outside a baked red earthen pavement for running water (Zhongguo 1983:22; Figure 6). The walls, supported by columns, were created out of a raw clay mixed with sand and soil. Inner and outer walls were apparently fired and then painted. Larger sets of inner columns supported the house and possibly further walls. A hearth lay at the center. Many similar large houses with fireplaces were excavated at Guanmiaoshan site in Hubei (Figure 8). The discovery of such large-scale houses not only exhibits the progress of construction technology but also the internalization of settlement and the differentiation of family, which is one major prelude of social complexity. The clear-cut distinction between large- and small-scale houses underscores the evolution of a settlement's internal unit and family differentiation.

With the expansion of the population and of settlements, tremendous changes occurred. During the Majiabang cultural phase, sites such as Changxing Jiangjiashan

FIGURE 9 Birds-eye view of Chengtoushan, Hunan (Hunan 2007:colorplate 1).

and Anji Zhili in Zhejiang developed what is known as trench settlement, or settlements surrounded by dug-out ditches (Zhejiang 2009b: 61, 64).

The earliest urban settlement in the Yangzi River Valley is the ancient city site of Chengtoushan in Song County, Hunan Province, dated to the Daxi cultural period. The ancient city is enclosed by a circular trench and short wall. The diameter is about 300 m and the city area is about 80,000 m². Three entrances open on eastern, southern, and northern sides. The settlement is equipped with a large altar; a sacrificial pit; and areas designed for burial, pottery workshops, residences, and other necessities. Rice fields lie to the northeast and south of the settlement. Boats, boat paddles, and other boat relics were unearthed from the trench surrounding this site, indicating that the trenches had an external transport function (Figure 9).

FIGURE 10 Remains of a canoe unearthed at Xiaoshan Kuahuqiao (Zhejiang and Xiaoshan 2007:colorplate 9).

As early as 6000 bce, a large canoe with a residual length of 5.6 m was unearthed at the site of Kuahuqiao, Xiaoshan in Zhejiang (Figure 10). Tianluoshan at Yuyao site also has a model canoe (Hemudu 2007). At Hemudu and Tianluoshan sites a considerable amount of wood pulp was unearthed. Evidently boat technology was advanced at this early date, allowing for the expansion and production of living space of the ancients. Communication and trade undoubtedly expanded with the convenience of river navigation.

During the Songze cultural period, in the lower reaches of the Yangzi River people living in mountainous and hilly areas of northwestern Zhejiang and Ningzhen began to migrate to the swamp plains on a larger scale due to the change of the natural environment, the cause of which is not entirely clear. Sites within the Hangzhou-Jiaxing-Huzhou plain increase in number and scale (Wang 2007:33). New architectural settlements resemble the popular man-made high earthen platform so well-known

FIGURE 11 Panoramic view of the Nanhebang altar, Jiaxing, Zhejiang (Nanhebang 2003).

during the Liangzhu cultural period. The earliest altar of the Songze culture exists at Nanhebang site in Jiaxing, Zhejiang (Figure 11). It lies in a slightly north-south direction, forms a rectangular pyramidal-shaped platform, with a top measuring 10 m wide from east to west, a remnant 10.5 m north-south, and an existing height of 1 m. Such raised earthen platforms are a quintessential feature of later Liangzhu cultural sites. Puanqiao site in Tongxiang, Zhejiang, dating to the late Songze to Liangzhu cultural eras, exemplifies an early intact settlement unit, which began with the construction of three man-made earthen platforms, upon which were constructed houses and burials (China Japan Joint Archeological Team 2014). Due to garbage and daily-use remains accumulating between these platforms, and the reconstruction of houses alongside tombs, the site eventually grew into a vast, east-west, pier-shaped large-scale platform. The settlement evolution of the Puanqiao site is representative of other Liangzhu-culture sites and settlements of the same and later periods (Figure 12).

ADVANCED HANDICRAFTS AND ART

To this author, Neolithic art represents a combination of economic needs and beliefs. Advanced handicraft art products also reflect the identity of the owner and social status. The arts of painting, sculpting, and engraving appear as early as 6000 bce, as represented, for example, by images of the sun on a ceramic shard from the site of Kuahuqiao (Figure 13). The subject is nature and its most revered object of worship—the sun (Zhejiang 2004:56–63).

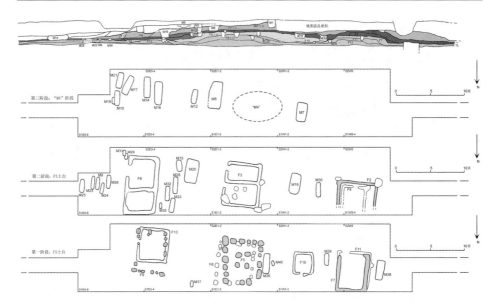

FIGURE 12 Three stages in the evolution of the Pu'anqiao site (Zhejiang and Pu'anqiao 2014:135, figure 1).

FIGURE 13 Image of the sun on a ceramic shard T202(2):9 from Kuahuqiao, Xiaoshan, Zhejiang.

During the Hemudu cultural period, the main artistic theme shows a combination of images, including the bird—the one with the obvious power to fly in the sky—and the circle, symbolizing light of the sky. The bone utensil from Hemudu T21(4):18 has engraved images of two groups of opposing-profile birds enclosing what has been identified most convincingly by Hayashi Minao as symbols of "daylight" and "moonlight" (Figure 14; Hayashi 1992). The two circles enclosed by the profile birds are differentiated: one is surrounded by emanating linear rays, and the other is without rays, suggesting the two images refer to the celestial symbols of sunlight and moonlight, respectively. This kind of double-bird image of light is also represented elsewhere on Hemudu-culture handicrafts of different materials and forms, for example on bone objects in butterfly

FIGURE 14 Bone carving, Hemudu site T21(4):18, 14.5 cm long (Zhejiang 2009:47).

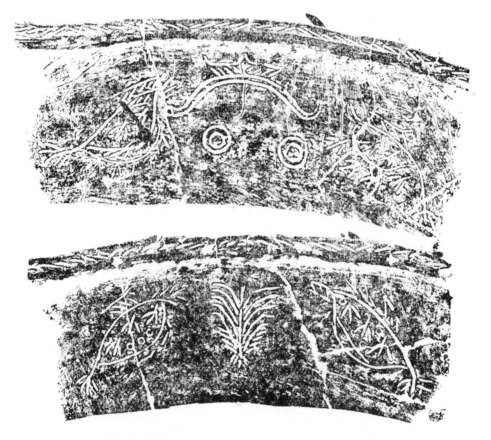

FIGURE 15 Rubbing of décor on ceramic bowl T29(4):46, Hemudu, Yuyao, Zhejiang.

shapes (editor's note: identified as atlatls, see Childs-Johnson and Major forthcoming). The products of light, which bring plant growth and fertility, are also represented by the image of luxuriantly sprouting leaves of cultivated plants (see for example Figure 15). The walls, inside, and outside of a ceramic bowl from Hemudu, T29(4):46, for example, are carved with various images: on the abdomen with birds and plants, and with birds and sun and moon symbols (also known as an "abstract human face"). This combination of images reflects three objects of worship: birds, light, and plant growth.

Another unique artistic product coming out of the Tangjiagang culture in the middle reaches of the Yangzi River is the deliberately chosen and meticulously decorated white clay ceramic. The largest number of stamped white ceramics come from the lower strata at Gaomiao site in Hongjiang, Hunan. White pottery, as represented at Tangjiagang site on the northwest shore of Dongting Lake in Anxiang, Hunan, are rich although not great in number and derive mostly from burials. In addition to a geometric stamped décor are other images representing various symbols and subjects, including the sun, birds, animal fangs, and other animal patterns. Representative of the geometric pattern is the octagonal star composition stamped into the center of the white clay bowl from Tangjiagang (Figure 16). These white clay ceramics were not for everyday use: they were status symbols of wealth and possibly functioned ritually. The white pottery décor and vessel types of the Tangjiagang culture are found throughout the Yuan River and the Xiangjiang River to the Pearl River Delta in Shenzhen and elsewhere; through the Han River, spreading as far as the Hanzhong Basin at Longzhengsi in Shaanxi; and along the Yangzi River all the way to the Taihu Basin and Tongxiangluo in Zhejiang. The spread and diffusion of white pottery describe a microcosm of Neolithic cultural exchanges in south China.

FIGURE 16   White clay bowl from Tangjiagang site, Hunan, M43:1 (Hunan 2013:colorplate 39).

The Songze cultural period is a vibrant and creative era, particularly as expressed in its public awareness and humor. Art from this period may be described as "liberated" 开放中的美术, but it is also a reflection of the close integration between belief and respect for artistic form. Ceramic vessels may be crafted in the form of an eagle and other living animal shapes. Images of a pair of turtles, as represented at Nanhebang site in Jiaxiang (Figure 17:1), were found below the corpse, as a pair, one slightly larger than the other. Both turtles have six feet and one has no tail. Their shells are decorated with raised nodules, numbering 11 in one case and 9 in the other. From large graves at Jiaxing art works also included human-headed gourd-shaped bottles and *he* pitcher vessels with incised bird motifs (Figure 17:2–5; Zhejiang 2005:118, 122; Zhejiang 2014:88; Zhejiang 2006:150; Changzhou 2012:143).

These bird motifs are similar to those more geometric and abstract motifs decorating spinning wheel whorls from Jiangjiashan at Changxing, Zhejiang as well as other art works from Xingang in Changzhou, Jiangsu (see Figure 17:5). Such widespread distribution and over such a long period of time underscores a profound belief in what could be represented both abstractly and representationally. The image appears, for example, as an abstract whirling bird with wings on a ceramic pig sculpture from the early Hemudu-Majiabang culture (Figure 17:5), on the bird ceramic, and around the edge of a white ceramic bowl (Figure 17:3–4). Since the pig was a significant part of meat production and the economy, it is only logical to connect it with the symbol of spirit sustenance in combination with the sun and bird symbol.

By the later phase of the Songze cultural period, the pattern of a circle framed by arching triangles appears as a popular motif decorating ceramics. Since this abstract motif emphasizes the center of the circle framed by what are simplifications of wing parts, the image most likely derives from the profile birds framing light symbols, and perhaps here primarily sunlight. According to an analysis of vessels unearthed in Huzhou, Zhejiang Province, the circle and arc pattern can be divided into five types of combinations that harmonize in form and rhythm (Zhejiang 2006:446–450). Although abstract and geometric, the image nonetheless is interchangeable with the more realistic interpretations of sun and light in combination with celestial birds, as represented on the bone carving from Hemudu (Figure 14).

The circle and arc pattern of Songze art also appears on openwork ceramic vessel stools from the Dawenkou culture in the Haidai region and may complement the circle and petal pattern painted on ceramics from the Yangshao culture. The suggestion is that the whirling symbol refers to the sun and its rotation, and thus probably to a practice of sun worship. This whirling sun pattern and symbol appears to have been transplanted during the era of the Liangzhu culture, with the large eyes of the face of the humanoid spirit power represented on jade art works.

Of course, the most important phenomenon in southern China during the period of 6000 to 5300 bce is the beginning of what has been identified as a "Jade Age" (Mou and Wu 1997; Childs-Johnson 2001:187–198, 2009:291–393). Jade products are represented at Kuahuqiao, Hemudu, and Pengtoushan sites and *huan* and *jue* jade rings had appeared in the Hemudu culture and Majiabang cultural periods. However, at this time stone

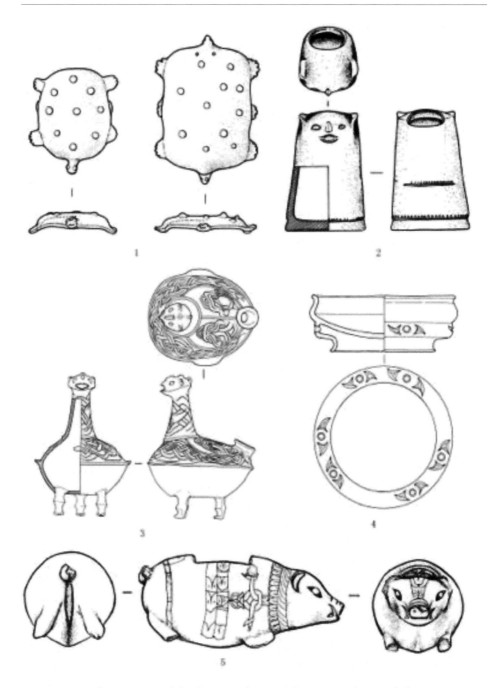

FIGURE 17 1. Ceramic arts of the Songze culture. 2. Ceramic turtles, Nanhebang, M27:14,15. 3. Animal-shaped *hu*, Nanhebang M59:22. 4. Bird-shaped *he* vessel (large grave). 5. *Pan* basin (Kunshan M47:9). 6. Ceramic pig (Xingang M39:5) (Zhejiang 2005:118–122; Zhejiang and Liangzhu Museum 2014:88; Zhejiang and Huzhou City Museum , 2006:150; Changzhou Museum 2012:143).

FIGURE 18   Anhui Lingjiatan Yizhi 87M11:7 Jade *huang*, front and back.

working mainly involved quartz, fluorite, and other stones. The exploitation and abrasive techniques of working "true jade" or tremolite nephrite began at Lingjiatan-Songze cultural sites (Qin 2014). Translucent nephrites are completely different from quartz, agate, fluorite, pyrophyllite, and related materials, since they have a very dense mineral structure, which can be polished to produce a moist and elegant luster. Furthermore tremolite nephrite resources are extremely scarce. The process of creating and using a rotary wheel are also completely different. One must use a slurry or solution in order to abrade the stone. The latter consumed much more time and labor than ceramic and bone working. This did not occur before or elsewhere than the Lingjiatan-Songze culture located in the lower reaches of the Yangzi River in southern China, where jade resources are located. Eight hundred and four pieces of jade were unearthed from 29 tombs in 1987 and 1999 (Anhui 2006). These jade ornaments include head ornaments, *huang* rings, sets of *huan* and *jue*, ax heads, human figurines, turtles, eagles, incised plaques, and large *huang* whose edges are incised with the zigzag symbol of sunlight. The latter type of jade *huang* is a typical Lingjiatan-culture jade (Figure 18) and is found spread amid cultures along the Yangzi River as far as Daxi sites, the Ningzhen region, and the area southwest of Lake Tai.

In 2007, 200 pieces of jade out of 330 objects were unearthed from tomb M23 at Lingjiatan 07M23 (Figure 19). Both ends of the coffin were decorated with groups of *huang* rings. The *huang* also decorated the owner's arms in bracelet sets. *Yue* ax heads

FIGURE 19 View of the burial 07M23 at Lingjiatan, Hanshan, Anhui.

also formed a major group of the burial's jades. In addition, a group of three jade turtles were carefully placed in the crotch of the deceased, and a jade pig weighing 88 kg was on the top of the body of the deceased.

Based on the analysis of human bones and burial goods within the cemetery at Chuoqun, Kunshan in Jiangsu, jades were primarily owned by the female sex—a very significant phenomenon of the Songze cultural period. Women at this stage occupied the main position within the community and society, maintaining social stability and cohesion (Shanghai 1987:98–105; Suzhou 2011:233–235). According to scientific and burial data of the Chuoqun cemetery, females (as opposed to males) were predominantly buried with jade *huang*, making it obvious that women at this stage occupied the main position of the community.

BIBLIOGRAPHY

Anhuisheng Wenwu Kaogu Yanjiusuo 安徽省文物考古研究所 2006. *Lingjiatan: No. 1 Field Archaeological Report* 凌家滩——田野考古发掘报告之一. Beijing: Wenwu chubanshe.

Bejing Daxue Zhongguo Kaoguxue Yanjiu Zhongxin, Zhejiangsheng Wenwu Kaogu Yanjiu suo 北京大学中国考古学研究中心、浙江省文物考古研究所 2011. *Comprehensive Research on the Natural Remains from Tianluoshan Site* 田螺山遗址自然遗存综合研究. Beijing: Wenwu chubanshe.

Changzhou 常州博物馆 2012. *Changzhou Xingang: Excavation Report on a Neolithic Culture Site* 常州新岗——新石器时代文化遗址发掘报告. Beijing: Wenwu chubanshe.

Childs-Johnson, Elizabeth 2001. "The Jade Age of Early China: Three Significant Jade Working Cultures during the Pivotal Period 4000–2000 bce." In *Haixia Liangan Guyu Xuehui Yilunwen Zhuankan*, vol. 1. 187–198. Taipei: Taiwan National University Press.

Childs-Johnson, Elizabeth 2009. "The Art of Working Jade and the Rise of Civilization in China." In *The Jade Age*. 291–393. Beijing: Kexue chubanshe.

Childs-Johnson, Elizabeth and John Major. Forthcoming. *Metamorphic Imagery in Early Chinese Art and Religion*.

Fengying et al 风英等 1984. "The Prehistoric Coastline based on Fengying et al," 石前海岸线依据潘凤英等 1984 "全世界以来苏南地区的古地李演变, *Dili yanjiu* 3.3.

Fuller, Dorian, Emma Harvey, and Ling Qin 2015. "Presumed Domestication? Evidence for Wild Rice Cultivation and Domestication in the Fifth Millennium BC of the Lower Yangtze Region." *Antiquity* 81(312):316–331. https://doi.org/10.1017/S0003598X0009520X.

Hayashi, Minao 林巳奈夫 1992. *"The Appearance of Rising and Twisting (推昂形) of 'qi [Life Breath' as Represented in Ancient China* "中國古代遺物上所表示的"氣"之推昂形的表現." Translated by Yang Meili. Gugong xuekan 9:31–74.

Hemudu Yizhi Bowuguan 河姆渡遗址博物馆 2007. *The Southeast's Dynastic Beginnings: Illustrations of the Hemudu Culture* 潮起东南——河姆渡文化图录. Hangzhou: Zhejiang sheying chubanshe.

Hunansheng Wenwu Kaogu Yanjiusuo 2006. 湖南省文物考古研究所 Pengtoushan and Bashidang 彭头山与八十垱. Beijing: Wenwu chubanshe.

Hunansheng Wenwu Kaogu Yanjiusuo 湖南省文物考古研究所 2007. *Lixian Chengtoushan: Neolithic Site Excavation Report* 澧县城头山-新石器时代遗址发掘报告. Beijing: Wenwu chubanshe.

Hunan 2014. 湖南省文物考古研究所编 *Anxiang Tang Jiagang: Neolithic Site Excavation Report* 安详躺家岗新石器时代报告. Beijing: Kexue chubanshe.

Luojiajiao Kaogudui 罗家角考古队, and Zhejiangsheng Wenwu Kaogusuo 浙江省文物 考古所 1981. *Excavation Report on the Remains at Luojiajiao in Tongxiangxian* 桐乡县罗家角遗址发掘报告. Beijing: Wenwu chubanshe.

Mou Yongkang 牟永抗, and Wu Naisong 吴汝祚 1997. "Analysis of the Era of the Jade Age: An Important Model for Production during the Age of Chinese Civilization 浅析玉器时代-中华文明时代的重要生产模式." In *Kaoguxue wenhua lunji*, vol. 4: 164–187. Edited by Su Bingqi. Beijing: Wenwu chubanshe.

Qin, L. 秦岭 2014. "The Early Phase Burials and Songze-Style Jade Objects from the Pu'anqiao Site, Tongxiang 同乡普安遗遗址早期墓葬及松泽风格土器。In *Collection of Excavation Reports of Songze Cultural Sites in Northern Zhejiang 1996–2014* 浙北崧泽文化考古报告集 1996–2014, 134–159. Ed by Zhejiang Provincial Institute of Cultural Relics and Archeology.

Shanghaishi Wenwu Baoguan Weiyuanhui 上海市文物保管委员会 1987. *Songze: Excavation Report on the Neolithic Remains* 崧泽——新石器时代遗址发掘报告. Beijing: Wenwu chubanshe.

Suzhoushi Kaogu Yanjiusuo 苏州市考古研究所 2011. *Remains of Chuoshan, Kundun* 昆山绰墩遗址. Beijing: Wenwu chubanshe.

Wang, Ningyuan 王宁远 2007. *Yaoyuan Village: Settlement and Residential Types of the Liangzhu Culture* 遥远的村落——良渚文化的聚落和居住形态. Hangzhou: Zhejiang sheying chubanshe.

Zhejiangsheng Wenwu Kaogu Yanjiushuo 浙江省 文物考古研究所 2003. *Hemudu: A Neolithic Archaeological Site* 河姆渡——新石器时代遗址考古报告. Beijing: Wenwu Chubanshe.

Zhejiangsheng Wenwu Kaogu Yanjiusuo 浙江省 文物考古研究所 2005. *Excavation Report on Songze Site Cultural Relics at Nanhebang: A New Era of Archaeology* 南河浜——崧泽文化遗址发掘报告. Beijing: Wenwu chubanshe.

Zhejiangsheng Wenwu Kaogu Yanjiusuo 浙江省 文物考古研究所 2009a. *New Age of Zhejiang Archeology* 浙江考古新纪元. Beijing: Zhongguo kexue chubanshe.

Zhejiangsheng Wenwu Kaogu Yanjiusuo 浙江省 文物考古研究所 2009b. *Neolithic Remains at Jiangjiashan, Changxing* 长兴江家山新石器时代遗 Beijing: Kexue chubanshe.

Zhejiangsheng Wenwu Kaogu Yanjiusuo 浙江省 文物考古研究所 2014. *Northern Zhejiang Songze Cultural Archaeological Report* (1996 ~ 2014) 浙北崧泽文化考古报告集. Beijing: Wenwu chubanshe.

Zhejiangsheng Wenwu Kaogu Yanjiusuo 浙江省文物考古研究所，湖州市博物馆 2012. *Pine Mountain* 崧山. Beijing: Wenwu chubanshe.

Zhejiangsheng Wenwu Kaogu Yanjiusuo, Huzhoushi Bowuguan 浙 江省文物考古研究所、湖州市博物馆 2006. *Kunshan* 毘山 Beijing: Wenwu chubanshe.

Zhejiangsheng Wenwu Kaogu Yanjiusuo, Liangzhu Bowuyuan 浙江省文物考古研究所、良渚博物院 2014. *Songze Art: Zhejiang Songze Culture Archaeological Exhibition* 崧泽之美——浙江崧泽文化考古特展. Hangzhou: Zhejiang sheying chubanshe.

Zhejiangsheng Wenwu Kaogu Yanjiusuo, Xiaoshan Bowuguan 浙江省文物考古研究所、萧山博物馆 2007. *Kuahuqiao* 跨湖桥. Beijing: Wenwu chubanshe.

Zhejiangsheng Wenwu Kaogu Yanjiusuo, Pujiang Bowuguan 浙江省文 物考古研究所、浦江博物馆2016. *Pujiang shangshan* 浦江上山. Beijing: Wenwu chubanshe.

Zhejiangsheng Wenwu Kaogu Yanjiusuo, Sushan Bowuguan 浙江省文 物考古研究所、萧山博物馆 2004. *Kuahuqiao* 跨湖桥. Beijing: Wenwu chubanshe.

Zhejiangsheng Wenwu Kaogu Yanjiusuo, Yuyaoshi Wenwu Baohu Guanlisuo, Hemudu Yizhi Bowuguan 浙江省文物考古研究所、余姚市文物保护管理 所、河姆渡遗址博物馆 2007. "*Excavation Report on the Neolithic Site of Tianluoshan in Yuyao, Zhejiang* 田螺山新石器时代遗址发掘简报." Wenwu 11: 4–24.

Zhongguo Kexueyuan Kaogu Yanjiusuo, Hubei Gongzuodui, Hubei Zhijian Guankiaoshan Yizhi Dierci Fajue 中国科学院考古研究 所湖北工作队，湖北枝江关庙山遗址第二次发掘1983. "*The Second Excavation Report on Remains at Guanmiaoshan, Zhijiang, Hubei* 湖北枝江关庙山遗址第二次发掘." Kaogu 1:17–29.

Zhongguo Shehui Keixueyuan Kaogu Yajiusuo, Hubei Gongzuodui, Hubei Zhijiang Tianmiaoshan Yizhi Di Erci Fajue 中国科学院考古研究 所湖北工作队，湖北枝江关庙山遗址第二次发掘 1983. "*The Second Excavation Report on Remains at Guanmiaoshan, Zhijiang, Hubei* 湖北枝江关庙山遗址第二次发掘." Kaogu 1:17–29.

Zhongguo Shehui Kexueyuan Kaogu Yanjiusuo 湖北考古研究所与中国社会科学院考古研究所1983. "*Second Excavation of the Miaoshan Site in Zhijianguan, Hubei* 湖北之间关庙山地儿子发掘报告." Kaogu 1.

Zhongguo Shehui Kexue Yuan Kaogu Yanjiusuo 中国 社会科学院考古研究所湖北工作队 2010. *Chinese Archeology: Neolithic Volume* 中国考古，新石器时代. Beijing: Zhongguo Kexue chubanshe.

Zhonggong Zhejiangsheng Weixuan Zhuanbu, Zhejiangsheng Wenwuju 中共 浙江省委宣传部、浙江省文物局 2016. *Zhejiang's National Treasures: Key Cultural Relics Protection* Unit *of Zhejiang* 浙江国宝:浙江省全国重点文物保护单位. Hangzhou: Zhejiang sheying chubanshe.

CHAPTER 3

THE NEOLITHIC JADE REVOLUTION IN NORTHEAST CHINA

BY CHUNG TANG, SHANDONG UNIVERSITY,
CHINA, MANA HAYASHI TANG, WASHINGTON
UNIVERSITY IN ST. LOUIS, GUOXIANG LIU,
INSTITUTE OF ARCHAEOLOGY, CHINESE
ACADEMY OF SOCIAL SCIENCES, AND YADI WEN,
SOUTHERN UNIVERSITY OF SCIENCE
AND TECHNOLOGY

JADE is a highly valued precious stone with an enduring history in East Asia (National Science Museum 2004; Childs-Johnson 2001; Keverne 1995; Tang 1998). The term "jade" collectively applies to compact aggregates of either nephrite or jadeite mineral species; the use of nephrite in particular can be traced as far back as the Upper Paleolithic in Russian Siberia (Derev'anko et al. 1998; Derevianko 2011; Okladnikov 1955). A systematic and stable relationship between nephrite and specific objects is not seen, however, until the early Neolithic Age. The earliest archaeological evidence of a nephrite jade assemblage is found in the Xinglongwa period (6200 to 5200 BCE) in northeastern China (Figure 1). Xinglongwa jades are significant for having neither contemporaneous nor preceding counterparts in their level of regional standardization. The sixth millennium BCE marks the beginning of nephrite being recognized as an exceptionally precious material; the established standards for nephrite jades in Xinglongwa would spread out and form the foundations for a long tradition of jade cultures in a wide region across East Asia. From the fifth millennium BCE, Xinglongwa nephrite slit rings, pendants, and beads spread into the Amur River region, coastal Far East Russia, and the Sea

FIGURE 1 Assemblage of Xinglongwa nephrite accessories.

of Japan region (Figure 2a–b). Further south, imitations made from quartzite, talcum, seashells, and other precious materials were discovered in major Neolithic cultural groups in the Yangtze River region, such as Hemudu and Majiabang. From a global perspective, the Xinglongwa slit rings are especially of interest, as they are the earliest archaeological evidence of earrings in prehistory. Slit rings, or *jue*, are circular rings with slits. They have been discovered from Yakutsk in the north to the Pearl River Delta in the south, and from Thailand and eastern India in the west to Japan, Kalimantan, and New Guinea in the Pacific. In South China, Southeast Asia, and the Pacific Islands, some ethnic minorities have continued to use slit earrings in recent times. Metal slit earrings worn by the Li group in Hainan are over 1 kg and more than 20 cm in diameter. Such examples give us rare ethnographic insights into the use of slit earrings in East Asia (Tang 2007a). Xinglongwa jades further reflect the achievement of a mature and intimate understanding of the properties of nephrite. Their craftsmen's knowledge in accessing, identifying, and processing nephrite was adopted by some of the most prominent jade-using Neolithic communities in China, including the Hongshan culture (fourth millennium BCE) in the Northeast, and the Liangzhu culture (third to mid-fourth millennium BCE) in the Yangtze River Delta (Tang 2014b).

The Xinglongwa nephrite jade assemblage was revolutionary and had long-lasting influence on later jade cultures. To understand the origins of jade cultures in prehistoric East Asia, and especially China, one must begin with an investigation of Xinglongwa

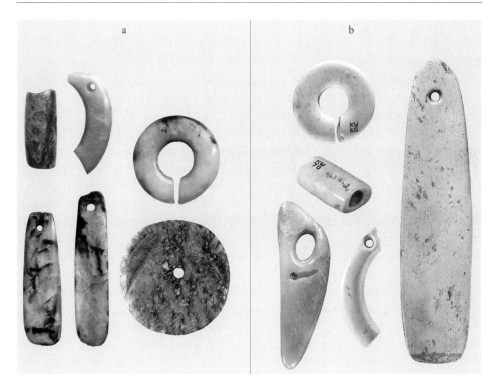

FIGURE 2A–B (a) Jade assemblage of Chertovy Vorota site, Russia. (b) Jade assemblage of Kuwano site, Japan.

and its nephrite jades. In the following, we will briefly review the societal background of Xinglongwa jades and discuss several representative case study sites.

Xinglongwa culture settlements are characterized by increased societal complexity and an emerging social hierarchy (Liu 2007b; Shelach 2000). In the sixth millennium BCE, they were the largest settlements in Northeast Asia. Beichengzi site is over 60,000 m² in total area, and at the type-site Xinglongwa settlement more than a hundred houses were discovered (Tang and Wen 2014). In some cases the settlements are surrounded by moats. Houses are semi-subterranean, generally rectangular, and largely arranged in rows and equidistant from each other. The sizes of houses within each settlement are generally consistent. Large central houses are more than twice the size of the other houses; they were likely used for communal assemblies or ceremonial activities and have been found in several settlements, such as at Chahai and Xinglongwa (Yang and Liu 1998). Overall there is evidence of sedentism and coordinated settlement planning. Evidence for hunted game worship is found at Xinglongwa site and Xinglonggou site; hunting and foraging were likely the primary modes of subsistence (Liu 2007b). Substantial millet consumption is inferred from analyses of the large quantities of charred domesticated millet remains and isotopic signatures of human bone collagen remains in Xinglongwa settlements (Liu et al. 2012). Though harvesting tools have not been discovered, stone spades are quite numerous, and mortars and pestles have been discovered in sets. Early forms of crop domestication may have been in practice. The following are examples of Xinglongwa-culture archaeological sites where nephrite jades have been excavated.

The eponymous type-site of the cultural period is located on the eastern bank of Mangniu River, which is a tributary of Daling River in eastern Aohan Banner (Figure 3). Six seasons of excavations were conducted between 1983 and 1993, unearthing a total area of 30,000 m^2. Over 180 houses, more than 400 ash pits, and 30 or so residential burials were discovered at the site. Three distinct periods in the Xinglongwa culture are identified at this site. The Xinglongwa phase 1 settlement is one of the earliest and most well preserved prehistoric settlements in China. It has an enclosing moat and many other residential features. All houses are oriented northwest-southeast and arranged in rows. Each row has a large central house, and the two largest houses are located in the settlement's central area. Fewer houses were found in Xinglongwa phase 2. The settlement maintains the general structure of Xinglongwa 1 but seems to have lost primary settlement status to the settlement at Xinglonggou (see the section on "Xinglonggou, Chifeng, Inner Mongolia"). In Xinglongwa phase 3, the houses are more densely packed and discernably smaller than before. Unfortunately, the overall structure of the Xinglongwa phase 3 settlement is hard to infer, as cultural layers from the Lower Xiajiadian period have cut through the settlement's west side. Most burials found at Xinglongwa site are residential burials (Liu 2001, 2007b; Yang and Liu 1998).

In Xinglongwa societies nephrite jades were rare, exquisite, and enduring objects, which are qualities that are in line with modern definitions of precious gemstones. The discovery of 23 jades has been reported so far at Xinglongwa site. They weigh a total of 319.9 g. Nearly half of the jades were found in residential burials: Burials 117, 130, and 135 each unearthed a pair of slit rings. Burials 118 and 142 each unearthed a pair of slit bead-shaped earrings. An arc-shaped accessory was found in Burial 109. Two pseudo-jade slit rings were found in Burial 108, one of which was identified as chalcedony. Another slit ring was found in an ash pit (Liu 2007c). A slit ring was found on the living surface of House 229. Houses 125, 128, and 201 each unearthed a scoop-shaped *bi* pendant from their living surfaces. A scoop-shaped *bi* pendant was found in House 113, and an arc-shaped accessory was found in House 250. Nephrite tools have been discovered at Xinglongwa as well: a chisel was found in House 260, and adzes were found in four houses and a test pit. Nephrite tools in Xinglongwa culture have use-wear consistent with practical use. They were rare commodities and, like the accessories, not readily accessible to all members of the community.

XINGLONGGOU, CHIFENG, INNER MONGOLIA

Another site that is representative of the Xinglongwa period is Xinglonggou, which is located on the western bank of Mangniu River, approximately 13 km northwest of

FIGURE 3 Location of Xinglongwa site, Inner Mongolia, China.

Xinglongwa site. The Location 1 site is approximately 1 km southwest of Xinglonggou village and corresponds in time period to the Xinglongwa phase 2 settlement. It is 50,000 m² in total area. In 2001–2003, over 5,600 m² was excavated. Thirty-seven houses were discovered, none of them cutting through each other. Twenty-eight residential burials were discovered as well. The houses are likely from the same time period; this site was likely a major settlement of its time (Liu 2007a; Liu et al. 2004; Yang et al. 2000).

Twelve jades were discovered at Xinglonggou site. Burials 4 and 7 each unearthed a pair of slit rings. In Burial 4, one of the slit rings was found in the right eyehole of a girl's skull, and the other was found in the burial's soil deposit. A large number of stone beads were also discovered in this burial. The slit rings in Burial 7 were found beside the left shoulder and right arm of the deceased. House 22 unearthed three scoop-shaped *bi* pendants and a slit bead semi-product. House 11 unearthed an arc-shaped accessory, and House 21 unearthed a chisel. Two adzes were surface-collected at the site (Liu 2007d; Yang et al. 2007).

Chahai site, Fuxin, Liaoning

Chahai site (6000–5000 BCE) is located in northwestern Liaoning. It was discovered in 1982 and excavated over seven seasons between 1986 and 1994. A total area of over 10,000 m² was unearthed. This site can be broken down into three cultural periods (Figure 4). The Early Chahai period corresponds in time to phase 3 at Xinglongwa site. Early Chahai–period houses were mostly found on the northwestern end of the site. An open space with numerous pits and stone piles was found between these houses. Houses from the Middle Chahai period were found in the northwestern portion of, and scattered across, the site. They cut through some of the earlier houses from the Early Chahai period. Houses from the Late Chahai period are mainly concentrated on the central to southeastern end of the site, cutting through earlier houses from the Middle Chahai period. The settlement is surrounded by a moat, and six residential burials have been identified within. The orientations and structures of the houses are generally consistent, regardless of time period. At the central area of the excavation site is a cemetery that is about 500 m² in total area. Features discovered here include 10 tombs, numerous burial pits, and a stone pile in the shape of a dragon. In general, the tombs are oriented north-south. The stone pile is located to the north of the cemetery tombs. It is 19.7 m long and made from a pile of basalt, which is reddish in color due to oxidation. Its head points southwest and its tail points northeast. Considering its size and context, it is speculated that this stone pile had ceremonial or religious significance (Xing 2012a).

Jades found at Chahai are relatively numerous. Out of 44 found at the site, a quarter were found within soil deposits of the cultural layers and mainly concentrated in the southwestern lowlands of the settlement. These include a chisel, an axe, rings, beads, and scoop-shaped *bi* pendants; a few of jades may have moved from their original contexts due to secondary disturbance. Two jade chisels and an axe were also found during surface surveying. For the others with clear archaeological contexts, 21 jades

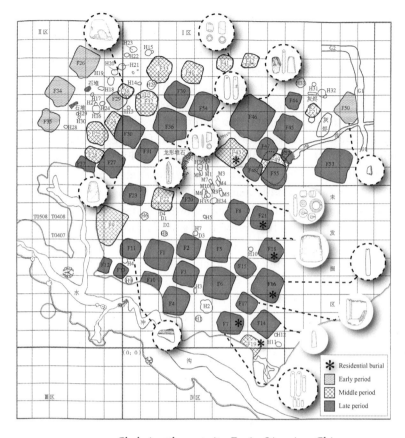

FIGURE 4 Chahai settlement site, Fuxin, Liaoning, China.

were excavated on the living surfaces of houses, eight were from residential burials, and one was from an ash pit. A jade axe fragment was found on the living surface of House 50 from the Early Chahai period. From the Middle Chahai period, jades were found on the living surfaces of Houses 38, 41, and 43. Jades were also found in the residential burial F43M in House 43. Jades were unearthed from 11 Late Chahai–period houses. In Houses 11, 14, 16, 17, 18, 20, 36, and 46 jades were found on the living floor, while in Houses 27 and 54 jades were found in their soil deposits. The residential burial, Burial F7M in House 7, unearthed six jade scoop-shaped *bi* pendants. A jade chisel was discovered with charred bones of a pig in ash pit 34 in the central cemetery (Xing 2012b).

Baiyinchanghan site is representative of the Late Xinglongwa period. It is located on the northern bank of the Xilamulun River in southern Linxi County in Inner Mongolia and was discovered during a national archaeological survey (Inner Mongolia 2004). A total area of 7,264.3 m² was excavated from 1988 to 1991. Two neighboring settlement areas were found. Each settlement is surrounded by a moat. The northern settlement is 4,772.5 m² and the southern settlement is 2,491.8 m² in total area, respectively. Three small-scale cemetery grounds were found in the vicinity. Cemetery 1 is the farthest, situated on a hilltop west of the northern settlement. Cemetery 2 is on a hilltop southwest of the southern settlement. Cemetery 3 is the smallest and rests on the saddle between the two hills. According to the stratigraphic relationships between the site's archaeological features, Baiyinchanghan can be divided into five periods and seven subperiods. Features from the 2b period are the most numerous and well preserved. There is much debate over the date of 2b, but the most commonly accepted is the late Xinglongwa period. Charcoal collected from the living surfaces of Houses 13 and 25 in the northern settlement is dated to 6590±85 ^{14}C BP and 7040±100 ^{14}C BP, respectively. No residential burial has been found at Baiyinchanghan. The northern settlement unearthed a total of 29 houses and the southern settlement 25. Fourteen burials in the cemeteries belong to the Baiyinchanghan 2b period. These are evenly distributed in Cemeteries 1 and 2. Most of these burials are stone-piled soil pits. Burial goods are not evenly distributed, ranging from one to more than a hundred objects per burial. Most of the burial goods are accessories; some are figurines. Only three practical tools were found in the burials (Inner Mongolia 2004; Suo 2005; Tang and Wen 2014).

Seven jades were found in burials from the Baiyinchanghan 2b period. All were polished and green in color. In Cemetery 1, a jade bead and a jade slit ring were found in Burial 2, which contained the remains of a male and a female (Qiao 2014). Two jade beads and a jade slit ring were found in Burial 4. A jade cicada figurine was found in Burial 7, which also unearthed a stone bear figurine. In Cemetery 2, a jade bead was found in Burial 11 (Inner Mongolia 2004).

Overview of archaeological context

These case studies are the most systematically excavated jades in the Xinglongwa period. Jade typologies and excavated contexts are generally consistent across the sites. None of the jade tools were found in the burials, while more than half of the accessories were. Jades excavated within houses were generally found together. The most n. merous accessories are the scoop-shaped *bi* pendants and the slit rings; the scoop-shaped *bi* pendants resemble bone accessories found in Upper Paleolithic Eurasia (Vanhaeren and d'Errico 2006), whereas the slit rings are unprecedented. Slit rings were almost exclusively found within burials, except for the oldest slit ring found in the Xinglongwa phase 1 settlement (Figure 5) and the slit ring discovered in the southwestern corner of House 43 at Chahai site. House 43 also hosted a residential burial, from which a pair of slit rings were discovered.

The positions of slit rings in the burials revealed that they were worn as earrings. In Residential Burials 117 and 135 at Xinglongwa site, a slit ring was found on each side of the tomb occupants' skulls, with the slits pointing downward (Figure 6) (Yang et al. 2007). Where bone remains were mostly or completely decomposed, the slit rings were found on the northern end of the burials, which is the direction in which the head was normally placed. A possible exception is the slit ring found in the right eye socket of the

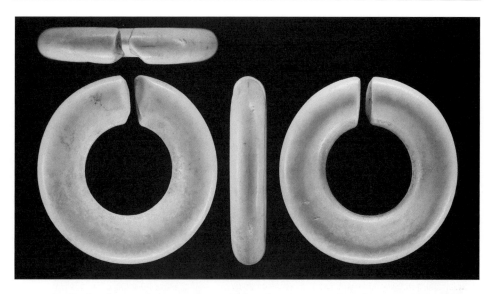

FIGURE 5 Earliest known slit ring in the world found in House 229 (Xinglongwa culture phase II), Xinglongwa site.

girl in Burial 4 at Xinglonggou. It is possible, however, that this circular ring was likely worn as an earring previously and was placed in her eye postmortem. The study of slit rings goes back at least a century in East Asia; the early documentation of slit rings found in pairs on either of the skulls in the six burials dated to 4000 BCE at Kofu site, Osaka, Japan in 1917–18 (Motoyama 1933). Thereafter, numerous pairs of slit rings have been discovered in comparable burial contexts in Initial Jomon–period Japan (Harunari 1997) and in Shang-period Hong Kong (Schofield 1935), confirming their function as earrings. Xinglongwa jade slit rings are the early confirmed jade earrings in the world (Yang et al. 2007), preceding Queen Pu-abi's lunate gold earrings found in the Ur royal tombs by at least 2,000 years.

Residential burials are characteristic but of relatively low occurrence in the Xinglongwa cultural phase. It is significant that jade accessories found in burials were exclusively discovered in residential burials (excluding Baiyinchanghan, where no residential burial has been found). Funerary practices are a reflection of beliefs concerning death, and variations between contemporaries are observed to be closely related to the social position of the deceased and their significance to the community in life (Keswani 1989; Wason 1994). Jades in burials were noticeably rare and associated with only a few members of Xinglongwa communities. Residential Burial 118 at Xinglongwa site was found in a large central house of the Xinglongwa 2 period settlement. The burial was created after the house had been inhabited for some time. A 50-year-old male was buried against the northeastern inner wall, which faces the central hearth and the entrance of the house. His elaborate burial goods include a pair of male and female pigs, pottery, microblades, bone spears, a circular shell accessory on the right wrist, a jade slit bead-shaped earring, and a pair of stone beads on the upper body.

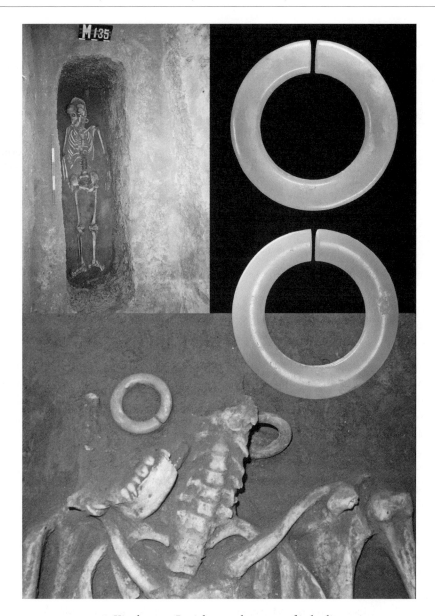

FIGURE 6 Xinglongwa Burial 135 and context of jade slit earrings.

Another jade slit bead-shaped earring was found in the backfill of the burial. The house was continued to be used post-burial, suggesting that the man was worshipped within the house after his death. Similarly, Residential Burial 7 at Xinglonggou site was found in a large central house of its settlement. An adult male was discovered here with a pair of jade slit rings on his upper body. Accessories made from human skull were also found on his right wrist and his chest. Xinglongwa's principal excavator Liu (2007c) hypothesizes that these men were among the chiefs of their settlements.

The spatial distribution of jades at Chahai site reveals that the accessories were possibly only shared exclusively within kin groups. Jades from the Early and Middle Chahai periods are relatively scattered and present no obvious spatial pattern, but those from the Late Chahai period are more numerous and concentrated within particular clusters of houses. Most jade tools and all jade accessories were found in the largest houses surrounding the central cemetery and in houses on the southeastern end of the settlement. Most of the residential burials found at Chahai are in the latter area. Four are confirmed child burials; only one child (Burial F7M) has burial goods, which are six jade scoop-shaped *bi* pendants. Preservation of body remains is relatively poor at Chahai site, but extrapolating from the position of the teeth in Burial F7M, the jade scoop-shaped *bi* pendants are arranged in pairs on where would have been the neck and torso of the child. Burial F7M is only one of two burials that unearthed jades at the site (the other being Burial F43M from the Middle Chahai period). It is also the only burial in the Xinglongwa period to have unearthed jade scoop-shaped *bi* pendants and presents an important clue to how they might have been worn. These clusters of houses are possibly "jade families" that had a preference for jades or had the ability to restrict the use of nephrite resources in their wider community (Tang and Wen 2014).

Residential burials are not known at Baiyinchanghan, which is the youngest site among our case studies. A change in attitude toward death may have occurred. Jades were only found within burials that had relatively rich burial goods, including an array of stone and shell beads. The jade cicada at Baiyinchanghan is the earliest known zoomorphic nephrite figurine found in China. Its discovery is fascinating in light of later Neolithic jade cultures in the region, such as Hongshan, in which nephrite was extensively used to produce zoomorphic and anthropomorphic figurines.

YELLOW-GREEN XIUYAN-TYPE NEPHRITE

The color and texture of Xinglongwa jades are some of their most strikingly noticeable characteristics. In this section we will discuss raw material preferences and explore the possibility of associated color symbolism.

Most of the Xinglongwa accessories with jade typologies are nephrite (Yang et al. 2007). Mineralogical analysis has been conducted on eight jades at Chahai site, including four slit rings, a slit bead, two scoop-shaped *bi* pendants, and a chisel (Wen 1990; Wen and Jing 1992). The seven accessories are identified as tremolite nephrite and the chisel as actinolite nephrite. Renowned nephrite specialist and mineralogist Wen notes that the accessories are not made from a single mother rock, suggesting that nephrite was being distinguished at high accuracy from similar-looking minerals, such as serpentine, and that the choice of nephrite was intentional. Nephrite comes in a variety of grain size and colors, the latter ranging from white, yellow-white, and green to black, with intermediate shades in between. Evenly textured, fine-grained yellow-green nephrite was carefully selected for the accessories, and especially so for the slit rings and slit beads. Most of the Chahai jades are white and opaque in appearance, but they were likely altered by post-burial weathering; yellow-green spots are still visible on several of the accessories (Xing 2012d). We speculate that the yellow-green nephrite in Xinglongwa was traded over a long distance, as there are no known local nephrite resources in southeastern Inner Mongolia to the west of the Liao River (Tang 2007d). The most widely accepted geological source for Xinglongwa jades is found several hundred kilometers to the southeast in eastern Liaoning. The Xiuyan region on the Liaodong peninsula is the only known prehistoric source of nephrite in northeastern China, and it has been extensively studied in numerous regional geological surveys (Hayashi 1999; Liu and Tang 2011; Tang 2007d; Tang and Liu 2011, 2012; Wang et al. 2007; Wen 1998). Wang (2011) points out that Xiuyan nephrite was widely used in Neolithic jade cultures of northeastern and northern China. The Hongshan culture (4500–3000 BCE) succeeded Xinglongwa as the most prominent jade culture in northeastern China, and they were likely able to more readily access nephrite than their predecessors, as there is significantly more nephrite products and materials found in Hongshan. Hongshan provides valuable clues to the nature of nephrite used in Xinglongwa. The largest and most elaborate Hongshan jades, including the famous anthropomorphic and zoomorphic figurines found at the Niuheliang cemetery, are made from fine-grained yellow-green Xiuyan-type nephrite (Tang and Liu 2012; Yang et al. 2007). Traces of rusty red cortices are often found on these elaborate Hongshan jades. The rusty red cortices are characteristic of fine-grained nephrite river gravels, which are even in texture and yellow-green within. Xinglongwa jades were likely made from such fine-grained Xiuyan-type nephrite river gravels as well. These gravels were likely obtained from riverbeds, flood plains, and fluvial terraces more than tens of kilometers from the primary geological sources (Guo 2011; Tang and Liu 2012).

In wider Northeast Asia, Xiuyan is not the only known prehistoric source of nephrite. Decisive mineralogical evidence is still necessary to confirm the geological provenance of Xinglongwa jades, but most geochemical methodologies in the past have failed to conclusively differentiate nephrite resources in the region (Zhou and Feng 2010; Wang et al. 2007; Liu and Cui 2002). Recent analyses of trace and rare earth elements show promising results (Lu et al. 2014; Burtseva and Murzintseva 2013; Zhong et al. 2013), and strontium stable isotope analysis may be applicable as well, as it has successfully determined nephrite provenance in other regions of the world (Adams et al. 2007). We mentioned earlier that prehistoric Russian Siberia has a long history of using nephrite. Okladnikov (1955) proposes that nephrite artifacts found in the Cis-Baikal region can be sourced back to the exposed northern cliffs of Munko-Sardyk in the Eastern Sayan Mountain. Several serpentine and nephrite discs, pendants, and a serpentine figurine have been discovered in the Upper Paleolithic Mal'ta-Buret' culture (Medvedev 1998). Nephrite adzes and knives are common burial goods in the early Neolithic Kitoi culture (6000–4800 BCE), and white translucent rings and disks are characteristic of early Bronze Age Glazkovo culture burials (3000–2000 BCE)

(Weber et al. 2006; Komissarov 1998, 2014). These white translucent nephrite rings and disks are also seen in the lower Amur region in the Russian Far East. Very little is known about the prehistoric exchange relationships between northeastern China and Russian Siberia. Kato (1998) is one of the earliest archaeologists to propose that the prehistoric white translucent nephrite accessories found in Heilongjiang province resemble those found in Cis-Baikal and the Russian Far East. The relative translucency of Cis-Baikal nephrite is easily distinguishable from that of the Xiuyan type, and we have since identified prehistoric white translucent nephrite accessories in Heilongjiang, Jilin, Inner Mongolia, and Liaoning provinces. We see them also in Hongshan culture sites, such as at the Niuheliang cemetery (Tang and Liu 2012). In terms of typology, however, this Cis-Baikal–type nephrite was not used to make slit rings or elaborate Hongshan jades. Instead, the typologies and production technologies closely resemble those of jades found in Russian Siberia, suggesting that these Cis-Baikal–type nephrite jades found in northeastern China were imported from the north. Cis-Baikal–type nephrite and jades have not been discovered in the Xinglongwa period, however. Considering Xinglongwa's use of its regional nephrite resources, and its unique jade typologies, we believe that the Xinglongwa jade tradition had developed independently of that found in Russian Siberia. This is not to suggest that their appreciation for nephrite occurred completely in isolation. North China belonged to a wider cultural group of microblade traditions in Northeast Asia, which had existed since approximately 25,000 years ago. As implied earlier, interactions between Neolithic to Bronze Age communities in Russian Siberia and northeastern China were likely. Scoop-shaped bone pendants were common in Russian Siberia during the Upper Paleolithic, and their Neolithic nephrite adzes and early Bronze Age nephrite scoop-shaped *bi* pendants closely resemble those found in northeastern China. Further international collaborations would surely benefit our collective understanding of prehistoric long-distance exchanges in the region.

For Xinglongwa, nephrite was a rare and exotic material with an extreme toughness that surpassed all of its other lithic resources (Tang 2007d). Considering the range of nephrite colors that we find in Xiuyan, and even just within Xinglongwa culture sites, the consistency we see in the slit rings was undoubtedly intentional. This preference for light yellow-green nephrite is not observed in prehistoric Russian Siberia, and it must be understood in the wider picture of a proliferation of greenstones during the early Neolithic Age. In the Near East, Bar-Yosef Mayer and Porat (2008) find that greenstones were used for the first time during the transition to agriculture, and they argue that the occurrence of green stone beads is directly related to this transition. We propose that the light yellow-green Xinglongwa jades represent a similar phenomenon in early Neolithic East Asia. From approximately 6000 to 4000 BCE, an appreciation for green slit rings had spread extensively from northeastern China to Japan, Far East Russia, and the Yangtze River region. It may be difficult to demonstrate a direct relationship between the green slit rings and the advent of agriculture. However, it is notable that the earliest confirmed archaeobotanical evidence of millet domestication has been identified in early Holocene in Neolithic northeastern and northern China (Zhao 2014). The surrounding regions to which green slit rings had spread had successively begun to practice crop domestication and early agriculture in the Neolithic as well (Aikens et al. 2009; Kuzmin et al. 1998; Kuzmin and Rakov 2011; Liu et al. 2009). In contrast, there is no evidence thus far of prehistoric agricultural practices in the Cis-Baikal region.

The Xinglongwa jade assemblage was often adopted in its entirety, and the choices in color and texture were closely imitated, regardless of whether or not these later cultural groups had access to the same geological resources. Where nephrite was less accessible, we see imitation jades made from similar-looking minerals, such as fluorite, which was used in Tashan site and Hemudu site in the lower Yangtze River region (Figure 7). It is evident from their imitation jades that green was an important quality. Furthermore, Hemudu is famous for discovering ample archaeobotanical evidence of rice cultivation approximately 7,000 years ago in the Yangtze River Delta. The adoption of nephrite working techniques in the making of such imitations, which do not necessarily require them, is proof that there was also a recognized set of knowledge associated with jade production. We will discuss these production techniques and technologies in the next section.

FIGURE 7   Imitation of Xinglongwa jade assemblage at Hemudu site, Zhejiang, China.

Xinglongwa nephrite technologies

Groundbreaking technologies were used in the production of Xinglongwa jades, and the quality of their craftsmanship was unsurpassed even in later time periods. At present, we do not have enough evidence from the Xinglongwa period to determine the identity of the jade artisans, as no jade workshop has been discovered yet. These artisans may or may not have been the pioneers of these technologies, but at the very least they are our early archaeological lead to those who revolutionized jade production for millennia to come.

Flexible sawing

String-sawing uses a flexible string, such as leather or hemp rope, to saw through an object by pulling abrasives back and forth against it (Figure 8a–b) (Kovachevich 2014; Lothrop 1955; Mou 1989; Tang 2007b). The use of abrasives has its foundations in the Upper Paleolithic, during which we begin to see a proliferation of polished artifacts made from bones and soft stone, including body accessories (Norton and Jin 2009; Pitulko et al. 2012; Sieveking 1971). The application of string-sawing to the production of nephrite accessories is thus not surprising. Though nephrite is not the hardest of

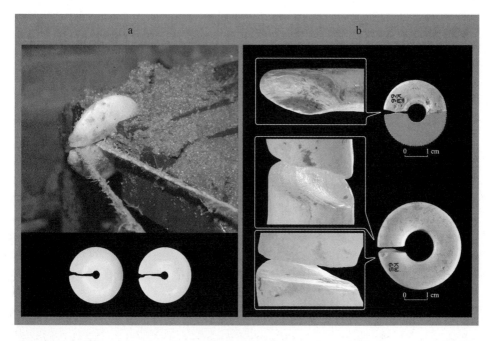

FIGURE 8 (a) Demonstration of string-sawing and the experimental slit ring product. (b) Slits of comparable slit rings KW65 and 66 from Kuwano site, Japan.

minerals—it has a Mohs scale hardness of 6–6.5—it is notoriously tough. At the micro-crystalline level, it is formed by randomly oriented fibrous bundles that can force propagating cracks to make drastic directional changes and form secondary crack branching (Wen 1998; Bradt et al. 1973). Considering these structural characteristics, the more commonly used lithic reduction such as free hand flaking techniques would have been inadequate to break the jades. Tang (2007b) argues that the artisans of Xinglongwa jades applied the malleable string-sawing technique specifically to achieve precise and minute control over the shaping of nephrite. Traces of string-sawing can be found on the slits of Xinglongwa slit rings, which are visible as a series of curved undulations that sometimes end with an abrupt breakage (Figure 9) (Tang 2007b). String-sawing is also used to slice sheets of nephrite. At Chertovy Vorota site, we have found traces of string-sawing on the surface of a nephrite disc found in a cultural layer dated to approximately 7,000 years ago. A jade slit ring found at this site was also produced using the string-sawing technique. Around this time period, string-sawing spread from northeastern China to wider East Asia, and its distribution largely corresponds with the dispersal of jades (Tang and Liu 2010). Later in the Neolithic, the Hongshan culture and the Liangzhu culture would inherit the string-sawing technique in their production of nephrite jades. Traces of string-sawing have been identified on many of the largest Hongshan jade objects, such as on the inner surfaces of the famous hoof-shaped *gu* (Tang and Liu 2012). Most Liangzhu jades were worked with string-sawing, notably when slicing large sheets of nephrite. Similar examples have been identified in

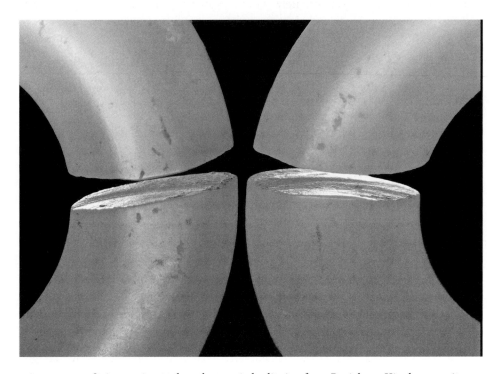

FIGURE 9   String sawing tool marks on a jade slit ring from Burial 130, Xinglongwa site.

the middle to lower reaches of the Yellow River and the Yangtze River; coastal eastern Guangdong; the Russian Far East; and Hokuriku, Japan (Tang 2007b). In the aforementioned Hemudu culture and nearby Majiabang culture, we have identified traces of string-sawing on imitations of jades as well.

The perfect circle

Considering how tough nephrite is, the incredibly precise handicraft of Xinglongwa rings has puzzled archaeologists for a long time. Xinglongwa slit rings are virtually perfect circles, each made from a circular disc with a concentric drilled hole. A noteworthy example is the pair of slit rings discovered in Burial M130 at Xinglongwa site, which are equal in size (diameters: 4.77 cm, inner diameters: 2.1 cm) and nearly identical in weight (23.0 g and 23.2 g). In Hongshan culture, we would further see a mass production of such nephrite rings, some of which are thinner than 1 cm and have inner diameters of up to 9 cm (Guo and Sun 2014). At Lingjiatan site (3600–3300 BCE) in the lower Yangtze River region, more than 300 nephrite rings were found, including stacks of near-identical rings (Anhui 2000; Zhang 2006). Drilling technologies that can maintain a stable center are required to mass produce such rings, which are essentially perfect annuli.

Drilling, like polishing with abrasives, was first observed in northeastern China during the Upper Paleolithic. Several bone needles, perforated animal teeth, and a fragment of an incised disc from approximately 30,000–20,000 BP were found in a cave site at Xiaogushan in Liaoning (Guo and Sun 2014; Huang and Bo 2009; Zhang et al. 1985). Drilled bone needles were discovered at Shandingdong site (18,000–11,000 BP) in Beijing as well (Guo and Sun 2014; Fang and Han 1992). The spatiotemporal distribution of prehistoric nephrite accessories and their production technologies brings to light two major drilling technologies in Neolithic East Asia (Tang 1998, 2003, 2013; Liu and Tang 2011). Largely in the north is Semenov's (1957) reconstructed drilling device, which is analogous to a beam compass. Tool marks consistent with the use of such a device were identified on nephrite jades in the Lake Baikal region and the Russian Far East. We further find nephrite jades made from this same technology in Heilongjiang, Inner Mongolia, and Jilin in China, where the distribution of Semonov's drilling technology partially overlaps with the distribution of Siberian -type nephrite rings and discs. To the south, C. Tang has reconstructed a high-speed rotary device from tool marks on jade products, as well as the use-wear and in situ context of excavated stone bearings (Figure 10) (Tang 2013, 2014b). The potter's wheel is a famous prehistoric rotary device that greatly increased the efficiency of pottery production (Roux and de Miroschedji 2009; Wood 1990, 1992). What we have found in prehistoric East Asia is another line of evidence to early rotary devices, which we hypothesize were used to assist tubular drilling in the production of nephrite jades (Figure 11). Bearings can reduce friction between mechanical parts of rotary devices to achieve high-speed true rotary motion. The stone bearings we have identified in the archaeological record were previously often categorized as stone drills. Tang argues that they are instead stone bearings based on the following evidence: (a) a lack of use-wear on the apexes, which is inconsistent with

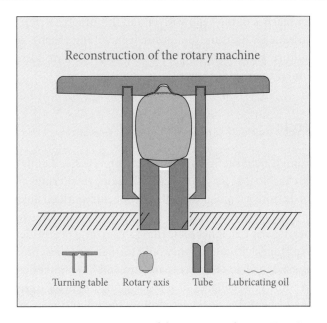

FIGURE 10 Reconstruction of the rotary machine in East Asia.

FIGURE 11 Distribution of stone bearings and rings in East Asia.

the way drills are used; (b) instead the shoulders are most worn out—at times even glassified—and have traces of concentric circles formed from the friction, heat, and pressure created between them and whatever objects they were pressed against; (c) the angle in which fractures propagated when it was damaged suggests that a strong force perpendicular to the axis was applied during use; and (d) the in situ context. In 2006, the excavation team of the Chinese University of Hong Kong unearthed a lapidary workshop from approximately 4,000 years ago at Hac Sa, Macau. It was the first systematic excavation of a prehistoric lapidary workshop, in which the in situ context of stone bearings and ring products was able to spatially demonstrate the function of the stone bearings (Tang 2013). Scanning Electron Microscope analyses (SEM) of the stone bearings from Hac Sa and other sites in the Pearl River Delta found that the stone bearings had undergone true rotary motion, and that their rotational force came from the rotating plate sitting above (Ye and Tang 2014). Tang's proposed rotary device would have made efficient mass production of successively smaller nephrite rings from a single piece of raw material possible (Tang 2013). The resulting smooth nephrite rings are also in contrast to the relatively irregular rings made from Semenov's drilling technology, which scrapes through the inner circumferences of nephrite rings in successive, short strokes.

The use of these rotary devices is still extremely understudied and would require broader awareness by the archaeological community to fully investigate their role in the production of exquisite nephrite jades, as well as their wider application in prehistoric pottery, lacquerware, and bronzeware production (Tang 2014a). At present, we have preliminarily identified the use of stone bearings within the following well-known prehistoric cultures in China.

Northeastern China

Evidence of prehistoric stone bearings in the Liao River region is sparse. No jade workshop has been discovered within the Xinglongwa and Hongshan cultures, though a possible stone bearing has been identified at Chahai site (Guo and Sun 2014; Tang 2013; Xing 2012c). Stone bearings have not been identified in the Hongshan culture, though the stone bearings from the Hongshan period were collected such as at Tuozi site in Tongyu County, Jilin.

Yellow River and Yangtze River region

From approximately 5000–4000 BCE, we begin to see evidence of stone bearings in the Yellow River region and the middle to lower reaches of the Yangtze River. At Beifudi site in the Bohai area of the Yellow River delta, 10 nephrite jades from approximately 5000 BCE were discovered in a ceremonial space. In the cultural layer dated to approximately 5000–4700 BCE, a stone bearing was discovered. Six more stone bearings were found in the next layer above (Duan 2006, 2014). Further west along the Yellow River, there is yet to be evidence of nephrite jades in the Xinglongwa period, but we begin to see the use of nephrite jades approximately 7,000 years ago, and stone bearings have been identified within some of the major cultural groups in the region. Nephrite jades were excavated from the Longgangsi site in Shaanxi (Shaanxi 1990), and pseudojade (serpentine and calcite) yues and a serpentine ring were found in the burials unearthed at Xipo site in Lingbao, Henan (Ma et al. 2006). Possible stone bearings have been identified within Yangshao culture sites such as Linshanzhai (T33) and Xiganggou (T4H4:3) (Tang 2013). At Dadiwan site in Gansu, nephrite rings were discovered from cultural layers dated to 5000–3000 BCE. Two stone bearings were discovered in Dadiwan cultural period 4 (3200 BCE). At Dongxiang Linjia site in Gansu, a large 16-cm-long stone bearing (3000 BCE) was discovered.

Further south along the lower reaches of the Yangtze River, as previously discussed, Liangzhu culture is famous for its discovery of a large number of nephrite objects. Lapidary rings and slit rings are seen in the earlier Hemudu and Majiabang cultures (approximately 5000 BCE), though they are not necessarily made from nephrite. On the northern side of Taihu Lake, nephrite beads and a slit ring were unearthed at Qitoushan site (4600–4300 BCE) of the Majiabang culture (Tang 2007c). On the southern side, two stone bearings were identified at Luojiajiao site (dated to 5000 BCE), also from the Majiabang culture (Shuo 2014; Tang 2013). At Fangjiazhou site (3900–3300 BCE) in Qiantangjiang, a lapidary workshop has unearthed many quartzite rings, along with over 40 stone bearings (Fang 2014; Tang 2013). In the aforementioned Lingjiatan site, a stone bearing was found in burial 98M23with a nephrite jade ring, three stone discs, two polishing stones, and some pottery. This burial was perhaps belonged to a jade lapidary.

Southern China and Southeast Asia

The use of stone bearings is not observed in the Pearl River Delta until approximately 2000 BCE. Examples include Baojingwan site in Zhuhai; Hac Sa in Macau; and many sites in Hong Kong, including Tung Wan, Sham Wan, Sha Lo Wan, and Lung Kwu Tan sites. Stone bearings continued to spread into Southeast Asia during the Bronze Age in 2000 BCE. They have been discovered in Vietnam, Taiwan, the Philippines, and Java Island. In particular, Trang Kenh site in northern Vietnam has revealed a nephrite jade workshop with several stone bearings and stacks of nephrite jade rings and discs of consistent sizes.

Joseph Needham (1965) says that mechanical engineering technology of China had already reached a very high level of development at the time, when engineering technology of the West was still in its primitive state. The existing data suggest that the production of jade rings in prehistory is closely related to the origin of rotary machinery in East Asia. Disc-shaped ornaments with drilled perforations at the center began to appear on the Eurasian continent approximately 20,000 to 10,000 years ago during the Upper Paleolithic. Xinglongwa jade slit rings represent a breakthrough in the production of circular ornaments in East Asia during the sixth millennium BCE, and we have been able to identify stone bearings from as early as then. Perhaps the ancient Chinese philosophy of "round heaven and square earth" is rooted in its jade culture. After all, the most sophisticated technology of Neolithic China was applied to its production of jades.

REMARKS

Xinglongwa jades were highly standardized in production technologies, material, color, and form. The assemblage was adopted by neighboring regions, and its influence on notable jade cultures across China is evident in the preservation of key characteristics that distinguish Xinglongwa jades from other prehistoric jade traditions, such as those found in Russian Siberia. There is no doubt that the foundations of jade traditions in East Asia can be found in the Xinglongwa jade assemblage. As of now, we do not have enough information to discern the social value of jades during the Xinglongwa period. However, we do know that Xinglongwa settlements were exceptionally large for their time period, and jades were associated with special members of these settlements. Those who were buried with jades often also had other exceptional burial goods, such as animal sacrifices and human skull accessories. Nephrite in the Xinglongwa period was a rare and exotic material with an enduring soft luster that has survived until the present. In later time periods, it was used to make zoomorphic and anthropomorphic figurines, most notably as a vessel of deities or spiritual beings during the Hongshan and Liangzhu periods. These prominent Neolithic jade cultures would not have existed without Xinglongwa. Interestingly,during the early Neolithic period in East Asia neither cultural group had technically surpassed the Xinglongwa period in the production of jades.

In particular, the influence of slit rings lasted beyond Xinglongwa and remained in East Asian jade cultures for longer than any other jade typology that originated in northeastern China. Evaluation of their symbolic significance is still only preliminary, but so far we see a very clear Upper Paleolithic influence on the pursuit of the true circle in the slit rings in East Asia . As mentioned before, the use of nephrite can be traced back to the Upper Paleolithic, but only in Xinglongwa do we begin to see intentional selection of yellow-green nephrite as the raw material and specialized technological advancements to produce desired jade typologies. Such rotary technologies were not used in the production of Xinglongwa pottery, however, suggesting that the rotary technologies developed in Neolithic northeastern China had a different purpose from the potter's wheel invented in western Asia. Considering its settlement sizes, Xinglongwa is an important cultural group for the prehistory of East Asia. Maybe more significantly, it also plays a significant role in the history of jades becoming preeminent in the East, as gold had come to reign supreme above other materials in the West.

ACKNOWLEDGMENT

This research is supported by the General Research Fund of the Research Grants Council Project No. 452812.

BIBLIOGRAPHY

Adams, Christopher J., Russell J. Beck, and Hamish J. Campbell 2007. "Characterisation and Origin of New Zealand Nephrite Jade Using Its Strontium Isotopic Signature." *Lithos* 97:307–322.

Aikens, C. Melvin, Irina S. Zhushchikhovskaya, and Song Nai Rhee 2009. "Environment, Ecology, and Interaction in Japan, Korea, and the Russian Far East: The Millennial History of a Japan Sea Oikumene." *Asian Perspectives* 48(2):207–248.

Anhuisheng Wenwu Kaogu Yanjiusuo 安徽省文物考古研究所, ed. 2000. *Jades Unearthed from Lingjiatan* 凌家滩玉器. Beijing: Wenwu chubanshe.

Bar-Yosef Mayer, Daniella E., and Naomi Porat 2008. "Green Stone Beads at the Dawn of Agriculture." *Proceedings of the National Academy of Sciences (PNAS)* 105(25):8,548–8,551.

Bradt, Richard C., Robert E. Newnham, and J. V. Biggers 1973. "The Toughness of Jade." *American Mineralogist* 58:727–732.

Burtseva, M. V., and A. E. Murzintseva 2013. "Mineralogical and Geochemical Properties of Nephrite in Eastern Siberia" (in Russian). Irkutsk, Russia: Vinogradov Institute of Geochemistry SB RAS. http://www.igc.irk.ru/Molod-konf-2013/Materiall/24-09-13/015.pdf

Childs-Johnson, Elizabeth 2001. *Enduring Art of Jade Age China: Chinese Jades of Late Neolithic through Han Periods.* Madrid: Turner.

Derev'anko, Anatoliy P., Demitri B. Shimkin, and W. Roger Powers, eds. 1998. *The Paleolithic of Siberia: New Discoveries and Interpretations.* Urbana and Chicago: University of Illinois Press.

Derevianko, Anatoly P. 2011. *The Upper Paleolithic in Africa and Eurasia and the Origin of Anatomically Modern Humans.* Novosibirsk: Institute of Archaeology and Ethnography SB RAS Press.

Duan, Hongzhen 段宏振 2006. "Excavation Report of Neolithic Beifudi Site in Yi County, Hebei 河北易縣北福 地新石器時代遺址發掘簡報." *Wenwu* 文物 9:4–20.

Duan, Hongzhen 段宏振 2014. "Prehistoric Stone Bearings and Jadeware Processing Technology at Beifudi 北福地史前遺址的輪軸石器和玉石器加工技術." In *Proceedings of the International Conference on Prehistoric Rotary Technology and Related Issues at Hac Sa, Macao* 澳門黑沙史前輪軸機械國際會議論文集. Edited by Tang Chung, 112–119. Macau: Instituto para os Assuntos Civicos e Municipais.

Fang, Xiangming 方向明 2014. "Production of the Rings and Slit Rings from Fangjiazhou Neolithic site, Tonglu 桐廬方家洲新石器時代遺址中的環玦製作及相關問題." In *Proceedings of the International Conference on Prehistoric Rotary Technology and Related Issues at Hac Sa, Macao.* Edited by Tang Chung, 156–201. Macau: Instituto para os Assuntos Civicos e Municipais.

Fang, Yan, and Renwei Han 方衍、韓任偉 1992. "Heilongjiang Early Human Activities 黑龍 江原始社會的人類活動." *Academic Exchanges* 5:112–114, 111.

Guo, Dashun 郭大順 2011. "Hongshan Jades and the Early Developmental History of Xiuyan Nephrite 紅山玉與岫玉早期開發史." In *Proceedings of the 2011 Symposium on Xiuyan Jades and the Jade Culture of China.* Edited by Tang Chung. Beijing: Kexue chubanshe.

Guo, Dashun, and Li Sun 郭大順、孫力 2014. "Application of Rotary Technology on Hongshan Culture Jades 旋轉技術在紅山文化玉器中的應用." In *Proceedings of the International Conference on Prehistoric Rotary Technology and Related Issues at Hac Sa, Macao*. Edited by Tang Chung, 128–155. Macau: Instituto para os Assuntos Civicos e Municipais.

Harunari, Hideji 春成秀樹 1997. *Excavation of History 4: The Spiritual Link, Ancient Ornaments* 『古代の装い』歴史発掘 4. Tokyo: Kodansha.

Hayashi, Minao 林巳奈夫 1999. *Review of Ancient Chinese Jades* 中國古玉器総説. Tokyo: Yoshikawa Kobunkan.

Huang, Weiwen 黃慰文 and Renyi Bo 博仁义 2009. "Bone Tools and Ornaments 骨角工具和垂飾." In *Xiaogushan: Comprehensive Study of Liaoning Haicheng Prehistoric Cave Site* 小孤山—遼寧海城史前洞穴遺址綜合研究. Edited by Weiwen Huang and Renyi Bo, 145–155. Beijing: Kexue chubanshe.

Inner Mongolia Autonomous Region Institute of Cultural Relics and Archaeology 內蒙古文物考古研究所, ed. 2004. *Baiyinchanghan: An Excavation Report on the Neolithic Site* 白音長汗—新石器時代遺址發掘報告. Beijing: Kexue chubanshe.

Kato, Shimpei 加藤晋平 1998. "The Use of Nephrite Ornaments in Prehistoric Lake Baikal Region 先史時代バイカル湖周辺の軟玉使用." In *East Asian Jade: Symbol of Excellence*, vol. 2 東亞玉器(第二冊). Edited by Chung Tang 鄧聰, 280–290. Hong Kong: Centre for Chinese Archaeology and Art.

Keswani, Priscilla Schuster 1989. "Dimensions of Social Hierarchy in Late Bronze Age Cyprus: An Analysis of the Mortuary Data from Enkomi." *Journal of Mediterranean Archaeology* 2(1):49–86.

Keverne, Roger 1995. *Jade*. London: Lorenz Books.

Komissarov, Sergei A. 1998. "The Ancient Jades of Asia in the Light of Investigations by the Russian Archaeologists." *East Asian Jade: Symbol of Excellence*, vol. 2. Edited by Chung Tang, 250–279. Hong Kong: Centre for Chinese Archaeology and Art, Chinese University of Hong Kong.

Komissarov, Sergei A. 2014. "Jade Implements in the Finds of Russian Archaeologists (within the Period of 2000s–2010s)." In *Proceedings of the International Conference on Prehistoric Rotary Technology and Related Issues at Hac Sa, Macao*. Edited by Chung Tang, 418–437. Macau: Instituto para os Assuntos Civicos e Municipais.

Kovachevich, Brigitte 2011. "The Organization of Jade Production at Cancuen, Guatemala." In *The Technology of Maya Civilization: Political Economy and Beyond in Lithic Studies*. Edited by Zachary X. Hruby, Geoffrey E. Braswell, and Oswaldo Chinchilla Mazariegos, 151–189. Sheffield, England: Equinox.

Kuzmin, Yaroslav V., and Vladimir A. Rakov 2011. "Environment and Prehistoric Humans in the Russian Far East and Neighbouring East Asia: Main Patterns of Interaction." *Quaternary International* 237(1–2):103–108.

Kuzmin, Yaroslav V., A. J. T. Jull, and Glenn A. Jones 1998. "Early Agriculture in Primorye, Russian Far East: New Radiocarbon and Pollen Data from Late Neolithic Sites." *Journal of Archaeological Science* 25(8):813–816.

Liu, Guoxiang 劉國祥 2001. "A Preliminary Probing into the Settlement Pattern of Xing Long Wa Culture 興隆窪文化聚落形態初探." *Kaogu yu wenwu* 考古與文物 6:58–67.

Liu, Guoxiang 劉國祥 2007a. "Excavations at the Xinglongwa and Xinglonggou Sites 興隆窪及興隆溝遺址發掘述要." In *The Origin of Jades in East Asia: Jades of the Xinglongwa Culture*. Edited by Hu Yang, Guoxiang Liu, and Chung Tang 楊虎、劉國祥、鄧聰, 14–17 and 28–32. Hong Kong: Centre for Chinese Archaeology of Art.

Liu, Guoxiang 劉國祥 2007b. "Characteristics of Xinglongwa Settlements 興隆窪文化聚落特徵." In *The Origin of Jades in East Asia: Jades of the Xinglongwa Culture*. Edited by Hu Yang, Guoxiang Liu, and Chung Tang, 18–20 and 33–35. Hong Kong: Centre for Chinese Archaeology of Art.

Liu, Guoxiang 劉國祥 2007c. "Residential Burials of the Xinglongwa Culture 興隆窪文化居室葬俗." *The Origin of Jades in East Asia: Jades of the Xinglongwa Culture*. Edited by Hu Yang, Guoxiang Liu, and Chung Tang, 21–23 and 36–38. Hong Kong: Centre for Chinese Archaeology of Art.

Liu, Guoxiang 劉國祥 2007d. "An Investigation into the Origin of Jade Culture in China: A Discussion of the Jades of the Xinglongwa Culture 中國玉文化起源探." In *The Origin of Jades in East Asia: Jades of the Xinglongwa Culture* 玉器起源探索—興隆窪文化玉器研究及圖. Edited by Hu Yang, Guoxiang Liu, and Chung Tang 楊虎、劉國祥、鄧聰, 217–223. Hong Kong: Centre for Chinese Archaeology of Art.

Liu, Guoxiang 劉國祥, and Chung Tang 鄧聰, eds. 2011. *Jades and the Foundation of Chinese Civilization I: Proceedings of the 2011 Symposium on Xiuyan Jades and the Jade Culture of China* 玉根國脈(一)—2011 "岫岩玉與中國玉文化學術研討會"文集. Beijing: Kexue chubanshe.

Liu, Guoxiang, Xiaobing Jia, Minghui Zhao, Guanglin Tian, and Guotian Shao 劉國祥、賈笑冰、趙明輝、田廣林、邵國田 2004. "2002–2003 Excavation of the Xinglonggou Settlement Site in Chifeng, Inner Mongolia 內蒙古赤峰市興隆溝聚落遺址 2002–2003 年的發掘." *Kaogu* 7:3–8.

Liu, Jing, and Wenyuan Cui 劉晶、崔文元 2002. "Study on Nephrite (Tremolite Jade) for Three Localities in China 中國三個產地的軟玉(透閃石玉)研究." *Baoshi yu Baoshi xue zazhi* 14(2):25–29.

Liu, Xinyi, Harriet V. Hunt, and Martin K. Jones 2009. "River Valleys and Foothills: Changing Archaeological Perceptions of North China's Earliest Forms." *Antiquity* 83:82–95.

Liu, Xinyi, Martin K. Jones, Zhijun Zhao, Guoxiang Liu, and Tamsin C. O'Connell 2012. "The Earliest Evidence of Millet as a Staple Crop: New Light on Neolithic Foodways in North China." *American Journal of Physical Anthropology* 149:283–290.

Lothrop, Samuel K. 1955. "Jade and String-Sawing in Northeastern Costa Rica." *American Antiquity* 21(1):43–51.

Lu, Li, Zhihong Bian, Fang Wang, Junqi Wei, and Xiaohong Ran 魯力、邊智虹、王芳、魏均啟、冉曉紅 2014. "Comparative Study on Mineral Components, Microstructures and Appearance Characteristics of Nephrite from Different Origins 不同產地軟玉品種的礦物組成、顯微結構及表觀特徵的對比研究." *Baoshi yu Baoshi xue zazhi* 16(2):56–64.

Ma, Xiulin, Xinwei Li, and Haiqing Yang 馬蕭林、李新偉、楊海青 2006. "Preliminary Study of Excavated Jades at Yangshao Culture Cemetery in Xipo, Lingbao 靈寶西坡仰韶文化 墓地出土玉器初步研究." *Zhongyuan wenwu* 2:69–73.

Medvedev, German 1998. "The Middle and Upper Paleolithic of Western and Central Siberia: 27 Upper Paleolithic Sites in South-Central Siberia." In *The Paleolithic of Siberia: New Discoveries and Interpretations*. Edited by Anatoly P. Derevianko, Demitri B. Shimkin, and W. Roger Powers, 122–131. Urbana and Chicago: University of Illinois Press.

Motoyama, Hikoichi, ed. 1933. *Catalog of the Motoyama Archeological Exhibit*. Masao Suenaga. Tokyo: Oka Shoin.

Mou, Yongkang 牟永抗 1989. "Three Topics on Liangzhu Jades 良渚玉器三題." *Wenwu* 5:64–74.

National Science Museum 2004. *Special Exhibition Jadeite: Treasure of the Orient*. Tokyo: Mainichi Shimbunsha.

Needham, Joseph 1965. *Science and Civilisation in China*, vol. 4: *Physics and Physical Technology, Part II: Mechanical Engineering*. Cambridge, UK: Cambridge University Press.

Norton, Christopher J., and Jennie J. H. Jin 2009. "The Evolution of Modern Human Behavior in East Asia: Current Perspectives." *Evolutionary Anthropology* 18:247–260.

Okladnikov, Alexander P. 1955. *Neolithic and Bronze Age of the Baikal Region (Glazkovo Period)*. Materials and Investigations on Archaeology of the USSR 43 (in Russian). Moscow-Leningrad: Nauka.

Pitulko, Vladimir V., Elena Y. Pavlova, Pavel A. Nikolskiy, and Varvara V. Ivanova 2012. "The Oldest Art of the Eurasian Arctic: Personal Ornaments and Symbolic Objects from Yana RHS, Arctic Siberia." *Antiquity* 86:642–659.

Qiao, Yu 喬玉 2014. "Questions on Gender Reflected in Xinglongwa Culture House Remains 興隆窪文化房屋內遺存所反映的性別問題." *Beifang wenwu* 4:23–27.

Roux, Valentine, and Pierre de Miroschedji 2009. "Revisiting the History of the Potter's Wheel in the Southern Levant." *Levant* 41(2):155–173.

Schofield, Walter 1935. "Implements of Palaeolithic Type in Hong Kong." *The Hong Kong Naturalist* 6(3–4):272–275.

Semenov, Sergei A. 1957. "Experimental Study of the Oldest Tools and Artefacts from Traces of Manufacture and Wear." *Prehistoric Technology*. USSR 54 (in Russian), 78–83. London: Cory, Adams & Mackay.

Shaanxi Institute of Archaeology 陝西省考古研究所 1990. *Longgangsi: Report on the Excavation of the Neolithic Site* 龍崗寺—新石器時代遺址發掘報告. Beijing: Wenwu chubanshe.

Shelach, Gideon. 2000. "The Earliest Neolithic Cultures of Northeast China: Recent Discoveries and New Perspectives on the Beginning of Agriculture." *Journal of World Archaeology* 14(4):363–413.

Shuo, Zhi 2014. "Lingjiatan Jade Slit Rings: Discussing the Function of the 'Stone Drill' and Evolution of the Rotary Bearing." In *Proceedings of the International Conference on Prehistoric Rotary Technology and Related Issues at Hac Sa, Macao*. Edited by Chang Tung, 202–233. Macau: Instituto para os Assuntos Civicos e Municipais.

Sieveking, Ann 1971. "Palaeolithic Decorated Bone Discs." *The British Museum Quarterly* 35(1/4):206–229.

Suo, Xiufen 索秀芬 2005. "Discussion of the Baiyinchanghan Type 試論白音長汗類型." *Kaogu yu wenwu* 考古與文物 4:48–53.

Tang, Chung ed. 1998. *East Asian Jade: Symbol of Excellence*, vols. 1–2. Hong Kong: Centre for Chinese Archaeology and Art.

Tang, Chung 鄧聰 2003. "Discussion of Prehistoric Jade Tubular Drilling Technology in East Asia 東亞史前玉器管鑽技術試釋." In *Prehistoric Jade Carving Techniques* 史前琢玉工藝技術. Edited by Tsien Hsien-Ho 錢憲和, 145–156. Taipei: National Museum of History.

Tang, Chung 鄧聰 2007a. "The Custom of Big Earlobes." In *The Origin of Jades in East Asia: Jades of the Xinglongwa Culture*. Edited by Hu Yang, Guoxiang Liu, and Chung Tang, 54–78. Hong Kong: Centre for Chinese Archaeology of Art.

Tang, Chung 鄧聰 2007b. "The String-Sawing Technique in Jade Processing." In *The Origin of Jades in East Asia: Jades of the Xinglongwa Culture*. Edited by Chung Tang, 80–85. Hong Kong: Centre for Chinese Archaeology of Art.

Tang, Chung 鄧聰 2007c. "The Dispersion of Slit Rings over the Past 8,000 Years." In *The Origin of Jades in East Asia: Jades of the Xinglongwa Culture*. Edited by Yu Hang, Chung Tang, and Guoxiang Liu, 125–131. Hong Kong: Centre for Chinese Archaeology of Art.

Tang, Chung 鄧聰 2007d. "Color Symbolism and Jade Use in Prehistoric East Asia." In *The Origin of Jades in East Asia: Jades of the Xinglongwa Culture*. Edited by Hu Yang, Guoxiang Liu, and Chung Tang, 278–302. Hong Kong: Centre for Chinese Archaeology of Art.

Tang, Chung 鄧聰 2013. *Archaeological Excavation of Prehistoric Lapidary Workshop in Hac Sa, Macao, China* 澳門黑沙玉石作坊. Macau: Instituto para os Assuntos Civicos e Municipais.

Tang, Chung, ed. 2014a. *Proceedings of the International Conference on Prehistoric Rotary Technology and Related Issues at Hac Sa, Macao*. Macau: Instituto para os Assuntos Civicos e Municipais.

Tang, Chung 鄧聰 2014b. "Typology, Origin and Development of Prehistoric Stone Rotary Bearings in East Asia 東亞史前輞轤軸承石器類型及源流." In *Proceedings of the International Conference on Prehistoric Rotary Technology and Related Issues at Hac Sa, Macao*. Edited by Tang Chung, 28–43. Macau: Instituto para os Assuntos Civicos e Municipais.

Tang, Chung, and Guoxiang Liu 鄧聰、劉國祥 2010. "Comparative Study of Slit Ring Technologies in East Asia: String-Sawing Technique from Xinglongwa to Kuwano 東亞玦飾工藝的對比研究—從興隆窪到 桑野的砂繩 切割技術." 1–9. Studies on Southeast China Archaeology series 4. Xiamen: Xiamen University Press.

Tang, Chung, and Guoxiang Liu 鄧聰、劉國祥 2011. "Hongshan Jade Technology and Formation of Chinese Civilization 紅山文化玉器 技術與中華文明的形成." In *Science for Archaeology series* 3 科技考古(第三輯). Edited by Yuan Jing 袁靖, 278–302. Beijing: Kexue chubanshe.

Tang, Chung, and Guoxiang Liu 鄧聰、劉國祥 2012. "Neolithic Jade Technology at the Niuheliang Site, Liaoning, China 牛河梁遺址出土玉器技術初探." In *Niuheliang: Excavation Report on A Hongshan Culture Site (1983–2003)* 牛河梁—紅山文化遺址 發掘 報告(1983–2003 年度). Edited by Guo Dashun 郭大順, 525–540. Beijing: Wenwu chubanshe.

Tang, Chung, and Yadi Wen 鄧聰、溫雅棣 2014. "Xinglongwa Culture Settlements and the Social Significance of Jades 興隆窪文化聚落與玉器的社會意義." In *Papers Presented at the International Conference on the Archaeology of Ancient Settlements and Cities in Northeast Asia*. Edited by Wei Jian 巍堅, 413–434. Beijing: Kexue chubanshe.

Vanhaeren, Marian, and Francesco d'Errico 2006. "Aurignacian Ethno-Linguistic Geography of Europe Revealed by Personal Ornaments." *Journal of Archaeological Science* 33:1,105–1,128.

Wang, Shiqi 王時麒 2011. "Gemological Characteristics of Xiuyan Nephrite and Its Significant Contribution to Chinese Jade Culture 岫岩玉的寶玉石學特徵及其對中華玉 文化的重 大貢獻." In *Jades and the Foundation of Chinese Civilization I: Proceedings of the 2011 Symposium on Xiuyan Jades and the Jade Culture of China*. Edited by Guoxiang Liu and Chung Tang, 3–9. Beijing: Kexue chubanshe.

Wang, Shiqi, Chaohong Zhao, Guang Yu, Xuemei Yun, and Tiyu Duan 王時麒、趙朝紅、 于洸、員雪梅、段體玉 2007. *Xiuyan Jades in China* 中國岫岩玉. Beijing: Kexue chubanshe.

Wason, Paul K. 1994. "Mortuary Data as Evidence of Ranking, Part I." In *The Archaeology of Rank*. Edited by Paul K. Wason, 67–86. Cambridge, UK: Cambridge University Press.

Weber, Andrzej W., Roelf P. Beukens, Vladimir I. Bazaliiskii, Olga I. Goriunova, and Nikolai A. Savel'ev 2006. "Radiocarbon Dates from Neolithic and Bronze Age Hunter-Gatherer Cemeteries in the Cis-Baikal Region of Siberia." *Radiocarbon* 48(1):127–166.

Wen, Guang 聞廣 1990. "A Study on Ancient Chinese Jade." *China Non-Metallic Minerals Industry* 2:2–10.

Wen, Guang 閏廣 1998. "Some Characteristics of Prehistoric Jades from Mainland China 中國 大陸史前古玉若干特徵." In *East Asian Jade: Symbol of Excellence*, vol. 3. Edited by Chung Tang, 217–221. Hong Kong: Centre for Chinese Archaeology and Art.

Wood, Bryant G. 1990. *The Sociology of Pottery in Ancient Palestine: The Ceramic Industry and the Diffusion of Ceramic Style in the Bronze and Iron Ages.* Sheffield, England: Sheffield Academic Press.

Wood, Bryant G. 1992. "Potter's Wheel." In *The Anchor Bible Dictionary*, vol. 5. Edited by David N. Freedman, 427–428. New York: Doubleday.

Xing, Yan 幸岩 2012a. "'Central' Cemetery and Residential burials 中心"墓地與居室墓." In *Chahai: Neolithic Settlement Site Excavation Report*, vol. 2 查海——新石器時代聚落遺址發掘報告 (中冊). Edited by Liaoning Institute of Cultural Relics and Archaeology 遼寧省文物考古研究所, 525–547. Beijing: Wenwu chubanshe.

Xing, Yan 幸岩 2012b. "Summary of Jades." In *Chahai: Neolithic Settlement Site Excavation Report*, vol. 2 玉器綜述查海–新石器時代聚落遺址發掘報告(中冊). Edited by Liaoning Institute of Cultural Relics and Archaeology 遼寧省文物考古研究所, 615–624. Beijing: Wenwu chubanshe.

Xing, Yan 幸岩 2012c. "Summary of Settlement at Chahai." In *Chahai: Neolithic Settlement Site Excavation Report*, vol. 2 聚落綜述.查海–新石器時代聚落遺址發掘報告(中):冊. Edited by Liaoning Institute of Cultural Relics and Archaeology 遼寧省文物考古研究所, 648–673. Beijing: Wenwu chubanshe.

Xing, Yan 幸岩 2012d. *Chahai: Neolithic Settlement Site Excavation Report*, vol. 3 查海—新石器時代聚落 遺址發掘報告(下冊). Edited by Liaoning Institute of Cultural Relics and Archaeology 遼寧省文物考古研究所 PAGES. Beijing: Wenwu chubanshe.

Yang, Hu 楊虎, and Guoxiang Liu 劉國祥 1998. "A Preliminary Discussion on Xinglongwa 興隆窪文化玉器初論." In *East Asian Jades: Symbol of Excellence*, vol. 1. Edited by Chung Tang, 128–139. Hong Kong: Chinese University of Hong Kong.

Yang, Hu, Guoxiang Liu, and Chung Tang, eds. 2007. *The Origin of Jades in East Asia: Jades of the Xinglongwa Culture I-II.* Hong Kong: Centre for Chinese Archaeology and Art.

Yang, Hu, Guoxiang Liu, and Guotian Shao 楊虎、劉國祥、邵國田 2000. "Survey of Neolithic Site at Xinglonggou, Aohan Banner, Inner Mongolia 內蒙古敖漢旗興隆溝新 石器時代遺址調查." *Kaogu* 考古 9:30–48.

Ye, Xiaohong, and Chung Tang 葉曉紅、鄧聰 2014. "SEM Analysis of Prehistoric Stone Bearings Used in the Production of Jades: A Pearl River Delta Region Case Study 史前玉工轆轤軸承器的 SEM 分析——以環珠江口地區為例." In *Proceedings of the International Conference on Prehistoric Rotary Technology and Related Issues at Hac Sa, Macao.* Edited by Chung Tang, 44–67. Macau: Instituto para os Assuntos Civicos e Municipais.

Zhang, Jingguo, ed. 張敬國 2006. *Lingjiatan* 凌家灘. Beijing: Wenwu chubanshe.

Zhang, Zhenhong, Renyi Fu, Baofeng Chen, Jingyu Liu, Mingye Zhu, Hongkuan Wu, and Weiwen Huang 張鎮洪、傅仁義、陳寶峰、劉景玉、祝明也、吳洪寬、黃慰文 1985. "A Preliminary Report on the Excavation of Paleolithic Site at Xiaogushan of Haicheng, Liaoning Province 遼寧海城小孤山遺址發掘簡報." *Renlei xue xuebao* 4(1):70–79 and 107–108.

Zhao, Zhijun 趙志軍 2014. "The Process of Origin of Agriculture in China: Archaeological Evidence from Flotation Results 中國古代農業的形成過程——浮選出土植物遺存證據." *Disiji yanjiu* 第四紀研究 34(1):73–84.

Zhong, Youping, Zili Qiu, Liufen Li, Xianzi Gu, Han Luo, Yao Chen, and Qiyun Jiang 鍾友萍、丘志力、李榴芬、谷嫻子、羅涵、陳瑤、江啟云 2013. "REE Composition of

Nephrite Jades from Major Mines in China and Their Significance for Indicating Origin 利用稀土 元素組成模式及其參數進行國內軟玉產地來源辨識的探索." *Zhongguo xitu xuebao* 31(6):738–748.

Zhou, Zhenhua, and Jiarui Feng 周振華、馮佳睿 2010. "A Petrological and Mineralogical Comparison between Xinjiang Nephrite and Xiuyan Nephrite 新疆軟玉、岫岩軟玉的岩石礦物學對比研究." *Acta Petrologica et Mineralogica* 29(3):331–340.

CHAPTER 4

THE JADE AGE REVISITED, CA. 3500–2000 BCE

BY ELIZABETH CHILDS-JOHNSON,
OLD DOMINION UNIVERSITY

As I proposed as early as 1988 and have been advocating since then, China experienced a Jade Age from ca. 3500–2000 BCE that preceded the Bronze Age. This cultural advancement of exploiting jade as a precursor to dynastic history is considered critical to understanding traditional "China" and its arts. Other late Neolithic cultures, such as the Yangshao culture, are not excluded but do not represent the power and cultural bravado that brought civilization to a climax in the East Asian Heartland. Exploiting jade and its concomitant symbols inaugurated an entirely new generation of what would define Chinese civilization.

As maintained, it is evident that major properties of traditional China were formulated long before the beginning of dynastic and imperial-period China. From approximately 3500–2000 BCE the stone jade was the major material symbol of cultural achievement and power, and a precedent for the later use of bronze as a cultural icon during the Xia, Shang, and Zhou eras. The three most important cultures working jade during the late Neolithic include the Hongshan, Liangzhu, and Longshan (the latter of which is represented by the Haidai Longshan in Shandong, the Northwest Longshan in Shaanxi and Shanxi, and the Shijiahe Longshan in Hubei, in addition to a successive early historic Erlitou period). These cultures comprise what in the present state of excavated finds are the most prominent in catalyzing China's early social and cultural development (Childs-Johnson 2009).

What these jade-working cultures achieved beyond other late Neolithic cultures were advances in socio-political life. As once argued, "China" did not experience a "Chalcolithic Age (Copper Age)" (Yan 1999; Childs-Johnson 2009). China never extensively worked copper but rather learned about bronze after exploiting jade.

During this period of jade exploitation major social changes emerged that would serve as the new direction for civilization in the East Asian Heartland. The monopoly of precious nephrite jade production gradually led to the creation of theocratic centers run by advanced cultures using jade as a cultural marker. One wonders if China had not discovered bronze molding and casting techniques whether their culture would have become a monolithic jade-working one similar to Olmec and Mayan-period Mexico, who did not use bronze or other metals. Although bronze-working eventually evolved during the dynastic phase of early China (Xia and Shang) and although stimulated by northwestern centers, working bronze became a strictly Chinese method of molding and casting—techniques that evolved subsequently to the use of the material nephrite jade and its cousins. The Jade Age era was essentially the predecessor of the historic period of the East Asian Heartland.

The Yangshao and other northern cultures in the ancient East Asian Heartland produced a wealth of ceramic and related arts but did not advance, according to the anthropological perspective, beyond a middle Neolithic social stage of early complex societies (Peterson et al. 2016; for a different point of view, see Li Boqian 2009). As Peterson and coworkers have emphasized, the "culture-historical conceptual approach" of past archaeology needs to be revised in taking a "lifeway" approach, searching through middens (household artifact assemblages) of discarded debris to learn about prestige and wealth differences, socio-economic practice, and inequality (Peterson et al. 2016:220, 200–225). Middle Neolithic cultures of the north did not create any thoroughgoing cultural iconography that was incorporated into the historic period nor did Yangshao settlements develop a rulership that depended on religious, political, or military seniority—the necessary catalyst leading to the creation of city-states, as in the case of Liangzhu- and Longshan-period China. The Yangshao and related pottery-working cultures died out about 3000 BCE (see chapter 1 by Andrew Womack on the northern Neolithic period), the time at which jade-working rose to an eminent position of creativity and authority, marked by the Late Hongshan, Liangzhu, and Longshan periods.

The significance of jade (primarily nephrite) to the identity of the East Asian Heartland during the late Neolithic period cannot be overstated. Jade evolved as a powerful symbol of wealth and power, not simply economically but spiritually as well. It is interesting that recent surface surveys of Hongshan sites, such as Dongshanzui and Fushanzhuang, revealed that they exhibit characteristic settlement patterns of other northern middle Neolithic communities (Peterson et al. 2010) while at the same time, in contradistinction, produced some of the most outstanding jade art works and artifacts that influenced not only central but also southern late Neolithic cultures and their development. Although it is not yet clear how residential settlement interacted socially and economically with the cultic Hongshan centers around Niuheliang, the latter are unprecedented in terms of funerary ritual monuments, large-scale circular and square stone constructed raised platforms, which in some cases are directly connected with rich underground pit burials full of jades (Childs-Johnson 2009; Nelson 1995). These cultic centers document a people's coordination to construct specialized monuments. Jade-working was simply another aspect of a major cultural advance, mastering the art of slicing and abrading *ruanyu*, soft jade, as opposed to *yingyu* or jadeite worked by early Mesoamerican cultures. The appreciation for a specialized material such as *ruanyu* would dominate the history of imperial and dynastic-period taste.

As pointed out, Hongshan, Liangzhu, and Longshan jade-working activities are sequential yet chronologically overlapping. Each produced jade works that were copied or imported for trade or other socially engaging activities. As provided in Figure 1.

Hongshan distinguished itself by manufacturing amuletic-type jade talismans, ornaments to be worn and displayed on a leader's chest or clothing. Tools or weapons had not yet appeared as attributes of the Hongshan jade assemblage. Stone awls or axes may appear in small burials, but as a rule forms of weapons had not yet been fashioned. Jades were primarily decorative, for personal display, and distinguished from later Liangzhu and Longshan types, which included new categories in the form of symbolic weapons and insignia blades. Nephrite jade, primarily locally available Xiuyan *yu*, was worked in pre-Hongshan contexts to create *jue* earrings (see chapter 3 by Chung Tang and colleagues). The same were worn in southern Yangzi cultures of comparable date (see chapter 2 by Xiangming Fang).

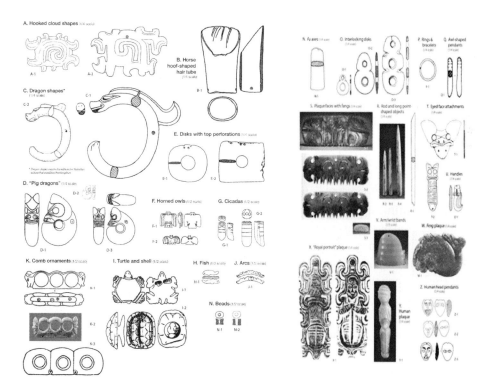

FIGURE 1 A–Z. Hongshan jade types. After Childs-Johnson 2009: Figure 8.

HONGSHAN JADE-WORKING

Hongshan jade-working is represented by approximately 20 types of jades, mostly from Hongshan burials and occasionally site remains. They may be classified according to three major categories: (1) mythic, the most prominent ("pig-dragon," eyed plaques with simplified "pig-dragon" forms, bird plaques, and plaques shaped as hooked cloud scrolls with bird head); (2) abstract and functional shapes (bracelets, beads, hair tubes, disks, arm guards, rods/pins, pendants, handles); and (3) representational forms (human figurines, scarified faces, frogs, turtle plastrons, cicadas, horned owls, and fish). By mythic is meant an image not of this world, as represented by the so-called "pig-dragon" and hooked cloud with profile bird or dragon head, two images that would become stereotypical Chinese images. A few jade types not found in burials but collected include the weaving spool and spindle, and utilitarian ax.

Hongshan social members were stratified, as told by burials with a richer assemblage of jades as opposed to assemblages with only a few or no jades. If an elite member of Hongshan society were imagined in full regalia, the person would have been bejeweled with jade paraphernalia including bracelets, armlets, necklaces, chunks of pig-dragon pendant sculptures, other pendants (cicada, turtle, turtle shells, owls, human heads), protective arm guards, hair tubes, hair combs, and a variety of broad flat cloud-scroll plaques.

The Hongshan leader of Mongolian blood was a hunter, as told by the arm guard jades that would have been strung with probably leather through holes around the arm to prevent backlash when an arrow was released from the bow. The chest plaques and sculptural images from Hongshan burials are self explanatory, hanging vertically at chest or girdle level. The hair accouterments are interesting, since functionally they appear identical to similar wares found in later Liangzhu- and Longshan-period contexts. Ornaments for hair control were likely attached with leather strings to comb parts that are no longer extant but probably were made of wood or bone. The hair tube is apparently unique to the Hongshan jade assembly, although jade hair attachments and ornaments are plentiful in later Chinese history. The tube is elliptical in shape and was probably secured by string through the bioncial holes at the base of the tube. Based on a Hongshan cultural image of a probable chieftain or deified image, the tube was vertically raised and to this author designed possibly to hold hair in ponytail fashion (Figures 1B, 1X, 2). The long pencil-shaped rods (Figure 1R) may also have been designed for holding the hair in place as stick pins, used by all generations of males and females throughout Chinese history.

It is likely that the flat plaque type of mythic and other jade images were sewn onto clothing, since most are characterized by what are described in archaeological literature as ox-nostril holes, double tear-shaped holes for attaching by sewing with thread or string on to another material (see for example back of Figure 1Z images). The jade ornaments with double holes are usually flat two-dimensional forms including small-scale faces, horned owls, turtles (Figure 1F, I, T, Z), large and flat plaques in the form of a bird with reverted "pig-dragon" head (Figure 1W), a bird head framed by symmetrical hooked cloud scrolls (Figure 1A), and a "pig-dragon" with sets of fangs framed by similarly symmetrical hooked cloud scrolls (Figure 1S).

The bracelets and pendants were worn on wrist or upper arm and were made to be suspended from string or thread around the neck or were hung at girdle level. The variety of pendants suggests that the wearer may have owned a large repertory of suspended ornaments ranging from the mythic heavy sculptural "pig-dragon" type to lighter cicada, fish, turtle, or frog types to linked or single disks.

The elaborate set of these Hongshan jades belonging to elite social members signified rank and wealth, if not a religious aura. The fact that nephrite jade (and sometimes serpentine) was singled out as the primary medium for accouterments of formal dress was intentional—something appreciated for its beauty and properties. The mythic image of succulently coiled fetal form ending in a large head with sizeable ear flaps and beady eyes can be identified with the earliest written graph for dragon, *qiu* 虯.

The cloud-shaped corner cusps framing a beady-eyed and fanged face—a variation of the head of the so-called "pig-dragon"—or framing an abstraction of the same or bird head may also be associated with the earliest pictograph for cloud, *yun* 云, the ubiquitous natural wonder and sky power that brings moisture and rain.

LIANGZHU JADE-WORKING

The second jade-working culture, Liangzhu marks the height of the movement of jade-working in the East Asian Heartland. Recent excavations of Mojiaoshan and environs in a triangular area encompassing Lake Tai and its surroundings place this second jade-working culture considerably ahead socially and economically beyond Hongshan. Some 200–300 sites have been identified as far east as Shanghai, as far south as Hangzhou, and as far west as the mountain ranges of Maoshan and Ningzhen. Geographically the area encompasses southeastern Jiangsu, southern Shandong, northern Zhejiang, and Shanghai municipality, an area of some 18,000 km² (Zhou Ying 2007). As related in chapter 5 by Liu Bin, Liangzhu represents the most advanced regionally consolidated culture during the era of 3200–2300 BCE and therefore is regarded as a major player in the birth of Chinese civilization. His excavations of the city site of Mojiaoshan in Zhejiang have uncovered a massive layout of some 8 million m² with an internal centralized palace area of some 300,000 sqm (=30 hectares). Fortification walls and waterway or moat surround the city-site. In addition, Liu discovered a vast water supply and conservancy system, large-scale astronomical observatories in connection with raised outdoor platform altars, and an extensive suburban settlement of some additional 1,000,000 km². The city evidently was a major military presence, as reflected by the abundant jade and stone weapons per elite burial as well as by the fortification walls surrounding the sacred compound center. Liangzhu rulers wielded power over not only their cultural center at Mojiaoshan but over communities of varying scales surrounding the center.

Social and economic stratification was pyramidal. The elite strata of Liangzhu society may be divided into four tiers (see Childs-Johnson 2009: Tables 3 and 4; Lu 1996: 195–215, 259–262) most likely composed of those who ruled (chieftain and family), those who were military personnel or property owners related to the ruler, and those who controlled jade-working and other highly skilled crafts such as ceramic-making. Laboring classes worked the fields and probably served when needed as foot soldiers. As with the Hongshan culture, the last phases of Liangzhu witnessed full cultural maturity. During Periods 3–4 (ca. 2800–2300 BCE) large-scale pyramidal platforms and theoretically astronomical observatories began to be constructed and flourished (see chapter 5 by Bin Liu). Sacrifice through burning animal and some human remains found on flat surface tops of the manmade platform altars apparently was common at these sacred Liangzhu sites (Huang 2000:43, 135; Lu 1996: 191). The burned sacrifices of animals corroborate the ceremonial use of these platform cemeteries in honoring what must have been a powerful dead elite. Although there was more than one site with a sacred outdoor altar center, Mojiaoshan was the biggest and most complex and is thus regarded as the "capital" of the Liangzhu people and culture.

The sophisticated expression emerging amid archaeological data reflects a large-scale central city-state (chiefdom) at Mojiaoshan with smaller surrounding cities, with their own sacred centers, suburbs, defensive moats, and competitive arts serving common socio-political interests. This mature expression of the Liangzhu culture may be described as the heart of the "Jade Age." Around 90% of goods from elite burials are jade works of art (Zhejiang 1988:7; see corroborative statistics as tabulated in Childs-Johnson 2009: Table 4, 327-338). Other burial goods may include lacquer vessels inlaid with jade, refined black and grey wares in eccentric shapes with delicately engraved designs, and ivory carvings (Huang 2000:Figures 70, p. 100; 76–77, pp. 112–113; 59, p. 75). Yet, the latter are consistently secondary to jades in terms of number per elite buried in these raised altar cemeteries.

Liangzhu peoples subscribed to a sophisticated and demarcated ritual system of belief in the spirit powers of nature. Culturally and stylistically their interests are entirely separate from precedent Hongshan ones, although this condition is not true regarding the transitional Lingjiatan culture of Anhui, as will be discussed. The Liangzhu peoples believed in a sophisticated cosmological system of four cardinal directions and central axis, with a preference for a northern orientation of outdoor earthen altars, human burials, and site settlements. The Hongshan favored a north-south orientation as well, but by the Liangzhu era there are clear-cut cosmological symbols of sun and moon worship, the power of a north-south axis, and belief in metamorphosis. The complexity of Liangzhu society and city settlement is reverberated in the complexity of jade types, their functions, and imagery. Although we still may not be clear how the most idiosyncratic jade types called *cong* and *bi* were used, it is clear the heart of the Jade Age rests firmly in the Liangzhu culture. The richest number and types of jades characterize this era.

This rich array of types is not limited to symbolic amuletic-type ornaments as typified the Hongshan culture. Liangzhu jade types include two new categories of specialized implements and symbolic weapons. This more complex assemblage of jades is connected with new interests in advertising military and social might, power over "ritual" and war. "Ritual" goes beyond status and power in suggesting something more specialized regarding ceremonial use. We tentatively use ritual to characterize not only certain jade types of eccentric shape and imagery but to define the sacrificial platforms that were used over an extended period of time. Burial jades fall into three major categories: specialized weapons (*yue*), specialized implements (*cong* and *bi*), and specialized costume and headdress ornaments. The latter is clearly a more sophisticated application of jade-working that supersedes that of the earlier Hongshan culture.

A reconstructed appearance of a Liangzhu elite leader differs from that of the Hongshan leader: striking differences appear in imagery and style, as well as in new types that are either symbols of weapons or ritual objects. The Liangzhu leader would have been covered by jade costume appurtenances, in addition to being accompanied by jade-studded weaponry (Figure 2C) and jade ritual implements (Figure 2AB).

Basic jewelry bedecking the body included bracelets, armlets, hair stickpins, and necklaces, in addition to multiple and numerous strands of pendant beads, pendant *huang* shapes, and pendant plaque types (Figure 2D:1–2, N). The jade belt hook is new to the jade repertoire of bodily ornaments (Figure 2O), as are certain headdress accouterments. One is the three-prong jade, theorized for setting a large-scale fan of peafowl feathers and a set of axially oriented D-shaped jades forming a diadem (Figure 2F:1–6). One jade crowned comb per burial, as with the Hongshan elite, is theorized to secure the individual's hair as it is to decorate (Figure 2:1–2). Similar to the Hongshan repertoire of small-scale pendant jades, the Liangzhu also may suspend small fish, frogs, turtles, birds of prey, cicadas, and a variety of bead types (Figure 2P–U). In addition to the jade belt hook, also new to the dress code is the presence of jade knee cap or boot pairs of ornaments (Figure 2E). One further and special pendant image includes the metamorphic image of a profile human in fetal position airborne by an attached bird (Figure 2S).

Entirely new to the jade repertoire are the shapes known in later literature as *cong* and *bi*. These two jades form a ritual pair that defies exact definition. The *cong* is a circular tube encased in a square sheath, and described therefore as a prismatic cylinder. The *bi* is on the other hand a flat disk with central hole. They appear in tombs in large numbers, sometimes more *bi* than *cong* and vice versa. Thirty-two *cong* were uncovered from Tomb 3 at Sidun as opposed to only four from Tomb 20 and three from Tomb 23. Forty-five and 54 *bi* were unearthed from tombs at Fanshan and 24 *bi* were unearthed from Tier 2 Tomb 3 at Sidun (Childs-Johnson 2009: Table 4, 327–338).

As maintained by Lu Jianfang almost 20 years ago, *cong* identify power, generation, and status among Liangzhu social members and clans (Lu 1996). He hypothesizes, for example, that the 32 *cong* from the 20-year-old's Tomb 3 at Sidun identify 32 clans (or families 家族) over which this male ruled. The 32 clans were bound as allies with common belief. At the time of the male's death these clans participated in some sort of ceremony by handing over to or requisitioning for this city's leader (at Sidun) their

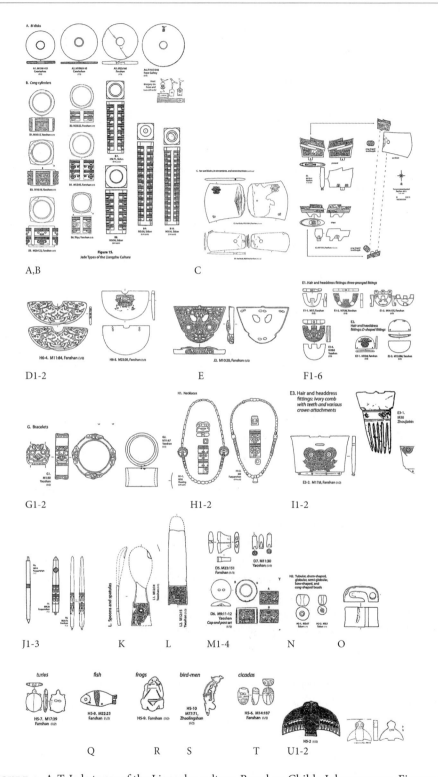

FIGURE 2 A-T. Jade types of the Liangzhu culture. Based on Childs-Johnson 2009 :Figure 15.

symbol of rank. In addition, each *cong* had generational significance. The levels of imagery up and down a *cong* signified the clan's age, which in this case had survived for five generations, since the *cong* had five levels of imagery. Similarly a *cong* with 15 layers of imagery stood for 15 generations of that clan. Thus, 32 different clans owed allegiance to the deceased in Tomb 3 at Sidun and each had different generational lifespans. The *cong* with a set of semi-human animal images within the same Tomb 3:43, found isolated next to the corpse's head, identified the deceased and his generational status—that the deceased died without offspring due to the single levels of animal and semi-human images. Communicating the number of generations or offspring apparently was also documented by the so-called "royal *cong*" 宗琮, also isolated in placement next to the head of the male buried in Tomb 12 at Fanshan (Figure 2B:3). Since the latter *cong* had two layers each of semi-human and animal images (four levels), the deceased died with one generation of offspring, according to Lu's theory (Childs-Johnson 2009). The shape of *cong* and *bi* and their imagery have often been described. The two functioned ritually in a context of cosmological significance, in addition to serving as wealth and status markers, as outlined by Lu. Ancient cultures, such as the Mesoamerican Olmec and Mayan, saw the world as dominated by what the early East Asian Heartland defines as a cosmic realm with axial extensions, defined by four directional axes, N, S, E, and W (see Childs-Johnson 2012), or as known in historic Shang time as *sifang* four-directional cosmology. The *cong* probably served as a late-Neolithic version of a cosmological tree (Hayashi), a circular sky tube encased by a directional square earth, rising indefinitely skyward as a variation on the axis-mundi theme. The *cong* is typically covered with a standardized program of mythic symbols, semi-human and zoomorphic animal, sometimes flanked by cosmic birds and repeated in cartouches at four corners. By contrast, the circular *bi* disk is traditionally limited to cosmological images of the bird perched in profile on a stepped altar.

Imagery is standardized and in this context may be read as ritually significant, documenting the power symbol of metamorphosis and spirit flight. The significance of these abstract stylized cartouche images up and down *cong* surfaces (Figure 2A) is underscored by the now well-published versions of the same masks on the celebrated "royal *cong*" from Fanshan (Figure 2B:3). The humanoid riding the large-scale zoomorph with whirling big eyes is a symbol of metamorphic ascension and transformation. Pairs of large cosmic eyes, symbolizing the natural power of sun and moon, whose cosmic rays define the breath of life, are equally comfortable defining the power of avian flight. Although we do not know the name of this demonic image, its significance is spelled out by the relationship of animal to human—the dominance of one over the other—and by the deity's attributes.

The focus of imagery on Liangzhu jades, although seemingly more complex and sophisticated than Hongshan imagery, is also dramatically different stylistically, although equally religiously powerful. The structure of iconic norms is a fundamental attribute of theocratic foundations and early complex societies. The two cultures, earlier Hongshan and later Liangzhu, nonetheless interacted independently as two precocious jade-working centers. The image of the "pig-dragon" or coiled *qiu* and later *long* versions of the dragon do not appear in the Liangzhu iconography.

LINGJIATAN JADE-WORKING

Yet, the symbiotic relationship of two powerful jade-working traditions forming theocratic settlements is eminently apparent in the pre-Liangzhu jade-working site of Lingjiatan in Hanshan, Anhui, related to both the Songze and later Liangzhu cultures in the eastern valley of the Yangzi River. Geographically, Anhui was a middle ground for interaction and influence between north and south, and in this case between Hongshan and Liangzhu. Pre-Liangzhu cultural traditions are well-represented by earlier Songze and Lingjiatan site finds and document what Li Boqian has qualified are early emanations of a theocratic city-state (Li 2012). Xiangming Fang in chapter 2 has also documented the contributions of the earlier Songze Neolithic culture on later Liangzhu cultural traditions in advancing social complexity. Key advances included not only rice cultivation; use of the stone plowshare; advanced wood technology; column architecture; surrounding dry trench settlement; high man-made platform structures and altars; and advanced crafts of painting, sculpting, and engraving but also use of the cosmological double bird symbols of moonlight and sunlight, and other light and fertility symbols, such as the rotating sun symbol with birds. And Fang notes, "The exploitation and abrasive techniques of working 'true jade' or tremolite nephrite [that] began at Lingjiatan-Songze cultural sites . . . did not occur elsewhere than the Lingjiatan-Songze culture located in the lower reaches of the Yangzi River in southern China where jade resources are located."

The major tomb find, M23 at Lingjiatan (Figure 3A), not only illuminates the abundance of jade but also various other major social dimensions that underline the significance of jade-working in the late Neolithic period. Firstly, Lingjiatan and Songze are comparable to Hongshan in date and represent independent jade-working centers of what were to emerge as city sites along the lower Yangzi. As illustrated (see Fang, chapter 2, Figure 15), 200 pieces of jade out of 330 objects in Lingjiatan burial No. 7M23 (Figure 3A) are exceptional for various reasons: not only in number but in the obvious preference for jade to the exclusion of other materials used in multiple contexts.

The corpse apparently was laid on two to six layers of jade and stone adzes, chisels, and axes—none showing use—and within a lacquer-painted coffin decorated with sets of suspended jade *huang* rings. The body was dressed with additional layers of sets of jade bracelets, jade armlets, and jade ornaments. Three turtles in fan array lay within the corpse's crotch, signifying fertility in the afterlife. A large jade sculpted pig weighing 88 kg in addition was placed on top of the body of the deceased (Figure 3B).

Of particular interest are the jades simulating Hongshan jade types (Figure 3C): the naked human with upheld arms (here apparently dressed), the archer's arm guard of semi-circular shape, the hair tube but here designed as a musical instrument with clapper, the coiled dragon, top and bottom carved parts of the turtle shell, variously decorated jade comb ornaments, and the peculiar pendant of a bird of prey with unfurled wings ending in matching heads of the "pig-dragon" and at the center of the

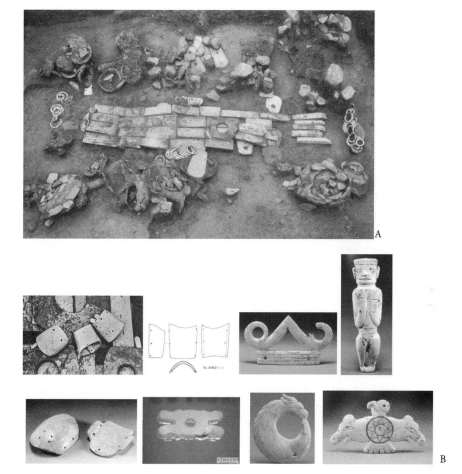

FIGURE 3 Jades from Lingjiatan, Anhui showing Hongshan influence, as represented by the following images: burial M23, Anhui Horse-hoof shapes as bells, crown of a comb, human with upraised arms, tortoise plastron and carapace, four-cusp cloud plaque, pig-dragon, raptor with boar headed wings and cosmological diagram. Based on images assembled in Childs-Johnson 2009: figures 26 A, B, C10, E, F, N2 and 16 E–F.

body a cosmological symbol of what is probably the sun as a circle with eight axially pointed rays. The latter image is directly related to the sun disk with sunbirds flying vigorously at four points extending axially from the disk on Liangzhu artifacts. It seems the Lingjiatan artisan or commissioner of the jade was mixing and matching symbols drawn from two different traditions, one northern (Hongshan) and the other southern. This is a clear case of one culture impacting another, in this example of northern Hongshan impacting Songze.

The celebrated discovery of the square jade plaque with a clearly delineated circular sun motif with axially extending rays in the center and four on the outer circle elsewhere at Liangjiatan (Figure 3A) is corroborative evidence for this common cosmological symbol. The square-shaped plaque lay over two hollowed halves of a turtle plastron, forming a composite image most likely in connection with some form of divination (Figure 3A). The image mimics the shape of the cosmological *cong* jade composed of circular inner tube framed by axial extensions at four corners of a square or rectangle exterior. The concepts of a domed sky and square earth are abundantly clear in this symbol.

In addition, what may be a singular interpretation of this advanced late-Neolithic settlement in Anhui is what takes the appearance of the Hongshan tubular headpiece but functions differently for the Lingjiatan member. The tube has turned into a musical instrument, as a bell with jade clappers (Figure 3C, 2nd row upper left).

Clearly these influences of the Hongshan on a southern site in Anhui associated with the later Liangzhu tradition of jade-working is no accident. Lingjiatan artisans simply adapted what they considered highly attractive and awesome to honor their deceased spirits in the afterlife. In addition, the second example of a carved jade boar (with upward-turning fangs)—the largest sculpture of its kind at this time in antiquity—shows a preference that is in keeping with the Hongshan emphasis on the wild boar and its domestic cousin, the pig, the main staple of both cultures' meat diet.

How extensive the influence of Hongshan jade-working was on southern practice and belief should be amplified with future excavations along the southern Yangze Valley. As supported in current scholarship, Lingjiatan, Songze, and Liangzhu cultures were firmly entrenched in a common course of chronological development. Again, core belief in *sifang* cosmology, symbols of spirit flight, and likely turtle divination tie these cultures closely together (see chapter 2 for further comparisons).

LONGSHAN JADE-WORKING

By the Longshan era, the Jade Age had metastasized and shifted into a final and sophisticated stage of city-state society and development. Hongshan was replaced by the Xiajiadian culture in the north and Liangzhu sites were gradually wiped out due to flooding and related disasters. Longshan-period city-states replaced those of Liangzhu with formidable fortifications and an equally formidable taste for jade. Cities were grander in size than Liangzhu city sites and were located in a geographically much more extensive area, covering most of today's northern and southern provinces. Oracle bone divination was omnipresent and writing began to appear. New specialized jade types define new ruling and competing elites. These new types are identified here as insignia jades, a type of status marker that undoubtedly had ceremonial use, not yet understood by any extant contemporary form of written data (Figure 4A–D) (Childs-Johnson 1995:64–90). The categories of symbolic *yue* blades and bodily and hair ornaments continued to thrive, although the ritual use of *cong* and *bi* gradually subsided in being replaced by jade blades signifying status and wealth.

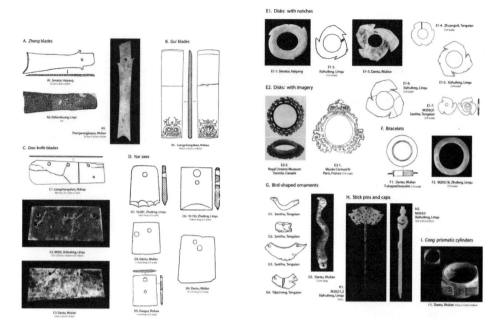

FIGURE 4 Shandong Longshan jade types. Based on Childs-Johnson 1999: Figures 24–25.

The insignia blades of jade—*gui, dao, zhang*—are all derived from utilitarian tool types and vary in number per tomb. The site of Shijiahe in Hubei and its jades serve as excellent illustration of interaction and contact between north and south, east and west settlements that explodes during this period, in continuing to employ jade as a cultural marker. In chapter 3 on *yazhang* Chung Tang explores the spread of the *zhang* jade blade, including the Erlitou period and beyond in Sichuan, Vietnam, and further south in Hong Kong and elsewhere. The Erlitou *zhang* blade is a product of an earlier Longshan-period invention that spreads throughout the northwest and southwest and, to a lesser extent, the southeast. The route that Shandong Longshan cultural influences take is inland, as represented by the rich finds at Shijiahe in Hubei and a variety of other destinations, particularly in the far northwest and far southwest.

The similarity between the three major icons of this period, the semi-human head, mythic *feng* bird, and heraldic bird of prey amid Shandong Longshan and Shijiahe Longshan has been mentioned and illustrated (see Figures 4A–C, E1–2). The two Longshan-period mask types worked on the well-known *gui* blade from Liangchengzhen in Shandong (Figure 4F) may be used as the classical standard to illustrate the movement of working jade and interpreting religious icons outside Shandong. Three blades of Longshan date are illustrative. One comes from a regional site of Licheng in Shanxi (Figure 4C). The Liangchengzhen semi-human mask may be varied in detail but basically consists of a semi-human with encircled eyes, a bared set of teeth, and an elaborate headdress formed by abstracted feather extensions and scrolls. This is

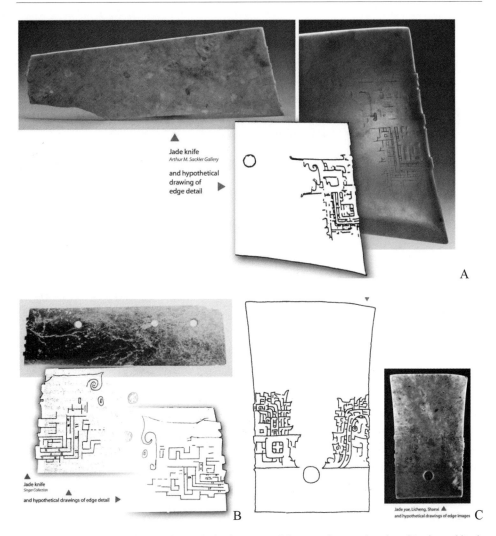

FIGURE 5 Longshan culture jades with dual images of the semi-human head and L-shaped limb extension. **A** *Dao* knife blade with identical image of a semi-human mask with extended limb at both ends. **B** *Dao* knife with identical semi-human mask with extended limb decorating the two short side ends. **C** *Yue* ax with two images, a semi-human profile with feathered headdress and an abstracted head with limb extension overlapping the two sides of the blade. Based on Childs-Johnson 2009 :Figure 27.

the type featured on the two *dao* blades in Washington, DC, yet also featured are bent L-shaped legs ending in talons (Figure 5B). The classical *dao* blade shape, although fractured in one case, is a long trapezoid or thin rectangle with holes perforated along the top edge (Figure 5AB). The image decorating these *dao* knife insignia blades is the same semi-human face represented on Shijiahe and Shandong Longshan jades. But the images on the museum blades fold over the short edge ends, so they may be read as profiles on either side. These images also differ in that a body part is represented by the L-shaped leg probably ending in talons, now worn over time, a feature that will characterize the Bronze Age image of the *yi* metamorphic mask. Both of these images correspond with the classical type represented on the Liangchengzhen *gui* blade and with many other museum works of jade art reflecting Shandong Longshan-period style. How these Longshan images carried on and advanced beyond their predecessors and prototypes of the Liangzhu culture has been previously reviewed (see Childs-Johnson 2009).

The image on the Licheng, Shanxi *yue* jade blade (Figure 4C) is the same profile head with an elaborate *feng* feathered headdress represented on the Liangchengzhen *gui* blade, with variations indicating local manufacture. Both profiles overlap both edges of the *yue* blade so that there are two images according to the Longshan standard of dual representation. Yet, one of these facial images is upside down and is marked by an internal cross instead of facial features. Is this a quadrant symbol of the semi-human unknown elsewhere or is this simply a local interpretation for a design? The *yue* blade itself is the type characterizing the many locally manufactured *yue* symbolic blades known throughout Longshan territory, and particularly in this far-northwest regional outpost in Shanxi. In any case, classical Longshan insignia blades and religious icons appear throughout a much more widespread realm in operating as legitimizing social and political symbols of power.

The cultural impact of the three jade-working cultures on early Chinese civilization from ca. 3500 to 2000 BCE extends well beyond the geographic origin and locus of each culture. The impact of the Hongshan culture on Liangzhu, Liangzhu on Longshan, and Longshan on most of north, central, and southwest areas has been illustrated. Although midden details are lacking to assess the lifeway of individual social members, the abundance and importance of jade is evident and all-important in assessing late Neolithic settlement and civilization.

IMPORTANCE OF JADE

Why the material nephrite jade, *ruanyu*, was elevated to a level affecting social and spiritual identity and cultural advancement is in part due to the belief that jade had special life-giving qualities, symbolic of not only social power and wealth but of spirit power, representing belief in the power of medium and the icons decorating the jade medium. We know, for example, that jade plugs (*han*) were inserted into the mouths of deceased members during the Songze era. What could this mean other than to seal and consume the "soul-spirit" of the once-living? The jade funerary bed made of countless jade blades at Lingjiatan; the jade costume and hair jewelry of Hongshan, Liangzhu, and Longshan elite; and later jade burial suits strung together with gold thread are all representative of this interest in the preciosity and spiritual associations of the material jade. It is, thus, without question that early China experienced a period that we proudly label Jade Age.

BIBLIOGRAPHY

Anhuisheng Wenwu Kaogu Yanjiusuo 安徽省文物考古研究所 2006. *Lingjiatan: Field Excavation Report* 凌 家滩: 田野考古发掘报. Beijing: Wenwu chubanshe.

Anhuisheng Wenwu Kaogu Yanjiusuo 安徽省文物考古研究所 2008. "New Discoveries in the Fifth Excavation of the Lingjiatan Site in Hanshan County, Anhui 安 徽省寒 县凌家滩 遗址第五次发掘的新发现." *Kaogu* 9:63–73.

Childs-Johnson, Elizabeth 1991. "Jades of the Hongshan Culture: The Dragon and Fertility Cult Worship." *Arts Asiatiques* 46:82–95.

Childs-Johnson 1995. "Symbolic Jades of the Erlitou Period: A Xia Royal Tradition," *Archives of Asian Art* XLVIII (1995): 64–90.

Childs-Johnson, Elizabeth 1998. "Jade as Material and Epoch." In *China: 5000 Years, Innovation and Transformation in the Arts*. Edited by, 55–68. New York: Solomon R. Guggenheim Museum.

Childs-Johnson, Elizabeth, ed. 2001–2002. *Enduring Art of Jade Age China*, vols. 1–2. New York: Throckmorton Fine Art.

Childs-Johnson, Elizabeth 2002. "Jade as Confucian Ideal, Immortal Cloak, and Medium for the Metamorphic Fetal Pose." In *Enduring Art of Jade Age China*, vol. 2. Edited by Elizabeth Childs-Johnson, 15–24. New York: Throckmorton Fine Art.

Childs-Johnson, Elizabeth 2009. "The Art of Working Jade and the Rise of Civilization in China." In *The Jade Age and Early Chinese Jades in American Museums*, 291–393. Beijing: Science Press.

Childs-Johnson, Elizabeth, with Gu Fang 2012. "Speculations on the Significance of the *Cong* and *Bi* of the Liangzhu Culture." In *Liangzhu Jades*. 5–12. New York: Throckmorton Fine Art.

Childs-Johnson, Elizabeth 2012. "Postscript to Big *Ding* and China Power- Shang *Sifang* Cosmology"對大鼎'和中國國王權力的後記:商代四方 (四個方向) 宇宙 學," in 紀念孫 作雲教授百年誕辰暨古代中國歷史與文化國際學術研討會論文集 (Proceedings in Honor of Professor Sun Zuoyun's Centennial and International Conference on Research on Ancient China History and Culture), Henan University Pub: 191–210.

Huang, Xuanpei 黄宣佩 2000. Fuquanshan福泉山. Beijing: Wenwu chubanshe.

Lei, Xiaoxun et al. 2016. "Green Mysteries." *China Daily E-Paper*, January 19, 2016. Beijing.

Li, Boqian 李伯谦 2009. "Two Modes of the Development of Chinese Ancient Civilization: On Observing of the Funeral Jades Unearthed from Large Graves of Hongshan Culture Liangzhu Culture, and Yangshao Culture 中国古代文明发展的两种模式 - 从红山文化 良渚文化,仰韶文化大墓出土观察葬礼." *Wenwu* 3:47–56. (Translated into English, *Chinese Archaeology* 10:136–142.)

Liu, Bin 刘斌 2018. *A Comprehensive Research Report on Liangzhu Ancient City* 良渚古城综 合研究报告. Beijing: Wenwu chubanshe.

Liu, Bin 刘斌 2016. *Eighty Years of Discovering the Liangzhu Culture* 良渚文化发现八十周. Beijing: Kexue chubanshe.

Liu, Bin, Wang Ningyuan, Chen Minghui 刘斌、王宁远、陈明辉 2015. *Liangzhu Ancient City: New Discoveries and Explorations; Rights and Beliefs; Archaeological Exhibition of Liangzhu Site Group* 良渚古城——新发现和探索，权利与信仰——良渚遗址群考古特展. Beijing: Wenwu chubanshe.

Lu, Jianfang 陆建方 1996。"A Study of Liangzhu Burials 良渚文化墓葬研究", In Xu Huping, ed., *Dongfang wenming zhi guang*, 176–217. Nanjing Museum with Hainan: Hainan International New Publishers.

Mou, Yongkang 牟永抗, and Wu Naizuo 吴汝祚 1997. "Analysis of the Era of the Jade Age: An Important Model for Production during the Age of Chinese Civilization 分析玉器时代 - 中华文明时代的重要生产模式." In *Kaoguxue wenhua lunji*, vol. 4. Beijing: Wenwu chubanshe.

Nelson, Sarah, ed. 1995. *The Archaeology of Northeast China Beyond the Great Wall.* London and New York: Routledge.

Peterson, Christian, Xueming Lu, Robert D. Drennan, and Zhu Da 2010. "Hongshan Chiefly Communities in Neolithic Northeastern China." *Proceedings of the National Academy of Sciences* 107:5,756–5,761.

Peterson, Christian E., Robert D. Drennan, and Kate L. Bartel 2016. "Comparative Analysis of Neolithic Household Artifact Assemblage Data from Northern China." *Journal of AnthropologicalResearch.*

Shaanxi Provincial Institute of Archaeology, Yulin Municipal Team of Cultural Relics and Archaeology, and Bureau of Culture and Sports, Shenmu County 陕西省考古所，神木县榆林市文物考古与文化体育局 2014. "The Shimao Site in Shenmu County, Shaanxi陕西神木县石卯遗址." *Chinese Archaeology* 14:18–26 (abridged version of the original report in *Kaogu* 2013.7:15–24).

Yan, Wenming 严文名 1999 "关于中国青铜并用石器时代 A Discussion of **the Chalcolithic Period** of **China**," *Shiqian Yanjiu* 1:36–44,3536-44, 35.

Yu, Pei 2015. "Jades Unearthed in Hubei Highlight the Highest Level of Jade-Working in Prehistoric China 湖北出土玉器彰显史前中国玉文化最高成就." Xinhua She 新华社 *Zhongguo kaogu baogao,* December 21, 2015.

Zhang, Chi 2013. "The Qujialing-Shijiahe Culture in the Middle Yangzi River Valley." In *A Companion to Chinese Archaeology*, edited by Anne P. Underhill. John Wiley.

Zhejiang 1988. Zhejiangsheng Wenwu Kaogu Yanjiusuo 浙江省文物考古研究所 1988. "Preliminary Excavation Report on the Cemetery at Fashan in Yuhang, Zhejiang 浙江余杭饭山良渚墓地发掘简报 Yuhang Fanshan Liangzhu mudi fajue jianbao", *Wenwu* 1988.1, 1–31.

Zhou, Ying 2007. *The Dawn of the Oriental Civilization: Liangzhu site and Liangzhu culture,* Beijing: China Intercontinental Press, Beijing.

CHAPTER 5

....

LIANGZHU CULTURE AND THE ANCIENT CITY OF LIANGZHU

....

BY BIN LIU, ZHEJIANG PROVINCIAL INSTITUTE OF CULTURAL RELICS AND ARCHAEOLOGY

CHINA geographically forms a relatively closed and independent vast area in East Asia. China is bordered on its east side by a vast sea; to the west by the Pamir Plateau; to the southwest by the Himalayas, the Qinghai-Tibet Plateau, and the Yunnan-Guizhou Plateau; to the northwest by the Tian Mountains, the Altai, the Mongolian Plateau, and the Gobi desert; and to the northeast by an uninhabited Siberia (Yan 2003). A number of independent geographical units evolved some 9,000 years ago within this land area of 9,600,000 km². Different geographical conditions gradually bred a number of different cultural types and different developmental stages. By around 4000 BCE a new era of accelerated development characterized these areas, leading to civilization and urbanization (Su 2000). From 3500 to 2000 BCE, cultures solidified, including the early Miaodigou, Hongshan, Liangzhu, Qujialing, Dawenkou and, subsequent to these, beginning around 3000 BCE the Longshan, Shijiahe, Taosi, and Qijia. Many of these cultures may be characterized as initial stages of regional civilizations, before unification.

The Liangzhu culture is a major example of these regional areas that I label "civilization," dating to the time period of ca. 3300–2300 BCE. Other cultures, including Miaodigou and Dawenkou in the Yellow River Basin, the Youziling and Songze cultures in the Yangzi River Basin, and the Hongshan culture in the north, after expanding and integrating also gradually consolidated into advanced regional cultures. The Liangzhu culture is the best example of regional consolidation. Its rise to this level of consolidation occurred at the same time civilization appeared in the West with ancient Egypt, Sumer, and Harappa. This era evidently not only witnessed the birth of Chinese but of world civilizations.

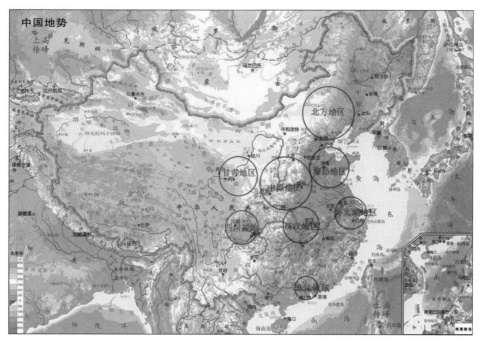

北地地区 Northern Area; 甘青地区 GanQing Area; 中原地区 Zhongyuan Area;
渤海地区 Bohai Area; 四川盆地 Sichuan Basin; 江汉地区 JiangHan Area;
环太湖地区 Huan Taihu Area; 珠江流域 ZhuJiang River Basin

FIGURE 1 Map showing major cultures of Neolithic China under one cultural system.

Thirty degrees north latitude appears to be a magical zone, including most of the significant natural and cultural landscapes of early civilizations. The latter include the ancient Egyptian civilization along the Nile River Valley, the Sumerian civilization along the Tigris and Euphrates Rivers, and the Harappa civilization along the Indus River Valley. The core area of the Liangzhu culture is distributed in the Lake Tai (Taihu) Basin in the lower reaches of the Yangzi River, lying between 30°–32° north latitude and 119° 10–121° 55 east longitude. The Taihu Lake Basin is surrounded by the Mao and Tianmu mountains in the west, with the Yangzi River and Qiantang River forming a boundary alongside the East China Sea in the east. The total area is about 36,900 km². The area is fertile with rivers and lakes and is suitable for human survival and reproduction.

The sequence of ancient cultural development around the Lake Tai Valley in the lower reaches of the Yangzi River in China is clear. The area was an independent cultural location with its own characteristics. From 5000 BCE to 2000 BCE, it experienced the cultures of Majiabang, Songze, and Liangzhu, and later the cultures of Qianshanyang and Guilin.

Characteristics of the Liangzhu civilization

The capital city: Its geographical location, structure, date, and engineering

The ruins of the city of Liangzhu lie at the core of the Liangzhu culture and identify the capital of the Liangzhu civilization. These ruins alongside the abundant burial jades serve as a hallmark of the material remains. Liangzhu is located in the Yuhang in area of Zhejiang. There it forms a crescent-shaped basin measuring some 800 km² in area. The city is located on high ground above a lower exterior and is surrounded by a cover of mountains to the north and south, and to the west by a series of low hills, all three of which lie at a distance of about 2 km from the ancient city. To the east is an open plain. Along the eastern side of the site the Tiao stream runs southwest to northeast and then flows into Lake Tai. The ancient city lies in a vast hinterland with a superior natural environment with rich resources and opportune communication conditions (Figure 2).

The core area of the ancient city of Liangzhu can be divided into three parts: a central or palace area of about 300,000 m²; an area surrounding the latter measuring about

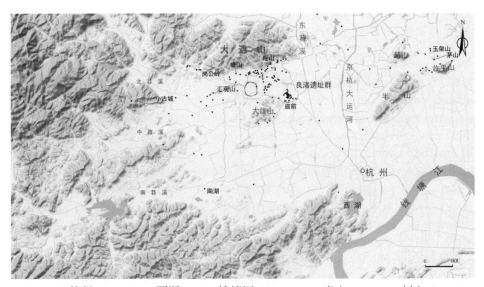

Map key: 杭州 Hangzhou, 西湖 Xihu, 钱塘河 Qiantanghe, 半山 Banshan, 赵山 Zhaoshan, 京杭大运河 JingHang Dayunhe, 良渚遗址群 Liangzhu Culture Sites, 庙前 Miaoqian, 大雄山 Daxiongshan, 汇观山 Huiguanshan, 岗公岭 Gangsongling, 塘山 Tangshan, 瑶山 Yaoshan, 东苕溪 Dongzhaoxi, 大痣山 Dazhishan, 北苕溪 Beizhaoxi, 中苕溪 Zhongzhaoxi, 小古城 Xiaogucheng, 南苕溪 Nanzhaoxi, 南湖 Nanhu

FIGURE 2   The distribution of Liangzhu-culture sites in a C-shaped basin, 3300–2300 BCE.

3,000,000 m^2 within fortified walls; and a third area, also surrounded by an outer citadel wall (*guo* 郭), of some 8,000,000 m^2. The city plan rises at the center and gradually diminishes in height as the site moves outward. This difference in heights of the city is significant. The site simulates the layout of later capital cities with a central palace compound, imperial city wall, and outer city wall, and thus may serve as the precedent for Chinese city and capital layouts. At the same time, the city site includes a vast water conservancy system to the north and northwest and a large-scale astronomical observatory related to altars at surrounding Yaoshan and Huiguan sites. The periphery of the city forms a vast suburb measuring a total area of some 1,000,000 km^2, indicating that the creation of this major settlement was extremely ambitious. The palace area along with other inner-city raised platforms, city wall, outer second citadel wall, peripheral water system, and outer suburbs are all man-made constructions. The city layout and design, peripheral water system, and suburbs are extremely vast in scale, which, statistically, in terms of the volume of soil and stone, includes some 8,400,000 cubic meters, a huge amount of work that must have required a large labor force and decades of work to complete.

Basic layout of the inner city, palace area, and outer citadel walls

Liangzhu forms a somewhat rounded rectangular city, oriented north to south measuring 1,910 m north-south and 1,770 m east-west, with a total area of nearly 3,000,000 m^2. The two hills, Fengshan and Zhishan, provide protection at the southwest and northeast corners of the site. The total length of the inner city wall is about 6 km with variations in width from 20–150 m. The best preserved remains measure 4 m high. The foundation of the wall, forming a stone layer 20–40 cm thick, reinforces the wall (see Figure 3). This wall was built with loess taken from nearby mountains and then rammed into layers. Apart from the south wall without an outer river, the other three have inner and outer rivers, forming a Jiahe-type fortified city. At present eight water gates have been identified, and two belong to each of the four walls, which interconnect with the inner and outer water system. One gate measures 10–60 m wide. The middle of the southern wall had a gate designed with a foundation of three small, rammed-earthen platforms.

FIGURE 3 View of a section of the south and north walls.

Planning and construction of the wall appear to have occurred simultaneously in preserving a unified vision. The city palace was located at the center of the Mojiaoshan city. Northwest and close to this center are the ruins of the royal cemetery at Fanshan. Other man-made earthen platforms also exist outside the city. A total of 51 inner-city rivers and streams may be added to the rivers running outside the city walls. The entire ancient city of Liangzhu is a "water city," with multiple crisscrossing waterways that provided a rich transportation system. According to our analyses the vast majority of these waterways were man-made, amounting to a total length of 31,562 m (Zhejiang 2015). Based on the layout of the earthen platforms and waterways, city building seems to have undergone two stages of construction (see Figure 4) (Wang and Yan 2014).

During the first phase, there were fewer earthen platforms and channeled waterways than in the second stage. As time passed, many river courses were buried by garbage, and in some places loess layers were rammed over garbage layers, forming new living areas and an expanded city. At this time, as the population increased living quarters also increased, both in and outside the city toward the north, east, south, and southwest, leading to the creation of a major citadel.

The Mojiaoshan Palace District, which is located in the center of the ancient city, represents the earliest "palace city" (*gongcheng* 宫城) known in China. It is a man-made rectangular structure, shaped like a pyramid flattened at the top. The rammed-earth platform consumes about 630 m east to west, and 450 m north to south, with an area of nearly 300,000 m². At the time Mojiaoshan was being constructed, builders took advantage of a natural wall formed by the hill girding its western side. In order to create the large-scale foundation of the earthen platforms, workers gathered green mud from the marshes to fill the low-lying sections east of the hill (Figure 5). Subsequently rammed layers of loess were stacked. The rammed layers of the eastern part measured about 10–12 m, whereas

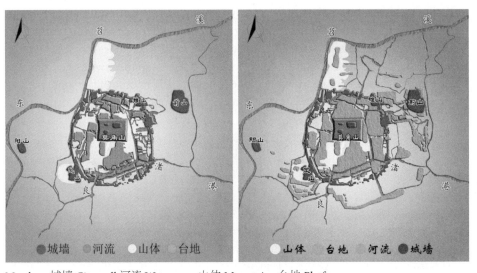

Map key: 城墙 City wall 河流 Waterways 山体 Mountains 台地 Platforms

FIGURE 4 Early and late phases of building inside and outside the city showing changes in land forms, ca. 3000 BCE.

Digital Elevation Model Key: 莫角山 Mojiaoshan; 东样家村 Dongyangjiacun; 凤山 Fengshan; 文家山 Wenjiashan; 杜山 Dushan; 中家山 Zhongjiashan; 扁担山 Biandanshan; 和尚地 Heshangdi; 雉山 Zhishan; 美人地 Meirendi; 里山 Lishan; 前山 Qianshan; 郑村Zhengcun; 高村 Gaocun; 卡家山 Kajiashan; 西杨家村 Xiyangjiacun.

FIGURE 5 DEM of citadel structure outside the ancient city.

the rammed-earthen layers of the western part measured only about 2–6 m thick. On the platform of the Palace District of Mojiaoshan were three additional small-scale earthen platforms, including Damojiaoshan, Xiaomojiaoshan, and Wuguishan. These consti-tuted the primary center of the main palace district. Damojiaoshan was the largest and thickest rammed-earth platform, the bottom of which measured about 180 m long and 97 m wide, with a surviving thickness of 16.5 m and relative height of about 5–6 m. In shape the platform formed a rectangular platform flattened at the top.

In the periphery of the ancient city of Liangzhu are long passages of highland, com-prising the Biandan mountains–Heshang area, the Li mountains–Zhengcun-Gaocun area, Bianjia mountains, and Dongyangjia town and Xiyangjialun, all of which had man-made constructions measuring some 60 m wide and about 1–3 m high. These sites formed intermittent strips surrounding the ancient city wall, in measuring an enclosure of some 8 km². Long-shaped residential areas also remain between the mentioned sites and the wall at Meirendi, Zhongjia town, and Zhou town. Due to the presence of a citadel wall (*waiguo* 外郭) that encircled the outermost part of the ancient city, it is evident that during the planning stages a residential area was definitely included, since it served not only as an integral part of the city and site but in its construction and use lasted from the middle to late phases of the Liangzhu cultural period.

In recent years, we identified a wider range of the water control system in the northwest of the ancient city of Liangzhu (Figure 6). Eleven dam sites have been discovered in the valley between the two mountain ranges. They may be divided into two groups, a northern and a southern group, that formed a protective system of water control. The lower dams in the south are at Tangshan, Shizishan, Liyushan, Guanshan, and Wutongnong, and the higher dams in the northern group are located at Ganggongling, Laohuling, Zhoujiafan, Qiuwu, Shiwu, and Mifenglong, respectively. In the north and northwest of the ancient city a water reservoir conserved an area of about 13 km². From our perspective we speculate that the water system may have been involved in flood control, transportation, water supply, irrigation, and other uses. According to historical legend water conservancy was believed to begin 4,000 years ago during the ages of Gong Gong, Gun, and Da Yu, yet the earliest surviving large-scale water conservancy project known had dated to the Late Springs and Autumns period. Now, due to the discovery at Tangshan and Ganggongling within the Liangzhu city site, water conservation and

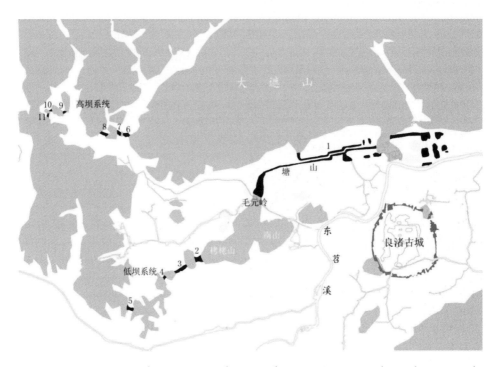

FIGURE 6 Water control system outside Liangzhu city. Lower southern dam controls: 1 Tangshan, 2 Laohushi, 3 Leishan, 4 Guanshan, 5 Wutongnong. Higher northern dam controls: 6 Ganggongling, 7 Laohuling, 8 Zhoujiafan, 9 Qiuwu, 10 Shiwu, 11 Mifenglong. Nos. 1–5: damned sections.

control facilities can now not only be dated much earlier, to 5,000 years ago, but can also be recognized as representing China's first and earliest large-scale water control system. This is the same time period that other ancient civilizations, such as ancient Egypt, were building dams. In 2650 BCE the ancient Egyptian kingdom southeast of Cairo, about 30 km southeast of Wadi Garawa, built the Sadd el Kafara Dam. The purpose was to collect the winter mountain water torrents to the east into a permanent reservoir. The dam measured 113 m long by 14 m high (it is also said the dam was 108 m long by 12 m high), with a storage capacity of 500,000 cubic meters (http://what-when-how.com/archaeology -of-ancient-egypt/urbanism-to-wadi-garawi-dam-archaeology-of-ancient-egypt/). Construction was estimated to take about 8~10 years. The volume is about the same as that behind the Ganggongling dam at Liangzhu city.

Also outside Liangzhu city are altars and aristocratic cemeteries, such as Yaoshan and Huiguanshan. Yaoshan is located about 5 km northeast of Mojiaoshan and is a natural hill that rises about 35 m above sea level (Figure 7). The first discovery of a Liangzhu-period outdoor altar was in 1987 at the top of this mountain (Zhejiang 2003), forming on its west and north faces what was once a sloping stone-encased pyramidal shape with flat top, with what appeared to be a trench forming a rectangular frame of lime earth around a mound shaped like the graph 回. From the inside to the outside a triple structure was formed out of an inner red earthen platform, an ash earthen frame, and a gravel stone platform. Thirteen large Liangzhu-period tombs were buried in two rows on the south side of the altar.

Huiguanshan is located about 2 km west of the Liangzhu city and is a natural hill rising 22 m above sea level (Zhejiang 1997, 2001). It is similar in shape and build to the Yaoshan altar. Four Liangzhu-culture tombs were excavated in the southwest part of the

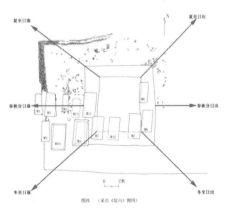

N north; 冬至日落 winter solstice sunset; 冬至日出 winter solstice sunrise; 春秋分日出 spring and autumn equinox sunrise; 春秋分日落 spring and autumn equinox sunset; 夏夏至日落 summer solstice sunset; 夏至日出 summer solstice sunrise. M = Burial, e.g. M12 is Burial No.12.

FIGURE 7 Yaoshan altar with aristocratic burials and diagrammatic view of the altar's orientation as a solar observatory.

Huiguanshan altar. After many years of observation and research, the director of excavations, Liu Bin, found that the direction of the sunrise and the orientation of the four corners of the altar are astonishingly consistent. Therefore, it is likely that the altar functioned as a solar observatory to date through observation the cycle of a regression year.

Outside the core of the ancient city of Liangzhu are two suburban class settlements with dense distribution (Liu 2006). One is at Xunshan as the center in the area of Liangchengzhen, and the other is in the northeast at the foot of Dashishan. The latter is the most important suburb of Liangzhu. The area of Xunshan comprises about 30 sites, and some 40 sites have been found at the foot of Dashishan. The hinterland of the ancient Liangzhu city, which forms a large C-shaped basin of about 800 km², contains a number of Liangzhu cultural sites, some forming clusters, such as the settlement of the Linping area about 30 km east of Liangzhu. Nearly 20 Liangzhu cultural sites are known as Linping ruins (Zhao 2012). In recent years Maoshan and Yujiashan sites have been excavated, with the result that Maoshan site revealed a model settlement favoring mountains and water, with rice paddies, tombs, residences, and other connected city attributes (Ding and Zheng 2010).

The site of Yujiashan covers about 15,000,000 m² in area (Lou et al. 2012). The site is richly endowed, comprising six trench rings of an intact Liangzhu cultural settlement. As an important archaeological discovery the site also includes aristocratic burials.

Liangzhu settlement clusters and regional centers with highly developed social differentiation

There are more than 600 Liangzhu settlement sites surrounding the Taihu Valley outside Liangzhu city center. The most concentrated sites are located in three major areas, namely southeast of Taihu in the area of Jiaxing, east of Taihu in Jiangsu and Shanghai, and north of Taihu in the region of Changzhou. Remains from these three areas are relatively high, as at Sidun and Luodun plus others north of Taihu; Fuquanshan, Zhanglingshan, Zhaolingshan, Caoxieshan, and other sites east of Taihu; and Yaojiashan, the area of Heye. All of these sites are large-scale man-made earth constructed platforms, and all contained burials with jade *cong*, jade *yue*, and jade *bi*. It is clear that Liangzhu-culture settlements had reached a staggering peak of development, with centers surrounded by large numbers of condensed habitation ranging from thousands to tens of thousands of small and medium-size villages.

Based on the variation of numbers and types of burial goods from these Liangzhu sites it is possible to distinguish differences in social status. The well-known archaeologist Zhang Zhongpei, in his study "Liangzhu Cemeteries and the Expression of Civilized Society" (Zhang 2012), divides the Liangzhu culture into six grades: the first grade focuses on Yaoshan cemetery as central. (For a detailed review of Liangzhu burials and social status also see Childs-Johnson 2009). This grade of burial contains jade *cong, bi, yue,* and so on and belongs to the royal elite and those with military power. The second grade includes as representative the third strata of Fuquanshan tombs. These burials typically have jade *cong,* jade *yue,* and stone *yue* and belong to the military class. The third grade is represented by the second strata of Fuquanshan burials. These usually contain jade *yue* and stone *yue* but are without jade *cong,* yet are of military rank.

The fourth and fifth grades belong to the lowermost level of Fuquanshan burials, with burials M3 and M8–10 at Maqiao as representative. These burials typically have only stone *yue* and belong to warriors. The sixth grade, represented by Maqiao burials M4–7, usually contain only a small amount of pottery and sometimes no funerary objects. These burials represent the poorest sectors of society.

A HIGHLY DEVELOPED JADE ART AND A THEOCRACY WITH SYMBOLS OF "ROYAL" POWER

Jade-working is one of the most important cultural assets to Chinese civilization during the Neolithic period. Instead of working copper at the end of the Stone Age, China made full use of another precious material—jade. As early as 6000–5000 BCE jade material types of actinolite-tremolite nephrite had begun to be worked into small-scale ornaments by members of the Xinglongwa culture (see Chung Tang and colleagues, chapter 3). One thousand years later, ca. 3500–2000 BCE, jade-working spread and was advanced by important cultures, such as Hongshan, Songze, Liangzhu, and Qijia. At this time jade was the material symbol par excellence and came to represent a phase during the Neolithic we now label the Jade Age (see chapter 4 in this volume by Childs-Johnson; Childs-Johnson 1988, 2001; Mou and Wu 1997). Jades functioned initially as ornaments and symbolic amulets, then as ritual implements and ritual insignia. This era also witnesses the first peak in the formation and development of regional civilizations in China. Jades of the Liangzhu culture represent the most significant achievement in China's Neolithic Jade Age.

The Liangzhu people created what were ritual jade sets of *cong, bi,* and *yue;* ornaments of a crown-shape, three-prong shape, and cone-shape; and *huang.* The latter were the most important jade types that came to represent a ritual jade set of the Liangzhu elite. Many of these jade art works were decorated with symbolic emblems and related symbolic images, as represented on jade *cong,* the crown-shaped ornament, and the jade attachments of the *yue* handle. The jade ritual program and symbolic emblems were consistent and uniform throughout the Liangzhu realm around Lake Tai, and in this respect served as a means of social and administrative control as well as tight social cohesion and a unified belief system. Disregarding number, volume, and form, jade-working of the Liangzhu and earlier Songze cultures are both advanced. This rapid leap forward artistically and culturally is accompanied by the phenomenon and rise of royal power. The Liangzhu king and elite classes were identified by emblems signifying status and rank as well as control of the spirit world, thus creating royal and military power and a monopoly of material wealth. A large number of these ritual jades are concentrated in large-scale burials belonging to Liangzhu elite and aristocratic classes. The Liangzhu culture that created the jade ritual system and the rule of governance by hegemonic power was developed and absorbed by later generations of Chinese civilization.

Based on the archaeology of the ancient city of Liangzhu, and especially the research on Liangzhu jades, it is evident that amid Liangzhu civilization control over the spirit realm is supreme and intimately connected with royal power. In general, Liangzhu civilization may be a type of civilization model with spirit power as the significant link, just as characterized the ancient Egyptian system.

This chapter will now introduce several of the most unique types of Liangzhu jades. Very characteristic of the Liangzhu culture is the jade *cong* and its engraved imagery of a spirit emblem, the very image of which is related to the origin and development of this special type of jade. The jade *cong* is the primary carrier of this symbolic emblem (Figure 8). There are also many ornaments and used implements that imitate the shape of the *cong* and carry this emblem, such as the *cong*-shaped jade bead, the *cong*-shaped jade post, and the rectangular-shaped jade awl ornament. Because the symbolic emblem is closely associated with the jade *cong*, it is evident that it was a ritual tool used in sacrifice to the spirit world. The one who presided over the ritual in turn was most likely a shaman (*wu* 巫).

There is usually only one jade *yue* ax per aristocratic tomb, and it serves as a symbol of a king's or a leader's power. Lin Yun, in his article "Defining Wang," pointed out the oracle-bone character for "king" is based on the form of the *yue* ax (Lin 1965). Thus, the jade *yue* serves as an important symbol of a ruler's power and military might. As is well known, the jade *yue* from Fanshan M12, the highest-ranking tomb of the Liangzhu culture, was decorated on both sides with two emblems of spirit power, indicating that spirit power and a leader's power were intimately related (Figure 9). The configuration at the top side of the jade *yue* takes the shape of a crown folded in two halves. In its location at the

FIGURE 8 The "royal jade" and its image of the complete spirit emblem from M12 at Fanshan.

FIGURE 9   The "royal jade" *yue* from Fanshan M12.

FIGURE 10   Fanshan jade *bi*, M23:23.

front end of the blade, this crowned ornament representing the spirit is none other than the symbol of "a leader's power received from the spirit realm 君神授"—the joining of ruler and spirit power.

Thus, in this context this jade transcends the category of weapon in serving as a form of insignia (Liu 2013).

The jade *bi* disk is a large-scale object in the Liangzhu ritual jade set (Figure 10). The quality of jade *bi* is generally different than that of other jades. Most reveal a mottled composition and to the naked eye a surface that looks like fibrous tissue. Jade *bi* most likely functioned as a sacrificial jade used in "serving the spirit realm 以玉事神." The more time elapsed the more frequent was the appearance of *bi* disks. By the end of the Liangzhu period the *bi* disk bore engraved symbols of the spirit bird and altar emblem.

Outside *cong*, *bi*, and *yue* other significant jades included three prominent types of ornaments: the crown-shape, the three-prong, and the awl-shape.

The discovery of a large number
of engraved emblems

No text has yet been deciphered from the Liangzhu civilization, although a large number of symbols have been discovered. Recently the latter were published by the editors of the Liangzhu Museum, titled *Engraved Signs of the Liangzhu Culture*, with a total of 554 pieces, of which 536 are ceramic, 11 stone, and 7 jade. The number of symbols totals 632, which is currently the most complete collection of Liangzhu signs or emblems. Many of the ceramic and stone-carved signs are pictorial signs (图符). Although they cannot be read, these characters were possibly used in the context of a text, as is the case with the five symbols or graphs engraved on an eared *hu* vessel found at Denghu in Suzhou (No. J127:1); the continuous text of graphs on a circular footed *guan* jar from Nanhu, Yuhangxian (Figure 11); and a number of consecutive signs or graphs on two stone *yue* from Zhuangqiao (T1012:10, H41:1).

In addition, a bird standing on a platform (altar) and other forms of special icons are engraved on a small number of jade *bi*, *cong*, and other artefacts, totaling seven jades and 10 symbols (Figure 12A,B,C). The icons or emblems feature two parts, a high platform and a profile bird. Most of the tall stepped platforms are filled with further emblems simulating eyes of a human and abstract bird shapes, suggesting reference to a shamanic image. It is worth noting that the image of a profile bird standing on a high platform is comparable to the ancient Egyptian image symbolizing the name of the king (Figure 12D). The names of kings and rulers of early dynasties, early states, and ancient

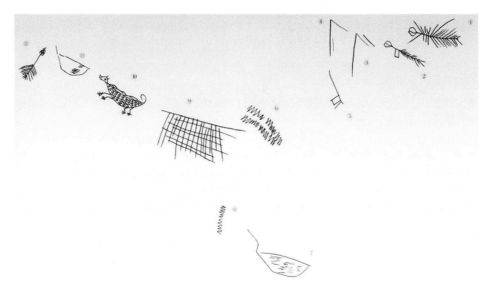

FIGURE 11 Ink rubbing of the engraved signs encircling the foot of a ceramic *guan* picked up at the site of Nanhu, Yuhang, Zhejiang.

何露斯神 ▷

国王的名字
（杰特，眼镜蛇）▷

宫殿正面图案 ▷

FIGURE 12 Erect birds on platform symbols engraved on three Freer Gallery jade *bi* and on the limestone stele of King Djet, also known as Cobra King or Cobra of Horus. A comparison between the bird emblems in the Liangzhu culture with the Egyptian name of a dynastic king on a limestone stele once in front of King Djet's tomb in the Umm el-Qa'ab, Abydos, now housed in the Louvre, Paris, France.

kingdoms were usually composed of birds (or bird and beast) on some form of platform. In the Egyptian case the bird represents the god Horus and the platform the palace, within which is a cobra symbolizing the name of the king, Djet, of the First dynasty. Djet's Horus name means "Horus Cobra" or "Serpent of Horus."

Advanced agriculture, handicrafts, and social stratification

Two ancient cities in the west, that of Uruk lying between the Euphrates and Tigris rivers and that of Mohenjo-Daro on the Indus River in India, are comparable chronologically with Liangzhu City. The Mesopotamian and Indian populations are both estimated to be some 40,000 or 30,000–40,000 people within over 2.5 km², respectively. Since the core area of the ancient Liangzhu city measures some 8 km², the population should not be less than the two Western ancient cities combined.

For such a large population agriculture must have been advanced. The origin of rice farming took place in the Yangtze River Basin (mainly in the middle and lower reaches of the Yangtze River; see chapter 2 in this volume by Fang Xiangming). Domestication of rice farming began more than 10,000 years ago. By the Liangzhu-culture period, rice farming had reached a high level. In the core area of Liangzhu civilization around Lake Tai there is no evidence that millet was farmed. Rice was the only staple food of the Liangzhu people. This is an important feature of Liangzhu civilization and differs from others in ancient China and the world. Therefore, to explore the economic development of Liangzhu civilization we first must discuss rice farming.

During the 2010–2012 season of excavations, a large pit, H11, was cleared at Mojiaoshan site where it slopes east, and reveals a major discovery. The pit had three layers of fill, of which the first and third layers were gray and black soil, including a large number of charcoal lumps, carbonized rice, lumps of burnt red earth, straw and wood ash, a small amount of grass rope, and ashes. A large number of carbonized rice remains underwent flotation analysis. The ash pit contained about 26,000 kg of rice. Such a large-scale accumulation of carbonized rice is rare. The accumulation suggested this was a granary site for storing rice that had at some point caught on fire, an accident that apparently occurred twice. In 2013, an additional significant accumulation of carbonized rice was also found while excavating the southwestern slope of Mojiaoshan. Drilling in the area of the "palace area" has also revealed areas rich in paddy-rice accumulation. These discoveries infer that the ancient palace of the city of Liangzhu had major rice reserves and large storage areas.

Around 2010 we carried out many drillings and investigations in and outside Mojiaoshan for signs of rice-field agriculture but to no avail. From the excavated evidence it is evident that in and outside the immediate citadel there was no rice agriculture. Rather rice was grown in the suburbs, outside Liangzhu city (Figure 13). This relationship demonstrates the probability that those living in and around the Liangzhu

FIGURE 13 Carbonized rice remains after flotation that were unearthed from pit H11 in the eastern slope of Mojiaoshan.

FIGURE 14 A large area for rice agriculture during the late Liangzhu phase from Maoshan site. 稻田口活动场地 = center of rice paddy activity; 田埂 = ridge edge of rice paddy; 稻田 = rice paddy; 水道 = water channel; 灌溉水道 = irrigation channels.

city proper were provided for by outer residents and farmers, and that such a relationship probably led to a tribute system.

Another discovery of rice production comes from the site of Maoshan in the Linping group of settlements, a situation informing us about agricultural production in a small village context at that time (Figure 14). Maoshan site is a typical sloping mound, exposing designated residential, burial, and rice-paddy field areas. The paddy field, located to the south of the foothills in the lowlands, covered 7 km² (approx. 83 acres). During the middle phase of the Liangzhu culture the scale of rice paddy was not large, in covering only a small area of the block, averaging from 1–2 to 30–40 m². By the late phase large rice fields were created, measuring 83 acres in area. Five north-south large burnt soil ridges measuring 17–19 m long and two east-west waterways defined a large block for paddy fields, divided into many sections of about 1 to 2 km², (1000–2,000 m²).

Handicrafts and arts

Advanced agriculture gave the Liangzhu ancient city and Liangzhu civilization a secure foundation and wealth in economic production and food security that led to a high level of cultivation of all sorts of handicraft arts. The latter include working jade, stone, lacquer, ceramics, and the craft of weaving. The diversification of handicrafts represents a high level of sophistication. Production of rich and multifaceted arts led to large numbers of stellar art works, including beautiful jades, lacquers, and decorated ceramics, and to an aristocratic level of these arts that created "royal" controlled workshops ("官营"), particularly in jade production (Figures 15–17).

FIGURE 15   Liangzhu lacquers. (a) Fanshan M12 multicolored lacquer cup, restored. (b) Fanshan M12 multicolored lacquer basin. (c) Cajiashan multicolored lacquer *gu*, detail, and (d) another lacquer fragment.

FIGURE 16   Animal-faced décor (left) and alligator images on ceramic fragments unearthed at Putaofan 葡萄畈.

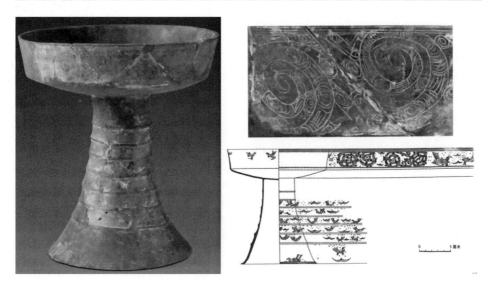

FIGURE 17 Engraved *dou* vessel with drawings of the vessel's imagery, M101:90, Fuquanshan, Shanghai.

THE IMPACT OF THE LIANGZHU CIVILIZATION ON CHINESE CIVILIZATION

Material finds of the Liangzhu culture have produced ongoing research, at the same time providing data for assessing the profound impact of Liangzhu on the formation of Chinese civilization.

The influence of the Liangzhu culture on cultures of the same period primarily manifests in the Dawenkou culture of northern Jiangsu and the Shixia culture in Guangdong. The most prominent influence of the Liangzhu culture in the north is documented in the remains from Huating in Xinyi, Jiangsu (Nanjing Museum 2003). Ceramics of Dawenkou origin and those of Liangzhu origin are both preserved in tombs at Huating. At the same time a sizeable amount of Liangzhu jades appear in the same tombs. To date the longest awl-shaped jade in Liangzhu cultural time comes from Huating. *Cong, bi, yue*, and crown-shaped ornaments of combs representing the Liangzhu jade ritual set are also represented at Huating and in Guandong. Among site finds from the more distant Shixia culture in Guangdong are typical Liangzhu jade types, including *cong, bi, yue*, and awl-shaped ornaments (Yang 1998; Guangdong Bowuguan 1978; Guangdong 2014). In addition, many Liangzhu ceramic types, such as the double-nosed *hu* and horizontal-eared *hu*, are also well represented. In addition, numbers of jade *cong, bi*, and *yue* of Liangzhu design are found amid Qijia cultural finds in the area of Gansu and Qinghai. A large amount of jade *cong, bi, yue*, and related jade items of the Qijia culture derive from the Ganqing region.

Liangzhu jade types during the slightly later Longshan period are also significant. Liangzhu-type jade *cong*, *yue*, *bi*, *zhang*, and V-shaped stone knives are well represented amid Longshan period ruins of the Taosi site in Shanxi (Shanxi Work Team 1990), and others including Yanan, Lushanmao in northern Shaanxi (Ji 1984), and Shimao and Xinhua in Shenmu, Shaanxi (Wang et al., 2001). In addition, Jade *cong* and *bi* of the Liangzhu type are also known amid Erlitou and Yinxu sites (Institute of Archeology 1981), and jade *yue* appear as well amid other Neolithic sites in the lower reaches of the Yangzi and Yellow Rivers. Liangzhu jade types including the *cong*, *bi*, and jade awl-shape are also found in Sanxingdui, Guanghan (Sichuan 1999) and Jinsha, Chengdu (Chengdu 2002) in Sichuan and in other Shang- and Zhou-dated dynastic sites. Based on ritual ceramic wares, including *ding*, *dou*, *hu*, and those of jade, including *cong*, *bi*, and *huang*, it is evident that the Liangzhu culture impacted the cultures of the Bronze Age and subsequent evolution of Chinese civilization.

BIBLIOGRAPHY

Chengdushi Wenwu Kaogu Yanjiusuo, Beijing Daxue Kaogu Wenwu Bowuguan 成都市 文物考古研究所,北京大学考古文物博物馆 2002. *Panning for Treasures at Jinsha* 淘 宝宝 藏在金沙. Beijing: Wenwu chubanshe.

Childs-Johnson, Elizabeth 1988. *Ritual and Power: Jades of Ancient China*. New York: China Institute in America.

Childs-Johnson, Elizabeth 2001. "The Jade Age of Early China: Three Significant Jade Working Cultures during the Pivotal Period 4000–2000 BCE." In *Haixia Liangan Guyu Xuehui Yilunwen Zhuankan*, vol. 1: 187–198. Taibei: Taiwan National University Press.

Childs-Johnson, Elizabeth 2009. "The Art of Working Jade and the Rise of Civilization in China." In *The Jade Age & Early Chinese Jades in American Museums*, 291–393. Beijing: Science Press:.

Dai, Yingxin 戴应新 1988. "Longshan Culture Jades from Shimao in Shenmu County 神木 县石卯龙山文化玉器." *Kaogu yu Wenwu* 5(6): 239–250.

Ding, Pin 丁品, and Zheng Yunfei 郑云飞 2010. "The Site of Maoshan, Linping, Yuhang, Zhejiang 浙江余杭临平毛衫的遗址." *Zhongguo wenwu bao* 3(12).: 4.

Guangdong Bowuguan, Qujiangxian Wenhuaju Fajue Xiaozu 广东省博物馆、曲江县 文化局石峡发掘小组 1978. "Preliminary Excavation Report on Shixia Tombs at Qujiang, Guangdong 广东曲江." *Wenwu*.7:1–16.

Guangdongsheng Wenhua Kaogu Yanjiusuo 广东省文化考古研究所 2014. *Preliminary Report on 1973-1978 Excavation Report on Shixia Site* 石峡 1973–1978.

Ji, Naijun 姬乃军 1984. "Ancient Jade Discovered at Yanan 延安市发现的古代玉 器." *Wenwu* 2: 84–87.

Lin, Yun 林云 1965. "Definition of *wang* '王'的说明." *Kaogu* 6: 311–312.

Liu, Bin 刘斌 2006. "A View on Dating the Sacrificial Mounds of the Liangzhu Culture 关于良渚化祭祀 代的观点." In *Academic Conference Papers Celebrating the 70th Year since the Discovery of Liangzhu Site Remains, Zhejiangsheng wenwu kaogu yanjiusuo xuekan 8*. Beijing: Kexue chubanshe.

Liu, Bin 刘斌 2013. *The World of Shamanism* 神巫的世界. Hangzhou chubanshe.

Liu, Bin 刘斌 2014. "*Looking for the Disappearing Kingdom: The Archaeological History of the Liangzhu Site (The Discovery of Liangzhu Ancient City)* 寻找消失的王国——良渚遗址的考古 历程(良渚古城发现记)》." In *Collected Papers Celebrating the 80 Birthday of Zhang Zhongpei* 庆祝张忠培先生八十岁论文集, 158–170. Beijing: Kexue chubanshe.

Liu, Bin 刘斌 2016. *Eighty Years of Discovering the Liangzhu Culture* 良渚文化发现八十周. Beijing: Kexue chubanshe.

Liu, Bin 刘斌 2018. *A Comprehensive Research Report on Liangzhu Ancient City* 良渚古城综合研究报告. Beijing: Wenwu chubanshe.

Liu, Bin, and Wang Ningyuan 刘斌、王宁远 2014. "2006–2013 Archaeological Excavation and Its Harvest at Liangzhu Ancient City 良渚古城的考古发掘与收获." *Dongnan wenwu* 2: 31–37.

Liu, Bin, Wang Ningyuan, and Chen Minghui 刘斌、王宁远、陈明辉 2015. *Liangzhu Ancient City: New Discoveries and Explorations, Rights and Beliefs; Archaeological Exhibition of Liangzhu Site Group* 良渚古城——新发现和探索，权利与信仰——良渚 遗址群考古特展. Beijing: Wenwu chubanshe.

Lou, Hang 楼航 et al. 2012. "The site of Yujiashan, Yuhang, Zhejiang: The Discovery of Intact Liangzhu Culture Group of Settlements Based on a Group of Six Adjacent Trenches." *Zhongguo wenwu bao* 2(24): 4.

Zhongguo Shehui Kexueyuan Kaogu Yanjiusuo, Luoyang Fajuedui 中国社会科学院考古研究所，洛阳发掘队 1965. "Preliminary Report of Erlitou Excavations at Yanshi, Henan 河南偃师二里头发 掘报告初步." *Kaogu* 5: 215–224.

Mou, Yongkang 牟永抗, and Wu, Naizuo 吴汝祚 1997. "Analysis of the Era of the Jade Age: An Important Model for Production during the Age of Chinese Civilization 分析玉 器时代 - 中华文明时代的重要生产模式." In *Kaoguxue wenhua lunji*, vol. 4, 164–187. Beijing: Wenwu chubanshe.

Nanjing Bowuyuan 南京博物院 2003. *Huating: Excavation Report on the Cemetery of the Neolithic Period* 新石器时代墓地的花厅 - 发掘报告. Beijing: Wenwu chubanshe.

Shaanxisheng Kaogu Yanjiusuo 陕西省考古研究所 2002. "1999 Preliminary Excavation Report on Xinhua Site in Shenmu, Shaanxi 陕西神木新华遗址1999发掘初步报告." *Kaogu yu Wenwu* 1: 3–12.

Sichuansheng Kaogu Yanjiusuo 四川省考古研究所 1999. *Sanxingdui Sacrificial Pit sanxingdui* 三星堆牺牲抗. Beijing: Wenwu chubanshe.

Su, Bingqi 苏秉琦 2000. *New Thoughts on the Origins of Chinese Civilization* 关于中华文明起源的新思. Sanlian shudian.

Wang, Ningyuan 王宁远 2013. *From Village Settlement to Royal City* 从村庄定居到皇家城.市 Hangzhou chubanshe.

Wang, Ningyuan 王宁远, and Yan, Kaikai 闫凯凯 2014. "Ancient Myths of Water Control and the Practice of Water Control by the Neolithic Residents of Liangzhu 良渚新石器时代居的水控古代神话与水利治理." In *Collected Papers from the Conference on the Civilization of the Huaihe River Valley and the Site of Yuhuicun*. 195–204.

Wang, Weilin, Sun, Zhouyong, and Xing, Fulai 王炜林, 孙周勇, 邢福来 2001. "The Site of Xinhua in Shenmu, Shaanxi 陕西神木新华遗址." In *Zhongguo Zhongyao Kaogu Faxian*, 21–25. Beijing: Wenwu chubanshe.

Yan, Wenming 严文明 2003. "The Origins of Chinese Civilization and Early Period Development 中华文明的起源与早期发展." In *Guoxueyanjiu*, vol. 12, 38–50. Beijing Daxue chubanshe.

Yang, Jianhua 杨建华 2014. *Two River Valleys: From Agricultural Villages to City-States* 两河流域:从农业村落走向城邦国家. Kexue chubanshe.

Yang, Shiting 杨式挺 1998. "Preliminary Analysis of Neolithic Jades from Guangdong 广东新石器时代的初步分析." In *East Asian Jade*. 304–315. Chinese University of Hong Kong and Research Center of Chinese Archaeology and Art.

Zhang, Binghua 张炳火, and Liangzhu Bowuguan 良渚博物馆, eds. 2015. *Incised Emblems/Graphs (fuhao) of the Liangzhu Culture* 良渚文化刻画符号. Shanghai Renmin chubanshe.

Zhang, Zhongpei 张忠培 2012. "The Liangzhu Culture Cemeteries and Their Representation of Civilized Society 良渚文化墓地及其文明社会的代表性." *Kaogu xuebao* 4: 401–422.

Zhao, Ye 赵晔 2012. "Analysis of the Settlements Groups at Linping Site in Yuhang, Zhejiang 浙江余杭临平遗址群的聚落考察." *Dongnan wenhua* 3: 31–39.

Zhejiangsheng Wenwu Kaogu Yanjiusuo 浙江文物考古研究所 2003. *Yaoshan* 瑶山. Beijing: Wenwu chubanshe.

Zhejiangsheng Wenwu Kaogu Yanjiusuo 浙江文物考古研究所 2015. "Investigation of the Water System Surrounding the Ancient City of Liangzhu 良渚古城周边水系的考察." *Kaogu* 1: 3–13.

Zhejiang Wenwu Kaogu Yanjiusuo, Hangzhou Wenhuahui 浙江文物考古研究所，余杭文化会 1997. "Preliminary Report on Excavations of the Cemetery and Liangzhu Culture Sacrificial Mound (*jitan*) at Huiguanshan in Yuhang, Zhejiang 浙江余杭汇观山祭坛及良渚文化祭祀遗址发掘初报." *Wenwu* 7: 4–19.

Zhejiang Wenwu Kaogu Yanjiusuo, Yuhang Wenhuahui 浙江文物考古研究所，余杭文化会 2001. "The Second Preliminary Excavation Report on Huiguanshan Site 汇观山遗址第二次初步发掘报告." *Wenwu* 12: 36–40.

Zhongguo Shehui Kexueyuan Kaogu Yanjiusuo 中国社会科学院考古研究所 1981. *Fu Zi Burial at Yinxu* 殷墟妇好(子)墓. Beijing: Wenwu chubanshe.发掘简报 Beijing: Wenwu chubanshe.

Zhongguo Shehui Kexueyuan Kaogu Yanjiusuo, Shaanxi Gongzuodui, Linfengqu Wenhuaju 中国社会科学院考 古研究所陕西工作队, 临汾区文化局 1983. "1978–1980 Preliminary Excavation Report on the Cemetery at Taosi, Xiangfeng, Shanxi 山西襄汾县陶寺遗址发掘初步报告1978–1980," *Kaogu* 1: 18–31.

Zhongguo Shehui Kexueyuan Kaogu Yanjiusuo, Shaanxi Gongzuodui, Linfengqu Wenhuaju 中国社会科学院考 古研究所陕西工作队, 临汾区文化局 1990. "Preliminary Excavation Report on Taosi Site in Xiangfen County, Shanxi 山西襄汾县陶寺遗址发掘报告简报." *Kaogu* 1: 30–42.

CHAPTER 6

LONGSHAN CULTURE ISSUES: TAOSI AND COSMOLOGY

BY NU HE, INSTITUTE OF ARCHAEOLOGY, CASS

THE cosmology of ancient China entails knowledge about and theoretical explanations of relationships among heaven, earth, and human beings, which develop and change within the framework of space and time. The cosmology consists of three parts, namely cosmogony, time, and space. Space deals with concepts such as the four directions, four poles, five quarters, the celestial north pole, and the magnetic north pole. Time comprises the four seasons, years, months, days, and hours. Cosmogony focuses on the origin, elements, evolution, regulation of movement, and change in the realms of heaven, earth, and humans (He 2012). Archaic cosmology affected various aspects of production and life in China's past societies. For instance, the design of districts within central settlement sites or capitals, the selection of sites for observatories and altars, the orientation of palaces, mortuary rituals, and the display of funerary furniture were all guided by cosmology. In this way, archaic cosmology is more or less preserved in the features of archaeological sites that preserve past behaviors. Relying on this, archaeologists can partially reconstruct the basic map of cosmology in past societies, by means of excavating and analyzing relevant archaeological materials.

The Taosi culture is an archaeologically defined culture referring to the final phase of the Longshan period, dating 4300 to 3900 BCE. It occupies the entire Linfen Basin and the northern part of the Yuncheng Basin in Shanxi Province (He 2004).The society of Taosi culture can be identified as an archaic state. As the capital of that archaic state, the Taosi site is located 7 km east of the county seat at Xiangfen. Based on archaeological excavation and research in last three decades, so far we have identified a city referred to the Early Taosi period (4300 to 4100 BCE), covering an area about 1,600,000 m², (including the main enclosure measuring about 200,000 m²) with an, orientation of 225°. The huge city of the Middle Taosi period (4100 to 4000 BCE) occupied an area at least

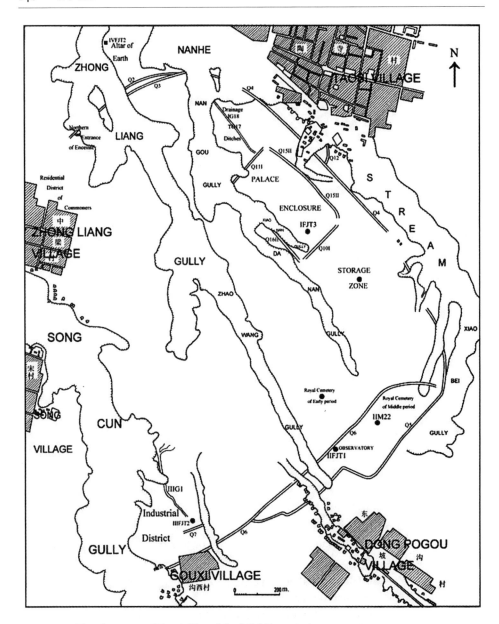

FIGURE 1 The plan map of Taosi City of the Middle period, ca. 2100 to 2000 BCE.

2,800,000 m², oriented also to 225°, which was divided into a palace district, royal cemeteries, a ceremonial center for the worship of heaven, an exclusive storage area, a residential district for lower elites, an industrial area, settlements for common citizens, and a ritual precinct for the earth lord (Figure 1). In the Late Taosi period, judging from the decay of the district design, the city appeared to decline, although it occupied an area over 3,000,000 m² (He 2018).

COSMOGONY

The archaeological evidence from Taosi indicates that the cosmogonic component of Taosi cosmology has two main concepts: one is Taiji Dualism, and the other one is lid-like heaven. Both of them entail knowledge of and explanations regarding the shapes and formation of heaven and earth.

Taiji Dualism (a reconstruction based on *yin-yang* dualism)

The outstanding cosmogonic theory of early China was *yinyang taiji*, or Taiji Dualism, a received theory of much later (Han) date than the Late Neolithic Taosi culture. It serves today nonetheless as the most essential philosophical theory explaining the formation of everything in the universe. Ancient documents such as the *Xici Shang* (Recapitulation, part 1) in *Zhouyi* (Book of changes); or the *Tianwen Xun* (Treatise on the patterns of heaven) in the *Huainanzi*, a preliminary materialistic theory about heaven-earth formation, articulate these views. Logically it was expressed as follows:

> Before heaven and earth were differentiated, there was turbulent nothingness. This state of affairs was called Taiji (the Great Monad). Taiji produced heaven and earth. These two systems originated in the nebulous void. The nebulous void produced the cosmos. In its midst was *qi* (matter-energy). *Qi* divided into the clear and the turbid. Between the two was a shoreline that took shape as a boundary. The clear and pure *qi*, shapeless and formless, rolled up and ascended to form heaven; this was called the Way of Heaven. The turbid and heavy *qi* whirled down to form earth, known as the Instruments of Earth. The Way of Heaven and the Instruments of Earth mutually conditioned and modified each other. Their smoothly rolling movements produced everything. Heaven rotated to the left, while earth rotated to the right.

The core part of the observatory at Taosi was composed of rammed clay and undisturbed soil in the shape of a *yin-yang* Taiji dualistic diagram.

Given the identification number IIFJT1, the observatory of Taosi is located in a small enclosure dating to the middle period at Taosi (Shanxi Team 2004, 2007, 2008; He 2013b), occupying what was identified as the heaven position or yang (sun) position according to Taosi cosmology.

The semi-round foundation of the observatory was constructed with small blocks made of rammed clay (Figure 2). Its arch orientates to the southeast. The entire structure involves a rim path and platform. The diameters of the entire structure, the platform, and its center of undisturbed soil are about 60, 40, and 28 m, respectively. The entire structure and the platform covered an area of about 1,740 and 1,000 m². The depth of the remaining rammed-clay foundation ranges from 1 to 6 m. According to archaeological stratum as well as artifacts, the structure can be dated from 2100 to 2000 BCE.

The platform has three terraces. The first terrace is located to the east of the platform, which is shaped as a crescent orientated due east, with an undisturbed soil core in the

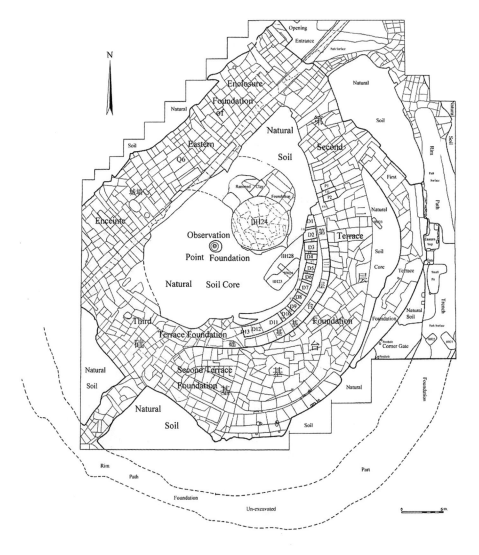

FIGURE 2 Plan of the observatory and Heaven Altar structures of the Middle period at Taosi, ca. 2100 to 2000 BCE.

crescent shape surrounded with rammed clay. It might have served as a ceremonial plot to the east. One formal rammed-clay step connects the rim path with the first terrace. The second terrace is formed in a semi-ring. Both ends are connected with the southern enclosure of the walled town. The crucial portion for the platform is the third terrace. It is constructed with an undisturbed soil core and rammed-clay counterfort wall. Between the core and counterfort wall, there is an arch system of basement wall composed of slots and rammed-clay pillars.

Inside the counterfort wall, there were 10 slots on the top of the basement wall. The slots were 4~17 cm in depth and most slots were 15~20 cm, but some were 30~50 cm in width (Table 1). The basement wall was around 1 m in width, and 1.9~3 m in depth.

Table 1 Data recording the observation slots

Slot No.	Plan	Length (cm)	Width (cm)	Remnant Depth (cm)	Orientation Angle of Slot's Center	Elevation
E1	Strip	120	30	6	131°04′4.7″	5°33′33″
E2	Strip	120	25	6	12°02′44.2″	5°48′34″
E3	Strip	130	20	4	118°52′18.″	5°31′43″
E4	Strip	130	20	9	112°40′47.2″	6°07′53″
E5	Strip	135	20	10	105°59′59.2″	7°11′56″
E6	Strip	125	20	9	100°38′16″	5°46′22″
E7	Trapezia	145	Inner 20, outer 50	16	94°27′52.2″	4°15′53″
E8	Strip	150	20	8	89°06′21.7″	3°19′28″
E9	Trapezia	165	Inner 15, outer 40	8	82°18′14.7″	2°15′41″
E10	TRAPEZIA	190	INNNER 14, OUTER 20	4	74°35′30″	1°54′23″
E11	GAP		50		66°4′31″	1°07′11″
E12	STRIP	160	40	17	60°20′54.7″	1°15′29″

(*Note*: The orientation angles are actual ones and do not include magnetic declinations).

On the second terrace, one slot was cut between two rammed-clay pillars for summer solstice observation. Based on such features the vertical pillars and slots were reconstructed on the original place. There are 12 slots in total, respectively focusing on a given point on the opposite Mountain of Chongshan.

The discovery of an observation point for the observatory is significant. The observation point was located almost on the center of the undisturbed soil core of the platform. Its GPS position is N35°52′55.9″, and E111°29′54.9″. It was composed of three concentric circles made by rammed clay. The diameters of the outer, middle, and inner circles were 86, 42, and 25 cm in turn. The observer could stand only within the inner circle, the radius from the center of the observation point to the outer and inner fringe of the slots was about 12.35 and10.1 m respectively (Shanxi 2007).

A total of 20 solar events of a tropical year (365 or 366 days) might have been marked on the skyline of the top of the Chongshan Mountain, while the sunlight shaft of the relative morning sunrise is narrowed by a given slot between the pillars, culminating at the core of the observation point. If the mist eliminated the sunlight, the hierophant would stand on the core of the observation point to view the half sunrise or the lower edge of the sun cutting the peak of the Chongshan Mountain, right in the middle of the particular slot or not. For a period from the winter solstice in 2003 to autumn equinox in 2005 we observed the sunrise 20 times through the slots. On the basis of observed data, it can be estimated that the Taosi ancestors observed winter solstice through the second slot on December 21 and summer solstice through the twelfth slot (the northernmost one) on June 21. On consideration of the long-term change of the ecliptic obliquity, it can be calculated that the horizontal point of sunrise on winter solstice 4,000 years ago should be at about 38′30.95″ south from the present point, which was in alignment with a peak of Chongshan Mountain.

According to this calculation, it is easily understood that the Taosi ancestors observed the sunrise on spring equinox and autumn equinox through the seventh slot on March 18 and September 25 separately. The seventh slot is set in the middle between the winter and summer solstice slots, with four slots in the interval. The first slot, at the southernmost position, demarcates the maximum southern excursion of the moon (18 2/3 year cycle). Chinese astronomers are convinced that the structure served as the earliest observatory in China about 4,100 years ago.

It is very striking that the core part of the observatory located in the third terrace is composed of rammed clay and undisturbed loess in a coiled 69 shape. This clearly illustrating an earthen diagram of Taiji Dualism ca. 2100–2000 BCE (Figure 2).

The earthen diagram implies a meaningful dialectic based on *yin-yang* dualism. Originally undisturbed loess without any shape, it was shaped by being given an outline of rammed clay. The undisturbed loess was considered as *dao*, namely heaven, a term applied to matter without shape. Because the rammed clay part was inserted into undisturbed loess, the outline was determined by the rammed clay, just like what is expressed by *Xici Shang* (Recapitulation, part 1) of the *Zhouyi*: when something was derived from nothing, its outline depended on *dao*. *Dao* was first, the outline was second.

As *dao*, heaven was regarded as matter without form, and it was so pure and holy that it could not be stained. Given this, in practice nobody would be allowed to stand on the undisturbed loess part of the observatory. One was obliged to stand on the rammed-clay part, representing earth. Therefore, the observer had to stand on the observation point made with rammed clay, and those carrying out the ritual of receiving sunrise must have stood on the rammed-clay core of the observatory (Figure 1). Such behavior symbolized the position of humans, standing under heaven and on the earth, exhibiting a typical mode of heaven-earth-human relationship in Chinese archaic cosmology. By symbolizing the axis point, the circle of the observation point also contributed to a Taiji Dualism diagram. It indicated the dialectic relationship between pure air and turbid dust in movement so that, as was explained in *Baihu tong* (Comprehensive discussions in the White Tiger Hall), heaven and earth moved together.

Lid-like heaven

If Taiji Dualism was the basic theory dealing with formation and movement of heaven and earth in cosmogony, the lid-like heaven was the first cognition and explanation concerning the shape of heaven and earth.

The observatory at Taosi is situated against the inner southern enclosure (Q6) of Middle-period (ca. 2,100 to 2000 BCE) Taosi and protrudes to the southeast in a semicircular shape (Figure 1). The treatise on astronomy in the *Jin Shu* said that heaven was like a round umbrella and earth was like a square chess board. The theory of lid-like heaven considered the heaven as an umbrella that inclined to one side. Therefore, the lower part of heaven, submerged under the horizon, was not visible. In this case, the heaven was actually experienced as a semicircle or arch shape over one's head. According to what *Xici Shang* in *Zhouyi* explained, matter appeared as phenomena in the sky, while it was shaped on the earth, parallel to the phenomena. It is estimated that the entire shape of the observatory at Taosi symbolized the dome of the sky being brought down to ground level, inclined to the northern sky, while the enclosure behind the observatory symbolized the chess-board-like earth or horizon.

TIME

Lacking significant evidence for calculating devices, we do not know how the people of the Taosi culture told and recorded time and how they divided the day and night. In contrast, a number of archaeological records have provided us with significant information to analyze the calendar and knowledge of the four seasons of Taosi culture. The calendar system of Taosi culture might have involved solar, lunar, and solar-lunar calendars.

There are a total of 12 observation gaps on the rim of the Taosi observatory. Among them, Gap E1 might not have been used for solar observation (Shanxi 2007, 2006). From Gap E2 to Gap E12, one could observe the half sunrise or the bottom edge of the sun cutting the top profile of a mountain that is located around 7 km east of Taosi, by standing on the observation point. This would enable an observer to identify the whole solar year as defined by 20 terms, including winter solstice, summer solstice, spring equinox, and autumn equinox. Based on the results obtained from observation or calculation, the astronomer would have been able to make a positional calendar for the Taosi ruling authorities. Taosi's solar calendar entailed 20 terms according to local seasonal change, cultivation schedules (He 2007), and ceremonial festivals. It is detailed in Table 2 as follows:

Table 2 Positional calendar derived from the observatory at Taosi

Date of Testing Observation	Date of Taosi Period	Gap No.	Seasonal Change	Ritual Festival	Cultivation Date	Interval Days
2005-12-22	1–7	E2	Winter solstice	Ritual for heaven and sun, ancestral ceremony		33
*2005-1-23	2–10	E3	Coldest			34
Calculation	2–28	E4	Spring begins	Receiving spring		18
2005-2-27	3–16	E5	Ice melts	Ritual for land and crops		18
2005-3-8	3–25	E6	Thaw, snow ends		Prepare to cultivate	9
2005-3-18	4–5	E7	Spring equinox		Brewing wine	11
2005-3-28	4–14	E8		Spring sacrifice to ancestors	Barley planting	9
Calculation	4–27	E9	Frost ends		Hemp planting	13
2005-4-26	5–14	E10	Summer begins	Receiving spring	MILLET PLANTING	17
2005-5-20	6–5	E11			Transplant rice seedlings	22

Date of Testing Observation	Date of Taosi Period	Gap No.	Seasonal Change	Ritual Festival	Cultivation Date	Interval Days
2004-6-21	7–11	E12	Summer solstice	Ritual for earth	Summer millet AND BROOMCORN MILLET planting	36
2004-7-23	8–15	E11	Hottest			35
Calculation	9–6	E10	Autumn begins	Receiving autumn	Spring millet harvest	22
2004-9-2	9–22	E9	Dew occurs		Summer millet tasseling	16
*2004-9-14	_____ 10–4 _____	_____ E8 _____	_____	Autumn sacrifice to ancestors	_____	_____ 12 _____
2005-9-25	10–13 _____	E7 _____	Autumn equinox _____		Metrologic calibration BROOMCORN MILLET HARVEST _____	9 _____
*2005-10-6	10–23	E6	Cold dew		Summer millet and rice harvest	10
2004-10-14	10–31	_____ E5	Frost occurs	Autumn sacrifice to heaven and earth		8
2004-10-31	11–16	E4	Winter begins	Winter sacrifice to ANCESTOR RECEIVING WINTER		16
2004-11-18	12–4	E3	FREEZE BEGINS	NEXT HARVEST PRAYING	CEASE FARMING	18

In the table, * refers to the date determined according to practical testing observation of earlier days before the sun rises in the middle of this gap.

In addition to the positional calendar obtained by observations at the Taosi observatory, the authorities also utilized a gnomon shadow template to derive the same solar calendar as a supplementary measure, in case sunrise was not visible on a foggy morning.

In 2002, a lacquered gnomon shadow template was recovered from the royal tomb No. 22 of the Middle Taosi period (ca. 2100 to 2000 BCE). It was put in the southeastern corner of the huge chamber. On the right side of the template, there was an alcove containing a red lacquered box, in which were placed three adjunct appliances for the template (Shanxi 2003; He 2009, 2011b). They include one nonius (supplementary scale) modified with a jade *cong* cube, one shadow definer utilized with a jade *qi*-ax, and one plumb bob utilized with a jade *qi*-ax. The *cong*, which is 4.4 cm in diameter, is just suitable to hitch the template, chasing the shadow of the gnomon moving on the template. The top and bottom collars of the *cong* had been cut off, in order to chase and precisely mark the movement of the gnomon shadow on the template. Combined with the jade *cong*, the jade *qi*-ax without the handle has a single hole, which is estimated to define the gnomon shadow on the template. Another jade *qi*-ax without the handle has double holes, which could not work as the shadow definer but could be utilized as plumb bob to judge the gnomon verticality. On June 21, 2009, we tested the replicas of the gnomon, template, shadow definer, and plumb bob at Taosi observatory. The results demonstrated what we had estimated of their functions (He 2015: 132).

The surviving part of the template is 171.8 cm long. The lower end was intact, while the upper end was slightly damaged, affecting less than 10 cm. In the middle of the template, one section measuring 26.4 cm was decayed (Figure 3).

With the assistance of Zhao Yongheng from the National Observatory of the Chinese Academy of Science, who precisely calculated shadow data of two solstices and two equinoxes from 2100 to 2000 BCE (He 2011a), I was able to convert such data into centimeters according to the foot of the Taosi culture, decoded by me, which is 1 Taosi *Chi* 尺 = 25 cm (He 2005). I compared such converted data to mark lengths on the template with a maximum error of ≤0.5 cm. I concluded that Mark No. 12 on the template might have served to identify the sun shadow of summer solstice at the Taosi site, and Mark No. 34 served for spring and autumn equinox identification. Mark No. 37 could work for identifying the sun shadow of the winter solstice at the Taosi site (He, 2010).

So far I have focused on the two solstices and two equinoxes identified by the gnomon shadow template from Taosi. Li Geng, also from the National Observatory of the Chinese Academy of Science, published his research on the Taosi template, concluding that the same solar calendar with 20 terms obtained by the template corresponded to what was obtained from the Taosi observatory. His argument is convincing (Li and Sun 2010). However, there are as many as 43 or 44 marks on the template; remarkably, this is many more than the 20 marks needed for the Taosi solar calendar. It suggests that the Taosi template might have not only served for calculating the local solar calendar but for establishing the calendar of other important sites or areas beyond Taosi. One thing is very clear: the Taosi people were aware of the four seasons before 4,000 years ago. Other uses of the gnomon shadow template as a scientific instrument included identifying the center of the (flat) earth and conducting astronomical geodesy.

Archaeological evidence from Taosi has indicated that the Taosi culture might have used a lunar calendar or even a solar-lunar calendar in addition to the solar calendar of 365 days and 20 solar periods.

FIGURE 3 Lacquered gnomon shadow template IIM22:43 粉紅pink; 綠green.

FIGURE 4 Copper gear-shaped wheel from grave No. 11 at Taosi.

One gear-shaped copper disk was unearthed from a small grave, designated No. 11, at a small cemetery located beyond and to the northwest of the northern wall of the Middle Taosi–period city (2100 to 2000 BCE). The cemetery is dated to the Late Taosi period (2000 to 1900 BCE) (Liang and Yan 2002). This copper disc is 12.4 cm in diameter, with a big central hole 7.5 cm in diameter. It is edged with 29 teeth (Figure 4) (PRC Ministry of Science and Technology and National Cultural Relics Bureau, 2009). It is only 3 mm thick.

Based on the archaeological context, I have argued that such a gear wheel with 29 teeth might have symbolized each day in a whole lunar month and could have been used in combination with a similar sun disk, engaging with the sun disk to calculate a solar-lunar calendar. Given this, the copper wheel with 29 teeth could be called a Small Moon Wheel (He 2010).

SPACE

In Taosi cosmology, spatial concepts consisted of Five Directions (east, west, south, north, and center), Five Quarters, and Eight Schematic Directions. The Five Directions system can be described as scientific; the five directions being determined by measurements with the gnomon shadow template, the celestial north pole, or even the less precise magnetic north pole. It mainly was utilized for scientific and secular purposes for scientific and secular purposes.

The Five Directions/Quarters system was established through the identification of five points using the gnomon shadow template, guided by the assumption that the observer's position represented the center, and thus an idea of centrality. It was an element in the ideological and political landscape. I call it the Five Quarters of Political Geography. Strikingly, the Five Quarters might have been a factor in Taosi politics. The Eight Schematic Directions system was based on heaven, earth, mountains, swamps, fire, water, wind, and thunder, as they related to eight directions surrounding the capital.

Such a system is exhibited by the district plan of inner Taosi City, which for the most part was involved with religion. It seems like there is not a central quarter or central point in the Eight Schematic Directions system, though one considers where the central point or central zone should have been localized according to the eight directions. In contrast, the concept of the center, namely the central point on the earth's surface, referred to the central point or central quarter of political geography and served political purposes.

DIRECTION IDENTIFICATION: THE SCIENTIFIC DIRECTION SYSTEM

The Taosi people had a concept of precise directions, and they could identify them in a scientific manner. This is demonstrated by the angle of the middle of observation slot E8 in the Taosi observatory. The angle is 89°06′21.7″, which was apparently selected deliberately, because it is very close to 90°—the true east. The error of less than 1° from true direction might have resulted from the construction techniques of 4,000 years ago. It is definite that east could be identified by the Taosi people.

As recorded in *Tianwen Xun* in the *Huainanzi*, the strategy for identifying the true direction was called "justifying morning and evening." One could move the gnomon pole along the circle with 10 steps in diameter, to confirm the positions both of sunrise and sunset, then connect these two points in order to identify the exact east. I pointed out that the length unit of Taosi culture is 1 *chi* = 25 cm, and 5 *chi* = 1 *bu* 步 (meaning "step as a length unit") = 1.25 m. The average distance from the center of the observation point to the outer edge of the arch of observation gaps is 12.3 m, which is very close to 10 steps equal to 12.5 m. It is not a coincidence that the middle line of the Gap E8 aligns almost to the exact east.

Given this, one can easily realize that the Taosi people already had the concepts of east, west, north, and south obtained by gnomon shadow observation. Accordingly, the four directions must establish the central direction. Eventually, the so-called four direction system came to be composed of five directions including the central one, which could be termed as the "scientific Five Directions system."

THE EIGHT SCHEMATIC DIRECTIONS SYSTEM ILLUSTRATED BY THE DESIGN OF TAOSI CITY

The most prominent manifestation of the spatial concept is illustrated by the planning of the Taosi City in the Middle period (2100 to 2000 BCE), which might have been directed by the Eight Schematic Directions (He 2013a). Originally they were considered eight natural gods, such as heaven, earth, mountains, swamps, fire, water, wind, and thunder, which were linked to eight directions with related religious meanings. Later, other meanings became attached to the eight directions, and accordingly they were respectively known by a second set of names, that is, the names of the Eight Trigrams of the *Zhouyi*: *Qian, Kun, Gen, Dui, Li, Kan, Zhen,* and *Xun.* At first this system was identified with heaven and earth.

On the basis of the actual relationship between archaeological features from Taosi and its micro-environment, and the contexts of artifacts compared to relevant historic documents, I concluded that the southeast district of Taosi City was heaven (*Qian*), the northwest was earth (*Kun*), the south was the mountain (*Gen*), the north was the swamp (*Dui*), the southwest was fire (*Li*), the northeast was water (*Kan*), the east was thunder (*Zhen*), and the west was wind (*Xun*) (Figure 5). I call that system the Spatial Mode of the Eight Schematic Directions. It was produced through a recognition that a given city must conform to the supernatural power of the universe, namely from the power of the

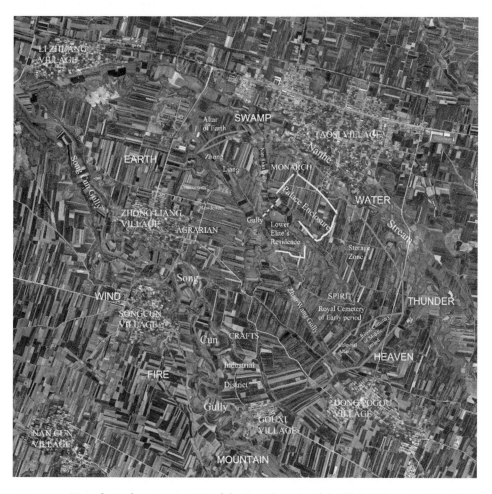

FIGURE 5 Hypothetical reconstruction of the spatial mode of the Eight Schematic Directions and district planning of Taosi City.

eight lords that control the eight directions. So the spatial mode of the Eight Schematic Directions mainly served religious purposes.

Based on the concept about "categorizing the relative matters into the same group according to their same attributes", as embodied in the *Xici Shang* of the *Zhouyi*, the functional heart of the inner city of the Taosi capital in the Middle period was divided into four quadrants: northwestern one for the monarch 人君, northeastern for the spirit (deities) 鬼神, 王陵, southeastern for the industries 工, and southwestern for farming 农. The Monarch Quadrant was categorized with the schematic directions relating to water such as the Swamp 泽, Water 水 or Canal 沟. The Spirit Quadrant was synthesed by the directions relating to supernatures including the Thunder 雷, namely the ancestral lord 帝, dragon 龙, and the Heaven/Sky Power 天. The Industry Quadrant was composed with the directions of the Mountain 山, the Fire 火, and the Wind 风. The Farm Quadrant was determined by the Earth 地 direction.

In *Zhouyi*, the Eight Schematic Directions were termed in another system as follows:. The Heaven is called as *Qian* 乾, the Earth as *Kun* 坤, the Mountain as *Gen* 艮, the Swamp as *Dui* 兑, the Fire as *Li* 离, the Water as *Kan* 坎, the Wind as *Xun* 巽, the Thunder as *Zhen* 震.

The palace district and residential district of lower aristocrats dominated this quarter, close to Water Direction and Swamp Direction (Figure 5), reflecting the human need for water to live.

As the spiritual quadrant, the southeastern walled-town contained the cemetery, the altar for heaven, and the observatory, in addition to secular residences and workshops. As such, the precinct was dominated by ghosts and spirits, close to the Heaven Direction, denoting the ruler's right and power to communicate with heaven (Figure 5).

As the industrial quadrant, the southwest was occupied with lithic- and ceramic-industry communities, close to the Wind and Fire Directions. According to the law of the Eight Schematic Directions interpreted according to the *Zhou Yi*, the Wind Direction was localized in the west and referred to craft production. Ceramic manufacturing needs fire (Figure 5).

As the agriculture quadrant, the northwest was occupied by farmer communities, according to the archaeological survey. Phytolithic data from this area have indicated that there might have been wide and flat fields for the cultivation of millet and rice (Figure 5; and see Yao et al. 2006).

The concept of the Center of the Earth derived from the Taosi gnomon shadow template

It is quite remarkable that the pink mark, No. 11, is abnormally inserted between the green ones, Nos. 10 and 12, on the gnomon shadow template from Taosi. It is very striking that the length of mark No. 11 is 39.9 cm, equivalent to 1.596 Taosi *chi* (with the length unit of Taosi, 1 Taosi *chi* = 25 cm); this is almost 1.6 *chi*, which was recorded in the *Zhou bi suan jing* (Classic of calculating with the Zhou gnomon) as the typical length of the gnomon shadow at the summer solstice observed in the Yuanqu region in Shanxi Province, the heartland of the Miaodigou II culture, the ancestral culture of Taosi culture. It hints that Taosi culture adopted the traditional criterion of the gnomon shadow at the summer solstice, which was clearly useless at Taosi. Such a complication can be explained by comparing it to another criterion specifying a gnomon shadow of 1.5 *chi* at the summer solstice observed at Dengfeng or Luoyang in Henan Province, which was recorded in *Zhou Li* (Rites of Zhou), and taking this as the criterion for the Center of the Earth. One can easily estimate that the striking mark No. 11 on the gnomon shadow template from Taosi might have indicated a designation of Taosi City as the Center of the Earth.

It is definitely the case that the Center of the Earth concept of the Taosi culture was based on the ruler's hegemonic right of speech with respect to regional political landscapes other than the center (He 2011a). The Center of the Earth was regarded as affording an exclusive passage connecting the plane of earth to the celestial zenith where the Supreme Lord resided. From this it is very clear that the concept of the Center of the Earth was set within the entire cosmological framework, and in that way it was rather different from the concept of center derived from the scientific Five Directions. The monarch selected his capital according to theory of the Center of the Earth, and so he tried to reside in the center to manipulate the exclusive passage between the earth and zenith, thus arrogating to himself the exclusive right and power of communicating with the Supreme Lord. Given this, one can easily realize that the concept of the Center of the Earth served politically as an ideologically specific concept of space.

The concept of the Political Five Quarters reflected by land surveys with the Taosi gnomon shadow template

I will try to draw a rough picture of the structure of the Political Five Quarters of Taosi culture by means of an analysis of the land survey using the gnomon shadow template.

Identification of four poles of Taosi culture

The gnomon shadow template with its gnomon pole could not only contribute to the establishment of a calendar but also to laying out territory by means of a land survey measure, based on the fact that the gnomon length depended on the latitude where the observation point was localized.

As described by *Yao dian* (Declaration of Yao) in the *Shang shu*, the civil virtue of King Yao shone over the four poles and ascended from the plane of earth to the celestial sphere. The scholars of the Han dynasty interpreted the four poles as four ending poles on the perimeters of the state territory by means of observation of gnomon shadows, taking the central pole as being established at the capital, namely at the Center of the Earth. Such a professional technique was detailed in the *Diguan situ* (Bureau of Terrestrial Offices, Superintendent of Public Affairs) chapter of the *Zhou Li* and explained by scholars of the Han dynasty. Based on that theory, I estimate that the central pole of the Taosi culture might have been placed in Taosi City, the contemporary Center of the Earth. Then the astronomers of Taosi identified the easternmost and westernmost poles of the Eurasia plane, along the latitude of Taosi City, N35°52′55.9″, almost N35°53′. Accordingly, they might have positioned the southernmost and northernmost poles of the Eurasia, along the longitude of Taosi City, E111°29′54.9″, about E111°30′.

Likewise, the southern pole of the Taosi culture might have been placed at Yueliangwan Beach, at Shapa, Wang Gang, Yangxi County, Guangdong Province, where the coordinates are N21°30′22.08″, and E111°29′21.42″, localized in the region called Jiaozhi (Sima Qian, *Shiji: Wudi benji*). This corresponds to descriptions in historical documents saying that the southern pole was positioned on the southern boundary of the territory referred to as the Jiaozhi region. The northern pole might have been placed on the beach of the Laptev Sea east of Nordvik in Russia, where the coordinates are N76°40′26.77″, E111°30′29.08″. Because it is located within the Arctic Circle, its attributes of cold and darkness truly correspond to descriptions in historical documents of Youdu (meaning the Dim Capital, the conceptual home base of spirits, see the *Shangshu Yaodian* and *Quyuan* 屈原 *Chuci* 楚辞 "*Zhaohun*招魂"). This phenomenon parallels the phenomenon of a polar night, as well as to the actual conditions near the pole at the northern periphery.

The eastern pole might have been located at the beach of Xinjian Cun in Jiaonan, Shandong Province, where the coordinates are N35°53′15.02″, E120°05′02.94″, southwest of Qingdao. This place was called Qingzhou in *Yu Gong* (Tribute of Yu, in the *Shangshu*) or Yu Yi in the *Yao Dian* (*Shangshu*). It corresponds to the attributes of the eastern pole on the eastern periphery of earth as described in historical documents. Accordingly, the western pole of the Taosi culture might have been calculated as being at the shore at Badrusiye in Ras al Basit, Syria, where the coordinates are N35°53′13.05″, E35°53′10.68″. Although such a hypothesis has not been demonstrated by any archaeological evidence, it may be attested indirectly by the four seas distance data, as recorded in documents.

Demonstration of the four seas' distance data, as recorded in documents

The dimensions of the world within the four seas (northern, southern, eastern, and western sea) were recorded in Chinese historical documents from the pre–Qin dynasty period as 28,000 *li* from east to west, and 26,000 *li* from south to north (*Huainanzi*: Dixingxun [淮南子·地形训]; *Guanzi*: Dishu [《管子·地数]; *Lushi Chunqiu*: Youshiguan [吕氏春秋· 有始览]; *Shanhaijing*: Zhongshanjing, Shizi [《山海经·中山经》,《尸子》]). Xu Fengxian reckoned that 28,000 *li* = 7,000 km and 26,000 *li* = 6,500 km, taking the unit of length of the Taosi culture as 1 *chi* = 25 cm, and 1,000 *chi* = 1 *li* = 250 m (Xu and He 2011).

Based on the latitude and longitude of Taosi City, I applied the formula provided by Xu Fengxian (Xu and He 2011) and recalculated the real distances between the four poles of Taosi culture. Taking into account of average radius of the globe as 6,371 km, the distance between the eastern and western poles of Taosi is 32,417×84°÷360°≈7,563 km, which is 563 km longer than the data of 28,000 *li* or 7,000 km. The deviation is 7.4%.

On the longitude circle of E111°30´, the distance between southern and northern 24 pole of Taosi is π×6,371×55°÷180°=6,113 km, which is 387 km less than 26,000 *li* or 6,500 km. The deviation is 6%. Clearly this analysis has demonstrated that the estimated four poles with a central pole of Taosi culture might have been the real story. And the data of distances within the four seas recorded in pre–Qin dynasty documents could be obtained by actual gnomon observations conducted by Taosi's astronomers (HE 2015:167–177).

Western Coast of the Pacific Eastern Coast of the Mediterranean

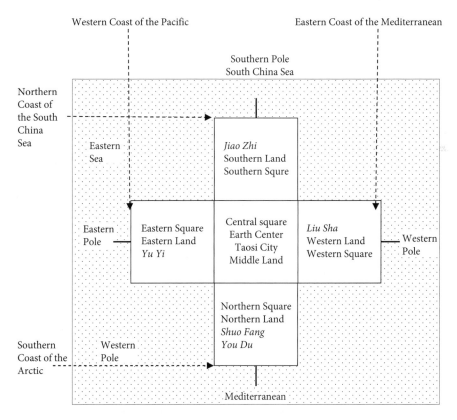

FIGURE 6 Diagram of the Political Five Quarters mode of Taosi culture.

Political Five Quarters of the Taosi culture

In the ideal territorial plan of the Taosi culture, the four poles not only bounded the state's territory but also laid out the boundaries of the four quarters, which were standardized as the eastern, western, southern, and northern quarters surrounding the central quarter where the Center of the Earth was located (Figure 6), in turn to form a *ya* 亞 shape. The central quarter was determined by the Center of the Earth, with the central pole at Taosi City, the capital situated at the Center of the Earth. The Five Quarters territory was believed to be surrounded by four seas. That was why it could be described as being "within four seas" (Figure 6).

In reality, the actual territory of Taosi state might have only covered the region of Southern Shanxi Province. Although the ideal presented here looks very ambitious, reality is another story.

Translated by John Major with Elizabeth Childs-Johnson.

BIBLIOGRAPHY

He, Nu 何 弩 2004. "A Summary of Studies of the Taosi Culture 陶寺文化谱系研究综论." *Gudai Wenming* 3:54–86. Beijing: Wenwu chubanshe.

He, Nu 何 弩 2005. "An Interpretation on the Length Unit of the Taosi Gnomon Template from IIFJT1 in Relation to the Observatory 从陶寺观象台 IIFJT1 相关尺寸管窥陶寺文化长度单 位从陶寺观象台 IIFJT1 相关尺寸管窥陶寺文化长度单位." *Zhongguo shehuikexue yuan Gudai Wenming Yanjiu Tongxun* 10(8):22–33.

He, Nu 何 弩 2007. "Preliminary Analysis of Data on the Observatory and Field Simulation 陶寺中期观 象台实地模拟观测资料初步分析." *Gudai Wenming* 6:83–115. Beijing: Wenwu chubanshe.

He, Nu 何 弩 2009. "On the Function of the '*guichi* 圭尺' Unearthed from the Large Tomb IIM22 at Taosi in Xiangfen, Shanxi 山西襄汾陶寺城址中期王级大墓 出土漆杆圭尺功能试探." *Ziran kexue shi yanjiu* 3:261–276.

He, Nu 何 弩 2010. "Analysis of the Use of the Bronze Toothed Wheel-Shaped Disk Unearthed at Taosi 陶寺出土铜齿轮形器功能辨析陶寺出土铜齿轮形器功能辨析." *Zhongguo wenwubao* 3(19):7.

He, Nu 何 弩 2011a. "A New Probe into the Origin of the Taosi Gnomon 'Zhong' in Relation to 'Zhongguo' 陶寺圭尺'中"与"中国"概念由来新探." *Sandai Kaogu* 4: 85–119.

He, Nu 何 弩 2011b. "Revisions on the *guichi* from Taosi 圭尺 陶寺圭尺补正." *Ziran kexueshii yanjiu* 3:278–287.

He, Nu 何 弩 2013a. "Preliminary Discussion on the Cosmologic Theory of the Layout of Capital-Like Settlements: With Taosi as an Example 试论都邑性聚落布局的宇宙观指导理论——以陶寺遗址为例 试论都邑性聚落布局的宇宙观指导理论——以陶寺遗址为例." *Sandai Kaogu* 5: 19–37.

He, Nu 何 弩 2013b. "The Longshan Period Site of Taosi in Southern Shanxi Province." In *A Companion to Chinese Archaeology*. Edited by Anne P. Underhill, 255–277. Blackwell.

He, Nu 何弩 2015. "How to read ancient thinking – intellectual archaeology and the practice of a spiritual culture, 怎探古人何所思——精神文化考古理论与实践探索》 Beijing: Kexue chubanshe.

He, Nu 2018. "Taosi: An archaeological example of urbanization as a politic center in Prehistoric China," *Archaeological Research in Asia* 14: 20–32.

Li, Gen and Sun, Xiaochun 黎耕、孙小淳 2010. "The Lacquer Stick and *guichi* to Measure Shadows of the Sun from Taosi IIM22, 陶寺 IIM22 漆杆与圭表测影." *Zhongguo kejishi zazhi* 31(4): 363–372.

Liang, Xingpeng and Yan Zhibin 梁星彭 and 严志斌 2002. "Taosi Culture City Remains from Xiangfen, Shanxi 山西襄 汾陶寺文化城址." In *2001-nian Zhongguo Zhongyao Kaogu Faxian*. Beijing: Wenwu chubanshe. 《2001 年中国重要考古发现》24–27.

PRC Ministry of Science and Technology and the National Cultural Relics Bureau 中华人民 共和国科技部，国家 物局 2009. *Early China and the Origin of Chinese Civilization* 中 国早期与中国 明起源. Beijing: Wenwu chubanshe.

Shangshu:Yao Dian.尚书:尧典 1980. In Shisanjing Zhushu十三经注疏", Vol. shang 上册, Beijing: Zhonghua shuju，117–124.

Sima, Qian 司马迁. *Shiji: Wudi benji* 史记:五帝本纪 1959. Beijing: Zhonghua Shuju, 1st edition. 16–17.

Xu, Fengxian 徐凤先 and He Nu 2011. "A new interpretation on the origin of the concept of gnomon shadow measuring one *cun* equivalent to a thousand *li* 里日影千里差一寸"观念 起源新解." *Ziran Kexueshi Yanjiu* 30(2): 155–157.

Yao, Zhengquan, Yan Wu, Changsui Wang, Nu He, and Zhijun Zhao, 姚 政权、吴妍、王昌 燧、何弩、赵志军 2006. "Phytolithic analysis on Taosi site in Xiangfen, Shanxi 山西襄汾 陶寺遗址植硅石分析," *Nongye Kaogu*, 4: 19–26.

Zhongguo Shehui Kexueyuan Kaogu Yanjiusuo, Shanxi Dui 中国社会科学院考古研究所山 西队. 2003 "Tombs of the Middle taosi Culture at Taosi City 陶寺城址发现陶寺文化中期 墓葬" Kaogu 9:3–6.

Zhongguo Shehui Kexueyuan Kaogu Yanjiusuo, Shanxi Dui 中国社会科学院考古研究所山 西队 2004. "Brief Excavation Report for the 2003 the Large-Size Building Foundations in the Sacrificial Area of the Taosi Site in Linfen, Shanxi 山西襄汾陶寺城址祭祀区大型建 筑基址 2003 年发掘简报." *Kaogu* 7:9–24.

Zhongguo Shehui Kexueyuan Kaogu Yanjiusuo, Shanxi Dui 中国 社会科学院考古研究所山 西队 2006. "Testing observation report deriving from IIFJT1 of the Middle Phase at Taosi 陶寺中期小城大型建筑基址IIFJT1实地模 拟观测报告." *Gudai Wenming yanjiu Tongxun* 29(6):3–14. Beijing Daxue Gudai Wenming Yanjiu Zhongxin.

Zhongguo Shehui Kexueyuan Kaogu Yanjiusuo, Shanxi Dui 中国 社会科学院考古研究所山 西队. "Preliminary Excavation Report 2004–2005 on the Large-Size Building-Foundations IIFJT1 at Taosi in Linfen County, Shanxi."

Zhongguo Shehui Kexueyuan Kaogu Yanjiusuo, Shanxi Dui, Linfenshi Wenwuju 中国社会科 学院考古研究所, 临汾文物局 2007. "The Large-Size Building-Foundations IIFJT1at the Walled-Town Site of 山 西襄汾县陶寺中期城址大型建筑 IIFJT1 基址 2004~2005 年发 掘简报." *Kaogu* 4:3–25.

Zhongguo Shehui Kexueyuan Kaogu Yanjiusuo, Shanxi Dui, Linfenshi Wenwuju 中国社会科 学院考古研究所山西工作队、山西省考古研究所、临汾市文 物局 2008. "The large-size rammed-earth building foundations of the Middle Taosi phase discovered at the Taosi city site in Xiangfen County, Shanxi." 山西襄汾县陶寺城址发现陶寺文 化中期大型夯土建筑基址." *Kaogu* 3: 3–6.

SECTION III

FIRST DYNASTY OF THE BRONZE AGE: XIA PERIOD

CHAPTER 7

INTRODUCTION: DEFINITIONS, THEMES, AND DEBATE

BY HONG XU, INSTITUTE OF ARCHAEOLOGY, CASS

THE general academic approach taken in China in studying its early history and civilization has been to deduce the unknown from the known. In order to probe for what characterizes such a social transformation, it is necessary to identify the origins and development of that early state. Due to China's rich literary and historiographical tradition, investigations have relied heavily on confirming the existence of specific dynasties known historically, without relying on modern archaeological methods new to China.

During the early twentieth century Wang Guowei studied oracle bone inscriptions unearthed at ancient Yinxu 殷墟 (Yin Ruins) and corroborated Shang king chronology related in *Shiji's Historical Records of Yin* (*Shiji: Yin Benji*,史记:殷本纪) (Wang 1959a, 1959b). His assessments appeared reliable in providing scholars and academe great promise for understanding early Chinese history. Wang Guowei himself optimistically deduced: "due to the actual lineage of Yin and Zhou kings, we can expect that a Xia royal lineage also existed" (Wang 1959a, 1959b). Based on the authenticity of the *Historical Records of Yin*, he further deduced that the history and records of the Xia 夏 dynasty could also be documented. Consensus amid academic circles in China led to an interest in not only analyzing Xia culture but in analyzing the division of Xia and Shang dynasties based on archaeological means.

Li Ji (Li Chi), known as "the father of Chinese archeology," visited the Zhongtiaoshan 中条山 area in southern Shanxi in 1926, the area where old legends of "Emperor Shun 舜 and the Xia dynasty were concentrated." In addition, he visited Xiaxian 夏县 which, according to legend, was the location of the royal capital and mausolea of the Xia dynasty. Based on clues provided in transmitted literature, Li Ji (Li Chi) sought to discover through survey and excavation in the Jinnan 晋南 area the ruins of Xia.

Subsequent discoveries of Yangshao-culture ceramics were associated initially with the Xia dynasty culture (Xu 1931; Ding 1935; Jian 1947). In the 1930s excavated remains of the Longshan cultural period, which succeeded those of Yangshao, gave rise to further speculation that the Longshan culture was equatable with the ruins of the Xia dynasty (Fan 1955; Wu 1956).

In 1928 excavations at Yinxu in Anyang confirmed that the remains belonged to the late Shang capital and from the standpoint of archaeology represented Shang civilization. During the 1950s the excavated remains of the Erligang culture and the Shang city of Zhengzhou 郑州 were similar but earlier than those of Yinxu, and thus based on archaeological data could be assigned to an early phase of the Shang culture (Li Ji 1990). After combing through the literature for a possible location of the "Ruins of Xia," Xu Xusheng (Hsü Hsü-shêng) in 1959 discovered the site of Erlitou and proceeded to excavate the site. The discovery in 1959 began the prelude to the study of the Xia culture, for which the Erlitou culture, named after the excavated site, has become key to explore.

Neither the Erligang or Erlitou culture has yet been documented by contemporary written texts or inscriptions. Thus, it has not been possible to confirm whether the Erligang culture belongs to the middle of the Shang dynasty or covers the entire first half of the Shang period. Although intimately related and earlier than the Erligang culture (Zou 1956; Henan 1977), the historical identity of Erlitou also cannot be confirmed. Early dynasties and clan lineages and archaeological cultures earlier than Yinxu of the late Shang have remained uncharted territory (Xu Xusheng 1959). Yet, scholars continued to debate the archaeological data used to identify Xia culture and the division of Xia and Shang, and what clan identity could be assigned the Erlitou culture. Despite indecision and decades of academic research, contemporary textual data to resolve these problems remains elusive.

Xia Nai, the well-known and leading figure of Chinese archaeology from the 1950s to 1980s, played a critical role in articulating his views on these pivotal periods of history. In 1977, the Longshan-culture site of Wangchenggang 王城岗 was excavated in Dengfeng 登封 county, Henan. The excavators considered that the city was the earliest capital of the Xia dynasty—Yangcheng 阳城. That year Xia Nai offered two hypotheses: "Firstly, that the Xia Dynasty was historical, unlike the theory of the school of doubters who say the Xia Dynasty never existed. Secondly, that the Xia culture had its own characteristics. Comrade spokespersons never debated these two hypotheses, yet almost everybody agreed with them" (Xia 1978). Xia Nai's two concepts may be summarized as follows: first, that cultural analysis is based on the premise that literature relating to the Xia dynasty may be viewed as historical documentation, and second, that in the absence of written contemporary material "Xia culture" may be characterized through archeological finds. Amid Chinese academic circles, these two primary theses formed the foundation of China's analytical approach.

The assumptions of Xia Nai are clearly based on the discovery of oracle bone inscriptions and the ancient Yinxu site. He states: "Since we recognize that the oracle bone inscriptions of the late Shang Dynasty fundamentally confirm the lineage history of the Shang as provided in the *Shiji: Yin Benji*, it is likely that the Xia royal lineage was also not fabricated. Conclusively, the existence of the Xia Dynasty is completely believable" (Zou 1980). The reasoning thus is that "since the dynastic lineage history of Shang is recorded in the *Shiji: Yin benji* and archaeological remains and oracle bone inscriptions identify the Shang culturally, it is reasonable that the Xia dynastic lineage may also be substantiated. The latter was the belief of the Chinese historian Wang Guowei and Chinese scholarship" (Zhongguo 2003). Such self-confidence and consensus-building regarding Xia culture apparently stems from the fundamental premise that confirmed the existence of the late Shang dynasty's Yinxu ruins according to archaeologist Zou Heng in 1978). Nonetheless, contemporary Xia-period texts do not exist (Zhongguo 2003).

The confidence and consensus taken in exploring Xia culture has obviously deviated from the basic premise that confirmed the historicity of the late Shang dynasty ruins at Yin—the mutual corroboration of excavated documents and classical documents. It is currently not yet possible to characterize the "Xia dynasty" as credibly historical until records contemporary with Xia are discovered or excavated.

In the aforementioned live speech at Dengfeng site in 1977, Xia Nai defined the official view of the Xia culture: "'Xia culture' refers to the Xia people's culture during the Xia dynasty" (Xia 1978). This definition determined the direction discussion took on the subject, including defining the political entities in a narrow historiography, the exact period of the "Xia dynasty," and specific clan associations of the "Xia people." These issues remain impossible to resolve without corroborative scientific data.

Since the 1970s most scholars accepted Xia Nai's definition or one close to it. Zou Heng, for example, stated: "Xia culture is an archaeological culture belonging to the Xia Dynasty" (Zou 1980). In the *Encyclopedia of China, Archaeology* section on "Xia Culture Questions" it is stated: "The goal of academic questions surrounding Chinese archaeological exploration with respect to the Xia Dynasty revolve around material remains from areas where Xia peoples have been active" (Yin 1986). Even in the twenty-first-century publication *Chinese Archeology: Xia and Shang*, "the Xia Culture" is still defined: "'the Xia Culture' refers to the material and spiritual cultural remains created by the Xia clan (or the population whose main body was the Xia clan) under the reign of the Xia Dynasty, the core of which is the historical relics of the Xia dynastic state.... What needs to be clarified is that the Xia Culture and Shang Culture, along with the later Zongzhou 宗周 Culture, Qin秦 Culture, and Chu楚 Culture, are historical periods defined by the names of the archaeological cultures" (Zhongguo 2003).

Xia Nai's definition not only laid the foundation for future discussions of the Xia culture in China but determined the conclusion of these discussions.

Premises and ways of thinking amid scholarly circles were misguided. Analytical parties adhered to the premise that the Xia dynasty existed, that later literature—mostly from the Eastern Zhou dynasty to the Han dynasty—was correct and trustworthy, and that archaeological remains could be assessed for use in identifying a certain clan or a specific rulership. Based on this contextual approach, relevant archaeological remains could be used to distinguish Xia from Shang and to attribute a specific individual or historical event, such as the Shang king Tang 汤defeating Xia. The difference lies only in what literature is reliable and should be cited, and what dynasty (or clan) is associated with what archaeological remains.

There are other problematic tendencies of scholarship. Authors, for example, often cite records yet lack necessary or sufficient research on the historical backgrounds of these citations. They represent the phenomenon of "just take it and use it 拿来就用."

Others use strongly emphatic, exclusive language, such as "can only," "affirms," and "undoubtedly." Such terms are abundantly used in articles reflecting self-confidence rather than hypothetical or inferential statements. The effect is often to shut out opposing theories or assessments of alternative historical possibilities. It is common to cite documentary evidence, dating data, and archaeological materials that are advantageous to the author's point of view.

With incomplete archaeological data, the main tendency has been for the Chinese archaeological community to focus on only the historical aspect of the findings, associating large settlements and specific cities with those recorded in received texts and some archaeological cultures with specific clans and dynasties. At the same time, in the absence of conclusive evidence, scholars revise or even change their views, or even start a new debate as new archaeological discoveries and dating data continue to emerge. The numerous articles with theories on Xia culture and the Xia dynasty cover a long period of time—the entire second half of the twentieth century BCE. The two in fact are a subject discussed more than any other academic issue.

When scholars refer to the existence of the Xia dynasty, they may rely on pre-Qin literary documents. The documents -甘誓, 汤誓, 召诰, 多士, 多方, 立政- in the *Book of Documents* (*Shangshu* 尚书), and the poem, 大雅·荡, in the *Classic of Poetry* (*Shijing* 诗经) include many references to the Xia dynasty, royal lineage, and the Shang conquest of Xia. In addition, there are plenty of other historical classics (see the *Zuozhuan* 《左传》:宣公三年,昭公元年,昭公四年,昭公十一年,定公四年,襄公四年,哀公元年; *Guoyu* 《国语》:周语,晋语; *Lunyu* 《论语》:为政; *Mengzi* 《孟子》:公孙丑,滕文公,告子; *Chushu Jinian* 《竹书纪年》; *Yizhoushu* 《逸周书》:度邑解,史记解; *Zhanguoce* 《战国策》:魏策; *Shiben* 《世本》; *Shangshu* 《尚书》:禹贡,吕刑; *Shijing* 《诗》:商颂·长发; *Mozi* 《墨子》:非攻; and *Chuce* 楚辞 《离骚》;《天问》) referring to Da Yu 大禹 and other historical figures and events (IA CASS 2003).

It also needs to be emphasized that none of the aforementioned pre-Qin transmitted corpuses was fully completed before the Eastern Zhou period. Furthermore, it is difficult to distinguish the original from the processed parts in these transmitted texts over such a long time period.

Recently excavated texts have provided little information on the Xia period or dynasty. An inscription on a middle-period Western Zhou vessel, the Duke Sui *xu* (遂公 盨), documents a passage stating "天命禹敷土, 堕山浚川 (Sky [Heaven] mandated Yu to till the land . . .)." It is the earliest account referencing the story of Great Yu (Da Yu 大禹) (Li Xueqin 2003). But, there is no reference to "Xia" or to Yu as a king of Xia. The reference is not to Yu as a king but as a divine being. This inscription is nonetheless "the earliest example of the legend concerning flood control by the Great Yu."

Based on textual data of transmitted literature and bronze inscriptions, we are led to conclude that "Xia" is first mentioned one thousand years later during the Eastern Zhou period. The inscriptions on the Duke Sui *xu* of middle-Western Zhou date and on earlier unearthed Duke Qin *gui* 秦公簋 and Shu Yi *zhong* 叔夷钟, nonetheless are historical references to "Yu" and "Xia" respectively of the Zhou period (Gu and Tong 1982).

LONGSHAN CONNECTIONS

The "Xia" referred to in texts is assessed to date to the twenty-first to seventeenth centuries BCE. The era of the Erlitou culture ranges from ca. 1900–1500 BCE. Preceding Longshan connections with the earliest phases of the "Xia" culture have advanced considerably over the last decades. In 1974, a preliminary report on No. 1 Palace remains at Erlitou was published in the journal *Kaogu* (Archaeology). The excavators used "Early Shang" in the title to affirm by their tone their opinion on the date and dynastic identity of these remains. This preliminary report said that "there was strong physical evidence that these remains belonged to the early Shang Dynasty palace of Western Bo 西亳 built by King Tang 汤" (Zhongguo 1974). The premise of this interpretation was that the "Erligang culture belonged to the Middle Shang period." And, because "Phase III stratigraphically dated before the Erligang period, it was possible to date the palace site to the early Shang period." The article also quoted a single passage in the *Geography Records of Han Shu* (《汉书·地理志》) that "Shixiang (which is in Yanshi County, Henan Province) was Yin Tang's capital." Subsequently two carbon dates for this identification were published. Since the date of Erlitou P3 (the date of the foundation of No. 1 Palace) according to dendrochronological calibration was from 1590 to 1300 BCE, Erlitou was considered to be "Early Shang." Erlitou Phase 1, based on tree-ring calibrations for dating, was assessed to be 2080 to 1690 BCE.

These data and publications quickly became a mainstream interpretation amid the academic community. Researchers would by inference conclude that "Wangwan Phase 3 and Erlitou Phase 1 were equivalent to the Xia Dynasty" (Tong 1975). Soon thereafter, based on four C^{14} specimens, Xia Nai maintained that "three of them dated to Erlitou phases I to IV of ca. 1900 to 1600 BCE" (Xia 1977). One calibration was excluded "because of potential error," and because it dated later than Phase 4. These dates formed the strongest proof to corroborate that Phase 3 was equivalent to "the early phase of Shang." Other scholars, however, reached a different conclusion in maintaining that "the span of 1900 to 1600 BCE matched the historical texts concerning the middle and late phase of the Xia Dynasty," namely that "Erlitou remains may be identified with important archaeological remains of the Xia Dynasty" (Li Min and Wen 1975).

In subsequent debates on the division of Xia and Shang cultures, many scholars selectively relied on ^{14}C dating, and often on just a single date, especially during the 1970s when these scientific data were first released. In fact, Xia Nai pointed out at the time "Only a series of consistent C^{14} dates is valuable. One or two isolated data, on its own terms, is of little significance" (Xia 1977). Dating experts warned academics that "solitary carbon[14] data are generally not believable," and "it is dangerous to draw conclusions based on individual carbon[14] data when discussing the Xia culture" (Qiu et al. 1983). Some scholars used tree-ring correction data, while others used the data without corrections; some used the half-life of 5,730 correction data, compared with the 5,570-year half-life data. The results of these dissimilar data are self-evident.

At the public meeting in 1977 at Dengfeng, Beijing University's Professor Zou Heng formally put forward his thesis that "Erlitou culture is the Xia culture." He said that "Zhengzhou Shang City was the capital Bo." He believed that "based on five aspects, including dating, geography, cultural characteristics, cultural resources, and social development, one can state that the Erlitou culture is the Xia Dynasty and the archaeological culture is namely the Xia culture" and that "Zhengzhou Shang City is Tang's capital Bo" (Zou 1978). In the subsequent publication of his *Collected Essays on the Archaeology of the Hsia, Shang and Chou Dynasties* (Zou 1980), Zou engaged in a more systematic and in-depth analysis of this point of view. This body of work by Zou has been held in high regard in the academic world and has had a profound impact on the academic community. Since this publication, an endless stream of publications of all kinds appeared. Using similar data for interpretation, scholars nonetheless reached entirely different conclusions. For example, changes in material goods in the face of social and political development were compared against various gradients and mutations, but the latter were primarily a matter of opinion. Academics also tried to cut a clean line between the Xia and Shang dynasties and between the late period of the Longshan culture, the Erlitou culture, and the early Erligang culture. Scholars used a variety of their own reasons for assessing this evolution.

An important site for understanding the Longshan era is Taosi 陶寺 in Xiangfen 襄汾, Shanxi. The Shanxi Team of the Institute of Archaeology of the Chinese Academy of Sciences (now part of the Chinese Academy of Social Sciences) carried out a large-scale archaeological survey in the 1950s and 1960s in the southern part of Shanxi Province (Jinnan), with the mission of exploring potential Xia culture sites (known as the Academic Mission to Explore Xia Culture) (Gao 2007; also see chapter 6 by He Nu on Taosi). The ruins found at Taosi were a major discovery leading to great academic excitement. The prevailing hypothesis at that time was that Erlitou and Dongxiafeng in Shanxi belonged to the Shang culture. According to ^{14}C dating at that time, the age estimate of Taosi culture was from 2500 to 1900 BCE, with a vacillation curve of hundreds of years from the beginning to the end of the Xia dynasty. Excavators selected the earliest and latest extreme values: the twenty-fourth ~ eighteenth centuries BCE for Taosi, with the estimate that middle- and late-period Taosi ruins were part of the Xia dynasty, and that the site and cemetery were probably the remains of Xia people (Gao et al. 1983).

The Taosi material was soon published, and various scholars expressed positions different from the excavators, recognizing, for example, that "much of the excavated material and transmitted textual data on Yao and Shun are actually comparable" (Li Min 1985). Subsequently, excavators embraced the "Erlitou-Xia culture thesis," which supported the one that the Taosi people and clans belonged to the Tao Tang clan [a different clan earlier than Xia people]" (Zhongguo 2003).

It became obvious that there was a direct relationship between the numerous clusters of settlements appearing in many places within the many small river valleys and basins located south of the Yellow River and in the area of Songshan during the Longshan period. It also became clear that many settlements were relatively independent yet inter-related (Liu and Chen 2007; Chen et al. 2003; Zhongguo 2005). Although separated geo-graphically, major settlements were large, surrounded with smaller to medium-sized settlements. Archaeological excavation uncovered data documenting different cultural backgrounds and practices of these Longshan settlements, and the discovery of a series of cities undergoing constant conflict represented by large-scale killing, and an increase in weaponry. This environment of inter-regional exchange and gradual integration ulti-mately contributed to the formation of a widespread Erlitou royal state.

Among the clusters of large and small settlements within the Central Plains, the most impressive are a dozen city sites (Wei 2010). These sites were only briefly occupied and differ greatly in this respect from others in Shandong and the middle and lower reaches of the Yangzi River that were occupied over a long time period. The sudden rise and fall of these cities is generally interpreted to represent military conflict. No large-scale cen-tral settlement with cross-regional influence appeared at this time in the Central Plains. Rather, this period witnessed small-scale settlements in intense conflict, turbulence, and warfare (Xu 2012).

So far 12 sites representing a common time period have been identified in the Dengfeng Basin, in the upper reaches of the Ying River upstream where the Dengfeng Wangchenggang city site is located. The majority form small-scale settlements, approxi-mating less than 10,000 m² in area, smaller than Wangchenggang. The larger size and higher location of the Wangchenggang site indicates it was a centralized settlement in this region.

This area of the Dengfeng Basin has a long history rich in Xia myth and legend. Due to the discovery of the nearby site of Yangcheng of Warring States date, academics asso-ciated the small fortified city at Wangchenggang with "Yu's Yangcheng" (Yu was the founder of the Xia dynasty) or with the "City Built by Gun" (Gun 鯀 was the father of Great Yu). The latest interpretation is that the small town at Wangchenggang may be the "City Built by Gun and that the large city is Yu's capital Yangcheng" (Zhongguo 2007).

The reliance on archaeological and historical data for understanding ancient China was thus continuously used to discover and deduce, and rediscover and re-deduce. Based on simulated recreations of a fortified wall and related statistics, the excavators estimated that it would require one year and two months and the mobilization of 1,000 people to complete the construction of the Wangchenggang fortifications. Based on local experience, if one village provided 50 to 100 young people to complete such a proj-ect, the manpower needed would require 10 to 20 towns for one year of labor. These numbers are consistent with the number of the Longshan culture settlements in the Dengfeng area. It is likely that the mobilization and collaboration of various groups within the larger settlement complex satisfied the construction of the Wangchenggang city (Beijing 2007).

Construction data indicate that building the fortification of the large city of Wangchenggang, measuring 300,000 m² in area, required a dozen or so surrounding small-scale settlements, indicating that large-scale mobilization of human labor from a vast territory was required to complete a city like Wangchenggang. Based on this hypothesis the site could be assumed to represent a Xia-dynasty capital.

Another possible city center settlement about the same period appears at Wadian 瓦店 in Yuzhou 禹州, only around 30 km away from Wangchenggang (Henan 2004). This area is also rich in legends associated with the Xia. Popular sayings about the area of Yuzhou include reference to "Yu's capital Yangdi 禹都阳翟" and to "the place where Yu's son Qi enjoyed worshipping heaven at Juntai at the beginning of the Xia 夏启有钧台之享."

Yet these associations were not made until two thousand years after the "Xia," as represented in texts of the Eastern Han and the Western Jin Dynasties (e.g., 地理志 Dilizhi in 汉书 *Hanshu* by Bangu; and 春秋左氏经传集解 *Chunqiu Zuoshi Jingzhuan Jijie*, by Du Yu, etc.). The large time gap of the two settings, one literary and one archaeological, still did not prevent people from connecting Wadian and legend. Based on the archaeological data, "the area of north of and south of Songshan had not yet formed a unified political order; settlement groups were relatively independent and mutual contentions and signs of violence were commonplace" (Wang Lixin 2006). The issue of how to regulate and coordinate tribal groups had not yet evolved during this transitional Late Longshan period.

About 40 km distant from Wangchenggang in Dengfeng is a third ancient walled city, Guchengzhai 古城寨 in Xinmi 新密, of similar date and pattern of settlement. More than 10 smaller settlements surrounded this central walled site (Henan 2002). The three fortified city centers of Wangchenggang, Wadian, and Guchengzhai city centers presiding over respective settlement groups were divided geographically; they were in turn separated by physical space suggesting they were independent governing bodies. Given such a settlement pattern created doubt about the emergence of a single unified polity or the birth of dynasty (Xu 2012).

When the three large independent city centers of Wangchenggang, Wadian, and Guchengzhai declined or were destroyed, a different large, ancient walled city called Xinzhai 新砦 rose as the center of this geographical locale. Xinzhai, which lay only 7.5 km away from Guchengzhai, is important in terms of dating and location. The city site began to flourish in the late Longshan era and thrived during the transition period leading to the Erlitou era. The latter two periods were labeled and identified as the "the Xinzhai period" designating two stages with an absolute age of 2050~1900 BCE and 1850~1750 BCE (Beijing 2008; Zhao 2009).

The Longshan era was a time of great conflict amid neighboring cultural settlements and was a time of decline and stagnation during its latest phase. It may be defined as a "breaking" point in terms of the process of developing an "early Chinese civilization" (Xu Hong 2001). It is also evident that this phenomenon of "breaking away" also took place, yet not so obviously around the birthplace of the Erlitou culture, in the area of

Songshan. Erlitou gradually emerged as the first core culture in Chinese history. The large city of Xinzhai and the remains of the Xinzhai type (which many scholars believe could be dated to the early phase of the Xia culture) is nonetheless critical in figuring out the reasons for the rise of the Erlitou culture and in understanding the transition of the turbulent Longshan era into a prosperous Erlitou cultural era.

The importance of the large city at Xinzhai is also reflected in its measurements and contents. The fortified site was 700,000 m² in area and thrived during the late Longshan era in the Central Plains. The Xinzhai site during the "Xinzhai period" formed a peninsula-shaped settlement of 1,000,000 m², with three trenches or walls: an outer moat, an intermediate moat, and an inner moat. The outer and intermediate trenches surrounded inner trenches; the area encircled by the inner trench in the southwest was on higher ground and enclosed an area of about 60,000 m², which was the center of the settlement. Excavations in this center area uncovered large building foundations, fragments of the bronze containers, and a ceramic cover with engraved motifs, which resemble the "dragon" created out of inlaid turquoise pieces at Erlitou.

"Xinzhai type remains" of the Xinzhai period appear to be distributed mainly in the area of Songshan, especially its eastern part (Zhao 2006). The unique plaque of a dragon form is a major link in the chain of the Central Plains civilization. Former traditions appear to have been inherited and incubated, leading to new cultural characteristics.

With respect to the "Xinzhai remains," academics agree on the following scenario: Xinzhai began to dominate the areas north and south of Songshan, in the process beginning to integrate former groups, to be influenced by external factors, and to enable cultures to further hybridize and solidify. If Erlitou is the "earliest China" in East Asia, the earliest core culture and royal state, then Xinzhai is clearly the beginning of that dawn (Xu 2009). It can be said that the emergence of the large-scale fortification at Xinzhai led to the destruction of the old order of the late Longshan era, where regional groups coexisted and constantly warred. The development during the Xinzhai period brought to a full stop the centuries of warring and struggle amid regional cities of the Central Plains.

According to the latest available dates, the Erlitou culture "cannot be earlier than 1750 BCE" (Zhang et al. 2007) and is not, as originally presumed, as early as 1900 BCE. According to these data, the mainstream point of view sees the early Xia culture as dating to the late Longshan. A symposium took place on this very topic (Beijing et al. 2012). Yet, we need to remind ourselves that these notions of so-called "mainstream views" or "consensus of academics" are not based on conclusive written evidence—that is, on unearthed written sources, such as oracle bone texts. Any transmitted textual data to verify the historicity of Xia is elusive, so the debate goes on.

ERLITOU EXCAVATION HISTORY AND FINDS

The Erlitou site at Yanshi, Henan, is one of the key historical sites in the history of China's early civilization. In the more than 50 years since the discovery and the first excavation in

1959, with the exception of several years (1965–1971) interrupted by the Cultural Revolution, excavations have been continuous, numbering 60 seasons in the past 30 years (spring and summer, and autumn and winter seasons). Excavations have covered a cumulative area of some 40,000 m² with a series of important results. The findings include a large area of rammed-earth foundations and remains of intersecting roads; a large number of palace building foundations; a large bronze casting workshop, along with workshops for making ceramics, bone artifacts, turquoise artifacts, and a number of architectural monuments related to religious sacrifices; and more than 400 small to medium-size tombs, including burials of ritual bronzes and jades (Zhongguo 1999). As an ancient civilization and large-scale dynastic capital of a state, the Erlitou site has achieved important academic status and recognition by academics worldwide.

In the summer of 1959, the famous historian of ancient history, Xu Xusheng (Hsü Hsü-shêng) led his team to investigate the "the ruins of Xia" and published his results (Xu 1959). That autumn, the Cultural Relics Task Force of Henan Province and the Luoyang Archaeological Team of the Institute of Archaeology of the Chinese Academy of Sciences (now the Chinese Academy of Social Sciences) separately continued to excavate (Zhongguo 1961). Thereafter the Institute of Archaeology (CASS) led excavations at Erlitou. Excavation and research can be divided into four stages: (1) From the autumn of 1959 to 1960. To understand the cultural setting pottery served as a pivot and basis for initially creating a framework. The first three seasons of excavation discovered a stratigraphical sequence from the late Longshan culture to the "Luodamiao Shang culture" (later named "the Erlitou type culture" and "the Erlitou culture") (Xia 1962, 1977). Initially, the cultural remains were divided into three periods, which later were identified as the Erlitou culture Phases 1-4. The size of the remains was estimated to be 2 to 2.5 km east to west and about 1.5 km north to south. Excavators in the fall of 1960 discovered a large rammed-earth area (foundation of palace No. 1).

(2) From the autumn of 1961 to 1978. This season comprised the major excavation of Palaces Nos. 1 and 2. Excavators uncovered more than 30 rammed-earth foundations; remains correlating with ceramic- and bronze-making and medium-sized tombs; further discoveries of jade, bronze, and other artifacts; and they confirmed a fourth period of the Erlitou culture. At the beginning and before digging began, the large area was presumed to be "a city," likely belonging to the "Shang capital of Tang." This assessment could not be assessed until the 1,000–10,000 m² area of No. 1 and No. 2 large-scale structures were fully exposed.

(3) From 1980 to 1997. This time period involved excavation of a bronze workshop site, small and medium-sized residences, and remains and burials documenting sacrificial areas, as well as bone and ceramic workshops. Continued excavation uncovered more bronzes, jades, lacquers, white pottery, turquoise stone, seashells, and other luxury goods from various burials. These findings revealed that the Erlitou site was not a simple settlement but a city with important cultural connotations.

(4) From the autumn of 1999 to the present. Comprehensive excavation addressed the structure and layout of the site. A trench-like deposit was discovered to form the eastern boundary. After large-scale drilling, the area and the road network around the palace

area were cleared. At the same time, large-scale excavation in the "palace area" revealed the central axis of the city layout of the large groups of rammed-earth foundations. The latter was executed in order to clarify the evolution of the east and west palace complexes. Then, the discovery of a "skeletal framework" of the city's network of roads led to the identification of the peripheral rammed-earth walls of the large-scale building area, a workshop area and its peripheral walls at the south of the city, as well as the workshop that specialized in making turquoise artifacts.

To summarize, the first three stages of site excavations and research focused on two major aspects with fruitful results. Firstly, a large area of excavations identified a wealth of relics, including ceramic remains that could serve as a framework for cultural evolution that would divide the Erlitou culture into four phases. The plotting of a ceramic evolution created an important basis for the study of the capital's ruins. Secondly, the excavations of the architectural foundations of Nos. 1 and 2 buildings, a bronze workshop, and medium-sized burials established that the Erlitou site was an important capital of China's earliest territorial state.

Since the Erlitou site has been found, several generations of scholars have achieved fruitful research results. A comprehensive study related to the site began during the late 1970s through the twentieth century. These researches covered the following subjects: archaeological cultural studies, chronological studies, urban construction studies, burial studies, relic analyses, decorative and engraved imagery analyses, macro-research (with focus on the evolution of civilization and the formation of a state, on cultural interaction and relationship between the center and the periphery, inter-regional exchanges, access to resources, etc.), geographic environment research, settlement morphology, and a combination of archaeological and historical data (e.g., the exploration of Xia culture and the division of Xia and Shang dynasties). In summary, more than 40 years of fieldwork and research have helped to identify the significance of the Erlitou site and the Erlitou culture. With regard to the history of civilization and emergence of state, Erlitou has not only the earliest known palace complex and royal relics, the earliest ritual bronze sets, and the earliest bronze workshop, but it was the largest urban settlement in early China and the East Asian Heartland during the early Bronze Age of China. Recognized as the capital of China's earliest territorial state, the Erlitou culture may be recognized as well as the earliest core culture in China, with highly developed cultural connotations and large-scale, cross-regional cultural absorption and expansion (see chapter 10 by Tang Chung and Fang Wang on Erlitou-period *yazhang*; Childs-Johnson 1995). The Erlitou culture and its successors, Shang and Zhou together may now be viewed as constituting mainstream Chinese civilization.

According to preliminary statistics, less than half of Erlitou studies relate to the first nine disciplines, as outlined in the above paragraph. Most, and over half—amounting to some 400 articles—have focused on the question of differences between Xia and Shang dynastic periods. Nonetheless, the overall academic orientation to research during the second half of the twentieth century, unfortunately remained concerned with the integration of the ancient literature with limited archaeological materials than with a strictly archaeological approach.

In conclusion, as we, Xu Hong and Liu Li recently pointed out: Erlitou is one of the most important early sites, which holds many answers to inquiries concerning the formation of state and civilization in ancient China. For more than 50 years of excavation at Erlitou, much attention has been placed on ethnic and dynastic affiliations. This approach has overshadowed other research orientations, such as craft production, agricultural practice, urban population parameters, and urban-rural interactions. As a result, we (still) know little about the political economy of this first urban center in China.

Archaeology and legendary history are different disciplines and need to be studied separately on their own terms. On the one hand, with no pre-Yinxu writing system apparent at present, there is no evidence to either prove or disprove the ancient textual accounts about the Xia and early Shang history. Historical inquiry needs to continue to separate historical facts from myth and legend in dynastic chronologies. Archaeological investigation, particularly addressing excavations of the early urban sites may on the other hand be subjected to multidisciplinary research to aid in defining state formation. Archaeological investigation remains the best tool to analyze spatial and temporal dimensions as well as the social development of urbanism in early China. Our assessment of archaeological data from Erlitou and surrounding settlements should remain the direction we take to deduce the unknown from the known (Liu and Xu 2007:886–901).

NOTES

1. For excavation from 1959 to 1978, see the Institute of Archaeology, CASS (1999).
2. For excavations from 1980 to 1997 consult works by the Erlitou Work Team, Institute of Archaeology, the Chinese Academy of Social Sciences Institute (1983, 1984a, 1984b, 1985, 1986, 1991, 1992; *Chinese Archaeological Yearbook* 1984~1988, 1990, 1993, 1995, 1996, 1998), and by Institute of Archaeology, Chinese Academy of Social Sciences (2003: 61-32).
3. For data from 1999 and thereafter see the Erlitou Team, IA CASS (2001, 2003).

Translated into English by Elizabeth Childs-Johnson with Xiang Li.

BIBLIOGRAPHY

Beijing Daxue Kaogu Wenbo Xueyuan, Henansheng Wenwu Kaogu Yanjiusuo 北京大学考古文博学院, 河南省文物考古研究所 2007. *Archaeological Discovery and Research on Dengcheng Wangchenggang (2002~2005)* 登封王城岗考古发现与研究 2002~2005. Zhengzhou: Daxiang chubanshe.
Beijing Daxue Zhendan (Aurora) Gudai Wenming Yanjiu Zhongxin, Zhengzhoushi Wenwu Kaogu Yanjiusuo 北京大学震旦古代文明研究中心,郑州市文物考古研究所 2008. *Field Report on Excavations from 1999-2000 at Xinmi Xinzhai* 新密新砦——1999~2000 年田野发掘报告. Beijing: Wenwu chubanshe.
Beijing Daxue Zhendan Gudai Wenming Yanjiu Zhongxin 北京大学震旦古代文明研究中心, Henansheng Wenwu Kaogu Yanjiusuo河南省文物考古研究所, Hebeisheng Wenwu

Yanjiusuo河北省文物研究所, and Zhengzhoushi Wenwu Kaogu Yanjiuyuan 郑州市文物考古研究院. eds. 2012. *Collected Studies on the Early-Xia Culture and Proto-Shang Culture*早期夏文化与先商文化研究论文集. Beijing: kexue Chubanshe.

Chen, Xingcan陈星灿, Li Liu 刘莉, Yun-Kuen Lee 李润权, Henry T. Wright 华翰维, Arlene Miller Rosen 艾琳. 2003. "Development of Social Complexity in the Central China: Research into the Settlement Pattern in the Yiluo River Valley 中国文明腹地的社会复杂化进程——伊洛河地区的聚落形态研究." *Kaogu Xuebao (Acta Archaeologica Sinica)*. 2003(2):161–218.

Ding, Shan丁山. 1935. "Analysis of Statehood Based on Three Generations of a City由三代都邑论其民族文化." In *Zhongyang yanjiu yuan lishi yanjiusuo jikan*国立中央研究院历史语言研究所集刊. First section, vol. 5, 第五本第一分册. 1935.

Fan, Wenlan 范文澜. 1955. "General History of China (Revised) 中国通史 (修订版) (1935)." Beijing: Renmin chubanshe.

Gao, Wei 高炜 2007. *Taosi, an Everlasting Issue: Research on Remains at Taosi in Xiangfen Xiangfen Taosi Yizhi Yanjiu* 陶寺 一个永远的话题襄汾陶寺遗址研究. Beijing: Kexue chubanshe.

Gao, Wei, Tianlin Gao, and Daihai Zhang 高炜, 高天麟, 张岱海 1983. "Several Issues Concerning the Taosi Cemetery 关于陶寺墓地 的几个问题." *Kaogu* 考古 6:531–536.

Gu, Jiegang, and Shuye Tong 顾颉刚,童书业 1982. "The Legend of Gun and Yu 鲧禹的传说." In *Gushibian*, vol. 7 (古史辨.七). Shanghai: Shanghai guji chubanshe.

Henan Wenwu Kaogu Yanjiusuo 河南文物考古研究所, and the Xinmishi Yanhuang Lishi Wenhua Yanjiuhui 新密市炎黄历史文化研究会 2002. "Report on Excavations of the Longshan City-Site of Xinmi in Guchengzhai, Henan 河南新密市古城寨龙山文化城址发掘简报." *Huaxia kaogu* 2:53–82.

Henan Wenwu Kaogu Yanjiusuo 河南文物考古研究所, and the Xinmishi Yanhuang Lishi Wenhua Yanjiuhui 新密市炎黄历史文化研究会 2004. *Yuzhou Wadian* 禹州瓦店. Beijing: Shijie tushu chuban gongsi.

Henansheng Bowuguan 河南省博物馆, and Zhengzhoushi Bowuguan 郑州市博物馆. 1977. "Zhengzhou Shangdaicheng Yizhi Fajuebaogao郑州商代城遗址发掘报告." In *Wen Ziliao Congkan* 文物资料丛刊, Edited by Wenwu Bianji Weiyuanhui 文物编辑委员会, vol. 1. Beijing: Wenwu Chubanshe, 1–47.

Jian, Bozan 翦伯赞 1947. "Distribution of the Xia and the Culture of Ding [and] Li 诸夏文化的分布与鼎鬲文化." In *Zhongguoshi Lunji* 中国史论集. Beijing: Wenfeng shuju.

Li, Ji 李济 1990. *Anyang: Discovery, Excavation, and Recovery of the Capital of Yin Shang* 安阳——殷商古都发现、发掘、复原记. Translated by Xiuju Su 苏秀菊. Beijing: Zhongguo Shehui Kexue chubanshe.

Li, Min 李民 1985. "The Legendary Era of Yao and Shun and the Archaeological Site at Taosi 尧舜时代与陶寺遗址." *Shiqian Yanjiu* 史前研究 4.

Li, Min 李民, and Wen Bing 文兵 1975. "The Formation and Development of Ancient China as Seen from Yanshi Erlitou Sites 从偃师二里头文化遗址看中国古代国家的 形成和发展." *Zhengzhou Daxue Xuebao* 郑州大学学报 4.

Li, Xueqin 李学勤 2003. "Suigong *Xu* Vessel and the Legend of Da Yu Controlling the Floods 遂公盨与大禹治水传说." *Zhongguo Shehui Kexueyuan Yuanbao* 中国社会科学院 院报. Jan. 23, 2003.

Liu, Li 刘莉, and Xingcan Chen 陈星灿 2007. *The Chinese Neolithic: Trajectories to Early States* 中国新石器时代:迈向早期国家之路. Beijing: Wenwu chubanshe.

Liu, Li, and Hong Xu 2007. "Rethinking Erlitou: Legend, History and Chinese Archaeology." *Antiquity* 81:886–901.

Qiu, Shihua仇士华, Lianzhen Cai蔡莲珍, Ziqiang Xian冼自强, and Guancheng Bo薄官成. 1983. "Youguan Suowei Xiawenhua De Tanshisi Niandai Ceding De Chubu Baogao有关所谓"夏文化"的碳十四年代测定的初步报告." *Kaogu*考古. 1983(10):923–928.

Tong, Zhuchen 佟柱臣. 1975. "Cong Erlitou Leixing Wenhua Shitan Zhongguo De Guojia Qiyuan Wenti从二里头类型文化试谈中国的国家起源问题." *Wenwu*文物. 1975(6):29–33.

Wang, Guowei王国维. 1959. "Yinbuci Suojian Xiangong Xianwang Kao 殷卜辞所见先公先王考." In Wang, Guowei. 1959. *Guantang Jili. Vol. 9* 观堂集林(卷九). Beijing: Zhongguo Shuju.

Wang, Guowei王国维. 1959. "Yinbuci Suojian Xiangong Xianwang Xukao 殷卜辞所见先公先王续考." In Wang, Guowei. 1959. *Guantang Jili. Vol. 9* 观堂集林(卷九). Beijing: Zhongguo Shuju.

Wang, Lixin 王立新 2006. "The Emergence of the Xia Dynasty from the Cultural Integration of North and South Songshan, Erlitou Site and Erlitou Culture 从嵩山南北的文化整合看夏王朝的出现." In *Erlitou Yizhi Yu Erlitou Wenhua Yanjiu* 二里头遗址与二里头 文化研究, Edited by Du, Jinpeng and Hong Xu. Beijing: Kexue chubanshe, 410–426.

Wei, Xingtao魏兴涛.2010. "Zhongyuan Longshan Chengzhi De Niandai Yu Xingfei Yuanyin Tantao中原龙山城址的年代与兴废原因探讨." *Huaxia Kaogu*华夏考古. 2010(1).

Wu, Enyu 吴恩裕. 1956. "The Origins of the Chinese Nation 中华族的起源." *Xinjianshe* 7.

Xia, Nai (Hsia Nai)夏鼐. 1962. "Xin Zhongguo De Kaoguxue新中国的考古学." *Kaogu*考古. 1962(9):453–458.

Xia, Nai (Hsia Nai) 夏鼐. 1977. "Tanshisi Ceding Niandai He Zhongguo Shiqian Kaoguxue 碳-14 测定年代和中国史前考古学." *Kaogu*考古. 1977(4): 217–232.

Xia, Nai (Hsia Nai) 夏鼐 1978. "Discussion of Several Issues Concerning Xia Culture: Again the Discovery of Dengfeng Gaocheng Remains; A Live Meeting 谈谈探讨夏文化的几个 问题——在〈登封告成遗址 发掘现场会〉闭幕式上的讲话." *Henan Wenbo Tongxun* 1.

Xu, Hong. 2001. "Disruption in Continuity: Thoughts on Formation of Chinese Civilization and Early State 连续"中的"断裂"——关于中国文明与早期国家形成过程的思考." *Wenwu* 2:86–91.

Xu, Hong 许宏. 2009. *The Earliest China* 最早的中国. Beijing: Kexue chubanshe.

Xu, Hong. 2012. "Archaeological Observations on the Historic Transition in the Central Plains ca. 2000 BCE 公元前 2000 年中原大变局的考古学观察." *Dongfang Kaogu* 9.

Xu, Xusheng (Hsü, Hsü-Shêng) 徐旭生 1959. "In Quest of Hsia Remains in Western Honan (Summer, 1958) 1958 年夏豫西调查"夏墟"的报告简报. *Kaogu* 11: 592–600.

Xu, Zhongshu 徐中舒 1931. "On Xiaotun and Yangshao再论小屯与仰韶." In *Anyang Fajue Baogao*, vol. 3 安阳发掘报告(第三期). Zhongyang Yanjiuyuan Lishi Yuyan Yanjiusuo.

Yin, Weizhang 殷玮璋 1986. "Xia Culture Questions 夏文化问题." In *Zhongguo Dabaike Quanshu: Kaoguxue*. Beijing: Zhongguo Dabaike Quanshu chubanshe.

Zhang, Xuelian 张雪莲, Shihua Qiu 仇士华, Lianzhen Cai 蔡莲珍, Guancheng Bo 薄官 成, Jinxia Wang 王金霞, and Jian Zhong 钟建 2007. "Establishment and Perfection of the Archaeological Chronological Sequence of Xinzhai-Erlitou-Erligang Cultures 新寨二里头 - 二里岗文化考古年 代序列的建立与完善." *Kaogu* 考古 8.

Zhao, Chunqing 赵春青 2006. "Some Questions about the Xinzhai Period and Erlitou First Period 关于新砦期与二里头一期的若干问题." In *Erlitou Yizhi Yu Erlitou Wenhua Yanjiu: Zhongguo Erlitou Yizhi Yu Erlitou Wenhua Guoji Xueshu Yantaohui Lunwenji* 二 里头遗址 与二里头文化研究:中国·二里头遗址与二里头文化国际学术研讨会论文 集, Edited by Du, Jinpeng 杜金鹏 and Hong Xu 许 宏. Beijing: Kexue Chubanshe, 279–303.

Zhao, Chunqing 赵春青 2009. "Practice and Methods of Settlement Archaeology at Xinzhai 新砦聚落考古的实践与方法." *Kaogu* 2.

Zhongguo Shehui Kexueyuan Kaogu Yanjiusuo 中国社会科学院考古研究所 1999. *Yanshi Erlitou: 1959 to 1978 Excavation Report* 偃师二里头:1959 年~1978 年考古发掘报告. Beijing: Zhongguo da baike quanshu chubanshe.

Zhongguo Shehui Kexueyuan Kaogu Yanjiusuo 中国社会科学院考古研究所 2003. *Chinese Archeology: Xia Shang Volume* 中国考古学•夏商卷. Beijing: Zhongguo Shehui kexue chubanshe.

Zhongguo Shehui Kexueyuan Luoyang Fajuedui. 1961. "1959 Nian Henan Yanshi Erlitou Shijue Jianbao 1959年河南偃师二里头试掘简报." *Kaogu*. 1961(2): 82–85.

Zhongguo Shehui Kexueyuan Kaogu Yanjiusuo, Erlitou Gongzuo Dui 中国社会科学院 考古研究所二里头工作队 1974. "Preliminary Report on the Early Shang Palace Remains at Erlitou, Yanshi, Henan 河南偃师二里头早商宫殿遗址发掘简报." *Kaogu* 4.

Zhongguo Shehui Kexueyuan Kaogu Yanjiusuo, Erlitou Gongzuodui 中国社会科学院 考古研究所二里头工作队 2005. "Preliminary Report on the 2001–2003 Survey of the Luoyang Basin in Henan 河南洛阳盆地 2001–2003 年考古调查简报." *Kaogu* 5:18–37.

Zou, Heng 邹衡 1956. "On the Newly Discovered Shang Cultural Sites at Zhengzhou 关于郑州新发现的商代文化遗址." *Kaogu xuebao* 3.

Zou, Heng邹衡. 1978. "Concerning Talking about the Journey of the Xia Culture 关于探索夏文化的途径." *Henan Wenbo Tongxun* (1).

Zou, Heng 邹衡. 1980. "Shilun Xiawenhua 试论夏文化." In *Xia Shang Zhou Kaoguxue Lunwenji*夏商周考古学论文集. Beijing: Wenwu chubanshe. 95–182.

CHAPTER 8

SETTLEMENTS, BUILDINGS, AND SOCIETY OF THE ERLITOU CULTURE

BY HONG XU, INSTITUTE OF ARCHAEOLOGY, CASS
AND XIANG LI, UNIVERSITY OF PITTSBURGH

DURING the first half of the second millennium BCE, the Erlitou culture stepped out of the late Longshan era that witnessed decline and stagnancy caused by warring factions competing for military and economic dominance, into an era witnessing the earliest core of civilization in China and the East Asian Heartland (Xu 2012).

Based on excavated data, the Erlitou culture covered a large area centered in the regions of Zhengluo 郑洛 (the western part of Henan province) and Yuncheng 运城-Linfen 临汾 Basins (southern Shanxi); Shangluo 商洛 (eastern Shaanxi) to the west; the Qinhe 沁河 River (across which the Erlitou culture was confronted with the Huiwei culture) to the northeast; and the Panlongcheng site (on the north bank of the Yangtze River) to the south. The eastern border lay alongside Qixian 杞县, Taikang 太康, Huaiyang 淮阳, Zhoukou 周口, and Xiangcheng 项城 in eastern Henan (Zhongguo 2003). The area covered the whole middle range of the Yellow River and more, with cultural radiation in all directions.

SETTLEMENTS OF THE ERLITOU CULTURE

Erlitou cultural settlements reveal a pyramid-like structure (Institute of Archaeology, CASS 2003; Nishie and Kuji 2006), with the Erlitou site, a settlement measuring over

3,000,000 m², as the vortex. Once Erlitou emerged as a first-level settlement (Grade 1 at the top of the pyramid according to settlement hierarchy theory), multiple new settlements sprung up throughout the Luoyang Basin (Figure 1). These newly born settlements, encircling the Erlitou site, collectively developed into a web that gradually and incessantly grew outward (Xu 2012).

The Erlitou site as a first-level settlement and capital

During Phase 3 of the Erlitou culture, the Erlitou site became a super settlement or a settlement complex with an area of over 1,000,000 m². The discovery and presence of prestige goods like bronze tools, bronze vessels, turquoises, art works, white ceramics, and incised symbols indicates that the Erlitou site grew into a major center in the Yiluo 伊洛 region, or across an even larger area. Due to inadequate preservation, settlement dating to Phase 1 is difficult to plot. Nonetheless, it is clear that the Erlitou settlement reached its heyday during Phase 2. The whole area expanded to more than 3,000,000 m², with construction of a building foundation complex covering 120,000 m². The turquoise and bronze-casting workshops were positioned to the south of the building foundation complex. All of these facilities continued to exist into Phase 4 (Figure 2).

After almost a half-century of fieldwork, no evidence of any fortifications had been found. In view of this phenomenon, the Erlitou site may be considered the earliest paradigm of a non-fortified primary capital (Xu 2013b). The defense pattern of "walls + wide moats," once extensively built during the Longshan era, changed during the Erlitou cultural period. If moats appear amid Erlitou cultural settlements they are divisible into

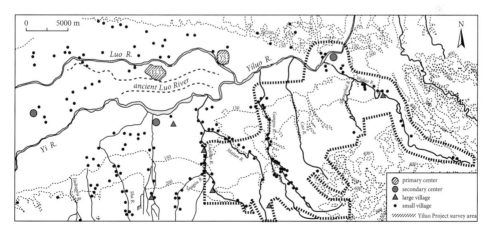

FIGURE 1 Distribution of Erlitou culture sites in the Yiluo region showing relationship between Erlitou (ELT) and Yanshi Shang City (YS). After Liu and Chen 2012:264, figure 8.3.

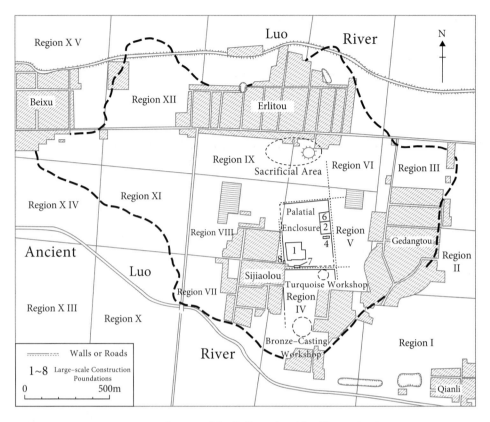

FIGURE 2   Layout of the Erlitou site. After Xu 2016:208.

two types: moats with a width of 5 m, found inside a settlement, were used to separate residents of different social status; and moats with a width of 10 m surrounding a settlement were built primarily as defenses located at distant frontier sites (Li 2011).

The Erlitou site is composed of a core area and ordinary residential areas. Most of the small aboveground and semi-subterranean dwelling sites and small tombs were found in ordinary residential areas. The core area formed the building foundation complex, positioned at the middle of the Erlitou site. With the construction of the building foundation walls, this complex became a "palatial enclosure" (宮城), which was surrounded outside by the earliest documented web of traffic lanes. A sacrificial area stretched some 200–300 m to the north of the building foundation enclosure. To the south of the building foundation area were the turquoise and bronze-casting workshops. Residences of the elite lay around the palace area. The construction and layouts of the building foundation enclosures, large-scale rammed-earthen buildings, and the traffic arteries were all oriented in the same direction, which means that the Erlitou site had a deliberate plan and design (Zhongguo 2014). The main functioning domains, such as the workshops, the "palace area," and the sacrificial area, ran south to north, forming the cultural axis of the Erlitou site (Du 2007).

Other levels among the settlements system

With the emergence and solidification of the Erlitou city site, the culture radiated and spread centrifugally and continuously outward, forming a web-like pyramid consisting of the Erlitou site at the middle surrounded by regional centers and primary settlements (Figure 3).

Regional centers usually comprised an area of 100,000–600,000 m². The Shaochai 稍 柴 site in Gongyi 巩义 and the Dashigu 大师姑 site in Zhengzhou 郑州, both with an area of 500,000–600,000 m², were exceptional. The Shaochai site, to the east of the Yiluo 伊洛 basin and at the crossing of the Yiluo 伊洛 and the Wuluo 坞罗 rivers, was an important connection point to the Erlitou site to the East in the lower range of the Yellow river. The Shaochai site was a significant fortress designed to protect the capital of Erlitou (Chen et al. 2003). The Dashigu city site with walls and moats was considered as a key military position or a different state's capital (Zhengzhou Municipality 2004). Pottery prestige goods were found in the regional centers, demonstrating that the Erlitou complex followed some sort of political design (Nishie and Kuji 2006).

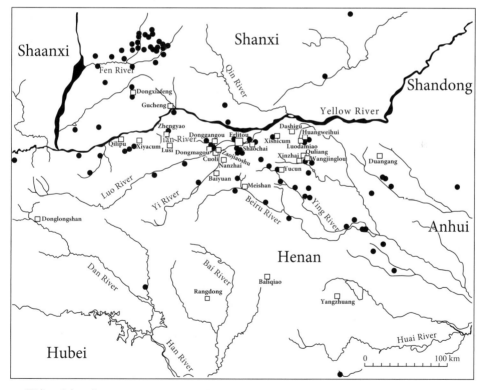

● Erlitou Culture Sites   □ Excavated Erlitou Culture Sites with Ritual Pottery

FIGURE 3 Erlitou cultural settlements. After Xu 2013:302, figure 15.1.

The majority of settlements of the Erlitou culture were less than 100,000 m², and virtually no prestige goods were found in these settlements or their burials.

The distribution and the number of settlements representing the Erlitou culture began to enlarge by Phase 2. The rapid expansion and growth documented not only a major increase in population, but also documented an increase in strategically locating newly built settlements for acquiring important resources like metal ores and salt.

Building constructions of the Erlitou culture

A number of residential buildings have been unearthed at the Erlitou site, and they can be divided into large-scale rammed-earth constructions and ordinary dwelling sites. The large-scale rammed-earth constructions—a feature resulting from the advancement of the social complexity (Xu 2013a)—are thought to be ancient palaces with high social rank used by elites. Some of the ordinary dwelling sites were built above-ground, while others were semi-subterranean.

Large-scale rammed-earth constructions

Large-scale rammed-earth constructions during the Erlitou period were mainly witnessed at the Erlitou site. The large-scale area of building foundations area and the surrounding traffic arteries were first developed in Phase 2, and during Phase 3 the palatial enclosure (Figure 4) with an area of 108,000 m² was solidified. After half a century of excavations, about 10 large-scale building constructions have been discovered, not only as independent structures but also as four-sided ones enclosing a courtyard, and some with multiple courtyards. Building complexes of the Erlitou area of large-scale buildings may be divided into two complexes lying to the east and west sides of the enclosure.

Nos. 3 and 5 buildings, constructed during Phase 2, comprised the early building complex. The archaeological material shows that both Nos. 3 and 5 were four-sided compounds with three inner courtyards. Nos. 3 and 5 were juxtaposed east to west and separated by roads and water channels.

The two complex groups (western: mainly including Nos. 1 and 7; eastern: mainly including Nos. 2, 4, and 6) that shared the same cultural axis were formed during the late phase of the Erlitou culture (Zhongguo 2014). No. 1 was a large-scale, irregular, rammed-earth foundation, forming a closed quadrangle of the main building, a south gate, and a courtyard with enclosed corridors. The whole area was about 9,585 m² (Zhongguo 1999). The main building was rectangular in shape, and at the north part of the foundation (20 m to the north and 70 m to the south gate) measured 900 m² in area. The south gate

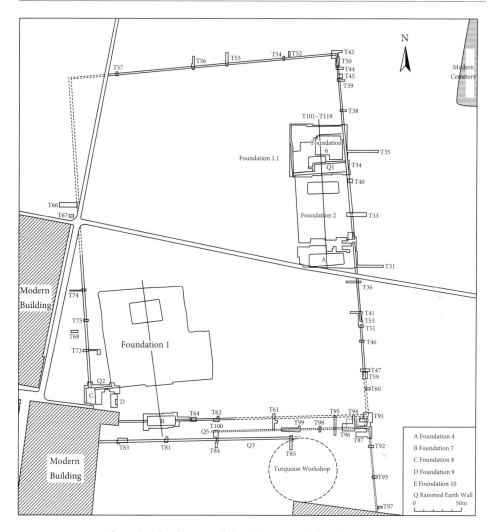

FIGURE 4 The palatial enclosure of the Erlitou site. After Xu 2013:310, figure 15.2.

had three passages, the middle of which was the widest, measuring 3.2 m, and the other two had a width of about 2.7 m.

Ordinary dwelling sites

The two main types of the ordinary dwelling sites include those that were above-ground and those that were semi-subterranean. They were either square or round in shape. During the early phase, most of the ordinary dwelling sites had only one room.

The above-ground type with usually only one room, sometimes several rooms, possibly belonged to the houses of the elite. These dwelling sites generally surrounded the palace area and were relatively large, measuring some tens or hundreds of square meters. The medium-size building IIIF1, excavated during the autumn of 1980 and the spring of 1981, was an above-ground rammed-earth raised platform divided into three rooms (Zhongguo 1984a). The foundation of 2003IIIF4 was a west-east oriented, rectangular, rammed-earth construction with only one room, and it is judged to belong to a medium- or lower-ranking elite (Zhongguo 2014). The semi-subterranean habitats belonging to labor classes were damp and dark rooms, lacking sunlight (Xu 2013a).

The construction techniques involved a house foundation that was rammed and flattened. Walls were variously constructed as wood-supported mud walls, rammed-earth walls, adobe walls, and even rammed-earth walls in conjunction with wood and mud. Additionally, the surface of the ground and walls of a house were commonly processed through baking, adding earth, and coating with lime or mud mixed with grass (Li 2007).

SOCIETY OF THE ERLITOU CULTURE

The Erlitou culture gave birth to the earliest territorial state with centralized power in China (Liu and Chen 2002). The following discussion focuses on the development of social complexity of the Erlitou culture as represented by architectural constructions, tombs, settlement patterns and their organization, and control of resources.

Social conditions represented by building construction

The size of housing for labor classes was about equal to or only slightly larger than that of the Wangwan Phase 3 cultural housing. Even though the rectangular multi-room houses were widely seen during the Longshan era, this type was abandoned during the Erlitou era. Rather, square single-room houses began to be prevalent. This trend demonstrates that the primary social unit was reduced to a more prevalent independent small family rather than the earlier lineage group bound by blood. As a result, labor forces became more specialized (Chang 2005).

The functions of the large-scale rammed-earth buildings at Erlitou, such as Nos. 1 and 2, have been variously explored. Some scholars consider these to represent the place where the rulers carried out different kinds of political events (Zhongguo 1984b), while others identify them as temples to memorialize the ancestors (Zou 1980). In ancient Chinese society, especially during the Bronze Age, sacrifice and political events were integrated and generally took place at the same place—"palaces" for the living and temples for the deceased were not separated (Tu 1987). Therefore, the large-scale rammed-earth constructions at the site of Erlitou may not only have been used by the administration to issue orders but also as a temple to sacrifice and memorialize forefathers and ancestors.

The scale of the large-scale buildings at Erlitou was larger than any other building at Erlitou. For example, the aforementioned No. 1 was as large as 9,585 m². In order to build such a large rammed-earth foundation, the state of Erlitou must have been able to mobilize adequate manpower and material resources, which means that the Erlitou society must have been highly stratified and administratively organized. The large-scale building foundations formed groups and in some cases complicated complexes. Each group had its own axis. The location of the large-scale building area in the middle of the core area of the Erlitou site served to display the importance of this area. The Erlitou site is the earliest paradigm of "palace construction" in Chinese history. It is noteworthy that in size and position the Erlitou palaces (large-scale building foundations) exceed contemporary living requirements. These buildings were closed, as was the enclosure proper. By contrast, during the Neolithic period houses were open and big to accommodate conventions and sacrificial events and did not require closed walls. Enclosure walls succeeded in separating and highlighting the "palace area" in contradistinction to other less important regions (Zhao 2006).

Social conditions reflected by tombs

Many scholars have analyzed the stratification system of the Erlitou cultural tombs through the tomb size, the number and types of the burial goods, and the prestige goods (Li 2008). Although a tomb's scale does not evidently reflect social differences at Erlitou, the combination of the prestige goods could be used to distinguish the social ranks. The largest tomb at Erlitou was found alone within an area of 6 m². Although no royal tomb has been identified, the largest tombs in the earlier Longshan era occupied areas as large as 27 m², and the largest medium tomb in the later Erligang culture was over 10 m². The ritual system of the Erlitou culture is reflected by the presence of groups of burial bronzes (Figure 5), lacquers, and ceramics (Li 2008).

According to size, type of coffins, and burial goods, the tombs of the Erlitou culture can be divided into four levels. The first rank is the shaft tomb with an area of over 2 m². The burial goods included ritual bronzes, jades, turquoise ornaments (Figure 6), and pottery. Coffins were made of wood, and some were painted. Cinnabar typically covered the bottom of tombs. The second rank includes shaft tombs with an area of 1–2 m². The burial goods included ritual pottery, jade, and turquoise ornaments in addition to occasional stonewares, such as, a hilt or axe blade. Wood coffins and cinnabar were also used. There are two types in the third rank: shaft tombs and underground chamber tombs. The shaft tombs of this rank generally were under 1 m² before Phase 4, and were over 1 m² during Phase 4. Ritual pottery was rare, although a few utilitarian ceramics may appear as burial goods in this third rank. There were no wooden coffins. The fourth-ranked shaft tombs measured under 0.8 m² in area and none had burial goods. Among a total of 265 tombs, 24 belong to the first rank, 60 the second rank, 76 the third rank, and 61 the

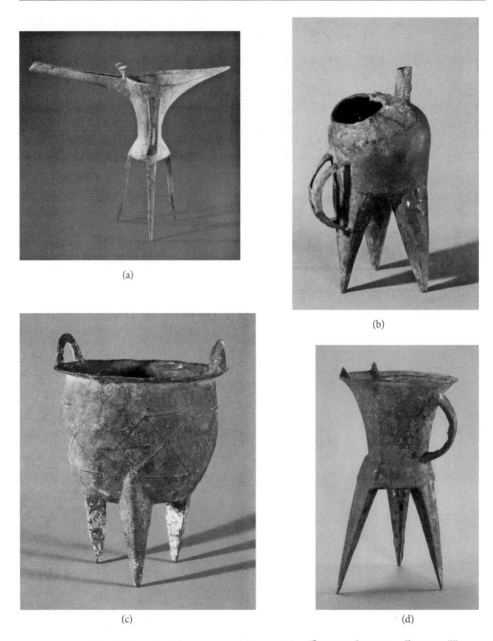

FIGURE 5 The Erlitou ritual bronze assemblage: **A** *jue* 爵, **B** *he* 盉, **C** *ding* 鼎, **D** *jia* 斝.

fourth rank. This pattern of tomb stratification exhibits another feature of this society's pyramidal structure (Li 2008).

Most tombs of the Erlitou culture to date have been found at the Erlitou site, especially the tombs of the highest rank. This implies that the Erlitou site as a capital attracted elites, resources, and administrative power. Unfortunately, no dedicated cemetery has

(a)

(b)

FIGURE 6 A "dragon" created out of inlaid turquoise pieces found in an elite's tomb. **A** full-length view; **B** close-up shot of the head part.

yet been uncovered at the capital. Those tombs in the site so far discovered are generally mixed in with the living quarters. This condition differs from other settlements. The tombs in the Erlitou site distributed amid several groups nonetheless exhibit features characterizing family type of ceremony. The coexistence of tombs with different ranks in the same region or the same group reflects that the social division also existed amid every family group. The social stratification was bound with the blood lineage. More mass graves appear now during the Erlitou phases than in the Longshan era, reflecting in turn that human sacrifice became more frequent and violent tactics became more institutionalized. Social stratification became more intense than earlier eras. The increase in burials for non-adults also signifies that the hereditary system had emerged (Li 2008).

Social conditions represented by settlement patterns

Erlitou society may be identified as a complex settlement system. Located at the top of the settlement system, being surrounded by the regional centers and the opulence in cultural artifacts demonstrate that the Erlitou site was the core settlement and the capital of the Erlitou culture, in addition to the institutionalization of a complex settlement web and the stratification amid the settlements. Erlitou society must have had an effective administration that could, on the one hand, adjust the population according to the social requirements and, on the other hand, manage the resources within the domain. Food could be redistributed to satisfy the needs of different regions caused by the imbalance in the productivity through a central settlement management (Wang 2014; Qiao 2010). The Huizui 灰嘴 site in Yanshi in the Luoyang Basin was very possibly a stone workshop during the Erlitou era, and the Gongyi Region very possibly a supplier of raw materials to fire white pottery (Chen et al. 2003).

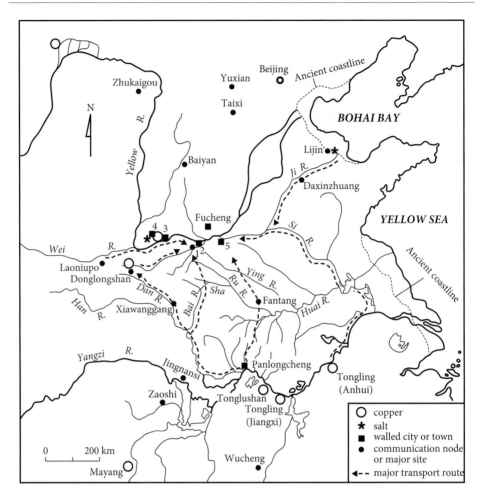

FIGURE 7 Locations of river channels in early dynastic times; locations of key natural resources; major transportation routes with communication nodes linking primary centers in the core area with the middle and lower Yangtze River Valley in the south, the Wei River in the West, and the coastal region in the east. **1** Erlitou, **2** Yanshi, **3** Yuanqu, **4** Dongxiafeng, **5** Zhengzhou. After Liu and Chen 2003:51, figure 10.

Social conditions represented by the control of resources

Early cities in China were political tools and symbols of political power (Zhang 1985, 1990). Since "the significant affairs of a state fall to ritual worship and the military," the rulers of the Xia, Shang, and Zhou dynasties all sought out metal resources like copper, tin, and lead. Because of the importance of the bronzes in the political contest during this period, Kwang-chih Chang (Zhang Guangzhi) once pointed out that the frequent capital moves should be ascribed to the need for sourcing copper and tin ores, which were key to maintaining political capital 政治资本.

Although the latest research reveals that the capital changes may not be related to the need for the resources, the population increases and the newly built settlements in fact represent the rulers' strong demand for these resources (Liu and Chen 2000). According to archaeological data, the metal ores from the Zhongtiao Mountains 中条山, and the mid and lower valleys of the Yangtze River were exploited earliest. During the period of the Erlitou culture, metal ingots from the area along the Yangtze River may have been transported to the Yiluo 伊洛 Basin through the sites of Jingnansi 荆南寺, Panlongcheng 盘龙城, and Xiawanggang 下王岗 (Figure 7) (Liu and Chen 2002).

Copper ores and pond salt were rich in southern Shanxi province. Mining and smelting were mainly executed locally. The Dongxiafeng 东下冯 site in Xiaxian 夏县 and the Nanguan 南关 site in Yuanqu 垣曲 served as control and transportation centers of the copper ores and salt because of their convenient location for communication and transportation. The egg-shaped urns and the mouth-contracted urns found in the Dongxiafeng site, for example, were probably used to store and transport salt. The convenience in obtaining the copper ingots allowed the Dongxiafeng and Nanguan sites to serve as the manufacturing centers in Erlitou Phase 3, especially for the purpose of casting bronze weapons and tools (Liu and Chen 2002; Zhongguo 2011; Dai 2010).

As for the impressed hard pottery and seashells, they must have been imported, suggesting that the Erlitou people engaged in long-distance trade. In conclusion, it is evident that Erlitou played a pivotal role in establishing the earliest major, probably "dynastic" capital and city center to emerge out of the warring and factional Longshan period.

BIBLIOGRAPHY

Chang, Huaiying 常怀颖 2005. "Development of Social Complexity in Central China: A Study Based on the Archaeological Materials Found in Central, Western and Southern Regions of Henan Province 龙山时期至二里头早期的社会复杂化进程初探——以河南中、西、南部 为观察中心." MA dissertation, Sichuan University, Chengdu.

Chen, Xingcan 陈星灿, Li Liu 刘莉, Lee Yun-Kuen 李润权, Henry Wright 华翰维, and Arlene Miller Rosen 艾琳 2003. "Development of Social Complexity in the Central China: Research into the Settlement Pattern in the Yiluo River Valley 中国文明腹地的社会复杂化进程—— 伊洛河地区的聚落形态研究." *Kaogu xuebao* 考古学报 2:161–218.

Dai, Xiangming 戴向明 2010. *Ceramic Production, Settlement Patterns and Social Change: The Yuanqu Basin during the Neolithic through Early Bronze Age* 陶器生产、聚落形态与社会变迁:新石器至早期青铜时代的垣曲盆地. Beijing: Wenwu chubanshe.

Du, Jinpeng 杜金鹏 2007. *Research on the City at Erlitou in Yanshi* 偃师二里头遗址都邑制度研究 *Xia Shang Zhou Kaoguxue Yanjiu* 夏商周考古学研究. Beijing: Kexue chubanshe.

Li, Hongfei 李宏飞 2011. "Moats in Fortified Settlements of the Erlitou Culture 二里头文化设防聚落 的环濠传统." *Zhongguo guojia bowuguan guankan* 中国国家博物馆馆刊 6:17–25.

Li, Zhipeng 李志鹏 2008. "Research on the Burial System of the Erlitou Culture 二里头文化墓葬研究," In *Complete Research on the Erlitou Culture: Early bronze culture of*

China 中国早期青铜文化-二里头文化专题研究, Edited by Zhongguo Shehui Kexueyuan Kaogu Yanjiusuo 中国社会科学院考古研究所. Beijing: Kexue chubanshe, 1–123.

Liu, Li 刘莉, and Xingcan Chen 陈星灿, 2000. "The City: The Problem of Controlling Natural Resources in the Xia-Shang Period 城:夏商时期对自然资源的控制问题," *Dongnan wenhua* 东南文化 3:45–60.

Liu, Li 刘莉, and Xingcan Chen 陈星灿, 2002. "The Form of Early States in China: A Discussion of the Relationship between the Center and Periphery in the Erlitou and Erligang Periods 中国早期国家 的形成——从二里头和二里岗时期的中心和边缘之间的关系谈起." In *Gudai Wenming*, vol. 1 古代文明(一). Edited by Center for the Study of Chinese Archaeology, Beijing University, and Center for the Study of Ancient Civilization, Beijing University 北京大学中国考古学研究 中心，北京大学古代文明研究中心. Beijing: Wenwu chubanshe, 71–134.

Liu, Li 刘莉, and Xingcan Chen 陈星灿, 2003. *State Formation in Early China*. London: Gerald Duckworth.

Li, Dong 李栋 2007. "Preliminary Research on the House Building Technology in Xia, Shang and Zhou Dynasties 夏商周时期房屋建筑技术初步研究." MA dissertation, Shandong University, Jinan.

Nishie, Kiyotaka 西江清高, and Daisuke Kuji 久慈大介 2006. "The Spatial Layout of the Central Plains Dynasty during the Erlitou Cultural Period 从地域间关系看二里头文化期中原王朝的空间结构," In *Erlitou Yizhi yu Erlitou wenhua yanjiu* 二里头遗址与二里头文化研究. Edited by J. Du and H. Xu. Beijing: Kexue chubanshe, 444–456.

Qiao, Yu 乔玉 2010. "Development of Complex Societies in the Yiluo Region: A GIS Based Population and Agricultural Area Analysis 伊洛地区裴李岗至二里头文化时期复杂 社会的演变——地理信息系统基础上的人口和农业可耕地分析." *Kaogu Xuebao* 考古学报 4:423–454.

Tu, Cheng-sheng 杜正胜 1987. "An Examination of the Origins and Early Development of the Central Plains States of Ancient China Based on Archaeological Data 从考古资料论中原国家的起 源及其早期发展." *Zhongyang yanjiuyuan lishi yuyan yanjiusuo jikan* 中央研究院历史语言研究所集刊 58(1):1–81.

Wang, Zimeng 王子孟 2014. "Controlling Network and Pattern of Erlitou Culture Settlements in the Luoyang Basin 洛阳盆地二里头文化聚落的控制网络与模式——基于遗址资源域 和泰森多边形的分析." *Huaxia Kaogu* 华夏考古 3:56–64.

Xu, Hong 许宏 2012. "A Dynamic Scan of Erlitou Cultural Settlement 二里头文化聚落动态扫描," In *Collected Studies on the Early-Xia Culture and Proto-Shang Culture* 早期夏文化与先商文化研究论文集. Edited by Aurora Centre for the Study of Ancient Civilizations, Beijing University 北京大学震旦古代文明研究中 心Beijing Daxue Chendan Gudai Wenming Yanjiu Zhongxin, Henansheng wenwu kaogu yanjiusuo 河南省文物考古研究所, Hebeisheng wenwu yanjiusuo 河北省文物研究所, and Zhengzhoushi wenwu kaogu yanjiusuo 郑 州 市 文 物 考 古 研 究 所. Beijing: Kexue chubanshe, 31–44.

Xu, Hong 许宏 2013a. "Palace Building and the Formation of the Central Plains Civilization 宫室建筑与中原国家文明的形成," In *Sandai Kaogu*, vol. 5 三代考古(五). Edited by Zhongguo Shehui Kexueyuan Kaogu Yanjiusuo Xia Shang Zhou Yanjiushi 中国社会科学院考古研究所夏商周研究室. Beijing: Kexue chubanshe, 3–18.

Xu, Hong 许宏 2013b. "Large Cities Are Not Fortified: On the Early Forms of Capitals of Ancient China 大都无城——论中国古代都城的早期形态." *Wenwu* 文物 10:61–71.

Xu, Hong 许宏 2016. *The Tradition of Non-Fortified Primary Capitals in Early China*大都无城. Beijing: Shenghuo·Dushu·Xinzhi Sanlian Shudian.

Zhao, Haitao 赵海涛 2006. "Preliminary Analysis of the Archaeological Rewards of Palace Remains at Erlitou 二里头遗址宫城区域考古收获初步综理," In *Sandai Kaogu*, vol. 2 三代考古 (二). Edited by Department of Xia, Shang, Zhou Archaeology, IA, CASS 中国社会科学院考古研究所夏商周研究室. Beijing: Kexue chubanshe, 159–169.

Zhang, Guangzhi (Chang Kwang-chih) 张光直 1985. "The Initial Stages of 'City' in Ancient China 关于中国初期"城市"这个概念." *Wenwu* 文物 2:61–67.

Zhang, Guangzhi (Chang Kwang-chih) 张光直 1990. "Similarities and Differences between Three Dynasties' Xia, Shang and Zhou Capital System and the Three Dynastic Cultures 夏商周三代都制与三代文化异同," In *Zhongguo Qingtong Shidai (Erji)* 中国青铜时代(二集), Edited by Zhang, Guangzhi (Chang Kwang-Chih). Beijing: Sanlian shudian, 15–38.

Zhengzhou. Zhengzhoushi Wenwu Kaogu Yanjiusuo 郑州市文物考古研究所 2004. *Dashigu in Zhengzhou* 郑州大师姑 (2002–2003). Beijing: Kexue chubanshe.

Zhongguo Guojia Bowuguan Tianye Kaogu Zhongxin, Shanxisheng Kaogu Yanjiusuo, Yunchengshi Wenwu Baohu Yanjiusuo 中国国家博物馆田野考古中心, 山西省考古研究所, 运城市文物保护研究所 2011. *Survey and Research on Settlement Archaeology in the Eastern Yuncheng Basin* 运城盆地东部聚落考古调查与研究. Beijing: Wenwu chubanshe.

Zhongguo Shehui Kexueyuan Kaogu Yanjiusuo, Erlitou Gongzuodui 中国社会科学院考古研究所二里头工作队 1984a. "Yanshi Erlitou Yizhi 1980~1981 Nian III Qu Fajue Jiangao 偃师二里头遗址 1980~1981 年 III 区发掘简报." *Kaogu* 考古 7:582–590.

Zhongguo Shehui Kexueyuan Kaogu Yanjiusuo, Erlitou Gongzuodui 中国社会科学院考古研究所二里头工作队 1984b. *Archaeological Excavation and Researches in New China* 新中国的考古发现和研究. Beijing: Wenwu chubanshe.

Zhongguo Shehui Kexueyuan Kaogu Yanjiusuo, Erlitou Gongzuodui 中国社会科学院考古研究所二里头工作队 1999. *The Erlitou Site in Yanshi: Excavations in 1959~1979* 偃师二里头:1959 年 ~1978 年考古发掘报告. Beijing: Zhongguo dabaike quanshu chubanshe.

Zhongguo Shehui Kexueyuan Kaogu Yanjiusuo, Erlitou Gongzuodui 中国社会科学院考古研究所二里头工作队 2003. *Chinese Archaeology: Xia and Shang* 中国考古学·夏商卷. Beijing: Kexue chubanshe.

Zhongguo Shehui Kexueyuan Kaogu Yanjiusuo, Erlitou Gongzuodui 中国社会科学院考古研究所二里头工作队 2014. *Erlitou (1999~2006)* 二里头(1999~2006). Beijing: Wenwu chubanshe.

Zou, Heng 邹衡 1980. *Essays on the Archaeology of the Hsia, Shang and Zhou Dynasties* 夏商周考古学论文集. Beijing: Wenwu chubanshe.

CHAPTER 9

··

THE BRONZE-CASTING
REVOLUTION AND THE
RITUAL VESSEL SET

··

BY HONG XU, INSTITUTE OF ARCHAEOLOGY, CASS
AND YU LIU, INSTITUTE OF ARCHAEOLOGY, CASS

METAL-WORKING in China occupies a very important place in the history of technology. During the Erlitou cultural period, by comparison to the Late Neolithic period, the amount and type of bronzes dramatically increased, and bronze melting and casting technology grew by leaps and bounds. A large number of bronzes have been unearthed from the Erlitou site, including vessels, weapons, tools, musical instruments, miscellaneous articles, and other types whose functions are not clear. According to recent estimates, over 160 specimens of bronze wares, among which 40 were from tombs, and 50 foundry remains, have been published (Chen 2008; Lian et al. 2011). Another 18 Erlitou cultural sites contributed 40 more bronzes and 50 more manufacturing remnants. Most of the vessels, bells, and large-scale weapons, such as *ge* 戈 dagger-axes and *yue* 鉞 flat axes, were found in tombs, whereas small bronzes and tools have been unearthed from various locations within the Erlitou-period remains.

One of the most important finds at Erlitou is the bronze-casting workshop. The workshop is located to the south of the site, overlooking a river edge and occupying an area of 10,000 m². The bronze workshop was in use for approximately 200 years, from Erlitou Phase 2 to Phase 4. This is the earliest known large-scale bronze workshop. Finds from this workshop included three "areas associated with casting"; several burials; one kiln; a massive amount of cast debris incorporating clay molds, stone molds, fragments of crucibles and furnaces, melting slags, copper ores, wood charcoal, and small bronzes (Zhongguo 2003).

At present 17 bronze vessels have been discovered at Erlitou. The majority are *jue* 爵 tripods (1 with projecting lip), numbering 13, in addition to 2 *jia* 斝, warming vessels, 1 *ding* 鼎 tripod, and 1 *he* 盉 pitcher (Table 1). Before the Erlitou culture, only a few

Table 1 The type and number of bronze vessels unearthed from the Erlitou site

Date of excavation	Place found	Bronzes type & number	Phase (former perspective	Phase (adopted by the authors of this paper)	Where published
1973	VIIIT22(3)	1 jue	3	3	Zhongguo 1999:195–196
1976	IIIKM6	1 jue	3	3	Zhongguo 1999:251–252
1978	VKM8	1 jue	3	3	Zhongguo 1999:252
1980	IIIM2	2 jue	3	3 late	Zhongguo 1983:202–203
1975	VIKM3	1 jue	3	4 early	Zhongguo 1999:251
1974	IVcollected	1 jue	4	4	Zhongguo 1999:299
1975	VIIKM7	1 jue	4	4	Zhongguo 1999:341–342
1983	IVM16	1 jue	4	4	Zhongguo 1998:32
1984	VIM6	1 jue	4	4 early	Zhongguo1986:319–320
1984	VIM9	1 jue、1 jia	4	4 early	Zhongguo1986:319–320
1984	VIM11	1 jue	4	4 late	Zhongguo1986:319–320
1987	VIM57	1 jue	4	4 late	Zhongguo1992:295–296
1987	VM1	1 ding, 1 jia, 1 gu (?)	4	4	Zhongguo1991:1138–1139
1986	IIM1	1 he	4	4	Zhongguo1992:120

examples of copper and copper alloy objects made by the piece-mold casting process had been known to exist in the entire East Asia region. These examples include the remains of a small piece of *pen* basin 盆 (?) from Taosi site in Xiangfen, Shanxi, dated to ca. 2100–2000 BCE; a copper bell from the late phase of Taosi site dated to ca. 2100~2000 BCE; fragments of a ternary alloy (tin-lead-copper) container from the Late Longshan–period site of Wangchenggang at Dengfeng, Henan dated to ca. 2050~1994 BCE; and fragments of a copper container from the Xinzhai site in Xinmi, Henan of the "Xinzhai period" dated to ca. 1850~1750 BCE (Xu 2012). Thus, the discovery of a ritual group formed by bronze vessels at Erlitou caused quite a stir.

Outside of the Erlitou site are several discoveries including, for example, 1 *jue* from the Wangjinglou site in Xinzheng (Xinzheng 1981), and 1 *he* and 1 *li* 鬲 in Zhengzhou (Zhongguo 2003) whose cultural affiliations appear related to the Erlitou period.

As evident from a review of Table 1, most of the bronze vessels discovered at Erlitou date from the late phases of the Erlitou culture, P3 and P4. It is also noteworthy that most of the bronzes were found in tombs, indicating that they were prestige goods (used in sacrificial rites before their owners' death). Maintaining this hypothesis, it is evident that a ritual system had developed by the Erlitou period (Zhu 2009).

The appearance of ritual bronzes was a landmark change, marking the beginning of the Bronze Age in China. Bronze production requires a sophisticated technology, high management skills, and a major input of labor and thus would reflect a control system of greater political, economic, and religious power than seen in earlier phases of the Late Neolithic period. The ritual use of bronze separates this metal industry of the Erlitou culture from the rest of China and the world (Liu 2004). Bronze ritual use becomes anew the core of early Chinese ceremony, which is different from the former practice of only using ceramics, lacquers, and jades during the Longshan era. Bronze serves as the precursor of Three Dynasties' (Xia, Shang, Zhou) ritual. Accordingly, there should be an initial system regulating which ritual vessels could be used in ceremonies and burials. Since it was still the beginning of the Bronze Age, ritual bronzes, although not yet widely used appeared commonly grouped with ritual jades, ceramics, and lacquers (Li Zhipeng 2008).

Bronze vessel types of the Erlitou culture include the *jue* 爵, *he* 盉, *jia* 斝, *gu* 觚 goblet, and *ding* 鼎 tripod. Standing out and at the center of these types is the ritual alcohol vessel, the *jue*. Although the *ding* tripod appears, only one example, dated late in the Erlitou period, is known. This example was collected by a villager, not excavated, suggesting it was not a significant part of a ritual bronze set. Alcohol vessels were the most common type of ritual vessels excavated, indicating that alcohol was all-important among the elites. There is little dispute about the function of the use of the *jue* as a ritual vessel to heat, not to drink fermented beverages (Childs-Johnson 1987). Due to the larger size of the bronze vessels—the *jia* and *he*—it is assumed that they were involved primarily in the pouring of alcohol.

The *jue* was the most important of the alcohol vessel set (*jue, gu, he, jia*). From tombs that had not been looted or decimated, if one vessel is to be found in a tomb, it would be the *jue*. The earliest appearance of bronze prestige goods occurred during Erlitou P3, and at this time there was only the *jue*. By Erlitou P4 the *jia, gu, ding* tripod, and *he* made their first appearance. It is clear that the ritual bronze *jue* was the symbol of the aristocratic class. The *jue* served as the core of the alcohol-oriented prestige goods and as the prelude of the ritual system of the Three Dynasties.

RESEARCH ON PRODUCTION TECHNOLOGY

About half of the bronzes unearthed were scientifically tested before 2006 (Chen 2008). The materials included pure copper and many kinds of alloys including copper-tin, copper-lead, copper-tin-lead, copper-arsenic, and copper-arsenic-lead (Zhongguo 1975; Archaeometallurgy group 1981; Feng et al. 1982; Li Minsheng 1984; Ma 1988:508; Qu et al. 1999:400; Jin 2000; Liang and Sun 2002). The results show that the matrix of the bronze material found amid Erlitou vessels is complex.

Compared with the late Neolithic and later Erligang-period bronzes, metallurgy technology during the Erlitou period can be seen as transitional in development. From Erlitou P1–4 the copper contents began to decline in proportion to the contents of bronze (Chen 2008:164–165). Specialists maintain that during the Erlitou period the composite of tin and lead forming the bronze alloy began to appear, although the separate appearance of these metal elements is not entirely clear. Tin and lead in bronze-casting at this time do not appear standardized (Jin 2000).

The research on slag and crucible fragments from Erlitou site shows that all the slags are melting slags generated during the preparation of the alloy. They were not smelting slags which were generated during the smelting process of the copper ore. The crucible has several layers with different metal remains, which means different alloys including Cu, Cu-Sn-As, Cu-Sn-Pb-As, Cu-Sn, Cu-Pb, and Cu-Sn-Pb were melted each time. The arsenic-bearing slag tends to decrease from earlier to later phases in the Erlitou period, although fluctuations also appeared. Erlitou P2 is likely the time for producing arsenical copper technology, but it was also the time that tin bronze began to appear (Li and Xu 2007).

Analysis of the slag shows that there was no smelting activity at the Erlitou site, just melting and blending of raw copper from other areas. The source of copper ore is still in the speculative stage, yet the four regions of Zhongtiaoshan, the middle and lower reaches of the Yangtze River, the western Henan mountains, and the Shandong Peninsula are considered to be possible sources of copper. Systematic and in-depth investigation of sources in these areas of ancient mining and smelting sites remains to be undertaken (Su et al. 1995:95–99).

The research on the production technology of Erlitou bronzes shows that although the bronzes are still relatively simple, and their shapes imitate earlier pottery and stone tools and retain a certain quality of primitivism, the basic framework for bronze production is established. The formation of the independent Chinese bronze-working tradition appears in the use of the piece-mold casting process. At this point the basic technical features of the piece-mold casting technique are intact: vertical and horizontal divisions of the piece-mold assembly are established, the orientation of design motifs following a horizontal direction is also established, and at that time the motifs were carved on the molds. The latter is one of the most important features of the Chinese bronze-casting technology, that is, the motifs are finished before the assembly completing and casting the final structure as a whole. This technical process and philosophical construct are very different from the technical tradition existing in Mesopotamia and the ancient Egyptian region, where designs were made after the bronzewares were formed (Zhang 2011). In addition, during the Erlitou period the piece-mold casting process went through using a single mold to bivalve molds to pieces of molds. From the early to late phases of this period, bronzes with no design developed to bronzes with simple décor consisting of chord lines, nail head motifs, square patterns, circle patterns, or openwork décor.

Although the Erlitou bronze vessels are not large or numerous, their thin and uniform wall shows a considerable level of casting technology. A sophisticated piece-mold casting technology incorporates a rigorous positioning technology during casting (cross and pin). Simple-shaped bronzes, such as tools and weapons created out of the piece-mold design, are known. Techniques were also well developed for making repairs of casting defects (Li Jinghua 1985; Lian et al. 2011). The specialized selection of soils and their treatment had reached a considerable level of achievement. Elutriated loess was used to create the molds, to which chaff and straw were added to improve the casting properties. Brushing the inner surface of the clay molds with a fine layer to alleviate separation of mold and final bronze after casting was also in evidence. Mold fragments sometimes appear burnt brown to red in color due to the remains of liquid bronze (Zhongguo 1999:81, 171, 270).

Other cast bronzes witnessed at Erlitou are the circular ornaments and the plaques inlaid in turquoise in a mosaic pattern. These bronze ornaments and plaques were all first cast then inlaid with turquoise pieces (Zheng 1993). Excavators have also identified a bronze knife whose surface they maintain has traces of gold (Zheng 1993, 1991), although this has not been scientifically tested and so awaits scientific determination.

The large-scale bronze workshop at Erlitou site lasted a long time and witnessed a high level of specialization in developing quarters for a casting workroom and the kiln for baking clay molds. The current findings show that bronze ritual vessels were only produced within this workshop. Bronze ritual vessel production requires sophisticated technology, a major input of labor, and high management skills. The manufacturing of bronze arrowheads nonetheless also reflects an organized level of standardized production. It appears that since production during the Erlitou period shows a high level of organization, this phase of working bronze does not represent an original stage of bronze industry but one that follows an earlier and probably longer period of development.

,Studies on the production technology of Erlitou bronzes need further research. Many issues remain, such as identifying the source of the minerals and understanding smelting and melting technology and equipment, turquoise inlay technology, and alloying technology.

Discussion on some problems in making bronzes

Alloy material

As of 2006, 53 bronze pieces from Erlitou were tested for their chemical composition and published, in addition to the publication of 1 piece of slag and 1 lead piece (Liang and Sun 2002, 2004). Out of the 53 bronze pieces, 7 are copper, 15 are tin bronze, 10 are leaded copper, 20 are leaded tin bronze, and 1 is arsenical copper. Zhao Chunyan and others who analyzed 18 of the bronze samples unearthed from the Erlitou 16 were identified as Erlitou P2–4, including 2 pieces of copper, 3 of bronze, 1 of leaded copper, 8 of leaded tin bronze, 1 of arsenical copper, and 1 of Cu-Sn-As ternary alloy (Zhao et al. 2009). Two came from the Erligang period, including 1 tin bronze and 1 leaded arsenical copper. Studies show that in Erlitou P4, tin and lead content increased, especially lead. The arsenic content of the arsenical copper is lower than 4%. As published in the archaeological report "Erlitou: 1999–2006 Archaeological Discovery and Research," 13 bronzes were tested, of which 2

Table 2 Analytical results of bronzes from the Erlitou site

Period	Cu	Cu-Sn	Cu-Sn-Pb	Cu-Pb	Cu-As	Cu-Sn-Pb-As	Cu-Sn-As	Total
Erlitou P1				1				1
Erlitou P2	3	3	1	1	2			10
Erlitou P3	3	8	8	3		1		23
Erlitou P4	5	11	24	6	1	1		48
Late Erligang	2	7			1		1	11
Total	13	29	33	12	4	1	1	93

pieces were pure copper (including one with slightly higher arsenic than the other), 4 were tin bronze, 5 were leaded tin bronzes, 1 was arsenical copper, and 1 was arsenic-bearing leaded tin bronze (Zhongguo 2014). Eight objects of the Erligang period were tested with the results identifying 1 as pure copper, 4 tin bronze, 2 leaded tin bronze, and 1 Cu-Sn-As ternary alloy. Out of 93 bronzes unearthed at Erlitou site, 13 pieces were pure copper, 26 tin bronze, 31 leaded tin bronze, 11 leaded copper, 3 arsenical copper, 1 arsenic-bearing leaded tin bronze, and 1 Cu-Sn-as ternary alloy. Eighty-two of these specimens are Erlitou in date, of Erlitou P1–4, yet the majority are from P3–4 and show an increase in use of the bronze alloy. The results of these different stages are shown in Table 2.

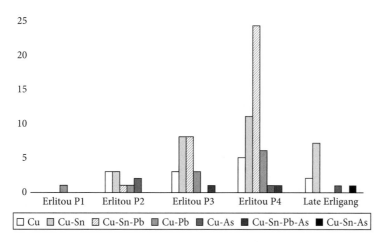

FIGURE 1 The evolution of bronze material from Erlitou culture period to Erligang culture period. Left: numerical amount; bottom of chart marks periods: Erlitou P1, P2, P3, P4, late Erligang; colors from the left include pure copper; tin bronze(Cu-Sn); leaded tin bronze(Cu-Sn-Pb); leaded copper (Cu-Pb); arsenical copper(Cu-As); arsenic-bearing leaded tin bronze9 (Cu-Sn-Pb-As); and Cu-Sn-As ternary alloy.

As can be seen from Figure 1, over the period of Erlitou P1–4 the proportion of copper objects decreased and bronze objects increased. The amount of arsenical copper objects is reduced, but there are fluctuations. Erlitou bronzes generally contain traces of arsenic, and some also contain traces of bismuth and silver. During Erlitou P3–4, the combination of lead and tin used to produce bronze was remarkable, especially in P4. The lead content was improved, and that changed the alloy material greatly. This may be due to the acquisition of the ore source and smelting technology. Li Yanxiang speculated that Erlitou tin material may come from a primitive lead-tin symbiotic ore, associated with arsenic, silver, bismuth, and antimony. The transition from arsenical copper to Cu-Sn-Pb-(As) alloy may be due to the fact that the lead-tin intergrowth deposits can produce different ores, and the evolution of smelting techniques can lead to the emergence of different alloys. Other relevant determinants of the bronze alloy may depend on the progress of smelting technology (e.g., enhancing the reduction of oxygen) (Li and Xu 2007). The results of the 19 bronze and slag tests partly support this observation.

There is also a correspondence of these processes in the production of other types of artifacts. For example, copper was initially used to produce tools, such as knives, chisels, awls, spinning whorls, and buttons. Yet tools, knives, chisels, and weapons (including *ge* daggers, *yue* ax heads, arrowheads, and vessels), and especially the weapons, were made of a bronze alloy of copper, tin, and lead. The relationship between metal content and object usage has certain requirements, yet in terms of the proportions of the alloy that standard was still very unstable. For example, of 20 tested knives, material varied from pure copper to leaded tin bronze, which has high lead content, and did not show a relatively fixed ratio.

The production technology of Erlitou-period bronze showed an early stage, where the material constituents were often complex. The relationship between the ratio of tin and of lead and the type of bronze is shows great variation of chemical contents, even in the same period. The difference in the material contents may be due to differences in the raw materials and technologies, which include both smelting, melting, and alloying techniques. In addition to individual objects, the Erlitou bronze tin content is still relatively low. A large number of diamond-shaped and needle-like tin dioxide crystals appear in the microstructure of these Erlitou bronzes samples, indicating that the tin is not completely alloyed with copper. In contrast, by the Late Erligang period tin bronzewares grew and arsenical copperwares decreased due to superior alloying technology.

Melting technology

Currently all the materials found at the Erlitou bronze workshop are melting slag from melting and casting activities with no evidence for smelting, which must have come from outside Erlitou. Melting slag is what is formed by the reaction of molten metal and the furnace wall (or crucible), producing fuel ash on the surface of the metal liquid during the melting and alloying process. Melting slag mainly contains silicon, aluminum, and other refractory silicate components; copper and other alloying elements are high, while iron and calcium content is low.

From the 20 slag specimens analyzed, the material is very diverse, including bronze, arsenic bronze, arsenic tin bronze, arsenic tin lead bronze, tin bronze, lead bronze, and tin lead bronze. These mineralogical constituents are the same as those found in alloys of Erlitou bronzes. Slag containing pure copper, bronze particles, SnO_2 crystals, and some high-lead phase, indicate that tin and lead contents have been able to combine in producing a true bronze.

SnO_2 crystals in the slag, along with copper particles or copper oxide, coexist mostly in the shape of a long strip, needle, square, diamond, and other forms. Morphologically speaking, some SnO_2 crystals have holes containing red copper. The presence of SnO_2 nanocrystals is a noteworthy phenomenon, suggesting that at least a portion of the alloy is prepared by direct use of copper and tin rather than tin ore. The SnO_2 crystal is formed by adding tin to the molten bronze. Bronze liquid flow is not good when reduction conditions are poor and tin is oxidized. As early as the Erlitou P2, the advanced process of adding tin to the copper directly instead of adding tin ore had appeared.

Craftsmanship

During the Erlitou period, most bronzewares were made by the piece-mold casting process, and they were formed just by pouring once. No objects are found using the cast-joint technique. Weapons, tools, and bells were cast using bivalves. In the past, a number of scholars analyzed the casting process of Erlitou bronzes and focused primarily on vessel types. Li Jinghua pointed out that the bronze bells were cast using two molds, one core, and two spacers that, when combined during casting, allowed two holes to form and for an even wall thickness (Li Jinghua 2004). The formation of the *jue* assembly has been the most controversial in determining mold and core formation for casting. For example, according to Li Jinghua the piece-mold technique used to create a *jue* comprised the use of two identical exterior belly molds, an internal clay core, three external foot molds, and the mold of a sprue, which was put under the spout of the *jue* or on the lower abdomen under the tail of the *jue* (Li Jinghua 2004). This is consistent with the view of Noel Barnard who mentioned the process of "sectionalism," now called "horizontal division" (Barnard 1993: 23–25). Su Rongyu said the process was not so complicated, and that the assembly included two exterior pieces of molds along the axis of the spout and tail of the *jue*; the handle core, which was single or coherent with the outer mold; and the sprue mold, which was put on the handle or the pole of the *jue* (Su et al. 1995:95–99). Namba Junko, in studying the evolution of the casting technology of bronze *jue* from the Erlitou to Erligang periods, divided the bronze-casting technology of the Erlitou period into two phases. In the early phase two mold pieces were used; in the late phase the outer molds included two pieces to form the cup part of the *jue* and three pieces to form the foot part, as described by Li Jinghua. In the Erligang period, one kind of assembly was the same as in the late phase, while the other one included three pieces for the cup part and three pieces for the foot part (Junko 1989). While Miyamoto Kazuo followed the argument of Su Rongyu (Kazuo and Xiang 2013:39–53), Lian

Haiping, after analyzing a few bronzewares, followed the process as articulated by Su Rongyu and Noel Barnard (Lian et al. 2011). Miyamoto Kazuo also discussed the process of casting a tripod and maintained that the T-shaped leg of a *jue* mold, if a triangular shape, may not belong to the Erlitou period but rather to the Erligang period (Kazuo 2013). This view differs from Su's and other advocates who maintain a two-piece mold assembly (Su et al. 1995:95–99).

Using bivalves to cast tools and weapons is relatively simple but involve different locations of the sprue; for example: for a knife the sprue is located on the handle, for a *ge* dagger it is on the handle, for a chisel on the striking side, for arrowheads on the collar end, and for the *yue* ax on the top (Liang and Sun 2002).

Since the microstructure of the Erlitou bronze had not been analyzed in the past, it was impossible to know whether forging or heating treatment was used. Based on the recent publication of 19 bronze metallographic analyses, it is evident that a majority of tools and weapons underwent annealing to increase the strength and toughness (Zhongguo 2014). The points of arrowheads may have been annealed. The smaller of two bronze knives was cold-forged, yet the large one was made by casting. These differences may be due to different functions, the former for utility and the latter for a more ritual function. Thus, what is witnessed during the Erlitou period is different skills in manufacturing bronzes—from the use of casting to forging, showing that in that era the production of bronzes made technological progress.

BIBLIOGRAPHY

Beijing Gangtie Xueyuan Zhi Jinshizu (BUIST) 北京钢铁学院冶金史组 1981. "A Preliminary Study of the Early Chinese Copper and Bronze Artefacts 中国早期铜器的初步研究." *Kaogu xuebao* 3:287–302.

Barnard, Noel 1993. "Thoughts on the Emergence of Metallurgy in Pre-Shang and Early Shang China and A Technical Appraisal of Relevant Bronze Artifact of the Time." *Bulletin of the Metals Museum* 19:3–48.

Chen, Guoliang 陈国梁 2006. "Overview of the Technology of Bronze Production at Erlitou 二里头文化铜器制作技术概述." *Sandai kaogu* 2:183–201.

Chen, Guoliang 陈国梁 2008. "*Research on Erlitou Bronzes* 二里头文化铜器研究." In *Early Bronze Culture of China: Special Study of the Erlitou Culture* 中国早期青铜文化——二里头文化专题研究, Edited by Institute of Archaeology, CASS:124–274. Beijing: Kexue chubanshe.

Childs-Johnson, Elizabeth 1987. "The *Jue*-Vessel and Its Ritual Use in the Ancestor Cult of Shang China." *Artibus Asiae* 48.3–4:171–196.

Feng, Fugen 冯富根, Zhenjiang Wang 王振江, Jueming Hua 华觉明, and Rongjin Bai 白荣金 1982. "Replication Study on the Casting Process of *Gu* Goblet from Yinxu in Shang Dynasty 殷墟出土商代青铜觚铸造工艺的复原研究." *Kaogu* 5:532–539, 527.

Henansheng Wenwu Kaogu Yanjiusuo 河南省文物考古研究所 2003. "Excavation of Several Shang Tombs at the Shangcheng Site, Zhengzhou 郑州商城新发现的几座商墓." *Wenwu* 4:4–20.

Jin, Zhengyao 金正耀 2000. "Scientific Research on the Bronzes of the Erlitou Culture and Exploration of the Xia Civilization 二里头青铜器的自然科学研究与夏文明探索." *Wenwu* 1:56–64, 69.

Junko, Namba 難波純子 1989. "Early Period Bronze Vessels 初現期の青铜彝器." *Shilin* 72.2:76–112.

Kazuo, Miyamoto 宫本 一夫 2013. "Formation of the Shang Civilization Viewed from the Bronze Production Technique in the Transitional Time between the Xia and the Shang Period夏商交替期的青铜器生产与商文化的形成." In *Radiance between Bronze and Jade-- Archeology, Art, and Culture in Shang and Zhou Dynasties*金玉交辉：商周考古、艺术与文化论文集, edited by Guangzu Chen 陈光祖：163–190. Taibei: Institute of history and language, Academia Sinica.

Kazuo, Miyamoto 宫本一夫, and Yunxiang Bai 白云翔, eds. 2009. *The Study of Bronze Culture in Early China* 中国初期青铜器文化の研究 *Tyugoku syoki seidoki bunka no kenkyu*. Fukuoka: Kyushu University Press.

Li, Jinghua 李京华 2004. "Discussion on Bronze Casting Technology in *The Erlitou Site in Yanshi* and Some Problems in the book 《偃师二里头》有关铸铜技术的探讨——兼谈报告存在的几点问题." *Zhongyuan wenwu* 3：29–36.

Li, Jinghua 李京华 1985. "A Few Ideas on Early Copper Smelting Technology and Related Issues of the Central Plains Region 关于早期铜冶炼技术及中原地区相关问题的几点思考." *Wenwu* 12：75–78.

Li, Minsheng 李敏生 1988. "The History Survey of the Use of Lead in Pre-Qin Period 先秦用铅的历史概况." *Wenwu* 10:84–89.

Li, Yanxiang 李延祥, and Hong Xu 许宏 2007. "Preliminary Research on the Foundry Remains at Erlitou Site 二里头遗址出土冶铸遗物初步研究." *Keji Kaogu* 2:59–82.

Li, Zhipeng 李志鹏 2008. "Research on the Tombs of Erlitou Culture二里头文化墓葬研究." In *Early Bronze Culture of China: Special Study of the Erlitou Culture*, Edited by Institute of Archaeology, CASS:55–60. Beijing: Kexue chubanshe.

Lian, Haiping 廉海萍, Derui Tan 谭德睿, and Guang Zheng 郑光 2011. "The Research and Exploration to the Bronze Casting Techniques in Erlitou Site 二里头遗址铸铜技术研究." *Kaogu xuebao* 4:561–575.

Liang, Honggang 梁宏刚, and Shuyun Sun 孙淑云 2002. "Report on the Analysis of the Bronze *Yue* Ax from Erlitou Site 二里头遗址出土青铜钺分析测试报告." *Kaogu* 11:33–34.

Liang, Honggang 梁宏刚, and Shuyun Sun 孙淑云 2004. "Summary of Research on Erlitou Bronzes 二里头遗址出土铜器研究综述." *Zhongyuan wenwu* 1:29–39, 56.

Liu, Li 刘莉 2004. "The Production of Early Ceremonial Instruments in the Neolithic Age of China 中国新石器和铜器时代早期礼器的生产." In *Essays in Honor of Professor AN Zhimin on the Occasion of His Eighties Birthday*桃李成蹊集：庆祝安志敏先生八十寿辰, edited by Chung Tang邓聪 and Xingcan Chen 陈星灿:98–111. Hong Kong: Centre for Chinese Archaeology and Art, The Chinese University of Hong Kong.

Ma, Chengyuan 马承源1988. *Chinese Bronzes* 中国青铜器. Shanghai：Shanghaigujichubanshe.

Qu, Changzhi 曲长芝, and Riqing Zhang 张日清 1999. "X-Ray Fluorescence Analysis of Erlitou Bronzes 二里头出土铜器 X 射线荧光分析." In *The Erlitou Site In Yanshi: Excavations in 1959–1978* 偃师二里头(1959 年～1978 年考古发掘报告), Edited by Institute of Archaeology, CASS: 243–268, Beijing: Zhongguo dabaike quanshu chubanshe.

Su, Rongyu 苏荣誉, Jueming Hua 华觉明, Kemin Li 李克敏, and Benshan Lu 卢本珊 1995. *The Metal Technology of Early Ancient China* 中国上古金属技术. Jinan：Shandong kexue jishu chubanshe.

Xinzhengxian Wenhuaguan 新郑县文化馆 1981. "Bronzes and Jades Unearthed at Wangjinglou Site in Xinzheng County, Henan Province 河南新郑县望京楼出土的铜器和玉器." *Kaogu* 6:556,580.

Xu, Hong 许宏 2012. "2000BC: Archaeological Observation of Historic Transition in the Central Plains 公元前 2000 年:中原大变局的考古学观察." *Dongfang kaogu* 9:186–201.

Zhang, Changping 张昌平 2011. "Interaction between Production Technology and Décor of Bronzes during Bronze Age in China.中国青铜时代青铜器装饰艺术与生产技术的交互影响." In *Research on the Casting Technology of Clay Molds for Shang and Zhou Bronzes*, edited by Jianli Chen 陈建立 and Yu Liu 刘煜: 1–22. Beijing: Wenwu chubanshe.

Zhao, Chunyan 赵春燕, Jinpeng Du 杜金鹏, Hong Xu 许宏, Guoliang Chen 陈国梁, Shuyun Sun 孙淑云, and Honggang Liang 梁宏刚 2009. "Analysis of Chemical Composition of Some Bronzes Unearthed from Erlitou Site in Yanshi, Henan Province 河南偃师二里头出土部分铜器的化学组成分析." In *Treatises on Exploration project of Chinese Civilization: Technology and Economics* 中华文明探源工程文集—技术与经济卷, vol. 1:372–380. Beijing: Kexue chubanshe.

Zheng, Guang 郑光 1991. "An Archaeological Pearl: the Erlitou Site 考古学上的一颗明珠—二里头遗址." *Zhongguo wenwu bao* 9(8).

Zheng, Guang 郑光 1993. "The Erlitou Site and Bronze Civilization in Early China. 二里头遗址与我国早期青铜文明." In *Treatises on Chinese Archaeology: The 40th Anniversary of the Founding of the Institute of Archeology* 中国考古学论丛—中国社会科学院建所四十周年纪念, edited by the Institute of Archaeology, CASS:190–195. Beijing: Kexue chubanshe.

Zhongguo Shehui Kexueyuan Kaogu Yanjiusuo 中国社会科学院考古研究所 1993. *The Essence of Archaeology: The 40th Anniversary of the Establishment of the Institute of Archeology of the Chinese Academy of Social Sciences* 考古精华——中国社会科学院考古研究所建所四十周年纪念, edited by the Institute of Archaeology, CASS. Beijing: Kexue chubanshe.

Zhongguo Shehui Kexueyuan Kaogu Yanjiusuo 中国社会科学院考古研究所 1998. *Chinese Academy of Social Sciences Institute of Archeology, Luoyang Branch of Archaeological Museum* 中国社会科学院考古研究所考古博物馆洛阳分馆. Luoyang: Wenhua meishu chubanshe.

Zhongguo Shehui Kexueyuan Kaogu Yanjiusuo 中国社会科学院考古研究所 1999. *The Erlitou Site in Yanshi: Excavations from 1959–1978* 偃师二里头 1959 年~1978 年考古发掘报告. Beijing: Zhongguo dabaikequanshu chubanshe.

Zhongguo Shehui Kexueyuan Kaogu Yanjiusuo 中国社会科学院考古研究所 2003. *Chinese Archaeology: Xia and Shang Volumes* 中国考古学·夏商卷. Beijing: Kexue chubanshe.

Zhongguo Shehui Kexueyuan Kaogu Yanjiusuo 中国社会科学院考古研究所 2014. *Erlitou (1999~2006)* 二里头(1999–2006). Beijing: Wenwu chubanshe.

Zhongguo Shehui Kexueyuan Kaogu Yanjiusuo, Erlitou Gongzuo Dui 中国社会科学院考古研究所二里头工作队 1975. "Excavation of Zones III and VIII at Erlitou site in Yanshi County, Henan Province 河南偃师二里头遗址三、八区发掘简报." *Kaogu* 5:302–309, 294.

Zhongguo Shehui Kexueyuan Kaogu Yanjiusuo, Erlitou Gongzuo Dui 中国社会科学院考古研究所二里头工作队 1983. "Brief Report on the Excavation at Erlitou Site in Yanshi County, Henan Province in Autumn 1980 1980 年秋河南偃师二里头遗址发掘简报." *Kaogu* 3:199–205, 219.

Zhongguo Shehui Kexueyuan Kaogu Yanjiusuo, Erlitou Gongzuo Dui 中国社会科学院考古研究所二里头工作队 1986. "Several Tombs Excavated at Erlitou Site in Yanshi County,

Henan Province in Autumn 1984 1984 年秋河南偃师二里头遗址发现的几座墓葬." *Kaogu* 4:318–323.

Zhongguo Shehui Kexueyuan Kaogu Yanjiusuo, Erlitou Gongzuo Dui 中国社会科学院考古研究所二里头工作队 1991. New Bronze Wares found at Erlitou Site in Yanshi County, Henan Province 河南偃师二里头遗址发现新的铜器." *Kaogu* 12:1,138–1,139.

Zhongguo Shehui Kexueyuan Kaogu Yanjiusuo, Erlitou Gongzuo Dui 中国社会科学院考古研究所二里头工作队 1992. "Brief Report on the Excavation of Tombs at the Site of Erlitou in Yanshi County in 1987 1987年偃师二里头遗址墓葬发掘简报." *Kaogu* 4:294–302.

Zhu, Fenghan 朱凤瀚 2009. *A Comprehensive Survey of Chinese Bronzes* 中国青铜器综论. Shanghai: Shanghaguji chubanshe.

CHAPTER 10

THE SPREAD OF ERLITOU *YAZHANG* TO SOUTH CHINA AND THE ORIGIN AND DISPERSAL OF EARLY POLITICAL STATES

BY CHUNG TANG, SHANDONG UNIVERSITY AND FANG WANG, JINSHA SITE MUSEUM

STATE formation is not an everyday phenomenon. It is well known that states have not appeared in either Oceania or Africa. Tribal societies also continue to exist into the modern eras, as represented in India, Afghanistan, and certain places in Southeast Asia. A national political system primarily includes the monopoly of an effective military force within a centralized, fixed territory. A political system has a decisive role in the formation of a state. In East Asia, what is today's China evolved as a state at an early stage.

Anthropologists and archaeologists divide the state into "primary" and "competitive" categories. The formation of a primary state refers to a state that evolved initially out of a tribal society. The formation of a "competitive state" refers to one that follows or imitates the lead of the first state. With the formation of the primary state, and the close association with a more powerful social structure by comparison to a tribal one, the state gradually assumes more influence in ultimately dominating a tribal society. However, the unwillingness of some tribal societies to be subdued by stronger states leads to copying or following the dominant political system in forming a secondary "competitive state."

Over the past half century, the Erlitou site in Yanshi, Henan has become a primary focus for scholars interested in identifying the origin of China's early state. Erlitou not only appears to be the birthplace of Chinese culture of later dynastic periods but may be regarded as the earliest known indigenous state, and in this respect effects the political and cultural evolution of the East Asian Heartland.

Addressing the issue of central versus regional jade-working traditions of Erlitou and Sichuan sites at Sanxingdui (Childs-Johnson 2010), Childs-Johnson has analyzed material data including *yazhang* and related insignia as symbols of a state equivalent in time and place to Xia (Childs-Johnson 1995).

Xu Hong has identified the Erlitou culture as the earliest representative of traditional China and the location of the earliest royal capital of the so-called Hua Xia 華夏. He characterizes this advanced and complex civilization as having several major features: (1) the earliest urban network, (2) the earliest royal city, (3) the earliest royal buildings on a planned axis, (4) the earliest formulation of ritual bronze vessel sets, (5) the earliest production of bronze weapons, (6) the earliest bronze-casting foundries, (7) the earliest turquoise workshops, and (8) the earliest use of a two-wheeled vehicle (Xu 2009).

Numbers one to three in Xu Hong's list signify the political manifestations of a centralized state and kingdom. Numbers four to eight reflect the military power of a dominant state.

Historical studies in the past have focused on Marxism and class struggle, yet currently there is a shift to understanding state ritual practice. Historians who study ancient history now tend to focus on the history of social ritual. The ritualistic evolution of society's common belief, we may say, in terms of governance and governance over time, is composed of an interdependent set of beliefs (Tōru 2013). As will be related in this chapter, we focus our analysis on what may be considered a new academic interest in the creation of the rites of an ancient state.

After investigating the site of Erlitou, Kyoto University's Professor Okamura Hidenori advocates that the most important indicator of early Chinese civilization is the maturity of royal ritual. And, the most significant symbol of ritual is represented by the material remains of bronze and jade. He maintains that the *yazhang* jade blade, for example, represents one core aspect of court ritual (Okamura 2012). Beyond the artistic significance of these remains is the light shed on the origin of what constitutes a political state system.

In order to illustrate the evidence for primary and secondary states, the evolution of the *yazhang* jade VM3:4 from Erlitou is initially analyzed and then compared typologically with examples from southern sites in China. For example, comparison of one of the earliest *yazhang* from Jinsha in Sichuan with that from Erlitou clearly illustrates that the former derives from Erlitou. The Erlitou *yazhang* serves as a primary material symbol of early China's state administrative system and in defining the southern site of Jinsha site as a representative of a "competitive, secondary state."

CHARACTERISTICS OF THE
ERLITOU VM3:4 *YAZHANG*

Significant differences in shape characterize *yazhang* from different periods (Figure 1) (Tang 2017; Childs-Johnson 1995, 2010). Standardized parts of this jade utensil, as measured with VM3:4 *yazhang* from Erlitou, include the body, toothed (serrated) part (*feiya* 扉 牙), and handle.

The part labeled "*feiya* 扉 牙," literally "gate-like teeth," is here translated "handle section with serrations (teeth)" (see Figure 2). ("Serrated" is used in this chapter alongside the translation "toothed" or *ya*; the two are one and the same feature.) Scholars have used both "*lan* 阑" and "*fei ya*" to describe the serrated protrusions on two sides of the inner middle part of the handle. Li Xueqin, for example, distinguishes two types of *yazhang*: those without a handle bearing protruding parts *lan* 阑 (Li 1994) and those with a handle bearing *lan*. The small protrusions lying within the *lan* Li calls "*chi* 齿 teeth." On the Erlitou VM3:4

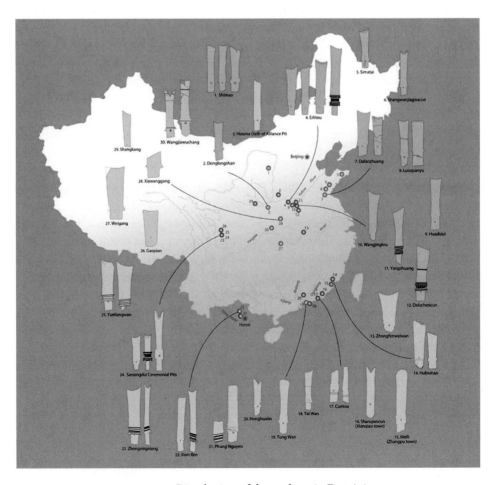

FIGURE 1 Distribution of the *yazhang* in East Asia.

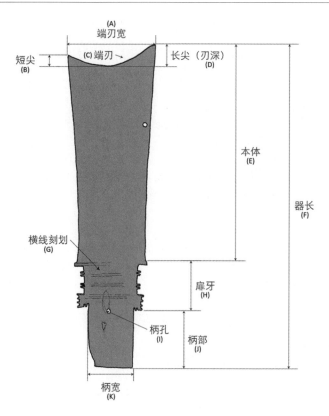

FIGURE 2 Names for the parts of the VM3:4 *yazhang* at Erlitou: **A** width of the blade tip, **B** short point height, **C** blade tip, **D** tall point height, **E** blade body, **F** length of *yazhang*, **G** horizontal incised lines, **H** *feiya*/dentil part of handle, **I** handle hole, **J** handle, **K** handle width.

yazhang two rows of opposing small teeth, each with four dentils, lie between two wider and longer set of protrusions also with teeth at top and bottom framing the handle. Zheng Guang considers the sets of teeth interchangeable (Zheng 1994). He maintains that "the *lan* parts appear to take the shape of an animal head with open mouth in profile," comparable to the head of a dragon (see e.g., Figure 8). Thus, *lan* to Zheng are an ornament featuring an animal head with open jaw. The author uses the term *feiya* to define both lateral decorative parts of the handle.

The four *yazhang* unearthed amid Erlitou site remains belong to cultural Periods 3–4 (Figure 3). KM6:8 *yazhang* belongs to Period 3; VM3:4 and VM3:5 *yazhangs* belong to Period 3; and VIIKM7:5 *yazhang* belongs to Period 4.

The *yazhang* VM3:4 was discovered in Area 3 in 1980, to the south of a public gravesite. A deep pit lay to the west about 350 m distant from the remains of Palace No. 1. This pit burial VM3 was 2.1 m long north to south, 1.3 m wide east to west, and 1.2–3 m deep. The burial probably originally had a second level ledge and remains of a coffin with a red lacquer skin. A pair of two *yazhang* lay at the middle of the tomb, one above the other. A pair of turquoise tubes lay nearby, close to the head (Yang and Liu 1983). The two *yazhang* apparently were centrally located in the area of the upper limbs of the tomb owner's body. Jades and ceramics of exquisite design also accompanied the deceased (Figure 4).

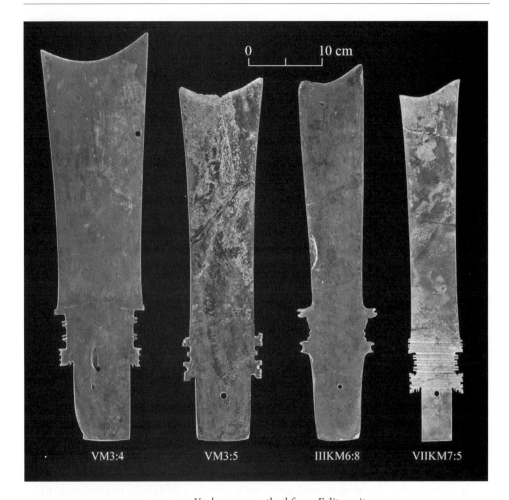

VM3:4   VM3:5   IIIKM6:8   VIIKM7:5

FIGURE 3 *Yazhang* unearthed from Erlitou site.

The *yazhang* VM3:4 measures 54 cm long by 14.9 cm wide. Amid the four discovered it is the largest. According to published finds, "the *zhang* color was light grey-green with a high polish. A hole was perforated from one side on the lower handle and another small hole of the blade was inlaid with turquoise. Both surfaces of the blade's edge were worked as concave in shape and the handle had flanking serrations" (Yang and Liu 1983).

Zheng Guang describes the VM3:4 *yazhang* similarly, as a blade divisible into three parts that diminish in width from the top of the blade edge to the bottom of the handle: blade, *feiya*, handle. The blade slopes downward from tip to handle. The tip takes a concave semi-circular shape, narrows along the blade, then terminates in a handle of two parts: a decorative section with opposing and matching sets of serrations and an end forming a more narrow rectangular haft. The upper handle part exposes one tooth-like projection, then narrows to two tiny sets of dentil projections and finally to a bracket with four tiny dentils. The multiple dentils or teeth section he describes as the open mouth of an animal head. To Zheng this blade is a form standardized during Erlitou P3

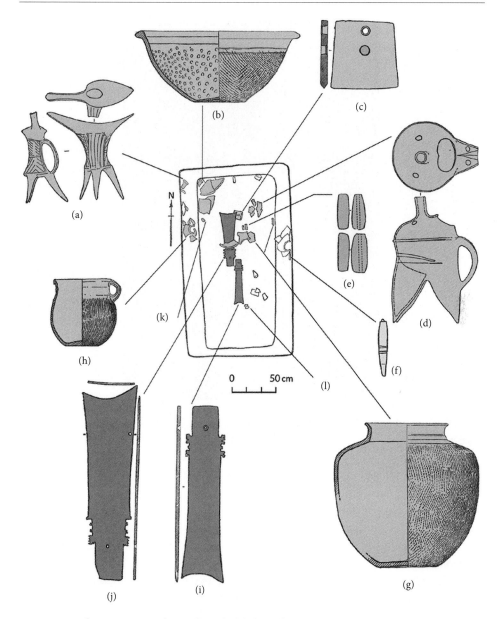

FIGURE 4 Erlitou remains of VM3 burial and their distribution. **A** Ceramic *jue* (VM3:7a) 1/6. **B** Ceramic *pen* (VM3:11) 1/6. **C** Jade *yue* ax head (VM3:3) 1/4. **D** Ceramic *he* (VM3:8) 1/6. **E** Turquoise tube ornaments (VM3:6) 1/4. **F** Jade pointed ornament (VM3:7b) 1/4. **G** Ceramic *guan* (VM3:10) 1/6. **H** Single eared ceramic *guan* (VM3:9) 1/6. **I** *zhang* (VM3:5) 1/8. **J** *zhang* (VM3:4) 1/8. **K** Circular ceramic piece. **L** Human bones.

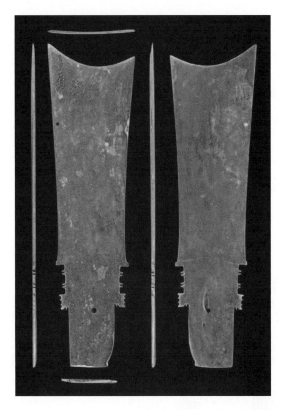

FIGURE 5   Front and back of the jade and drawing of the same with side view of the Erlitou VM3:4 *yazhang.*

(Zheng 1994). In the winter of 2005, our preliminary investigation of the VM3:4 *yazhang* showed that between the dentils of teeth were additional engraved lines (Tang 2007) (Figures 5 and 6). Visible on opposing surfaces, both sides show serrations and incised straight lines. The linear incisions are faint and camouflaged in part by a cinnabar skin. The linear incisions measure 0.5 mm wide, and upon close examination these lateral incisions form miniscule raised ridges.

The length of the serrations or *feiya* is 8.19 and 7.5 cm, respectively, with one slightly larger than the other in thickness and shape (Figure 7).

The creation of large-scale stone *zhang* from Jinsha

At present the largest number of stone and jade *zhang* from China are found amid the remains at Jinsha, in Chengdu, Sichuan. Zhang Qing pointed out that the number of unearthed *yazhang*, both small and long, amounts to over several hundred from Jinsha

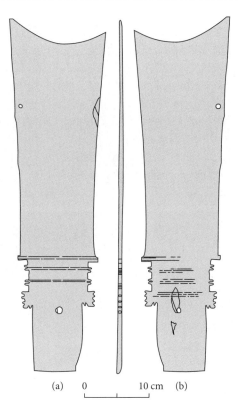

(a)   0   10 cm   (b)

FIGURE 6 Front and back of the jade and drawing of the same with side view of the Erlitou VM3:4 *yazhang.*

and some 96 from Sanxingdui. According to reports the majority of the earliest examples are created out of stone and the latest out of jade. Zhang Qing has published a comprehensive study of these finds in his "Preliminary Research on the *Yazhang* Unearthed at Jinsha" (2006).

According to the reports, there are 66 large stone *yazhang* with serrated handle décor. The most concentrated number come from No. 3 sacrificial pit (Figure 9). Zhang Qing analyzed 28 of these large-sized stone *zhang* and divided them into A and B types. Type A, represented by only one example, has a concave arched blade tip. Type B, comprising 16 examples, has blade tips forming oblique arcs suggesting a wide mouth that leads to slender bodies. The serrated edges of the handle comprise an inner set of two small teeth and a lower set of four, with an upper slightly wider single serration, as characterizes the Erlitou model example already discussed. In addition to these features, incised horizontal bowstring lines filled with cinnabar dust align the handle. Surfaces reveal rough grinding of the original stone, leaving flaking and scar marks and many uneven concave and convex worked parts (Zhang 2006). Differences of the handle décor are categorized into subtypes, BI and BII.

One of the stone *zhang*, 2001CQJ No. C261 (Figures 10–11), measures 48.8 cm long by 10 cm wide at the tip. The body is narrow, measuring 8.8 cm wide, with a handle length

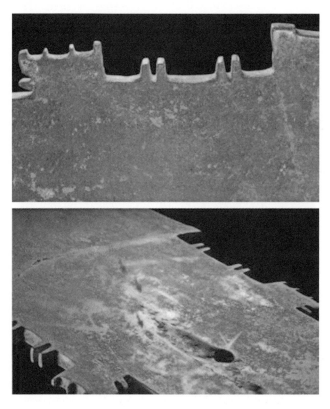

FIGURE 7 *Feiya* (above) and multiple incised straight lines on both sides of Erlitou VM3:4 *yazhang* (below).

FIGURE 8 Dragon-shaped turquoise burial cover unearthed from Erlitou, Henan.

of 8 cm to 6.2 cm wide. The widest part is at the top, with a slightly tapering long body that narrows to a handle with a stepped outline forming small horizontal dentils and a round haft. Both sides of the *zhang* were completely ground into flat planes. One side has well-preserved evidence of scars signifying surface grinding (Figures 10 and 11). The direction of grinding is longitudinal, as revealed in several crude linear marks that have not been ground to a refined smooth surface, especially on one side of the blade. A second group of processing scars are worked from the edge of the teeth to the middle of the

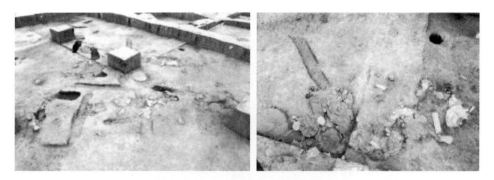

FIGURE 9   Unearthed stone *zhang* from Jinsha remains (left) and close-up detail (right).

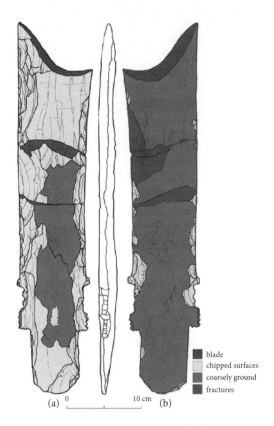

blade
chipped surfaces
coarsely ground
fractures

(a)   0 — 10 cm   (b)

FIGURE 10   Stone *zhang*, C261, Jinsha C261.

zhang blade. Based on the gouged and worked surfaces from edge to face, the edges appear to have been worked to a thinner surface than the handle proper. The thickest part of the entire blade is the serrated portion of the handle. Striking points of flaking are easily visible, as are points of grinding. Serrations are similar in size, about 6.8 cm, which after being roughly ground were refined by additional tooling. Yet, since the technical production of C261 stone *zhang* is still quite crude and the faces and shape of the *zhang*

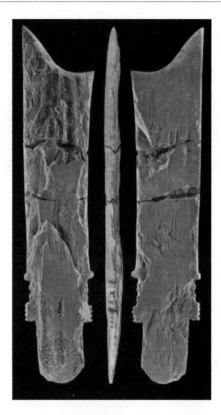

FIGURE 11 Drawing showing abrasion and flaking marks of stone *zhang* side view, Jinsha.

body are only roughly worked through grinding, this stone probably is a semi-finished product. Technically, steps taken may be summarized as follows: before determining the body thickness appropriate for working the stone it was necessary to complete the design of serrations. After this stage, the craftsperson roughly constructed both sides of the stone *zhang* and chiseled until the body of the *zhang* was reduced to a thin plane. Lastly, the blade tip was worked to a pointed edge, yet one side of the serrations remained only roughly worked. No horizontal incised lines or ridges were worked. The original stone appears to have originated from a large stone flake.

A second example, 2001CQJ No. C260, although with a damaged tip, measures about 50 cm long, with a residual thickness of 9 cm (Figures 12 and 13). The widest part of this blade is the serrated handle. The *zhang* body typically narrows and ends in a handle formed as two cross-like beams framing an aperture of small pairs of serrations. Sides A and B were separately worked. The surface of side A is incomplete, whereas that of side B is meticulously executed. Working of sides A and B evidently involved different steps of the process. As with example No. 261, this stone exhibits several phases of working. Initially the stone slab was worked into a flat rectangular surface with tip, body, and serrated handle area. The preliminary stage of chiseling the surface is represented by cracked and ruptured areas, particularly on side A. Serrated dentils matching horizontal

blade
chipped surfaces
coarsely ground
polished facets
fractures

(a)   0   10 cm   (b)

FIGURE 12 C260 stone *zhang*, Jinsha.

lines characterize only one side, side B, indicating that one side received more processing than the other and evidently was groomed to represent the front. The serrated handle section appears to be worked directly on the grinding stone. Other processing scars on side A show free-hand flaking where the thickness of the blade was adjusted. The tip was worked to a thin edge by grinding primarily side A. It is estimated that while working the tip to an even surface, edge of the tip broke off.

As witnessed on side B, the ground surface is meticulously worked, and although not all surfaces are evenly milled, the direction of grinding is uniformly longitudinal. It is evident, thus, that A and B surfaces of *zhang* were worked at different stages, one side before the other and one side before the serrated handle was finalized (see Figure 14). It is also evident that incised lines were horizontally worked on the handle after finely working side B. The incised lines form six different groups of two and in one case three lines, all extremely light, measuring under 0.5 mm in width.

Another, third stone *zhang*, 2001CQJ No. C258, is broken at the upper and lower ends and has several fissures and scars on its surface. Although the blade was initially ground, many roughly worked horizontal scars and several raw unworked surfaces still appear on the surface of side A. The last area to be worked was evidently the tip of the blade. The area below the handle serrations retains the original rough surface of the stone, with, as exposed on the right, a number of chipped areas still visible (Figure 15, 3rd row on the

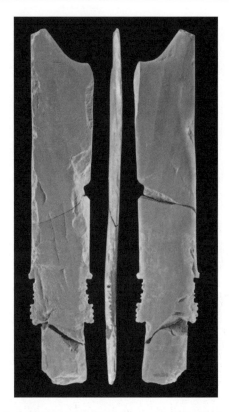

FIGURE 13 Side views of C160 stone *zhang*, Jinsha, showing the blade, chipped surfaces, coarse grinding, and fractures.

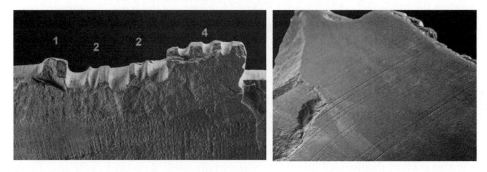

FIGURE 14 Jinsha Ruins C260 *Yazhang*: *Feiya* (serrations) (upper) on side A, and inner lines between the opposing serrations (lower) on side B.

left). On the latter blade the shank clearly narrows, yet the *feiya* have not been completely ground. Although the handle remains coarse on side B, this side of the blade is otherwise refined and polished and the grinding direction is longitudinal. The crack on side A, visible at the tip, is not completely polished. Seven groups of horizontally incised lines transverse the serrated section of the handle, divided into four groups of three horizontal lines

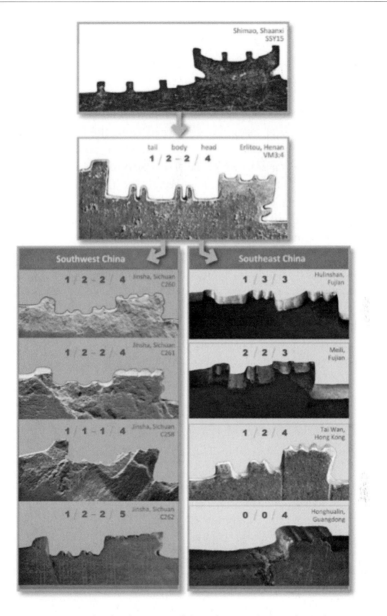

FIGURE 15 The development of the Erlitou VM3:4 *yazhang feiya*.

and three groups of two horizontal-line combinations. The serrations were roughly ground after creating what is another semi-finished blank.

Stone *zhang* 2001CQJ No. C267 is broken into three parts, with the bottom and tip missing. After refining the grinding of side A, the point and edge of the blade tip were worked and side B was ground into a refined surface. Again, the direction of the grinding moves longitudinally. The serrations remain incomplete, although transverse incised straight lines are still visible, with 3-1-2 combinations, and another of unclear combination.

Although the tip is partially broken, cracks appear on the front left side and grinding remains incomplete, indicating again a semi-finished blank. Raised ridges of the serrated handle are missing, yet the two pairs of teeth and horizontal top and bottom parts remain.

The *yazhang* C262, measuring 52 cm long, 10.63 cm wide, and 1.6 cm thick, is on exhibit at the Jinsha Museum (Figure 15. 5th row on left side). It has been published and is considered one of the best examples unearthed from the sacrificial pits at Jinsha. Although side A remains coarse, the surface of side B is exquisitely ground and only slightly uneven. The body part is composed of two pairs of double teeth and is framed by an upper serration and a bottom section of serrations. The two inner teeth have three and two incised combinations of straight lines. Three horizontal-line combinations are framed as three groups, and two horizontal-line combinations include five groups, comprising altogether eight groups of dentils.

Yazhang blade C263, with similar measurements to C262 (53.8 cm long, 11.06 cm wide, and 1.44 cm thick), is also on exhibit. The display shows that after the A side of the blade was ground flat, the craftsperson began working the right edge with particular refinement, especially in the area of the serrated portion of the handle. On the left side of the serrated portion long marks and strips of grinding are visible. Two groups of paired teeth were created, after which the tail end was formed.

Based on on-sight analyses of the Jinsha stone blades, the steps in the production of stone *yazhang* at Jinsha may be understood as follows:

(1) The initial preparation of preforms of the *yazhang*. Through bifacial retouching large stone flakes are created into rectangular preforms.

(2) Formation of *yazhang* blanks. Chipping and polishing techniques are used to process the preforms into blanks.

(3) Production of serrations. Stick-shaped polishing sandstones appear to have been then used to form the serrations and end of the blade.

(4) Coarse to fine sanding equipment is then used sequentially to polish the surfaces of the *yazhang* blanks.

(5) The thin edge of the tip of the mouth and the incised lines on the handle surfaces of the *yazhang* are subsequently formed.

DISSEMINATION OF THE ERLITOU VM3:4 *YAZHANG*

Erlitou is the core culture of the earliest advanced civilization in East Asia, and one with a strong impact and influence on surrounding and long-distance regional cultures. The proliferation of the Erlitou culture may be regarded as the integration of multiple settlements and movements into one Huaxia state, or the embryonic form of an empire.

By analyzing Erlitou cultural characteristics and their dissemination, the spread of the ritualized politics associated with the *yazhang* may be identified. Based on a case study of the typological and technical characteristics of the Erlitou VM3:4 *yazhang*, we illustrate not only the spread of the Erlitou *yazhang* culture to the south but identify its specific properties. Xu Hong noted that "by the Erlitou era, jade *zhang* spread from the Central Plains region to the upper reaches of the Yangtze River, and even as far as Lingnan" (2009).

In order to the illustrate the history of the early Chinese political state system and the proliferation of the archetype represented by Erlitou VM3:4 *yazhang* over different periods, the following points need to be considered: Firstly, how do we identify "fingerprint characteristics" of the Erlitou *yazhang* VM3:4 and the process of transmission. Secondly, what is the relationship between the Yellow River Valley Longshan cultural stage and the spread of the Erlitou VM3:4 *yazhang*. Thirdly, what are the means of transmission and acceptance of the Erlitou VM3:4 *yazhang* model in the south China region. We initially review the characteristics of the Erlitou *yazhang* VM3:4 and compare these with Shaanxi, Shangdong Longshan, and Xinzhai culture *yazhang* in Henan. Following, we identify how the Jinsha stone *zhang* relate to the spread of the Erlitou VM3:4 *yazhang* in the Sichuan Basin. Finally, we examine the stone *yazhang* from the southeast areas of Fujian, Guangdong, and Hong Kong in documenting the spread of the *yazhang* type of Erlitou VM3:4. Although the four *yazhang* excavated from Erlitou P3–4 have slightly different forms, they belong to the standard *yazhang* type represented by *yazhang* Erlitou V3:4.

The characteristics of the Erlitou VM3:4 *yazhang* are summarized as follows: (1) Erlitou *yazhang* are large in size, as represented by the VM3:4 *yazhang* measuring over 54 cm long, whereas those from earlier Longshan and Xinzhai cultures are shorter, approximately 20–30 cm long. The larger scale of Erlitou period examples signifies a change, yet it becomes a standard feature of the Erlitou type. (2) The eccentric outline of the blade and the detailed carvings exhibit a new sophisticated expression of refinement beyond the Longshan *zhang* type. (3) The upper part of the *yazhang* is typically the widest part of the blade, and the narrowest part is the handle, with two-sided serrations and multiple fine line décor, unlike the Shandong Longshan type. (4) The serrations of the handle typically vary from one longer projection at the top and four dentils of two pairs at the middle, to four to five dentils at the top, totaling altogether nine dentils on the Erlitou VM3:4 type, as opposed to the type of Longshan date.

Although the East Asian prehistoric *yazhang* of Longshan date evolves from a smaller to larger size of Erlitou date, the most distinctive stylistic change occurs in the morphology of the *feiya*. The standard variation of serrations of the archetypal Erlitou V3:4 *yazhang* from 4 to 2 and 2 to 1 serves as a "fingerprint" for this specialized insignia blade. Thus far, the *yazhang* from Shandong dating to the Longshan period are the earliest known type of this insignia form. Interestingly, Erlitou-period influence is not apparent in any post-Longshan-period site in Shandong. In analyzing the *yazhang* from Shandong with Shandong University, archaeologists identified certain differences in terms of toothed décor (Tang et al. 2014). For example, *yazhang* recovered from Luoquanyu village ruins, YL:12, have primarily two *feiya*-style serrations, larger at the bottom than at the top in line with that of the Erlitou V3:4 *yazhang*. The style of the tips, blade shape, and handle extension of another *yazhang* from the same site of Luoquanyu, YL:11, and others from Tafanzhuang, L:211, and Simatai are, in turn, similar in having top and bottom dentils but no inner-handle smaller dentils.

Two additional *yazhang*, one complete, one broken but with preserved handle and serrations, from the Central Plains and earlier in date than the Erlitou examples, have been discovered in Huadizui, Henan (Gu and Zhang 2007). The example from Huadizui, T17H40:1, is 30 cm long with stylistic characteristics of the Shandong type, carrying an opposing pair of protrusions (one dentil type each side) that stick out and slope downward, in distinction from those at Erlitou and Jinsha.

The recent excavation of the large-scale Longshan to the Erlitou-period site of Shimao in Shaanxi has attracted much discussion and attention. Over 20 jades have been discovered, and two have been securely dated to the Late Longshan through Erlitou periods (Liu and Liu 2014). The latter and Erlitou *yazhang* are directly related typologically. In 1975 Dai Yingxin collected over 35 jade *yazhang* from other Shimao areas in Shaanxi. Amid these, four had the characteristic handle serrations in separate groups and linear horizontal incisions of the Erlitou archetype. One, SSY15, is described as like the forehead of a water buffalo with two outward-turning curling horns, at the center of which protrude two small ears. The latter jade, decorated with three separate sets of small dentil teeth, measuring 30.6 cm long by 9.3 cm wide and 0.4 cm thick (Dai 1994), is closely comparable to the Erlitou V3:4 *yazhang*. The handles of the *yazhang* SSY16, 17, and 18 from Shimao also have "teeth." Differences nonetheless exist between the Shimao and Erlitou examples. The serrations of the Shimao *yazhang* in some cases curve upward, as if in simulation of the Erlitou type. The two serrations located inside the indented part of the handle are, furthermore, not paired and protrude as individual verticals, unlike the Erlitou model.

Most of the *yazhang* from Shimao average 30 cm in length, in contrast with the more than 50-cm-long *yazhang* from Erlitou VM3:4. The authors suggest that the Erlitou VM3:4 *yazhang* is probably influenced by the *yazhang* from Shimao. The influence of the Erlitou VM3:4 *yazhang* is omnipresent in south China, as represented by examples in the Sichuan Basin and in the southeast coastal areas of Fujian and Guangdong, and is probably the prototype for the Shimao versions. The Erlitou VM3:4 *yazhang* predates the examples from the south and is certainly the prototype for Sanxingdui and Jinsha versions. Nonetheless, the specific process of how Erlitou impacted the Sichuan Basin is not yet clear. It is also unclear why there are so many *zhang* at Jinsha and not Sanxingdui. Some scholarly circles date the used stone *yazhang* of Jinsha to Yinxu Periods 1–2 and maintain they belong to the state (方国) of Sanxingdui. According to Zhang Qing (2006) the large-scale remains at Jinsha site in which jade *yazhang* were used primarily date to Yinxu Periods 3–4 and early Western Zhou. By that time the state of Sanxingdui had weakened and disappeared. Thus, it is possible that Jinsha replaced Sanxingdui and adopted the ritual use of jade *yazhang* (2006).

As pointed out by Zhang Qing,

> Part of the remains of *zhang* from Jinsha consisted of remnants from the manufac-
> turing process and the other included those unearthed primarily from Pit No. 3. The
> former consisted of stone *bi*, half worked stone *zhang* and stone buttons. The mound
> was 19 m long west to east, 14 m wide and covered an area of 300 m². The majority
> of stones worked formed only the body of the *zhang* blade, and some carried han-
> dles. Most were found next to stone *bi* disks or under the latter, without any particu-
> lar order.... [C]onsidering the context of the sacrificial area and collected stone
> *zhang* it is probable that these remains date to early Shang and Yinxu Period 1.
>
> (Zhu et al. 2004; Wang 2014)

The large number of stone *zhang* from Jinsha date to the first phase of settlement, but
whether or not these finds may be dated to Yinxu P1 or even earlier remains for future
research. Many of the over 60 stone *zhang* have not yet been published. Yet whether
these represent the whole 60 or more *zhang* typologically and stylistically remains for
later analysis. Analysis here of six *zhang* shows stylistic consistency, and we suspect
they date to the same time period. The characteristics of these six correspond surprisingly close in type to the prototype of Erlitou VM3:4 *yazhang*. The question persists:
are the working techniques of Erlitou and Jinsha comparable? Presently the resolution
of this issue remains in limbo. Since little is known about the production process of
the Erlitou *yazhang*, comparison may be made only from the point of view of style and
typology.

As illustrated, Erlitou VM3:4 and the six Jinsha *zhang* are similar in shape, style, and
décor. And, although the Erlitou *zhang* was excavated from a tomb and the Jinsha examples came from a sacrificial pit, the examples are generally similarly worked. The Erlitou
zhang exhibits superiority in the meticulous detail of dentils and incisions and thus
stands out by contrast with the cruder Jinsha examples. The Jinsha stone examples are
largely not worked to a smooth plane and the linear markings appear on only one side.
One side is polished and the other left rough. Gouged areas also remain on the Jinsha
examples. These phenomena probably reflect the social and cultural background of
Jinsha rather than the high or low quality of working the stone (Figure 15). The major
differences between the cruder Jinsha examples and the Erlitou archetype are listed as
follows:

(1) *Large scale*: Both the Erlitou VM3:4 jade *zhang* and the six Jinsha stone *zhang* are
    approximately 50 cm long, thus the six approximate the size of Erlitou *yazhang*.
(2) *Yazhang shape*: The three-part shape with blade body, *feiya*, and handle and
    thinning profile of the Jinsha *zhang* approximate in shape that of Erlitou VM3:4.
    The widest portion continues to be at the tip of all blades, in approximating that
    of Erlitou. The Jinsha examples appear relatively advanced in taking on the
    eccentric shape of the Erlitou example.
(3) *Surface décor of incised shallow lines*: Sawed serrations of the handle typify both
    the Erlitou VM3:4 *yazhang* and Jinsha *zhang* C260, C262, C258, and C267. The

creation of these 1-mm-wide shallow lines was most likely executed with a very fine stone saw, although this is barely visible.

(4) *Grouping of incised shallow lines in horizontal groups:* Three or two horizontal lines per group and four to eight different groups characterize the Erlitou VM3:4 *yazhang* and Jinsha *zhang* C260, C262, C258, and C267.

(5) *Feiya design:* A three-part composition characterizes the Erlitou VM3:4 *yazhang* and Jinsha *yazhang* C260, C262, C258, and C267. The design of Erlitou VM3:4 and that of C260 and C261 are particularly similar. The latter also have comparable proportions of 4, 2–2, and 1, comprising 9 protruding teeth. C258 has a balance of 4/11/1 and C252 has a balance of 5/2–2/1.

The Erlitou VM3:4 *yazhang* is dated to Erlitou P3 and is clearly the model for C260 and C261 *yazhang* at Jinsha. Erlitou P4 is represented by Erlitou VIIM7:5 and Wangjinglou and Daluchencun *yazhang*. It is also apparent that the *yazhang* from Yueliangwang Sanxingdui date later than the stone *yazhang* from Jinsha. Examples of the latter type of *yazhang* in turn scarely appear in Southeast Asia's Vietnam. We recognize that the stone material of *yazhang* from Jinsha currently represents the earliest type known in the Chengdu Basin. Thus, whether these date to the early Shang or even earlier must await more field data.

The dissemination of the Erlitou VM3:4 *yazhang* type further afield to Fujian, Guangdong, and Hong Kong may be identified by several examples. In 2001 stone *yazhang* were unearthed from two tombs, M13 and M19 in Hulinshan in Zhangzhou, Fujian province. The former *yazhang* measured 51.4 cm long, 13.8 cm wide, and 1.5 cm thick and corresponds well in size with the Erlitou examples from VM3:4 (Chen and Yang 2003). The difference from the Erlitou-type *yazhang* is in the proportion of 3/3/1 of the *feiya* serrated handle section and in the simplification of the handle butt. Another *yazhang*, from Meli in Fujian, has serration proportions of 3/2/2.

In 1990 we excavated a *yazhang*, although small, from the Tai Wan site of Lamma Island in Hong Kong. It measured 21.8 cm long and 4.6 cm wide (Tang 1994). The type has the familiar *feiya*, with two areas of small dentils. Proportions of the serrations are 4/2/1 and 3/2/1. A shallow diamond-shaped pattern is incised on the handle. The small-scale *yazhang* from Guangdong collected at the Honghualin site measured 21 cm long and 6 cm wide. The proportions measure 4/0/0 (Hong Kong Museum 2014).

From these analyses it is evident that the Erlitou VM3:4 *yazhang* had a significant impact on cultural settlements well beyond its borders. The influence on southwestern Jinsha was direct, whereas the influence on southern Fujian and Guangdong appears indirect due to differences in scale and numbers of dentils and the shape of handles.

Our conclusions may be summarized as follows: (1) Erlitou site constitutes the earliest "royal capital of China," with a mature royal ritual system and the earliest state model. (2) Over the past half century research on the relationship of Xia and Shang *yazhang* and their development has had tremendous results, particularly with regard to dating and typological categorization. Here, however, the analysis is different in focusing on the detailed attributes of one major *yazhang* and its interpretation elsewhere in the East

Asian Heartland. We distinguish particular features of the *yazhang* and maintain that the blade probably had a specific function. (3) This case study of the Erlitou VM3:4 *yazhang* characteristics shows that it served as the prototype for the evolution of this blade in the rest of East Asia, and in turn defined a macrozone area of the royal political system over some thousands of kilometers. This symbolic blade served as a symbol of a new political culture and of leadership over the macrozone. (4) Through comparisons of the Erlitou V3:4 jade *yazhang* and Jinsha stone *yazhang*, the Jinsha stone *yazhang* imitate the Erlitou V3:4 prototype, reflecting the political influence of Xia-Shang Central China on regional political entities. (5) The duplication of the Erlitou serrated jade *yazhang* in southern China may be regarded as a reflection of a primary state's influence on a secondary state. Political systems are necessary for the development of nation states, yet the emergence of nation states is not inevitable. The *yazhang* is thus an early material symbol of the formation of state politics in East Asia.

EARLY PERIOD GOVERNANCE AND THE *YAZHANG*

The spread and expansion of the Erlitou influences occurred well south of the Yellow River Valley, including the Yangzi River Valley, and even into the north region of Vietnam. The Erlitou site probably belonged to the capital of the late phase of the Xia dynasty, and the archaeological finds from this site are sufficient evidence for identification a royal state dynasty tradition. Thus, instead of seeking written evidence only, one seeks material evidence to provide clues to the existence of the Xia dynasty…, as initially proposed by Childs-Johnson in 1995.

ACKNOWLEDGMENTS

The author Tang is indebted to Wang Wei, Gong Wen, Xu Hong, Du Jinpeng, Zhu Naicheng, and Zhao Haitao of the Institute of Archaeology of the Chinese Academy of Social Sciences for the opportunity to analyze Erlitou and related materials; to Wang Yi, Jiang Zhanghua, Zhu Zhangyi, and Zhang Qing of the Sichuan Archaeology Museum, Sichuan Archaeology Relics Research Institute and Jinsha Site Museum for the opportunity to study Jinsha and related materials; and to Chen Zhaoshan of Fujian Museum of Cultural Relics and Archaeology for the opportunity to study Fujian excavated data. He deeply appreciates their considerate advice and assistance and owes them heartfelt appreciation and thanks.

This chapter is revised from the essay in the *Journal of the National Museum of China* (*Zhongguo Guojia Bowuguan Guankan*) in 2015, volume 5, issue 142. Translated by Elizabeth Childs-Johnson.

Bibliography

Chen, Zhaoshan, and Lihua Yang 陈兆善、杨丽华主编, eds. 2003. *Hulinshan Site Remains: One of Fujian's Zhangzhou Shang Zhou Excavation Reports* 虎林山遗址——福建漳州商周遗址发掘报告之一. Haichao sheying yishu chubanshe.

Childs-Johnson, Elizabeth 1995. "Symbolic Jades of the Erlitou Period: A Xia Royal Tradition." *Archives of Asian Art* 48:64–90.

Childs-Johnson, Elizabeth 2010. "An Introduction to the Spectacular Jades Discovered in Sichuan Province, China." In *Shang and Western Zhou Jades.* 9–22. New York: Throckmorton Fine Art.

Childs-Johnson, Elizabeth, with Fang Gu 2009. *The Jade Age and Early Chinese Jades in American Museums* (Chinese and English). Beijing: Kexue chubanshe.

Dai, Yingxin 戴应新 1994. "Shimao *Yazhang* and Recarving: Notes on Research on the Shimao Longshan Culture Jades 石峁牙璋及其改作——石峁龙山 文化玉器研究札记." In *Ancient Cultures of South China and Neighbouring Regions* 南中国及邻近地区古 文化研究. Edited by Tang Chung, 79–86. Hong Kong: Chinese University Press.

Fukuyama, Francis 弗朗西斯·福山 (毛俊 杰译) 2011. *The Origins of Political Order: From Prehuman Times to the French Revolution* 政治秩序的起源——从前人类时代 到法国大革命. Farrar, Straus and Giroux (干 西师 范大学出版社).

Gu, Wanfa 顾万发, and Songlin Zhang 张松林 2007. "Analysis of the Black Jade *Yazhang* from Huadizui 论花地嘴遗址所出墨玉璋." *Shangdu Wenming* 4.

Hidenori, Okamura 冈村秀典 2012. *China's Oldest Royal Ritual: The Evolution of Xia Shang Civilization* 中国最古の宫廷仪礼をする. Kodansha 講談社.

Li, Xueqin 李学勤 1994. "On the *Yazhang* Jade and Its Cultural Background 试论牙璋及其文化背景》." In *Research on the Cultural History of South China and Neighboring Areas* 南中国及邻近地区古 文化研究. Edited by Tang Chung, 5–7. Hong Kong: Chinese University of Hong Kong Publication Society.

Liu, Xiubing 刘修兵, and Liyu Liu 刘黎雨 2014. "Shimao Site: Searching for the Origins of Chinese Civilization 石峁遗址 :探寻中华文 明起源的窗口." *Zhongguo wenwubao*, July 15, 2014.

Tang, Chung 邓聪 1994. "Preliminary Report on the Shang *Yazhang* Unearthed at the Tai Wan Site, Hong Kong 香港大湾出土商代牙璋串饰初论." *Wenwu* 12:54–63.

Tang, Chung [Deng Cong] 2017. "*Yazhang* and an Incipient Stage of the Political World Order of Early China." In *Xu Gu Heng Jin: 110th Anniversary of the Birth of Professor Cheng Te-k'un.* 30–33. Centre for Chinese Archaeology and Art, CUHK.

Tang, Chung 邓聪, Fengshi Luan 栾丰实, and Qiang Wang 王强 2014. "Early *Yazhang* in East Asia: Discussion of Shandong Longshan Type *Yazhangs* 东亚最早的牙璋——山东龙山式牙璋初论." In *Jades in the East, Yu Run Dong Fang* 玉润东方. Edited by Yang Bo杨波, 51–62. Beijing: Wenwu chubanshe.

Tang, Chung, Hong Xu, and Jinpeng Du 邓聪、许宏、杜金鹏 2007. "Analysis of Jade-Working and Related Questions of the Erlitou Culture 二里头文化玉工艺相 关问题试释." *Keji Kaogu* 2:120–132.

Tōru, Ootsu 大津透 2013. "Foreword はしめに." In *Japanese History*, vol. 1: *Prehistory and Ancient Times* 日本歷史.第 1 卷·原始·古代1. Iwanami岩波书店.

Wang Fang 王方 2014. "Analysis of the Stone-Working Craft of the Ancient Shu Culture in the Chengdu Plain 试 论成都平原古蜀文化时期的石器制作技术." In *Collected Papers of the International Conference on the Civilization of the Xia Shang Zhou States.* in press.

Wang, Fang 王方, and Qing Zhang 张擎 2004. "Brief Report on Period 1 Excavations at 'Meiyuan' Area 1 at Chengdu's Jinsha Site 成都金沙遗址I区"梅苑"一期发掘简报." *Wenwu* 4:4–65.

Xianggang Lishi Bowuguan (Hong Kong History Museum) 香港历史博物馆 (香港历史博物馆专题展览), ed. 2014. *Collected Essays of the International Conference on Historical Imprints of Lingnan: Major Archaeological Discoveries of Guangdong, Hong Kong and Macao* 岭南印記:粤港澳考古成果展. Leisure and Cultural Services Department, HKSAR.

Xu, Hong 许宏 2009. *Early China* 最早的中国. Beijing: Kexue chubanshe.

Yang, Guozhong 杨国忠、, and Zhongfu Liu 刘忠伏 1983. "Preliminary Report on Excavation during the Fall of 1980 at the Erlitou Site, Yanshi, Henan 1980 年秋河南偃师二里头遗址发掘简报." *Kaogu* 3:199–205.

Zhang, Qing 张擎 2006. "Preliminary Study of the *Yazhang* at the Jinsha Site 金沙遗址出土牙璋的初步研究." In *Zhongguo yuwenhua Yuxue Luncong* 中国玉文化玉学论丛. Edited by Yang Boda 杨伯达, 516–519. Beijing: Zijincheng chubanshe.

Zheng, Guang 郑光 1994. "Analysis of the *Yazhang* 略论牙璋." In *Ancient Cultures of South China and Neighbouring Regions* 南中国及邻近地区古文化研究. Edited by Tang Chung, 9–17. Hong Kong: Chinese University Press.

THE FIRST HEIGHT OF THE BRONZE AGE: THE SHANG PERIOD

CHAPTER 11

....

THE CULTURAL AND HISTORICAL SETTING OF THE SHANG

....

BY JONATHAN SMITH, CHRISTOPHER NEWPORT UNIVERSITY, WITH YUZHOU FAN, NANJING UNIVERSITY

TRADITIONAL Chinese historiography, oriented as it is in terms of the received textual record, has long regarded the mid-to-late second millennium BCE Shang 商 dynasty as the second of China's great hereditary monarchies. Evidence for the putative first—the Xia 夏—has remained limited to written accounts of the much later Warring States (475–221 BCE) and early imperial periods. By contrast, the historical reality of Shang was conclusively and spectacularly demonstrated by archaeological evidence unearthed beginning around the turn of the twentieth century in and around the village of Xiaotun 小屯, Anyang, in northern China's Henan province. Decisive among this material has been a large body of written inscriptions on some 130,000 pieces of bone and turtle shell, products of an elaborate pyro-osteomantic tradition. These so-called oracle bone inscriptions (OBI) bear direct witness to the reigns of nine named kings whom the later textual record holds to have been the final rulers of Shang. By consolidation of these parallel indications, the lifetime of the Xiaotun site has come to be called "Late Shang." This era, spanning something less than two centuries near the close of the second millennium BCE, is now represented by a number of related archaeological sites of the middle and lower Yellow River Valley regions and further afield. However, the Anyang type site in particular, and the inscriptions there uncovered, have become key foci for historians of the Shang period. This is in part because the evidence from Anyang constitutes a relatively secure piece of our still dim and unsettled picture of the formative period of Chinese civilization.

PRE-ANYANG SHANG

How early and middle second millennium BCE sites of the same general region might by extension be keyed to the earlier period of Shang hegemony to which texts attest, or even to Xia, is a much contended question. Associations of this kind are sought because, to many scholars, it is only natural to consider archaeological discoveries through the lens afforded by the received tradition. That is, these two bodies of evidence—excavated artifacts and later written histories—are presumed to offer generally complementary views onto a single historical reality. Among the earliest of the sites felt to demand such historiographical resolution is Erlitou 二里頭, near Luoyang in central Henan, marking the beginning in earnest of the Chinese Bronze Age. With its associated archaeological horizon extending across the North China Plain, much or all of the Erlitou period (ca. 1900–1500 BCE) has by many authors been tentatively associated with Xia. Also debated are the great walled cities at Yanshi 偃師, close to and largely postdating Erlitou, and slightly later at Zhengzhou 鄭州 as well as closely related Panlongcheng 盤龍城 to the south.[1] Might any of these have been pre-Anyang Shang "capitals"?

But the question of how, or whether, to seek to reconcile an archaeological view with the written tradition is a messy one (see Brown 2011; and chapter 7 on Erlitou in this volume, by Hong Xu). To consider an obvious example, the name scholars have bestowed upon the Anyang site itself, Yinxu 殷墟 ("Yin Ruins"), reflects a somewhat uncertain text-driven assumption regarding the site's nature. This designation derives from classical-era anecdotes describing Shang king Pan Geng's 盤庚 relocation of his capital to a city Yin 殷, with slightly different accounts found in, for instance, the *Records of the Historian* (*Shi ji* 史記) and the *Bamboo Annals* (*Zhushu jinian* 竹書紀年). However, the inscriptions themselves seem to name the area "Da yi Shang" 大邑商 ("great settlement Shang"), and suggest also that occupation of the Xiaotun site began only somewhat later with the king Wu Ding 武丁. It is certainly possible that these discrepancies will be resolved by the recovery of Pan Geng–era inscriptional evidence at the more recently discovered and only briefly occupied Huanbei 洹北 site, immediately predating and lying just to the north of Xiaotun. Still, the most skeptical view would reject even the name "Late Shang" for this era in favor of a purely archaeological term such as "Anyang

---

[1] To some researchers, Yanshi has represented "Early Shang" (in particular, the first capital at Xibo 西亳, named in early texts), with Zhengzhou marking a middle period. Now, more commonly, "Early Shang" is used to refer to the whole of the expansive Erligang 二里崗 archaeological culture (ca. 1600–1400 BCE), including Yanshi, Zhengzhou, Panlongcheng, and others, with later (ca. 1400–1250) sites, including Xiaoshuangqiao 小雙橋 near Zhengzhou, representative of a so-called "Middle Shang" (see Liu and Chen 2012:278–294). Due to material and archaeological finds, Huanbei 洹北 (just north of the Xiaotun site) is frequently associated with an initial settlement of the area under "Late Shang" kings Pan Geng, Xiao Xin, and Xiao Yi; see, for example, He 2006.

period." After all, while there are clear continuities in terms of material culture, no earlier site can yet be concretely linked to a Shang polity by written evidence.[2]

Nevertheless, given the desire to develop systematic early chronologies, combined with clear points of agreement between received and inscriptional evidence, interest in classical-era reflections of formative periods remains strong. For the very earliest years of Shang—even prior to a storied conquest of Xia—many scholars have focused upon the traditional list of leaders or rulers provided within the "Annals of Yin" ("Yin benji" 殷本紀) chapter of the *Records*, adjusting this sequence in light of partially corresponding information from the OBI to produce a tentative genealogy of 14 "pre-dynastic" kings. Such a sequence proceeds from a semi-legendary founder, Xie 偰, of the received texts, to incorporate in its later portions the earliest kings of the inscriptionally-attested sacrificial roster (see Figure 1 Kings 1–6)—that is, putative ancestors belonging to an epoch far more ancient than Anyang "Late Shang" itself.[3]

"Dynastic" Shang, classical texts report, began with the overthrow of Xia and its tyrannical final ruler, Jie 桀, by the virtuous Shang king Tang 湯. The same figure, it is held, is Da Yi 大乙 of the inscriptions, where he stands as successor to Shi Gui. By a similar procedure to the above but now arguably on surer footing, this period, considered to have lasted some 500 years from the founding of the dynasty through its conquest at the hands of neighboring Zhou 周, is often presented in terms of 29 kings beginning with Da Yi ~ Tang and terminating with Di Xin 帝辛, i.e., Zhou 紂 ~ Shou 受 of the texts (Figure 1 Kings 7–35).[4] Via attention to fluctuation between direct and collateral descent, as indicated by received descriptions, scholars have generated detailed reconstructions of the Shang kingly succession like that shown in Figure 1.[5] Evidence is naturally strongest for the Yinxu period proper, with inclusion of the Huanbei site giving a slightly longer "Anyang period".

[2] A very small number of inscribed bones resembling those of Anyang have been recovered from other sites, including four apparently of late Shang date from Zhengzhou. This evidence is reviewed in Takashima 2011.

[3] These 14 "kings" are Xie 偰, Zhao Ming 昭明, Xiang Tu 相土, Chang Ruo 昌若, Cao Yu 曹圉, Ming 冥, Wang Hai 王亥, Wang Heng 王恒, Shang Jia 上甲, Bao Yi 報乙, Bao Bing 報丙, Bao Ding 報丁, Shi Ren 示壬, and Shi Gui 示癸. Beginning with Shang Jia, regarded as the first inscriptionally attested king, discrepancies in name (some minor, some more substantial) are dealt with via co-definition: the "Annals of Yin" king Zhen 振 is identified with inscriptional Wang Hai; Wei 微 with Shang Jia, etc.

[4] Di Xin 帝辛 is the posthumous title, or "temple name," of the final Shang king; his birth name is given in the "Annals of Yin" as Zhou 紂, apparently a corruption (?) of the ancient script rendering of the character *shòu* 受. The latter form of the name is found, for instance, in the *Book of Documents* (*Shang shu* 尚書).

[5] Figure 1 shows Shang kings by posthumous title with ascension order and reconstruction of direct vs. collateral descent following A. Smith 2010:4 who in turn relies on Chang 1987:134. Regarding both inheritance patterns and specific names and written characters, received and inscriptional indications are at odds in numerous details; cf. also Keightley 1978:185–187, Loewe and Shaughnessy 1999:234–235; and Li 2013:55. Here, G# = Generation number; indents break generations and show sons inside fathers, with bolded King (i.e., succession order) numbers marking eldest brothers. Cognomens, always preceding Heavenly Stem name, are translated at first appearance where meanings seem transparent.

G# King# and title			(continued from left; King 18 = son of 15)	
(Beginning of succession suggested by OBI sacrificial roster)				
1	1 Shang (Higher) Jia 上甲		13	18 Zu (Ancestor) Yi 祖乙
2	2 Bao Yi 報乙		14	20 Qiang Jia 羌甲
3	3 Bao Bing 報丙		15	22 Nan Geng 南庚
4	4 Bao Ding 報丁		14	19 Zu Xin 祖辛
5	5 Shi Ren 示壬		15	21 Zu Ding 祖丁
6	6 Shi Gui 示癸		16	23 Yang Jia 陽甲
(Proposed beginning of "Dynastic" Shang)			(Proposed beginning of "Anyang period")	
7	7 Da (Greater) Yi 大乙			24 Pan Geng 盤庚
8	10 Wai (Outer) Bing 外丙			25 Xiao Xin 小辛
	8 Da Ding 大丁			26 Xiao Yi 小乙
9	9 Da Jia 大甲		(Beginning of Yinxu /Xiaotun period proper)	
10	11 Da Geng 大庚		17	27 Wu (Martial) Ding 武丁
11	12 Xiao (Minor) Jia 小甲		18	28 Zu Ji 祖己
	14 Yong Ji 雍己			29 Zu Geng 祖庚
	13 Da Wu 大戊			30 Zu Jia 祖甲
12	16 Wai Ren 外壬		19	31 Kang Ding 康丁
	17 Jian Jia 戔甲		20	32 Wu Yi 武乙
	15 Zhong (Central) Ding 中丁		21	33 Wenwu (Cultured-Martial) Ding 文武丁
(continued at right)			22	34 Di (Lord) Yi 帝乙
			23	35 Di Xin 帝辛

FIGURE 1 Shang kingly succession after A. Smith 2010:4.

In a parallel effort, as has been noted, Shang capital cities reflected in texts—the "Annals" claim five shifts to have occurred over the course of the dynastic period—are tentatively mapped to this or that early archaeological site. Indeed, there are interesting correspondences here to apparent irregularities in patterns of collateral descent (see Li 2013:103–104), and in general there is probably no good reason to reject such suggestions out of hand or to doubt that Tang ~ Da Yi and other "early dynastic" Shang kings were flesh-and-blood historical figures. Certainly, their status is more secure than that of the early pre-dynastic rulers named in the "Annals." At the same time, the notion of "dynastic" Shang, and more generally of a linear succession of powers—Xia, Shang, and Zhou—each taking its rightful turn at dominion over the Central Plains region, is now frequently seen as a historiographical construct beginning from the Zhou and later notion of strictly successive, heaven-conferred legitimacy (the passing of *tianming* 天命 "heaven's mandate"). While the timeline of the emergence of early states as told by the archaeological record corresponds in very general terms to received traditions regarding the so-called "Three Dynasties" (Li 2013:51–52), the history of Bronze Age China and of Shang in particular as told by that record naturally turns out to be far more complex than a straightforward genealogy of kings and kingdoms can allow.

THE ANYANG PERIOD

The Yinxu phase as such, lasting between 150 and 200 years, can be approached relatively directly, though still not as precisely as we would wish. The earliest universally accepted absolute date in Chinese history remains 841 BCE, from which begin the regular annual accounts of the *Records*. A key goal in the investigation of early periods has been to extend this absolute chronology back through the Western Zhou and into Shang, with numerous past studies seeking relevant evidence within the inscriptional record.[6] Such efforts have thus far failed to generate much consensus. At least, it is noteworthy that the final, momentous conquest of Shang by Zhou is now dated by most investigators to the mid-eleventh century BCE.[7] Indeed, a conquest date of 1046 BCE has been put forward first by David W. Pankenier, in a series of studies of astronomical phenomena as reflected in textual records and the relationship of such phenomena to dynastic change, and more recently by scholars working under the auspices of the Xia-Shang-Zhou Chronology Project (1996–2000) on the basis of a range of archaeological, astronomical, and textual evidence.[8] For the Anyang period, though, we must for now make do with the more general indications provided by contemporaneous archaeological evidence, key among this material being the oracle bone inscriptions.

THE ORACLE BONE INSCRIPTIONS

As we have seen, it is generally assumed by reference to received accounts that Xiaotun and environs, straddling the Huan 洹 River and covering an area of approximately 30 square kilometers, was the location of a Late Shang royal capital Yin. If Pan Geng's generation is included—for he is believed to have relocated the capital to the area—this ancient complex would have been home to eight royal generations and 12 kings, nine during the period of occupation of the Xiaotun site proper. Following the defeat of Shang by Zhou, and the Duke of Zhou's quelling of the Shang loyalist uprising remembered as the Rebellion of the Three Guards, the area seems to have been abandoned, again to become the focus of the world's attention only with the discovery of the oracle bone inscriptions—a breakthrough to usher in a fundamental shift in the study of early Chinese history. "Dragon bone" or *longgu* 龍骨, a substance associated in traditional *materia medica* with the treatment of a variety of medical complaints, is most typically the powder of fossilized vertebrate remains. In the final years of the Qing dynasty, curiously marked shell and bone fragments began to circulate among these materials at pharmaceutical markets in Beijing and nearby towns. In or around 1899, in a discovery

---

[6] This is a hotly debated topic celebrated by the study sponsored by the Xia-Shang-Zhou Chronology Project titled *Xia, Shang Zhou Gongcheng* 夏商周斷代工程, commissioned by the PRC in 1996 and heavily criticized by David Nivison, among others (see e.g., Nivison 2002).

[7] Proposals regarding the date of King Wu of Zhou's 周武王 conquest of Shang now number in the dozens and are too numerous to cite here. For a brief synopsis of the arguments see Li Feng 2008: 31–32.

[8] Pankenier (1981–1982, 1992a, 1992b, 1995) has focused largely on early accounts of planetary portents found within the *Bamboo Annals*, the *Yi Zhou shu* 逸周書, and the *Moil* 墨子. See also Xia-Shang-Zhou Chronology Project Group 2000.

that has since acquired the sheen of legend, the Qing official and scholar of bronze and stone inscriptions Wang Yirong 王懿榮 recognized these markings as an early form of Chinese writing.[9] It fell to associates of Wang, including scholar Luo Zhenyu 羅振玉, to trace the source of these fragments to Henan province and the village of Xiaotun, in the northwestern outskirts of the city of Anyang. Thanks to the efforts of Wang, Luo, and many others, these inscriptions were before long recognized as records of ritual queries to spirits and ancestors offered up some three millennia prior by the Shang royals. The painstaking excavation and organization of this vast collection of individual inscribed pieces means that research into all aspects of the Shang world now rests upon the foundation of contemporaneous written records.

Pyro-osteomancy using turtle shells is older than the Anyang period and geographically widespread. However, the term "oracle bone inscriptions" tends to refer specifically to the inscribed bones associated with Late Shang and unearthed at Xiaotun. The most significant finds date to the first scientific excavations of the site in the late 1920s and 1930s. Additional caches include some 5,000 inscribed bones recovered in 1973 at the southern periphery of the site (Xiaotun nandi 小屯南地), and an additional 1,500 or so that emerged east of the neighboring village of Huayuanzhuang 花園莊 in 1991, these last important in part for providing indications of divinatory practice outside direct royal purview. During the Anyang period, materials used for divination included a variety of animal bones, with bovine scapula and turtle shells employed frequently; bovine ribs and scapula of deer, sheep, and pigs are also in evidence.

In the preparation of turtle shells, it was necessary first to separate carapace from plastron along the bridge—the structure joining upper to lower shell—such that the flat portion of the bridge remained integrated with the plastron (see Figures 2–4). The outermost portion of the bridge was subsequently sawed away so as to leave a clean, slightly curved border. The carapace was typically split into roughly symmetrical halves along the spine. On occasion, the more extreme convex portions at the spinal edge and at the head and tail were also cut away, leaving a form resembling that of the sole of a shoe. Boring a hole through the center of such a piece left an element scholars term the "modified carapace (see Figures 5–7)."

Bovine scapulae were also processed prior to use (see Figures 8–10). Typically, between half and one-third of the longer face of the glenoid cavity (or socket) was cut away, leaving a crescent shape. Downward and outward cuts were then made at the socket end, leaving an approximately right-angled notch. This initial processing phase was completed with the grinding down of the scapular spine and of the protruding areas just beneath the socket, along with the smoothing of the entire bone face.

A series of round and elongated ovoid depressions, deepest at their centers and tapering upward, were dug or bored into the undersides of either plastron or scapula such that when heat was applied to the hollows during divination, cracks would appear

---

[9] Typically, the initial discovery of the oracle bone inscriptions is dated to the twenty-fifth year of the reign of the Guangxu 光緒 emperor of Qing, 1899, a date which still seems most likely based on Wang Xiang's 王襄 1933 statements on the matter.

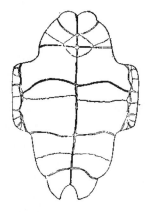 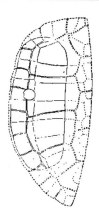 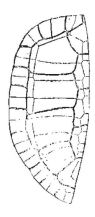

FIGURE   2 Processed
turtle plastron, bridge
retained at left and right.

FIGURE 3 Processed car-
apace, hole at center left.

FIGURE 4 Split
carapace.

on the opposite face. Longer, ovoid "troughs" tend to be approximately 1 cm in length, relatively wide at the mouth and narrowing to the bottom, while rounder and slightly smaller "pits" are usually bored directly alongside the troughs. Both were bored such that only a thin layer of bone or shell separated them from the facing side. These depressions are arranged in ordered arrays on bone fragments, with quantity a function of the size of the piece (see Figures 11-14).

Inscriptions on the bones served a number of different purposes, not all immediately related to the divinatory act itself (see Figures 11–14). For instance, processed pieces, prior to their use in divination, were designated to the care of particular functionaries. As part of their curatorial role, these officials used the peripheral areas of the shell or bone to inscribe information concerning the pieces' source and status. Such administrative accounts appear in one of five different positions: (1) the bridge portion of the plastron's reverse side (Figure 15); (2) the margins of the carapace's reverse side (Figure 16); (3) the bridge portion of the plastron (Figures 10 and 17); (4) the scapular socket surface (Figure 18); and (5) the broad end of the scapula (Figure 19). Such documentary inscriptions themselves comprise a meaningful body of inscriptional evidence.

Also, the divinatory act itself had apparently during late Shang become the province of a functionary responsible for applying the lit end of a wooden rod to the bone or shell depressions. The T-shaped cracks produced by the application of heat in this manner, read as portents in some still-unknown manner, became the basis for determination of the favorability or unfavorability of the oracle's response. In samples from relatively early periods, we often find inscribed beneath these "portent cracks" numbers indicating the position in sequence of each charge, these forming another component of the available inscriptional evidence.

The main body of evidence is of course the records, inscribed upon the bone or shell, of individual divinatory procedures and their results. These are in most cases written on the obverse face, though in some cases inscriptions appear on the reverse side, typically

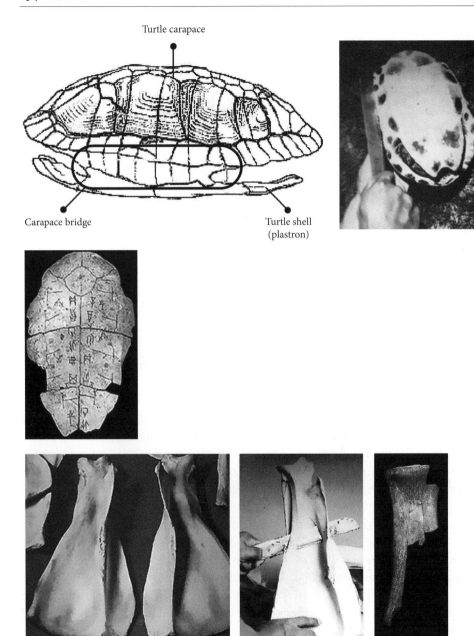

Turtle carapace

Carapace bridge

Turtle shell
(plastron)

FIGURES 5–10 illustrating preparation of turtle plastron (lower shell) and carapace (upper shell) and of the ox scapula. After Guoli Gugong Bowuyuan: 22,26 top left two and bottom left two) and Cai: cover page (top and bottom right).

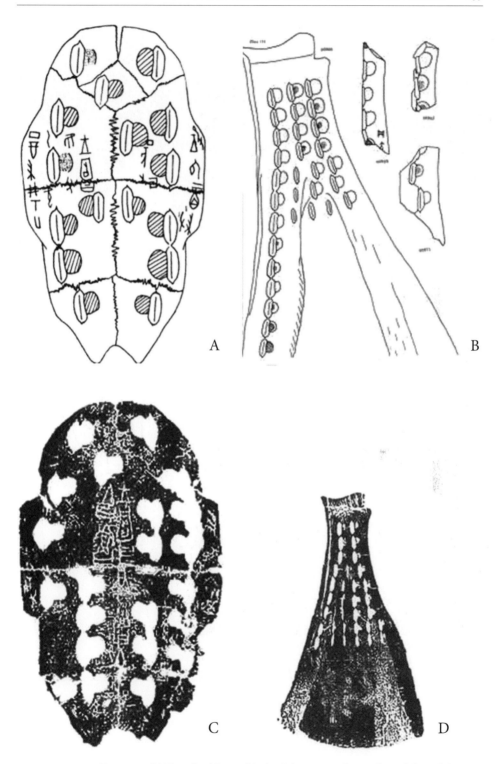

FIGURES 11–14 Drawings (AB) and rubbings (CD) of plastron and scapula with bored depressions. After Hsü: plates 125 (S0053) (C), 131 B0966-24(B), 4 S0053b (CD).

Que entered in 500
[turtle shells]

FIGURE 15 Reverse plastron bridge ("Que entered in 500 [turtle plastrons]").

FIGURE 16 Turtle carapace edge ("Official Fou…").

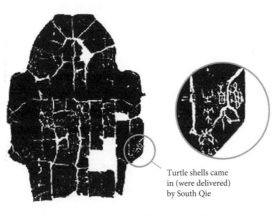

Turtle shells came in (were delivered) by South Qie

FIGURE 17 Plastron bridge ("Turtle shells came in (were delivered) by South Qie").

FIGURE 18 Scapular socket ("On day *jisi* Nu Shi (and delivered)red] 100 scapula").

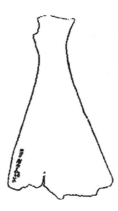

FIGURE 19 Lower scapular face.

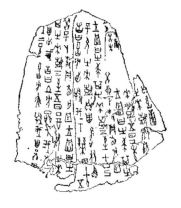

FIGURE 20 A fully inscribed oracle bone fragment.

when writing from the front surface is carried over to the back. A maximally complete divinatory inscription is made up of what may be treated as four discrete components. These are (1) the *preface*, generally containing the sexagenary date and the name of the diviner reciting the charge; (2) the *charge*, in which the question at issue is posed; (3) the *prognostication*, in which the king or diviner offers an interpretation of the oracle's response; and (4) the *verification*, generally consisting of later remarks on a prognostication borne out by events.

A relatively complete inscription from the reign of Wu Ding is shown above (Figure 20), with a rough translation of a portion of the bone as follows:

> In a divination on the day *guimao* (Day 40 of 60) Zheng divined: During the next ten-day week, will misfortune come to [Name]? The Shang king prognosticated: misfortune will arrive, perhaps from without. Seven days following [the prognostication], on the day *jisi* (Day 6 of 60), misfortune indeed arrived from the west. Zhi Fa reported that the Gong Fang had appeared, harassing the border and abducting seventy-five people.

The total number of characters employed within the Late Shang inscriptions is around 4,000, though given that the inscriptional language is specialized in nature, it is possible that this number understates the full scope of the writing system of the time. Certainly, given what we know of its use, the OBI constitute a mature writing system, and one based on the same organizing principles that govern the script in its later stages. For instance, there are both iconic ("pictographic") characters—*xiangxing* 象形, lit. "resembling the form"—and characters that employ phonetic components—*xingsheng* 形聲, lit. "form (and) sound." Indeed, it appears that the proportion of this latter type steadily increases over time, reaching its peak during the dynasty's final years under Di Yi and Di Xin. We also detect in late Shang writing the beginnings of the specialization of certain character forms in the subordinate role played by later phonetic and semantic indicators, or "radicals" (Anderson 2015). Most importantly, it is clear that the Shang writing system is the direct antecedent of the Western Zhou inscriptional script, the later clerical script, and in turn the writing system of the present day.

PERIODIZATION

It is doubtful that the OBI were the only written records of the time. The inscriptions offer fairly clear indication that books of wooden or bamboo strips (*ce* 冊) were also in use, and the occasional brush-written character on bone also points to the existence of alternative media. However, as far as we know, the inscriptions are the only surviving contemporaneous records, meaning they are of unparalleled importance for periodization. Archaeological tools have rightly come to play a more and more prominent role in addressing this question: differences in the physical features of bone pieces—as different modes of boring and burning divination holes and cracks—can be significant for chronology (Song and Liu 2006; Fan 2010). Site stratigraphy and ceramic seriation are also critical considerations (see e.g., Zhongguo 1994). Li and Peng (1996) reminds us, though, that neither are these infallible, pointing for instance to the importance of undisturbed pit contexts as opposed to imposed sector numbers, and to the fact that stratigraphic layer tends to provide an early limit but not a late one. Other features of the pieces, most significantly inscriptional content, thus become essential to consider.

One such early key—noticed by scholars including Wang Guowei 王國維, Luo Zhenyu, and James Menzies—were kinship terms employed in association with posthumous titles to name a king's ancestors and living relatives: *fu* 父 'father; paternal uncle'; *bi* 妣 'paternal grandmother; paternal great-aunt', and so on.[10] These titles, found to shift in a regular fashion to reflect the relation of a new king to fixed deceased relatives, permitted the reconstruction of inscription–internal generational relations. Slightly later, Dong Zuobin's 董作賓 insights came to form the basis for most subsequent discussion of inscription periodization (see Dong 1931, 1933). Perhaps most significantly, Dong observed that the formulaic style of many charges included as one component the name of the individual diviner responsible for issuing the charge. These diviner names, on present evidence numbering some 120, could be arranged into groups based on, for instance, cases in which multiple names occurred on single bones, and subsequently fitted into a relative chronology by reference to kinship terms or other proper nouns (names of officials, places, etc.) appearing on the same samples. The diviner names recorded in the bone inscriptions have been grouped by various scholars. Dong provided a well-known division of the OBI material into five periods numbered 1 through 5, while this chapter prefers a simpler scheme of three periods 2 through 4 (Li and Peng 1996; Hwang 1991). As noted, thus far, no inscriptions clearly date to the reigns of the three kings—Pan Geng, Xiao Xin 小辛, and Xiao Yi 小乙—who received texts would indicate were the first to rule at Yin ("Period 1"). Period 2 on such a scheme, further divided as A

---

[10] Such titles were made up of a kinship term combined with a posthumous name consisting of one of the so-called Heavenly Stems (*jia* 甲, *yi* 乙, [...] *gui* 癸) reused and applied apparently idiosyncratically. Where earlier scholars focused on the possibility that these might reflect birthday, clan name, or some such, the best evidence seems to point to their having been fixed via divination after the king's death: see e.g., Chen 1956; A. Smith 2011.

and B, is associated with kings Wu Ding and Zu Geng 祖庚 and diviner groups including Li 曆, Shi 自, and Bin 賓. Period 3 includes the reigns of the kings Zu Jia, Lin Xin, Kang Ding, and Wu Yi, and diviner groups Chu 出 and He 何 (as well as some inscriptions from the "Without Name{Wuming]" 無名, or "anonymous," group). Finally, Period 4 indicates the final three Shang kings, Wen Ding 文丁, Di Yi, and Di Xin, with diviner groups Huang 黃, Wu ming, and others. There is naturally some overlap between periods, however they are delineated. For example, the Li group of diviners worked during the reign of both Kings Wu Ding and his son, Zu Geng. In the same way, the Chu group overlapped the reigns of kings Zu Geng of Period 1B and Zu Jia of Period 2.

A key debate regarding inscriptional periodization has concerned the placement of inscriptions of the Li 歷 diviner group and the related Shi 自 (or Dui), Zi 子, and Wu 午 groups (Li and Peng 1996; Hwang 1991; Liu and Cao 2002). While Chen Mengjia assigned such material to Wu Ding's reign—that is, to the earliest strata of OBI material—Dong placed much of the same material in the later Wen Ding period (his Period 4), proposing to explain certain anachronistic features in terms of a Wen Ding–era revival of earlier divinational practices. The stratigraphy of the 1973 Xiaotun nandi finds, for instance, seemed to provide contradictory indications (see Liu and Cao 2002). The tomb of Fu Zi

Late Shang diviners and their date

Number	Diviner Name	Diviner Name Transcribed	Period Date	Number	Diviner Name	Diviner Name Transcribed	Period Date	Number	Diviner Name	Diviner Name Transcribed	Period Date
1		扶	SHI 自	30		定		59		先	CHU 出
2		自	SHI 自	31		者 (沐)		60		㠱	
3		勺	SHI 自	32		樂		61		寅	
4		叶	SHI 自	33		卯		62		骨	
5		卤		34		㝵	BIN 賓)	63		歲	HE 何
6		盧		35		子	ZI 子	64		何	HE 何
7		徝		36		余	ZI 子	65		卹	HE 何
8		設 (殻)	BIN 賓)	37		我	ZI 子	66		彭	HE 何
9		宁 (賓)	BIN 賓)	38		狐 (逫)	ZI 子	67		口	HE 何
10		爭	BIN 賓)	39		䶂	ZI 子	68		專	HE 何
11		亘	BIN 賓)	40		亞	YA 亞	69		羅	HE 何
12		内	BIN 賓)	41		歷	LI 歷	70		寧	HE 何
13		出 (古)	BIN 賓)	42		出	CHU 出	71		順	HE 何
14		冘	BIN 賓)	43		兄	CHU 出	72		壴	HE 何
15		品	BIN 賓)	44		大	CHU 出	73		狄	HE 何
16		亩	BIN 賓)	45		逐	CHU 出	74		教	HE 何
17		吏 (事)	BIN 賓)	46		中	CHU 出	75		逆	HE 何
18		箙	BIN 賓)	47		㠱	CHU 出	76		剡	HE 何
19		永	BIN 賓)	48		即	CHU 出	77		弔	HE 何
20		爭	BIN 賓)	49		喜	CHU 出	78		徬	
21		韋	BIN 賓)	50		旅	CHU 出	79		卲 (卬)	
22		亘	BIN 賓)	51		洋	CHU 出	80		名 (合)	
23		己		52		尹	CHU 出	81		黃	HUANG 黃
24		佣	BIN 賓)	53		行	CHU 出	82		䢅 (通)	HUANG 黃
25		絀	BIN 賓)	54		猳	CHU 出	83		泳 (派)	HUANG 黃
26		摔		55		冎	CHU 出	84		立	HUANG 黃
27		焱	SHI & BIN 自賓)	56		渁	CHU 出	85			HUANG 黃
28		琢		57		陟					
29		釣		58		堅					

FIGURE 21 Chart documenting oracle bone periodization and diviners according to group. Based on Song and Liu 2006.

(popularly known as Fu Hao), among other evidence including common names and events, allowed Li Xueqin to demonstrate the close contemporaneity of the Li and the Dong Period 2 Bin inscriptions, thus making an apparently definitive assignation of this material to the early period. In sum, diviner groups may thus be periodized as follows: Period 2: Shi 自, Bin 宾, Li 历; Period 3: Chu 出, He 何, anonymous/Wuming 无名; and Period 4: Huang 黃, anonymous/Wuming 无名 (see Figure 21).

Finally, language and writing at a more general level are also significant for relative dating. For instance, the opening portions of many charges take one of several highly formulaic arrangements. These structures, several characters in length, tend to include such features as a two-character date in terms of the sexagenary Heavenly Stem–Earthly Branch (*gan–zhi* 干支) cycle; diviner name; the verb *bu* 卜 "crack" > "divine"; the verb *zhen* 貞 "query"; and a place name where the divination was performed, all in characteristic combinations and orders that vary regularly in part by era. Scholars also attend to subject matter; to syntax more generally; to word choice; and to the forms taken by particular written characters, including calligraphic tendencies or idiosyncrasies.

Culture background

In terms of sheer scope and scale, Shang Anyang represents on current knowledge the pinnacle of civilization in East Asia at the time (Campbell 2014:130). Late Shang cultural reach appears at its greatest extent to have touched a significant portion of the East Asian Heartland (Childs-Johnson and Major, forthcoming; for the term see Mair 2006), extending approximately from northern modern-day Hubei province in the south to southern Liaoning in the north, and from Shaanxi and Gansu provinces in the west to the Bohai Bay coast and northern Shandong province in the east. The sites marked on the following map provide a general indication of an Anyang archaeological horizon. Outlying regions referenced within the OBI by the cardinal directions—northern, southern, eastern, and western "lands" (土)—cannot be demarcated with any precision, though the close study of inscriptional toponyms offers hope for a clearer understanding of geography. Other evidence sheds some firmer light on the reach of Shang cultural practices: inscribed bone fragments akin to the OBI (though extremely limited in quantity) are now available from areas to the south, east and west of Anyang—at Zhengzhou in central Henan province south of the Yellow River; at Daxinzhuang 大辛莊 in Shandong on the east coast; and at Zhouyuan 周原 in western Shaanxi (see e.g., Takashima 2011; Song 2005; Yang 1992; Wang 1984). (Figure 22).

Because the Shang Dynasty as represented by the Anyang period, especially for students of Chinese history, is all too easy to see as a beginning, it is useful to consider the era also as a consequence of what came before. Particularly following the birth of a native Chinese archaeological practice in the early twentieth century, much attention has been paid to the gradual emergence of a Shang "state" from late Neolithic and early

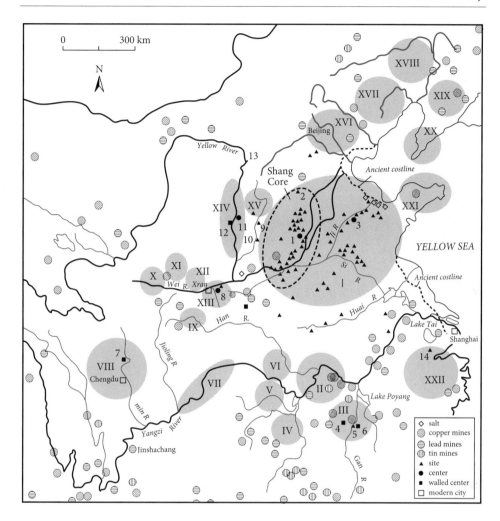

FIGURE 22 Geographical extent of late Shang according to surveyed and excavated site finds. *Cultures*: I Shang; II Panlongcheng; III Wucheng; IV Duimenshan- Hejiahe; V Baota; VI Zhouliangyuqiao; VII Lujiahe; VIII Sanxingdui; IX Baoshan (Chengyang Bronze Asemblage); X Lujia; XI Proto-Zhou; XII Zhengjiapo; XIII Laoniupo; XIV Lijiaya; XV Guangshe; XVI Weifang III; XVII Weiyinzi; XVIII Gaotaishan; XIX Miaphoushan; XX Shuangtuozi III; XXI Zhenzhumen; XXII Hushu. *Sites*: 1 Yinixu; 2 Taixi; 3 Daxinzhuang; 4 Wucheng; 5 Dayangzhou; 6 Niucheng; 7 Sanxingdui; 8 Laoniupo; 9 Jingjie; 10 Qiaobei; 11 Gaohong; 12 Lijiaya; 13 Xicha; 14 ceramic kilns in the Dongtiaoxi River region. (After Liu and Chen 2012:351, figure 10.1 and Chinese Institute of Social Sciences 2003).

Bronze Age communities of the region. This endeavor is of course an intellectual one, with new ideas reflecting shifting interpretations of the available archaeological record. At the same time, it is unavoidably part of a national historical project that is informed and confined by attitudes regarding the first nature and essential character of "China." In the earliest studies of Chinese Neolithic cultures, Western researchers, and thus

Western perspectives, took a central position. The 1921 excavation of the Yangshao 仰韶 type site in Henan, for instance, was spearheaded by the Swedish archaeologist Johan Gunnar Andersson. However, the conclusions of Andersson and others were ultimately perceived by some Chinese scholars to focus unduly on the possibility of a trans-Eurasian eastward cultural transmission (see e.g., Chang 1993). The significance of Li Ji 李濟 and his associates' 1930–1931 excavation of the Chengziyai site, near the village of Longshan 龍山 in coastal Shandong province, was thus in part in appearing to furnish incontrovertible evidence for Chinese civilization's indigenous roots. The most characteristic material product of what came to be understood as "Longshan culture" was a wheel-turned and thin-walled polished black pottery markedly distinct from the painted products of Yangshao.

At first, on the basis of these two geographically opposed ("western" Yangshao versus "eastern" Longshan) late Neolithic cultural areas, scholars including Fu Sinian 傅斯年 (1933) and Liang Siyong 梁思永 (1933) proposed that Shang represented a merger of earlier groups they termed "Xia" 夏 and "Yi" 夷, here borrowing nebulously defined ethnocultural terms from the classical tradition. Somewhat later, in light of stratigraphical evidence from the Miaodigou 廟底溝 (Henan) site that suggested instead a temporal relationship between an earlier Yangshao and a later Longshan, the standard view shifted to one of a central nuclear zone, with later eastward spread from this center seen to account for the distribution of Longshan cultural remains in regions like Shandong (Chang 1959; 1993:56). Deeper understandings of Central Plains Bronze Age cultures like Erligang at Zhengzhou and earlier Erlitou, widely interpreted as China's first state-level polities, seemed in general to validate this emphasis on the central Yellow River Valley, with Shang appearing a more-or-less direct outgrowth of what were in origin "nuclear-zone" developments.

More recently, this picture of Shang cultural heritage has been considerably complicated. Archaeologists have had to come to grips with an expanding body of evidence for previously unsuspected levels of social and technological sophistication throughout Neolithic and Bronze Age China—in the remote northeast, in the highlands of southwestern Sichuan, in the middle as well as the lower Yangtze valley, and yet further south. Newer understandings have thus put less stock in the idea of a single nuclear area, instead arguing that over the course of the late Neolithic and early Bronze Age a number of developments at first confined to distinctive regional cultural contexts gradually became more widely distributed via emergent interregional "interaction spheres" (Chang 1993:59). The Longshan archaeological horizon of the mid-fourth to third millennia BCE is now generally seen as just such a cross-cutting phenomenon. Key developments of the time, visible all across the Chinese landscape, include the beginnings of small-scale metallurgy in copper and bronze and, perhaps most importantly, hierarchical settlement patterns and burial configurations suggestive of increasingly complex social structures (Liu and Chen 2003, 2012; Li 2013; Flad 2015; Underhill et al. 2008; Chang et al. 2005). In some cases, widespread Longshan-horizon features can be assigned particular, local histories (e.g., the ritual role of bronze or of jade); others (the Bronze Age "city") take the form of cross-regional developments. Recently, Childs-Johnson (1988, 2001–2002, 2009) has construed much the same "Longshan period" as a Jade Age (ca. 3500–2100 BCE), implicating chronologically overlapping cultures including Hongshan 紅山 (mid-fifth to third millennium BCE; northeastern Liaoning and Inner Mongolia), Liangzhu 良渚 (ca. third millennium BCE; Yangtze delta), and Longshan proper (Yellow River Valley), with developments of the period setting the stage for the epochal developments of the subsequent Bronze Age.

Livelihood

These newer analytical approaches, along with an ever-expanding body of material evidence, mean that at Shang Anyang we can perceive a range of features from, at one end of the scale, the highly archaic and relatively "indigenous" to, at the other, cosmopolitan reflections of what were (in relative terms) more recent cross-regional contacts. The civilization of the Anyang period, as reflected by the archaeological record at Yinxu (critically including the OBI) and associated sites, was a settled, predominantly agricultural one, with many of the era's variety of food crops having long local histories. For instance, the first domestication of the key staple, foxtail millet (*Setaria italica*), likely occurred in this very heartland some millennia prior, with early evidence available from sites associated with the sixth-millennium Peiligang 裴李崗 culture of the Yi-Luo basin in Henan. Other crops, like wheat, had arrived from points west rather later as part of larger-scale Eurasian dispersals. Naturally enough, agricultural concerns are clearly reflected in the Anyang period evidence (see esp. Yang 1992). Agricultural implements in stone—spades, scythes, sickles, and so on—as well as ceramic cooking implements directed to the storage and preparation of grains, for instance, are abundant. Within the inscriptions are found supplications for harvest and for rain, reference to inspections of agricultural yield at particular named sites or cardinal quadrants, and accounts of sacrificial presentation of crops to spirits and royal ancestors. The OBI also suggest that the Shang king personally oversaw agricultural activities within the immediate royal domain and outlying regions, whether personally or via delegates, and we hear the king directing subordinates to activities like clearing, planting, monitoring of stores, and the harvest, as well as to the distribution of land among lords or nobles—transactions which, the inscriptions suggest, were at times recorded in physical documents.

Among animal domesticates, another important piece of the Anyang-era cultural milieu, both dog and pig are traceable to the local Neolithic and were apparently domesticated in the region. Sericulture, based on harvesting and eventual domestication of the silkworm, has also earned attention as a defining feature of a Middle Yellow River Valley culture, with cocoon remains available from the Yangshao Xiyincun 西陰村 site in Shanxi (Chang 1986; Shelach-Lavi 2015:94). On the basis of such discoveries, the critical domestication event is generally associated with the Central Plains region and dated to the third millennium BCE, and the practice does continue to Shang, with the OBI apparently referring on several occasions to offerings to a "silkworm spirit" (Kuhn 1988:250–252). Caprid and cattle would have arrived somewhat later as they spread east across the continent (Yuan 2008); pastoralism based upon these two animals was a significant piece of the Anyang-period economy, a key indicator being the striking quantities of these animals that appear in sacrificial contexts (Yang 1992:203). The horse, and slightly later the horse-drawn chariot, would have arrived closer to the dawn of the Anyang period via the steppes of Central Asia. The chariot in particular was to transform the nature and efficacy of military campaigns (Sawyer 2011); as this technology would have contributed significantly to the military advantage the late Shang kings enjoyed over their neighbors to the south and east, it is natural that the chariot became a key symbol of elite status—a fact reflected in burial practices of the time, with whole chariots interred along with their owners.

Hunting served as an additional source of meat, of raw materials for handicrafts, and of sacrificial victims, though it was to be transformed in parallel fashion by the arrival of the drawn chariot.[11] Wild animal bones and hunting implements, including arrowheads, are well-represented in the Anyang-era archaeological record. Large numbers of OBI charges also refer to methods of hunting (pit-traps, nets, etc.) and to hunting expeditions, with the Shang king often seen to play a personal prominent role. The specific references of the many toponyms involved here, numbering in the hundreds, have been the subject of much debate, with early geographical terms of the received textual record providing an essential point of reference. We also appear to have in the OBI the names and titles of local officials responsible for reporting on local wildlife and playing key roles in the royal hunt (Yang 1992:315–316; Childs-Johnson 1998:32–42; Fiskesjö 2001). Seasonal fishing catch would have provided both sustenance and sacrificial and burial offerings: OBI character forms provide evidence for nets, and still more informative are the fishhooks of copper, bone, and shell recovered from Anyang-period sites as well as net weights of stone and ceramic, from the late Shang period but also from local Neolithic contexts. Recovered remains do offer some evidence for cross-regional interaction, as it appears that fish were derived not only locally, as from the Huan and other Yellow River tributaries, but from as far afield as the Yangtze and the eastern seaboard, perhaps acquired in the form of tribute (Yang 1992).

Certain ceramic vessel types are ancient in the region, with the full-blown industries in ceramic and stone of the Anyang period having direct predecessors at Erligang sites. Workshops at the Anyang site include those devoted to ceramics as well as to bronze and bone, with indirect yet extensive evidence for the carving of jade, textiles, and woodworking. Bone workshops produced for the most part large quantities of quotidian artifacts like arrowheads, awls, and pins (Campbell et al. 2011; Li 2013; He 2006). There is

---

[11] Both Yang (1992:319–323) and Lewis (1990:21) have considered the shared vocabulary of hunting and warfare; Yang is interested in the literal connection and shared vocabulary, Lewis in their shared religious character. Childs-Johnson (1998) reviews the royal hunt, the king as hunter supreme, and evidence for the hunted animal in Shang royal imagery.

evidence for separate centralized ("royal") and distributed ("lineage") production centers (He 2015; Childs-Johnson forthcoming). Notably, Neolithic distribution patterns suggest ultimately eastern origins for vessel shapes including the tripod (*dǐng* 鼎) and goblet-bowl (*dou* 豆) (Chang 1999:50). Similarly, the Hongshan culture and associated Neolithic cultures of the northeast anticipate Shang-era jade-working traditions as well as particular iconographic elements, most significantly including the dragon (Childs-Johnson 1991:82–95). The most remarkable Neolithic specimens are products of the Hongshan, Liangzhu and Longshan cultures; the ceremonial role of jade appears to have spread from points of origin in the north, south and northeast (Childs-Johnson 1995). A number of distinctive forms—like rings (of various proportions) and the *yazhang* 牙璋 "ceremonial jade blade," both ubiquitous throughout modern-day China as in the Longshan period—bear clear witness to the early and wide distribution of these traditions (see chapter 10 on the *yazhang* in this book, by Tang Chung and Fang Wang).

The bronze industry of the Central Plains, seen in its infancy at Erlitou, reaches a spectacular peak within the Erligang and Anyang phases, when we begin to find the massive cast-bronze vessels that are the most iconic products of the industry. In part as the material is an alloy of copper, tin, and lead, a development that was to produce greater durability, large-scale work in bronze is considered to require a relatively high degree of social and technological sophistication. The technology as such may have arrived from points west, as the earliest, small-scale bronze artifacts in China are from upper Yellow River late Neolithic sites like those associated with Majiayao in modern-day Gansu. However, the material was soon to be adapted to local material cultural and ritual traditions: production methods, unique to the Central Plains tradition, have been described in detail by a number of authors (K. C. Chang 1980:98). Piece-mold casting techniques involved the crafting of a (positive) model from which a (negative) mold was derived; the pouring process required in addition an inner mold or "core," often derived by reduction of the model (see Chapter 14 by Chanping Zhang). Variation of several kinds is observed—as with carving on the model versus on the mold, or cast rather than carved inscriptions. The complexity of these processes would seem to point to the specialization and organization of labor in service of a political elite. Some scholars consider present evidence insufficient to support the common presumption of close centralized control of raw materials and finished products (Liu 2003; Campbell :137–138), though it is clear that ritual bronzes were exclusive to Shang society's highest social strata (see E. Childs-Johnson's chapter 13 in this volume).

Copper deposits are widespread in the region with a number of early mines identified, while Yang (1992: 393–394) suggests that Shang and Western Zhou rulers may have looked to the south for access to tin in particular; Jin Zhengyao (2008) documents the import of high-radiogenic lead from far southern sources. The distribution of these industries at the Anyang site, along with inscriptional indications, provide clear evidence for the division of labor in person and in space. Kuo Pao-chun observed a major industrial complex in the northern part of the middle group of ground houses as early as 1933. In some cases foundries for the production of weapons and tools were separate from those producing ritual objects.

The monumental rammed-earth construction found at Anyang is familiar from, for instance, the large walls of Erligang sites—Yanshi, Zhengzhou, Panlongcheng—but also late Neolithic sites throughout the Longshan-period horizon, as at Chengziyai in Shandong. The relative sequence and arrangement of the Xiaotun site's superstructures are not always well-understood (see E. Childs-Johnson chapter 15 in this volume). The central and largest built precinct apparently featured a northern and a southern courtyard. Du Jinpeng (2007:572–602) suggests the northern of these as residential and the middle section as an ancestral temple complex due to associated sacrificial pits. A network of roads is centered on this area, often termed a "palace-temple." Reading, this term provides a useful degree of ambiguity regarding function, though more often, authors are pointing to the probable conflation of political and spiritual authority, with king and court both organizing pinion of Shang society and conduit between the human realm and a world of ancestors and nature spirits. A typical view of the relationship between state and cult holds that Late Shang represents a "Bronze Age theocracy" (Wheatley 1971; Childs-Johnson forthcoming) in which "it is hard to separate the activities and interests of the state from those of the king and the royal lineage" (Keightley 1983:523).

Material to spiritual

Burial practices in evidence at Anyang have ancient histories: most directly, large elite shaft-tomb burials with accompanying sacrifice are found at Zhengzhou and Panlongcheng, these directly prefiguring the monumental tombs of the Anyang royals including that of Wu Ding's consort Fu Zi 婦子 (traditionally Fu Hao 妇好), excavated intact in 1976. Shaft burials with "waist pits" go back to late Neolithic Longshan sites like nearby Taosi and also Liangzhu in the Yangtze delta, with burial goods at both sites pointing to the new emergence of a class of religious-political elite. A distinctive feature of the Anyang site are the outlying clusters of what are interpreted as residences, some partly subterranean, associated with burials in a manner that has suggested an additional aspect of social structure in relation to religious attitudes—the "lineage." Also at Anyang, heating and drinking implements make up a key portion of burial paraphernalia: food and also alcohol—an undistilled grain-derived brew akin to ale—held prominent positions in Shang ritual. There is of course a perfunctory dimension to the most distinctive ritual element of all—the massive cast bronze, previously mentioned—but these speak more to the religious practice of ritual feasting and offering. Such bronzes, now numbering in the hundreds and widely distributed, were the marker of elite status and political power par excellence. For the most convincing interpretations of bronze iconography as it related to religious belief, see the work of Childs-Johnson (1998; 2016).

Pyro-osteomancy plus inscription is also a defining feature of Shang religious culture. Famously, a few symbols inscribed mostly on turtle plastrons have been recovered at Jiahu 賈湖, Wuyang, Henan, a Central Plains Neolithic site dating to around the seventh millennium BCE, but these are not the products of an osteomantic tradition (nor can the symbols be directly connected with Anyang writing). More significant for the origins of the Shang practice is early evidence for the association of the burning of bone with divination. Such traditions, usually involving animal scapulae or turtle plastrons, appear to have been relatively widespread during the Chinese Neolithic: the earliest known samples are from the Fuhegoumen 富河溝門 site in modern-day Liaoning province (formerly Inner Mongolia) in the extreme northeast (Song 2005; Flad 2015). Other pieces also derive from the north and east, as the burned and cracked deer scapulae of Chengziyai. Aside from a very small number of debated pieces from Zhengzhou and earlier Dinggong in Shandong, Taosi in Shanxi, and Longlazhuang in Jiangsu (see Chapters 7 and 8 by Hong Xu, and Hong Xu and Xiang Li in this volume), however, subsequent inscription of burnt pieces is so far unique to the Anyang materials. Certainly, to all appearances, late Shang represents the high-water mark of an inscriptional pyro-osteomantic practice, with the OBI testifying in abundance to the use of divination of this kind by Shang royals to gauge the auspiciousness of all manner of circumstances and hypothetical courses of action. Most significant and all-encompassing of these concerns was the proper manner of offering sacrifice; divination and sacrifice, related in the manner of negotiation and payment, stand as complementary elements of a single religious attitude. Other topics of inquiry include military campaigns, hunting expeditions, the harvest, meteorological conditions, sickness, and much else, in many cases with duplicated testings of a single proposition organized symmetrically across a plastron.

Somewhat less concrete is the suggestion that Shang religion was characterized by "shamanistic beliefs and practices" (Chang 1999:50), an idea based most generally on the clear possibility that the Shang king played a direct role in spiritual identification (yi 異) between the royal family and the domain of spirits and ancestors (see Childs-Johnson 2008). Different understandings of what constitutes shamanism have produced scholarly differences of opinion here: on traditional approaches to Chinese religion, the idea of an early ecstatic shamanistic practice can seem an exotic and thus suspicious intrusion; on the other hand, more generalist approaches would see the shaman-as-medium as part of a common, indeed near-ubiquitous, mode of traditional religiosity. As far as material remains are concerned, "shamanism" is at times invoked in reference to archaeological discoveries like the Erlitou tomb M1 in Yanshi, Henan from PII, where the deceased is covered by turquoise mosaics in the life-size image of a dragon (Liu and Xu 2015), which suggests a spiritual guide or avatar (Childs-Johnson, personal communication 2017). Such ideas would indeed point to deep indigenous roots—but there is reason for concern that such speculations rely rather too much on cosmological conceptions explicitly attested only as of the much later classical period. More cautiously, it should not be hard to accept that Shang ritual centered on a figure of special religious status engaged in negotiation with spiritual forces (Childs-Johnson 2008). It appears that the king alone had the capacity to receive spirits (bin 賓) via communication or identification (Childs-Johnson 2008:29–50), a notion buttressed by what is seen in the growing body of "non-royal" inscriptions—in particular the Huayuanzhuang corpus—associated with a Shang "prince" (though for another recent interpretation, see Chao 2016). The most complete argument for a Shang spiritual metamorphosis is that of

Childs-Johnson (2008; see also K. C. Chang 1983), working from Shang-period data including bronze iconography and, critically, related epigraphical observations.

The Shang calendar as attested within the inscriptions is also a key to the period's religious life, as the drive toward ever-greater precision here would not have been motivated by purely mundane—as agricultural—concerns. The OBI employ a lunisolar calendar; thus, while the year generally contained twelve *yue* 月 "moons, lunar months," intercalary (*run* 閏 "smoothing") months were added so as to effect coordination with the seasonal cycle. Generally, months are held to have been of 29 and 30 days, allowing close coordination with the synodic lunar month of ~29.5 days. Further study of specific aspects of cosmology and calendrics as reflected within the OBI will allow for more specific characterization of Shang practice, and perhaps ultimately more specific conclusions regarding its likely mixed origins. The OBI-era seasonal terms, for instance, remain poorly understood, with competing claims resting on problematic assumptions of close homology with later traditions. As regards the year, it is noteworthy that three inscriptional words come close to this meaning via metonymy. *Nian* 年, later "year," is an agricultural word in the OBI ("harvest"); *si* 巳~祀 names the cyclical sacrificial schedule providing for timely sacrifice to deceased kings and their wives, toward the end of Shang dominion to grow in length to approximate the solar year (Chang Yuzhi 1987:191–200; Yang Shengnan 1992:89–90); and *sui* 歲 is seasonal in the OBI ("end of the year") but ultimately calendrical astronomical in origin (J. Smith 2012). Also of importance for Shang cosmology, Sarah Allan has considered the myth of 10 suns (1991) and Childs-Johnson (1998) the sun more generally; both scholars have seen the Shang world to have been conceived as four directional quadrates surrounding a center, as proposed long ago by the eminent bone specialist Chen Mengjia (1956) and followed by others (Wheatley 1971, Song and Liu 2006).

The ritual underpinnings of timekeeping (Pankenier 1981–1982) are especially clear as regards the 10- and 12-day cycles, in later periods called the "Heavenly Stems" (*tian gan* 天干) and "Earthly Branches" (*di zhi* 地支), which from the earliest Shang inscriptions are seen to run in parallel to produce a larger series of 60 days. It is the Stems, also employed to name deceased kings, that were a central ordering mechanism for the ritual schedule previously noted, though both series are plainly archaic as of the Anyang period (A. Smith 2011). As the origins of these two systems have recently begun to be considered to constitute the origins of Chinese writing itself (Pankenier 2012), clear etymological understandings may provide telling indications regarding the cultural and ethnolinguistic roots of the Shang. Recent studies of the Stems and Branches have focused in particular on the possibility of a connection to formative calendrical astronomy: Pankenier (2009, 2012) has offered a solution for Ding 丁, the fourth of the Stems; J. Smith attempts the same for Wu 戊 (2012) and, more speculatively, for other members of the series (J. Smith 2010). The question of whether Anyang-era writing might have undiscovered antecedents that will speak to this issue is crucial and unanswered (Keightley 2006; Bagley 2004; A. Smith 2008). Certainly, as higher-resolution understandings of the Chinese late Neolithic and Bronze Age have rendered the notion of indigeneity increasingly relative, it is natural to entertain the possibility that Shang writing itself was born of cultural exchange, one of a number of cross-regional developments associated with the melding of the great Yellow and Yangtze River Valleys into a unified "Longshan" interaction sphere.

BIBLIOGRAPHY

Allan, Sarah 1991. *The Shape of the Turtle: Myth, Art, and Cosmos in Early China.* Albany, NY: State University of New York Press.

Anderson, Matthew McCutchen 2015. "Change and Standardization in Anyang: Writing and Culture in Bronze Age China." PhD dissertation, University of Pennsylvania.

Brown, Shana 2011. "What Is Chinese about Ancient Artifacts? Oracle Bones and the Transnational Collectors Hayashi Taisuke and Luo Zhenyu." In *Collecting "China": The World, China, and a Short History of Collecting.* Edited by Vimalin Rijavacharakul, 63–72. Newark: University of Delaware Press.

Campbell, Roderick B. 2014. *Archaeology of the Chinese Bronze Age: From Erlitou to Anyang.* Monographs 79. Los Angeles: University of California at Los Angeles Cotsen Institute of Archaeology Press.

Campbell, Roderick B., Zhipeng Li, Yuling He, and Jing Yuan 2011. "Consumption, Exchange and Production at the Great Settlement Shang: Bone-Working at Tiesanlu, Anyang." *Antiquity* 85: 1,279–1,297.

Cao, Dingyun 曹定雲 1983. "Analysis of Sacrifices to Wuyi and Wending Mentioned in Bone Inscriptions論武乙，文丁祭祀卜辭." *Kaogu* 3: 238–243.

Chang, Kwang-Chih (Zhang Guangzhi) 張光直 1959. "Dating the Neolithic cultures of China中國新石器時代文化斷代." *Bulletin of the Institute of History and Philology, Academia Sinica,* 中央研究院歷史語言研究所季刊 20: 259–309.

Chang, Kwang-Chih 1980. *Shang Civilization.* New Haven, CT and London: Yale University Press.

Chang, Kwang-Chih 1983. *Art, Myth, and Ritual: The Path to Political Authority in Ancient China.* Cambridge, Mass.: Harvard University Press.

Chang, Kwang-Chih 1986. *The Archaeology of Ancient China,* 4th ed. New Haven, CT and London: Yale University Press.

Chang, Kwang-Chih 1999. "China on the Eve of the Historical Period." In *The Cambridge History of Ancient China: From the Origins of Civilization to 221 BC.* Edited by Michael Loewe and Edward L. Shaughnessy, Cambridge, UK: Cambridge University Press.

Chang, Kwang-Chih, Pingfang Xu, Liancheng Lu, and Sarah Allan, eds. 2005. *The Formation of Chinese Civilization: An Archaeological Perspective.* New Haven, CT: Yale University Press.

Chang, Yuzhi 常玉芝 1987. *Sacrificial System of the Shang Dynasty* 商代周祭制度. Beijing: Zhongguo shehui kexue chubanshe.

Chao, Fulin 晁福林 2016. "Brief Discussion of Sacrifices in Shang Bone Inscriptions 卜辭所見商代里浅谈." *Kaogu xuebao* 3:343–364.

Chen, Mengjia 陈梦家 1956. *A Comprehensive Study of the Divination Inscriptions from the Ruins of Yin* 殷墟卜辭综述. Beijing: Kexue chubanshe.

Childs-Johnson, Elizabeth 1988. *Ritual and Power: Jades of Ancient China.* New York: China Institute in America.

Childs-Johnson, Elizabeth 1998a. "The Metamorphic Image: A Predominant Theme in Shang Ritual Art." *Bulletin of the Museum of Far Eastern Antiquities* 70:5–171.

Childs-Johnson, Elizabeth 1998b. "Postscript to Big *Ding* and China Power-Shang *Sifang* 對'大鼎'和中國國王權力的後記:商代四方(四個方向)宇 宙 學." In *Proceedings in Honor of Professor Sun Zuoyun's Centennial and International Conference on Research on Ancient China History and Culture* 紀念孫作雲教授百 年誕辰暨古代中國歷史與文化國際學術研討會論文集, 191–210. Kaifeng: Henan daxue chubanshe.

Childs-Johnson, Elizabeth 2008. *The Meaning of the Graph Yi* 異 *and Its Implications for Shang Belief and Art*. East Asia Journal Monograph 1. London: Saffron.

Childs-Johnson, Elizabeth 2009. "The Art of Working Jade and the Rise of Civilization in China." In *The Jade Age [and] Early Chinese Jades in American Museums*, 291–393. Beijing: Kexue chubanshe.

Childs-Johnson, Elizabeth, and John S. Major. *Metamorphic Imagery in Early Chinese Art and Religion*, forthcoming.

Dong, Zuobin 董作賓 1931. "Study of four plastrons" 大龜四版考釋. In *Anyang fajue baogao* 安陽發掘報告 No. 3, Guoli zhongyang yanjiuyuan lishi yuyan yanjiusuo Special Volume 1 國立中央研究院歷史語言研究所專刊之 1, 440–441. Beijing: Guoli zhongyang yanjiuyuan lishi yuyan yanjiusuo.

Dong, Zuobin 董作賓 1932. *Research on oracle-bone inscriptions* 甲骨文斷代研究例. Beijing: Guoli zhongyang yanjiuyuan lishi yuyan yanjiusuo.

Du, Jinping 杜金鵬 2007. *Research on the Archaeology of Xia, Shang and Zhou* 夏商周考古学研究. Beijing: Kexue chubanshe.

Fan, Yuzhou 范毓周 2010. "Several Questions Concerning the Periodization of the Yinxu Culture 关于殷墟文化考古分期的几个问题," *Zhongyuan wenwu* 中原文物 2010(4) :

Fiskesjö, Magnus 2001. "Rising from Blood-Stained Fields: Royal Hunting and State Formation in Shang Dynasty China." *Bulletin of the Museum of Far Eastern Antiquities* 73:48–191.

Fu, Sinian 傅斯年 1933. "Theory of the Yi in the East and the Xia in the West 夷夏東西說." *Bulletin of the Institute of History and Philology, Academia Sinica, Chung-yang Yen-chiu-yuan Li-shih Yu-yan Yen-chiu-suo chi-kan* 中央研究院歷史語 言研究所季刊 1:1,093–1,134.

He, Yuling 何毓灵 2006. "Tomb No. 60 at Huayuanzhuang East, Yinxu, Anyang, Henan 河南安阳殷墟花园庄东地 60 号墓." *Kaogu* 1:7–17.

He, Yuling 何毓灵 2015. "Remains of a Bone Factory of the Yinxu Culture at Tiesanlu, Anyangshi, Henan 河南安阳市铁三路殷墟文化时期制骨作坊遗址." *Kaogu* 8:37–62.

Flad, Rowan 2015. "Divination and Power: A Multi-Regional View of the Development of Oracle Bone Divination in Early China." *Current Anthropology* 49(3):403–437.

Hwang, Tianshu 黃天樹 1991. *Chronology and Periodization of the Royal Bone Inscriptions of Yinxu* 殷墟卜辭的分類與斷代. Taibei: Wenjin chubanshe.

Jin, Zhengyao 金正耀 2008. *Lead Isotope Archaeology in China* 中國鉛同位素考古. Hefei: University of Science and Technology of China.

Keightley, David N. 1978. *Sources of Shang History: The Oracle-Bone Inscriptions of Bronze Age China*. Berkeley: University of California Press.

Keightley, David N. 1983. "The Late Shang State: When, Where, and What?" In *The Origins of Chinese Civilization*. Edited by David N. Keightley, 523–564. Berkeley: University of California Press.

Kuhn, Dieter 1988. "Textile Technology: Spinning and Reeling." In Part 9 of *Science and Civilisation in China*, vol. 5: *Chemistry and Chemical Technology*. Edited by Joseph Needham, Cambridge, UK: Cambridge University Press.

Li, Feng 2008. *Bureaucracy and the State in Early China, Governing the Western Zhou*. Cambridge, UK: Cambridge University Press.

Li, Feng 2013. *Early China: A Social and Cultural History*. New Approaches to Asian History 12. Cambridge, UK: Cambridge University Press.

Li, Ji [Li Chi] 李濟 1977. *Anyang*. Seattle: University of Washington Press.

Li, Xueqin 1989. *Collected Works of Li Xueqin* 李學勤集 (殷墟甲骨兩系說與歷組卜辭). Harbin: Heilongjiang jiaoyu chubanshe.

Li, Xueqin 李学勤, and Yushang Peng 彭裕商 1996. *Research on Oracle Bone Periodization of Yinxu* 殷墟甲骨分期研究. Shanghai: Shanghai guji chubanshe.

Liang, Siyong 梁思永 1933. "Longshan and Yangshao at Xiaotun 小屯龍山與仰韶." *Bulletin of the Institute of History and Philology, Academia Sinica Waibian, The Institute of History and Philology, Academia Sinica Celebrates Tsai Yuan-pei's 65 year of his Collected Works* 中央研究院歷史語言研究所季刊外篇:555–567.

Liu, Li, and Xingcan Chen 2003. *State Formation in Early China*. London: Gerald Duckworth.

Liu, Li, and Xingcan Chen 2012. *The Archaeology of China*. Cambridge, UK: Cambridge University Press.

Liu, Li, and Hong Xu 2015. "Rethinking Erlitou: Legend, History and Chinese Archaeology," *Antiquity* 81(314):886–901.

Liu, Yiman and Dingyun Cao 刘一曼, 曹丁云 2002. "The Oracle Bone Inscriptions from the eastern section of Huayuanzhuang, Yinxu 殷虚花园庄东地的甲骨 *Kaogu Xuebao* 1993(3).

Loewe, Michael, and Edward L. Shaughnessy, eds. 1999. *The Cambridge History of Ancient China: From the Origins of Civilization to 221 BC*. Cambridge, UK: Cambridge University Press.

Mair, Victor H., ed. 2006. *Contact and Exchange in the Ancient World*. Honolulu: University of Hawai'i Press.

Nivison, David 1999. *Key to the Chronology of the Three Dynasties: The "Modern Text" of the Bamboo Annals*. University of Pennsylvania: Department of Asian and Middle Eastern Studies.

Nivison, David 2002. "The Xia-Shang-Zhou Chronology Project: Two Approaches to Dating." *Journal of East Asian Archaeology* 4:359–366.

Nivison, David 2009. *The Riddle of the Bamboo Annals* 竹書紀年解謎. Taipei: Airiti Press.

Pankenier, David W. 1981–1982. "Astronomical Dates in Shang and Early Zhou." *Early China* 7:2–37.

Pankenier, David W. 1992a. "The Bamboo Annals Revisited: Problems of Methodology in Using the Chronicle as a Source for the Chronology of Early Zhou, Part 1." *Bulletin of the School of Oriental and African Studies* 55(2):272–297.

Pankenier, David W. 1992b. "The Bamboo Annals Revisited: Problems of Methodology in Using the Chronicle as a Source for the Chronology of Early Zhou; Part 2; The Congruent Mandate Chronology in *Yi Zhou shu*." *Bulletin of the School of Oriental and African Studies* 55(3):498–510.

Pankenier, David W. 1995. "The Cosmo-Political Background of Heaven's Mandate." *Early China* 20:121–176.

Sawyer, Ralph 2011. *Ancient Chinese Warfare*. New York: Basic Books.

Shelach-Lavi, Gideon 2015. *The Archaeology of Early China: From Prehistory to the Han Dynasty*. Cambridge, UK: Cambridge University Press.

Smith, Adam 2011. "The Chinese Sexagenary Cycle and the Ritual Foundations of the Calendar." In *Calendars and Years II: Astronomy and Time in the Ancient and Medieval World*. Edited by John M. Steele, 1–37. Oxford: Oxbow.

Smith, Jonathan 2011. "The 'Di Zhi' 地支 as Lunar Phases and their Coordination with the 'Tian Gan' 天干 as Ecliptic Asterisms in a China Before Anyang," *Early China* 33: 199–228.

Smith, Jonathan 2012. "The Old Astronomical Significance of the Glyph <歲> and the Word Suì < *Swats," *Journal of the American Oriental Society*, 132.1:41–60.

Song, Zhenhao 宋镇豪 2005. *Xia Shang Zhou Social History* 夏商周社会生活史, 2 vols. Beijing: Zhongguo Shehui Kexueyuan.

Song, Zhenhao 宋镇豪, and Yuan Liu 刘源 2006. *Oracle Bone Studies of Shang History* 甲骨学殷商史. Fuzhou: Fujian renmin shehui.

Takashima, Ken-ichi 2011. "Literacy to the South and the East of Anyang in Shang China: Zhengzhou and Daxinzhuang." In *Writing and Literacy in Early China*. Edited by Li Feng and David Branner, 141–172. Seattle: University of Washington Press.

Tsai, Che-mao 菜哲茂 1999. *Collection of bone inscription rejoinings* 甲骨綴合集. Taipei, Taiwan: Lexue shuju.

Underhill, Anne P., Gary M. Feinman, Linda M. Nicholas, Fang Hui, Luan Fengshi, Yu Haiguang, and Cai Fengshu 2008. "Changes in Regional Settlement Patterns and the Development of Complex Societies in Southeastern Shandong, China." *Journal of Anthropological Archaeology* 27(1):1–29.

Wang, Changming 汪常明, and Zhengyao Jin 晋正耀 2010. Copper isotope analyses applied to archaeological studies: A review 铜同位素分析法在考古研究中的应用探讨. *Wenwu baohu yu kaogu kexue* 文物保护与考古科学 22(1): 83–88.

Wang, Yuxin 王宇信 1984. *Analysis of Western Zhou Oracle Bones* 西周甲骨探论. Beijing: Zhongguo shehui kexueyuan.

Wheatley, Paul 1971. *The Pivot of the Four Quarters: A Preliminary Enquiry into the Origins and Character of the Ancient Chinese City*. Chicago: Aldine.

Xia-Shang-Zhou Duandai Baogao 2000. 夏商周断代工程 1996–2000. *Short Edition of the Report on Results of the 1996–2000 Work on the Chronology of the Xia, Shang and Zhou* 年阶段成果报 告: 简本. Beijing: Shijie tushu chubanshe.

Xu, Hong 许宏 2009. *Earliest China* 最早的中國. Beijing: Kexue chubanshe.

Yang, Shengnan 杨升南 1992. *The Economic History of the Shang Dynasty* 商代经济史. Guiyang: Guizhou renmin chubanshe.

Yuan, Jing 袁靖 2008. "The Origins and Development of Animal Domestication in China." Translated by Rowan K. Flad. *Chinese Archaeology* 8(1): 1–7.

Zheng, Zhenxiang 鄭振香 1994a. *Research on and discovery of Yinxu* 殷墟的发现与研究. Beijing: Kexue chubanshe (reprinted 2001 and 2007).

Zheng, Zhenxiang 鄭振香 1994b. "Chronology and Periodization of the Yinxu Culture." 殷墟文化的分期与年代. In *Research on and discovery of Yinxu* 殷墟的发现与研究, 25–39. Beijing: Kexue chubanshe.

Zhongguo Shehui Kexueyuan Kaogu Yanjiusuo 2003. Institute of Archaeology, CASS 中国社会科学院考古研究所 2003. *Chinese Archaeology: Xia Shang Volume* 中国考古学：夏商卷。Beijing: Zhongguo shehui kexue yuan chubanshe.

Zou, Heng 鄒衡 1980–2001. *Collected Works on Xia, Shang, Zhou Archaeology* 夏商周考古学论文集, vols. 1–3. Beijing: Wenwu chubanshe.

CHAPTER 12

··

EARLY AND MIDDLE SHANG PERIODS

··

BY GUODING SONG,
BEIJING NORMAL UNIVERSITY

ZHENGZHOU SHANG CITY

ZHENGZHOU Shang City is located in the eastern area of the current Zhengzhou City in Henan Province. The site is situated east of the Jingguang (Beijing-Guangzhou) Railway and north of the Longhai (Lianyungang to Lanzhou) Railway; the Jinshui River lies to the north of the site; and the Xionger River lies to the south and runs through the site from west to east and into the city moat. Zhengzhou Shang City sits at the junction of the hilly Loess Plateau region and the lake-swamp plain area. In antiquity, this area had always been an artery for traffic and trade.

The discoveries of Zhengzhou Shang City and Erligang sites are inseparable. Zhengzhou Erligang site was discovered in autumn of 1950, and multiple related sites, such as Nanguanwai and Baijiazhuang, were also discovered and excavated within that decade (Henan 2001). The overlapping types of Erligang culture and Yinxu (Yin Ruins) proved that the Erligang culture predated that of Yinxu (Henan 1959).

In the autumn of 1955, the foundations of Zhengzhou Shang City were identified. The discovery of 11 openings on the surrounding walls were believed to be city gates. From 1950 to the early 1990s, additional rammed-earth walls were found a few hundred meters outside of Zhengzhou Shang City, on the south and west sides. These earth walls were considered to belong to an additional outer city wall. During the 1970s, a building foundation area was excavated in the northeastern part of the Zhengzhou Shang City site. A number of rammed-earth platforms were found in this area, and they were determined to have been built around the same time as the outer city walls. In addition, from September 1974 to February 1996, three bronze pits were unearthed at Duling site on Zhangzhai South Street, in Xiangyang Muslim Food Factory on Chengdong Street, and

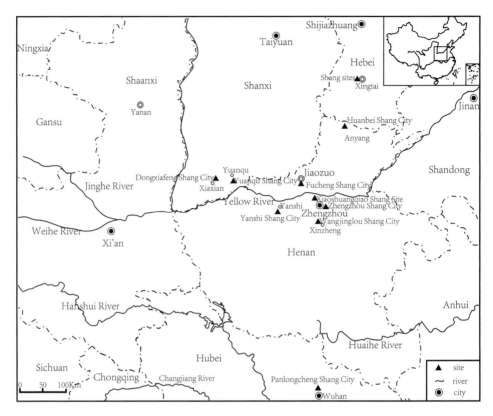

FIGURE 1 The distribution map for the cities and sites of early through middle Shang date.

at Nanshuncheng Street site (Henan 1999). The 28 Shang royal bronze vessels unearthed from these pits provide valuable evidence for understanding the nature of the Zhengzhou Shang City and dating of the site. One of the bronze vessels is depicted in Figure 2. Based on this discovery and related finds, it is apparent that Zhengzhou Shang City was indisputably the largest-scale city in the Early Shang Dynasty, rich in remains and valuable artifacts, and was a capital city site at that time.

Walls

The layout of Zhengzhou Shang City resembles a rectangle, with an inner wall that is 6,960 m encompassing the city in circumference. The east and south walls are both over 1,700 m long, the west wall 1,870 m long, and the north wall 1,690 m long. The highest extant inner wall averages approximately 9 m and the lowest roughly 1 m. The walls were constructed out of strongly enforced rammed-earth layers and built as segments pressed between wood boards. Each tamped layer is about 8–10 cm thick, and each ram impres-

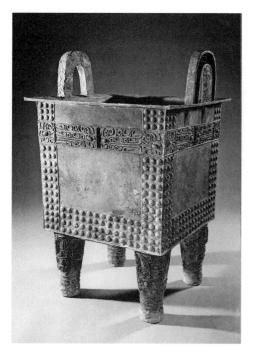

FIGURE 2 A large-scale tetrapod *ding* excavated at Zhengzhou Shang City.

sion is 2–4 cm with a depth of 1–2 cm. The cross-sections of the walls are trapezoidally shaped. Remains of moats were also found outside parts of some walls.

As of 2015, the walls excavated include an additional outer one that extends from the southeast corner to the northwest corner and is over 7,000 m in length and 12–17 m in width. Foundation ditches were constructed before the walls were built, and their method of construction is distinct from the inner walls. Considering the shape of the walls, it is clear that the outer walls were built to surround the Zhengzhou Shang City in forming fortified periphery around the city site.

Building foundation area

The building foundation area, located in the northeast part of the inner city, covers an area some 750 m long from east to west and 500 m wide from north to south. Dongli Road is at the center of the area and intersects with Shunhe Road to the north, with the north side of Chengbei road to the south, Zijingshan Road to the west, and the East wall to the east (Henan 1983a). Some rammed-earth foundations were found outside this range, though they are more scattered. Dozens of rammed-earth foundations were found since the beginning of the 1970s (Song 1993). Small foundations measured 100 m², while large ones were more than 2,000 m². Two foundations in the building foundation area, C8G15 and C8G16, are the largest in scale and relatively well preserved. C8G15, estimating from the observed foundation ditches, was over 65 m long from east to west and 13.6 m wide from north to south. Only one row of eave columns was found on the outside of this foundation site. The building foundation could be reconstructed as a long rectangle within an enclosed cloister, indicating that C8G15 was probably a large-scale residential hall. On the other hand, C8G16 was constructed differently; its construction method is as follows: firstly, foundation ditches were dug, earth filled and rammed, and a platform constructed; secondly, column base holes were dug, column base and wood pillars were placed in the middle of the holes; finally, earth was filled and rammed firmly around them. The column base pits were structured in three rows: inside, middle, and outside. The distance among each wood pillar ranged from 2.05–2.5 m to 1.6–2.45 m. Estimated from the edges of the foundation ditches, C8G16 is 38.4 m long from north to south and 31.2 m wide from east to west. Judging from the three rows of pillar remains, the original design was a building foundation with double gallery and roof without walls. This building foundation is thought to be an administration center.

In addition to the Jinshui River and Xionger River, the major water source of Zhengzhou Shang City was well water. Wells found within the city site can be divided into two categories: one, the most basic and common type forming a rectangular-shaped shaft found throughout the city site and the other, a more sophisticated pit, found in the building foundation area. The latter is represented by three wells: two that are square with rounded corners and one that is round in shape. Foundations were constructed with wooden shafts in sets and the shafts were lined with rounded wood beam crossovers, which overlapped and climbed upward. Tenons made the wood beams connect together. At the bottom, large square wood beams were used to make the base of the well. Storage facilities and pipelines inside the building foundation area document a rather complete system for water supply (Henan 1993).

Craft workshops

All craft workshops were located within the area between inner and outer city walls. Major workshop sites include the bronze-casting site at Nanguanwai; the bronze-casting site north of Zijingshan; the pottery workshop at Minggong Road, and the bone pit north of Zijingshan.

The bronze-casting site at Nanguanwai, located 700 m distant from the south edge of the fortification wall, is 100 m in length from south to north and 80 m in width from east to west. Remains included a kiln for firing molds; a bronze-casting facility; a storage pit; fragments such as copper, crucible parts, slag from the melting process, charcoal, clay molds; and objects made of bronze, pottery, stone, bone, and mussel shell. The site's age, when dated, corresponded to the city site's age.

The bronze-casting workshop site north of Zijingshan was located 300 m away from the north wall in the Zhengzhou Shang City. The workshop contained remains of a housing foundation; a storage pit; detritus such as copper, lead, crucible, slag from the melting process, charcoal, clay molds; and remains of bronze artifacts, ceramics, stone, bone, and mussel shell (Henan 1989).

The pottery workshop at Minggong Road was located inside today's Fourteenth Middle School, 1,300 m west of the inner city. Excavated remains included a pottery kiln foundation, burials, ash pits, lime-lined floors, large amounts of utilitarian ceramics, unfired clay bodies, unsuccessfully fired ceramics, and ceramic tools (Henan 1991).

The bone pit north of Zijingshan was located inside today's Henan branch of Xinhua News Agency and outside the north wall of Zhengzhou Shang City. More than 1,000 bone objects, finished and unfinished, along with related bone materials and bone waste were excavated. Grind stones and small bronze knives used to process bone objects were also discovered, demonstrating that the site constituted a bone-manufacturing workshop.

Residential housing

Although years of archaeological investigation have been carried out at Zhengzhou Shang City, due to the destruction of Eastern Zhou, Han, Tang, and Song dynastic buildings little evidence of residence housing remains. Small-scale housing foundations have been discovered mostly between inner and outer city walls.

Burials

Burials in Zhengzhou Shang City were distributed around the inner city and in the area between the inner and outer parts of the city. Representative examples exist at Baijiazhuang, Yangzhuang, Longhai East Road (Zhengzhou Tobacco Factory), Beierqi Road (Henan 1983b), Peoples' Park, and Minggong Road sites (Zhengzhou 1965). Inside the inner city, very few burials were found, yet several have been discovered near the fortified walls.

Large burials associated with Shang rulers have not yet been found in this city site. Burials found here are all single vertical pits. Frequently, traces of a coffin and use of the second-ledge platform were discovered. Both supine and prone burials were found. Waist pits, mostly buried with dogs, frequently lined the bottom of tombs. Human sacrifices appear in burials of medium size. Smaller burials were mostly accompanied by several pottery vessels of the following types: *li, jia, jue, dou, pen,* and *gui*. Round-shaped painted red ceramics were also frequently found in the smaller burials. Richer burials included bronze objects (Yang et al. 1981), proto-porcelain *zun* (Figure 3), and jades. The most commonly found bronze vessels are *jue, jia,* and *gu*, while the most commonly found jade objects are handle-shapes. Other burials formed simple pits, in which corpses were scattered in ash pits or in cultural layers, and some were buried with animal bones.

FIGURE 3 Proto-porcelain *zun*, West Minggong Road, Burial M2:1, Zhengzhou.

Dating and chronology

The building foundation of the Zhengzhou Shang City "building foundation" began no later than the early Shang Phase 1 (Erligang Lower Phase 1). The scholars who excavated the site suggest dating the construction of the wall to be around Erligang Lower Phase 1. The Shang City continued to be occupied through the early Shang Phase 2 and prospered through early Shang Phase 3. By the middle Shang Phase 1, equivalent to the Baijiazhuang Phase, Zhengzhou Shang City started to decline. By the middle Shang Phase 2, the city site had been completely abandoned. We categorize the Erligang Culture at Zhengzhou into four phases based on cultural strata, their overlapping relationships, and detailed studies of excavated pottery and bronze objects from representative layers. The four phases are as follows.

The first phase is represented by two locations including Erligang H9 and Dianxiao H6 (at Zhengzhou Electric Power College). The majority of ceramics are gray sandy-wares and coarse sand-tempered gray pottery. Reddish-brown pottery, also found in considerable proportions was estimated to occur in the same amount as the grey pottery at certain sites. Bronze objects had thin walls and were few in both variety and number. During this phase, the only type of bronze found is the *jue*. Bronze *jue* of this phase have the following characteristics: a long round body in the cross-section, a wide and short silhouette, a long pointed tail with outward-turning walls, and tapered feet. Judging from known materials, the Shang people had settled in this area and also practiced building foundation large-scale constructions, such as the "building foundation."

The second phase is represented by three locations, including Erligang H19, the ash layer above the rammed earth of C8T62 in the building foundation area, and C8M32. Bronze objects have thicker walls than before and were both more diverse and numerous in type. The body of the bronze *jue* vessel becomes slightly rounder, with thinner and taller silhouette, shortened tail, protruding pillars, flat bottom, and hollow feet with a rectangular-shaped cross-section. This phase represents a period of prosperity of Zhengzhou Shang City.

The third phase is represented by four locations including Erligang H2 Yi, Erligang H1, Beierqi Road M1, and Minggong Road M2. The bronzes excavated here increased in both variety and number. During this phase bronze *jue* take on short tails, mushroom-shaped protruding pillars, abdominal walls that are straight yet slanting, and a cross-section of feet that change to triangular prisms. Bronze *gu* vessels have flat bottoms, with no apparent protruding abdominal walls. Bronze *jia* are rough and short, with more apparent protruding bottoms and feet that form triangular prismatic shapes. This phase was the most prosperous period of Zhengzhou Shang City.

The fourth phase is represented by five locations including Shang City CNM5, the second layer of Baijiazhuang, Baijiazhuang M2 and M3, and Minggong Road M4. Large amounts of bronze artifacts were found in three storage pits and new types of artifacts were unearthed. Previously unseen bronze types include *lei*, *zun*, *you*, flat-footed *pan*-shaped *ding*, square *ding* with four feet, ring-footed *pan*, and *yu* basins with a pillar in the center. Bronze *jue* have shorter tails, with abdominal walls changed from a straight slant to one that protrudes outward and with bottoms that also slightly protrude. Bronze *gu* vessels have more apparent protruding abdominal walls and slightly protruding bottoms. In addition, a slender type of *gu* also appears. From a stylistic, decorative, and casting technological standpoint, it is clear that bronzes found in these storage pits are not all from the same period of time. Different characteristics distinguish earlier- and later-period examples. Storage pits at Zhangzhai South Street and the Muslim Food Factory may be dated to the fourth phase (Table 1).

Nature

The series of discoveries at Zhengzhou Shang City demonstrate that it was a capital site. Some scholars have proposed that the Zhengzhou Shang City is the historical capital "Ao" where the early Shang king Zhongding moved. During the late 1970s, other scholars suggested that Zhengzhou Shang City was the historical capital "Bo" where king Tang (Shang Tang) first settled. The latter theory is based on transmitted texts stating that Bo city resided in the Zheng region (see *Zuozhuan*, Xianggong 11th year) and that this record corresponded to the written references on late Warring States pottery excavated from local nearby sites. This theory is generally accepted in scholarly circles. In addition, scholars consider that Zhengzhou Shang City is associated with another early Shang site—the Yanshi Shang City. The importance of Zhengzhou Shang City cannot be overstated. Zhengzhou Shang City not only has major, large-scale inner and outer wall

Table 1 Dating and chronological phases of Zhengzhou Shang City
(1630 BCE to 1400 BCE)

Phase	Representative locations	Archaeological remains
1	Erligang H9 and Dianxiao H6	Thin and few bronze objects, *jue* (only type), large-scale constructions (building foundation)
2	Erligang H19, the ash layer above the rammed earth of C8T62 in the building foundation area, and C8M32	Thicker bronze objects more diverse and numerous in type, representing a period of prosperity for Zhengzhou Shang City
3	Erligang H2 Yi, Erligang H1, Beierqi Road M1, and Minggong Road M2	Bronzes increasing in both variety and number, including *jue*, *gu*, and *jia*, representing the most prosperous period of Zhengzhou Shang City
4	Shang City CNM5, the second layer of Baijiazhuang, Baijiazhuang M2 and M3, and Minggong Road M4	Large amounts of bronze artifacts in various types, including *lei*, *zun*, *you*, *ding*, *pan*, *yu*, *jue*, and *gu*

remains but also dozens of rammed-earth platforms for a building foundation-temple complex, well used bronze-casting sites, and valuable ceremonial bronze vessels. This evidence appears sufficient to state that the Zhengzhou Shang City is the ruins of the first capital, "Bo," of the historical Shang Dynasty (Wang 1998).

YANSHI SHANG CITY

The discoveries and excavations of Yanshi Shang City (Zhongguo 2003) originated in cooperation with the site selection of Shouyang Mountain Power Plant. Excavations of the Yanshi Shang City began in the spring of 1983 under the supervision of the Han-Wei Luoyang Ancient Capital Team of the Institute of Archaeology, Academy of Social Sciences. In the spring of 1983, after examining and exploring the ruins of Yanshi Shang City, three walls on the west, north, and east sides were confirmed and three large-scale rammed-earth building complexes were located. The research team proposed that Yanshi Shang City had characteristics of a capital city and was very possibly the historical capital "West Bo," which, according to transmitted texts, was established by Shang King Tang after he overthrew the Xia Kingdom. In the late 1980s, eastern and western gates of the Yanshi Shang City were discovered and excavated. In addition, partial ruins of a building foundation center and some small and medium-size residential foundations were discovered, followed by another north-central city center, large amounts of waste pits, storage pits, pottery kilns, water wells, and burials. A series of seasons of fieldwork were pursued in order to establish the date of the city and its layout, in addition to determining the relationship between smaller and bigger building foundations. These efforts resulted in a historical landmark, as well as in defining the cultural boundary and dynastic alteration between the Xia and Shang kingdoms.

Layout

The city walls, city gates, moats, and roads at Yanshi Shang City (Figure 4) were not built at the same time. They were built over a number of different periods during which various changes and expansions took place (Zhongguo 2013).

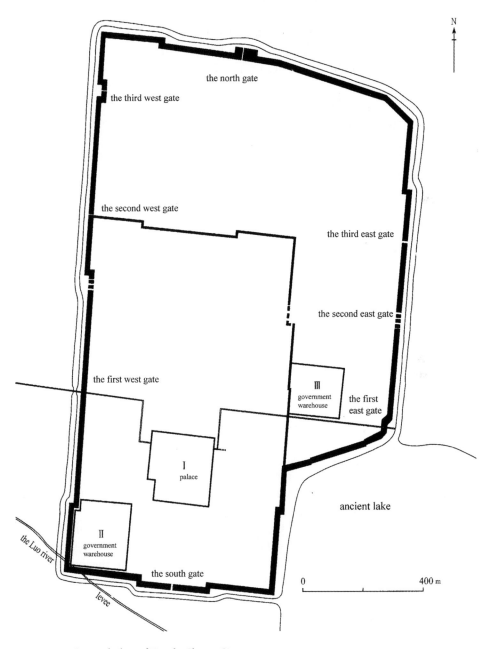

FIGURE 4 Ground plan of Yanshi Shang City.

The earliest smaller complex was rectangular in shape with an area of over 810,000 m², running 1,100 m from north to south and 740 m from east to west. The orientation of the city was 7 degrees off due north. The city walls measured mostly 6–7 m thick. None of the walls were perfectly straight, while some sections were concave and some convex. Foundation ditches were shallow with depths of less than 0.5 m. Remains of the wall were not well preserved, with subsidiary accumulations found on both the inner and the outer layers of the wall.

City walls of the second larger complex of Yanshi Shang City take the shape of a butcher's knife. The southern side of the city is narrower, resembling the handle of the knife. The orientation of the city is also 7 degrees off due north. The total length of the city walls is 5,500 m, and the area is close to 2 million m². Some parts of the city walls are slightly bent. The east wall measures about 1,770 m in total length. The total horizontal distance covered by the west walls is about 1,710 m, that of the north wall roughly 1,240 m, and that of the south wall 740 m. The top of the wall measures approximately 16–18 m wide and the foundation is 18–19 m wide. The east, west, and north walls are preserved in good shape, and the thickness of the rammed-earth layers is about 1–3 m. The construction process of making these rammed-earth walls was to dig the foundation ditch first and then apply a layer of rammed earth. The opening of the ditches was wider than the base of the foundation.

The number of city gates identified in the larger complex of Yanshi Shang City totaled five: two each on east and west walls and one on the north wall, with three gates verified by archaeological excavation. The symmetrical layout of Yanshi Shang City is corroborated by the locations of these city gates. Gates of the West Wall clearly divide the west wall into three equal portions, and eastern and western gates are located directly opposite each other. Later, a gap was found in the mid-section of the north wall, and judging from the stratigraphy of the gap, it must have the remains of a gate. The earthen level underneath the gap dates to the early Shang period. The excavated city gates were similarly constructed with single-door pylons. The width of each pylon was different, but both sides of each pylon were equipped with wood-framed rammed earth between 0.8 to 1 m thick. It is assumed that architectural remains stood above the pylons.

A moat surrounding the larger city complex stretches more than 10 m distant from the city walls. The moat measures approximately 20 m wide and about 6 m deep, with a very steep outside slope and a smooth and vertical inside slope. Silted soil remained stacked at the bottom of the moat.

Roads existed inside and outside the city and fall into four categories: the first type was the major thoroughfare that passed through the city gate. The second type was the road outside the city, mainly surrounding the outside of the city wall. The third type was the road that followed the inside of the city wall. The fourth type included roads that led to major buildings and connected different building complexes.

Pools of water, water supply facilities, and a drainage system were all identified at Yanshi Shang City (Figure 5). The waterway system in the Yanshi Shang City was divided into two parts: one that served the outside and another the inside of the city. The water-

FIGURE 5 A man-made pool found in the northern part of the building foundation area of Yanshi Shang City.

ways outside the city constitute the moat surrounding the city wall and rivers near the site. Inside the city, three types of waterways may be distinguished: the first type was the water supply and drainage system that connected the building foundation garden pool to the outside of the city, the second type was the drainage system that supported the large building complex, and the third type was a simpler system of shallow trenches for drainage.

An artificial pool, found in the northern part of the building foundation site, was assembled with stones. It formed a long rectangular-shaped water pond 130 m long from east to west, 20 m wide from north to south, and roughly 1.5 m deep. Some pottery or marble-made net sinkers were found inside the pool, suggesting that this pool was possibly associated with a royal garden. Both east and west ends of the pool had a channel, built with piled-up stones, that connected to the pool. And, judging from the data measured, the west channel was a water supply channel and the east channel was for drainage. Both channels ran through the east and west walls of the building foundation, then turned two corners, went underneath through the West 1 and East 1 city gate, and finally passed through the pylon to connect with the moat outside of the city.

The Building foundation Area of Yanshi Shang City comprised a complex of buildings located in the south of the city center and covered an area of over 45,000 m² (Wang and Gu 2006). More than nine structural foundations, all facing southwest, were discovered in the south side of this building foundation area. The area was almost square in shape, with the north wall measuring 200 m long, the east wall 180 m, the south wall roughly 90 m, and the west wall 185 m long. The wall itself was about 1.95–2.15 m thick, and the remaining height was about 0.35–0.5 m. The foundation ditch was about 1 m deep and slightly wider than the wall. There was a 2-m-wide doorway in the middle of the south wall. Five complexes, Nos. 1, 4, 8, 7, and 9, have been confirmed archeologically. Terrain on the northern side in the building foundation area is lower than the south. A long ditch, which is over 100 m, runs from the east to west outside a rammed-earth wall to the north of the No. 8 building foundation complex and is dated to the early phase of Yanshi Shang City of Yanshi 1.

A number of renovations and expansions were executed after the second phase of the Yanshi Shang City. However, the building foundation area maintained an encircled and self-contained layout with minimal change throughout the occupation. Each building foundation complex was built in a unique fashion.

No. 4 building foundation complex foundation complex covers an area of 1,632 m²: 51 m long east to west, 32 m wide from north to south, with an orientation of 8 degrees off due north. The complex was centered with a main hall facing south; the east, west, and south sides each had a veranda (gallery). The west wall was built at the north end of the west gallery; the north and west walls were directly behind the main hall and connected with the east wall. This complex appears to have been an enclosed *siheyuan* (four-sided courtyard) structure.

The foundation of No. 5 building foundation complex covers an area of 9,769 m²: 107 m long from east to west, 91.3 m wide from north to south, with an orientation of 10 degrees off due north. The overall layout is very similar to that of No. 4 building foundation complex. However, No. 5 covers an area nearly six times larger than No. 4 building foundation complex. Northern and southern galleries framed each side of the main hall. The northern gallery was longer than the main hall but they both faced the same direction. There was a large and open room in the middle of the south gallery. The building foundation platform of the main hall was 54 m long from east to west and 14.6 m in room depth. Remains of the pillars were found surrounding the four sides of the platform. By reconstructing the original placement of the pillars, it shows there should have been 48 pillars originally, and 35 of those were found in the remains, with a distance between each pillar of approximately 2.2–3.1 m. Remains of stairs were seen in four locations at the south side of the main hall, with spacing over 6.5 m. Rectangular pits, with dogs buried inside, were found on both sides of each stair foundation.

The foundation for No. 6 building foundation complex was underneath the remains of No. 5. The shape of this platform was special: the layout formed an open square and covered an area of 1,638 m²: 38–39 m wide from east to west, 42 m long from north to south. The platform on the northern side was wider and the other three sides slightly narrower. Four long buildings interlocked with each other, forming the shape of "□" with a courtyard in the center. A doorway stood in the middle of the east building for access.

A full understanding of the Yanshi Shang City building foundation area as well as the discovery of the royal garden in the north side of the building foundation area aid in understanding the consistency and variation of Shang architectural types, designs, and layouts during the early Shang dynasty (Figure 6).

Yanshi Shang City handicraft workshops include not only bronze-casting but also pottery and bone ones. The remains associated with bronze-casting include three pot-shaped pits, H8–H10, found under a pile of subsidiary accumulation at the northeast corner city wall of the large city. The three pits are dated to Yanshi Shang City Phase 1. Remains include charcoal, pieces of pottery molds, and copper-smelting slag. Other pits (diameter of 0.3 m) with burnt soil were found near the workshop pits. These signs clearly indicate these remains were associated with bronze-casting.

In Yanshi Shang City, 10 pottery kilns were found in the northern part of the big city. Near the pottery kilns, some simple housing, trampled ground, and water wells were also discovered. The pottery kilns were all vertical pits with a diameter of 1–1.5 m. Pottery kiln chambers that were above ground level were made of a mud and grass mixture, but unfor-

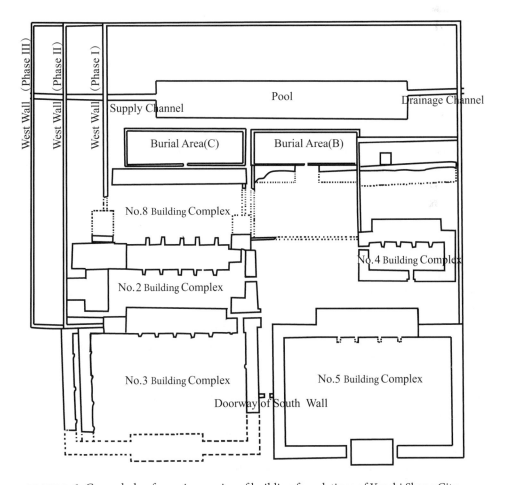

FIGURE 6 Ground plan for main remains of building foundations of Yanshi Shang City.

tunately these chambers have all collapsed. Remains of pottery grids, fire chambers, fire doors, a furnace column, and an operating pit have been found below ground level.

Remains of bone workshop comprise animal bones buried inside pit- and groove-like formations on the west side of the building foundation area. The majority of the animal bones belonged to sheep and pig. Due to the accumulation of numerous bones, it is clear that a bone workshop once existed in this area. A large amount of bone parts remained, including homogenous types of tools made out of bones, such as arrowheads, spoons, and hairpins.

Residential housing in Yanshi Shang City was mainly found in the central and northern part of the city, including four types of small-size housing. The first type typically contained a single room, which covered about 10 m², built above the ground with wood-framed walls; a second type comprised multiple rooms divided by walls, which covered roughly 20–30 m², built above ground with wood framed walls; a third type formed semi-subterranean dwellings, which covered an area of 10 m², constructed with post holes in the center of the house; and a fourth type, a few small houses built within a pit whose floor had been leveled.

Wells found outside the building foundation area were usually located close to the residential housing area and nearby workshops. The opening of a well was generally rectangular, about 2 m long and 1 m wide. The depth of the well was usually more than 5–6 m. On both sides of the well wall were semicircular foot impressions simulating stairs.

More than a hundred burials have been found in Yanshi Shang City. Most burials were earthen vertical pits associated with low economic status and without traces of coffins. Waist pits were rarely dug. Nearly half or more of these burials had no funerary objects. Household pottery was the only funerary object. Bronze and jade objects were seldom seen. No area has yet been identified in association with a cemetery.

In 1996, one burial area was found inside the city wall at the northeast corner of the city. Seventeen graves belonging to male and females were excavated, with 11 excavated underneath the first layer of road soil and six found under the second layer of road soil. Three prone and extended burials were males. Six of the burials had funerary objects. The majority of the objects were pottery, and only one had a bronze *jue*. The excavated pottery was diverse, with groups made up of *li*, *pen*, and *zeng*; *ding*, *gui*, *dou*, and *zun*; and *li*, *pen*, *dou*, and *weng*.

The duration of the construction of the early Shang City of Yanshi to the time of its abandonment was approximately 200 years. It was suggested by the "Xia-Shang-Zhou Chronology Project" that the beginning of the Shang Dynasty was around 1600 BCE. Comparing collected data of Yanshi and Zhengzhou Shang cities, Early Shang culture Period 3 (representing Yanshi Shang City early and middle part of Phase 3) represents a period of transition to the Middle Shang culture Period 1 (Yanshi Shang City late part of Phase 3) around 1400 BCE. Shang cultural remains in the Yanshi Shang City can be divided into three phases based on the relationship of strata and development in pottery. Construction of the city also progressed through three phases of changes in the city layout and structure.

Table 2 The chronological phases of Yanshi Shang City (1600 BCE to 1400 BCE)

Phase	Character of the phase	Archaeological remains
1	The initial construction and in-use period of the Yanshi Shang City	Building Foundation Complex Nos. 1, 4, 7, and 8 and the bronze-casting workshop located northeast, outside of the small city
2	The large-scale expansion and continued use of the Yanshi Shang City	The city walls of the large city built on the foundation of the small city, the rapidly expanded city, and the simultaneous change of building foundation area
3	Another prosperous but short phase of the Yanshi Shang City (by its late period, Yanshi Shang City had been abandoned)	The overall layout of the city without major changes, several more large-scale building complexes built

Phase 1: The initial construction and in-use period of the Yanshi Shang City includes the early phase of the building foundation area; Building foundation Complex Nos. 1, 4, 7, and 8; and the bronze-casting workshop located northeast, outside of the city.

Phase 2: The large-scale expansion and continued use of the Yanshi Shang City involves the city walls of the large city that were built on the foundation of the small city. The city expanded rapidly and the layout of the building foundation area simultaneously changed.

Phase 3: Another prosperous phase of the Yanshi Shang City, though this period is relatively short. The overall layout of the city did not have major changes. The most prominent changes occurred inside the building foundation area, with several more large-scale building complexes being built. By the late period of this phase, Yanshi Shang City had been abandoned and became just another settlement (Table 2).

As provided by archaeological exploration and excavation, Yanshi Shang City began as a small-scale town and expanded into a large-scale city, evolving from a simple to complex construction. Based on the scale, content, and layout of the city, it is clear that the Yanshi Shang City was a political center and state-level capital during the early Shang dynasty.

CITY REMAINS OUTSIDE THE CAPITAL CITY IN THE EARLY SHANG DYNASTY

One major site outside the capital cities of Zhengzhou and Yanshi is Yuanqu Shang City, located in the ancient town of Nanguan of Yuanqu County in Shanxi Province (Zhongguo Guojia Bowuguan 1996). It sits on a raised loess plateau at the point where the Haoqing River joins the Yellow River. Based on current excavated data the city remains take the shape of an irregular square of approximately 1,470 m in perimeter. The walls stretch 400 m from north to south and 350 m from east to west. The overall surface area is over 130,000 m². There are numerous foundation ditches underneath the city wall. Both the north and east walls are single-walled structures, while the south section of the west wall and western section of the south wall are dual-layered due to an apparent reinforcement of the defenses. The existence of a moat was discovered outside the west wall. The gap found in the middle of the west wall, slightly to the north, was confirmed to be a city gate. A major avenue runs through this city gate, extending southeast toward the central building complex, that was located in the middle of the city slightly to the east side. Six rammed-earth platforms were found, and the southeast part of the city is considered to be the residential area.

Twenty Shang tombs, mostly dated to the early Shang period, were excavated within Yuanqu Shang City: three pit burials (special burials), four child or urn burials, and 13 adult burials. Bronze objects were found in the adult burials M1 and M16. Pottery objects were found in M3, M6, and M19. Burials were not found in one concentrated area.

Erligang culture remains in the Yuanqu Shang City can be divided into four phases. The characteristics of objects associated with each phase are parallel to those found in Zhengzhou Shang City, and the chronology line also resembles that of Zhengzhou.

Panlongcheng Shang City is located in Huangpi County, Wuhan City, Hubei province (Hubeisheng Bowuguan 2001). The City rests on a peninsula extending into Panlong Lake, surrounded by water on the east, south, and west sides. Shang cultural remains are abundant and rammed-earth walls were found in the southeast part of the site. The shape of the city wall layout resembles a parallelogram with the axis about 20 degrees east of due north. The city site covers an area of 75,400 m², with a total of 1,100 m in perimeter: 290 m from north to south and 260 m from east to west. City walls are steep on the outside and slope gently inside. The foundation of the city wall is 21 m in width. These walls, trapezoidal in cross-section, were built by stamping earth between board frames section by section, then put together to construct the wall and the sloping protective parts. A moat was dug surrounding four sides of the city wall. In the center of each wall was a gap that is judged to be a city gate. Walls remained at 1.8–2 m high and 20 m thick at the west city gate. At the bottom of the city gate, a stone paved path, 3 m in width and 7 m in partial length, probably served as a doorway (Figure 7). The major building complex, located in the northeastern part of the city, included three buildings sitting on a large-scale rammed-earth platform. This platform was more than 100 m long from north to south and above 60 m wide from east to west. All three buildings were aligned in the same direction along a front-center-back orientation and parallel with each other on the platform. Among the buildings, F1 was probably the "sleeping chamber." F2 seems to have been a large hall with open space and presumably served as the main hall among the three buildings.

Yangjiawan site in the north side of the city is rich in finds: three to five pottery vats and crucibles were often found clustered together, with an accumulated layer of charcoal ash. It has been suggested that the site is the remains of a ceramic workshop.

The cemetery was located outside of the city. Tombs of aristocracy are mainly those discovered at Lijiazui site, whereas middle- and small-sized burials are located in

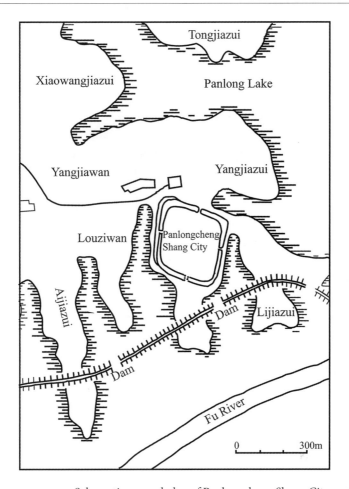

FIGURE 7 Schematic ground plan of Panlongcheng Shang City.

Louziwan, Yangjiazui, and Yangjiawan sites. All tombs were rectangular earth-pit burials. Lijiazui M2 was a rectangular earthen-pit burial (Figure 8) with a direction of
20 degrees east of due north. The pit is filled with pounded rammed earth, narrow in the
opening and wide at the bottom: the opening measures 3.67 × 3.24 m and the bottom
measures 3.77 × 3.40 m. Originally there was an outer chamber placed adjacent to the
outer wall of the burial. The chamber wood facing inside was painted with red lacquer,
and the outside was carved with delicate décor in red and black lacquer. Impressions of
images included animal masks and multiple cloud patterns. In the middle bottom area
of the tomb, close to the east side, a waist pit was discovered. Inside the waist pit, remains
of bones had already turned into powder, no longer identifiable as human or dog.
Within the bone powder remains, a piece of a jade dagger, intentionally broken into
three pieces, was excavated. The funerary objects in this tomb were rich, including
bronze, jade, lacquer, and pottery objects. There were 63 bronze objects including
23 vessels such as *ding*, *li*, *yan*, *gui*, ring-footed *pan*, small *pan*, *lei*, *he*, *gu*, *jia*, and *jue*

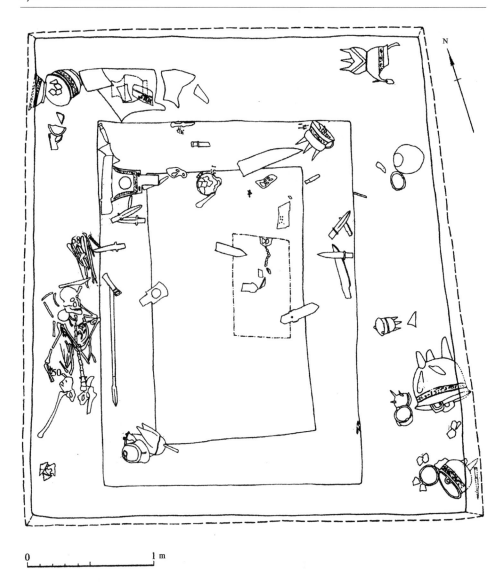

0 ————————————————— 1 m

FIGURE 8 Burial M2 at Lijiazui, Panlongcheng Shang City, Huangpi District, Hubei Province.

(Hubei 1976). The largest bronze vessel was the bronze tripod *ding* with a diameter of 55 cm (Figure 9). In addition, 40 bronze weapons and tools were found, such as *yue*, *ge*, *mao*, *dao*, *fu*, *zu*, *ben*, *zao*, *ju*, and *dun*. The large *yue* (axe) was 41 cm long with a blade as wide as 26 cm, and imagery of a dragon and cloud-scroll patterns appeared at the top of the axe head. This type of weapon was a symbol of a commanding military leader, the tomb owner. Jade objects, including the prominent large jade dagger, handle-like objects, and hairpins, were all placed either inside the coffin or between the coffin and the chamber. Lacquer objects were concentrated in the northwest corner outside of the

FIGURE 9 Bronze tripod *ding* excavated from M2, Lijiazui, Panlong Shang City.

coffin. Some lacquers were carved with patterns, though none of the lacquer objects' type could be identified. Pottery objects included *li*, *guan*, small *guan* with spout, sand-tempered red pottery cylinder, hard pottery *zun* with impressed patterns, and an urn. Three human sacrifices were found in the tomb, and one of the three was a child.

Panlongcheng Shang City was first built in Phase 2 of the early Shang period and was abandoned by Phase 2 of the middle Shang dynasty. This city probably served as a southern center for military and political control of the Shang dynasty. It is also possible that this city was a capital of a non-Shang state, such as a *fang*-state, in the southern region of the Shang kingdom.

Another northwestern early Shang city is Dongxiafeng Shang City. The site rests on a plateau by Qinglong River, toward the northeast of Dongxiafeng village in Xian county, Shanxi province (Institute of Archaeology CASS). The city walls on all four sides were badly damaged. Though the north wall has not been found, the other three city corners, relatively rounded, have been located—structures with rammed-earth walls with protective slopes on both sides, which were about 8 m wide at the bottom of the foundation. All walls were built from the ground level and moats existed outside the walls.

A group of circular building platforms were found in the southwest corner of the city. These 40–50 circular buildings were lined up horizontally and vertically. A platform was located underneath each building foundation and cross-shaped grooves were found on all platforms. There were 30–40 postholes surrounding the platform foundation. No doorway was found. It is speculated that these buildings were stilt-style storage facilities.

All burials found at the site were rectangular rammed-earth vertical pits. Funerary objects included ceramic vessels such as *li*, *pen*, *jia*, *dou*, and *guan*. Only one type of bronze vessel, the *jue*, was found. Stone objects included *fu* (axes), *ben* (adzes), *chan* (shovels), *dao* (knives), *lian* (sickles), *zao* (chisels), *zu* (arrowheads), and *fanglun* (spinning wheels). Bone, horn, and ivory/shell objects found included *chan* (shovels), *zhen* (needles), *bi* (ladles for rice), *ji* (hairpins), *zhui* (awls), *dao* (knives), *lian* (sickles), and *zu* (arrowheads), and so on. The variety of types in this category was similar to those found at Erligang. A few differences were marked by more stone *chan* (shovels) and more stone knives than sickles. There were only a few small bronze objects, such as *dao* (knives) and *zu* (arrowheads).

The Early Shang culture of Dongxiafeng can be divided into four successive cultural phases, corresponding to those four of the Zhengzhou Shang City.

The early Shang site Fucheng Shang City is located in the southwest suburbs of Jiaozuo City in Henan Province (Yuan 2000). Each wall measures approximately 300 m long in forming a square citadel. The east wall has been restored to its original length of 300 m. The south wall remains only as a foundation ditch. The foundation ditches measure 15 m wide and 0.9 m deep. This city with rammed-earth walls was built in the Early Shang Dynasty.

Four rammed-earth platforms were found inside the city. Among them, Nos. 1 and 2 are well preserved. No. 1 platform forms a rectangle measuring 70 m long from north to south and 55 m wide from east to west. The layout is composed of three halls and two form enclosed open courtyards (Figure 10).

Wangjinglou Shang City is located on the east side of Wangjinglou Reservoir, 6 km north of Xinzheng City, Henan Province (Zhengzhoushi 2011). The Huang River flows through the western side of the site. The Wangjinglou Shang City was first discovered in 1965. In 2010, a reconstruction project of the Zhengxin Expressway cut through the east side of the remains leading to the discovery of the site dating to the early Shang, Erligang culture (Gu 2016).

Since the walls were mostly buried below ground surface, the city remains were relatively well preserved (Figure 11). The square city was oriented 15 degrees east of north and covered an area of about 370,000 m^2: the north wall was about 802 m long, the east wall 590 m, the south wall 630 m, and the recovered west wall roughly 560 m. The city walls were constructed out of three parts: foundation ditch, the wall, and protective slope. Three city gates were found, two on the east wall and one on the south wall. The east city gate covered an area of 2,000 m^2 and has been identified as forming a "*weng*," an additional extension of the fortification outside the city gate. Evidently the fortified site exhibits an interest in a strong military defense. Remains from the city site also include roads, large rammed-earth platforms, ceremonial pits, housing foundations, stoves, pottery kilns, pits, wells, and burials. Small burials were randomly scattered within the city. City walls were first built in the Lower Erligang Phase 1, flourished in the Lower Erligang Phase 2 and Upper Erligang Phase 1, and were discarded in the Upper Erligang Phase 2. Wangjinglou City site of the Erligang culture of the early Shang period provides valuable data for analyzing cities, possibly of a non-Shang state (*fang* state) associated Swith the early Shang dynasty.

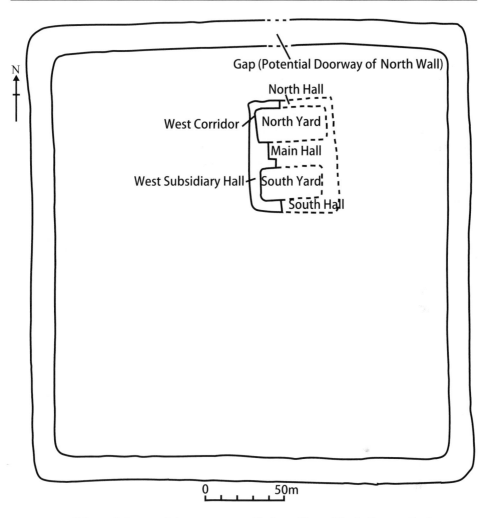

FIGURE 10 Schematic layout of the structures at Fucheng Shang City in Jiaozuo, Fucheng, Henan.

MIDDLE SHANG PERIOD

The Yanshi Shang City and the Zhengzhou Shang City are the most important representatives of the Early Shang culture. Late Shang is represented by the Yin Ruins in Anyang. The important stage between these two periods is currently called by its archaeological label, "Middle Shang period." According to published scientific articles, the relics belonging to this stage have been found at representative sites, such as Baijiazhuang locale in Zhengzhou; Xiaotun in Anyang, Henan; Xingtai in Hebei; and Jinan in

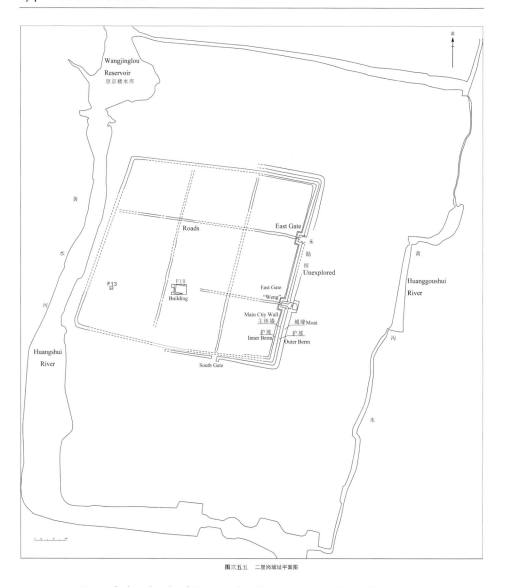

图三五五　二里岗城址平面图

FIGURE 11 Ground plan sketch of Wangjinglou Shang City, Xinzheng, Henan.

Shandong. The discovery and excavation of Xiaoshuangqiao in Zhengzhou and Huanbei Shang City in Anyang gradually led to the solidification of this identification of a Middle Shang period.

Huanbei Shang City and other remains of the same period in adjacent areas

Huanbei Shang City of Anyang was discovered in 1999 and lies on the north bank of Huan River in Anyang, Henan (Anyang Gongzuodui 2003). The southwest part of the city abuts the Yin Ruins heritage site. City remains are buried 2.5 m underground and take the layout of a square covering an area of more than 4,000,000 m², with each side of the wall close to 2,000 m in length.

Based on the perspective of a cross-section, only the foundation ditches of the city wall remain extant and average about 9 m wide. During the 1960s, a survey of the Huan River Basin uncovered city remains of Shang date. Subsequently, bronzes of the Middle Shang period were excavated at Sanjiazhuang and Dongwangducun sites, outside the city wall. Many rammed-earth platforms were discovered throughout the site and particularly large-scale ones in the south-central part of the city. The latter were presumed to be ancestral temples or royal buildings. Other house foundations, wells, ash pits, burial pits, and layers of settlement were also excavated.

Archaeological discoveries at Huanbei Shang City since the 1960s have been used to create significant datasets for understanding the layout and design of this Shang city. The ancient tradition of planning the structures around a major axis was confirmed based on the layout of this city. The building foundation area of Huanbei Shang City was built on the south part of an axis running from north to south. Densely packed settlements were seen in the northern part of the city. These housing foundations were clustered together, with a large plaza or courtyard space separating each. The remains of road soil were also found between each structure. Regularly used roads connected settlement clusters and were found as well as skirting large rammed-earth platforms that stood alone. The latter platforms were usually larger in size and better built than others. Judging from the spacing arrangement, it is suggested that these were shared public buildings for multiple settlements (Tang 1999).

Huanbei Shang City building foundation area

The building foundation area was located in the southeast and shaped as a rectangle with an orientation of 13 degrees off due north. It covered about 410,000 m² and was 795 m long and over 515 m wide. The foundation ditch of the walls around the building foundation was 6–7 m wide, and the main wall was 5–6 m thick. The surveyed large rammed-earth platforms lie within the excavated wall of the site, and those in the east, north, and mid-section of the southern outer wall are clearly visible. Only the east section of the south wall has been explored. The location of the west wall was determined by the existence of rammed earth. The impression, direction, width, soil quality, and ramming technique of rammed earth found elsewhere also help show the positioning of the west wall. Building Foundation buildings were located in the north part of the building foundation area in Huanbei Shang City. More than 30 rammed-earth platforms were found, and all were oriented east to west and arranged in a north to south order with an orientation of 13 degrees off due north. The overall layout was very precise with no overlap between the platforms. Most of No. 1 and all of No. 2 platform foundations were explored (Figure 12) (Tang 2010). The plan of No. 1 was apparently an enclosed courtyard building foundation, or *siheyuan* 四合院. The structure of this building foundation complex comprised a main hall in the north and a hall with covered corridors and rooms next to the hall in the south, alongside stairs set in the west. Although the east has not yet been excavated, it is clear that with surveys the structure extended symmetrically in line with the west side. The total area covered by the building complex was close to 16,000 m², with east to west being 173 m long and from north to south 85–91.5 m wide. Rooms next to the hall in the south and the main hall in the north are wider than those elsewhere. The courtyard in the center covers an area of about 10,000 m². The plan of No. 2 platform was shaped as a "*hui* 回" character with a double enclosed courtyard building. The com-

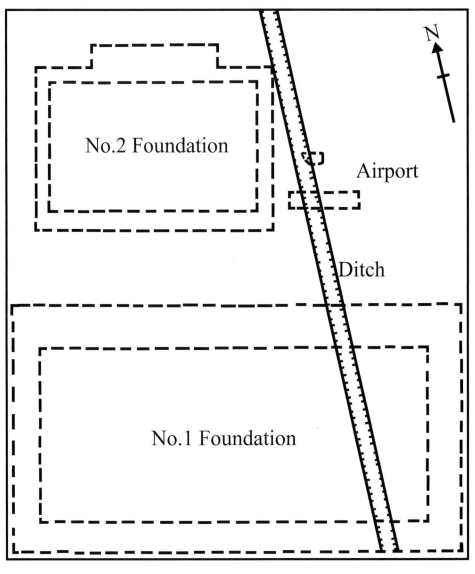

FIGURE 12 Schematic drawing for the spatial relationship between No. 1 and No. 2 rammed-earth foundations at Huanbei Shang City, Anyang, Henan.

plex covered an area of 5,992 m², was 92 m wide from east to west, and the north-south span was between 61.4 and 68.5 m (Anyang Gongzuodui 2010). All south, east, and west side buildings were covered corridors, and the north side was the main hall with "er-wu 耳屋" (side-rooms) on both sides. The No. 2 platform foundation had structures including a main hall with flanking side-rooms, a west side-room, south side-room, doorway, east side-room, and attached structures on the northeast of the east side-room, in addition to wells. Nos. 1 and 2 platform foundations were both critical parts of the building foundation area in the Huanbei Shang City. The two platforms were adjacent to each other, one in the north and one in the south, with 29 meters distance from each other. The difference in scale and structure reflects the different nature and function of these two buildings, yet the close spatial relationship indicates the two platforms were linked. A large number of sacrificial pits were found in front of the main hall and side-rooms of the No. 1 platform, and sacrificed dogs were found inside the main chamber of the main hall. It is thus suggested that No. 1 platform was associated with ritual activities and could very possibly have functioned as an ancestral temple (Figure 13). In the Shang dynasty, it was common practice to combine the building foundation used for administrative purposes and the ancestral temple used for ceremonial rites into one building foundation. There were no large-scale sacrifices found near the No. 2 platform. In addition, wells were found in the attached structures in the southeast, so it is reasonable to assume No. 2 platform was for residential use.

After excavating burials in Huanbei Shang City, it seems the majority were distributed around residential areas. This indicates that the Shang people were not only living in the city but also buried in the neighboring area of the settlements. Dozens of burial types were found in Huayuanzhuang, Dongwangdu, and east of Sanjiazhuang sites in the northwest of Huanbei Shang City. Burial types can be categorized into an earthen-pit type, a foundation layer burial, a pit burial, and an urn burial. The latter three types were more likely sacrificial in function. The majority of earthen-pit burials were medium or small in size, and if wooden coffins were used, the deceased faced upward with straight limbs. Sacrificial dogs were located either on the inner surrounding burial ledge or in the waist pit. Funerary objects include: bronze, jade, lacquer, pottery, stone, bone, turquoise, clam shell objects, and so on. Certain combinations and types of objects were seen in funerary findings, such as more ceramic food vessels including *li*, *dou*, and *gui*, and bronze wine vessels such as *gu*, *jue*, and *jia*.

According to ¹⁴C dating and the Accelerator Mass Spectrometer dating (AMS) data recorded in the "1996–2000 Phase Progress Report of the Xia-Shang-Zhou Chronology Project," Huanbei Shang City may be dated 1350 to 1250 BCE (Xia Shang Zhou 2000). Huanbei Shang City can be divided into two phases based on ceramic characteristics. Chronologically, the early phase is close to the middle Shang Phase 1 or a bit later and should be dated to middle Shang Phase 2; the later phase is associated with the middle Shang Phase 3. Phases 2 and 3 are represented by early and late stratigraphic remains found in 1997 inside Huanbei Shang City (Anyang Gongzuodui 1998). The Daxinzhuang site in Jinan proves that middle Shang Phase 2 is later than 1 (Shandong Daxue 1995). The relationship between Middle and Late Shang cultures is based on stratigraphic evidence

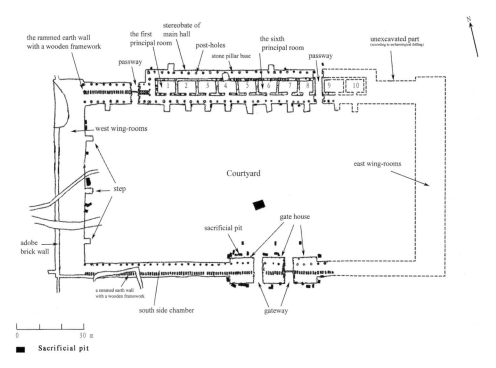

FIGURE 13 Ground plan of the platform foundation No. 1 at Huanbei Shang City, Anyang, Henan.

of the 1980s—on a pit excavated to the east of Sanjiazhuang site (Anyang Gongzuodui 1983). The Middle Shang period at Huanbei went through three phases of development (Table 3).

As a large-scale site with major rammed-earth platform foundations identifying major buildings, Huanbei Shang City site may be equated with a capital settlement. Some scholars believe that the site may be the settlement created after Shang Emperor "Pangeng 盘庚" moved to "Yin 殷" (Yang 2000); some scholars also propose that Huanbei Shang City is in fact Shang King "Hedanjia's 河亶甲" capital, "Xiang 相," of the Middle Shang period (Wen 1998).

Zhengzhou Xiaoshuangqiao

The site is located in Xiaoshuangqiao village on a southwestern river terrace with a gentle alluvial plain, about 20 km northwest of Zhengzhou City in Henan Province. A series of comprehensive investigations along with large-scale excavations took place after 1990 (Henan 2012). The site area covers about 1,500,000 m². Excavated remains include a number of rammed-earth platform foundations; bronze-casting sites; sacrificial areas; storage pits; pits; stoves; trenches; a rich wealth of ceramics; and bronze, stone, bone, and clamshell objects. Cultural remains include architectural foundations of a building foundation or temple, sacrificial pits, storage pits, miscellaneous other pits, trenches,

Table 3 The dating and chronological phases of Huanbei Shang City (1400 BCE to 1250 BCE)

Phase	Period	Archaeological remains
1	Middle Shang Phase 2	The early stratigraphic remains found in 1997 inside Huanbei Shang City
2	Middle Shang Phase 3	The late stratigraphic remains found in 1997 inside Huanbei Shang City

burials, and wells. Northeast of the site was the area for the "building foundation cum ancestral temple" complex. Shang remains include a foundation ditch for the city wall, high raised platforms made of rammed earth for ceremonial use, building platform foundations, residential sites, groups of sacrificial pits, foundation pits, a moat, and much more. Close to 10 rammed-earth platform foundations were found in the center of the site within the walls of the building foundation. Sacrificial remains close to the building foundations suggest a building related to an ancestral temple. One high, raised rammed-earth platform measures 50 m long east to west, 40 m wide north to south, and stands more than 12 m high. It appears to have functioned as a large altar for Shang royal members to conduct sacrifice and worship activities. Remains associated with sacrifice are abundant in this site: a sacrificial field, multiple animal sacrifice pits, human and animal sacrifice pits (Figure 14), pits with ox heads, pits with ox horns (Figure 15), human sacrifice pits, foundation pits, object pits, and evidence of the fire ceremonials (*liao* 燎). "*Yimai* 瘗埋" sacrifices (earthen burials) are the main type of sacrifice, with the largest number of sacrificial victims directly buried into the soil—a practice probably offered in honor of the "Spirit of the Soil and the Ground." The content of these sacrificial pits may be divided into three types: (1) human and animal sacrificial pits, including group burial pits, human skull pits, multiple human burial pits, double sacrificial pits, single sacrificial pits, human and animal co-burial pits, ash pits, and ash layer burials; (2) animal sacrifice pits of cattle, sheep, dogs, pigs, deer, and other livestock; and (3) multi-animal pits. Other ritual objects used included bronze, jade, stone, ceramic, proto porcelain, clam shell, gold foil, oracle bones, and so on.

Writing in cinnabar was also discovered amid Xiaoshuangqiao site remains. Characters, written with a soft brush dipped in cinnabar, were discovered on the surface and vessel openings of ceramic jars found in a sacrificial area and among sacrificial remains. Judging from the writing style and character structure, these cinnabar writings of sacrificial intent are similar to those words carved into oracle bones of the Late Shang period (Figure 16). They are one and the same writing style, and the ceramic writing in cinnabar is related to sacrificial activities. In addition, scribal symbols were also found on ceramic vessels. Two kinds of scribal symbols were found: one that may have functioned as ideographic symbols and the other as décor.

Excavated bronze objects survived mostly as fragments. Types of bronze objects with identifiable shapes comprised *ding, jia, jue, zu, gou, zan,* carving knives, and round-shaped objects. Yet bronze architectural fittings were also found for the first time.

FIGURE 14 Sacrificial pit with human and animal bones, Xiaoshuangqiao, Zhengzhou.

FIGURE 15 Pit with ox horns, Xiaoshuangqiao, Zhengzhou.

FIGURE 16 Characters, written on the surface of ceramic jars, Xiaoshuangqiao Site, Zhengzhou (left is the original picture; right is processed by photoshop).

Excavators initially dated the Xiaoshuangqiao site with early and late phases, equivalent to the Middle Shang culture Phases 1 and 2. According to the "Xia, Shang and Zhou Chronology Project," the latest dating data show that the absolute age of Zhengzhou Xiaoshuangqiao site is equivalent to 1435–1412 BCE (Xia Shang Zhou 2000). Dating is complicated by the fact that the Yueshi culture is a part of the cultural setting at Xiaoshuangqiao (Henan 2012). After a comprehensive study of the remains from the site, it is suggested that the occupation of Xiaoshuangqiao site is relatively short, and that the site dates to the earlier stage of the middle Shang dynasty, parallel with the Baijiazhuang period or the last phase of Zhengzhou Shang City Erligang phase (An Jinhuai 1988). Xiaoshuangqiao site prospered at the same late phase of Zhengzhou Shang City (Henan 1996). Although the scale of remains at Xiaoshuangqiao is considerably smaller, cultural connotations indicate that the site was a capital city. Historically, the occupation of the site would tally with the records of the ancient "Ao 隞" ("Xiao 嚣") capital of the Shang king "Zhongding 仲丁" of the Middle Shang period.

Cultural remains and relics of the Middle Shang period excavated in Xingtai area of Hebei Province have gradually caught the attention of academia (Hebei 1995). The sites associated with this Middle Shang culture forming an interconnected group include Caoyanzhuang, Dongxianxian (Tang 1959), Xiguanwai (Tang 1960), Jiacun (Hebei 1958b), Nandaguozhuang (Tang 1957), Yinguocun (Hebei 1960), and others. Only Caoyanzhuang has undergone a large-scale excavation (Hebei 1958a). This site is located inside Xingtai City and is overlapped by Xingtai Railway Station and nearby buildings. It was discovered in 1954, and excavated Shang remains were divided into two strata. The lower strata is dated slightly earlier than the Late Shang culture at Yinxu and later than the Middle Shang culture Phase 1. Surveyed remains at the site are not only large in scale but should be extremely valuable in archaeological studies due to their geographical location in the northeast and their dating. Based on historical literature and excavation results, various scholars have speculated that the cultural remains of this area are associated with the historical capital "Xing 邢" where Shang king "Zuyi 祖乙" set up his capital (Zou 1999). Political disruption and competition nonetheless defined the Middle Shang period as one of turbulence marked by constant moves of a capital's location.

To conclude, the three Shang city sites of Zhengzhou, Xiaoshuangqiao, and Huanbei Shang City are very possibly remains of capital cities, as indicated by not only fortified walls but large-scale building structures and related finds. Though these associations cannot be proved currently through contemporary written data, the locations correspond to historical records, and excavated remains in terms of scale and chronology support the possibility. It is anticipated that future archaeological excavations will provide continued proof and further conclusions.

BIBLIOGRAPHY

An, Jinhuai 安金槐 1988. "A Further Study on the Staging of Pottery in Erligang Period of Shang Dynasty in Zhengzhou 关于郑州商代二里岗期陶器分期问题的再研究," *Huaxia Kaogu* 4: 104–108.

Anyang Gongzuodui, Zhongguo Shehui Kexueyuan Kaogu Yanjiusuo 中国社会科学院考古研究所安阳工作队 1983. "The Excavation of East of Sanjiazhuang Site in Yin Ruins, Anyang 安阳殷墟三家庄东的发掘." *Kaogu* 2: 126–132.

Anyang Gongzuodui, Zhongguo Shehui Kexueyuan Kaogu Yanjiusuo 中国社会科学院考古研究所安阳工作队 1998. "Archaeological Excavation Report of Huayuanzhuang site in Anyang, Henan, 1997 河南安阳市洹北花园庄遗址 1997 年发掘简报," *Kaogu* 10: 23–35.

Anyang Gongzuodui, Zhongguo Shehui Kexueyuan Kaogu Yanjiusuo 中国社会科学院考古研究所安阳工作队 2003. "The Survey and Trial Excavation of Huanbei Shang City in Anyang, Henan. 河南安阳市洹北商城的勘察与试掘," *Kaogu* 5: 387–400.

Anyang Gongzuodui, Zhongguo Shehui Kexueyuan Kaogu Yanjiusuo 中国社会科学院考古研究所安阳工作队 2010. "No. 2 Foundations in Huanbei Shang City's Palace Area, Anyang, Henan 河南安阳市洹北商城宫殿区二号基址发掘简报," *Kaogu* 1: 9–22 + 97–100.

Gu, Wanfa 顾万发 2016. *Xinzheng Wangjinglou: Archaeological Excavation Report from 2010 to 2012* 新郑望京楼：2010–2012年田野考古发掘报告. Beijing: Kexue chubanshe.

Hebeisheng Wenwu Guanli Weiyuanhui 河北省文物管理委员会 1958a. "The Excavation Report of Xingtai Caoyanzhuang Site 邢台曹演庄遗址发掘报告," *Kaogu xuebao* 4: 43–50.

Hebeisheng Wenwu Guanli Weiyuanhui 河北省文物管理委员会 1958b. "A Brief Report of the Jiacun Shang Site in Xingtai 邢台贾村商代遗址 试掘简报," *Wenwu cankao ziliao* 10: 29–31.

Hebeisheng Wenwu Fuchadui, Hebei Xingtaidui 河北省文物复查队邢台 分队 1995. "A Brief Report on Archaeological Investigation in Xingtai County, Hebei 河北邢台县考古调查简报," *Wenwu chunqiu* 1: 1–13.

Hebeisheng Wenwuju Wenwu Gongzuodui 河北省文化局文物工作队 1960. "A Brief Report of the Yinguocun Shang Site and Tombs of Warring States Period in Xingtai 邢台尹郭村商代遗址及战国墓葬试掘简报," *Wenwu* 4: 20–23.

Henansheng Wenwu Kaogu Yanjiuyuan 河南省文物考古研究院 1959. *Zhengzhou Erligang Site* 郑州二里岗. Kexue chubanshe: Beijing.

Henansheng Wenwu Kaogu Yanjiuyuan 河南省文物考古研究院 1983a. "The First Archaeological Excavation Report of the Palace Area of Zhengzhou Shang City 郑州商代城内宫殿遗址区第一次发掘报告," *Wenwu* 4: 1–28.

Henansheng Wenwu Kaogu Yanjiuyuany 河南省文物考古研究院 1983b. "The New Discoveries of Three Tombs of the Shang Dynasty in Zhengzhou's Beierqi Road 郑州北二七路新发现三座商墓," *Wenwu* 3: 60–77.

Henansheng Wenwu Kaogu Yanjiuyuan 河南省文物考古研究院 1989. "The Bronze-Casting Workshop of Shang Dynasty's Erligang Period in Zhengzhou 郑州商代二里岗期铸铜基址," *Kaoguxue jikan* 6. Beijing: Kexue chubanshe.

Henansheng Wenwu Kaogu Yanjiusuo 河南省文物考古研究院 1991. "Report on the Pottery Workshop of Zhengzhou Shang City 郑州市商代制陶遗址发掘简报," *Huaxia Kaogu* 4: 1–19.

Henansheng Wenwu Kaogu Yanjiusuo 河南省文物考古研究院 1993. "The Archaeological Excavation Report of the Zhengzhou Electric Power College 郑州电力学校考古发掘报告," *The New Discovery and Research of Zhengzhou Shang City* 郑州商城考古新发现与研究. Zhengzhou: Zhongzhou guji chubanshe.

Henansheng Wenwu Kaogu Yanjiusuo 河南省文物考古研究院 1996. "Excavation of the Xiao Shuangqiao Site in Zhengzhou in 1995 1995 年郑州小双桥遗址的发掘." *Huaxia Kaogu* 3: 1–56.

Henansheng Wenwu Kaogu Yanjiusuo 河南省文物考古研究院 1999. *The Shang Dynasty Cellar-Stored Bronze in Zhengzhou* 郑州商代铜器窖藏. Beijing: Kexue chubanshe.

Henansheng Wenwu Kaogu Yanjiusuo 河南省文物考古研究院 2001. *Zhengzhou Shang City: 1953–1985; Archaeological Excavation Reports* 郑州商城：1953–1985 考古发掘报告. Beijing: Wenwu chubanshe.

Henansheng Wenwu Kaogu Yanjiusuo 河南省文物考古研究院 2012. *Zhengzhou Xiaoshuangqiao: The Archaeological Excavation Report from 1990–2000* 郑州小双桥：1990–2000 年考古发掘报告. Beijing: Kexue chubanshe.

Hubeisheng Bowuguan 湖北省博物馆 1976. "The Bronze Artifacts of Erligang Period in Panlongcheng Shang City 盘龙城商城二里冈期的青铜器." *Wenwu* 2: 26–41.

Hubeisheng Bowuguan, Hubeisheng Wenwu Kaogu Yanjiusuo 湖北省博 物馆，湖北省文物考古研究所 2001. *Panlongcheng Shang City: The Archaeological Excavation Report from 1963 to 1994* 盘龙城：1963–1994 年 考古发掘报告。Beijing: Wenwu chubanshe.

Shandong Daxue Lishixi, Kaogu Zhuanye 山东大学历史系考古专业等 1995. "A Report about Trial Excavation of the Daxinzhuang Site of Jinan in the Autumn of 1984, 1984 年秋济南大辛庄遗址试掘述要." *Wenwu* 6: 12–27.

Song, Guoding 宋国定 1993. *Overview of Zhengzhou Shang City's Archaeological Research from 1985–1992,* 1985–1992年郑州商城考古发现综述. Zhengzhou: Zhongzhou guji chubanshe.

Tang, Jigen 唐际根 1999. "Research on the Middle Shang Culture 中商文化研究." *Kaogu xuebao* 4: 393–420.

Tang, Jigen 唐际根 2010. "Research on the Construction and Restoration of the No. 1 and No. 2 Rammed Earth Foundations in Huanbei Shang City's Palace Area 河南安阳市洹北商城宫殿区二号基址发掘简报." *Kaogu* 1: 9–22+97–100.

Tang, Yunming 唐云明 1957. "A Brief Report on the Site of the Nandaguo Shang Site of Xingtai 邢台南大郭村商代遗址探掘简报." *Wenwu Cankao Ziliao* 3: 61–63.

Tang, Yunming 唐云明 1959. "A Survey of the Dongxianxian Shang Site of Xingtai, Hebei 河北邢台东先贤村商代遗址调查." *Kaogu* 2: 108–109.

Tang, Yunming 唐云明 1960. "Trial Excavation of the Xiguanwai site in Xingtai 邢台西关外遗址试掘." *Wenwu* 7: 69–70.

Wang, Lixin 王立新 1998. *Research on the Early Shang Culture* 早商文化研究. Beijing: Gaoji jiaoyu chubanshe.

Wang, Xuerong, and Gu Fei 王学荣，谷飞 2006. "The Research of Yanshi Shang City's Layout and Change 偃师商城宫城布局与变迁研究." *Zhongguo guojia bowuguan* 6: 4–15.

Wen, Yu 文雨 1998. "Huayuan Zhuang Site of Huangbei and Hetanjia's Capital 'Xiang' 洹北花园庄遗址与河亶甲迁相." *Zhongguo wenwu bao* November, 25.

Xia-Shang-Zhou Duandai Gongcheng Zhuanjiazu 夏商周断代工程专家组 2000. *Xia-Shang-Zhou Chronology Project: The Report of Phase Achievements from 1996 to 2000 (Abridged Version)* 夏商周断代工程 1996–2000 年阶段成果报告(简本). Beijing: Shijie tushu chuban gongsi.

Yang, Xizhang et al. 杨锡璋等 2000. "On Pangeng's Move to Yin 盘庚迁殷地点蠡测." *Zhongyuan Wenwu* 1: 15–19.

Yang, Yubin et al. 杨育彬等 1981. "New Discoveries of Bronze Artifacts from Zhengzhou Shang City in Recent Years 近几年来在郑州新发现的商代青铜器." *Zhongyuan wenwu* 2: 1–3.

Yuan, Guangkuo 袁广阔 2000. "The Excavation Report of Fucheng Shang City in Jiaozuo 河南焦作市府城遗址发掘简报." *Huaxia kaogu* 2: 16–35.

Zhengzhou Bowuguan 郑州博物馆 1965. "Two Shang Tombs Located at the West of Minggong Road in Zhengzhou 郑州市铭功路西侧的两座商代墓." *Kaogu* 10: 500–506.

Zhengzhoushi Wenwu Kaogu Yanjiusuo 郑州市文物考古研究院 2011. "A Report on the Preliminary Investigation and Excavation of Erligang Culture at Wangjinglou 望京楼二里岗文化城址初步勘探和发掘简报." *Zhongguo guojia bowuguan* 10: 19–28.

Zhongguo Guojia Bowuguan, Shanxisheng Kaogu Yanjiusuo, Yuanquxian Boquguan 中国国家博物馆，山西省考古研究所，垣曲县博物馆 1988. *Xiaxian Dongxiafeng* 夏县东下冯. Beijing: Wenwu chubanshe.

Zhongguo Guojia Bowuguan, Shanxisheng Kaogu Yanjiusuo, Yuanquxian Boquguan 中国国家博物馆，山西省考古研究所，垣曲县博物馆 1996. *Yuanqu Shang City*, vol. 1 垣曲商城(一). Beijing: Kexue chubanshe.

Zhongguo Guojia Bowuguan, Shanxisheng Kaogu Yanjiusuo, Yuanquxian Boquguan 中国国家博物馆，山西省考古研究所，垣曲县博物馆 2013. *Yanshi Shang City* vol. 1 偃师商城(第一册). Beijing: Kexue chubanshe.

Zhongguo Shehui Kexueyuan Kaogu Yanjiusuo 中国社会科学院考古研究所 2003. *Chinese Archeology: Xia and Shang* 中国考古：夏商卷. Beijing: Kexue chubanshe.

Zou, Heng 邹衡 1999. "Research on the Predynastic Shang Culture in Xingtai and Zuyi's Migration to Xing 邢台与先商文化、祖乙迁邢研究." *Sandai Wenming Yanjiu* 三代文明研究 I: 33–40.

....

CHAPTER 13

SHANG BELIEF AND ART

....

BY ELIZABETH CHILDS-JOHNSON, OLD DOMINION UNIVERSITY

THE art of Shang, primarily ritual in function, is dominated by "shamanic" trappings. The primary remains are small in scale, yet as art they include technically brilliant cast and polished bronzes, refined carved bone, ivory vessels, and stone and jade worked forms. Large-scale art and architecture once existed in the form of perishable materials, primarily wood, as in lacquer-painted, wood-carved performance sculptures and insignia, alongside extensive rammed-earth citadels on high-rising platforms, stretching south to north in a series of rectangular and square—now lost—one- or two-story halls and outdoor pyramidal altars. Shang belief and religious practice reveal themselves in visual formats and oracle bone terminology. As outlined in this chapter, the Shang lived a form of what I label "institutionalized shamanism." The Shang embraced metamorphic belief, worshipped an empowered dead, and created a visual vocabulary of mnemonic royal power symbols.

REVIEW OF METAMORPHISM AND METAMORPHIC ART STANDARDS

I take an approach that few scholars have taken in studying Shang ritual art. I approach the field from a holistic point of view exploring Shang contemporary data, which is threefold in comprising written, archaeological, and visual materials. Past attempts are primarily represented in categorizing imagery or in explaining representations with concepts prevalent in post-Shang classical texts. Stylistic analyses have also grown moribund and stagnant. As with other ancient cultures, the creation of royal art and architecture of early China was profoundly interlocked with religious belief and practice. One manifested the other. As evinced in bone divinations, the Shang depended on spirits for sustenance and for a natural order.

"Institutionalized shamanism" fused with the need to incorporate the ruling party of Shang and their royal claim to authority.[1] The origin of royal ancestor worship began with the establishment of the state and the need to anchor state power. Kings cohabited at death with the cosmological deity Di or Shang Di, "Di on High," a pervasive sky power. In afterlife the royal dead gradually coalesced with the cosmological power of Di, and the dead forbears became divinities accompanying Di. Di controlled all that was natural. Shang kings assumed superhuman powers—not as mediators[2] but as a manifestation, as divinities with quasi-equal powers. These powers reinforced the king's legitimacy to rule.[3] Metamorphism or *yi* 異, as known in bone inscriptions, defines Shang belief and the power of the king to *bin* 賓 or "to identify with the spirit world" (Childs-Johnson 2008). As defined in various articles, the imagery of the Shang era is dominated by the rendering of transformation or *yi*, the power to metamorphose or spiritually transcend in communicating and identifying with the spirit world. Shang imagery is royal imagery. And the power to *bin* was the prerogative of the king. Through spirit power *yi* 異 and awesome threat *wei* 畏/威 (Childs-Johnson 1995) the king maintained control of his dominion. The predominant theme of metamorphosis is based on the belief in the power of one to identify with the spirit world. In representation the image is the semi-human animal mask, here labeled metamorphic power mask, and its variants, which may be complete or abbreviated, featured as images of display or semi-abstract renderings. Other royal power images may accompany this mask as subordinate images of metamorphosis. Representative are the *feng* bird and *long* dragon in various conformations. Others include the cicada, snake, owl, and mythic combinations. The mask and its connotation of change from human to spirit realms is the basis of Shang imagery.

As reviewed recently, I define the vocabulary of metamorphic imagery by several conventions of representation.[4] These standards of representation or modules were formulated by the beginning of the Early Shang period and continued to be present through the prime of the Shang cultural period.

The standard conventions and traditions used to represent the metamorphic semi-human animal mask of Shang are present in the earliest early Shang images and continue to be present and dominate, as summarized in this chapter. They appear in the earliest of images, as mentioned, from Zhengzhou, Erligang, and Xiaoshuangqiao sites. It should be clarified that the term used in many past publications to describe the ubiquitous face and extensions decorating ritual Shang art works, that of *taotie*, is inappropriate since it is a

[1] The archaeologist K. C. Chang (1983) took a generalized approach to Shang institutions, dominated by a sort of politically unified panhellenic shamanism, based primarily on late transmitted texts dating well after the Shang period.

[2] Childs-Johnson notes that "It is a repeated misconception that the royal dead interceded with Di on behalf of the living" (2012:176) as once proposed by Keightley (1978:212–213) and followed by others (e.g., Wang 2000:36, 39). The king is not a supernatural intermediary but one with divine power. As proposed by Hu Houxuan in 1944 "dead royal spirits [that] accompanied Di, *pei di* 配帝, resided with Di in the empyrean above" (1944:298–299).

[3] For a review of Di's power in relation to others see Childs-Johnson, forthcoming.

[4] Standardization of imagery may also be defined generically, as a process of modular building (see Ledderhose 2001 for an analysis of the concept of modular in Chinese art).

label of much later time, of late Warring States and Han periods, and therefore cannot be used to identify anything from the Shang period of at least 1,000 years earlier (for a review of the misnomer see Childs-Johnson 1998:11–17). The recommended term to describe the major image of Shang time, and used throughout this chapter, is "metamorphic power mask" or "semi-human animal mask." A summary of points made in several earlier publications are numbered here as 1–8 (Childs-Johnson 1998, 2016):

1. The ubiquitous mask image in Shang art varies on a scale from simple to more complex body parts and is consistently composed of variable numbers of human and animal parts, from early through late Shang time. Representative cast images on ritual bronzes, dating to early through middle and late Shang time, are frontal and displayed images, consistently composed of two eyes, ears, headdress extension, and abbreviated body extending to left and right of the face in bas-relief, sunken relief, or raised-line relief (see Figure 1). Eyes may be rendered as ovals or as circles within sockets. Sometimes the image has human features, such as eyebrows, or a complete human head but is always part of a larger composition featuring a wild animal, whether identified through ears of a tiger or inward-curling horns of a bighorn sheep or flanking profile renderings of the actual animal, usually the tiger, although bighorn sheep, stag, and buffalo are also known to be represented in a displayed position.

2. The animal part of the mask image is consistently a hunted animal, as signified by the shape of ear, horn, or antler referencing tiger, buffalo, bighorn sheep, and stag/deer. As represented in the chart, the most common mask types include hunted wild animals (see Figure 2), all of which are known in faunal remains at Anyang and in bone inscriptions as objects of the royal hunt. These wild animal features are usually limited to ear or horn types, although, as will be clear, the whole animal may also be represented. Additional attributes of the mask image include variations of the oval, round, or human-type eye with headdress excrescences identifying peafowl plumage along the central meridian (usually abstractly rendered), ears variously rendered, nasal ridge, mouth, and frequently a body extension in the form of displayed flanking arms ending in bird claws opposite the upper jaw and a headdress display at ear or horn level

3. Hieratic (adhering to a religious program) and hierarchical properties are observed in a composition in which the frontal mask is dominant, and subsidiary symbols usually flank the mask in subordinate positions. The mask, when part of a larger composition of flanking images, whether the ubiquitous dragon or bird in profile, is consistently larger by comparison with flanking subordinate images (see Figure 3). This hierarchical position of supplementary images is also characteristic of subordinate images in circumscribing bands flanking upper or lower edges of the frontal mask. Flanking subordinate images are consistently mythical *long* dragons or *feng* birds, both imaginary beings, yet symbolic images in other contexts, such as bands, may include cicada, snake, and additional bird and dragon types.

4. The mask has interchangeable semi-human and animal attributes. When rendered more elaborately the mask is oftentimes characterized by more clear-cut human than animal attributes. Human attributes may appear in facial details, such as human-shaped

FIGURE 1 Semi-human animal mask with abbreviated body dating from Early through Middle and Late Shang periods. Top row: Early Shang period; second row: Early and Middle Shang periods; third row: Middle and Late Shang periods; fourth row: Late Shang period.

eyes, mouth, nose, ears, and limbs, yet these consistently appear in the context of a frontal face of a mask with animal ears or horns, a central bird feather plume, and flanking body limbs ending in bird claws (see Figure 4). The image on the upper left is drawn from an ivory carving excavated from the royal tomb M1001 at Xibeigang: the human attributes of mouth, eyes, and ears are obvious and the central meridian plume ends in "literal" abstractions of the eyed peafowl feather; the body extension of limbs are abstracted as inward-curving forms. Decorating the turquoise inlaid ivory beaker from Fu Zi's tomb, M5 (upper right), similar human attributes of the face are identifiable, yet the horns identifying the animal attribute turn inward as abstractions of the buffalo horn, limbs end in bird claws, the headdress and central feather plumes extend

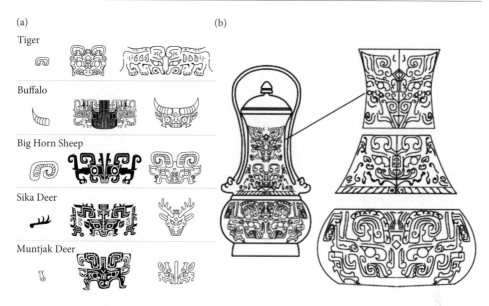

(a)   (b)

Tiger

Buffalo

Big Horn Sheep

Sika Deer

Muntjak Deer

FIGURE 2 A-B Chart with abstract and representational versions of the semi-human animal mask.

FIGURE 3 Subordinate images of profile birds and dragons flanking the metamorphic power mask.

upward to the frame of the mask, and the triangular body extension alludes to the cicada.

5. Representational and abstract versions of images are interchangeable, as are whole animal and abbreviated versions of images. As represented in the four levels of imagery (see Figure 5), it is apparent that there are two modes of representing the feature of the wild hunted animal: one that is abstract and another that is more representational. In the case of the buffalo (bottom level), the horn may represent the wrinkled upward-shaped horn, as interpreted on the royal tetrapod *ding* from M1004 on the left, or may

FIGURE 4 Images showing varying, interchangeable human and animal features of the meta-morphic power mask.

represent the same horn abstracted as an inward-curling horn, as represented on the lidless "*lei*" bronze container on the right. Moving upward, the same treatment is wit-nessed with the bighorn sheep horn that turns the opposite direction of the buffalo horn; it turns inward as simply and abstractly represented on the Zhengzhou tripod *ding* band of décor or as represented more representationally on the bighorn-sheep-shaped alcohol container from Fu Zi's M5 tomb at Xiaotun. The representation of a tiger's ears abstractly as C-shapes may be varied as a representational version, as a full-bodied profile tiger squatting as would a human in the guise of a tiger. The stag horn is similarly treated, as an abstract extension with tines flowing outward in length on the small tetrapod *ding* (middle example) or flowing outward representationally, as on the royal tetrapod *ding* from M1004 (top left level). Significant here is that the wild animal when represented may be abstract or complete in the form of a ritual bronze vessel. Abstract and represen-tational renderings, and simple and more full-bodied renderings, are interchangeable.

6. Other conventions symbolizing metamorphosis include easily understood ones, such as the cicada, sometimes a snake, as a body extension of the mask. The cicada is a well-known symbol of natural metamorphosis and is used to symbolize spirit meta-morphosis in Shang art. The cicada symbol may appear in various ways in Shang ritual art, as a body symbol or extension, or as a small-scale symbol on its own decorating a bronze vessel or related ritual utensil. As provided in these illustrations, the cicada may be represented abstractly or more representationally (see Figure 6). As apparent in the drawing of imagery on the Fu Zi owl-shaped bronze, the cicada appears in two primary ways: as a small-scale representational version seen in outline from above with eyes, triangular body, and flanking legs or the same as an extension of the buffalo horned mask with marked ears and oval eyes. On the second drawing of a buffalo horned mask, the cicada body extension is abstracted as a triangular shape. On the third object, a jade, the cicada body is rendered as a representational extension of a semi-human buffalo-horned mask with arm limb extension ending in claws. The fourth to the far right is the familiar image decorating front and back of the bronze simulating a leather drum from

FIGURE 5 Four types of wild animals featured in the metamorphic power mask based on horn, ear, or antler type. Living examples of tiger, stag, bighorn sheep, and wild buffalo are based on images available on: **A** variations of the stag mask and living stag; **B** variations of the tiger mask and living tiger; **C** variations of the bighorn sheep mask and living bighorn sheep; **D** variations of the buffalo mask and living wild buffalo.

the Sumitomo collection. The semi-human wears a headdress in the form of abstract bighorn sheep horns and has feathered arms ending in bird claws, a feathered body defined by the abstract transformational symbol of the cicada body, and a phallus. The

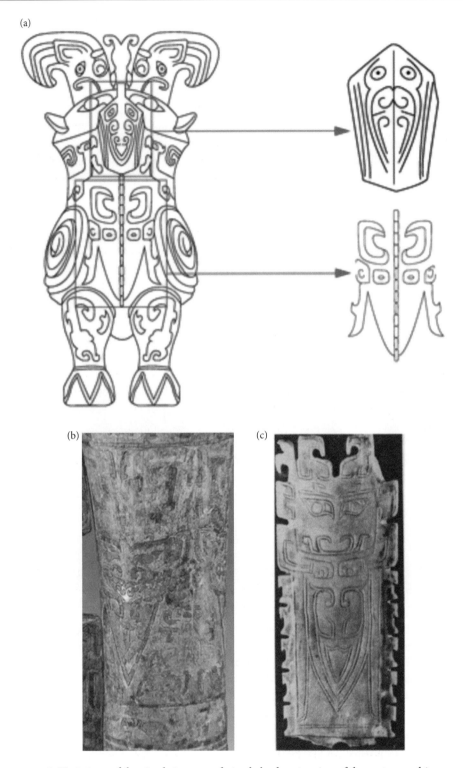

FIGURE 6 Variations of the cicada image and cicada body extension of the metamorphic power mask.

cicada is used more prominently in Shang imagery than the snake, who in nature sheds its skin, to symbolize change or metamorphosis. The snake, nonetheless, is also used as a body extension, with the implied symbolism of transformation and change.

7. The displayed mode or displayed animal devouring a human is used to signify spirit metamorphosis (from human to animal). As is revealed in all of these images, the displayed two-dimensional one is the most common means of representation in Shang art, whether the image is the representational tiger or human or the more abstract version of the same image (see Figure 7). As characterizes most other early historic cultures two-dimensional rendering is standard and may be expressed in variations of profile and frontal interpretations. The displayed type is the most ubiquitously used in Shang art and typically is composed of a frontal face and profile extensions to left and right of the face.

Occasionally a more story-telling rendering appears, as is the case in the pair of tiger-shaped *zun* vessel bronzes with tiger embracing a human with head turned in profile. The latter almost certainly describe a mythical narrative perhaps close to what is represented by the Romulus and Remus legend of ancient Rome or the supernatural birth of the founders of the Shang or Zhou lineages, respectively. The tiger played a significant role in Shang metropolitan imagery and gradually was selectively emphasized in representations on southern, more regional bronzes manufactured in the Shang domain.

8. In addition to conventions of representation identifying metamorphic imagery is written evidence, associated with the term for spirit metamorphosis, *yi* 異, in divinatory inscriptions. As I demonstrated in a recent book (2008), belief in metamorphism and the king's power to transcend or identify with spirit powers is reflected by semantic and graphic use of *yi* in bone inscriptions. *Yi* 異 is used in the following representative inscriptions to mean "to metamorphose," "to undergo metamorphosis," or "to be metamorphically empowered." It is the major term along with a variety of others that I cite to document the belief in spirit transformation from human to the non-human realms, dominated by daemonic spirits of dead ancestors and the world of the wild and hunted prey. See, for example, the following inscriptions:

Heji: 2,274 abbrev. Crack-making on the *bingzi* day Bin divined: If Father Yi (26th king) metamorphoses/causes spirit empowerment will it mean bestowing the power of the tetrapod *ding* vessel on the king (his eldest son)? Second auspicious announcement. Second auspicious announcement! If Father Yi does not cause spirit empowerment will it mean not bestowing the tetrapod *ding* upon the king?

   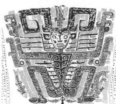 

FIGURE 7 Early and late Shang versions of the devouring or displayed image of metamorphism.

Heji: 11,921 Crack-making on the *gengxu* day Zheng divined: If it doesn't rain will [that] be caused by Di's spirit empowerment?

Heji: 29,395 It was divined:...from Mai place...dog(s) would [they] be without danger? Crack-making on the *xinchou* day Peng divined: On the next day *ren* if the king is spirit empowered will [he, the king] when hunting at Mai on a cloudy day be without danger?

Yi may be defined as a logogram, a word based on a pictorial counterpart, a human wearing a mask. The graph is equivalent to what is interpreted to be the representational interpretation of *yi* in Shang art, as illustrated in Figure 8.

Both the graph and ritual image represent a displayed human donning a mask. The graph is drawn as a simplified displayed stick-like human with upraised arms and splayed legs, both of which end, if represented, in three claws. The mask radical varies, as does imagery, from a more representational version to a more abstract version, from a head with horns to a head over human-shaped eyes to the more common shape of a box with an internal cross-shape, and is sometimes open at the top. *Yi* in bone inscriptions may be used as a transitive or intransitive verb or adjective, describing ritual *ding*-meat offering vessels or alcohol offered to a royal-house dead member. The subject of *yi* is either a dead royal spirit or the king, and in the context of the king is usually used at the time of a royal hunt or "when communicating with the royal dead power on earth through demonstrations of celestial approval of their status..." (Krupp 1997:34). Hunting was a major demonstration of kingly power and celestial approval—the ability to exercise physical prowess in taming and subordinating the wild. Although we are aware that the Shang worshipped a variety of natural forces, such as clouds, certain rivers, certain mountains, and the earth, in addition to the royal dead, the ruler was the one and only supreme power who could tame the wild, whether it was through the royal hunt and the royal hunted sacrifices that were offered directly to the royal dead or through donning or flaunting the wild animal mask. Wild hunted animals were a major symbol of power that were transmuted from the inherited semi-human mask symbol of the Late Neolithic period into the semi-human wild animal mask in Shang time. In this sense what the king hunted and celebrated were also his "spirit helpers" populating the four directions of the greater cosmos. His spirit helpers were those who could help in taming the wild.

These characteristics govern the repertoire of Shang ritual imagery decorating bronzes, ivories, bones, and other media. Some motifs are more aesthetically defined than others, and some are larger in size and composition. By the end of the Wu Ding, Zu Jia, and Zu

FIGURE 8 Variations of the graph *yi* 異 in bone inscriptions.

Geng periods (P2), imagery gradually disintegrates into what may be defined as a zoo-morphic hodge-podge without rules or classical rigor. This phase is equivalent to Late Shang OBI (oracle bone inscriptions) Periods 3 and 4. Stylistically, imagery evolves in stages from one of formulation (Early Shang) and development (Middle Shang) to one of classical expression (Late Shang 2) and ultimately one of dissolution (Late Shang 3–4).

METAMORPHISM, EXORCISM, AND CYCLICAL ANCESTOR RITES OF WORSHIP

The ritual worship of ancestors originated in the worship of royal house members, the king and consorts that bore royal offspring. Worship was codified as a ritual system with ongoing sacrifices and eventually spread as a practice followed by other lineages of the Shang ruling house and elite. Two issues surface: one is the fusion of "shamanic" belief with the institution of rulership and its power mechanisms. The second is the development of a ritual system of worship based on exorcistic practices and their evolution as primarily flesh and other foodstuffs offered on a daily regimen to the dead, royal and elite. Exorcism is "the religious or spiritual practice of purportedly expelling daemons or other spiritual entities from a person or an area they are believed to have possessed" (Jacobs 1999). In bone inscriptions, to exorcise is written with two primary variations: 彳, 𢔍, *yu* 禦 the exorcism rite is Da Yu 大禦, and the lesser exorcism rite is *yu* 禦 (simplified).[5] Serruys identifies 土卩 as the probable original form of the graph, a kneeling person before an earthen mound (Serruys 1953:86n3). The graph was expanded by adding signifiers *shi* 示, and *tu* 土 was replaced by the phonetic *yu* 禦 (also see Chang Tsung-tung 1970:51; Shirakawa 1977:91, figure 16:10, p. 90). The word *yu* 御 御 御 elsewhere in bone inscriptions refers to "to drive a chariot and horse," possibly an extension of the original concept of "to drive out noxious influences," as interpreted by Chang Tsung-tung. As typifies numerous bone graphs, one graph frequently functions as a noun or as a verb, and *yu* therefore may mean "exorcism," "to exorcize," or "to be exorcized."

Following the suggestion of Serruys, the earthen mound may have been the *beng* 祊, or the square rammed-earth outdoor altar in pyramidal shape that is located at the northernmost end of Yi (B) ritual architectural remains at Xiaotun, Anyang, or one of the many other square earthen altars associated with the Bing (C) ritual architectural remains (see chapter 15 of this book by Childs-Johnson). Examples of the Great Exorcism rite that serve as the precedent for the *zhouji* 周祭 rites addressed to royal ancestors are as follows:

> *Heji* 32,329 front and reverse: It was divined on the *guichou* day: Should on the *jiayin* day [the king] undertake the Great Exorcism rite beginning with Shang Jia by offering

---

[5] I follow the definition of *yu* 禦 by Paul Serruys' (1953:86n3).

alcohol and six small penned sheep through burning? This was used. Shang Jia did not cause rain to arrive. [The king prognosticated stating:] "Da Yi did not cause rain to arrive. Da Ding did not cause rain to arrive." On the *gengshen* day it was divined (again): If the king on the coming *jiazi* day undertakes the Great Exorcism rite by offering alcohol and six small penned sheep through cult burning, and nine ox through *mao*-cutting to Da Jia will it not rain? It was divined: Should the king on the coming *jiazi* day undertake the Great Exorcism rite by offering alcohol and six small penned sheep through cult burning, and nine ox through *mao*-cutting to Da Jia?

Heji 32,847: On *x-hai* day it was divined: Should [the king] undertake the Great Exorcism rite to the High Ancestor Wang Hai with …

Heji 32,330: On the *jiachen* day it was divined: Should the king carry out the Great Exorcism rite with blood offering of nine white oxen beginning with [Shang Jia] and to the Xia Shi (Lesser Lineage of Rulers) by offering [sprinkled blood]? It was divined on the *dingwei* day: Should the king carry out the Great Exorcism rite with blood offering of nine white oxen beginning with Shang Jia and to the Xia Shi (Lesser Lineage of Rulers) by sprinkling blood of oxen? It was divined in Fu Ding's temple. It was divined on the *guichou* day: Should it be the *jiazi* day when [the king] carries out the Great Exorcism rite with alcohol offering?

Power of the royal elite was recognized by the power of a day, *ri* 日, a 24-hour day of sun and moon light. The dead were believed to be spirits with the power over a day, which equates with the passage of the solar star in terms of cosmic space. The Shang did not distinguish past and present, thus the concept of time from the point of view of history had not been formulated (Vogelsang 2014). Dead kings were assigned worship on a specific day, and that day served as that spirit's source of power, thus royal ancestral rites were consolidated as an extension of royal prestige and authority. Exorcistic rites and sacrifices continued but within the context of a rigid calendar of rites codified and standardized. In several cases, one royal dead may be assigned the same ritual day name as another. Some days were luckier than others and therefore tended to be the most popular choice for ritual allocations. Exemplary bone inscriptions illustrating a sun's association with a ten-day name of an ancestor spirit and the power of that day's sun appear as follows:

Heji Bu 535 Period 1: Crack-making on the *dingzi* day it was divined: If the king carries out the *bin* rite of receiving the sun spirit will it not rain?

Heji 27,446 Period 3: Crack-making on the *jiyou* day Ming divined: Should [the king] offer one ox to the sun spirit of Fu Jia on the next *jiayou* day?

Heji 1,248 front Period 1: [Que] divined: On the next *jiashen* day should the king not *bin* (receive) Shang Jia's sun? Crack-making on the *guiwei* day Que divined: Should the king on the next day *jiashen bin*/receive in sacrifice Shang Jia's sun? The king prognosticated saying: "Auspicious, [the king] will *bin*/receive [Shang Jia's sun]. [The king] indeed *bin*/received [Shang Jia's sun]."

To the Shang, the sun and moon were essentially orbiting constellations, mysteriously rising and sinking, shining and shrouding light and spawning night. Royal dead spirit powers waxed beyond that of individual nature powers, such as He Yellow River; Qiu

Mountain(s); or other less powerful nature powers, such as *yun* clouds, *fang* directional territories, and *tu* earth. Nature was always all-important, and danger or loss of control lurked in all territories, as expressed in the mythic terrains of the post-Shang text, the *Shanhaijing*.[6] Although the north polar star had been plotted and the gnomon had become a well-established tool for orientation (see chapter 6 by He Nu), nature was wild and needed to be tamed. Large-scale human and animal slaughter were lavishly deployed as sacrifices to both nature and human spirits, and order and control by the supreme ruler were perpetuated by ritual performances who were part of the greater Natural Relam.

SIFANG COSMOLOGY AND THEOCRATIC HEGEMONY

Sifang or four-directional cosmology is recognized as a basic philosophical concept of Shang thinking, as represented in oracle bone divinations.[7] The Shang lived in a universe that emanated outward in four directions and was controlled by a divine ruler at the center. For the Shang, the universe was a cosmos that could be controlled by a pyramidal structure, dominated at the center by the ruler who maintained spirit control within a centralized state, soon to be known as Zhong guo 中国, as documented in the inscription of the He *zun* and often translated "Middle Kingdom" instead of Kingdom at the Center, as translated here. (For a transcription of the vessel's text, see Zhongguo 2001:275, no. 6,014; Cook and Goldin 2016 :13–15.) the state at the center, but as Zhong Shang 中商 (Shang at the Center) in bone inscriptions. The Shang ruled as hegemonic theocrats. The concept and meaning of *fang* have long been misunderstood in identifying *fang* as an enemy state (see e.g., Keightley 1983; Chang Kwang-chih 1983; Wang Aihe 2000; Allan 1991). *Fang* in bone inscriptions of late Shang time and certainly earlier meant territory, which could be referred to specifically and generally, as land outside the capital that was occupied by both foe and friend of the Shang (see e.g., Chen Mengjia 1956). It is incorrect to identify *fang* as strictly enemy powers or "outsiders" who attacked the insider Shang state. There was no distinction in Shang time between outsider and insider.[8] There was distinction between powers, nonetheless, of a Shang hegemon and his minions who had to be under constant supervision, constant inspection, and constant surveillance. Rebellion and attacks were common during the Shang, but *fang* was not specifically a word for enemy during the Shang. *Fang*

---

[6] It is tempting to use myth as an explanation for the origin of day names. As noted by Chen (1956:574), Shang Di's wife Xihe 羲和 gave birth to 10 suns (*shi ri* 十日), as related in the *Shanhaijing*: Dahuang Nanjing section 山海经大荒南经.

[7] Most Shang oracle bone specialists have addressed this issue, beginning with Chen Mengjia (1956) and followed by Song Zhenhao and Yang Shengnan, Sarah Allan (1991), and Childs-Johnson (2012).

[8] In bone inscriptions *wai* may be associated with one of the names of the past rulers, Wai Bing, yet the translation of wai 外 or of bu 卜 are both possible. *Wai* does not appear in bone inscriptions in reference to the concept of inner or inside.

referred to lands beyond the center. These sometimes were enemy powers and at other times were awarded territories and also tributaries (Childs-Johnson 2012).

The Shang lived at a time of constant warfare and the king lived a life of constant royal peregrination. The four directions had to be controlled, and that involved fervent maintenance by the king and his staff within and without the royal household. For this reason the king had a substantial staff to help execute his needs and commands in presiding over almost every aspect of his kingdom. In understanding the hegemonic pattern of Shang control, probably some of the most important members of the king's staff were the ones in charge of livestock and animal husbandry, called *mu* 牧. As a graph and word, *mu* may act verbally and nominally with two functions, as a place name or as an official name. It also should not be forgotten that according to transmitted texts the Shang were defeated by the Zhou at Mu Ye, the Field of Mu 牧野, south of the capital (Yang 1992:235, 237). Meanings of both verb and noun are connected with animal husbandry, breeding, and herding of primarily cows and sheep. Citations in bone inscriptions most commonly refer to the name of the person in charge of what is represented taking place on these lands: managing livestock breeding and herding. *Mu* 牧 are cardinally referenced in bone inscriptions and may be described as *mu bi* 牧鄙, as grazing lands and probably gated pastures located in the suburbs, in the vicinity of *dian* 奠 but also well beyond as documented by archaeological discoveries and paleographic references from a variety of locations.

Based on an extensive analysis of these Shang officials, it is evident that they were not only owners of bronze vessel sets but very significant members of Shang society (Yang 1992:235–259). Yang demonstrates that these *mu* were functionaries of an advanced and autonomous industry under Shang influence; they, as with other aristocrats, were both independent and dependent, fluctuating as many territories did between allegiance and vengeance, as typifies what is defined here as theocratic hegemony and display of power and control through force. *Mu* polities independently managed their respective position but were beholden to the central authority by requisition of their produce. In some cases *mu* clearly were royalty or Shang elite, since they were also entitled *ya* 亞 elder royal brothers and in other cases as *ce* 冊 scribes. These Shang *mu* are documented by a rich number of records of their activities, by geographically diverse locations of their settlements, by an overwhelming number of livestock remains excavated at Tiesanlu and elsewhere at Anyang and earlier sites, and by the overwhelming numbers of livestock used in ritual sacrifices. The Shang were extremely sophisticated livestock handlers who raised excessively large numbers of cattle and sheep but also horses, deer, and many other animals (Yang 1992:84–202).

Based on inscriptions from excavated bronzes, the Shang officials named *mu* are known from a broad stretch of territory extending far to the west, north, east, and south of the Shang capital. Inscribed bronzes are represented in the far southwest province of Sichuan at Chuwajie in Pengxian (Wang Jiayou 1961; Yang 1992 :246), the far northwest, Gansu and Shaanxi border area at Weijia in Longxian (*Jicheng* 5,575); at Laoniupo in Shaanxi (*Jicheng* 28,769; Song 2005:41; Yang 1992:244); at Baoji, Zhuyuangou No. 7 tomb in Shaanxi (Shaanxi Chutu 1980; Yang 1992 :247); and from Yanshan in the southern corner of Fengning county in Hebei (*Jicheng* 456). Titles inscribed on these bronzes include Mu Zheng 牧正, You Mu 右牧, and Ya Mu 亞牧. These three refer to three different titles. Zheng 正 references a manager or director. *You* 右 refers to one of three *mu* (*you mu* 右牧, *zhong mu* 中牧, *zuo mu* 左牧) in charge of breeding and herding in a particular area, and Ya Mu 亞牧 refers to a royal-house male in charge of a particular area for husbandry. Evidently these livestock officials were extensively represented throughout the Shang kingdom, and often at great distance from the Shang capital. Long-distance control and tribute of such lands clearly documents widespread Shang hegemony and influence extending through the northwest of Shaanxi and Gansu, north to Hebei, and southwest to Sichuan.

Yang has identified over 40 *mu* lands in bone inscriptions, covering some that are well documented through archaeological discoveries and others through geographical associations. For example, Zi Gua Zhu 子瓜竹 is a Shang state located in today's Fengning county in Hebei. This is where a pipe-footed tripod *ding* was found inscribed Ya Mu/ Elder Royal Brother [General] Livestock Manager (Li Xueqin 1983; Yang 1992:245n2). Most likely the Mu owner of this vessel was stationed by the Shang king to supervise livestock breeding in this area of Hebei; he stayed to continue to nurture and supervise these lands as well as to protect them as a Ya, a royal house member who typically ranked as a general. In bone inscriptions, Gua Zhu state members are referred to as Zhu Chu 竹芻, hay thrashers and collectors.[9] Zhu 竹 is well known as a tribute-bearing member of the Shang kingdom (see *Heji* 902 reverse; Yang 1992:239), and evidently they were a significant part of the Shang domain in the north in southern Hebei province.

Mu frequently interacted with other officials including *bo* 伯 landed title, *hou* 侯 landed title, *quan* 犬 dog managers, *ma* 馬 horse managers, *chen* 臣 official, *shu* 戍 officers, *zheng* 正 directors, and slaves and laborers identified as Qiang 羌 and *chu* 芻.[10] Such interaction may be identified on the basis that *mu* and other officials work within the same states, cities, and towns (Yang 1992:238–240, 252). These interconnections and associations indicate that *mu* were animal husbandry managers who worked in the company of others and, as with these others, were often solicited in divinations to aid on hunts, since hunts often took place in areas associated with livestock breeding, land acquisition, and other official posts (Yang 1992:238, 246–254).

Apparently Mu livestock managers also moved around, as did *chu* 芻 laborers. Some of the areas for raising livestock were close to the Shang capital at Anyang, and others were further afield in the Wei and Han River Valleys and elsewhere, as documented by the extensive presence of *mu* cited in inscriptions. One of the areas for raising livestock close to the capital is associated with the landed estate of one named lord, You Ye (You Hou Ye 攸侯葉) in Henan. These inscriptions concern whether or not the Right, Left, or Center Mu Livestock Manager should undertake work in the suburb estate of Lord Ye of

[9] See, for example, the following inscription, "取竹芻于丘 Should [we] obtain hay field labor (slashers and collectors) from the state of Zhu 竹 at Qiu?" (at *Heji* 108; Yang 1992:239).

[10] Not listed here are *hou* 后, possibly small-time managers in charge of raising dogs, sheep, pigs, boar, and other types of swine on lands within the domain of *mu* (see Yang 1992:248).

You, indicating again the flexibility of the king who could exercise an order seemingly at whim within his extended domain (inscriptions cited in Yang 1992 :241, 254).

> *Heji* 119: "貞零 X 取雍芻? *Heji* 114: 貞取克取?貞取般芻? It was divined: Should [we] order X to obtain *chu* of Yong? It was divined: Should [we] obtain [*chu*] of Ke? Should [we] obtain *chu* of Pan?"
>
> *Heji* 93: "乙丑卜殻貞即致芻其五百唯六?貞即致芻不其五百唯六? Crack-making on the *yichou* day Ke divined: Will Ji deliver 506 *chu*? It was divined: Will Ji not deliver 506 *chu*?"
>
> *Heji* 32,982: "戊戌貞右牧于片攸侯鄙。中牧于义(?)攸侯葉鄙。[左牧于口攸鄙] It was divined on the *wuxu* day: Should the You Mu at Pian serve at the suburbs of You Hou? Should the Zhong Mu at Yi serve at the suburbs of [You] Hou? [Should the Zuo Mu at X serve at You Hou Bi]?"[11]

These and other representative inscriptions demonstrate that although *mu* do not own land they supervise raising and breeding livestock on another, senior land owner's property, in this case the Lord Ye of You. It is also evident that on large estates, such as that belonging to Lord Ye of You, three different Mu officiated, one Zhong Mu at the center, and two others, Left and Right Mu officials, all appointed by the Shang king. The evidence for other Mu named by title of right, left, or center within different landed estates corroborates the sophisticated administrative operation under the hegemonic control of the Shang king.

Although *mu* do not appear to own land, they evidently occupied a strategic and significant position as livestock supervisors on the site of their origin of work. The importance of cattle, including a percentage acquired by tribute and the rest coming from royal and subservient lands, can be easily underscored by the extremely large number of that breed's bones assembled at Tiesanlu. Tiesanlu was located in the southern suburbs of the royal center at Anyang, near Miaopudi. As reported by the excavators at Tiesanlu, this was a huge bone-working center, mostly for the production of bone "perforators" or pins that in part functioned as hairpins and were made from cattle leg parts (Campbell et al. 2007). Although other bones from deer antler to pig tusks were also found, humerus bones of cattle were by far the major bone material worked or partially worked. It is apparent that the bones from the site were selectively used and designed, and despite their seemingly humble role as artifact, the scale of production was mammoth. As reviewed, it is estimated that "if we consider that TSL is only one of three major bone-working areas (Li *et al.* forthcoming), and if our back-of-the-envelope calculation of over four million artefacts for TSL is accurate, then bone workshop production outstripped local consumption, perhaps by as much as 300%. Clearly, breeding and raising cattle was important business, and to most early China specialists, it would be considered a reflection of a centralized redistributive production model (Chen and Liu)" (Campbell et al. 2007).

---

[11] Pian, Yi, and You belong to the three Mu stationed within the land of Ye You Hou (Lord You of Ye). For similar inscriptions see *Heji* 32,982 (口卯貞右牧「于片攸侯」 葉鄙); Yang 1992:241.

Although *mu*, as with other appointed members of Shang nobility, did not own land or livestock, their sense of obligation to the "crown" reflects the profound influence of the center of command. Numbers of raised sheep and cattle far outnumber pigs, dogs, horses, chickens, birds, and other domesticated species, including buffalo and deer.

The enormous numbers of cattle raised and sacrificed corroborates the sophisticated level that livestock breeding had reached at this point in history. Cattle and sheep were the primary domestic species offered in ritual sacrifices to spirits ranging from dead kings and queens to the Four Directions and other nature spirits. Other animals sacrificed include dogs and pigs but not to the same degree as cattle and sheep (Yang 1992:208). Some of the highest numbers (a total of 600 and 1,000) offered are recorded in samples of bone inscriptions, as cited in Yang 1992:212, 213, 215):

Heji 20,699:... 五百牢 (written 羊)...? [should sacrifice] 500 pairs (=1,000) sheep?

Heji 301,302: 禦[于大丁]，大甲，祖乙百鬯百羌卯三百牢(羊)? Should [we] offer in exorcism [to Da Ding], Da Jia, Zu Yi 100 [*you*] of *chang* alcohol, 100 Qiang tribesmen, and 600 penned sheep (300 pairs)?

Heji 301,302: 禦[于大丁]，大甲，祖乙百鬯百羌卯三百牢(羊)? Should [we] offer in exorcism [to Da Ding], Da Jia, Zu Yi 100 [*you*] of *chang* alcohol, 100 Qiang tribesmen, and 600 penned sheep (300 pairs).

Heji 22,274 (Y213):... 兄丁延三百牢?... [to] Brother Ding up to (?) 300 penned oxen?

Heji 39,531 and Ying Zang 1,240: 乙亥[卜]內冊大[乙]五百牛百伐? Crack-making on the *yihai* day Nei [divined]: If a royal proclamation is made to Da [Yi] should we offer 500 beheaded oxen?

Heji 1,027 *zheng*: 丁巳卜爭貞其降冊(口)千牛?不其降冊(口)千牛千人? Crack-making on the *dingsi* day Zheng divined: If a proclamation descended [should we] offer 1,000 cattle? If a proclamation does not descend [should we] not perhaps offer 1,000 cattle and 100 men?

Heji 20,699:... 五百牢 (written 羊)...? [should sacrifice] 500 pairs (=1,000) sheep?

Although such large numbers seem impractically high, they may be matched physically by sacrifices of these animals to spirits of dead kings buried in the field next to the royal burial ground at Xibeigang and in sacrificial ditches located within palace compounds at Yinxu, Zhengzhou, and Yanshi Shang capitals.[12] Based on available excavated remains, it is apparent that not only cattle but also sheep were bred and raised in numbers at a scale well beyond the capacity of the Shang population. The importance of the livelihood of *mu* and their direct relationship with the capital thus is strategic for the stability of Shang kingship, command near and far in the kingdom, and evidently for trade. Ritual offerings also operated under influence and stigma of a central chief.

---

[12] Yang (1992: 208–209) doubts that such large numbers of animals were actually sacrificed.

Conclusions

Based on the combination of data from oracle inscriptions, archaeological finds, and visual material, it is evident that the Shang believed in spirit metamorphism and a religio-social system of "institutionalized shamanism," the power of the king as spirit receiver supreme who from the Center of Shang ruled the *sifang* realm extending in four directions.

Bibliography

Allan, Sarah 1991. *The Shape of the Turtle: Myth, Art and Cosmos in Early China*. Chinese Philosophy and Culture Series. Albany, New York: SUNY Press.

Campbell, Roderick B., Zhipeng Li, He Yuling, and Yuan Jing 2007. "Consumption, Exchange and Production at the Great Settlement Shang: Bone-Working at Tiesanlu, Anyang." *Antiquity* 85 (330) :1,279–1,297.

Chang, Kwang-chih (Zhang Guangzhi) 1983. *Art, Myth, and Ritual: The Path to Political Authority in Ancient China*. Cambridge, MA: Harvard University Press.

Chang, Tsung-tung 1970. *Der Kult der Shang Dynastie im Spiegel Orakelinschriften (Eine palaographische Studie zur Religion in Archaaischen China)*. Wiesbaden: Otto Harrassowitz.

Chen, Mengjia 1956. *Yinxu Buzi Zongshu* 殷墟卜字綜述. Beijing: Kexue chubanshe.

Childs-Johnson, Elizabeth 1995. "The Ghost Head Mask and Metamorphic Shang Imagery." *Early China* 20:79–92.

Childs-Johnson, Elizabeth 1998. "The Metamorphic Image: A Predominant Theme in Shang Ritual Art." *Bulletin of the Museum of Far Eastern Antiquities* 70:5–171.

Childs-Johnson, Elizabeth 2008. *The Meaning of the Graph Yi* 異 *and Its Implications for Shang Belief and Art*. East Asia Journal Monograph. London: Saffron Books.

Childs-Johnson, Elizabeth 2012. "Postscript to Big *Ding* and China Power-Shang: *Sifang* Cosmology." In *Proceedings of the International Conference for Commemorating 1 Century after Sun Zuoyun's Birthday* 纪念孙作云教授百年延长 及古代中国历史与文化国际学术研讨会论文集, 91–210.

Childs-Johnson, Elizabeth 2016. "Urban daemons of the early Shang," *Urbanism in ancient China,Archaeological Research in Asia*, Online 9.19.2016:1–16, Elsevier Ltd; Volume 14, June 2018:135–150.

Childs-Johnson, Elizabeth. Forthcoming. *Great Settlement Shang (Shang at the Center): Art, Religion and Culture*.

Cook, Constance A., and Paul R. Goldin, eds. 2016. *A Source Book of Ancient Chinese Bronze Inscriptions*. Early China Special Monograph Series 7. Berkeley, CA: Society for the Study of Early China.

Heji 1978–1982. *The Complete Set of Oracle Bone Inscriptions* 甲骨文合集, vols. 1–13. Beijing: Kexue chubanshe.

Heji 1999. *The Complete Collection of Oracle Bone Inscriptions: Translations*, vols. 1–4 甲骨文合集釋文 vols 1–4, and *The Complete Collection of Oracle Bone Inscriptions: Their Sources and References* 甲骨文材料来源 *Cailiao Laiyuan Biao* vols. 1–2, compiled by Guo Moruo. Beijing: Kexue chubanshe.

Hsü Chin-hsiung 許進雄 1965. "*Shi yu* 試禦." *Chung-kuo wen-tz'u* 12. Taibei.

Jacobs, Louis 1999. "Exorcism." *Oxford Reference Online*. Oxford University Press. Accessed January 24, 2011.

Hu, Houxuan 1989 [1944]. *Collected Writings on Shang History in Oracle Bone Studies* 甲骨学商史论丛, vols 1–2. Shanghai: Shanghai shudian. Originally published Chengdu: Jilu daxue.

Jicheng 2012. Shang and Zhou Bronze Inscriptions Collected and Illustrated 商周青铜器铭文圖 像集成, 35 vols. Edited by Wu Zhenfeng 吳鎮烽. Shanghai: Guji chubanshe.

Keightley, David N. 1978. *Sources of Shang History: The Oracle-Bone Inscriptions of Bronze Age China* . Berkeley and Los Angeles: University of California Press.

Keightley, David N. 1983. "The Late Shang State: When, Where, and What?" In *The Origins of Chinese Civilization*. Edited by David N. Keightley, 523–564. Berkeley: University of California Press.

Krupp, E. C. 1997. *Skywatchers, Shamans and Kings*. Hoboken, New Jersey: John Wiley & Sons.

Ledderhose, Lothar 2001. *Ten Thousand Things: Module and Mass Production in Chinese Art*. Princeton: Princeton University Press.

Li, Xueqin 李学勤 1959. *Brief Discussion of Yin Dynasty Geography* 殷代地理简论. Beijing: Kexue chubanshe.

Serruys, Paul L. M. 1953. "Studies in the Language of the Shang Oracle Inscriptions." *T'oung Pao* 59:12–83.

Shaanxi 1980. Shang and Zhou Bronzes Unearthed from Shaanxi 陕西出土商周青铜器, vol. 3. Beijing: Kexue chubanshe.

Shirakawa, Shizuka 白川靜 1977. The World of Oracle Bone Inscriptions: Construction of the Ancient Dynasty of Yin 甲骨文的世界—古殷王朝的締構. Chinese translation of *Kôkotsubun No Sekai—Kodai In Ochô No kôz* by Cai Zhemao and Wen Tianhe. Taipei: Chu-liu tu-shu kung-tse.

Song, Zhenhao 宋镇豪 2005. *The Social History of the Xia and Shang Shi* 夏商社會生化史, 2 vols. Beijing: Kexue chubanshe.

Vogelsang, Kai 2014. "The Shape of History: On Reading Li Wai-yee." *Early China* 37:579–599.

Wang, Aihe 2000. *Cosmology and Political Culture in Early China*. Cambridge: Cambridge University Press.

Wang, Jiayou 王家祐 1961. "Discussion of the bronzes unearthed from Zhuwajie, Pengxian, Schuan记四川彭县竹瓦街的同器," *Wenwu* 1961.11:28–31.

Yang, Shengnan 杨升南 1992. *The Economic History of the Shang Dynasty* 商代经济史. Guizhou: Guizhou renmin chubanshe.

Zhongguo Kexueyuan Kaogu Yanjiusuo 中国科学院考古研究所, ed. 2001. *Translated Texts of Collected Shang and Zhou Bronze Inscriptions* 殷周金文集成釋文. Hong Kong: Xianggang Zhongwen Daxue chubanshe.

CHAPTER 14

SHANG BRONZE CASTING TECHNOLOGY AND METALLURGY ISSUES

BY CHANGPING ZHANG,
WUHAN UNIVERSITY

THE Shang period refers to three archaeological culture phases, including Erligang (Early Shang), Zhong Shang (Middle Shang), and Yinxu (Late Shang). However, the development of bronzes does not entirely synchronize with these archaeological phases. For example, the characteristics of the bronzes of the early Erligang culture contrast with the Late Erligang culture in aligning more closely with the bronzes of Erlitou. Late Yinxu (Late Shang) bronzes including those from Fu Zi's (Fu Hao's) tomb are in turn close in type to those of the Early Western Zhou period. For these reasons the development of the bronze vessel may be classified into three periods, including early Erligang, late Erligang to early Yinxu Phase 1, and after late Yinxu 1. Taking into account that the characteristics of bronzes of the Early Erligang culture reflect those of the Erlitou cultural period, discussion here focuses on the latter two stages only. For the sake of simplicity, these two phases are referred to as the late Erligang phase and the late Yinxu phase. The spatial scope of this discussion draws on the culture of the Central Plains and directly related areas.

The two important phases, as noted, the Late Erligang culture and Late Yinxu culture, are intimately related to the technological development of Chinese bronze manufacturing. Bronze production of the Late Erligang culture is of considerable importance. Bronzes from burials include many different types, ranging from *gu*, *jue*, *jia*, and other alcohol types to a small number of food-related vessels, such as *ding* and *li*. During this period, the variety in type and shape of bronzes is minimal, the volume remains small, and the walls remain thin, yet décor mostly appears in the form of a narrow single register of the animal face (兽面). By the beginning of the late Shang phase, Yinxu 2, examples of bronzes, represented from the tomb of Fu Zi (Fu Hao) (M5), surge in number and type, although the majority still remain focused on alcohol types. During this period bronze vessels have thicker walls and are heavier in weight. Décor is more complex with multiple levels of imagery, including the appearance of flanges, high-relief decoration, and embossed animal-head protomes. Besides the animal face, bronze imagery is rich and varied, accompanying by *kuilong* dragon and *feng* phoenix images. This second phase, a luxurious and rich style, compared with that of the Erligang period, reflects a peak in the development of bronze foundry technology.

Following the shape and décor of the bronze, we will discuss the technology of bronze-casting and its evolution through the Late Erligang and Yinxu periods.

THE TECHNOLOGY OF BRONZE-CASTING AND ITS EVOLUTION

Alcohol vessel types occupy the most prominent position and illustrate the most dramatic changes that occur in production during the late Yinxu phase. Casting technology is standardized and based on the use of clay molds. The use of piece-molds in casting, represented, for example, by the tripod *ding*, relies initially on legs as the pivot for arranging three modular parts to create the outer mold. Circular footed vessels without ears are also created out of three outer mold parts. *Gui*-type vessels with ears differ in their mold composition, relying on two- or four-piece outer mold parts. The technological development of bronze vessels is based on several standardized means of casting, as follows.

Balancing the position of attachments

Before the Middle Shang period, molds forming the legs were positioned so that one ear faced one of the three legs or one ear was positioned between two legs (Figure 1:A, B, and C on *ding*, *jia*, *yan*, and other three-legged vessels with two ears. From whatever direction these vessels are viewed, the two ears and three legs are not visually symmetrical or balanced (Figure 2:A). However, after the middle Shang phase, legs and ears of the three-legged vessels (Figure 1:B) become balanced.

Owing to technological interests, legs of tripod vessels are positioned along the joints of the outer molds. As noted, three legs of *ding*, *li*, *jia*, and *jue* are all incorporated at the center of joints, and one ear of *jia*, *jue*, and *he* typically faces one leg. Even base openings, protruding animal heads and flanges of *zun* and *lei*, are also positioned evenly along piece-mold joints. As represented by the bases of Erligang-phase *jia* vessels, spacer pieces are used to join the three-part mold.

At this stage of the Late Erligang period, piece-mold parts forming the tripod legs of *ding* and *li* were not joined, so that the placement of the two ears and three legs corresponded. Since the two handles were not positioned at the joins of the piece-molds as were the three legs, they created an imbalanced distribution (Figure 2). After the Middle Shang period craftsmen nonetheless sought to rectify this imbalance. Casting adjustments were made. On ring-footed vessels, such as the *zun* and *lei*, animal-head protomes also changed according to these aesthetic requirements. Initially they were awkwardly positioned straddling the line of the mold joins, yet after the late Erligang phase this positioning of animal-head protomes changed in aligning with the images of the animal face of the vessel proper. By the Late Shang period animal-head imagery corresponded with the position of the animal-head protomes on vessel shoulders.

(a)   (b)   (c)

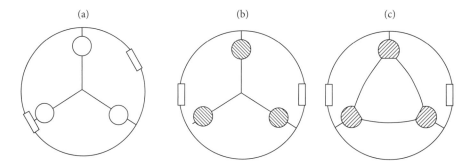

FIGURE 1 A, B, C Drawing of the three piece-mold design for a Shang-dynasty bronze tripod.

(a)   (b)

FIGURE 2 Early Shang bronze vessels illustrating uneven correspondence between the two handles or the three animal head protomes and band imagery. **A** Cache H1: 1 tripod ding from Xiangyang Moslem Grocery, Zhengzhou. **B** Zun from Xiangyang Moslem Grocery, Zhengzhou.

During the Erligang phase, the number of outer piece-molds did not correspond with the number of attachments. If one of the ears was placed at the joint of molds, then how could the additional ear be coordinated to balance with the other joint? The same problem occurs when casting a *gu* goblet as a two-part mold assemblage with three base openings (Figure 3:(a)). This phenomenon also occurs when bronze vessels are cast in imitation of what is mainstream. As represented by the *gui* vessel from Panlongcheng, the two loop handles do not harmonize with the layout of the three-part mold joints and base openings (Figure 3:(b)). One ear aligns with one mold joint yet does not align with the three belly images of the animal face. The ears were cast on after the vessel was cast, thus this was a conscious choice of the craftsmen to copy mainstream interpretations of Zhengzhou Erligang, even if the ears were imbalanced.

Positioning blind cores

One of the major changes in bronze production during the Yinxu Phase 1 is the change from a hollow leg to a solid leg. Early-period *ding*, *yan*, *li*, and other cooking vessels, in addition to *jia* alcohol vessels, had legs that were hollow in connecting foot and belly of the vessel. For cooking this appears inconvenient, however, having a solid foot would

(a)   (b)

FIGURE 3 Early Shang period bronze décor flush with the vessel surface but out of balance with the placement of two handles or two blind foot perforations. **A** M3:2 *gu* from Yangjiawan, Panlongcheng. **B** M1:5 *gui* from Lijia, Panlongcheng.

allow for greater cooling and a decrease in defects from casting. As represented by tripod *ding* from Fu Zi's (Fu Hao's) tomb of the Yinxu period, the legs of tripod *ding* and of the *jia* are solid. The technique used to create hollow legs is abandoned. Ceramic cores now remain in the leg and all openings between leg and vessel belly disappear. Leaving the fired ceramic core in the leg also avoided creating casting holes in the legs. The change of casting solid "blind" core legs also gave rise to other changes. Handles of *ding* and *yan*, as represented by the *yan* from Erligang cache H1 at the Moslem Grocery in Zhengzhou, were also cast as hollow spaces. Yet this changed during the Yinxu period when ears of large rectangular vessels were cast with "blind cores" (cast ceramic cores), as were the legs of other vessels.

The use of blind-core technology for handles and ears of bronze vessels lasted from the Yinxu period and thereafter through the Warring States, Qin, and Han periods. Because blind cores needed to be suspended in the outer mold pieces, the bronze liquid when poured needed to surround the blind clay core. From the point of view of design this is a complex challenge. The use of blind cores in round *ding* and *jia* witness a long period of developing this casting technique.

The open space of the late Erligang *ding* typically extend to the tip of the leg (Figure 4:(a)). By the end of the Middle Shang period, during the Yinxu Phase 1, as represented by Hubei M10 and Xiaotun M388 tripod *ding*, the leg changes in having only a partially open leg (see Figure 4:(b)). The open space of the leg begins to shrink and the bottom of the leg contains more of the ceramic core. By Yinxu Phases 1 and 2 the open space of the leg begins to close and eventually will completely close so that the top of the leg is even with the belly of the *ding* (Figure 4:(c)). The leg gradually takes on a solid circular tube shape, filled with the fired ceramic core, as represented by Wuguancun M1 and Xiaotun M331 *ding* (Figure 4:(d)). The latter signifies the end of the cast hollow leg.

The evolution of the leg of the *jia* from hollow to solid casting follows the same path of the *ding*. Yet, in addition to the disappearance of the empty area between belly and leg, the leg of *jia* takes a different form, one that is T or one that is prismatic in shape. The T-shape of the leg reveals slightly grooved inner sides, so that it looks like a T-shape in cross-section. The inside of the leg has shallow grooves, yet the T-shape is created out of a solid ceramic core. The translation from empty to T-shape involved experimentation. Examples include a rather simple version, represented by the *jia* from Xiaotun M333:R2045 and slightly later more sophisticated examples represented by *jia* from Xiaotun M331 and Huadong M60:8. The sides of the leg of the latter bronzes widen in incorporating the two grooves in creating a more solid, completely prismatic shape. The prismatic foot of the *jia* from Wuguan M1 burial is exemplary of what is now a prismatic-shaped leg (三棱形), filled with a solid ceramic core, as are legs of *ding* vessels. In addition there is new evidence of small holes representing the use of spacers (clay/bronze pieces) to separate wall and core during the time of pouring the bronze. This change from a T-shaped leg to a prismatic shape reflects the evolution and perfection of the art of "blind core" technology. This evolution from T- to prismatic-shaped leg, typifying *jia*,

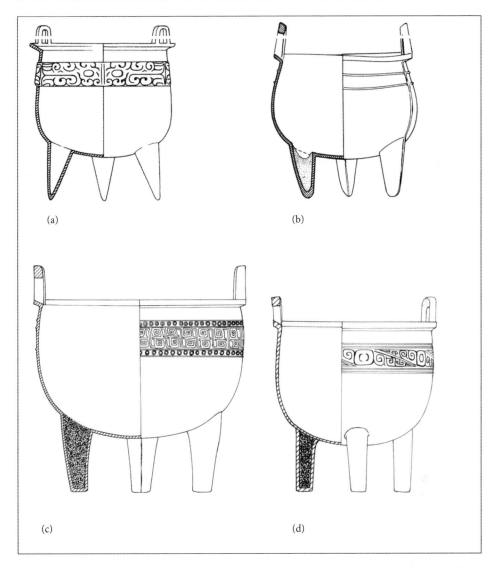

FIGURE 4 Shapes of the blind core foot part of round belly tripod ding bronze vessels. **A** C8M2:4 Zhengzhou Shang City. **B** M388:R2054 Xiaotun. **C** M60:1 HuadongYinxu. **D** M1:2 Wuguancun.

compares with the evolution of the *ding* leg from open to solid form. (A clear evolution of the *jia* leg may be traced from Xiaotun M333:R2045 → Xiaotun M388:R2046 → Xiaotun M331:R2043 → Huadong M60: 8.)

Regarding the evolution of the two ear-shaped handles of *ding* and *li* and the position of the three legs, or the creation of a solid leg out of one that was originally hollow, the evolution of bronze technology improved and functionality was enhanced over the course of the late Erligang to late Yinxu periods.

RITUAL VESSELS OF THE LATE ERLIGANG THROUGH THE LATE YINXU PHASES

The latter gradually take on imagery that covers the entire vessel. Types and placement of imagery are diverse in including primarily images of the animal face, and dragon and bird forms. Additional imagery includes cloud motifs, triangles, circles, string lines, and various other patterns as if to emphasize decorative interests. Over different periods the animal face may be rendered in intaglio, bas-relief, or high relief, which reflects again the interest in décor (Bagley 1990). In addition to imagery on a flat surface and the emergence of raised imagery, the decorative patterns become gradually more sophisticated in relation to the evolution of casting technology. For example, the position of an individual motif gradually evolves by expanding in cooperation with the division of the mold parts and their division lines. Since the division of individual units of décor is oriented toward the viewer, the goal is to create imagery that is technically perfected with clarity and precision.

In the interest of imagery, there are three aspects of development of bronze-casting techniques from late Erligang to Yinxu, as follows.

(a)   (b)

FIGURE 5 *Fang yi* bronze vessel with animal face and detail, Metropolitan Museum of Art.

THE GROWING COMPLEXITY
OF MOLD DIVISIONS

The basic image in the creation of a multi-level decorative program is the bas-relief motif, protruding on the surface against a background of *leiwen* (cloud-scroll motifs), which also may decorate in small scale the bas-relief parts of the image. The latter we label a "three-layer pattern" (Figure 5:(a-b)). The technique of transferring and impressing these multi-level and densely refined designs from the surface of the model onto the surface of the ceramic mold parts was technically difficult. One major difficulty was how to release the ceramic mold parts from the model and how to increase refinement of designs of small parts in decorative bands. For example, the early round belly *ding* was initially created out of the three outer mold parts that may require six and in some cases nine or 12 units of mold imagery. These mold units of imagery increased exponentially along with the increased technical casting expertise, as represented by the numerous remains at Xiaomintun (Li, Yue, Liu 2007), and in particular by mold fragments of one round *lei* vessel. Mold units could use five bands made of six horizontal units, bringing the total number to some 30 outer molds to create the image (Zhongguo 2006; Yue et al. 2008). This type of multiple-level casting involved improved technology in the assembly of the pieces and in this respect reflects a peak in perfection of casting technology.

THE COMPOSITE MOLD SET

From the Erlitou through early Erligang period, bronze imagery was quite simple. By the late Erligang phase imagery began to appear in the context of a flat surface and animal-head protomes decorating shoulders of *zun* and *lei* vessels. Great strides were reached by the late Shang phase, appearing, for example, in the sculptural and relief effects of imagery. Beyond the imagery of *zun*, *lei*, and other alcohol vessels, *ding* and *gui* were also decorated with relief imagery of more than one type of animal head. Attachments or accessories, such as handles, legs, caps, and lugs, were also decorated with relief imagery and sculpted animal-head protomes.

With the advent of relief and sculptural imagery new challenges included how to separate mold parts from model parts, and how to attach appendages. The method that was devised for attaching the animal head involved the independent creation of a cast head that could then be embedded into the outer piece-mold, thus creating the composite mold set. This means of casting the animal head by embedding it in the outer mold not only resolved the question of how to remove the piece mold parts but how to maintain the integrity of the vessel. If we had not excavated such composite sets of molds of clay heads at Xiaomintun, it would have been impossible to understand how the composite mold was assembled.

CASTING-ON AND PRE-CASTING TECHNOLOGY

Late Erligang bronzes over time became more complex in shape, and vessel imagery in relief became increasingly advanced. In order to create more complex shapes or clay casts forming ears and handles on vessels, the technique of casting-on or pre-casting evolved and grew in use.

The earliest use of the casting-on technique is witnessed in the Panlongcheng Lijiazui M1:5 *gui* vessel with animal-face imagery (Hubei 2001) (Figure 3:(b)). Because the joints of the three mold parts and handle protomes did not align, the ears were first cast and later cast-on. In order to cast the handles directly on the wall of the vessel a hole was created for insertion, thus creating a tenon-type connector with the remains of this connector on the inner wall forming a fissure-like extension of the tenon-type nail.

By the late Yinxu phase several of the more complex ears and caps, especially decorating *jia* posts, used this method of casting-on. Many of the *jia* from Fu Zi's (Fu Hao's) tomb have sculptural animal-head attachments. In all cases these are cast and then recast on the vessel proper. The eight elephant and animal-head protomes on the shoulder of the square *zun* from Guojiazhuang M160 also employ this method of direct casting-on of a separate element by inserting it into a tenon-type opening on the shoulder (Hua and Feng 1981) (Figure 6:B).

Bronze-casting in the Yangzi River Valley area during the Yinxu period tends to use casting-on or pre-casting techniques. In this context deeply undercut sculptural and high-relief images take different forms of casting-on. Décor attachments are initially cast and then placed directly into cavities of the vessel body; subsequently molten bronze was poured, forming the entire bronze vessel incorporating the animal parts, which differs from the composite casting method of Yinxu. Vessel examples include the

(a)

(b)

FIGURE 6 Animal head protomes and flanges on Shang *zun* bronze vessels. **A** Xiaotun M18 *zun*. **B** Guojiazhuang M160 *zun*.

well-known four-ram square *zun* from Ningxiang and the *zun* from Funan. Four ram heads with horns decorate the shoulder of the square *zun*, and dragon and tiger heads decorate the shoulder of the Funan *zun*. Casting in this format creates a more homogenous image, as if the animal heads were formed uniformly with the vessel. Flanges decorating Xingan bronze vessels were also formed in the way Yangzi bronzes were created (Su et al. 1997:260–262): firstly cast and then inserted into the vessel molds to receive the final one-time bronze pour and casting of all parts of the vessel. This method contrasts with the method employed at Anyang.

These different techniques of casting complex shapes and decorative programs evidently varied from secondary casting-on, pre-casting, or casting in one piece (with bisque-fired models [*hunzhu*]). These multiple variations of casting illustrate that the technology grew and matured from the late Erligang phase to the late Yinxu phase.

Editor's note: 婦子 should be translated Fu Zi, not Fu Hao. Animal face/head is also used in place of the inaccurate term, *taotie*, a Han-inspired word.

BIBLIOGRAPHY

Bagley, Robert W. 1990. "Shang Ritual Bronzes: Casting Technique and Vessel Design." *Archives of Asian Art* 43: 6–20.

Hua, Jueming 华觉明, and Feng Fugen 冯富根 1981. "Research on the Casting Technology of the Vessels from Fu Hao's [Fu Zi's] Tomb 妇好墓的青铜器铸造技术研究." *Kaoguxue jikan* 1.

Hua, Jueming 华觉明, and Feng Fugen 冯富根 1999. *Ancient Chinese Metal Technology: Creating Civilization with Bronze and Iron*. Zhengzhou: Daxiang chubanshe.

Hubeisheng Wenwu Kaogu Yanjiusuo 湖北省文物考古研究所 2001. *1963–1994 Archaeological Report on Panlongcheng* 盘龙城-1963–1994 发掘报告. Beijing: Wenwu chubanshe.

Li, Yongdi, Zhanwei Yue, and Yu Liu 李永迪, 岳占伟, 刘煜 2007. "New Data Based on the Excavation of Ceramic Molds Discovered at Xiaomintun 从孝民屯东南地出土陶范谈对殷墟青铜器的几点新认识." *Kaogu* 3: 52–63.

Ma, Chengyuan 马承源 1996. "China's Bronze Art 中国青铜器艺术." In *Complete Volume of Chinese Bronzes*, vol. 1 全中国青铜器 1. Beijing: Wenwu chubanshe.

Su, Rongyu 苏荣誉等 et al. 1995. *China's Ancient Metal Technology* 中国上古金属技术. Jinan: Shandong Kexue jichubanshe.

Su, Rongyu 苏荣誉等 et al. 1997. "Research on the Casting Technology Used to Create Bronze Vessels from the Large Tomb at Xingan 新干大洋洲商代青铜器群铸造工艺研究." In *Xingan Shangdai Damu*. Edited by Jiangxisheng bowuguan et al., 260–262. Beijing: Wenwu chubanshe.

Yue, Zhanwei, Hongbin Yue, and Yu Liu 岳占伟, 岳洪彬, 刘煜 2008. "Research Report on Casting Technology and the Use of Ceramic Piece-Molds from Yinxu 殷墟铸造技术及陶瓷片模具应用研究报." In *Yinxu Xin Chu Qingtongqi* 殷墟新出青铜器. Kunming: Yunnan renmin chubanshe.

Zhang, Changping 张昌平 2003. "Preliminary Study of the Bronzes Unearthed at Panlongcheng 盘龙城商代青铜容器初步研究." *Jianghan Kaogu* 1: 45–51.

Zhongguo ShehuiKexueyuan Kaogu Yanjiusuo 中国社会科学院考古研究所 2006. "2000–2001 Excavation Report on the Yin Dynasty Bronze Casting Remains at Southeast Xiaomintun 2000–2001 年殷代孝民屯东南地青铜铸造遗址发掘报告." *Kaogu Xuebao* 3: 351–384.

CHAPTER 15

LATE SHANG RITUAL AND RESIDENTIAL ARCHITECTURE AT GREAT SETTLEMENT SHANG, YINXU IN ANYANG, HENAN

BY ELIZABETH CHILDS-JOHNSON,
OLD DOMINION UNIVERSITY

THE Late Shang cultural presence is primarily known by one major excavation at the site of modern-day Anyang in northern Henan. The site is known as Yinxu 殷墟, Yin Ruins, in transmitted texts and as Da Yi Shang 大邑商, Great Settlement Shang, in Shang bone divinatory inscriptions. The site has undergone excavation since 1928, when formal digging first began under the then newly founded auspices of the Academia Sinica. The Late Shang capital city and its environs reveal a large settlement of some 30–36 km², larger in size than the first capital of the Early Shang Period, Zhengzhou Shang City, or any other major Shang city or capital site. The layout of this metropolis with extensive surrounding communities is unparalleled in excavations elsewhere during the Shang period. Great Settlement Shang may be viewed as representing the center of the East Asian Heartland region during the fourteenth through eleventh centuries BCE.

Newly excavated cemetery and burial finds of all social classes and numerous workshop and architectural configurations allow for a general assessment of social and ritual distinctions and for cultural and artistic periodization. As with Zhengzhou Shang City of the Early Shang period, Anyang Shang City is characterized by similar but much more complex and grander properties that define the site as a capital center of the East Asian Heartland region. The site boasts the following: large-scale bronze vessels belonging to

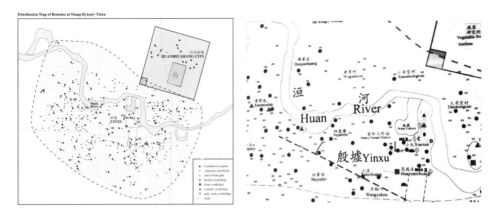

FIGURE 1 Map of settlements at Late Shang–period Yinxu and enlarged detail. After Yinxu Gongzuozhan, large-scale chart, Dept. of Archaeology, Yinxu, Henan. Detail of layout at Yinxu, Late Shang period, showing workshops, inscription caches, cemeteries, and settlements distinguished by shape (triangle: bronze workshop; square: bone workshop; half circle: pottery workshop; diamond: jade and stone workshop; rectangle: cemetery; dot: settlements; plastron: oracle bone inscription cache repositories). After Zhongguo Shehui 2016:84; and Zhu 2016:84 figure.

royalty; a large-scale and richly diverse layout without fortified walls; numerous satellite sites with royal and non-royal workshops for making different types of artifacts; numerous settlements of military- and labor-class residents; large-scale human and animal sacrifice; palace-temple and non-royal architecture; and a classical metropolitan artistic style. Unlike earlier Shang cities, excavations reveal many aristocratic, clan, and lineage burial grounds, in addition to a royal cemetery. The latter is well known through excavations at Xibeigang 西北岡 or Northwest Terrace, however, due to heavy looting remains are piecemeal. The reach of the Shang state may also be measured by the extensive settlement outside the capital (Jing et al. 2013;Tang et al. 1998). For example, partially excavated remains of an aristocratic cemetery exist at Sufutun (Yin 1977) and Qianzhangda (Zhongguo 2005) in northeastern Shandong. Recent excavations have uncovered burials and settlement south of Anyang in the Luoyang area at Luyi near the Anhui border (Henan 2000); the same at Luoshan near the Hubei border (Zhongguo Anyang 1979; Henan 1986); and also within Lingshixian in Shanxi province (Shanxi 2006; Dai 1980). Certain Early and Middle Shang sites, such as Laoniupo in Shaanxi (Liu Shi'e 2001) continued to thrive during the Late Shang period. Extensive site excavations of Late Shang date are few, yet the probability that the Late Shang maintained control over much of what belonged to the realm of the Early and Middle Shang periods is suggested by remains other than ceramics, mostly bronzes from burials and caches. Although it is not always clear whether a bronze vessel found in Hubei or Hunan was captured and brought there, gifted to a southerner, or whether it was produced there, bronze vessel distribution points to widespread communication in a realm that represents cultural and political Shang hegemony. A classical metropolitan style of the Late Shang at Anyang, on the basis of available archaeological data, extends geographically as far as the realm did during Middle and Early Shang periods, with the exception of northern and eastern Jiangxi province where the local Wu culture superseded the occupation of early and middle Shang peoples.

Periodization of the Late Shang period is still fraught with debate among archaeologists, historians, and art historians. Certain archaeologists favor a ceramic evolution that follows bronze periodization (Zhongguo 1985); others follow oracle bone periodization, as first proposed by Dong Zuobin (Song and Liu 2006); and a third group creates a new ceramic periodization (Meng 2003). As will be presented in this chapter, based on oracle bone, ceramic, and bronze data from Yinxu, the Late Shang period as a cultural whole may be divided into four phases, Phases 1–4, associated with the Late Shang Kings Pan Geng through Di Yi and Di Xin (Zhongguo 1994). Phase 1, as identified in previous research, corresponds to an earliest phase, identified with the settlement of the three kings Pan Geng, Xiao Xin, and Xiao Yi, preceding Wu Ding at Yin and currently associated by some scholars with remains at Huanbei of ancient Yinxu (Tang et al. 2010; 2016; Meng 1991). The cultural height and climax of the Late Shang capital occurred during Phase 2, the long reign of King Wu Ding, and that of his son and successor, Zu Geng. Phase 3 includes Kings Zu Jia, Kang Ding, and Wu Yi, and Phase 4 includes the last three kings, Wen Ding, Di Yi, and Di Xin. Phase 3 carries on the classical material tradition of Phase 2 but with an evolution by Phase 4 that exhibits repetition and gradual degradation of ceramic, bronze, and other crafts. Although this periodization system may require tweaking and revisions with new excavations and discoveries, the four phases are employed here to represent the cultural and historical evolution of the Late Shang period:

Table of Late Shang phases and kings: P1 = Pan Geng, Xiao Xin, Xiao Yi; P2 = Wu Ding (Zu Ji and royal family group), Zu Geng; P3 = Zu Jia, Kang Ding, Wu Yi; P4 = Wen Ding, Di Yi, Di Xin.

Shang capital criteria

As recently proposed, criteria identifying a site as a Shang capital include six major characteristics: (1) the presence of monumental tetrapod *ding* and related royal bronze vessels; (2) a royal city center; (3) an extensive urban settlement; (4) royal and urban workshops; (5) large-scale ritual sacrifice; and (6) a classical metropolitan artistic style (see *Great Settlement Shang, the State at the Center: Art, Religion and Culture*, forthcoming), one of which, a royal city center, is analyzed here. In analyzing the royal city center at ancient Yinxu, Anyang, several issues are raised. Questions asked include whether there was a planned city layout, a royal cemetery, and inner city with residential/administrative quarters, or ritual centers for worship and sacrifice. Dating of excavated remains at Anyang Shang City have been considerably revised in the past decade (see e.g., Zhongguo 2003a; Liu and Chen 2012) to include all historic periods documented in transmitted texts, which, as mentioned comprise Phases 1–4, from Pan Geng to Di Xin.

The royal city center of the Late Shang capital, Great Settlement Shang

Since 1928, the year that excavations began at Anyang, the site has been recognized as the Late Shang capital, known locally as Yinxu, or Yin Ruins. The name Yin derives from transmitted historical texts yet may be traced to nomenclature in the latest phase of bone inscriptions, primarily belonging to the Zhou (Wang Yuxin 1984). Shang is the name that the Shang peoples gave to themselves, in referring to their kingdom and capital as Great Settlement Shang (Da Yi Shang 大邑商) in divinatory inscriptions (Tang and Jing 2009). The site was initially identified as a capital due to its association with the source for the famous, popularly labeled "dragon bones," primarily oxen shoulder bones and tortoise plastron shells bearing divinatory inscriptions that were initially traced and identified by Wang Yi in 1899 and studied and collected by a succession of well-known specialists (see the review by Cao 2007:174–188). Li Ji (Li Chi) (1997), intermittently in charge of excavations at Anyang from 1928–1937, recounts the discovery and history of excavations at Yinxu before the governmental change in 1948 that created Taiwan and the People's Republic of China and led to the transfer of most of the excavated material from Anyang to Nangang (Nan-kang), Taiwan within the Academia Sinica.

The major contribution of several seasons of excavations at Anyang before 1948 includes the excavation of a royal cemetery north of the Huan River at Xibeigang and a royal architectural complex at Xiaotun, on the bank south and west aligning the Huan River (Figures 1–3) (Zhongguo 1987).

The Institute of Archaeology of the Chinese Academy of Social Sciences (abbreviated IA, CASS), established in 1950 in the PRC, has carried out additional seasons of excavations. The latter major excavations and discoveries have been published by Yang and Liu (1995; 2007a) and by Liu and He (2007). What has revolutionized our understanding of the Late Shang capital are the overwhelming number of further finds revealed by continuous excavation of previously known and new sites surrounding Anyang, as well as the more recent discovery in 1987 of the southern extension of the royal palace-temple complex at Xiaotun (Zhongguo 1994a; 1994b; Zhongguo Anyang 2001; 2009; National Chinese Cultural Relics Bureau 2001). The recent discovery of several intact burials, including the now famous burial M5 at Xiaotun belonging to the woman warrior (Zhu 2016; Zhongguo 1977; Childs-Johnson 1983) and the intact burials from Guojiazhuang (Zhongguo 2011; 1998a) and Liujiazhuang (He et al. 2012; Yue and Yue 2009b; Zhongguo 2007b), and the cemetery at Qijiazhuang East (Zhongguo Anyang 2015) are just a few of the new finds that add considerably to our understanding of the social and ritual context of the Shang bronze-working tradition.[1]

Major excavations from 1958–1961 occurred at peripheral sites south of the Huan River, at Miaopu North and Xiaomintun, where site remains and bronze-casting centers were identified (Zhongguo 2010; Yue and Yue 2009a); at Dasikongcun and Beixinzhuang, where site remains, burials, and bone workshops were identified (Zhongguo 2014); at various other sites with stratigraphically dated remains, including Xiaotun West (Zhongguo 1979), Zhangjiawen, Meiyuanzhuang, Baijiawen Northeast, Wangyukou West, and Baijiawen West (Zhongguo 2010); and at Hougang, where a large-scale circular sacrificial pit and large-scale inscribed tripod *ding* were discovered (see Zhongguo 1987).

Recent book publications documenting some of these excavations at Anyang, mostly undertaken after the Cultural Revolution (1966–1976), from the late 1970s through 1990s and through 2004, include the site report of the now well-known intact burial belonging to Fu Zi, entitled *Yinxu Fu Hao (Zi) Mu* (1980) and a series of other reports.[2] Several new discoveries of oracle bone caches have also been published, as illustrated in Figure 1 including library pits discovered in 1973 at Xiaotun South (Zhongguo 1980a) and at Huayuanzhuang East in 1991 (Schwartz 2013), both of which belong to royal house members excluding the king (also see, Zhongguo 1983, 2003b; Cao 2007:174–189; Yang and Liu 2007a, 2007b; Zhongguo 2007c; Song and Liu 2006).

City layout

As at Yanshi and the Shang capital city of Zhengzhou, the Late Shang capital city at Anyang is characterized by a large-scale and rich diversity of buildings. The city comprises a complex purposefully perched on high ground (79.2 m above sea level), high above the adjacent Huan 洹 River (Figure 1). Settlements extend outward in all directions

[1] An issue of *Kaoguxue Jikan* 考古学季刊 14 (2007) is devoted to a review of Anyang excavations and issues, including articles covering the history of excavations and an Anyang bibliography, as provided for example by two appendices: Yang Xizhang and Liu Yiman, 2007, "The Chronological Table of Archaeological Excavations at the Yinxu Site in the Past Seventy Years," *Kaoguxue Jikan* 考古学季刊 14:391–394; and Liu Yiman and He Yuling, 2007, "Bibliography of the Yinxu Archaeology," *Kaoguxue Jikan* 考古学季刊 14:395–415.

[2] See the site report on the cemetery excavated from 1982–1992 at Guojiazhuang, south of Xiaotun, entitled *Anyang Yinxu Guojiazhuang Shangdai Mucang* (1988); the study and illustrated publication of tomb bronzes from southern sites at Anyang, entitled *Anyang Yinxu Qingtongqi* (1993) by Meng Xianwu et al.; the analysis and publication of selected bronzes excavated from 1958–1982 from 35 sites at Anyang, entitled *Yinxu Qingtongqi* (1985) by three sets of authors, Zheng Zhenxiang and Chen Zhida; Yang Xizhang and Yang Baocheng; and Zhang Xiaoguang; a review of new finds of the 1980s titled *Yinxu de Faxian yu Yanjiu* by archaeologists of The Institute of Archaeology, CASS, in 1994; a publicly sponsored government report of excavation, legal, and conservation history at Yinxu site with new maps and a bibliography, entitled *Yinxu* (2001); and Meng Xianwu's *Anyang Yinxu Kaogu Yanjiu* (2003), where he introduces unpublished new finds and data, particularly from cemetery burials on the western and southern periphery of Yinxu, outside the protected limits of Yinxu proper.

beyond the Huan River to the northeast and south, and to the northwest lies a large-scale royal cemetery and sacrificial center (Zhongguo 2004; Zhongguo 2007a). It is questionable whether Anyang Shang City was surrounded by city walls, although fortified city walls are in ready supply at earlier Shang cities, including Zhengzhou, Yanshi, Yuanqu, Panlongcheng, Laoniupo, Xiaoshuangqiao, and Huanbei (Childs-Johnson forthcoming).

An enigmatic ditch *haogou* 壕溝, as drawn on the map in Figures 2–3 was once identified as flanking the western side of the royal center at Xiaotun in an L-shape that mirrors the inverted L-shape of the Huan River on its opposite side. The current assessment is that the ditch is an inexplicable phenomenon due to the fact it was only in use for a short period, was abandoned in P2, and is far too small to have served as a fortified wall (He Yuling, personal communication 2016).[3] The Huan River has changed its course since the Shang period in flowing further west and south, so that a major eastern portion of the royal buildings have been flooded and submerged. The original course of the Huan River naturally defended the Shang city on northern and eastern flanks, since it curves south at the northeastern corner of the Shang City and is considered to have followed this general course in antiquity (Figure 1) (see Yang and Liu 2004:21).

An alternative, shrewd suggestion is that one or more other outer fortified city "wall(s)" originally extended further west as far as Sipanmo, well beyond the western and southern parts of the ditch and more in conformity with the size of citadel walls of other Shang capitals and cities (Meng 2003; Yue and Yue 2009a; Tang Jigen 2009). Increasing the probability that another more extensive wall may have been constructed further west beyond Sipanmo and probably as far south as Xuejiazhuang and Guozhuang are the facts that these areas were densely settled in the Shang period, and a precedent existed for defense and for protection against flooding of the large-scale urban setting at earlier Zhengzhou and most other early and middle Shang city sites. A novel and different interpretation, proposed by Xu Hong is that major capital sites did not need fortifications. This situation is explained as being due to security from nearby states with allegiance, who served as guard assets for capitals (大都无城, 卫军不守民), including Da Yi Shang at Yinxu (Xu 2013; 2016; 2017). One needs to keep in mind that flanking the western face of Xiaotun was a vast lake and swamp (see map Figure 1), only recently identified archaeologically (Du 2010). In addition and further south between Fu Zi's burial M5 and the *siheyuan* structure of Huayuanzhuang was another, yet smaller lake. Clearly water was not in short supply; flooding was a constant concern, thus the likelihood that the L-shaped ditch may have been momentarily constructed to prevent flooding and that a more comprehensive wall or walls (*cheng-guo* 城郭), one surrounding the royal center and an outer one the Shang settlement) once existed seems tenable.

[3] Meng states the use is "still up in the air" (Meng 2003:10), whereas Zheng Zhenxiang states that if it functioned as a moat it must pass over two locations, Angang Avenue and Zhongzhou Road. Since it does not, it is unlikely a moat or wall foundation (Zheng 2010). The so-called L-shaped moat forms a discontinuous 3–10 m deep ditch along the western and southern edges of the inner city and measures 1,100 m long north to south and 650 m long west to east. It incorporates Huayuanzhuang in the south and runs east as far as the Huan River (see Du 2010:5; Yang and Liu 2004:21). It was labeled by Meng as a Shang-dynasty *haogou* (see Meng 2003:Figure 1, p. 67).

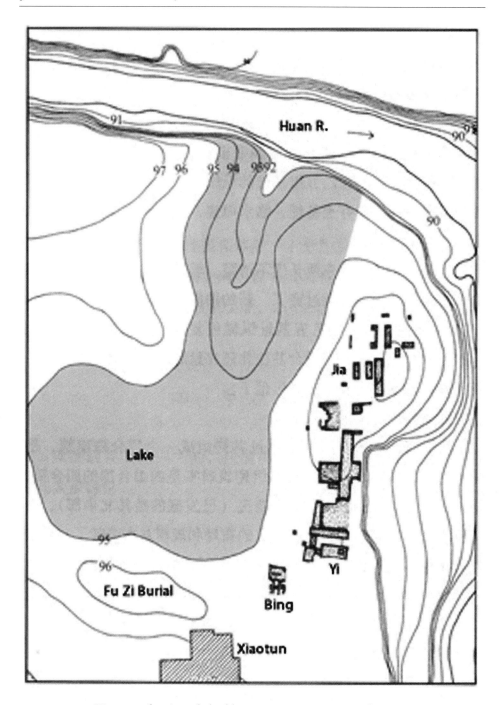

FIGURES 2–3 Xiaotun palace/temple building remains at Yinxu site showing western extent of the lake (left) and L- shape of the "trench" surrounding the palace-temple complex (right).

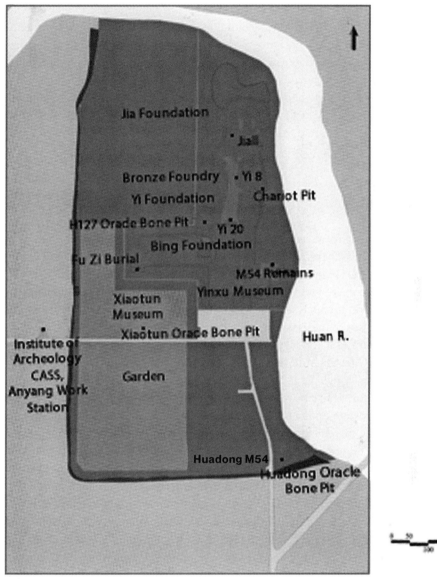

Jia Foundation

• Jia

Bronze Foundry • Yi 8

Yi Foundation Chariot Pit

H127 Oracle Bone Pit • Yi 20

Bing Foundation

Fu Zi Burial
•

M54 Remains

Yinxu Museum

Xiaotun
Museum

Xiaotun Oracle Bone Pit Huan R.

•
Institute of
Archeology
CASS, Garden
Anyang Work
Station

Huadong M54 •

Huadong Oracle
Bone Pit

FIGURES 2–3 (*Continued*)

As at earlier fortified capitals, the palace-ritual complex was located in the northeast of the citadel proper.

Although the question about the existence of fortifications remains anomalous, unless Xu Hong's theory rings true, the foresight in planning the capital layout is apparent not only in its geographical location but in the disposition of inner-city structures. For the Shang, high ground above or near a river or waterway was requisite for founding a city. The orientation strictly observed is south to north or vice versa, although structures may align slightly off several degrees from the position of magnetic due north.

And, as is characteristic of all royal Chinese architectural complexes, a gateway with walls leads from formal to more informal building types as one proceeds from the gateway in the south to the north. Entrances were systematically designed in leading primarily from south to north. Gateways of fortifications, however, could be numerous, lying in different directions, north, south, east, or west. Although an inner citadel wall has not been identified, the likelihood that one once existed is based on other Shang citadels at earlier Panlong, Zhengzhou, and Yuanqu Shang cities. As mentioned, royal burials are consistently separate from the inner royal center. Workshops were located outside the citadel yet within the city outskirts.

Royal cemetery

Thus far the only Shang royal cemetery discovered and identified is the Late Shang one at Xibeigang (Northwest Terrace), northwest of the royal architectural complex at Xiaotun and across the Huan River (Figure 4). The looted burials have frequently been analyzed with an attempt to identify which large cruciform burial belongs to which Late Shang king (see the recent analyses of Mizoguchi and Uchida 2018 and Gao 2011). The present author follows the thesis that the cemetery was once much more extensive than presently known, and that the layout of certain of the tombs, including M1001 surrounded by M1004, M1002, and M1550, may be associated with King Wu Ding and his three royal offspring, Kings Zu Ji, Zu Geng, and Zu Jia (Soper 1966). It is also highly likely that the cruciform burials were crowned by mounds or shrines for worship, as is the case for several extant Shang tombs at Xiaotun including M5 and Dasikongcun, as well as Qianzhangda in Tengzhou, Shandong, and elsewhere during the Shang period (see Figure 17) (He Yuling 2016). There is little reason for building such large-scale tombs that continued to be actively honored through constant sacrifice and dedication by descendants unless the burials could be recognized externally, by what probably originally was a field of at least 11 circular-shaped mounds above underground cruciform-shaped burials, by the end of the Late Shang period. The existence of the latter would agree with the cosmological interests of the Shang, who believed in an umbrella-shaped canopy of the sky and a square earth radiating axially in four or eight directions (Zhongguo 1994).

The cruciform-shape is formed as four radial sloping tunnels extending east, west, north, and south, with the southern typically longer than the rest. The burial proper lay in a square pit dug deeply at the center with one or more dog pits and a panoply of human sacrifices in earthen pits or occasionally in an individual wood-constructed tomb. These burials have been frequently described, as have the sacrifices accompanying them (see e.g. Zhongguo 1994). The number of human sacrifices outside the tomb is equally stunning and has been addressed at length and most recently in several analyses by Roderick Campbell, who describes what he calls Shang rites of blood (Campbell 2013).

Several recent excavations have augmented our understanding of the royal burial system and its history at ancient Yinxu. Current data indicate, for example, that Xibeigang cemetery indeed probably housed tombs of the earliest royal settlers at Yinxu, Kings Pan

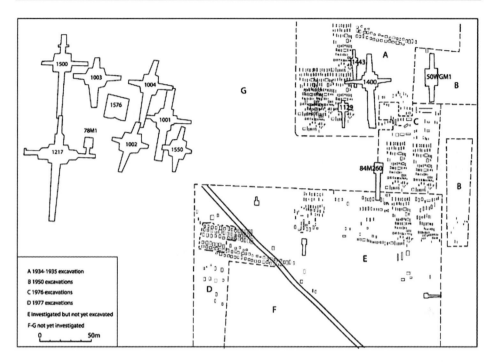

FIGURE 4 Ground plan of "royal cemetery," Xibeigang, Anyang, Late Shang period. Keys: After Guojia Wenwuju 2001:special figure, p. 57.

Geng, Xiao Xin, and Xiao Yi of Yinxu P1. Several phenomena of early date document this probability. For example, the small tomb M1, with southern extension lying below the largest Xibeigang West royal burial, M1217, dates to Yinxu P1 (for illustration and analysis see He 2012:35–36, Figures 1–2; Chinese National 2001:66, Figure 11) (see Figure 4). Tomb M60 from the Huayuanzhuang cemetery at Anyang (Zhongguo 2007a) and the series of tombs (M188, M238, M331, M232) below buildings at Xiaotun in Locus Bing also date to Yinxu P1 (Zhongguo 1994). The settlement in Locus Ding dates to Yinxu P1 and P2 (Du 2010). Although not published nor thoroughly excavated, the area of Wuguancun just southeast of Xibeigang (see Figure 4) appears not to be settled by residences of any kind but rather was occupied by extensive burial groups, suggesting that the area along with Xibeigang had long been used for burial purposes throughout the Late Shang era, from P1 to P4. The suggestion is that a pre–Wu Ding settlement belongs to at least his three predecessors, including Wu Ding's father King Xiao Yi and others who, as related in transmitted texts, settled this area south of the Yellow River. It is difficult nonetheless to hypothesize that the large cruciform tomb M1400 belongs to Wu Ding and M1001 to Wu Ding's father King Xiao Yi on the basis of the socio-political argument that three sets of relationships (X, Y, and Z: one of respect, disrespect, and pairing) govern the layout of big burials (Mizoguchi and Uchida 2018). The chronology proposed by Zheng Zhengxiang, 1001 → 1550 → 1400 → 1004 → 1003 → 1002 → 1500 → 1217, and others for the dating of large-scale burials is followed here until more evidence for King Xiao Yi becomes available (IA 1994a).

Huanbei Shang City aligning the north edge of Yinxu unquestionably dates to a pre–Wu Ding period, although more data need to be published in order to clarify this identification and its relationship with the rest of the Yinxu settlement. Tang Jigen earlier hypothesized that Huanbei Shang City dated to a brief so-called "mid-Shang" era (Tang and Jing 2016:340; also see Meng 1991; IA 2003c; IA 2007b). (Author's note: Middle Shang is used in preference to "mid-Shang," in keeping with the terms Early and Late Shang). Since Huanbei was short lived as a capital, ending through burning, it is probable that the site was occupied by Wu Ding predecessors and possibly even earlier, yet the latter remains to be revealed through future excavations.

The newly documented small tomb with southern entrance extension (*jia* 甲 in shape), M1, lying below the large cruciform-shaped royal tomb, M1217, is considerably smaller than M260, also *jia* 甲 in shape (total length < 35 m) (Yang Baocheng 1982). The latter is identified with Queen Mother Wu, King Wu Ding's third wife, who produced King Zu Jia who ruled during P3.[4] Ceramics from the small *jia*-shaped tomb M1 compare to those falling between a pre–Wu Ding and post-Erligang early Shang era (He 2012; IA 1994: 267–276 [M232, M331, M333, M388, Wu Guan M1]. For other P1 burials at Dasikongcun and Miaopubeidi see IA 1994a: 135-136). This piece of dateable data makes it extremely likely that the whole area of Xibeigang and Wuguancun once served as a large-scale burial ground, primarily for royalty during the Shang occupation of Yinxu. Although there are countless sacrificial burials and retainer burials within and outside the cruciform-shaped tombs, only some of these are dateable to Phase 1, or pre–Wu Ding. The majority represent animal and human sacrifices made to the royal dead, including one queen buried in M260.

Inner city layout

The inner city layout at Yinxu, as with the royal cemetery, is also typified by excavated finds of pre–Wu Ding through Di Xin date, suggesting that the transmitted histories may be right about the chronological occupation from Kings Pan Geng through Di Xin. Certain Anyang archaeologists adhere to the theory that the walled site of Huanbei just northeast of Xiaotun belongs to a late Middle Shang period whereas Xiaotun Shang City corresponds to the Late Shang Phases 1–4 (Pan Geng through Di Xin) (Tang and Jing 2016). The chronological coverage of Phase 1 currently vacillates amid those who assign it to pre–Wu Ding and early Wu Ding and those who do not include the first three Late Shang kings. Due to limitations of space Huanbei and new finds will not be analyzed here (for analysis of Huanbei finds see Tang et al. 2010; Childs-Johnson forthcoming); rather, the focus is on Xiaotun Shang City and new architectural data that help fill out the picture of Late Shang kings and their capital buildings.

---

[4] In size M1 lies 7.2 m deep, is 7.7 m long by 5.4 - 5 m wide. The southern ramp, cut off by M1217, extends more than 6.9 m long.

The layout of major royal buildings excavated north of today's Xiaotun town is attributed to the construction and reconstruction of Wu Ding through Di Xin eras and now, due to new finds, includes the pre–Wu Ding era of Pan Geng, Xiao Xin, and Xiao Yi. Few architectural structures, nonetheless, have been identified below those built allegedly during the Wu Ding through Di Xin era, other than the remains in the area labeled Bing and burials identified through stratigraphical analysis by Anyang archaeologists (Zheng et al. 1985; Zheng 2001). Because finds are still quite piecemeal at Yinxu, it is not possible to clarify whether the complex was designed with a compound wall, as testified by earlier structures at Erlitou and Erligang, or whether parts of it were constructed during a pre–Wu Ding era or not. Nonetheless the layout adheres to the architectural precedent of earlier Shang cities in the sense that there is a consistent architectural complex that begins in the south and continues north, not vice versa. At these royal cities, multiple rectangular columned halls erected on sunken and raised rammed-earthen platforms are normative, as is the emphasis on a substantial water supply system and widespread sacrifice at the time of construction. For example, at Zhengzhou and Huanbei Shang cities (Tang et al. 2016), it is clear from the partially excavated remains that an extensive water channel system and series of large-scale columned halls once stood within a northeastern sector of all three inner cities. At Xiaotun, the plan published since 1959 is that provided in 1976 and 1977 by Shi Zhangru (1976; Li Ji 1977) and updated in 2009 and 2010 by Anyang archaeologists (see Figure 3) (Zheng 2001:9.27; Du 2010).

The royal city of Yinxu has traditionally been identified as composed of three parts, Jia (A), Yi (B), and Bing (C), and stated to be chronologically successive from north to south. Locus Jia was considered the earliest and Loci Yi and Bing were considered to follow in construction during Wu Ding's era. Contrary to these old hypotheses, archaeological evidence of pre–Wu Ding date may be identified not only within Locus Jia and the whole area of Locus Bing but also at the new site recently labeled Locus Ding (D). Furthermore, ceramics dateable to Phase 1, pre–Wu Ding, underlie most architectural foundations of Jia and Yi structures. So the old dating may be turned upside down. Dating of the Late Shang capital is revised to begin with a pre–Wu Ding phase associated with the first three Late Shang kings, followed by a classical phase covering the reign of Wu Ding with occupation continuous until the end of the dynasty and demise of the last Shang king, Di Xin (Du 2010). Due to new research, it is evident that the Xiaotun architectural center was repaired, refurbished, and expanded during several different eras, including the last by Kings Wen Wuding, Di Yi, and Di Xin, as illustrated in different shaded sections of Figure 5.

Residential and palace center: Jia section

Scholars generally agree that the northernmost part of the royal center architecturally probably belonged to palaces—residential architecture referred to as *qin* 寢, *xiqin* 西寢 (west *qin*), *dongqin* 東寢 (east *qin*) in bone divinations, bronze inscriptions, and

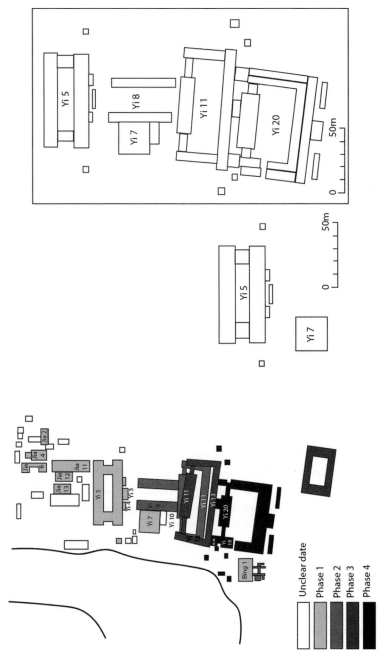

FIGURE 5 Layout of Xiaotun buildings (Loci Jia, Yi, Bing, Ding) from P1–4 (left) and additions to Locus Yi (four on right) over Periods 1–4. After Du 2010:Figure 11.2, p. 47. Chronological evolution of Jia 甲, Yi 乙, Bing 丙, Ding 丁 buildings at Yinxu by Du Jinpeng (white: unclear date; black: P4; charcoal gray: P3; gray: P2; light gray: P1). After Du 2010:Figures 11.2, 11.1.1, 11.1.4.

transmitted texts. *Qin* refers to a household and specifically to the residence of the king and staff, including queen, concubines, and retainers.

The primary evidence demonstrating that these buildings belonged to a residential quarter is inscriptional and textual but also archaeological. As Du elaborates, citing various divinatory inscriptions with reference to *qin* 寢, this was where *fu* 婦, royal women, and the king resided (Du 2010:89–93). Apparently more than sleeping, cooking, and eating occurred in the residential quarters. Divinations were sought (占卜), awards made (錫賞), ancestral offerings made (祭祀), and births were deemed lucky or unlucky (婦娩嘉), all by the king assisted by his staff. Such data would corroborate the scholarly view that religio-ritual and administration were not distinguished by location or different architectural forms (see Xu and Li, Chapter 8 in this volume). Divinatory inquiries about constructing new residences are documented, as are numerous references to different locations of *qin*, as east or west or as big or small. *Qin* also had welcoming hall(s) (堂室) and officials in charge of business in these residential quarters, who, as noted, were called *qin* by name, occasionally also including a personal surname, such as Qin Yu 寢魚. Yu we know was a son of Wu Ding who did not ascend to the throne and in this case functioned as an (or one of the) inner house official(s) in charge of the royal residence. Corroborative excavated data indicating that this northern portion may identify a royal residence is the lack of animal or human sacrifice associated with ritual, as is typically found in sections of the complex further south.[5]

Shang royal centers adhere to a standardized architectural layout that begins at the south with a gateway, leading to public buildings and reception halls and extending north with an administrative and ritual center and ultimately to private residential palaces at the very back. This is the pattern reflected in Beijing's Forbidden City and the Ming complex of Daming Palace, as it is in earlier Han and Tang palace complexes in ancient Changan, the earlier Western Zhou center of Zhouyuan and Fengchu, and the Shang City complexes at Zhengzhou and Huanbei. It is difficult to reconstruct the remains excavated from 1927–1938 and the following 1950s at Yinxu, particularly in the northernmost part of the complex (Locus Jia) where excavated remains are piecemeal. Certain architectural properties may be identified in following the recent research published by Du Jinpeng (2006, 2007a, 2007b, 2007c, 2010).

Based on current assessments, Locus Jia (A)—reportedly the palace residential component—survives with 20 foundations (Du 2010; Zhongguo 1994:53 says 15 foundations) and symmetrical flanking east and west structures lying on a north to south axis, but how and if they link together cannot be plotted. Long rectangular buildings with multiple rooms and doors survive but with no clear ground plan of the common *siheyuan* 四合院 or four-sided enclosed courtyard with building structures, as typifies other build-

---

[5] Most of these Jia foundations overlaid refuse-type pits dating to a pre–Wu Ding phase, according to Li Chi (1977:179; Institute of Archaeology 1994:54) and architectural analyses of Du Jinpeng (2010). Du generously amplifies the original ground plan (1959) and the more recent archaeological evidence (2008) in identifying and clarifying old and new structures. .

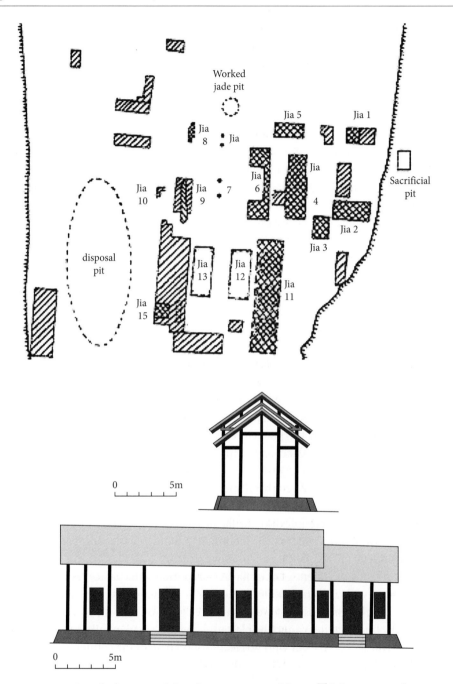

FIGURES 6–7 Detail of piecemeal foundation remains of the Jia 甲 (A) section and reconstruction of side and front elevation plan of Locus Jia 4 甲四 at Xiaotun, Anyang, Late Shang period. After Du 2010:Figures 1.1.3, 2.6.4.

ings in Yi, Bing, and Ding sections as well as earlier capital sites of Zhengzhou and Huanbei. This different layout may be due to the limitations of initial excavations (Zhongguo 1994), hiding northern and southern building walls, which would have enclosed a large-scale *siheyuan*.

In any case innermost building doors face inward, whereas secondary, outermost building doors face outward. Complementarity of west and east buildings dictates the layout of these and most other aristocratic and royal buildings.

The architectural remains cover an area of approximately 9,000 sqm (100 m north to south and 90 m east to west) with over 20 building foundations, the most significant of which are those at the center (Jia 4, 6, 11–13), in addition to the probability that others, such as piecemeal foundations of Jia 9, 10, and 15, relate to no longer fully extant complemented buildings on flanking western sides of the area. Small subordinate structures with shallow foundations were built around these, suggesting that these belonged to quarters of personnel connected with duties in the inner and larger palatial structures. Most of the central structures are deep, with buried rammed-earth foundations rising on high rectangular platforms that support look-alike structures oriented east to west. Construction is dated to the beginning of the Wu Ding era, if not earlier, with a continued occupation lasting through the end of the late Shang era (Du 2010).

Four types of buildings within Locus Jia may be reconstructed, although not connected. Du reconstructs several of the Jia foundations with superstructures. Jia 4 and the comparable mirror structure Jia 10 face opposite directions and may be surmised to comprise staff structures serving royal quarters of Jia 6 and 9: the doors of Jia 4 open to the east (facing outside) and the doors of Jia 6 open to the west (facing inside). As types the two also differ: Jia 6 rests on a considerably higher platform of rammed earth than Jia 4 (Figures 6–7) (Du 2010:59–61).[6] Jia 6 is reconstructed as a massive one-story structure on a wide platform flanked by two spacious northern and southern corner rooms, possibly with staircases (Figure 8). This storied rectangular structure is divided into five units by three rows of columns, two of which (front and back) were embedded in a pisé wall, thus leaving the center an open yet enclosed and roofed rectangular room. Narrow colonnades flanked outer long sides of the structures. Jia 4 and reconstructed mirror Jia 10, as noted, differ in function from Jia 6 and 9. They are more modest and humble due to a less massive supporting platform; narrower stairs opening to the east in the opposite direction of Jia 6; and by a division into more numerous, smaller rooms with walls and no outer colonnades. The two Jia 4 and opposing Jia 10 probably served as residences for personnel or lesser members of the royal house (Figure 9). The fact that doors open east as opposed to the center of the complex also indicates a subordinate role, again probably connected with residential staff, known in bone inscriptions by the term *qin* 寢. The opposite western side (Jia 10) hypothetically had a similar structure, perhaps called the

---

[6] Many of Shi Zhangru's early reconstructions of the Jia foundations are based on the combined data of archaeological remains, descriptions of columned halls in the *Kaogongji* of the *Zhouli*, and local architecture of Yunnan and Sichuan (see Du 2010:56, figure 18; and Li Ji 1977:183, figure 17).

western *qin*, and perhaps in practice was professionally managed by another aristocrat *qin*, the official household manager.

Complementarity of buildings is also exhibited by the largest and longest building foundation of the Jia group, Jia 11, and its symmetrical yet not extant copy, Jia 15 (see Figure 10), just south and in front of the smaller complementary pair of Jia 4 and Jia 6. Jia 11 measures 46.7 m long by 10.7 m wide, with an area of almost 500 sqm (Zhongguo 1994:53, figure 16). It was likely mirrored by a comparable opposing structure at Jia 15, although this structure has not been preserved. Two shorter, mirror structures, Jia 12 and 13, rest between Jia 11 and Jia 15. Thirty-four pillar base supports survive and 10 of these were decorated with cast bronze circular-to-oval floor-level fittings, functioning as decorative column supports (Zhongguo 1994:54). The latter fittings help document the function of those surviving at the earlier, Middle Shang–period site of Xiaoshuangqiao (Henan 2012; Childs-Johnson 2016). Doors open to the west so they face the central courtyard, and the expected opposing similar structure would have similar doors facing east. These sets of long rectangular buildings facing each other with 12 separate rooms, matching yet smaller end rooms, and matching staircases may once have formed living or administrative quarters for the royal house. There appear to be no outer sets of colonnades.

A fourth type, the two smaller rectangular structures, Jia 12 and 13 (Figure 11) (Zhongguo 1994:51, figure 17; 56, Figure 18) rest between the considerably longer Jia 11 and

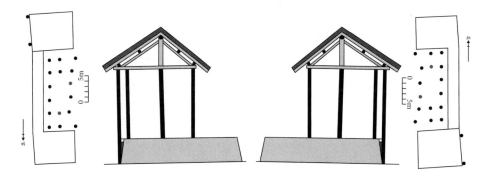

FIGURE 8 Ground plan and reconstruction of Jia 6 building, and duplicated is the no longer extant matching Jia 9 building at Xiaotun, Anyang, Late Shang period;, both face inwards. After Du 2010: 21.

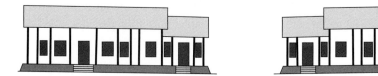

FIGURE 9 Reconstruction of Jia 4 East (right) and duplicated copy simulating no longer extant Jia 10 (?) West (left);, both face outwards, away from the center. After Du 2010:Figure 2.6.4.

15 halls. The two represent a third type of building and in this case carry eave columns, and in the case of Jia 12 clearly support two tent-shaped roofs of thatch. No tile remains were discovered (Li Ji [Li Chi] 1977:184). The latter is hypothesized as two-storied due to the presence of a deeply embedded underground, rammed-earth foundation, as reconstructed by Du. Although these two inner structures differ in type from the flanking outer longer structures (Jia 11 and Jia 15), whether or not they were specific ancestral halls of primary and secondary lineages, as once hypothesized by Shi, or welcoming administrative halls is not possible to confirm (Du 2010:69–71). A central ridge-pole inside Jia 12 building was supported by columns at five points. Plastering with a shell-lime mixture for walls is similar to that used at earlier and other Shang city sites. Stepped entrances are located at two points along the western wall, indicating that the primary orientation of the building was inward toward the central courtyard.[7] The latter complementary structures

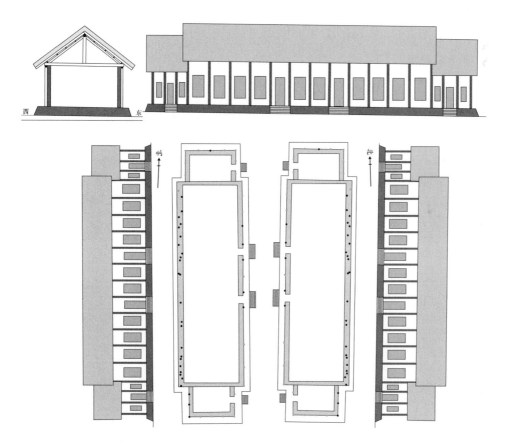

FIGURE 10 Ground plans and reconstruction of Jia 11 building ground plan and duplicated copy representing opposing non-extant Jia 15 (?), facing inwards. After Du 2010:Figure 2.17.3.

---

[7] Although Shi and Du hypothesize a different configuration for Jia 13 building, remaining data are not convincing to demonstrate an original appearance (see Du 2010:72–74).

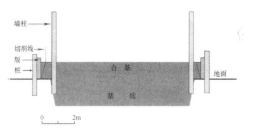

FIGURE 11 Illustration of foundations of Jia 12 building, its reconstruction, and duplicated copy representing no longer extant opposing structure. After Du 2010.

represented amid surviving Jia building foundations identify a third type that was two storied, a type probably more common than revealed by current remains.

Ritual sacrificial center: Yi (B) section

Locus Yi (B), the second group of buildings and most numerous in terms of archaeological remains, is most likely ritual in function, due to various, primarily archaeological- and architectural-related phenomena. This section is separated geographically from Jia (A) buildings by a back wall behind a platform with a pyramidal altar, Yi 1–2 (B); by an underground library of divinatory texts (at Daliankeng 大連坑) dating to Wu Ding P2; and by 21 building foundations grander in scale and size than Jia or Bing, covering some 20,000 sqm in measuring 200 x 100 m in length and breadth (Figure 12). The buildings differ from those remaining at Locus Jia in that they may be identified as unified in layout, from south to north and entirely enclosed within surrounding walls embracing multiple platforms. Locus Yi (B) may be reconstructed as a ground plan, as drawn in Figure 12 with the exception of the rear structure. At the very rear is the climax—what appears to be an outdoor pyramidal altar prefaced by a concatenation of extraordinary long *ting* halls and wide horizontal platforms, spacious courtyards, and corridors, all rising higher than the other preceding structure, with the highest of all, the pyramidal earthen altar, at the back. The structure as a whole is composed of primarily two parts: a spacious grand southern gateway (extended and

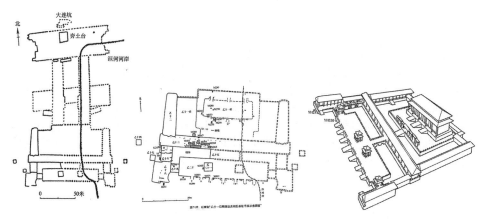

FIGURE 12 Ground plan of Locus Yi architectural complex, Xiaotun, Anyang (the black line represents flooding by the Huan River), late Shang P2. Yi 7–10 ritual buildings at Xiaotun (with black line showing destruction through flooding), Anyang, Late Shang P2. Reconstructed ground plan of the "southern gate," Yi 11–21 building foundations according to refurbished and revised designs by Kings Wen Wu Ding and Di Xin at the end of the site's occupation, as reconstructed by Shi (middle) and (right) by Du 2010.

refurbished several times), opening north to long flanking wing extensions aligned and divided into nine different rooms, with the focus of the ritual, the high raised outdoor altar, at the very center back. The reconstructed southern gateway occupies one-third of the enclosed complex.

The southernmost section of buildings, representing a monumental gateway, most likely sat before an impressive platform and a reception hall that led further back to another higher platform, a ritual complex forming two long colonnaded halls punctuated by an intersecting horizontal section of building wings (Figure 13). Stairs provided access to the multiple platforms that rose higher the further one ventured north. Doors primarily opened on south and north sides. Compound activities must have been pompous and glorious as one made way along a formidable breadth of platforms, moats, and open courtyards stretching 50 m to a centralized high-rising rearmost rectangular platform on its own highest raised platform, once plastered with brilliant white polished stone and crowned with apparently the jewel, the open-air altar mound that formed a flat-topped pyramidal shape. As noted, Locus Yi (B) buildings were entirely contained within surrounding walls open only to the inside. Although the east side of the site was washed away by the Huan River, the layout can be separated into three major parts: (1) an entrance with matching towers on top of a long raised horizontally oriented rammed-earthen platform, which gives way to a long bracket C-shaped moat, which in turn connects to a narrow central and raised bridge and walkway leading to a horizontally oriented reception hall entered by three front stairways and exited by three rear stairways (Jia 11–21); (2) next, a formidably long passageway composed of two symmetrical, longitudinally constructed colonnaded buildings divided into small rooms (Jia 7–10); and (3) the crescendo, a centrally aligned rear platform with the open-air pyramidally shaped altar, once rising much higher than neighboring structures.

The architectural design of the final Shang era comprises a dramatically expansive southern entrance crowned by two tall towers with two stories and hip-shaped roofs, and all other buildings (Jia 1–5) (Zhongguo 1994) were supported at ground level by an outer set of pillars, with foundation stones measuring 7 m wide (Li Ji 1977:186). The large size and height of seven sets of stairs on the south side of the tower platform aid in identifying the two towers preserved above the stairs as watchtowers. Platform stairs are widest and longest in the middle and diminish in size as they move outward (see Yi 11–13). Shi imagined that the door of the tower's second story opened northward, whereas the door of the first floor opened eastward so "the guards might watch the entrance directly" (Li Ji 1977:187). Small pillar stones[8] identified on the top back edge of the platform indicate that this long rectangular entrance platform was enclosed by balustrades (Li Ji 1977:185).

The reconstruction of the twin entrance watch towers encircled by imposing sets of balustrades on a large rectangular platform is reinforced by the fact that the platform is deeply planted two meters into the soil, and by the fact that a further smaller rammed earthen platform was constructed below each tower—for support of Yi 20, although Yi 21 was destroyed by flooding in antiquity. Apparently this southern end of the ritual center was extended several times with additional enclosed courtyard structures, once during P3 and the last during P4 of the Wen Wuding, Di Yi, and Di Xin era (Du 2010).

This grandiose structure rising high on a raised, paved platform evidently served as the major entrance with rear welcoming hall to the inner complex of what most likely was the capital's ritual center, as already hypothesized. The massively broad southern entrance with watch towers proceeds along a narrow path across a bridge over a long horizontally-bracket-shaped pool of water, and equally long east to west corridors divided into 14 small rooms. Moving further north one ascends a staircase to a higher platform with a massive rectangular welcoming hall, on its own higher platform with three sets of steps in front and rear. Fronting this hall are a series of six short screen walls. The entire structure is enclosed within courtyards and surrounding walls, with colonnades and additional small-scale rooms on flanking sides (Figure 13).

The second set of buildings includes long colonnaded corridor foundations, reconstructed according to the layout of Yi 8. They extend south to north 50 m and measure only 7.5 m wide. This architectural type is described as *banfengbi shi jianzhu* or "half-closed-style architecture" (Zhongguo 2010:25). Since the eastern hall has been destroyed by flooding, this portion (without number) is reconstructed as an identical mirror structure of Yi 8 (Figure 13).

These long corridor halls are punctuated by a wide horizontal foundation (Yi 7) at approximately the center, but this building foundation has not been retrieved or published in archaeological restorations. Yet, due to the abundance of pits with animal and human sacrifice in this area, the structure as a whole has been identified as the

---

[8] These measured 2.5 m apart on east and west sides and 8 m apart on north and south sides.

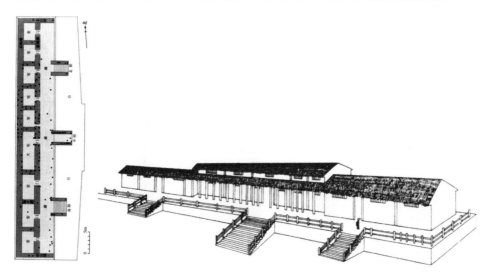

FIGURE 13 Ground plan and reconstruction of Yi 8 building foundations with three stairways open to a central courtyard and duplicated with no longer extant opposite-facing version that has flooded. After Du 2010:6–15.

major center of ritual activity. The multitude of small-scale rooms most likely served various functions connected with ritual equipment and sacrificial offerings, which in turn may have been processed in the central courtyard. Three stairs provide access to the inner courtyard.

The third component of building foundations includes Yi 1–5, focused on the rearmost raised rectangular earthen platform (Figure 14). The latter foundation stretches 21.5 to 25 m west to east and 33 m wide north to south, and it forms a *siheyuan*, a large courtyard surrounded on four sides with a central door opening at the south (Du 2010:136–137). On top and center rear of this raised rammed-earthen platform is the major feature of this enclosure, a square altar, Yi 1, surviving in measuring only 11.30 by 11.80 m, an almost-square structure covering an area of 133.34 sqm (approx. 38 m), with a surviving depth of only 1.00 m (Du 2010:101). Although the altar has been severely reduced in structure and thus cannot be entirely restored to its original appearance and size, it almost certainly measured considerably more—at least three times the size of 33 x 33 m. The uniqueness of this square structure has been underscored by Li Ji: "The top of the pure yellow earth (*huang tu*)... [is] distinguished by its yellow color... [all] sides were bounded by pounded earth somewhat different in color... [and] the orientation of this nearly square altar [lay] exactly to the magnetic south" (Li Ji 1977:188–189). After the construction of these platforms during the early part of Wu Ding's era, the altar must have been maintained and elevated. The structure Yi 2, which slopes down from Yi 1, was probably originally connected with it as a sloping side of an original larger pyramidal outdoor rammed-earth structure, most likely as part of what once stood originally as a wide pyramidal structure with flat top. There is no evidence of any superstructure or

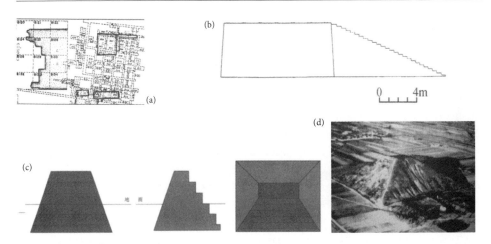

FIGURE 14 Detail of ground plan of foundations of Yi 1, 2, 3, 5 ritual buildings at Xiaotun by Shi Zhangru and hypothetical reconstruction of Yi 1 by Du. For A see Du 2007:Figure 2, p. 605 (after Shi); B possible original extension of pyramidal altar, drawing after Shi who once imagined these stairs and platform led to a further top building (removed from drawing), once associated with a temple; C hypothetical reconstructed shape of Yi square altars at Yi 15; D Photograph of flat-topped pyramid-mound at Xian, Shaanxi (Han period), 210' tall 720' taken after end of WWII. The hypothetical reconstruction for the structure at Xiaotun Locus Yi, now measuring only 38 sqm possibly once measuring many times the size if the stairs as hypothesized by Shi extended the full length of the mound on all four sides.

columns.[9] The raised square stands alone unhindered by walls or columns, and because it combines at least two different types of packed earth, yellow and ashen, the structure undoubtedly had ritual significance.

The special features of the Late Shang outdoor altar include: (1) a construction predating the raised rectangular platforms surrounding it; (2) an alignment that is oriented at exactly magnetic north;[10] (3) a mound that is stepped and made out of specialized earth that is yellow in the center with different-colored earth surrounding it in different layers; (4) a raised square platform with no evidence of a superstructure—no walls or pillar holes (Du 2010:111); (5) a fore-hall with five bays without doors and a screened entrance (see Du 2007:Figure 7 top, p. 614, based on Shi); and (6) buried remains representing domestic and wild hunted sacrifices, many of which were pigs and pig parts at various depths throughout the eastern side,[11] in addition to antlers and skull of a stag and a skull of a tiger (Yi 1 and 2) (Du 2010:112). The latter numerous sacrificial beasts led to the identification of this area as the 臭台 "fetid platform" (Du 2007:574–576).

---

[9] Shi speculated in his reconstruction that the altar was an ancestral temple approached by a long stair and enclosed by a balustrade. Also see Shi's other speculations reviewed by Du 2010:122–149.

[10] Other buildings tended to be slightly off due north, indicating that their orientation was based on another means of measurement, the angle of the sun at high noon.

[11] These data are based on excavations of 1931; see Du 2010:111 chart 3–1.

Clearly this was a cosmologically significant focal point of Late Shang ritual, maintained during the reigns of some 11 to 12 Shang kings (Du 2010:149–150). Since the altar was not housed within a roofed structure but was completely exposed, it must have served either as the outdoor *beng* 祊 (口) altar, well known in inscriptions as a location for offering sacrifices and worshipping nature and other spirits—from Di, the High Cosmological Spirit, to the He River Spirit and ancestral ones (Liu Yuan 2008)—or it may be an earthen altar dedicated to the local earth god (社). We may recall comparable outdoor altars forming centralized platforms for outdoor worship constructed of multiple colors of rammed earth at Late Neolithic Liangzhu culture sites in Zhejiang and Jiangsu, an influential pace-setting culture of the Jade Age preceding Xia and Shang. The precedent of Jade Age Hongshan square altars should also not be overlooked in considering the origins and the evolution of outdoor altars. The distinctive multiple-colored square mound is such a distinctive characteristic of precedent Jade Age Liangzhu city sites, such as Mojiaoshan, that it seems more than likely that this practice of worship grew out of the late Jade Age in the south. Large-scale mounds are currently identifiable at certain Shang burial sites and, since the excavated remains here at Xiaotun have been almost irredeemably destroyed, it is highly likely that this different-colored square earthen outdoor altar once measured considerably larger. It was after all the focal point of the long architectural stretch of buildings beginning with a formidable gateway.

Other ritual buildings: Bing (C) and Ding (D) sections

The layout of the capital proper has recently become entangled due to recent excavations of substantial architectural remains far south of Jia (A) and Yi (B) areas, extending south about 130 m to the large gate of today's Yinxu Museum and beyond (Zhongguo 1994; Zheng 2001:18). The area encompasses what had been previously documented as Area Bing, with outdoor earthen altars of considerably smaller scale than those at Yi 1. These Locus Bing remains, just south and west of those at Yi, may not necessarily be directly related to the ritual center and residences of Jia and Yi buildings to the north, since much of these remains are pre–Wu Ding in date. Further south and west lies the famous intact burial, M5, belonging to the woman warrior Fu Zi, and a host of some five other aristocrat burials, including M17 belonging to Royal Son Yu and further southeast M54 belonging to General Ya Chang.

Since reports on architectural remains have been published, it has been assumed that the southern area remains labeled Bing (C) were dated to a period after the primary occupation at Anyang, thus after Di Xin. As recently demonstrated, ceramic remains and divinatory inscriptions point to a much earlier date, to Yinxu P1. Interestingly, the layout of the structures simulate on a smaller scale, one-tenth the size, of building types recorded by the Yi complex of ritual buildings, namely long flanking colonnaded halls leading to a sacrificial center prefaced by a rectangular "reception hall" and backed by earthen altars exposed to the air. Two further small outdoor altars, numbered Bing 14 and Bing 15, are identified at a further south location, in the front, flanking east and west

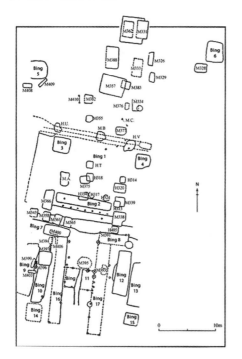
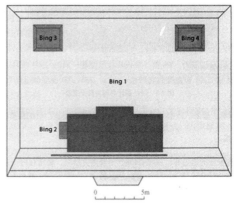

FIGURE 15 Ground plan of Bing foundation remains and reconstruction of Bing 1, 2, 3, 4 buildings by Du (2010). Reconstruction of buildings Bing 2 superimposed on Bing 1 rammed-earth foundation and flanking open-air rammed-earth altars, Bing 3 and 4, lying just behind the Bing 2 entrance. After Du 2010:299, figure 9-1; 304, figure 9-4-1.

sides of two long colonnaded halls. All buildings are slightly off-center of due north. Reconstructions indicate that the altars had four sloping or stepped sides (Figure 15), a pyramidal stepped shape that is likely the design of the larger altar Yi 1, copying and maintaining the precedent of earlier Jade Age–period sites. No walls or columns are extant. Du speculates that these altars relate to the sacred earthen altar, *tu* 土 or *she* 社, cited in bone inscriptions as an object of sacrifice (Du 2010). They just as likely served as eastern and western *beng* outdoor altars for lineage sacrifice to ancestral spirits and nature powers by the first three late Shang kings ruling at Yinxu.

The multiple numbers of rammed-earthen, pyramidal-step-shaped altars may differ from the centralized earthen altar at the back of Yi building remains. Two lay at the back and two lay at the front of the open-colonnaded Bing structure. As stated, these remains date to the earliest settled strata at Anyang, to Yinxu P1, and therefore are associated with the pre–Wu Ding group of burials (M238, M331, M338), dating to the reigns of the first three kings, Pan Geng, Xiao Xin, and Xiao Yi, who according to transmitted histories moved and settled the capital at Yin before Wu Ding ascended the throne. Wu Ding was the son of Xiao Yi.

Royal and aristocratic burials and settlements beyond Jia, Yi, Bing, and new Area Ding

The inner royal city is defined by the natural borders of the Huan River and a massive lake to its west, and by a complex of various architectural structures: gateways with towers, rectangular residences or palaces, sacrificial courtyards, and outdoor pyramidal altars. To the south of this nucleus are additional buildings and burial clusters honoring royal lineages, of which Yu 鱼 and Zi 子 were some of its members. Some of these burials in turn were crowned by superstructures in the form of columned halls without walls— a new fifth type of architecture signifying a focus for outdoor worship of the deceased buried below. Superstructures constructed above burials belonging to aristocrats lying in BM4 at Qianzhangda, Shandong (Figure 16A) and in M311 at Dasikongcun, Anyang (Figure 16B) and to Fu (Noble Woman) Zi lying in M5 at Xiaotun (Figure 16C) are exemplary as foci designed to honor royal house lineages with ongoing ancestral sacrifices, as elaborately documented by cyclical rites recorded in bone divinatory inscriptions. Fu Zi's temple is mentioned in bone inscriptions as Mu Xin's Zong 母辛宗, Mother Xin's Temple, her posthumous temple name. Fu Zi's tomb and temple were built during P2, while King Wu Ding was alive. Why she was buried in this area and not in the royal cemetery at Xibeigang is still unclear, yet with the report and excavation of the new Area Ding at Xiaotun (see ground plan Figure 5), her relation to other aristocrats may eventually be unraveled. Sacrificial buildings or halls crowning M311 at Dasikongcun (Figure 16B) and the burial BM4 at Qianzhangda in Shandong (Figure 16C) undoubtedly typified many more elite burials whose open halls have disappeared over time of some 3,000 years. It becomes clear from archaeological and paleographic evidence that spirits of the dead could be honored at their tomb, as characterized tombs of post-Shang date and as highlighted by the well-known Qing Ming festival or "Sweeping the Tombs" holiday today in China.

At this stage of excavations it appears that the southern and western parts of the "royal enclave" were more extensive than presently understood. On the basis of currently available data, this phenomenon, particularly represented by Bing remains, may be correlated with an earlier settlement dating to Wu Ding's predecessor kings, which should become even more clear with future excavations and the publication of data.

Buildings other than those of Jia, Yi, and Bing have recently been uncovered in an area newly labeled Ding (D), to the south and east. The picture of the royal city center at Anyang is considerably more complex than witnessed just five years ago, with the excavation of Fu Zi's and neighboring Zi Yu's tombs (Zhongguo 1980; Zhongguo 1981). Although residential and ritual parts of the capital are documented, however spotty and incomplete, the settlement of inner and outer compounds at Yinxu is far more extensive

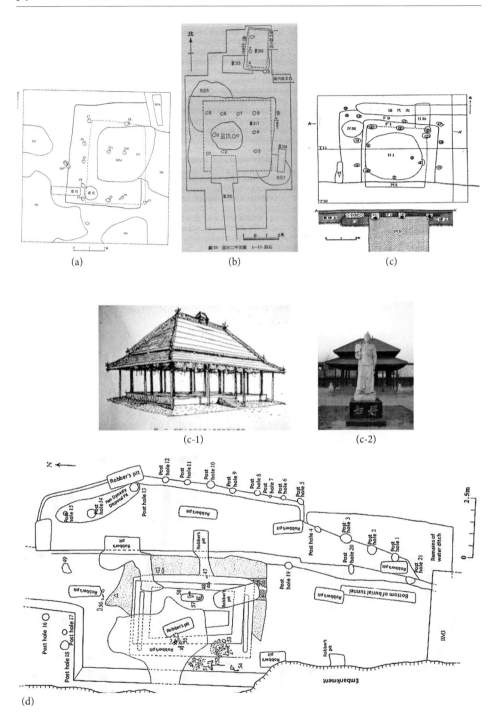

(a)

(b)

(c)

(c-1)

(c-2)

(d)

FIGURE 16 Extant remains of temples crowning Shang-period burials: (a) M54 at Huayuanzhuang (Xu 2004); (b) M315 and M31 at Dasikongcun (Cheng 1960); (c) M5 at Xiaotun, Late Shang period, with superimposed temple chambers, either hip and gable or double hip in style of roof (IA 1980) and (d) BM4 at Qianzhangda, Shandong (IA 2005: 57, Figure 44).

than originally documented in 1927. The additional area south of the "royal compound" now appears to have been densely settled by peoples throughout P1–4 (P1 = pre–Wu Ding; P2 = Wu Ding and Zu Geng; P3 = Zu Jia and others; and P4 = Wen Wu Ding, Di Yi, Di Xin). As noted, aristocrat members of the Shang royal house are documented by burials of the first queen of Wu Ding, son Yu (Zi Yu) of Wu Ding of P2, and Ya Chang (collateral line surname Chang, son of father Ya Chang of the Wu Ding period) of P3 but as well by an extensive cemetery inclusive of non-elite burials and other residential constructions.

This additional area currently labeled Locus Ding was once labeled Huayuanzhuang Locus East (Figure 17). The area not only includes a large cemetery (Zhongguo 2007c) but also two major caches of divinatory inscriptions (Zhongguo 2003b) and a major residential component. As with certain burials underlying the royal center at Locus Yi, remains at Locus Ding may also be dated to a pre- through Wu Ding era, although major occupation appears to have lasted from the Wu Ding through post–Wu Ding eras. One pre–Wu Ding burial, M60, has been unearthed within the cemetery and stratigraphically dates to Late Shang Yinxu P1 (Zhongguo 2006). A series of other smaller excavated tombs belonging to non-aristocrats also date from Late Shang P1 through P4. The largest tomb, M54 (Xu and He 2004), belongs to a Ya Chang of Yinxu P3, King Zu Jia's era, as previously mentioned. The other stellar finds, including the two caches of divinatory bone inscriptions, come from Xiaotun Locus South and Huayuanzhuang East, both belonging to the Royal Sons 子 Group rather than the king. In addition, an enormous *siheyuan* on rammed-earth foundations has been discovered well north of the M54 burial and related cemetery. These and other architectural remains within Locus Ding, north of the Huayuanzhuang cemetery area, cover a 5,000 sqm compound (IA 2010). The once-enigmatic structure, F1–F8, recently surveyed and excavated, is now identified as a *siheyuan* with four longitudinal row-house-like components: northern and southern matching ones and western and eastern, although the easternmost section is missing due to flooding by the Huan River (Figure 18). The structure of "row-house" types forms an almost square, measuring some 53 m long on the north opening to the south by some 50 m wide on the west facing east (IA 2010). Based on reports, this was a large-scale *siheyuan* constructed on sunken and raised rammed-earthen foundations supporting a closed four-walled compound with central courtyard. According to reports, only one door exits the rear of northernmost F1 "row-house," and no doorways have been reported exiting F2 on its south wall, thus it is unclear how one entered or exited the complex, or whether there were other unexcavated, further northern or southern parts to the structure. The complex is difficult to characterize primarily due to the fact the structure remains isolated, unattached to contemporary or related buildings, as represented, for example, by halls within the Jia and Yi complexes of the "royal city" further north at Xiaotun. As reported (IA 2010), the *siheyuan* building lay on earlier constructed buildings, from which pisé wall material was borrowed, but none of these earlier structures has been reconstituted or reconstructed, thus leaving it unclear what structures preceded the Wu Ding–era building.

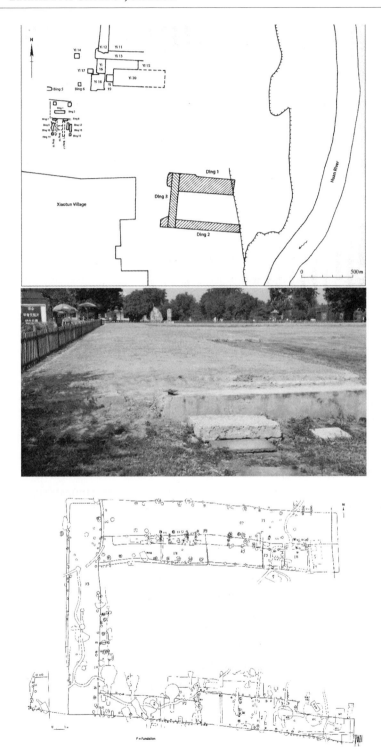

FIGURE 17 **A.** Photograph of no longer extant *siheyuan*, facing east (enclosed within gated fence), author's photograph. **B.** Preliminary ground plan, not including matching eastern building completely destroyed by flooding of the Huan River. The open space without drawn wall of Locus Ding *siheyuan* has also been destroyed by flooding. After Zhongguo 2010:17, figure 4.

FIGURE 18 Bronze *he* inscribed "Wu Fu Yi 武父乙," Martial Father Yi, possibly commissioned by son King Wu Ding, from foundation remains of F1. After Zhongguo 2010: 28, figure 7.

The four structures communicated with each other via doors and steps.[12] No. 7 doorway is the only example of a columned step leading outward to the north. The other six doorways, Nos. 1–6, all similarly constructed and comparable to No. 7, are evenly spaced in leading up to the terraced F1 (F = foundation of a building) building, which was internally supported by further pillar supports thicker than others (only one, No. 28, is assigned a number). The colonnaded fore-chamber of F1 is divided into row-house-style rooms, F7, F5, F4, and F8, as represented on the published ground plan.

A multitude of sacrificial human burials (thus far totaling 20) dominate the fore and back walls of F5, F6, and also F7 and also the entire raised stairway platform along the fore of this F1 structure. Most framed the two sides of doorways leading up to the raised hall F1. The human sacrifices are hypothesized to symbolize offerings at the time construction was finalized (Zheng 2001).

F2 mimics F1 and was a part of it, a long engaged columned structure with eave colonnades. In addition, at the rear of F2 is a central porch leading north. Due to a lack of human sacrifices in this section and multiple disposal pits with ceramics, the excavator theorizes this part of the *siheyuan* or *banfengbishi* 半封闭式 (half-closed-style architecture) was residential in function, designed for extended residences (Zhongguo 2010: 37–39). A series of water channels corroborate this function.

Characteristic of all Shang eras is the propensity to offer sacrificial humans and animals at the time of a building's construction. The sacrificial victims found at F1 foundation were usually three humans in one tomb pit without coffin, accompanied by intentionally broken ceramic vessels (Zhongguo 2010:67–106). Near one of these

---

[12] The northernmost structure comprises two sections, a front open and wide colonnaded eave that gives way to a long rear component, with a total of seven identified doorways with steps between them.

burials, between pillar Nos. 23 and 24 of F1, in a small pit, lay the inscribed bronze *he*, identifying Wu Fu Yi 武父乙 (see Figure 18B), Wu's father Yi, hypothetically Wu Ding, who had cast the *he* bronze vessel in honor of his father Fu Yi (Zheng 2001). The reconstructed ceramics from the sacrificial human burials consistently comprise *zun*, *pen*, and *lei*-type vessels, all utilitarian examples. This custom of breaking ceramics at the time of burial is also witnessed in burials from Huayuanzhuang East cemetery and others and is translated as a prophylactic gesture that prevented the influence of noxious, malevolent spirits. Due to the appearance of these numerous sacrifices and to the inscribed ritual bronze *he* vessel, Zheng maintains that F1 was a temple dedicated to Fu Yi, constructed by Wu Ding, and F2 was a residence. Here it is assumed that the building forms a *siheyuan* structure whose function cannot be precisely assigned until more data are available. It may turn out that this construction was a preliminary to the large-scale Jia and Yi structures, further north, that lasted from Wu Ding through Di Xin.

Archaeologists date the *siheyuan* structure to the early Wu Ding P2 of Yinxu stratigraphy, based not only on the inscribed evidence of the bronze *he* vessel but on ceramic types and certain weapon paraphernalia from burials and disposal pits (Zhongguo 2010: 26–28). Although smaller than the largest hall at Huanbei (measuring 85 to 91.5 m long), in size and type the Ding structure is comparable to some of the royal halls characterizing Xiaotun, particularly Yi 11–3 (see Figure 15) and also Yi 20 (Zhongguo 2010:27–28). The latter structure and Ding one are similar in size (Yi 20 is estimated to measure over 50 m long), and both have similarly located and constructed doorways. Clearly this large-scale structure, comparable to royal ones further north, is a significant component of royal architecture at Xiaotun. Just how it is related to surrounding settlements should become clear with further excavation. With more data, we should be able to characterize more closely residential and ritual structures and their interrelationships. What isn't yet apparent is how this *siheyuan* is related to the Xiaotun finds of royal use. Presently it occupies an isolated architectural area in this southern extension of Xiaotun finds.

Conclusions

The extensive remains of royal artifacts and architectural remains document that Yinxu served as the major capital during the late Shang period. Although we haven't been able to review data revealing major-scale bronze and other factories producing late Shang goods or the extensive urban settlement outside the royal center, the extensive settlements documenting aristocratic lineages forming professional work units associated with bronze, ceramic, bone, or other types of manufacturing and the presence of massive units of laborers indicate that Yinxu at this time in history may be considered the central economic and cultural hub of the East Asian Heartland region in East Asia and what would become China.

BIBLIOGRAPHY

安阳市文物工作队, and 安阳市博物馆, eds. 2015. *Anyang Yinxu, Excavation Report on the Shang Cemetery at Qijiazhuang East* 安阳殷墟，戚家庄东商代墓地发掘报告. Zhengzhou: Zhongzhou guji chubanshe.

Campbell, Roderick 2013. "Transformation of Violence: On Humanity and Inhumanity in Early China." In *Violence and Civilization*. Edited by Roderick Campbell, 96–104. Brown University: Joukowsky Institute for Archaeology and the Ancient World Publication.

Cao, Dingyun 曹丁云 2007. "Field Excavation and Chronology of Oracle Bone Inscriptions at the Yinxu Site 殷墟甲骨文的田野考古与断." *Kaoguxue jikan* 14:174–188.

Chang, Kwang Chih 1980. *Shang Civilization*. New Haven: Yale University Press.

Cheng Te K'un 1960. *Archaeology in China vol. II: Shang China*. Cambridge: Heffer)

Childs-Johnson, Elizabeth 1983. "Identification of the Tomb Occupant and Periodization of M5." Excavation of Tomb No. 5 at Yinxu, Anyang," *Chinese Sociology and Anthropology* 15:1–37.

Childs-Johnson, Elizabeth 2016. "Urban daemons of the early Shang." In *Urbanism in ancient China, Archaeological Research in Asia*, Online 9.19.2016 1-16, edited by Li Liu. Elsevier Ltd; Volume 14, June 2018:135–150.

中华人民共和国国家文物局 2001. Yinxu 殷墟 。Beijing: Zhonghua renmin gongheguo guojia wenwuju.

Dai, Zunde 戴尊德1980. "Shang Burial and Bronzes at Jingjiecun in Lingshi, Shanxi 山西灵石县七届村商代墓和青铜器." *Wenwu ziliao congkan* 3:46–49.

Du, Jinpeng 杜金鹏 2006. "Excavation History and Research on of the Architectural Remains in the Palace Area of Yinxu 殷墟宫殿区建筑基址的发掘与研究综述." In *Chinese Archaeology in the 21st Century: Celebrating Mr. Zhu Zhuchen's Eighty-Five Early Learning Academic Papers*. Edited by Zhongguo shehui kexueyuan kaogu yanjiusuo. Beijing: Wenwu chubanshe.

Du, Jinpeng 杜金鹏 2007a. *Archaeological Research on the Xia, Shang, and Zhou* 夏商周考古学研究. Beijing: Kexue chubanshe.

Du, Jinpeng 杜金鹏 2007b. "Questions Concerning Yi Remains at Yinxu 殷墟乙-基址及其相关问题." In *Archaeological Research on the Xia, Shang, and Zhou* 夏商周考古学研究. 603–623. Beijing: Kexue chubanshe.

Du, Jinpeng 杜金鹏 2007c. "Research on Yi 3, Yi 4, and Yi 5 at Yinxu 殷墟乙三，乙四，乙五基址研究." In *Archaeological Research on the Xia, Shang, and Zhou* 夏商周考古学研究., 624–650. Beijing: Kexue chubanshe.

Du, Jinpeng 杜金鹏 2010. Studies on the Architectural Foundations of the Palace-Temple District at Yinxu 殷墟宫殿区建筑基址研究. Beijing: Kexue chubanshe.

Gao, Xiangping 郜向平 2011. *A Study of the Shang Burial System* 商戏墓葬研究. Beijing: Kexue chubanshe.

GB (Global Times) Times *tjhx0526/360doc.com* "The mystery behind China's giant pyramid hills," by Geni Raitisoja Aug 09, 2016 16:29.

He, Yuling and Jigen Tang 何毓灵, 唐际根 2010. "A Brief Report of the Excavation of Compound 2 within the Palace-Temple District at Huanbei Shang City in Anyang, Henan 河南安阳市洹北商城宫殿区二号 基址发掘简报." Kaogu 1:9–22.

He, Yuling, Hongbin Yue, and 何毓灵, 岳洪彬, 岳占伟 2012. "Preliminary Excavation Report on Liujiazhuang North at Yinxu in Anyang County, Henan 河南安阳市殷墟刘家庄北地 2010~2011 年发掘简报." Kaogu 7:6–31.

He, Yuling, Hongbin Yue, and 何毓灵, 唐际根, 岳占伟 and Shishan Niu 牛世山 2012. "The excavation at Liujiazhuang Locus North at Yinxu Site in Anyang City, Henan in 2010–2011 河南安阳市殷墟刘家庄北地 2010~2011 年发掘简报." *Kaogu* 2012. 12:26–42.

Henan Wenwu Kaogu Yanjiusuo 河南省文物考古研究所 2012. *1990–2000 Archaeological Excavation Report* 郑州小双桥 1990–2000 发掘报告 Zhengzhou Xiaoshuangqiao. Beijing: Kexue chubanshe.

Henansheng Wensu Kaogu Yanjiusuo and Zhoukoushi Wenwuju 河南省文 物考古研究所，周口市文化局, eds. 2000. *Taiqinggong Changzikou Tomb in Luyi* 鹿邑太清宫长子口墓. Zhengzhou: Zhongzhou guji chubanshe.

Hehansheng Xinyang Diqu Wenguanhui, Luoshanxian Wenhuaguan 河南省信阳地区文管会 罗山县文化馆1986. The Shang Zhou Cemetery at Tianhu, Luoshan 罗山天湖商周墓地," *Kaogu xuebao* 1986.2:153–197.

Jing, Zhichun, Tang Jigen, George Rapp, and James Stoltman 2013. "Recent Discoveries and Some Thoughts on Early Urbanization at Anyang." In *A Companion to Chinese Archaeology*. Edited by A. Underhill, 343–366. Wiley-Blackwell.

Li, Ji [Li Chi] 1977. *Anyang*. Seattle: University of Washington Press.

Liu, Li, and Xingcan Chen 2012. *The Archaeology of China*. Cambridge: Cambridge University Press.

Liu, Shi'e 刘士莪2001 *Laoniupo, Field Report of Archaeology Program, Northwest University* 老牛坡, 西北大学考古专业田野发掘报告. Xian: Shaanxi renmin chubanshe.

Liu, Yiman and He Yuling 刘一曼, 何毓灵 2007. "Bibliography of Yinxu Archaeology 殷墟考古参考." *Kaoguxue jikan* 14:395–415.

Liu, Yuan 刘源 2008. "Another Discussion of the Character '口' in Yinxu Huadong Divinations 再谈殷墟花东卜辞中的"口"." In *Oracle Bone Script and Yin Shang History*, vol. 1 甲骨文与殷商史》新一本. Edited by Song Zhenhao 宋镇豪, 131–160. Beijing: Xianzhuang shuju.

Meng, Xianwu 孟宪武 1991. "Determination of the Date of the Shang Bronzes Discovered at Dongwangdu Village and Sanjiazhuang at Anyang 安阳三家庄，董王度村发现的商代青铜器及其年代推定." *Kaogu* 10:932–938.

Meng, Xianwu 孟宪武 2003. Archaeological Research on the Yin Ruins in Anyang 安阳殷墟考古研究. Zhengzhou: Zhongzhou guji chubanshe.

Schwartz, Adam Craig 2013. *Huayuanzhuang East I: A Study and Annotated Translation of the Oracle Bone Inscriptions*. Chicago: University of Chicago, Division of the Humanities, Department of East Asian Languages and Civilizations Pub.

Shaanxisheng Kaogugu Yanjiusuo, Hai Jinle and Han Binghua 陕西省考古研究所, 海金乐, 韩炳华，eds. 2006. *The Shang Cemetery at Jingjie, Lingshi*灵石旌介商墓. Beijing: Kexue chubanshe.

Shi, Zhangru (Shih, Chang-ru) 石璋如 1959. *Xiaotun First Volume: Discoveries and Excavations; First Fascicle; Architectural Remains* 小屯。第一本。遗址地发现与发掘.一 遍.建筑遗存. Taibei: Zhongyang yanjiu yuan lishi yuyan yanjiu suo.

Song, Zhenhao 宋镇豪, and Liu Yuan 刘愿 2006. *Research on Oracle Bones and Shang History* 甲骨学殷商史研究. Fuzhou: Fujian renmin chubanshe.

Soper, Alexander C. 1966. "Early, Middle, and Late Shang: A Note." *Artibus Asiae* 28.1:5–38.

Tang, Jigen 唐际根, and Jing Zhichun 荆志淳 2009. "Shang Settlements and Great Settlement Shang in Anyang 安阳的"商邑"与"大商邑"." *Kaogu* 9:70–80.

Tang, Jigen 唐际根, Jing Zhichun 荆志淳, George Rapp 瑞拉, and Xu Guangde 徐广德 1998. "Preliminary Report on the Regional Archaeological Survey in the Huan River Valley 洹河流域区域考古研究初步报告." *Kaogu* 10:13–22.

Tang, Jigen 唐际根, Jing Zhichun, and Liu Zhongfu 刘忠伏 2010. "A Brief Archaeology Report of the 2005–2007 Years of Investigation of Huanbei Shang City in Anyang, Henan河南安阳市洹北商城遗址 2005–2007 年发掘简报." *Kaogu* 1:3–8.

Tang, Jigen 唐际根 et al. 2016. "The Road and Water Networks of Huanbei Shang City and Yinxu Sites 洹北商城与殷墟遗址的道路和水道." *Kaogu Xuebao* 3:319–342.

Xu, Hong 许红 2013. "Large Cities Are Not fortified: On the Early Forms of Capitals of Ancient China 大都无城—论中国古代都城的早期形态." *Wenwu* 10:61–71.

Xu, Hong 2016. Capitals without Fortifications 大都无城. Beijing: Sanlian shudian.

Xu, Hong 2017. Pre-Qin Cities and Capitals from an Archaeological Perspective 先秦城邑考古. Beijing: Jincheng chubanshe.

Xu, Guangde 徐广德 and He Yuling 何毓灵 2004. "Excavation of Tomb M54 at Huayuanzhuang in Anyang, Henan 河南安阳花园庄54号墓的发掘," *Kaogu* 2004.1:7–19.

Yang, Baocheng 杨宝成 1982. "Brief Excavation Report on M1 at Anyang Houjiazhuang North 安阳侯家住北地一号墓发掘简报." *Kaogu xuebao jikan* 2:35–40.

Yang, Xizhang杨西璋, and Yiman Liu,刘一曼 1995. "Major Achievements of 70 Years Archaeological Excavations in Yinxu七十年殷墟考古发掘的主要收获," *Zhongyuan wenwu* 1999.2.

Yang, Xizhang and Liu Yiman 杨西璋,刘一曼 2007a. "The Chronological Table of Archaeological Excavations at the Yinxu Site in the Past Seventy Years." *Kaoguxue jikan* 14:391–394.

Yang, Xizhang and Liu Yiman 杨西璋,刘一曼 2007b. "Major Archaeological Achievements of the Past Seventy Years at Yinxu 殷墟七十年来的主要考古成就." *Kaoguxue jikan* 14:18–30.

Yin, Zhiyi 殷之彝 1977. "The Ancient Cemetery at Subutun in Yidu County, Shandong Province, and the Group of Bronzes Bearing the Inscription Ya Chou 山东益都苏埠屯墓地和亚醜铜器." *Kaogu xuebao* 2:23–34.

Yue, Hongbin and Yue Zhanwei 岳洪彬, 岳占伟 2009a. "A Preliminary Report on the Excavation of a Large Shang Tomb in Xiaotun West at Yinxu, Anyang, Henan 河南安阳殷墟小屯西的巨大 墓葬发掘报告." *Kaogu* 9:54–69.

Yue, Hongbin and Yue Zhanwei 岳洪彬, 岳占伟 2009b. "2008 Preliminary Excavation Report at Locus North of Liujiazhuang at the Yin Ruins, Anyang County 2008 河南安阳市殷墟刘家庄北地 2008 年发掘简报." *Kaogu* 2009.9:54–69.

Zheng, Zhenxiang 郑振香 2001. "Excavation of Large-Scale Architectural Remains at Yinxu, Anyang, Henan 河南安阳殷墟大型建筑基址的发掘." *Kaogu* :5.

Zheng, Zhenxiang 郑振香, Chen Zhida 陈志达, Yang Xizhang 杨西璋, Yang Baocheng 杨宝成, and Zhang Xiaozhuang, 1985. *Yinxu Bronze Vessels* 殷墟青铜器. Beijing: Kexue chubanshe.

Zhongguo Shehui Kexueyuan, Kaogu Yanjiusuo 中国社会科学 院, 考古研究所, eds. 1980a. *Oracle Bones from Xiaotun South* 小屯南地甲骨. Beijing: Zhonghua shuju.

Zhongguo Shehui Kexueyuan, Kaogu Yanjiusuo 中国社会科学院, 考古研究所 1980b. *Tomb of Noble Woman Zi (Hao)* 殷墟妇好墓. Beijing: Wenwu chubanshe.

Zhongguo Shehui Kexueyuan Kaogu Yanjiusuo, Anyang Gongzuodui 中国社会科学院,考古研究所, 安阳工作队 1981. "Two Yin Burials from Xiaotun North at Anyang安阳小屯村北的两座殷代墓," *Kaogu xuebao*1981.4:491–499.

Zhongguo Shehui Kexueyuan Kaogu Yanjiusuo 中国社会科学 院,考古研究所 1983. *Oracle Bone Inscriptions from Xiaotun South* 小屯南地甲骨，下册第一分册. Beijing: Zhonghua shuju.

Zhongguo Shehui Kexueyuan Kaogu Yanjiusuo 中国社会科学 院,考古研究所 1987. *Yinxu Excavation Report 1958–1961* 殷墟发掘报告 1958–1961. Beijing: Wenwu chubanshe.

Zhongguo Shehui Kexueyuan Kaogu Yanjiusuo. 中国社会科学 院,考古研究所 1988a. 安阳殷墟郭家庄商代墓葬 *The Shang Dynasty Burial at Guojiazhuang at Yinxu*, Anyang. Beijing: Wenwu chubanshe.

Zhongguo Shehui Kexueyuan Kaogu Yanjiusuo. 中国社会科学 院,考古研究所 1994a. *Discoveries and Research at the Ruins of Yin* 殷虚的发现与研究. Beijing: Kexue chubanshe.

Zhongguo Shehui Kexueyuan Kaogu Yanjiusuo. 中国社会科学 院,考古研究所 1994b. *Report on Yinxu Excavations* 殷墟发掘报告. Beijing: Wenwu chubanshe.

Zhongguo Shehui Kexueyuan Kaogu Yanjiusuo. 中国社会科学院,考古研究所 2003a. *Chinese Archaeology: Xia Shang* 中国考古学:夏商卷. Beijing: Zhonguo shehui chubanshe.

Zhongguo Shehui Kexueyuan Kaogu Yanjiusuo. 中国社会科学 院,考古研究所 2003b. Oracle Bones from Huayuanzhuang East at Yinxu 殷墟花园庄东地甲骨 6 卷, 6 vols. Kunming: Renmin chubanshe.

Zhongguo Shehui Kexueyuan Kaogu Yanjiusuo. 中国社会科学 院,考古研究所 2003c. "Henan Anyang City Huanbei Shang City Survey and Excavation 河南安阳洹北商城检查与发掘." *Kaogu* 5:17–23.

Zhongguo Shehui Kexueyuan Kaogu Yanjiusuo. 中国社会科学院,考古研究所 2004. *Xiaotun Anyang* 安阳小屯. Beijing: Shijie tushu chubanshe.

Zhongguo Shehui Kexueyuan Kaogu Yanjiusuo. 中国社会科学 院,考古研究所 2005. *The Cemetery at Qianzhangda Tengzhou I–II* 滕州前掌大，上下. Beijing: Wenwu chubanshe.

Zhongguo Shehui Kexueyuan Kaogu Yanjiusuo. 中国社会科学 院,考古研究所 2007a. *Shang Tombs at Huayuanzhuang Locus East in Anyang* 安阳殷墟花园庄东地商代墓葬. Beijing: Kexue chubanshe.

Zhongguo Shehui Kexueyuan Kaogu Yanjiusuo. 中国社会科学 院,考古研究所 2007b. "Tomb M1046 to the North of Liujiazhuang at the Yinxu Site in Anyang 安阳殷墟遗址刘家庄北地 1046 号墓." *Kaoguxue jikan* 14:359–390.

Zhongguo Shehui Kexueyuan Kaogu Yanjiusuo. 中国社会科学 院,考古研究所 2007c. "Excavation Report on Huayuanzhuang Locus East at Huanbei Shang City in Anyang 安阳洹北商城花园庄东地发掘报告." *Kaoguxue jikan* 14:296–358.

Zhongguo Shehui Kexueyuan Kaogu Yanjiusuo. 中国社会科学 院,考古研究所 2010. *Architectural Remains at Xiaotun, Yinxu in Anyang* 安阳殷墟小屯建筑遗存. Beijing: Wenwu chubanshe.

Zhongguo Shehui Kexueyuan Kaogu Yanjiusuo. 中国社会科学 院,考古研究所 2014. *Dasikongcun in Anyang: Report of the Excavation in 2004, I–II* 安阳大司空-2004 年发掘报告,上下. Beijing: Wenwu chubanshe.

Zhongguo Shehui Kexueyuan Kaogu Yanjiusuo. 中国社会科学院,考古研 究所, and Anyang Work Team 安陽工作/考古 1979. "1969–1977 Excavation Report on the Western Sector Cemetery at Xinxu 1969–1977 年殷墟西区墓葬发掘报告." *Kaogu Xuebao* 1:27–146.

Zhongguo Shehui Kexueyuan, Kaogu Yanjiuwuo, Anyang Gongzuodui中国社会科学院,考古研 究所, 安陽工作考古 2001. "Excavation of the Large-Scale Building Foundations at Yinxu, Anyang, Henan 河南安阳殷墟大型建筑基址的发掘." *Kaogu* 5:18–26.

Zhongguo Shehui Kexueyuan, Kaogu Yanjiuwuo, Anyang Gongzuodui中国社会科学院,考古研 究所, 安陽工作/考古 2006. "M60 Burial from Huayuanzhuang East at Yinxu, Anyang, Henan 河南安阳殷花园庄东地 60 号墓." *Kaogu* 1:8–18.

Zhongguo Shehui Kexueyuan Kaogu Yanjiusuo. 中国社会科学院,考古研 究所, and Anyang Work Team 安陽工作考古队 2007a. "Shang Building Remains at Xiaomintun in Anyang

City 安阳小屯商代建筑遗址." *Kaogu* 1:3–13; English translation in Chinese Archaeology 2008.1:8–15.

Zhongguo Shehui Kexueyuan Kaogu Yanjiusuo. 中国社会科学院,考古研 and Anyang Work Team 安陽工作/考古 2007b. "Excavation Report on the Locus East of Huayuanzhuang of the Shang Period City at Huanbei in Anyang in 1998–1999, 1998–1999 安阳花园庄东地商城发掘报告." *Kaoguxue Jikan* 14:296–358.

Zhongguo Shehui Kexueyuan Kaogu Yanjiusuo. 中国社会科学院,考古研 究所, and Anyang Work Team 安陽工作/考古 2009. "Survey and Excavation of the Palace-Temple District at Xiaotun in Yinxu 2004–2005 殷墟小屯调查发掘宫庙区 2004–2005." *Kaogu Xuebao* 2:217–249.

Zhu, Naicheng 朱乃成, ed. 2016. *Queen, Mother, and General: 40th Anniversary of Excavating the Shang Tomb of Fu Hao [Zi]* 王后母親女將. Beijing: Kexue chubanshe.

CHAPTER 16

···

LATE SHANG: FU ZI AND M5 AT XIAOTUN

···

BY DINGYUN CAO, INSTITUTE OF ARCHAEOLOGY, CASS

THE 1970S WAS the most important decade for Yinxu excavations. In 1971, inscriptions carved on cattle scapulas were discovered in western Xiaotun site. In 1973, 4,600 pieces of oracle bones were found south of the Xiaotun site. In 1976, 1,900 objects, including numerous bronzes and jades, were excavated from Fu Zi's tomb at Xiaotun. In 1976, 191 sacrificial pits were excavated in the Yinxu royal cemetery. These data from the excavations have greatly enriched our understanding of and further glorified the Yinxu culture, especially the discovery of the Fu Zi tomb. The latter was preserved intact and is the most richly furnished royal tomb discovered to date in the history of Yinxu excavations. These valuable materials are an extremely important reference for the study of the Shang dynasty, in particular for studying the Wu Ding era in its various aspects, including political, economic, and cultural. These data are also essential for dating Yinxu bronzes and oracle bone inscriptions and for carrying out research on jades.

Twelve inscribed relics from Fu Zi's tomb are significant. Only one inscription is unreadable due to corrosion and remains to be verified. The 11 legible inscriptions include: Fu Zi 婦 好; Hou Mu Xin 司 母 辛; Hou Xin 司 辛; Hou 䍃 Mu 司䍃母; Ya Qi 亞 其; Ya 亞弜; Ya Qi 亞 啟; Ge 𠂤戈𠂤; Ren Zhu ru shi 妊 竹 入 石; Zi 㯥 Quan 子㯥泉; Lu Fang Gua ru ge wu 盧 方 刕 入 戈 五.

These inscriptions on excavated objects are confirmation of names dating to the era of Shang King Wu Ding. The names provided in these inscriptions mostly concern upper-ruling-class figures, such as royal members or leaders of important vassal or regional states (*fangguo*) from the Wu Ding era. Most descendants of these figures continued to be officials, inheriting their ancestors' titles or acquiring new ones. It is vital to clarify the meaning of these inscriptions and their evolution not only for the study of the Fu Zi tomb but also for the study of the entire Yin Shang history.

My book, *Yinxu Fuhao mu ming wen yan jiu* (Studies of inscriptions from Yinxu Fu Zi [Fu Hao] tomb) (Cao 2007), is devoted to an analysis of the quoted inscriptions. These inscriptions might seem simple, but they all contain a wealth of historical information, thus each will be analyzed individually in this chapter.

INSCRIPTION 1: FU ZI 婦好

This inscribed title, Fu Zi, is the name of the owner of objects made for her. A total of 196 inscribed objects were excavated from Fu Zi's tomb, and 111, more than half the total, were inscribed "Fu Zi." Catalogues of these relics are now available, and the majority are medium-size bronzes often unearthed in pairs. Bronze objects inscribed "Fu Zi" are the main components of her funerary objects. Inscription variations of the graphs include the following:

1. Two *nu* (female) characters facing each other and *fu zi* characters in the center. An example is M5:790 three-linked steamer (*yan*) vessels (Figure 1:1).
2. *Nu* (female) character on the right and "Fu Zi" character on the left. An example is M5:796 *pou* vessel (Figure 1:2).
3. *Nu* (female) character on the left and "Fu Zi" character on the right. An example is M5:856 square *lei* vessel (Figure 1:3).
4. "Zi," "Fu," and "*nu*" comprise three characters in one straight line. An example is M5:682 *jue* vessel (Figure 1:4).

Two large-scale bronze *yue* axes inscribed "Fu Zi" unearthed from the tomb were objects symbolic of power and authority. Average individuals did not possess them. It is reasonable to assume that objects inscribed "Fu Zi" were made for Fu Zi, the tomb owner. The relationship among political figures revealed in inscriptions from this tomb is obviously centered on her, Fu Zi, and peoples around her who were important.

Fu Zi was no ordinary female figure. Because of her position as a leading warrior who participated in a series of battles with the Qiang Fang, Tu Fang, Ba Fang, and Yi state and her established glorious military achievements, she was promoted to head concubine and became the legal spouse of Shang King Wu Ding. Fu Zi was not only involved in military and political affairs but also presided over ritual ceremonies. She was an important figure of power in the early era of King Wu Ding.

The "Fu" character in Fu Zi means *shi fu* 世婦, or "a generational female," a position passed through generations and always hereditary for females who held state positions. As Zhang Zhenglang correctly pointed out, the meaning of *shifu* (generational female) is the same as *shichen* (generational official), a position passed from generation to generation. Female figures and official figures occupied political positions both inside and

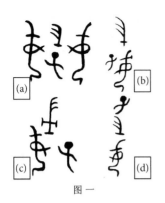

FIGURE 1 Variations of the oracle bone graphs for Fu Zi (Fu Hao).

图 一

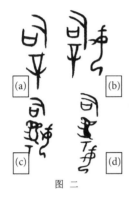

FIGURE 2 Variations of the oracle bone graphs for Hou Mu Xin (1,2) and for Hou 🐟 Mu (3,4).

图 二

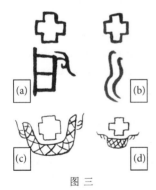

FIGURE 3 Variation of the oracle bone graph for Ya Qi 亞啟 (1), Ya 弜 (2), and Ya Qi 亞其 (3-4).

图 三

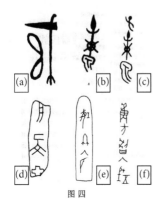

FIGURE 4 Variations of other signatures on artifacts from Fu Zi (Fu Hao) burial M5: Ge 自 (戈 自) *(hewen)* 𠂤 (1); Zi 㑚 Quan (子 㑚 泉) ⃛ (2-3) 㞢 Ya ⃛ (4); Ren Zhu entered in qing stone chime (妊 竹入磬) ⃛ (5); Lu Fang Gua entered in 5 *ge* daggers", 盧方刞入戈五 ⃛ (6).

图 四

outside the power center, and these were passed on to future generations of relatives (Zhang 1983). This is the reason why the characters for *fu mou* 婦某, a female named something, appeared repeatedly in oracle bone inscriptions through different periods. This is the fundamental reason for the phenomenon of different generations of females with the same name. Fu Zi was the spouse of Shang King Wu Ding. "Fu" is a title of position. "Zi" is the name of a female from the Zi state. "Zi" is not a surname but a state name; it refers to the state (*fang*) Zi. Wu Ding and Fu Zi did not marry within the same surname group. According to transmitted histories the surname of Shang people is not 子 Zi but 姒 Si. I have discussed this issue in depth elsewhere and will not repeat it here (Cao 1989b).

INSCRIPTION 2: HOU XIN 司辛

This inscription appears on sacrificial objects made by King Wu Ding for his wife Fu Zi. The title Hou Xin appears on a mandible, for example, of a small sculpture of a white marble cow in a prostrate position (M5:315), measuring 25 cm long by 14 cm tall (Figure 2:1). The inscription is carved in a thick and powerful font close in style to the set of graphs known from the "Wu Ding" Bing group. "Hou Xin" is used to address a figure of the same generation. It is reasonable, therefore, to assume that the marble sculpture was ordered by the Shang King Wu Ding to pay homage to Fu Zi after her death.

Fu Zi was one of Wu Ding's three legal spouses. While alive she was special to King Wu Ding and was the object of his praise. It is possible that Wu Ding offered more gifts to Fu Zi. However, without inscriptions, this assumption is unable to be corroborated. The only evidence is the one inscribed sculpture. "Hou" is a title of a position. Only she who is a legal spouse who had given birth to a child who inherited the throne may be called "Hou." "Xin" is a temple name. Reference to Fu Zi as "Hou Xin" was appropriate for King Wu Ding to use.

This marble cow, facing south, was placed at the center top of the outer coffin at 5.7 meters from the opening of the tomb. The special placement of King Wu Ding's funerary gift to his wife Fu Zi underscores the special relationship between them. Therefore, some scholars suggested "this marble sculpture of cattle carries the same function and significant meaning as a tomb stone" (Chen 1991). This statement in fact is quite true.

INSCRIPTION 3: HOU MU XIN 司母辛

This reference is used by Fu Zi's son, Xiao Ji, in addressing his deceased mother. Five works were inscribed "Hou Mu Xin" or Hou Mother Xin, including a pair of large tetrapod *ding*, M5:789 and M5:809; a pair of tetrapod *gong*, M5:803 and M5:1163; and a square vessel with a tall ring-shaped foot, M5:850. Hou Mu Xin is inscribed such that the *mu* (mother) character is most times located on the right side of the two characters "Hou Xin" (see Figure 2:2, M5:809). Such placement is elegant and dignified and is comparable to the two graphs "Fu Zi" inscribed on the steamer set. It should be clear that the patron of the set of bronzes inscribed "Hou Mu Xin" was someone in a position of power.

The character "Hou" in the Hou Mu Xin denotes position. Only one who was a legal spouse and had given birth to a child or children qualified to inherit the throne could be addressed "Hou" (Cao 2012). "Hou Mu" was how a royal son addressed his mother, and "Xin" was Fu Zi's temple name. Works inscribed with "Hou Mu Xin" characters were executed by a son of King Wu Ding and the king's wife Fu Zi. The question as to which son requires careful investigation. As examined in the article "Analyzing the Relationship between Fu Zi and Xiao Ji," the patron for Hou Mu Xin burial sets of art works is the same *wang* 王 (king) who appears among Wu Ding oracle bone inscriptions and there is referred to as *xiao wang* (small king). He is named Xiao Ji (Small Ji) in historical records (Cao 1993). Xiao Ji was birthed by Fu Zi and was recorded as the crown prince of King Wu Ding. It is evident that Xiao Ji of the transmitted histories, as crown prince, was the person who held the memorial ceremony for his birth mother Fu Zi. It is also recorded in the histories that after the death of Fu Zi, Xiao Ji was victimized by his stepmother and sent into exile by King Wu Ding, after which he died in misery. Xiao Ji's crown prince position was given to his younger brother instead.

INSCRIPTION 4: HOU 嬳 MU, 司嬳母

This inscribed title was used for sacrifices made by another legal spouse of King Wu Ding. Twenty-eight artifacts from Fu Zi's tomb—all exquisite—were inscribed with the three characters "Hou 嬳 Mu," including, for example, large round-shaped *zun* (M5:867), square *hu* (M5:807), *gu* (M5:617), and *jue* (M5:689). Two forms of inscriptions were used: (1) the three characters "Hou 嬳 Mu" were inscribed in a straight vertical line, as represented on large round-shaped *zun* (M5:867; see Figure 2:4); and (2) the *nu* 女 female character was inscribed to the right side of Hou 司, as represented on a *gu* (M5:617; see Figure 2:3). In terms of quality and quantity this group of bronzes is second to the sets inscribed "Fu Zi." This patron was evidently significant and had a close relationship with the tomb owner Fu Zi. "Hou 嬳 Mu" and "Hou Mu Xin" are addressed by the same title, Hou, and thus are of equal rank. The son of Hou 嬳 Mu was thus equally qualified to inherit the throne.

King Wu Ding had three legal spouses: Bi Xin 妣辛, Bi Wu 妣戊, and Bi Gui 妣癸. Bi 妣 is the graph signifying a legal female spouse. Fu Zi is already confirmed to be Bi Xin, legal spouse Xin.

INSCRIPTION 5: YA QI 亞啟

This title is used by prince Ya Qi, another son of King Wu Ding. Three bronzes from Fu Zi's tomb were inscribed with the two graphs Ya Qi, including one square *yi* (M5:823) and a set of two bronze *yue* (M5:1156, etc.). The two characters were consistently inscribed with the "Ya" character placed on top of the graph "Qi" (Figure 3:1). According to the general practice in Yin-Shang inscriptions, "Ya" is a title for a position of a military official generally used by royal family princes. These princes addressed with the title "Ya" were more powerful and higher in status than those without the title. "Qi" was the name for a vassal state. It is therefore evident that Ya Qi was an important prince of a vassal state during the King Wu Ding era.

As analyzed in an earlier article, "Deciphering 'Ya 亞' and 'Ya Qi 亞 啟,'" Ya Qi was the person "Qi" appearing in oracle inscriptions of the Wu Ding era. Ya Qi was also referred to as Zi Qi 子啟 (Prince Qi), who was the legitimate and fourth son of King Wu Ding (Cao 1983). There is no evidence yet to state whether Prince Ya Qi was a son of Fu Zi or not. Judging from the fact that Fu Zi died at an early age and her son Prince Xiao Ji was the prince to inherit the throne, it is very possible that Ya Qi was not Fu Zi's son but a son of another legal spouse of King Wu Ding. Nonetheless, Ya Qi must have had a tight relationship with Fu Zi through his close involvement as a warrior and participation in official matters. This close relationship is shown by the fact that Ya Qi offered two bronze *yue* (axes) inscribed with his name, a symbol of Ya Qi's power and status, to Fu Zi in honor of her death and burial.

INSCRIPTION 6: YA QI 亞其

This title and name identifies the prince of the state Qi. Twenty-one bronzes, mostly alcohol vessels, were inscribed with the two graphs "Ya Qi," including a pair of large round-shaped *jia* (e.g., M5:1197), 10 *gu* (e.g., M5:630), and 9 *jue* (e.g., M5:682). Two forms of inscriptions include: (1) a "Ya" enclosing the character "Qi," as exhibited on the large round-shaped *jia* (M5:1197; see Figure 3:3); and (2) a "Ya" character placed above the character "Qi," as shown on the *gu* (M5:630; and Figure 3:4). Based on a comparison of the types of funerary objects, the status and personal relationship between Ya Qi and Fu Zi was less than other royal members, Prince Xiao Ji and Prince Ya Qi (啟).

Who exactly was Ya Qi? In an earlier article, "Examining 'Ya Qi 亞 其,'" I determined that this prince was likely the diviner (*zhen ren* 貞人) named "𡘋" whose name appears in oracle inscriptions of the King Wu Ding era. However, because of Fu Zi's death at a young age and the fact that the diviner "𡘋" was in his youth during the King Wu Ding era, it is possible that the Fu Zi burial Ya Qi was not the diviner "𡘋" himself but was rather Ya Qi's father or elder brother (Cao 1980). Ya Qi was an important vassal during the Shang dynasty, entitled to his own land and with official status in court, as explained by his position as a diviner.

Coincidentally, during 1986–1987 excavations in the southern area of Huayuanzhuang site in Yinxu (Shang Ruins) uncovered ceramic fragments of wide-mouth jars inscribed with two characters, "[illegible] Ya." The fragments were found in the fourth strata of Unit 16 (T16; see Figure 4:4; Institute of Archaeology, CASS 1992). "[illegible] Ya" is the same as "Ya [illegible]." Utilitarian ceramics could be easily broken and not carted from one location to another. These fragments with "[illegible] Ya" inscriptions in the southern area of Huayuanzhuang site in Yinxu are further documentation of the relatives and descendants of the diviner "[illegible] Ya" and serve as proof of their continued official positions in late Shang history.

Regarding research on the two characters "[illegible] Ya," I maintain elsewhere that "[illegible] Ya" is equivalent to "Ya Yan 亞燕." "[illegible] " is a variant character for "Yan" and refers to the "Yan" state in the Shang dynasty (see Cao 2003).

Based on various analyses, it should be clear that Ya Qi was very likely the diviner "[illegible]" whose name appears among oracle inscriptions dated to the era of King Wu Ding. He was an official historian (as diviner) and also a military official. As an official at court, he was entitled to his own land and therefore maintained an important position in both military and state administration.

Inscription 7: Ya Jiang (亞弜)

This title and name refers to another landowner, Ya Jiang (亞弜). Six bronzes were inscribed with the title and state name "Ya 弜," including one large round-shaped *ding* (M5:808) and a set of five *nao* (e.g., M5:839). Soot marks found on the *ding* tripod's belly and feet show the vessel was used over time. The style of writing the two characters "Ya 弜" may also be associated with the early Wu Ding period (see Figure 3:2).

Ya 弜 was a prince with military and ministerial rank, as characterized Ya Qi (亞啟) and Ya Qi (亞其). Evidence from oracle inscriptions indicates that Ya 弜 was an important general who maintained a close relationship with Fu Zi and was under her command. These six bronzes inscribed with "Ya 弜" characters were undoubtedly a gift offered by Ya 弜 to Fu Zi before her death and placed in her tomb after her death.

Inscription 8: Ren Zhu 妊竹

This inscribed name was found in Fu Zi's tomb on a musical stone chime *qing* (磬) commissioned by the leader of Gu Zhu state. The inscription appears cast on a long strip, narrow on top and wider below on the musical stone (M5:316; 44 cm long by 8.5–12 cm wide and 2.4–3.2 cm thick) and could be suspended by means of a hole perforated at the stone's center top. The four characters "Ren Zhu *ru shi* 妊竹入石" were inscribed on the upper part of one side. This inscription, as with others, functioned as a record chronicling important events. This inscription documents a gift offered to Fu Zi from "Ren Zhu."

Some scholars transcribe the character "*zhu*" as "*ran* 冉." Interpreting this character as "*zhu* 竹" is not only in line with the character shape but also corresponds to divination records. "*Zhu*" is frequently mentioned in oracle bone divinations and in inscriptions on Yin Shang bronze objects. The differing interpretation of the character "*ren*" in *ren zhu* suggest that "Ren 妊" is the surname "Ren 任" as used in "Ren *xing* 任姓." According to this analysis, "Zhu" may be explained as "*ran* 冉," and "Ren Ran 妊 冉" refers to a woman with surname Ran who married into Ren family (Jao 306–307). According to this explanation, two surnames were used together as overlapping with husband's surname first and then the wife's family name following. A similar example, Jiangmi 江芈, a Chu female who married into Jiang family, thus was called Jiang-Mi, as recorded in the Wenyuan chapter of *Zuozhuan* (Commentary of Zuo). This explanation is improbable. (In inscription No. 1,545 "*yi duo tian ya ren*" and "*tian, ya, ren*" all appear as honorific titles; see Guo 2002:no.1,545.) Among oracle bone and bronze inscriptions of Shang date, the use of the surname is rare; most often state names and clan names are used. Two surnames for a female do not appear. Furthermore, one cannot apply examples found in the Autumns and Springs period to the Shang. Another reason the graph "*ren* 妊" in "Ren Zhu" is not "*ren* 任," a surname, is that it is an honorary title. In "Duo *tian ya ren* 多 田 亞 任" inscriptions found in oracle bones from Yinxu, "*tian*," "*ya*," and "*ren*" are all honorary titles. In inscriptions from Fu Zi's burial, figures "Qi 其," "Qi 啟," and "Ya" with an honorary title "Ya 亞": "亞其," "亞啟," and "亞." It is likely thus that "Zhu 竹" is also paired with an honorary title, in which case "Ren 妊" may be equated with "任" yet remains transcribed "Ren Zhu 妊竹."

"Zhu 竹" is the diviner "Zhu" of oracle bone inscriptions of the Wu Ding era. Diviner Zhu was related to diviners of the "Bin group 宾组," "X group," and "[illegible] group," who continued to work during the eras of Shang Kings Zu Geng and Zu Jia (Cao 1987:3, 2007:46). These diviners were contemporaries who worked together over a long period of time. It is hypothesized that the diviner Zhu was titled with the honorific "Ren" yet ranked in a lower position than those titled "Ya 亞."

Inscription 9: Ge 自, 戈自

This two-character name was found on only one object in Fu Zi's tomb, a large round tripod *ding* (M5:1173) made by diviner 自 of the Wu Ding era. This combination of two characters, "ge 戈" and "自," is a composite emblem 戈 (see Figure 4:1). More than a few examples are found in bronze inscriptions from the Shang and Zhou periods. "Ge 戈" is a clan emblem of Ge state, often associated with descendants of the Xia dynasty (Cao 1989, 2007:61). At some later date the name of state became the name of the Ge clan. The graph "X" is the name of the diviner who also served as a military commander, as recorded in detail in oracle bone divinations. Evidently a close connection existed between diviner Ge 自 and Fu Zi.

INSCRIPTION 10: LU FANG GUA
*RU GE WU*盧方刟入戈五

This six-character inscription records the event when a gift of five jade *ge* daggers were offered by Gua of the Lu state. Representative is jade *ge* M5:580 from Fu Zi's tomb. The character "*gua* 刟" is a combination of "X" and "口," which are interchangeable in use, and therefore the character is read as 刟. " on the top and "日" on the bottom. "日" " are all recorded

Although without inscriptions the four other daggers are similar in style and form a group. The character "*wu* 五 (five)" in the inscription cites the number in the set. This inscription records the event, hypothetically ordered by Fu Zi (or another Shang royal house member), to record the leader of Lu State's tribute of five jade daggers. The six characters are read as "Lu Fang Gua presented five *ge* daggers."

Evidently the relationship between the Lu state and Shang royal members, although not referenced in bone inscriptions, was cooperative. The fact that leader Gua of the Lu state sent five jade daggers as tribute to Fu Zi portrays a good relationship between Shang kingdom and Lu state. It is known from transmitted histories that later the Lu state rebelled by supporting Zhou King Wu at the Battle of Muye, which resulted in the downfall of the Shang dynasty and establishment of the Zhou dynasty.

Many suggestions have been proposed regarding the location of Lu state. In my book *The Lu Fang during Yin Dynasty*, I suggested that the Lu state was active around the upper course of the Jing River, located in modern Pingliang County, Gansu province (Cao 1981, 2007:32). This conclusion is based on historical and archaeological data.

INSCRIPTION 11: ZI 㯥 QUAN, 子㯥泉

This nomenclature was found on tributary bronzes offered by a leader of Zi Fang, Fu Zi's home state. Twenty-two bronzes, mostly alcohol vessels, were inscribed with the three characters, "Zi 㯥 Quan." The vessels included a pair of round *zun*, one *jia*, nine *jue*, and 10 *gu*. As represented by the inscription on the round *zun* (M5:320), the second graph combines "*mao*" (矛) and "*shu*" (束) and can be transcribed "㯥" (see Figure 4:3). The inscription "𣏗泉" (Figure 4:2) is an abbreviated version of "子𣏗泉." "Mao 矛" is found among many Shang and Zhou bronze inscriptions (Rong 1939:851). The character "𣏗" represents a branch within the Mao clan, combining *shu* 束 and *mao* 矛.

How to decipher "Zi 子" in "子𣏗泉" has long been a puzzle for those attempting to read this inscription. Some scholars suggest *zi* be read "son" (Institute of Archaeology, CASS 1980:100). Among oracle bone and bronze inscriptions, names associated with Zi have primarily been a single character following Zi, as represented, for example, by "Zi Qi" and "Zi Yang." Double characters following "Zi" character are rarely found. Moreover, if the *zi* were sons of Wu Ding, they typically appear with honorary titles, as is the case of "Zi Qi" who was also recorded as "Ya Qi." "子 泉" has no corresponding honorary title. It is suggested that "子𣏗泉" was not a son of Shang King Wu Ding.

I would like to propose that the Zi in "子𣏗泉" was the same Zi in "Fu Zi." I maintain the *zi* stood for the "Zi" *fang* (state), the home country of Fu Zi. Sometimes "子𣏗泉" was abbreviated in the bronze inscriptions as "𣏗泉." In this case, the state name was omitted, but the clan name "泉" was never omitted. The number of 22 bronze vessels with the "子泉" inscription was only surpassed by the ones inscribed "Fu Zi (婦好)" and "Hou Mu (司𤔅母)." For this reason, this figure 子𣏗泉 stands out as having a probable close relationship with Fu Zi. It is possible that 子𣏗泉 was a leader in Fu Zi's home country, the Zi state, and was in fact a relative (a father or sibling) of Fu Zi. It is my conclusion that 子𣏗泉 was a powerful figure in the Zi state who shared a close kinship with Fu Zi. It is also possible that the 22 alcohol vessels were not just gifts from 子𣏗泉 but part of her dowry, thus they were buried with her in death.

Conclusion

We have discussed figures associated with the 11 sets of inscriptions found on burial objects in Fu Zi's tomb: Fu Zi, Wu Ding, Xiao Ji, Ya Qi1, Ya Qi2, Ya X, Hou 𤔅 Mu, Ren Zhu, Ge 𠦝, Lu Fang Gua, and Zi 𣏗 Quan. These were important figures within the Shang ruling house who were centered around Fu Zi: Wu Ding was king and husband of Fu Zi. Xiao Ji was Fu Zi's son and crown prince. Hou 𤔅 Mu was probably another legal wife of Shang King Wu Ding and Fu Zi's peer. Ya Qi1, Ya Qi2, Ya 弜, and Ge 𠦝 were military officials and princes of the Shang kingdom. Lu Fang Gua, Ren Zhu, and Zi 𣏗 Quan were leaders of different states and gathered together around Fu Zi due to the fact she was a high commander in the military. The close relationship of these figures shaped and reflected a microcosm of what must have served as a supreme military group during the early Wu Ding era. The geographical areas associated with this group of figures as known through the inscriptions were widespread. Ya Qi1 probably resided in present-day Xiaqiyuan area of Hebei and neighboring Shandong province. Ya 弜 probably resided in present-day southeastern Shaanxi and northwestern Henan areas. Ya Qi2 was assigned in the north where the Yan state peoples later settled. Ren Zhu's land was later called Gu Zhu in present-day Lulong area of Hebei province. Ge 白 was located near the present-day Zhengzhou area. Zi Fang (state) was very possibly within the present-day Shandong province. Lu Fang was most likely located in the far west near present-day Pingliang in Gansu Province.

Regions associated with these royal members and neighboring states covered the Yellow River Basin from west to east, north to the North China Plain, and over the Yan Mountains range reaching to northern Hebei and southern Liaoning. Tributes to Fu Zi came from princes and other state leaders from a vast area. The powerful position that Fu Zi held was not simply achieved from her own individual influence but was more a reflection of political power of the Shang kingdom. In the "Xuanniao (Swallow, black bird)" chapter in the Shang Song section of the *Book of Songs*, Shang King Wu Ding's kingdom was described as a "royal domain of a thousand miles... where the people rest; there commence the boundaries that reach to four seas." Inscriptions from the Fu Zi tomb reflect precisely this description of that prosperous era.

Written on December 18, 2013, at Waweili, Zhaoyang District, Beijing and translated by Elizabeth Childs-Johnson.

BIBLIOGRAPHY

Cao, Dingyun 曹丁云 1980. "Studies on 'Ya Qi' 亚启"亚启'研究." *Wenwu Jikan* 2: 143–150.

Cao, Dingyun 曹丁云 1981. "Lu Fang in the Shang Dynasty 商代盧方." *Social Science First Bimonthly* 社会科学前两个月 2: 121–122.

Cao, Dingyun 曹丁云 1983. "Studies on 'Ya Qi 启,' 'Ya Qi 其, "亞其,亞 研究." *Oracle Bone Inscriptions in Yin Shang History* 殷尚历史上的甲骨文 3.文章多少页数.

Cao, Dingyun 曹丁云 1987. "'Zhu 竹' and 'Zhu 古竹' in Shang Dynasty 商代'竹'與'古竹?" *Huaxia Kaogu* 3: 71–84.

Cao, Dingyun 曹丁云 1989a. "The Clan Symbol 'Ge' in the Shang Dynasty and as a Descent Clan from the Xia Dynasty 商代的氏族象征'Ge'和夏朝的血统氏族." *Kaogu yu Wenwu* 1: 72–79.

Cao, Dingyun 曹丁云 1989b. "Fu Zi Was a Daughter of the Zi State 婦子是梓国的女儿." In *Essays in Celebration of Professor Su Bingqi's Fifty-Five Years as an Archaeologist*, 381–385. Beijing, China: Wenwu chubanshe.

Cao, Dingyun 曹丁云 1993. "Researches on the Relationship between Fu Zi and Xiao Ji 婦子与萧集小己关 系研究." *Zhongyuan wenwu* 93:80–89.

Cao, Dingyun 曹丁云 2003. "Studies on the Yan State in the Shang Dynasty 商代燕国研究." *Journal of Social Sciences and Philosophy* (Taiwan) 文张多少页数?

Cao, Dingyun 曹丁云 2007. *Studies on Inscriptions from the Yinxu Fu Zi Tomb* 殷墟府子墓铭文研究. Kunming, China: Yunnan Renmin Chubanshe.

Cao, Dingyun 曹丁云 2012. "Si Mu Wu Ding Should Not Be Renamed Hou Mu Wu Ding [司母戊鼎]不得更 名[后母戊鼎]." *Zhongguo shehui kexue bao* 2012.3.27.

Chen, S. 1991. "Writing Found on Jade and Stone Objects from the Shang Dynasty 写作发现于商代的玉器和石器上." *Huaxia kaogu* 2:67–68.

Guo, Moruo 郭沫若 2002 [1937]. "Yinqi Cuibian 殷契粹編." *Yindu xuekan* 4:1549.

Jao, Tsung-I 饒宗頤. "Studies on Clan Names and Neighboring States on Bronze and Jade Objects Excavated from the Fu Zi Tomb 从妇子墓出土的青铜器和玉器上的氏族名称和邻国研究." *Guwenzi yanjiu* 12:303–307.

Rong, Geng 容庚 1939 [1938]. *A Collection of Inscriptions on Ancient Bronze Objects* 金文编. Changsha, Hunan: Shangwu yinshuguan.

Zhang, Zhenglan 张正蓝 1983. "A Brief Introduction to Fu Zi 妇子简介." *Kaogu* 6. 文章多少页数?

Zhongguo Shehui Kexueyuan Kaogu Yanjiusuo, Anyang Gongzuodui 中国社会科学院考古研究所安阳工作队 1992. "Huanyuanzhuang South site 1986–1987 安阳花园庄南发掘报告." *Kaogu xuebao* 1. 文章多少页数?

Zhongguo Shehui Kexueyuan Kaogu Yanjiusuo 中国社会科学院考古研究所 1980. *Fu Zi Tomb in Yinxu* 殷墟妇子. 墓 1st ed. Beijing: Wenwu chubanshe.

Zhongguo Shehui Kexueyuan Kaogu Yanjiusuo 中国社会科学 院考古研究所, 安阳工作队 1992. "1986–1987 Excavation Report on the Anyang."

Zhongguo Shehui Kexueyuan Kaogu Yanjiusuo 中国社会科学院考古研究所安阳工作队 1992. "Huanyuanzhuang South site 1986–1987 安阳花园庄南发掘报告." *Kaogu xuebao* 1. 文章多少页数?

SECTION V

THE SECOND HEIGHT OF THE BRONZE AGE: THE WESTERN ZHOU PERIOD

CHAPTER 17

....

WESTERN ZHOU CULTURAL AND HISTORIC SETTING

....

BY MARIA KHAYUTINA, LUDWIG-MAXIMILIANS
UNIVERSITY OF MUNICH

ACCORDING to early Chinese traditional historiography, in the mid-eleventh century BCE the Zhou 周 polity, located in the present-day Shaanxi province, headed a coalition of allies and seized the capital of the Yin 殷 dynasty, Shang 商. The last Shang king, Zhou 紂, committed suicide, and the Zhou ruler proclaimed himself king. Thus the Zhou royal dynasty was founded. The present chapter summarizes what is known about Zhou before the conquest of Shang, outlines the "Western Zhou period" ending with the death of King You 幽 (r. 780–771 BCE) touching upon the problem of its chronology, and discusses the political organization of this epoch.

SOURCES

Written sources for the Western Zhou period include transmitted literature and epigraphy. Traditionally, Chinese historians gave (and many of them still give) priority to transmitted texts, regarding epigraphy as a complementary source. However, transmitted texts, produced at various intervals after the events on which they reflect and modified many times during the process of editing and copying, represent only secondary and even tertiary historical sources.

Among the earliest transmitted texts, the "Major Elegantiae" (Da ya 大雅) of the *Book of Odes* (*Shi jing* 詩經) glorify early Zhou rulers of the twelfth to eleventh centuries BCE, while the *Book of Documents* (*Shang shu* 尚書) includes speeches ascribed to the rulers of the eleventh to tenth centuries BCE.[1] These texts were traditionally regarded as first-hand evidence from the earliest Zhou reigns. Recent investigations reveal their commemorative ritual nature and point to the fact that they were probably written several centuries later.[2] Some major events of the ninth to eighth centuries BCE are reflected in the *Guo yu* 國語 (*Conversations of the States*), composed during circa the fourth to third centuries BCE, and are referred to in various other texts written before the Qin dynasty (221–206 BCE).

The *Book of Odes*, the *Book of Documents*, the *Conversations of the States*, and other pre-Qin texts, preserved until today, constitute the basis of the "Basic Annals of Zhou" in the *Grand Scribe's Records* (*Shi ji* 史記, translated alternatively as *Historical Records*, or *Records of the Grand Historian*).[3] This text, drafted by Sima Tan 司馬談 (died 110 BCE) and completed by his son Sima Qian 司馬遷 (ca. 145-90 BCE), is regarded as the standard account of the Zhou history. Counting slightly more than 8,000 words, it summarizes what was known about the Zhou royal house from its legendary origins until its end in 256 BCE. Although this work enjoys traditional authority, it is itself based on relatively late secondary sources and should be treated with caution.[4]

Authentic written materials from the Western Zhou period are mostly available in the form of inscriptions on bronze ritual vessels and musical instruments made for ancestral sacrifices and burials and unearthed from tombs or hoards.[5] Nearly 7,000 bronze inscriptions have been transcribed in modern characters and made accessible through publications in inscription compendia and online databases.[6] The first edited collection of English translations of 82 inscriptions, including 62 Western Zhou pieces, was published in 2016.[7] More translated bronze inscriptions can be found in individual scholarly publications.[8] Several caches of Zhou oracle bone inscriptions have also been found.[9] Epigraphic texts, not altered by editorial processes and available as originals, today qualify as primary sources at least in the sense that they reflect contemporaneous views. Their ritual and commemorative functions should be considered while using them as historical sources.[10]

[1] *Shi jing, Shang shu*. For translations, cf. Legge 1991a, 1991b; Karlgren 1950, 1974; Waley and Allen 1996.
[2] See Kryukov 2000:407; Vogelsang 2002; Kern 2007:109–176; Kern 2009:143–151; Kern 2017.
[3] *Shi ji* 4 ("Zhou ben ji" 周本紀), pp. 111–170; Nienhauser et al. 1994:55–86. For other Western translations of the *Shi ji*, see Chavannes 1895; Watson 1961; Vyatkin et al. 2001: 179–217.
[4] Ess 2003–2004, 2014; Khayutina 2009a.
[5] For an introduction into Western Zhou bronze inscriptions see Shaughnessy 1991.
[6] *Yin Zhou jinwen jicheng* (hereafter *Jicheng*) is the standard edition of bronze inscriptions used by most scholars since 1990s. Chong and Ch'en 2006 comprises inscriptions published after 1990. The most comprehensive compendium of inscriptions up to today is Wu Zhenfeng 2012. Online databases include password-protected Academia Sinica "Digital Archives of Bronze Images and Inscriptions" and *Chinese Ancient Texts Database* (CHANT), as well as the freely accessible *Lexicon of Pre-Qin Oracle, Bronze Inscriptions and Bamboo Slips* (Ch'en and Chong).
[7] *A Source Book of Ancient Chinese Bronze Inscriptions* (following, *A Source Book*) (Cook and Goldin 2016).
[8] See Shaughnessy 2001-2002; 2016.
[9] For publications of the oracle bones from Fengchu see Cao Wei 2002, Chen Quanfang 2003. Oracle bones from Zhougongmiao 周公廟, discovered in 2004, have not been published yet.
[10] For scholarly approaches to inscriptions, cf. Shaughnessy 1991, 2001–2002; Falkenhausen 1993; Wang Ming-ke 1999; Li Feng 2006; Khayutina 2010, 2014, 2019.

Archaeological excavations have unveiled further evidence for investigations of material culture, technology, economy, historical geography, social structure, and religious representations.[11] However, planned excavations are still rare. Salvage excavations are launched either in connection with development projects or as a measure to prevent tomb-looting.

LEGENDARY ORIGINS OF THE ZHOU

According to several texts from the *Major Elegantiae* section of the *Book of Odes*, on which the "Basic Annals of Zhou" rely, the Zhou progenitor *Hou* Ji 后稷 (Lord Millet) was born by Jiang Yuan 姜嫄 (Jiang-surnamed female progenitor) after she stepped in a footprint of Di 帝 deity (Chinese titles and kinship terms will be italicized throughout this chapter). *Hou* Ji resided in Tai 台 and practiced agriculture. *Gong* Liu 公劉 (Patriarch Liu) was warlike and resided in Bin 豳. Gu *gong* Dan *fu* 古公亶父 (Ancient Patriarch Father Dan) led his people across Ju 沮 and Qi 漆 Rivers to the place beneath the Mount Qi 岐 called Zhou Plain 周原 and built there a new settlement, referred to as Qi Zhou 岐周 (Zhou-under-Qi) in some other texts. His son *Wang ji* 王季 (Royal Junior, also known as *Ji* Li 季歷, Junior Li) begot Wen *wang* 文王 (Adorned King, also known as *bo* 伯 [Elder] Chang 昌).[12] The latter conquered the Lord of Chong 崇, seized his territory and built a settlement in Feng 豐. His son Wu *wang* 武王 (Martial King, also known under his personal name Fa 發) built a residence in Hao 鎬 and conquered Shang.[13] Written for rituals of royal ancestor worship, the odes reverently call the early Zhou rulers by the royal title *wang*, even if they probably did not call themselves "kings" during their lifetime.

The "Basic Annals of Zhou" state that *Gong* Liu, *Gugong* Dan *fu*, and King Wen were direct descendants of *Hou* Ji in the third, twelfth, and fourteenth generations, respectively.[14] Western Zhou bronze inscriptions reflect the cult of King Wen and King Wu but almost never mention earlier ancestors.[15] It is thus unclear how many generations of

[11] Hsü and Linduff 1988; Rawson 1999; Falkenhausen 2006; Li Feng 2006; Jing and Wang 2014; Shelach-Lavi 2015:264–305; Jaffe 2016.

[12] Siblings were distinguished according to their birth sequence as *bo* 伯 (Elder, or First-Born), *zhong* 仲 (Second-Born), *shu* 叔 (Third-Born), and *ji* 季 (Junior). See *Baihutong*, 415 ("Xing ming" 姓名); cf. Falkenhausen 2006:70; Gassmann 2006:321. "Wen," translated here as "Adorned" based on the meaning of *wen* as "pattern, decorum," is often understood as "Civil" as a counterpart to Wu, "Martial," the title of King Wen's successor. Translations "Civilized" and "Cultivated" are also often seen, but they project Eastern Zhou, Han, and modern concepts back to the archaic past. For other suggestions, see Falkenhausen 1996 ("Accomplished"); Schaberg 2001:57–86 ("Patterned").

[13] See the odes Nos. 245, 250, 237, 241, 244, 240, 236 of the Mao Tradition of the *Shi jing* (Mao shi 毛詩), arranged according to the citation order, in *Shi jing* pp. 483, 469, 459, 470, 480, 468, 455. Cf Legge 1991b:465–471, 483–488, 437–441, 448–455, 460–464, 446–447, 432–436; Waley and Allen 1996:244–245, 252–253, 232–233, 236–239, 241–242, 235–236, 229–230.

[14] *Shi ji* 4, pp. 111–120, cf. Nienhauser et al. 1994:55–58.

[15] Khayutina 2019.

Zhou leaders prior to Dan *fu* were actually remembered. Several texts in the *Book of Odes* represent *Hou* Ji as an addressee of prayers for harvest, while Warring States–period texts regard him as an administrator of agriculture who served legendary emperors of antiquity. Chang Kwang-chih (1931–2001) supposed that, as a mighty royal ancestor, *Hou* Ji later transformed into a communally worshipped agricultural deity.[16] A reversed transformation of a communal deity into an early progenitor of the ruling lineage is equally conceivable.

Ji and Jiang surnames and Zhou marital policies

Relying on the *Conversations of the States*, Sima Qian traced back to *Hou* Ji the origin of the Ji 姬 surname. This was the surname of the Zhou ruling house and all lineages that descended from it but also of some lineages that split from the common stem before or at the time of Dan *fu*. Surnames (*xing* 姓) served in Early China for regulating marital relationships.[17] Marriages with persons of the same surname were prohibited. Dan *fu* and several Zhou kings married women of Jiang 姜 surname. The Ji- and Jiang-surnamed ruling houses of two Zhou dependencies in the east, Lu and Qi, regularly intermarried during the Springs and Autumns period.[18] The overlapping of some designations of patrilineal and marital relatives in the early Chinese kinship terminology points to the practice of cross-cousin marriage.[19] The veneration of Hou Ji's mother, Jiang Yuan, possibly reflects the tradition of preferential marital alliances between Ji- and Jiang-surnamed lineages.

Opinions vary regarding the nature of social groups who identified themselves by the Ji and Jiang surnames before the beginning of the Zhou dynasty. Jiang (*kaŋ or kjaŋ in old Chinese) is phonetically and graphically similar to *qiang* 羌 (*khaŋ or khjaŋ).[20] In Shang oracle bone inscriptions, the term *qiang* referred to captives taken in military campaigns that often took place somewhere in the west from Anyang. Qiang 羌 appears as a proper noun in the list of participants of the conquest of Shang in the Oath at Mu (Mu shi 穆誓) chapter of the *Book of Documents*.[21] These coincidences brought about assumptions that Qiang was a name of a specific polity, culturally and ethnically distinct from both Shang and Zhou, while Shirakawa Shizuka (1910–2006) suggested that the surname Jiang derived from this ethnonym.[22] Some authors even attempted relating the Shang period's Qiang with the Qiang people that lived in western China during the Han dynasty and, possibly, were the ancestors of the present-day Tibetan-speaking Qiang minority.[23]

---

[16] Chang 1976:180.
[17] Kryukov 1967:128–154.
[18] Pulleyblank 1983; Gassmann 2006.
[19] Granet 1930:157; Kryukov 1972:151; Chang 1976:89–92.
[20] For Old Chinese phonetic reconstructions, see Schuessler 2009:No.3-5a, 3-6a.
[21] *Shang shu*, p. 109 ("Mu shi"); cf. Legge 1991a:300; Karlgren 1950:29.
[22] Shirakawa 1958.
[23] Hsü and Linduff 1988:55–59.

However, *qiang* in oracle inscriptions may have been a general term for captives whom the Shang regarded as suitable to be used for human sacrifices.[24] Relationships between the *qiang* of the Shang and the Qiang of the Han periods are questionable given the great chronological and geographical gap between them.[25] The comprehensive list of foreign polities mentioned in the Oath at Mu in the *Book of Documents* may be a retrospective fiction.[26] Thus, the hypothesis about a connection between the Jiang surname and a distinctly foreign ethno-cultural entity cannot be verified. The surnames Ji and Jiang, related phonologically, morphologically and, possibly, semantically, may designate two exogamic (marrying outside a patrilineal kinship group) intermarrying moieties within one culturally and ethnically homogenous group.[27]

Beginning at least from the rule of Dan *fu*'s son *Ji* Li, Zhou rulers diversified their marital relationships, thus extending their political network. *Ji* Li's Ren-surnamed spouse from Zhizhong 挚仲 lineage "came from Yin Shang to get married in Zhou."[28] King Wen's spouse was a Si 姒–surnamed lady whose place of origin is not known.[29] She was the mother of King Wu and most of the founders of Zhou colonies in the east.[30] These females were commemorated in the *Major Elegantiae* in the *Book of Odes* and worshiped as female ancestors of the royal house and most important Ji-surnamed lineages.

ARCHAEOLOGICAL SEARCH FOR PRE-DYNASTIC ZHOU

Places where the Zhou resided before the conquest were traditionally localized in the central part of present-day Shaanxi province: Tai in the Wei 渭 River Valley in Wugong 武功 County, Bin in the middle flow of Jing 泾 River, Zhou Plain on the edge of Qishan 岐山 and Fufeng 扶風 counties, and Feng and Hao on the western and eastern banks of Feng 澧 River near the provincial capital Xi'an 西安. The three latter centers were continuously used during the Western Zhou period, and their locations are confirmed by archaeology and inscriptions.[31] The earlier centers, Tai and Bin, cannot not be precisely identified. The location of Bin is particularly hotly debated. Shortly after the discovery of oracle inscriptions mentioning Zhou in Anyang, Qian Mu 钱穆 (1895–1990) questioned the traditional localization of Bin in Shaanxi and argued that Zhou probably did not reside that far from Shang. He suggested that Bin was in the lower flow of the Fen 汾 River in Shanxi province. His interpretation relies on a reference in the Warring States

[24] Shelach 1996; Fiskesjö 2001:143; Liu and Chen 2012:380.
[25] For a critical overview of sources relating the Qiang to Tibetans, see for example Ban and Xie 1985.
[26] Kern 2017.
[27] Pulleyblank 1983:419–421.
[28] Mao *shi* No. 236 in *Shi jing*, p. 455; cf. Legge 1991b:432–436; Waley and Allen 1996:229–230.
[29] Mao *shi* No. 240 in *Shi jing*, p. 468; cf. Legge 1991b:446–447, Waley and Allen 1996:235–236.
[30] *Shi ji* 35 ("Guan Cai shijia" 管蔡世家), p. 1563.
[31] Zhang and Yin 2004:56–62; Khayutina 2010.

period's book *Mengzi* 孟子, where Bin was transcribed not as 豳 as in the *Shi jing*, but as 邠 (a combination of *fen* phonetic and *yi* "settlement" radical). Qian further stressed that according to this text—incorporated in the "Basic Annals of Zhou"—on the way from Bin to the Zhou Plain, Dan *fu* passed by a certain Mount Liang 梁. This place name can be matched either with Lüliang 呂梁 mountains in western Shanxi or Liang 梁 on the western bank of the Yellow River in eastern Shaanxi.[32] Thus, Qian Mu suggested that Bin should have been located eastward of the Yellow River, and his view remains influential until today.[33] However, during the Shang period, inter-regional interactions sometimes extended to distances of over a thousand kilometers. Thus, the early Zhou needed not to be located much closer to Anyang to be able to interact with the Shang. Archaeological materials reflect that although the presence of the Shang culture in the central Shaanxi reduced during the Late Shang period, some communication between this region and the Central Plains was still maintained.[34] The place-name Bin 豳 in Western Zhou bronze inscriptions pertains to an area in Jing River Valley, supporting the traditional localization.[35] On the other hand, Mount Liang was not mentioned in the account about Dan *fu* in the *Shi jing*, the oldest source of early Zhou history. Besides, the place-name Liang, literally "roof-beam," was not a unique name and, therefore, not a secure orientation point. Further evidence in favor of the "eastern origin" hypothesis is still missing, although the evidence supporting the "western origin" theory remains similarly ambiguous and inconclusive.

Archaeologists attempt to find traces of the early, pre-conquest Zhou in central Shaanxi. In the Chinese archaeological literature, ceramic typology is regarded as the most distinctive element of archaeological "cultures" (*wenhua* 文化), whose local variants are referred to as "cultural types" (*wenhua leixing* 文化類型). The sphere of distribution of one ceramic tradition is often regarded as the area of settlement of certain population groups or even political entities.[36] Ethno-archaeological investigations in other parts of the world warn us that "pots do not equal people." In many cases, spatial distributions of certain types of material objects or even of some cultural practices may cut across ethnic and political boundaries, whereas boundaries between such traditions may eventually fall in areas with no particular cultural or political significance.[37] Studying mortuary and other ritual practices, construction of dwellings and organization of production sites, and layout and spatial distribution of settlements is necessary in order to reveal cultural identities and boundaries. Such investigations are gradually progressing, but there is still much work to be done. Even when cultural entities can be distinguished, connecting these to the names of peoples or polities mentioned in transmitted texts is methodologically problematic in the absence of written materials among archaeological findings.

---

[32] Qian Mu 1931.
[33] Hsü and Linduff 1988:34–35; Shaughnessy 1999:303–307.
[34] See Zhang Tian'en 2004.
[35] Khayutina forthcoming; see also See Li Feng 2006:160-161.
[36] See for example Liu and Chen 2003, 2012.
[37] Dietler and Herbich 1994:460; see also Campbell 2009:831.

Surveys and excavations reveal that during the late second millennium BCE different ceramic traditions were distributed in central Shaanxi in the valleys of Wei and Jing Rivers. Materials available today suggest that this region experienced influences from the metropolitan Shang centers: first Zhengzhou and later Anyang. During the upper Erligang phase, the Beicun 北村 variant of the Erligang ceramic tradition spread to the eastern central Shaanxi, reaching to the area of the present-day provincial capital Xi'an.[38] The Laoniupo 老牛坡 site in the eastern suburbs of Xi'an was continuously in use from the lower Erligang period until the last phase of Yinxu.[39] During the Yinxu period, the Laoniupo variant developed independently from Anyang. The Laoniupo bronze assemblage includes both vessels made after Anyang models and implements from non-Shang traditions distributed farther in the south.[40] In the Jing River Valley, the Zhumazui 朱馬嘴 site, occupied between the upper Erligang and the second phase of Yinxu, similarly displays the gradual weakening of the Shang factors and strengthening of a local tradition.[41] On the Zhou Plain, Shang features are witnessed in a group of sites, dated between the upper Erligang and the early part of the second phase of Yinxu at the latest.[42] Thus, in general, the Shang influence in central Shaanxi faded around 1200 BCE.

Archaeologists debate which local ceramic tradition can be recognized as the "proto-Zhou culture" (*xian Zhou wenhua* 先周文化). One major condition for its identification is that the choice and shapes of pottery vessels in archaeological complexes in question should display continuity with the standard pottery repertoire of the Early Western Zhou period, as it is manifested in Fengxi in Chang'an county, presumably corresponding to the Feng settlement, founded by King Wen. On this site, joint-crotch *li* tripods without handles and *guan* jars with angular shoulders represent the main pottery types both in the early Western Zhou and in the underlying layers, whereas pocket- and separated-crotch *li* tripods and ring-footed *gui* bowls are seen there in a smaller number. Similar pottery types are characteristic of several pre–Western Zhou sites in the Wei Valley, including Zhengjiapo in Wugong county, Hejiacun in Qishan county, Nanzhihui in Fengxiang county, and Doujitai in Baoji county (see Figure 1 and Table 1). Some authors regard all these sites as "proto-Zhou," while others distinguish "Zhengjiapo culture type" and "Doujitai culture type."[43] Other scholars attempt to trace the source of the "proto-Zhou culture" to the middle flow of the Jing River, where the ancient Bin area was located according to the "western origin" theory. The best-explored archaeological site in this region is Nianzipo in Changwu county, dating from the second phase of Yinxu up to the Early Western Zhou period.[44] The excavators and some other archaeologists

---

[38] See Campbell 2014:83–84 with further references.

[39] For the dating and external connections of Laoniupo, see Liu Shi'e 2001:329–336; Campbell 2014:122, 153; cf. Childs-Johnson forthcoming.

[40] Zhang Tian'en 2004:30–31; Jing and Wang 2014:170–172; Campbell 2014:154–155.

[41] Zhang Tian'en 2004:52–55.

[42] Zhang Tian'en 2004:55–56.

[43] Cf. Wang and Xu 2000; Zhang and Yin 2004:20–26; Lei Xingshan 2010.

[44] Zhongguo 2007.

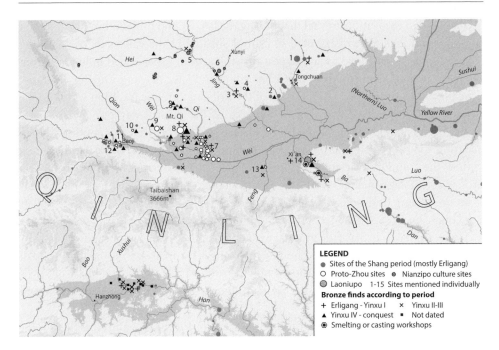

FIGURE 1 Map of Shang and Proto-Zhou archaeological sites in Wei River valley (ca. 13–11 C. BCE).

consider that burial rites, dwelling forms, and pottery types in Nianzipo were similar to those in Wei River Valley and regard it as a "proto-Zhou" site.[45] Other scholars point out that in Nianzipo, the pocket- and crotch-shaped *li* prevail over the joined-crotch *li* and often have handles, which was not typical of Western Zhou ceramic tradition. They observe that the Nianzipo pottery manifests strong connections to the Xindian and Siwa traditions of the upper Jing River Valley in the present-day Gansu province and suggest treating Nianzipo as a separate "culture."[46] A more recently excavated site, Zaoshugounao in Chunhua county, is also discussed in connection to the search for "proto-Zhou."[47] On this site, joined-crotch *li* are predominant, but *li* with idiosyncratic snake designs and egg-shaped jars with three pocket-legs (*sanzuweng*) point to the relationships between the local residents and cultures of the Steppe zone of northeastern Shaanxi.[48] Finds of bronze weapons and golden earrings in Chunhua county suggest that this area was within the reach of the Lijiaya cultural tradition, which, in its turn, was connected to cultures of Central Asia and Southern Siberia.[49] Another cultural tradition characterized by catacomb burials was identified in Liujia in Fufeng county. It shows strong connections to cultures of Gansu and Qinghai provinces. The excavators and some other authors interpret it as "the culture of the Jiang."[50] Chronological correspon-

[45] Li Feng 1994; Hu Qianying 1993, 2005; Zhongguo 2007.
[46] Cf. Zhang and Yin 2004:17–26; Zhang Tianen 2004:196–197; Cao Bin 2007; Ma Lingwei 2014.
[47] Xibei et al. 2012.
[48] For *sanzuweng*, see Khayutina 2016:91.
[49] Cf. Wu En Yuesitu 2007:141–169; Rawson 1999:403.
[50] Shaanxi 1984; Liu Junshe 1994.

Table 1 Archaeological cultures of central Shaanxi during the second part of the second millennium BCE[51]

Representative sites	Distribution	Distinct features	External connections
Zhengjiapo 鄭家坡 in Wugong 武功 county; Hejiacun 賀家村 tombs in Qishan county, Fengxi 灃西 in Chang'an 長安 county, Nanzhihui 南指揮 in Fengxiang 鳳翔 county, Doujitai 斗雞台 in Baoji 寶雞 county,	Wei Valley from Baoji to Feng Valley	Pottery: joint-crotch *li* tripod, pocked-legged *li* tripod with high neck, angular *guan* jar, *yan* steamer, ring-footed bowl *gui* Bronze: *ding* tripod, *gui* bowl (Fengxi) Burial: vertical pit tombs, *ercengtai*, coffins, pottery *li*, and *guan* as burial goods	Erligang and Yinxu Shang culture Xindian 辛店 culture of Qinghai and Gansu provinces, Siwa 寺洼 culture of Gansu province, Liujia culture
Nianzipo 碾子坡 in Changwu 長武 county; Duanjing 斷涇 in Binxian 彬縣 county	Middle Jing Valley	Pottery: pocked-legged *li* tripod with high neck, often with handles; joint-crotch *li* tripod; various *guan* jars; *yan* steamer; basin with high foot *dou* Bronze: *ding* tripod, *pou* 瓿 jar (Nianzipo) Burial: vertical pit tombs, *ercengtai*, stone slabs as covers or walls, pottery *li* as burial goods	Wei Valley cultures, Xindian and Siwa cultures, Yinxu Shang culture
Zaoshugounao 棗樹溝腦 site, Heidouzui 黑豆嘴 tombs in Chunhua 淳化 county	Middle Jing Valley	Pottery: joint-crotch *li*, narrow-mouth *guan*, *yan*-steamer, *li* and *yan* with snake design, *sanzuweng*, basin with high foot *dou* Bronze: *ding* tripods, *jue* drinking cup, *hu* jar, hafted axe, halberds, rounded-blade knives (Heidouzui) Gold: flat earrings (Heidouzui) Burial: shallow pits, wooden slabs as covers, pottery *li* as burial goods	Cultures of Wei valley, Cultures of northern Steppe belt, Yinxu Shang culture
Liujia 劉家, Fufeng 扶風county, Shizuitou 石嘴頭 in Baoji county	Wei Valley from Baoji to Meixian and Fufeng counties	Pottery: high necked pocket-legged *li* tripod with and without handles, one- or two-handled jars with high neck Burial: catacomb tombs, niches in walls, pottery *guan* with stones inside as burial goods	Xindian culture, Zhengjiapo-Doujitai type cultures of Wei Valley

[51] The table summarizes the data from Zhang and Yin 2004:20–26 and adds the data for Zaoshugounao based on Xibei 2012.

dences and relationships between the sites in Jing and Wei Valleys are a matter of ongoing debate, and association of archaeological complexes with the "Ji-surnamed Zhou," "Jiang," or other cultural and political units mentioned in transmitted sources remains problematic in the absence of written materials on these sites.

ZHOU RELATIONSHIPS WITH SHANG
BEFORE THE CONQUEST

The "Yin benji" 殷本記 ("Basic Annals of Yin") in the *Historical Records* state that *Ji* Li's son Chang ruled at the beginning under the title Xi *bo* 西伯 (Elder of the West) and held the office of one of the "Three Excellencies" (*san gong* 三公) at the court of Shang King Zhou but was later dismissed. Deriving from the third-to-second-century-BCE collection of anecdotes, *Stratagems of the Warring States* (*Zhanguoce* 戰國策), the latter account is ahistorical, since the institution of the "Three Excellencies" was established at the beginning of the imperial age nearly a millennium later. The story in the "Basic Annals of Zhou" that the Shang king imprisoned Chang in Yuli 羑里 but released him for bribes, circulated during the fourth to second centuries BCE, but is not seen in earlier accounts.[52] Whether the Shang king actually bullied Chang, or such legends emerged as to serve moral justification of his "rebellion" against the Shang in the eyes of posterior generations, remains unclear.[53] The "Basic Annals of Zhou" further state that the Shang king later officially conferred on Chang a "mandate" (*ming* 命).[54] The already-mentioned text from the *Book of Odes* mentions that *Ji* Li married a woman from Shang. Although she did not belong to the Shang royal house, this marital alliance could signify a rapprochement between the Zhou and the contemporary political and cultural paragon.

There are several dozen mentions of Zhou in oracle inscriptions from Anyang. One inscription from the second half of the thirteenth century BCE mentions Zhou *fang* 周方.[55] *Fang* was the Shang generic term for polities or territories.[56] The mention of *fu* Zhou 帚(婦)周 "Zhou Spouse" in a further contemporaneous inscription indicates that

[52] *Shi ji* 3 ("Yin benji" 殷本紀), p. 106, 116; cf. *Zhuangzi* 9:29, p. 919; *Hanfeizi* 37, p. 824; *Zhanguoce* 20:3, vol. 2:74.

[53] See Pines 2008.

[54] *Shi ji* 4, p. 116.

[55] Hsü Chin-hsiung 1979:No. 427.

[56] As pointed out by Childs-Johnson (2012), earlier publications mistake *fang* as enemies of the Shang (see e.g., Keightley 1979–1980, 27–28; Allan 1991:79). *Fang* as states or territories could be friendly or unfriendly. They were not strictly enemies as mistaken by past scholarship. Childs-Johnson analyzes various uses of *fang* in identifying the macro and micro meanings with regard to Shang cosmology and belief systems. Sun and Lin 2010:254, 258 present a statistic clearly revealing that relationships between the Shang and the *fang* could change yet could be cooperative. Hence, they suggest that *fang* was a generic term for political entities, rather than a specific term for alien or inimical ones. In one oracle inscription Shang itself is referred to as a *fang* (*Heji* No. 7,982).

at least once, Zhou provided a spouse to the Shang king.[57] An inscription from the mid-to-late twelfth century BCE mentions Zhou *hou* 侯 (Lord of Zhou). This title is understood as identifying leaders subordinate to the Shang king. In a few other inscriptions Zhou was referred to as a recipient of royal commands *ling* 令 (*ming* 命).[58] However, there are also a few inscriptions concerned with *fa* Zhou 伐周 ("striking Zhou") or *jian* Zhou 翦周 ("seizing Zhou"), showing that hostilities did exist between Shang and Zhou long before the ultimate clash of the mid-eleventh century BCE.[59] The example of Zhou may illustrate the generally unstable character of relationships between the Shang and other entities, where alliances may be supported by marital ties that could result in a hierarchical subordination of a foreign leader, who—or whose descendants—might revolt or disregard the earlier contract at any time.[60]

Archaeology corroborates that before the conquest of Shang, the Zhou relied on Shang ritual practices, including osteo-pyromancy (divination by applying fire to specially pretreated bones of animals). Although osteo-pyromancy per se was widespread in China already since the Late Neolithic period, the systematic ways of selecting and pre-treating the divinatory media as well as the divinatory record-making were likely inspired by Shang examples.[61] A cache of inscribed and uninscribed oracle bones, predominantly tortoise plastrons, was found in the ruins of a palace or temple in Fengchu 鳳雛 on the Zhou Plain. Another cache was discovered near a cemetery of the royal lineage in Zhougongmiao 周公廟 ca. 30 km to the west. Some inscriptions from Fengchu mention sacrifices to the Shang progenitor Cheng Tang 成湯 and other Shang royal ancestors.[62] According to transmitted texts of the Eastern Zhou period, only patrilineal descendants could perform ancestral sacrifices.[63] Therefore, scholars are puzzled as to who performed sacrifices to Shang ancestors in the Zhou heartland. Some authors argue that these inscriptions were produced by the Shang people.[64] However, certain Zhou oracle bone graphs and terms, the use of tiny characters, as well as the shapes of hollows chiseled to control the crack-making differ from those used by the Shang in Anyang. This suggests that the Fengchu corpus developed at the Zhou court during several decades before and after the conquest of Shang. Hence, no matter how this could have been legitimated, pre-conquest Zhou rulers venerated and sought support from Shang ancestral spirits and, probably, imitated royal rites.[65]

[57] *Heji* Nos. 22,264, 22,223.

[58] *Heji* Nos. 4,885, 8,854, 20,074, 32,885.

[59] *Heji* Nos. 22,294, 353.

[60] Cf. Keightley 1983:529–532.

[61] Such systematic pre-treatment methods included, among other things, the choice of the media, bovine scapulae or turtle plastrons; removing of some parts of the bones; then drilling and chiselling of equally sized hollows, arranged in rows; as well as chiselling of additional grooves as to control the production of cracks. For the spread and evolution of osteo-pyromantic techniques from the Neolithic to the Zhou period, see Flad 2008.

[62] Cao Wei 2002:No. H11:1, 82, 112.

[63] *Zuo zhuan* 309 (Xi: 5), 487 (Xi: 31), cf. Durrant et al. 2016:277–279 and 411.

[64] Wang Yuxin 1985–1987.

[65] For the summary of various opinions regarding the makers of the Fengchu oracle bones see Cao Wei 2002:8–9. See also Xu Xitai 1987:130–131; Chen Quanfang 2003:125–126; Shaughnessy 1985–1987a and b with further references.

In an inscription from Fengchu dating from the first half of the eleventh century BCE, the Zhou leader was referred to as Zhou *fang bo* 周方伯, "the *bo* of the Zhou *fang*." Specialists working on the Shang period regard *bo* as a title used by leaders of *fang*.[66] During the Western Zhou period, the Zhou used *bo* as a generic kinship-cum-political term identifying a lineage's elder.[67] Some scholars, therefore, suspect that it could be used in the same way during the Shang period too.[68] The inscriptional sample is too small to rule out either option. The same inscription records that "the king" (possibly referring to the Shang king) "*ce* (冊口)-ed" the Zhou leader.[69] *Ce* (冊口) possibly corresponds to *ce* 冊. In oracle inscriptions, *ce* was used in the senses "to pledge / to announce through prayer," "to stab / to chop off," and "to enclose, to confine."[70] In Shang bronze inscriptions, the graph *ce* often appears together with monograms of lineages in the frame of composite emblems. In Western Zhou bronze inscriptions, *ce ming* 冊命 "*ce*-ing of a command" represented a standard element in the ritual of appointments of officials.[71] In this context, *ce* is understood either as "writing down" or "reading aloud" a written command.[72] This use suggests that the *ce* character may designate wood or bamboo strips bound together and used for writing. It is plausible that the Fengchu inscription refers to a comparable ritual award of a written charge, possibly of military character.[73] A version that the Zhou inscription may refer to the slaughtering of the Zhou ruler *Ji* Li by the Shang king Wen Ding 文丁, mentioned in the Warring States period's text *Bamboo Annals* (*Zhushu jinian* 竹書紀年), seems less plausible.[74] Another hypothesis suggests that Zhou *fang bo* was a Zhou lineage ancestor who was the recipient of the *ce* sacrifice.[75] This seems problematic since *bo* was a lifetime title, whereas dead ancestors were normally referred to as *fu*, "Fathers." Although interpretations are controversial, the Fengchu find suggests that the relationship between Zhou and Shang during the first half of the eleventh century BCE was intense.

THE ZHOU CONQUEST OF SHANG

According to tradition, after Chang's death, his son Fa posthumously declared his father and two previous Zhou rulers "kings." Fa called himself *taizi* 太子 (crown prince), not daring to assume the royal title, and launched a campaign against the Shang, pretending

---

[66] Li Shaolian 1999; Jiang Yude (Campbell) 2011; Childs-Johnson forthcoming.
[67] Li Feng 2008b:114; Khayutina 2014:9–11; Khayutina forthcoming.
[68] Keightley 1979–1980:28.
[69] Cao Wei 2002:No. H12:84. For an overview of interpretations see Cao Wei 2002:8.
[70] Matsumaru and Takashima 1994:31:259–262, 585; Kern 2007:153–154 with further references.
[71] He Jingcheng 2013:40–45; Feng (Venture) 2014.
[72] Kern 2007:152–157.
[73] Wang Hui 1998:7. Feng (Venture) 2014 demonstrates a connection between *ce* and military tasks and points out that there might be a transformation of the *ce* ritual between the Shang and Zhou periods.
[74] Yu Xingwu 1979:172–174; cf. Wang Guowei 2008:235–256 (Wu Ding: 11).
[75] Cf. Xu Xitai 1987:60; Shaughnessy 1985–1987a:155–160.

to act upon King Wen's orders. Fa marched to Mengjin 孟津/盟津, the ford over the Yellow River, and took there an oath with his allies, but did not proceed to attack the Shang capital immediately.[76] The "Tai shi" 太誓/泰誓 (Great Oath), allegedly pronounced by Fa at Mengjin and accusing the Shang king of many crimes, circulated widely during the Eastern Zhou period. The extant text in the *Book of Documents* was forged during the Han dynasty.[77]

Next time, Fa gathered his allies at the Muye 牧野 field in the suburbs of the Shang capital Yin and led them in the final attack. The Oath at Mu in the *Book of Documents*, fully quoted in the "Basic Annals of Zhou," vividly portrays Fa holding a yellow battle-axe and raising a white banner while addressing Zhou functionaries and representatives of foreign peoples.[78] This commemorative text, probably written centuries after the respective events, praises the overwhelming military power and the broad recognition of the Zhou ruler.[79] The "Shi fu" 世俘 (The Great Capture) chapter of the *Yi Zhou shu* 逸周書 (Leftover Writings of the Zhou Dynasty) seems closer to the language and spirit of Western Zhou bronze inscriptions and is plausibly written earlier. It offers a chilling account about hostilities committed during the war against the Shang.[80] Various texts of the Warring States period mention the conquest of Shang, making clear that political and intellectual elites of that time treated the memory of the conquest as a shared ground of their common cultural and political history.[81] However, the authors of these texts were concerned "with interpretation of this history rather than its facts, its relevance rather than its substance, and the lessons it offered rather than its content."[82] What exactly provoked a war between Shang and Zhou, who else participated in it, and how the conquest was technically achieved cannot be adequately reconstructed based on late and biased transmitted texts, while contemporaneous descriptions are not available.

Following the conquest of Shang, Fa assumed the royal title *wang*. He was posthumously venerated as King Wu (Martial). After his death—only three years after the conquest—his brothers, installed as "overseers" (*jian* 監) over former Shang territories, allied with the Shang descendant Wu Geng 武庚 in an attempt to exempt eastern regions from Zhou control. Further polities or groups in the east and southeast arose against the Zhou at the same time.[83] The Zhou were able to suppress these upheavals. This can be understood as the "Second Conquest," which targeted not only Shang but also some other goals further to the east.[84] These events serve as the historical setting for several chapters in the *Shang shu*, including the "Da gao" 大誥 (Grand Proclamation), "Duo

---

[76] *Shi ji* 4, p. 120.

[77] *Shang shu*, pp. 318–321; cf. Kern 2017 for a translation of *shi* as "harangue."

[78] *Shang shu*, pp. 109–113; cf. *Shi ji* 4, p. 122–123.

[79] See Kern 2017.

[80] For analysis and translation see Shaughnessy 1997; cf. Grebnev 2018.

[81] See Khayutina 2019 with further references. For a collection of passages related to the conquest of Shang in transmitted texts, see Sawyer 2013.

[82] Knoblock 1990:4.

[83] *Shi ji* 4, pp. 126–132; 35, 1563–1565; cf. Shaughnessy 1999:310–311.

[84] Li Feng 2006:65.

Table 2 Essential facts about the "Western" Zhou rulers according to "Basic Annals of Zhou"[85]

Rulers/interregna	Personal names and other titles	Achievements and other events
Gu gong 古公 (Ancient Patriarch), later Tai wang 太王 (Great King)	Dan fu 亶父 (Father Dan)	Founded the Zhou settlement 周邑 in the Zhou Plain (Zhouyuan 周原).
Gong ji 公季 (Patriarch the Junior), Wang ji 王季 (Royal Junior)	Ji Li 季歷 (Li the Junior)	Son of Dan fu.
Wen wang 文 (Adorned King)	Chang 昌; Xi bo 西伯 (First-Born of the West)	Son of ji Li. Founded a residence in Feng 豐. Was recognized as one who received the Mandate of Heaven.
First conquest of Shang, followed by the adoption of the lifetime title wang ("King") by all Zhou rulers		
Wu 武 (Martial)	Fa 发; taizi (Crown Prince)	Son of Chang. Founded a residence in Hao 鎬. Conquered Shang, assumed the royal title and founded the Zhou dynasty. Created colonies Lu 魯, Yan 燕, Cai 蔡, Guan 管, and Qi 齊 with his brothers and a marital relative as princes. Enfeoffed Lu fu 祿父, a.k.a. Wu Geng 武庚, the son of the late Shang King, in Yin.
Cheng 成 (Accomplished)	Song 誦	Son of King Wu. Founded the eastern residence Luoyi 洛邑, a.k.a. Chengzhou 成周. Led wars against the Yi of Huai 淮夷 and the Yi of the East 東夷. Founded Jin 晉 and some other colonies, installed there his brothers.
Kang 康 (Prosperous)	Zhao 釗	Son of King Cheng. Ruled in peace. "Weapons were not used for longer than forty years."
Zhao 昭 (Illustrious)	Xia 瑕	Son of King Kang. Lost his army and died during a military campaign toward the south.
Mu 穆 (Solemn)	Man 滿	Son of King Zhao. Led a war against Quan Rong 犬戎. "Ruled fifty five years."
Gong 共 (Steady)	Yihu 緊扈	Son of King Mu.
Yi 懿 (Exemplary)	Su 譟	Son of King Gong.
Xiao 孝 (Pious)	Bi 辟	Youngest son of King Mu. Enfeoffed Feizi 非子 (d. 858 BCE) in Qin 秦.
Yi 夷 (Peaceful)	Xie 燮	Son of King Yi.
Li 厲 (Terrible) (d. 827 BCE; r.?–841/828 BCE)	Hu 胡	Son of King Yi. Ruled despotically. Was banned from Zhou in his "thirty-seventh year" (842 BCE). Spent the rest of his life in exile in Zhi 彘.
Gonghe 共和 Interregnum 841–828 BCE		Joint government of the Duke of Zhou 周公 and Duke of Shao 召公. King Li's son Jing 靜 was raised in the family of the Duke of Shao.

[85] Rulers' designations consist of their posthumous names and generic kinship and political terms. Generic terms have been italicized to distinguish them from proper nouns.

Rulers/interregna	Personal names and other titles	Achievements and other events
Xuan宣 (All-Embracing) (827–782 BCE)	Jing 靜	Son of King Li. Reconsolidated power. Led wars against northern and southern neighboring peoples. Enfeoffed his younger brother in Zheng 鄭. Ruled forty-six years.
You 幽 (Gloomy) (781–771 BCE)	Gongsheng 宮湦	Divorced his wife, Lady Jiang of Shen 申姜. Lord of Shen 申 rebelled with the help of Rong peoples. Quan Rong invaded western Zhou territories and killed King You in 771 BCE.

fang" 多方 (Many Regions), "Duo shi" 多士 (Many Officers), and the "Bi shi" 柴/費誓 (Oath [or Harangue] at Bi), all of which became integrated in the "Basic Annals of Zhou" with slight alterations.[86]

In the "Basic Annals of Zhou" Sima Qian compiled everything he could find about the consequent Zhou kings, including their personal names and posthumous titles, and accounts about their achievements and failures (see Table 2). Since the chapters of *Book of Documents* were mostly related to earlier reigns, Sima used the *Conversations of the States* as his main source about later reigns starting from King Mu until King You (781–771 BCE). The *Lai pan* 逨盤 inscription, commissioned during the reign of King Xuan (827–782 BCE), excavated in 2003 in Licun in Meixian county, Shaanxi, corroborates Sima's list of 11 Zhou kings from King Wen to King Li.[87] Other bronze inscriptions substantially complement but also often shed different light on the early Zhou history, as represented by Sima Qian.

THE "WESTERN" ZHOU PERIOD

Although King Cheng founded the eastern royal residence Luoyi (Settlement on the Luo River), referred to in inscriptions as Chengzhou (Accomplished Zhou) in present-day Henan province as suitable to "rule the world," Zhou kings stayed there only occasionally. Until the end of King You's reign, they spent most of their time moving between their western royal residences Zhou (Zhou-under-Qi) and Zongzhou 宗周 (possibly corresponding to Feng-Hao) in Shaanxi (see Figure 2). In 771 BCE Quan Rong (Hound-Rong), a group of northern neighboring peoples, invaded the western metropolitan areas and killed King You. The Zhou dynasty was restored with King You's son Yijiu 宜 臼 as King Ping 平 (770–720 BCE) in Luoyi, called later Luoyang 洛陽 (North of Luo River). Today, the relocation of the royal residence to the east is usually regarded as the

---

[86] Cf. *Shang shu*, p. 300 ("Shu xu" 書序); cf. Khayutina 2017.

[87] Chong and Chen 2006:No.757. For the full translation see *A Source Book*, pp. 230–238; cf. Sena 2005:81–86.

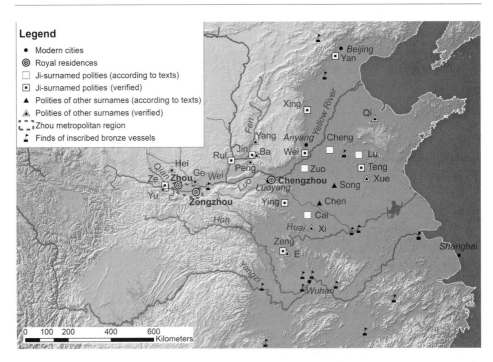

FIGURE 2   Map of Early Chinese polities of the Western Zhou period (ca. 900 BCE).

watershed between the "Western" and "Eastern" Zhou periods, the former characterized by the strong royal power and the latter by the establishment of the "multi-state system," at which time the Zhou kings played the role of just a symbolic authority.[88] Some authors even go so far as to distinguish between the Western and Eastern Zhou "dynasties." However, the murder of King You did not cause an interruption of the Zhou dynasty, and the early Chinese historiography regarded it as a crisis but not as the essential "turning point." In pre-Qin and Han thought, the nearly eight-hundred-years-long Zhou dynasty was perceived as a continuity, marked by a gradual but not abrupt weakening of the royal power. It should be therefore kept in mind that the western-eastern dichotomy is a modern, but not a traditional concept. The present chapter follows the current scholarly convention and uses the term "Western Zhou" yet with reservations.

The date of the conquest and the chronology of early Zhou reigns

The date of the conquest of Shang and the beginning of the Zhou royal dynasty represents one of the big puzzles of early Chinese history. In absence of a continuous annual

---

[88] Creel 1970; Hsü and Linduff 1988; Shaughnessy 1999; Li Feng 2006, 2008a, 2013. For the term "multi-state system" see Walker 1953.

calendar, the Zhou court recounted years beginning after the ascension of a new king. The official annals of the Western Zhou kings, if they ever existed, did not survive. Sima Qian was able to reconstruct the Zhou chronology only staring from 841 BCE, the year of King Li's exile. Any dates prior to 841 cannot be easily traced.

Chapters of the *Book of Documents* related to the conquest do not record years but contain other calendric information, possibly relevant for commemorative rituals. They identify days according to the sexagesimal counting system of Heavenly Stems and Earthly Branches (*tian gan di zhi* 天干地支, abbreviated as *gan zhi* 地支). According to the "Mu shi," the battle at Muye happened on the day *jia-zi* 甲子. The *jia-zi* date is corroborated by the inscription on the bronze ritual vessel *Li gui* 利簋 excavated in 1976.[89] The lost "Wu cheng" 武成 chapter of the *Book of Documents*, quoted in the *Han shu* 漢書 (History of the [Western] Han Dynasty), stated that "King Wu attacked Shang King Zhou on *jiazi*, the fifth day after *jisiba* 既死霸 in the second month."[90] Terms *chuji* 初吉 (first auspiciousness), *jishengba* 既生霸 (after the new-born brightness), *jiwang* 即望 (after the fullness), and *jisiba* 既死霸 (after the dying brightness) often appear in Western Zhou bronze inscriptions and specify the days' positions within the lunar month. It has been debated whether these "lunar terms" refer to fixed days, to short intervals including several days, to longer intervals of different length, or to four equal quarters of the month. One passage in the *Guo yu* identifies the positions of Jupiter and other celestial bodies at the time of the conquest. If this information is true, knowing the sidereal period of Jupiter (11 years and ca. 314 days) and understanding the meaning of the four lunar terms, it is theoretically possible to identify all years in which day *jiazi* may be found in the *jisiba* part of the second month. Different choices of sources to rely on, and conflicting opinions about the Zhou calendar in general and about the meaning of the four "lunar terms" in particular, resulted in 22 different dates of the conquest ranging from 1122 to 1025 BCE.[91]

The traditionally accepted date 1122 BCE was deduced by the calendar specialist and astronomer Liu Xin 劉歆 (46 BCE–23 CE). He calculated it, based on the *Guo yu*, while erroneously estimating Jupiter's cycle to 11 years and 336 days and understanding *siba* and *shengba* as the days of new moon and full moon respectively. Liu Xin's hypothesis was seldom questioned before the twentieth century and is often seen in older Western publications (see Table 3). Today it is unanimously regarded as invalid.[92]

Two other influential hypotheses, dating the conquest back to either 1050 or 1027 BCE, derive from one manuscript, discovered in the third century CE in the tomb of King Xiang'ai 襄哀 of Wei 魏 (r. 318–296 BCE). Written on bamboo strips, it became known as the *Bamboo Annals* (*Zhushu jinian*). It includes a chronologically arranged collection of excerpts from the official annals of the Jin 晉 (second part of eleventh century to 403 BCE) and Wei 魏 (403–221 BCE) states, starting from 770 BCE up to the late fourth century BCE. Another part contains similarly arranged records about ascensions and deaths

[89] *Jicheng* No. 4,131; for translation see *A Source Book*, pp. 10–12.
[90] *Han shu* 21, p. 1,615.
[91] Zhu and Zhang 1998:432.
[92] Cf. Pankenier 1981-1982:9-13; Shaughnessy 1991:219; Xia Shang Zhou 2000:40.

Table 3 Variants of Zhou king chronology in transmitted sources and scholarly reconstructions

Periods	Kings	Chronologies				
		1	2	3	4	5
		Traditional (after Liu Xin, Han dynasty)	*"Modern Text" Bamboo Annals,* Eastern Zhou	Chen Mengjia, 1955	Edward Shaughnessy, 1991	Xia Shang Zhou Periodization, 2000
Early	Wu 武	1122–1116	1050–1045	1027–1025	1049/1045–1043	1046–1043
	Cheng 成	1115–1079	1044–1008	1024–1005	1042/1035–1006	1042–1021
	Kang 康	1078–1053	1007–982	1004–967	1005/1003–978	1020–996
	Zhao 昭	1052–1002	981–963	966–948	977/975–957	995–977
Middle	Mu 穆	1001–947	962–908	947–928	956–918	976–922
	Gong 共	946–935	907–896	927–908	917/915–900	922–900
	Yih 懿	934–910	895–871	907–898	899/897–873	
	Xiao 孝	909–895	870–862	897–888	872–866	899–878
	Yi 夷	894–879	861–854	887–858	865–858	
Late	Li 厲	878–842	853–842	857–842	857–842	877–841
	Gonghe 共和	841–828	841–828	841–828	841–828	841–828
	Xuan 宣	827–782	827–782	827/825–782	827/825–782	827–782
	You 幽	781–771	781–771	781–771	781–771	781–771
Total length		352	280	257	275	276

of kings, wars, other state affairs, and astronomical and atmospheric phenomena starting from the time of the legendary Yellow Emperor until 771 BCE. Most entries can be traced back to the *Book of Documents*, the *Book of Odes*, and some other Eastern Zhou texts. The *Bamboo Annals* dates the conquest of Shang to 1050 BCE and identifies the lengths of all kings who ruled before 841 BCE. The imperial court of the Jin 晉 dynasty (265–420) appointed a commission of scholars in order to arrange and to transcribe the manuscript. Striving to determine the absolute chronology of the Chinese past, the editors introduced *gan zhi* symbols in order to numerate years, as this became usual starting from the Eastern Han dynasty (25–220 CE) and, possibly, manipulated some other data. The original and the first copies of the third century BCE do not survive. The earliest extant copy dates from ca. 1570.[93] Since the eighteenth century, the authenticity of

[93] Shaughnessy 2006:136, 255, 155.

this *"Modern Text" Bamboo Annals* (*Jin ben Zhushu jinian* 今本竹書紀年) edition was put in question. Scholars began to reconstruct the *"Old Text" Bamboo Annals* (*Gu ben Zhushu jinian* 古本竹書紀年) by collecting early quotations from the original in other texts. One such quotation brought about the "short chronology" of the Western Zhou period starting with 1027 BCE. This date from the "genuine" *Bamboo Annals* was preferred by Chen Mengjia and some other scholars and is accepted in many Western publications prior to 1990s.[94] However, it derives from an incomplete quotation of the same passage that appears in the *"Modern Text"* version, resulting in 1050 BCE as the conquest's date. Modern astronomy and computing technology allowed scholars to verify that the dates of the major celestial phenomena of the Shang and Western Zhou periods recorded in the *"Modern Text" Bamboo Annals* differed from the true ones by 4–12 years. Such considerably small errors plausibly resulted while the authors of this compilation, working during the Eastern Zhou period, attempted to reconstruct the true dates based on the contemporary astronomical knowledge. Thus, many authors regard the *"Modern Text" Bamboo Annals* as an authentic Eastern Zhou text and assume that its date of the conquest differed from the true one by only a few years.[95]

New plausible dates of the conquest of Shang have been proposed during the 1980s. Combining the information of Sima Qian's *Historical Records, Bamboo Annals*, and other transmitted texts with astronomical data, and accepting Wang Guowei's (1877–1927) hypothesis that the four previously mentioned "lunar terms" referred to the four quarters of the lunar month, David Nivison (1923–2014) suggested January 16, 1045 BCE as the conquest's date.[96] This date has been accepted by several leading Western scholars of the Western Zhou period.[97] Alternatively, David Pankenier has accepted the assumption, currently shared by most Chinese scholars, that only three of the four "lunar terms" refer to the appearance of the moon, whereby *jishengba* and *jisiba* designate the first and the second halves of the month, and the meaning of *jiwang* is somewhat broader, referring to "full moon." The term *chuji* to a certain extent overlaps with *jishengba* and, possibly, refers to the first auspicious heavenly stem (*gan*) of the month.[98] Based on the astronomical data in the *Bamboo Annals* and in the *Guo yu*, Pankenier has dated the conquest to January 20, 1046 BCE.[99] During 1996–2000, the "Xia-Shang-Zhou Periodization Process" chaired by Li Xueqin (1933–2019) brought together historians, bronze inscription specialists, astronomers, and archaeologists who, following the same lines of reasoning, but apparently unaware of Pankenier's publication, have also dated

---

[94] Chen Mengjia 1955; Hsu and Linduff 1988:390.

[95] Cf. Nivison 1983; Pankenier 1981–1982; 1992b, c; Shaughnessy 1986, 1991:257 with further references.

[96] Nivison 1983:517. Shortly afterwards, Nivison repudiated his 1045 date in favor of 1040. See Nivison 1982.

[97] Shaughnessy 1999; Li Feng 2006, 2008a.

[98] Pankenier 1981–1982:25; Xu Fengxian 2010–2011:192–198. For the criticism of the "four quarters" theory see Pankenier 1992a.

[99] Pankenier 1981–1982:16.

the conquest to January 20, 1046 BCE.[100] This date is currently accepted as standard in most Chinese publications and is gradually gaining recognition in the West.

The chronology of individual reigns represents an even more complex puzzle. During the 1930s, scholars began to systematically use the data of bronze inscriptions in order to countercheck the traditional chronology and to reconstruct the true one. Groups of inscriptions belonging to one reign have been identified based on names of persons or references to particular events.[101] The methodology for the periodization of bronze vessels judging by their shapes, decorations, and inscriptions paleography gradually progressed.[102] New excavations brought to light more and more inscriptions with "full dates," including a *ganzhi* designation of a day, a "lunar term," a month, and a year number. Combining all available data, it is now theoretically possible to identify whether the dates of the sets of such "fully dated" inscriptions are compatible with the reconstructed lunisolar calendar of the eleventh to eighth centuries BCE[103] and to verify the assumptions about individual reign lengths. Again, different hypotheses about the "lunar terms" result in conflicting chronologies. Accepting Wang Guowei's "four quarters theory," Edward Shaughnessy has accommodated 55 "fully dated" inscriptions for his chronology of Western Zhou reigns reconstructed based on the *"Modern Text" Bamboo Annals*.[104] The participants of the Xia-Shang-Zhou Periodization Team, disregarding the *Modern* and using only the data from the *"Old Text" Bamboo Annals*, while understanding *jishengba* and *jisiba* as two halves of the month, *jiwang* as the days around the full moon, and *chuji* as the first auspicious stem, have accommodated in their chronology 66 fully dated events of the Western Zhou period, including three in the *Book of Documents* and 63 bronze inscriptions.[105] However, only few inscriptions with "full dates" are available prior to the late 10th c. BCE, as the royal year-count did not become yet a standard reference for recording events.[106] The official Xia-Shang-Zhou chronology should still be regarded as provisional and the problem of the Zhou reigns' dates as not yet fully resolved.[107]

WESTERN ZHOU POLITICAL DOCTRINE AND THE POLITICAL SYSTEM

The *Book of Documents* and the *Book of Odes*, legitimating the conquest of Shang, various decisions of the Zhou Kings, or the rule of the Zhou dynasty in general, repeatedly

---

[100] Xia Shang Zhou 2000:47; Liu Ciyuan 2000:134.
[101] Guo Moruo 1932, 2002; Wu Qichang 1936; Shirakawa 1966–1983; Tang Lan 1986.
[102] Zhang Guangzhi 1973; Guo Baojun 1981; Rong Geng 1984; Ma Chengyuan 1988; Li Xueqin 1990; Rawson 1990; Wang Shimin 1999; Peng Yushang 2003, Zhang Maorong 2008; Zhu Fenghan 2009.
[103] For reconstructions cf. Dong Zuobin 1960; Zhang Peiyu 1987.
[104] Shaughnessy 1991:284–285.
[105] Xia Shang Zhou 2000.
[106] See Khayutina 2009.
[107] See Shaughnessy 2009, 2016.

refer to the "Mandate of Heaven" (*tian ming* 天命). According to the doctrine of the "Mandate," Heaven, which gradually and ultimately was worshipped by the Zhou as the supreme political deity, dismissed the Shang dynasty because of its moral degradation and transferred power to the virtuous King Wen.[108] Consequent Zhou kings inherited the Mandate but were aware of the risk that it can be terminated should they behave improperly.[109] The "Bei shan" 北山 (Northern Mounts) ode of the *Minor Elegantiae* (Xiao ya 小雅) section of the *Book of Odes* states: "Under the vast Heaven there is no land that is not the king's, within the borders of these lands there is no one who is not the king's servant" (溥天之下，莫非王土，率土之濱，莫非王臣).[110] Certainly a product of the Eastern Zhou period, this text is often quoted as evidence of universal political and land ownership claims of the Zhou kings from the beginning of the dynasty.

The genuine official political doctrine of the royal court during this epoch is manifested in speeches of kings, often quoted in Western Zhou bronze inscriptions. They show that already from early on, the Zhou royal house claimed that King Wen received the Great Command (*da ling* 大令) from Heaven.[111] Starting either from King Kang or King Zhao, reigning kings were venerated as Sons of Heaven.[112] One bronze inscription states:

> The King approvingly said: Yu! Illustrious King Wen received Heaven's blessings [and] the great Mandate. When King Wu succeeded King Wen, he created the *bang*, eliminated his foes, broadly possessed the Four Quarters, [and] greatly governed the people *min*...(Figure 3).[113]
>
> 王若曰:「盂，丕顯文王受天有(佑)大令，在武王嗣文作邦,闢厥慝，匍有四方，畯正厥民。」<...>

Bang 邦 was a Zhou political concept designating a polity with hereditary rulers.[114] The term *min* 民, referring to common people in contrast to elite in more modern contexts, more likely refers to members of external lineages or polities.[115] It should be noted that the kings were aware of the limits of their power and did not treat the whole

---

[108] For Heaven as a political deity see Pines 2009:17.

[109] Creel 1970:81–100. For the 1059 BCE conjunction of the five (visible) planets as the manifestation of heaven's mandate in 1059 BCE, see Pankenier 1995. Cf. also Allan 2007.

[110] *Mao shi* No. 205, cf. Legge 1991b:360–362; Waley and Allen 1996:189–190.

[111] The earliest inscription mentioning the Great Mandate is the He *zun* 何尊, *Jicheng* No. 6014, translated in *A Source Book*, pp. 16–18. Many scholars date it to the reign of King Cheng, although King Kang's or King Zhao's dates are also possible. See Khayutina 2019:165.

[112] King Kang's dates are based on the inscription on the *Da Yu ding* 大盂鼎 bronze cauldron, *Jicheng* No. 2837; for translations, see Dobson 1962:221–226; *A Source Book*, pp. 30–35. This vessel, however, may date considerably later (cf. Khayutina 2016:129n105; Khayutina 2019:165). Next oldest inscriptions operating with the title Son of Heaven date from the reign of King Zhao.

[113] *Da Yu ding* 大盂鼎, *Jicheng* No. 2837.

[114] *Bang* is often translated "state" or even "nation," which leads to anachronistic interpretations of Zhou political organization. It is not clear whether *bang* is used in the singular or in the plural in this inscription, referring either to the Zhou *bang* or to all the *bang* units created after the conquest of Shang. Cf. Khayutina forthcoming.

[115] Crone 2014.

FIGURE 3 Rubbing of the inscription on the *Da Yu ding* bronze cauldron mentioning the great Mandate issued to the first Zhou kings. After *Jicheng* No. 2837.

population of the "Four Quarters" as their "servants." Inscriptions witness grants of lands, situated in the Zhou metropolitan area in Shaanxi or located elsewhere and previously conquered by kings, to their relatives or other subordinates.[116] But there are no indications that the kings claimed ownership of all lands. However, they claimed to "protect" (*bao* 保) or to "stabilize" (*dian* 奠) "ten thousand *bang*" (*wan bang* 萬邦) in the "Four Regions" (*si yu* 四或/域).[117]

At the beginning of the dynasty, Zhou kings created colonies in conquered areas. In most of them they established their brothers, sons, or nephews as hereditary rulers, referred to collectively as "All the Lords" (*zhuhou* 諸侯). The book *Xunzi* 荀子, written

[116] For translations and a study see Lau 1999.
[117] Cf. Li *zun* 盉尊, *Jicheng* No. 6,013; Lai *pan*, translated in *A Source Book*, 77–79.

during the third century BCE, states that among 71 principalities known to its author, 53 were conferred on princes with the surname Ji.[118] Some important colonies, including Qi in present-day Shandong province, were entrusted to Jiang-surnamed allies, possibly because of the marital ties between Ji and Jiang, previously mentioned. Sites of some colonies of the Western Zhou period including Jin, Yan, Ying, Wei, and Qi have been identified and investigated archaeologically.[119] In the space between and around principalities founded by the Zhou colonists, other polities existed. Some of them were in place already during Shang time, others emerged later. Sites of Yu, Peng, and Ba polities not mentioned in early Chinese literature and possibly founded by foreign peoples have been found during recent decades.[120] New finds indicate that political relationships in the Western Zhou world were very complex.

For much of the second half of the twentieth century, the Western Zhou political system was interpreted as "feudal." Historians supposed that the *zhuhou* accepted the terms of subordination and entered a personal contract with the king in the course of "investiture ceremonies," while this contract had to be renewed in each generation.[121] Inscriptions confirm that Zhou kings installed rulers of some principalities, but this evidence is limited to the Early Western Zhou period and only concerns Ji-surnamed princes.[122] The ceremonies of *ce ming* (writing down or reading aloud the mandate) reflected in bronze inscriptions of the Middle and Late Western Zhou periods and regarded by earlier scholars as feudal "investitures" have been correctly recognized as appointments of officials in the Zhou metropolitan areas.[123] Contractual elements may be distinguished in the relationship between the royal house and the Ying 嬴–surnamed Qin 秦 principality.[124] But in general, there was no "feudal-vassal institution" during the Western Zhou, and thus the term "feudal" is unsuitable for the Chinese context.[125]

Chinese scholars traditionally supposed that the authority of the king toward the principalities ruled by Ji-surnamed lineages was legitimated by the so-called *zong fa* 宗法 ("lineage order"). In a "conical" lineage structure, branches founded by younger relatives were hierarchically subordinated to the trunk lineage, in which the direct descent line from the eldest ancestors was secured by the rule of primogeniture. The head of the trunk lineage alone was entitled to perform sacrifices to the eldest ancestors, representing the whole group before them and thus enjoying high ritual authority.[126] Inscriptions

[118] *Xunzi* 8, p. 144.

[119] See Rawson 1999:403–413; Li Feng 2006:300–342; Falkenhausen 2006.

[120] Cf. Zhang and Yin 2004:78–118; Lu and Hu 1988; Shanxi et al. 2006; Shanxi 2011; for studies, see Rawson 1999:397–401, 419–423; Sun Yan 2013; Khayutina 2016.

[121] Qi Sihe 1947; Creel 1970:317–387; Hsü and Linduff 1988:147–185; Vasil'ev 1995:257–267.

[122] For examples, see Mei *situ* Yi *gui* 沫司徒疑簋, *Jicheng* No. 4,059; Yi *hou* Ze/Yu *gui* 宜侯夨簋, *Jicheng*, No. 4,320, translated in *A Source Book*, pp. 23–27; Mai *zun* 麥尊, *Jicheng* No. 6,015, translated in *A Source Book*, pp. 42–44; see Khayutina 2014:52–53.

[123] Kane 1982–1983:14–28.

[124] Cf. *Shi ji* 5 ("Qin Benji" 秦本紀), pp. 177–179.

[125] Cook 1997:282–290; Li Feng 2003:122–124.

[126] Cf. Hsü and Linduff 1988:163–171; Qiang Zongfan 1989; Qian Hang 1991:1–2; Falkenhausen 2006:66; Gassmann 2006:103.

commissioned by Ji-surnamed *zhuhou* and their close associates commemorate that they executed commands and performed services for the kings or traveled over long distances in order to meet the kings personally.[127] Although inscriptions commissioned by rulers of other surnames have also been found, they do not contain comparable commemorations. Thus, the relationships between Zhou kings and patrilineally related principalities were closer than those with principalities ruled by lineages of other surnames. Acknowledging kinship, ancestral cult, and *zong fa* as organizing principles in the Zhou society, Li Feng has recently suggested understanding the Western Zhou political organization as a "delegatory kin-ordered settlement state."[128] Whereas kinship was plausibly a major organizing principle in the Zhou world, assessing the Western Zhou political organization as a "state" appears problematic in absence of an integrated administrative and economic structure that bound principalities to the Zhou royal house,. The idea of a universal polity, comparable to the empire of the later periods, had not yet fully developed during the Western Zhou period. It seems therefore more suitable, following the suggestion of Roderick Campbell pertaining to Shang, to define this conglomeration as a kin-ordered political "network."[129]

FACTORS OF INTEGRATION IN THE ZHOU POLITICAL SYSTEM

The military strength of the Zhou kings was based on their ability to control 14 or more *shi* 師 units located in the metropolitan areas in Shaanxi and Henan provinces and engaging in military campaigns in various other places. The *shi* are sometimes seen as royal "standing armies," but armies composed of recruits could hardly exist without a regular taxation system. The same term *shi* also referred to individuals. Since the latter are often mentioned in a military context, they are also seen as "captains" or "marshals," although *shi* can be translated more generally as "master."[130] Some inscriptions mention "*shi* lineages" (*shi shi* 師氏), suggesting that the *shi* represented local lineages entrusted by the king with defensive or offensive tasks.[131] Indeed, most *shi* mentioned in inscriptions are identifiable as members of a group of prominent Ji-surnamed lineages residing in the Wei River Valley.[132]

---

[127] See Khayutina 2010:11-28.
[128] Li Feng 2008:294–298.
[129] See Campbell 2009; Campbell 2018:139 and 174–177.
[130] Cook 1995; Li Feng 2008a:122, 232; Khayutina 2016:109.
[131] In bronze inscriptions, the term *shi* 氏 usually appears together with lineage names or surnames of persons, males or females alike. It points at these persons' position as a member of a certain lineage and can be translated either as "sir" or "lady." The designation *shi shi* 師氏 is usually applied not to individuals but to a group of people. The "sirs-captains" are often mentioned together with (and distinguished from) *you si* 有司, "administrators" or "managers."
[132] Khayutina 2018. A detailed analysis of inscriptions pertaining to the *shi* units will be given in Khayutina forthcoming.

Some scholars suppose that the *shi* were either indispensable for protecting principalities from external threats or ready to suppress any disobedience of the network's members. At the same time, inscriptions show that Zhou principalities recruited their own warriors, supported the king in military campaigns, or led such campaigns on their own. The military capacities of the royal *shi* and of principalities cannot be measured against each other due to the lack of evidence. It is likely that principalities stayed within the Zhou political network not because of the fear of punishment but rather because of the benefits of cooperation. Successes of commanders from metropolitan Zhou, fighting upon the king's orders against some foreign peoples' groups, sometimes motivated leaders of other groups to declare their loyalty and to join the Zhou network.[133]

Western Zhou inscriptions mostly attest to Zhou kings' role not as military leaders, but as hosts of receptions. The kings performed various sacrificial ceremonies, banquets, hunts and archery competitions. Even more inscriptions commemorate individual audiences held in royal palaces and temples, as well as in a variety of other locations. Probably, the kings spend a great amount of time while regularly touring around the region between their western and eastern residences Zhou, Zongzhou and Luoyi and meeting people.[134] During royal receptions, kings usually distributed gifts. Gift-giving, especially donations of prestige objects by the Zhou king, represented a significant factor of integration and regulation in Western Zhou society and politics. Inscriptions witness that within the Zhou metropolitan area, royal gifts, especially items of ceremonial gear and decorations for chariots, were used for recruiting people into service and rewarding them for loyalty.[135] Rulers of allied polities also commemorated royal gifts, especially bows and arrows, chariots and alcoholic beverages.[136] Prestige gifts further facilitated acquisition of new allies among foreign peoples' groups.[137]

Both inscriptions and archaeological evidence point to the fact that marital alliances represented a substantial form of cooperation in the Western Zhou world.[138] Most ritual bronzes commissioned by Zhou kings and by rulers of principalities of various surnames were made in connection with marriages. By taking wives from distant places, once defined as parts of the Zhou political network through conquest and colonization, Zhou kings inhibited the drifting away of non-Ji-surnamed principalities. Marrying women from polities founded by foreign groups, the kings secured peace on the cultural periphery. Marital alliances were also concluded without mediation of the king between the ruling lineages of individual Zhou principalities, and between the latter and various non-Zhou units. The king-centered and decentralized marital networks complemented each other over a long period of time and represented an important factor in maintain-

[133] Cf. Kryukov 1967:73–74; Creel 1970:305–310; Vasil'ev 1995:264; Shaughnessy 1999:329; Li Feng 2003:136–139; Li Feng 2006:98–99; Lau 1999:161; Li Feng 2008a:264–268; Khayutina 2014:93.

[134] See Khayutina 2010.

[135] Kryukov 1997; Cook 1997.

[136] Kryukov 1997:252–258.

[137] Khayutina 2014:93-94, 2016:113.

[138] See Hsu and Linduff 1988:159; Ch'en Chao-jung 2004; Falkenhausen 2006:74–126.

ing integration and stability.[139] Not by chance, the dynastic crisis of 771 BCE was caused by King You's violation of marital norms. Namely, he dismissed his Jiang-surnamed spouse from Shen in favor of a Si-surnamed concubine from Bao and replaced the heir apparent.[140] The succession conflict was ended by the joint efforts of the rulers of major Ji-surnamed principalities, Jin, Lu, and Zheng, who supported King You's father-in-law, the Jiang-surnamed ruler of Shen, who was the grandfather of the legitimate heir.[141] Together they enthroned King Ping in Luoyang and the falling apart of the Zhou political network was prevented.

Sima Qian's "Basic Annals of Zhou," written some 150 years after the end of the Zhou dynasty, represents eight hundred years after the time of the charismatic king-founders Wen and Wu as a history of progressing decay. This pessimistic view, still dominating the understanding of the Zhou history,[142] was to some extent a product of the Zhou official memory policy.[143] The veneration of the "Former Kings" (xian wang 先王), propagated orally through royal speeches or in written form through commemorative odes and documents, helped to keep together the network of Ji-surnamed lineages, the most important of whom descended from Kings Wen and Wu.[144] At the same time, it lifted the dynasty's founders to an unattainable height. In their shadow, any posterior king appeared as a dwarf even if he had merits, not to speak if he made errors. Contrary to this view, many facts signal that during circa 275 years since the beginning of the dynasty, Zhou kings achieved significant successes in the institutionalization of statecraft and territorial consolidation of the metropolitan areas.[145] The crisis of 771 BCE prevented extending the royal control over the whole network of principalities. Nevertheless, the royal house was successful in the propaganda of its own role as the central stabilizing element and the paramount ritual authority in the Zhou world, which permitted it to stay in place during another half millennium.

TRANSMITTED TEXTS AND TRANSLATIONS

Baihutong 白虎通, after Chen Li 陳立, ed. 1994. *The Comprehensive Discussions in the White Tiger Hall with Explanations and Verifications* 白虎通疏證. Beijing: Zhonghua shuju.

Chavannes, Édouard 1895. *Les mémoires historiques de Se-ma-Ts'ien. Tome premier.* Paris: E. Leroux.

[139] See Khayutina 2014.
[140] *Shi ji* 4, p. 149; Nienhauser et al. 1994:73–74.
[141] Wang Guowei 2008:262–283; Li Xueqin 2011.
[142] Cf. Li Feng 2006.
[143] For Western Zhou memory culture, see Wang Ming-ke 1999; Kern 2009; Khayutina 2019. For an example of Eastern Zhou misinterpretations of Western Zhou political institutions see Li Feng 2008b.
[144] *Chunqiu Zuo zhuan zhu* pp. 307 (Xi: 5), 421 (Xi: 24), 1,160 (Xiang: 29); *Shiji* 31, p. 1,446 ("Wu tai bo shijia" 吳太伯世家), 34, p. 1549 ("Yan Shao gong shijia" 燕召公世家), 35, p. 1,563 ("Guan Cai shijia" 管蔡世家); 44, p. 1,835–1864 ("Wei shijia" 魏世家).
[145] Li Feng 2004, 2008a; Khayutina 2009a, 2010.

Durrant, S. W., Wai-yee Li, and D. Schaberg 2016, trans. *Zuo tradition = Zuozhuan* 左傳: *Commentary on the "Spring and Autumn Annals,"* 3 vols. Seattle: University of Washington Press.

Han shu 漢書 1962. Beijing: Zhonghua shuju.

Hanfeizi 韓非子, Wang Xianshen 王先慎, ed. 1998. *Hanfeizi with Collected Explanations* 韓非子集解. Beijing: Zhonghua shuju.

Karlgren, Bernhard 1950. *The Book of Documents.* Stockholm: Museum of Far Eastern Antiquities.

Karlgren, Bernhard 1974. *The Book of Odes.* Stockholm: Museum of Far Eastern Antiquities.

Legge, J., trans. 1991a [1865]. *The Chinese Classics,* vol. 3: *The Shoo King.* Taipei: SMC.

Legge, J., trans. 1991b [1871]. *The Chinese Classics,* vol. 4: *The She King.* Taipei: SMC.

Nienhauser, William H., et al. 1994. *The Grand Scribe's Records,* vol. 1: *The Basic Annals of Pre-Han China by Ssu-ma Ch'ien.* Bloomington: Indiana University Press.

Shi ji 史記 1959. Beijing: Zhonghua shuju.

Shang shu 尚書, Qu Wanli 屈萬里 1983. *Shang shu with Collected Annotations* 尚書集釋. Taibei: Lianjing.

Shi jing 詩經, Qu Wanli 屈萬里 1983. *Shi jing with Interpretations and Annotations* 詩經詮釋. Taibei: Lianjing.

Waley, Arthur, and Joseph R. Allen, trans. 1996. *The Book of Songs: The Ancient Chinese Classic of Poetry.* New York: Grove Press.

Wang, Guowei 王國維 2008. "Modern Text Zhushu jinian with Explanations and Verifications "今本竹書紀年疏證. In *Ancient Text Zhushu jinian with Collected Verifications* 古本竹書紀年輯證, 2nd ed. Edited by Fang Shiming 方詩銘 and Wang Xiuling 王修齡, 188–290. Shanghai: Shanghai guji chubanshe.

Watson, Burton 1961. *Records of the Grand Historian of China: The Shih chi of Ssu-ma Ch'ien.* New York: Columbia University Press.

Xunzi 荀子, Li Tiaosheng 李滌生 1981. *Xunzi with Collected Annotations* 荀子集釋. Taibei: Taiwan xuesheng shuju.

Zhanguoce 戰國策. Gao You 高誘, comm. 1937. *Zhanguoce* 戰國策, 3 vols. Shanghai: Shangwu yinshuaguan.

Zhuangzi 裝子. Guo Qingfan 郭慶藩 1961. *Zhuangzi with Collected Explanations* 裝子集釋. Beijing: Zhonghua shuju.

Zuo zhuan 左傳. Yang Bojun 楊伯峻 1981. *Annotated Chunqiu Zuo zhuan* 春秋左傳注. Beijing: Zhonghua shuju.

INSCRIPTION PUBLICATIONS AND INSCRIPTION TRANSLATIONS

Academia Sinica. "Digital Archives of Bronze Images and Inscriptions 殷周金文及青銅器資料庫." http://www.ihp.sinica.edu.tw/~bronze/, last accessed on 01.02.2020.

A Source Book. Cook, Constance A., and Paul R. Goldin, eds. 2016. *A Source Book of Ancient Chinese Bronze Inscriptions.* Early China Monograph Series 7. Berkeley: Society for the Study of Early China.

Cao, Wei 曹瑋 2002. *Oracle Bone Inscriptions from Zhouyuan* 周原甲骨文. Beijing: Shijie tushu.

Ch'en, Chao-jung 陳昭容, and Chong, Po-sheng 鍾柏生, eds. "Lexicon of Pre-Qin Oracle, Bronze Inscriptions and Bamboo Slips 先秦甲骨金文簡牘詞彙資料庫." http://inscription.asdc.sinica.edu.tw/c_index.php, last visited on 01.02.2020.

Ch'ong, Po-sheng 鍾柏生, and Ch'en, Chao-jung 陈照容 2006. *A Compilation of Inscriptions and Images of Newly Collected Bronze Vessels from Shang and Zhou Periods* 新收殷周青銅器銘文暨器影彙編, 3 vols. Taipei: Yiwen.

Chen, Quanfang 陳全方 2003. *Western Zhou Turtle Plastrons Inscriptions with Explanations* 西周甲文注. Shanghai: Xuelin.

Chinese Ancient Texts Database (CHANT). The Chinese University of Hong Kong. http://www.chant.org, last accessed on 01.02.2020.

Heji 合集 Zhongguo shehui kexueyuan lishi yanjiusuo 中國社會科學院歷史研究所, ed. 1978–1982. *A Combined Compendium of Oracle Bone Inscriptions* 甲骨文合集, 13 vols. Beijing: Zhonghua shuju.

Hsü, Chin-hsiung 許進雄 1979. *Oracle Bones from the White and Other Collections* 古文物懷特氏等收藏甲骨文集. Toronto: Royal Ontario Museum.

Jicheng. Zhongguo kexueyuan kaogu yanjiusuo 中國科學研究院考古研究所, ed. 1984–1994. *Jicheng: An Integrated Compendium of Yin and Zhou Bronze Inscriptions* 殷周金文集成, 18 vols. Beijing: Zhonghua shuju.

Wu, Zhenfeng 吳鎮烽 2012. *An Integrated Compendium of Inscriptions and Images on Shang and Zhou Bronze Objects* 商周青銅器銘文 圖像集成, 35 vols. Shanghai: Guji chubanshe.

BIBLIOGRAPHY

Allan, Sarah 1991. *The Shape of the Turtle: Myth, Art, and Cosmos in Early China.* New York: State University of New York Press.

Allan, Sarah 2007. "On the Identity of Shang Di 上帝 and the Origin of the Concept of a Celestial Mandate (Tian Ming 天命)." *Early China* 31:1–46.

Ban, Mawen 班马文, and Xie Reshi 谢热译 1985. "A Preliminary Discussion of the Origin of the Tibetan People 藏族族源初探." *Zangzu yanjiu* 4:94–98.

Campbell, Roderick B. 2009. "Toward a Networks and Boundaries Approach to Early Complex Polities: The Late Shang Case." *Current Anthropology* 50(6):821–848.

Campbell, Roderick B. 2014. *Archaeology of the Chinese Bronze Age from Erlitou to Anyang.* Los Angeles: Cotsen Institute of Archaeology Press.

Campbell, Roderick B. 2018. *Violence, Kinship and the Early Chinese State: The Shang and Their World.* Cambridge, UK: Cambridge University Press.

Cao, Bin 曹斌 2007. "An Explanatory Discussion of the Scholarship on the Proto-Zhou Culture 先周文化研究述论." *Jianghan kaogu* 3:60–66.

Chang, Kwang-Chih [Zhang Guangzhi] 1976. *Early Chinese Civilization: Anthropological Perspectives.* Cambridge, MA: Harvard University Press.

Chen, Mengjia 陳夢家 1955. *A Study of the Chronology of the Western Zhou* 西周年代考. Shanghai: Shangwu yinshuguan.

Chen, Chao-jung 陳昭容 2004. "Marital Relationships between Various Polities of the Han-Huai Region as Seen from Inscriptions on Bronze Objects 從青銅器銘文看兩周漢淮地區諸國婚姻關係." *Lishi yuyan yanjiusuo jikan* 75(4):635–697.

Childs-Johnson, Elizabeth 2012. "Shang *Sifang* (Four Directional) Cosmology." In *Commemorating the Centenary of Professor Sun Zuoyun's Birthday Proceedings of the International Symposium on Ancient Chinese History and Culture*, 191–210. Kaifeng: Henan daxue.

Childs-Johnson, Elizabeth. *Great Settlement Shang: Art, Belief and Culture*. Forthcoming.

Cook, Constance A. 1995. "Scribes, Cooks, and Artisans: Breaking Zhou Tradition." *Early China* 20:241–277.

Cook, Constance A. 1997. "Wealth and the Western Zhou." *Bulletin of the School of Oriental and African Studies* 60(2):253–294.

Creel, Herrlee G. 1970. *The Origins of Statecraft in China*, vol. 1: *The Western Chou Empire*. Chicago: Chicago University Press.

Crone, Thomas 2014. "Der Begriff mín 民 in Texten der Westlichen Zhōu-Dynastie (1050–771 v. Chr.)." *Orientierungen* 1:33–53.

Dietler, Michael, and Ingrid Herbich 1994. "Ceramics and Ethnic Identity: Ethnoarchaeological Observations on the Distribution of Pottery Styles and the Relationship between the Social Contexts of Production and Consumption." In *Terre cuite et société: La céramique, document technique, economique, culturel, XIVe Rencontre Internationale d'Archéologie et d'Histoire d'Antibes*. Edited by Didier Binder and Jean Courtin, 459–472. Juan-les-Pins: Editions APDCA.

Dobson, W.A.C.H. 1962. *Early Archaic Chinese: A Descriptive Grammar*. Toronto: University of Toronto Press.

Dong, Zuobin 1960. *Chronological Tables of Chinese History*. Hong Kong: Chinese University of Hong Kong.

Ess, Hans van 2003–2004. "The Tradition of the Scribe: Introduction." *Oriens Extremus* 44:1–2.

Ess, Hans van 2014. *Politik und Geschichtsschreibung im alten China: Pan-ma i-t'ung* 班馬異同. Wiesbaden: Harrassowitz.

Falkenhausen, Lothar von 1993. "Issues in Western Zhou Studies." *Early China* 18:139–226.

Falkenhausen, Lothar von 1996. "The Concept of Wen in the Ancient Chinese Ancestral Cult." *Chinese Literature: Essays, Articles, Reviews (CLEAR)* 18:1–22.

Falkenhausen, Lothar von 2006. *The Chinese Society in the Age of Confucius (1000–250 BC): The Archaeological Evidence*. Los Angeles: Cotsen Institute of Archaeology, UCLA.

Feng, Yicheng 風儀誠 (Olivier Venture) 2014. "Discussing again the 'ce' Graph in Shang and Zhou Lineage Emblems 再談商周族徽中的「冊」." *Rao Zongyi guoxue yuankan* 饒宗頤國學院院刊 4:225–232.

Fiskesjö, Magnus 2001. "Rising from Blood-Stained Fields: Royal Hunting and State Formation in Shang China." *Bulletin of the Museum of Far Eastern Antiquities* (73):49–191.

Flad, Rowan 2008. "Divination and Power: A Multiregional View of the Development of Oracle Bone Divination in Early China." *Current Anthropology* 49(3):403–437.

Gassmann, Robert 2006. *Verwandtschaft und Gesellschaft im alten China: Begriffe, Strukturen und Prozesse*. Bern: Peter Lang.

Granet, Marcel 1930. *Chinese Civilization*. Translated by Kathleen E. Innes and Mabel R. Brailsford. London: K. Paul, Trench, Trübner.

Grebnev, Yegor 2018. "The Record of King Wu of Zhou's Royal Deeds in the Yi Zhou shu in Light of Near Eastern Royal Inscriptions." *Journal of the American Oriental Society* 138(1):73–104.

Guo, Baojun 郭寶鈞 1981. *A Comprehensive Investigation of a Group of Shang and Zhou Bronze Objects* 商周銅器群綜合研究. Beijing: Wenwu chubanshe.

Guo, Moruo 郭沫若 1932. *An Examination of Bronze Inscriptions of the Both Zhou Periods* 兩周金文辭考釋. Tōkyō: Bunkyūdō Shoten Taishō.

Guo, Moruo 郭沫若 2002 [1957]. *A Compendium, an Illustrated Catalogue and an Examination of Bronze Inscriptions of the Both Zhou Periods* 兩周金文辭大系圖錄考釋. Beijing: Kexue chubanshe.

He, Jingcheng 何景成 2009. *An Investigation of Inscriptions with Lineage Emblems of Shang and Zhou Bronze Objects* 商周青铜器族氏铭文研究. Jinan: Qi Lu shushe.

Hsü, Cho-yun, and Katheryn M. Linduff 1988. *Western Chou Civilization.* New Haven: Yale University Press.

Hu, Qianying 胡谦盈 1993. "Discussing the periodization of the sites (cemeteries) of the Proto-Zhou Culture in Nianzipo, Qi yi and Feng yi 论碾子坡与岐邑、丰邑先周文化遗址(墓葬)的年代分期." In *Kaoguxue yanjiu: Shaanxi sheng kaogu yanjiusuo chengli sanshi zhounian jinian wenji* 考古学研究: 陕西省考古研究所成立三十周年纪念文集. Edited by Shi Xingbang 石兴邦, 332–55. Xi'an: Sanqin.

Hu, Qianying 胡谦盈 2005. "An Analysis of the Nature of the Remains of the Proto-Zhou Culture from Nianzipo in the Southern Bin 南邠碾子坡先周文化遗存的性质分析." *Kaogu* 6:74–86.

Jaffe, Yitzchak 2016. "Colonialism in the Time of Globalization: The Western Zhou State Revisited." In *The Routledge Handbook of Globalization and Archaeology.* Edited by Tamar Hodos, 438–453. London: Routledge, 2016.

Jiang, Yude 江雨德 (Roderick B. Campbell) 2011. "The Great Affairs of the State: The Improvement of the Ritual Regulations of the Late Shang Period 国之大事: 商代晚期中的礼治改良." In *Yinxu and the Shang Culture: The Collected Writings Commemorating the Eighty Years of Scientific Investigations of Yinxu* 殷墟与商文化—殷墟科学发掘 80 周年纪念文集. Edited by Zhongguo shehui kexue yanjiuyuan kaogu yanjiusuo, 267–276. Beijing: Kexue chubanshe.

Jing, Zhongwei 井中伟, and Wang Lixin 王立新 2014. *The Archaeology of Xia, Shang and Zhou* 夏商周考古学, 2nd ed. Beijing: Kexue chubanshe.

Kane, Virginia C. 1982–1983. "Aspects of Western Chou Appointment Inscriptions: The Charge, the Gifts, and the Response." *Early China* 8:14–28.

Kern, Martin 2007. "The Performance of Writing in Western Zhou China." In *The Poetics of Grammar and the Metaphysics of Sound and Sign.* Edited by Sergio La Porta and David Shulman, 109–176. Leiden: Brill.

Kern, Martin 2009. "Bronze Inscriptions, the *Shangshu*, and the *Shijing*: The Evolution of the Ancestral Sacrifice during the Western Zhou." In *Early Chinese Religion, Part One: Shang Through Han (1250 BC to 220 AD).* Edited by John Lagerwey and Marc Kalinowski, 143–200. Leiden: Brill.

Kern, Martin 2017. "The 'Harangues' (Shi 誓) in the Shangshu." In *The Classic of Documents and the Origins of Chinese Political Philosophy.* Edited by Martin Kern and Dirk Meyer, 281–319. Leiden: Brill.

Keightley, David N. 1979–1980. "The Shang State as Seen in the Oracle-Bone Inscriptions." *Early China* 5:25–34.

Keightley, David N., ed. 1983. *The Origins of the Chinese Civilization.* Berkeley: University of California Press.

Khayutina, Maria 2009a. "Western 'Capitals' of the Western Zhou Dynasty (1046/5–771 BC): Historical Reality and Its Reflections until the Time of Sima Qian." *Oriens Extremus* 47:25–65.

Khayutina, Maria 2009b. "The Royal Year-Count of the Western Zhou Dynasty (1045–771 BC) and Its Use(r)s: A Sociological Perspective." In *Time and Ritual in Early China.* Edited by

Xiaobing Wang-Riese and Thomas O. Höllmann, 125–151. Asiatische Forschungen Monographienreihe. Wiesbaden: Harrassowitz.

Khayutina, Maria 2010. "Royal Hospitality and Geopolitical Constitution of the Western Zhou Polity (1046/5–771 BC)." *T'oung Pao* 96(1–3):1–77.

Khayutina, Maria, ed. 2013. *Qin: The Eternal Emperor and His Terracotta Warriors*. Zurich: NZZ Libro.

Khayutina, Maria 2014. "Marital Alliances and Affinal Relatives (*sheng* 甥 and *hungou* 婚購) in the Society and Politics of Zhou China in the Light of Bronze Inscriptions." *Early China* 37:39–99.

Khayutina, Maria 2016. "The Tombs of the Rulers of Peng and Relationships between Zhou and Northern Non-Zhou Lineages (until the Early Ninth Century B.C.)." In *Imprints of Kinship: Studies of Recently Discovered Bronze Inscriptions from Ancient China*. Edited by Edward L. Shaughnessy, 71–132. Hong Kong: Chinese University of Hong Kong Press.

Khayutina, Maria 2017. "The 'Bi shi' 柴誓, Western Zhou Oath Texts, and the Legal Culture of Early China." In *The Classic of Documents and the Origins of Chinese Political Philosophy*. Edited by Martin Kern and Dirk Meyer, 416–445. Leiden: Brill.

Khayutina, Maria 2018. "The Six and Eight 'Camps' (liu shi ba shi 六師八師) and Zhou Military Cooperation." Paper presented at the Bronze Inscriptions Workshop, the University of Chicago Center, Paris.

Khayutina, Maria 2019. "Reflections and Uses of the Past in Chinese Bronze Inscriptions from ca. 11th to 5th Centuries BC: The Memory of the Conquest of Shang and the First Kings of Zhou." In *Historical Consciousness and the Use of the Past in the Ancient World (3000 B.C.– A.D. 600)*. Edited by John Baines, Tim Rood, Henriette van der Blom, and Samuel Chen, 157–180. Sheffield and Bristol: Equinox.

Khayutina, Maria. *Kinship, Marriage and Politics in Early China (ca. 13–8th c. BCE) in the Light of Ritual Bronze Inscriptions*. Forthcoming.

Knoblock, J. H. 1990. *Xunzi: A Translation and Study of the Complete Works*, vol. 2. Stanford, CA: Stanford University Press.

Kryukov, Michail V. 1967. *Formy sozial'noi organizazii v drevnem Kitae* [Forms of the social organization in ancient China]. Moscow: Nauka.

Kryukov, Michail V. 1972. *Sistema rodstva kitajzev* [The system of kinship of the Chinese]. Moscow: Nauka.

Kryukov, Vassili M. 1997. *Ritualnaya kommunikaziya v drevnem Kitae* [Ritual communication in ancient China]. Moscow-Taibei: Institut Vostokovedeniya RAN.

Kryukov, Vassili M. 2000. *Tekst i Ritual: Opyt interpretazii drevnekitaiskoi epigrafiki epohi Yin-Zhou* [Text and ritual: An attempt of interpretation of ancient Chinese epigraphy of the Yin-Zhou epoch]. Moscow: Pamyatniki istoricheskoi mysli.

Lau, Ulrich 1999. *Quellenstudien zur Landvergabe und Bodenübertragung in der Westlichen Zhou- Dynastie (1045?–771 v. Chr.)*. Monumenta Serica Monograph Series 41. Sankt Augustin: Monumenta Serica.

Lei, Xingshan 雷兴山 2010. *An Exploration of the Proto-Zhou Culture* 先周文化探索. Beijing: Kexue chubanshe.

Li, Feng 李峰 1994. "An Inquiry about the Content and the Origin of the Proto-Zhou Culture 先周文化的内涵及其渊源探讨." *Kaogu xuebao* 3:265–284.

Li, Feng 2003. "'Feudalism' and Western Zhou China: A Criticism." *Harvard Journal of Asiatic Studies* 63:115–144.

Li, Feng 2004. "Succession and Promotion: Elite Mobility during the Western Zhou." *Monumenta Serica* 52:1–35.

Li, Feng2006. *Landscape and Power in Early China: The Crisis and Fall of the Western Zhou, 1045–771 BC.* Cambridge, UK: Cambridge University Press.

Li, Feng 2008a. *Bureaucracy and State in Early China.* Cambridge, UK: Cambridge University Press.

Li, Feng 2008b. "Transmitting Antiquity: The Origin and Paradigmization of the 'Five Ranks.'" In *Perceptions of Antiquity in Chinese Civilization.* Edited by Dieter Kuhn and Helga Stahl, 103–134. Heidelberg: Edition Forum.

Li, Feng 2013. *Early China: A Social and Cultural History.* Cambridge, UK: Cambridge University Press.

Li, Shaolian 李绍连 1999. "A Question Concerning the Political Form of the Shang Kingdom: Supplementary Archaeological Verifications of the Kingdom's Territorial Extent 关于商王国的政体问题——王国疆域的考古佐证." *Zhongyuan wenwu* 2:28–35.

Li, Xueqin 李学勤 1990. *Investigations of New-Coming Bronze Objects* 新出青铜器研究. Beijing: Wenwu chubanshe.

Li, Xueqin 李学勤 2011. "Discussing 'The Command to the Lord Wen' in the Light of the Qinghua Manuscript 'Xinian' 由清华简《系年》论《文侯之命》." *Wenwu* 3:70–74.

Liu, Ciyuan 刘次沅 2000. *From the Double Dawn to King Wu's Conquest of [the Shang King] Zhou: The Questions of Astronomic Chronology of the Western Zhou* 从天再旦到武王伐纣：西周天文年代问题. Beijing: Shijie shudian.

Liu, Junshe 刘军社 1994. "Periodization and Nature of the Zhengjiapo Culture and the Liujia Culture 郑家坡文化与刘家文化的分期及其性质." *Kaogu xuebao* 1:25–62.

Liu Li, and Chen Xingcan 2003. *State formation in Early China.* London: Duckworth.

Liu Li, and Chen Xingcan 2012. *The Archaeology of China: From the Late Paleolithic to the Early Bronze Age.* Cambridge, UK: Cambridge University Press.

Liu, Shi'e 刘士莪 2001. *Laoniupo: The Report of the Field-Archaeological Excavation by the Chair of Archaeology of the North-Eastern University* 老牛坡——西北大学考古专业田野发掘报告. Xi'an: Shaanxi renmin chubanshe.

Lu, Liancheng 卢连成, and Hu Zhisheng 胡智生 1988. *The Cemetery of the Yu State in Baoji* 宝鸡鱼国墓地. Beijing: Wenwu chubanshe.

Ma, Chengyuan 马承源 1988. *Chinese Bronze Objects* 中国青铜器. Shanghai guji chubanshe.

Ma, Lingwei 马林伟 2014. "A Preliminary Discussion of the Nianzipo Culture 碾子坡文化初论." *Longdong xueyuan xuebao* 7:37–40.

Matsumaru, Michio 松丸道雄, and Kenichi Takashima 高嶋謙 1994. *A Comprehensive Survey of Interpretations of Oracle Bone Characters* 甲骨文字字釋綜覽. Tokyo: Tokyo daigaku shuppansha.

Nivison, David S. 1982. "1040 as the Date of the Chou Conquest." *Early China* 8:76–78.

Nivison, David S. 1983. "The Dates of Western Chou." *Harvard Journal of Asiatic Studies* 43(2):481–580.

Pankenier, David W. 1981–1982. "Astronomical Dates in Shang and Western Zhou." *Early China* 7:2–37.

Pankenier, David W. 1992a. "Reflections of the Lunar Aspect on Western Chou Chronology." *T'oung Pao*, Second Series 78(1–3):33–76.

Pankenier, David W. 1992b. "The Bamboo Annals Revisited: Problems of Method in Using the Chronicle as a Source for the Chronology of Early Zhou, Part 1." *Bulletin of the School of Oriental & African Studies* 55(2):272–297.

Pankenier, David W. 1992c. "The Bamboo Annals Revisited: Problems of Method in Using the Chronicle as a Source for the Chronology of Early Zhou, Part 2: The Congruent Mandate Chronology in Yi Zhou Shu." *Bulletin of the School of Oriental & African Studies* 55(3):498–510.

Pankenier, David W. 1995. "The Cosmo-Political Background of Heaven's Mandate." *Early China* 20:121–176.

Peng, Yushang 彭裕商 2003. *A Comprehensive Investigation of the Chronology of Western Zhou Bronze Vessels* 西周青铜器年代综合研究. Chengdu: Ba Shu shudian.

Pines, Yuri 2008. "To Rebel Is Justified? The Image of Zhouxin and the Legitimacy of Rebellion in the Chinese Political Tradition." *Oriens Extremus* 47:1–24.

Pines, Yuri. 2009. *Envisioning Eternal Empire: Chinese Political Thought of the Warring States Era.* Honolulu: University of Hawai'i Press.

Pulleyblank, E. G. 1983. "The Chinese and Their Neighbors in Prehistoric and Early Historic Times." In *The Origins of Chinese Civilization.* Edited by David N. Keightley, 411–466. Berkeley: University of California Press.

Pulleyblank, E. G. 2000. "Ji and Jiang: The Role of Exogamic Clans in the Organization of the Zhou Polity." *Early China* 25:1–27.

Qi, Sihe 齐思和 1947. "An Investigation of the Investiture during the Zhou Dynasty 周代锡命礼考." *Yanjing xuebao* 32:197–226.

Qian, Hang 钱杭 1991. *Investigations of the History of the System of Lineage Rules during the Zhou Dynasty* 周代宗法制度史研究. Shanghai: Xuelin.

Qian, Mu 錢穆 1931. "An Investigation of the Geography of the Beginning of Zhou 周初地理考." *Yanjing xuebao* 10:195–200.

Qian, Zongfan 钱宗范 1989. *Investigations of the System of Lineage Rules during the Zhou Dynasty* 周代宗法制度研究. Kuilin: Guangxi shifan daxue.

Rawson, Jessica 1999. "Western Zhou Archaeology." In *The Cambridge History of Ancient China*, edited by Michael Loewe and Edward L. Shaughnessy. Edited by Loewe und Shaughnessy, 352–449. Cambridge: Cambridge Univ. Press.

Rawson, Jessica 1990. *Western Zhou Ritual Bronzes from the Arthur M. Sackler Collections, II.* New York: Arthur M. Sackler Foundation.

Rong, Geng 容庚, and Weichi Zhang 张维持 1984. *A Thorough Discussion of Yin and Zhou Bronze Objects* 殷周青铜器通论. Beijing: Wenwu chubanshe.

Sawyer, R. D. 2013. *Conquest and Domination in Early China.* Charleston, SC: Published by the author.

Schaberg, David 2001. *A Patterned Past: Form and Thought in Early Chinese Historiography.* Harvard East Asian Monographs. Cambridge, MA: Harvard University Asia Center.

Schuessler, Axel. 2009. *Minimal Old Chinese and Later Han Chinese: A Companion to Grammata Serica Recensa.* Honolulu: University of Hawai'i Press.

Sena, David 2005. "Reproducing Society: Lineage and Kinship in Western Zhou China." PhD dissertation, Chicago: University of Chicago.

Shaanxi Zhouyuan Kaogudui 陕西周原考古队 1984. "A Brief Report of the Excavation of the Cemetery of Jiang-Surnamed Rong People in Liujia in Fufeng County 扶风刘家姜戎墓葬发掘简报." *Wenwu* 7:16–29.

Shanxisheng Kaogu Yanjiusuo Dahekou Mudi lianhe Kaogudui 山西省考古研究所大河口墓地考古队 2011. "山西翼城县大河口西周墓地." *Kaogu* 7:9–18.

Shanxisheng Kaogu Yanjiusuo 山西省考古研究所, Yuncheng shi wenwu gongzuozhan 运城市文物工作站, Jiang xian wenhuaju 绛县文化局 2006. "The Western Zhou Cemetery in

Hengshui in Jiang County of Shanxi Province 山西绛县横水西周墓地." *Kaogu* 考古 7:16–21.

Shaughnessy, Edward L. 1985–1987a. "Zhouyuan Oracle-Bone Inscriptions: Entering the Research Stage?" *Early China* 11–12:146–163.

Shaughnessy, Edward L. 1985–1987b. "Extra-Lineage Cult in the Shang Dynasty: A Surrejoinder." *Early China* 11–12:182–194.

Shaughnessy, Edward L. 1986. "On the Authenticity of the Bamboo Annals." *Harvard Journal of Asiatic Studies* 46(1):149–180.

Shaughnessy, Edward L. 1991. *Sources of Western Zhou History: Inscribed Bronze Vessels*. Berkeley: California University Press.

Shaughnessy, Edward L. 1997. " 'New' Evidence of the Zhou Conquest." In *Before Confucius: Studies in the Creation of the Chinese Classics*. Edited by Edward L. Shaughnessy, 31–67. New York: State University of New York Press.

Shaughnessy, Edward L. 1999. "Western Zhou History." In *The Cambridge History of Ancient China*. Edited by Michael Loewe and Edward L. Shaughnessy, 292–352. Cambridge: Cambridge Univ. Press.

Shaughnessy, Edward L. 2001–2002. "New sources of Western Zhou History: Recent Discoveries of Inscribed Bronze Vessels." *Early China* 26–27:73–98.

Shaughnessy, Edward L. 2006. *Rewriting Early Chinese Texts*. New York: State University of New York Press.

Shaughnessy, Edward L. 2009. "Chronologies of Ancient China: A Critique of the 'Xia-Shang-Zhou Chronology Project.'" In *Windows on the Chinese World: Reflections by Five Historians*. Edited by C. Ho Wing-chung, 15–28. Lanham, MD: Lexington Books.

Shaughnessy, Edward L. 2016. "Newest Sources of Western Zhou History: Inscribed Bronze Vessels, 2000–2010." In *Imprints of Kinship: Studies of Recently Discovered Bronze Inscriptions from Ancient China*. Edited by Edward L. Shaughnessy, 133–188.Hong Kong: Chinese University of Hong Kong Press.

Shelach, Gideon 1996. "The Qiang and the Question of Human Sacrifice in the Late Shang Period." *Asian Perspectives* 35(1):1–26.

Shelach-Lavi, Gideon 2015. *The Archaeology of Early China: From Prehistory to the Han Dynasty*. Cambridge, UK: Cambridge University Press.

Shirakawa, Shizuka 白川靜 1958. "An Investigation about the Qiang Tribe 羌族考, *Kōkotsu kinbungaku ronshū*." 甲骨金文学論叢 9.

Shirakawa, Shizuka 白川靜 1966–1983. *Commentaries of Bronze Inscriptions* 金文通釈. *Hakutsuru bijutsukanshi* 白鶴美術館誌 56. Bände, Kobe.

Sun, Yabing 亚冰, and Lin Huan 林欢 2010. *The History of the Shang Dynasty*, vol. 10: *Shang Geography and Regional States* 商代史卷 10: 商代地理与方国. Beijing: Zhongguo shehui kexue chubanshe.

Sun, Yan 2013. "Material Culture and Social Identities in Western Zhou's Frontier: Case Studies of the Yu and Peng Lineages." *Asian Archaeology* 1:52–72.

Tang, Lan 唐兰 1986. *Historical Verification of the Periodization of Inscriptions on Western Zhou Bronze Objects* 西周青铜器铭文分代史徵. Beijing: Zhonghua shuju.

Vasil'ev, Leonard S. 1995. *Drevnij Kitaj*, vol. 1: *Period Zapadnogo Zhou* [Ancient China, vol. 1: Western Zhou period]. Moscow: Vostochnaya literatura.

Vyatkin, Rudolf, et al., trans. 2001. *Sima Qian, Istoricheskie zapiski. Tom 1. Izdanie vtoroe, ispravlennoe i dopolnennoe*. Moscow: Vostochnaya literatura.

Vogelsang, Kai 2002. "Inscriptions and Proclamations: On the Authenticity of the 'gao' Chapters in the Book of Documents," *The Bulletin of the Museum of Far Eastern Antiquities* (74): 138–209.

Waley, Arthur, and Joseph R. Allen, trans. 1996. *The Book of Songs: The Ancient Chinese Classic of Poetry.* New York: Grove Press.

Walker, Richard Louis 1953. *The Multi-State System of Ancient China.* Westport, CT: Greenwood Press.

Wang, Hui 王晖 1998. "Properties of Oracle Bones from Zhouyuan and Transformations of Sacrificial Rituals at the Edge of Shang and Zhou Dynasties 周原甲骨属性与商周之际祭礼的变化." *Lishi yanjiu* 3:5–20.

Wang, Ming-ke. 1999. "Western Zhou Remembering and Forgetting." *Journal of East Asian Archaeology* 1:231–250.

Wang, Yuxin 1985–1987. "Once again on the New Period of Western Zhou Oracle-Bone Research: With a Brief Description of the Zhouyuan Sacrifice Inscriptions." *Early China* 11–12:164–172.

Wang, Shimin 王世民, Chen Gongrou 陈公柔, and Zhang Changshou 张长寿 1999. *Investigations of the Periodization and Dating of Western Zhou Bronze Objects* 西周青铜器分期断代研究. Beijing: Wenwu chubanshe.

Wang, Wei 王巍, and Xu Lianggao 徐良高 2000. "An Exploration of the Proto-Zhou Culture 先周文化的考古学探索." *Kaogu xuebao* 3:285–310.

Wu, En Yuesitu 乌恩岳斯图 2007. *Investigation of Archaeological Cultures of the Northern Steppes* 北方草原考古学文化研究. Beijing: Kexue chubanshe.

Wu, Qichang 吴其昌 1936. *Verifications of New Moon Records in Bronze Inscriptions* 金文歷朔疏證. Shanghai: Shangwu yinshuguan.

Xia Shang Zhou Duandai Gongcheng Zhuanjiazu 夏商周断代工程专家组 ed., 2000. *The Report of the Results of the 1996–2000 Period of the Work Process of Reconstructing the Chronology of the Xia, Shang and Zhou Dynasties: A Concise Edition* 夏商周断代工程 1996/2000 年阶段成果报告: 简本. Beijing: Shijie tushu.

Xibei Daxue Wenhua Yichan and Kaoguxue Yanjiu Zhongxin 西北大学文化遗产与考古学研究中心, Shaanxi sheng kaogu yanjiuyuan 陕西省考古研究院, Chunhua xian bowuguan 淳化县博物馆 2012. "The Remains of the Proto-Zhou Period on the Zaoshugounao Site in Chunhua County of Shaanxi Province 陕西淳化县枣树沟脑遗址先周时期遗存." *Kaogu* 3:20–34.

Xu, Fengxian 2010–2011. "Using Sequential Relations of Day-Dates to Determine the Temporal Scope of Western Zhou Lunar Phase Terms." Translated by D. Pankenier. *Early China* 33–34:172–198.

Xu, Xitai 徐锡台 1987. *A Summary of the Oracle Bones from Zhouyuan* 周原甲骨文综述. Xi'an: Sanqin.

Yu, Xingwu 于省吾 1979. *A Collection of Interpretations of Inscriptions on Oracle Bones* 甲骨文释林. Beijing: Zhonghua shuju.

Zhang, Changshou 张长寿, and Yin Weizhang 殷玮璋, eds. 2004. *The Archaeological Scholarship of Shang and Zhou* 商周考古学: 两周卷. Beijing: Zhongguo shehui kexue.

Zhang, Guangzhi 張光直 [Chang Kwang-chih] 1973. *A Comprehensive Investigation of Shang and Zhou Bronze Objects and Bronze Inscriptions* 商周青銅器與銘文的綜合研究. Taibei: Academia Sinica.

Zhang, Maorong 张懋镕 2008. "On the Question of Unbalance of the Evolution of Western Zhou Bronzes 试论西周青铜器演变的非均衡性问题." *Kaogu xuebao* 3:337–352.

Zhang, Peiyu 张培瑜 1987. *Calendrical Tables of the Pre-Qin History of China* 中国现秦史历表. Jinan: Jilu shushe.

Zhang, Tian'en 张天恩 2004. *Investigations of Cultures of the Shang Period in the Guanzhong Area* 关中商代文化研究. Beijing: Wenwu chubanshe.

Zhongguo Shehui Kexueyuan Kaogu Yanjiusuo 中国社会科学院考古研究所 2007. *Nianzipo in the South of the Bin Region* 南邠州·碾子坡. Beijing: Shijie shudian.

Zhongguo Tianwenxue Shi zhengli Yanjiu Xiaozu 中国天文学史整理研究小组 1981. *The History of Chinese Astronomy* 中国天文学史. Beijing: Kexue chubanshe.

Zhu, Fenghan 朱凤瀚 2009. *A Comprehensive Discussion of Chinese Bronze Objects* 中国青铜器综论, 3 vols. Shanghai: Guji chubanshe.

Zhu, Fenghan 朱凤瀚, and Zhang, Rongming 张荣明, eds. 1998. *Investigations of the Chronology of Western Zhou Kings*. Guiyang: Guizhou renmin chubanshe.

CHAPTER 18

WESTERN ZHOU GOVERNMENT AND SOCIETY

PAUL NICHOLAS VOGT, INDIANA UNIVERSITY

THE importance of the rise of Zhou in shaping the political and social development of what is now China can hardly be overstated. The Western Zhou period saw the spread of a common (elite) written language across the entirety of north China and well into the south; the incorporation of far-flung and diverse communities into a common sphere of elite interaction; and the establishment of modes of familial and governmental organization that would dominate the early Chinese political scene until at least the rise of the Qin empire. The attainments of the Zhou remained a key point of cultural memory in later centuries of early Chinese history, especially as portrayed in sources, such as the *Grand Scribe's Records* and the *Rites of Zhou*, which attained recognition during the Han dynasty (206 BCE–220 CE).[1] Through these sources, idealizations of the Zhou social and governmental model influenced the conduct of Chinese governance down into the modern era.[2]

The very ubiquity and normative power of such classic treatments, however, complicate efforts to uncover the "real" social and political history of the Zhou period beyond what is typically endemic to the historical project. Fortunately, as is the case with so many aspects of early Chinese history, the growth of scientific archaeology in China over the last century and a half has furnished substantial contemporary evidence on society and politics under the Zhou. This evidence includes both material-cultural

---

[1] Dates for the Han are derived from the tables in Twitchett and Fairbank 1986:xxxix–xli. On the history of these two texts see Hulsewé 1993:405–409; Boltz 1993:25–29.

[2] For a history of the influence of the *Rites of Zhou* in East Asian governance, see the essays collected in Elman and Kern 2009.

remains—weighted heavily toward mortuary remains, but including in a few exceptional cases full settlement sites—and contemporary texts in the form of inscriptions on bronze vessels, the study of which has advanced by leaps and bounds in recent decades. The latter, despite their limitations as sources, have provided the foundation for a relatively rich understanding of Western Zhou institutions, based both on the information they themselves include and on the considered reexamination of traditional historical sources in the light of archaeologically attested materials.[3] The depth and breadth of this understanding is regularly augmented by new discoveries.[4]

This chapter provides a summary of the image of Western Zhou government and social organization that has emerged from the ongoing cooperation between archaeology, paleography, and classical history. The first section addresses the general nature of the Western Zhou state and society and the organizational principles that theoretically underlay it, including the nature and basis of royal authority as well as the organization of lineages and their role in interactions among Zhou-adherent elites. The structure and vocabulary of Zhou state administration are taken up in the second section, with brief consideration given to continuity with later textual depictions. A final section introduces the regional states that were established during the Western Zhou; their general role in the ideological construct of Zhou authority is considered, and a few example states are briefly described. (For other chapters on the Western Zhou see Chapters 17, 19, 20).

THE BASIC NATURE OF THE WESTERN ZHOU STATE

In short, and in its ideal form, the Western Zhou state consisted of a royal court, with two main headquarters at the sites of Feng and Hao (near modern Xi'an, Shaanxi Province) and Chengzhou (modern Luoyang, Henan Province), which administered, directly or indirectly, a broad domain reaching across much of what is now north and

[3] On the limitations of the Western Zhou archaeological record, see Falkenhausen 2006:17. On the inscriptions of bronze vessels as sources, see Shaughnessy 1991; Falkenhausen 1993:167–171; Li Feng 2008:11–20. For an example of the reevaluation of the received textual tradition on Western Zhou based on bronze inscriptions, see Kern 2009. All bronze inscriptions cited in this chapter are accompanied by their index numbers in the Academia Sinica's "Digital Archives of Bronze Images and Inscriptions" (see the references section). Identifiers from that work containing only numbers correspond to those in Institute of Archaeology CASS 1984–1994, while those prefaced with the letters "NA" are unique to the Digital Archives.

[4] Major discoveries of Western Zhou bronzes in recent years are too numerous to list but include, for example, the bronze hoard from Yangjiacun, Mei County, Shaanxi, on which see Shaanxi et al. 2003 (summarized in English in Shaanxi Provincial Institute et al. 2004); the cemetery of the polity Ba 霸 at Dahekou, Yicheng County, Shanxi, on which see Shanxi sheng Dahekou 2011 (abridged version published in English as Joint Archaeological Team 2012); and the marquesal tombs of Zeng 曾 at Yejiashan, Hubei, treated extensively in Hubei 2012 (summarized in English in Hubei 2013).

central China.[5] This court claimed the allegiance and obedience of a large and diverse population of elite families, some of which were spin-off branches of the royal house itself, and many of which had participated, or were descended from participants, in the overthrow of the prior hegemonic power known as Shang.[6] Certain of these families enjoyed a special status within the structure of state administration, exercising direct and comparatively independent control over large areas outside the immediate vicinity of the royal strongholds; these regional states or sub-states had their own hereditary dynasties but were understood to exercise their authority only through the will and at the pleasure of the king.[7] Many, though not all, of these states were created by royal fiat during the early stages of the Western Zhou period.[8]

In practice, the early Zhou state seems to have consisted of a core area under the direct control of the royal house, married to a network of settlements tied together by the common allegiance of their controlling parties to the king; by the presence in greater or lesser degree of a common elite culture; and by a suite of shared administrative techniques.[9] Many of these settlements were home to elite lineages that organized their local hierarchies in ways common throughout the sphere of Zhou influence, with the royal house as the rhetorically understood source of their authority; thus Li Feng has recently characterized the Western Zhou state as a "delegatory, kin-ordered settlement state" (Li Feng 2008:294–299). Over the course of the Western Zhou period, the control of land within the royal domain in particular intensified, possibly due to demographic pressures created by population expansion and the continued use of land grants as a

---

[5] See Li Feng 2006:30, 43–46, the latter providing a summary of the archaeological evidence on the western capitals. This is not to say that those two were the only sites of royal activity or of ideological importance to the Zhou group identity; on the sphere of mobility of the Western Zhou kings, see in particular Khayutina 2010.

[6] The precise balance of power between aristocratic lineages and the royal house at different points in the Western Zhou period, and the role of lineage structure and kinship in the operation of the Western Zhou state, is still debated. See Li Feng 2008:155–156; Falkenhausen 2014:260–265.

[7] On the assignment of regional states as part of the establishment and expansion of the Zhou state, see Yang 2003:373–404; Shaughnessy 1999:311–313; Li Feng 2006:70–76; Hsu and Linduff 1988:153–158; Li Feng 2008:30–34. On the theoretical subordination and practical autonomy of the regional states, see Li Feng 2008:98–99, 256–270.

[8] The Zuozhuan, the traditional received history of the subsequent Springs and Autumns period, proposes a list of states with the royal surname Ji 姬 that were created early in the Western Zhou period; see Ruan 1980:2,119 (tabulated in Li Feng 2006:71). Many of the populations in the Zhou political network are traditionally supposed to have predated the conquest of Shang and establishment of the Zhou-centered state, however; see Ruan 1980:182–183 ("Mu shi"); Yang 2003:373–374. The best overall source on the early Chinese regional states in general remains Chen Pan 1969 (along with Chen Pan 1970).

[9] On the existence of a central royal domain, see Li Feng 2008:49, 159–189. In Chinese, this area is generally referred to with the term wangji 王畿, which appears in the "Xia guan—Sima" chapter of the Zhouli; see Ruan 1980:863. For a short introduction to this phenomenon, see Lü Wenyu 1990b; other treatments include Lü Wenyu 1990a; Yu Wei 2008. A critical treatment of the idea of a royal domain appears in Creel 1970:363–366.

medium of royal patronage.[10] The conception of state (or local) authority over complete territories of land may have resulted. If so, that change was but one aspect of a set of sea changes in Zhou government, religion, and social organization in general that many researchers have postulated as occurring sometime in the Middle-Late Western Zhou period (Falkenhausen 1996:56–64; Falkenhausen 1999:149–155; Liu Yu 1989: 514–515; Rawson 1989:89–93; Rawson 1990:93–110; Rawson 1999:433–446; Shaughnessy 1997:184–186; Shaughnessy 1999:323–328; Vogt 2012:321–334).

The degrees of involvement of individual polities or lineages in Zhou politics and in the Zhou elite culture in general likely varied. A meaningful distinction can be drawn between the Zhou government, a political and ideological construct organized around the administrative authority of a specific hereditary line; and a Zhou elite culture comprising features such as the creation of bronze vessels for ancestral devotion, the use of a writing system derived from Shang, and so on. It is possible that some Western Zhou–era polities that participated in Zhou-style elite culture nonetheless paid only occasional lip service to the authority of the Zhou kings and the principles that justified their rule. Recent work has highlighted other factors—notably the creation of political ties through marriage—contributing to the coherence of a Zhou interaction sphere beyond the activities of the central government.[11] However, since the extant written sources capture mainly emic viewpoints from within the Zhou ideological construct, much of the available evidence concerning Western Zhou–era politics and governance focuses on ways in which the Zhou state conformed to, rather than departed from, an idealized image of perfect royal control. The descriptions of governmental structure, administrative techniques, and official positions provided in this chapter should be understood to refer to the times and areas in which that image was most nearly achieved, without implying that all populations participating in the Zhou interaction sphere adopted them in their entirety.

The question of feudalism

The feudal model of European medieval history long exercised substantial influence in characterizations of early Chinese governance in general and the Western Zhou period, as the putative cradle thereof, in particular.[12] Never uncontroversial even in the context

---

[10] On the likelihood of systemic demographic changes beginning by the Middle Western Zhou period, see Shaughnessy 1999:323; Li Feng 2006:115–116, 121–129; Zhu 1990:413–427; Falkenhausen 2006:66–70. Li Feng 2006 discusses the "piecemeal granting" (125) of royal land to aristocratic supporters, noting that Western Zhou land grants seem to have been measured in smaller units. See also Itō (1975, 53–54), cited therein.

[11] See for example Khayutina 2014, which explores the role of affinal relations in maintaining the social coherence of the Zhou realm.

[12] In Western languages, examples include Maspero 1950:111–146; Granet 1952; Creel 1970:317–387; Bodde 1981; Hsu and Linduff 1988:147–185. This is a separate phenomenon from the influence of the Marxist model of feudalism, as a social-historical stage, in the study of the Western Zhou, for which see, for example, Zhao Guangxian 1980 (cited in Gassmann 2006:22); Yang Kuan 2003 (e.g., 268–282). I am indebted to Li Feng for this observation.

of European studies, the feudal interpretation as applied to early China prompted negative reactions virtually since its introduction.[13] Nonetheless, the support of the eminent
Sinologist Herrlee Creel kept feudalism in the conversation within English-speaking
scholarship on early China.[14] However, recent work, particularly that of Li Feng, has
thoroughly discounted the applicability of the feudal model to the Western Zhou
period, to say nothing of its utility in the study of European history in general.[15] It is
not unusual to see the title of the famed "Duke of Zhou" (*Zhougong*) in particular
appear in the work of modern authors of the Western Zhou (the present chapter
included), despite the fact that any systematic analogy between the aristocratic terms
of address of the Western Zhou period and those of the English aristocracy, for example, has been proved thoroughly anachronistic.[16] The use of this now conventional
term should, however, not be taken as an indication of a belief in the analogy between
ancient China and "feudal" Europe.

WESTERN ZHOU KINGSHIP

The ideology of Zhou royal authority

The rulers of the Western Zhou period adopted the term of address *wang* 王, usually
translated as "king," by which the Shang rulers had also been called. According to classical sources, the change of rulership was justified by the selection of the Zhou royal line
in general and Wen, father of the conquering King Wu, in particular as the next rightful
ruler of the world by the Zhou high "god" Tian (usually translated as "sky" or "Heaven")
on moral grounds.[17] Wen was thus considered to have borne the title of "King," despite
the fact of his death before the final defeat of the Shang royal faction. This direct yet

---

[13] Creel 1970:317 notes the existence of such objections, and Gassmann 2006:11 cites Gernet 1983 in
this regard; later negative reactions include Blakeley 1976; Li Feng 2003 (revisited in Li Feng 2006).
[14] Creel 1970:317–387. For a proximate objection to Creel's characterizations, see Loewe 1972.
[15] Li Feng 2003; Li Feng 2008:277–278, 288–290. An alternate view of the scholarship on European
feudalism appears in Falkenhausen 2014:274–276.
[16] Examples of the Duke of Zhou in writings on the Western Zhou include Shaughnessy 1991:45–46
and throughout; Lau 1999:189 (as "Herzog von Zhou"); Li Feng 2006:11 and throughout. The index to
Shaughnessy 1991 lists more than 20 different "dukes" (*gong* 公) treated in the work; on the customary
nature of that translation for the title, see 91n33. This translation is no longer universal; Cook and
Goldin 2016, for example, uses "Patriarch of Zhou" (see e.g., Cook 2016c, 37; Cook 2016e, 123; but not
Cook 2016d, 98, where the transliterated "Zhou Gong" is used). "Patriarch" also appears in
Khayutina 2014:47.
[17] *Shijing*, "Wen wang," "Da ming"; *Shangshu*, "Wu cheng," "Da gao," "Kang gao," "Shao gao," "Luo gao,"
"Duo shi," "Duo fang" (Ruan 1980:502–505, 506–509, 183–185, 197–200, 202–205, 211–214, 214–217, 219–221,
227–230). The nature of Tian, and its relationship to the Shang religious entity Shang Di ("the High
Lord"), is the subject of a voluminous body of literature, including but not limited to Creel 1970:493–506;
Takayama 1980; Toyota 1980; Hu 1989; Eno 1990:19–29, 181–189; Li Xiangping 1991:40–81, 206–215; Zhang
Guangming 1993; Zhu Fenghan 1993; Pankenier 1995; Allan 2007.

transferable sanction of a certain hereditary ruling line by the forces guiding the cosmos came to be known in the later textual tradition as the *tianming*, or "Mandate of Heaven," under which name it constituted a basic principle of early Chinese governmental thought.[18]

Judging from the inscriptional sources, the state of affairs during the Western Zhou period was, unsurprisingly, somewhat less cut-and-dried than the classical model might suggest. The Zhou king was not the only power-holder in the Western Zhou milieu who laid claim to the title *wang*, and its use to describe other figures in relatively official Zhou inscriptions of the period suggests that such claims were sometimes tacitly accepted, if not embraced, even by the representatives of the Zhou royal house.[19] The designation *tianzi*, or "Son of Heaven," seems to have been exclusive to the Zhou kings but took hold only once the Zhou state project was well underway.[20] The nature of the Zhou king's role in state ritual likewise changed over time, as the emphasis on camaraderie, leading by example, and situational patronage endemic to the ritual of the early Western Zhou gave way to a regulated and naturalized image of the king as conceptual center of the state and origin point of key resources (Vogt 2012:321–334; for another detailed analysis of Western Zhou ritual, see also chapter 19 by Constance A. Cook in this volume). Generally speaking, the idea of a qualitative distinction between the king and other elites seems to have developed over the course of the Western Zhou period.[21]

The communication of Zhou royal authority

To project their authority over an unprecedentedly large area of ancient China, the Zhou kings relied on a powerful and sophisticated suite of administrative, ritual, and technological methods. Early in the period, after the galvanizing threat of Shang no longer offered an external impetus to preserve the Zhou coalition, the royal faction leveraged the power of ritual to bring its adherents under the umbrella of a shared cultural identity. Early Zhou ritual, it has often been noted, was derived largely from that of the Shang royal house, with whom the Zhou kings has a long history of association.[22] A variety of early-middle Western Zhou inscriptions show in detail how the Zhou kings combined

[18]   See e.g., *Lunyu*, "Ji shi" 8 (Ruan 1980:2,522); *Mengzi*, "Li lou shang" 7 (Ruan 1980:2,719); *Liji*, "Biao ji" (Ruan 1980:1,640–1,641), etc. During the Western Zhou period, the legitimizing sanction of the Zhou royal house was known simply as the "Great Mandate" (*da ming*); for a relatively complete list of this idea's appearances in the Western Zhou inscriptions, see Kern 2008:148.

[19]   On the use of the title *wang* among Western Zhou elites outside the royal line, see Khayutina 2014:46–49. In particular, the Guaibo *gui* 乖伯簋 (4331) and the Sanshi *pan* 散氏盤 (10176) situate individuals claiming that title in contexts of political interaction.

[20]   On the chronological distribution of occurrences of the term *tianzi* 天子, see Kern 2009:144.

[21]   Vogt 2012:191–192, 226–231. Here I do not mean to imply that the concept of a *wang* as fundamentally different from his subjects began with the Zhou royal house; the Shang kings undoubtedly had already benefited from such a conception.

[22]   A famous early statement of this idea appears in *Lunyu*, "Wei zheng" 23 (Ruan 1980:2,463). Classic treatments of Western Zhou ritual and the degree and quality of its connections with Shang practice include Chen Mengjia 1935; Liu Yu 1989; Liu Yuan 2004.

various ritual techniques, many of Shang provenance, in the context of major ceremonial events attended by elites from across the Zhou sphere of control. These "ritual assemblies" incorporated specific elites into idealized narratives of relations between the Zhou king and his adherents, thus encouraging the conceptualization of Zhou as a coherent political and cultural entity through which personal status was arbitrated (Vogt 2012:290–307).

Direct royal patronage, in the form of public recognition, official titles, sumptuary accoutrements, grants of land and subordinates, and raw wealth (most often in the form of cowry shells, metal, or cloth) was unsurprisingly vital in creating and maintaining the Zhou political network as centered on the king.[23] Royal grants and recognition dominate those Western Zhou bronze inscriptions long enough to contain narrative content; in particular, a practice called *mieli*, interpreted by many scholars as an official acknowledgment of merit, often provided a context for the conferral of royal gifts.[24] By the Middle Western Zhou period, a standardized ceremony of official appointment to government positions came to dominate the inscriptional records of royal patronage.[25]

From a material-cultural standpoint, the Western Zhou period is well known as the heyday of inscribed bronze vessels. Though these were cast, sometimes on a very large scale, under the Shang, the sheer quantity of examples from the Western Zhou testifies to their prevalence in contemporary elite culture; and the length and diversity of content of Western Zhou bronze inscriptions overshadows that of both the preceding and following eras.[26] Aristocrats across the Zhou realm used these vessels for ancestral offerings and other hospitality activities, in which context local interaction partners from both within and outside their lineages would have been exposed to them and, in all likelihood, to their inscriptions, including the royal appointments, gifts, and so on that they

---

[23] Treatments of royal patronage and official appointment as reflected in Western Zhou bronze inscriptions include Huang Ranwei 1978; Musha 1980; Cook 1997; Chen Hanping 1986; Jing Hongyan 2006; Wu Hongsong 2012, among others.

[24] The ceremony *mieli* 蔑歷—whose reading is still somewhat controversial—is treated in detail in e.g., Tang Lan 1995:224–235; Shirakawa 1959; Li Feng 2011, Yan Yiping 1962; Cook 1997:278–280; Li Feng 2011:277–279; Vogt 2012:233–248.

[25] Li Feng 2008:36. On the standardized appointment ceremony of the Middle-Late Western Zhou period, see e.g., Chen Hanping 1986; Musha 1980; Yoshimoto 1991; He Shuhuan 2007; Kane 1982–1983; Kern 2007:140–151; Li Feng 2008:103–114; Vogt 2012:274–284. Vogt 2012:274–275 offers a more complete list of studies.

[26] A casual search of the Academia Sinica's *Digital Archives of Bronze Images and Inscriptions* (http://www.ihp.sinica.edu.tw/~bronze/), a relatively complete database of inscribed bronzes, produces 6,313 cases of likely Shang date, 6,756 of likely Western Zhou date, 1,763 of likely Springs and Autumns date, and 1,911 of likely Warring States date (though these figures will contain some overlap between bronzes of ambiguous date; figures retrieved July 7, 2017). Index numbers appearing in parentheses after the names of bronze vessels throughout this chapter – for example, the Hu *gui* (NA0633), cited below – are the identifiers from this database (itself originally based on The Institute of Archaeology, CASS, ed. 1984-1994; identifiers containing only numbers refer also to that work). Though the figures for Shang and Western Zhou are close, Shang bronze inscriptions are generally shorter; compare for example the Shang vs. Western Zhou entries in Shanghai bowuguan Shang Zhou qingtongqi mingwen xuan bianxiezu 1986–1990:3.

recorded.[27] It is a notable peculiarity of the early Chinese milieu that, despite the accomplishments of contemporary craftsmen in both clay and metal, the Zhou were apparently not in the habit of depicting their kings realistically in statuary or relief sculpture.[28] The portrayals of kings to which most Western Zhou aristocrats would have been exposed were therefore textual, in the form of bronze inscriptions and quite possibly of perishable documents on which they were based.[29] Inscribed bronzes, and their customary use in the lineage cults of aristocrats, thus constituted one of the chief vehicles through which the Zhou kings could make their influence felt, ideologically speaking, within local contexts and without needing to be physically present (Vogt 2012:63–67). This crucial role as material manifestations of Zhou royal ideology may have contributed to their prevalence during the Western Zhou period.[30]

The communication of the Zhou royal will did not, however, rely entirely on ritual manifestations of royal ideology and their technological effluvia. As noted, the Zhou probably composed documents on more perishable materials with some regularity— indeed, if even a fraction of the received texts traditionally so dated were actually written down during the Western Zhou period, the Zhou must have made extensive use of such documents—and some hints exist of the use of documents to convey royal commands.[31] The kings also regularly dispatched representatives on short-term missions to allies' territories and apparently maintained a core of "inspectors" (*jian* 監) to oversee the proper implementation of policy in the regional states.[32] The most direct and forceful means of conveying the royal majesty, however, was perhaps the presence of the king himself. Judging from the opening statements of bronze inscriptions, the Zhou kings frequently traveled to the territories of adherents to carry out ceremonies.[33] Moreover,

[27] For example, the Hu *gui* 虎簋 (NA0633) records that the king appointed its commissioner Hu to a position of service and gave him luxurious accoutrements for professional use. Translations of this inscription appear in Li Feng 2008:194–197; Cook 2016b. This model of elite interaction with bronzes taps into an ongoing debate in Western Zhou studies about the nature of bronze vessels, the purposes for which they were produced, and the contexts in which their inscriptions were read or heard. At stake is whether and how bronze inscriptions could reasonably be seen (and used) as historical documents, by modern scholars or among those who produced them. For statements on both sides of this debate, see Falkenhausen 1993; Li Feng 2008:11–20.

[28] This gap in the art-historical record is all the more notable given that we know the Zhou were capable of realistic three-dimensional representation inac plastics, as shown, for example, by the famous Li *juzun* 盠駒尊 (6011), cast convincingly in the shape of a horse.

[29] For evidence on the use of perishable documents during the Western Zhou period and their relationship to bronzes, see Falkenhausen 1993:161–167; Li Feng 1997:140–141; Kern 2007; Li Feng 2011:esp. 273–287.

[30] On material manifestations of ideology in the archaeological record, see DeMarrais et al. 1996.

[31] On the written forms of Western Zhou royal commands, see Falkenhausen 2011:esp. 268–270; Li Feng 2011:273–279.

[32] The Wei *ding* 衛鼎 (2733), for example, cites the entertainment of royal representatives (*shi* 使, written as *li* 吏) as part of the purpose behind its creation; for a translation see Vogt 2012:81. On Western Zhou royal inspectors, see Zhang and Liu 2003:49; Li Feng 2008:251–252, 314.

[33] For a few likely examples, see the inscriptions of the Da *gui* 大簋 (4165); the Duan *gui* 段簋 (4208); and the Ling *ding* 令鼎 (2803). Khayutina 2010 offers a comprehensive list of such inscriptions as of the date of its publication.

rather than remaining in a single, defended stronghold, the kings were in the habit of moving regularly between a series of key governmental and ceremonial centers, including the capitals at Feng and Hao, near modern Xi'an; the eastern capital of Chengzhou, built under King Cheng to secure Zhou rule in the east; Pangjing, apparently a ceremonial center; and others (Khayutina 2010). Local potentates, including regional rulers and their representatives, also visited the centers of Zhou power for appointment to new territories and to attend state ritual events.[34] These movements presumably facilitated regular contact, and thus the maintenance of established relations, between the king and his adherents within the core regions of Zhou control.

Agriculture and land management

The importance of agriculture in the Zhou self-concept is clear from the earliest strata of received sources, which, in addition to their frequent depictions of farming activities, record the Zhou claim of descent from the divine figure Hou Ji 后稷, "the Millet Lord," as well as the story of the royal ancestor Gugong Danfu's settlement beneath Mount Qi and institution of a sedentary lifestyle.[35] The management of land is a reasonably frequent subject of Western Zhou bronze inscriptions, many of which record the conferral of lands (measured as *tian*, "fields," or in *li* 里, a unit of length or area) by the king upon his subjects or the exchange of land between aristocratic lineages.[36] It has been suggested that the central government administered a certain amount of land directly, which supported the operations of the state government and provided the basis for further land grants when such were needed to maintain the loyalty of adherents (Li Feng 2008:158–159). One of the most famous textual manifestations of Zhou royal ideology holds that the Zhou king was in fact considered the ultimate owner of all land, implicitly granting only use-rights thereof (*Shijing*, "Bei shan," in Ruan 1980:463). In practice, however, the exchange of land between aristocrats, if not exactly frequent, was common enough to suggest that lineages enjoyed practical ownership of their land, including exchange rights (Li Feng 2008:155).

As with so many aspects of Western Zhou governance, the Zhou management of farmland became an object of idealization and imitation in certain texts of the subsequent classical and early imperial periods. An influential construct called the *jingtian*,

[34] The inscription of the Mai *fangzun* 麥方尊 (6015), for example, commemorates the visit of a potentate to the royal territories upon his appointment to rule a new territory; the Xiao Yu *ding* 小盂鼎 (2839) describes a triumph of sorts, hosted by the king, which accommodated a wide range of high-ranking guests.

[35] On the descent of the Zhou from Hou Ji, see *Shijing*, "Sheng min" (Ruan 1980:528–532); "Bi gong" (Ruan 1980:614–618); *Shiji*, "Zhou ben ji," 111–113; on Gugong Danfu, see "Mian" (Ruan 1980:509–512); *Shiji*, "Zhou ben ji," 113–116.

[36] See Chen Hanping 1986:259; Hsü and Linduff 1988:275–279; Lau 1999; Yang Kuan 2003:212–223; Li Feng 2008:36–37, 154–158. On *li*, see Li Feng 2008:180–181. The most famous land exchange inscriptions are probably those produced by an individual by the name of Qiu Wei 裘衛, to wit, the Qiu Wei *he* 裘衛盉 (9456), Fifth-Year Wei *ding* 五祀衛鼎 (2832), and Ninth-Year Wei *ding* 九年衛鼎 (2831).

or "well-field," model—which held that the men of old had divided areas of farmland into tic-tac-toe grids of nine squares (resembling the Chinese character *jing* 井, or "well"), of which the outer eight were privately held by individual families, while the center field was worked cooperatively for the common good—became prominent in the moral construct of the Confucian classic *Mencius* and, through it, in understandings of the Western Zhou period in general.[37] Wang Mang, the powerful official whose usurpation of the Han throne constitutes the traditional touchstone between the Western and Eastern Han dynasties, is said to have tried to implement the well-field system, with little success (Watson 1999:363–366).

Agriculture and ritual

Besides its importance as a subsistence activity, its direct connection to ritual practices lent agriculture a special ideological significance in the Western Zhou milieu. As portrayed in the *Book of Songs* in particular, the assumed end of the agricultural cycle was not simply the sustenance of the living but also the provision of consumables for ancestral offerings after various degrees of processing (that is, in the form of raw grains and livestock sacrifices, as well as grain alcohol, mincemeats, and pickles).[38] Supporting ritual offerings was considered so crucial to the Zhou state that, in later texts, the royal house is said to have dedicated and maintained a special agricultural territory, known by the toponym "Thousand Acres" (*qianmu* 千畝), specifically for the purpose of ensuring the supply thereof. That this facility was seen as directly connected with the well-being of the state can be seen from accounts in which its neglect by King Xuan of the late Western Zhou implicitly led to a major Zhou military loss at the site.[39] The Thousand Acres are also connected, in the corpus of received texts, with a tradition holding that the Zhou kings conducted an annual ceremonial ploughing of the fields, in which they and their adherents broke ground on the agricultural season in a sequence symbolizing the unity and hierarchy of the upper-level Zhou aristocracy.[40] This practice is attested, albeit sparsely, in the Western Zhou bronze inscriptions, though the details of the ceremony are not discussed, and the implications thereof seem in context not to coincide precisely with those discussed in the received textual record. Still, the fact of the royal

[37] *Mencius*, "Teng Wengong shang" (Ruan 1980:2,702–2,703) (wherein the term *jingdi* 井地, rather than *jingtian*, is used); see also e.g., *Guliang zhuan*, "Xuangong 15th year" (Ruan 1980:2,415); Yang Kuan 2003:185–211; Hsu and Linduff 1988:350. Creel (1970:154n87) notes the lack of attestation of this phenomenon in the Western Zhou sources. Lewis (1999:604–605) suggests that Mencius's inspiration might have come from Li Kui, a minister in the state of Wei during the fifth century BCE.
[38] *Shijing*, "Feng nian" (Ruan 1980:594); "Zai shan" (Ruan 1980:601–602). On the components of the early Chinese diet and sacrifices, see Sterckx 2005:esp. 35–38.
[39] *Shiji* 144–145; Wang Xianqian 1984:710; Legge 1960:156. The *Xi nian*, part of the recently acquired Tsinghua University corpus of Warring States manuscripts, contains a passage that elaborates on this theme; see Tsinghua University 2011:136–137.
[40] For references to this ceremony in classical texts, see e.g., Chen Qiyou 1984:2–14; 11–17; 23–43, esp. 42. For recent scholarship on the topic, including treatments of the relevant Western Zhou bronze inscriptions, see Yang Kuan 2003:268–282; Vogt 2012:206–214.

ceremonial ploughing implies the desire to foster a conceptual connection between royal authority and the natural order during at least part of the Western Zhou period (Vogt 2012:206–214, 226–231).

SOCIAL DIVISIONS

Kinship

Per the traditional construct of ancient Chinese history, the *zongfa* 宗法, or "ancestral temple model," paradigm of kinship has long been considered one of the great contributions of the Zhou to Chinese civilization at large. Briefly, the *zongfa* model is a system of patrilineal primogeniture in which the first son by the first wife inherits, while the descendants of later sons are seen as belonging to the same kinship unit down unto the fifth generation of separation from the inheriting lineage, at which point each son's descendants achieve the status of a separate lineage and are no longer represented in the lineage temple of the originating family.[41] The *zongfa* system of kinship in its ideal form thus achieves the dual goal of maintaining bonds between recent generations of a family in the face of potential separation—important in the early Western Zhou governmental context of the foundation of regional states based often on shared kinship with the royal house—and control of the volume of targets admissible to, and thus the habituating effectiveness of, the activities of the ancestral cult, a key factor in Western Zhou elite identity at both the lineage and state levels.[42] Substantial evidence, both paleographical and archaeological, has made clear that the patrilineal kinship principles idealized in the *zongfa* construct were present in the organization of the core lineages of Western Zhou society from relatively early on.[43] Certain aspects thereof were, however, less neatly organized than the later textual constructs might suggest, and even their perfect

---

[41] Treatments of the *zongfa* system are too numerous to list, but include Zhao Guangxian 1980:99–110; Hsu and Linduff 1988:163–171; Qian Hang 1991; Yang Kuan 2003:426–452; Falkenhausen 2006:66–69. The preeminent treatments of early Chinese kinship in general to date are, in Chinese, Zhu Fenghan 1990, and in German, Gassmann 2006. The term *zongfa* itself, as noted in Li Feng 2008, 248n25, is of later pedigree.

[42] On the process of foundation of the regional states, see the final section of this chapter as well as Khayutina, chapter 17 of this volume; on the control of the ancestral cult in the face of an expanding elite population, see Falkenhausen 2006:67–69.

[43] Hsü and Linduff (1988:166–171) summarizes much of the evidence on lineage organization from Western Zhou elite cemeteries. On the paleographical front, the inscriptions on bronze vessels from hoards found in the Zhou heartland have allowed scholars to trace family relationships across generations as manifested in the accoutrements of the ancestral cult. The most spectacular, and most complete, sequence of such bronzes was recovered from a hoard at Zhuangbai, Fufeng County, Shaanxi; see Shaanxi Zhouyuan 1978; Falkenhausen 2006; Yin Shengping 1992, cited therein. One of the most famous bronzes from this find, the Shi Qiang *pan* 史牆盤 (10175), contains a genealogy of the caster's ancestors along with one of the Zhou royal house, supporting a relatively detailed reading of the family relationships represented in the hoard as a whole. This inscription is notably translated in Shaughnessy 1991:1–4, 183–192.

implementation could still lead to ambiguities that confound modern investigators. For example, Western Zhou elites were, generally speaking, strongly in the habit of using a codified set of birth-order terms (*bo, zhong, shu, ji* 伯、仲、叔、季) to indicate seniority within lineages.[44] These terms constituted a regular part of elite modes of nomenclature as understood from the Western Zhou bronze inscriptions; thus a particular individual might be referred to as, for example, "Shaobo Hu" ("Hu, Elder of the Shao [Lineage]) or "Tangzhong Duo" ("Duo, Second Son of the Guo [Lineage]").[45] As a lineage grew in both antiquity and size, the descendants of its non-inheriting scions split off into "branch lineages" related but no longer identical to the "trunk lineage," thus creating a hierarchy of elite lineages organized by seniority; under the classic *zongfa* construct, this was understood to happen in the fifth generation of separation from a common ancestor.[46] In practice, the nomenclature of such a new lineage was apparently based on the seniority relationship claimed by its founder within his own generation. An ambiguity was thus created between modes of address for individuals within their own generation of a main lineage and those for members of a branch lineage; for example, a "Guoshu X" might be either "X, Third (or Later) Son of the Guo (Lineage)" or "X of the Guoshu (Branch Lineage of the Guo Trunk Lineage)." Such issues of nomenclature complicate efforts to describe interfamilial relationships and obscure to what degree the idealized classical construct of *zongfa* reflected Western Zhou practice.[47]

Classically speaking, again, the kinship identity of an elite individual of the Western Zhou consisted not merely of a patriline (*zong* 宗, "temple lineage," or *shi* 氏, though the latter term began to be used in reference to kinship identity only late in the Western Zhou period) but also of an affiliation known as *xing* 姓, often translated as "clan," but perhaps more precisely rendered as "marriage group."[48] *Xing* identity was determined by the patriline to which one belonged, but individual instances of the category could reach across multiple patrilines, especially those that traced their ancestry back to a

---

[44] Falkenhausen 1993:185; Li Feng 2006:112. Falkenhausen (2006:70) notes an increase in this practice from the Middle Western Zhou period on. On these seniority terms see also Gassmann 2006:202–203, 320–322, 445–446, 507–513; Sena 2012:67n12.

[45] See the inscriptions of the Shaobo Hu *xu* 召伯虎盨 (NA0374), Diaosheng *gui* 琱生簋 (4292-4293), and Tangzhong Duo *hu* 唐仲多壺 (9572).

[46] *Liji*, "Da zhuan" (Ruan Yuan 1980:1,508); Falkenhausen 2006:66–70. Even in times closer to the composition of these ideal expressions of lineage and cult organization, rules concerning the elimination of particular ancestors from the lineage cult had a way of being circumvented when faced with the social pressures surrounding individual cases. On this phenomenon in the context of the Han imperial cult see Brashier 2011:esp. 103–183.

[47] Falkenhausen 1993:185n92; Sena 2005:123–124, 123n94. Sena lists a number of additional relevant sources.

[48] On the basic nature of the *xing* 性 category, see Zhu Fenghan 1990:19–22; Pulleyblank 2000:esp. 4–11; Sena 2005:7–10; Gassmann 2006:37–62; Chen Jie 2007:21–36. Like much of the common body of terminology concerning Western Zhou kinship, the term *xing* itself was not regularly used during the Western Zhou (Sena 2005:7). For a diachronic analysis of the use of the term *shi* 氏 in the Western Zhou inscriptions, see Vogt 2012:54–62. I favor the translation "temple lineage" for *zong* on the grounds that, in the Western Zhou inscriptions, it could refer both to locations associated with the ancestral cult and to patrilines; for examples, see Vogt 2012:36–48.

common trunk; *xing* identity, unlike lineage identity, did not change with time and distance from a perceived origin (see e.g., Gassmann 2006:40–42, 55–56). The Zhou royal house, for example, belonged to a *xing* known as Ji 姬, and since many of the Zhou regional states were conferred upon lesser scions of the royal house, the division between Ji-surnamed states and non-Ji-surnamed states became a traditional one (Li Feng 2006:71–72 comprises the main lists of Ji-surnamed states in the classical texts). A normative prohibition against endogamy was the defining characteristic of *xing* groups (Creel 1970:333–334n56; Pulleyblank 2000:4–7). The set of *xing* classifications thus encouraged the creation of affinal connections between lineages, thereby contributing to the coherence of the geographically broad Zhou political and cultural sphere. (On the political importance of marriages, see Pulleyblank 2000:7–12; Hsu and Linduff 1988:224–225; Khayutina 2014.)

In addition to temple lineages and marriage groups, the Western Zhou sources contain traces of a kinship category called *zu* 族. *Zu* appear to have been somewhat smaller than lineages as previously described, and perhaps served in the Western Zhou context as sub-units thereof, though in some cases they functioned as lineages in their own right.[49] In Western Zhou bronze inscriptions, *zu* are referred to mostly in their role as units of military organization, apparently customarily led by, or at least closely associated with, persons addressed as *gong* 公 (on this term see note 16). The low degree of overlap between the term *zu* and the narratives of ancestral ritual in the bronze inscriptions suggests that *zu* organization, while potentially kinship-based, perhaps stood independently from the system of temple lineages. In the later classics, however, the words *zong* and *zu* were combined into the phrase *zongzu*, a term for patrilineal kinship relations writ large.[50]

Social roles of women

A classic late source on the *zongfa* model of elite interaction suggests that a married woman's status was determined as a member of the patriline of her husband (*Liji*, "Da zhuan," Ruan 1980:1,507). In practice, it appears that Western Zhou elite women could potentially carry out offerings within both their birth and marriage lineages. To support this involvement, elite women were often furnished with vessels cast on their behalf by either fathers or husbands. The bulk of readily discernible contemporary references to elite women come from the inscriptions of such vessels.[51] Women in the inscriptions are frequently called by their clan surnames (*xing* 姓; see previous section) in combination

[49] Falkenhausen 2006:23–24, 66, 69, 555; Gassmann 2006:173–174; Khayutina 2014:40n2. Falkenhausen (2006:23–24) offers an excellent account of the difficulty inherent in trying to establish correspondences between ancient Chinese social-organizational terminology and modern English.

[50] Vogt 2012:48–50. Vogt (2012:48n46) offers a sampling of occurrences of the term *zongzu* 宗族 in the Chinese classics. The rendering "patriarch" for *gong* follows Khayutina 2014:47.

[51] Khayutina 2014:69; Falkenhausen 2006:119. On inscribed Western Zhou bronzes produced for women, see Li Zhongcao 1991; Chen Zhaorong 2006; Li Feng 2006:186n26.

with terms referring to their seniority within their birth lineages, the lineages or states into which they married, or both, depending on the perspective of the vessel commissioner.[52] Women played an indispensable role in the Zhou political network as marriage partners. The exchange of brides across long distances maintained kinship connections among the Zhou center and the various Zhou-adherent states of greater or lesser independence, helping to preserve the ideological power of kinship ties as an aspect of Zhou state organization. Such ties must have been of particular importance in integrating polities or populations without preexisting blood ties to the royal house into the Zhou political and cultural sphere.[53]

Beyond these roles, some powerful women of the Western Zhou wielded personal influence as both political and devotional figures. The Zhou queen is unsurprisingly the best attested such case; multiple inscriptions refer to her (by the term *Wang Jiang*, "the king's [lady of the surname] Jiang") in capacities including director of activities in the royal household and patron of other aristocrats.[54] One elite lady known as Geng Ying was important enough to host the king at her own eponymous facility and to record the event in the inscriptions of multiple bronze vessels for posterity.[55] During the Late Western Zhou period, the consort of the ruler of the important Shao lineage apparently took an active role in receiving official business and conveying official messages.[56] In the realm of the ancestral cult, ancestresses often received devotions in pairs with their husbands; but in at least one case, a Western Zhou aristocrat singled out his deceased mother to thank her specially for her protection in battle (see Dong *gui* 或簋 [4322]). Though such influential elite women are little remembered in the received historical record (beyond the special, rhetorically limited roles of the wife and mother of King Wen), the contemporary sources make clear that such figures contributed to the operation of Western Zhou society in multiple ways and on multiple levels.[57]

[52] Chen Zhaorong 2001:398; on this practice in the received texts, see Pulleyblank 2000:5–6. See also Khayutina 2014:42.

[53] For a nuanced approach to the role of marital alliances in maintaining connections among the various lineage polities participating in the Zhou state, see Khayutina 2014:esp. 88–99.

[54] E.g., the Zuoce Huan *you* 作冊睘卣 (5407); the Shu *gui* 叔簋 (4132, 4133); the Zuoce Ze Ling *gui* 作冊夨令簋 (4300–4301); the Cai *gui* 蔡簋 (4340) (the latter employing the term of address *Jiangshi* 姜氏). See also Creel 1970:129–132, 394–395. A tradition, apparently real, holds that the Zhou royal house, which bore the surname Ji 姬, customarily intermarried with the surname group Jiang 姜. See Khayutina 2014:43; for a detailed treatment of the two surnames, see Pulleyblank 2000.

[55] Geng Ying *ding* 庚嬴鼎 (2748); Geng Ying *you* 庚嬴卣 (5426). For the identification of Geng Ying as female, see e.g., Ma 1986–1990:3:37n1. In other contexts, facilities called by the term *gong* 宮 (often translated as "temple" or "palace") in combination with the name of a living individual have been interpreted as facilities for the individual's work-related activities; see Li Feng 2001–2002.

[56] Zhousheng *gui* 琱生簋 (4292, 4293); Zhousheng *zun* 琱生尊 (see Baoji and Fufeng 2007, available in English as Baoji and Fufeng 2008; for the relevant interpretation of the role of Shao Jiang, see 103).

[57] The classical sources on King Wen's mother Tai/Da Ren and wife Tai/Da Si include most notably *Shiji* 115, 1,967–1,969; *Shijing*, "Da ming"; "Si zhai" (Ruan 1980:506–509, 516–517). For English-language introductions to these figures, see Cook 2007; Lee and Stefanowska 2007:74–75.

Non-elite status

Some contemporary sources provide an image of the division of labor among non-elite individuals during the Western Zhou period. The received text of the *Book of Songs* offers a few potentially idealized details about the activities of agricultural laborers and their families.[58] Inscriptions make clear that there were dedicated craftsmen whose activities were separately managed by the state, as well as permanent military staff attached to the king.[59] The existence of professional merchants is suggested obliquely by a very small range of sources.[60] The nature of the Western Zhou government necessitated the existence of a substantial volume of professional clerical officials spread throughout the various units of Zhou society (Li Feng 2008:309).

Western Zhou materials describe certain persons, often referred to by terms such as *chen* 臣, *pu* 僕, and *li* 吏, in such a way as to suggest that they had less than complete autonomy. Various inscriptions note the inclusion of such people in royal gifts or their transfer as part of the creation of new rulers or states. (See for example the Fu *zun* 復尊 [5978]; the Da Yu *ding* 大盂鼎 [2837]; the Zuoce Ze Ling *gui* 作冊夨令簋 [4300], etc.) The Hu *ding* 曶鼎 (2838) inscription records the use of individuals, referred to as *fu* 夫, as exchange commodities; it is somewhat unclear, however, whether the people themselves or the fruits of their labor were being exchanged, as well as whether their relationship to the royal household affected the terms of their status under the agreement.[61] During a triumphal ceremony recorded in the famous Xiao Yu *ding* 小盂鼎 (2839) inscription, the military leader Yu claimed to have taken well in excess of 10,000 prisoners on campaign.[62] The same figure once received a royal gift that included hundreds of people of different statuses, including some that apparently held positions of administrative responsibility.[63]

There were thus various social and political contexts in the Western Zhou that occasioned the treatment of people of various statuses as transferable assets, whether in terms

[58] These sources are treated in Hsü and Linduff 1988:345–355; Sun Zuoyun 1966:esp. 185–203.

[59] The former are referred to in bronze inscriptions as the *baigong*, or "Hundred Craftsmen"; see Ling *fangzun* 令方尊 (6016) Ling *fangyi* 令方彝 (9901); Zhang and Liu 1986:49; Li Feng 2008:51–52, 154. A group called the "Tiger Servants" (*huchen* 虎臣) is commonly understood in the latter sense; see Creel 1970:107, 111, 304; Hsu and Linduff 1988:245; Li Feng 2008:90.

[60] Creel (1970:137–150) devotes substantial space to the question of trade under the Western Zhou, suggesting that certain units of what was most likely silk may have developed into a unit of accounting; see esp. 149–151.

[61] For a statement of the latter view, see Skosey 2016:131–132. The inscription specifies that these individuals were to remain on the lands that they had been working. On the inscription see also Lau 1999:368–383; Skosey 1996:99–101. Glahn (2016:35–36) offers a detailed discussion of the issue and its implications for the status of farmers in the Western Zhou.

[62] Eno, "Inscriptional Records of the Western Zhou," http://www.indiana.edu/~g380/3.10-WZhou_Bronzes-2010.pdf (accessed July 7, 2017), 20, notes the implications of this number for the debate about the nature and role of slavery in Western Zhou society.

[63] Da Yu *ding* 大盂鼎 (2837). The descriptor applied to these persons, *si* 司, is the same term often used in the title of the "Three Supervisors" discussed later in this chapter. Translations of the relevant part of the Da Yu *ding* inscription appear in Li Feng 2006:127–128; Cook 2016a.

of their actual location or the direction of their allegiance. The practical differences in relative status between categories of persons in the Western Zhou period are thus still less than clear.[64] The effort to unpack status has been complicated in past scholarship by the influence of the Marxist historiographical paradigm, in which the distinction between slave society and feudal society, and therefore the social status of slave versus servant, are of ideological as well as historical significance.[65] Meanwhile, the Western Zhou archaeological record is dominated by mortuary remains (Falkenhausen 2006:17). Very little thus remains to be seen of those who were not in a position to commission the digging of rammed-earth graves or the production of inscribed bronzes. The role of the subaltern, so to speak, is nearly invisible in the Western Zhou archaeological record.

MILITARY AFFAIRS

Military organization

Zhou elite culture was to an extensive degree what might be referred to as a "military aristocracy"; the traces of this character appear at various levels of Zhou social organization. The kinship unit of Shang pedigree known as the *zu* may in the Western Zhou have been adopted as a basic unit of military organization, with individual *zu* contributing troops for common military endeavors (see Creel 1970:91n36, 315n257; Hsu and Linduff 1988:148–150, 164). The title *shi* 師, "Captain" or "Marshal," was a common component in Western Zhou forms of address even among parties singled out for civil promotion, suggesting that past military experience played a role in the personal and professional identities of Zhou elites (Li Feng 2008:229–232). The institutional positions of the "Three Supervisors"—a high-level administrative mechanism duplicated locally in communities across the Zhou area of control—included a dedicated official responsible for military affairs (*Sima* 司馬, or "Master of Horse") who stood on a par with the managers of agricultural issues, craftsmen, and so on.[66] Large-scale royal ceremonies from at least the first half of the Western Zhou period, attended by officials and rulers from across the Zhou realm, honored accomplished Zhou war leaders and symbolically portrayed the military might of the king himself.[67]

Military readiness was also a guiding principle of Zhou organization on the state level. The existence of standing royal armies has been proposed as one of the key points differentiating Zhou government from the feudal model (Li Feng 2008:290). The Zhou royal

[64] Glahn (2016:34–36) addresses the ambiguity in the Western Zhou vocabulary of subordinate station.

[65] Notable Marxist-informed approaches to Zhou society include Yang Kuan 2003:283–295; Guo Moruo 2005. See also Glahn 2016:34.

[66] On the "Three Supervisors" in general, see Li Feng 2008:305–306; on the office called *sima* 司马, or "Master of Horse," in particular, see Zhang and Liu 1986:12–13; Li Feng 2008:307–308.

[67] See in particular the inscriptions of the Xiao Yu *ding* 小盂鼎 (2839) and the Mai *fangzun* 麥方尊 (6015), the latter of which is analyzed in detail in Vogt 2012:295–311.

house apparently enjoyed the service of two separate groups of standing armies, divided into six and eight units, respectively; the frequent use of the qualifier *Yin*—which, among other meanings, served as the name of the last capital of Shang—for the latter has led to the suggestion that the "Six Armies" were maintained in the vicinity of the western capitals of Feng and Hao, while the "Eight Armies" were likely stationed near Chengzhou and perhaps composed at least in part of soldiers of former Shang allegiance.[68] Some Western Zhou inscriptions mention place names with military implications, suggesting that the Zhou and their associates maintained a network of settlements with military affiliations across much of north China, or, at least, that military concerns had informed the distribution of settlements during the Zhou expansion.[69] Apart from the forces under its direct control, the royal house also claimed, in principle, the right to call on the rulers installed in regional sub-states to join it on the battlefield (Li Feng 2008:246–247, 264–268).

Military practices

Archery

The ideological importance of archery in the Western Zhou period is hard to overstate. Later texts and Western Zhou inscriptional materials accord with one another in identifying archery as a key skill of an accomplished aristocrat. (Adamski 2014 offers a comprehensive survey of Western Zhou bronze inscriptions that record archery events.) Royally sponsored archery competitions emerged relatively early in the Western Zhou as a venue for official recognition and political exchange, and by the reign of the middle Western Zhou King Mu, the central court saw fit to maintain a dedicated facility for teaching archery to elite scions.[70] The accoutrements of archery

[68] On the various interpretations of the "Six Armies [of the West]" and the "Eight Armies [of Yin (Shang)]/[of Chengzhou]" that appear frequently in the Western Zhou inscriptions, see Creel 1970:305–310; see also Yu Xingwu 1964; Li Xueqin 1987.

[69] The term *shi* 師, used in the names of the "Six Armies" and the "Eight Armies," is, as noted, a common term of address in the Western Zhou bronze inscriptions, but it also appears in place names— for example, Jingshi 京師, a locale of importance during the war against western populations during the later years of the Western Zhou period (see the inscription of the Duoyou *ding* 多友鼎 [2835]). Less common, but still relevant, is the term *shu* 戍, "garrison," more often a verb, but potentially appearing as a noun in the inscriptions of the Zuoce Ze Ling *gui* 作冊矢令簋 (4300–4301) and the Shan *ding* 善鼎 (2820). In fact, these two terms are used together in the latter, in the phrase *Binshi shu* 圖師戍, "the garrison at Binshi" (transcription from Zhongyang yanjiuyuan shiyusuo jinwen gongzuoshi, "Digital Archives of Bronze Images and Inscriptions"); the simple place name *Binshi* appears in the inscription of the Qi *gui* 簋 (4266).

[70] This was the *Shexuegong* 射學宮, in charge of which a figure named Jing was at one point placed, as depicted in the inscription of the Jing *gui* 靜簋 (4273). Judging from the urgency with which Jing's performance as an archery instructor is described in the inscription, the social stakes of archery exhibitions would seem at that point to have been very high indeed. The political dimensions of royal archery competitions are perhaps best captured in the inscription of the Chang Xin *he* 長盉 (9455), in which representatives of the central court are paired with local figures as shooting teams; see e.g., Barnard 1960; Vogt 2012:248–273, esp. 257–258. For the identification of this vessel as a dating standard for the reign of King Mu, see also Shaughnessy 1990:110–111. On the later understanding of archery as one of the "Six Arts" of an accomplished classical gentleman, see e.g., *Zhouli*, "Diguan situ" (Ruan 1980:707, 731).

appear consistently in royal rewards as symbols of the recognition of elite status (Chen Hanping 1986:255–257). The very title borne by the regional rulers appointed by the Zhou king to settle outlying lands and protect the Zhou core appears to have been a reference to the practice of archery, suggesting a general understanding of archery as metonymic for military endeavor in general.[71] Archaeological discoveries corroborate the importance of bows and arrows as Zhou elite accoutrements, whether ceremonial or for actual use.[72]

Chariots in warfare

The predilection of the Zhou for chariots is well documented in the full gamut of received, inscriptional, and material-cultural sources.[73] As with archery equipment, chariots and their accoutrements were a key symbol of aristocratic status during the Western Zhou, in which capacity they often formed part of royal gifts accompanying acknowledgments of meritorious service or appointments of elites to new offices (Chen Hanping 1986:239–250). Chariots also sometimes accompanied elite burials, typically in separate pits nearby (see for example Lu and Hu 1988:388–407). In one particular case, an accomplished official was recognized with the privilege of riding in the king's chariot, or, perhaps, of employing a chariot fit for a king (see Mai *fangzun* 麥方尊 [6015]).

The efficacy of chariots as a primary vehicle of warfare has in the past been called into question; it has thus been suggested that the Zhou might instead have used chariots as "mobile command platforms" for overseeing the deployment of infantry.[74] Inscriptions such as that of the Duoyou *ding* 多友鼎 (2835), however, suggest that both the Zhou and certain of their opponents did in fact field chariots in large numbers, and moreover that they were considered dangerous enough that, if necessary, it was preferable to destroy captured chariots rather than risk the chance that they might fall back into enemy hands.[75]

---

[71] On the etymology of the title *hou* 侯, often rendered "Marquis" in translations of later sources, see Yu and Yao 1996:2,542–2,545; Zhou Fagao 1974-1975:3,464–3,465; Li Feng 2008:27, 44.

[72] To cite but a single example, a tomb of probable early Western Zhou date excavated at Taiqinggong, Luyi county, Henan, in 1997 included 32 arrowheads among its grave goods; see Henan and Zhoukou 2000:20, 22.

[73] Detailed treatments are available in e.g., Dewall 1964; Shaughnessy 1988. Creel (1970:262–296) reviews much of the relevant evidence from received texts.

[74] Shaughnessy 1988:208–210. Creel 1970 devotes a great deal of space to the question of chariots in Western Zhou warfare; see 262–293, esp. 270. Creel is strongly reliant on the information in Dewall 1964.

[75] See Shaughnessy 1988:225–226. Li Feng (2006:147–150) offers a translation of the Duoyou *ding* inscription and a summary of ongoing arguments about its date; on this question see also Shaughnessy 1983–1985. In a nutshell, the vessel dates to either the early or the late phase of the Late Western Zhou period.

ADMINISTRATIVE STRUCTURE
OF THE ZHOU STATE

State administrative hierarchy

Perhaps the most basic division of the Zhou state was between areas under the more or less direct control of the royal house and those subject to the intermediary authority of aristocratic lineages.[76] The ground-level administrative unit within both of these divisions was the *yi* 邑, a term construed to include both a settlement (regardless of size) and the resource-producing lands immediately surrounding it. Between the royal court and the *yi*, the Zhou heartland contained mid-level administrative subdivisions called *li* 里, overseen by dedicated officials, which could comprise multiple *yi*-settlements; and there appear to have been hierarchical relations between groups of settlements as well (Li Feng 2008:171–182, 280–283, 297; see also Matsumaru 1970; and Itō 1978, cited therein). A set of settlements known as the "Five Cities" (*wuyi* 五邑), however, which were of particular importance in the ideology of Zhou royal power, had their own separate administrative structures; these could perhaps be compared with Berlin in the modern Bundesrepublik Deutschland or the various provincial-level cities in the PRC (Li Feng 2008:165–167; Hsu and Linduff 1988:247–249). Locations referred to as "encampments" or "garrisons" (*shi* 師) may perhaps also have been administered separately, whether under military authority or under the direct supervision of the king.[77]

Outside the area of direct royal control, in areas in which other aristocratic lineages held sway, the situation was slightly more complex. Traditionally, the constitu-

---

[76] The model put forth in this section is based heavily on Li Feng 2008, which offers the most complete vision of the operations of the Western Zhou state to date. For alternate takes on some aspects of this vision, see Falkenhausen 2014. It should be noted that the administrative structure of the Western Zhou state, like most other aspects of its operation, underwent changes over the course of the period, and that the structures described here are most clearly visible for the middle-late Western Zhou onward, when the volume of inscriptions dealing with administrative affairs increased; see Li Feng 2008:49–95 for a diachronic approach to this issue. The proposed existence of a demarcated "royal domain" under the direct control of the royal house and its own administrative apparatus is not uncontroversial. Creel in particular objected to the "royal domain" vs. "outlying fiefs" model, noting the degree to which it became systematized and idealized in later (but still early) treatments; see Creel 1970:363–366; Guo Moruo 1954:36a–39a, cited therein. Creel notes, however, that the royal house must have possessed its own holdings from which it derived wealth (364n167). Li Feng 2008 has described an administrative distinction between properties, including both estates and building complexes belonging directly to the royal house, and others administered by the central government of the Western Zhou state in general; the former, he suggests, were mostly associated with large population centers, while the latter were found throughout the less populated areas of the Zhou heartland (149–189, esp. 159).

[77] Creel (1970:310–315) notes that the "Eight Armies" (see "Military organization" above; the "armies" in question were also designated with the term *shi* 師) could be appointed their own administrative officials. See also Yu Xingwu 1964, cited therein; Li Feng 2008:79–82.

ent units of the Western Zhou state are meant to have been divided between lineage politics falling within the royal domain, which were subject to direct administration by the royal house; and the regional states falling outside the royal domain proper, which, though their authority ultimately derived from that of the king, possessed separate administrative apparatuses.[78] The nomenclature used for the various states in both received and inscriptional sources suggests that the central government, at least, observed a division between polities located in the eastern and western portions of the Zhou area of control. Within the heartland of the realm, powerful lineages, often referred to as *bang* 邦, occupied a similar structural position to the *li*-units previously mentioned, ranking as subordinate to the king but holding administrative sway over groups of *yi*-settlements (Li Feng 2008:44–48, 183–188). In the outlying areas, regional states, their rulers frequently referred to as *hou* 侯, operated essentially as freestanding administrative realms, with the understanding that the authority of the *hou* to administer their states, though hereditary, was entirely contingent upon the approval of the royal house (Li Feng 2008:236–238, 245–248). In both cases, whether the individual lineages subordinate to the royal house in turn interacted hierarchically—that is to say, whether certain lineages and certain regional states were in practice subordinate to others, or all were directly answerable to the royal house—remains unclear.[79]

Governmental divisions and officials

The Zhou kings appear to have taken an active role in the administration of their state—presiding over diplomatic and religious events, taking a personal role in the appointment of officials, and perhaps even leading armies themselves—throughout most of the Western Zhou reigns.[80] They were assisted in this by an extensive body of appointed

---

[78] This is the substance of the "royal domain" model to which Creel objected; see note 77. Li Feng (2008:43–49) identifies these with the western and eastern portions of the Western Zhou realm, respectively, suggesting that the two regions were managed in appreciably different ways. See in particular 49n13, 15, which list much of the prior scholarship on the royal domain.

[79] It is quite likely that hierarchical relationships pertained between what may now be called "branch lineages" and "trunk lineages" as conceived of under the *zongfa* model (on which see above, "Social divisions"), judging from the continued use of individual seniority terms to differentiate between related lineages (see Sena 2005:123–124). Likewise, it appears that individual settlements interacted hierarchically; see Matsumaru 1970, cited in Li Feng 2008:280–283. However, whether the politics of the Western Zhou period accommodated the existence of hierarchical relations between mid- to upper-level political entities that were not expressed through kinship relations remains to my mind an open question.

[80] A convenient reign-by-reign summary of the events of the Western Zhou period appears in Hsu and Linduff 1988:112–146; compare also Shaughnessy 1999; Yang Kuan 2003:549–576, 840–843.

officials, most with relatively well demarcated areas of responsibility.[81] Though the Zhou administrative apparatus evolved over the course of the period, it seems to have employed such means from relatively early on, such that the birth of the extensive bureaucracy for which the later empires were famed has often been pinpointed in the Western Zhou period.[82] A full account of the variety of official government positions attested in the Western Zhou materials is beyond the scope of this chapter and, at any rate, is readily available in multiple other sources.[83] Instead, the following account will discuss some of the organizing principles of the Zhou officialdom and its relationship to state operations, characterizing a few key positions in more detail along the way.

Early in the Zhou dynasty, a general term, *qingshiliao* 卿士寮, or "Bureau of Ministerial Affairs," had arisen that basically indicated the uppermost layer of central government officials for the Zhou state; this body of officials seems, like cases such as "the White House," "the Kremlin," and so on, to have been referred to by the name of the location in which it was headquartered. The *qingshiliao* came to encompass subdivisions concerned with particular fields of administration, among them the Three Supervisors (*sanyousi*) for the central government, discussed later in this section (Li Feng 2008:52–54, 70–75; cf. Creel 1970:106n15; Hsu and Linduff 1988:237–238; Yang Kuan 2003:321–331). By the middle Western Zhou, a second such institution, the *taishiliao* 太史寮, or "Bureau of the Grand Scribe," had come to be, comprising perhaps a separate division of clerical officials; based on its pairing with the *qingshiliao* in certain key inscriptions, the *taishiliao* came to be seen as a basic division of Western Zhou officialdom. In the meantime, as Li Feng has shown, the royal house and the assets subject to its regular use maintained a separate body of officials; these came to be headed by a figure known as the *zai* 宰 but included also a separate clerical body under the command of the *neishi* 內史, or "Interior Scribe" (Li Feng 2008:53, 63–70, 76, 85–90).

A key organizing principle of the Zhou officialdom was the grouping of posts known as the "Three Supervisors" (*sanyousi* 三有司). These consisted of a trio of official postings focused on the management of (especially human) resources: the "Supervisor of Land" or "Supervisor of the Multitudes" (*situ*, written in different cases with the characters 司土 or 司徒), probably responsible for the organization of agricultural activities; the "Supervisor of Works" (*sigong* 司工 or *sikong* 司空), a manager of buildings;

---

[81] It is to be noted that from each of the customary divisions of the Western Zhou period—that is, early, middle, and late—we have an inscription that records the awarding of control over a broad swath of the government to one powerful minister. These are the Zuoce Ling *fangyi* 作冊令方彝 (9901), the Fansheng *gui* 番生簋 (4326), and the Maogong *ding* 毛公鼎 (2841) inscriptions, respectively, which form the core of Li Feng's reconstruction of the structural evolution of the Western Zhou government; see Hsu and Linduff 1988:237–238; Li Feng 2008:50–54, esp. 53n19, 63–67, 85–90. There does not seem to have been a specific title for these prime ministers, so to speak, as in later times; and it is less than clear that the naming of such an official was a general practice of Western Zhou governance rather than a response to specific historical contingencies.

[82] On the development of bureaucracy during the Western Zhou period, see Hsu and Linduff 1988:249, 254–257, 380; Li Feng 2008:esp. 94–95. Creel (1970:419–420) offers a now out-of-date objection to this idea.

[83] The primary sources for this are Zhang and Liu 1986 and, more recently and in English, Li Feng 2008.

and the "Supervisor of Horses" (*sima* 司馬, sometimes translated as "Master of Horse"), somehow associated with military affairs. The institution of the *sanyousi* was apparently modular, such that not only the central government but also regional states, the Five Cities, and lesser settlements all had their own sets of Three Supervisors to manage affairs.[84]

The Western Zhou government produced a great deal of writing—in the form of bronze inscriptions but almost certainly also in the form of more perishable documents—and so naturally relied upon a large body of clerical officials. Notable among these were the positions of "Document Maker" (*zuoce* 作冊)—a title with an old Shang pedigree, referring possibly to officials responsible for the production of official royal communications, which seems to have been phased out by the late Western Zhou—and *shi* 史, generally translated as "Scribe," likely used for those responsible for recording events and, in certain contexts, for reading written commands attributed to the king. The title of *shi* developed both horizontal and vertical distinctions over the course of the Western Zhou period, such that in addition to simple "Scribes" and the "Grand Scribe" (*taishi* 太史, as in the *taishiliao*), there were among other types "Interior Scribes," responsible specifically for internal documents used at the royal court, who frequently announced the royal commands as part of the standardized official appointment ceremony that held sway during the Middle-Late Western Zhou period.[85] The title of "Scribe" seems early on to have become an accepted part of the construction of identity for Zhou elites, perhaps as a civil counterpart to the militarily tinged *shi* 師; thus many commissioners of Western Zhou bronzes bore the title *shi* 史 as part of their names (see e.g., the Shi Lai *jiao* 史 速角 [9063]; the Shi Mi *gui* 史密簋 [NA0636]; the Shi Qiang *pan* 史牆盤 [10175]; and many bronze inscriptions. See also Li Feng 2008:55).

The most detailed treatment of the Western Zhou government in the later classical canon, the *Zhouli* ("Rites of Zhou"), makes much of the importance of ancestral devotions as an organizing principle of Western Zhou governance; an entire subdivision of the text describes a detailed hierarchy of Zhou religious officials, and many of the specific positions treated in the other sections are meant to have performed duties that supported ritual offerings (*Zhouli*, "Chunguan dazongbo," Ruan 1980:752–829 and throughout). Ancestral rites clearly contributed in a vital manner to the coherence of Zhou elite society and the operation of the Zhou state, particularly through the royal

---

[84] Zhang and Liu 1986:8–9, 12–13, 22–24, 102–105; Li Feng 2008:81, 305–308, 187, 255, 168–169, 71–74. See also Creel 1970:107–108, 302. Both Creel (302) and Zhang and Liu (13) note that the *sima* does not in general seem to have been directly involved in campaigns; the precise sphere of this office's responsibility under the Western Zhou government remains somewhat vague.

[85] Zhang and Liu 1986:26–36; Li Feng 2008:55–57, 75–78, 109, 308–311. See 57–58, in particular, for the suggestion of a qualitative distinction between the positions of *zuoce* and *shi*. As noted in Li Feng 2008:310–311, there was at one point during the middle Western Zhou also a "Document Maker Interior Scribe" (*zuoce neishi* 作冊內史). On the use of perishable documents during the Western Zhou, see note 29.

performance and patronage thereof.[86] From contemporary inscriptions, however, only one major religious office is known, namely that of the Invokers (*zhu* 祝), of whom the Grand Invoker (*taizhu* 太祝) was presumably the head.[87] One holder of that latter office, known by name the Grand Invoker Qin, was the heir of the famous Duke of Zhou and the future first sitting ruler of the powerful regional state of Lu (see below, "States"), suggesting that it was a position of some prestige.[88] Generally, however, the importance of ancestral ritual in the ideological construct of the Zhou state does not seem to have been matched by a state-supported religious bureaucracy. Religious duties on the state level may have been distributed between more general offices; alternately, they may have been seen as the independent purview of individual lineages (with the royal line of course numbering among them).

STATES

From apparently humble beginnings, the Zhou royal house and their adherents were able to extend their influence over an unprecedentedly vast swath of the Chinese landmass (cf. Tan Qixiang 1982:15–16; Hsu and Linduff 1988:15). Outside a core area that lay under the direct control of the royal house, they accomplished this through the creation and incorporation of a number of smaller polities, creating a network of subordinate states with military obligations to the royal house; this sentiment is expressed in both the classical texts as the exhortation to "screen" (*ping*) the Zhou kings (*Shangshu*, "Kang wang zhi gao," Ruan 1980:244; *Zuozhuan*, Duke Xi 24th year, Ruan 1980:1,817; Pulleyblank 2000:7). The influence of this practice on both the practical and intellectual aspects of early Chinese governmental history was enormous. The creation of an interaction network of regional states—differing, sometimes wildly, in environment and even language but bound by a shared elite material culture, writing system, and professed allegiance to the Zhou royal government—set the political stage for the subsequent Springs and Autumns and Warring States periods, the complex interstate relations of which form the backdrop for many of the great surviving works of early Chinese philosophy.

The Zhou practice of establishing regional states in its classically depicted form—that is to say, the granting of a state to a lesser scion or ally of the royal house in recognition of

---

[86] In addition to the role played by royal ancestral rites in politico-religious assemblies, certain inscriptions suggest that some Zhou kings patronized the ancestral rites of others (see for example the inscriptions of the Da gui 大簋 [4165] and the Ren *ding* [NA1554]). These issues are discussed in depth in Vogt 2012:290–311 and throughout; a translation of the Da *gui* inscription appears on pages 98–99.

[87] Zhang and Liu 1983:36–37; Li Feng 2008:311. Zhang and Liu specify the existence of an office in charge of crack-divination (*Sibu*, or "Supervisor of Cracks"); see 37. Whether that position could be described as specifically religious is, however, debatable.

[88] See the inscriptions of the Qin *gui* 禽簋 (4041) and the Dazhu Qin *ding* 大祝禽鼎 (1938); on the rulership of Qin see *Shiji*, "Lu Zhougong shijia" (Ruan 1980:1,518).

services rendered, in order to maintain peace in outlying areas and defend the Zhou center from attack—came later to be known by the term *fengjian* 封 建, which eventually came to denote feudalism in general and the feudal stage of Marxist historiography in particular in modern Chinese.[89] In reality, the logic of the relations between Zhou and the various states under its control seems to have varied substantially from case to case. The following section briefly introduces a series of examples, considering in each case the extant evidence for the state and its cultural and political relations to the Zhou center, as well as its relationship to the received historical record.

Lu魯

The state of Lu is the prototypical example of the early Zhou practice of the foundation of regional states, thanks largely to its special relationship to the classical Confucian textual tradition. Of all of the regional states founded by the Zhou, Lu is perhaps the best attested in the received historical record, thanks to its association with both Confucius and his favored moral exemplar, the Duke of Zhou.[90] The core text of Springs and Autumns–period history, the *Spring and Autumn Annals*, is a line-item record of the history of Lu, and so the canonical histories of the Springs and Autumns period (the *Zuozhuan* chief among them), construed in the main as commentaries to that text, center around the official activities of the representatives of that state (Cheng 1993). Lu is also the only regional state to have achieved the singular distinction of the inclusion of poems associated with its activities in the *song*, or "Hymns," section of the *Book of Songs* (Ruan 1980:608–619). As such, certain aspects of the history of Lu are extraordinarily well documented in comparison with other states of Western Zhou provenance, so to speak. Nonetheless, the history of Lu has been vulnerable to polemical distortion and instrumentalization, as for example with the understanding of its unusual sequence of ducal successions.[91]

Lu in the form it took for most of early Chinese history was granted to a figure known from the classical texts as Bo Qin, eldest son of the famed Duke of Zhou, as a reward for

---

[89] In fact, the terms *feng* and *jian* appear, in the Western Zhou inscriptions, to have referred to the establishment of a state in the Zhou heartland vs. in the eastern reaches of Zhou control, respectively; see Li Feng 2008:45–49. On the history and etymology of the term *fengjian*, see Creel 1970:322–323; Li Feng 2006:110–111; McMullen 2011. For the *locus classicus* of the term, see *Zuozhuan*, Duke Xi, 24th year (Ruan 1980:1,817–1,818). For an example of its application in Marxist historiography, see Li Yachen 1954.

[90] Confucius is said to have been born in Lu, to have spent much of his life there, and to have served for some time at the court thereof; see e.g., Eno 1990:37–38 for an accessible introduction to the subject. Confucius's famous personal admiration for the Duke of Zhou is portrayed in *Analects*, "Shu er" (Ruan 1980:2,481), "Tai bo" (Ruan 1980:2,487).

[91] Yang and Wang 2008:31–33. Briefly, Lu experienced an equal number of filial and fraternal successions during the Western Zhou period, such that it was later suggested that the pattern could be taken as the rule; see *Shiji*, "Lu Zhougong shijia," 1,532. As Yang and Wang point out, this should be understood as a justification.

the latter figure's exemplary accomplishments and devoted service.[92] This grant came in the wake of what has been called the "second conquest of Shang" during the early Western Zhou, in which the Zhou fought former Shang adherents and local populations all the way to the coast of modern Shandong province.[93] Lu was thus situated on the site of a settlement of great significance to the Shang, and the original population of Lu was historically understood to have consisted largely of persons of former Shang affiliation.[94] The religious traditions of Lu thus supposedly included certain unusual elements syncretizing these two traditions.[95]

As one of the states founded after the second conquest, and occupying the strategically significant location that it did, Lu was well situated to fulfill the vaunted role of "screen for Zhou" (see "States" above). However, relations between Lu and the Zhou royal court seem to have cooled over the course of the Western Zhou period, judging from the lack of references to communications between Lu and the kings in later bronzes (Li Feng 2006:119); and during the later reigns of the Western Zhou period, a conflict reportedly arose between the royal and ducal houses over the succession in Lu (Li Feng 2006:138; *Shiji*, "Lu Zhougong shijia," 1,527–1,528).

Ba 霸

In 2007, an elite cemetery was discovered in northern Shaanxi, the rich furnishings of which turned out to include a number of inscribed bronzes of Western Zhou date (Shanxi 2012). The inscriptions of these bronzes make clear that the polity to whose

---

[92] *Shiji*, "Lu Zhougong shijia," 1,518; Yang and Wang 2009:23–27. Bo Qin is generally identified with the Qin mentioned in the inscriptions of the Dazhu Qin *ding* 大祝禽鼎 (1937–1938) and the Qin *gui* 禽簋 (4041); see e.g., Ma 1986–1990:18.

[93] Li Feng 2006:304–314, 306 quoted. There is a strain of thought that holds that the Lu famous from the ancient Chinese histories was in fact the second state of that name, the first being located in the vicinity of Lushan, modern Henan province, and having been granted to the Duke of Zhou by his brother King Wu; the Lu located in Shandong and granted to the Duke and his descendants by King Cheng, the story goes, kept the name of the original grant. On this point see *Shiji*:126–128; Liu Zongxian 2007:39; Li Feng 2006:306n20. Hsu and Linduff 1988:158–159 follows this tradition in part (citing Chen Pan 1969); Li Feng (2006:306n20) notes evidence opposing this chronology. On the early history of the Western Zhou, see also Khayutina, this volume.

[94] Lu is said to have occupied the original location of a polity called Yan or sometimes Shang Yan (to distinguish it from the state of Yan founded during the early Western Zhou period, on which see the section on Yan below); see e.g., Liu Zongxian 2007:35–37. For the classic historical statement on this foundation of Lu and its inclusion of several *zu* 族 of Shang affiliation, see *Zuozhuan*, Duke Ding, 4th year (Ruan 1980:2,134; translated in e.g., Creel 1970:91–92), with the caveat that that source is of later date (see Cheng 1993). On the Qufu site, capital of Lu from the late Western Zhou period on, see Shandong et al. 1982. Note, however, that Cui 1992 has shown that the remains at Qufu begin with the late Western Zhou rather than the early Western Zhou, as suggested by the preparers of the official Qufu report; see also Li Feng 1006:314–315, and Falkenhausen 2006:176.

[95] In particular, Lu is said to have maintained separate altars to the earth (*she* 社) in the styles of, or perhaps intended for the use of, both the Zhou and Shang peoples; on this tradition see Yang and Wang 2009:29–32.

ruling family the cemetery belonged was called Ba 霸 and that the ruling family of Ba engaged in occasional public expressions of subordination to the Zhou royal house.[96] A bronze produced by the leader of this apparently relatively small polity was once previously discovered in a tomb associated with the powerful state of Jin, within whose area of influence Ba undoubtedly fell (Shanxi 2011:18; Beijing University 2000:9; Babo *gui* 霸伯簋 [NA0939]). The grave goods of Ba show distinct regional characteristics (Shanxi 2011:18; Beijing University 2000:9; Babo *gui* 霸伯簋 [NA0939]), suggesting the influence of a local tradition of bronze production. Given the importance of bronzes as a symbol of participation in the elite culture of Zhou, this fact suggests that the state of Ba was in a position of divided loyalties, so to speak, enjoying political and cultural connections with both the Zhou royal house and its nominal local representatives, the rulers of Jin. In all likelihood, this state of affairs held true for many of the small local states founded and incorporated during the Western Zhou.[97]

Zeng 曾

The state of Zeng, located in modern Hubei province, is best known from the gorgeous bounties recovered by modern archaeologists from the tomb of Marquis Yi, a potentate of Zeng who lived and died during the Early Warring States period.[98] Until recently, the archaeological discoveries associated with Zeng dated back no further than the late Western Zhou, suggesting that the state might have come into existence around that time.[99] However, recently, archaeologists have uncovered additional complements of tombs of Zeng rulers, ranging in date all the way back to the early Western Zhou.[100] The extraordinarily rich contents of these tombs include inscribed bronzes that hint at the details of the political situation in the Suizhou region.[101] These new discoveries have

---

[96] In particular, the inscription of the Shang *yu* 尚盂 (M1017:6) specifies that the Zhou king dispatched a representative to carry out the *mieli* (recounting of merits) ceremony for Shang, probably the Elder of Ba (*Babo* 霸伯), i.e., the head of the Ba polity; see Li Xueqin 2011; Shanxi 2011:16–17, figs. 7.2, 8). Whether this act of patronage reflected an ongoing subordination of Ba to the Zhou kings, or whether it simply provided a convenient pretext for an occasional expression of political relations between the ruling families of Zhou and Ba, is difficult to determine.

[97] Though sources disagree on the total number of states created by or integrated into the Zhou political system, it was certainly over 100; see Hsu 1999:547–548; Chen Pan 1969.

[98] On the tomb of Marquis Yi, see Hubei Provincial Museum 1989; Falkenhausen 2006:306–308.

[99] Yang Kuan 2003:642; interpretation recalled in Hubei and Suizhou 2012. An exception may have been the Zhong *yan* 中甗 (949), dating in all likelihood to the reign of King Zhao, in which the Zeng in question is perhaps mentioned (Ma 1986–1990:76; Li Feng 2006:328–329). Mortuary sites associated with the rulers of Zeng are quite numerous; Fang Qin 2014 provides a convenient summary.

[100] The recently discovered Yejiashan cemetery in Suizhou, Hubei, dates to the early Western Zhou period; see Hubei and Suizhou 2012 (summarized in English as Hubei Provincial Institute et al 2013), as well as Hubei and Suizhou 2013. Another Zeng cemetery was recently discovered at Wenfengta, Suizhou, the tombs of which are of mid- to late Springs and Autumns date; see Hubei and Suizhou 2014.

[101] Hubei and Suizhou (2012:51) notes that the inscriptions from Yejiashan contain references to 16 various lineages or states.

necessitated a rethinking of the geographic distribution of military and economic power in the southern reaches of the Zhou cultural sphere during the early Western Zhou. Likewise, the relative absence of the apparently wealthy and influential state of Zeng from the canonical sources on the Western Zhou casts into sharp relief the endemic biases of the received textual record.[102]

Yu

Near the city of Baoji, at the western end of the Wei River Valley as it flows through Shaanxi Province, three cemeteries are to be found that belonged to the ruling family of a polity called Yu. From a material-cultural standpoint, the elite population of Yu clearly enjoyed very close relations with Zhou but appears also to have maintained certain independent mortuary traditions, including in particular the use of chamber-side niches for consort burials of accompaniment (see Lu and Hu 1988:esp. 45–46, 48, 94–95, etc.; Sun Yan 2012:54). Based on the inscriptions of bronzes recovered from the Yu tombs, Yu was closely integrated into the Zhou political network writ large, inasmuch as the ruling lineage thereof exchanged marriage partners with both influential families from the Zhou heartland and nearby states sharing the Ji surname with the Zhou royal house (Sena 2005:228–229; Falkenhausen 2006:80; Sun Yan 2012:53, 62–63; Khayutina 2014:50). However, Yu is not proven to have been directly subject to the Zhou kings (Khayutina 2014:48). Instead, Yu may have been an example of a polity near the Zhou heartland that chose, despite its independence, to participate at least partially in the Zhou cultural and political sphere.

BIBLIOGRAPHY

Academia Sinica's Bronze Inscriptions Studio 中央研究院史語所金文工作室. "Digital Archives of Bronze Images and Inscriptions 殷周金文暨青銅器資料庫." http://www.ihp. sinica.edu.tw/~bronze/. Accessed July 7, 2017.
Adamski, Susanne Jenny 2014. "The Depiction of Archery in Bronze Inscriptions from the Western Zhou Period (1045–771 BCE) Die Darstellung des Bogenschießens in Bronzeinschriften

---

[102] On the apparent absence of Zeng from the classics, see Hsu and Linduff 1988:130. The relationship of Zeng to the received historical tradition is the subject of a longstanding debate in early China studies, centering around the question of whether the Zeng known from the sites previously cited was the same polity as a Sui 隨 referred to in the received histories (see e.g., *Zuozhuan*, Duke Huan, 6th year, 1,749, cited in Yang Kuan 2003:643). The literature on this debate is too extensive to list here; for an efficient summary, see Wang Xinchun 2013. The extension of the chronology of Zeng back into the Early Western Zhou period, as demanded by the Yejiashan find, has changed the terms of this debate. Recent work based on the Yejiashan materials has begun the effort to situate Zeng within the network of early Western Zhou political and kinship relations; see e.g., Huang and Hu 2014a; Huang and Hu 2014b. The recent discovery of a *ge*-blade bearing an inscription that mentions a "Grand Master of Horse of Sui" (*Sui da sima* 隨大司馬; see Hubei and Suizhou 2014:30–31, 33) has added new evidence to this debate; however, I concur with Wang Xinchun (2013:55) that the discovery is not enough to settle the matter.

der West-Zhōu-Zeit (1045–771 v.Chr.): Eine philologische Quellenanalyse." PhD dissertation, Westfälische Wilhelms-Universität Münster, Münster, Germany.

Allan, Sarah 2007. "On the Identity of Shang Di 上帝 and the Origin of the Concept of a Celestial Mandate (*tian ming* 天命)." *Early China* 31:1–46.

Barnard, Noel 1960. "A Recently Excavated Inscribed Bronze of the Reign of King Mu of Chou." *Monumenta Serica* 19:67–113.

Baoji and Fufeng. Baoji Municipal Institute of Archaeology and Fufeng County Museum 2008. "The Cache of Valuable Western Zhou Bronzes at Wujunxicun, Fufeng, Shaanxi." Translated by Nick Vogt. *Chinese Archaeology* 8:96–103.

Baoji and Fufeng. Baoji Municipal Institute of Archaeology and Fufang County Museum 宝鸡市考古研究所, 扶风县博物 馆 2007. "Preliminary Report on the Excavation of a Cache of Western Zhou Bronzes at Wujunxicun, Fufeng, Shaanxi 陕西扶风五郡西村西周青铜器窖藏发掘简报." *Wenwu* 8:4–27.

Beijing University Department of Archaeology Shang and Zhou Group and Shanxi Institute of Archaeology 北京大学考古学系商周组, 山西省考古研究所 2000. *Tianma-Qucun 1980–1989* 天马—曲村 1980~1989. Beijing: Kexue.

Blakeley, Barry 1976. "On the 'Feudal' Interpretation of Chou China." *Early China* 2:35–37.

Bodde, Derk 1981. "Feudalism in China." In *Essays on Chinese Civilization*, edited by Charles Leblanc, 85–131. Princeton, NJ: Princeton University Press.

Brashier, Kenneth 2011. *Ancestral Memory in Early China*. Cambridge, MA and London: Harvard University Press.

Chen, Hanping 陈汉平 1986. *The Western Zhou System of Documents of Command* 西周册命制度研究. Shanghai: Xuelin.

Chen, Jie 陈絜 2007. *The Western Zhou System of Surnames* 商周姓氏制度研究. Beijing: Shangwu.

Chen, Mengjia 陈梦家 1935. "Shang and Zhou Sacrifices in Paleographical Materials 古文字中的商周祭祀." *Yanjing xuebao* 18–19(1):91–155.

Chen, Pan 陳槃 1969. *Collated Noble Surnames and Durations of the Various States in the Tables of the Great Affairs of the Spring and Autumn Period* 春秋大事表列國爵姓及存滅表譔異. Taipei: Academia Sinica.

Chen, Pan 陳槃 1970. "Regional States Not Appearing in the Tables of the Great Affairs of the Spring and Autumn Period 不見於春秋大事表之春秋方國稿." Taipei: Academia Sinica, 1970.

Chen, Qiyou 陳奇猷 (Lü Buwei呂不韋) 1984. *Collated Explanations of the Springs and Autumns of Master Lü* 呂氏春秋校释. Shanghai: Xuelin.

Chen, Zhaorong 陳昭容 2001. "The Status of Women in Zhou Dynasty Sacrifices: Gender, Status, and Role in Bronze Inscriptions [Part 1] 周代 婦女在祭祀中的地位-青銅器銘文中的性別、身份與角色研究(之一)." *Qinghua xuebao* 清華學報 31(4): 395–440.

Chen, Zhaorong 陳昭容 2006. "'Dowry' and 'Dowry Vessels' in the Marriage Relations of the Zhou Dynasty: Gender, Status, and Role in Bronze Inscriptions, Part 2 兩週婚姻關係中的'媵'與媵器-青銅器銘文 中的性別、身分與角色研究之二." *Zhongyang yanjiuyuan lishi yuyan yanjiusuo jikan* 77(2):193–278.

Cheng, Anne 1993. "*Ch'un ch'iu* 春秋, *Kung yang* 公羊, *Ku liang* 穀梁 and *Tso chuan* 左傳." In *Early Chinese Texts: A Bibliographical Guide*. Edited by Michael Loewe, 67–76. Berkeley, CA: Society for the Study of Early China.

Cook, Constance A. 1997. "Wealth and the Western Zhou." *Bulletin of the School of Oriental and African Studies* 60(2):253–294.

Cook, Constance A. 2007. "Tai Ren." In *Biographical Dictionary of Chinese Women: Antiquity through Sui, 1600 B.C.E.–618 C.E.* Edited by Lily Xiao Hong Lee and A. D. Stefanowska, 74–75. Armonk, NY and London: M. E. Sharpe.

Cook, Constance A. 2016a. "Da Yu *ding* 大盂鼎." In *A Source Book of Ancient Chinese Bronze Inscriptions.* Edited by Constance A. Cook and Paul R. Goldin, 30–35. Berkeley: Society for the Study of Early China.

Cook, Constance A. 2016b. "Hu *guigai* 虎簋蓋." In *A Source Book of Ancient Chinese Bronze Inscriptions.* Edited by Constance A. Cook and Paul R. Goldin, 74–76. Berkeley: Society for the Study of Early China.

Cook, Constance A. 2016c. "Shenzi Ta *guigai* 沈子它簋蓋." In *A Source Book of Ancient Chinese Bronze Inscriptions.* Edited by Constance A. Cook and Paul R. Goldin, 36–38. Berkeley: Society for the Study of Early China.

Cook, Constance A. 2016d. "Shi Qiang *pan* 史墙盤." In *A Source Book of Ancient Chinese Bronze Inscriptions.* Edited by Constance A. Cook and Paul R. Goldin, 93–100. Berkeley: Society for the Study of Early China.

Cook, Constance A. 2016e. "Xing *zhong* 癲鐘 and Related Inscriptions." In *A Source Book of Ancient Chinese Bronze Inscriptions.* Edited by Constance A. Cook and Paul R. Goldin, 115–125. Berkeley: Society for the Study of Early China.

Cook, Constance A., and Paul R. Goldin, eds. 2016. *A Source Book of Ancient Chinese Bronze Inscriptions.* Early China Special Monograph Series 7. Berkeley, CA: Society for the Study of Early China.

Creel, Herrlee G. 1970. *The Origins of Statecraft in China*, vol. 1: *The Western Zhou Empire.* Chicago and London: University of Chicago Press.

Cui, Lequan 崔乐泉 1992. "The Sequence of Eastern Zhou Archaeological Cultures from the Shandong Region 山东地区东周考古学文化的序列." *Huaxia kaogu* 华夏考古 4:72–97.

De Bary, William Theodore, and Irene Bloom 1999. *Sources of Chinese Tradition*, vol. 1: *From Earliest Times to 1600.* New York, Chichester: Columbia University Press.

DeMarrais, Elizabeth, Luis Jaime Castillo, and Timothy Earle 1996. "Ideology, Materialization, and Power Strategies." *Current Anthropology* 37(1):15–31.

Dewall, Magdalene von 1964. *Pferd und Wagen im frühen China.* Bonn: Rudolf Habelt Verlag.

Elman, Benjamin A., and Martin Kern, eds. 2009. *Statecraft and Classical Learning: The Rituals of Zhou in East Asian History.* Leiden: Brill.

Eno, Robert 1990. *The Confucian Creation of Heaven: Philosophy and the Defense of Ritual Mastery.* Albany: State University of New York Press.

Falkenhausen, Lothar von 1993. "Issues in Western Zhou Studies: A Review Article." *Early China* 18:139–226.

Falkenhausen, Lothar von 1999. "Late Western Zhou Taste." *Etudes Chinoises* 18(1–2):143–178.

Falkenhausen, Lothar von 2006. *Chinese Society in the Age of Confucius (1000–250 BC): The Archaeological Evidence.* Los Angeles: Cotsen Institute of Archaeology.

Falkenhausen, Lothar von 2011. "The Royal Audience and Its Reflections in Western Zhou Bronze Inscriptions." In *Writing and Literacy in Early China.* Edited by Li Feng and David Prager Branner, 239–270. Seattle: University of Washington Press.

Falkenhausen, Lothar von 2014. "Review of Li Feng, 'Bureaucracy and the State in Early China: Governing the Western Zhou.'" *Zhejiang daxue yishu yu kaogu yanjiu* 浙江大學藝術與考古研究 1(10):252–277.

Fang, Qin 方勤 2014. "An Archaeological Perspective on the History of the State of Zeng 曾国历史的考古学观察." *Jianghan kaogu* 江汉考古 133(4):109–115.

Gassmann, Robert H. 2006. *Kinship and Society in Early China: Terms, Structures, and Processes, Verwandtschaft und Gesellschaft im alten China: Begriffe, Strukturen und Prozesse.* Bern: Peter Lang.

Gernet, Jacques 1983. *The Chinese World: The History of China from the Beginnings to the Present, Die chinesische Welt: Die geschichte Chinas von den Anfängen bis zur Jetztzeit.* Frankfurt: Insel Verlag.

Glahn, Richard von 2016. *The Economic History of China: From Antiquity to the Nineteenth Century.* Cambridge, UK: Cambridge University Press.

Granet, Marcel 1952. *La Féodalite chinoise.* Oslo: Institut pour l'Étude Comparative des Civilisations.

Guo, Moruo 郭沫若 1954. *Jinwen congkao* 金文从考. Beijing: Renmin.

Guo, Moruo 郭沫若 2005. "The Age of Slavery *Nulizhi shidai* 奴隶制时代." Beijing: Zhongguo renmin daxue.

He, Shuhuan 何樹環 2007. *Xi Zhou ximing mingwen xin yan* 西周錫命銘文新研. Taibei: Wenjin.

Henan and Zhoukou. Henan Provincial Institute of Cultural Relics and Archaeology, and Zhoukou Area Cultural Relics Bureau 河南省文物考古研究所, 周口地区文化局 2000. "A Western Zhou Tomb Excavation at Taiqinggong, Luyi County, Henan 河南鹿邑 县太清宫西周墓的发掘." *Kaogu* 9:9–23.

Hsü, Cho-yun 1999. "The Spring and Autumn Period." In *The Cambridge History of Ancient China: From the Origins of Civilization to 221 B.C.* Edited by Michael Loewe and Edward L. Shaughnessy, 545–586. Cambridge, UK: Cambridge University Press.

Hsü, Cho-yun, and Katheryn M. Linduff 1988. *Western Chou Civilization.* New Haven, CT and London: Yale University Press.

Hu, Houxuan 胡厚宣 1989 [1944]. "Veneration of the Sky/Heaven during the Yin Period Yin 殷代之天神崇拜汇." In *Collected Writings on Shang History in Oracle Bone Studies* 甲骨学商史论丛, vol. 2. Edited by Hu Houxuan, 1–29. Shanghai: Shanghai shudian. Originally published Chengdu: Jilu daxue.

Huang, Fengchun 黄凤春, and Gang Hu 胡刚 2014a. "On the Figure 'Nangong' in Western Zhou Bronze Inscriptions and the Affiliation of the Western Zhou Zeng State Cemetery at Yejiashan, Suizhou 说西周金文中的"南公"—兼 论随州叶家山西周曾国墓地的族属." *Jianghan kaogu* 131(2):50–56.

Huang, Fengchun 黄凤春, and Gang Hu 胡刚 2014b. "Further Discussion on the Figure 'Nangong' in Western Zhou Bronze Inscriptions: A Second Discussion of the Affiliation of the Western Zhou Zeng State Cemetery at Yejiashan 再说 西周金文中的'南公'—二论叶家山西周曾国墓地的族属." *Jianghan kaogu* 134(5):41–45.

Huang, Ranwei 黃然偉 1978. *Reward Inscriptions of the Yin and Zhou Periods* 殷周青銅器賞賜銘文研究. Hong Kong: Longmen.

Hubei Provincial Institute of Cultural Relics and Archaeology, and Suizhou Museum 2013. "The Yejiashan Cemetery of the Western Zhou Dynasty in Suizhou City, Hubei." Translated in *Chinese Archaeology* 13:1–10.

Hubei Provincial Museum 湖北省博物馆 1989. *The Tomb of Marquis Yi of Zeng* 曾侯乙墓, 2 vols. Beijing: Wenwu chubanshe.

Hubei and Suzhou. Hubei Provincial Museum, Hubei Provincial Institute of Cultural Relics and Archaeology, and Suizhou Municipal Museum 湖北省博物馆, 湖北省文物考古研究

所, 随州市博物馆, eds. 2013. *Yejiashan, Suizhou: An Early Western Zhou Cemetery of the State of Zeng* 随州叶家山——西周早期曾国墓地. Beijing: Wenwu chubanshe.

Hubei and Suzhou. Hubei Provincial Institute of Cultural Relics and Archaeology and Suizhou Municipal Museum 湖北省文物考古研究所, 随州市博物馆 2012. "The Western Zhou Cemetery at Yejiashan, Suizhou, Hubei 湖北随州市叶家山西周墓地." *Kaogu* 7:31–52, 101–104.

Institute of Archaeology, Chinese Academy of Social Sciences中国社会科学院考古研究所, ed. 1984–1994. *Compendium of Yin and Zhou Bronze Inscriptions* 殷周金文集成, 18 vols. Beijing: Zhonghua.

Itō, Michiharu 伊藤道治 1975. *The Formation of the Royal Court in Early China* 中国古代王朝の形成. Tokyo: Sōbunsha.

Itō, Michiharu 伊藤道治 1978. "On the Qiu Wei Bronzes: Private Land Rights in the Western Zhou Period 裘衛諸器考—西周期土地所有形態に関する私権." *Tōyōshi kenkyū* 37(1):35–58.

Jing, Hongyan 景红艳 2006. "The Western Zhou System of Rewards *Xi Zhou shangci zhidu yanjiu* 西周赏赐制度研究." PhD dissertation, Shaanxi shifan daxue 陕西师范大学, Xi'an, China.

Joint Archaeological Team of Shanxi Provincial Institute of Archaeology 2012. "The Western Zhou Cemetery at Dahekou in Yicheng County, Shanxi." Translated by Nicholas Vogt. *Chinese Archaeology* 12:1–12.

Kane, Virginia 1982–1983. "Aspects of Western Zhou Appointment Inscriptions: the Charge, the Gifts, and the Response." *Early China* 8, 14–28.

Kern, Martin 2007. "The Performance of Writing in Western Zhou China." In *The Poetics of Grammar and the Metaphysics of Sound and Sign*. Edited by Sergio La Porta and David Shulman, 109–176. Leiden: Brill.

Kern, Martin 2009. "Bronze Inscriptions, the *Shijing*, and the *Shangshu*: The Evolution of the Ancestral Sacrifice during the Western Zhou." In *Early Chinese Religion, Part 1: Shang through Han (1250 B.C.–220 A.D.)*. Edited by John Lagerwey and Marc Kalinowski, 143–200. Leiden: Brill.

Khayutina, Maria 2010. "Royal Hospitality and Geopolitical Constitution of the Western Zhou Polity (1046/5–771 BC)." *T'oung Pao* 96.1/3 :1–77.

Khayutina, Maria 2014. "Marital Alliances and Affinal Relatives (*sheng* 甥 and *hungou* 婚媾) in the Society and Politics of Zhou China in the Light of Bronze Inscriptions." *Early China* 37:1–61.

Lau, Ulrich 1999. *Sources on the Distribution and Transfer of Land in the Western Zhou Dynasty (1045?–771 B.C., Quellenstudien zur Landvergabe und Bodenübertragung in der westlichen Zhou-Dynastie (1045? - 771 v.Chr.)*." Sankt Augustin: Institut Monumenta Serica.

Lee, Lily Xiao Hong, and A. D. Stefanowska, eds. 2007. *Biographical Dictionary of Chinese Women: Antiquity through Sui, 1600 B.C.E.–618 C.E.* Armonk, NY and London: M. E. Sharpe.

Legge, James 1960 [1865]. *The Chinese Classics*, vol. 3: *The Shoo King or the Book of Historical Documents*. Hong Kong: Hong Kong University Press. Originally published London: Henry Frowde.

Lewis, Mark Edward 1999. "Warring States Political History." In *The Cambridge History of Ancient China: From the Origins of Civilization to 221 B.C.* Edited by Michael Loewe and Edward L. Shaughnessy, 587–650. Cambridge, UK: Cambridge University Press.

Li, Feng 1997. "Ancient Reproductions and Calligraphic Variations: Studies of Western Zhou Bronzes with 'Identical' Inscriptions." *Early China* 22:1–41.

Li, Feng 2001–2002. "'Offices' in Bronze Inscriptions and Western Zhou Government Administration." *Early China* 26–27:1–72.

Li, Feng 2003. "'Feudalism' and Western Zhou China: A Criticism." *Harvard Journal of Asiatic Studies* 63(1):115–144.

Li, Feng 2006. *Landscape and Power in Early China: The Crisis and Fall of the Western Zhou, 1045–771 BC.* Cambridge, UK: Cambridge University Press.

Li, Feng 2008. *Bureaucracy and the State in Early China: Governing the Western Zhou,* Cambridge, UK: Cambridge University Press.

Li, Feng 2011. "Literacy and the Social Contexts of Writing in the Western Zhou." In *Writing and Literacy in Early China: Studies from the Columbia Early China Seminar.* Edited by Li Feng and David Prager Branner, 277–279. Seattle and London: University of Washington Press.

Li, Xiangping 李向平 1991. *Royal and Spiritual Authority: Government and Religion in the Zhou Dynasty* 王權與神權-周代政治與宗教研究. Shenyang: Liaoning jiaoyu.

Li, Xueqin 李学勤 1987. "On the Six Armies and the Eight Armies in Western Zhou Bronze Inscriptions 论西周金文中的六 师、八师." *Huaxia kaogu* 华夏考古 2:207–210.

Li, Xueqin 李学勤 2011. "A Preliminary Explanation of the Inscription of the Shang *yu* from Dahekou, Yicheng 翼城大河口尚孟铭文试释." *Wenwu* 9:67–68.

Li, Yachen 李亚辰 1954. *Slavery and Feudalism in China* 中国的奴隶制与封建制. Huadong renmin.

Li, Zhongcao 李仲操 1991. "Terms of Address for Women in Western Zhou Bronze Inscriptions 西周金文中的妇女称谓." *Baoji wenbo* 1:35–39.

Liu, Yu 刘雨 1989. "Ancestral Rites in Western Zhou Bronze Inscriptions 西周金文中的祭祖礼." *Kaogu xuebao* 4:495–522.

Liu, Yuan 刘源 2004. *Shang and Zhou Rites of Ancestor Worship* 商周祭祖礼研究. Beijing: Shangwu.

Liu Zongxian 刘宗贤, ed. 2007. *The Culture of the State of Lu* 鲁文化研究. Jinan: Qi Lu shushe.

Loewe, Michael 1972. "Review of Herrlee G. Creel, *The Origins of Statecraft in China. Vol. One. The Western Chou Empire.*" *Bulletin of the School of Oriental and African Studies* 35(2):395–400.

Lu, Liancheng 卢连成, and Hu Zhisheng 胡智生 1988. *The Cemetery of the Yu State at Baoji* 宝鸡 㠪国墓地, 2 vols. Beijing: Wenwu chubanshe.

Lü, Wenyu 吕文郁 1990a. "On the Royal Territory in the Zhou Dynasty Zhoudai wangji kaoshu 周代王畿考述." *Shehui kexue jikan* 社会科学辑刊 5:108.

Lü, Wenyu 吕文郁 1990b. "The System of Fiefs in the Zhou Dynasty 周代的 采邑制度." *Wenxian* 文献 4:74–82.

Ma, Chengyuan 马承源) [and Shanghai Museum Shang Zhou Bronze Inscription Selection Group 上海博物馆商周 青铜器铭文选编写组] 1986–1990. *Selected Inscriptions from Shang and Zhou Dynasty Bronzes* 商周 青铜器名文选, 4 vols. Beijing: Wenwu chubanshe.

Maspero, Henri 1950. "Feudal Rule and Land Ownership in Ancient China, Le régime féodale et la propriété foncière dans la Chine antique." In *Miscellaneous Posthumous Writings on the Religions and History of China III: Historical Studies, Mélanges posthumes sur les Religions et l'Histoire de la Chine III: Études Historiques.* Edited by H. Maspero, 111–146. Paris: Musée Guimet, Bibliothèque de Diffusion.

Matsumaru, Michio 松丸道雄 1970. "The Structure of the Yin and Zhou States 殷周国家の構造." In *Iwanami Lectures: World History* 岩波講座:世界歴史. Edited by Kabayama Kōichi 樺山紘一, 49–100. Tokyo: Iwanami shoten.

McMullen, David L. 2011. "Devolution in Chinese History: The Fengjian Debate Revisited." *International Journal of China Studies* 2(2):135–154.

Musha, Akira 武者章 1980. "A Tentative Categorization of Western Zhou Appointment Inscriptions 西周冊命金文分類のこころみ." In *Bronzes and the Western Zhou State, Sei Shū seidōki to sono kokka* 西周青銅器とその国家. Edited by Michio Matsumaru 松丸道雄, 241–324. Tokyo: Tokyo daigaku.

Pankenier, David W. 1995. "The Cosmo-Political Background of Heaven's Mandate." *Early China* 20:121–176.

Pulleyblank, Edwin G. 2000. "Ji and Jiang: The Role of Exogamic Clans in the Organization of the Zhou Polity." *Early China* 25:1–27.

Qian, Hang 钱杭 1991. *The History of the "Lineage Model" System of the Zhou Dynasty* 周代宗法制度史研究. Shanghai: Xuelin.

Rawson, Jessica 1989. "Statesmen or Barbarians? The Western Zhou as Seen through Their Bronzes." *Proceedings of the British Academy* 75 (1989), 71–95.

Rawson, Jessica 1990. *Western Zhou Ritual Bronzes from the Arthur M. Sackler Collections.* 2 vols. Washington, DC: Arthur M. Sackler Foundation.

Rawson, Jessica 1999. "Western Zhou Archaeology." In *The Cambridge History of Ancient China: From the Origins of Civilization to 221 B.C.,* ed. Michael Loewe and Edward L. Shaughnessy, 352–449. Cambridge: Cambridge University Press.

Ruan, Yuan 阮元 1980. *Commentary and Subcommentary on the Thirteen Classics Shisanjing zhushu* 十三經註疏. Beijing: Zhonghua.

Sena, David 2005. "Reproducing Society: Lineage and Kinship in Western Zhou China." PhD dissertation, University of Chicago, Chicago, IL, USA.

Sena, David 2012. "Arraying the Ancestors in Ancient China: Narratives of Lineage History in the 'Scribe Qiang' and 'Qiu' Bronzes." *Asia Major* 25(1):63–81.

Shaanxi Provincial Institute of Archaeology et al. 2004. "The Discovery of the Western Zhou Bronze Hoard at Yangjiacun in Meixian, Shaanxi, and Its Implications." Translated by Zhang Liangren. *Chinese Archaeology* 4:34–38.

Shaanxi Provincial Institute of Archaeology, Joint Baoji Municipal Archaeology Work Team and Yanjiacun Archaeology Team, and Meixian Cultural Station 陕西省考古研究所, 宝鸡市考古工作对杨家村联合考古队 眉县文化馆 2003. "Preliminary Report on the Excavation of a Cache of Western Zhou Bronze Vessels at Yangjiacun, Mei County, Shaanxi 陕西眉县杨家村西周青铜器窖藏发觉简报." *Wenwu* 6:4–42.

Shaanxi Zhouyuan Archaeology Team 陕西周源考古队 1978. "Preliminary Report on the Excavation of Western Zhou Bronze Vessel Cache No. 1 at Zhuangbai, Fufeng, Shaanxi 陕西扶风装白一号西周青铜器发掘简报." *Wenwu* 3:1–18.

Shandong Provincial Institute of Cultural Relics and Archaeology 山东省文物考古研究所 et al. 1982. *The Old City of the Lu State at Qufu* 曲阜鲁国故城. Jinan: Qilu.

Shanxi sheng kaogu yanjiusuo Dahekou mudi lianhe kaogudui 山西省考古研究所大河口墓地聯合考古隊 2011. "The Western Zhou Cemetery at Dahekou, Yicheng County, Shanxi 山西翼城县大河口西周墓地." *Kaogu* 7:9–18, plates 3–6.

Shaughnessy, Edward L. 1983–1985. "The Date of the 'Duo You Ding' and Its Significance." *Early China* 9.1 (1983–1985):55–69.

Shaughnessy, Edward L. 1988. "Historical Perspectives on the Introduction of the Chariot into China." *Harvard Journal of Asiatic Studies* 48(1):189–237.

Shaughnessy, Edward L. 1991. *Sources of Western Zhou History: Inscribed Bronze Vessels.* Berkeley: University of California Press.

Shaughnessy, Edward L. 1997. *Before Confucius: Studies in the Creation of the Confucian Classics*. Albany: SUNY Press.

Shaughnessy, Edward L. 1999. "Western Zhou History." In *The Cambridge History of Ancient China: From the Origins of Civilization to 221 B.C.* Edited by Michael Loewe and Edward L. Shaughnessy, 292–351. Cambridge, UK: Cambridge University Press.

Shirakawa Shizuka 白川静 1959. "Explaning *mieli* 蔑曆解." *Kōkotsugaku* 甲骨學 4–5:89–104.

Skosey, Laura A. 1996. "The Legal System and Legal Traditions of the Western Zhou (1045 B.C.E.–771 B.C.E.)." PhD dissertation, University of Chicago, Chicago, IL, USA.

Skosey, Laura A. 2016. ""Hu *ding* 曶鼎." In *A Source Book of Ancient Chinese Bronze Inscriptions*. Edited by Constance A. Cook and Paul R. Goldin, 129–135. Berkeley: Society for the Study of Early China.

Sterckx, Roel 2005. "Food and Philosophy in Early China." In *Of Tripod and Palate: Food, Politics, and Religion in Traditional China*. Edited by R. Sterckx, 34–61. New York and Houndmills: Palgrave Macmillan.

Sun, Yan 2012. "Material Culture and Social Identities in Western Zhou's Frontier: Case Studies of the Yu and Peng Lineages." *Asian Archaeology* 1, 52–72.

Sun, Zuoyun 孫作雲 1966. *The Book of Songs and Zhou Dynasty Society* 詩經與周代社會研究. Beijing: Zhonghua.

Takayama, Setsuya 高山節也 1980. "The Function of the 'Mandate of Heaven' in the Western Zhou State 西周国家における 「天命」の機能." In *Bronzes and the Western Zhou State* 西周青銅器とその国家. Edited by Michio Matsumaru 松丸道雄, 325–390. Tokyo: Tokyo daigaku.

Tan, Qixiang 譚其驤, ed. 1982. *Historical Atlas of China* 1 中國 歷史地圖集 vol. 1. Shanghai: Ditu.

Tang, Lan, and Gugong bowuyuan 故宮博物院, ed. 1995. *Collected Writings of Mr. Tang Lan on Bronze Inscriptions* 唐兰先生金文论集. Beijing: Zijincheng.

Toyota, Hisashi 豊田久 1980. "On the Structure of Ruling Authority in the Zhou Dynasty: With the 'Recipients of the Mandate of Heaven' 周王朝の君主権の 構造について一「天命の膺受」者を中心に." In *Bronzes and the Western Zhou State* 西周青銅器とその国家. Edited by Michio Matsumaru 松丸道雄, 391–456. Tokyo: Tokyo daigaku.

Tsinghua University Centter for Excavated Literature Research and Protection 清華大學出土文獻研究與保護中心 2011. *The Warring States Bamboo Slips in the Collection of Tsinghua University* 清華大學 藏戰國竹簡, vol. 2. Edited by Xueqin Li 李學勤 ("Xi nian" 系年). Shanghai: Shanghai wenyi.

Twitchett, Denis, and John K. Fairbank, eds. 1986. *The Cambridge History of China*, vol. 1: *The Ch'in and Han Empires, 221 B.C.–A.D. 220*. Cambridge, UK: Cambridge University Press.

Wang, Xianqian 王先謙 1984. *Collected Explanations of the* Book of the Later Han (*Hou Han shu*) 後漢書集解. 2 vols. Beijing: Zhonghua, 1984.

Wang, Xinchun 王新春 2013. "The Archaeological Riddle of the Century: The Conflict between the States of Zeng and Sui 考古学世纪之谜-曾国与随国之争." *Guojia renwen lishi* 国家人文历史 77(5):54–55.

Watson, Burton 1999. "The Economic Order." In *Sources of Chinese Tradition*, vol. 1: *From Earliest Times to 1600*. Edited by William Theodore De Bary and Irene Bloom, 353–366. New York, Chichester: Columbia University Press.

Wu, Hongsong 吳红松 2012. "The Western Zhou System of Rewards: From the Perspective of the Quantitative Analysis of Items Conferred in Western Zhou Bronze Inscriptions 西周赏

赐制度研究———以对西周金文赏赐物的量 化分析为视角." *Anhui nongye daxue xue-bao (shehui kexue ban)* 安徽农业大学学报 (社会科学版) 21(6):66–69.

Yan, Yiping 嚴一萍 1962. "The Old Meaning of *Mieli* 蔑曆古意." *Zhongguo wenzi* 10:1–13.

Yang, Chaoming 杨朝明, and Wang Qing 王青 2008. *Exploring the History and Culture of the State of Lu* 鲁国历史与文化探秘. Beijing: Wenwu chubanshe.

Yang, Chaoming 杨朝明, and Wang Qing 王青 2009. *The History and Culture of the State of Lu* 鲁国历史与文化. Beijing: Wenwu.

Yang, Kuan 杨宽 2003. *Western Zhou History* 西周史. Shanghai: Shanghai Renmin.

Yoshimoto, Michimasa 吉本道雅 1991. "Sei Shū satsumei kinbun kō 西周冊命金文考." *Shirin* 史林 74.5, 38–66.

Yin, Shengping 尹盛平 1992. *The Western Zhou Bronze Vessels of the Wei Lineage* 西周微氏家族青铜器群研究. Beijing: Wenwu.

Yu, Wei 于薇 2008. "Approaching the Question of Royal Territory in the Zhou Dynasty through the Conflict between the Royal House and the Su Lineage 从王室与苏氏之争看周王朝 的王畿问题." *Shehui kexue jikan* 社会科学辑刊 2:152–156.

Yu, Xingwu 于省吾 1964. "An Outline of the 'Six Armies' and 'Eight Armies' in the Western Zhou Bronze Inscriptions and Their System of Assignment to Land 略论西周金文中的"六师" 和"八师"及其屯田制." *Kaogu* 3:152–155.

Yu, Xingwu 于省吾, and Yao Xiaosui 姚孝遂, eds. 1996. *Collected Explanations of Oracle Bone Characters* 甲骨文字诂林, 4 vols. Beijing: Zhonghua.

Zhang, Guangming 张荣明 1993. "Evidence against the 'Sky/Heaven' Spirit of the Zhou Dynasty 周代 '天'神说驳证." *Tianjin shida xuebao* 天津师大学报 3:42–48.

Zhang, Yachu 张亚初, and Liu Yu 刘雨 1986. *Official Posts in Western Zhou Bronze Inscriptions* 西周金文管制研究. Beijing: Zhonghua.

Zhao, Guangxian 趙光賢 1980. *An Analysis of Zhou Dynasty Society* 周代社會辨析. Beijing: Renmin.

Zhou, Fagao 周法高, ed. 1974–1975. *Jinwen gulin* 金文詁林. 15 vols. Hong Kong: Xianggang zhongwen daxue.

Zhu, Fenghan 朱風瀚 1990. *Patterns of Kinship in the Shang and Zhou Dynasties* 商周家族形态研究. Tianjin: Tianjin guji.

Zhu, Fenghan 朱風瀚 1993. "The Veneration of the Sky/Heaven in the Shang and Zhou Dynasties 商周时期的天神崇拜." *Zhongguo shehui kexue* 中国 社会科学 4:191–192.

CHAPTER 19

WESTERN ZHOU RITES AND MORTUARY PRACTICE (INSCRIPTIONS AND TEXTS)

BY CONSTANCE A. COOK, LEHIGH UNIVERSITY

WARRING States–period classicists and adherents of Confucian ideals promoted an idealized notion of Zhou ritual (li 禮) based on their memory of Western Zhou–period norms. They helped to preserve ancient practices but also changed them radically to fit the exigencies of their changed social era; no longer did a king, designated the Son of Heaven, rule through a network of aristocratic lineages. The scholars refashioned the literary expression of practices originally associated with ancestor worship, transforming them into lessons for civil behavior. With the advent of modern archaeology, we now know that the transmitted texts documenting earlier rituals often were affected by later biases. While the transmitted texts record detailed rites for many aspects of political, domestic, and religious life, the excavated tombs generally reflect contemporary funerary practices rather than ones articulated many centuries earlier. Since many objects placed in Western Zhou tombs are not mentioned in the transmitted texts (for example, the small half-bird or dragon / half-man jade figurines in fetal-like positions analyzed by Childs-Johnson 2002 and in chapter 13; Allan 2010), it seems difficult to know their social meaning or ritual function based on texts. Fortunately, one type of item, bronze, more clearly reflects the political and religious rituals not only in its distribution in the wealthier ancient tombs and caches but also in the occasional inscribed text.

Western Zhou bronze inscriptions reveal some continuities with later documented rites, but more often than not scholars find many disparities between the actual and the idealized. For example, two major aspects of Confucian practice—the use of ritual music for self-cultivation and the emphasis on proper mortuary display as symbols of social rank and fealty—can be traced back to Western Zhou evidence, but contexts of the rites were quite different. For example, the use of music for self-cultivation in the earlier period was less associated with personal advancement to a sage-like mental state than it was with lineage advancement in the context of Zhou ancestor worship (Cook 2017; see chapter 21 by Scott Cook). Proper burial according to political rank and social status was particularly important to Confucians. This fundamental concept reflects a concern with social hierarchy that goes back to the late Neolithic. But the details of the rituals, the implements employed in them, the human and spiritual agents engaged, and even the expected results of the rituals no doubt varied over time and place. Where the Confucians' stated focus was secular social order, the Western Zhou concern, particularly early on, seemed to be with the supernatural order. For example, both groups worshipped *tian* 天 (the sky, heaven) as the source of life energy and political authority, but for the Confucians it evolved away from the star-filled/ancestor-filled court of the judgmental high god, Shangdi 上帝, into an abstract cosmic force, Nature, that could be embodied as a supreme mental and physical state of moral empowerment (see Csikszentmihalyi 2004). Transmitted texts presume to dictate the number of vessels, types of foods, clothing, and other such details for the conduct of funerals, but Western Zhou tombs and texts do not reflect the texts' focus on precisely differentiated sumptuary laws according to political rank. In fact, it seems that lineage rank during the Western Zhou determined wealth and power and that interment practices might have varied in the regional courts despite their tributary and political connections to the central court. Finally, the idealized versions of Zhou ritual may reflect only those late Western Zhou practices carried on in the local court of Lu 魯 (or other nearby eastern states, such as the powerful Qi 齊), where the Confucian group initially formed in the late fifth century BCE, or even those practices as they were consolidated and reevaluated by Han classicists towards the end of the BC era and beginning of the CE era.

Another factor to consider is that tombs clearly dating to the Western Zhou period may include only token items from the central court; this is particularly the case for regional courts that made up the larger Western Zhou tributary state. In some cases the evidence, such as a historically important inscribed bronze, may have been carried over time and place by forces unknown. A prime example of this is the early period vessel discovered in the southern Yangzi River Valley, a locale with weak to non-existent loyalty to a Zhou state (Shaughnessy 1999:319). In a cache of vessels of different dates (some much later) and origins, the Yi Hou Ze *gui* 宜侯夨簋 details the gifts of lands and people of Yi to a Lord Yu 虞 by the king when he was inspecting the maps of the eastern regions captured from the Shang (Cao 2007:5–9; Li 2008:238–241).

Indeed, it is controversial how safely one can label archaeological sites distant from the Zhou homeland as "Zhou." Even if a distant tomb reveals material objects symbolic of Zhou cultural domination, how do we really know what rituals the local elite employed in their use and placement? Some courts, even located quite close to the Western Zhou cultural center along the Wei River, may have maintained their cultural independence. For example, in the burial grounds of the small polity of Yu (強), outside modern Baoji 寶雞, Shaanxi, in the western section of the Wei River Valley, we find double burials, a male primary occupant with one female (Lu and Hu 1988). Except for the Jin 晉 royal tombs in modern Shanxi, Zhou tombs were generally single tombs and, indeed, during a Warring States–period controversy over Zhou burial recorded in the "Tangong" 壇弓 chapter of the ritual text, the *Liji* 禮記, it was claimed that a tradition of double burials (*hezang* 合葬) began with Zhou Gong (the patron saint of the eastern state of Lu, and the uncle, teacher, and regent for King Cheng whose father died when he was a small child).

The Yu burial grounds revealed other anomalies. The top of the heads faced south, not north as is considered typical of Zhou. Some tombs also included human sacrifice (men, women, and children), a practice seemingly diminished after the end of the Shang period. Odd pieces, such as an inlaid bronze cowrie-shaped highly decorated animal face with prominent nostrils, were also included with the typical ritual sets of sacrificial vessels, in this case food vessels, 5 bronze *ding*, 3 bronze *gui*, and 2 lacquer *dou* (Rujiazhuang M1, the female half of a double tomb). The primary tomb chambers generally included a larger range of ritual sets, including bells and drinking and libation vessels, suggesting adherence to the Shang-Zhou–style mortuary practices of feasting and music. Pits with chariots and horses too suggest a shared belief in travel conveyances as prestige items or perhaps as items necessary in the afterlife (Cook 2006). The richest tombs belonged to men of the status of *bo* 伯, lineage elders and local leaders. They intermarried with the Zhou yet maintained some of their own traditions. It is ironic that the richest Western Zhou–period tombs have been found outside of the Zhou homeland, which was located in the Zhouyuan area, in the central northern section of the Wei River Valley region. No clearly marked royal tombs have yet been found, and only the bronze inscriptions of one king, those of the renegade late-period King Li (r. 877–841 BCE), are known. At the same time, large caches of valuable bronzes collected by aristocratic lineages over the generations have been found in the Zhouyuan area. The most famous, buried in the Late Western Zhou period, belonged to the Wei family, who traced their heritage back to the Shang, when their educated ancestors, like other Shang officials after the conquest, were incorporated into the newly formed Zhou state (Yin 1992; Rawson, 1999:385, 390). From these hoards, we now understand that many of the most outstanding sacrificial vessels, particularly the ones that inscribe aspects of lineage history, were stored above ground, possibly in shrines, and not buried with the dead.

Bronzes, beginning in the Shang period, were the predominate symbol of prestige, both because of the circumstances of their manufacture and of their use. Access to the minerals and technical knowledge to produce a bronze vessel implied control over a vast supply chain and manufacturing centers (Childs-Johnson 2013). Through their use in sacrifice to the ancestral spirits, they functioned as a primary conduit of communication between the parallel natural and supernatural spheres. As symbols of power, they represented Heaven-ordained royal authority, what the Zhou called the "Heavenly Mandate" (*tianming* 天命). While the majority of bronze vessels were not inscribed, many of the surviving inscriptions record a system of gift-giving and award in which one of the primary gifts was the bronze itself (Kane 1982–1983; Cook 1997). For example, in the Yi Hou Ze *gui* previously mentioned, the first gift awarded Yu Hou was a *you* 卣 container of fermented grain ale (a type of *chang* 鬯). The *gui* vessel itself was for grain, bean, and vegetable offerings, which Yu Hou dedicated for use in sacrifice to his father Yu Gong Fu 虞公父. (The title *gong*, often used for dead patriarchs during the Western Zhou, was in later times, like *bo*, interpreted to be strictly a political title.) As far as we

can tell from tomb structure, the type and design of ritual objects, and the rare inscription, early Western Zhou rites and mortuary ritual were primarily adapted from the earlier waves of cultural influence from first the central and then the eastern Yellow River
Valley cultures, particularly the late Shang culture with its large mortuary production
center in modern Anyang, Henan. The center of power moved westward with the rise of
the Zhou royal house. The sophistication of what would become known as Zhou civilization, considered the golden age by later Confucians, evolved slowly over the three
hundred years of Zhou royal domination. The importance of bronze inscriptions and
the rise of longer and longer texts that were limited to simply recording ritual dedications to particular ancestral spirits provide insight into a culture that would otherwise
remain unknown and subject to later historical reimagining of earlier texts and tales.
The peak of central Zhou innovation occurred during the late tenth and ninth centuries
BCE. By the end of the Western Zhou period in 771 BCE, cultural memes that had fluo-
resced as a vibrant Zhou metropolitan style during the Middle Western Zhou period
had already deteriorated into stale, alienated symbols copied into local scenarios.

Ultimately, the decadence of high Zhou culture would ironically prove to be a key
catalyst for its lasting contribution as a basis for the later Chinese civilization. As the grip
of the Zhou royal house declined, literacy spread to local courts, which had risen in
wealth and power, taking over and strengthening their holds over chunks of the former
Zhou enterprise. During this time, literary production increased in type and length,
including both ceremonial and legal texts (Li & Branner 2011). Some ceremonial texts
would evolve into genres that would eventually be captured in the transmitted classics,
most famously as "documents" (*shu* 書) or "odes" (*shi* 詩)—the core Confucian curricu-
lum (Kern 2009). In the process of evolution, however, the Western Zhou ceremonial
frames contextualizing the performance and use of the narratives would fall away as
irrelevant to the society that had evolved away from worship of an interconnected network of aristocratic and royal ancestral spirits (Cook 2017).

RITES

Rites in ancient China helped to reaffirm social hierarchy as well as to ease transitions
during times of change in people's lives, particularly among the aristocracy. Birth, death,
and taking up positions that symbolize adulthood (marriage for girls, politics for boys)
all affected lineage relationships and the structure of society in the linked natural and
supernatural spheres (Cook 2017). If there was a celebration of birth during the Western
Zhou period, it left no record (earlier and later divination records preserved on bone
and bamboo suggest a continued concern with successful births, infant survival, and the
alignment of gender with certain days of the calendar and other signs). Death, on the
other hand, as the clear portal into the spirit world, was a major concern, as clearly
shown in the proliferation of sacrificial vessels, grave goods, and inscriptions (see the
next section on Mortuary Rites). In fact, the surviving bronze records of Western Zhou

rites, even politically based awards and promotions, were cast on vessels and bells used primarily in ceremonies for use in honor of ancestral spirits (Falkenhausen 1993; Cook 2017; see chapter 21 by Scott Cook).

The fact that our most important records of Western Zhou ritual exist at all is almost incidental. The vast majority of bronze vessels had no text at all, and the majority of those that did preserved simple names or dedications, documenting lineage status in both spheres. Except for those kept above ground in shrines (and discovered later in caches), many of these were buried with the dead and were never expected to be seen by the living again (see Venture 2004). Many bronzes were likely melted down by warring factions over the years for weapons or other implements, or even as an active way to terminate communication of a people with their ancestral spirits, thus culturally disenfranchising them. Despite these limitations, we find that over the course of the Western Zhou, longer and longer texts began to emerge. The increasing length and variety of examples suggest that the reading public had also expanded beyond a closed system of priests, scribes, and ancestral spirits.

Ceremonies were held outdoors near sacred sites or structures, or inside ancestral shrines on auspicious days of the sixty-day ritual calendar inherited from the Shang. It is likely that the days were chosen according to key ancestral cult days as well as through divination. The audience included the king, lords, elite relatives, and honored guests. Amid activities such as divination, animal sacrifice, prayer, and feasting, the king (or a functionary speaking on the king's behalf) made an announcement to the ancestral spirits. He introduced first himself, his merits and right to rule, and then the awardee, his merits, and gifts awarded. Gifts generally consisted of ritual vessels, special alcohols, and ritual and military clothing and equipment. Promotions came with new responsibilities over land and peoples or other government chores, including military and ritual activities (Cook 2017).

Several early inscriptions provide examples of early ceremonies that took place in shrines and outside. The Ling 夆 *zun* and *yi*, a set of square alcohol storage vessels, record the combination of a political promotion rite with sacrifices performed on different days in the lunar year (Shaughnessy 1991:193–216; Cook 1997:268–269; Li 2008:50–54). The first event occurred in the eighth month on Day 21 marked with an astral sign (called *chen* 辰). This day belonged to an endlessly repeating 60-day ritual calendar inherited from the Shang. These day signs, recorded with a set of 10 sun or day signs associated with Shang royal dead combined with 12 signs of unknown origin (and used later for different sectors of time, such as months or hours), may have retained at that time period the earlier Shang system of auspicious and inauspicious days. Day 21 began with a *jia* 甲, the first of the ten sun signs and a notably auspicious term throughout the bronze age and later. On this day, the Zhou king (unnamed but most likely King Zhao), commanded the son of Zhou Gong to take up the Three Affairs (control over artisans, horses, and land) in the Four Regions (a term for the combined natural and supernatural world; see Allan 1991:74–111; Childs-Johnson 2012). On Day 24, the king's command was announced formally to Zhou Gong or to Zhou Gong's spirit in his sacred enclosure or building (*gong* 宮), and then he or his son went off to join his officers. Day 24, Dinghai

丁亥, is an auspicious Zhou day, and is found most commonly claimed as the day in which the inscribed bronze vessels were cast. Then, on a Lunar Auspicious Guiwei 月吉癸未 day (most likely referring to the time of the month when the moon was waxing), Zhou Gong's son came to the dawn court of the king's in the newly constructed more central city of Chengzhou to take up his duties and command his subordinates. Then on the next Day 21, he performed an animal sacrifice at the sacred capital enclosure, the Jing Gong 京宮, possibly the shrine to the Zhou founder kings, Wen and Wu. The next day, Day 22, he performed an animal sacrifice at the sacred enclosure for (the spirit of) King Kang, the Kang Gong 康宮. Then he performed animal sacrifice to the present king (perhaps in the royal city). After that, he awarded first Master Kang 亢師, possibly his tutor and mentor, and then Ling each a quantity of sweet ale, metal, and a calf for use in prayer. They received his commands, and then Ling extolled Duke Zhou's son for his beneficence and dedicated the vessel to his father's spirit. Presumably Master Kang also made a vessel with his gift of metal to pray to his own father's spirit, but that vessel has not survived.

One of the rare records of an outside ceremony is preserved on the Mai 麥 *zun*, a square alcohol vessel (Cook 1997:267–268; Li 2008:260–263). This inscription records the safe travel of a local ruler and Zhou ally, Lord Xing 邢候 from Xing, located in modern Hebei, to the ancestral Zhou capital, Zongzhou 宗周, located in the Zhouyuan region, in the second month. He joined the king's group (possibly King Kang's) in performing a *rong* 肜 sacrificial offering (most likely a sliced meat or libation ritual of some sort). The next day, he followed the king in a boat with red banners on the sacred jade-like circular pool called the *biyong* 璧灘 to celebrate the Great Harvest (or "Great Sweet Ale") ceremony by shooting large birds with arrows. This may have been to provide game for a feast or perhaps for apotropaic purposes. The fact that birds had been sacred symbols decorating ritual bronzes and jades for eons before and after this event along with the fact that the shooting of birds with arrows was depicted in pictorial bronzes hundreds of years later strongly supports an association of flight with the spirit world (Childs-Johnson 1989; Allan 2010). Once the king shot down a bird, he took the Lord of Xing into his private quarters and awarded him with a decorated black dagger axe. Then in the evening, at a place called An 斥, the king gave him gifts of slaves, a chariot, metal bridles, and an outfit consisting of a cap, jacket, kneepads, and shoes. After his successful return to Xing, he extolled the king's beneficence and reported it to his ancestors.

The increase in the recording of the ritual of appointment evident in middle Western Zhou inscriptions reflects the growing complexity of the state. These took place in a variety of locales, always inside buildings, but the grandest seemed to occur at Zongzhou, Ancestral Zhou, where the foundations for a number of structures have been excavated (see Rawson 1999:392, 394; Li 2008:Figure 13). Drawing from a number of the inscribed records, we can understand the general choreography of the ceremony, although details no doubt varied. The king takes up his position formally on a dais of some sort, facing south. The awardee comes into the building escorted by an important official, perhaps with some relationship to him, who is at his right. Judging from descriptions of court meetings and feasts in a text that presumes to record local events from the period following the fall of the Zhou (the *Zuozhuan*), it is likely that to the sides are seated other officers and guests according to rank and their relationship to the king or, in some cases, another powerful official when the king wasn't available. The times for these appointment ceremonies, like other ceremonies involving the rearrangement of social status or adjustment in the hierarchy, would have been determined by divination or timed to coincide with the memorial feast of relevant ancestral spirits. The awardee received a new or renewed charge, gifts, and a text of the charge, which he accepted, and he then left, returning to express his thanks. He then took the written charge back to his own ancestral shrine, where he extolled the gift-giver and memorialized the event with an inscription on a bronze for use in sacrifices to his own ancestors (Cook 1995–1996, 1997:279–282; Falkenhausen 2011; see esp. the Lai *pan* in Cook and Goldin 2016:230–240). In the following example, the awardee was a man named Wang 望 and the memorial of the event was inscribed on a *gui* food vessel:

It was in the king's thirteenth year, in the sixth month, *chuji*, on *wuxu* day [no. 35], when the king resided at Kang Hall and New Hall of Zhou, when at dawn the king arrived at the Grand Room. Once the king had taken his position, Chief Domestic Officer Peng Fu guided Wang in from the right, who then entered the gate and took his position in the center of the court facing northward toward the king. The king called Archivist Nian to record the command to Wang on a bamboo ledger: "Take on the responsibility of supervising the King of Bi's family. I award you crimson-circlet-patterned kneepads and a pennant fringed with bells to use in military and ritual service."

I, Wang, clapped my hands together and knocked my head on the ground, and in response extolled the Son of Heaven's manifest grace. I, Wang, take this opportunity to make for my Brilliant Ancestor Elder Jia (?) Fu a treasured tureen. May I for ten thousand years have sons of sons and grandsons of grandsons to eternally treasure and use it.

Another inscription by a man of the same name from around the same time period, perhaps the King Gong reign, describes a different type of promotion ritual. This involved proving that the subject (referred to often as the "youth," possibly relating to his relationship to a particular ancestor spirit) had earned enough merit through the performance of Zhou ritual and military deeds to take over the position vacated by a deceased father or ancestor. Wang had already achieved the "Grand Master" (*dashi* 大師) status of accomplishment, so the timing of the ritual may have to do with the mortuary ritual schedule associated with that particular ancestor. He recorded his accomplishment on a sacrificial bronze tripod *ding* vessel (Cook 2017: 64–69).

Grand Master and Youth Master Wang said: "Greatly Manifest and Brilliant, my Deceased Father Patriarch Jiu, gravely, so gravely, was able to make his heart luminous and to carefully attend to his *de* in order to aid the Former King, and [thus] achieve wealth without being harmed.

"I, Wang, from the first followed and modeled myself upon my Brilliant Deceased Father [and likewise], respectfully from morning to night, carried the king's charge in and out [of the court], not daring to forgo pursuing [enemies] to the end. The king takes this opportunity not to forget the descendant of the Sage Man, increasing his record of accumulated merit and awarding gifts.

"I, Wang, dare in response to extol the Son of Heaven and the greatly manifest and abundant grace, and take this opportunity to make for my Brilliant Deceased Father, Patriarch Jiu, a tripod *ding* for expressing reverence. May I, Master Wang, for ten thousand years [have] sons of sons and grandsons of grandsons to forever treasure and use it."

Merit, referred to as *de*, while invisible, except as manifested in bronze gifts, had a substance-like quality in that it could accumulate over time if Heaven and the Zhou ancestral spirits approved of the behavior of the king (the gift-giver) and the subject (recipient). Merit, in the form of an intangible substance, *de*, originated from the supreme sky-power Shangdi or Tian. That deity gave it to the first Zhou king as an award for punishing the evil last Shang king, who according to legend had ceased to provide adequate sacrifices to the Shang royal ancestors. Every Zhou king thereafter had to earn the right to carry on that ancestral *de* through military and ritual performances as well as through prescribed sacrifices to the earlier Zhou kings. Officials who worked for the Zhou kings could also receive a measure of *de*, and their heirs also had the right to earn and carry on lineage *de* (Cook 2017). Increased rank and wealth symbolized royal award and the accumulation of *de*.

The concept of *de* continued up through the Warring States period, but by that time it had nothing to do with lineages of kings, aristocrats, ancestral spirits, or even the Zhou polity per se. For disciples practicing Confucian "Zhou"-style rituals transformed into individual self-cultivation practices, it was a natural substance that everyone was born with and was capable of nurturing with proper training. It also took on a moralistic quality and hence is often translated as "virtue." Even in later times, only those with this cultivated inner power were considered worthy to rule (Cook 2017).

During the Early Western Zhou period, feasts followed most ceremonies, even those involving legal situations such as land negotiations (see the Wusi Wei *ding* in Cook and Goldin 2016:84–92. Increasingly, ritual feasts included musical performances involving instrumentals, group dancing, and singing. This was particularly the case with promotion rituals where the heirs succeeded to their ancestral positions, symbolically "grasping" the ancestral *de*, singing rhymed eulogies to their ancestors and their past accumulation of *de*. Sets of bells recorded the blessings from the ancestors that descended in cascades of musical notes (Cook 2017; see chapter 21 by Scott Cook on Zhou music).

Although the Confucian practitioners of later times cultivated their inner *de* through the practice of ritual music, including odes associated with legends of the early Zhou kings, their contexts might be classrooms, private shrines, or local courts rather than a ruler's ancestral shrine (Cook 2011; 2017). The performers would also be elite men, but they were not brought together to celebrate lineage events. And, although like the elite celebrants of Western Zhou times, they considered having enough *de* a prerequisite to working in government, the Confucian practitioners were on their own, individual agents competing for the attention of local rulers of what had become essentially independent states rather than a single king. This transition from group to individual *de*, while symptomatic of the era after the Western Zhou collapse, likely began during the

Late Western Zhou period when the Zhou kings had clearly already begun to lose their authority, appearing less and less often in bronze inscriptions.

Drought and famine, a sign of Heavenly disapproval, combined with political upheaval during the last century of Zhou rule. Rarely do bronze inscriptions from this period document the king's role. Increasingly, the narratives of local lords were recorded without the ceremonial context of the king's court. Ironically, these texts are longer and more lyrical than any before (see the Shi Qiang *pan* in Cook and Goldin 2016; Cook 2017:69–80). The eating or contact surfaces of vessels for food and ablution provided the largest areas for documents, which included by then everything from records of shifts in wealth (through land or goods exchanges, awards, and punishments) to somber declarations of proper governorship (see the Mao Gong *ding* in Cook and Goldin 2016; Cook 2017:127–130). The striking surfaces of bells were utilized to record the ecstatic musical ceremonies in honor of the descended ancestral spirits during sacrificial feasts. Parts of texts found in the *Shangshu* (Classic of documents) and the *Shijing* (Classic of odes) may have begun to be codified during this time, as there is some shared language with Zhou rhetoric found on inscriptions of this time period, although no inscriptions record copies or even versions of the transmitted texts. Such versions were unknown before the discovery of Warring States–period bamboo texts from tombs. Examples include versions of chapters from the *Liji*; scraps of odes embedded in other texts; and chapters from the *Shangshu*, such as the version of the tale of Zhou Gong's prayers for the ill King Cheng hidden in a metal casket.

Mortuary practices

Mortuary practices included preparations for burial, the funeral performance, interment, and sacrifices to the deceased spirit in the lineage shrine and perhaps in the graveyard. Bronze vessels, although used in the sacrifices to powerful ancestors and often buried with the dead, are silent about the other aspects of mortuary ritual. Their inscriptions reinforce the idea that the existence and power of an ancestor relied on the memories of the living as reinforced through sacrifice and rituals performed after their death. Most inscriptions by the end of the Western Zhou period included prayers that the vessel or bell would be used for tens of thousands of years. The following example is from a large set of bells dated to the Late Western Zhou period:

> I, Xing, perform with a martial step from dawn to dusk for the Sage Lights; pursuing in memory and presenting filial offerings to High Ancestor Patriarch Xin, Accomplished Ancestor Patriarch Yi, and Brilliant Deceased Father Patriarch Gong. With harmonious chime bells, I summon their spirits and make them arrive, giving the Former Accomplished Ones pleasure and musical entertainment. I take this opportunity to exorcise bad luck to gain longevity and beg for eternal life, and have extended to me a purging of noxious influences and emoluments in abundance. So,

Brilliant Ancestors and Deceased Father on High, I respond to you, blazing and
stern, residing above—so fruitful and mighty—calmed by the fragrance of cooked
food, you provide blessings and good fortune, expand and open my person, so that
I can rejoice in eternal life and can embrace and receive in me your fine good fortune. May I, Xing, for ten thousand years perform the sacrifices of horned animals,
who glitter with light, present the meat sacrifices to the Accomplished Spirits without limit, and so illustrate my good fortune, taking this opportunity to lodge the
radiance in my, Xing's, person so as to make eternal my treasuring of it (Cook and
Goldin 2016:115–125; Cook 2017:80–86).

The fact that caches of inscribed vessels, such as the Wei family cache in which the
Xing bell set was found, were collected by a lineage over generations and existed outside
of tombs reconfirms that not only were continuous lineage-based ceremonies at shrines
key to the ancestral cult survival but that likely powerful individuals spent much of their
accumulated wealth over a lifetime preparing for lavish burials. Scholars, such as Jessica
Rawson (1999:433–440), document a shift in the bronze ritual sets and style around the
ninth century BCE. This "ritual revolution" was an attempt to codify ritual during the
time of political reform (Yu and Gao 1978; Childs-Johnson 2013; Cook and Goldin 2016:
xxx–xxxv, xlix–l). This reform coincided with the spread of power and wealth to the
nominal allies of the Zhou court. Despite a seeming uniformity, in fact there are many
internal inconsistencies in mortuary displays between individual tombs within burial
grounds and even more between regional burial grounds themselves (Falkenhausen
2006:111). So while sumptuary rules for burial may have been consolidating into a "Zhou
style" there remained flexibility in the individual manner of their execution.

A comparison of two burial grounds, Gaojiabao 高家堡 and Sanmenxia 三門峽, one
from the earliest period of the Western Zhou, closer to the Zhou homeland in Shaanxi,
and one from the latest phase of the Western Zhou, located in the middle Yellow River
Valley and to the east of the administrative center in Chengzhou, can reveal general
changes in burial style. Gaojiabao, located in the lower Jingyang 涇陽 River Valley, may
have originally been occupied by people who identified themselves as part of a larger Ge
戈 clan or tribal network, probably first established in the late Shang capital of Anyang
(Shaanxi 1995). A number of the ancestors marked to receive sacrifices in the short
inscriptions found on food and drink vessels in this burial ground were labeled as Ge
members. However, typical of early Zhou tombs, vessels marked with the signs of other
networks were also included in the ritual sets, reflecting that the exchange and collection
of vessels from different origins was a key aspect of early ritual. Indeed, Ge-manufactured
vessels and weapons are among the most widely distributed in the Late Shang–Early
Zhou period. The tombs at Gaojiabao date to this transition period between the former
eastern and later western centers of power. Basic attributes of mortuary ritual, established
by the late Shang people, were carried on by the Zhou: rammed-earth vertical rectangular
pits with the body pointed northward and placed supine over a "waist pit" (*yaokeng* 腰坑)
containing a deer or dog (dogs were preferred by the people at Gaojiabao), with the ritual
vessels placed near the head on a rammed-earthen terrace (called an *ercengtai* 二層台)

that encircles the wooden coffin. These features remain constants for most Western Zhou–period tombs. Some tombs also included the burial of sacrificial dogs and humans (possibly buried alive). The Gaojiabao tombs, like many Zhou tombs, had a layer of cinnabar, a preservative associated with long life in later times, on the floor of the tomb. There were remains of mats under the coffins and cloth around the ritual vessels.

The disposition of the bodies in the rich tombs in the late Western Zhou graveyard at Sanmenxia continued the tradition of supine placement with the head to the north (Henan 1999). But the wooden coffins now consisted of several nesting layers of inner coffins with an outer wooden coffin around the terrace. There were no waist pits, but the floors might be covered with tiny bronze fish among other small items. Mats were placed under the coffin, and layers of cloth, some red, yellow, or patterned, were draped between and over the embedded inner coffins. The bodies were wrapped in layers of cloth; the faces covered with masks inlaid with jade pieces; and the bodies were decorated with multiple layers of long jade necklaces composed of agate and jade beads, together with semicircular and circular flat rings of jade. Other jades, such as flat jade staffs or tiny carved jades representing animals, silkworms, or cowries, were placed around the waists and elsewhere under and around the body. The surrounding terrace was loaded with bronze ritual vessels, musical instruments, weapons (including some meteoric iron blades), tools, and horse-and-chariot fittings. Some of the ritual vessels were clearly manufactured only for the tomb and not used for life above ground. (Such articles made especially for burial in tombs were called *mingqi* 明器, "bright objects.") There were no sacrificed dogs or people, but large pits for horses and horse-and-chariot combinations might be found to the east and west of the main tomb.

Excavated tombs can provide evidence of belief structures at the time of internment but tell us very little about the funeral rituals performed before, during, and after burial. We can see from the examples that the amount and variety of goods buried with the dead reflect the prestige and rank that the survivors accorded the deceased at the time of interment. Also, we can understand that powerful people accumulated goods during their lifetime precisely to take with them into the afterlife. The importance of proper burial to the ancestral cult suggests that many of the awards commemorated in the inscriptions, the manufacture of bronze vessels, and even the gifts of land for hunting and agriculture associated with political appointments were essential aspects of ritual maintenance of the ancestral cult—accumulating the wealth required for proper interment and sustaining the required sacrifices thereafter. Some items, such as tools, sacrificial vessels, and horses-and-chariots, may have been used in the funerals, or envisioned as used for protection in the after-life.

Although impossible to verify simply from tomb data, aspects of the funeral arrangements are suggested by later texts. Since a death qualified as a disruption in the normal cycle of ritual activities, divination would have been necessary to determine auspicious days in the 60-day ritual calendar for determining when best to hold the funeral and for the interment. Cult days were associated with sacrifices for powerful state ancestors and perhaps on which days what spirit was most influential. The importance of this calendar and the auspiciousness of certain days (such as *dinghai*, number 24, for casting bronzes) is clear from bronze inscriptions throughout the Western Zhou period. After the burial, the periodic sacrifices performed over the next few years to ascertain the position of the deceased in the ancestral spiritual line-up were formally prescribed although no doubt varied from region to region.

Since little remains of Western Zhou–period corpses but the occasional bone, we do not know specifically how the bodies were prepared for burial. Drawing from later archeological and textual data, we can speculate about some aspects of the body preparation and funeral (see Cook 2006). The existence of vessels for ablution support later textual information that a key step in the preparation involved ritual cleansing of the corpse before dressing it. Later texts indicate that at this point a piece of the deceased's old clothing was waved, perhaps from a corner of the rooftop in a particular direction, to symbolically summon back the wandering soul of the deceased. In later burials, the corpses were wrapped in multiple layers of finely embroidered cloth over plain outfits consisting of jackets; skirts; feet coverings; and head coverings, including ties for binding the jaws shut. Rich patrons may have been placed in nested wooden coffins. It is unclear if the coffin was stored in a specially built room or perhaps in a section of the ancestral shrine until time for the funeral procession and interment.

The symbolism of weave, design, and color for the skirt, jacket, belts, and caps worn by mourners likely reflected rank and closeness to the deceased. Near relatives, as expressions of sadness, may have worn coarse un-dyed plain hemp wraps tied with rope, with the chief mourner using a staff to hobble along. The burial goods, including clothing, food, fine bronzes, ceramics, lacquerware, jewelry, and other items, may have been displayed during rites in the shrine before being loaded onto the chariots for the procession to the burial ground. The most elaborate tombs had ramps to accommodate the movement of that portion of the goods that would actually be buried in the tomb versus those later displayed, or perhaps stored, in the shrine.

After the coffins were tied shut tightly and tombs sealed under layers of different-colored muds, the ceremonies of the mourners continued above ground. Rituals recorded on the bronze inscriptions took place in shrines and often seemed more festive than the somber Confucian versions recorded in later texts. Although drinking was excoriated as having caused the downfall of the Shang royal house, texts extolling the communal feasts suggest that everyone—relatives by lineage and marriage, honored guests, ancestral spirits, and the newly deceased represented by a lineage heir acting as the "corpse" (*shi* 尸)—ate and drank their fill, followed by dancing and song. Although burial evidence in Western Zhou tombs shows a shift away from a focus on displays of drinking vessels to displays of meat and grain vessels, the prominence of vessel sets for storing, pouring, and drinking fruit-infused grain ales continued throughout the Bronze Age (Cook 2005).

The ritual vessel displays inside the tomb replicated the ceremonies above ground. Scholars suggest that some aspect of the deceased spirit was thought to emerge from the coffin and live in the tomb. That feast layout—including cooking, heating, storing, serving, eating, and drinking vessels in bronze, ceramic, and lacquer—inside the tomb may have had a double purpose. It both fed the deceased once it was able to shed its corpse and provided the means to continue to serve lineage ancestors and communicate with the eternal world. Scholars debate whether the Zhou people understood that the body contained more than one type of soul, and whether one of them, perhaps liked to the person's social identity, left the tomb. In some conceptions, it traveled to a corner of the world where it could climb to Heaven, where it would join the ranked spirit bureaucracy surrounding the former Zhou kings and Shang Di (Cook 2006; Brashier 2011; Lai 2015; Cook 2017: 112–16).

The preservation of memory through ritual led to the rise of literature and history in ancient China. While the actual rituals performed over the three hundred years of the Western Zhou period differed radically from those performed by Confucian practitioners many centuries later, their attempt to preserve the past and teach it to others was fundamental to the rich texture of later Chinese civilization.

BIBLIOGRAPHY

Allan, Sarah 1991. *The Shape of the Turtle: Myth, Art, and Cosmos in Early China*. Albany: State University of New York.

Allan, Sarah 2010. "He flies like a bird; he dives like a dragon; who is that man in the tiger mouth? Shamanic Images in Shang and Early Western Zhou Art," *Orientations* 41 (2010) 3: 45–51.

Brashier, K. E. 2011. *Ancestral Memory in Early China*. Harcard-Yenching Institute Monograph Series 72. Cambridge, MA: Harvard University Asia Center.

Cao, Jinyan 曹錦炎 2007. *Wu Yue lishi yu kaogu lunye* 吳越歷史與考古論業. Beijing: Wenwu chubanshe.

Childs-Johnson, Elizabeth 1989. "The Bird in Shang Ritual Art: Intermediary to the Supernatural." *Orientations* November 1989:53–60.

Childs-Johnson, Elizabeth 2002. "Jade as Confucian Ideal, Immortal Cloak, and Medium for the Metamorphic Fetal Pose." In *Enduring Art of Jade Age China*, vol. 2. Edited by , 15–24. New York: Throckmorton Fine Art.

Childs-Johnson, Elizabeth 2012. "Postscript to Big *Ding* and China Power: Shang *Sifang* Cosmology 對大鼎'和中 國國王權力的後記:商代四方(四個方向)宇宙 學, "紀念孫作雲教授百年誕辰 暨古代中國歷史與文化國際學術研討會論文集." In *Proceedings in Honor of Professor Sun Zuoyun's Centennial and International Conference on Research on Ancient China History and Culture*. Edited by , 191–210. Henan University Publishers.

Childs-Johnson, Elizabeth 2013. "The Big *Ding* and China Power: Divine Authority and Legitimacy; The Monumental Royal Tetrapod *Ding* of the Shang Period." *Asian Perspectives* 52(1):164–220.

Cook, Constance A. 1995–1996. "Scribes, Cooks, and Artisans: Breaking Zhou Tradition." *Early China* 20:241–277.

Cook, Constance A. 1997. "Wealth and the Western Zhou." *Bulletin of the School of Oriental and African Studies* 60(2):253–297.

Cook, Constance A. 2005. "Moonshine and Millet: Feasting and Purification Rituals in Ancient China." In *Of Tripod and Palate: Food, Politics, and Religion in Traditional China*. Edited by Roel Sterckx, 9–33. New York: Palgrave Macmillan.

Cook, Constance A. 2006. *Death in Ancient China: The Tale of One Man's Journey*. Leiden: Brill.

Cook, Constance A. 2009. "Ancestor Worship during the Eastern Zhou." In *Early Chinese Religion, Part One: Shang through Han (1250 BC–220 AD)*. Edited by John Lagerwey and Marc Kalinowski, 237–279. Leiden: Brill.

Cook, Constance A. 2011. "Education and the Way of the Former Kings." Edited by Li and Branner, 302–336.

Cook, Constance A. 2017. *Ancestors, Kings, and the Dao*. Cambridge, MA: Harvard University Asia Center.

Cook, Constance A., and Paul R. Goldin, eds. 2016. *A Source Book of Ancient Chinese Bronze Inscriptions*. Early China Special Monograph Series no. 7. Berkley, CA: Society for the Study of Early China. Revision published 2020.

Csikszentmihalyi, Mark 2004. *Material Virtue: Ethics and the Body in Early China*. Leiden: Brill.

Falkenhausen, Lothar von 1993. "Issues in Western Zhou Studies." *Early China* 18:139–226.

Falkenhausen, Lothar von 2006. *Chinese Society in the Age of Confucius (1000–250 BC): The Archaeological Evidence*. Los Angeles: Cotsen Institute of Archaeology, University of California, Los Angeles.

Falkenhausen, Lothar von 2011. "Royal Audience and Its Reflections." Edited by Li and Branner, 239–270.

Henansheng wenwu kaogu yanjiusuo 河南省文物考古研究所 and Sanmenxiashi wenwu gongzuodui 三門峽市文物工作隊. 1999. *Guo State Cemetery at Sanmenxia* 三門峽虢國墓, 2 vols. Beijing: Wenwu chubanshe.

Kane, Virginia 1982–1983. "Aspects of Western Chou Appointment Inscriptions: The Charge, the Gifts and the Response." *Early China* 8:14–28.

Kern, Martin 2009. "Bronze Inscriptions, the *Shijing* and the *Shangshu*: The Evolution of the Ancestral Sacrifice during the Western Zhou." In *Early Chinese Religion, Part One: Shang through Han (1250 BC–220 AD)*. Edited by , 143–200. Leiden: Brill.

Lai, Guolong. 2015. Excavating the Afterlife: The Archaeology of Early Chinese Religion. Seattle: University of Washington Press.

Li, Feng 2008. *Bureaucracy and the State in Early China*. Cambridge, UK: Cambridge University Press.

Li, Feng 2011. "Literacy and the Social Contexts of Writing in the Western Zhou." Edited by Li and Branner, 271–301.

Li, Feng, and David P. Branner, eds. 2011. *Writing and Literacy in Early China: Studies from the Columbia Early China Seminar*. Seattle: University of Washington Press.

Li, Yujie 李玉潔 1991. *Research on Burial Systems of Pre-Qin Era* 先秦喪葬制度研究. Zhengzhou: Zhongzhou shudian.

Lu, Liancheng 盧連成, and Hu Zhisheng 胡智生 1988. *Cemetery of the Yu State Baoji* 寶雞彊國墓 地, 2 vols. Beijing: Wenwu chubanshe.

Rawson, Jessica 1999. "Western Zhou Archaeology." In *The Cambridge History of Ancient China: From the Origins of Civilization to 221 BC*. Edited by M. Loewe and E. Shaughnessy, 352–449. Cambridge, UK: Cambridge University Press.

Shaanxisheng kaogu yanjiusuo 陝西省考古研究所, ed. *Gaojiabao Ge guo mu* 高家堡戈國墓. Xi'an: Sanqin chubanshe, 1995.

Shaughnessy, Edward 1991. *Sources of Western Zhou History: Inscribed Bronze Vessels*. Berkeley: University of California Press.

Shaughnessy, Edward 1999. "Western Zhou History." In *The Cambridge History of Ancient China: From the Origins of Civilization to 221 BC*. Edited by Michael Loewe and Edward Shaughnessy, 292–351. Cambridge, UK: Cambridge University Press.

Thote, Alain 2009. "Shang and Zhou Funeral Practices." In *Early Chinese Religion, Part One: Shang through Han (1250 BC-220 AD)*. Edited by J. Lagerwey and M. Kalinowski, 103–142. Leiden: Brill.

Venture, Olivier 2004. "L'écriture et la communication avec les esprits en Chine ancienne." *Bulletin of the Museum of Far Eastern Antiquities* 74:34–65.

Wu, Hong 1988. "From Temple to Tomb: Ancient Chinese Art and Religion in Transition." *Early China* 13:86–90.

Yin, Shengping 尹盛平 1992. *Research on the Western Zhou Bronze Vessels of the Chengshi Family* 西周微氏家族青銅器群研究. Beijing: Wenwu chubanshe.

Yu, Weichao 俞伟超, and Gao Ming 高明 1978. "Research on the Use of *Ding* Vessels in the Zhou Dynasty 周代永定制度研究." *Beijing Daxue xuebao, Shehui kexue* 1:84–98.

CHAPTER 20

BRONZE VESSELS: STYLE, ASSEMBLAGES, AND INNOVATIONS OF THE WESTERN ZHOU PERIOD

YAN SUN, GETTYSBURG COLLEGE

CURRENT scholarship in general employs a three-phase chronological scheme: Early, Middle, and Late Western Zhou (1049/1045–771 BCE) to characterize the evolution of Western Zhou bronze vessel style. Inscribed bronzes, particularly those bearing important dating information, are singled out as "standard vessels" 标准器in establishing a framework for the stylistic evolution of Western Zhou bronzes. Uninscribed vessels are in turn assigned dates through comparison of their shape and decoration with these "standard vessels." In following this approach, this analysis will initially use securely dated essels to illustrate the general stylistic transition of Western Zhou bronzes in the Zhou metropolitan center—the region in the Wei River Valley in central Shaanxi and Luoyang area, where the eastern capital of the Zhou was situated. Additionally, this chapter will also discuss the Zhou interaction with communities of diverse cultural and social backgrounds, as revealed by recent archaeological discoveries of vessel types that originated on the periphery of the Zhou.

THE EARLY WESTERN ZHOU PERIOD

The Early Western Zhou generally refers to the reign of four kings, Wu 武, Cheng 成, Kang 康, and Zhao 昭, roughly from the mid-eleventh to mid-tenth centuries BCE (also see chapter 17 by Maria Khayutina for dating and chronology of the Western Zhou period). The style of bronze vessels during this century-long period is characterized by the continuation of the shape and decoration from the Shang capital at Anyang and the emergence of limited new types that can be attributed to the newly founded Zhou state. The persistence of Shang bronze characteristics could be related to an influx of skillful Shang casters into the Zhou casting foundry at Zhouyuan in the west and Beiyao in the east (Luoyangshi 1983; Zhang 2013:235–255). These places were Zhou power centers after the downfall of the Shang. The Shang casters, now working for the new Zhou regime, brought with them not only the knowledge and skill of Shang bronze-casting but also Shang aesthetics and artistic sensitivity. There is also a possibility that the foundry at Anyang continued to be in operation and produced bronzes for the newly rising Zhou elite after the downfall of the Shang (Li et al. 2018: 97-105). The Xianhou (献侯) *ding* tripod, which according to its inscription dates to King Cheng's reign (1005/1003–978), for example, shows the continuation of late Shang style into the early Zhou time (Figure 1). This *ding* type, characterized by a three-lobed body and solid cylindrical legs, is commonly seen in late Shang tombs such as M1046 and M1713 at Anyang (Figure 2). The body of the Xianhou *ding* is completely decorated with three pairs of animal faces

FIGURE 1 Xianhou *ding* Early Western. Zhou. Taiwan. (http://catalog.digitalarchives.tw/item/00/0c/c0/00.html).

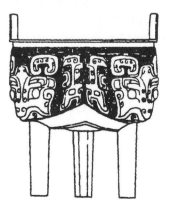

FIGURE 2 Three-lobed *ding* from M1046 at Anyang, late Shang. Zhongguo Shehui 2004.

against a square spiral background (see Childs-Johnson 2016 for a new definition of the meaning of the Shang animal-based image). Incised lines are further superimposed on raised facial features of animal faces. The shape, motif, and decorative scheme of the *ding* are clearly reminiscent of late Shang bronze style.

The adoption of late Shang vessel types continued into the later phase of the Early Western Zhou period. A group of four bronze alcohol vessels, a square *yi*, a *jia*, a *zun*, and a *gong*, commissioned by Zhe from the well-known Wei lineage represented by the cache find at Zhuangbai, Fufeng, is a classic example of the reinterpretation of late Shang style during the Early Western Zhou period (Figure 3). Historical information in inscriptions on Zhe *fangyi* allows dating the vessel to the end of the early Western Zhou, around mid-tenth century BCE (Yin 1992:90; Wang et al. 1999:143). Prototypes of Zhe bronzes can be traced back to the Late Shang period. The square *yi* of architectural form, for instance, has been reported in tombs Nos. 5 and 238 at Xiaotun, Anyang. The Zhe *zun*, *gong*, and square *yi* are fully decorated with the Shang animal imagery on the principal

FIGURE 3   Zhe vessels, mid-11th c.eleventh century BCE, hoard 1 at Zhuangbai, Fufeng, Shaanxi. **A** Zhe *yi*; **B** Zhe *jia*; **C** Zhe *zun*; **D** Zhe *gong*. Cao 2005.3: 567, 575, 547, 554

exterior of the vessels. Hooked flanges in more fluid and expansive forms than those of the Shang are applied on Zhe *yi*, *zun*, and *gong* to accentuate their shapes.

One of the most distinctive bronze vessel types of the Early Western Zhou period is the newly designed square-base upholding a round *gui* bowl 方座簋. Current archaeological evidence indicates that the emergence of square-based *gui* was closely associated with the Zhou culture in Baoji area, the western periphery of the Zhou metropolitan center during the Late Shang and Early Western Zhou periods, around mid-eleventh century BCE (Zhang 1999). The well-known inscribed Li *gui*, cast seven days after the downfall of the Shang, is an early example of such a *gui* (Figure 4). The principal image on the bowl and four sides of the square base of the *gui* are large animal faces of late Shang style. Another famous *gui* of the same type of the Early Western Zhou period is the Tianwang *gui* 天亡簋 (Figure 5). Different from Li *gui*, the Tianwang *gui* is decorated with a new motif of a coiled dragon (known in Chinese as snail-bodied animal 蜗体兽纹), which emerged and became popular during the early Western Zhou. The motif is presented as a pair confronting in profile in one register. This kind of decorative theme breaks away from the convention of the late Shang animal face, in forming an independ-

FIGURE 4 Li *gui*, early Western Zhou, Lintong, Shaanxi, eleventh century BCE 11th c. Zhongguo Qingtongqi: colorplate 49.

FIGURE 5 Tianwang *gui*, early Western Zhou, Licun, Qianshan, Shaanxi (National Museum of China) eleventh century BCE 11th c. Zhongguo Qingtongqi: colorplate 50.

ent individual decorative unit rather than crossing the entire surface of the vessel. The emergence of this new motif and its layout forecast the Zhou departure from relying on late Shang bronze imagery.

Debut of new shapes and decorations in the Middle Western Zhou period

One of the defining stylistic features of bronzes of the beginning of the mid-Western Zhou period—King Mu 穆 (956–918 BCE) and King Gong's 恭 reign (917/915–900 BCE)—is the squat drooping body of the vessel belly. The angular form of the vessel popular in the early Western Zhou gives way to round and smooth shapes. Bronze vessels in the tomb of Bo Dong 伯 㦱 at Zhuangbai, Fufeng, Shaanxi are good examples to illustrate this change. Eight out of 14 bronze vessels in this tomb were commissioned by the same patron, Dong. The silhouette of the body of these four-legged *ding* gently bulges toward the bottom of the vessel, a departure from the design of the tetrapod *ding* with perpendicular walls of the Shang and Early Western Zhou period (Figure 6). Below the rim of both *ding* are two pairs of confronting relief dragons in a narrow band, each with a curved S-shaped extended body and reverted head, a decorative scheme that was in vogue during this time.

The naturalistic, representative imagery on a lidded *gui* commissioned by Dong is also worth mentioning. The body and lid are fully covered with pairs of confronting birds featuring upward- and inward-turning tails and fancy plumed crests with small hooks smoothly bent toward ground level (Figure 7). The representational style here also differs from the symmetrically arranged animal faces seen on Shang and early Western Zhou bronzes. On Dong's lidded *gui*, individual birds in profile form individual

FIGURE 6 A pair of tetrapod *ding* by Dong, Zhuangbai, Fufeng, mMiddle Western. Zhou, 10th ctenth century BCE. Cao 2005.7: Line drawing 0101, 0100.

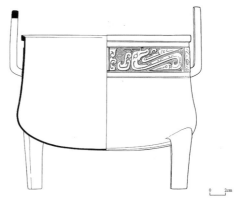

FIGURE 7 Dong *gui*, Zhuangbai, Fufeng, Middle Western Zhou, King Mu and King Gong, tenth century BCE. Cao 2005:00961367.

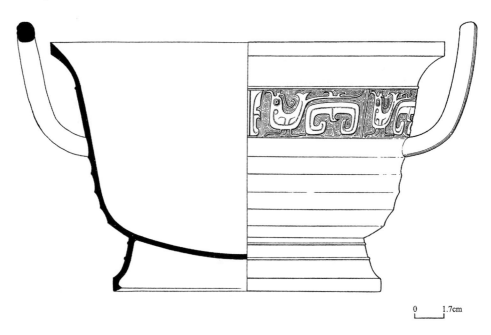

FIGURE 8 Bodong *gui*, Zhuangbai, Fufeng, Middle Western Zhou, King Mu and King Gong, tenth century BCE. Cao 2005:0097.

units in symmetrical pairs. A modest miniature version of small birds facing one direction lining up in a narrow register can be observed under the rim of another *gui* (Bo Dong *gui*) in the same tomb commissioned by Dong (Figure 8).

Meanwhile, abstract geometric motifs, such as grooves (瓦纹) and interlocking square spirals (窃曲纹) make their debut as main decorations on bronzes in the early

FIGURE 9 Shihu *gui* 师虎簋 of King Yih's reign (899/97–873). Chen 2004: 282.

FIGURE 10 Shishi gui of late phase of the middle-Western Zhou, the second half of 9th cthe ninth century BCE. Zhongguo Qingtongqi 1996: colorplate 64.

mid-Western Zhou and then proliferate in the late Middle Western Zhou. Groove patterns are often featured on part or on the whole body of the vessel. Below the band of the bird motif on the bowl of Bo Dong *gui*, for instance, are horizontally laid grooves. The Shihu *gui* 师虎簋 of King Yih's 懿 reign (899/897–873), by contrast, is fully covered with horizontally laid grooves (Figure 9). The standard vessel of King Xiao's reign in the later part of the Middle Western Zhou, the first year of Shishi *gui* 元年师 旗簋, for instance, features groove patterns on the body and squared interlocking spirals in three narrow bands on the lid, right below the rim and on the ring foot (Figure 10). In addition, simple raised lines were also favored as principal motifs, as seen on the fifth-year Shishi *gui*, one of the so-named "standard vessels" of King Yi's 夷 reign (865–858 BCE). This decorative simplification during the later part of the Middle Western Zhou continued into the Late Western Zhou period.

Simplification and standardization of Late Western Zhou bronzes

The style of Late Western Zhou (reigns of Kings Li 历, Gonghe 共和, Xuan 宣, and You 幽) bronzes from the mid-ninth century to the fall of the Zhou power in 771 BCE shows a fundamental departure from that of early periods. The variety seen in earlier vessel types and subtypes has been significantly reduced. Food vessels, especially the *ding* and *gui* of identical style, are favored, and each type is intimately grouped into a set. The *ding* is often cast in the same style and, when represented in a series of *ding*, cascade in size, yet the *gui* are often identical in both size and style. The emphasis on uniformity and standardization of the vessels may reflect a change in concept and practice in rituals during the time, but one must recall that individual vessel types as sets are represented in late Shang period at Anyang (Childs-Johnson 2014). Despite the reduction and disappearance of some vessel types, food vessels become increasingly prominent and varied in design, and this is a major departure from the emphasis on alcohol vessel sets in Shang time. Varieties include *li*, *dou*, *xu*, and *fu*, formerly made of ceramic, lacquer, and bamboo but not bronze. In contrast, vessels such as *zun*, *you*, *jue*, *zhi*, *jia*, *fangyi*, and *gong* used in connection with millet ale (*jiu*), an undistilled fermented beverage, common in the Early and Middle Western Zhou period and earlier Late Shang time, faded away in vessel assemblages found in tombs and hoards. Abstract animals with only eyes visible and geometrical motifs such as horizontally and vertically laid waves and scale-like patterns dominate the surface ornament on the exterior of vessels. In terms of decorative schemes, surface design is frequently represented in a consecutive fashion rather than confined in compartmented registers.

Ding and *gui* remain the most prominent food vessels but with limited variations. Two types of *ding* become popular. One type, such as the Maogong *ding*, has a deep globe-shaped body contracted at the bottom and three splayed legs bulging at the top, narrowing in the middle and ending in wide feet (Figure 11). Its surface décor, consisting of a narrow band of horizontally laid oval patterns and a bow string below the rim, is limited and simple. The other type, exemplified by Da Ke 大克 *ding*, has a wide, shallow, and oval body in cross section (Figure 12). The legs of this *ding* are similar to those of the first type except for the flange used as the central ridge dissecting an animal face. Wave patterns executed with thick bands decorate the main body of the vessel. Abstract animal motifs separated by solid short ridges encircle the body below the rim.

FIGURE 11 Maogong *ding*, lLate Western Zhou. Zhongguo Qingtongqi 1996: colorplate 36.

Two popular types of *gui* during the late Western Zhou include the *gui* with a square base and body decor. A good example of this type of gui is the Hu *gui* 㝬簋 commissioned by King Li in the twelfth year of his reign. The body of Hu *gui* has a smoothly bulging silhouette and sits on a sloped ring foot (Figure 13). Vertical flutings encircle the bowl between horizontal bands of interlinking geometric hooked curls below the rim and on the ring foot. Flutings are further repeated on the four sides of the square base. The only representational motif is a sculptural dragon-like motif featured on each handle. The other type of *gui* is the Shi Song *gui* 师颂簋 with a short, wide body supported by three legs (Figure 14). Horizontally laid grooves cover the body and the lid of the vessel. On the rim of the lid and body are abstract interlocking square spiral patterns in relief. The ring foot encircled by U-shaped patterns is elevated by three legs in the shape of elephant trunks issuing from high relief animal heads.

Large square *hu* wine flasks, often found in pairs, become the most prominent alcohol containers during the period. Their impressive size (often over 50 cm) and solid appearance project a steady yet heavy impression, perhaps as a way to compete with richly assembled food vessels and to win the attention of ritual participants. A pair of *hu* from a richly furnished cache discovered in 2003 at Yangjiacun, Meixian best illustrates the shape and decoration of the square *hu* of the Late Western Zhou period (SW ZSY 2003:20-21). The bronze cache belonged to the prominent Shan 单 lineage. A pair of squared *hu* features

FIGURE 12 Dake *ding* of Late Western Zhou period. Zhongguo Qingtongqi 1996: colorplate 31.

FIGURE 13 Hu *gui*, lLate Western. Zhou, 12th year of King Li. Zhongguo Qingtongqi 1995: colorplate 68.

FIGURE 14 Song *gui*. Lu 2004: p.22.

FIGURE 15 A pair of square *hu* from a cache at Yangjiacun, Meixian, Shaanxi province. Shaanxisheng 2003: colorplates 20–21.

an S-shaped profile, slightly contracted neck, and a wide body of round to rectangular shape in cross section (Figure 15). Each side of the body is fully covered with two dragons with a shared sculptural head and intertwined bodies; the neck is encircled with wave-like patterns composed like ribbons. A sculptural animal head surmounted by a dragon-like animal is featured on both handles, each holding a ring.

Bronze assemblages in burials and caches

Bronze vessels are indispensable components of ritual paraphernalia in ancestral sacrifices during the Zhou era. Studies of their type, function, and assemblage in tombs and caches are crucial for modern scholars seeking to understand the nature of ritual practice and its evolution through time. Chinese scholar Guo Baojun in the 1960s was the first to use the concept of "group" or "assemblage" to study bronze vessels in tombs and caches, particularly those that were scientifically excavated. Building on comprehensive examinations of their shape, decoration, assemblage, casting method, inscription, and residues or traces of use, Guo characterized the assemblage of ritual bronzes in the early Western Zhou prior to King Mu's reign (mid-tenth century) as "alcohol-focused assemblages" 重酒组合, and the late Western Zhou as "food-focused assemblages" 重食组合 (Guo 1981:44–69). This dichotomy has served as a fundamental guiding principle for later studies on bronze assemblages.

In the past several decades, increasing archaeological materials, especially those beyond the Zhou metropolitan center, have been brought to light. These new materials reveal a complex picture of Western Zhou bronze assemblages, indicating that the transition from a focus on alcohol to food assemblages did not necessarily follow a unilateral evolution, especially during the early part of the Western Zhou. It seems the choice of "alcohol-focused assemblage" or "food-focused assemblage" was contingent on the social and cultural background of their patrons (Huang 2012). In the following discussion, Guo's terminology will be employed, yet the emphasis will be on different implementations of food and alcohol vessel assemblages among people of different cultural backgrounds.

Co-existence of "alcohol-focused assemblages" and "food-focused assemblages" in the Early Western Zhou period

A prominent characteristic of a bronze assemblage in late Shang tombs is the overwhelming emphasis on vessels used for undistilled fermented beverage known as *jiu* or *changjiu*, primarily *jue* and *gu* (Zhang 1979; Guo 1981; Zheng and Chen 1985:27-78; Yang and Yang 1985: 79-102; Yue 2006:274–309). A recent statistical analysis of late Shang tombs at Yinxu showed that 55 to 100% of the bronze vessels in most of the tombs are alcohol vessels (Huang 2012). This alcohol-vessel-dominated Shang sacrificial tradition did not die out abruptly with the downfall of the dynasty; instead, it was maintained by leftover subjects of the Shang period, some of whom continued to live in their homeland, while others were relocated to Zhou power centers and regional states. Simultaneously, the Zhou emphasis on food vessels, which originated in the western region of the Wei River Valley, made their way into the bronze assemblage. Consequently, the bronze assemblage of the early Western Zhou is characterized with the juxtaposition of these two distinctive practices.

Emphasis on the alcohol assemblage among remnants of the Shang

Though remnants of the Shang continued to bury alcohol vessels with their deceased in their tombs, the type and quantity of them underwent noticeable changes. The *gu* goblet often paired with the *jue* in late Shang tombs largely disappears in Western Zhou period tombs from its very beginning; the *jue* survives but experiences a dramatic reduction in its popularity. The downward trend regarding the use of *gu* and *jue* in tombs is often regarded as a decrease in alcohol consumption at the time of feasts and sacrifices, revealed by Zhou constructed prejudicial historical texts, such as the "Jiugao" 酒诰in *Shangshu* 尚书 and the inscription on the famous Da Yu *ding* 大盂鼎 (King Kang's reign). Although traditional Zhou texts attribute excessive alcoholism to the Shang and their decline, the gradual disuse in the number of *jue* (or *jiao* or *zhi*) in funeral contexts could in fact reflect Zhou policy to restrict alcohol consumption among the remnants of the Shang.

Although excessive consumption of alcohol may have been prohibited, remnants of the Shang continued their alcohol focused sacrificial practices well into the early part of the Western Zhou, until the transformation of bronze assemblage in tombs during the reign of King Gong (917/915–900 BCE). An early example can be seen in tomb M52 at Liulihe, the cemetery of the Zhou regional state Yan, whose subjects included a number of lineages historically associated with the Shang ruling power (Sun 2003). The tomb is dated to King Cheng and King Kang's reign, from the mid-eleventh to the early part of the tenth centuries BCE. Its occupant has been identified as Fu, a member of the Ju 举 lineage derived from the Shang era. The tomb contained six bronze vessels, of which four (or 66.7%) are alcohol vessels, including 2 *jue*, 1 *zhi*, and 1 *zun*. Inscriptions on four vessels (1 *ding*, 1 *jue*, 1 *zhi*, and 1 *zun*) have the ancestral temple name Fu Yi, indicating the patron cast the vessels for his deceased father Yi (Fu Yi).

Dong's tomb, dating to King Mu's reign (956–918 BCE), at Zhuangbai, Fufeng, Shaanxi, offers a later example for the continuation of alcohol sacrifice among remnants of the Shang. The tomb contained 12 bronzes, including 6 *jiu* vessels (2 *jue*, 1 *zhi*, 2 *yinhu* and 1 *hu* flask) and 6 food ones. Inscriptions on the vessels indicate that Dong used both Shang and Zhou practices of naming ancestors. Dong referred to his deceased parents as Cultured Father Jia Gong 文父甲公 and Cultured Mother Ri Geng 文母日庚, and his grandparents Cultured Ancestor Yi Gong 文祖乙公 and Cultured Grandmother Ri Wu 文姒日戊. Father, mother, and ancestral day name follows Shang practice of nomenclature. Adding *wen* or "cultured" is a Western Zhou innovation. The vessels and inscriptions on them reveal that as a remnant of the Shang, Dong adopted contemporary Zhou ritual practice but at the same time still held onto elements of Shang ritual.

Zhou emphasis on food assemblage

The emphasis on food vessels, particularly *ding* and *gui* in a funerary context, is considered a hallmark of Zhou sacrificial practice. Such practice likely originated in the Late Shang period in the Wei River Valley where the Zhou clan and their affiliates were active (Zhang 2009; Childs-Johnson 2014, 2018). After the Zhou succeeded the Shang, the emphasis on food-focused assemblages, particularly *ding* and *gui*, can be widely observed in tombs in the Zhou metropolitan area and its regional states.

A richly furnished tomb, M253, of the Yan state at Liulihe provides a good illustration for this new emphasis in the Early Western Zhou period. The tomb occupant, according to inscriptions on the vessels, has been identified as Yu 圉, a high-ranking official at the Yan court. His tomb contained 22 bronze vessels, including 13 food vessels (6 *ding*, 4 *li*, 2 *gui*, and 1 *yan*), 7 *jiu* vessels (2 *jue*, 2 *you*, 1 *zun*, 1 *hu*, and 1 *zhi*), and 2 water vessels (1 *pan* and 1 *he*). The food vessels numbered over 59% of the entire vessel assemblage.

Bronze assemblages in the tombs of Yu Bo, the lineage head, and his wife Jing Ji of King Mu's reign at Rujiazhuang, Baoji, epitomize the emphasis on food sacrifice practiced by the Yu lineage in the Wei River Valley in the beginning of the Middle Western Zhou period. Yu was a non-Ji lineage member who had close ties with the Zhou. In Yu Bo's tomb, 55% of the 36 bronze vessels are food types, including 8 *ding*, 5 *gui*, 2 *li*, 1 *yan*, and 4 *dou*. In Jing Ji's tomb, the wife of Yu Bo, no alcohol-type vessels were buried. Of the 17 vessels in her tomb, 15 (88%) are food types (6 *ding*, 5 *gui*, 1 *yan*, 3 *li*), and the other 2 are water ones.

Changes of bronze assemblage in the Middle and Late Western Zhou periods

A prominent transition of the bronze assemblage during the Middle and Late Western Zhou phases, roughly King Gong's (917/915–900) and King Yih's reigns (899/897–873), was long ago noticed by Chinese scholars (Guo 1981:44–69; Yu and Gao 1978–1979). Central to this transition is the use of *ding* and *gui* sets in elite tombs. This change has been regarded as a material indication of a "ritual reform" or "ritual revolution," although opinions differ on how to characterize this change and when this change took place (Cao 1993:443–456; Luo [Falkenhausen] 1997; Rawson 1990:93–125, 1999:352–449). More recently studies have also noted that there is a lack of substantial written or archaeological data documenting the formation of a new ritual system (Li 2010–2011; Childs-Johnson 2014). Yu and Gao pointed out that what appears new in systematizing ritual texts is the delineation of number of vessels allowed per set according to social rank. Historical studies point to a series of reforms in military, land, and court offices launched by the Zhou court in response to the waning power of the royal family (Shaughnessy 1999; Yu and Gao 1978–1979). On top of the internal crisis, Zhou's borderland was also seriously threatened by the aggressive Rong in the northwest and the Huaiyi in the south. This challenging socio-political environment could have prompted an emphasis on uniformity and standardization of ritual vessel sets.

Bronze vessel assemblages in tombs and hoards exhibit a number of noticeable changes. The use of alcohol vessels continues to decline, with the eventual complete disappearance of *jue*, *zhi*, *zun*, and *you*. Yet the alcohol sacrifice is not abandoned, as is told by the new and emerging emphasis on pairs of *hu*-type containers of alcohol vessels. The most significant other change nonetheless is the simplification of the *ding* and *gui* and their use in matching groups of vessels. *Ding* in a set are designed similar in shape and decoration and may descend in size; the *gui* in a set are often of the same size and style. This change is a departure from Shang ritual assemblage in which a vessel type was designed similar in size and shape in sets but not as different vessels forming sets because of a common imagery program (Childs-Johnson 2013). It is also different from the early part of the Western Zhou, which often featured *ding* and *gui* of widely diverse types and decoration. The adoption of similarly shaped, decorated, and sometimes inscribed *ding* and *gui* not only creates a visual uniformity in temples and tombs, but in a simple and direct way conveys information on the status of their owners.

The wide use of the standardized bronze *ding* and *gui* set after the reign of King Yih can be observed in both tombs and caches. An intact tomb of King Yih dating to Xiao's reign at Qiangjiacun, Fufeng, for example, contained 18 bronze vessels, 24 bronze horse and chariot fittings, 5 ceramic vessels, and 550 pieces of jade. The bronze vessels placed on the secondary ledge next to the head of the deceased include 4 *ding* (2 identical and 2 with the same shape but slightly different decoration), 4 identical *li*, 5 *gui*, 2 identical *yi*, Bo Yi *gui* and 2 Bo Ji Fu *gui*, a plain *gui*, 2 identical *hu*, 1 *pan*, and 1 *he*. The plain *gui* and *pan*, coarsely cast, were likely used as *mingqi* or replacements of authentic ones.

Bronzes from caches in Zhouyuan provide another important line of evidence for the practice of duplicating certain ritual bronze vessels as sets in late Western Zhou. These bronzes, the largest group of late Western Zhou bronzes that so far have been found, were likely interred and hidden by Zhou nobles in a hurry before they fled the area during the Quanrong invasion. The lengthy inscriptions on the bronzes indicate that the vessels belonged to individual nobles of different aristocratic families or to several generations in a single family. Near those caches are architectural remains identified as temples or residences of Zhou nobles (Cao 2004:55-65). For instance, bronze caches at Qijiacun are spread around remains of a large structure, either a temple or residence, and two bronze caches at Yuntangcun are near the remains of a temple. The spatial proximity between caches and temples or residences suggests that those cached bronzes could have originally been displayed at ancestral altars and used for ritual activities in lineage temples before their deposition.

Cached bronzes, therefore, reflect to some degree the use of bronze vessels in temple ritual in late Western Zhou. Bronzes from Pit 1 at Zhuangbai in Fufeng and a hoard at Yangjiacun in Meixian are two of the best examples to examine in this regard. Pit 1 at Zhuangbai contained 103 bronzes commissioned by at least four generations of the Wei family (Yin 1992). Among 22 bronze vessels bearing the name Wei Bo Xing 微伯癏, the last generation of the family who were active from the reign of King Xiao to King Li, are 8 identical *gui*, 5 identical *li*, 2 identical square *hu* (the third year Xing *hu*), 2 identical *pen*, 3 *jue* (2 identical and 1 similar in style), and 2 spoons. The 8 *gui* vessels were all fashioned with simple ridges on the belly, lid, and square base. Their lid and belly were encircled with a band of horizontally laid oval patterns. The *li* with a squat body and accented ridges on the belly above three legs were decorated with shallow relief lines. These vessels show the typical preference for simplicity and uniformity in bronze design prevalent during this period.

The Xing ritual assemblage does not include the *ding*, one of the core types of food vessels. Luckily, the discovery in 2003 at Yangjiacun helps us fill that gap (SW ZSY 2003). The hoard contained 27 magnificently cast bronze vessels, all bearing inscriptions. The majority of them were commissioned by one noble named Lai 逨, a prominent figure of the Shan lineage 单氏. Ten of the *ding*, based on the long inscriptions on them, can be dated to the forty-third year of King Xuan, and the other 2 to the forty-second year of the same king. These 12 *ding*, extremely similar in shape and decoration, bear stylistic features typical of late Western Zhou *ding*: a wide and shallow bowl supported by three splayed legs. Wave patterns decorate the body and a band of abstract distorted dragon motifs decorate the band below the rim. The lengthy inscriptions repeatedly document glorious moments during Lai's life when he received promotions, lands, and symbolic gifts from King Xuan at royal ceremonies. One can imagine a great sensation those 12 *ding* would create in ritual occasions at the ancestral temple. It is an extravagant and proud display of Lai's prestigious status. The increasing centrality of *ding* and *gui* sets in elite tombs has led scholars to investigate whether the number of the *ding* and *gui* in a set is consistently associated with the rank of the elite, as ritual texts state (Yu and Gao 1978–1979). The Zhou King presumably used a 9-*ding* set; rulers of regional states, a 7-*ding* set; followed by ministers and upper magnates, lower magnates, and gentlemen with 5, 3, and 1 *ding*, respectively. Bronze assemblages in tombs display diverse and often inconsistent practices, as a study pointed out (Falkenhausen 2006:100). In the Guo state cemetery at Shangcunling, for instance, the lineage head was accompanied with a 7-*ding* set; at the Jinhou cemetery at Beizhao, the ruler of the Jin was only supplied with a modest 5-*ding* set. The difference in terms of the magnitude of the *ding* set between the Guo and the Jin is particularly interesting, since both lineages were branches of the Zhou royal family. The discrepancy and regional variation exemplified by these two lineages suggest that even if there were a regulation defining a universal standard on the scale of the *ding* and *gui* set for each level of the elites in principle, such regulation was not uniformly implemented in practice.

The last, but not the least, conspicuous change of bronze assemblages in the Middle and Late Western Zhou periods is the increasing incorporation of a set of bronze bells. The earliest archaeological evidence of the Western Zhou set of bronze bells in the Wei River Valley comes from the Yu lineage tombs at Baoji. Tomb M7 at Zhuyuangou of King Zhao's reign and M1 at Rujiazhuang of King Mu's reign each contained a set of three bronze bells. They were placed with other bronze vessels between the inner and outer coffins aligned with the direction of the head of the deceased, suggesting they could have been treated with similar importance as bronze vessels in funerary practice. A set of bronze bells had become increasingly popular in the Wei River Valley after the end of the tenth century (King Gong and King Yih's reigns). This phenomenon may be a reflection of elites' desire to expand the scope and sophistication of their sacrificial ritual. Indeed, in the following Eastern Zhou period, bronze bells became indispensable ritual paraphernalia of local lords.

Exotic vessel shapes beyond the Zhou metropolitan center

The newly founded Zhou consisted of people of diverse social and cultural backgrounds. The installation of regional states beyond the Zhou political center further brought Zhou into communication with local communities, many of which had adopted typical Shang and Zhou bronze vessels in their ritual practices. At the same time, bronzes of idiosyncratic style, though limited in type and number, began to emerge. These bronzes are often based on local ceramic prototypes outside the Shang and Zhou cultural tradition. Depending on the social and cultural background of their patrons, the presence of exotic bronzes implies the attempt to elevate and perpetuate local cultural traditions.

Miniature bronzes in the Yu lineage cemetery at Baoji

The Yu 弓鱼 was a non-Ji royal lineage active in the western periphery of the Zhou metropolitan center from early to the beginning of mid-Western Zhou. Yu lineage tombs feature a set of four miniature bronzes, including flat- and pointed-bottom *guan* jars, rectangular shallow *pan*-shaped plates, and ladle-shaped bronzes with curved handles. What makes the four types so special is not only their distinctive style but also their exclusive presence in Yu tombs in the Early Western Zhou period. All four vessels are of modest sizes: the flat- and pointed-bottom jars about 4 to 8 cm tall; the ladle-shaped bronzes between 4 cm and 6 cm tall with the handle; and the largest plate, from Yu Bo's burial, M7, only 13.4 cm long (without handles) and 6.7 cm wide. They were used widely in Yu tombs: 6 of the 12 early Western Zhou tombs each contain all four types and the rest each one to three types. They were likely gender-neutral artifacts offered to both male and female deceased, as shown in tombs M4, M7, and M13, each of which contains a male lineage member and his female consort. Undecorated and crudely cast with visible marks of imperfection, these objects were often placed together near the head of the deceased, along with bronze hairpins and comb-like ornaments. They could have been toiletry items for personal beautification.

The provenance of these four types of vessels is still a matter of debate (Lu and Hu 1988:451; Sun 2000:2–46; Rawson 2013:357-398). Accidental discoveries of three waste pits at a Yu residential site at Rujiazhuang yielded rich information regarding the prototype of bronze flat- and pointed-bottom jars. Pottery shards recovered from those pits are mainly composed of two types: flat-bottom jars (about 60%) and pointed-bottom jars (about 25%) (Lu and Hu 1988:7–8). Published examples indicate that jars of both types are also small. Their presence in the residential site suggests that at least the ceramic version of both types of vessels was used in the daily life of the Yu lineage. Their transformation from ceramic into bronze vessels further indicates their significant role as a material indicator of Yu's distinctive cultural identity (Sun 2013).

Bronze three-foot jars and double-handled jars in the state of Jin

Jin was a regional state installed in southern Shanxi by the Zhou court during the early Western Zhou. Its history since its establishment was closely intertwined with the bronze-using groups in the Northern Zone, who were broadly named Rong in contemporary bronze inscriptions and later historical texts. Two types of vessels, a bronze three-foot jar (*sanzuweng*) and a double-handled jar (*shuang'er guan*) provide material evidence of Jin's contact with their neighbors in the north and west.

Both vessels were discovered in tomb M113 at Jinhou's cemetery at Beizhao (BKW SKY 2001). The tomb, dated to a late phase of the early Western Zhou, has been attributed to a wife of Jin Hou. Besides bronze vessels of typical Shang and Zhou–style *ding*, *gui*, *yan*, *zun*, and *you*, the tomb yields a bronze three-foot jar and a double-handled jar unseen in other Western Zhou–date tombs. The bronze three-foot jar is characterized by an oval-shaped belly bulging toward the bottom and three short pointed feet (Figure 15). Interestingly, a ceramic three-foot jar of the same style but twice the size of the bronze jar was also found in the same tomb. The former likely serves as the prototype of the latter.

Though the ceramic three-foot jar is rare in Jin tombs throughout the Western Zhou period, this type of vessel had a long history in northern Shaanxi, north-central Shanxi, and south-central Inner Mongolia from the Late Neolithic Longshan period to the early Bronze Age (ca. 2300–1900 BCE) (Jing 2006). It remained as a core type of pottery assemblage in the following Lijiaya culture (ca. 1400–1000 BCE), active west and north of southern Shanxi where the Jin was later established. Recent typological studies proposed that ceramic egg-shape *sanzuweng* in Jin tombs derived from the Lijiaya culture, but the type exemplified by the ceramic one in tomb M113 is stylistically different from the egg-shaped ones and therefore could be a creation by the Jin (Jing 2006). If this claim is plausible, it shows that the Jin not only adopted the northern-style three-foot jar but modified it into a new type to suit their needs.

FIGURE 16 Bronze *sanzuweng* and *shuang'er guan* from tomb M113 at Jinhous' cemetery, Beizhao, Shanxi. Beijing Daxue 2001: Plate 21; Shanghai Museum 2002: colorplate 55.

The bronze, double-handled *guan* jar is characterized by a collared neck slightly flaring to the mouth, sloped shoulders, and a contracted body. A circle of roped design decorates the ridge where the body and shoulder join (Figure 16). The two handles first extend horizontally then slightly curve to rest on the shoulders. No ceramic version of such bronze has been reported in Jin tombs excavated so far. Pottery *guan* jars of the same style, however, were popular in the Qijia culture (2500–1500 BCE) in Gansu, northwestern China, and could have spread eastward over time, since the jar type has been found in a number of early Bronze Age sites in Inner Mongolia, northern Shanxi, and Shaanxi (Zhao 2008). The strong morphological connections of the bronze *guan* from the Jin cemetery with the ceramic ones from the Jinshan Plateau and further north suggest that the *guan* could also have northern cultural roots.

BIBLIOGRAPHY

Anonymous. Taiwan E-learning and Archives Programs. http://catalog.digitalarchives.tw/item/00/0c/c0/00.html, accessed on July 17, 2014.

BKW SKY. Beijing Daxue Kaogu Wenboyuan 北京大学考古文博院 and Shanxisheng kaogu yanjiusuo 山西省考古研究所 2001. "The sixth excavation campaign at the Beizhao cemetery of the Marquises of Jin at the Tianma-Qucun site 天马-曲村遗址北赵晋侯墓地第六次发掘". *Wenwu* 8: 4–21; 55.

Cao, Wei 曹瑋 1993. "The Change in Ritual Regulation during the Transition of Early and Late Western Zhou as Witnessed in the Change of Bronze Artifacts 從青銅器的演化試論西周前後期之交的禮制變化." In *Proceedings of the Conference on Zhou and Qin Culture* 周秦文化學術討論會 論文集. Xi'an: Shaanxi renmin chubanshe, pp. 443–456.

Cao, Wei 曹瑋, ed. 2004. "The Excavation of the Zhouyuan Sites and the Discovery of Cached Bronzes 周原遺址的發掘與窖藏銅器的發現." In *The Zhouyuan Site and Studies of Western Zhou Bronzes* 周原遺址與西周銅器研究. Beijing: Kexue chubanshe, pp. 55–65.

Cao, Wei 曹瑋 2005. *Bronzes Unearthed in Zhouyuan* 周原出土青铜器, vols. 3 and 7. Chengdu: Bashu shushe.

Chen, Peifen 2004. *Research on Xia, Shang and Zhou Bronzes* 夏商周青铜器研究. Shanghai: Shanghai guji chubanshe.

Childs-Johnson, Elizabeth 2018. "Urban Daemons of the Early Shang: Urbanism in Ancient China." *Archaeological Research in Asia* 14: 135–150.

Childs-Johnson, Elizabeth 2014. "The Big *Ding* and China Power: Divine Authority and Legitimacy; The Monumental Royal Tetrapod *Ding* of the Shang Period." *Asian Perspectives* 52(1):164–220.

Falkenhausen, Lothar von 2006. *Chinese Society in the Age of Confucius: The Archaeological Evidence*. Los Angeles: Cotsen Institute of Archaeology, University of California.

Guo, Baojun 郭宝钧 1981. *A Comprehensive Study on Shang and Zhou Bronzes* 商周铜器综合研究. Beijing: Wenwu chubanshe.

Huang, Mingchong 黃銘崇. 2012. "A study of "Fenqi" or vessel distribution in Western Zhou date tombs and the type and phase of Western Zhou Ritual Practice (Part 1) 从考古发现看西周墓葬的 '分器' 现象与西周时代礼器制度的类型与阶段(上篇)." *Zhongyang yanjiuyuan lishi yuyan yanjiusuo jikan* 83(4):607–670.

Jing, Zhongwei 井中偉 2006. "A Study on Egg-shaped *Weng* 蛋形瓮研究." *Kaogu xuebao* 3:419–446.

Li, Feng 2010–2011. "A Response and a Methodological Confession on the Study of Western Zhou History." *Early China* 33–34:287–306.

Li, Yungti, Zhangwei Yue and Yuling He 2018. "Annihilation or Decline: The Fall of Anyang as an Urban Center." *Archaeological Research in Asia* 14: 97–105.

Lu, Liancheng 卢连成, and Zhisheng Hu 胡智生 1988. *The Yu State Cemetery at Baoji* 宝鸡弓鱼国墓地. Beijing: Wenwu Press.

Lu, Wensheng, ed. 2004. *Treasures from the Shandong Museum: Bronzes* 山东省博物馆藏珍:青铜器. Ji'nan: Shandong wenhua yinxiang chubanshe.

Luo, Tai 羅泰 (Falkenhausen, Lothar von) 1997. "New Thoughts Concerning the Late Western Zhou Ritual Revolution and the Date of the Zhuangbai Bronzes 有关西周晚期礼制改革及庄白微氏青铜年代的新假设:从世系铭文说起." In *Zhongguo kaoguxue ji lishixue zhi zhenghe yanjiu*, vol. 2. Edited by Cheng-hua Tsang. Taipei: Institute of History and Philology, Academia Sinica, pp. 651–75.

Luoyangshi Wenwu Gongzuodui 洛阳市文物工作队 1983. "The Excavation of Bronze Casting Site at Beiyao, Luoyang between 1975 and 1979. 1975–1979 洛阳北窑西周铸铜遗址的发掘." *Kaogu* 5:430–441.

Rawson, Jessica 1990. *Western Zhou Ritual Bronzes from the Arthur M. Sackler Collections*. Cambridge, MA: Harvard University Press.

Rawson, Jessica 1999. "Western Zhou Archaeology." In *The Cambridge History of Ancient China: From the Origins of Civilization to 221 BC*. Edited by Michael Loewe and Edward Shaughnessy. Cambridge, UK: Cambridge University Press, pp. 352–449.

Rawson, Jessica 2013. "Miniature Bronzes from Western Zhou Tombs at Baoji in Shaanxi Province." In *Radiance between Bronze and Jade: Archaeology, Art, and Culture of the Shang and Zhou Dynasties*. Edited by Guangzu Chen. Taipei: Institute of History and Philology, Academic Sinica, pp. 357–398.

SW ZSY. Shaanxisheng Wenwuju and Zhonghua Shijitan Yishuguan 陕西省文物局，中华世纪坛艺术馆 2003. *Shengshi Jijin* 盛世吉金. Beijing: Beijing chubanshe.

Shanghai Museum 上海博物館 2002. *Jinguo Qizhen* 晋国奇珍. Shanghai: Shanghai renmin meishu chubanshe.

Shaughnessy, Edward L. 1999. "Western Zhou History." In *The Cambridge History of Ancient China: From the Origins of Civilization to 221 BC*. Edited by Michael Loewe and Edward Shaughnessy. Cambridge, UK: Cambridge University Press, pp. 292–351.

Shui, Tao 2001. "Research on the Formation and Cultural Organization of the Bronze Age in the Xingan Area甘青地区青铜时代的文化结构和形态研究." In *Zhongguo xibei diqu qingtong shidai kaogu lunji*. Bejing: Kexue chubanshe, pp. 193–327.

Sun, Hua 孙华 2000. "A Preliminary Study on Bronze Cultures in Sichuan Basin 四川盆地青铜文化初论." In *The Bronze Age in the Sichuan Basin*四川盆地的青铜时代. Edited by Sun Hua. Beijing: Kexue chubanshe, pp. 2–46.

Sun, Yan 孙岩 2003. "Bronzes, Mortuary Practice and Political Strategies of the Yan during the Early Western Zhou Period." *Antiquity* 77:761–770.

Sun, Yan 孙岩 2013. "Material Culture and Social Identities in Western Zhou's Frontier: Case Studies of the Yu and Peng Lineages." *Asian Archaeology* 1: 55–74.

Taiwan E-learning and Archives Programs. http://catalog.digitalarchives.tw/item/00/0c/c0/00.html

Wang, Shimin, Gongrou Chen, and Changshou Zhang 1999. *The Periodization of Western Zhou Period Bronzes* 西周青铜器分期断代研究. Beijing: Wenwu chubanshe.

Yang, Xizhang 杨锡璋, and Baocheng Yang 杨宝成 1985. "The Dating and Assemblage of Shang Period Bronze Vessels 殷代青銅禮器的分期与组合." In *Yixu Qingtongqi*. Edited by the Institute of Archaeology, Chinese Academy of Social Science. Beijing: Wenwu chuban-she, pp. 79–102.

Yin, Shengping 尹盛平 1992. *Studies on Wei Family Bronzes of the Western Zhou* 西周微氏家族青銅器群研究. Beijing: Wenwu chubanshe.

Yu, Weizhao 俞偉超, and Ming Gao 高明 1978–1979. "Sumptuary Regulations Concerning the Use of Tripods during the Zhou Dynasty (section I) 周代用鼎制度研究 (上)." *Beijing daxue xuebao* 1978(1): 84–98.

Yu, Weizhao 俞偉超, and Ming Gao 高明 1978–1979. "Sumptuary Regulations Concerning the Use of Tripods during the Zhou Dynasty (Section II) 周代用鼎制度研究 (中)." *Beijing daxue xuebao* 1978(2): 84–97.

Yue, Hongbin 岳洪彬 2006. *Studies on Bronze Vessels from Anyang* 殷墟青銅禮器研. Beijing: Zhongguo shehui kexue chubanshe.

Zhang, Changshou 张长寿 1979. "Yin Shang Bronze Vessels 殷商時代的青銅容器." *Kaogu xuebao* 3:271–300.

Zhang, Maorong 张懋镕 1999. "Study of the *Gui* with Square Stand 西周方座簋研究." *Kaogu Xuebao* 12:69–76.

Zhang, Maorong 张懋镕2009. "New Thoughts on the Emphasis on the Food Culture of the Western Zhou Based on the Ganquan Yanjiagou Bronzes 西周重食文化新认识—从甘泉阎家沟青铜器谈起." *Kaogu yu wenwu* 1:32–38.

Zhang, Tian'en 张天恩 2013. "Observations on the Rnterrelationship of Bronze Manufacturing during the Shang and Zhou Dynasties 商周之际青铜制造迁移的观察." In *Radiance between Bronze and Jade: Archaeology, Art, and Culture of the Shang and Zhou Dynasties*. Edited by Guanzu Chen, 235–255. Taipei: Institute of History and Philology, Academic Sinica, pp.235–255.

Zhao, Meiju 赵梅菊 2008. "Study on the Archaeological Culture Pattern of the Shanxi-Shaanxi Plateau 晋陕高原考古学文化格局研究." In *North and Sof the Jinshan Plateau during the 2nd Millennium BCE* 公元前 2 千纪晋陕高原与燕山南北. Edited by Jianhua Yang and Gang Jiang. Beijing: Kexue chubanshe, pp. 3–43.

Zheng, Zhenxiang 郑振香, and Zhida Chen 陈志达 1985. "Periodization and Chronology of Yinxu Bronzes 殷代青銅禮器的分期与年代." In *Yinxu Qingtongqi*. Edited by the Institute of Archaeology, Chinese Academy of Social Science. Beijing: Wenwu chubanshe, pp. 27–78.

Zhongguo Qingtongqi Quanji Bianji Weiyuanhui 中国青铜器全集编辑委员会 1996. *The Complete Set of Chinese Bronzes*, vol. 5 中国青铜器全集 5. Beijing: Wenwu chubanshe.

Zhongguo Shehui Kexueyuan Kaogu Yanjiusuo, and Anyang Gongzuodui 中国社会科学院考古研究所，安阳工作队 2004. "Anyang Yinxu Liujiazhuangbei No. 1046 Burial 安阳殷墟刘家庄北 1046 号墓." *Kaoguxue jikan* 考古学集刊15. Beijing: Wenwu chubanshe, pp. 359–390.

CHAPTER 21

BELLS AND MUSIC IN THE ZHOU

BY SCOTT COOK, YALE-NUS COLLEGE

An early Zhou ode from the "Zhou song" 周頌 section of the *Shi jing* describes a sacrificial scene as follows:

> Blind musicians, blind musicians,
> in the courtyard of the Zhou;
> set up beams and set up stands,
> raised mounting hooks adorned with feathers;
> hanging drums, both small and large,
> swivel-drums, chimestones, wood blocks, and scrapers.
> All prepared, the performance commences,
> panpipes and flutes raised in full array.
> Resounding are the tones!
> Calling forth in solemn harmony,
> our ancestral fathers intently listen.
> We the guests here come to rest,
> eternally observing their great achievements. ("You gu" 有瞽)

From large state sacrifices to small rural gatherings, music played a central and indispensable role in the lives and ritual practices of the Zhou. Music by its nature encapsulated a message of social harmony, and its performance at sacrifices was no less essential to the mollification of the departed spirits than the alcoholic libations that served to make them drunk with feelings of goodwill toward the living. And such performance was equally important to the latter, for whom music symbolized the eternal promise of concordant interaction with both their ancestral forebears and the disparate members of their own intricate social networks.

THE ZHOU'S MUSICAL HERITAGE

Sound is by its nature ephemeral, and the lack of recording capabilities in ancient times means that we will never be able to reconstruct what actual music in the Zhou may have sounded like with any degree of fidelity. However, enough remains in the archaeological and textual records to give us some sense of the broad instrumental and theoretical parameters in which music of the time was composed and performed.

The Zhou of course had a long tradition of musical practice upon which to draw. Evidence from the Neolithic era is scattered, and with any possible wooden, bamboo, or other more perishable instruments having long since disappeared from the archaeological record, the picture that emerges from it is naturally one dominated by relatively crude percussion instruments, ranging from alligator-skin pottery drums to pottery shakers and pottery clapper-bells. A number of chimestones coarsely chiseled from limestone and other sonorous rocks have been unearthed from this period, but they are never found in sets and thus would not seem to have served melodic purposes. To that end, the most remarkable find is that of over 30 polished bird-bone flutes unearthed from various tombs in Jiahucun 賈湖村, Wuyang 舞陽, Henan, that date from around 8,000 years ago, each drilled with five to eight fingering holes. Pitch-testing on the most well preserved of the flutes suggests an instrument designed to play a six- or perhaps seven-note scale; while the pitch relationships are far from precise and the overall intervallic structure is not entirely clear, it has sufficient capacity to recognizably play a modern folk tune (Liu Zaisheng 2006:3–10). The same might be said of the various pottery egg-shaped ocarinas excavated from different sites as far west as modern-day Gansu, which bear from between one to three fingering holes, and the more complex of which seemed designed to produce four-note scales (Li Chunyi 2005:35–36). The flutes and some of the other instruments were usually found buried adjacent to the body of a male tomb occupant, suggesting they may have been markers of special status and perhaps played an important role in religious rites. At the same time, they clearly reveal a long-term engagement with intervallic structures and pitch relationships, punctuated rhythmically by a variety of crude yet effective percussion instruments.

The Bronze Age ushered in advances in both instrumental design and the quality of manufacture, as social stratification presumably yielded an entire new class of both craftsmen and musicians, not to mention increased cultural interchange in the form of coerced musical and instrumental tributes. Excavations from Erlitou 二里頭, Yanshi 偃師, Henan show, for instance, that smooth, polished chimestones of uniform thickness and capable of producing pitches of considerable sustaining power had begun to replace the roughly chiseled and more quickly decaying instruments of the Neolithic past, and that bronze clapper-bells with marked tonal qualities had likewise come to replace their

pottery counterparts. Whether such clapper-bells were used for strictly musical purposes is unclear, but their design and manufacture certainly paved the way for the grand
orchestral bells of the Shang and Zhou (Li Chunyi 2005:26).

By the end of the Shang dynasty, we have evidence of both great refinements in
instrument manufacture and at least the beginnings of a full-fledged musical system.
The most noteworthy of Shang musical artifacts are bells that most archaeologists
label *nao* 鐃, which are often found in sets of two to five instruments of varying size
and pitch, each crafted with tonal precision at the casting stage of the process, which
employed a piece-mold technique. These are bells of almond-shaped cross-section
with cylindrical shaft-handles and prominently curved rims, designed to be struck
with a mallet and, usually, mounted upright in a stand. The common three-bell sets
tend to appear in relatively consistent intervallic patterns that suggest either T-M3-P5
(*do-mi-sol*, e.g., C, E, G or D-F#-A, etc.) or M3-P5-T (*mi-sol-do*) (Li Chunyi 2005:57;
for a differing assessment, see Falkenhausen 1993:228–229). A five-bell set from the
tomb of Fu Zi (Hao) 婦好 at Yinxu 殷虛, Anyang 安陽, Henan appears to reveal a
four-pitch scale of G-A-C-E-G, which would likely suggest a tonic of C and thus a
major pentatonic scale minus the major second, starting at the low end from the perfect fifth, namely P5-M6-T-M3-P5 (*sol-la-do-mi-sol*) or, in Chinese terms, *zhi* 徵, *yu*
羽, *gong* 宮, *jue* 角, *zhi* 徵. There is no doubt that these were instruments of melodic or
quasi-melodic function, and they display a tonal structure which, in incipient form, is
entirely consistent with Zhou musical practices.

Shang chimestones, too, begin to occasionally appear in sets of up to three, and in
some cases show great advances in their exacting levels of manufacture and decidedly
more resonant tonal qualities. Ocarinas reveal similar levels of refinement, having now
developed into a common type with three fingering holes in the front and two in the
back, the easiest fingerings of which, much like the Fu Zi (Hao) bells, suggest tetratonic
scales, with full major pentatonic (or even hexatonic) scales possible with somewhat
more intricate fingerings; some of the tombs even yield ocarinas in large-and-small
pairs a major third apart, a fact that would appear to demonstrate a certain practical
understanding of keys and absolute pitch (Li Chunyi 2005:64).

In addition to these durable tonal instruments, a number of sizeable, decorative
drums have been unearthed from Shang tombs, which are of a curved barrel shape that
suggests derivation from a more common wooden model. These had mutually resonating alligator-skin heads at both ends and were meant to be played horizontally; the presence of either upper rings or feet suggests that they could alternately be hung or placed
on the ground (Li Chunyi 2005:45–47). To date, no perishable Shang instruments of
wood or bamboo have survived, but certain oracle-bone graphs suggest the existence of
panpipes, and some have even speculated—not without controversy—that the early
form of the graph *yue* 樂, "music," may have itself been a kind of ideographic representation of a zither-like instrument.

INSTRUMENTAL TYPES AND ENSEMBLES
IN THE ZHOU

The Zhou has long been associated with court music in the historical minds of the Chinese, with tradition having it that the Duke of Zhou 周公 was in fact the one who initially "fashioned ritual and created music" 制禮作樂. While Zhou musical practices must have to a great degree followed Shang precedent, the Zhou also certainly refined such practices and brought them to an entirely new level and, as the statement suggests, music became one of the primary means through which power and privilege was displayed as part of an intricate ritual system. As evidenced through both textual and archaeological records, bronze bells were often given as gifts of honor to meritorious relatives or ministers in recognition of their services (occasionally bearing dedicatory inscriptions proclaiming them as such), and these in turn became part of musical ensembles performed in devotional sacrifice to one's departed ancestors, extolling their virtue while making them drunk with spirits and song. Let us first briefly examine the types of instruments that made up such assemblages.

Bells

Perhaps the most prototypical Zhou court instruments are sets of bronze bells, which count among the most intricately manufactured artifacts from early China, having developed substantially from their Shang counterparts. The *nao* bells that predominate the Shang archaeological record quickly fade from existence once we reach the Zhou, though some larger solitary *nao* of a southern regional variety continue to be found in Western Zhou tombs of the mid-to-lower Yangtze region. These latter have developed acoustically from their earlier predecessors, now bearing rows of bosses, which served the function of eliminating upper harmonics and hum and allowed the bells to vibrate with more stability (Li Chunyi 2005:82). The mid-to-lower Yangtze is also the region where the earliest *bo* 鎛 bells have been found, a kind of ovular, flat-rimmed bell hung from a highly ornate upper handle, which often bore decorative wings as well. Like the southern variety of *nao*, these were originally solitary instruments, but by the early Zhou they had found their way to the northern states—where they became important symbols of status for nobility—and in some cases these northern *bo* bells even begin to appear in sets, perhaps showing the influence of their new locale (Li Chunyi 2005:82–84).

The disappearance of the Shang *nao*, however, is most probably due to the emergence of a superior type of bell that would become the quintessential Zhou instrument: the *yong* bell 甬鐘.

The earliest known *yong* appear in the north, but this type may have originated in the south; in any case, by the middle of the Western Zhou these bells are already found throughout much the Chinese world, from modern-day Shaanxi to Hunan and

Zhejiang. *Yong* bells were constructed with a long shaft above the resonating, almond-shaped, curved-rim body of the bell, and they were designed to be hung at a slanted angle from a ring cast into the lower part of the shaft, to be struck with a pole or mallet; these bells also consistently had rows of bosses cast into the surface of their resonating bodies. Typologically, they are closely related to the *nao* they replaced, though now suspended rather than mounted, and may be thought to have derived directly therefrom (see Falkenhausen 1993:153–157). Western Zhou examples are often found in sets, with three being the most common number early on (much like their Shang *nao* antecedents), but by the end of the period they are frequently found in sets of up to eight bells (Li Chunyi 2005:85–92). *Yong* bells particularly flourished during the Chunqiu period, developing into three somewhat distinct regional design-types and found in sets of anywhere from three to nine or eleven bells, and they would continue to thrive throughout much of the Warring States period—as seen especially in the Marquis of Zeng find to be discussed later in this chapter—but would eventually witness a dramatic decline during its latter years (Li Chunyi 2005:119–120, 186; for a more detailed treatment of the *yong*'s development over time, see Falkenhausen 1993:159–168).

By the beginning of the Chunqiu period, a new type of relatively simple handle-hung bell begins to emerge, the *niu* 鈕 bell—similar in shape to more ancient varieties of *ling* clapper-bells but designed to be struck with a mallet. *Niu* bells become increasingly prevalent by the middle of the Chunqiu period, and while there tends to be little variation in structure, a good deal of regional differences in décor may be observed; by the Warring States period, the *niu* have become just as prevalent as the *yong*. Commonly found in sets of five or nine, these somewhat smaller bells presented an upper-register counterpart to the lower-register *yong* bells and most probably carried a more pronounced melodic function; some even carry inscriptional names like *yong ling* 詠鈴, "singing bells" (Li Chunyi 2005:124, 129, 190).

In addition to the *yong*, *niu*, and *bo* bells, other varieties of Zhou bells include a large, shaft-handled, clapper-bell known as the *duo* 鐸, a vertically suspended shaft-handled bell called the *zheng* 鉦, and a hung, curved bell roughly in the shape of an upside-down vase, known as the *chunyu* 錞于—located most prominently in the southwest. Though some of these instruments are occasionally found together with bell-sets—possibly suggesting a musical function—these acoustically penetrating bells all appear to have served primarily as military signaling instruments and are more often unearthed together with military paraphernalia. In the Chunqiu period, another type of bell known as *goudiao* 鉤鑃 appears in the lower Yangtze region and areas further south; these were long, shaft-handle bells played with the mouth facing upward, found in sets ranging from two to seven and apparently used in banquets and sacrifices. Finally, large *tong gu* 銅鼓, "bronze drums," are to be found from the Chunqiu period onward throughout southwestern China, but these probably functioned more as ritual instruments than musical ones per se (Li Chunyi 2005:130–139).

A particular feature of many *yong* and *niu* bells is their capacity to produce two distinct tones, depending on whether they are stuck at the center of the striking portion or at an alternate location to one of its sides. This may initially have been an accidental feature of bells resulting from their almond-shaped cross-sectional design, which also gave the bells fast attenuation and a concentrated pitch (Bagley 2005:55); a number of Shang bells also have such two-tone capabilities but with little exactitude in interval and no signs of any intended usage of the alternate pitch. With Zhou bells, however, it is common for such pitches to be spaced either a minor third or major third apart, and such capacity appears to have been consciously utilized, at least in some cases, by the late Western Zhou, as exhibited by such *yong* bells as the Marquis of Ying bell 應侯鐘 from Lantian 藍田, Shaanxi, which has a distinct bird design cast into the lower-right, alternate striking portion, precisely at the point where a secondary tone a minor-third higher than the primary tone can be produced (Li Chunyi 2005:87). Such bells usually have long, narrow troughs scraped into the interior of the resonating body for the purpose of fine pitch adjustments, most likely in order to lend greater exactitude to the intervallic distance of the two tones (Falkenhausen 1993:83–84; Li Chunyi 2005:87). Whether or not such alternate pitches were utilized in any given case naturally complicates our understanding of the tonal structure of bell sets, an issue we will return to shortly.

By far the most impressive display of bells is to be found in the early–Warring States tomb of Marquis Yi of Zeng 曾侯乙 (d. ca. 433 BCE), excavated at Leigudun 擂鼓墩, Suizhou 隨州, Hubei, in 1978. This well-preserved set of bells formed part of a larger ensemble of instruments found in the tomb's central chamber, which included a variety of wind and string instruments, along with drums and chimestones; a smaller chamber ensemble in the east chamber consisted of a small drum, a pair of mouth organs, and seven zithers (see Major and So 2000). The bell set comprised some 65 individual bells laid out on a large L-shaped rack in three tiers; the bells consist mostly of a mix of *niu* and *yong* types, with different parts of the rack displaying bells of different configurations and décor. As Falkenhausen puts it, the assembler of the Zeng bells appears to have "purposefully combined elements of preexisting chimes so as to create a musical assemblage that, as a whole, was more comprehensive and versatile than any of its parts" (1993:249). Three pairs of wooden mallets and two wooden poles found together with the bells suggest they may have been played by a team of five performers. In addition to their sheer immensity and high quality of manufacture, the Marquis of Zeng bells are most remarkable for bearing detailed inscriptions situating them tonally within a complex music-theoretical system, which we shall detail further in this chapter.

Chimestones

The archaeological record contains some early–Western Zhou examples of solitary chimestones, but most instances from this point forward are found in sets. While early inscriptional materials make note of gifts of chimestones in sets of at least five, no full sets of more than three from the Western Zhou have been found intact. What does remain of these often highly decorative stones demonstrates further advancements from Shang manufacture, with slight adjustments to the stone's angularity and the length of each top side enhancing both the durability and playability of the instruments, and with greater precision in the initial cutting of the stone obviating the need for anything more than minor grinding of the stone's base to achieve the desired pitch (Li Chunyi 2005:75–79). By the Chunqiu period, all chimestones are now found in sets and appear to have developed into a fixed design, sharply angular at the top end but now with a pronounced curvature on the bottom. Made mostly of a less-than-durable form of limestone, no well-preserved sets from the period remain, though at least one set of originally 10 chimestones (Shangmacun 上馬村, Houma 侯馬, Shanxi) seems to reveal an arrangement that most likely constituted a major pentatonic scale in the key of C (Li Chunyi 2005:115–116). By the Warring States period, chimestones are found in sets of 25 or more, the most impressive being those of the Marquis of Zeng tomb.

The Marquis of Zeng chimestones are somewhat damaged and so provide no accurate pitch measurements, but they bear inscriptional notations of their tones and pitches along their sides and edges. The stones are numbered from 1–41 in pitch order, forming a chromatic scale over the span of three-and-a-half octaves. However, their storage boxes reveal that they were sorted in sets forming major pentatonic scales, one starting on C (C D E G A), another starting a tri-tone away on F# (F# G# A# C# D#), and a third containing the remaining notes of B and F (Falkenhausen 1993:270–274; Bagley 2005:61–63). The two-tiered rack itself holds only 32 stones at once (and indeed, the remaining 9 stones were not found in the tomb) and appears to have been designed to hang three octaves of one pentatonic scale on the top rack (with all the *sol* and *do* notes to the left, and the *re*, *mi*, and *la* to the right), and three of another on the bottom rack—the particular stones arrayed during interment coming in the keys of B (*zhuo guxian* 濁姑洗) and C (*guxian* 姑洗), respectively (Li Chunyi 2005:183–184). The red-inlaid inscriptions on the stones are given in Chu nomenclature (see the section on "Musical theory and practice" below), and these in each case tell us (among other information) which tone the stone would play in each of the five pentatonic scales to which it could belong, such as the "*do* of *guxian*" 姑洗之宮, the "*re* of *muzhong*" 穆鐘之商, and so on (Bagley 2005:71–72). The Marquis of Zeng chimestones are not the only ones to include pitch inscriptions; remnant stones of an incomplete set from the partially looted tomb of Jincun 金村, Luoyang 洛陽, Henan bear inscriptions that speak to each stone's absolute pitch, its position on the rack, and the particular subset of which it is a part (Li Chunyi 2005:181–182).

Drums, winds, and strings

The archaeological record is largely incomplete for these instruments made out of more easily perishable materials. The earliest Zhou drums found to date come from the late-Chunqiu tomb of Hougudui 侯古堆, Gushi 固始, Henan, which yields a pair of small flat drums, one with a handle (Li Chunyi 2005:114–115). Somewhat later, the Marquis of Zeng assemblage produces a large, lacquer, barrel-shaped drum with skinned heads at each end; the drum was erected with a long wooden pole bored through its center and situated in an ornate stand. A similarly impressive specimen is a large, two-headed flat drum from Tianxingguan 天星觀, Jiangling 江陵, Hubei, which was suspended perpendicularly from an elaborate stand consisting of two outward-facing bird figures each perched atop a seated tiger. These and other tombs of the region have given us a variety of smaller, hand-held drums as well (Li Chunyi 2005:178–182).

Among wind instruments, even the more durable ocarina is not found in great quantities during the Zhou, and the few scattered examples from Western Zhou tombs follow the same basic design and fingering layout of their Shang predecessors. More important to the orchestras of the time were flutes, panpipes (*xiao* 簫), and mouth organs (*sheng* 笙). The mouth organ was an instrument composed of a hollow gourd, shaped during growth to form a vertical shaft toward its stem, with sets of bamboo pipes, each drilled with fingering and air holes and fitted with a bamboo reed inside, inserted into holes drilled into the gourd's body (see Feng Guangsheng 2000:95–98). Among the earliest examples of this droning instrument is one found in the late-Chunqiu tomb of Caojiagang 曹家崗, Dangyang 當陽, Hubei; only the gourd body remains, with three rows of holes where some 22 pipes had once been fixed (Li Chunyi 2005:142). A few scattered Warring States examples have been unearthed mostly from tombs in and around the Chu region, including a Marquis of Zeng remnant artifact that originally bore some 18 pipes; a tomb from Lijiashan 李家山 in Jiangchuan 江川, Yunnan has even yielded a gourd-shaped mouth organ made of bronze (Li Chunyi 2005:202–204). Almost nothing in the way of Zhou flutes has thus far been unearthed, save for a couple of transverse flutes known as *chi* 篪 found in the Marquis of Zeng tomb. These were each made of a bamboo shaft closed off at both ends; along with a blowing hole and venting hole, the surface also included five fingering holes (Feng Guangsheng 2000:91–92; Li Chunyi 2005:200–201). In addition to these flutes, the Marquis of Zeng tomb also produced a couple of panpipes, each of which consisted of 13 bamboo pipes of different lengths and diameters (Feng Guangsheng 2000:93–94; Li Chunyi 2005:200–201). Naturally, none of these instruments is preserved well enough to provide anything in the way of accurate pitch measurements, even supposing the proper blowing technique could be duplicated.

Much like the flutes and other wind instruments, string instruments may also have had a long history in early China, but their materials of manufacture were not well suited to preservation. Such instruments took the form of zithers: long, hollow wooden instruments roughly in the shape of a rectangular (or trapezoidal) box with resonating holes in the floorboard, but with a slightly arched top over which any number of strings were suspended via bridges and tied to posts or tuning pegs at one end or the other. These came mainly in two varieties: the *se* 瑟, a larger instrument with moveable frets (internal bridges) and between 19–26 strings, some of which may have been tuned in unison; and the *qin* 琴, a smaller, fretless instrument with fewer strings and less sonorous, likely not well suited to larger orchestral contexts. The earliest examples of the former are two *se* from the late-Chunqiu tomb of Caojiagang, which bore 21 and 26 strings respectively, and between them average around 200 cm in length, 30-plus cm in width, and close to 17 cm in height. Warring States *se* appear to have seen a decrease in length but an increase in the size of the resonating body, as evidenced from limited finds mainly from the Chu region and vicinity, such as the dozen highly decorative *se* of the Marquis of Zeng tomb, one typical example of which is 167 cm in length and had once fitted 25 strings running across three separate bridges in groups of 9, 7, and 9; a similar configuration is found in a 134-cm *se* unearthed from Changtaiguan 長台關, Xinyang 信陽, Henan (Li Chunyi 2005:205; see also Lawergren 2000:69–70). The *qin* makes its first archaeological appearance only in the Warring States, with a short 67-cm, ten-string *qin* from the Marquis of Zeng tomb and an 80-cm, possibly 9-string *qin* from Wulipai 五里牌, Changsha 長沙, Hunan. These instruments, however, are rather different from the 7-string *qin* of later times, with the neck in both cases protruding over a third of the length beyond the resonating body. Given that rough resemblance in shape to the central Asian lute, along with the peculiar ornamentation found on some of these instruments' tuning pegs, some suspect that the early *qin* may have derived in part from foreign influences (Lawergren 2000:74–77). Nonetheless, by the end of the Warring States, the *qin* would come to be seen as the quintessential instrument of the noble man, and the high level of artistry that *qin* (and sometimes *se*) performance had attained is attested by the fact that texts of the period take note of famous practitioners of the instrument, the most famous being Bo Ya 伯牙 (Li Chunyi 2005:144; see esp. the "Ben wei" 本味 chapter of the *Lüshi chunqiu* 呂氏春秋). In addition to the *qin* and *se*, a long, thin-stringed instrument identified by some as the *zhu* 筑 appears within the Marquis of Zeng assemblage, and remnants of an instrument that may be a prototype of the moveable-fret *zheng* 箏 have been found at a few scattered sites in southeastern China.

Although the accidents of preservation give us a somewhat incomplete record of the instrumental inventory of Zhou-period China, what has been unearthed, combined with the orchestral depictions of early texts, nonetheless serves to demonstrate the richness and variety of the timbral tapestry the orchestras of the time were capable of weaving. Let us now turn to the parameters by which such instruments were made to sound in harmony with one another.

MUSICAL THEORY AND PRACTICE

At some point in time—certainly by the end of the Warring States—early Chinese thinkers discovered that music conformed to principles of numerical regularity that lay at the basis of the natural order. Much like their early Greek counterparts, they discovered that the basic intervals of music could be generated through the simplest of mathematical ratios, revealing an inherent order of numerical organization within the very nature of music itself. But the experience of what sounds musically pleasing must always come prior to the discovery of why it sounds so pleasing, and in the Chinese case it was the pentatonic scale (*wu yin* 五音) that, over time, eventually proved most well suited to the ears of early Chinese music makers and had become the basis of early Chinese melodies long before it ever came to be isolated by theorists and subjected to analysis. It was a set of aurally accepted intervallic relationships that crystallized well before the notion of interval had even begun to be understood, and it could be keyed to any pitch long before the need was felt to invent standards for such pitches.

Whether the pentatonic scale was the norm by the early Zhou, however, is somewhat uncertain. Early Zhou bell ensembles in fact reveal a preference for the same four-tone scale as their Shang predecessors, at least when we take the alternate striking tones into account. For instance, the late–Western Zhou Zhongyi *yong* bell set 中義鐘 from Fufeng 扶風, Shaanxi, produces on the main striking portions only three distinct tones over the span of three octaves: *la-do-mi-la-mi-la-mi-la*; but assuming the right striking portion was also intended for playing, the *mi* and *la* bells also produce *sol* and *do* notes (each a minor third higher), suggesting the use of a four-note scale of T-M3-P5-M6 (*do-mi-sol-la*; or 宮角徵羽). Given that bells and chimestones were most likely used for melodic punctuation rather than as carriers of the melody per se, their tonal array may certainly have been more limited than that of other instruments of the ensemble, such as flutes or mouth organs, which may well have still utilized the pentatonic scale (on this point, see also Falkenhausen 1993:265). By the time of the Chunqiu period, however, the pentatonic scale (including the M2, i.e., 商, or *re*) appears to predominate in bells and chimestones as well, as evidenced perhaps from the Shangmacun chimestone set previously mentioned. Pitch testing on some of the larger *niu*-bell sets also tends to suggest the use of the standard major pentatonic scales on the main striking portions, with the lowest bell often a *sol* tone, or P5 (so, for instance, D E G A B), with the possibility of even producing heptatonic scales with major sevenths and raised fourths once the alternate striking portions are taken into account. A heptatonic scale may well indeed have been in use by the end of the Chunqiu, judging from the nine-piece late-Chunqiu Chu *yong* bell set from Xiasi 下寺, Xichuan 淅川, Henan, which appears capable of playing a complete major scale (with some inexactitude in pitch) on the main striking portions alone (see Li Chunyi 2005:124, example 4). Notably, however, Warring States texts speak only of pentatonic scales and never of heptatonic ones, and it seems safe to assume that the pentatonic scale was at least the basic building block of musical compositions throughout the Chunqiu and Zhanguo periods, if not earlier. The Marquis of Zeng chimestones and bells, to be discussed further in this chapter, also reveal a clear rootedness in the pentatonic scale.

Texts of the late Warring States tell us that early music theorists eventually came around to the remarkable discovery that each of the five tones of the scale stood in relation to one of the other five by a single interval, or what we know as the perfect fifth: *zhi* (*sol*) lay a fifth above (or, equivalently, a fourth below) the tonic *gong* (*do*); *shang* (*re*) a fifth above *zhi*; *yu* (*la*) a fifth above *shang*; and *jue* (*mi*) a fifth above *yu*. In other words, they discovered that the entire scale could be generated from the primary tone by a series of multiplications of the frequency of vibration of each tone by the simplest (excluding the octaval 2:1) of numerical ratios: 3:2. Concretely, this meant that if the length of a strung silk string, or a hollow bamboo tube, were multiplied by two-thirds (that is, by subtracting one third of its length), it would produce a pitch a fifth higher than the original pitch; if this second length were again multiplied by two-thirds, the third pitch would be produced, and so on until we arrived at the fifth pitch. But since such a series of ascending fifths would stretch over more than two octaves, every other multiplication by two-thirds would have to be changed to multiplication by four-thirds (i.e., adding rather than subtracting a third of the length) to keep the scale within a single octave. So if we started with a string-length of 81 inches that happened to produce the note of C, we would derive lengths of 54 (G), 72 (D), 48 (A), and 64 (E) inches, yielding the pentatonic scale (see Figure 1).

FIGURE 1 Zeng bell rack, side view.

This could well have been the first step in advancing musical practice into the realm of musical theory, paving the way for the next significant step in the development of the musical system: the creation of pitch-standards, *lü* 律. In their rudimentary form, pitch-standards must have appeared long before, with the advent of instrumental ensembles—at least once these had advanced beyond combinations of voice and one or two tunable instruments such as zithers, which could always be adjusted together on the basis of relative pitch alone, without any concern for whether the "key" in which they played corresponded to anything absolute. For once fixed-pitch instruments are combined—flutes and ocarinas, for instance—they must be crafted according to a single pitch-standard in order to work together, and the need for absolute pitch standards becomes all the more acute once manufacture and trade reaches a level of specialization in which instruments are brought together from different locales. As the inherent demand for musical variety entails the necessity of different keys, a single pitch standard would never satisfy the human ear, thus necessitating the creation of a full *set* of pitch-standards. In order to facilitate musical exchange and transposition, such a set of pitch-standards clearly had to be organically related to the musical system already in practice, which is to say the pentatonic scale. Modulation and transposition are only possible in a system wherein the octave is divided into a series of equidistant notes, and such a series must simultaneously be inclusive of the scales upon which the music is composed or performed. While not all of the early Chinese instruments were capable of sounding the full gamut of tones, some degree of overlap was certainly desired, so that an ocarina keyed to one pitch could play some of the notes of the pentatonic scale produced

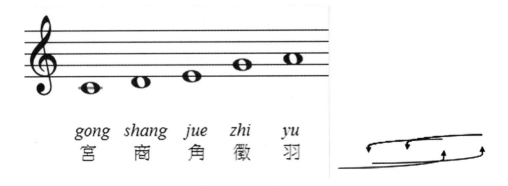

by a flute keyed to another. This is only possible if the pitch-standards to which the two were keyed were organically derived from the pentatonic scale itself (Cook 1995:87–93, 101–102).[1]

---

[1] For a somewhat different, yet roughly compatible scenario in which the concept of absolute pitch was introduced when signaling bells were gradually added to a pentatonic-playing ensemble, and the chromatic scale arose from the need to transpose within the context of such sets of fixed-pitch instruments, see Bagley 2005:74–79.

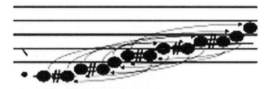

Generation of the twelve-tone gamut by
spiral of fifths

The fact that the pentatonic scale could be generated via a series of ascending fifths (and descending fourths) naturally led to these pitch-standards being composed of 12 equidistant pitches—equivalent to the chromatic scale—which was derived by extending this series of generations onward until it closed itself off by reaching an octaval equivalent of the initial note, which would happen (more or less) after the twelfth generation (see figure 2). The final note of the series is not the exact 2:1 octaval equivalent of the initial note, differing, as it does, by a margin of 23.5 cents; but it is close enough to be perceived by the human ear as the same note. This method of "circle of fifths" pitch generation is essentially the same as that ascribed to Pythagoras in the West, where the discrepancy in question is known as the "Pythagorean comma" (see DeWoskin 1982:49–52). This process is well documented in Warring States texts and is known as the "three-parts addition-subtraction method" (*sanfen sunyifa* 三分損益法). In all such accounts, the primary pitch-standard from which the other 11 are generated is known as *huangzhong* 黃鐘 ("Yellow Bell"), the determination of which would eventually become a matter of the utmost gravity. The "Yinlü" 音律 chapter of the *Lüshi chunqiu* 呂氏春秋 contains a description of this process in which the names of the 12 pitch-standards are given, as in Figure 3.

While the 12 pitch-standards were always conceived of as in some sense deriving from the natural world, it is interesting to note that philosophical texts would also view them as a sagely creation that utilized cosmic principles to construct standards by which to harness nature itself, including its music. Thus in the "Gu yue" 古樂 chapter of the *Lüshi chunqiu*, we are told of how the music master of the Yellow Emperor 黃帝 "distinguished the 12 pitch-standards by listening to the calls of the phoenixes, the calls of the males giving six, and the calls of the females also giving six" 聽鳳皇之鳴, 以別十二律;其雄鳴為六, 雌鳴亦六, all of which corresponded in perfect proportion to the *huangzhong* pitch he had previously derived from a segment of bamboo. Subsequent to this, the Yellow Emperor orders his music officials to "cast a set of 12 bells" to these pitch-standards, "in order to bring harmony to the five tones" 鑄十二鐘，以和五音, thus creating a set of uniform standards in the image of nature through which the rulers might exercise control over the powerful and influential medium of music. Conversely, the division of the 12 pitches into six paired sets of "male" *lù* 律 and "female" *lü* 呂, ostensibly borrowed from nature, likely represented a further attempt to organize the pitch standards into a rational scheme. The terms *liu lù* 六律 and *liu lù* 六呂 are seen in texts from the *Zuo zhuan* 左傳 onward, and these correspond to the pitches found on the right and left of

FIGURE 2 Zeng *niu* bell.

Figure 3, respectively, such that the six pitches of either set are each spaced a whole tone apart; as the set of six "female" pitches was seen as in some sense subordinate to the "male" set, the pitch standards are sometimes referred to collectively as simply *liu lü*. This sort of codification of the pitch standards into a dominant set of six is in fact reflected in the inscriptions from the Marquis of Zeng bell set, which, along with the chimestones from the same tomb, give us the first reliably accurate information on excavated bell-sets in terms of the music-theoretical practices under which they were performed.

The Marquis of Zeng bells are the only complete set of bells from pre-imperial China on which are inscribed the names of the actual tones they are capable of sounding, and they are the only set capable of playing the full gamut of 12 tones—at least for some three-plus octaves of their five-octave range. In terms of the basic solfège nomenclature, the Zeng bells (and chimestones) primarily use a system in which the four basic tones of *gong, shang, zhi,* and *yu* are nominally the primary tones, and to each of these are added two tones a major third above and a minor third below (or perhaps two major thirds above), respectively labeled with the affixes of *jue* 角 and *zeng* 曾. The combination of the four primary tones and their permutations yields precisely 12 distinct tones, equivalent to the chromatic scale (Falkenhausen 1993:295; Bagley 2005:65–68), and arguably suggests that a method of intonation closely akin to the Western system

wuyi 無射 F# ▾▸	G 應鐘 *yingzhong*
yize 夷則 E ▸	F 南呂 *nanlü*
ruibin 蕤賓 D ▴◂	D# 林鐘 *linzhong*
guxian 姑洗 C ▴	C# 仲呂 *zhonglü*
taicou 太簇 A# ▴▴	B 夾鐘 *jiazhong*
huangzhong 黃鐘 G# ▴▸	A 大呂 *dalü*

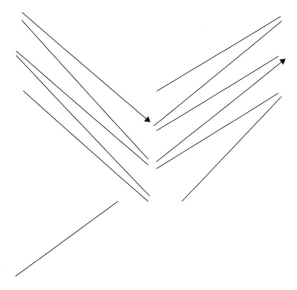

FIGURE 3 The Twelve Pitch Standards: *liu lü* 六律 (left) and *liu lü* 六呂 (right) (*huangzhong* given here as G#).

of "just intonation" was employed in the manufactured tuning of these bells (Cook 2020). In bells of the lower racks, however, the term *jue* is often used to indicate a tone in its own right, suggesting once again that the pentatonic scale was the primary building block in the music of these bells, and certain other notes of the chromatic scale are indicated in these lower bells by use of the prefix *bian* 變, "altered," to indicate their flattening by one semitone.

The *niu* bells on the long arm of the upper rack, which are all capable of sounding two tones a minor third apart, present an especially interesting arrangement: as these bells are consecutively spaced a whole tone apart, playing them at the alternate striking portions in a zigzag manner neatly yields a chromatic scale, showing an unusual interest in mathematical regularity and precision (see the description in Bagley 2005:65; see also Falkenhausen 1993:249–250). Tones of the five different octaves spanned by all the bells are further indicated by a somewhat irregular series of prefixes or affixes. For instance, while the *gong* in the middle register is simply *gong*, the same note an octave lower is labeled *da gong* 大宮, whereas one an octave higher might be labeled *xiao gong* 少(小)宮 or *gong fan* 宮反, and one an octave further above that *xiao gong zhi fan* 少(小)宮之反; a few of the tones an octave above the middle register even have entirely different names altogether in lieu of the prefixes or affixes.

Pitch standards are likewise indicated on the bells, and the scale tones and pitch standards are named in relation to one another in terms of "equivalency formulas," in which a bell whose A-tone (primary striking tone) produced the pitch C might have inscribed at that spot "the *gong* of *guxian*" 姑洗之宮, "the *shang* of *taicu*" 太簇之商, "the *jue* of *huangzhong*" 黃鐘之角, and so on.

FIGURE 4 Zeng *yongzhong.*

In the upper tier, the front of each bell gives its solfège tones (in the key of *wuyi* 無射) for each of the two striking points, for example *shang* 商 (*re*) and *yuzeng* 羽曾 (*fa*); the back of each inscription tells us in which key the note would function as tonic—namely, the absolute pitch standard to which the bell corresponds: for example, the "*do of huang-zhong*" 黃鐘之宮 for one bell, the "*do of ruibin*" 蕤賓之宮 for another (Figure 4). The primary names for these pitch standards are close to the terms found for the equivalent pitches in received texts, except that only those corresponding to the six *lü* 律 are given. In addition to these six, variant names are listed for one or more of the pitches according to how they are referred to in states such as Zhou 周, Jin 晉, and Qi 齊. Only for the state of Chu 楚, Zeng's powerful neighbor, are the names of all 12 pitch-standards mentioned, but these also show evidence of grouping into six pairs, as they consist of unique names for each of the six *lü*, with the names for their six *lü* counterparts formed by attaching the prefix *zhuo* 濁 ("turbid," i.e., flattened) to the names of the corresponding *lü* pitches lying a half-step above (for charts of the various state nomenclatures, see Falkenhausen 1993:286; DeWoskin 1994:358).

Taken as a whole, the inscriptional and pitch-measurement evidence suggests that musical pieces based on the pentatonic scale were to be performed in a variety of keys—namely, all those listed in the first half of the equivalency inscriptions. A closer look at specific patterns of tonal distribution within certain keys also suggests, moreover, that a number of hitherto unattested types of scales (both pentatonic and otherwise) may have tended to be performed in those keys (Cook 2020). It is certainly worth speculating as to why, in the base nomenclature of pitch standards adopted for the Zeng bells, only the names of the six "male" pitch-standards are ever stated in the inscriptions, but in any case it is probably not necessary to assume that this sort of division of the octave into six equidistant pitches was anything other than a systematizing move designed to provide a particular framework upon which to utilize the 12 pitch-standards into which the octave had most likely—for the inherently musical reasons stated previously—already been divided.[2]

Aside from bell and chimestone sets, there is also a badly damaged set of bamboo pitch-pipes excavated from a late–Warring States tomb in Yutaishan 雨台山, Jiangling 江陵, Hubei, upon which are inscribed in ink Chu names for the pitch standard of each pipe as tonic (*do*) along with its intervallic relation to some other pitch standard, such as "the *do* of *zheng xinzhong*, which is the [*la*] of *zhuo mu*[*zhong*]" 定(正)新鐘之宮為濁穆[鐘之羽], wherein *zheng xinzhong* sounds equivalent to F# and *zhuo muzhong* to A. A reconstruction of the pipes, along with their remnant inscriptions, suggests that the names correspond precisely to the Chu nomenclature of the Marquis of Zeng bells and chimestones (Figure 5), save for the addition here of *zheng* ("proper") before each of the primary, unflattened pitches (Li Chunyi 2005:218–219).

---

[2] For an alternate view, in which these six pitch standards are only later divided into 12 and gradually "conflated" with the five tones, see Falkenhausen 1993:299–307.

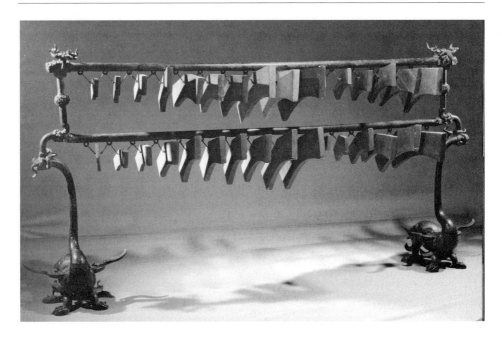

FIGURE 5 Zeng chimestones.

MUSICAL INSTITUTIONS AND REGULATIONS

Understanding the theoretical basis of the music, however, tells us relatively little about how the music was actually composed and performed. With no surviving scores from early China, we know next to nothing about how melodies were constructed, how such melodies may have been punctuated and supported by non-melodic instruments in the ensemble, or the rhythmic patterns to which such instrumentation was set. What we do know is that the more intricate rituals of state often involved a detailed liturgy of songs (some of which are partially preserved in the *Shi jing* 詩經), instrumental pieces, and even full-scale dance repertoires, and that these all constituted an important part of the practices and institutions by which hierarchical status was proclaimed and claims to allegiance were promulgated. As much as the colorful insignia woven into courtly garments or the gradations of livestock offered in ancestral sacrifices, musical regulation played a vital role in defining the hierarchical social relations that formed the core of ritual culture. This was natural enough, given that music was viewed as one of the primary means of communication with and influence upon the ancestral spirits, but music was also unique in terms of its capacity to reinforce one's social status and political power both visually and audibly. In visual terms, the elaborate instruments of an orchestra were aligned to all sides before the audience of ruler and his guests, each crafted to exacting proportions, and all hung out the night before

FIGURE 6 Zeng *se*-zither.

in strict accordance with detailed ritual precepts, while elaborately costumed singers, dancers, and musicians all performed in visually rhythmic tandem. Audibly, an array of sonorous instruments provided a feast for the ears: lofty pole drums boomed forth across the space at regular intervals while a variety of smaller drums punctuated in between; large sets of massive bronze bells and chimestones resounded in dialogue as they built the core melodic framework of the composition; great numbers of reeded mouth-organs droned out pitches to provide a collective ostinato; while, in front, bamboo flutes and stringed zithers (Figure 6) filled in the spaces with meandering melodic ornament. At the same time, costumed singers would recount to those assembled in harmonious voice a plaintive tale, such as the heroic deeds of King Wu and his conquest of the Shang, as down below several rows of colorful dancers bearing spears and shields acted out the various stages of the conquest in a fully choreographed rhythmic display of unified motion.

Such musical performances being as powerful as they were, they were quite naturally the subject of strict, if largely unenforceable, sumptuary regulations. According to early received literature, the makeup of the orchestras themselves was to be divided along the lines of hierarchical status, wherein the number of sides of an orchestral square one was allowed have occupied by musical instruments was ostensibly to be determined by rank (see Yang Yinliu 1980:39; Falkenhausen 1993:32–39). Whether such orchestral arrangements, or "musical suspensions" (*yuexuan* 樂懸), were in fact employed in precisely the manners described, however, is somewhat doubtful, given that the four-sided "palace suspension" (*gongxuan* 宮懸), for example, would have resulted in an orchestra that was effectively closed off to its audience; more practical is the type of arrangement suggested by the Marquis of Zeng assemblage, in which an L-shaped bell stand stands at the south and west, forming a three-sided enclosure with the chimestones along the north side, with the quieter winds and strings arrayed in front (Li Chunyi 2005:102). Texts likewise speak of regulation of the number of dancers one was allowed to have perform in his troupe, with the Zhou king's dance troupe supposedly set at eight rows of eight dancers each, while the regional lords were allowed six rows of eight, and so on down the line (see Liu Baonan 1990:77–79). The power and prestige accorded by a performance of civil or military dance by row upon row of rhythmically conjoined, costumed dancers bearing the emblems of feathers and flutes or shields and axes was recognized then as it still is today—the opening ceremony of the Beijing Olympics being only the most recent manifestation of a long and enduring tradition. Given the power of such displays, open usurpation of such prerogatives in dance performance became emblematic of the decline of the ritual system itself; as Confucius is given to lament over the head of the Ji 季 ministerial family: "Eight rows dancing in his courtyard—if he can bear to do this, what could he not bear to do?" 八佾舞於庭, 是可忍也, 孰不可忍也 (*Lunyu* 論語 3.1). Even the specific odes to be sung atop the raised hall during ritual occasions were considered an issue of important ritual concern, yet another matter in which Confucius is given cause for complaint (see *Lunyu* 3.2).

As properly crafted music was thought to embody a semblance of virtue within its very makeup, while the lyrics of its songs and costumed enactments of its dances could proclaim such ethical values in more overt forms, the ancient Chinese state did everything it could to incorporate music into its educational institutions. According to the *Zhou Li* 周禮, the high-ranking Grand Directors of Music, *Da Siyue* 大司樂, were charged with the task of teaching the principles of governance to the Sons of State 國子 in the official academy, with an array of music masters under their direction instructing these young members of the nobility in all aspects of a proper musical education, including musical virtue, musical language and rhetorical devices, and patriotic dances, thereby inculcating the finer points of established orthodoxy to the future members of the ruling class. While this work certainly represents something of an idealization of the true situation, it is far from the only text to make mention of influential music officials, who appear in a variety of names and ranks. Western Zhou inscriptions speak of a "Lesser Tutor" (*shao fu* 少傅) serving simultaneously as the "Drum and Bell [Master]" (*guzhong* 鼓鐘), thus already suggesting some sort of intrinsic connection between music and education at an early time (see the *Shili gui* 師嫠簋, as cited in Li Chunyi 2005:74). In texts from the *Zuo zhuan* and *Guoyu* 國語 on down, the most general name is that of "master" (*shi* 師) or "music master" (*yueshi* 樂師), which come in both "greater" (*da* 大) and "lesser" (*shao* 少) varieties, whereas "music chief" (*yue zheng* 樂正) appears as a high-level music official, and various musical "craftsmen" are presented by such general terms as *gong* 工 or *ling* 伶. As many of these officials were recruited from among the ranks of blind men, they are also often referred to by such terms as *gu* 瞽, *meng* 矇, and *sou* 瞍 (Li Chunyi 2005:108–110). In addition to their more strictly educational roles, music masters also seem to have been highly valued for the unique insights they might contribute to the affairs of state, and they are sometimes depicted as playing an important role as advisors to the ruler. Music officials are also seen involved in the establishment of standards and measures, and in certain military contexts as well (Li Chunyi 2005:111–112). Aside from all these educational, advisory, and military activities, music officials were also in charge of arranging the performance of the various musical offerings, in different keys at different times of the year, to the ancestral spirits and natural deities, who together constituted a key source of ritual legitimacy.

MUSIC AND PHILOSOPHY

Given the great importance attached to music and its roles in ancestral sacrifices and other major ritual functions, it naturally became a crucial focal point for the philosophical masters of the Warring States. This was especially true of the Confucians, who viewed music as an indispensable aspect of self-cultivation and saw the spontaneous flow of fully embodied musical mastery as representative of the highest state of moral attainment. Accordingly, they also recognized music's unique capacity to channel human affections directly and immediately and thereby extolled music as the perfect counterpart to ritual in its ability to educate the populace and lead it in the direction of an ordered society, while also warning against the social dangers posed by licentious forms of music. Finally, they saw in the natural order of music itself an embodiment of the notion of harmonious balance among disparate constituents, the five tones and eight timbres working in tandem representing an ideal society in which well-defined, hierarchical roles functioned together in the name of order and stability. Of course, the excessively lavish musical displays and indulgent performances to which many royal courts of the time were inclined—as evidenced by the Marquis of Zeng assemblage—gave others, namely the Mohists 墨家, cause to take a stance against court music altogether. This gave rise to further debate, beginning with the staunch defense of the role of state music by Xun Zi 荀子, and coming to its pre-imperial conclusion with an attempt to reconcile these competing views by the Lüshi chunqiu, which put forth a vision for the emerging empire in which music would continue to play a vital and significant role. Details of these debates, however, require a treatment that goes well beyond the scope of the present chapter (for more on musical thought in early China, see DeWoskin 1982; Cai Zhongde 1993; Cook 1995; Brindley 2012).

Rich in its variety of instrumental timbre; advanced in its degree of technological precision and manufacturing capabilities; grounded in a complex yet harmonically sound system of musical theory and practice; performed within a rationally designed institution of ritually prescribed contexts; and profoundly articulated in terms of its role, impact, and significance by the era's most influential thinkers, the music of early China presents us with a melodious orchestral tapestry of cultural achievement that finds few parallels in human history. Though its musical instruments, as found in the archaeological record, may no longer be capable of yielding the abundant diversity of tones and rhythms they once could, enough remains by which to give us an appreciation for the vast and intricate resources that went into the creation of music in ancient China, in the attempt not only to satisfy the eyes and ears of the listening audience but to ensure a sense of harmonious communion among all members of the social order, and with the departed ancestors as well.

BIBLIOGRAPHY

Bagley, Robert 2005. "The Prehistory of Chinese Music Theory." In *Proceedings of the British Academy 131 (2004 Lectures)*. Edited by P. J. Marshall, 41–90. Oxford: Oxford University Press.

Brindley, Erica Fox 2012. *Music, Cosmology, and the Politics of Harmony in Early China*. Albany: State University of New York Press.

Cai, Zhongde 蔡仲德 1993. *A History of Chinese Musical Aesthetics* 中國音樂美學史. Taipei: Landeng.

Cook, Scott Bradley 1995. "Unity and Diversity in the Musical Thought of Warring States China." PhD diss., University of Michigan, Ann Arbor.

Cook, Scott 2020. "Technology in a New Key: Toward a Reexamination of Musical Theory and Practice in the Zeng Hou Yi 曾侯乙 Bells." *T'oung Pao* 106.3 (forthcoming).

DeWoskin, Kenneth J. 1982. *A Song for One or Two: Music and the Concept of Art in Early China*. Ann Arbor: The University of Michigan Center for Chinese Studies.

DeWoskin, Kenneth J. 1994. "Picturing Performance: The Suite of Evidence for Music Culture in Warring States China." In *La pluridisciplinarité en archéologie musicale*, vol. 2. Edited by la Masion des sciences de l'homme, 351–364. Paris: Centre Français d'archéologie musicale Pro Lyra.

Falkenhausen, Lothar von 1993. *Suspended Music: Chime-Bells in the Culture of Bronze Age China*. Berkeley: University of California Press.

Feng, Guangsheng 2000. "Winds." In *Music in the Age of Confucius*. Edited by Jenny F. So, 87–99. Washington, DC: Freer Gallery of Art and Arthur M. Sackler Gallery, Smithsonian Institution.

Lawergren, Bo. 2000. "Strings." In *Music in the Age of Confucius*. Edited by Jenny F. So, 65–85. Washington, DC: Freer Gallery of Art and Arthur M. Sackler Gallery, Smithsonian Institution.

Li, Chunyi 李純一 2005. *A History of Pre-Imperial Chinese Music* 先秦音樂史, rev. ed. Beijing: Renmin yinyue chubanshe.

Liu, Baonan 劉寶楠 (1791–1855) 1990. *The Analects, with Corrected Meanings* 論語正義. Edited by Gao Liushui 高流水. Beijing: Zhonghua shuju.

Liu, Zaisheng 劉再生 2006. *A Concise History of Ancient Chinese Music* 中國古代音樂史簡述, rev. ed. Beijing: Renmin yinyue chubanshe.

Major, John S., and Jenny F. So 2000. "Music in Late Bronze Age China." In *Music in the Age of Confucius*. Edited by Jenny F. So, 13–33. Washington, DC: Freer Gallery of Art and Arthur M. Sackler Gallery, Smithsonian Institution.

So, Jenny F., ed. 2000. *Music in the Age of Confucius*. Washington, DC: Freer Gallery of Art and Arthur M. Sackler Gallery, Smithsonian Institution.

Wu, Zhao 吳釗, and Liu Dongsheng 劉東升, eds. 1993. *A Brief History of Chinese Music* 中國音樂史略, rev. ed. Beijing: Renmin yinyue chubanshe.

Yang, Yinliu 楊蔭瀏 1980. *A Draft History of Ancient Chinese Music* 中國古代音樂史稿, rev. ed. Beijing: Renmin yinyue chubanshe.

THE THIRD HEIGHT OF THE BRONZE AGE: SPRINGS AND AUTUMNS PERIOD

CHAPTER 22

··

HISTORICAL BACKGROUND DURING THE SPRINGS AND AUTUMNS PERIOD

··

BY YURI PINES, HEBREW UNIVERSITY
OF JERUSALEM[1]

> When the Way prevails under Heaven, rites, music, and punitive
> expeditions are initiated by the Son of Heaven; when there is no Way
> under Heaven, rites, music, and punitive expeditions are initiated by
> regional lords. If they are initiated by regional lords, few [states] will not
> be lost within ten generations; if they are initiated by nobles, few will not
> be lost within five generations; when retainers hold the state's [power to
> issue] commands, few will not be lost within three generations. (*Analects*)

THE Springs and Autumns (Chunqiu 春秋, 770–453 BCE) period was the heyday of China's aristocratic age. It was the age when a few noble lineages monopolized social, economic, political, and cultural power in each of the polities that comprised the Zhou 周 world, effectively preventing outsiders from ascending the ladder of power. It was also the age of one of the deepest systemic crises in China's long history. The aggravating weakness of the rulers—both of the Zhou kings and of regional lords—brought about political disintegration, the pace of which accelerated by the sixth to fifth centuries BCE. Confucius's (Kongzi 孔子, 551–479 BCE) saying cited in the epigraph (*Lunyu* 16.2:174) may serve as a brief summary of the devolution of political power during that age. The inability of policy-makers to curb the powers of disintegration stands at the background of profound reforms that ensued in the subsequent Warring States period (Zhanguo 戰國, 453–221 BCE), and which redirected the Zhou world toward the new, imperial era (Chapter 27).

---

[1] This research was supported by the Israel Science Foundation (grant No. 568/19) and by the Michael William Lipson Chair in Chinese Studies.

THE RISE AND FALL OF MULTISTATE ORDER

The Springs and Autumns period was the only age in China's long history during which efforts were made to create a viable multistate system. Back then, in marked distinction from other periods of political fragmentation, coexistence of multiple independent polities was not considered an aberration but rather a fait accompli. Statesmen of that age invested considerable efforts in solidifying and perfecting the multistate system. They even tried to create a proxy for an interstate law and developed diplomatic codes. It is only in the aftermath of the fiasco of these efforts that the search for multistate order was discontinued and the quest for political unification of All-under-Heaven (*tianxia* 天下) turned into the central feature of traditional Chinese political culture (Pines 2000).

The formation of the multistate system of the Springs and Autumns period was a by-product of the malfunctioning of the Zhou dynasty. Nominally, throughout this period and much beyond, the Zhou kings, the self-proclaimed "Sons of Heaven" (*tianzi* 天子), remained the supreme locus of political legitimacy. The kings inherited the immense prestige of the founders of the Zhou dynasty: they symbolized political order; stood at the apex of the ritual pyramid; and, most importantly, acted as exclusive mediators between the supreme deity, Heaven, and humankind. Practically, however, the Zhou dynasty had never recovered from the disastrous collapse of its western power-base in the Wei River Valley in 771 BCE. Never again could its economic and military prowess match its ritual prestige. Gradually but inevitably, the Sons of Heaven lost the ability to impose their will on regional lords (*zhuhou* 諸侯), who turned into independent political actors. Regional polities waged wars, concluded alliances, and maintained diplomatic relations with each other, while the Zhou kings were mostly hapless spectators of these developments, granting them post-factum approval and being unable to actively influence interstate dynamics. As time passed, the locus of political gravity shifted irreversibly from the Zhou royal court at Chengzhou 成周 (near modern Luoyang) toward the courts of powerful regional leaders.

The decline of the royal power was a complex process with manifold ebbs and flows. The dynasty reached its weakest point shortly after the collapse of its power in 771 BCE. According to the newly available information from the bamboo manuscript *Xinian* 繫年 (*String of Years*) from the Qinghua/Tsinghua University collection, after one of the contenders for the throne was killed in 750 BCE, "for nine years (749–741 BCE) Zhou was without a king, and the rulers of the states and regional lords then for the first time ceased attending the Zhou court" (*Xinian* 2, slip 8). Only in 741 BCE did Marquis Wen of Jin 晉文侯 (r. 780-746 or 770-736 BCE) establish the new incumbent, King Ping 周平王 (r. 770/741–722 BCE) on the throne, and in 738 BCE transferred him to Chengzhou (Chen and Pines 2018). There, under the protection of Jin 晉 and Zheng 鄭, the dynasty started to recover its prestige. According to *Zuo zhuan* 左傳, our major source for Springs and Autumns period history (see this chapter and chapter 23), in the late eighth century BCE the kings could even initiate punitive expeditions against minor polities whose leaders behaved disrespectfully. However, maintaining the semblance of the royal house's authority would not be possible without the ongoing support of powerful regional lords, and this support could not be taken for granted. In 707 BCE, the coalition army, personally led by King Huan of Zhou 周桓王 (r. 719–697 BCE), was defeated by the king's protector-turned-foe, Lord Zhuang of Zheng 鄭莊公 (r. 743–701 BCE). The king was wounded in the battle, and although Lord Zhuang refused to continue his assault on royal forces and even sent an envoy to express his condolences to the king, the renewed blow to the Zhou prestige was harsh. This defeat marked the end of the kings' military activism.

In the early seventh century BCE the first attempt was made to restructure the interstate system so as to reflect a new power balance between the kings and regional lords. This was the establishment of the institution of hegemony (*ba* 霸), under the aegis of Lord Huan of Qi 齊桓公 (r. 685–643 BCE). Lord Huan's hegemony was based on a combination of Qi's military superiority together with the lord's ability to position himself as a surrogate and protector of the Zhou kings. Although Lord Huan redirected some of the interstate ceremonies, such as court visits, from the Zhou court to himself, he continued to display reverence to the kings, assisting them in their conflicts with external and internal foes and invoking their name in his incursions against other regional lords, most notably against the rising superpower of Chu 楚 in 656 BCE.

Moreover, Lord Huan acted resolutely against the Rong 戎 and Di 狄 incursions into the Zhou lands and, in a remarkable display of selflessness, restored in 659 BCE the statelets of Xing 邢 and Wei 衛 that were earlier annihilated by the Di invaders. All these actions, in addition to Lord Huan's carefully orchestrated display of adherence to the Zhou ritual norms of interstate intercourse, served as a useful veneer to Lord Huan's blatant military superiority, turning him from a powerful local potentate into a protector of the Zhou-mandated interstate order.

Lord Huan's success notwithstanding, the institution of hegemony, based as it was on the combination of unilateral military superiority of a regional lord and the ritual prestige of the Zhou king, was not sustainable in the long run. By the late seventh century BCE it was replaced by a bi-polar system of two competing alliances, each led by a powerful state (Jin in the north, Chu in the south). The alliance system can be considered the second major device developed by the Springs and Autumns period statesmen as a means of stabilizing the multistate system, at least within each alliance. The alliance leaders tried to maintain order within their coalitions, acting as arbiters in inter- and intra-state conflicts and protecting domestic order within the allied states. They maintained vibrant diplomatic activities, convening the allied lords for periodic meetings and swearing solemn alliance covenants. Jin leaders also tried to emulate Lord Huan's role as protectors of the Zhou house, although in reality their actions often deviated from this role. Thus, the first of the Jin hegemons, the illustrious Lord Wen 晉文公 (r. 636–628 BCE), arrogantly demanded of his protégé, King Xiang 周襄王 (r. 651–619 BCE), to grant him royal sumptuary privileges; when refused, Lord Wen retaliated by *summoning* the king to an interstate meeting in 632 BCE. This appalling disregard of ritual norms dealt another blow to royal prestige, foreshadowing further marginalization of the Sons of Heaven during the second half of the Springs and Autumns period.

The system of alliances could temporarily ensure intra-alliance stability, but in the long term it proved woefully ineffective. The alliance leaders were often prone to pursue narrow interests of their polities at the expense of the allies, betraying their solemn oath obligations and sacrificing the trust of their protégés for the sake of immediate gains, particularly territorial expansion. Worse, the century-long struggle between Jin and Chu, which culminated in three major—but indecisive—battles of Chengpu 城濮 (632 BCE), Bi 邲 (597 BCE), and Yanling 鄢陵 (575 BCE), served as the permanent destabilizing factor in interstate relations. The fierce inter-alliance competition amid ongoing military deadlock caused the leaders of both major powers to seek expansion of their alliances by alluring or forcing the enemy's allies to switch sides. This, in turn, generated repeated invasions of intermediate polities, sandwiched between Jin and Chu. The situation of these polities, according to a contemporary testimony, was grave indeed:

> With the domain cut to pieces and thrown topsy-turvy, there is no place to turn to for appeal. Those among the people who perished were either fathers and older brothers or sons and younger brothers. Everyone is in sorrow and pain, not knowing where to find protection. (*Zuo zhuan*, Xiang 8.7b; translation borrowed from Durrant et al. 2016: 947).

This plight of the tiny states generated the final and the most curious attempt to stabilize the multistate system: namely, two "disarmament conferences" in 546 and 541 BCE. The organizers proposed the creation of a mega-alliance, led simultaneously by Jin and Chu, legitimating thereby the bipolar world. This initiative, however, failed miserably owing to the lack of mutual trust between major powers. After a short period of de facto hegemony by a ruthless King Ling of Chu 楚靈王 (r. 540–529 BCE), the internal crises in both Chu and Jin opened the way to the rise of new major powers. By the late sixth century BCE, the center of political gravity shifted to the peripheral southeastern states of Wu 吳 and Yue 越. Wu, loosely allied with Jin, had inflicted a major blow on Chu, briefly occupying Chu's capital, Ying 郢, in 506 BCE. Later, as Chu recovered its power, Wu shifted its attention northward, expanding robustly into the direction of Shandong. This strategy backfired, though, as Wu's southern rival, the state of Yue, assaulted Wu from the south, eventually eliminating it in 473 BCE. In the aftermath of this illustrious success, King Goujian of Yue 越王句踐 (r. 496–464 BCE) inherited Wu's policy of a loose alliance with Jin and continued northward expansion into Shandong.

Their occasional military success notwithstanding, neither Wu, nor Yue, nor the resurrecting powers of Chu and Jin were able to maintain even a semblance of stability that existed under earlier hegemons. By the end of the Springs and Autumns era, erstwhile alliances disintegrated and the war of all against all ensued. The very idea of a sustainable multistate system had eventually lost its appeal. The period following the breakup of the state of Jin in 453 BCE, and prior to the imperial unification of 221 BCE, is ominously known as the age of the Warring States: the age when no rules of interstate intercourse were maintained. It was during that age that the dictum of political unification as the only way toward peace and stability ensued, becoming the cornerstone of Chinese political culture for millennia to come (Pines 2000 and 2012:11–43).

ETHNOCULTURAL IDENTITIES
IN FRAGMENTED WORLD

The Late Warring States–period text, the *Gongyang* 公羊 commentary on the canonical *Springs and Autumn Annals* (*Chunqiu* 春秋), famously hails Lord Huan of Qi as the defender of Chinese civilization against the southern state of Chu and against the northern Di and Rong tribesmen:

> Chu is the country that is the last to submit when there is a True Monarch, and the first to rebel when there is no True Monarch. It belongs to Yi 夷 and Di 狄 ["barbarians"] and extremely hates the Central States ["China"]. When southern Yi and northern Di communicated, China was on the verge of being cut off like a thread. Lord Huan rescued the Central States and repelled the Yi and the Di, and finally had pacified Jing (Chu): this is considered the undertaking of the True Monarch. (*Gongyang zhuan*, Xi 4:203)

The idea that Lord Huan saved China from mortal peril is echoed in a few other texts from the Warring States and early imperial periods; when read in tandem with harsh pronouncements in contemporaneous texts that emphasize the alleged bestiality of the "barbarians" and their impaired humaneness, it creates an impression of a clearly pronounced "Sino-barbarian" dichotomy. Not a few scholars picked up these citations to argue that already during the Springs and Autumns period seeds of Chinese exclusive nationalism or even of racism were sown (e.g., Dikötter 1992:1–30). These scholars furthermore uncritically accept the picture of a clear-cut spatial and cultural separation between the proud bearers of Chinese civilization (self-named Xia 夏 or Huaxia 華夏) and the culturally backward "barbarians of the four quarters." This picture is largely false though. Careful reading of early textual sources, such as the *Zuo Tradition* or *Zuo Commentary on the Springs-and-Autumns Annals* (*Zuo zhuan*, see chapter 23), coupled with analysis of material data and of relevant paleographic sources creates a radically different picture. Ethnocultural identities of the pre-imperial age appear much more malleable and flexible than the authors of later systematizing texts and some modern scholars would want us to believe (Di Cosmo 2002; Pines 2005).

To begin with, pace the *Gongyang Commentary*, the "Central States" were not surrounded by belligerent "barbarians"; rather, the latter were often settled in between "Chinese" polities, sometimes at the very heartland of the Central Plains. For instance, in 478 BCE the ruler of the centrally located state of Wei 衛 was surprised to discover a Rong settlement at the sight distance from the walls of his capital. Moreover, wars were only one—and arguably not the most significant—aspect of Sino-alien interactions. Although the mid-seventh-century-BCE Rong and Di incursions into the northeastern part of the Zhou world caused serious devastation and clearly increased "anti-barbarian" sentiment, these were exceptions rather than the rule. Non-Sinitic polities were involved in a complex web of relations with their Xia neighbors, which included alliances, inter-marriage, and even forging fictitious kinship ties through adopting the clan names of the Zhou royal house or of other Xia polities. When military conflicts occurred, more often than not the Rong and the Di acted as the allies of one Xia polity against another; alternatively they are often depicted as victims of the Xia expansion rather than insatiable belligerents. Actually, the alarmist tone of the cited *Gongyang* statement is highly exceptional in pre-imperial texts. Ethnicity or kinship could be invoked to justify a war or an alliance, but they were never the major determinant of the polity's course.

To illustrate the latter point let us briefly focus on the behavior of the leaders of Sui 隨 (or Zeng 曾),[2] once the major stronghold of the Zhou ruling clan in the eastern part of the Han River Valley. Since the late ninth century BCE, most Zhou-related polities in this area were conquered by Chu, and Sui became the Chu satellite. In 506 BCE, following the disastrous defeat by the Wu forces, the beleaguered king of Chu fled to Sui. The Wu commanders requested the Sui leaders to hand the fugitive king over and avenge therewith the fate of their Ji 姬 (Zhou-related) clansmen (recall that the kings of Wu claimed, like many non-Sinitic rulers, to be members of the Zhou royal Ji clan). The Sui leaders refused. Their position is explained in a recently unearthed inscription on the Marquis Yu of Zeng bells 曾侯與編鐘. The marquis of Zeng (Sui) tells that although he is proud of his ancestors' service of the Zhou dynasty, by now the Zhou house had declined and the Mandate of Heaven had shifted to Chu. The Marquis boastfully proclaims, "The restoration of the King of Chu is thanks to the numinous power of the Marquis of Zeng" (Khayutina 2019; Pines 2020:86). Namely, what matters is the new configuration of power, not the ancestral memories.

An additional reason for the relative marginality of ethnicity as a political factor in the Springs and Autumns period is that cultural belonging back then was remarkably malleable, defying the simplistic "us-versus-them" dichotomy. To illustrate the latter point, suffice it to trace briefly the cultural trajectories of several major polities of that age. For example, states such as Wu and Yue in the lower Yangzi region came into close contact with the states of the Central Plains only in the sixth century BCE. Archeological data and textual evidence alike clearly testify to the cultural otherness of the Wu and Yue elites, and yet this otherness was in the process of being eroded (Falkenhausen 2006:271–284). The rulers of Wu and Yue forged genealogies that made them descendants, respectively, of the Zhou royal progenitors and of the sage Thearch Yu 禹, thereby acquiring a respectable Xia pedigree; their elites were absorbing mortuary practices of their Zhou peers; advisors from other Zhou polities flocked to their states; and their leaders became active participants in interstate assemblies and covenants of the Late Springs and Autumns period. A similar tendency toward cultural integration is observable with regard to a few other polities associated with Rong and Di, although in these cases the dearth of reliable data prevents us from making far-reaching conclusions.

---

[2] The question of identity between Zeng and Sui has aroused numerous controversies since the 1970s, but with the new discoveries it may be considered positively settled. For a cautious summary, see Venture 2017. For an updated analysis that takes into account 2019 discoveries, see Pines 2020: 85–88.

While some of the aliens were in the process of becoming "Chinese," a few Xia states were moving in the opposite direction. Two major examples of this alienation from the Zhou realm are the states of Qin 秦 in northwest and Chu in the south. Texts of the Warring States period and later often (even if not unanimously) identify both major polities as "barbarian" entities; the cited *Gongyang Commentary* statement is representative of this trend. However, this image of the otherness of Qin and Chu does not fit the realities of the Springs and Autumns period. Elite burials from both Qin and Chu share major characteristics with those of other Zhou states in terms of the shape and furnishing of the tombs, assemblages of sacrificial vessels, inscriptions on some of these vessels, and social hierarchy as reflected in burial practices and the like (Falkehnausen 2006). There are certain local idiosyncrasies to be sure—such as a higher frequency of flexed (as opposed to supine) burial in Qin tombs or the appearance of new shapes of bronze vessels in Chu—but these are indicative, to cite Lothar von Falkenhausen (2014:39) of a "regional phase" of the Zhou culture and not of a separate culture. The material evidence shows then that despite their distinctiveness, both Chu and Qin were full members of the Zhou cultural *oikouménē*. A similar picture comes from *Zuo zhuan*, the major textual source for the history of the Springs and Autumns period. Although the text does refer to Qin's "remoteness" (from the viewpoint of the eastern state of Lu 魯; *Zuo zhuan*, Wen 12.5) and to Chu's being "not of our kin" (i.e., not ruled by the same Ji 姬 clan as Lu, Jin, or Zhou; *Zuo zhuan*, Cheng 4.4), it never refers to either Qin or Chu as "barbarians." Elite members of Qin and Chu appear as equal participants in the common aristocratic ritual culture, which was defined in *Zuo zhuan* and elsewhere as the hallmark of cultural belonging to the Zhou world.

The "barbarian" image of Qin and Chu appears then to be the product of the Warring States cultural milieu: a mark of their estrangement from the states of the Central Plains. This process of estrangement started earlier in the state of Chu, the heads of which claimed the royal title (*wang* 王) already in the Springs and Autumns period, thereby defying the Zhou norms (although they were careful not to claim the title of Son of Heaven, leaving the Zhou kings a semblance of ritual superiority). In the case of Qin, the shaping of a new identity was a later process, which started in the Warring States period and will not be discussed here (Shelach and Pines 2005). Yet differences aside, both cases of Chu and Qin demonstrate that aside from acculturation into the Zhou world, elites in at least some of the Zhou polities were engaged in the opposite process of forging a distinctive cultural identity.

The malleability of cultural identities in the Springs and Autumns period is duly reflected in the multifaceted presentation of the Other in contemporaneous texts. Aside from pejorative remarks about the alleged bestiality of the "barbarians," we find many other cases in which the aliens are treated neutrally, or even positively, as being culturally and intellectually superior to the dwellers of the Central States (Schaberg 2001:132–133). Yet what is really remarkable—and what critically distinguishes pre-imperial Chinese historical texts from those in, for example, the Greek or Roman world—is the relative marginality of the aliens as a topos. More often than not, the cultural otherness of a statesman is not an issue at all, and it is frequently ignored altogether (Pines 2011).

For instance, only a few careful readers of *Zuo zhuan* would notice that the leading Jin statesman, and the architect of Lord Wen's hegemony, Zifan 子犯 (also known as Hu Yan 狐偃, fl. 650–630 BCE), was a person of the Rong stock. Nor would many readers pay attention to the fact that Lord Wen himself was born of a Rong mother. This lack of interest in cultural otherness of important political figures is not incidental. It seems that, pace the *Gongyang Commentary*, statesmen of the Springs and Autumns period were much more preoccupied with struggles against their peer polities than in defending the Xia against the "barbarians."

THE HEYDAY OF ARISTOCRATIC RULE

In 522 BCE a conflict erupted between Lord Yuan of Song 宋元公 (r. 531–517 BCE) and two leading ministerial lineages in his state, Hua 華 and Xiang 向. The conflict turned into a major domestic war, which started with the massacre of many of Song princes and ended with the partial extermination and partial expulsion of both rebel lineages. It generated manifold dramas, such as that of Grand Marshal Hua Feisui 華費遂, who first assisted Lord Yuan in quelling the rebellion of his kinsmen, driving one of his own sons into exile, but then was forced to join the rebels almost against his will because of a fratricidal struggle between two of his remaining sons. The war lasted for three years and involved military forces from all the major powers of the age, including Jin 晉, Chu 楚, Qi 齊, and Wu 吳, in addition to Song's tiny neighbors, Cao 曹 and Wei 衛.

This dramatic story is just one of dozens of similar events narrated in the latter half of *Zuo zhuan*. Clashes between regional lords and ministerial lineages, coupled with perennial inter- and intra-lineage struggles, plagued most polities of the Springs and Autumns period. They reflected the major distinctive feature of the political structure of that age: the shift of power from the regional lords to their underlings, members of the powerful ministerial stratum. By the end of the Springs and Autumns period, only a few rulers succeeded in preserving the reins of power in their hands.

The power of nobility was embedded in the very foundations of the Zhou system, in which a noble lineage acted as the fundamental socioeconomic, religious, military and, naturally, political unit (Zhu Fenghan 2004), but by the middle of the Springs and Autumns period it reached new dimensions. By then, ministerial (*qing* 卿) lineages formed a new social segment distinguishable from the rest of the nobles (*dafu* 大夫). The emergence of this new stratum derived from two major peculiarities of the political structure of the Springs and Autumns period, namely the systems of hereditary office holding and of hereditary allotments. Both systems are traceable to the Western Zhou period, but it was only by the late seventh century BCE that they outgrew their original scope and turned into the major threat to domestic stability (Qian Zongfan 1989). Of the two, the system of hereditary allotments was the most consequential. Originally it was designed as a means of compensating an official for his services. Upon appointment, a new official was granted an allotment comprising of several settlements (or several dozen settlements for top appointees) and their adjacent fields. The allotment's master commanded all of its economic and human resources; the allotment's inhabitants paid him taxes, served as auxiliaries in his military forces, and owed him their exclusive allegiance. The allotment was ruled by the master's personal appointees, mostly his kin and retainers. In principle, the allotment was alienable: upon cessation of service, the official was supposed to return his territory to the lord, preserving just a few settlements as his hereditary possession.

In the short run the system of hereditary allotments was sustainable, but it was undermined by the system of hereditary ministerial positions. Whereas in the early Springs and Autumns period it was still customary for every new ruler to replace his predecessor's appointees with new ministers, mostly from among his closest kin, gradually this situation changed (Hsu 1965). Should a single minister succeed to preserve his position during the reigns of two or more rulers, he could amass sufficient power to manipulate succession of the office in favor of his son. In that case the office itself and the related allotment would become a hereditary possession of a ministerial lineage, and the ruler could not but acquiesce. Specifics of this process varied in place and time, but the overall direction was clear: slowly but steadily the rulers were losing their administrative power, and with it the ability to command the resources of their state.

Transformation of allotments from ad hoc possessions of individual ministers into hereditary holdings of ministerial lineages had profound implications on the nature of the polities of the Springs and Autumns period. Most fundamentally it meant dispersal of political, economic, and military authority. Having monopolized material and human resources of the allotment, powerful ministers could rival their nominal superiors, the regional lords, in terms of wealth and military prowess; gradually their allotments turned into mini-states in their own right. Allotments were run by the master's courts patterned after the regional lord's court; they had an independent administrative system, their own weights and measures, a cultic center (the ancestral temple of the allotment's master), and their own military forces that were only indirectly subordinate to the regional lord. Some allotments began emulating regional polities seeking territorial expansion, and it was not uncommon for some of the ministers to conduct independent foreign policy in the interest of their allotment, invading minor polities or concluding alliances so as to expand the territory under their direct control. The desire to expand an allotment at the expense of one's neighbors exacerbated tensions among ministerial lineages, aggravating the domestic turmoil that plagued the polities of the Springs and Autumns period.

The empowerment of ministers meant progressive devolution of economic, military and, most notably, political authority. As the rulers were eclipsed by their underlings, the very pattern of centralized rule was profoundly challenged, and most polities were in the process of being transformed from monarchies into de facto aristocratic oligarchies, run by coalitions of powerful ministers. These coalitions rarely could ensure stability, being perpetually undermined by internecine struggle among rival lineages. In the state of Jin, for instance, followers and supporters of Lord Wen formed the core of the new leadership: since the end of the seventh century BCE they rotated among themselves the all-important positions of commanders and vice-commanders of the country's six (later three) armies. Yet as time passed, inter-lineage struggles decimated the number of power-sharers: by the mid-sixth century BCE only six ministerial lineages remained. Two of these were annihilated in 497–490 BCE and another one in 453 BCE; the remaining three (Wei 魏, Han 韓, and Zhao 趙) eventually divided the state of Jin among themselves. Similar decimation of ministerial lineages took place in the state of Qi 齊, in which a single victor emerged: the Chen 陳 (Tian 田) lineage, the members of which had ruled the state since 481 BCE on behalf of puppet lords, until finally usurping the Qi throne in 386 BCE. The Qi example appears exceptional insofar as a single lineage succeeded in consolidating power; elsewhere the collateral branches of the ruling lineage rotated the power among themselves. In the state of Zheng 鄭 these were the seven lineages of descendants of Lord Mu 鄭穆公 (r. 627–606 BCE); in the state of Lu 魯, the triumvirate of descendants of Lord Huan 魯桓公 (r. 711–694 BCE) under the supremacy of the head of the Jisun 季孫 lineage; and similar coalitions emerged in Song 宋, Wei 衛, and elsewhere. The only major exception to this pattern of dispersed authority was the state of Chu, which maintained a higher degree of centralized control and stronger monarchic authority than any other comparable polity (Blakeley 1992). Some scholars suggest that a similar centralized pattern characterized Qin as well, although the precise situation there remains debatable (Thatcher 1985; cf. Yoshimoto 1995).

Not all the rulers accepted their position as figureheads; some tried to fight back and regain political initiative. A few succeeded, most notably King Zhuang of Chu 楚莊王 (r. 612–591 BCE), whose smashing of the Ruoao 若敖 lineage in 605 BCE ensured the lasting dominance of Chu kings over their ministers. Others failed miserably. Lord Ling of Jin 晉靈公 (r. 620–607 BCE) tried to get rid of his powerful prime minister, Zhao Dun 趙盾, but was killed by Zhao's henchmen. A generation later, Lord Li of Jin 晉厲公 (r. 580–573 BCE) tried to replace chief ministers with his personal favorites and even succeeded to wipe out the powerful Xi 郤 lineage, but other ministers retaliated, and the hapless lord was murdered and posthumously humiliated. His heir, Lord Dao 晉悼公 (r. 572–558 BCE), dared not punish the assassins and retained the reins of power only by carefully maneuvering among his haughty underlings. In the state of Wei 衛, in 559 BCE the coalition of powerful nobles expelled Lord Xian 衛獻公 (r. 576–559 and 546–544 BCE) and ruled through a puppet. In the state of Lu, an attempt by Lord Zhao 魯昭公 (r. 541–510 BCE) to eliminate the overbearing Jisun lineage failed; the lord was expelled in 517 BCE and died in exile. For seven years, the triumvirs of the "Three Huan" lineages ruled their state without even bothering to appoint a new lord, creating thereby an unprecedented situation of direct rule by powerful aristocrats. These examples can be easily multiplied.

To aggravate the ruler's situation, even the ideological realm, as reflected in *Zuo zhuan*, was firmly controlled by the members of the ministerial stratum, who eagerly provided justifications for their elevated position vis-à-vis the regional lords (see more in chapter 23). At times it seems that even some of the rulers had internalized the realities of the new balance of power. Nothing exemplifies more the regional lords' humility than an offer made in 547 BCE by the ousted Lord Xian of Wei to Ning Xi 甯喜, the son of his former enemy, Ning Zhi 甯殖: "If you let me return [to Wei], all the administration will be in the hands of the Ning lineage, while I shall [only control the] sacrifices" (*Zuo zhuan*, Xiang 26.2). De facto, the lord acquiesced to the position of a ritual figurehead. Although this was an exceptional offer, it suffices to indicate that the ruler's authority was approaching its nadir.

The lack of effective rulership both within the Zhou *oikouménē* and within individual polities aggravated political crisis in the Zhou world, leading to a series of odd situations. For instance, in Confucius's home state of Lu, after the expulsion of Lord Zhao by the "Three Huan" lineages in 517 BCE, the scheming steward of the Jisun lineage, Yang Hu 陽虎 (fl. 510–490 BCE), a member of a lowly *shi* 士 (low nobility) stratum, turned for a few years (505–502 BCE) into a de facto dictator of his state, with both the nominal lord and the head of the Jisun lineage being his puppets. Elsewhere, powerful states discovered that the territories recently acquired from the neighbors could immediately after the annexation become a power base of rebellious ministers, thereby annulling the advantages of territorial expansion. States were decimated due to intermittent struggles between the lords and their ministers, among ministerial lineages, and among rival branches of major lineages. Some of the states—like the major superpower, the state of Jin—had completely disintegrated. Alternatively the ruling lineage could be replaced, as happened in the state of Qi after the Chen (Tian) usurpation. The outcomes differed, but malfunctioning of the political system was evident in every case.

Given the obviously negative consequences of the ruler's weakness, it is remarkable that throughout the entire Springs and Autumns period we have no evidence of significant reforms aimed at recreating effective centralized control.[3] It seems that leading ministers, who were in charge of restoring stability, remained torn between their conflicting public commitment to the state's well-being, which required re-empowerment of the ruler, and their private responsibilities toward their lineages, which would have to pay a price in case of renewed centralization. Unwilling either to cede their power to the lords or to institutionalize it, these ministers—and the rulers' courts run by them—remained paralyzed. The odd situation of the de facto ministerial oligarchy had not been legitimated, but no viable alternative to it had been proposed either.

This said, the seeds of recentralization were sown outside the rulers' courts. Some of the ministers began experimenting with a more centralized form of rule within their allotments. They discontinued the system of hereditary office holdings, paid their servants salaries in kind or in precious metals instead of further parceling the allotment, and maintained effective control over the entire territory under their rule. When some of the allotments turned into full-fledged states—such as happened to the successor states of Jin, namely Wei, Han, and Zhao, and to the new state of Qi, reconstituted by the "usurpers" from the Chen/Tian family—the new rulers continued with centralized forms of control. In due time these measures were emulated elsewhere, and a new state was born (Zhao Boxiong 1990; Lewis 1999). By the fourth century BCE

---

[3] It should be noted that the supposed reforms in the state of Qi under the aegis of Guan Zhong 管仲 (d. 645 BCE) are definitely an invention of Warring States–period thinkers and are not related to actual political situation in Qi during the Springs and Autumns period (Rosen 1976).

newly centralized territorial states under powerful monarchs replaced the loose aristocratic polities of the Springs and Autumns period. China started its drive toward the centralized "universal" empire.

"CAPITAL-DWELLERS" AND POLITICAL ACTIVISM FROM BELOW

Political instability was the major curse of the Springs and Autumns era, but for some people it might have been a blessing. In particular, it benefitted commoners and minor nobles (*shi* 士), who formed an increasingly vociferous group of capital-dwellers (*guo ren* 國人).

Capital-dwellers were a broad social group that comprised most of the male inhabitants of the capital, including farmers, whose plots were located outside the walls, in addition to petty nobles and their retainers, merchants, and artisans. During the Springs and Autumns period, capital-dwellers emerged as a highly influential political force. Two factors contributed to their high visibility. First, they were a major source of auxiliary manpower for the ruler's armies. Although infantry soldiers recruited from among the capital-dwellers could not match the chariot-riding professionals of aristocratic descent, they were of huge importance not just as auxiliaries but primarily as the last-ditch (or, more properly, last-wall) defenders of the capital during times of siege. Second, and more importantly, their proximity to their ruler could become a major asset at times of domestic turmoil. When battles were waged on the streets of the capital, aristocrats had no particular advantage, and military intervention by capital-dwellers could become decisive.

Even a brief survey of *Zuo zhuan* shows how significant capital-dwellers were during domestic conflicts. The text identifies no less than 25 cases in which they actively influenced the outcome of internal struggles, such as succession conflicts or inter- and intra-lineage feuds. Their importance was duly recognized; the *Zuo zhuan* cites many speeches in which contemporaneous statesmen reiterate the need to cater to the needs of "the people" (i.e., capital-dwellers), in particular by taking care of their material interests. Without that, the speakers warn, the fighting spirit of the people will be impaired or, worse, they will side with the ruler's enemies. Whatever the authenticity of these speeches, it seems that they reflect a common political awareness of rulers and ministers alike. The *Zuo zhuan* repeatedly tells how contenders for power adopted a variety of "populist" measures to endear themselves to capital-dwellers: they cut taxes, cancelled old debts, supported the needy, displayed frugality, and the like. Thus, we read of Prince Bao 公子鮑 of Song who distributed grain to the starving population during a famine, securing thereby the capital-dwellers' assistance in a coup against his elder brother, Lord Zhao 宋昭公 (r. 620–611 BCE), in 611 BCE. Similar steps ensured the survival of the Han 罕 lineage in the state of Zheng and the Yue 樂 lineage in the state of Song during the tensest period of inter-lineage feuds in those states. Probably the most famous example of a scheming minister employing populist measures was the policy adopted by the Chen (Tian) family in the state of Qi. The Chen leaders used a double system of measures and weights so that they lent the people more grain than the people had to repay. This policy, which reportedly caused the people to "sing and dance" in praise of the Chen (*Zuo zhuan*, Zhao 26.11), allowed them not only to overcome rival lineages but ultimately to usurp the power in their state.

In addition to eliciting economic benefits from the lord or from his rivals, capital-dwellers sometimes intervened directly in policy-making. Their opinion was influential enough to determine the course of interstate policy of their country or to influence certain promotions and demotions. There were even certain arrangements that institutionalized the input of capital-dwellers in policy-making. In cases of exceptional emergency, such as disastrous defeats, domestic turmoil, or just before a fateful decision such as relocation of the capital, rulers assembled capital-dwellers, apologized for "humiliating the altars," or performed a religiously significant covenant ceremony (*meng* 盟) to reconfirm their ties with the populace. This kind of a "people's assembly" encouraged certain scholars (e.g., Lewis 2006:136–150) to suggest that capital-dwellers were "citizens" rather than mere "subjects" and even to assert that the Springs and Autumns–period polities bore strong similarities to the ancient Greek city-states. This comparison is somewhat far-fetched though, since in the Chinese case, unlike in the Greek *poleis*, the people's assemblies were an extraordinary ad hoc measure and not a normal political institution. Nonetheless, their existence, even if marginal, is indicative of much broader popular participation in politics than was the case in any subsequent period in Chinese history. And yet, these practices of popular assemblies and of political participation from below discontinued in subsequent centuries. Why?

To answer this question we should be reminded that political participation of the commoners was a direct by-product of political turmoil that plagued the polities of the Springs and Autumns period. Covenants between the rulers and the population were akin to the covenants occasionally made between the ruler and his rivals from among ministerial lineages: an abnormal solution to the abnormal situation of the ruler's weakness. As an ad hoc means, such covenants, or assembling the capital-dwellers and soliciting their opinion on matters of vital importance, were tolerable, but they were never considered desirable and no attempt was ever made to institutionalize them. Actually, manifold speakers, cited in the *Zuo zhuan* and elsewhere, repeatedly express concern with the people's livelihood, but we know of not a single voice that advocated increase in the people's political participation. If such demands were ever made, they might have been inconsequential enough to disappear from historical accounts and from political rhetoric without leaving any trace. The people's sentiments had to be taken into account, but it was up to the elites to understand the people's needs and to respond to them. The commoners' direct impact on political life, associated as it was with unruly capital-dwellers of the Springs and Autumns period, was a symptom of political malady and not the remedy (Pines 2009:187–214).

Summary: Cultural unity
at the age of fragmentation

Politically speaking, the Springs and Autumns period was a disastrous age. Fragmentation of the Zhou realm, the collapse of the multistate order, and perennial turmoil in major polities turned this period into a paradigmatic negative example, the mistakes of which should never be allowed to recur. In particular, the lesson of the unruly ministerial stratum was properly learned: the political system should never again allow a few lineages to monopolize political, economic, and military power. To a significant extent, bureaucratization, centralization, and empowerment of the monarch, which ensued in the subsequent Warring States period (Lewis 1999), and which remained the hallmark of Chinese imperial polity, should be understood as a conscious negation of the turmoil of the Springs and Autumns era.

And yet, the Zhou world did not disintegrate completely in the aftermath of three centuries of aristocratic rule. Its cultural ties appear even stronger by the end of the period under discussion than they were at the beginning, and the elite Zhou culture even expanded further into the lower Yangzi basin and, somewhat superficially, into the Sichuan basin as well (Falkenhausen 2006:244–288). Moreover, as time passed, the idea that the dwellers of the Zhou realm shared a common destiny became ever more pronounced, as can be judged from the increasing usage of the term All-under-Heaven (*tianxia*), the common designation of the Zhou *oikouménē*. This term is marginal in the Western Zhou texts and in the first half of the *Zuo zhuan* narrative, but its usage intensifies in the second half of the *Zuo zhuan*, and it becomes ubiquitous in the texts of the Warring States period (Pines 2002). What are the reasons for this increasing awareness of the commonality of the sub-celestial realm? Why did political fragmentation not affect negatively the sense of common cultural belonging?

To answer this question we should revisit the hereditary aristocracy—the very stratum whose unruliness contributed so much toward the political divisiveness of the Springs and Autumns period. It appears that whereas the nobles were the major factor behind political disintegration, culturally they were the major integrative force. The very mode of their life transcended the parochial limits of their allotment or of their polity. Under the mandatory rules of clan exogamy, the nobles often had to marry daughters of aristocratic clans from neighboring polities, creating thereby a web of cross-Zhou marital ties. More importantly, the nobles routinely had to depart from their country on military or diplomatic missions, during which they interacted with their peers from other states thus, perpetuating common aristocratic identity. Judging from the *Zuo zhuan*, at these meetings they conversed in "eloquent language" (*ya yan* 雅言), the lingua franca of the Zhou world; performed common ceremonies; and were expected to be versatile in the *Canon of Poems* and understand ritual music. Even military encounters were a means of perpetuating common cultural links, as they gave participants a chance to demonstrate adherence to common rules of chivalry. These rules required not just display of martial spirit and personal courage but also courtesy to the rival: hence, one was not expected to attack an unprepared enemy or to benefit from the rival's dire straits; even an exchange of arrows presupposed shooting in turns. The *Zuo zhuan* (and later texts) is often critical of excessive adherence to the rules of chivalry at the expense of pursuing military victory, and it is clear from the text that these rules were not uniformly observed, but there is little doubt that the wars of the Springs and Autumns period were conducted in an incomparably more gentlemanly way than during the subsequent Warring States era.

One may suspect the *Zuo zhuan* of exaggerating the degree of the Zhou elites' cultural cohesiveness, but archaeological evidence supports this picture. Cultural diversity in the Zhou world notwithstanding, in most essential aspects of burial customs we observe uniform rules throughout the entire *oikouménē*. Such status-defining parameters as the size of the tomb, the amount of inner and outer coffins, mortuary assemblages of bronze vessels (or of their ceramic imitations, the *mingqi* 明器), and the like all reflect adherence to common rules (Falkenhausen 2006; Yin Qun 2001). Similar uniformity is observable in the inscriptions on the ritual bronze vessels, the authors of which employ similar formulaic language throughout the Zhou world (Mattos 1997). To be sure, the uniformity was not absolute: one can observe manifold infractions of ritual regulations, local modifications of burial customs, and the appearance of new ritual assemblages. However, these modifications were performed within the commonly accepted parameters. The fundamental idea of the Zhou ritual system, namely strict observance of social hierarchy as reflected in strict sumptuary rules, was maintained unwaveringly in every polity of the Zhou world throughout the entire Springs and Autumns period.

The subsequent Warring States period witnessed the demise of hereditary aristocracy, which was absorbed into a broader meritocratic elite based on the *shi* 士 stratum. And yet the idea of the cultural unity of All-under-Heaven became even stronger. The *shi* inherited not just the political power of the aristocrats and their pride; more consequentially, they inherited and further strengthened the notion of common belonging to All-under-Heaven and of common cultural values that transcend the boundaries of individual states. This was the background for their quest for political unification of the entire sub-celestial realm, the quest that became the perennial feature of Chinese political culture from the Warring States period onward.

Bibliography

Blakeley, Barry B. 1992. "King, Clan, and Courtier in Ancient Ch'u." *Asia Major* (3rd series) 5(2):1–39.

Chen, Minzhen 陳民鎮, and Yuri Pines 2018. "Where Is King Ping? The History and Historiography of the Zhou Dynasty's Eastward Relocation." *Asia Major* (3rd series) 31(1):1–27.

Chunqiu Gongyang zhuan yizhu 春秋公羊傳譯注 2010. Annotated by Liu Shangci 劉尚慈. Beijing: Zhonghua shuju.

Chunqiu Zuo zhuan zhu 春秋左傳注 1981. Annotated by Yang Bojun 楊伯峻. Beijing: Zhonghua shuju.

Di Cosmo, Nicola 2002. *Ancient China and Its Enemies: The Rise of Nomadic Power in East Asian History*. Cambridge, UK: Cambridge University Press.

Dikötter, Frank 1992. *The Discourse of Race in Modern China*. Stanford, CA: Stanford University Press.

Durrant, Stephen W., Li Wai-yee, and David Schaberg 2016. *Zuo Tradition/Zuozhuan: Commentary on the "Spring and Autumn Annals."* Seattle: University of Washington Press.

Falkenhausen, Lothar von 2006. *Chinese Society in the Age of Confucius (1050–250 BC): The Archeological Evidence*. Los Angeles: Cotsen Institute of Archaeology at UCLA.

Falkenhausen, Lothar von, with Gideon Shelach 2014. "Introduction: Archaeological Perspectives on the Qin 'Unification' of China." In *Birth of an Empire: The State of Qin revisited*. Edited by Yuri Pines, Lothar von Falkenhausen, Gideon Shelach, and Robin D. S. Yates, 37–52. New Perspectives on Chinese Culture and Society. Berkeley: University of California Press.

Gongyang zhuan. See *Chunqiu Gongyang zhuan*.

Hsü, Cho-yun 1965. *Ancient China in Transition: An Analysis of Social Mobility, 722–222 BC*. Stanford Studies in the Civilizations of Eastern Asia. Stanford, CA: Stanford University Press.

Khayutina, Maria. 2019. "Reflections and Uses of the Past in Chinese Bronze Inscriptions from ca. 11th to 5th centuries BCE: The Memory of the Conquest of Shang and the First Kings of Zhou." In *Historical Consciousness and the Use of the Past in the Ancient World*. Edited by John Baines et al. 157–180. Sheffield: Equinox.

Lewis, Mark E. 1999. "Warring States: Political History." In *The Cambridge History of Ancient China: From the Origins of Civilization to 221 BC*. Edited by Michael Loewe and Edward L. Shaughnessy, 587–650. Cambridge, UK: Cambridge University Press.

Lewis, Mark E. 2006. *The Construction of Space in Early China*. Albany: State University of New York Press.

Lunyu yizhu 論語譯注. 1992. Annotated by Yang Bojun 楊伯峻. Beijing: Zhonghua shuju.

Mattos, Gilbert 1997. "Eastern Zhou Bronze Inscriptions." In *New Sources of Early Chinese History: An Introduction to Reading Inscriptions and Manuscripts*. Edited by Edward L. Shaughnessy, 85–124. Berkeley, CA: Society for Study of Early China.

Pines, Yuri 2000. "'The One That Pervades All' in Ancient Chinese Political Thought: Origins of the 'Great Unity' Paradigm." *T'oung Pao* 86(4–5):280–324.

Pines, Yuri 2002. "Changing Views of *tianxia* in Pre-Imperial Discourse." *Oriens Extremus* 43(1–2):101–116.

Pines, Yuri 2005. "Beasts or Humans: Pre-Imperial Origins of Sino-Barbarian Dichotomy." *Mongols, Turks and Others: Eurasian Nomads and the Sedentary World*. Edited by Reuven Amitai and Michal Biran, 59–102. Leiden: Brill.

Pines, Yuri 2009. *Envisioning Eternal Empire: Chinese Political Thought of the Warring States Era*. Honolulu: University of Hawaii Press.

Pines, Yuri 2011. "Where Had the Barbarians Gone? The Cultural Other in Early Chinese Historiography." In *Noctes Sinenses: Festschrift für Fritz-Heiner Mutschler zum 65. Geburtstag*. Edited by Andreas Heil, Matthias Korn, and Jochen Sauer, 235–240. Heidelberg: Universitätsverlag.

Pines, Yuri 2012. *The Everlasting Empire: Traditional Chinese Political Culture and Its Enduring Legacy*. Princeton, NJ: Princeton University Press.

Pines, Yuri. 2020. *Zhou History Unearthed: The Bamboo Manuscript* Xinian *and Early Chinese Historiography*. New York, NY: Columbia University Press.

Qian, Zongfan 錢宗范 1989. *Study on the Kinship-Based Political System of the Zhou Dynasty* 周代宗法制度研究. Guilin: Guangxi shifan daxue chubanshe.

Rosen, Sydney 1976. "Search for the Historical Kuan Chung." *Journal of Asian Studies* 35(3):431–440.

Schaberg, David 2001. *A Patterned Past: Form and Thought in Early Chinese Historiography*. Cambridge, MA: Harvard University Asia Center.

Shelach, Gideon, and Yuri Pines 2005. "Power, Identity and Ideology: Reflections on the Formation of the State of Qin (770–221 BCE)." In *An Archaeology of Asia*. Edited by Miriam Stark, 202–230. Oxford: Blackwell.

Thatcher, Melvin P. 1985. "Central Government of the State of Ch'in in the Spring and Autumn Period." *Journal of Oriental Studies* 23(1):29–53.

Venture, Olivier 2017. "Zeng: The Rediscovery of a Forgotten Regional State." In *China across the Centuries: Papers from a Lecture Series in Budapest*. Edited by Gábor Kósa, 1–32. Budapest: Department of East Asian Studies, Eötvös Loránd University.

Yin, Qun 印群 2001. *Burial System of the Eastern Zhou Period in the Middle and Lower Basin of the Yellow River* 黃河中下游地區 的東周墓葬制度. Beijing: Shehui kexue chubanshe.

Yoshimoto, Michimasa 吉本道雅 1995. "Preface to the Study of Qin History 秦史研究序說." *Shirin* 史林 78(3):34–67.

Zhao, Boxiong 趙伯雄 1990. *Research on the State Morphology during the Zhou Period* 周代國家形態研究. Changsha: Hunan jiaoyu.

Zhu, Fenghan 朱鳳瀚. 2004. *Research on Shang and Zhou Kinship Morphology* 商周家族形態研究, 2nd rev. ed. Tianjin: Tianjin guji chubanshe.

Zuo zhuan. See *Chunqiu Zuozhuan zhu*.

CHAPTER 23

···

HISTORIOGRAPHY, THOUGHT, AND INTELLECTUAL DEVELOPMENT DURING THE SPRINGS AND AUTUMNS PERIOD

···

BY YURI PINES, HEBREW UNIVERSITY OF JERUSALEM[1]

IN terms of intellectual flowering, the Springs and Autumns period cannot be compared with the subsequent age of the Warring States, frequently dubbed the age of the Hundred Schools of Thought. The only truly towering thinker from the Springs and Autumns period, Confucius 孔子 (551–479 BCE), should be considered a transitional figure: in terms of his pedigree, his career, and the focus of his intellectual pursuits, Confucius is much closer to the Warring States–period Masters (zi 子) than to his aristocratic contemporaries. Yet the Springs and Autumns period occupies the place of pride in the history of Chinese historiography. Suffice it to mention that it is the only age in China's lengthy history that got its name from the title of a book, namely the *Springs and Autumns Annals* (*Chunqiu* 春秋, hereafter the *Annals*) of the state of Lu, which is traditionally, even if inaccurately, considered as the fountainhead of China's immensely rich historiographical tradition. More importantly, one of the commentaries on the *Annals*, namely the *Zuo Tradition* or *Zuo Commentary* (*Zuo zhuan* 左傳), exercised immense impact on subsequent history writing. These two texts may be justifiably considered the singularly important legacy of the Springs and Autumns period to posterity.

[1] This research was supported by the Israel Science Foundation (grant No. 568/19) and by the Michael William Lipson Chair in Chinese Studies.

FORMATION OF THE HISTORIOGRAPHICAL TRADITION

The *Springs and Autumns Annals* may well compete for the designation as the most boring and the least inspiring of Chinese classics. A text some 17,000-odd characters in length, it comprises short entries that record major events from the life of the state of Lu and of related polities from 722 to 481 (or 479) BCE. Every year has at least four seasonal records; only exceptionally there are more than 10 records per year. The records are very brief, mostly consisting of one to two short sentences. There is no narrative in the text, no mention of causality or of broad background of the events. Few if any texts in the entire corpus of early Chinese literature can be less engaging for an average reader.

This problematic setting notwithstanding, the *Annals* were eventually elevated to the position of one of the most profound and sophisticated texts in the entire Chinese intellectual tradition, the summa of the wisdom of Confucius, the blueprint for properly running the empire. This interpretation was first put forward by Confucius's famous follower, Mengzi 孟子 (also known as Mencius, ca. 380–304 BCE). In a famous passage, Mengzi narrates the creation of the *Annals*:

> When All-under-Heaven declined and the Way fell into obscurity, deviant doctrines and violence again arose. There were instances of regicides and patricides. Confucius was apprehensive and composed (*zuo* 作) the *Springs and Autumns Annals*. The *Annals* are the matter for the Son of Heaven. Hence Confucius said: "Those who understand me will do so through the *Annals*; those who condemn me will also do so because of the *Annals*." . . . When Confucius completed the *Annals*, regicidal ministers and patricidal sons were overawed. (*Mengzi* 6.9:155)

This passage defined the dominant view of the *Annals* for millennia to come. The text is explicitly attributed to Confucius; its composition was an almost sacrosanct undertaking, which normally should have been initiated by the Son of Heaven alone; and when composed, the text turned into a potent weapon to overawe the evildoers. The *Annals*, then, have profound meaning and unusual political potency. This view was shared by two of the major commentaries on the *Annals*—the *Gongyang Commentary* 公羊傳 and *Guliang Commentary* 穀梁傳. Both traditions consider the *Annals* as a blueprint for the ideal political order. This blueprint is built on the combination of unshakeable ritual norms, inherited from King Wen of Zhou 周文王 (d. ca. 1047 BCE), coupled with their flexible adaptation to ever-changing political circumstances. The *Annals* not just embed King Wen's norms but also show how these norms should be applied. They are based on strict "rules of recording," any deviation from which, for example by altering personal appellations or by adding or omitting dates or place names, is not incidental but rather is done to present Confucius's praise or blame of historical personalities and of their actions (Gentz 2001, 2015). The "subtle words" (*weiyan* 微言)

of the *Annals* epitomize Confucius's unrivaled political wisdom; understanding them will immensely benefit policy-makers.

The popularity of the *Annals* peaked under Emperor Wu of the Han dynasty 漢武帝 (r. 141–87 BCE), when the *Annals*, in their *Gongyang* interpretation, were briefly elevated to the position of the empire's foundational text. This adoration of the *Annals* receded later, although their position among the canonical scriptures was never questioned throughout the imperial millennia.[2] Yet in the twentieth century, when the former canonical texts lost their primacy as the quintessence of traditional wisdom, and Confucius himself was dethroned from his position as the ultimate sage and relegated to that of an average thinker, the *Annals* lost their appeal almost entirely. Even in the scholarly community only a very few continue to investigate them, while for the general public they remain almost unknown. Yet once we rid ourselves from attempts to comb the *Annals* for Confucius's wisdom, we can start analyzing the text for what it is: a product of the Springs and Autumns historiography.

For a contemporary researcher the *Annals* are still a riddle. First, what was the nature of Confucius's connection—if any—to the *Annals*? Although nobody considers him a composer, as is possibly implied by the verb *zuo* in *Mengzi*, it is unclear whether he edited the *Annals*, just promoted circulation of an extant version, or was simply erroneously identified as their editor by later followers. Second, how should we read the *Annals*? Does their formulaic language convey praise and blame of historical personages, and if yes then how? For instance, it is highly likely that different naming patterns of historical personages may be used to criticize their actions, but should we interpret other irregularities (e.g., in dating or location of the event) in a similar way? Yet before we answer these and related questions, we should address the third and, arguably, the most intriguing question: who was the intended audience of the *Annals*?

The last question may sound odd: intuitively, we tend to identify the *Annals* as a historical text directed at the members of educated elite, much like any other product of China's immensely rich historiographic tradition. Yet the problem is that even a cursory reading of the *Annals* will identify numerous records that could have no meaningful value for either contemporaries or posterity. For instance, no less than 63 of the *Annals'* entries record only the season and its first month without any event reported for this period of time (e.g., "Spring, the first month," or "Autumn, seventh month"). Who was the addressee of these records? How important for a reader would it be to know that in winter 696 BCE the walls were built for the town of Cheng 成, and that in autumn 688 BCE snout moth's larva (*ming* 螟) was reported? Is there any didactic or entertaining value for these records? Were these events considered exceptionally worthy of commemoration? A modern reader remains perplexed.

Not all of the *Annals'* records are so boring; but many others are unintelligible to the people lacking proper scribal education. How a lay reader was expected to understand,

---

[2] Among a few statesmen who reportedly suggested expurgation of the *Annals* from the list of the classics, one may mention the famous Song reformer, Wang Anshi 王安石 (1021–1086), although whether or not he really denigrated this text is debatable. See Zhao Boxiong 2004:460–468.

for example, that the phrase "In the third year, in spring, in the royal first month, Ni met with a Qi army to make an attack on Wei" (Zhuang 3.1) was meant to criticize Prince Ni 溺 of Lu who supported the Qi 齊 assault on Wei 衛 without receiving the command of the lord of Lu (this criticism is hinted at by omitting the designation of "ducal son" [*gongzi* 公子] before Ni's name)? Even more confusing are the cases of concealment in the *Annals*. For instance, whenever a ruler or an heir-apparent in Lu was assassinated, the *Annals* invariably reported them as "passing away" (*hong* 薨; *Zuo zhuan*, Yin 11.8, Huan 18.1, Min 2.3), or "dying" (*cu* 卒) for the heir (*Zuo zhuan*, Zhuang 32.5; and Wen 18.5). Records are modified to avoid unpleasant news when the lord of Lu was detained or otherwise humiliated by foreign powers (*Zuo zhuan*, Xi 17.4; Wen 2.3; Cheng 10.7; Zhao 16.1; see also Van Auken 2016a:59–61). And, when in 517 BCE rebellious ministers expelled Lord Zhao 魯昭公 (r. 541–510 BCE), the *Annals* laconically recorded: "Ninth month; on [the day] *jihai*, the lord left for Qi" (*Chunqiu*, Zhao 25.5; when other dignitaries or foreign rulers went into exile, the *Annals* report them as "fleeing" [*ben* 奔]). Needless to say, a reader would not properly understand these entries without an additional explanation.

The peculiar language of the *Annals* makes them into a singularly incomprehensible historical text in China's lengthy tradition of recording the past. A Han-dynasty scholar, Huan Tan 桓譚 (ca. 20 BCE–56 CE) sighed: "Should the [*Annals*] classic lack the [*Zuo*] commentary, the sage would close the door and ponder over it for ten years, and even then he would not understand it!" (*Xin lun* 9:39). It is likely indeed that the text was not originally prepared for broad circulation; according to the *Zuo zhuan* anecdote it was normally stored at the scribe's office of the state of Lu and shown to a visiting dignitary from the state of Jin 晉 only as a sign of an extraordinary favor (*Zuo zhuan*, Zhao 2.1). It is even possible that the readers of the text were not human beings but ancestral spirits of the state of Lu, to whom periodic reports had to be made in the ancestral temple (Pines 2009b:318–323). If so, then omissions of unpleasant news from the *Annals* may reflect the same tendency in the bronze inscriptions, which are also overwhelmingly directed at the donors' ancestors and avoid disturbing news (Falkenhausen 1993:152). Although this supposition of the cultic context of the *Annals* cannot be unequivocally proven or refuted, it is clear that the text was not designed to serve as a plain factual record of events for the use of educated elite members.

Terseness and partial incomprehensibility aside, the *Annals* are also an informative and a highly meaningful political text. Their entries are never whimsical. They invariably derive from the records of the Lu scribes or from reports to Lu from other polities, whose scribes routinely updated the Lu court about major events in the lives of their states, such as wars, covenants, rulers' successions, or cases of internal turmoil (Van Auken 2016a:43–52). Hence, the *Annals* are rich in details about "who, what, when, and where," leaving only the question of "why" outside their concern. Moreover, the *Annals* provide an invaluable glimpse into the ritual conventions of their age. These ritual norms dictate the *Annals*' terse records. For instance, the image of the superiority of Zhou kings is preserved through careful placing of the kings' representatives ahead of even the most powerful regional lords whenever an inter-state meeting or a covenant are reported. The *Annals* furthermore uniformly refer to foreign dignitaries according to their ranks within the Zhou original hierarchy, stubbornly refusing to recognize the ritual "upgrading" of powerful rulers of such states as Qin 秦, Chu 楚, Wu 吳, and Yue 越 and from their original *bo* (伯, earl) or *zi* (子, viscount) to the *gong* (公, duke) and *wang* (王, king) rank. This ritual precision of the *Annals* explains perhaps their importance in the eyes of Confucius and the members of his circle: if indeed they were responsible for the broader circulation of the *Annals*, this was probably done to disseminate knowledge of the ritually correct language—and mutatis mutandis of ritual in general—among the elite members.

The *Annals* exercised tremendous influence on subsequent Chinese historiography in terms of their language—the precision in the usage of official titles, personal names, and the like became the hallmark of official histories. Yet it was the *Annals*' major commentary, the *Zuo zhuan*, which can be justifiably considered the fountainhead of traditional Chinese historiography. Its style, language, adherence to chronological framework with only minor digressions and, most of all, its combination of being highly informative on the one hand and didactic—both explicitly and implicitly—on the other turned the *Zuo zhuan* into a source of inspiration for the father of Chinese official histories, Sima Qian 司馬遷 (ca. 145–90 BCE) and for his countless successors (Durrant et al. 2016: LXIX–LXXVII).

The *Zuo zhuan* is one of the most contestable texts in the entire pre-imperial lore: countless generations debated its authorship, dating, reliability, and its relation to the *Annals*. Sima Qian identified its author as a "superior man from Lu," Zuo Qiuming 左丘明, who allegedly created his work so as to explicate the message put into the *Annals* by Confucius (*Shiji* 14:509–510). Later scholars added many details regarding the transmission of the *Zuo zhuan* from the times of Zuo Qiuming (supposedly, Confucius's contemporary) into the Han, but their claims, just as Sima Qian's assertion of Zuo Qiuming's authorship, remain unverifiable. What is clear is that during Sima Qian's times the recognition of the *Zuo zhuan* as the *Annals*' commentary remained lackluster: the text was treated as a repository of the knowledge of the past and not as an exegesis on the canonical work. Only by the end of the Former Han 前漢 (206 BCE–9 CE) did the situation change, when the court archivist, Liu Xin 劉歆 (ca. 50 BCE–23 CE), demanded establishing an official position for the *Zuo zhuan* exegetes among the court academicians. It took many years of bitter controversies before the *Zuo zhuan* was approved as an official commentary of the *Annals* by the Han court, but doubts about its relation with the *Annals* were not dispelled. In the late eighth century CE the controversies over the *Zuo zhuan* renewed: first, several scholars argued that it should be treated as a pure historical text and not a commentary on the classic; then, by the Song 宋 dynasty (960–1279) others began pointing at alleged anachronisms in the *Zuo zhuan*, suggesting that it was produced much later than implied by Sima Qian. This broadened the controversy: not only the text's relations to the *Annals* but its dating and authorship were henceforth questioned.

Debates over the *Zuo zhuan* intensified in the late nineteenth century, when the famous reformist statesman, Kang Youwei 康有爲 (1858–1927), eager to dismiss once and for all the *Zuo zhuan*'s position as a commentary to the *Annals*, argued that the entire text was a forgery by Liu Xin and hence is of no relevance to the Springs and Autumns period whatsoever. Despite the obvious weakness of Kang's argumentation (van Ess 1994), his views were endorsed by the so-called "Doubters of Antiquity" current (*yigu pai* 疑古派), centered around Gu Jiegang 顧頡剛 (1893–1980). The controversy expanded to involve a full range of questions concerning the nature, dating, and historical reliability of the *Zuo zhuan*; it encompassed dozens of scholars in China, Japan, and the West and continued throughout much of the twentieth century. For a sample of different views, see Schaberg 2001; Pines 2002; Li 2007; and Durrant et al. 2016:I-XCV and see there for further references.

Not all of the past debates are relevant nowadays. For instance, the question of the text's authorship lost much of its relevance. The idea of an active author who is engaged in a dialogue with his readers, expresses his personal feelings, and hints at his hidden or overt agendas did start in China only with Sima Qian (Kern 2016), and as such it is irrelevant to the *Zuo zhuan*, whose author(s) hide(s) himself/themselves behind the neutral designation of "a noble man" (*junzi* 君子; Henry 1999; cf. Van Auken 2016b). The question of the *Zuo zhuan*'s relations to the *Annals* also seems to have become less acute. At the very least scholars who deal with the *Annals*' exegesis overwhelmingly accept the *Zuo zhuan* as its earliest commentary (e.g., Zhao Shengqun 2000; Van Auken 2016a; but see also Wang He 2011 for an opposing view). Nor would a serious scholar today dismiss the *Zuo zhuan* as a "historical romance" as was once common (Gu Jiegang 1988:16; Maspero 1927:chapter 7) or as Liu Xin's forgery.

In contrast to the question of the *Zuo zhuan*'s authorship, the question of its dating continues to arouse heated polemic. To demonstrate the difficulty to arrive at a convincing answer, suffice it to consider a single example of an irresolvable contradiction. The *Zuo zhuan* contains no less than five predictions that were based on calculations of Jupiter's position (*Zuo zhuan*, Xiang 28.1, 30.10, Zhao 8.6, 9.4, 11.2). As paleo-astronomers had demonstrated, these calculations were retroactively produced after 375 or 365 BCE and then incorporated into the text (Hu Nianyi 1987:57–61; for the possibility that these entries were forged by Liu Xin, see Qiao Zhizhong 2016). At the same time, the *Zuo zhuan* contains a famous prediction by the "noble man," according to which "Qin will never again march eastward" (*Zuo zhuan*, Wen 6.3). This prediction could not have been made after the 360s BCE, when Qin renewed its eastward expansion. These examples of mutually contradictory dates can easily be multiplied. How can we understand them?

The riddle of the text's dating will be resolved once we dismiss the erroneous (even if popular) idea according to which a single date can be offered for the *Zuo zhuan*'s composition. Actually, there are at least four or five dates of the materials in *Zuo zhuan*. The earliest is the date of the composition of its component materials, local histories of the Springs and Autumns–period states (see below in this section). Then at a certain point (either in the fifth or fourth century BCE) these histories were put together, arranged chronologically, and probably supplemented with the commentarial layer, providing the earliest version of the *Zuo* commentary on the *Annals*. Then came a lengthy period of transmission, during which unknown redactors of the text may have intervened into its content: this includes an obvious instance of Han-dynasty redaction,[3] with some modifications continuing till the age of Liu Xin (Qiao Zhizhong 2016; Xu Jianwei 2017:181–246) to the text's major exegete, Du Yu 杜預 (222–285) (Durrant et al. 2016: LVII). However, the fact that the fallacious prediction about Qin was not edited out may suggest that the editorial efforts of the fourth century BCE and later were of limited nature: the transmitters might have added sections or sentences that would serve their ideological needs or would flatter their patrons, but they did not comb the text for editing out earlier content. This scenario may explain, for instance, why the effusive—and probably spurious—panegyrics of, for example, ancestors of the Ji 季 lineage in Lu or the Wei 魏 lineage in Jin (Pines 2002:234–242) coexist with other narratives that are highly critical of the members of these lineages. A reader of the *Zuo zhuan* must be doubly cautious in discerning the dating of many of its segments.

Going from the dating of the *Zuo zhuan* to its nature, we may immediately notice that the text resembles the *Annals* in terms of presenting an abundance of minute details about "who, what, when, and where." Yet the *Zuo zhuan* is much more detailed than the terse *Annals*. Its meticulous records that include a wealth of information about personal and place names, the events' dates, the participants' official titles, and the like were surely not invented but rather introduced from the text's primary sources. The reliability of some of this information can be furthermore independently verified by the newly unearthed paleographic sources, including contemporaneous bronze inscriptions.[4] Yet *Zuo zhuan* is not a dry chronicle. In distinction from the *Annals*, the text is concerned primarily with the question "why." This preoccupation with the event's causality is visible most immediately through the ubiquitous illative expressions *gu* 故 (because of, hence) and *shiyi* 是以 (therefore), which recur in the text well over 800 times. Yet by far more important are speeches of wise statesmen and post-factum observations of the "noble man" and Confucius, which allow the reader to draw proper historical lessons. It is this explicit didacticism that distinguishes the *Zuo zhuan* dramatically from the *Springs and Autumns Annals* (Schaberg 2001; Li Wai-yee 2007; Durrant et al. 2016:LX-LXIX).

One of the crucial questions concerning the reliability of the *Zuo zhuan*—in particular with regard to the intellectual history of the Springs and Autumns period (discussed in the next section)—is whether or not a variety of interpretative devices encountered in the text are the product of its compilers and transmitters (which means that they come from the Warring States period or even from the Han age) or rather were introduced into the text from its original sources (which means that they reflect the intellectual milieu of the Springs and Autumns period). The dominant answer until recently was the former: the *Zuo zhuan* was read as a polemical treatise aimed "to validate Ru teachings . . . through writing them into a narrative of the past" (Lewis 1999:132). Now, with a

---

[3] The most obvious indication of the Han redaction of the current version of the *Zuo zhuan* is its avoidance of the tabooed bang 邦, the name of the Han dynastic founder, Liu Bang 劉邦 (d. 195 BCE).

[4] See for instance the recently discovered Zifan-*bianzhong* 子犯編鐘 inscription, which narrates the Jin victory over Chu and celebrations in the Zhou royal palace. The date of the ceremony of rewarding the Jin commanders, *dingwei* 丁未 (10th day) of the fifth month, is identical to the one recorded in *Zuo zhuan* (Xi 28.3h). See more in Pines 2020: 82–84.

wealth of new materials, which allow a better understanding of the *Zuo zhuan*'s sources, this assertion can be disputed. Of particular value is the bamboo manuscript *Xinian* 繫年 (*String of Years or Linked Years*) from the Qinghua/Tsinghua University collection (composed ca. 370 BCE). Since it is evidently based on the same primary sources as the *Zuo zhuan*, the comparison between the texts allow meaningful reconstruction of these sources (Pines 2014, 2020).

From this reconstruction and from renewed scrutiny of the *Zuo zhuan* itself, it may be tentatively averred that the text's primary sources were not short annalistic accounts but rather much longer local histories from several contemporaneous polities. These histories were in all likelihood produced by the same court scribes, who were responsible for the preparation of the *Annals*-like ritualistic chronicles. However, unlike the *Annals*, these lengthy histories were aimed to teach the elite members about the past of their countries and lineages and also edify and entertain the readers (see more in Pines 2020). It is highly likely that many—most?—of the interpretative devices employed in the *Zuo zhuan* derive from the text's primary sources. This may explain the multiplicity of voices and perspectives in the *Zuo zhuan*. Thus, some of the narratives go against the moral messages enunciated in other parts of the text, creating considerable tension over the bottom line of the text's didactic message (Li 2007).

The sophistication of the *Zuo zhuan*'s primary sources reflects the importance of historiographic tradition in the Springs and Autumns–period Zhou world. *Zuo zhuan* itself is self-referential in its insistence on the importance of mastering the past to cope with current challenges. Its protagonists routinely invoke the past in a variety of court or interstate debates, and their superior knowledge of former events becomes a useful polemical weapon. References to successes and failures of previous rulers and ministers, analyses of historical developments in a rival state, or invocations of earlier precedents to justify a policy choice are recurrent rhetorical strategies in the *Zuo zhuan*. The past is a tool in the statesmen's hands, and to make it more accessible the text aims at providing the reader with as much useful information about important events in the life of major states and lineages as possible. This attitude toward the past was in all likelihood not invented by the *Zuo zhuan*'s compiler(s) but reflected common attitudes of the age.

It was the importance of mastering the past that gave rise to the flourishing history-writing during the Springs and Autumns period. The discovery of *Xinian*, another quasi-historical text from the Qinghua University collection, *Chu ju* (楚居, "Chu residences"; see Asano 2012; Cook and Luo 2017; Pines 2020); and the still-unpublished Chu historical manuscripts, one from the Anhui University collection (Huang Dekuan 2017 and another excavated in 2019 from the cemetery at the northern shore of Longhui River 龍會河, Jingzhou [Hubei]; see Li Huibo and Wu Yaxiong 2019) demonstrate the richness and heterogeneity of contemporaneous historiographic tradition. Accounts of the past were prepared to edify and entertain, to teach the statesmen about ritually important sites and to communicate with the ancestors, to provide the policy-makers with the background of contemporaneous inter-state situations, and for many other reasons (Pines 2020). However, it seems that at a certain point between the Springs and Autumns and the Warring States periods a change in usages of the past had occurred. The *Zuo zhuan* combination of being highly informative and sophisticatedly didactic is not matched in later texts. When the Zhou world entered the age of bitter ideological disputes, the so-called age of the Hundred Schools of Thought, the thinkers' priorities changed. What was prized now was not historical accuracy but a didactic message: through retelling, twisting, or inventing the narratives of the past, thinkers could provide compelling justifications for their policy proposals. Detailed narratives of the past had all but disappeared from the contemporaneous texts; instead, the overwhelmingly dominant historical genre was henceforth that of didactic anecdotes.

Didactic anecdotes—short vignettes valued for their moralizing messages or amusing features—are ubiquitous in Warring States–period writings. They permeate most texts later classified as either "histories" (like *Guoyu* 國語, Discourses of the States and *Zhanguo ce* [戰國策, Stratagems of the Warring States]) or "philosophies" (e.g., *Han Feizi* 韓非子, or *Lüshi chunqiu* 呂氏春秋). In an excellent study, David Schaberg (2011) had summarized some of the essentials of the anecdotal genre. Anecdotes are normally short and easily detachable textual units of several hundred characters length. Most anecdotes contain an exchange of speech and either a confirmation of one of the speakers' prescience or judgment by a later commentator. Schaberg concludes: "The early Chinese historical anecdote is a fundamentally didactic form, as valuable for instructing rulers and peers as for training young students" (Schaberg 2011:396; see also Van Els and Queen 2017).

Whether the anecdotes serve as the primary building blocks of historical knowledge in pre-imperial China as asserted by Schaberg (2011), or they are derivative of earlier longer sources as asserted by myself (Pines 2020) remains to be seen. What is clear is that the proliferation of the anecdotes was accompanied by their progressive dissociation from informative aspects of history writing and overwhelming focus on didacticism. In the Warring States–period texts, not only the interest in minute details is lost but even the basic concern with historical accuracy. Many anecdotes, the earliest versions of which appear in the *Zuo zhuan*, were retold repeatedly from the Warring States to the Han periods, with later versions becoming progressively dissociated from the factual background of the anecdote. In these late versions we can encounter such features as the same speech attributed to different personalities from different periods, proliferation of purely fabricated speeches, and abundance of blatant anachronisms (Henry 2003; cf. Van Els 2017).

It should be recalled here that more detailed historical records continued to be produced by scribal offices in each of the competing states, yet their circulation remained limited. Eventually they perished during the infamous Qin biblioclasm of 213 BCE (*Shiji* 15:686). What survived was only segments of the Wei 魏 chronicle, the so-called *Bamboo Annals* discovered in 279 or 280 CE (Shaughnessy 2006), and Qin's own "scribal records," which were later utilized by Sima Qian in sections of his *Shiji*. Judging from the relevant portions of *Shiji*, the Qin records were not anecdotal in their nature but more information-oriented (Yoshimoto 1995; Fujita 1997; Pines 2005–2006). However, we still lack a full understanding of non-anecdotal aspects of historical writing in the Middle to Late Warring States periods. It can be only hoped that new discoveries will bring to light more historical documents from that age.

THE WORLD OF THOUGHT BEFORE CONFUCIUS

Moving from the realm of historiography to the realm of political and ethical thought of the Springs and Autumns period, we stand on more shaky ground. The major problem of reconstructing the world of thought before Confucius is our overwhelming indebtedness to a single source, namely the *Zuo zhuan*, which records speeches of contemporaneous statesmen. Many of these speeches are highly interesting in terms of the light they shed on the speaker's worldview, but how reliable are they? To recall, not all of the *Zuo zhuan* comes from the Springs and Autumns period; it contains later interpolations and, possibly, embellishments and other redactional efforts by the composer and the transmitters. How can we be sure that ideas pronounced by the *Zuo zhuan* speakers are reflective of the Springs and Autumns period's intellectual milieu and were not put into their mouths later? This question remains highly controversial (cf. Schaberg 2001; Pines 2002).

We cannot ascertain the authenticity and dating of each of the hundreds speeches scattered throughout the *Zuo zhuan* but, when read systematically, these speeches provide us with a highly peculiar ideological picture, which does not have clear parallels in any of the transmitted texts from the Warring States or later periods. Most notably, the speeches in the *Zuo zhuan* reflect a distinctively aristocratic outlook of the vast majority of protagonists. This aristocratic mindset evidently reflects the power and self-confidence of hereditary aristocrats during the heyday of their power (see more in chapter 22), and it is highly unlikely that it would be post-factum invented by a Warring States–period forger and put in the mouths of dozens of the speakers. It is similarly unlikely that other peculiar approaches that permeate the *Zuo zhuan* speeches, such as, for example, approval of the multistate order or treating the ministers rather than the rulers as the true masters of the state, were fabricated by the Warring States–period thinkers, who lived under very different sociopolitical conditions. It is plausible then that the *Zuo zhuan* as a whole reflects the intellectual milieu of the aristocratic Springs and Autumns period, later editions and embellishments notwithstanding.

To introduce the world of thought depicted in the *Zuo zhuan*, we can conveniently contrast it with that of the subsequent Warring States period by focusing on three major topics: the views of the interstate order, the ruler's authority and ruler-minister relations, and the nature of social hierarchy. With regard to the first of these, what distinguishes the *Zuo zhuan* protagonists from the later ideologues is their indifference toward the idea of political unity of the Zhou realm. In the Warring States period and thereafter the quest for unification became the common conviction of competing thinkers (Pines 2000), but judging from the *Zuo zhuan*, it did not exist at all during the Springs and Autumns period. The protagonists discuss at length the means of perpetuating a viable multistate order, address the nature of hegemony and of alliances, and debate advantages of peace and war, but they never propose unification either through restoration of an effective rule of the Zhou Sons of Heaven or through other means. In the late years of the Springs and Autumns period we encounter brief references to the desire of the Chu kings to "attain All-under-Heaven," but this desire is presented as exceptional and unreasonable (e.g., *Zuo zhuan* Zhao 13.2g). The solution to the interstate turmoil, according to the *Zuo zhuan*, is perfection of the multistate system rather than its dismantling (see also chapter 22).

A reader may discern increased frustration with the ongoing failures in creating a viable multistate order. This frustration is well palpable in the changing attitudes toward the institution of hegemony. Early hegemons, such as Lord Huan of Qi, Lord Wen of Jin, and Lord Wen's descendants, are repeatedly urged to maintain their position through adherence to ritual norms, display of magnanimity and trustworthiness, refraining from annexations, and through displaying "kindness" (*de* 德) along with "awesomeness" (*wei* 威). In the later half of the *Zuo zhuan*, these admonitions fade away. New leaders, including such respectable statesmen as Zichan 子產 (d. 522 BCE) of Zheng 鄭 and Sima Hou 司馬侯 (d. ca. 535 BCE) of Jin, candidly advocate annexations and resort to force as inevitable and legitimate means of maintaining interstate leadership (*Zuo zhuan*, Xiang 25.5; Xiang 29.11). These voices reflect a sober understanding that the age of trustworthiness and kindness is gone forever. Even more revealing is a Late Springs and Autumns–period speech by Wu Zixu 伍子胥 (d. 484 BCE), one of the most prominent statesmen of his age. Wu Zixu urges his patron, the king of Wu, to eliminate the rival state of Yue, not because of the depravity of the Yue ruler but precisely because the latter is a model sovereign, who is able to attract his subjects: this makes him an even bitterer adversary:

> [Yue] has existed on the same lands as we do, and for generations they have been our enemy. Therefore, to overcome it but not to seize its territory, and moreover to preserve its existence, is to contradict Heaven and prolong [the life of] the adversary. Even if you repent later, you will be unable to reverse the case. (*Zuo zhuan*, Ai 1.2)

This prescient speech (Yue indeed eliminated Wu in 473 BCE) might not have been pronounced by Wu Zixu himself, but those who put it into his mouth wanted to indicate the coming of a new age. It suggests that the multistate order is not sustainable; the rival polities are engaged in a life-and-death struggle with each other, and the only way for maintaining hegemony is to mercilessly smash the enemy. This sober recognition of the impossibility to maintain lasting peace in a fragmented world would serve a precondition for the voices that demanded political unification as the only viable means of stabilizing the sub-celestial realm. Mengzi's dictum "stability is in unity" (*Mengzi* 1.6) is never articulated in the *Zuo zhuan*, but it sounds like a reasonable conclusion from reading its speeches, which convince the reader that the multistate order is doomed.

The *Zuo zhuan* differs from later texts not only in its avoidance of the issue of political unification but also in its views of the monarchic order. As mentioned in chapter 22, the Springs and Autumns period marked the nadir of the ruler's power—both the Zhou Son of Heaven and most of the regional lords were eclipsed by their underlings. From the perspective of later monarchic thought, this situation should be considered a grave aberration (Pines 2009a:25–53), but in the *Zuo zhuan* it is often treated as a fait accompli.

Although the text does contain a few sayings that compare the ruler's authority to that of Heaven (*Zuo zhuan*, Xuan 4.3b; Ding 4.3e), these are exceptional. Normally, the protagonists are eager to provide rationalizations for the decline of the ruler's power. For instance, in one of the most ideologically significant speeches in the entire text, Master Kuang 師曠 of Jin justifies the expulsion of the lord of Wei 衛 in 559 by implicitly blaming the lord himself. Kuang explains that while theoretically the ruler should be revered as Heaven and Earth, this reverence is not unconditional: it depends on the ruler's ability to take care of the people's needs. Otherwise, the ruler loses his legitimacy:

> The ruler is the master of the deities, the hope of the people. But if he fatigues the people's lives, neglects the deities, and ignores the sacrifices, then "the hundred clans" will lose their hope, and the altars of soil and grain will have no master. What use is [such a ruler]? What can one do but expel him? (*Zuo zhuan*, Xiang 14.6)

The idea that the ruler's right to his position should be subordinated to proper performance of his tasks is not novel: its roots can be found already in the Western Zhou documents that elaborate the idea of Heaven's Mandate (*tian ming* 天命). Yet Master Kuang goes further. Those who should act on Heaven's behalf and supervise the ruler are his high ministers, namely precisely the members of the stratum that repeatedly challenged the lords. In Kuang's eyes, rulers are given "helpers to teach them and protect them and to prevent them from exceeding [proper] measures. . . . When [the ruler] is good, he is rewarded; when he exceeds, he is corrected; when he is in distress, he is rescued; when he loses [the proper way], he is replaced" (*Zuo zhuan*, Xiang 14.6). This conclusion puts the right to replace the ruler in the hands of his ministers, making them singularly powerful political actors and severely undermining the ruler's authority.

The *Zuo zhuan* speakers' willingness to justify expulsion and replacement of the rulers is matched by their high esteem of the ministers. Those are considered not the ruler's servitors but rather companions, who share with him responsibility for the "altars of soil and grain" (*sheji* 社稷), namely the collective entity of the state. The leading ministers are proudly designated "masters of the people" (*min zhi zhu* 民之主), a term normally reserved for the rulers alone. They repeatedly argue that they owe allegiance to the altars of soil and grain rather to the ruler personally, and in the name of the altars they have the right to defy the sovereign's orders and even to depose him (Pines 2002:136–163). This haughty ministerial discourse was by itself one of the manifestations of the power of the ministerial stratum and the weakness of the rulers, which plagued the world of the Springs and Autumns period (see chapter 22).

Ministerial self-confidence as depicted in the *Zuo zhuan* is related to the overall self-confidence of hereditary aristocrats, which permeates the book. The nobles were immensely proud of their status, which was defined primarily, if not exclusively, by their pedigree. The term "noble man" (*junzi* 君子), the most respectable designation of the elite members, is applied in the *Zuo zhuan* exclusively to the members of upper (*qing* 卿) and middle-rank (*dafu* 大夫) nobility but never to the members of the *shi* 士 stratum, which will become so prominent in the age of the Warring States (Pines 2017). The term *shi* itself is marginal in the *Zuo zhuan*: it is employed to define the low-rank nobles (or, in other contexts, soldiers or males) but is never used either as a generic elite designation or as a referent to a morally and intellectually superior individual, as is common in later texts (Pines 2009a:115–135). It is clear that for the *Zuo zhuan* protagonists the elite is confined to the upper ranks of hereditary aristocracy; *shi* are not its members.

The Springs and Autumns period aristocrats were not prone to open the ruling stratum to newcomers from below. Hence, many common topoi of the Warring States–period discourse are either absent or marginal in the *Zuo zhuan*. For instance, the meritocratic principle of "elevating the worthy" is normally not articulated. If individual's worthiness is mentioned at all in the context of one's appointment, it is invariably done either in the context of choosing a better heir or selecting a more suitable candidate from among highest aristocrats—but never in the context of promoting a *shi* person. This differs dramatically from the Warring States-period discourse (Pines 2013). Similarly, self-cultivation and learning are rarely discussed: after all, the aristocrats owed their position to their pedigree rather than to self-acquired skills. At the same time, the single most important concept that repeatedly resurfaces in dozens of speeches is ritual (*li* 禮)—the best panacea from social ills, a universal stabilizer of hereditary aristocracy. A leading thinker, Yan Ying 晏嬰 (d. ca. 500 BCE), explains:

> According to *li*, the family's favors do not exceed those of the state; the people do not drift; peasants do not move [to new lands], artisans and merchants do not change [their occupation], *shi* do not overflow, officials do not exceed [their responsibilities], and the nobles dare not seize the lord's profits. (*Zuo zhuan*, Zhao 26.11)

Ritual is supposed to stabilize society. Everybody will perform his ancestral tasks; everybody will be satisfied with his hereditary position; then the *shi* will not "overflow" the nobles, while the nobles, in turn, will not endanger their rulers. This conservative vision epitomizes the expectations of the Springs and Autumns–period aristocrats as reflected in the *Zuo zhuan*. Fixing the society once and for all according to rigid hierarchic norms is the only means to save it from ongoing disintegration.

Social values of the Springs and Autumns–period nobles were fundamentally conservative; yet seeds of change were sown already then, as is reflected in a gradual reconceptualization of the nature of the elite status. Rather than justifying their elevated positions in terms of pure pedigree, aristocrats of the Springs and Autumns period increasingly tended to emphasize abilities and morality as the true foundation of their power. This change is visible in the increasing tendency to imbue the term "noble man" (*junzi*) with ethical content. Although the pedigree connotation of the term remained clear (hence, in the *Zuo zhuan* this designation is never applied to a *shi*), *junzi* was gradually reinterpreted as pertaining to one's qualities rather than pure pedigree. Only the noble who was impeccably moral and intelligent deserved his elevated position; otherwise he could be designated "a petty man" (*xiao ren* 小人), indicating thereby his unworthiness of the noble status. In the age of frequent downfall of powerful ministerial lineages, this emphasis on personal inadequacy of those who were supposed to be "superior men" provided contemporary aristocrats with convenient explanations of the ever-accelerating downward mobility of the members of their stratum (Pines 2002:165–171).

This shift away from one's lineage and one's pedigree to one's individual qualities as a major determinant of one's status is visible in the Late Springs and Autumns period, from both textual and paleographic sources.[5] Yet this "ethicization" of the "superior men's" self-image had unexpected consequences for the nobles. Even if in the short term it was designed to provide further legitimation for the aristocrats' dominant position, in the final account it paved the way for the upward mobility of the *shi* stratum. In due time, the rising *shi* began emulating the behavior of the "noble men," thereby laying claim to their eligibility for the *junzi* status. The aristocrats remained powerless in the face of this challenge. Ironically, those who imbued the term *junzi* with ethical meaning were unable to find ideological justifications to repel the *shi* assault on their hereditary privileges. Thus, by downplaying the importance of the pedigree in obtaining high political status, aristocrats of the Springs and Autumns period contributed to the dismantling of the very social order that had ensured their elevated position. The new age belonged to the new men.

Bibliography

Asano, Yūichi 淺野裕一 2012. "A Preliminary Study of Tsinghua Bamboo Manuscript 'Chu Ju' 清華簡《楚居》初探." *Qinghua jian yanjiu* 清華簡研究 1:242–247.

Chunqiu Zuo zhuan zhu 春秋左傳注 1981. Annotated by Yang Bojun 楊伯峻. Beijing: Zhonghua shuju.

Cook, Constance A., and Luo Xinhui 2017. *Birth in Ancient China: A Study of Metaphor and Cultural Identity in Pre-Imperial China*. Albany: State University of New York Press.

Durrant, Stephen W., Li Wai-yee, and David Schaberg 2016. *Zuo Tradition/Zuozhuan: Commentary on the "Spring and Autumn Annals."* Seattle: University of Washington Press.

Els, Paul van 2017. "Old Stories No Longer Told: The End of the Anecdotes Tradition of Early China." In *Between Philosophy and History: Rhetorical Uses of Anecdotes in Early China*. Edited by Paul van Els and Sarah Queen, 331–356. Albany: State University of New York Press.

Els, Paul van, and Sarah Queen, eds. 2017. *Between Philosophy and History: Rhetorical Uses of Anecdotes in Early China*. Albany: State University of New York Press.

Ess, Hans van 1994. "The Old Text/New Text Controversy: Has the 20th Century Got It Wrong?" *T'oung Pao* 80:146–170.

Falkenhausen, Lothar von 1993. "Issues in Western Zhou Studies: A Review Article." *Early China* 18:139–226.

Fujita, Katsuhisa 藤田勝久 1997. *Research on Historical Materials from the Warring States Period in the Shiji* 史記戰國史料の研究. Tōkyō: Tōkyō University Press.

Gentz, Joachim 2001. *Das Gongyang zhuan: Auslegung und Kanoniesierung der Frühlings und Herbstannalen (Chunqiu)*. Wiesbaden: Harrassowitz Verlag.

[5] Thus, as pointed by Gilbert Mattos (1997:86–87), bronze inscriptions of the Springs and Autumns period turn away from the ancestors and focus on the individual attainments of the donor; for similar analysis of the inscriptional evidence, see Pines 2002:171–175.

Gentz, Joachim 2015. "Long Live the King! The Ideology of Power between Ritual and Morality in the *Gongyang zhuan* 公羊傳." In *Ideology of Power and Power of Ideology in Early China*. Edited by Yuri Pines, Paul R. Goldin, and Martin Kern, 69–117. Leiden: Brill.

Gu Jiegang 顧頡剛 1988. *Lectures Concerning Ancient Chinese History* 中國上古史研究 講義. Beijing: Zhonghua shuju.

Henry, Eric 1999. "'Junzi yue' and 'Zhongni yue' in *Zuozhuan*." *Harvard Journal of Asiatic Studies* 59(1):125–161.

Henry, Eric 2003. "Anachronisms in *Lüshi chunqiu* and *Shuo yuan*." *Early Medieval China* 1:127–138.

Hu, Nianyi 胡念貽 1987. "On the Authenticity Time of the '*Zuo zhuan*' 《左傳》的真偽和寫 作時代考辨." In *Zhongguo gudai wenxue lungao* 中國古代文學論稿. Edited by Hu Nianyi, 21–76. Shanghai: Shanghai guji chubanshe.

Huang, Dekuan 黃德寬 2017. "Overview of the Bamboo Slips of the Warring States Period Kept at Anhui University 安徽大學藏戰國竹 簡概述." *Wenwu* 9:54–59.

Kern, Martin (柯馬丁) 2016. "The Concept of Author in the *Shiji* 《史記》裡的'作者'概念." In *Shiji xue yu shijie hanxue lunji xubian* 史記學與世界漢學論集續編. Edited by Martin Kern and Lee Chi-hsiang 李紀祥, 23–61. Taipei: Tangshan chubanshe.

Lewis, Mark E. 1999. *Writing and Authority in Early China*. Albany: State University of New York Press.

Li, Huibo 李慧博, and Wu, Yaxiong 吳亞雄 2019. "Precious Western Han Bamboo Slips and Wooden Boards and Warring States-Period Chu Slips Unearthed in Hubei, Jingzhou Have High Scholarly Value" 湖北荊州發現珍貴西漢簡牘和戰國楚簡极具学術价值. http://culture.people.com.cn/BIG5/n1/2019/0507/c1013-31071897.html (accessed November 9, 2019).

Li, Wai-yee 2007. *The Readability of the Past in Early Chinese Historiography*. Harvard East Asian Monographs. Cambridge, MA: Harvard University Asia Center.

Maspero, Henri 1965 [1927]. *La Chine antique*. Reprint. Paris: Les Presses universitaires de France.

Mattos, Gilbert L. 1997. "Eastern Zhou Bronze Inscriptions." In *New Sources of Early Chinese History: An Introduction to Reading Inscriptions and Manuscripts*. Edited by Edward L. Shaughnessy, 85–124. Berkeley, CA: Society for Study of Early China.

Mengzi yizhu 孟子譯注 1992. Annotated by Yang Bojun 楊伯峻. Beijing: Zhonghua shuju.

Pines, Yuri 2000. "'The One That Pervades All' in Ancient Chinese Political Thought: Origins of the 'Great Unity' Paradigm." *T'oung Pao* 86(4–5):280–324.

Pines, Yuri 2002. *Foundations of Confucian Thought: Intellectual Life in the Chunqiu Period, 722–453 BCE*. Honolulu: University of Hawai'i Press.

Pines, Yuri 2005–2006. "Biases and their Sources: Qin history in the *Shiji*." *Oriens Extremus* 45:10–34.

Pines, Yuri. 2009a. *Envisioning Eternal Empire: Chinese Political Thought of the Warring States Era*. Honolulu: University of Hawai'i Press.

Pines, Yuri 2009b. "Chinese History-Writing between the Sacred and the Secular." In *Early Chinese Religion: Part One; Shang through Han (1250 BC–220 AD)*, vol. 1. Edited by John Lagerwey and Marc Kalinowski, 315–340. Leiden: Brill.

Pines, Yuri 2013. "Between Merit and Pedigree: Evolution of the Concept of 'Elevating the Worthy' in Pre-Imperial China." In *The East Asian Challenge for Democracy: Political Meritocracy in Comparative Perspective*. Edited by Daniel Bell and Li Chenyang, 161–202. Cambridge, UK: Cambridge University Press.

Pines, Yuri 2014. "Zhou History and Historiography: Introducing the Bamboo *Xinian*." *T'oung Pao* 100(4–5):287–324.

Pines, Yuri 2017. "Confucius's Elitism: The Concepts of *junzi* and *xiaoren* Revisited." In *A Concise Companion to Confucius*. Edited by Paul R. Goldin, 164–184. Chichester: Wiley- Blackwell.

Pines, Yuri 2020. *Zhou History Unearthed: The Bamboo Manuscript* Xinian *and Early Chinese Historiography*. New York, NY: Columbia University Press.

Qiao, Zhizhong 喬治忠 2016. "An Iron Proof that Liu Xin Made Interpolations in *Zuo zhuan* and *Guoyu*: Expounding the Explanation of the Historical Chronologist Liu Tan" 《左傳》《國語》被劉歆竄亂的一項鐵證——歷史年代學劉坦之說申論. *Beijing shifan daxue xuebao* (shehuikexue ban) 北京師範大學學報(社會科學版) 3:68–78.

Schaberg, David 2001. *A Patterned Past: Form and Thought in Early Chinese Historiography*. Cambridge, MA: Harvard University Asia Center.

Schaberg, David 2011. "Chinese History and Philosophy." In *The Oxford History of Historical Writing*, vol. 1: *Beginnings to AD 600*. Edited by Andrew Feldherr and Grant Hardy, 394–414. Oxford: Oxford University Press.

Shaughnessy, Edward L. 2006. *Rewriting Early Chinese Texts*. Albany: State University of New York Press.

Shiji 史記 1997. By Sima Qian 司馬遷 et al., annotated by Zhang Shoujie 張守節, Sima Zhen 司馬貞, and Pei Yin 裴駰. Beijing: Zhonghua shuju.

Van Auken, Newell Ann. 2016a. *The Commentarial Transformation of the Spring and Autumn*. Albany: State University of New York Press.

Van Auken, Newell Ann 2016b. "Judgments of the Gentleman: A New Analysis of the Place of *junzi* Comments in *Zuozhuan* Composition History." *Monumenta Serica* 64(2):277–302.

Wang, He 王和 2011. "The Various Segments Added by Latter Personalities into the *Zuozhuan* 《左傳》中後人附益 的各種成分." *Beijing shifan daxue xuebao* (shehuikexue ban) 北京師範大學學報(社會科 學版) 1:82–95.

Xin jiben Huan Tan Xin lun 新輯本桓譚新論. Collated by Zhu Qianzhi 朱謙之. Beijing: Zhonghua shuju.

Xin lun. See *Xin jiben Huan Tan xin lun*.

Xu, Jianwei 徐建委 2017. *Textual Revolution: Liu Xiang, "Bibliographic Treatise" of the* Hanshu, *and Research of Early Texts* 文本革命:劉向 、《漢書.藝文志》與早期文本研究. Beijing: Zhongguo shehui kexue chubanshe.

Zhao, Boxiong 趙伯雄 2004. *History of the Studies of the Spring and Autumn Annals* 春秋學史. Ji'nan: Shandong jiaoyu chubanshe.

Zhao, Shengqun 趙生群 2000. *Research on the Springs and Autumns Classic and Commentaries* 春秋經傳研究. Shanghai: Shanghai guji chubanshe.

Zuo zhuan. See *Chunqiu Zuozhuan zhu*.

....

CHAPTER 24

CULTURES AND STYLES OF ART DURING THE SPRINGS AND AUTUMNS PERIOD

....

BY XIAOLONG WU, HANOVER COLLEGE

THE first part of the Eastern Zhou period (770–256 BCE) in China's early history is the Springs and Autumns period (770–476 BCE), named after the *Chunqiu* (*Springs and Autumns Annals*), the official annals of the state of Lu. This period is ushered in by the forced relocation of the Zhou capital to present-day Luoyang, Henan Province in 770 BCE. The nearly three hundred years of the Springs and Autumns period is an era marked by profound transformations in various aspects of the society. Although the bronze industry continued to develop, iron tools started to be widely used, which led to major changes in agriculture and crafts.[1] Social structures and political systems also experienced dramatic changes, mainly characterized by the unraveling of the Zhou system based on kinship and lineage, the diminishing authority of the Zhou court, and the rising power of the regional states originally established by Zhou. Large states vied with each other to become the next dominant power, or hegemon,

---

[1] The earliest smelt iron artifacts, an iron sword with a bronze and jade handle and a *ge* dagger axe with iron blades, were found in M2001 and M2009 of the Guo state cemetery at Shangcunling, Sanmenxia, Henan, dated to the beginning of the Springs and Autumns period (Henan 1999:530). Carburizing steel and cast-iron artifacts have been found in various sites of the Late Springs and Autumns period. Over 80 iron and steel artifacts have been found in Springs and Autumns sites (Gu and Zhu Shunlong 2003:164–173). Also see Chapter 26 on the iron industry by Wangcheong Lam in this book.

through reforms, diplomatic relations, and annexing smaller states. Within the regional states, the Zhou system of aristocratic ranks was challenged, and the new elite from the lower ranks of the aristocracy took over as rulers of many states, such as Jin 晋, Qi 齐, Lu 鲁, Song 宋, and Zheng 郑. Meanwhile, changes in the world beyond the Zhou regional states, specifically the fast development of various forms of pastoralism in the western and northern parts of China, had created a keener consciousness of a collective identity among the Zhou regional states, reflected by the emerging concept of "Huaxia."

Material culture of this period seen through archaeological discoveries reflects the same trend toward regionalism described in historical sources. A spirit of rivalry and innovation can be noticed in finds of different regional states, which started to develop their own characteristic artistic traditions and tastes. Meanwhile, the traditions of the centuries-long Zhou material culture and ritual practices lingered on and became a shared heritage that provided a discourse for internal and interstate politics and a group identity vis-à-vis others. Therefore, it is appropriate for a survey of the material culture of this period to be organized by individual states, while keeping in mind the common threads of development for comparisons both with the Western Zhou and among Springs and Autumns states themselves.

The roughly three hundred years of the Springs and Autumns period are traditionally divided into three historical periods: Early (770–670 BCE), Middle (670–570 BCE), and Late (570–476 BCE). Chronologies established by archaeological studies, especially those based on the study of bronze vessels, however, do not precisely coincide with this division: some studies divide the tombs of this period into three phases (see e.g., Gao 1981; Zhu Fenghan 2009; Peng 2011), while some use a four-phase periodization (see e.g., Li Xueqin 1984; Liu Binhui 1995). Among the studies that divide the tombs of this period into three phases, some coincide roughly with the historical division of Early, Middle, and Late (Table 1), while some differ significantly from it (Zhu Fenghan 2009). This chapter will use the traditional tripartite historical division of this period, shown in Table 1.

Table 1 Early, middle, and late phases of springs and autumns period bronzes

Periodization of bronze vessels of the Central Plains area	Historical division and absolute dates
Phase 1	Early (770–ca. 650 BCE)
Phase 2	Middle (ca. 650–ca. 550 BCE)
Phase 3	Late (ca. 550–ca. 453 BCE)

The Central Plains area: Zhou, Guo, Zheng, and Jin

The Central Plains in this chapter refers to the Zhou royal domain around modern-day Luoyang and the surrounding states of the royal Ji 姬 clan, such as Guo 虢, Zheng 郑, and Jin 晋, located in northern Henan and southern Shanxi provinces. Due to their close lineage connections and geographical proximity those states share many features in the development of material culture (Table 2). The state of Jin rose to be one of the most lasting hegemons of the Springs and Autumns period and played an important role in Chinese history of the Zhou period. Jin archaeological discoveries are equally impressive.

Table 2 Representative burial sites and tombs: The Central Plains area

Site Name	State Affiliation	Date of Site: E (Early), M (Middle), or L (Late) Springs and Autumns	Significant Tombs	Important Features or Main Assemblage (m=mingqi)	Date of Tombs Mentioned: E (Early), M (Middle), or L (Late) Springs and Autumns
Beizhao cemetery, Quwo, Shanxi	Jin	E	M93	5 ding (+1m), 6 gui (+1m), 16 bells	E
			M102		
Yangshe cemetery, Quwo, Shanxi	Jin	E	M1		E
			M2		
Shangcunling cemetery, Sanmenxia, Henan	Guo	E	M2001	7 ding (+3m), 6 gui (+2m), 8 li, 8 bells	E
			M2012		
Shangguo cemetery, Wenxi, Shanxi	Jin	E-M	M49, M374, 89WSM7, 76M1, 76M4		E-M
Shangma cemetery, Houma, Shanxi	Jin	E-L	61M13	7 ding, 4 dui, 9 bells	M/L
			M1004	5 ding	
			M5218	5 ding	
			M1006, M1026, M2008		L

Site Name	State Affiliation	Date of Site: E (Early), M (Middle), or L (Late) Springs and Autumns	Significant Tombs	Important Features or Main Assemblage (m=*mingqi*)	Date of Tombs Mentioned: E (Early), M (Middle), or L (Late) Springs and Autumns
Beizhicun Pingdingshan, Henan	Ying	E	M1	5 *ding*	E
			M8	5 *ding*	
Taipuxiang, Jiaxian, Henan	Zheng	E		5 *ding*	E
Gaochengzhen, Dengfeng, Henan	Zheng	E	M3	5 *ding*	E
Zhongzhoulu, Luoyang, Henan	Zhou	E-L		Ceramic vessels: E: *li, pen, guan*; M: *li, pen, guan,* and *mingqi ding*; L: *mingqi ding, dou, guan*	E-L
Tiyuchanglu, Luoyang, Henan	Zhou	E	C1M10122	Four ramps	E
Chengcun, Linyi, Shanxi	Jin	M-L	M0003, M1002, M1023, M1064, M1082		L
Tombs in Huixian, Xinzheng, and Weishi Counties, Henan		M			M
Lijialou, Xinzheng, Henan	Zheng	M		16 *ding*, 7 *gui*, 4 *fang hu*	M
Ritual bronze vessel caches, Xinzheng, Henan	Zheng	M		9 *ding*, 8 *gui*, 9 *li*, 1 *dou*, 2 *fang hu*, 1 *yuan hu*, 1 *jian*	M
Miaoqiancun, Wanrong, Shanxi	Jin	L	58M1, 62M1, 62M5		L
Fenshuiling, Changzhi, Shanxi	Jin	L	M269, M270		L

(Continued)

Site Name	State Affiliation	Date of Site: E (Early), M (Middle), or L (Late) Springs and Autumns	Significant Tombs	Important Features or Main Assemblage (m=mingqi)	Date of Tombs Mentioned: E (Early), M (Middle), or L (Late) Springs and Autumns
Liulige, Huixian, Henan	Jin or Wey	L	Jia Mu,	15 *ding*, 1 *yan*, 4 *li*, 4 *gui*, 4 *fu*, 8 *dou*, 2 *lei*, 6 *fang hu*, 6 *yuan hu*, 1 flat *hu*, 1 *zun*, 3 *jian*, 1 *zhou*, 1 *pan*, 1 *yi*, 30 bells	L
			Yi Mu	10 *ding*, 1 *yan*, 4 *li*, 4 *gui*, 4 *fu*, 1 *dou*, 1 *fang hu*, 2 *jian*, 2 *zhou*, 1 *pan*, 1 *yi*, 29 bells	L
			M60	24 *ding*, 1 *yan*, 6 *li*, 6 *gui*, 4 *fu*, 1 *dou*, 2 *lei*, 3 *fang hu*, 1 *he*, 3 *j'ian*, 1 *zhou*, 2 *pan*	
Jinshengcun, Taiyuan, Shanxi	Jin	L	M251	27 *ding*, 2 *yan* 5 *li*, 2 *fu*, 14 *dou*, 6 *fang hu*, 1 *zun*, 2 *lei*, 6 *jian*, 4 *zhou*, 2 *pan*, 2 *yi*	L

Table 2 Representative burial sites and tombs: The Central Plains area   (Continued)

EARLY SPRINGS AND AUTUMNS PERIOD

The Tianma-Qucun 天马-曲村 site in Shanxi, discovered in 1962, is identified as the seat of the Jin ruling house during the Western Zhou and Early Springs and Autumns periods. The cemetery of commoners and low-ranking aristocrats was found at Qucun village. The cemetery located at the Beizhao 北赵 village in the center of the site contains nine pairs (with an exception of three tombs) of large tombs with one or two ramps; inscriptions on bronzes from these tombs suggest they are burials of Jin lineage heads (Jin hou 晋侯) and their consorts. A pair of tombs at the northwest corner of the cemetery, M93 and M102, are probably those of Wen Hou 文侯, the first ruler of Jin in the Springs and Autumns period, and his consort (Beijing 1995). In 2005, another cemetery of Jin rulers was found at the Yangshe 羊舌 village some 4,500 meters to the south, and five large tombs with two ramps were located, along with dozens of tombs of smaller sizes. Unlike the Beizhao cemetery, at Yangshe Jin rulers and people of lesser ranks were buried in the same cemetery. M1 and M2 at Yangshe were excavated, but the artifacts were limited mainly to jade pendants and pottery due to damage caused by severe looting in antiquity. Hundreds of small sacrificial pits, each containing remains of cattle, sheep, or goat, were found around the southern ramps of the two tombs, which could either represent "grave sacrifice" (Song 2007:159) or remains of "oaths of alliance" ceremonies (Sun 2012). The authors of the report proposed that this cemetery was the continuation of the Beizhao cemetery, and M1 and M2 were tombs of Wen Hou and his consort (instead of M93 and M102 at Beizhao), thus placing them at the beginning of the Springs and Autumns period (Shanxi 2009). It is probable that both M93 and M102 at Beizhao and M1 and M2 at Yangshe are Early Springs and Autumns–period tombs. All four tombs contain a layer of rocks and a layer of charcoal around the wooden burial chamber (*jishi jitan* 积石积碳); this structure was limited to the tombs of Jin lineage heads during this period but was widely adopted by large tombs during the Late Springs and Autumns period and the Warring States period (Song 2007:145–146).

The Guo state cemetery, located at Shangcunling in the city of Sanmenxia 三门峡, Henan Province, was discovered and partially excavated in the 1950s (Zhongguo 1959b). This excavation revealed 234 tombs and three chariot-and-horse pits in the southern section of the cemetery. Work resumed in the 1990s and 18 tombs and four chariot-and-horse pits were excavated in the northern section (Henan 1999). The cemetery contains over 500 tombs of various sizes that belong to different social ranks; the northern section, separated by a ditch from the southern section, is the area where the rulers of the Guo state and their families were buried. Tombs of different sizes scatter amid each other, indicating that this is a clan cemetery where tombs were grouped by lineage rather than social rank. The Lijiayao 李家窑 site about one mile south of the cemetery was probably the Guo capital of Shangyang 上阳 (Zhongguo 1959b:50).

Based on the style of bronze vessels and historical texts, the Guo cemetery is dated between the relocation of the Zhou capital in 770 BCE and the destruction of Guo by the state of Jin in 655 BCE, therefore falling into the Early Springs and Autumns period (Zhu Fenghan 2009:1,544–1,545; Wang Entian 2012; Ning 2000; Gao 1981; Yin 2006). Alternative arguments hold that the absolute chronology of the Guo cemetery straddled the Late Western Zhou and Early Eastern Zhou periods (Henan 1999). It is argued that the state of Guo in modern-day Sanmenxia was established by the Xi Guo 西虢, who migrated eastward from Shaanxi after the fall of Western Zhou (Zhu 2009:1,541–1,547). Xi Guo was a state established by a brother of King Wen, and Guo belonged to the same Ji lineage of the Zhou kings. M2001 and M2012 are two neighboring large tombs excavated in the northern section; each has a chariot-and-horse pit. Among the 2,487 bronze items from M2001, the ritual bronze assemblage includes seven *ding* 鼎, six *gui* 簋, eight *li* 鬲, and eight *zhong* 钟 bells. The seven *ding* are similar in shape and decoration and graduated in size, thus forming a set of *ding* for presenting sacrificial meat, or *lieding* 列鼎 (Figure 1), the number of which often reflect the aristocratic rank of the deceased in the Springs and Autumns period. In addition to this ritual vessel set, three *ding* and two *gui* of different sizes and styles were added and probably used as *mingqi* 明器 (funerary objects made for burial). Fifty- two bronze inscriptions from this tomb stated that Guo Ji 虢季 was the person who commissioned the bronzes, thus identifying him as the owner of this tomb. Guo Ji is probably a ruler and lineage head of the Guo, although some consider him an aristocratic member of the next lesser rank, similar to those buried in M1052 and M2011, both identified as Guo princes or heirs apparent

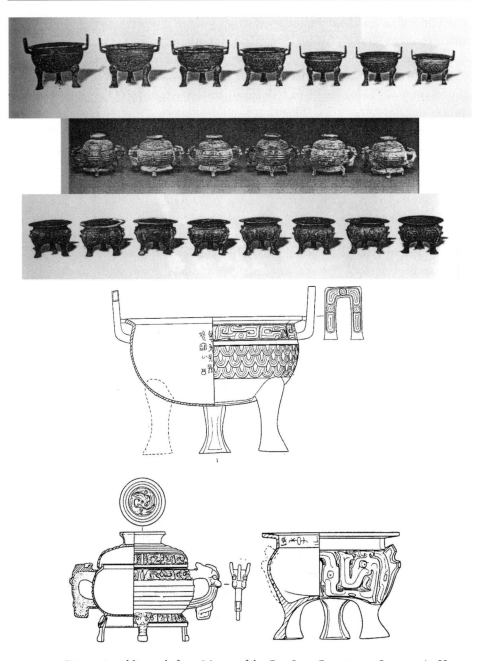

FIGURE 1 *Ding*, *gui*, and *li* vessels from M2001 of the Guo State Cemetery at Sanmenxia, Henan, Early Springs and Autumns period. Modified after *Sanmenxia Guoguo mu*. Beijing: Wenwu Chubanshe, 1999: colorplates 3.1, 4.1, 5.1; figures 22, 30, 34.

(Taizi 太子). M2012 was further identified as the tomb of Guo Ji's wife based on its location and bronze inscriptions containing Liang Ji 梁姬, or lady of the Ji clan from Liang, although some contending opinions maintain that the Guo rulers, who belonged to the Ji clan, could not marry women from the same clan. The assemblages of bronze vessels in those tombs indicate a system of hierarchy among the aristocracy close to that described in the later ritual classics. Different sumptuary rules distinguish the Guo state cemetery at Shangcunling and the late Western Zhou tombs at the Jin state cemetery at Beizhao village in Shanxi Province, since the ritual furnishings at the Guo tombs are more opulent (Falkenhausen 2006:109). When compared to the early Springs and Autumns tombs of Jin rulers at Beizhao, the same observation still stands. For instance, tombs of Guo rulers were furnished with seven *ding*, while those of Jin rulers were afforded only five. This difference was probably due to the seniority of the Guo ruling house within the Zhou genealogical hierarchy in comparison to that of Jin (Falkenhausen 2006:110). In addition, Guo lineage heads also served as high-ranking officials at the Zhou court in the Late Western Zhou and Early Springs and Autumns periods.

Three seasons of excavation at the Shangguo 上郭 cemetery in Wenxi 闻喜, Shanxi have yielded 76 rectangular earthen-pit tombs, most of which are smaller than 15 square meters (except M55, 31.2 m²) and date to the Early and Middle Springs and Autumns period (Zhu Hua 1994; Shanxi 1994a, 1994c). Modern-day Wenxi County is the Quwo 曲沃 of Jin during the Springs and Autumns period, the seat of a minor lineage of the Jin ruling house that later replaced the main lineage at Yi 翼 as Jin rulers in 679 BCE. The Shangguo cemetery might be related to this minor lineage and its polity. Twenty-seven of these tombs yielded bronzes, usually a spouted *ding* and some water vessels (*pan* 盘 and *yi* 匜). The innovative nature of the tomb patrons is betrayed by three small box-shaped bronze vessels decorated with dragons, tigers, birds, and monkeys in both relief patterns and sculptural forms, one supported by four human figures (from M49) and two shaped like chariot boxes on movable wheels (from M374 and 89WSM7). Many bronze vessels indicate interaction with mobile pastoralist cultures on the Eurasian steppe, such as the *fu* 鍑 from tomb 76M1, and the rope-shaped handles on the *ding* from tomb 76M4 (Shanxi 1994a:138).

Excavations at the Shangma 上马 cemetery in Houma 侯马, Shanxi have yielded 1,387 tombs, all medium- or small-sized earthen-pit tombs dated from the end of the Western Zhou to the end of the Springs and Autumns (Shanxi 1994b, 1963). The cemetery probably became part of the Jin capital Xintian 新田 (also called Xinjiang 新绛 in historical texts) at Houma after Duke Jing (Jing Gong 景公) of Jin moved the capital here in 585 BCE. Since the absolute chronology of these tombs spans the entirety of the Springs and Autumns period, and because this cemetery is basically intact and fully excavated, it provides an invaluable set of statistically representative data for the study of the material culture and social structure and their changes in this region (Shanxi 1994; Falkenhausen 1999:482). The typological sequences for both bronze and pottery vessels established for Shangma cemetery also provide a chronological framework for dating other tombs in the Central Plains area. Among the 23 tombs with bronze vessels, only one tomb (61M13) contains an assemblage with seven *ding* (two of which have inscriptions and were made by Geng'er 庚兒 from the State of Xu), and only two tombs have an assemblage with five *ding*, while most tombs contain only one pottery vessel (880 tombs, usually a *li*); small ornaments of bone, stone, or jade (220 tombs); or no grave goods at all (230 tombs). The cemetery probably represents the lower aristocracy and commoners and was organized spatially according to lineages and families. Paired tombs for husband and wife appeared during the end of this period and were limited to the aristocracy (tombs with bronze vessels); although all tombs of males in the four paired tombs at Shangma were furnished with bronze vessels, three out of the four tombs of females lack any bronze vessels, suggesting gender inequality in social status (Shanxi 1994:302–303).

Other tombs dated to the Early Springs and Autumns period include M1 and M8 at the Ying 应 State cemetery at Beizhicun 北滍村 in Pingdingshan 平顶山, Henan (Henan 1988, 2007). Both tombs have a bronze assemblage marked by five *ding*, although those in the smaller tomb M1 are *mingqi* funerary vessels. A tomb at Taipuxiang 太仆乡, Jiaxian 郏县 (Henan 1954), and M3 at Gaochengzhen 告城镇, Dengfeng 登封 (Zhengzhou 2006), both in Henan Province, are tombs of the Zheng state, both with a five-*ding* assemblage. During the Early Springs and Autumns period, tomb sizes and those furnished with bronze vessels basically correlate with numbers of *ding* vessels. Tombs with three or more *ding* are usually larger than 10 square meters in size. The assemblage usually contains *ding*, *gui*, *li*, *fang yan* 方甗, and *pu* 铺 for food vessels; wine vessels only include *fang hu* 方壶 (Figure 2), seen in pairs in almost all of the tombs with three or more *ding*. The number of *ding* in each tomb varies from 9 (seven if only *lie ding* is counted) to one, all in odd numbers. The number of *gui* in a tomb correlates with that of *ding* and is usually the even number above or below the number of *ding*.

The *ding* sets are usually *lie ding*, namely a set of *ding* identical in shape and style but graduated in size, yet some may show minor differences in shape within the set, indicating that they were probably not cast as one batch. In some cases where *gui* outnumber *ding* by one, two extra *ding* of different shapes and decoration were added to the set of *lie ding* to form an assemblage of a higher rank, as represented in M2010 and M2011 at Shangcunling. In other cases the number of *gui* remain higher than that of *ding*, such as M93 at Beizhao and M1 at Pingdingshan, which yielded five *ding* and six *gui*, and M8 at

FIGURE 2 *Hu* with dragon patterns, Early Springs and Autumns period. Photograph by the author.

Pingdingshan and M2010 and M1820 at Shangcunling, which contain three *ding* and four *gui*. Some tombs in the early phase of this period contain a set of coarsely made *mingqi* vessels in addition to the regular assemblage. These *mingqi* vessels often have an archaic air: many are similar to vessel types and styles seen in the Early Zhou period, as represented by the presence of *fang yi* 方彝, *jue* 爵, and *zhi* 觯. This practice stopped during the later phase of this period (Zhu 2009:1,557–1,587). These irregularities in assemblage of ritual vessels suggest certain flexibility or changes in the sumptuary rules among the ranked elite, probably initiated by regional rulers instead of the Zhou court.

The shape and decoration of bronze vessels of this period basically continued the style of the Late Western Zhou period with only minor changes. For instance, the *ding* usually have bowl-shaped bellies and thick legs that bulge out on the top and flare out on the bottom. Decor usually forms horizontal bands on the belly, with typical late Western Zhou patterns such as waves, scales, double rings, long-plumed birds, and squared dragon patterns (*qiequ wen* 窃曲纹) (Figure 3). The bodies of vessels of this period tend

Loops

Scales

Squared dragon patterns

FIGURE 3 Some typical decorative patterns on bronzes during the Early Springs and Autumns period. Modified after *Shangcunling Guoguo mudi*. Beijing: Kexue Chubanshe, 1959: figures 8 and 9.

to grow shorter and wider in proportion, and some new decorative designs appear, such as the dragon pattern with upturned snouts and curled bodies, often arranged in symmetrical rectangular units, in addition to linked dragons arranged into bands.

MIDDLE SPRINGS AND AUTUMNS PERIOD

If the bronzes of the Early Springs and Autumns period appear to be vestiges of the late Western Zhou style and even a decline in quality of production, those of the Middle Springs and Autumns period display signs of innovation and revitalization in assemblage, shape, and decoration. The vessel types in the assemblage become more standardized across different ranks of the aristocracy, and the often-sagging, rigid shapes and static, geometric patterns are replaced by more intricate and energized forms. The new casting technologies surely contributed to these changes: body and attachments were often cast separately and then welded together, and pattern blocks were used to print identical relief designs to cover large areas of the surface of bronze vessels. These new techniques not only transformed their shape and decoration but also improved the efficiency and quality of production and encouraged wider consumption of bronze artifacts due to their reduced cost. These new features reflected and facilitated the changes in social and economic structure of the period and embodied the energy and taste of the rising lower strata of the aristocracy.

The finds from foundry sites at Houma, Shanxi, including over 50,000 pieces of ceramic molds, illustrate many of the newly developed casting techniques and designs of the sixth and fifth centuries BCE, including pattern blocks and an efficient system of standardized and commercialized production (Shanxi 1993:441–452). The casting techniques and decorative vocabulary developed at Houma had a great impact on the surrounding regions in the Jin cultural sphere, which can be illustrated by bronzes found in Jin-affiliated states that have similar or identical decorative designs as those seen on the molds from Houma, such as the *hu* from Liyu 李峪, Hunyuan 浑源, Shanxi province (Figure 4). The Houma foundry site is part of the Jin capital site of Xintian (Shanxi 1996), occupied between the early sixth and early fourth centuries BCE. Tests and excavations since the 1950s have discovered eight walled cities, building foundations, cemeteries (including the Shangma cemetery), sacrificial sites, workshops, and residential sites. The scattered individual cities form a unique model of capital design that is different from the more common capital layout of this period, with one large walled city divided into a *gongcheng* 宫城 (palace city) and a *guocheng* 郭城 (outer city). It is possible that the three adjacent cities at Niucun 牛村, Pingwang 平望, and Taishen 台神 were used as palace cities, and the one at Chengwang 呈王 could be ancestral temples, while the smaller cities further away belonged to powerful ministers of the Jin (Xu 2000:88).

The site of the Wangcheng 王城 capital of the Eastern Zhou kings is situated near the confluence of the Luo 洛 and the Jian 涧 Rivers in present-day Luoyang, Henan Province. Archaeological work on this site has continued since the 1950s. Only partially

FIGURE 4 Bronze *hu* vessel from Liyu, Hunyuan, Shanxi province, Late Springs and Autumns period. Photograph by author.

explored, the city is roughly a square with the northern wall measuring 2,890 meters. Two large areas of pounded-earth platforms in the southwestern part of the city were identified as palace structures dated to the Springs and Autumns period (Zhongguo 1989:138–140; Xu 2000:31).

Since the Luoyang area was the Zhou royal domain during the Eastern Zhou period, discoveries in Luoyang are representative of the characteristics of the Central Plains area discussed in this section. So far over 7,000 tombs of the Eastern Zhou period have been excavated at Luoyang, most of which were located within the capital Wangcheng site (Jing and Wang 2013:308). One early and important discovery is the Zhongzhoulu 中州路 site excavated in 1954–1955. The 260 Eastern Zhou tombs excavated at the site span the entirety of the Eastern Zhou period. Nine tombs yielded bronze vessels, and 161 tombs contained ceramic vessels. The ceramic vessels were divided typologically into seven phases, the first three of which correspond to the Springs and Autumns period. The bronze vessels were divided into four phases, corresponding with the first four phases of the ceramic typology (Zhongguo 1959a). (For a more comprehensive and updated typological study of the ceramic vessels from the Luoyang area, see Zhang Xin 2002.) The chronological sequence established with the Zhongzhoulu material had been an important guiding reference for dating and study of other Eastern Zhou finds. Typical ceramic assemblages of the Early Springs and Autumns period (Phase 1) at Zhongzhoulu included *li* 鬲, *pen* 盆, and *guan* 罐, mostly practical utensils; during the middle period (Phase 2), the typical assemblage remained the same, but ceramic *mingqi* in imitation of bronze *ding* started to appear, and the practical utensils began to decline. This trend continued in the late period (Phase 3), when the typical assemblage changed to *ding*, *dou* 豆, and *guan* (Zhongguo 1989:140–145). This change indicates that starting from the Middle Springs and Autumns period, the privilege of using *ding* in funerary rituals had expanded to the common people outside the traditional aristocracy, and more burial customs were shared among tombs across all ranks. Later in the Warring States period, even the highest-ranking members of the aristocracy were buried with ceramic *mingqi* imitating bronze vessels.

More recent discoveries in the Luoyang area (Zhongguo 1985, 2002; Luoyang 1983, 20 01, 2009, 2011, 1999, 2002, 2003, 1981) include a looted large tomb with four ramps that is considered the tomb of King Ping (Ping Wang 平王), the first Zhou king to have ruled in the Wangcheng capital at Luoyang (Luoyang 2011). Based on their sizes and the number of ramps, these tombs were divided into five categories. All tombs are rectangular earthen-pit tombs. Tombs of the highest rank have four axial ramps; tombs of lesser ranks have two ramps (on the short sides), one ramp, or no ramp. Most tombs were equipped with from one to three layers of wooden chambers (*guo* 椁) or coffins (*guan* 棺), although some small tombs do not have any (Jing and Wang 2013:309). The size, number of ramps, layers of *guan* and *guo*, and richness of tomb offerings correlate and mark different ranks in the social hierarchy.

In addition to some tombs at the Shangguo and Shangma cemeteries discussed earlier, tombs dated to this Middle Springs and Autumns period include nine tombs from the Chengcun 程村 cemetery in Linyi 临猗, Shanxi (Zhongguo et al. 2003). Chengcun cemetery contains 226 tombs, 50 of which were excavated in the 1980s. The cemetery belonged to an aristocratic lineage in the state of Jin. Some other bronze-yielding tombs were found in Huixian 辉县 (Zhongguo 1956), Xinzheng 新郑 (Henan 2005), and Weishi 尉氏 (Zhengzhou 1982), all in Henan province.

The famous large tomb discovered by the locals at Lijialou 李家楼, Xinzheng 新郑, Henan in 1923, one of the earliest sensations of Eastern Zhou archaeology, also dates to this period. Due to the unscientific nature of its excavations and later political turmoil, the surviving bronze artifacts from this tomb were scattered in four different museums, totaling 102 items. The 63 ritual vessels from this tomb cover 10 vessel types, including 16 *ding*, 11 *gui*, and 4 *fanghu*. The richness of the furnishings and the size of the assemblage suggest that this tomb probably belonged to a ruler of the state of Zheng (Henan 2001). Bronze vessels from this tomb exhibit two distinct styles: the conservative style is similar to earlier examples such as those from Shangcunling, such as *li*, *yan*, and two sets of lidless *ding*. One set of 7 *ding*, however, all have lids, starting a new style of *ding*. The bodies of a pair of *fanghu* are decorated with intricately intertwined serpentine bodies of dragons and phoenixes; fantastic tigers support the base, and dragons climb up 4 edges of the body. The lids flare out into double rows of openwork lotus petals, with a naturalistically sculpted crane standing in the middle. The flamboyant new style of the Xinzheng bronzes contrasts sharply with the solemn appearance of the late Western Zhou and early Springs and Autumns vessels and suggests a different nature of the rituals involved and a more direct display of power and status among the regional rulers.

Other important finds of the Zheng state come from its capital city at Xinzheng, located at the confluence of the Shuangji River 双洎河 and the Huangshui River 黄水河. Zheng was annexed by Han in 375 BCE, and Han used the city as the capital until its own demise under the attacks by Qin in 230 BCE. The irregular, oblong walled city is divided into west or inner city (*cheng* 城) and east or outer city (*guo* 郭). Dense distribution of pounded-earth foundations in the north central part of the west city suggest that this is the palace city of this Zheng and Han capital. The large pounded-earth platform to their north, with wells and ceramic plumbing pipes, is a structure built during the Springs and Autumns period. Bronze, ceramic, and bone workshops are mainly located in the east city. Four cemeteries of the Springs and Autumns period have been found at the site; the two within the city mainly contain large tombs and the two to east and south include mostly small tombs (Henan 1980).

An important discovery at the Zheng capital at Xinzheng is 29 caches of bronze ritual vessels found at three locales. One of these sites includes 18 caches and yielded 142 bronze vessels and 206 bronze *zhong* bells. Four of the five intact caches with bronze vessels contain the same assemblage: nine *ding*, eight *gui*, nine *li*, one *dou*, two square *hu*, one *round hu* 圆壶, and one *jian* 鉴; the other cache only has nine *ding* and nine *li*. The similarities in their combination and style suggest that they were interred within a short period of time from each other. The 11 caches for bells seem to be arranged in groups of three, with each group matched to a vessel cache. Forty-five sacrificial pits were also found at the site, each with two or four horses buried inside. Based on its location and the surrounding features (lack of buildings nearby and enclosing walls), the excavators considered that this is probably a sacrificial site where the Zheng ruler worshiped the deities of earth and grain (*sheji* 社稷) (Henan 2000, 2006). This group of bronze vessels and bells is a good representative of the middle Springs and Autumns style of the Central Plains area because of its large quanitiy, high quality, and the completeness of vessel assamblages of the highest rank for state rituals.

Compared with the early period, the lower strata of the aristocracy seem to have acquired more ritual privileges, and their assemblage of bronze vessels became more standardized. In tombs with only one *ding*, the assemblage usually comprised *ding* 鼎, *dui* 敦, *he* (*zhou* 舟), *pan* 盘, and *yi* 匜, a complete assemblage with all four vessel categories: meat containers (*ding*), grain containers (*dui*), vessels for fermented alcoholic beverages (*he*), and water or washing vessels (*pan* and *yi*). In contrast, the typical bronze vessel assemblage among larger tombs is comprised of *ding, gui, he* (*zhou*), *pan*, and *yi*, and tombs with five or more *ding* often have *hu* 壶 in addition to *he* (*zhou*) for alcoholic beverage vessels (Gao 1981:79). Members of the upper ranks of the aristocracy buried in large tombs have more conservative vessels types, such as *li, yan*, and *gui*, and their styles still follow the late Western Zhou prototypes. Lower ranks of the aristocracy used *dui* to replace *gui* as grain containers in the assemblage. The bronze vessel assemblages for different ranks grew increasingly homogeneous, and by the end of the Springs and Autumns period tombs of all ranks usually contain the typical assamblage of *ding, dou, hu, pan*, and *yi* (Gao 1981:79). This trend suggests the rigid boundaries between the different aristocratic ranks started to be blurred since the Middle Springs and Autumns period, and the lower strata of the elite, especially the *shi* class, started to play more significant roles in the social-political system. (For an analysis of the *shi* class see chapter 30 by Andrew Meyer).

Unlike the *ding* of previous centuries, *ding* vessels of this period usually have lids, and large tombs often have more than one set of *ding*, each set in a different shape and style. *Hu* vessels (both square and round) still have a long neck with two handles with rings, and a drooping body sitting on a ring-foot. Some *hu* lid rims are decorated with open-work interlaced patterns (*panchi wen* 蟠螭纹) or lotus petals. Relief patterns of interlacing serpents and dragons (*panchi wen* and *panhui wen* 蟠虺纹), rendered in thin lines, started to become the dominant decorative vocabulary, usually arranged in horizontal bands on the body surface of bronze vessels (Zhu Fenghan 1994:158). The thick intertwining dragon relief patterns (*long wen* 龙纹) were still seen, as represented on square *hu* from the caches at Xinzheng.

LATE SPRINGS AND AUTUMNS PERIOD

During the first half of the Late Springs and Autumns period (ca. second half of the sixth century BCE), the basic bronze vessel assemblage and style remained the same as the previous period, while certain trends of change started in the previous period continued to develop. Major discoveries dated to this period include three tombs (M2008, M1006, M1026) at the Shangma cemetery in Houma; five tombs (M0003, M1002, M1023, M1064, M1082) at Chengcun, Linyi; three tombs (58M1, 62M1, 62M5) from Miaoqiancun 庙前村, Wanrong 万荣; and two tombs (M269, M270) from Fengshuiling 分水岭, Changzhi 长治, all Jin tombs in Shanxi province. Zhou tombs include two tombs (LBM4, C1M7258) in Luoyang (Shanxi 1994b; Zhongguo et al. 2003; Shanxi 1996b; Bian and Li 1974; Zhongguo 1985; Zhu Fenghan 1994:1,618). Although tomb size and the number and type of vessels buried in each tomb varied significantly, a core assemblage of *ding*, *dui*, *he* (*zhou*), *pan*, and *yi* was shared across different ranks, continuing the homogenizing trend in ritual activities performed by different ranks of the aristocracy. The number of lidless *ding* continued to dwindle and only appeared in large tombs (such as Fengshuiling M269 and M270).

Among bronze-yielding tombs dated to the second half of the Late Springs and Autumns period (ca. first half of the fifth century BCE), the two large tombs (*jia mu* 甲墓 and *yi mu* 乙墓) excavated in the 1930s at Liulige 琉璃阁, Huixian 辉县, Henan probably belong to a ruler of Wey 卫 and his consort (Guo 1959; Guoli 2003; Henan 2011; Guo 1981). Another opinion maintains that the Liulige tombs belong to the Jin ministers from the Fan lineage (Song 2007: 17–21; Yu 1985). Other tombs include M55 and M60 at Liulige (Guo 1959, 1981); five tombs at Shangma (M12, M1001, M1004, M1072, M4006; Shanxi 1994); four tombs from Linyi (Zhongguo et al. 2003); four tombs from Luoyang (M2729, Zhongguo 1959a; M439, Luoyang 2002; M535, Zhongguo 2002; C1M7039, Luoyang 2003 after Zhu 1994:1,632); and one tomb from Shangguo. In terms of the ritual vessel assemblage, the most important change is the rising dominance of the lidded *dou*, which was almost ubiquitous in all assemblages. It replaced *dui* as the main grain container, although *dui* can still be found in tombs with five or more *ding*. Thus, a new core assemblage was formed and shared by tombs of all different ranks: *ding*, *dou*, *he* (*zhou*), *pan*, and *yi*. It also appears that *hu* vessels were often added to the *he* (*zhou*) as wine containers among the middle- and lower-ranking aristocracy (tombs with three *ding* or less). Among these, the round belly *hu* became more popular than the square belly *hu* (*fanghu*). By the Early Warring States period *hu* already replaced *he* (*zhou*), and *ding, dou, hu, pan,* and *yi* became the constituents of the new standard assemblage. Meanwhile, more conservative vessel types and shapes were still used in addition to the new ones in the largest tombs, such as the lidless *ding,* the *gui* with three short legs, and *fanghu* seen in the large tombs at Liulige. These observations suggest that changes and innovations in assemblage, vessel type, style, and decoration were initiated by the lower strata of the aristocracy, and the aristocracy of the highest rank reluctantly followed the lead while hanging on to the old ritual privileges embodied by archaic vessel types and styles. These changes were not only results of, but also a means for, the modification of the existing ritual system, and the rising influence of the new elite who served as ministers and officials of the traditional ruling houses.

The position of the bulbous belly's girth gradually moved upward through this period, relieving the sagging feeling of earlier examples, and lids decorated with lotus-petals grew more popular. The thin and dense *panchi* pattern is still the most common decoration, and variations of the *panchi* pattern started to become more popular, including the thick-bodied forms (such as Liulige M55 *jian*) and the angular forms (such as Liulige Jia mu 甲墓 *dou* and Shangma M1004 *ding*). Colored inlay started to appear as a new decorative technique, such as the copper inlay seen on the flat *hu* from Jia mu at Liulige. Another new decorative method that became popular during this period was engraving thin lines with a sharp tool (probably a steel needle) on surfaces of thin-walled water containers, mostly *jian* and *yi,* to depict pictorial scenes such as archery, hunting, banquets, and ritual ceremonies (for examples see Ye 1983; Zhang Guangli 1983; Song 2002; Weber 1966). This is one of the earliest forms of pictorial art in China known to us through archaeological remains.

It is fitting to wrap up this period with the rich and exquisite finds from M251 at Jinshengcun 金胜村, Taiyuan 太原, Shanxi, an intact rectangular earthen-pit tomb dated to the mid-fifth century BCE (end of the Springs and Autumns period or beginning of the Warring States period) (Shanxi 1996; Hou 1989; Qu 1989). The tomb chamber was lined with rocks and charcoal and was accompanied by an L-shaped pit filled with 44 horses and 15 chariots. Among over 3,000 artifacts from this tomb are 99 bronze ritual vessels, 2 sets of bronze bells, and a large number of weapons. The bronzes were decorated with masterfully executed designs in low and high relief and probably represent the best examples of the production from the foundry at Houma due to their similarity to excavated ceramic molds from that site. The deceased, around 70 years old, was probably a lineage head of the Zhao clan. one of the powerful ministerial families that would replace the Jin ruling house derived from the Ji clan at the end of this period. The tomb owner could be either Zhao Jianzi 赵简子 (d. 475 BCE) or his son Zhao Xiangzi 赵襄子 (d. 425 BCE) (Shanxi 1996; Hou 1989; Qu 1989), Among the 27 *ding* found in this tomb are 3 sets of *sheng ding* (7, 6, 5 *ding* each); the largest set of 7 *ding* signifies a rank below regional ruler (*zhuhou* 诸侯) of the Middle and Late Springs and Autumns period. The numbers of chariots, horses, and weapons, however, greatly exceed those of other tombs of regional rulers. By the end of this period, the content, quantity, and quality of grave furnishings were no longer determined by aristocratic rank but by the amount of power and resources at the patron's command.

THE SHANDONG AREA: QI, LU, JÜ, AND OTHERS

Qi 齐 and Lu 鲁 were the two most important regional states in the east established by the Zhou at the beginning of the Western Zhou period (Table 3). Qi was the fief of the Jiang 姜 clan in modern-day Shandong 山东 Province, ruling from the capital city of Linzi 临淄 (ca. 859 to 221 BCE), located in Linzi 临淄 District, Zibo 淄博, Shandong (Shandong 1961; Qun 1972; Shandong 2013). Flanked by two rivers and covering around 20 square kilometers, Linzi has a large walled city with a small walled city embedded in its southwest corner. The small city and its large building foundations probably belong to the new palace city built by the Tian 田 clan rulers who replaced the Jiang clan in the early fourth century BCE during the Warring States period, while the earlier palaces were probably located at the north-central part of the large city (Xu 2000:99–100). In addition to various foundry and workshop sites and settlements, the cemetery of the Qi ruling house of the Jiang clan was found at the Heyatou 河崖头 site at the northeast part of the large city, where more than 20 large tombs were found, some with two ramps. One of them, M5, is a large tomb (chamber size 614 m²) with one ramp and a tomb chamber

Table 3 Representative burial sites and tombs: The Shandong area

Site Name	State Affiliation	Date of Site: E, M, or L Springs and Autumns	Significant Tombs	Important Features or Main Assemblage (m=mingqi)	Date of Tombs: E, M, or L Springs and Autumns
Heyatou cemetery, Linzi, Shandong	Qi		M5	Over 600 horses	L
Qufu, Shandong	Lu	E-L			
MD2 and Dongxiaogong, Tengzhou, Shandong	Xue	E-L			
Dadian, Jünan, Shandong	Jü		M2	Human sacrifices	M
			M1	Human sacrifices	L
Liujiadianzi, Yishui, Shandong	Jü		M1	11 *ding* (including a set of 9 *ding*), human sacrifices	M
Dongjiangcun cemetery, Zaozhuang, Shandong	Xiao Zhu			Human sacrifices	
Xianrentai cemetery, Changqing, Shandong	Shi		M5	Human sacrifices 3 *ding*, 2 *dui*, 2 *zhou*, 1 *hu*, 1 *pan*, 9 bells	M

encased with rocks. Although the tomb chamber and the storage pit to its north were both looted, the unique U-shaped sacrificial pit around the tomb contains over 600 horses. Dated to the Late Springs and Autumns period based on pottery, this large tomb must have belonged to a Qi ruler, probably Jing Gong 景公 (Shandong 1984a). Large Qi tombs of the Eastern Zhou period usually have ramps, a stone chamber, and horse or horse-and-chariot pits near the tomb. Starting from the Late Springs and Autumns period, Qi tombs usually have wooden boxes or storage pits for grave goods on the raised earthen ledges (*ercengtai* 二层台) built along the walls of the chamber, and human sacrifices with their own coffins and grave goods were often put on the ledge (Jin 1994). Some of those burial practices, such as human sacrifices and storage pits around the tomb chamber, as well as certain ceramic vessel types in Qi tombs, were results of contacts with Yi 夷 cultures in eastern Shandong (Wang Xun 1994:103–105). During the Early Springs and Autumns period, bronze vessel assemblages from Qi tombs resemble those in the Central Plains area, such as *ding, li, fu* 簠, *pan*, and *yi*, but certain vessel types were missing, such as *gui, pu* 铺, and *hu*. By the Late Springs and Autumns period, although part of the Qi bronze assemblage still resembled those of the Central Plains area (*ding, dui,* and *he; pan* and *yi* were often missing), more unique Qi-style vessels started to appear, such as the *ding* with tall legs and flat lids, and round *hu* with chain handles (Zhu 1994:1,680–1,683).

Sites for salt production were found in various locations in the coastal area in northern Shandong, mostly in Weifang 潍坊 and Binzhou 滨州. Many pots with round or pointed bottoms found at these sites, from Late Shang through Eastern Zhou periods, were probably used as boilers for making sea salt and were probably also used for the transportation and measuring of salt as a commodity (Fang 2004; Liu and Lan 2009). Archaeological finds and historical texts both suggest that salt production and trade played an important role in the Qi economy.

The capital city of Lu is located in the city of Qufu 曲阜, Shandong. The walled city, around 10 square kilometers, is shaped as an irregular rectangle, with three gates on each side of the city wall (except the south side, which has two gates), and five avenues running north-south and five running east-west (Shandong 1982). Lu was the fief awarded to the Duke of Zhou, King Wu's brother who also acted as the regent during the early years of King Cheng's reign (1042–1006), but his son Boqin 伯禽 was the one who actually ruled in Lu. Due to the lack of early Western Zhou remains in the city, some scholars maintain that Qufu did not become the capital until the second half of the tenth century. The concentration of large building foundations at the center of the city suggests the location of the palaces, but no palace city wall has yet been identified, suggesting a different layout from other capitals of this period. However, a small city was probably partitioned out at the southwest part of the city as the palace city during the Warring States period (Xu 2000:95–97). Ten workshops for iron, bronze, ceramic, and bone artifacts, six cemeteries, and 11 settlement sites have been found within the city, spanning the whole period of its occupation from middle Western Zhou to 249 BCE, when Lu was annexed by Chu.

The 158 Zhou-period tombs in the Lu capital city of Qufu were divided into two groups (Jia 甲 and Yi 乙) based on differences in their location, burial practices, and grave goods. Group Jia tombs are more numerous, and are mostly small tombs (early tombs usually have waist pits and sacrificial dogs) with a rich variety of pottery vessels. Group Yi tombs have no waist pits or sacrificial dogs and usually only have *li* and *guan* ceramic vessels. Group Yi tombs of the late Western Zhou or Springs and Autumns include some large tombs furnished with bronze vessels (M48, M30) (Shandong 1982).

Reflecting two different groups of population in the city, the Jia group tombs are believed to belong to descendants of the local Yi 夷 peoples which were non-Zhou groups who lived in this region and further to the east even before Lu was established, and the Yi group tombs probably belonged to the aristocratic Ji clan of the Zhou (Zhang Xuehai 1985). Patrons of Group Yi tombs enjoyed higher social status compared to those of Group Jia. The distinction between the colonizing Zhou lineages and Yi peoples at Qufu continued throughout the Western Zhou and Springs and Autumns periods. Most Lu bronzes of the Springs and Autumns period were found in and around the capital, and most are dated to the eighth and seventh centuries (Qi 1972; Zhu Hua 1973; Shandong 1982). The basic assemblage and shape of bronze vessels are similar to those of the Central Plains, except for a type of *hu* vessel with short neck, egg-shaped body, and loop-handle attachments, which probably was formed due to the influence of the Yi "aboriginal" groups in Eastern Shandong (Zhu 1994:1,654–1,659).

Many recent, exciting discoveries in southern Shandong, south of Qi and Lu, belong to the ancient states of the Yi 夷 groups in this region, such as Xue 薛, Zhu 邾, and Jü 莒, known in historical texts and bronze inscriptions as local states that existed since the Shang period. The old city of Xue in Tengzhou 滕州, Shandong, 5 km by 3.5 km in size, was probably built during the Middle Springs and Autumns period; a smaller city is located at the southeast corner inside the larger city and could be as early as the Late Shang or Early Western Zhou periods. Various settlements, workshops, and cemeteries were found in the city (Shangdong 1991, 1994). The cemetery MD2 north of the small city was probably that of the Xue lords and aristocratic lineages. Smaller tombs were also found at Dongxiaogong 东小宫 in Tengzhou (Shandong 2000). Xue tombs are mostly earthen-pit tombs with wooden coffins and chambers; many have ledges on one side, storage pits, and sacrificial humans, which are considered characteristics of burial practices of the Yi culture (Wang Xun 1994:110). Xue bronze assemblages and styles are similar to the Central Plains finds of the same period, indicating strong influences of Zhou culture, but some vessels started to show unique characters since the Middle Springs and Autumns period, such as pairs of one short and one tall *ding* with flat lids, *li* with pointed legs, and a flat *hu* with loop handles (Zhu Fenghan 1994:1,659–1,6563).

Jü was the most powerful of the Yi states in southeastern Shandong during the Springs and Autumns period. We still know little of the Jü capital city found in Jüxian 莒县 County, but many tombs of the Jü state have been excavated, including the large tombs at Dadian 大店 in Jünan 莒南 County (Shandong 1978), and Liujiadianzi 刘家店子 in Yishui 沂水 County (Shandong 1984b). During the Early Springs and Autumns period, Jü bronzes are similar in style to the Central Plains examples (see e.g., finds from the tomb at Xidazhuang 西大庄, Jüxian; Jüxian Bowuguan 1999).

The bronze trident-shaped objects from M1 at Xidazhuang 西大庄, Jüxian were probably a type of coffin decoration called *sha* 翣 in later ritual texts. Jü bronzes exhibited strong local characteristics during the Middle Springs and Autumns period, including the Yi-style *li* with tall, pointed, hollow legs; *dou* with openwork stems and flower-petal-shaped lids; and little jars with a bird cast in the round on the lid. In addition, the nine *ding* vessels from M2 at Liujiadianzi are identical in shape, decoration, and size, differing from the graduated size of the *ding* sets in the Central Plains area (Zhu Fenghan 1994:1,702–1,719). During the Late Springs and Autumns period, Jü bronzes exhibit a strong influence of Chu-style bronzes due to the advance of Chu power in southern Shandong. Jü tomb chambers were often divided into two parts: a burial chamber with coffins and a wooden storage chamber for grave goods. Most tombs were oriented to the east, and large tombs often have sacrificial humans and waist pits with a dog, all features characterizing Yi-culture burials. Late Springs and Autumns Jü tombs also show Chu features, as in the use of fine clay to seal wooden chambers.

The two large tombs at Jiwanggu 纪王崮 in Yishui excavated in 2012–2013 are an unusual discovery yet to be published; both tombs were excavated from living rock on the flat top of a rocky hill, and one of them is unfinished and unoccupied. The chamber of the occupied tomb, 40 by 13 meters in size with a ramp on the southeast side, probably belonged to a high-ranking member of the Jü aristocracy (Quanguo 2014). Another rather unique feature of this tomb is that both the tomb chamber and the horse-and-chariot pit are located in the same pit, and one of the four chariots carried three ritual vessels: a *ding*, a *li*, and a *dui*. The over 200 artifacts found in the tomb include bronze ritual vessels, *zhong* bells, and jade items. The presence of ledges, storage boxes, three sacrificial humans, and a waist pit with a dog are typical Jü tomb features. Another regional culture is located further east in the Jiaodong 胶东 peninsula, in counties such as Longkou 龙口, Penglai 蓬莱, Qixia 栖霞, and Haiyang 海阳. These finds probably were associated with the indigenous Lai 莱 state of the local Yi people in historical records (Wang Xun 1994:96–102). A city with a heavily fortified outer city and a smaller L-shaped inner city, measuring 10 square kilometers in size, found near the coast in Longkou 龙口 (Li and Lin 1991; Zhongmei 2011), was probably the center of the Lai state, a rival of the Qi until the end of the Middle Springs and Autumns period (Lai was conquered by Qi in 567 BCE). Just like other finds of the Yi peoples, the burial practice and material culture are a continuation of the Yi culture of the Shang period in this region, and the pottery and bronzes contain many local characteristics, suggesting the existence of a local bronze-casting industry (Zhu 1994:1,702).

In addition to Xue, Jü, and Lai, other finds in Shandong belonging to the Yi states include six tombs at Dongjiangcun 东江村, Zaozhuang 枣庄 (Zaozhuang 2007), and six tombs at Xianrentai 仙人台, Changqing 长清 (Shandong 1998; Ren 1998), related to the states of Xiao Zhu 小邾 and Shi 邿, respectively. Those tombs usually contain sacrificial humans; the vessel types in assemblages often appear in even numbers; and their grave goods often contain vessel types unseen in other regions, such as the little bronze jar with a chain handle and lid, often topped by a bird cast in the round, features considered characteristic of the Yi peoples (Wang Qing 2002). Nonetheless, that the elite adopted status symbols of the Zhou culture in their own society is shown through some Zhou-style bronze vessel types and styles in large tombs. The Zhou ritual system and bronzes were not simply adopted but modified in creating a new, hybrid culture.

The Yangzi and Huai River Valleys: Chu, Wu, and others (Table 4)

According to statistics of 10 years ago, over 6,000 Chu tombs have been excavated, constituting 75% of excavated Eastern Zhou–period tombs. Today, excavated Chu tombs exceed over 10,000 in number (Jing and Wang 2013:379). Only a small portion of them are dated to the Springs and Autumns period, and most of them are located in southern Henan and Northern Hubei along the middle reaches of the Han River. Chu power quickly expanded to the south and east during the Warring States period, and areas where Chu tombs were found extended to Hunan and Anhui provinces.

Chu moved its capital six times during the Eastern Zhou period (Li Xueqin and Chang 1985:163–164). Sixty-six Chu cities have been found, and among them the city of Chuhuangcheng 楚皇城 in Yicheng 宜城 (Chuhuangcheng 1980), and the city at Jijiahu 季家湖 in Dangyang 当阳 (Hubei 1980), both in Hubei province, were probably capital cities of Chu during the Springs and Autumns period. Although the city walls at Chuhuangcheng (2.2 km²) were dated to the Warring States period, the city was built on a large settlement of the Eastern Zhou period comprised of over 80 residential sites and cemeteries, and this region could have been the location of Ying 郢, an early Chu capital recorded in historical texts (Hubei 1992:160–216). Ying is actually a general name used by Chu for all its capital cities. The city at Jijiahu (2.24 km²) is further south near the Yangzi River. A large Chu cemetery was found 10 kilometers to its north at Zhaojiahu 赵家湖 in Dangyang, and several kilometers to its west in Zhijiang 枝江 were some large Chu tombs covered with huge mounds. In addition to those cemeteries, other scattered Chu tombs of the Springs and Autumns period were found in Yunxian 郧县, Dangyang, Zhijiang, Jiangling, and Macheng 麻城 (Jing and Wang 2013:373–375).

Chu tombs of the Springs and Autumns period excavated so far are earthen-pit tombs without ramps or tomb mounds, and the large tombs usually have a wooden chamber and a coffin (some have nested coffins or side-by-side coffins). Around 300 tombs were excavated at the Zhaojiahu cemetery, spanning continuously from the Late Western Zhou to Late Warring States periods, establishing a chronological sequence of tombs of the lower strata in the social hierarchy (Zhu 1994:1,789–1,797). Most are small tombs for commoners; the nine tombs with bronze vessels dated to the Springs and Autumns period belong to low-ranking aristocrats. In addition to bronze vessels, five of those nine tombs also contained a set of polished black ceramic mingqi vessels (ding, ding-shaped vessel, gui, li, dou, guan) or a set of utilitarian red-brown ceramic vessels. By the Late Springs and Autumns period tombs with bronze vessels no longer contained polished black ceramic mingqi vessels, and tombs furnished with only black ceramic vessels

Table 4 Representative burial sites and tombs: The Yangzi and Huai River Valleys

Site Name	State Affiliation	Date of Site: E, M, or L Springs and Autumns	Significant Tombs	Important Features or Main Assemblage (m=mingqi)	Date of Tombs: E, M, or L Springs and Autumns
Zhaojiahu, Dangyang, Hubei	Chu	E-L			
Shanwan, Xiangyang, Hubei	Chu	M-L			
Xiasi, Xichuan, Henan	Chu	M-L	M1		
			M2	19 *ding* (including a set of 7 *sheng ding*)	M/L
Heshangling, Xichuan, Henan	Chu		M1	6 *ding*	M
			M2	7 *ding*, 17 bells	L
Xujialing, Xichuan, Henan	Chu		M3, M9		L
Guojiamiao, Zaoyang, Hubei	Zeng	E			
Wenfengta cemetery, Suizhou, Hubei	Zeng	M-L	M1, M21, M33		
Baoxiangsi, Guangshan, Henan	Huang		Tombs of Huang Jun Meng and Meng Ji	Huang Jun Meng's chamber: 2 *ding*, 2 *dou*, 2 *hu*, 2 *lei*, 1 *pan*, 1 *yi*; Meng Ji's chamber: 2 *ding*, 2 *dou*, 2 *hu*, 2 *lei*, 2 *he*, 2 *li*, 1 *pan*, 1 *yi*	E
Shouxian, Anhui	Cai		Tomb of Cai Hou Shen	17 *ding* (including a set of 7 *sheng ding*), 8 *gui*, 8 *li*	L
Caijiagang, Huainan, Anhui	Cai		Tomb of Cai Hou Chan M2	Looted/incomplete	L
Jiuxian, Yexian, Henan	Xǔ		M4		L
Yuehe,Tongbai, Henan	Yang		M1		L
Zhiyangling, Pingdingshan, Henan	Ying		M301		L
Wangpo, Xiangfan, Hubei	Deng				E
Shucheng, Anhui	Qun Shu				
Dafudun, Danyang, Jiangsu	Wu				E

(Continued)

Table 4 Representative burial sites and tombs: The Yangzi and Huai River Valleys (Continued)

Site Name	State Affiliation	Date of Site: E, M, or L Springs and Autumns	Significant Tombs	Important Features or Main Assemblage (m=*mingqi*)	Date of Tombs: E, M, or L Springs and Autumns
Liangshan, Dantu, Jiangsu	Wu		M2		M
Beishanding, Dantu, Jiangsu	Wu				L
Zhenshan, Suzhou, Jiangsu	Wu		D9 M1	Jade face covering and funerary shroud	L
Hougudui, Gushi, Henan	Wu		M1	9 *ding* (3 sets of 3 *ding*), 17 bells	L
Chengqiao cemetery, Liuhe, Jiangsu	Wu		M1, M2, M3		L
Jiunüdun, Pizhou, Jiangsu	Xú		M3		L
Potang, Shaoxing, Zhejiang	Yue		M306	Looted/incomplete	L
Yinshan, Shaoxing, Zhejiang	Yue			Looted/incomplete	L

have a different assemblage (*li, yu* 盂, *dou, guan*; for further references see Zhu 1994:1,789–1,797). These differences suggest a cultural change that was probably caused by the shift of Chu power from the region to the new capital of Ying 郢 in Jingzhou 荆州 (Hubei 1992:160–216), which was first built in the Late Springs and Autumns period (Falkenhausen 1999:514–516). Starting from the Warring States period, ceramic vessels in imitation of bronze ritual vessels became the main tomb furnishing at Zhangjiahu. The cemetery at Shanwan 山湾 in Xiangyang 襄阳, Hubei also contained 14 tombs dated to the Middle and Late Springs and Autumns periods, and the five bronze-yielding tombs, with two or less *ding* in the assemblage, belong to low-ranking aristocrats (Hubei 1983).

Excavations at the Xiasi 下寺 cemetery in Xichuan 淅川, Henan in 1978 revealed nine large tombs, 15 small tombs, and five horse-and-chariot pits. The adjacent tombs M1 and M2 are the largest among them and were considered paired tombs of husband (M2) and wife (M1) based on grave goods and inscriptions. The smaller tomb on the other side of M2 probably belonged to another consort. No ceramic vessels were found in the nine large tombs. Bronzes from M2 include two sets of seven identical *ding*. One set of seven large *ding* (Figure 5) have flat bottoms and concave contours, and their bodies bear inscriptions identifying the patron as Wang Zi Wu 王子午, or "Prince Wu," while the inscriptions on their lids include the name Peng 佣, which also appeared on many other

FIGURE 5 *Ding* of Wang Zi Wu from M2 at the Xiasi cemetery, Xichuan, Henan, mid-sixth century BCE. Photographs by author.

bronze vessels from M2, as the owner (Henan 1991). The tomb-owner Peng was identified as Yuan Zifeng 薳子冯, a *lingyin* 令尹 or chief minister of Chu who died in 548 BCE (Li Ling 1981). M2 also yielded a *ding* with an oval contour and a small opening with a lid, and the inscription reads "Chu Shu zhi sun Peng 楚叔之孙佣" or "the descendant of a minor branch of the Chu ruling lineage." The Xiasi tombs probably belonged to the Yuan family, a high-ranking aristocratic lineage. The bronzes from M2 of Yuan Zifeng were impressive not only due to their number and "monumental" size but also because of their rather flamboyant, baroque style with intricate writhing animals attached on the bodies of *ding* and *li* vessels; the bronze *jin* 禁 altar table from M2 is the earliest example of the use of the lost-wax casting technique, which reached its full-fledged expression in the *zun* 尊 and *pan* from the tomb of Zeng Hou Yi of the Warring States period. The innovative energy seen in those bronzes suggests not only the rising power of Chu but also the personal aspiration and power of their patrons.

Two large tombs (M1 and M2) were found at Heshangling 和尚岭, 400 meters east of the Xiasi tombs (Henan 2004b). Six *ding* were the primary remaining artifacts in the looted M1, and the intact M2 yielded a bronze vessel assemblage including seven *ding*, a set of nine *niuzhong* 钮钟 bells, a set of eight *bo* 镈 bells, and a set of 12 *qing* 磬 chime stones. Based on studies of inscriptions on bronzes from both tombs, they were considered tombs of the same Yuan lineage buried at Xiasi and were dated to the end of the Springs and Autumns period. The date of the two tombs at Heshangling is still under debate (Henan 2004b:118–119). The 10 tombs excavated at the Xujialing 徐家岭 cemetery, three kilometers north of Heshangling, include two Springs and Autumns–period tombs (M3 and M9) (Henan 2004b:118–119), with bronze inscriptions suggesting this is another cemetery of the Yuan (or Wei 蒍) lineage. Many bronzes from M3 and M9 bear the name Yuan Zishou 薳子受 as the patron, the same name appearing on many bronzes from M2 at Heshangling. It is not clear why bronzes commissioned by Yuan Zishou were scattered in three different tombs; they were probably given to or inherited by his family members.

Noteworthy here are two copper-inlaid bronze *hu* from M2 at Heshangling and a pair of bronze feline-like animals cast in the round from M9 at Xujialing. The simple copper inlay of individual animal patterns and geometric forms seen on the *yu fou* 浴缶 from M2 at Xiasi had developed into multiple registers of designs covering the whole surface of the two *hu*, representing fantastic animals and birds and combats between humans and animals. The bronze feline figures, probably bases for a drum, have dragon heads with lolling tongues, tiger bodies, and flat flipper-like feet. They each have six dragons writhing on their heads and support a smaller feline on their back, which in turned holds a horned serpent in their mouth. Both were inlaid with turquoise in patterns of birds, serpents, and tigers.

The variety of Chu bronze vessels is slightly different from those in the Central Plains area, and the bronze assemblage is slightly different too. The bronze vessels in tombs of the first half of the Springs and Autumns period are simple, incomplete assemblages, usually consisting of a *ding* and a *gui* and sometimes a *zhan*, a vessel type rarely seen outside the Chu cultural sphere. In the second half of this period the assemblage became more diverse, and *fu* and *zhan* became popular; by the end of this period *fu* and *dui* had replaced *gui* and *zhan* as the main food vessels to match the *ding*. However, the *dou*, which became the main food container in the assemblages of the Late Springs and Autumns period in the Central Plains area, are not seen in Chu tombs. In addition to water vessels *pan* and *yi*, the *yu fou* 浴缶 was added as a water container (Figure 6), while *jian* was not included.

FIGURE 6 *Yu fou* excavated at Xiaojiayuan, Yunxian, Hubei, Middle Springs and Autumns period. Photograph by author.

Food vessel *yan* and *li* and wine vessels *lei* 罍, *hu*, and *he* are rarely seen (Zhu 1994:1,797–1,798). *Ding* is the most important type of ritual vessel in Chu tombs, and they can be divided into five to seven different types (Gao Chongwen 1983; Liu Binhui 1995:110–139). The most characteristic Chu vessel is the *sheng ding* 升鼎 with a squeezed waist and a flat bottom, a type of *ding* only found in Chu tombs and areas with strong Chu influence, such as tombs of Zeng 曾 and Cai 蔡 states. The earliest example of this type of *ding* is probably the Ke Huang 克黄 *ding* from M1 at Heshangling, which can be dated shortly before 605 BCE. Some scholars believe that the Chu style *sheng ding* has roots in the form of a *ding* from Liujiaya in Suizhou and even older roots in late Western Zhou *ding* of the flat-bottomed type (see Zhang Changping 2009:208–224). The largest examples are the aforementioned Wang Zi Wu *ding* from M2 at Xiasi. This Chu-style *sheng ding* continues to be popular during the Warring States period. Another unique type of Chu *ding* was the *tang ding* 汤鼎, such as the one from M2 at Xiasi with the inscription "Chu Shu zhi sun Peng." They were also found in M1 and M3 at Xiasi and the tomb of Cai Hou Shen 蔡侯申 in Shouxian 寿县, Anhui, but their origin can probably be traced to similar *ding* in tombs further east along the Yangzi River in Anhui (Anhui 2006; Liu Binhui 1995:132–133; Zhu 1994:1,798). They were probably used for boiling hot water for ritual baths (see Liu 1995:130–133; Li Ling 1983). These features indicate that although Chu adopted the Zhou system of ritual and symbols of social status, the Chu elite started to emphasize some local characteristics in ritual activities and aesthetic preferences that were different from those of the Zhou and the Ji clan states. Those trends indicate a strong sense of cultural confidence, autonomy, and even rivalry vis-à-vis the Zhou court at Luoyang and the Ji clan states. Nevertheless, Chu finds participated in the same Huaxia culture (see Falkenhausen 2006:166–167; Li Feng 2013:180–182) that started to form during this period among the regional states that shared the heritage left by the Western Zhou.

Zeng, a polity located in Suizhou 随州, Hubei along the Yunshui 涢水 River, is an ancient state that existed since the Late Shang period (Zhang Changping 2009:372). The most renowned discovery of this polity is the early Warring States tomb of Zeng Hou Yi 曾侯乙 at Leigudun 擂鼓墩 in Suizhou (Hubei 1989). Earlier Zeng finds, including 29 tombs excavated at Guojiamiao 郭家庙 in Zaoyang 枣阳, Hubei in 2002, prove to be Zeng tombs of the Late Western Zhou and Early Springs and Autumns periods (Xiangfanshi 2005). The tombs include a pair of looted large tombs with one ramp on the east side, one of which contains a bronze ax with an inscription identifying Zeng Bo Yi 曾伯陭 as the patron. Other tombs exhibit a great variety of different sizes and richness in grave goods, indicating that this cemetery was used by members of different social ranks associated with this Zeng aristocratic lineage. A cemetery was discovered at Yejiashan 叶家山 in Suizhou in 2011, and the ensuing work at the site has excavated 140 tombs of the Early Western Zhou period, including three pairs of tombs of Zeng rulers and their consorts, including Zeng Hou Jian 曾侯谏 and Zeng Hou Kang 犺 (Hubei 2013). In 2009, two disturbed late Springs and Autumns tombs (M1 and M2) were excavated at the Wenfengta 文峰塔 cemetery in Suizhou. The remaining bronze artifacts of M1 include bronze bells with long inscriptions, one of which bears 169

FIGURE 7 Detail of the inscription on the bronze bell from M1 at the Zeng state cemetery at Wenfengta, Suizhou, Hubei province. Late Springs and Autumns period. Photograph by author.

characters (Figure 7). The inscriptions suggest that the bells were cast by Zeng Hou Yu 與 (Marquis Yu of Zeng), and the text also recounts a historical event that took place in 506 BCE: the state of Wu attacked Chu and entered the Chu capital Ying, and the Chu king fled to Zeng for refuge. The location of Zeng Hou Yu's tomb (M1) suggests that the Wenfengta cemetery is the burial place for Zeng rulers of the Springs and Autumns period (Hubei 2014a). The excavations at Wenfengta in Suizhou in 2012 and 2013 revealed 54 Eastern Zhou tombs that are part of a Zeng cemetery from the Middle Springs and Autumns to the Early Warring States periods. A bronze *pan* with traces of flowing wax from M33 gave new evidence for the use of the lost-wax casting technique in the state of Zeng during the Springs and Autumns period (Hubei 2014b). The *ge* dagger from M21 with the inscription 隨大司馬嘉有之行戈, "the traveling *ge* dagger ax of Jia You, Grand Minister of War of Sui," was found with bronzes inscribed with 曾孫 邵 "Shao, descendent of the (house of) Zeng" (Hubei 2014b; Huang 2014). As the first known bronze inscribed with the state name Sui 隨, this will surely stir up new debates on the mysterious relationship between two polity names that seem to overlap with each other both spatially and temporally, namely the Zeng known through archaeological finds, and the Sui known in historical texts. Most scholars now believe that Zeng and Sui were one and the same polity. Zeng was a polity established by the Ji clan, and Zeng bronzes of the Early and Middle Springs and Autumns period conform largely to those of the Central Plains area in style and combination but by the Late Springs and Autumns period started to show stronger similarities with Chu bronzes. This growing affiliation with Chu style indicates the gradual domination of Zeng by Chu during the Springs and Autumns period.

Zeng was one of the dozens of small polities located in the Han 汉 and Huai 淮 River Valleys that were annexed by Chu during the Eastern Zhou period. A neighboring state that intermarried with Zeng is Huang 黄 located in the Huang 潢 River Valley in Henan, a tributary of the Huai. Unprovenanced inscribed bronze vessels made by Huang aristocrats have been known to us, but more information about the Huang was provided by archaeological finds in the 1970s and 1980s, especially the tomb of the Huang ruler Meng 孟 and his wife at Baoxiangsi 宝相寺, Guangshan 光山 County, Henan (Henan 1984). The wooden burial chambers for Meng and his wife Meng Ji 孟姬 were located in the same tomb, and both contained a set of bronzes vessels consisting of two *ding*, *dou*, *hu*, and *lei* as well as some other vessels types. The wife was actually buried with more bronze vessels than Meng, indicating either her higher social status by birth or more wealth at the time of her death. Huang was conquered by Chu in 648 BCE; most Huang remains belong to the Early Springs and Autumns period. The even numbers for all major ritual vessels and the comparatively small number of *ding* were characteristic, as well as the *li* and *yan* with a spout and a curled-tail-shaped handle, showing cultural connections with polities between the Hui and Yangzi Rivers further south (see the following discussion on the Qun Shu in this section).

Further north and east of Huang was the state of Cai 蔡 of the Ji clan of the royal Zhou lineage, conquered by Chu in 447 BCE. The largest group of Cai finds is the large tomb in Shouxian, Anhui discovered in 1955 (Anhui 1956), identified as the tomb of the Cai ruler Zhao Hou 昭侯 named Shen 申. The 486 bronze artifacts from this tomb, dated to the Late Springs and Autumns period, were often covered with dense *panchi* patterns and resemble Chu vessels of the time in both shape and decoration (Figure 8). Meanwhile, several bronze vessels bear inscriptions concerning marriage relations between Cai and the state of Wu 吴. Those vessels demonstrate the strong impact Chu culture had on Cai and the political gestures Cai rulers made in relation to their powerful neighbors Chu and Wu (Zhongguo 2004:388–389). The two looted large tombs at Caijiagang 蔡家岗, Huainanshi 淮南市, Anhui—one of which (M2) is identified as that of Cai ruler Sheng Hou 声侯 named Chan 产 (d. 457 BCE)—are dated to the Late Springs and Autumns or Early Warring States periods (Anhui 1963).

Another polity of the Ji clan, Xu 许, was located in central Henan. The tomb found in Yexian 叶县 County in 2002 (Pingdingshan 2007), identified with the Xu ruler Linggong 灵公 named Ning 宁 (r. 591–547) based on inscriptions, yielded an assemblage of bronze vessels very similar to that of M2 at Xiasi in combination, shape, and decoration. The strong Chu flavor in Xu bronzes shows that although Xu was a Ji clan polity enfiefed by Zhou, its culture had a strong Chu flavor due to its status as a Chu affiliate (Zhu 1994:1,756–1,757). Nevertheless, some unique weapons such as the multi-pronged *ge* 戈 and *ji* 戟 decorated with animals cast with the newly popular lost-wax method demonstrate some cultural distinctness and independence of the Xu rulers. Other Huai River Valley polities include Yang 养, represented by 26 tombs excavated at Yuehe 月河, in Tongbai 桐柏, Henan (Nanyang 1997), and Ying 应, represented by a cemetery at

Zhiyangling 滍阳岭, in Pingdingshan 平顶山, Henan (Henan 2012). Early remains of Yang and Ying bronzes also conform to Central Plain forms, but those of the Late Springs and Autumns period show clear affinity to Chu-style vessels. In addition, four Springs and Autumns–period tombs at Wangpo 王坡, Xiangfan 襄樊, Hubei can also be put into this category of small polities absorbed by the expansion of Chu during the Middle and Late Springs and Autumns periods. Belonging to the polity of Deng 邓, which was annexed by Chu in 678 BCE, the finds at Wangpo exhibit Central Plains features and some local characteristics and are not affected by the Chu characteristics, which were not formed until the Middle Springs and Autumns period (Hubei 2005).

Further east in Shucheng 舒城 and the surrounding areas in central Anhui province, some scattered finds were identified with the Qun Shu 群舒, or "the many Shu," polities

ding   *ding*   *gui*

dou   *zun*   *fang hu*   *jian*

FIGURE 8 Bronze vessels from the tomb of Cai hou Shen, in Shouxian, Anhui province, Late Springs and Autumns period. Photographs by author.

established by various branches of the Shu clan. In addition to some vessels still clinging to the archaic Western Zhou prototypes such as *ding* and *yi*, some vessels indicate strong local styles, such as *yan* and *li* with spouts and curled-tail-shaped handles, *ding* with rims terminating into an animal head in sculptural form, and *fou* with flat lids (Zhu 1994:1,798–1,809). Bronzes found in southern Anhui south of the Yangzi River are similar to those from the Shucheng area but exhibit more connections with the Wu state in the lower Yangzi River Valley (Anhui 2006).

Wu 吳 and Yue 越 were the two states controlling the lower Yangzi River Valley during the Western and Eastern Zhou periods. Although the origin and early history of the Wu ruling house is still under debate, both Wu and Yue arose in the area of the so-called "Yue barbarians" beyond the Shang and Zhou realms of political control. Wu was established during the early Zhou period and was centered in southern Jiangsu province, although at the height of its power Wu controlled most of Jiangsu and Shanghai and parts of Anhui and Zhejiang. Wu was conquered by the state Yue in 473 BCE. Yue, originally from south of the Taihu 太湖 Lake, took over the Wu territory and expanded further north into southern Shandong. Yue declined during the Warring States period and was conquered by Chu during the late fourth century BCE. Remains of Wu and Yue were often grouped together as the Wu Yue culture due to their cultural similarities and geographical proximity.

Small tombs in this region during the Early and Middle Springs and Autumns period maintained the earlier practice of burying the dead under a mound piled on the ground instead of in an earthen pit. Large tombs during the Late Springs and Autumns period, by contrast, started to have a burial chamber dug into the ground before being covered up with a large mound (in some cases up to 70 meters across at the base and 8 meters tall), probably a result of interacting with Chu culture and the Central Plains area. Some tombs in Zhejiang province and around the Taihu Lake in Jiangsu have a chamber built with rocks and stone slabs under the mound, a structure used in central Zhejiang since the Middle Western Zhou period. Small tombs usually contain grave goods made of hard-fired stoneware with impressed patterns (fired above 1,000 C) and the so-called "primitive porcelain" (stoneware with a greenish glaze; fired above 1,200 C). Large tombs for the aristocrats were usually dug into the living rock on hilltops; covered with mounds; and furnished with bronze vessels, bells, horse-and-chariot fittings, and weapons as well as ceramics (Feng 2007:71–115; Zhongguo 2004:396).

Large Wu tombs dated to the Early and Middle Springs and Autumns period include the tomb at Dafudun 大夫墩 in Danyang 丹阳, Jiangsu (Daifudun 1994), and M2 at Liangshan 粮山 in Dantu 丹徒, Jiangsu (Liu Jianguo 1987). The tomb chamber of M2 at Liangshan, excavated from living rock, required the removal of 1,000 cubic meters of rock and has a sacrificial human on a stone ledge and bones of a sacrificed horse along with stoneware vessels around the main occupant. Large Wu tombs of the Late Springs and Autumns period include the one at Beishanding 北山顶 in Dantu 丹徒 (Jiangsu 1988) and D9M1 at Zhenshan 真山 in Suzhou 苏州 (Suzhou 1999). The Beishanding tomb is one of many mound tombs located on hills along the banks of the Yangzi River in Dantu. Although the tomb was a rectangular pit with a ramp, the tomb mound and the three sacrificed humans exhibit strong Wu characteristics. It was probably the tomb of a Wu king of the Late Springs and Autumns period (probably Yumo 余眜). Tomb D9M1 at Zhenshan was dug into living rock, and the lacquered nested coffins, now decomposed, were placed on raised platforms built with mixed rocks and earth. The jade plaques and over 10,000 beads of turquoise and malachite were probably remains of a jade face covering and funerary shroud and could be the prototype of the later jade funerary garments for royal figures. This tomb was probably also the burial for an earlier Wu king (probably Mengshou 梦寿) (Feng 2007:81; Suzhou 1999).

Tomb M1 at Hougudui 侯古堆, Gushi 固始 County, Henan is a large earthen-pit tomb with one ramp and two layers of wooden chambers and one coffin, but around and inside the outer chamber are 17 sacrificed humans, each in their own coffins. Inscriptions on a bronze *fu* from this tomb suggests that the main occupant was the sister of the Song ruler (Song Gong, 宋公, probably Song Jing Gong 宋景公) named Luan 欒 and the wife of a Wu ruler (Gou Wu Furen 勾敔夫人, namely the wife of Wu) of the Late Springs and Autumns period (probably Fuchai 夫差) (Henan 2004a). Although nine *ding* were found in the tomb, they belong to three different sets of three, and the largest *ding* was probably used as *huo ding* 镬鼎 (large *ding* used for the actual cooking of sacrificial meat), as suggested by the cattle bones inside and the soot on the bottom. The reasons for the remote location of her burial might have been related to Fuchai's military expedition against Chu in this region. She was probably on the expedition with Fuchai when she died, and the three shoulder-carried sedan chairs found in the tomb were probably the means of her travel (Henan 2004a). Her unusually high ritual privilege (such as the nine *ding*, a set of eight *bo* bells, and a set of nine *zhong* bells) might also be explained by such unusual circumstances. The inscriptions on the *bo* and *zhong* bells indicate that they belonged to a Chu general; the *ding* vessels are also in Chu style, similar to those found at Xiasi and Shouxian. These tomb offerings were probably war booties that Fuchai lavished on his wife's funeral.

The three tombs discovered at Chengqiao 程桥 in Liuhe 六合 north of the Yangzi River can also be grouped as outlying aristocratic Wu tombs beyond the core of Wu culture in southern Jiangsu (Jiangsu 1965; Nanjing 1974; Nanjing 1991). Also worth noting are two tombs excavated at Jiunüdun 九女墩, Pizhou 邳州 in northern Jiangsu (Kong and Chen 2002; Nanjing 1999). Tomb M3 at Jiunüdun has a tomb mound, a chamber and coffin with two occupants, and sixteen sacrificed humans around the chamber in the earthen pit, a practice similar to the Yi-culture tombs in Shandong. The inscriptions on the nine bronze bells suggest that the owner was probably a descendent of a ruler of the ancient state of Xu 徐 (Zhu 1994:1,831–1,834). The bronzes in the tomb are a mixture of vessels of Central Plains, Wu, and Qun Shu ("the many Shu") features, exhibiting the hybrid nature of the aristocratic culture of Xu as a small polity surrounded by powerful states.

Major Yue tombs include M306 at Potang 坡塘 (Zhejiang 1984), and the large tomb at Yinshan 印山 (Zhejiang 1999), both in Shaoxing 绍兴, Zhejiang 浙江 province. The Yinshan tomb was probably built for a Yue ruler, mostly likely Yuchang 允常 (d. 497

BCE), the father of Yue king Goujian 勾践. Like the large Wu tombs, this tomb was also dug into living rock on a hill and covered with a mound about nine meters in height, but it exhibits some unique features of Yue royal tombs. The tomb is surrounded by a wide ditch that forms a square covering some 85,000 sqm. The wooden burial chamber is not a box-like structure but a corridor with walls slanting inward to form an isosceles-triangle-shaped cross section, and it is divided into front, middle, and rear rooms. The chamber was then sealed with 5,700 cubic meters of fine clay (青膏泥), and 1,400 cubic meters of charcoal. The coffin, six meters long, was carved out of a single piece of tree trunk. The protective ditch around the tomb and the combined use of charcoal and *qinggaoni* for preservation were prominent features of the earlier funerary structures of the Qin rulers at Yongcheng, Shaanxi province, thus indicating cultural borrowing from Qin in the west (Zhejiang 1999).

All of these large tombs of Wu and Yue excavated so far were looted, and the scattered remaining grave goods do not provide a clear picture of the complete assemblages of bronze vessels or of the offerings in general. The Wu bronzes from scattered chance finds show influence from the Central Plains area, reflected by the presence and style of *ding*, *fu*, *dou*, and *jian*. Chu influence was not strong but can be seen in the presence of *fou*. Many vessels exhibit strong local character, such as the shallow, cylindrical-bodied *ding* with thin walls and flat legs that flare out, the deep-bodied *pan*, and *li* with two attached handles and long hoof-end legs (Zhu Fenghan 1994:1,818–1,822). Although bronze artifacts were generally only found in large tombs belonging to individuals of high social status, bronze vessels were used in a more haphazard way compared to other regions where a more defined hierarchy can be seen through bronze assemblages (Falkenhausen 1999:531). The Wu Yue region was best known for the highly developed techniques for crafting bronze swords, one of which was found in M1 at Wangshan 望

山 in Jiangling, Hubei (Figure 9). The dark net pattern of rhombus shapes was formed by a type of sulphide to protect the blade from erosion. The beautiful gold inscription written in the decorative bird-script identifies this sword as one originally owned by the Yue king Goujian.

The cultural distinctiveness shown in the burial practices and bronzes of the Wu and Yue can also be seen in city design. Among the Wu and Yue city sites the best preserved is Yancheng 淹城 in Wujin 武进, Jiangsu. Built during the Late Springs and Autumns period, this Wu city has roughly an oval shape measuring 850 meters east to west and 750 meters north to south, enclosed by three concentric rings of city walls. Each layer of city wall was surrounded by a moat 30 to 60 meters wide. The walls were not constructed with pounded earth but were formed simply by piling the earth excavated from the moats. Each ring of wall has one gate, and the city can only be accessed on boats. Mounded tombs scatter in the outer city and in the area surrounding the city. A well, a canoe, and bronze and ceramic artifacts were found in the innermost part of the city, suggesting some form of settlement. The function of the city is not clear: it may have been used as a military stronghold, a ritual center, or a city for an enfiefed lord of Wu (Xu 2000:123–124; Jiangsu 1994).

FIGURE 9 Bronze sword with inscriptions in gold inlay, from M1 at Wangshan, Jiangling, Hubei province, Late Springs and Autumns period. Photograph by author.

QIN AND THE GUANZHONG AREA (TABLE 5)

Similar to Chu, Wu, and Yue, Qin 秦 was not one of the affiliated states established by the Zhou at the beginning of the Western Zhou period, and the origin of the Qin is still under debate. Based on both textual and archaeological evidence, studies on Qin origin can be grouped under the "west origin theory," which maintains that Qin was rooted in the Rong 戎 cultures in Eastern Gansu, and the "east origin theory," which traces Qin ancestors to the Yi groups in the east. (For an archaeological analysis of the development of Qin culture and a more detailed discussion on Qin's origin, see Teng 2002.) An eclectic opinion holds that Qin ancestors migrated to the west from the east, went through a cultural change under the influence of Rong cultures, and rose in power but were recognized by the Huaxia as one of the Rong (Huang Liuzhu 1995). The excavation of the Maojiaping 毛家坪 site in Gangu 甘谷, Gansu 甘肃 province in 1980 reveals two groups of coexisting remains, A and B. The A group remains, covering the Western Zhou through the Springs and Autumns periods, were identified as Qin culture because although their tomb structure and ceramic style resemble those of the Zhou culture in the middle Wei 渭 River Valley in Shaanxi and differ from the Rong cultures further

Table 5 Representative burial sites and tombs: Qin and the Guanzhong area

Site Name	State Affiliation	Date of Site: E, M, or L Springs and Autumns	Significant Tombs	Important Features or Main Assemblage (m=mingqi)	Date of Tombs: E, M, or L Springs and Autumns
Maojiaping cemetery, Gangu, Gansu	Qin	E-L	A group tombs		
Baqitun cemetery, Fengxiang, Shaanxi	Qin	E-L			
Dengjiaya, Fengxiang, Shaanxi	Qin	E-L			
Dabuzishan cemetery, Lixian, Gansu	Qin		M2 M3	Looted/incomplete	E
			Sacrificial Pit	3 *bo zhong* bells, 8 *yong zhong* bells	
Yuandingshan cemetery, Lixian, Gansu	Qin	M-L		Looted/incomplete; human sacrifices; waist pit; bronze *ding, gui,* and *hu*	
Qin Royal cemetery, Yongcheng, Fengxiang, Shaanxi	Qin	M-L	M1	Looted/incomplete; chamber of cypress logs; 166 sacrificed humans	L
Liangdaicun, Hancheng, Shaanxi	Rui	E	M26	5 *ding*, 4 *gui*, 5 *li*, 2 *hu*, 1 *yan*, 1 *he*, 2 *fu*, 2 *pen*	E
			M27	7 *ding*, 6 *gui*, 2 *hu*, 1 *yan*, 1 *he*, 1 *you*, 1 *zun*, 1 *zhi*, 1 *jiao*, 8 bells	
			M28	5 *ding*, 4 *gui*, 4 *li*, 2 *hu*, 1 *yan*, 1 *pan*, 1 *he*, 8 bells	

west, their treatment of the body with an extremely flexed position (with legs drawn to the body) was different from the Zhou tradition, in which the body was in supine extended position. The coexisting B group remains were identified with the Rong in this region (Gansu 1987). Therefore, the archaeological remains at Maojiaping do not seem to support the west-origin theory (Teng 2002:47–57), which is mainly based on historical texts. Meanwhile, the recently published texts on the Warring States–period bamboo slips in the Qinghua University collection include a passage mentioning that King Cheng of Zhou relocated the Shang-period polity Shang Yan 商奄 or Shang He 商盍 in the east to Zhuyu 朱圉 (also in Gangu County, close to Maojiaping) in the west, from where the Qin derived. Therefore the Shang Yan people might have been one of the ancestral lineages of Qin in addition to the lineage of Qin that already existed in eastern Gansu in Shang times, as recorded in the *Shiji* (Chen 2013:273–277). In discussions concerning ethno-genesis, be it Qin culture or pre-Zhou culture, we need to caution ourselves not to simply equate patterns in material culture (including burial customs) with ethnic identity, because ethnic identity is more complicated, subjective, and fluid than ceramic style or tomb structure. It also needs to be noted that the ruling lineage, the aristocracy, and the commoners may belong to different ethnic groups and maintain different traditions.

The middle- and small-sized tombs (tombs other than those of the Qin rulers and their family members) of the Springs and Autumns period were mainly found in several Qin cemeteries, including Baqitun 八旗屯 (Wu and Shang 1980; Shaanxi 1986) and Dengjiaya 邓家崖 in Fengxiang 凤翔 (Shaanxi 1991), and Dianzi 店子 in Longxian 陇县 (Shaanxi 1998). Those tombs are typically rectangular earthen-pit tombs oriented east to west, with the head of the deceased pointing to the west. In most cases the body is extremely flexed. The bodies from seven tombs at Dengjiaya excavated so far, however, are all in the supine position. The content and richness of grave goods nonetheless are not different from those cemeteries with deceased in the flexed body position, such as Baqitun. Both Dengjiaya and Baqitun were a few miles south of the Qin capital Yongcheng 雍城 at Fengxiang. It is possible that the Dengjiaya cemetery represents a group of people who were distinct from the Qin in burial practice, but they lived in the capital with the Qin people, adopted the Qin material culture, and were not treated differently in terms of social status (Teng 2002:94–95). Among tombs with bronze ritual vessels, *ding*, *gui*, *hu*, *pan*, and *yi* (or *he* 盉) are a typical combination, having become standardized since the Middle Springs and Autumns period.

Ceramic ritual vessels in imitation of bronze vessels started to appear in middle Springs and Autumns Qin tombs; they are similar in shape to their bronze prototypes, and most were painted to imitate decor. Utilitarian ceramic tomb offerings include *li*, *pen*, *dou*, and *guan* with large flaring rims as the main combination. The presence of bronze vessels coincides with large tomb sizes, and they sometimes coexist with the two categories of ceramic vessels, suggesting social status of high-ranking aristocracy. Smaller tombs contain ceramic ritual vessels, and the smallest tombs contain only utilitarian vessels or no grave goods at all. During the Early Springs and Autumns period, Qin bronzes were largely homogeneous with Zhou-style bronzes of the Late Western Zhou period, such as lidless *ding* with handles standing on rims, the square *fang yan* and *fang hu*, and the *gui* with ring feet; this archaic style continued through the Middle Springs and Autumns period in Qin bronzes, when the assemblage in the Central Plains area had transitioned to lidded *ding*, *dui*, and round *hu*. The typical Qin-style *ding* feature straight handles on the rim, shallow bodies, and thick muscular legs attached rather high on the belly; this type of *ding* lasted till the end of the Springs and Autumns period. In contrast to this conservative trend, the use of ceramic ritual vessels is quite innovative, since they were not seen in tombs in other regions until the Warring States period. In addition to maintaining certain Zhou cultural elements, Qin remains of this period also show interactions with the northern steppe cultures, reflected by appearance of straight-edge short swords and bronze *fu* cauldrons (Teng 2002:94–95). (For more details about the middle- and small-sized Qin tombs and the style of Qin bronze vessels see Zhu 1994:1,858–1,885.) Bronze-yielding tombs with northern-style artifacts were probably those of a new military elite who gained aristocratic status through military interactions with the northern non-Huaxia groups. Their newly acquired status was different from the hereditary Qin elite or the previous indigenous Zhou elite under Qin rule. Military merit continued to be the most important factor in acquiring social status (Teng 2002:72–74).

The largest Qin tombs, by contrast, seem to differ in many significant ways from the middle- and small-sized tombs. The two large tombs, M2 and M3, in the Qin cemetery at Dabuzishan 大堡子山, Lixian 礼县, Gansu, for example, are 88 meters and 115 meters long, respectively (including the two ramps at the east and west ends). The deceased were buried in lacquered coffins and a wood chamber in supine position, instead of the flexed position of smaller Qin tombs. The seven sacrificial humans on the ledge in the tomb chamber of M2 were also buried in the supine extended position, while those buried in the ramps of both M2 and M3 were in a flexed position (Dai 2000:75). The nine middle- and small-sized tombs (2–5 meters long) excavated in this cemetery also contain deceased in coffins in supine position. Although M2 and M3 and most of the around 200 smaller tombs in the cemetery were looted (M2 and M3 were looted in 1992–1993 and excavated in 1994), the bronze vessels and bells (Figure 10) were retrieved by the authorities as well as some others that recently turned up in private and museum collections (22 in total). The latter bear inscriptions identifying them as ritual objects cast by Qingong 秦公, or lineage head of the Qin (Li and Ai Lan 1994; Li Chaoyuan 1996, 2002). Based on bronze style and inscriptions, M2 and M3 can be dated to the Late Western Zhou or Early Springs and Autumns periods and are probably tombs of two Qin rulers (probably Zhuang Gong 庄公 and Xiang Gong 襄公, due to the fact that they were the only two Qin rulers who ruled in the Lixian area; see Li Feng 2011; for another interpretation see Dai 2000).

A sacrificial site was excavated about 20 meters southwest of M2 and M3, which includes a rectangular pit with three *bo zhong* 镈钟 bells, eight *yong zhong* 甬钟 bells, two sets of stone chimes, and a decomposed wooden support (Zaoqi Qin 2008c). Since a set of three *bo zhong* and seven *yong zhong* were also found in Baoji in 1977 (Baoji 1978), it seems that ritual music for Qin rulers used three *bo zhong* as a standard. One of the *yongzhong* has an inscription of 26 characters, which identifies the patron as a Qin ruler who called himself Qin Zi 秦子. Unlike the caches of Zheng bronze bells discovered at Xinzheng, the Qin Zi bells were found in a rectangular sacrificial pit near tombs of Qin rulers. Although the nature and recipient of this sacrificial event are not clear, they could have been sacrifices to the earth god rather than to the deceased in the large tombs (Zhao et al. 2008; also see the latter for other opinions concerning the identity of Qing Zi and the owners of M2 and M3). Based on the ratio of the height to the width of the bronze bells, studies of the Qin Zi bells arrived at different conclusions about their date. Li Feng argued that the bells were cast at least 75 years later than the date of M2 and M3. After the Qin ruling house moved to the Baoji area in the middle Wei River Valley in 763 BCE, the earlier center of Qin territory in Lixian in the Xihanshui 西汉水 River Valley was lost to invading Rong groups. The bells were cast in a period when Qin had regained control over the upper Wei River Valley and Xihanshui River Valley (Tianshui and

gui

bo   *ding*

FIGURE 10 Bronze vessels and bells with "Qin Gong" inscriptions, from the Qin royal cemetery at Dabuzishan, Lixian, Gansu province. Collections of the Shanghai Museum. Early Springs and Autumns period.

Lixian), and Qin Zi was a Qin ruler (probably Xuan Gong) in his mourning period after the death of the preceding ruler and before ascending the throne himself, hence the self-appellation Zi (Li Feng 2011).

The relatively later date of the excavated smaller tombs at Dabuzishan (Zaoqi Qin 2008d) as well as a large building foundation identified as a storage facility (Zaoqi Qin 2008a) corroborate Li Feng's conclusion by suggesting frequent activities at this site during the Middle and Late Springs and Autumns period. The two tombs of Qin rulers (M2 and M3) previously discussed are located in a walled city of an irregular oblong shape on top of a hill at the confluence of the Xihanshui 西汉水 River and its tributary Gucheng 固城 River. The city is enclosed with pounded-earth walls covering an area around half a million square meters, and building foundations, settlement sites, and cemeteries have been found in and surrounding the city. The Dabuzishan city site is one of the over forty Qin sites at the upper Xihanshui River Valley identified by an archaeological survey that started in 2004. Across the Xihanshui River from Dabuzishan is another smaller city (around 80,000 square meters) on a hill called Shanping 山坪; at Yantuya 土崖 around two kilometers to the northwest is a large Qin cemetery. Around three kilometers further east is the Yuandingshan 圆顶山 cemetery. These sites, in a three-kilometer radius from Dabuzishan, are the largest complex of Qin sites in this region (Zaoqi Qin 2008b). Excavations at Yuandingshan in 1998 and 2000 salvaged four looted tombs; all four tombs have sacrificed humans in niches carved on the sides of the burial chamber, and the large ones also have a dog inside a waist pit, all conservative vestiges of Shang culture rarely seen in the Central Plains area by this time. (Burying sacrificed humans in niches is a unique feature for some Qin tombs.) The bronze artifacts from these tombs are combinations centered on *ding*, *gui*, and *hu*, and most of them have beautiful decorations in the Late Western Zhou style but with some unique features, such as the symmetrically arranged animal-shaped relief decorations attached on some vessels. Those tombs, dated to the Middle and Late Springs and Autumns period, belonged to the Qin aristocracy of various ranks (Gansu 2002, 2005).

The Qin capital city of Yongcheng 雍城 (capital between 677 and 383 BCE) is located at the city of Fengxiang in Shaanxi province. The remaining sections of the city wall show that the city is an irregular square 3.3 by 3.2 kilometers in size; the southern wall was built against the Yongshui 雍水 River, and a protective ditch runs along the west wall. Four avenues running east to west and four avenues running north to south divide the city into a grid. Remains of large buildings are lined up east to west in the center section of the city. A large palace foundation (20,000 square meters) was found near the Yaojiagang 姚家岗 village in the central west part of the city, along with ceramic tiles and tile decorations (Shaanxi 1991). Three caches discovered near the foundation contained 64 bronze ornaments used on wooden beams and pillars, probably the *jingang* 金釭 ornaments mentioned in ancient texts (Yang 1976; Fengxiang 1976). The dense *panchi* pattern on the bronze beam ornaments demonstrates that certain decorative images were shared between bronze ritual vessels and architectural elements. The luxury of the Qin palace is also reflected by a square underground ice storage chamber discovered at the west side of the Yaojiagang palace site, which can hold 190 cubic meters of ice (Shaanxi 1978; Wang Xueli 1994:84–88). The ancestral temple area is located in the center of Yongcheng, and to the north of Majiazhuang 马家庄 village. One of these temples is the building complex No. 1, excavated between 1981 and 1984; it is a rectangular walled compound facing south, arranged symmetrically along a roughly north-south central axis, with the *zumiao* 祖庙 temple (for the founding member of the royal lineage) in the north, the *zhaomiao* 昭庙 temple (for the royal grandfather) in the east, and the *mumiao* 穆庙 temple (for the royal father) in the west, all facing a central courtyard. Each of the three buildings has a central hall, flanking side-rooms, and antechambers in the back. Along the central axis, a gateway is located at the southern entrance, and a smaller building is added at the north end behind the *zumiao*. In the central courtyard are 181 sacrificial pits (a few of which disturbed the *zumiao* foundation), containing either cattle, sheep, humans, or chariots, or a mixture of cattle and sheep or humans and sheep. Their arrangement suggests that those ritual activities continued over a long period of time, and some took place after the temple was deserted (Shaanxi 1985; Yongcheng 1986; Wang Xueli 1994:79–84). Building complex No. 3 at Majiazhang is the remains of a narrow compound consisting of five courtyards aligned one behind another on a central north to south axis, of which the second, third, and fifth has building foundations. This structure was identified as the residential palace of the Qin ruler, with the audience halls in the front and the residential area in the back (Shanxi 1985; Wang Xueli 1994:88–90). A roughly rectangular walled area (around 34,000 square meters) was found near the north wall in the city; the Qin currency and other artifacts found there suggest that this was a market. Its location behind (to the north of) the palace area conforms to a feature of the Zhou royal cities as described in a much later text (third century BCE), the Kaogongji chapter in the *Zhouli*, and suggests the centralized control over commercial activities in the Qin city (Wang Xueli 1994:90–92).

The Qin royal cemetery across the Yongshui River from Yongcheng is also part of the city. The royal cemetery is located six kilometers south of the city of Fengxiang, covering an area of 12 by three miles, enclosed by a protective ditch. Eighteen large tombs with two ramps on the east and west sides were found, and they were divided into 13 groups, each surrounded by another ditch that is either rectangular or trapezoid in shape (called a *lingyuan* 陵园 or funerary park by excavators). Some of these large tombs have a third layer of ditch around the burial chamber. The practice of using rectangular protective ditches continued during the Warring States period in Qin royal cemeteries in Xianyang 咸阳 and Lintong 临潼. Those 18 large tombs were also accompanied by 23 horse-and-chariot pits and six smaller tombs with one ramp. Although no tomb mound was detected, remains of buildings were found on these tombs, probably used as sacrificial halls (*xiangtang* 享堂) (Shaanxi 1983, 1987; Wang Xueli 1994:256–258; Jing and Wang 2013:395, 403). Those large tombs obviously belonged to the 19 Qin rulers who reigned from Yongcheng. Being placed outside of the capital city and organized into funerary parks for better management, the Qin royal cemetery at Yongcheng appears to be unique and advanced in design compared to their counterparts in the Central Plains area, as represented by Jin and Zheng (Teng 2002:110). Tomb No. 1 in funerary park No. 1 when excavated turned out to be the largest tomb of the Eastern Zhou period, measuring 300 meters long (tomb chamber measuring 59.4 by 38.5 by 24 meters in length, width, and depth). Although looted many times, the tomb stilled yielded over 3,000 small artifacts, including 30 pieces of stone chimes whose carved inscriptions help identify the tomb owner as Jing Gong 景公 (reigned 576–537 BCE). The wooden chamber, sealed in a layer of charcoal and a layer of fine clay, was built with interlocking cypress logs (later known as *huangchang ticou* 黃腸題湊 in the Han period); this L-shaped chamber was divided into a front room, a rear room, and a side chamber for grave goods. On a six-meter-wide ledge in the tomb shaft were 166 sacrificed flexed humans; 72 were buried with two nested coffins, and the rest of them only had one thin coffin. The large number of sacrificial humans is another important feature of Qin elite tombs during this period (Wang Xueli 1994:270–273; Jing and Wang 2013:395).

Early Springs and Autumns–period Qin bronze vessels and their inscriptions, such as those from Dabuzishan, were experimental versions imitating Zhou products. Their execution and arrangement of inscriptions had not been perfected and standardized. Qin rulers started to borrow phrases from bronze inscriptions on late Western Zhou vessels cast in the Zhou domain. Meanwhile, Qin rulers also participated in the process of constructing a Qin royal lineage that shared with dynastic Xia, Shang, and Zhou the same origin in the legendary kings of prehistory. This was a means for the Qin, an entity rising among the Rong barbarians, to be accepted within the Huaxia geopolitical network (Chen 2013). By the end of the Early Springs and Autumns period, Qin rulers started to challenge and appropriate the authority of the Zhou king; this challenge is revealed in the inscription on the *bo* bells of Qin Wu Gong (r. 697–678) from Baoji (Baoji 1978; Falkenhausen 1999:487), which claimed that Qin ancestors received the Mandate of Heaven (*shou tian ming* 受天命, *yan shou da ming* 𧅢受大命), and that Qin rulers were charged to carefully deal with the barbarians (*xi shi man fang* 虩事蠻方) and to dutifully govern the Four Quarters of the world (*pu you si fang* 匍有四方). All of these phrases were borrowed directly from inscriptions recounting the charge of a Zhou king to a subject. The ambition of Qin rulers to unite the Huaxia world can be detected in the material culture dated to as early as this period. The unprecedented size of the tomb of Jing Gong and scale of the royal cemetery at Fengxiang further attest to this early aspiration.

The cemetery at Liangdaicun 梁帶村 in Hancheng 韓城 County, Shaanxi is located on the west bank of the Yellow River and includes around 1,300 tombs dated to the Late Western Zhou and Early Springs and Autumns periods. Archaeological works between 2005 and 2007 excavated five large tombs with ramps (M27, M26, M19, M28, M502), eight middle-sized tombs, and 26 small tombs, and proved that this is the cemetery of the state of Rui 芮 (Shaanxi 2008, 2007a, 2007b, 2010). All the large tombs except M502 are dated to the Early Springs and Autumns period. The largest tomb, M27, the only tomb with two ramps, yielded an assemblage of bronze vessels headed by seven *ding* and six *gui*, similar to the combination in tombs of state rulers in the Central Plains area, such as M2001 at Shangcunling. The inscriptions on the *gui* prove that these vessels were made by a Rui ruler (Rui Gong 芮公); the large tombs were tombs of Rui rulers and their family members (Shaanxi 2007b). M27 also contained *gu* 觚, *jiao* 角, *you* 卣, and *zun* 尊 vessels, which can be dated to the Early Western Zhou period; M26, which is the tomb of Rui Jiang 芮姜 from the Jiang clan, the main consort of a Rui ruler, yielded many pieces of jade artifacts of Hongshan, Shang, and Western Zhou production (Shaanxi 2008). These antiques were probably precious collections of the Rui ruler and his consort as symbols of the prestige of their lineages. The Rui was a political entity with the same royal Ji clan name of Zhou kings, while the Jiang clan was a powerful ally of the Zhou. The bronze assemblage and their style and decoration are all similar to those of the Central Plains area of the same period. Although Rui was dominated by Qin during the Early Springs and Autumns period until its demise under Qin attacks in 650 BCE, Rui material culture showed little influence from Qin culture.

CONCLUSION

These discussions of archaeological cultures within the Zhou cultural sphere underscore the divergent as well as convergent developments in the material cultures of different regions and political entities. In the first century following the fall of Western Zhou, bronze vessels of polities in all those regions still largely maintain the late Western Zhou standards of content and style and suggest that the earlier Zhou political and ritual system was preserved and followed. The Middle Springs and Autumns period witnessed the flourishing of innovations in the type, style, and combination of bronze ritual vessels in the Central Plains area, and strong local characteristics started to come into full expression in the "regional states" as represented by Chu and Qin. Those changes on the one hand reflect the dissolution of the Zhou political and economic structure based on kinship. (For more details of social, political, and economic changes during this period, see Hsü 1999; for an archaeological analysis of the social changes during this period see Falkenhausen 1999.) On the other hand these changes mirror the growing confidence among rulers of large states and the rising sense of local identity after the weakening of an overarching Zhou identity. Of course, technological advances, a topic not explored in this chapter, must have facilitated innovations in, and popularization of, material symbols of social status among the new elite, especially those acquired through service in the military (for a review on acquiring aristocratic status through military merits see Teng 2002:68–74; Hsü 1999:570–572). At the same time, a centripetal cultural force was at work due to the assimilation of conquered lands by large states, intense interactions in the multistate system that came into being by the sixth century BCE, and the rejection of the non-agrarian groups in the north and west, which all contributed to the formation of a new cultural identity called the Huaxia (Li F 2013:180–182). This unifying cultural force further developed during the following Warring States period, which is reflected by the ever more homogenous sets of bronze and ceramic vessels as symbols of social status in mortuary rituals. Under such a convergent political identity, regional cultural identities were never lost, and those can be best observed in remains of the middle and lower strata of the society, reflected by idiosyncratic tomb structures, burial practices, vessel types, and decorative styles. The Springs and Autumns period is an era of rich and diverse cultures and profound social changes whose material remains warrant many more interesting future studies.

Bibliography

Anhui Daxue and Anhuisheng Kaogu Yanjiusuo 安徽大学, 安徽省考古研究所 2006. *Bronzes of the Late Shang and Zhou Periods in the South Anhui* 皖南商周青铜器. Beijing: Wenwu chubanshe.

Anhuisheng Wenwu Guanli Weiyuanhui and Anhuisheng Bowuguan 安徽省文物管理委员会, 安徽博物馆 1956. *Excavated Artifacts from the Cai Hou Tomb at Shouxian* 寿县蔡侯墓出土遗物. Beijing: Kexue chubanshe.

Anhuisheng Wenhuaju Wenwu Gongzuodui 安徽省文化局文物工作队 1963. "Warring States Tombs at Zhaojiaguadui, Caijiagang, Huainanshi, Anhui 安徽淮南市蔡家岗赵家孤堆战国墓." *Kaogu* 4: 204–212.

Baojishi Bowuguan and Baojishi Wenhuaguan 1978. "The Discovery of the Qingong Bells from Taigongmiaocun, Baojixian, Shaanxi 陕西宝鸡县太公庙村发现秦公钟、秦公镈." *Wenwu* 11: 1–5.

Beijing Daxue Kaoguxi 北京大学考古系 and Shanxisheng Kaogu Yanjiusuo 陕西省考古研究所 1995. "The Fifth Excavation of the Cemetery of Jin Rulers at Tianma-Qucun 天马-曲村遗址北赵晋侯墓地第五次发掘." *Wenwu* 7: 4–39.

Bian, Chengxiu and Li, Fengshan 1974. "Eastern Zhou Tombs 269 and 270 at Fengshuiling, Changzhi 长治分水岭 269–270 号东周墓." *Kaogu xuebao* 2: 63–85.

Chen, Chao-jung 陈昭容 2013. "The Evolution of the Integration of the Early Qin Kingdom into Mainstream Huaxia as Seen from Textual and Archaeological Data 从出土文献与出土文物看早期秦国融入华夏的历程, in *Unearthed Materials and a New Perspective* 出土材料与新视野." Edited by Li Zong-kun 李宗焜, 271–310. Taipei: Zhongyang yanjiuyuan.

Chuhuangcheng Kaogu Fajuedui 1980. "Brief Report on the Finds from Chuhuangcheng at Yicheng, Hubei 湖北宜城楚皇城勘察简报." *Kaogu* 2: 108–113.

Dai, Chunyang 2000. "Issues Concerning the Cemetery of Qin Rulers at Dabaozishan in Lixian 礼县大堡子山秦公墓地及有关问题." *Wenwu* 5: 74–80.

Daifudun Kaogudui 大夫墩考古队 1994. "Excavation Report on Dafudun, Heyang, Dayang City 丹阳市河阳大夫墩发掘报告." *Dongnan wenhua* supplementary issue 2.

Falkenhausen, Lothar von 1999. "The Waning of the Bronze Age: Material Culture and Social Developments, 770–481 BC." In *The Cambridge History of Ancient China: From the Origins of Civilization to 221 BC*. Edited by Michael Loewe and Edward L. Shaughnessy, 450–544. Cambridge, UK: Cambridge University Press.

Falkenhausen, Lothar von 2006. *Chinese Society in the Age of Confucius (1000–250 BC)*. Los Angeles: Cotsen Institute of Archaeology, University of California, Los Angeles.

Fang, Hui 方辉 2004. "Archaeological Studies of the Marine Salt Industry in the Lubei Area during the Shang and Zhou Dynasties 商周时期鲁北地区海盐业的考古学研究." *Kaogu* 4: 53–67.

Feng, Puren 2007. *Wu Yue Cultures* 吴越文化. Beijing: Wenwu chubanshe.

Fengxiangxian Wenhuaguan and Shaanxisheng Wenguanhui 1976. "Excavation of the Pre-Qin Palace at Fengxiang and Its Bronze Building Components 凤翔先秦宫殿试掘及其铜质建筑构件." *Kaogu* 2: 121–128.

Gansu 1987. Gansusheng Wenwu Gongzuodui 甘肃省文物工作队 and Beijing Daxue Kaoguxi 北京大学考古系 1987. "Excavation Report of Maojiaping Site in Gangu, Gansu 甘肃甘谷毛家坪遗址发掘报告." *Kaogu Xuebao* 3: 359–396.

Gansusheng Wenwu Kaogu Yanjiusuo 甘肃省文物考古所 et al., 2002. "The Springs and Autumns Qin Burials at Yuandingshan, Lixian 礼县圆顶山春秋秦墓." *Wenwu* 2: 4–30.

Gansusheng Wenwu Kaogu Yanjiusuo 甘肃省文物考古所 et al., 2005. "The Springs and Autumns Qin Burials 98LDM2 and 2000LDM4 at Yuandingshan, Lixian, Gansu 甘肃礼县圆顶山 98LDM2、2000LDM4 春秋秦墓." *Wenwu* 2: 4–27.

Gao, Chongwen 高崇文 1983. "Analysis of the Chu Style Ding of the Eastern Zhou 东周楚式鼎形态分析." *Jianghan Kaogu* 1: 1–18.

Gao, Ming 高明 1981a. "Research on the Bronze Ritual Vessels of the Eastern Zhou Period in the Central Plains Area, Part 1 中原地区东周时代青铜礼器研究-上 *Kaogu yu wenwu* 2: 68–82.

Gao, Ming 高明 1981b. "Research on the Bronze Ritual Vessels of the Eastern Zhou Period in the Central Plains Area, Part 2 中原地区东周时代青铜礼器研究-下 *Kaogu yu wenwu* 4: 82–91.

Gu, Derong and Zhu, Shunlong 顾德融, 朱顺龙 2003. *Chunqiu History* 春秋史. Shanghai: Shanghai renmin chubanshe.

Guo, Baojun 1959. *Shanbiaozhen and Liulige* 山彪镇与琉璃阁. Beijing: Kexue chubanshe.

Guo, Baojun 1981. *Research on the Grouping of Ritual Bronzes of the Shang and Zhou Periods* 商周铜器群综合研究. Beijing: Wenwu chubanshe.

Guoli Lishi Bowuguan and Henan Bowuyuan 博 国历史博物馆，河南博物院 2003. *The Reappearance of Treasures: Catalog of Artifacts fromthe Jia and Yi Tombs from Liulige in Huixian County* 瑰寶重現:輝縣琉璃閣甲乙墓器物圖集. Taibei: Guoli lishi bowuguan.

Henan Bowuyuan and Taibei Lishi Bowuguan 河南博物院,台北歷史博物館 1954. "Ancient Bronze Vessels Discovered in Jiaxian, Henan 河南郏县发现的古代铜器." *Wenwu cankao ziliao* 3: 60–62.

Henan Bowuyuan and Taibei Guoli Lishi Bowuguan 河南博物院，台北歷史博物館 2001. *Bronze Vessels from the Large Tomb of Duke of Zheng in Xinzheng* 新郑郑公大墓青铜器. Zhengzhou: Daxiang chubanshe.

Henan Bowuyuan and Taibei Lishi Bowuguan 河南博物院,台北歷史博物館 2011. *Two Burial of Jia and Yi from Liulige, Huixian* 辉县琉璃阁 甲乙二墓. Zhengzhou: Daxiang chubanshe.

Henansheng Bowuguan Xinzheng Gongzuozhan, et al. 河南省博物馆新郑工作站 1980. "Drilling and Trial Digging at the Ancient City of Zhenghan inXinzheng, Henan, 河南新郑郑韩故城的钻探和试掘." In *Wenwu ziliao congkan* 3 文物资料丛刊 3. Edited by Wenwu Bianji Weiyuanhui. Beijing: Wenwu chubanshe.

Henansheng Wenwu Yanjiusuo 河南省文物研究所, and Pingdingshanshi Wenguanhui 平顶山市文管会 1988. "Excavation Briefing on Tomb No. 1 at the Zhou Cemetery in Beizhi Village, Pingdingshan City 平顶山市北滍村两周墓地一号墓发掘简报." *Huaxia kaogu* 1.

Henansheng Wenwu Yanjiusuo 河南省文物研究所, and Pingdingshanshi Wenwu Guanliju 平顶山市文物管理局 2007. "Brief Excavation Report on Tomb No. 8 at the Yingguo Cemetery, Pingdingshan, Henan 河南平顶山应国墓地八号墓发掘简报." *Huaxia kaogu* 1: 30–44.

Henansheng Wenwu Kaogu Yanjiusuo 河南省文物考古研究所 2000. " Excavation Briefing of Zheng State Sacrifice Site in Zhenghan Ancient City, Xinzheng City, Henan 河南新郑市郑韩故城郑国祭祀遗址发掘简报." *Kaogu* 2: 61–77.

Henansheng Wenwu Kaogu Yanjiusuo 河南省文物考古研究所 2004a. *Tomb No. 1 at Hougudi, Gushi* 固始侯古堆一号墓. Zhengzhou: Daxiang chubanshe.

Henansheng Wenwu Kaogu Yanjiusuo 2004b. *Chu Tombs at Heshangling and Xujialing in Xichuan* 淅川和尚岭与徐家岭楚墓. Zhengzhou: Daxiang chubanshe.

Henansheng Wenwu Kaogu Yanjiusuo 河南省文物考古研究所 2006. *Sacrificial Sites of the Zheng State atXinzheng* 新郑郑国祭祀遗 址. Zhengzhou: Daxiang chubanshe.

Henansheng Wenwu Kaogu Yanjiusuo 河南省文物考古研究所 2012. "Brief Excavation Report on the Late Springs and Autumns Period Tomb M301 at Pingdingshan, Henan 河南平顶山春秋晚期 M301 发掘简报." *Wenwu* 4: 4–28.

Henansheng Wenwu Kaogu Yanjiusuo and Samenxia Shi Wenwu Gongzuodui 三门峡文物工作队 1991. *Chu tombs of the Springs and Autumns Period at Xiasi, Xichuan* 淅川下寺春秋楚墓. Beijing: Wenwu chubanshe.

Henansheng Wenwu Kaogu Yanjiusuo and Samenxia Shi Wenwu Gongzuodui 三门峡文物工作队 1999. *Guo State Burials at Sanmenxia* 三门峡虢国墓. Beijing: Wenwu chubanshe.

Henansheng Wenwu Kaogu Yanjiusuo and Tongbaixian Wenwu Guanli Weiyuanhui 桐柏现文物管理委员会 2005. "*The Second Excavation of the Yuehe Cemetery in Tongbai, Henan* 河南桐柏月河墓地第二次发掘." *Wenwu* 8: 21–38.

Henansheng Wenwu Yanjiusuo and Xinzheng Gongzuozhan 河南省文物研究所, 新郑工作站 2005. "Springs and Autumns Period Tomb No. 6 at Zhenghganlu, Xinzhengshi 新郑市郑韩路 6 号春秋墓." *Wenwu* 8: 39–46.

Henan Xinyang Diqu Wenguanhu and Guangshanxian Wenguanhui 河南信陽地區文官戶, 光山縣文管會 1984. "Excavation Report on the the Early Springs and Autumns Period Tombs of the Huang State Ruler Meng and His Wife 春秋早期黄君孟夫妇墓发掘报告." *Kaogu* 4: 302–332.

Hou, Yi 1989. "On the Identity and Status of the Tomb No. 251 at Jinsheng Village, Taiyuan 试论太原金胜村 251 号墓墓主身份." *Wenwu* 9: 90–94.

Hsu, Cho-yun 1999. "The Springs and Autumns Period." In *The Cambridge History of Ancient China: From the Origins of Civilization to 221 BC.* Edited by Michael Loewe and Edward L. Shaughnessy, 545–586. Cambridge, UK and New York: Cambridge University Press.

Huang, Fengchun 2014. "The Eastern Zhou Cemetery at Wenfengta, Suizhou, Hubei 湖北随州文峰塔东周墓 地." Zhongguo Shehui Kexueyuan Kaogu Yanjiusuo. http://www.kaogu.cn/html/cn/xueshuhuodongzixun/2013nianquanguoshidakaoguxinfaxian/2014/0411/45829.html, accessed 7/19/2014.

Huang, Liuzhu 1995. "On the Two-Origin Theory of Qin Culture 秦文化二源说." *Xibei daxue xuebao (zhexue shehui kexue ban)* 3: 28–34.

Hubeisheng Bowuguan 湖北省博物馆 1980. "Chu City Remains at Jijiahu, Dangyang 当阳季家湖楚城遗址." *Wenwu* 10: 31–41.

Hubeisheng Bowuguan 湖北省博物馆 1983. "Excavation Report on the Eastern Zhou Cemetery in Fuyang, Shanwan, Xiangyang 襄阳山湾 东周墓地发掘报告." *Jianghan Kaogu* 2: 1–35.

Hubeisheng Bowuguan 湖北省博物馆 1989. *The Tomb of Marquis Yi of Zeng* 曾侯乙墓. Beijing: Wenwu chubanshe.

Hubeisheng Bowuguan, Hubeisheng Wenwu Kaogu Yanjiusuo, and Suizhoushi Bowuguan, 湖北省考古研究所 随州市博物馆 2013. *The Zeng State Cemetery of the Early Western Zhou Period at Yejiashan, Suizhou* 随州叶家山西周早期曾国 墓地. Beijing: Wenwu chubanshe.

Hubeisheng Wenwu Kaogu Yanjiusuo 湖北省考古研究所 et al. 2005. *Eastern Zhou, Qin, and Han Tombs at Wangpo, Xiangyang* 襄阳王坡东周秦汉墓. Beijing: Kexue chubanshe.

Hubeisheng Wenwu Kaogu Yanjiusuo 湖北省文物考古研究所, and Suizhoushi Bowuguan 随州市博物馆 2014a. "Brief Excavation Report on M1 (Tomb of Marquis Yu of Zeng) and M2 at Wenfengta, Suizhou 随州文峰塔 M1(曾侯與墓)、M2 发掘简报." *Jianghan Kaogu* 4: 3–51.

Hubeisheng Wenwu Kaogu Yanjiusuo and Suizhoushi Bowuguan 湖北省文物考古研究所, 随州市博物馆 2014b. "Eastern Zhou Tombs at Wenfengta, Suizhoushi, Hubei 湖北随州市文峰塔东周墓地." *Kaogu* 7: 18–33.

Hubeisheng Yichang Diqu Bowuquan and Beijing Daxue Kaoguxi 湖北宜昌地区博物馆,北京大学考古系 1992. *Chu Tombs at Zhaojiahu, Dangyang* 当阳赵家湖楚墓. Beijing: Wenwu chubanshe.

Jiangsusheng Dantu Kaogudui 江苏丹徒考古队 1988. "Excavation Report of the Springs and Autumns Tomb at Beishanding, Dantu, Jiangsu 江 苏丹徒北山顶春秋墓发掘报告." *Dongnan wenhua* 3–4: 13–56.

Jiangsusheng Wenwu Guanli Weiyuanhui and Nanjing Bowuyuan 1965. "Eastern Zhou Burials at Chengqiao, Lliuhe, Jiangsu 江蘇文物管理委員會, 南京博物院." *Kaogu* 3: 105–115.

Jiangsusheng Yancheng yizhi kaogu fajue dui 1994. "Major Achievements from Excavations at the Yancheng Site 江苏省淹城遗址考古发掘队." In *Nanjing Bowuyuan jianyuan 60 zhounian jinian wenji (1933–1993)* 南京博物院建院 60 周年纪念文集 (1933–1992). Edited by Nanjing Bowuyuan. Nanjing: Nanjing Bowuyuan.

Jin, Guiyun 靳桂云 1994. "Studies on the Burial System of the Qi State Nobles in the Eastern Zhou Period 东周齐国贵族埋葬制度研 究." *Guanzi xuekan* 3: 59–63.

Jing, Zhongwei and Wang, Lixin 井中伟, 王立新 2013. *The Archaeology of Xia, Shang, and Zhou Periods* 夏商周考古学. Beijing: Kexue chubanshe.

Juxian Bowuguan 莒县博物馆 1999. "Western Zhou Tombs at Xi Dazhuang, Jü County, Shandong Province山东莒县西大庄西周墓葬." *Kaogu* 7: 38–45.

Kong, Lingyuan and Yongqing Chen 孔令远 , 陈永清 2002. "Excavation of MoundNo. 3 of Jiuduandun, Pizhou, Jiangsu 江苏邳 州九女墩三号墩的发掘." *Kaogu* 5: 19–30.

Li, Buqing 李步青 and Lin Xianting 林仙庭. "Investigation and Excavation of the Ruins of Guicheng in Huangxian, Shandong Province 山东黄县归城遗址的调查与发掘." *Kaogu* 10: 910–918.

Li, Chaoyuan 2002. "Studies on the Newly Acquired Qin Bronzes by the Shanghai Museum 上海博物馆新藏秦器研究." *Shanghai Bowuguan jikan* 9: 38–52.

Li, Chaoyuan 1996. "Studies of the Newly Acquired Bronzes at the Shanghai Museum 上海博物馆新获秦公器研究." *Shanghai Bowuguan jikan* 7: 23–33.

Li, Feng 2011. "An Outline of the Studies on Early Qin Bronzes and Sacrificial Sites Unearthed in Li County 礼县出土早期秦国铜器及祭祀 遗址论纲." *Wenwu* 5: 55–67.

Li, Feng 2013. *Early China: A Social and Cultural History*. London, UK: Cambridge University Press.

Li, Ling 李零 1981. "Who Is 'Chu Shu Zhi Sun Peng'? '楚叔之孙佣'究竟是谁." *Zhongyuan Wenwu* 4: 36–37.

Li, Ling 李零 1987. "The Classification of Chu State Bronzes 楚国铜器类说." *Jianghan Kaogu* 4: 69–78.

Li, Xueqin 1984. *The Civilizations of the Eastern Zhou and Qin Dynasties* 东周与秦代文明. Beijing: Wenwu chubanshe.

Li, Xueqin and Ai Lan (Sarah Allan) 1994. "The Recently Discovered Hu of the Duke of Qin 最新出现的秦公 壶." *Zhongguo wenwu bao* October 30, 1994.

Li, Xueqin and Kwang-chih Chang 1985. *Eastern Zhou and Qin Civilizations*. Early Chinese Civilizations Series. New Haven, CT: Yale University Press.

Liu Binhui 刘彬徽 1995. *Studies on Chu Bronzes* 楚系青铜器研究. Wuhan: Hubei jiaoyu chubanshe.

Liu, Jianguo 1987. "The Stone-chamber Tombs at Liangshan, Dantu, Jiangsu 江苏丹徒粮山石穴墓." *Kaogu yu wenwu* 4.

Liu, Yanchang 刘延常 and Lan Yufu 兰玉富 2009. "New Progress in Zhou Dynasty Archaeology in Shandong Province 山东地区周代考古的新进展." *Dongnan wenhua* 6: 61–67.

Luoyang Shi Wenwu Gongzuodui 洛阳市文物工作队 2001. "Clearance of the Eastern Zhou Tomb (C1M5269) at Zhenzhichang, Luoyangshi. 洛阳市针织厂东周墓 (C1M5269) 的清理" *Wenwu* 12:41–59.

Luoyangshi Bowuguan 洛阳博物馆 1981. "Brief Report on the Clearance of the Tomb of Ai Cheng Shuin Luoyang 洛阳哀成叔墓清理简报." *Wenwu* 7: 65–67.

Luoyangshi Di'er Wenwu Gongzuodui 洛阳第二文物工作队 2002. "Brief Excavation Report on the Eastern Zhou Tomb (JM32) at Yaochang Road, Luoyang City 洛阳市纱厂路东周墓 (JM32)发掘简报." *Wenwu* 11: 31–37.

Luoyangshi Wenwu Gongzuodui 洛阳文物工作队 1983. "Two Eastern Zhou Period Bronze-yielding Tombs at Luoyang 洛阳两座东周铜器墓." *Zhongyuan Wenwu* 4: 17–18.

Luoyangshi Wenwu Gongzuodui 洛阳文物工作队 1999. "Luoyangshi 613 suo dongzhou mu 洛阳 613 所东周 墓." *Wenwu* 8: 14–18.

Luoyangshi Wenwu Gongzuodui 洛阳文物工作队 2003. "Clearance of Several Late Springs and Autumns Tombs at Xigongqu, Luoyangshi 洛阳市西工区几座春秋墓的清理." *Kaogu yu wenwu* 2: 9–15.

Luoyangshi Wenwu Gongzuodui 洛阳文物工作队 2009. *Eastern Zhou Tombs at Wangcheng Guangchang, Luoyang* 洛阳王城广场东周墓. Beijing: Wenwu chubanshe.

Luoyangshi Wenwu Gongzuodui 洛阳文物工作队 2011. "Brief Report on the Excavation of the Horse and Chariot Pits at the Springs and Autumns site at Tiyuchang Road, Luoyang 洛阳体育场路春秋车坑马坑发掘简报." *Wenwu* 5: 12–24.

Nanjing Bowuguan 南京博物院 1974. "The Eastern Zhou Tomb No. 2 at Chengqiao, Liuhe, Jiangsu 江苏六合程桥二号东周墓." *Kaogu* 2: 116–120.

Nanjing Bowuyuan et al. 1999. "Brief Excavation Report on Mound No. 2 at Jiunüdun, Pizhoushi, Jiangsu 江苏 邳州市九女墩二号墩发掘简报." *Kaogu* 11: 28–34.

Nanjingshi Bowuguan and Liuhexian Wenjiaoju 六合县文教局 1991. "The Eastern Zhou Tomb No. 3 at Chengqiao, Liuhe, Jiangsu 江苏六合程桥东周三号墓." *Dongnan wenhua* 1: 204–211.

Nanyangshi Wenwu Yanjiusuo and Suizhoushi Bowuguan 南阳市文物研究所, 桐柏贤文馆办 1997. "A Brief Excavation Report on the Springs and Autumns Period Tomb No. 1 at Yuehe, Tongbai 桐柏月河一号春秋墓发掘简报." *Zhongyuan Wenwu* 4: 8–23.

Ning, Huizhen 宁会振 2003. "Discussions on the Date of the Guo State Cemetery at Shangcunling 上村岭虢国墓地时代刍 议." *Huaxia kaogu* 3: 55–57.

Peng, Yushang 彭裕商 2011. *Comprehensive Studies on the Date of Springs and Autumns Period Bronze Vessels* 春秋青铜器年代综合 研究. Beijing: Zhonghua shuju.

Pingdingshan 2007. Pingdingshanshi Wenwu Guanliju 平顶山市文物管理局, and Yexian Wenhuaju 叶县文化局. "Brief Report on the Springs and Autumns Period Tomb No. 4 in Jiuxian, Yexian, Henan Province 河南叶县旧县四号春秋墓发掘简报." *Wenwu* 9: 4–37.

Qi, Wentao 1972. "Overview of Shang and Zhou Bronzes Unearthed in Shandong in Recent Years 概述近年来山 东出土的商周青铜器." *Wenwu* 5: 3–18.

Qu, Chuanfu 1989. "Hypothesis on the Date of the Large Tomb at Jinshengcun in Taiyuan 太原金胜村大墓年代的推定." *Wenwu* 9: 87–89.

Quanguo Shida Kaogu Xinfaxian Pingxuan Huodong Bangongshi, Zhongguo Shehui Kexueyuan Kaogu Yanjiusuo 全国十大考古新发现评选活动办公室, 中国社会科学院

考古研究所 2014. "Springs and Autumns Tombs at Jiwanggu, Yishui, Shandong 山东沂水纪王崮春秋墓葬." http://kaogu.cn/html/cn/xueshuhuodongzixun/2013nianquanguoshidakaoguxinfaxian/2014/0411/45828.html, accessed 07/19/2014

Qun, Li 群力 1972. "Exploration summary of the Qi State Capital City of Linyi 临淄齐国故城勘探纪要." *Wenwu* 5: 45–54.

Ren, Xianghong 1998. "A Preliminary Study on the Zhou Dynasty Cemetery of Xianrentai in Changqing County, Shandong Province 山东长清县仙人台周代墓地及相关问题初探." *Kaogu* 9: 26–35.

Shaanxisheng Kaogu Yanjiusuo 陕西生考古研究所，Yongcheng Gongzuozhan 雍正工作站 1991. "Brief Report on Excavations of the Qin Tombs at Dengjiaya, Fengxiang 凤翔邓家崖秦墓发掘简报." *Kaogu yu wenwu* 2.

Shaanxisheng Kaogu Yanjiusuo 陕西省考古研究所 1998. *Qin Burials at Dianzi, Longxian* 陇县店子秦墓. Xi'an: San Qin chubanshe.

Shaanxisheng Kaogu Yanjiusuo et al. 陕西省考古研究所 2007a. "Brief Excavation Report on M19 at Liangdaicun, Hancheng, Shaanxi 陕西韩城梁带村遗址 M19 发掘简报." *Kaogu yu wenwu* 2.

Shaanxisheng Kaogu Yanjiusuo et al. 陕西省考古研究所 2007b. "Brief Excavation Report on M27 at Liangdaicun, Hancheng, Shaanxi 陕西韩城梁带村遗址 M27 发掘简报." *Kaogu yu wenwu* 6: 3–14.

Shaanxisheng Kaogu Yanjiusuo et al. 陕西省考古研究所 2008. "Brief Excavation Report on M26 at Liangdaicun, Hancheng, Shaanxi 陕西韩城梁带村遗址 M26 发掘简报." *Wenwu* 1: 4–21.

Shaanxisheng Kaogu Yanjiusuo et al. 陕西省考古研究所 2010. *Report of the 2007 Excavation of the Rui State Cemetery at Liangdaicun* 梁带村芮国墓地—2007 年度发掘报告. Beijing Wenwu chubanshe.

Shaanxisheng Wenguanhui Yongcheng Kaogudui 陕西省文管会雍城考古队 1978. "Brief Excavation Report on the Springs and Autumns Period Ice Storage Site of the Qin State in Fengxiang, Shaanxi 陕西凤翔春秋秦国凌阴遗址发掘简报." *Wenwu* 3: 43–47.

Shaanxisheng Wenguanhui Yongcheng Kaogudui 1985. "Brief Excavation Report on Building Foundation No. 1 at Majiazhuang, Fengxiang 凤翔马家庄一号建筑群遗址发掘简报." *Wenwu* 2: 1–29.

Shaanxisheng Yongcheng Kaogudui 1986. "Brief Report on the 1981 Excavation of the Baqitun Cemetery in Fengxiang 一九八一年凤翔八旗屯墓地发掘简报." *Kaogu yu wenwu* 5.

Shaanxisheng yongcheng Kaogudui 1987. "Brief Report on The Second Drilling at the Furnarery Parkof Qin Rulers in Fengxiang 凤翔秦公陵园第二次钻探简报." *Wenwu* 5: 55–65.

Shaanxisheng Yongcheng Kaogudui and Han Wei 1983. "Brief Report on the Drilling and Excavation at the Funerary Park of Qin Rulers in Fengxiang 凤翔秦公陵园钻探与试掘简报." *Wenwu* 7: 30–37.

Shandong Daxue Kaoguxi 山东大学考古系 1998. "Zhou Dynasty Cemetery at Xianrentai, Changqing County, Shandong Province 山东长 清县仙人台周代墓地." *Kaogu* 9: 11–25.

Shandongsheng Bowuguan 山东省博物馆 et al. 1978. "Springs and Autumns Period Tombs of the Jü State with Sacrificed Humans at Dadian, Jünan 莒南 大店春秋时期莒国殉人墓." *Kaogu xuebao* 3: 317–336.

Shangdongsheng Jiningshi Wenwu Guanliju 山东省济宁市文物管理局 1991. "Report on the Investigation and Excavation of the Ancient City of the Xue State and its Tombs 薛国故城勘查和墓葬发掘报告." *Kaogu xuebao* 4: 449–495.

Shandongsheng Wenwu Guanlichu 山东省文物管理处 1961. "Brief Report on the Test Excavation of Qi State City at Linzi, Shandong Province 山东省临淄齐故城试掘简报." *Kaogu* 6: 289–297.

Shandongsheng Wenwu Kaogu Yanjiusuo 1982. *The Ancient City of Qufu of the State of Lu* 曲阜鲁国故城. Ji'nan: Qilu shushe.

Shandongsheng Wenwu Kaogu Yanjiusuo 山东省文物考古研究所 1984a. "Excavation of the Eastern Zhou Tomb No. 5 and the Large Sacrificial Pit of Horses at the Ancient City of Qi 齐故城五号东周墓及大型殉马坑的发掘." *Wenwu* 9: 14–19.

Shandongsheng Wenwu Kaogu Yanjiusuo 山东省文物考古研究所 1984b. "Brief Report on the Excavation of the Springs and Autumns Period Tomb at Liujiadianzi, Lishui, Shandong 山东沂水刘家店子春秋墓发掘简报." *Wenwu* 9: 1–10.

Shandongsheng Wenwu Kaogu Yanjiusuo 山东省文物考古研究所 1994. "Major Achievements in the Exploration and Excavation of the Ancient City of Xue 薛故城勘探试掘重大成果." *Zhongguo wenwu bao* June 26, 1994.

Shandongsheng Wenwu Kaogu Yanjiusuo 山东省文物考古研究所 2000. "The Zhou and Han Dynasty Cemeteries at Dongxiaogong, Tengzhou, Shandong 山东滕州东小宫周代、两汉墓地." *Kaogu* 10: 66–80.

Shandongsheng Wenwu Kaogu Yanjiusuo 山东省文物考古研究所 2013. *The Ancient Capital City of Qi State at Linzi* 临淄齐故城. Beijing: Wenwu chubanshe.

Shanxisheng Kaogu Yanjiusuo and Houma Gongzuozhan 山西省考古研究所, 侯马工作站 1993. *The Houma Bronze Foundries* 侯马铸铜遗址. Beijing: Wenwu chubanshe.

Shanxisheng Kaogu Yanjiusuo and Houma Gongzuozhan 山西省考古研究所, 侯马工作站 1996. *The Jin Capital of Xintian* 晋都新田. Taiyuan: Shanxi Renmin chubanshe.

Shanxisheng Kaogu Yanjiusuo 1994a. "The Salvage Excavations of Zhou Dynasty Tombs at Shangguocun, Wenxi in 1976 1976 年闻喜上郭村周代墓葬清理记." In *San Jin kaogu*. Edited by Shanxisheng Kaogu Yanjiusuo. Taiyuan: Shanxi Renmin chubanshe, 123–138.

Shanxisheng Kaogu Yanjiusuo 1994b. *Shangma Cemetery* 上马墓地. Beijing: Wenwu chubanshe.

Shanxisheng Kaogu Yanjiusuo 1994c. "Brief Report on the Excavation at Shangguocun, Wenxi County in 1989 闻喜县上郭村 1989 年发掘简报." In *San Jin kaogu*. Edited by Shanxisheng Kaogu Yanjiusuo. Taiyuan: Shanxi Renmin chubanshe, 139–153.

Shanxisheng Kaogu Yanjiusuo 山西省考古研究所 1996a. *The Tomb of a Jin Minister of the Zhao Family at Taiyuan* 太原 晋国赵卿墓. Beijing: Wenwu chubanshe.

Shanxisheng Kaogu Yanjiusuo 山西省考古研究所 1996b. "Results of the Excavation of Eastern Zhou Tombs at Miaoqian, Wanrong 万荣庙前东周墓葬发掘收获." In *San Jin Kaoguo, vol. 1* 三晋考古 第一辑 Edited by Shanxisheng Kaogu Yanjiusuo 山西省考古 研究所. Taiyuan: Shanxi Renmin chubanshe: 218–250.

Shanxisheng Kaogu Yanjiusuo and Quwoxian Wenwuju 曲沃县文物局 2009. "Brief Report on the Excavation of the Cemetery of Jin Rulers at Yangshe, Quwo, Shanxi 山西曲沃羊舌晋侯墓地发掘简报." *Wenwu* 1: 4–14.

Shanxisheng Wenwu Guanli Weiyuanhui Houma Gongzuozhan 山西省文物管理委员会 侯马工作站 1963. "The Eastern Zhou Tombs at Shangma, Houma, Shanxi 山西侯马上马村东周墓 葬." *Kaogu* 5: 229–245.

Shanxisheng Yongcheng Kaogudui 山西省雍城考古队 1985. "Brief Report on the Drilling and Excavation of the Qin Capital Yongcheng 秦都雍城 钻探试掘简报." *Kaogu yu wenwu* 2.

Song, Lingping 宋玲平 2002. "An Analysis of the Regional Styles of the Eastern Zhou Narrative Pictorial Patterns on Bronze Vessels 东周青铜器叙事画像纹 地域风格浅析." *Zhongyuan Wenwu* 2: 46–50.

Song, Lingping 宋玲平 2007. *Studies on the Burial System of Jin Tombs* 晋系墓葬制度研究. Beijing: Kexue chubanshe.

Sun, Qingwei 孙慶偉 2012. "Sacrifices or Alliance Oaths: A New Discussion on the Nature of Sacrificial Pits in the Cemeteries of Jin Rulers at Yangshe and Beizhao 祭祀還是盟誓:北趙和羊舌晉侯墓地 祭祀坑性質新論." *Zhongguo bowuguan jikan* 106(5): 25–38.

Suzhou, Bowuguan 苏州博物馆1999. *Eastern Zhou Cemeteries at Zhenshan-- Excavation and Research of the Elite Tombs of the Wu and Chu States* 真 山东周墓地—吴楚贵族墓地的发掘与研究. Beijing: Wenwu chubanshe.

Teng, Mingyu 滕铭予 2002. *Qin Culture: Archaeological Observations from Vassal State to Empire* 秦文化: 从封国到帝国的考古学观察. Beijing: Xueyuan chubanshe.

Wang, Entian 王恩田 2012. "'The Two Kings Side by Side' and the Terminus Post Quemof the Guo State Cemetery '二王并立'与虢国墓地年代上限." *Huaxia kaogu* 4: 85–91.

Wang, Qing 王青 2002. *Studies on Zhou Dynasty Tombs of the Haidai Area* 海岱地区周代墓葬研究. Jinan: Shandong Daxue chubanshe.

Wang, Xueli 王学理 et al., eds. 1994. *The History of the Material Culture of Qin* 秦物质文化史. Xi'an: San Qin chubanshe.

Wang, Xun 王迅 1994. *Studies on the Eastern Yi and Huai Yi Cultures* 东夷文化与淮夷文化研究. Beijing: Beijing Daxue chubanshe.

Weber, Charles D. 1966. "Chinese Pictorial Bronze Vessels of the Late Chou Period: Part II." *Artibus Asiae* 28(4):271–311.

Wu, Zhenfeng 吴镇烽 and Shang Zhiru 尚志儒 1980. "Brief Report on the Qin State Cemetery at Baqitun, Fengxiang, Shaanxi 陕西凤翔八旗屯秦国墓葬发掘简报." *Wenwu ziliao congkan* 3.

Xiangfanshi, Kaogudui 襄樊市考古队, et al. 2005. *Zeng State Cemetery at Guojiamiao, Zaoyang* 枣阳郭家庙曾国墓地. Beijing: Kexue chubanshe.

Xu, Hong 许宏 2000. *Archaeological Studies on Pre-Qin Cities* 先秦城市的考古学研究. Beijing: Beijing Yanshan chubanshe.

Yang, Hongxun 1976. "Springs and Autumns Period Bronze Architectural Components from Qin Palaces Unearthed in Fengxiang: Jingang 凤翔出土春秋秦 宫铜构---金釭." *Kaogu* 2: 103–108.

Ye, Xiaoyan 叶小燕 1983. "Eastern Zhou Engraved Bronzes 东周刻纹铜器." *Kaogu* 2: 158–164.

Yin, Qun 印群 2006. "On the Date of the Tombs of a Royal Consort and a Crown Prince in theCemeteryoftheGuoStateandtheOriginofTheirRelatedClans论虢国墓地新出夫人及太子墓的年代及相关族氏的来源." In *Sandai kaogu, vol. 2* 三代考古(二). Edited by Zhongguo shehui kexueyuan kaogu yanjiusuo, Xia Shang Zhou kaogu yanjiusuo. Beijing: Kexue chubanshe.

Yongcheng, Kaogudui 雍城考古队 1986. "Supplements on the Brief Report on Building Group No. 1 at Majiazhuang, Fengxiang 凤翔马家庄一号建筑群遗址发掘简报补正." *Wenbo* 1: 11–13.

Yu, Weichao 俞伟超 1985. *Collected Papers of Pre-Qin and Han Archaeology* 先秦两汉考古学论文集. Beijing: Wenwu chubanshe.

Zaoqi Qin Wenhua Lianhe Kaogudui 早期秦文化联合考古队 2008a "Brief Report on the 2006 Excavation of Building Foundation No. 21 at Dabaozishan, Li County, Gansu Province 2006 年甘肃礼 县大堡子山 21 号建筑基址发掘简报." *Wenwu* 11: 4–13.

Zaoqi Qin Wenhua Lianhe Kaogudui 早期秦文化联合考古队 2008b. "Report on the Survey of Three City Sites in Lixian, Gansu 甘肃礼县三座城址调查报告." *Gudai wenming* 7: 323–362.

Zaoqi Qin Wenhua Lianhe Kaogudui 早期秦文化联合考古队, 2008c. "Brief Report on the 2006 Excavation of the sacrificial site at Dabaozishan, Li County, Gansu Province 2006 年 甘肃礼县大堡子山祭祀遗址发掘简报," *Wenwu* 11: 14–29.

Zaoqi Qin Wenhua Lianhe Kaogudui 早期秦文化联合考古队 2008d. "Brief Report on the 2006 Excavation of the Eastern Zhou tombs at Dabaozishan, Li County, Gansu Province 2006 年甘肃礼县大堡子山东周墓葬发掘简报," *Wenwu* 11: 30–49.

Zaozhuangshi Bowuguan 枣庄市博物馆 et al., eds. 2007. *Remains of the Xiaozhu State* 小邾国遗址. Beijing: Zhongguo Wenshi chubanshe.

Zhang Changping 张昌平 2009. *Studies on Zeng State Bronzes* 曾国青铜器研究. Beijing: Wenwu chubanshe.

Zhang, Guangli 张广立 1983. "Engraved Décor of Eastern Zhou Bronzes 东周青铜器刻纹." *Kaogu yu wenwu* 1.

Zhang, Xin 张辛 2002. *Studies on Eastern Zhou Tombs with Ceramics in the Central Plains Area* 中原地区东周陶器墓葬研究. Beijing: Kexue chubanshe.

Zhang, Xuehai 张学海 1985. "On the Types and Ethnic Affiliations of Zhou Burials at the Lu Capital and Related Issues 试论鲁城两周墓葬的类型族属及其反映的问题." In *Zhongguo kaogu xuehui disici nianhui lunwenji (1983)* 中国考古学会第四次年会论文集 *(1983)*. Beijing: Wenwu chubanshe, 81–97.

Zhao, Huacheng, Wang Hui, and Wei Zheng 2008. "Discussion of Related Issues Concerning the Qinzi Musical Instrument Pit at Dabaozishan in Li County 礼县大堡子山秦 子乐器坑相关问题探讨." *Wenwu* 11: 54–66.

Zhejiang Wenwu Kaogu Yanjiusuo and Shaoxingxian Wenwu Baohu Guanlisuo 浙江文物考 古研究所, 绍兴县文物保护管理所 1984. "A Brief Excavation Report of the Warring States Tomb No. 306 in Shaoxing 绍兴 306 号战国墓发掘简报." *Wenwu* 1: 10–26.

Zhejiang Wenwu Kaogu Yanjiusuo, and Shaoxingxian Wenwu Baohu Guanlisuo 浙江文物考 古研究所, 绍兴县文物保护 管理所 1999. "A Brief Excavation Report of the Large Tomb at Yinshan, Shaoxing, Zhejiang 浙江绍兴印山大墓发掘简报." *Wenwu* 11: 4–16.

Zhengzhoushi Bowuguan 郑州市博物馆 1982. "A Group of Springs and Autumns Period Bronze Vessels Unearthed in Weishi 尉氏出土一批春 秋时期青铜器." *Zhongyuan Wenwu* 4: 32–35.

Zhengzhoushi Wenwu Kaogu Yanjiusuo and Dengfengshi Wenwuju 郑州文物考古研究所, 登封市文物局 2006. "Tomb No. 3 at the Eastern Zhou Cemetery at Gaocheng in Dengfeng, Henan河南登封告城东周墓地三号墓." *Wenwu* 2006.4: 4–16.Zhongguo Shehui Kexueyuan Kaogu Yanjiusuo 2002. "The Clearing of Eastern Zhou Tombs at Zhongzhoulu North, Luoyang, Henan 河南洛阳市中州路北 东周墓的清理." *Kaogu* 1: 29–33.

Zhongguo Shehui Kexueyuan Kaogu Yanjiusuo 1989. *Luoyang Excavation Reports—Archives of the 1955–1960 Excavations at Jianbin, Luoyang* 洛阳发掘报 告—1955–1960 年洛阳涧滨 考古发掘资料. Beijing: Yanshan chubanshe.

Zhongguo Shehui Kexueyuan Kaogu Yanjiusuo 1959a. *Luoyang Zhongzhoulu* 洛阳中州路. Beijing: Kexue chubanshe.

Zhongguo Shehui Kexueyuan Kaogu Yanjiusuo 1959b. *Guo State Cemetery at Shangcunling* 上村岭虢国墓地. Beijing: Kexue chubanshe.

Zhongguo Shehui Kexueyuan Kaogu Yanjiusuo et al. 2003. *The Cemetery at Chengcun, Linyi* 临猗程村墓 地. Beijing: Zhongguo Dabaike Quanshu chubanshe.

Zhongguo Shehui Kexueyuan Kaogu Yanjiusuo Luoyang Tangchengdui 中国社会科学院考古研究所洛阳唐城队 1985. " Brief Report of the 1983 Excavation at Luoyang's Xigong District." 年洛阳西工区墓葬发掘简报." *Kaogu* 6: 508–521.

Zhongguo Shehui Kexueyuan Kaogu Yanjiusuo 中国社会科学院考古研究所 1956. *Huixian Excavation Reports* 辉县发掘报告 Beijing: Kexue chubanshe.

Zhongguo Shehui Kexueyuan Kaogu Yanjiusuo 中国社会科学院考古研究所 2004. *Chinese Archaeology: Western Zhou and Eastern Zhou, Monographs of Chinese Archaeology, Zhongguo kaoguxue—liang Zhou juan* 中国考古学—两周卷. Beijing: Zhongguo Shehui Kexue chubanshe.

Zhongmei Lianhe Guicheng Kaogudui 中美归城联合考古队 2011. "Brief Report on the Survey of the Zhou City of Guicheng in Longkou City, Shandong Province山东龙口市归城两周城址调查简报." *Kaogu* 3: 30–39.

Zhu, Fenghan 朱凤翰 2009. *Comprehensive Studies of Chinese Bronzes* 中国青铜器综论, 2 vols. Shanghai: Shanghai guji chubanshe.

Zhu, Hua 朱华 1994. "Text Excavations of the Ancient Tombs at Shangguocun, Wenxi 闻喜上郭村古墓群试掘." In *San Jin kaogu*. Edited by Shanxisheng Kaogu Yanjiusuo. Taiyuan: Shanxi Renmin Chubanshe, 95–122.

Zhu, Huo 朱活 1973. "The Lu Bo Da Fu Ying Ji Ji *Gui* Unearthed from Licheng, Shandong 山东历城出土鲁伯大父媵 季姬簋." *Wenwu* 1: 64.

THE IRON AGE–WARRING STATES PERIOD

CHAPTER 25

....

THE WARRING STATES PERIOD: HISTORICAL BACKGROUND

....

BY YURI PINES, HEBREW UNIVERSITY OF JERUSALEM[1]

AT first glance, the political situation of the Chinese world during the Warring States period (453–221 BCE) seems to continue the basic trend of the preceding Springs and Autumns period (chapter 22), namely the ongoing political fragmentation. This fragmentation brought about ever more prolonged, large-scale, and devastating wars, which post-factum gave the period under discussion its gloomy name. Historians who focus on this—admittedly, singularly important—feature of the Warring States era consider it one of the nadirs in the history of Chinese civilization.

A closer look, however, will show fundamental differences between the Warring States period and the preceding age. First and most notable is the trend toward territorial integration of individual states. Loose aristocratic polities of the past were gradually replaced by a centralized bureaucratic state that maintained a much higher degree of domestic order than was attainable during the Springs and Autumns period. Second, the Warring States period was marked by unprecedented dynamism. Armies marched hundreds and even thousands kilometers; peasants migrated—voluntarily or not—to new lands far away from their places of birth; and ambitious statesmen routinely crossed the borders in search of better employment, "serving Qin in the morning and Chu in the evening" (*zhao Qin mu Chu* 朝秦幕楚). This was the age rife with opportunities for skilled individuals of whatever pedigree; the age of painful conflicts but also of manifold new departures, especially in the realm of thought (see chapters 30–33); and the age in which the male's career was determined by his worth rather than birth. Third, this was the age of considerable expansion of the Chinese world. In search for new material and

[1] This research was supported by the Israel Science Foundation (grant No. 568/19) and by the Michael William Lipson Chair in Chinese Studies.

human resources, the competing "hero-states" of the Warring States period were engaged in conquest and incorporation of areas previously on the margins or outside the reach of the Zhou civilization. This territorial expansion shaped the geopolitical contours of much of "China proper" as it is known in the imperial era.[2]

TEXTS AND SOURCES

In 213 BCE, just a few years after the establishment of the first unified empire on Chinese soil, the First Emperor of Qin 秦始皇帝 (emp. 221–210 BCE) heeded the advice of his prime minister, Li Si 李斯 (d. 208 BCE) and issued an infamous order to burn the impractical books from private collections. Among the books to be burned were histories composed at the courts of the vanquished Warring States. A century later the historian Sima Qian 司馬遷 (ca. 145–90 BCE) lamented the loss:

> The historical records were stored only in the Zhou archives, and hence were all destroyed. How regrettable! How regrettable! All we have left are the Qin historical records, though they do not record days and months and the text is sketchy and incomplete. (*Shiji* 15:686; Watson 1993:87)

This complaint encapsulates the major problem faced by the historians of the Warring States period. The *Qin Records* salvaged by the future Han chancellor, Xiao He 蕭何 (257–193 BCE), from the Qin archives became the backbone of Sima Qian's own reconstruction of the Warring States history and especially of its chronology (Fujita 2008). Yet the sketchiness and laconism of this source made Sima Qian's task extremely challenging. The historian was able to utilize fragments of other materials in addition to *Qin Records*, such as genealogies of the ruling houses of rival states as well as a few surviving non-Qin chronicles, but these remained of secondary importance. Not a single surviving historical work of the Warring States period could match in comprehensiveness, details, or accuracy the major source for the preceding Springs and Autumns period, *Zuo zhuan* (for which see chapter 23). As a result, the Warring States–period sections in Sima Qian's *Records of the Historian*—our major source for the history of that age—contain not a few lapses, especially with regard to chronology and sequence of major events (Yang Kuan 1998:14–16; Pines 2020).

To augment the paucity of reliable historical sources, Sima Qian resorted to multiple anecdotal and quasi-anecdotal collections, most notably those currently incorporated in the *Stratagems of the Warring States* (*Zhanguo ce* 戰國策). The *Stratagems* is a heterogeneous compilation put together by the Han archivist, Liu Xiang 劉向 (79–8 BCE) from several disparate collections. The text comprises hundreds of vignettes, most of which

---

[2] The single most detailed study of the Warring States history is by Yang Kuan (1998); for an excellent English summary of parts of Yang's discussion, see Lewis 1999.

center around a speech by one of the so-called peripatetic persuaders (*youshui* 遊説) who dominated the inter-state relations of the Warring States period. These vignettes and speeches contain rich information about military history, diplomacy, and court intrigues of that age; but the reliability of this information is often questionable. The *Stratagems* were not designed as a historical treatise, and historical accuracy was not the goal of the text's authors and compilers. References to the past events in the *Stratagems* usually appear in the context of political argumentation, which makes the speakers prone to embellish certain events, gloss over others, and at times invent their information altogether. To aggravate matters, the currently available text of the *Stratagems* suffers from considerable textual corruption, which brings about confusion concerning the identity of certain speakers and of the events to which they refer. All these diminish the historical value of the *Stratagems* and of those related anecdotes that were incorporated in the *Records of the Historian* (He Jin 2001).

Another important source of historical information about the Warring States period are the texts of the contemporaneous Masters (or Philosophers, *zi* 子) discussed in chapters 31–33. As historical argumentation was extremely common in the ideological debates of that age, philosophical texts contain references to hundreds of events from the recent and distant past. This is particularly true of the texts from the third century BCE, such as *Han Feizi* 韓非子 or *Lüshi chunqiu* 呂氏春秋, whole sections of which are dedicated to analyzing events of the past and deducing proper lessons from attainments and failures of former statesmen and rulers. These texts may become invaluable in augmenting Sima Qian's data, but utilization of their information requires utmost caution. The overt polemical nature of the Masters' texts makes them even more susceptible to the author's tampering with historical facts than is the case of the *Stratagems*. Moreover, the Masters' texts are not concerned with either historical accuracy or even with systematic presentation of the past. Relating the information in these texts to that in the *Records of the Historian* is an arduous task.

Transmitted texts aside, a historian of the Warring States period may benefit from two additional sources of information. The archeological revolution of recent decades brought to light thousands of contemporaneous sites—from cemeteries to residential areas, from fortifications to ritual structures, from palaces to workshops, from remnants of hydraulic works to roads, long walls, and military installations. These rapidly expanding data allow us to reassess many factors in the lives of contemporaneous societies, ranging from demography and economy to arts, technology, social history, changing cultural identities, and the like (see, e.g., Falkenhausen 2006; Barbiery-Low 2007; Shelach-Lavi 2015 and chapters 26, 28, 34, 35). Although by their nature the archeological data are less pertinent to political history per se, they can be useful in some respects. For instance, they allow tracing with relative precision phases in the territorial expansion of the state of Qin from its original location in the upper Wei 渭 River basin to the middle reaches of the Yellow River and beyond to the Loess Plateau in the north and toward Sichuan Basin in the south (Teng Mingyu 2003, 2014; Falkenhausen 2004:110–115). Similarly, mortuary data allow us to trace the southward expansion of Chu settlements, a topic that is barely mentioned in our sources (Yang Kuan 1998:297n1).

Another and more important source of information about the history of the Warring States period are paleographic sources. The *Bamboo Annals* (*Zhushu jinian* 竹書紀年), looted ca. 279–280 CE from the tomb of King Xiang of Wei 魏襄王 (r. 318–296 BCE), became the earliest historical text unbeknown to Sima Qian that came to light after the publication of the *Records of the Historian*. This annalistic text, akin in its structure to the *Springs and Autumns Annals* of the state of Lu (chapter 23) allowed correction of some of Sima Qian's mistakes and even spurred interest in historical criticism in general.[3] In contrast to this spectacular discovery, paleographic findings of recent decades primarily comprise administrative, legal, and religious texts. These greatly expanded our knowledge of the Warring States social, economic, and administrative structure but were less informative in terms of political history. This situation changed in 2011 with the publication of the bamboo manuscript *Xinian* 繫年 (*String of Years* or *Linked Years*) from the collection of the Tsinghua (Qinghua 清華) University (Pines 2014, 2020). The last four sections of this text provide precious information about the history of ca. 450–396 BCE, which is not adequately covered in the extant sources. More information about the Warring States–period history can be extracted from several other bamboo manuscripts and a few lengthy bronze inscriptions. Among the latter, the most notable come from the royal cemetery of the state of Zhongshan 中山. Their publication in the 1970s brought to light the previously much neglected cultural trajectory and history of this polity (Wu Xiaolong 2017).

FORMATION OF THE MULTISTATE WORLD: THE RISE AND DECLINE OF WEI

In 453 BCE, the state of Jin became engulfed in a bitter conflict among four major aristocratic lineages, the heads of which for generations occupied top positions in the Jin government. After twists and turns, the coalition of the Wei 魏, Han 韓, and Zhao 趙 lineages eliminated their rival, the Zhi 知 lineage, finalizing thereby the partition of the state of Jin into three independent polities. Although it will take another fifty years before the status of the three "usurping ministers" as independent regional lords will be officially confirmed, the year 453 can serve as a convenient starting point of the Warring States history.

Eager to solidify their position and bolster their legitimacy, the heads of the newly formed "Three Jin" polities started implementing a series of social, administrative, military, and economic reforms. The details of these reforms (as of fifth-century-BCE history in general) are sketchy, but their direction—centralization, strengthening the ruler's

---

[3] For the complex nature of the *Bamboo Annals* see Shaughnessy 2006; cf. Nivison 2009; Cheng Pingshan 2013. For their historiographic impact see Qiu Feng 2013.

authority, increasing the state's control over its material and human resources, and bolstering agricultural production—is clear enough. Of particular importance was the readiness of new leaders, most notably Lord Wen of Wei 魏文侯 (r. 445–396 BCE), to employ in top positions men-of-service (*shi* 士) instead of hereditary nobles. The state of Wei attracted a stellar group of advisers, including the military genius Wu Qi 吳起 (d. 381 BCE); an economic reformer, Li Kui 李悝 (fl. 400 BCE); and several disciples and followers of Confucius. Thanks to these men the state of Wei quickly rose to the position of superiority within the Zhou cultural realm.

In the immediate aftermath of the victory over the Zhi lineage, the heads of Wei, Han, and Zhao continued to act in the name of the puppet lord of Jin, which ensured their ongoing cooperation in struggling against external foes. Wei benefitted most from these amicable relations with the two fraternal states. In the late fifth century BCE its armies expanded westward into the eastern reaches of the Wei River, repelling the Qin resistance; northeastward, where they occupied the state of Zhongshan in 406 BCE; and, together with Han and Zhao allies, southward, where they inflicted a series of defeats on the state of Chu. The Three Jin states benefitted in particular from cooperation with the southeastern kingdom of Yue 越, which by the late fifth century BCE had reached the peak of its power. In 441 and 430 BCE the coalition armies inflicted heavy defeats on the state of Qi 齊 in the east, causing its rulers to erect the Long Wall along Qi's southern border, probably the first ever construction of a Long Wall in China's history (Pines 2018). In 405–404 BCE the Jin armies again invaded Qi, completely overpowering it. Triumphant, heads of the Wei, Han, and Zhao houses presented the war captives to the Zhou king. The ceremony was attended by the humiliated lord of Qi as well as rulers of several medium-sized states, such as Lu 魯, Zheng 鄭, Song 宋, and Wei 衛. It was out of gratitude for this manifestation of respect that the Zhou Son of Heaven decided in 403 BCE to recognize the position of the Three Jin leaders as regional lords.

The Three Jin states continued a series of victories in 398–396 BCE, inflicting a heavy defeat to their major rival, the southern superpower of Chu. The southerners lost three top generals and the Chu chronicle admitted: "the Chu forces threw away their banners, tents, chariots and weapons, and returned, running like fleeing dogs" (*Xinian* 23, translated in Pines 2020:238). Yet these successes proved to be short-lived. Soon after the death of Lord Wen of Wei the erstwhile cooperation among the Three Jin states gave place to competition and mutual struggle. The expansion stopped, and some of the neighbors, most notably the state of Qin (see the next section), inflicted several defeats on the Wei armies. Wei also lost control over the state of Zhongshan, which was separated from the core Wei land by the territories of the state of Zhao. Only the southern expansion continued: the apex of it was the elimination of the state of Zheng by Han armies in 375 BCE and parallel conquest of Chu territories to the south of the Yellow River by Wei armies. In 361 BCE the Wei state felt confident enough to relocate its capital to Daliang 大梁 (currently Kaifeng), on the southern bank of the Yellow River. Parallel to this relocation it exchanged lands with Han and Zhao, allowing each of the states to attain a higher degree of territorial integration.

The major problem of Wei was its location: this state (just like its ally, the state of Han) was surrounded by formidable enemies on all sides. A chapter of *The Book of Lord Shang* (*Shang jun shu* 商君書) penned in a state of Wei 魏 explains this predicament:

> The state that has to fight on four fronts values defensive warfare; the state that borders the sea values offensive warfare. If the state that has to fight on four fronts is fond of raising troops to repel the four neighbors, it will be imperiled. The four neighbors raise an army [each] for just one campaign, while you have to raise four armies [to repel them]; hence you are called the imperiled state. (*Book of Lord Shang* 12.1)

This passage encapsulates the problems that brought about the decline of Wei. In 354 BCE, when the Wei armies laid a siege to the Zhao capital of Handan 邯鄲 in the north, Qi and Qin seized this opportunity to attack Wei from east and west. Wei survived this double assault, but the writing was on the wall. Yet, Lord (later King) Hui of Wei 魏惠王 (r. 369–319 BCE) remained adamant. In 344 BCE he assembled the leaders of many medium-sized polities and representatives of major powers, bringing them to the audience with the Zhou Son of Heaven; in return he was recognized as king (*wang* 王), a title that according to the Zhou ritual norms was an exclusive possession of the Zhou royalty. This hubris backfired: in two years Wei fell victim to coordinated incursions by Qi from the east, Qin from the west, and Zhao from the north. The results were disastrous: Wei armies suffered a series of humiliating defeats; the heir apparent was imprisoned by the Qi armies, and another prince of blood was seized by the Qin forces. This was the end of Wei's hegemony in the Central Plains. Hereafter this state survived only as a secondary actor on the inter-state arena.

Ephemeral alliances: Qin and its rivals

The collapse of Wei hegemony ca. 340 BCE brought about major reconfiguration in the balance of power in the Zhou world. First, it marked the shift of the center of political gravity from the Central Plains to the periphery, most notably to the states of Qin and Chu, and to a lesser extent to the states of Qi and Zhao. Second, insofar as no state could subjugate its major rivals militarily, they turned greater attention to diplomacy, making the Middle Warring States period into the golden age of traveling persuaders. Third, diplomacy aside, rival states sought ways to increase land and population under their control, in particular through expansion into the peripheral territories inhabited by non-Sinitic tribes. The story of wars and alliances of that period is extremely messy, but behind the ever-changing power configurations one can distinguish the single process of gradual but steady increase in the power of Qin at the expense of its rivals.

The state of Qin entered the Warring States period when it was at the nadir of its power. Domestic struggles and a series of military setbacks turned Qin into a marginal player, causing Sima Qian to observe: "Qin originally was a small and remote state, all the Xia [=Chinese] shunned it, treating it as Rong and Di [='barbarians']" (*Shiji* 15:685). Albeit historically inaccurate (Pines 2005–2006), this assessment grasps well Qin's low position at the beginning of the fourth century BCE. It was then that Lords Xian 秦獻公 (r. 384–362 BCE) and Xiao 秦孝公 (r. 361–338 BCE) launched their reforms, reinvigorating their polity and turning it into one of the "hero-states" of the Zhou world.

Qin reforms, especially those associated with Shang Yang 商鞅 (d. 338 BCE) and his followers, are discussed in chapter 27 and will not be addressed here; suffice it to say that they allowed this state to fully mobilize its human and material resources, turning its army into the most formidable force in the Zhou world. Starting with the 360s BCE the Qin forces repeatedly emerged victorious in their battles against Wei and Han, allowing Qin eventually to absorb the Wei territories to the west of the Yellow River bend and then to cross the River eastward, expanding simultaneously along its southern and northern shores into Shanxi and Henan. In 325 BCE, Lord (later King) Huiwen of Qin 秦惠文王 (r. 338–311 BCE) elevated himself to the position of a king. This was a symbolic act: Qin was no longer subordinate to the Zhou house but considered itself its equal and potentially its replacer. Qin was not the first to adopt the royal title; Chu's rulers did it centuries ago, while Wei and Qi monarchs recognized each other's position as kings back in 334 BCE. Yet it was Qin's adoption of this title and its forsaking of amicable relations with the Zhou kings (Pines 2004:12–20) that dealt the mortal blow to the semblance of Zhou superiority in the sub-celestial realm. As rulers of Yan 燕, Zhao, Han, and even the tiny Zhongshan followed the Qin pattern by recognizing each other as "kings," the once-prestigious title of *wang* lost its erstwhile aura of exclusivity. The Zhou kings retained the exclusive appellation as "Sons of Heaven," but their ritual superiority vis-à-vis the newly proclaimed kings diminished.

In the aftermath of King Huiwen's assumption of the royal title, Qin increased its pressure on the eastern states. For Qin's immediate neighbors, Wei and Han, this menace became unbearable. Unable to withstand the Qin assault militarily, leaders of these two states became engaged in vibrant diplomatic activities fluctuating between allying themselves with Qin and receiving thereby a degree of protection from its assaults, and joining the anti-Qin alliance, which was supposed to counterbalance the Qin military might. For a few decades thereafter the political arena of the Zhou world was dominated by the competition between the so-called Horizontal (pro-Qin) and Vertical (anti-Qin) alliances.

Fluctuations of these alliances stand at the core of the anecdotes in the *Stratagems of the Warring States*. Sima Qian made his best to put these anecdotes in a convincing chronological framework, but his efforts were only partly successful. Significant segments of the *Stratagems* present the history of competing alliances as a heroic struggle between two individuals: Zhang Yi 張儀 (d. ca. 309 BCE) and Su Qin 蘇秦 (d. 284 BCE). Su Qin reportedly tried to find employment in Qin but was rejected; to punish this state for this humiliation he invested all his efforts in forming the anti-Qin Vertical Alliance. Zhang Yi, in contrast, acted for the sake of Qin, trying to convince kings of the Warring States to ally with the superpower rather than fighting it and suffering inevitable defeat.

The *Stratagems* record a series of speeches by the two statesmen pro and contra alliances with Qin. The historical veracity of many of these speeches is minuscule, and their attribution to Zhang Yi and Su Qin is more than disputable; the very fact that a whole generation separates the lives of both statesmen shows that they could not compete with each other. Yet inventions and embellishments aside, the factual skeleton remains valid: several anti-Qin coalitions were formed following King Huiwen's ascendancy, causing Qin much concern. For instance, in 318 BCE the united forces of Wei, Han, Zhao, Chu, the northeastern state of Yan, and even, if our sources are reliable, the Xiongnu 匈奴 tribesmen attacked the Qin but were repelled suffering huge casualties (*Shiji* 5:207). In 296 BCE the coalition of Han, Wei, Zhao, Qi, and Song launched a more successful attack on Qin, causing the latter to give up some of its recent conquests (*Shiji* 5:210). A joint attack on Qin was repeated in 287 BCE. Qin, in turn, was successful at times in forming counteralliances either with Wei and Han, or with Chu and Qi.

There is no doubt that the anti-Qin Vertical Alliance thwarted some of Qin's attempts to expand eastward; yet the viability of this alliance (as well as that of its antipode, the Horizontal Alliance) remained limited. As Han Fei 韓非 (d. 233 BCE) with the advantages of hindsight explained, neither "serving one strong [country, i.e., Qin] to attack many weak" nor "allying with many weak to attack one strong" was an efficient strategy (*Han Feizi* 49:452 ["Wu du" 五蠹]). What each country sought was lands, and insofar as territories could be acquired by timely betrayal of erstwhile allies this course of action was considered entirely legitimate. To aggravate the atmosphere of mistrust, the diplomats of that age more often than not acted not just for the sake of their employer but for their own sake, seeking material and territorial gains for themselves, even if this meant effectively betraying the country they represented. In an attempt to cement alliances, some diplomats gained simultaneous positions in several polities; Su Qin reportedly was employed at the same time by no less than six states that allied against Qin (*Shiji* 69:2,261). Naturally, each of the employers had good reasons to suspect that Su Qin was not completely loyal to him but actually served his rivals, which further complicated the possibilities of effective cooperation.

Perhaps the single most significant impact of the alliances on Qin's trajectory was the temporary shift of its expansion from eastward to a southward direction. In 316 BCE, the Qin courtiers decided to abandon assaults on its eastern neighbor of Han and focus instead on its weak southern neighbors, Shu 蜀 and Ba 巴 located in Sichuan. To attain this goal Qin had to invest heavily in building roads in mountainous terrain that separates the Wei River basin from the fertile Sichuan basin; but once the logistical challenge was dealt with, the conquest was relatively smooth. This was a major strategic gain. Not only was Sichuan rich in natural resources, such as iron and salt, but, once the raging waters of the Min 岷 River had been controlled through the efforts of the governor of the region, Li Bing 李冰 (fl. 250 BCE) and his son, the Chengdu Plain produced an enormously abundant and reliable harvest of grain, which the Qin used to supply its armies. The colonization of Sichuan through the establishment of military settlements and through sending to the region many thousands of convicts to exploit its mineral and natural resources provided the Qin rulers with a viable model of effective incorporation of the newly conquered territories into their expanding realm (Sage 1992; Korolkov 2010).

Qin's conquest of Sichuan brought about major strategic change in its position vis-à-vis its southeastern neighbor, Chu. For centuries both countries maintained a loose alliance, only infrequently violating it for the sake of territorial gains in the Dan 丹 River Valley that separated their territories. Traditionally, Chu's major rival was the state of Jin and later its successors, particularly Wei. Chu had the broadest territories of all the Warring States, although in terms of population it apparently fell behind its northern rivals. It was also less centralized than other Warring States. Early in the fourth century BCE the statesman and military commander Wu Qi, who relocated to Chu from Wei, tried to strengthen the power of the Chu kings at the expense of the nobles but failed; in 381 BCE Wu Qi was killed and his reforms discontinued. Chu's nobles were more powerful than their peers elsewhere in the Warring States world, but still they were not in a position to directly threaten their king; rather they acted as the king's trusted lieutenants (Zheng Wei 2012). And whereas Chu was less successful in its northward expansion, it compensated these setbacks with active incorporation of southern and southeastern territories. Its major achievement came by ca. 306 BCE when it was able to utilize internal strife in the eastern kingdom of Yue and absorb much of Yue's territories.

The *Stratagems of the Warring States* cite the Qin statesman Zhang Yi: "In general, the most powerful states under Heaven are either Qin or Chu. If both are engaged in battle in which they are matched, only one would be able to survive" (*Zhanguo ce* 14.18:514). Indeed, Chu was the most potent of Qin's rivals. The Qin conquest of Sichuan increased the tension between the two countries. Henceforth, Qin outflanked Chu from the east and potentially threatened the Chu capital, Ying 郢, located just north of modern Jingzhou, Hubei province. During the last decade or so of the fourth century BCE Qin and Chu were engaged in complex diplomatic maneuvering, once renewing their alliance, once going to war. The results were gloomy for Chu: if our sources are to be trusted (and this is a big *if*), Qin not just repeatedly duped King Huai of Chu 楚懷王 (r. 328–299 BCE) but eventually seized him during the king's visit to Qin and prevented his return back. This mean act made the two erstwhile allies into mortal enemies, as is known from the frequently cited Chu promise: "even if only three households left in Chu, Chu will be the one to extinguish Qin" (*Shiji* 7:300).

The third major power that contested the supremacy in the Zhou world was the state of Qi. At the beginning of the Warring States period this immensely rich and densely populated state was in a relatively weak position, suffering from internal struggle within the ruling Tian 田 lineage. By 386 BCE the Tian house finalized its century-long usurpation of the supreme power in the state of Qi, deposing the last legitimate ruler from the Jiang 姜 clan. For a generation or so thereafter, the Tian rulers refrained from military activism, focusing on solidification of their domestic power. In particular, they become renowned patrons of scholars who gathered in Qi, turning it into the most thriving center of learning in the Zhou world. Gradually under King Wei 齊威王 (r. 356–319 BCE) and his successors Qi resumed assertive military policies, scoring several successes in battles with Wei and other rivals. And yet, the ambitions of Qi rulers to unify All-under-Heaven were not easily realizable. Mengzi 孟子 (ca. 380–304 BCE) plainly compared their desire to unify the realm through military means to "looking for fish by climbing a tree" (*Mengzi* 1.7).

Qi's policies were to a significant degree determined by its peculiar geographic location. Bordering the sea was expedient in terms of protecting one's rear, but it also limited the country's possibility to expand into the non-Sinitic periphery. For Qi, any territorial expansion could come only on behalf of powerful or medium-sized Zhou polities, which would inevitably cause a backlash from the country's multiple rivals.[4] Qi received a precious opportunity to improve this situation in 314 BCE, when King Kuai of the neighboring state of Yan 燕王噲 (r. 320–314 BCE) decided to emulate ancient Thearch Yao, yielding the throne to his meritorious minister, Zizhi 子之. King Kuai's motivations for this extraordinary step are not clear, but the results of his decision were both unequivocal and disastrous: the state of Yan sank into a bloody conflict between Zizhi and the legitimate heir, Ping 平, and the eventual turmoil allowed Qi to occupy much of the Yan territory. The results were disappointing from the point of view of Qi though. The Qi army failed to solidify its control over Yan and was driven out of this state, allowing restoration of the legitimate Yan dynasty. The state of Yan, once an amicable neighbor of Qi, became its mortal enemy, although its rulers reportedly concealed their ambitions for revenge, waiting for an appropriate opportunity.

By the year 300 BCE it seemed that Qi approached the apex of its power. Prudent diplomacy ensured its cooperation with Wei and Han against Qin; and when Chu failed to join the anti-Qin coalition, Qi orchestrated an assault on this state as well, inflicting a major defeat on it in 301 BCE. Under the rule of King Min 齊閔王 (r. 301–284 BCE) Qi started absorbing small polities in southern Shandong. Even Qin back then felt unable to check the rise of Qi; in 288 BCE the king of Qin agreed to share the new title of "thearch" (*di* 帝) with King Min. Although both rulers had to yield to the pressure of other regional lords and relinquish the new title, King Min felt confident enough to pursue his assertive course further. His decision to annex the state of Song in 286 BCE proved to be fateful.

Song was the largest and richest among the medium-sized polities of the Warring States period, and its position as a focus of contest among Chu, Qi, and Wei secured for several generations its independence. Once Qi annexed it, this was an open challenge to other regional lords, and they did not procrastinate in their reaction. A powerful coalition led by Zhao and Yan and joined by Qin, Han, and Wei led an assault on Qi in 284 BCE. The primary forces of the coalition were Yan armies led by the general Yue Yi 樂毅, who struck from the barely protected northern frontier of Qi, across the Ji 濟 River. Qi's collapse was complete: its armies were routed, King Min fled and was killed by the Chu general who was nominally dispatched to save him, and Qi was on the verge of extinction. Although in 279 BCE, the Tian house succeeded to restore its rule over the core

---

[4] One exception to this rule was the situation in southern Shandong, particularly in the Si 泗 River Valley, where many tiny polities survived without being conquered by Qi. For a possibility that Qi refrained from southward expansion because of its reluctance to advance too far away from the protective Long Wall, see Pines 2018.

territories of Qi, this country never resumed its position as a potential leader of All-under-Heaven.

It is worth noting here that numerous Warring States–period anecdotes attribute the misguided policy of King Min to the plot by Su Qin, who clandestinely acted on behalf of the king of Yan. By directing Qi to conquer Song, Su Qin had effectively alienated Qi's erstwhile allies and prepared the ground for Yan's deadly assault. Needless to say, the veracity of this version of events is unverifiable. What matters though is the implicit irony in the story: Su Qin, the staunchest enemy of the state of Qin, played a crucial role in the demise of the only state that might have been sufficiently powerful to combat Qin's expansion. By 284 BCE, Qin emerged as the major beneficiary of the new power configuration in the Zhou world.

TOWARD UNIFICATION: THE AUTUMN OF TRAVELING PERSUADERS

The last decades of the Warring States history were marked by an almost unstoppable expansion of the state of Qin at the expense of its major rivals. The collapse of Qi as an effective superpower allowed Qin to increase its pressure on the neighboring Wei and Han, which were battered by almost annual incursions. Although these incursions failed to bring about decisive victories—in particular Qin's repeated sieges of Wei's capital, Daliang, were unsuccessful—they still inflicted huge casualties on Qin's rivals. Su Qin's brother, Su Dai 蘇代, is said to have observed: "Qin killed several million people of the Three Jin [states]. Those who are alive today all are the orphans of those who died by Qin" (*Zhanguo ce* 30.1:1,130 ["Yan 燕 ce 2"]).

Parallel to its pressure eastward, Qin focused on expansion in a southeast direction, against the state of Chu. In 279–278 BCE the campaign led by one of Qin's most brilliant generals, Bai Qi 白起 (d. 257 BCE), inflicted a major defeat on Chu. First the Qin army captured Chu's major stronghold on the Han 漢 River, the city of Yan 鄢, which it flooded through diverting the water of the nearby Yi River夷水; reportedly, "hundreds of thousands" of civilians and military personnel perished. This was followed by the rapid assault on Chu's capital, Ying, which was conquered and looted. The victorious Qin armies advanced further southward, well into modern Guizhou and Hunan; and although these southernmost territories were ultimately returned to Chu, Chu's erstwhile heartland remained henceforth under Qin's control. This campaign effectively neutralized Chu as a competitor of Qin.

By the second quarter of the third century BCE only one state was able to effectively withstand the Qin armies, the state of Zhao. Initially the least important among the three successors of Jin, Zhao steadily improved its position, particularly through expanding northward toward the steppe belt where it became engaged in steady conflicts with nomadic tribes. The tribal method of mounted warfare impressed the Zhao leaders, especially King Wuling 趙武靈王 (r. 325–299 BCE), who ordered his subjects in 307 BCE to adopt "northern tribesmen's clothes" (i.e., trousers), thereby facilitating usage of cavalry. Zhao proved its military prowess in 296 BCE when it eliminated the kingdom of Zhongshan, established by a Sinicized branch of the White Di 白狄 tribesmen (for this state's history, see Wu Xiaolong 2017). Throughout the first decades of the third century BCE, Zhao was able to withstand the Qin assault, inflicting occasional defeats on the Qin armies and simultaneously expanding its territories at the expense of Wei and Qi. The decisive battle between Zhao and Qin seemed inevitable.

This battle finally ensued in 262–260 BCE in the vicinity of Changping 長平, in the hilly terrain of southern Shanxi. Both sides committed most of their military forces to the campaign, which reportedly involved almost one million combatants. Unable to defeat each other, both armies remained entrenched in fortified encampments in the hills separated by just a few kilometers of the valley. After two years of standoff, a Zhao commander was lured to strike the Qin troops. A carefully preplanned Qin cavalry maneuver split the Zhao forces into two, and additional Qin forces dispatched through an emergency conscription succeeded to cut off the supply routes of Zhao soldiers. After 46 days the starved Zhao troops surrendered to the Qin commander, Bai Qi, who ordered the massacre of over 400,000 prisoners, erecting a terrace made of their sculls (*Shui jing zhu* 9:835). The state of Zhao faced imminent annihilation.

Luckily for Zhao, Qin was too exhausted to immediately utilize its victory, and when it resumed a campaign against Zhao's capital, Handan (259–257 BCE), the latter was unsuccessful. Wei and Chu, fearful of excessive empowerment of Qin, abandoned their neutrality and sent troops to save Zhao from extinction. The renewed anti-Qin coalition succeeded in slowing the pace of Qin expansion. However, it was not a viable alliance. Soon enough, rival Warring States were re-engaged in mutual conflicts, allowing Qin to prepare for its final assault.

In 256 BCE, after the death of King Nan 赧 of Zhou the royal house fell in turmoil and Qin intervened, annexing the Zhou royal principality (Pines 2004:19–23). Militarily it was a minor event, but its symbolic implications were huge. The cessation of the eight-centuries-old dynasty of the Sons of Heaven meant that the ritual center of the Zhou civilization had been lost. The authors of *Lüshi chunqiu* 呂氏春秋, composed ca. 240 BCE in the state of Qin, lamented:

> Nowadays, the house of Zhou has been destroyed, [the line of] the Sons of Heaven has been severed. There is no turmoil greater than the absence of the Son of Heaven; without the Son of Heaven, the strong overcome the weak, the many lord it over the few, they use arms to harm each other, having no rest. (*Lüshi chunqiu* 13.5)

The authors' gloomy estimate that without a singular locus of power the entire sub-celestial realm is doomed to sink in endless turmoil reflects a common conviction of the thinkers of the Warring States period: to attain peace, All-under-Heaven should be uni-fied (Pines 2000). By mid-third century BCE Qin was the only candidate to attain this goal. Its ultimate realization was delayed due to a variety of factors: either machinations of powerful courtiers who utilized the victories of Qin armies to aggrandize their allot-ments rather than to benefit the state; or inter-ministerial conflicts and succession cri-ses; or insufficient manpower in Qin, which, demographically speaking, lagged behind its eastern neighbors; or sporadic successes of anti-Qin coalitions to thwart its leaders' efforts to subjugate the neighbors.[5] Yet none of these factors could in the long term save the fate of Qin's rivals. A young scholar, Li Si 李斯 (d. 208 BCE), who decided in the 240s BCE to seek a career in Qin, observed: "This is the time for swift move by the plain-clothed [i.e., poor but ambitious men-of-service like himself]; it is the autumn of travel-ling persuaders." Indeed, gone was the age of diplomats: the realm was due to be unified.

Li Si's eventual employer, King Zheng 政 of Qin (king from 246 to 221 BCE; emperor from 221 to 210 BCE), was determined to translate Qin's superiority into ultimate success. Heeding the advice of Li Si and likeminded statesmen, he started campaigns of annihila-tion against the rival "hero-states." Han was subjugated first in 230 BCE, followed by Zhao (228 BCE, last resistance smashed in 222 BCE), Wei (225 BCE), Yan (226–222 BCE), Chu (224–223 BCE), and finally Qi (221 BCE). Having accomplished within just ten years the subjugation of "All-under-Heaven," King Zheng, proud of his achievements, in 221 BCE proclaimed himself emperor (*huangdi* 皇帝, literally "August Thearch"). Gone was the age of the Warring States. A new era in Chinese history had begun.

Bibliography

Barbieri-Low, Anthony J. 2007. *Artisans in Early Imperial China*. Seattle and London: University of Washington Press.

The Book of Lord Shang: Apologetics of State Power in Early China. Translated and edited by Yuri Pines. New York: Columbia University Press.

Cheng, Pingshan 程平山. 2013. *The First Part of Studies of the Bamboo Annals and Unearthed Texts: Research on the Bamboo Annals* 竹書紀年與出土文獻研究之一: 竹書紀年考. Beijing: Zhonghua shuju.

Falkenhausen, Lothar von 2004. "Mortuary Behavior in Pre-imperial Qin: A Religious Interpretation." In *Religion and Chinese Society*, vol. 1: *Ancient and Medieval China*. Edited by John Lagerwey, 109–172. Hong Kong: Chinese University of Hong Kong Press.

Falkenhausen, Lothar von 2006. *Chinese Society in the Age of Confucius (1050–250 BC): The Archeological Evidence*. Los Angeles: Cotsen Institute of Archaeology at UCLA.

Fujita, Katsuhisa 藤田勝久 2008. *Research on Historical Materials from the Warring States Period in the Shiji* 《史記》戰國史料研究. Translated by Cao Feng 曹峰 and Hirose Kunio 廣瀬薫雄. Shanghai: Shanghai guji chubanshe.

Han Feizi jijie 韩非子集解 1998. Compiled by Wang Xianshen 王先慎 (1859–1922). Beijing: Zhonghua shuju.

He, Jin 何晉. 2001. *Study of Zhanguo ce* 《戰國策》研究. Beijing: Beijing daxue chubanshe.

Korolkov, Maxim 2010. "Zemel'noe zakonodatel'stvo i kontrol' gosudarstva nad zemlej v epokhu Chzhan'go i v nachale ranneimperskoj epokhi (po dannym vnov' obnaruzhennykh

---

[5] For the list of these factors, see, for example, *Han Feizi* 17.43:398 ("Ding fa" 定法); *Book of Lord Shang* 15; and narrations scattered throughout the *Stratagems of the Warring States* and *Records of the Historian*.

zakonodatel'nykh tekstov)." PhD dissertation, Moscow: Russian Academy of Sciences, Institute of Oriental Studies.

Lewis, Mark E. 1999. "Warring States: Political History." In *The Cambridge History of Ancient China*. Edited by Michael Loewe and Edward L. Shaughnessy, 587–650. Cambridge, UK: Cambridge University Press.

Lüshi Chunqiu jiaoshi 呂氏春秋校釋 1990. Compiled and annotated by Chen Qiyou 陳奇猷. Shanghai: Xuelin.

Mengzi yizhu 孟子譯注 1992. Annotated by Yang Bojun 楊伯峻. Beijing: Zhonghua shuju.

Nivison, David S. 2009. *The Riddle of the Bamboo Annals*. Taipei: Airiti.

Pines, Yuri 2000. "'The One That Pervades the All' in Ancient Chinese Political Thought: The Origins of 'The Great Unity' Paradigm." *T'oung Pao* 86(4–5):280–324.

Pines, Yuri 2004. "The Question of Interpretation: Qin History in Light of New Epigraphic Sources." *Early China* 29:1–44.

Pines, Yuri 2005–2006. "Biases and Their Sources: Qin History in the *Shiji*." *Oriens Extremus* 45:10–34.

Pines, Yuri 2014. "Zhou History and Historiography: Introducing the Bamboo Manuscript *Xinian*." *T'oung Pao* 100(4–5):325–359.

Pines, Yuri 2018. "The Earliest 'Great Wall'? Long Wall of Qi Revisited." *Journal of the American Oriental Society* 138.4:743–762.

Pines, Yuri. 2020. *Zhou History Unearthed: The Bamboo Manuscript* Xinian *and Early Chinese Historiography*. New York, NY: Columbia University Press.

Qiu, Feng 邱鋒 2013. "The *Bamboo Annals* and Historiography from Jin to Tang Dynasties 《竹書紀年》與晉唐閒的史學." *Shixue shi yanjiu* 史學史研究 1:24–32.

Sage, Steven F. 1992. *Ancient Sichuan and the Unification of China*. Albany: State University of New York Press.

Shaughnessy, Edward L. 2006. *Rewriting Early Chinese Texts*. Albany: State University of New York Press.

Shelach-Lavi, Gideon 2015. *The Archeology of Early China: From Prehistory to the Han Dynasty*. Cambridge, UK: Cambridge University Press.

Shiji 史記 1997. By Sima Qian 司馬遷 et al. Annotated by Zhang Shoujie 張守節, Sima Zhen 司馬貞, and Pei Yin 裴駰. Beijing: Zhonghua shuju.

Teng, Mingyu 滕銘予 2003. *Qin Culture: Archaeological Observations from an enfeoffed polity to Empire* 秦文化: 從封國到帝國的考古學觀察. Beijing: Xueyuan chubanshe.

Teng, Mingyu 2014. "From Vassal State to Empire: An Archaeological Examination of Qin Culture." Translated by Susanna Lam. In *Birth of an Empire: The State of Qin revisited*. Edited by Yuri Pines, Lothar von Falkenhausen, Gideon Shelach, and Robin D. S. Yates, 71–112. Berkeley: University of California Press.

Watson, Burton, trans. 1993. *Records of the Grand Historian*, vol. 3: *Qin Dynasty*. Hong Kong: Chinese University of Hong Kong.

Wu, Xiaolong 2017. *Material Culture, Power, and Identity in Ancient China*. Cambridge, UK: Cambridge University Press.

Yang, Kuan 楊寬 1998. *History of the Warring States* 戰國史, rev. ed. Shanghai: Renmin chubanshe.

Zheng, Wei 鄭威 2012. *Research on the Enfeoffed Rulers from the State of Chu* 楚國封君研究. Wuhan: Hubei jiaoyu chubanshe.

CHAPTER 26

....

IRON TECHNOLOGY AND ITS REGIONAL DEVELOPMENT DURING THE EASTERN ZHOU PERIOD

....

BY WENGCHEONG LAM, CHINESE UNIVERSITY OF HONG KONG

DURING the Warring States period (456–221 BCE), Chinese society witnessed remarkable transformations in various domains (e.g., Lewis 1999; Yang 2004a:89–187), and iron production is unquestionably the most essential one in the field of technology. The earliest iron industry in ancient China was based on bloomery iron, used primarily in manufacturing elite weaponry. From the seventh to fifth centuries BCE, cast iron technology was gradually established in the Central Plains as well as in different peripheral states (Han and Chen 2013; Lam 2014). By the dawn of the Qin unification (221 BCE), the rapid increase in the use of iron resulted in the innovation of both decarburized steel and malleable iron in various territorial states, as documented by the discovery of iron objects (Han and Duan 2009; Han and Ke 2007:604). The point has been made (Wagner 2008:144–146, 210–220) that in the ancient world manufacturing iron, particularly cast iron, required not only large amounts of fuels and raw materials, but also a complex system to organize substantial labor is also applicable to understanding ancient Chinese society and production.

In the literature, the contributions of cast-iron technology in various social domains, such as in stimulating the manufacture of more useful agricultural tools, have been well recognized and extensively discussed (e.g., Yang 2003:42–57, 2004a; Hsu 1980; Bai 2005). Unfortunately, the developmental process of iron technology in ancient China has not yet been scrutinized and subjected to further fine-grained analysis. As a result, two critical issues have long been overlooked and under-addressed. First, where did local iron technology first appear? How did the transition to cast-iron-based industry and associated techniques happen? Although some Chinese scholars had suggested the Chu state in the Middle Yangtze River Valley was the center of cast-iron technology (Huang 1999; Yang 2004b), Donald Wagner (1993, 2008) tentatively suggested that the technology was innovated in the Wu state in the Lower Yangtze River Valley. No matter which one is more likely to be the case, no one has critically examined the argument by integrating the long-term development of technology in the region. Moreover, these ideas were basically proposed a few decades ago; it is time to reinvestigate these proposals given the large volume of data recently published.

The second critical issue is how the technology integrated into various divided states of the Warring States period, and the extent that the technology contributed to the social development of these regions has been inadequately addressed. Previous literature (e.g., Barnard and Satō 1975; Li 1975; Lei 1980; Yang 2004a) agrees that the appearance of iron objects in tombs represents a hallmark of the arrival of a large-scale cast-iron industry that characterized the era of the Warring States. Nonetheless, these studies do not illustrate how the industry was developed in each state and how this development was relevant to the cultural, economic, and even historical background of the region. Some scholars suggest that iron technology, or the organization of iron production, might have been an important factor in the unification of the Qin state (e.g., Trousdale 1977; Wagner 2008:146–147; for criticism of this idea, see Keightley 1976; Barnard 1978–1979), but no comparative evaluation between the Qin and other states has been conducted.

Since voluminous site reports of the Warring States period have been published in recent decades, updated data offer a timely opportunity to re-evaluate the nature of technological change and social development of iron in ancient China. Therefore, this chapter attempts to review iron technology in ancient China while offering some new insights on these issues. In order to explain the developmental trajectory of the iron industry, I initially review previous critical studies on iron metallurgy (Han and Duan 2009; Han 1998; Han and Ke 2007; Han and Chen 2013) and iron typology (Bai 2005) during the first millennium BCE. Then I explore the difference of iron assemblages and technological variations between three major territory states: Jin (or the Three Jin states: Han, Zhao, and Wei), Qin, and Chu; all three states have much better published data than the other two major states, Qi and Yan. At the end I provide multiple lines of evidence to illustrate an image of the iron industry that is different from that in previous literature. During the Early Eastern Zhou period, the tradition of using iron in the manufacturing of bimetallic weapons appeared to be widely practiced in the north but not in the south. Shortly thereafter, cast-iron technology quickly developed in both the Jin and Chu states. But in archaeological records, cast-iron technology was more likely to be triggered by the demand of agricultural tools and did not entirely replace the bronze in the weaponry industry of most major states. Moreover, the iron industry appeared to be operated on different scales between the three major states, Jin, Qin, and Chu. A regional perspective is essential to illustrate the impacts of iron technology during the Warring States period.

DEVELOPMENT OF IRON TECHNOLOGY BEFORE THE FIFTH CENTURY BCE

To contextualize iron technology in its historical background for readers who are not familiar with the issue, this chapter will first clarify how early iron-smelting technology was developed in ancient China. So far, the earliest iron products in ancient China are the two iron pieces (one is an iron bar while the other one is an iron lump) from the Mogou 磨沟 cemetery in Gansu province associated with the Qijia culture (Chen et al. 2012), dating to about the fourteenth century BCE. Results of metallurgical analysis of these two iron pieces showed that they are bloomery iron products. Since a handful of early iron objects falling within the range of ninth to eighth century BCE (Chen 2014:220) have been found before, the discovery of these early iron pieces from Mogou reiterates previous speculation (e.g., Tang 1993; Zhao 2012) that early iron technology (i.e., bloomery iron) was the result of cultural exchange or interaction from Central or West Asia, rather than a local invention (cf. Bai 2005:42–43). However, the link in archaeological evidence is still missing to demonstrate how iron technology was spread through the Hexi corridor to the Central Plains[1] and how the technology led to the manufacturing of bimetallic weapons dating to the Shang dynasty, as represented by the bimetallic *yue* axe from the Taixi site in Hebei (Hebei 1985).

The widespread adoption and employment of iron technology in craft production appeared more clearly during the transition between the Western Zhou and Eastern Zhou dynasties, or about the ninth and eighth centuries BCE. The evidence of smelting iron employed in the manufacture of bimetallic weapons such as *ge* halberd and daggers was widely found in elite funeral contexts[2] in northern China during this period, particularly in the part of the Central Plains including Jingjiazhuang 景家庄 (Liu and Zhu 1981) in Gansu; Bianjiazhuang 边家庄 (Shaanxi & Baoji 1988), Yimencun 益门村 (Tian and Lei 1993), and Liangdaicun 梁带村 (Chen et al. 2009) in Shaanxi; Shangcunling 上村岭 (Henan and Sanmenxia 1999) in Henan; Jundushan 军都山 (He et al. 2004) in Hebei, and Xianrentai 仙人台 (Shandong 1998) in Shangdong (Figure 1).

In southern China, bimetallic weapons are generally missing in the archaeological literature; only one piece of an iron dagger mounted on a jade shaft has been found from

---

[1] We define the Central Plains as referring to area of the middle Yellow River Valley and the southeastern edge of the Loess Plateau.

[2] According to the metallurgical analyses that have been conducted so far, all these products were made of either bloomery iron or meteoric iron. These objects sometimes were also made by meteoritic iron and fitted with bronze handles.

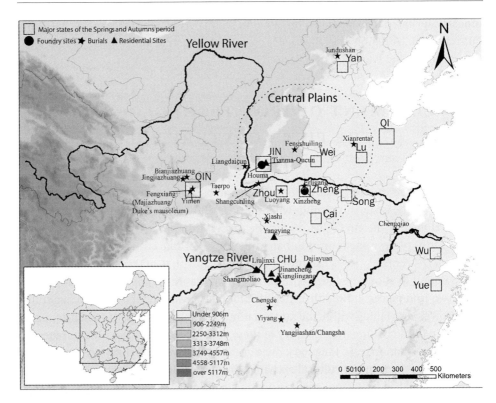

FIGURE 1 Distribution map of bimetallic weapons, early cast-iron objects, and cemeteries that are mentioned in the chapter.

tomb No. 10 at Xiaxi 下寺 (Henan et al. 1991), an elite cemetery associated with the Chu state, in the Xicun River Valley, Henan. As this tomb is usually dated to the Late Spring and Autumn period, this piece represents the last example of the bimetallic or biomaterial tradition in the manufacture of iron weaponry in the core of ancient China.[3] Except for the case of Jundushan, which was associated with a non-Sinitic occupant, all other cases were either marquises or high-rank elite tombs with substantial numbers of bronze vessels. Metallurgical analyses also demonstrate that most of these items were either bloomery iron or meteoric iron (Chen 2014; Wang et al. 2019). Even though the provenance of these objects has not been addressed, the widespread distribution of materials implies the value of iron should have been appreciated by elites as prestige goods in most of the Eastern Zhou states in the Central Plains. The Early and Middle Spring and Autumn period therefore might have staged the period for experimenting with iron-smelting techniques in ancient China. According to the context of these early iron objects, the development of bloomery iron in ancient China also embodies Cyril Smith's

---

[3] Bimetallic weapons were also found in "peripherals" alongside the "crescent shaped cultural communication belt" coined by Tong Enzheng (1990) from Guyuan, Ningxia to Kunming, Yunnan. But these examples will not be discussed here, because they might belong to the tradition different from the core in ancient China.

(1970) famous argument that the innovation of using new materials was usually not triggered by practical need but rather by the interests of art. The invention of iron-casting was one of the indirect results of elite patronage in the craft industry.

It is worthwhile to clarify beforehand the two basic types of iron: cast iron and bloomery iron. Cast iron refers to the smelting or melting of iron to its liquid stage for casting, which implies the control of a high temperature and strong reducing atmosphere inside the furnace.

Bloomery iron means reducing iron ores in a relatively low temperature and weak-reducing environment. The final products were sponge-shaped mixtures of iron, since slag was not completely separated from the metallic iron. Cast iron is in fact an iron-carbon alloy, which is extremely hard and lacks flexibility. Annealing and decarburizing processes are necessary in order to make cast-iron tools practical (i.e., to convert cast iron into steel) in production (For detailed definition of the terminologies, see Table 1). In contrast, bloomery iron is relatively soft; ironsmiths need to carburize bloomery iron to steel during the hammering and forging process to shape an iron tool. Almost all experiments with iron in ancient society started with the manufacture of bloomery iron (Rehren et al. 2013), and China was not an exception.

Archaeological records also show that the initial cast-iron production immediately followed the widespread use of bloomery iron in the manufacture of prestige weaponry. The early evidence of cast-iron production came from the Tianma-Qucun 天马-曲村 (Beijing and Shanxi 2000) site in Houma, Shanxi. Two pieces of cast iron were unearthed from midden contexts dating to the Early Spring and Autumn period. Nonetheless, the shape of these objects are so irregular that it imposes a big challenge to identify whether these pieces are iron products or just by-products of the smelting process of bloomery

Table 1 Definition of basic technical terminologies

Terminology	Definition
Cast iron	Iron that was melted and cast, usually with about 4% of carbon (Wagner 1993:336)
Bloomery iron	Iron was smelted by reduction of the ore to solid iron at a low temperature in what is called a bloomery (a small-scale hearth or a shaft furnace). Final products usually are wrought iron (iron with carbon content in the range 0.1–0.3%) (Wagner 1993:274; 2008:89)
Solid-state decarburization of cast iron	The annealing of a cast iron object in an oxidizing atmosphere in order to produce wrought iron or steel (iron with carbon content in the range 0.5–1%) for smithing (Wagner, 1993:291)
Malleable cast iron	An object was cast in its intended final form and annealed at a high temperature for a period of days to decarburize or graphitize the casting (Wagner 1993:291)
Fined iron	The operation of converting cast into wrought iron or medium-carbon steel in a hearth or open fire, facilitated by a blast of air with charcoal as the fuel (Wagner 1993:290–291)

iron (Han and Chen 2013). In northern China there is also some evidence showing the emergence of cast-iron production during the Late Spring and Autumn period (Lam 2014), as represented by the iron tools from the sacrificial pit at Majiazhuang 马家庄, the Duke Jing's Mausoleum of the Qin State (Han and Jiao 1988) in Shaanxi, and tomb No. 7 at Tanghu 唐户 of the Zheng state (or present-day Xinzheng) (Kaifeng et al. 1978) in Henan, though cast-iron remains are generally sporadic in archaeological contexts during the entire Spring and Autumn period.

In contrast to the practice witnessed in the Central Plains, cast-iron technology was more widely documented in the Yangtze River Valley in southern China about the same time.

Agricultural implements[4] and remains related to cast-iron production were found in the middle Yangtze River and Han River Valleys, including Shanmoliao 上磨垴 (Hubei 2000), Liulinxi 柳林溪 (Guowuyuan and Guojia 2003), Dajiayuan 大家园 (Hubei and Hubei 2006), Xianglinggang 响岭岗 (Jingmen 1990), and Yangying 杨营 (Hubei 2003)[5] (Figure 1). All these locations were considered to date to the Late or even the Middle Spring and Autumn period.[6] Only samples from Yangying have been subject to metallurgical analysis (Chen 2014), but all these objects are very likely to be cast iron according to typological comparison. Nonetheless, the most significant discovery of early cast iron is from further south. One decarburized steel sword and a cast-iron cauldron were unearthed from a Chu tomb in Changsha dating to the Late Spring and Autumn period[7] (Changsha 1978); similar objects have not been found in any contemporary contexts.

Other early cast-iron objects were also found in the lower Yangtze River Valley. Two lumps of iron and an iron bar were discovered in two burials dating to the Late Spring and Autumn period at the Chengqiao 程桥 site in Jiansu. One of them is cast iron, whereas the other one is reported to be bloomery iron according to metallurgical analysis (Jiangsu and Nanjing 1965; Nanjing 1974). As already mentioned, the distribution pattern did lead some scholars to suggest that cast-iron technology—which involved a different and complicated technical settling—might have first been invented in this part of ancient China (Wagner 1993, 2008). Nonetheless, controversies still exist due to the fact that no other iron pieces were reported among the enormous data in the region (e.g., Zhejiang and Deqing 2011). No matter which region was the first to invent

---

[4] Although some scholars (e.g., Yang 2004a) suspected that some items might have been made of bloomery iron, the result of metallurgical analysis has not been fully published, and it is yet to be clear whether these southern states employed bloomery iron technology in the production.

[5] According to published site reports, (cast) iron agricultural implements were also found at Bojiawang 薄家湾 (Hubei 2011) in Danjiankou 丹江口, Zhangjiaping 張家坪 (Hubei and Hubei 2010) in Yuanxi 郧西, and Xiangzikou 巷子口 (Hubei and Guangshui 2008) in Suizhou 隨州. But the dates of these remains are not very clear-cut, and they usually date to the Late Spring and Autumn and Early Warring States periods.

[6] Among these sites, only Yangying has AMS-C14 data, which show that iron objects were made between 518–350 BCE (after calibration, 2σ) (Chen 2014:223). We suspect that the date based on ceramic typology might be too early.

[7] Even though some scholars cast doubt on the date of the tomb in which the iron objects were found, one of the editors of the site report, Yang Quanxi, reiterated in a more recent work that the tomb (Yangjiashan M65) should date to the Late Spring and Autumn period; see Gao 2012:27.

the iron-casting technique, the widespread evidence of cast-iron production should date to the Late Spring and Autumn period starting before the fifth century BCE.

The technique of annealing seems to be closely allied with the widespread arrival of agricultural implements. Annealing is an essential fabrication technique used to enhance the physical property of cast-iron tools by heating iron implements in a relatively low temperature for a long time to reduce carbon content. This technique appeared before the Warring States period and probably was developed by multiple states simultaneously. Two early pieces of evidence come from burial contexts, one at Tanghu in the Zheng state (Li 1975) and the other in Luoyang, controlled by the Eastern Zhou royal family. During the Warring States period, iron objects—either agricultural implements or weaponry—were commonly discovered in burial contexts and widely processed by the annealing technique (e.g., see the results in Li 2006). The annealing technique provides an important means to transform brittle cast iron into a practical material for making weaponry. The sword from the Chu tomb at Yangjiashan previously mentioned is claimed to be made of decarburized steel (Changsha 1978), and in this respect may be the earliest evidence showing the essential step using cast iron in the manufacture of weaponry.

The discovery of iron tools in residential sites usually was rare throughout the Spring and Autumn period. Their discovery, especially amid Central Plains burials, also seems to be sporadic. Unlike bimetallic weapons, cast-iron objects were not exclusively found associated with elite as prestige items. Also, given the various locations reported as having cast-iron wares, it is possible that the new technique appeared simultaneously in multiple centers or states covering both the Central Plains and Yangtze River Valley.

Based on the evidence published thus far, the entire technical transition to iron-casting seems to have been achieved in less than 400 years (Table 2). We have reliable evidence from the Central Plains showing the techniques of decarburizing and annealing in archaeological contexts no later than the Late Spring and Autumn period. The quick adoption of cast iron did lay down an essential technical foundation for the widespread distribution of iron technology and the start of the massive production of iron objects in

Table 2 Major development and innovation of iron technology

Techniques	Time frame	Dynastic Chronology
Adoption of iron smelting technology	11th–8th century BCE	Western Zhou (1046–771 BCE)
Innovation of cast iron technology	8th–6th century BCE	Spring and Autumn (771–454 BCE)
Large-scale manufacturing of agricultural implements	5th century BCE	
Appearance of decarburization and annealing	5th–3rd century BCE	Warring States (454–221 BCE)

most divided states during the Warring States period. The beginning of cast-iron production had already focused on commoners' needs and fueled the production of daily-use goods, especially those consumed on a very large scale, such as digging tools or agricultural implements. The cast-iron industry might have been triggered by the huge demand for bronze agricultural tools by initially serving as a supplementary source (Lam 2014). The latter phenomenon is documented at the Houma foundries (Shanxi 1993), in which extraordinary numbers of tool-making molds for bronze-casting were unearthed.

REGIONAL VARIATIONS IN THE DEVELOPMENT OF IRON-CASTING DURING THE SECOND HALF OF THE FIRST MILLENNIUM BCE

With the understanding of the foundations of iron technology, I now turn to explore regional developments and variations on the basis of burial data represented in the Jin, Qin, and Chu regions. During the past several decades, large numbers of archaeological reports of the Eastern Zhou period, most of them associated with burials, have been published, which provide a solid database for comparative study. This growing dataset allows us not only to draw more robust conclusions through interregional comparison but also to evaluate textual records via material evidence. From a textual perspective, Chu and Han (one of the Three Jin states) were often depicted as major iron manufacturing centers[8] with advanced techniques in the manufacturing of iron weaponry. Archaeological excavations have primarily focused on excavating cemeteries and large-scale building structures; residential sites or settlements associated with commoners are remarkably underexplored. Thus, burial goods are the only available data for the evaluation of the iron industry at this stage.

In certain previous studies (e.g., Yang 2004a), the development of iron and steel technology was portrayed as relatively homogenous among different states. For instance, after the invention and widespread use of cast-iron technology, it was considered that these territorial states adopted the technology at more or less the same time, and that most states controlled access to sources and achieved the ability to manufacture advanced steel agricultural implements. Based on archaeological data, I suggest on the contrary that there was more heterogeneity in terms of regional development among these states, as the following interregional comparison reveals.

---

[8] These texts include: *Xunzi* chapter 15; *Yi bing*; and *Shiji* chapter 79. A summary of these texts can be found in Lewis 1999.

Jin states

As other scholars have demonstrated (Han and Duan 2009), Jin states (i.e., Han, Zhou, Wei) comprised a relatively well-understood center for cast-iron technology and its iron industry. The most useful statistical figures for comparisons are provided by the systematic research of Han Rubin and Duan Hongmei (2009). In their study of iron technology of the Jin state, they recorded a total of 751 iron artifacts from more than 1,000 graves of commoners in various areas such as Changzi and Houma. Iron weaponry was particularly few in number (about 50 pieces), and iron objects usually included belt-hooks and agricultural implements such as axes, shovels, sickles, and pickaxes (Figure 2). Their metallurgical analysis showed that 90% of selected iron samples (a total of 60 pieces) were cast from the liquid state, including 22 white iron samples softened by annealing. In other words, the majority of these iron tools were made of cast iron. In addition, a number of iron tools were identified in workshop contexts. From the bronze foundries (Shanxi 1993) in the Houma capital of the Jin state, 2 iron pieces, probably belonging to iron knives, were found in a stratum dating to the Early Warring States period. From the ceramic workshop in the capital of the Han state, 1 sickle and 9 knives were discovered alongside remains and manufacturing waste of daily-use and architectural ceramics (Henan 1991). As Han and Duan maintain, the high quality and large scale of production may be key factors contributing to the widespread use of iron tools in daily life during the Warring States period.

The scale of the iron industry represented by cemetery burials information at the Fengshuiling (Shanxi 2010) 分水岭 in Changzi (Figure 1) belonging to the Han state[9]

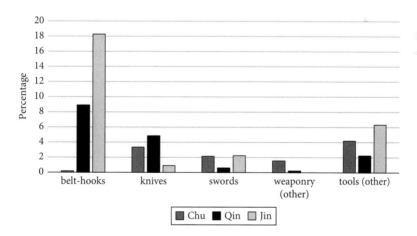

FIGURE 2 Statistic figures of the percentage of tombs including major types of ironwares in the three regions during the Warring States period. Please note that the data for the Chu state only come from the Changsha and Yiyang areas, not including the Jiangling area.

---

[9] According to the site report, the cemetery first belonged to the Zhou state, but later the area was occupied by the Han state, by 358 BCE.

will now be introduced as a representative example for further comparison. Among the 165 published tombs primarily dating to the Early and Middle Warring States period, 29 pieces of iron were identified: 5 belt-hooks, 16 axes, and 4 spades, with some representing tools remaining after the tomb was constructed. Another representative Late Warring States–period site is the Erligang 二里冈 (Henan 1959) cemetery in present-day Zhengzhou city belonging to the Han state. Fifty-two iron belt-hooks in addition to 2 knives, 3 hoes, 2 spades, and 7 *jue* axes were identified from 212 tombs. This assemblage approximates those from the Fengshuiling cemetery, yet iron objects are more frequently included in the former case (at least 24% of tombs included at least 1 iron object).

Amid the Jin states, large-scale iron foundries (e.g., Henan 2007; Henan and Zhongguo 1992; Zhang and Huang 1993) specializing in manufacturing agricultural tools were found within walled capitals and towns. Iron belt-hooks in turn were common in the burial assemblages during the Warring States period. It is possible that those iron objects from burials might not represent the whole assemblage of ironware in contemporary life. However, in the Jin state iron weaponry did not seem to be popular in archaeological contexts. Even in the Fengshuiling cemetery that included at least 25 elite tombs with bronze vessels of various types, iron weaponry was barely represented. From almost all the highest-ranking tombs that were identified so far, iron objects were primarily related to agricultural implements. Bronze weaponry, in contrast, was commonly identified in elite male tombs; at least 15 bronze daggers were found, indicating the industry of iron weaponry might not have been equally full-blown in the three Jin states.

Qin state

In previous decades, large numbers of site reports (e.g., Xianyang 2005; Shaanxi 2008, 2006; Xi'an 2004) on Qin tombs have been published and provided a relatively comprehensive view (Teng 2013; Teng 2002) about the Qin society based on burial data and funeral practices. Most of the excavations concentrated in the Xianyang area dating to the Late Warring States period. For residential sites, however, only two ceramic workshops have been published, one in Yongcheng (Shaanxi et al. 2013), Baoji, and the other in Xianyang (Shaanxi 2004). Of note, no iron implements were reported from residential refuse pits[10] according to site reports, unlike the scenario in the three Jin states.

In contrast to the scenario in habitation contexts, ironwares commonly served as burial goods (or leftover remains). In a previous study (Lam et al. 2017), I had collected all published data during the Warring States and Qin unification periods—which include about 1,500 tombs—to understand how iron objects were adopted in assemblages and how those reflect social change. This dataset, including 118 belt-hooks,

[10] Only from the workshops associated with the Qinshihuang mausoleum (Shaanxi and Qinshihuang 2007)—which date to relatively after the Qin unification—did iron tools start to be frequently found. Also, some iron objects were made by either bloomery or refined pig iron (Liu et al. 2010), a tradition that was different from cast-iron manufacturing.

65 knives, and 30 digging tools, shows an assemblage similar to what was identified in Jin tombs but with much fewer objects.

In general, the percentages of tombs including these major types of ironwares are lower by comparison with the statistic figures of the Jin states (Figure 2). In addition, iron weapons were not commonly found in burials. Only eight iron swords and daggers were identified from various locations[11] so far. By comparison with the total number of burials identified, the number of iron weapons still appears to be very limited. It is important to note that elite tombs (i.e., tombs with bronze ritual vessels) have been rarely found in the Qin state. In most cases, commoners' tombs did not contain substantial numbers or various types of iron products. Agricultural implements were identified in tombs, but they were primarily spades and, more often than not, were found in refilled soil, indicating they are likely left over after a tomb's construction. Burying iron digging tools or wood-working implements seems to be a rare practice in Qin tombs.

In order to enhance the understanding about the Fengshuiling and Erligang cemetery, I select data from the Ta'erpo cemetery 塔儿坡 (Xianyang 1998) (Figure 1) to compare with the Jin dataset. This cemetery is one of the well-excavated commoner cemeteries within the area of Xianyang. Since this cemetery includes a total of 391 tombs, this dataset should be representative of the assemblage of iron objects during the Late Warring States period. From all these burials, 67 belt-hooks, 40 knives, 5 swords, and 10 other types of tools were found. For those burials with iron objects, each one usually contained 1 knife or 1 belt-hook. Even though the percentage of tombs with iron belt-hooks (17%) is still lower than that in the Erligang cemetery (24%), iron knives appeared to be more frequently found in the assemblage.

Similar to the Jin states, Qin tombs rarely contained iron weapons. Only small amounts have been identified. There is no evidence for a large-scale production of iron weapons. Also, the absence of iron tools in habitation contexts and the lower amounts of iron objects in burials implies that the scale of the Qin iron industry was relatively small by comparison with the Jin states. Although the Qin people more often placed iron knives in tombs as burial goods, this difference in funeral practices might have been related to funeral customs rather than the scale of production.

Chu state

Although the discovery of early steel products in the Changsha area has attracted substantial attention and debates (Huang 1999), the iron products discovered from tombs within the core of Chu territory, known as the Jiangling area, were surprisingly rare. As Wagner (2008:106–107) and Bai (2005:378) pointed out, only one iron axe and one spade were identified from the Yutaishan 雨台山 (Hubei 1984) cemetery—one of the largest cemeteries excavated so far, which included 500-plus tombs dating from the

---

[11] These locations include Gaozhuang 高莊, Taerpo 塔兒坡, Youjiazhuang 尤家莊, Xi'an northern suburbs, Dali 大荔, and Yangling 杨凌.

Middle Spring and Autumn to the Middle Warring States periods. Similarly, iron objects were rarely found at the Jiudian 九店 (Hubei 1995) cemetery, another large commoner cemetery contemporary to Yutaishan in the same area. Among 590-plus excavated burials, only seven iron objects—including one decarburized steel sword,[12] one iron axe, one knife, and four other unknown objects—were discovered from seven tombs. Even in elite tombs such as Tianxinguan 天星观 tomb Nos. 1 (Hubeisheng Jingzhou1982) and 2 (Hubei 2003) and Baoshan 包山 Tomb No. 2 (Hubei 1991), iron objects were very few, with just several simple forms of tools. The pattern in the assemblage presents a remarkable difference compared to the scenario in the Jin and Qin states. What is more intriguing is the fact that no clues of large-scale iron foundries were identified within Jinancheng 纪南城, the capital of the Chu state, dating from the Middle Spring and Autumn to the Middle Warring States periods. The organization of the iron industry in the Chu state seems therefore much less present than in the Jin states. Nonetheless, from residential contexts (e.g., gates and houses), some iron implements were found, including spades, sickles, chisels, axes, and other tools (Hubei 1982a, 1982b). Even though it is puzzling that a cast-iron foundry has not yet been reported, cast-iron production unlikely took place on a very small scale.

The discovery of few iron objects from tombs in the southern territory of the Chu state seems to stand in remarkable contrast with the north. As previously explained, Changsha (Changsha 1978) is one of the areas yielding the earliest[13] steel (probably decarburized steel) weaponry in ancient China. In addition, iron weapons were frequently identified within commoner's cemeteries[14] in this region. In the Greater Changsha area, for instance, among 2,048 tombs published in the site report that date primarily to the Warring States period, there are 135 pieces of iron tools and 39 iron weapons. Meanwhile, bronze weaponry still played an essential role; 960 pieces of bronze weapons were found from the same dataset.

To the west of Changsha, iron objects were also commonly found in Chu tombs in the Yiyang 益阳 area (Yiyang 2008) (Figure 1) dating to the Early and Middle Warring States period. According to the site report, a total of 126 pieces of iron, including 23 swords and various types of tools, were found from 89 tombs. Iron belt-hooks were rarely found in the assemblage. Two iron sword samples were analyzed and identified as cast iron.[15] Although iron weaponry was still not as common as bronze counterparts in the assemblage (there are 99 bronze swords yielded from 650-plus burials), iron tools and weap-

[12] This iron sword was identified as 铸钢剑 with large ferrite grains and widmanstatten structure. But I think this term should refer to "decarburized steel" instead of "cast-steel," according to the microstructure described.

[13] Scholars (e.g., Gao 2012:35–36, 265–278) working in Hunan province recently reconfirmed the dates of these pre–Warring States iron and steel discoveries and emphasized the development of the iron industry in the production of agricultural implements and weaponry.

[14] Commoner cemeteries here refer to the burial grounds containing mostly commoner tombs. But this type of cemetery sometimes includes tombs with bronze ritual vessels.

[15] The report mentioned they were cast iron, but I suspect they might have been incompletely decarburized steel.

onry clearly are more ubiquitous than the assemblage either in the Chu core or in other contemporary states (Figure 2).

The reason underlying the regional difference is yet to be clarified (cf. Bai 2005:377), but the relatively abundant iron objects in the assemblage in the Hunan region cast doubt on the previous idea that the iron industry in the Chu state was underdeveloped or operated on a small scale (Wagner 2008:126–128). The absence of ironware in the core Jiangling-area burial context perhaps was due to other cultural preferences or political restriction on using iron objects for funeral rites rather than the shortage of iron supply. By comparison with the Jin and Qin states, the Chu state appeared to focus more on manufacturing iron weapons.

DISCUSSION OF THE IRON INDUSTRY DURING THE EASTERN ZHOU PERIOD

Archaeological data are always subject to various biases, particularly when using excavated data to analyze historical changes. But the investigation of iron technology within a long-term perspective reveals several critical aspects in the development of the iron industry in ancient China.

First, the development of early iron technology might have been triggered by the manufacturing of elite ritual weaponry; it has been documented in northern China but might not have been as widely adopted in the south. Cast-iron technology was probably inspired by the metallurgical process of smelting bloomery iron, but the manufacture of bimetallic weapons did not seem to directly result in the arrival of cast-iron technology. Archaeological evidence clearly suggests that cast-iron technology was widely used in the manufacturing of agricultural implements from the fifth century BCE onward. However, in the Central Plains, so far there is no evidence documenting the transformation of cast-iron technology into military or warfare hardware (cf. Wang and Liang 2000:246). Except for Chu and Yan states[16] (which, strictly speaking, did not belong to the Central Plains), the discovery of iron in both elite burials and "weaponry pits" is generally very sparse. The large-scale manufacturing of iron weaponry did not seem to arrive until the innovation of the refined pig iron (also known as *caogang* 炒钢) technique during the Western Han period (Beijing and Xuzhou 1997). Therefore, at least for the Central Plains states, the social-economic significance of cast-iron is not so much in the production of weapons as it is in the production of utilitarian and agricultural implements (Lam 2014).

[16] From the Wuyangtai 武阳台 location at Yanxiadu (Hebei 1996), a substantial amount of iron weaponry was discovered; some items were subject to metallurgical analysis and belong to bloomery iron. The site report even mentions that iron armies were commonly found at the Gaomocun and Langjincun locations. In addition, fragments of iron armors and 51 pieces of iron weaponry were discovered in a mass grave (tomb No. 44) (Beijing 1975).

Second, even though bimetallic weapons in general are missing in the south, archaeological evidence seems to suggest a simultaneous development of cast-iron technology in multiple states (both Central Plains and the Yangtze River Valley regions) during the first half of the first millennium BCE. Once the cast-iron technology was invented, the knowledge and techniques of smelting and casting were rapidly adopted among multiple different states. The distribution of cast iron among the major divided states was rapid, covering less than two hundred years. The annealing technique followed, having been invented by the beginning of the fifth century BCE in multiple centers, including simultaneously at Xinzheng in the Jin state and the Changsha region. Nevertheless, the Yangtze River Valley appeared to adopt the cast-iron production more widely than other regions; evidence of cast-iron production is more ubiquitous from sites associated with the Chu state or Chu culture. Perhaps due to this reason, it is not surprising that the iron industry of manufacturing agricultural implements in the region was more well developed or slightly ahead than other states at least by the Late or even the Middle Springs and Autumns period.

Having recognized the foundation of regional variations in the iron industry (for the summary of the variations, see Table 3), we suggest that the iron industry in the Qin state during the Warring States period should be more carefully scrutinized in the future, because it might have operated on a relatively smaller scale than presently understood. As the Qin assemblage of cast-iron objects (e.g., belt-hooks, digging tools, etc.) is more or less similar to the Jin states, ironworks controlled by the Qin state might employ similar techniques and manufacture a similar assemblage of iron products. But the total amount of iron objects was much less than the assemblage in the Three Jin states.

In contrast, the iron industry of the Chu state seems to show a trajectory different from the Qin and Jin states. In certain parts of the Chu state, such as Changsha and Yiyang areas, large numbers of iron weapons were found, which clearly indicate that the local iron industry focused more extensively on the manufacture of weapons. Such a phenomenon has not been identified in either the Jin or Qin states. Even though iron objects were very few in the Chu core area (Jianling) and no large ironworks have been reported, the scale of iron production might have been underrepresented by our current archeological evidence.

Table 3 Summary of the iron industry in each state represented by archaeological evidence

States	Characteristics of the Iron industry during the Warring States period
Jin	More developed in the production of tools, implements, and ornaments
Qin	Produce tools, implements, and ornaments but in a smaller scale
Chu	Most developed in the production of iron weaponry

Apparently regional development appears to be an underestimated issue in addressing iron technology and untangling the relationship between iron and its contribution to overall social development. Regional differences in the iron industry existed not only in terms of the types of products but also the scale of manufacturing between each territorial state during the Warring States period. In particular, for the Qin and perhaps the Jin states, there is no one indictor to show iron technology led to military superiority. Based on this comparative study, drawing any connection between the Qin unification and the iron technology, which has been proposed in some studies, would seem to lack a credible basis.

It is important to note that several important pieces are still missing in the puzzle of understanding the iron industry. One problem is the underexplored region of the Yangtze River Valley. The arrival of new technology, cast iron and decarburized weaponry, in the Chu state appeared to be slightly earlier and ahead of other territorial states. In addition, we witness the large-scale production of iron weapons in the southern frontier of the Chu state during the Warring States period. And a good number of these weapons were accessible to commoners, indicating a unique condition in the Warring States era. Unfortunately, no iron foundry has yet been excavated within the Chu territory. The lack of evidence also impedes a thorough comparison regarding various domains of craft specialization (e.g., see Costin 1991) between different states. But still, archaeological evidence clearly challenges the simplistic assumption that there was a simple one-to-one correlation between the development of iron technology and the superiority of weaponry during the second half of the first millennium BCE. We tend to be in line with other scholars (e.g., Lewis 1999) who attribute the major driving forces for the unification to the way the Qin state mobilized residents instead of the physical military superiority supplied by iron implements and armors. In this regard, the study of iron at this point has made significant contributions to the history of science as well as to our understanding about the differences in the economic and political structures of states during this tumultuous Eastern Zhou period.

ACKNOWLEDGMENTS

I am grateful to Prof. Jianli Chen and Prof. Elizabeth Childs-Johnson for their comments and editing help. This research was made possible by support from The Chinese University of Hong Kong Direct Grant (project title: The Archaeology of Iron and the Han Sovereignty in the Guangzhou Region) and the Hong Kong Government RGC-Early Career Scheme (RGC Ref. No. CUHK 24607916).

BIBLIOGRAPHY

Bai, Yunxiang 白云翔 2005. *Archaeological Study on Iron Works before 3rd Century AD in China* 先秦两汉铁器的考古学研究. Beijing 北京: Science Press.
Barnard, Noel 1978–1979. "Did the Swords Exist? Rejoinder." *Early China* 4:60–65.
Barnard, Noel, and Tamotsu Satō 1975. *Metallurgical Remains of Ancient China*. Tokyo: Nichiōsha.

Beijing Daxue Kaogu Xuexi Shang Zhou Zu 北京大学考古学系商周组, and Shanxi Sheng Kaogu Ynajiusuo 山西省考古研究所 2000. *The Tianma Qucun Site 1980–1989* 天马—曲村 1980–1989, 4 vols. Beijing: Kexue chubanshe.

Beijing Gangtie Xueyuan Yali Jiagong Zhuangye 北京钢铁学院压力加工专业 1975. "Preliminary Report on the Metallurgical Analysis of Iron Objects from Tomb No. 44 at Yanxiadu in Yixian 易县燕下都44号墓葬铁器金相考察初步报告." *Kaogu* 4:241–243.

Beijing Keji Daxue Yajingshi Yanjiusuo 北京科技大学冶金史研究所, and Xuzhou Hanbing-mayong Bowuguan 徐州汉兵马俑博物馆 1997 "Metallurgical Report on the Analysis of Iron Objects from the Mausoleum of the Chu State at Shizishan in Xuzhou 徐州狮子山楚王陵出土铁器的金相实验研究." *Wenwu* 7:146–156.

Changsha Tielu Chezhan Jianzao Gongcheng Wenwu Fajiedui 长沙铁路车站建造工程文物发掘队 1978. "The New Discoveries of Spring and Autumn Steel Swords and Iron Products in Changsha 长沙新发现春秋晚期的钢剑和铁器." *Wenwu* 10:44–48.

Chen, Jianli 陳建立 2014. Exploration of the Metal Smelting and Casting Civilization in Ancient China 中国古代金属冶铸文明新探. Beijing: Kexue chubanshe.

Chen, Jianli 陈建立, Junchang Yang 杨军昌, Binjun Sun 孙秉君, and Yan Pan 潘岩 2009. "Manufacturing Technique of Bronze-Iron Bimetallic Objects Found in M27 of Liangdaicun Site 梁带村遗址M27出土铜铁复合器的制作技术." *Science in China Series E: Technological Science, Zhongguo Kexue E ji* 中国科学E 辑 52(10):3,038–3,045.

Chen, Jianli 陈建立, Ruilin Mao 毛瑞林, Hui Wang 王辉, Honghai Chen 陈洪海, Yan Xie 谢焱 and Yaopeng Qian 钱耀鹏 2012. "Iron artifacts unearthed from burials of the Xiwa Culture at the Moguo site in Lingtan, Gansu, and the origin of Iron smelting technology in China 甘肃临潭磨沟寺洼文化墓葬出土铁器与中国冶铁技术起源." *Wenwu* 8:45–53.

Costin, Cathy L. 1991. "Craft Specialization: Issues in Defining, Documenting, and Explaining the Organization of Production." In *Archaeological Method and Theory*, vol. 3. Edited by M. Schiffer, 1–56. Tucson: University of Arizona Press.

Gao, Zhixi 高至喜 2012. *Chu Tombs in Hunan and Chu Culture* 湖南楚墓与楚文化. Changsha: Yuelu shushe.

Guowuyuan Sanxia Gongcheng Jianshe Weiyuanhui Bangongshi 国务院三峡工程建设委员会办公室, and Guojia Wenwuju 国家文物局 2003. *The Liulinxi Site in Zigui* 秭归柳林溪. Beijing: Kexue chubanshe.

Han, Rubin 韩汝玢 1998. "A Metallographic Study on Early Iron Objects of China, 5th c BCE 中国早期铁器(公元前5世纪以前)的金相学研究." *Wenwu* 2:87–96.

Han, Rubin, and Hongmei Duan 2009. "An Early Iron-Using Center in the Ancient Jin State Tegion (8th–3rd century BC)." In *Metallurgy and Civilisation: Eurasia and Beyond: Proceedings of the Sixth International Conference on the Beginnings of the Use of Metals and Alloys (BUMA VI)*. Edited by J. Mei and T. Rehren, 99–106. London: Archetype.

Han, Rubin, and Jianli Chen 2013. "Casting Iron in Ancient China." In *The World of Iron*. Edited by J. Humphris and T. Rehren, 168–177. London: Archetype.

Han, Rubin 韩汝玢, and Jun Ke 柯俊 2007. *China Science and Technology History (Volume of Mining and Smelting)* 中国科学技术史(矿冶卷). Beijing: Kexue chubanshe.

Han, Wei 韩伟, and Nanfeng Jiao 焦南峰 1988. "A Summary of the Excavation and Research on the Qin Capital Yongcheng 秦都雍城考古发掘研究综述." *Kaogu yu wenwu* 5–6:111–126.

He, Tangsheng 何堂坤, Jihong Wang 王继红, and Fengyi Jin 靳枫毅 2004. "Scientific Analysis of the Bimetallic Dagger from the Yanqing Site 延庆山戎文化铜柄铁刀及其科学分析." *Zhongyuan wenwu* 2:71–75.

Hebeisheng Wenwu Yanjiusuo 河北省文物研究所 1985. The Shang site of Taixi in Gaocheng 藁城台西商代遗址. Beijing: Wenwu chubanshe.

Hebeisheng Wenwu Kaogu Yanjiusuo 河南省文物考古研究所, and Sanmenxia Shi Wenwu Gongzuodui 三门峡市文物工作队 1999. Guo State Tombs at Sanmenxia 三门峡虢国墓. Beijing: Wenwu chubanshe.

Hebeisheng Wenhuaju Wenwu Gongzuodui 河南省文化局文物工作队 1959. Erligang in Zhengzhou 郑州二里冈. Beijing: Kexue chubanshe.

Henansheng Wenwu Yanjiusuo 河北省文物研究所 1996. Lower Capital of the Yan state 燕下都. Beijing: Wenwu chubanshe.

Henansheng Wenwu Yanjiusuo 河南省文物研究所 1991. "Preliminary Report on the Excavation of Remains at the Ceramic Workshop in the Zheng-Han Capitals, Xinzheng, Henan 河南新郑郑韩故城制陶作坊遗迹发掘简报." Huaxia kaogu 3:33–54.

Henansheng Wenwu Kaogu Yanjiusuo 河南省文物考古研究所 2007. The Sacrificial Site of the Zheng State in Xinzhen 新郑郑国祭祀遗址. Zhengzhou: Daxiang chubanshe.

Henansheng Kaogu Yanjiusuo 河南省文物研究所, and Zhongguo Lishi Bowuguan Kaogubu 中国历史博物馆考古部 1992. The Wangchenggang Site at Dengfeng and the Ancient Cities of Yangcheng 登封王城岗与阳城. Beijing: Wenwu chubanshe.

Henansheng Kaogu Yanjiusuo 河南省文物研究所, Henan Sheng Danjiang Kuqu Kaogu Fajuedui 河南省丹江库区考古发掘队, and Xichuan Xian Bowuguan 淅川县 博物馆 1991. The Spring and Autumn Period Chu Tombs at Xiasi, Xichuan 淅川下寺春秋楚墓. Beijing: Wenwu chubanshe.

Hsü, Cho-yun 1980. Han Agriculture: The Formation of Early Chinese Agrarian Economy (206 BC–AD 220). Edited by J. L. Dull. Seattle: University of Washington Press.

Huang, Zhanyue 黄展岳 1999. "The Origin of Iron-Metallurgy and Earliest Use of Iron-Tools 关于中国开始冶铁和使用铁器的问题." In The Archaeology and Culture of the Pre-Qin and Two Han Periods 先秦两汉考古与文化. Edited by Zhanyue, Huang 15–28. Taibei: Yunchen wenkua.

Hubeisheng Wenwu Kaogu Yanjiusuo 湖北省文物考古研究所, and Guangshuishi Bowuguan 广水市博物馆 2008. "Preliminary Report of the Excavation at the Xiangzikou Site in Guangshui, Hubei 湖北广水巷子口遗址发掘简报." Jianghan Kaogu 1:15–36.

Hubeisheng Wenwu Kaogu Yanjiusuo 湖北省文物考古研究所, and Hubeisheng Wenwuju Nanbei Shuidiao Biangongshi 湖北省文物局南水北调办公室 2010. "An Excavation Report of Zhangjiaping Site in Yunxi County 湖北郧西张家坪遗址发掘简报." Jianghan Kaogu 3:3–19.

Hubeisheng Wenwu Kaogu Yanjiusuo 湖北省文物考古研究所, Hubeisheng Xiaoganshi Bowuguan 湖北省孝感市博物馆 2006. "Brief Report on the Excavation of Eastern Zhou Dynasty Site at Dajiayuan, Xiaogan 孝感大家园东周遗址发掘简报." Jianghan Kaogu 2:12–16.

Hubeisheng Jingsha Tielu Kaogudui 湖北省荆沙铁路考古队 1991. Chu Tombs at Baoshan 包山楚墓. Beijing: Wenwu chubanshe.

Hubeisheng Jingzhou Diqu Bowuguan 湖北省荆州地区博物馆 1984. Chu State Tombs at Yutaishan of Jiangling 江陵雨台山楚墓. Beijing: Wenwu chubanshe.

Hubeisheng Wenwu Kaogu Yanjiusuo 湖北省文物考古研究所 1995. Eastern Zhou tombs at Jidian, Jiangling 江陵九店东周墓. Beijing: Kexue chubanshe.

Hubeisheng Wenwu Kaogu Yanjiusuo 湖北省文物考古研究所 2003. "Brief Report on Excavation of Spring and Autumn Period Site in Yangying, Laohekou, 湖北老河口杨营春秋遗址发掘简报." Jianghan Kaogu 3:16–31.

Hubeisheng Bowuguan 湖北省博物馆 1982a. "The Survey and Excavation of Jinancheng, the Chu Capital 楚都纪南城的勘察与发掘(上)." *Kaogu xuebao* 3:323–350.

Hubeisheng Bowuguan 湖北省博物馆 1982b . "The Survey and Excavation of Jinancheng, the Chu Capital 楚都纪南城的勘察与发掘(下). *Kaogu xuebao* 4:477–507.

Hubeisheng Jingzhou Bowuguan 湖北省荆州博物馆 2003. *No. 2 Chu Tomb at Tianxingguan in Jingzhou* 荆州天星观二号楚墓. Beijing: Wenwu chubanshe.

Hubeisheng Jingzhou Diqu Bowuguan 湖北省荆州地区博物馆 1982. "Excavation of the No.1 Chu Tomb at Tianxingguan in Jianling 江陵天星观1号楚墓." *Kaogu xuebao* 1:82–103.

Hubeisheng Wenwu Kaogu Yanjiusuo 湖北省文物考古研究所 2000. "The Excavation of the Western Zhou Site at Shangmoliao in Yichang County, Hubei 湖北宜昌县上磨垴周代遗址的发掘." *Kaogu* 9:22–35, 99.

Hubeisheng Wenwu Kaogu Yanjiusuo 湖北省文物考古研究所 2011. "An Excavation Report of the Bojiawan Site in Danjiangkou City, Hubei Province 湖北丹江口市薄家湾遗址发掘简报." *Jianghan Kaogu* 1:42–58.

Jiangsusheng Wenwu Guanli Weiyuanhui 江苏省文物管理委员会, and Nanjing bowuyuan 南京博物院 1965. "The Eastern Zhou Tomb at Chengqiao, Liuhe, Jiangsu 江苏六合程桥东周墓." *Kaogu* 3:105–115.

Jingmenshi Bowuguan 荆门市博物馆 1990. "A Brief Report on the Excavation of Residential Area and Cemetery at Xianglinggang, Jingmen City 荆门市响岭岗东周遗址与墓地发掘简报." *Jianghan Kaogu* 4:12–55.

Kaifeng Diqu Wenguanhuai 开封地区文管会, Xinzheng Wenguankai 新郑县文管会, and Zhengzhou Daxue Lishixi Kaogu zhuanye 郑州大学历史系考古专业 1978. "A Preliminary Report on the Tombs of the Zhou Dynasty in XinZheng Country, Henan 河南省新郑县唐户两周墓葬发掘简报." Edited by Wenwu bianji weiyuanhui 文物编辑委员会, 45–65. Wenwu Ziliao Congkan Series 2. Beijing: Wenwu chubanshe.

Keightley, David N. 1976. "Where Have All the Swords Gone? Reflections on the Unification of China." *Early China* 2:31–34.

Lam, Wengcheong 2014. "Everything Old Is New Again? Rethinking the Transition to the Cast Iron Production in the Central Plains of China." *Journal of Anthropological Research* 70(4):511–542.

Lam, Wengcheong 林永昌, et al. 2017. "The Population of Iron Ware in the Qin State and the Distribution of Iron Ware in the Guanzhong Basin 论秦国铁器普及化与关中地区战国时期铁器流通模式." *Zhongguo guojia bowuguan guankan* 3:36–51.

Lei, Congyun 雷从云 1980. "Discovery and Its Significance of Iron Agricultural Tools in the Warring States Period 战国铁农具的考古发现及其意义." *Kaogu* 3:259–260.

Lewis, Mark Edward 1999. "Warring States Political History." In *The Cambridge History of Ancient China: From the Origins of Civilization to 221 BC*. Edited by M. Loewe and E. Shaughnessy, 587–650. Cambridge, UK: Cambridge University Press.

Li, Xiuhui 李秀辉 2006. "Metallographical Report of Irons from the Xinzheng Sacrificial Site 郑国祭祀遗址出土部分铁器的金相实验研究." *The Sacrificial Site of Zheng State in Xinzheng* 新郑郑国祭祀遗址. Edited by Henansheng Wenwu Kaogu Yanjiusuo, 1,050–1,057. Zhengzhou: Daxiang chubanshe.

Li, Zhong 李众 1975. "The Development of Iron and Steel Technology in Ancient China 中国封建社会前期钢铁冶炼技术发展的探讨." *Kaogu xuebao* 2:1–21.

Liu, Dezhen 刘得祯, and Jiantang Zhu 朱建唐 1981. "The Spring and Autumn Tomb at Jingjiazhuang in Lingtai, Gansu 甘肃灵台县景家庄春秋墓." *Kaogu* 4:298–301.

Liu, Jiangwei 刘江卫, Yin Xia 夏寅, Kun Zhao 赵昆, et al. 2010. "Preliminary Report on the Analysis of Iron Objects from the Stone Workshop at Zhengzhuang 郑庄秦石料加工场遗址出土铁器的初步研究." *Zhongyuan wenwu* 5:100–103.

Nanjing Bowuyuan 南京博物院 1974. "The Eastern Zhou Tomb at Chengqiao, Liuhe, Jiangsu 江苏六合程桥二号东周墓." *Kaogu* 2:116–120.

Rehren, Thilo, et al. 2013. "5,000 Years Old Egyptian Iron Beads Made from Hammered Meteoritic Iron." *Journal of Archaeological Science* 40:4,785–4,792.

Shaanxisheng Kaogu Yanjiuyuan 陕西省考古研究院, and Baojishi Kaogu Gonguodui 宝鸡市考古工作队 1988. "Preliminary Report on the Excavation of the No. 5 Spring and Autumn Tomb at Bianjiazhuang in Longxiang, Shaanxi 陕西陇县边家庄五号春秋墓发掘简报." *Wenwu* 11:14–23.

Shaanxisheng Kaogu Yanjiusuo 陕西省考古研究所 2004. *Archaeological Report on the Investigations and Excavations at the Ancient Qin Captial Xianyang* 秦都咸阳考古报告. Beijing: Kexue chubanshe.

Shaanxisheng Kaogu Yanjiusuo 陕西省考古研究所 2006. *Qin Tombs in Northern Suburb of Xi'an* 西安北郊秦墓. Xi'an: Sanqin chubanshe.

Shaanxisheng Kaogu Yanjiusuo 陕西省考古研究所 2008. *Qin Tombs at Youjiazhuang, Xi'an* 西安尤家庄秦墓. Xi'an: Shaanxi kexue jishu chubanshe.

Shaanxisheng Kaogu Yanjiusuo 陕西省考古研究所, and [Qinshihuang Bingmayong Bowuguan 秦始皇兵马俑博物馆 2007. *Report on Archaeological Researches of the Qin Shihuang Mausoleum Precinct (2001-2003)* 秦始皇帝陵园考古报告 2001~2003. Beijing: Wenwu chubanshe.

Shaanxisheng Kaogu Yanjiusuo 陕西省考古研究院, Baojishi Kaogu Yanjiusuo 宝鸡市考古研究所, and Fengxiangxian Bowuguan 凤翔县博物馆 2013. *Ceramic Workshop of the Warring States Period at Doufucun Site in Qin Yongchen* 秦雍城豆腐村战国制陶作坊遗址. Beijing: Kexue chubanshe.

Shandong Daxue Kaogudui, 山东大学考古队 1998. "Excavation of Zhou Dynasty Cemetery at Xianrentai in Changqing Country, Shangdong 长清仙人台周代墓地." *Kaogu* 9:11–25.

Shanxisheng kaogu yanjiusuo 山西省考古研究所 1993. *Bronze Foundry Sites at Houma* 侯马铸铜遗址. Beijing: Wenwu chubanshe.

Shanxisheng Kaogu Yanjiusuo 山西省考古研究所, Shanxi Bowuguan 山西博物院, and Changzhishi Bowuguan 长治市博物馆 2010. *The Eastern Zhou Cemetery at Fengshuiling in Changzhi* 长治分水岭东周墓地. Beijing: Wenwu chubanshe.

Smith, Cyril Stanley 1970. "Art, Technology, Science: Notes on Their Historical Interaction." *Technology and Culture* 11:493–549.

Tang, Jigen 唐际根 1993. "The origin of Chinese iron metallurgy 中国冶铁术的起源问题." *Kaogu* 6:563–564.

Teng, Mingyu 滕铭予 2002. *Qin Culture in Archaeological Perspective: From a Feudal State to Great Empire* 秦文化: 从封国到帝国的考古学观察. Beijing: Xueyuan chubanshe.

Teng, Mingyu 2013. "From Vassal State to Empire: An Archaeological Examination of Qin Culture." Translated by Susanna Lam. In *Birth of an Empire: The State of Qin Revisited*. Edited by Y. Pines, S. Gideon, L. von Falkenhausen, and R. D. S. Yates, 113–140. Berkeley: University of California Press.

Tian, Renxiao 田仁孝, and Xingshan Lei 雷兴山 1993. "Preliminary Report on the Excavation of the No. 2 Tomb in the Spring and Autumn Period in Yimencun, Baoji 宝鸡市益门村二号春秋墓发掘简报." *Wenwu* 10:1–14.

Tong, Enzheng 童恩正 1990. "On the Crescent-Shaped Cultural Communication Belt 试论我国从 东北至西南的遍地半月形传播带." In *Zhongguo Xinan minzu kaogu lunwenji* 中国西南民族考古论文集. Edited by Tong Enzheng, 252–278. Beijing: Wenwu chubanshe.

Trousdale, W. 1977. "Where All the Swords Have Gone: Reflections on Some Questions Raised by Professor Keightley." *Early China* 3:65–66.

Wagner, Donald B. 1993. *Iron and Steel in Ancient China*. Handbuch der Orientalistik 4:9. Leiden: E. J. Brill.

Wagner, Donald B. 2008. *Ferrous Metallurgy 5: Chemistry and Chemical Technology, Science and Civilization in China*. Cambridge, UK: Cambridge University Press.

Wang, Xueli 王学理, and Yun Liang 梁云 2000. *Qin Culture* 秦文化. Beijing: Wenwu chubanshe.

Wang, Yingchen 王颖琛, Yaxiong Liu 刘亚雄, Tao Jiang 姜涛, and Kunlong Chen 陈坤龙 2019. Scientific Research of Bimetallic Objects Unearthed from M2009 in the Guo State Cemetery at Sanmenxia 三门峡虢国墓地M2009出土铁刃铜器的科学分析及其相关问题. *Spectroscopy and Spectral Analysis* 39(10):3154–3158.

Xi'anshi Wenwu Baohu Kaogusuo 西安市文物保护考古所 2004. *Qin Tombs in Southern Outskirts of Xi'an* 西安南郊秦墓. Xian: Shaanxi renmin chubanshe.

Xianyangshi Wenwu Kaogu Yanjiusuo 咸阳市文物考古研究所 1998. *Qin Tombs in Taerpo* 塔儿坡秦墓. Xi'an: Sanqin chubanshe.

Xianyangshi Wenwu Kaogu Yanjiusuo 咸阳市文物考古研究所 2005. *Qin Tombs in Renjiazui* 任家咀秦墓. Beijing: Kexue chubanshe.

Yang, Kuan 杨宽 2003. *History of Warring-States* 战国史. Shanghai: Shanghai renmin chubanshe.

Yang, Kuan 杨宽 2004a. *History of Ferrous-Metallurgy Development in Ancient China* 中国古代冶铁技术发展史. Shanghai: Shanghai renmin chubanshe.

Yang, Quanxi 杨权喜 2004b. "The Utilization and Development of Iron Tools and Wares in the Chu State 试论楚国铁器的使用和发展." *Jianghan kaogu* 2:70–77.

Yiyangshi Wenwu Guanlichu 益阳市文物管理处, Yiyangshi Bowuguan 益阳市博物馆. 2008. *Yiyang Chu Tombs* 益阳楚墓. Beijing: Wenwu chubanshe.

Zhang, Tongxing 张童心, and Yongjiu Huang, 黄永久 1993. "A Brief Report on the Warring States Handicraft Workshops at Miaohou Xinzhuang in Yuwangcheng, Xiaxian 夏县禹王城庙后辛庄战国手工业作坊遗址调查简报." *Wenwu Jikan* 2:11–16.

Zhao, Huacheng 2012. "The Application and Production of Iron." In *The History of Chinese Civilization*, vol. 1. Edited by X. Yuan, W. Yan, C. Zhang, and Y. Lou, 312–346. Cambridge, UK: Cambridge University Press.

Zhejiangsheng Wenwu Kaogu Yanjiushou 浙江省文物考古研究所, and Deqingxiang Bowuguan 德清县博物馆 2011. *Deqing Tiangziqiao: Excavation Report on the Proto-Porcelain Kilns* 德清亭子桥:战国原始瓷窑址发掘报告. Beijing: Wenwu chubanshe.

CHAPTER 27

....

INSTITUTIONAL REFORMS AND REFORMERS DURING THE WARRING STATES PERIOD

....

BY YURI PINES, HEBREW UNIVERSITY OF JERUSALEM[1]

THE Warring States period was the age of profound institutional changes. A loose aristocratic polity of the Springs and Autumns period was replaced with a highly centralized territorial state, run by professional bureaucrats, who penetrated the society down to the smallest hamlets. The new state, which was able to fully mobilize its human and material resources, turned into a formidable military machine. Forceful unification of the entire sub-celestial realm, unthinkable in the Springs and Autumns period, became henceforth possible.

Later tradition associates the reforms of the Warring States period with a few outstanding statesmen, but this is inaccurate (Lewis 1999). In most cases the reforms were not devised by a single individual but evolved through a lengthy process of trial and error, which spanned generations. They occurred, albeit at a different pace, in each of the states that comprised the Zhou world and, differences aside, they invariably contributed toward the empowerment of the state apparatus and of the monarch. As such, the reforms may be understood primarily as the rejection of the Springs and Autumns–period legacy of political fragmentation and weak rulers (see chapter 22). Moreover, a variety of additional economic and military factors made the Warring States–period reforms much broader in their scope than just political readjustment. These reforms contributed toward profound bureaucratization of the society, in the wake of which the assertive state apparatus intervened into the socioeconomic lives of subjects to an extent unthinkable before.

[1] This research was supported by the Israel Science Foundation (grant No. 568/19) and by the Michael William Lipson Chair in Chinese Studies.

In discussing the Warring States–period reforms it is convenient to focus on the state of Qin, which eventually unified the Chinese world in 221 BCE, bequeathing its political system on the unified empire.[2] Putting aside manifold idiosyncrasies in Qin's trajectory, we are justified to say that this trajectory's basic parameters—a transformation from a loose aristocratic polity to an assertive bureaucratic and highly centralized state—were shared by each of the major political entities of the Warring States period. Furthermore, a Qin-focused discussion may benefit from the fact that the Qin reforms can be studied much better than those of other states due to a fortunate combination of rich textual, paleographic, and material evidence (Pines et al. 2014). In particular, a series of paleographic discoveries of the recent decades brought to light many thousands of legal and administrative documents from the state of Qin. Although the majority of these documents date from the Imperial Qin (221–207 BCE), such as those from Tomb 11 at Shuihudi, Yunmeng 雲夢睡虎地 (Hubei); from the archive of the Qianling 遷陵 County, discovered in a well and in a defense moat at the town of Liye, Longshan 龍山里耶 (Hunan); and from the Yuelu Academy 岳麓書院 collection, they provide a good testimony to the functioning of the pre-imperial state of Qin as well.

Qin reforms are usually associated with the towering figure of Shang Yang 商鞅 (aka Lord Shang 商君 or Gongsun Yang 公孫鞅, d. 338 BCE). This statesman arrived at Qin soon after the ascendancy of Lord Xiao 秦孝公 (r. 361–338 BCE) and remained in command for two decades, during which Qin was propelled to the position of supremacy in the Zhou world. Shang Yang was executed soon after the death of his patron, but the reforms initiated by him continued and evolved for generations to come. It is not always possible to discern which reforms were initiated by Shang Yang himself, which he inherited from his unnamed predecessors, and which were wrongly attributed to him (Yoshimoto 2000), but his overall impact on Qin's history is beyond doubt (Pines 2017:7–24).[3] It was Shang Yang who orchestrated the transformation of Qin from an aristocratic Zhou-type polity into an awesome Warring State, and his arrival at Qin may be considered the turning point in the history of the Warring States period in general.

Shang Yang's most daring reform was the overhaul of Qin's social structure. Old aristocratic ranks were abolished, and a new system ensued, based on 20 (initially less) ranks of merit for which most males were eligible, regardless of pedigree or economic status. The eight lowest ranks were distributed in exchange for military achievements, particularly decapitation of enemy soldiers, or could be purchased by wealthy individuals; successful rank-holders could be then incorporated into the military or civilian administration and thereafter be promoted up the social ladder. Each rank granted its holder economic, social, and legal privileges (Yates 1995; Loewe 2010). This new rank system, which eventually incorporated a majority of the male population, effectively transformed the society from one based on pedigree, in which the individual's position was determined primarily by his/her lineage affiliation, into an open one, in which

---

[2] Much of the discussion that follows is based on Pines et al. 2014:18–32.

[3] For the archeological data that confirm a radical change in Qin's social composition in the aftermath of Shang Yang's reforms, see Shelach and Pines 2005; Teng 2014.

individual merits, especially military merits, determined social position (Yates 1987; Teng 2014). The ranks were not fully inheritable; under normal circumstances a man could designate one heir to his rank, but the heir received one or two ranks lower than his father, and the decrease was sharper for the holders of higher ranks (except for the one or two highest ones; Barbieri-Low and Yates 2015: 850–851). This system generated therefore much higher social mobility than was possible in the aristocratic age (Pines et al. 2014:25–26). Moreover, it had effectively eliminated hereditary aristocracy as an autonomous elite group, incorporating former nobles into an expanding bureaucraticized nobility of merit. Although it is doubtful that Qin succeeded fully to unify one's rank, one's wealth, and one's societal power, the very desire of its leaders to attain this situation is indicative of their remarkable assertiveness.

Shang Yang's reforms aimed not just at eliminating aristocracy but, primarily, at directing the entire population at the mutually reinforcing occupations of agriculture and warfare. It was during his age that widespread introduction of iron tools revolutionized agriculture, in particular through making it possible to turn virgin soils and swampy areas into rich farmland (see chapter 26). Henceforth, the state could intervene much more actively in economic life, turning Qin into what Karl A. Wittfogel (1957) aptly named an "agro-managerial state." Qin leaders invested considerable effort into bolstering agricultural productivity, especially through developing the wastelands. Peasants were encouraged to resettle to the new lands through a mix of coercion and tax incentives, and the state apparatus assisted them in disseminating iron tools, lending draft animals, and initiating large-scale irrigation projects. Archeologically observable expansion of Qin's settlements beyond the original core of the Wei River basin testifies to the success of these efforts (Falkenhausen 2004:110–115; Teng 2014).

Parallel to encouraging agricultural production on the macro level, the Qin officials were doing so through active intervention into the lives of agricultural communities. Even a brief look at Qin administrative regulations discovered at Shuihudi, Liye, and elsewhere discloses an amazing degree of state activism. The officials were concerned with everything: from the fitness of the oxen, which were measured every season to the inch, with punishment inflicted on local officials and village heads if the oxen decreased in girth, to the number of rat holes in the granaries, to the amount of offspring of cows and ewes—the overseers were punished for insufficient birth rates among the animals. They closely supervised the life of rural hamlets, where even an appointment of a hamlet head and a postman required the approval of the county authorities. They collected information about any imaginable aspect of rural life, from weather conditions, which were to be reported regularly by the county authorities to authorities in the capital, to the quality of iron tools and of draft animals. They maintained registration of the plots, prepared cadastral maps, and closely supervised annual harvest yields, adjusting tax quotas accordingly (Pines et al. 2014; Hulsewé 1985; Yates 1995; Korolkov 2010 and 2020:68–136; Yates 2012–2013); Yates, forthcoming.

Economic activism of the state was not confined to farming and to production of iron utensils alone. To assess its breadth, suffice it to read a list of evaluations submitted to higher authorities by the Qin Bureau of Finance of Qianling County (Liye): reports on lacquer and on workshops, on bamboo cultivated in groves and on ponds, on orchards and on markets, on convict laborers who died or absconded and on financial transactions, on mining and on ironworks, on arrows and on weapons, on chariots and on craft materials and equipment, and so on (Hunan 2012:8–454, 8–493, etc.; Yates 2012–2013 and forthcoming). The state officials were engaged in manufacture, transportation, and market transactions; few if any areas of economic life remained outside their interest.

The third pillar of Shang Yang's reforms was mobilizing population for war. Military developments of the Warring States period are depicted elsewhere (chapter 29); here suffice it to say that the transformation of the army into a large infantry-based entity, filled by peasant conscripts, necessitated overall adjustment of the government policies. In particular, establishment of universal conscription, ensuring the soldiers' loyalty, and preventing their absconding had become a major source of concern for Qin leaders. Shang Yang is quoted as saying that the soldiers will become valiant fighters only when "there is nowhere to flee from the army ranks, and migrants can find no refuge" (*Book of Lord Shang* 18.3).To achieve this situation, the authorities had to establish tight control over the population, including its mandatory registration and surveillance over its movements.[4]

Shang Yang is attributed with dividing the population into groups of five households, the members of which were connected by the system of mutual responsibility; this system served both for the purposes of mutual surveillance and military recruitment (one man was taken from each family to fill a squad of five soldiers in the army). The members of five-family units, just like the members of the squads, were obliged to denounce each other's crimes, particularly absconding from the battlefield (Lewis 1990:53–96; Yates 1999, 2007, 2009c). Other measures were undertaken to prevent free movement of individuals, such as the system of passports and checkpoints. While absconding remained a major problem for Qin policy-makers (Shi Weiqing 2004; Zhang Gong 2006), the overall system of population control appears impressively efficient.[5]

The Qin government's activism would not have been possible without an elaborate bureaucratic apparatus. Although we lack precise data on the evolution of Qin's bureaucracy, it is clear that by the end of the Warring States period it was impressively sophisticated and mature. Elaborate rules governed selection, promotion, and advancement of officials, their ranks and salaries. The superiors had to meticulously monitor their underlings' performance, keeping records about the precise amount of time, down to the day, they spent serving in each office (Yates 1995). Everything had to be reported to the superiors: from the amount of spoilt and worn iron tools loaned by the government

---

[4] The registration of the population is fully exemplified in samples of registers from the Liye defense moat (Hsing 2014). For the monitoring of population movements, the best example is the early Han "Ordinances on Fords and Passes" (*Jinguan ling* 津關令), discovered among the hoard of legal texts in Tomb 247, Zhangjiashan 張家山 (Hubei), are translated and analyzed in Barbieri-Low and Yates (2015:1112–1166). The Liye documents published to date yielded many examples of what appears as rudimentary passports.

[5] A series of Liye documents demonstrate the ability of local authorities in Qin to trace debtors, even when those were relocated from one county to another (Sanft 2015).

to the peasants; to deaths of government horses and cattle; to transactions of grain, hay, and straw (Hulsewé 1985:A8 and A9:27, A19–A22:34–39). In addition to an annual check, officials' performance was investigated at the end of their term; those responsible for inaccurate records were fined (Yates 1995). The state supervised strictly even the small-est financial transaction by the officials and mercilessly punished violators of discipline, imposing manifold fines.

Supervision of officials was part of an elaborate legal system that facilitated control over all the segments of the population. Qin is notorious for the severity of its laws, which imposed harsh penalties even for the slightest offences. These laws were indeed draconic in many respects. For example, they stipulated a variety of mutilating punish-ments, from shaving the beard and side whiskers to tattooing, cutting off the nose, amputation of a foot, and castration; for many crimes, the entire property of the convict could be confiscated and his family members enslaved by the state. Yet punishments were not arbitrary: Qin statutes demanded careful investigation of legal cases, punished officials for failure to follow proper legal procedure, discouraged abuse of torture, and distinguished between intended and accidental offenses (Hulsewé 1985:1–18; Yates 2009a, 2009b). Moreover, in many cases Qin statutes allowed remittance of mutilations by forced labor for the state's needs, and it is conceivable that one of the aims of the harshness of the laws was to create an additional pool of involuntary laborers to aug-ment the regular labor conscripts.

The political, social, economic, and legal system of Qin required a high degree of cen-tralization, which evolved as the reforms progressed. Although pockets of autonomous allotments remained a salient feature of the Qin system until relatively late into the Warring States period, overall the country was administered through a two-tier system of commanderies (*jun* 郡) and counties (*xian* 縣), run by professional bureaucrats on the state's payroll.[6] The appointees were responsible to the central government, which closely supervised their activities; they were routinely rotated and promoted (or demoted) according to their performance. The county was in charge of cantons (*xiang* 鄉), which formed the third, lower tier of administration; below the cantons were hamlets, the heads of which were selected by a canton chief from among the local inhab-itants (Bu Xianqun 2006). The already sizable administrative machine employed high number of part-time auxiliaries, such as runners, guards, wardens, and so forth; many of these were conscripted on an ad hoc basis or drafted from among convicts and bond-servants. It is difficult to estimate the overall cost of this elaborate administration sys-tem, but it appears to be relatively high, and it is possible that high administrative costs were among the factors contributing toward the ultimate crisis of the Qin Empire (Shelach 2014).

The Qin rulers who presided over this centralized bureaucratic machine—as their counterparts in other Warring States—were incomparably more powerful than their

---

[6] The uppermost tier, that of a commandery, evolved only slowly from a military to bureaucratic entity; this process started in the Warring States period and ended during the unified empire. See more in You Yifei 2014.

predecessors from the aristocratic age. Mark E. Lewis (1999:597) is fully justified to call the Warring State a "ruler-centered" polity. The rulers controlled appointments to the upper tiers of bureaucracy, they supervised their administrators, and their executive powers were immeasurably higher than those of even the most powerful officials. The adoption of the royal title by Lord (later King) Huiwen of Qin 秦惠文王 (r. 337–311) in 325 marked yet another step in the monarch's elevation above the rest of the elite. This elevation is fully visible archaeologically: both in the huge size of the tombs of Qin kings (such as Tomb 1 at the Zhiyang 芷陽 Necropolis in Lintong 臨潼 [Shaanxi]; Falkenhausen 2004:120–121) as well as in the layout of the last Qin capital, Xianyang 咸陽 (350–207 BCE), which was dominated by towering palatial buildings (Lu Qingsong 2010). This tendency for the rulers to engage in an ever-escalating "giganto-mania" (Falkenhausen 2014) peaked in the aftermath of the imperial unification, as is evident from various famous projects associated with the First Emperor of Qin (秦始皇帝, r. 246–221 BCE as a king, 221–210 BCE as an emperor), such as his mausoleum complex and the never-completed Epanggong 阿房宮 palace (Sanft 2008; Shelach 2014).

The state of Qin epitomizes the bureaucratic revolution of the Warring States period. Its historical trajectory demonstrates both positive and negative aspects of this revolution. Qin was arguably the best organized polity of the Warring States period, which allowed it to triumph over its rivals. Yet in the aftermath of the imperial unification, the "state organized for war" (Lewis 2007) lacked clear goals, and the system aimed at attaining utmost efficiency in mobilizing human and material resources outlived itself. It continued to mobilize the population at an ever-accelerating scale until the rebellion broke out. The sudden collapse of the first imperial dynasty taught its successors a useful lesson: a "fuzzy" and less efficient system may be more viable in the long term than the Qin system with its strive for extraordinary precision and efficiency (Shelach 2014).

BIBLIOGRAPHY

Barbieri-Low, Anthony J. and Robin D. S. Yates 2015. *Law, State, and Society in Early Imperial China: A Study with Critical Edition and Translation of the Legal Texts from Zhangjiashan Tomb No. 247*. Leiden: Brill.

Bu, Xianqun 卜憲群. 2006. "A Study on the Canton and Hamlet-Level Officials during Qin and Han Dynasties: A Discussion Based on Liye Qin Bamboo Slips 秦漢之際鄉里吏員雜考——以里耶秦簡為中心的探討." *Nandu xuetan* 南都學壇 1:1–6.

The Book of Lord Shang. See Pines 2017.

Falkenhausen, Lothar von. 2004. "Mortuary Behavior in Pre-Imperial Qin: A Religious Interpretation." In *Religion and Chinese Society*, vol. 1: *Ancient and Medieval China*. Edited by John Lagerwey, 109–172. Hong Kong: Chinese University of Hong Kong Press.

Falkenhausen, Lothar von, with Gideon Shelach 2014. "Introduction: Archaeological Perspectives on the Qin 'Unification' of China." In *Birth of an Empire: The State of Qin revisited*. Edited by Yuri Pines, Lothar von Falkenhausen, Gideon Shelach, and Robin D. S. Yates, 37–52. Berkeley: University of California Press.

Hsing, I-t'ien 邢義田. 2014. "Qin-Han Census and Tax and Corvée Administration: Notes on Newly Discovered Materials." In *Birth of an Empire: The State of Qin Revisited*. Edited by

Yuri Pines, Lothar von Falkenhausen, Gideon Shelach, and Robin D. S. Yates, 155–186. Berkeley: University of California Press.

Hulsewé, A. F. P. 1985. *Remnants of Ch'in Law: An Annotated Translation of the Ch'in Legal and Administrative Rules of the 3rd Century* BC *Discovered in Yün-meng Prefecture, Hu- pei Province, in 1975*. Leiden: Brill.

Hunansheng wenwu kaogu yanjiusuo 湖南省文物考古研究所. 2012. *Liye Qin jian (One)* 里耶秦 簡(壹). Beijing: Wenwu chubanshe.

Korolkov, Maxim. 2010. "Zemel'noe zakonodatel'stvo i kontrol' gosudarstva nad zemlej v epokhu Chzhan'go i v nachale ranneimperskoj epokhi (po dannym vnov' obnaruzhennykh zakonodatel'nykh tekstov)." PhD dissertation, Moscow: Russian Academy of Sciences, Institute of Oriental Studies.

Korolkov, Maxim. 2020. "Empire-Building and Market-Making at the Qin Frontier: Imperial Expansion and Economic Change, 221–207 BCE ," PhD dissertation, New York: Columbia University.

Lewis, Mark E. 1990. *Sanctioned Violence in Early China*. Albany: State University of New York Press.

Lewis, Mark E. 1999. "Warring States: Political History." In *The Cambridge History of Ancient China*. Edited by Michael Loewe and Edward L. Shaughnessy, 587–650. Cambridge, UK: Cambridge University Press.

Lewis, Mark E. 2007. *The Early Chinese Empires: Qin and Han*. Cambridge, MA: Harvard University Press.

Loewe, Michael. 2010. "Social Distinctions, Groups and Privileges." In *China's Early Empires: A Re-Appraisal*. Edited by Michael Nylan and Michael Loewe, 296–307. Cambridge, UK: Cambridge University Press.

Lu, Qingsong 陸青松. 2010. "Viewing the Politics of Rulership in the State of Qin from the Perspective of Ritual Reform 從禮制變革看 秦國的君主政治." *Wenbo* 1:39–43.

Pines, Yuri, trans. and ed. 2017. *The Book of Lord Shang: Apologetics of State Power in Early China*. New York: Columbia University Press.

Pines, Yuri, with Lothar von Falkenhausen, Gideon Shelach, and Robin D. S. Yates. 2014. "General Introduction: Qin History Revisited." In *Birth of an Empire: The State of Qin revisited*. Edited by Yuri Pines, Lothar von Falkenhausen, Gideon Shelach, and Robin D. S. Yates, 1–36. Berkeley: University of California Press.

Sanft, Charles 2008. "The Construction and Deconstruction of Epanggong: Notes from the Crossroads of History and Poetry." *Oriens Extremus* 47:160–176.

Sanft, Charles 2015. "Population Records from Liye: Ideology in Practice." In *Ideology of Power and Power of Ideology in Early China*. Edited by Yuri Pines, Paul R. Goldin, and Martin Kern, 249–269. Leiden: Brill.

Shelach, Gideon. 2014. "Collapse or Transformation? Anthropological and Archaeological Perspectives on the Fall of Qin." In *Birth of an Empire: The State of Qin revisited*. Edited by Yuri Pines, Lothar von Falkenhausen, Gideon Shelach, and Robin D. S. Yates, 113–140. Berkeley: University of California Press.

Shelach, Gideon, and Yuri Pines. 2005. "Power, Identity and Ideology: Reflections on the Formation of the State of Qin (770–221 BCE)." In *An Archaeology of Asia*. Edited by Miriam Stark, 202–230. Oxford: Blackwell.

Shi, Weiqing 施偉青. 2004. "On the Phenomenon of Absconding in the State of Qin after Shang Yang's Reform 論秦自 商鞅變法後的逃亡現象." *Zhongguo shehui jingji shi yanjiu* 中國社會經濟史研究 2:39–46.

Teng, Mingyu. 2014. "From Vassal State to Empire: An Archaeological Examination of Qin Culture." Translated by Susanna Lam. In *Birth of an Empire: The State of Qin revisited*. Edited by Yuri Pines, Lothar von Falkenhausen, Gideon Shelach, and Robin D. S. Yates, 71–112. Berkeley: University of California Press.

Wittfogel, Karl A. 1957. *Oriental Despotism: A Comparative Study of Total Power.* New Haven, CT: Yale University Press.

Yates, Robin D. S. 1987. "Social Status in the Ch'in: Evidence from the Yün-meng Legal Documents: Part One; Commoners." *Harvard Journal of Asiatic Studies* 47(1):197–236.

Yates, Robin D. S. 1995. "State Control of Bureaucrats under the Qin: Techniques and Procedures." *Early China* 20:331–365.

Yates, Robin D.S., 1999. "Early China." In *War and Society in the Ancient and Medieval Worlds: Asia, the Mediterranean, Europe, and Mesoamerica*. Edited by Kurt Raaflaub and Nathan Rosenstein, 9–46. Washington D.C.: Center for Hellenic Studies, Trustees for Harvard University and Harvard University Press.

Yates, Robin D. S. 2007. "The Rise of Qin and the Military Conquest of the Warring States." In *The First Emperor*. Edited by Jane Portal, 30–57. Cambridge, MA and London: Harvard University Press.

Yates, Robin D. S. 2009a. "Chinese Law, History of: Eastern Zhou, Ch'in State and Empire." In *The Oxford International Encyclopedia of Legal History*, vol. 1. Edited by Stanley N. Katz, 406–412. Oxford: Oxford University Press.

Yates, Robin D. S. 2009b. "Mutilation in Chinese Law." In *The Oxford International Encyclopedia of Legal History*, vol. 4. Edited by Stanley N. Katz, 196–197. Oxford: Oxford University Press.

Yates, Robin D. S. 2009c. "Law and the Military in Early China." In *Military Culture in Imperial China*. Edited by Nicola Di Cosmo, 23–44, 341–343. Cambridge, MA: Harvard University Press.

Yates, Robin D. S. 2012–2013. "The Qin Slips and Boards from Well No. 1, Liye, Hunan: A Brief Introduction to the Qin Qianling County Archives." *Early China* 35–36:291–330.

Yoshimoto, Michimasa 吉本道雅. 2000. "Preface to the Lord Shang's Reform 商君變法研究序說." *Shirin* 史林 83–84:1–29.

You, Yifei 游逸飛. 2014. "Reform in the Institute of the Commandery from the Warring States Period to the Early Western Han Dynasty 戰國至漢初的郡制變革," PhD dissertation, Taibei: National Taiwan University.

Zhang, Gong 張功. 2006. *Study on the Crime of Absconding in Qin and Han Times* 秦漢逃亡犯罪研究. Wuhan: Hubei renmin chubanshe.

CHAPTER 28

....

CHANGE AND CONTINUITY AT THE INTERSECTION OF RECEIVED HISTORY AND THE MATERIAL RECORD DURING THE WARRING STATES PERIOD

....

BY CHARLES SANFT, UNIVERSITY
OF ARIZONA

RECENT decades have brought tremendous advances in our understanding of early China. Archaeologists have uncovered an astounding array of artefacts, buildings, and paleographic documents and have thereby fundamentally changed our understanding of the past. These discoveries provided examples and details about places and institutions, information that provides new and more accurate understandings of the complexity, variety, and processes of change that characterized the past in China. This chapter treats four things represented in both received texts and the archaeological record: capital cities, the registration of the populace, oaths, and tallies used as signs of authority or permission. Our current understanding of each derives from both traditional texts and archaeological excavation and differs from previous understandings.

CAPITALS

The origins of capital cities in China lie with the beginnings of urbanism, which precede reliable history. Archaeological excavations have shown that certain design characteristics of later capitals were present already in Neolithic settlements. The most enduring of these was the tendency to align important structures with the cardinal directions. During the earliest identified dynasties this developed into a pattern of rectangular structures with primary entrances to the south. Palace buildings were often located to the north in walled towns and cities, a pattern that reappeared frequently throughout the imperial period. The relative position of palaces led to the expression "facing south" (*nanmian* 南面), a metonym for rulership that occurs already in bronze inscriptions from the Western Zhou period (Pankenier 2013:83, 86, 123; Yates 1997:86–87).

Many pre-imperial Chinese capitals followed one of two main layouts. The "concentric" form featured an exterior wall surrounding the city, which had within it a smaller walled area containing palaces and other significant buildings. In the "double" structure, two separate but connected walled precincts formed one city, with the smaller section containing the ruler's dwellings and primary government buildings. Both the concentric and double forms of cities existed already in the period before the Shang dynasty and reappeared throughout the Warring States period (Wu 2001:243–44; Steinhardt 1990:43–50).[1]

The concentric form seems like a natural development, in which multiple encircling walls provided improved security. The prototypical Jade Age city of the Liangzhu culture and the Early Shang city of Zhengzhou 鄭州 are early examples of the double structure (see chapters 5, by Liu Bin, and 12, by Song Guoding, in this volume). Yang Kuan 楊 寬 (1993) suggests the form strengthened defense and concentrated government administration around the ruler, reinforcing his authority. The double form was widespread among Springs and Autumns city-states and Warring States capitals. As the economy developed in pre-imperial times, the larger sections of these cities came to contain workshops and the residences of bureaucrats, merchants, and others. The smaller sections generally held government offices and elite residences, though they also contained workshops and markets. The earliest cities in China established a pattern of integration, in which cities—especially capitals—were populated by both elites and commoners and constituted centers of political activity, ritual, and economic production (see in this volume chapters 5 by Liu Bin; 7–9 by Xu Hong; 12 by Song Guoding; and 13, section 1, by E. Childs-Johnson; as well as Liu and Chen 2012:295–296; Falkenhausen 2008:218–222; Wu Hung 2001:239; Trigger 1999; Yang 1993:88–91; Steinhardt 1990).

Erlitou 二里頭 (ca. 1900–1500 BCE) is probably the earliest identifiable capital in the area. Some archaeologists suggest it may represent a Xia dynasty capital, because its main period of use roughly coincides with the presumed dates of the Xia. The limitations on written evidence from Erlitou culture sites, nonetheless, discourages historians from

---

[1] Steinhardt (1990:43–50) proposes three main structures to be found among Warring States capitals, which Wu Hung (2001) revises to just two.

definitively identifying the Erlitou site with the Xia. Yet Erlitou seems sure to have been the central city of a complex state with a broadly instantiated social hierarchy. And while determining the exact extent of Erlitou's political authority is becoming possible, archaeology shows that the influence of its material culture was extensive. The rectangular city was laid out along the cardinal directions, and evidence identifying specific buildings is limited. Archaeologists point to an area in the middle of the site that holds a number of packed-earth foundations of various sizes, including those believed to have supported palaces. The evidence reflects the presence of workshops for casting bronze and working jade, as well as pottery kilns. The population is estimated to have been 18,000 to 30,000 persons at its peak. Notably, there is no evidence that Erlitou was walled (see Xu Hong 2015; in this volume chapters 7–9, by Xu Hong, and 10, by Chung Tang; and see also Falkenhausen 2008:218; Allan 2007; Liu and Chen 2003:34, 57–64; Xu 2000:53–54). The earliest historically attested dynasty is the Shang, famous for its highly mobile form of government, the center of which followed the Shang king on his frequent travels. Shang rule was in all likelihood loose and the boundaries of its power fuzzy. The Shang are supposed to have had a number of capitals, perhaps as many as eight. There are extensive walled towns at a number of Shang sites containing packed-earth plinths for buildings, including those for large buildings that may have been palaces. Some of these towns— particularly Yanshi 偃師 and Zhengzhou 郑州—may have been Shang capitals. Their cultural affiliation with the Shang seems clear, and archaeological data suggest their identity as major cities and thus possibly capitals (see chapters 13, by Childs-Johnson, and 12, by Song Guoding, in this volume; and Childs-Johnson 2017). There has been some contention about this, however (see Liu and Chen 2012:278, 352–353, 389; Keightley 2012:200–202; Lewis 2006:136–137; Wu 1998:9–10; Keightley 1983; Chang 1980:5–7).

The one Shang city that is universally accepted as a capital is at modern Anyang 安陽 (Henan). Inscribed oracle bones were recovered in large quantities there in modern times and they identify the site as Yin 殷, the final Shang capital. Anyang is thus the earliest site that received and paleographic texts confirm was a capital in China. Occupied for more than 270 years, the site is large, covering approximately 24 square kilometers and comprising a large number of remains. These include an identified palace complex of more than 50 packed-earth foundations. Commoners' residences occur in numerous smaller groups, and there is extensive evidence of workshops that made items of bronze, pottery, bone, jade, and stone (see Childs-Johnson, chapter IV.4 in this volume; Liu and Chen 2012:256, 355–358; Liu and Chen 2003:144; Xu 2000:58–59).

The Western Zhou took over the general form of Shang government and oversaw a loose group of smaller territories governed by Zhou royal relatives. The Western Zhou rulers moved their capital multiple times, never investing a specific capital city or place with a unique and immutable political significance. Tradition identifies the primary capitals of Zhou as Feng 澧 and Hao 鎬, both in the vicinity of modern Xi'an (Shaanxi), Qishan 岐山 (Shaanxi), and Chengzhou 成周 (Henan). Li Feng (2006:43–46) uses Western Zhou bronze inscriptions to argue for the central role of Feng and Hao in Zhou governance and ritual. Feng and Hao are believed to have developed complementary functions, with Feng the location of the ancestral temple and its sacrifices and Hao the center of government administration and military command. Although there is no debate about the general location of these two cities, archaeologists and historians have disagreed about their exact positions (see Khayutina, chapter 17 in this volume; Falkenhausen 2008:218–219, 223; Khayutina 2008; Wu 2001:247; Lewis 2006:137–138; Wu 1998:11–14; Yang 1993:65–66).

The Springs and Autumns period is characterized by the existence of more than two hundred city-states, a situation that emerged out of the dissolution of the Zhou dynasty's dispersed governance. Each city-state governed a territory that was small and linked closely to the city, which was surrounded by the agricultural land that supported it. As such, they were not capitals of extensive states. Yet as larger polities developed during the Warring States period, certain of the city-states became capitals (Lewis 2006:137–140; Trigger 1999:46–47).

The picture of capital cities is clearer in the Warring States period due to the wealth of information available from textual sources and archaeological research. Cities in Warring States times were generally constructed on top of previous settlements. Cities were ever-evolving products of building and rebuilding. Each of the more than 140 states known to have existed during the Warring States period had a capital, which typically combined political and economic functions. Archaeologists have examined about 50 of these capitals to differing degrees. Their results indicate that over the course of the period and as part of the general trend toward territorial consolidation, certain of these cities grew in size, their populations becoming larger and their encircling walls higher and longer (Wu 2001; Wu 1998:14–18). The capitals of Qi 齊 and Qin 秦 are representative examples. The capital of Qi was Linzi 臨淄 (today Shandong), in its time the most famous city in China and an important center for trade. Linzi's population at its height was ca. 500,000, the largest of any city then in existence. At the high point of its development, Linzi was a double city, with a smaller walled enclosure that was added on the southwest corner of the larger enclosed city. The larger section may date as far back as the Western Zhou period, while the smaller section was a Warring States construction. The smaller section of Linzi was rectangular and surrounded by a packed-earth wall approximately 2,200 m long on its east and west sides, and about 1,400 m on the northern and southern sides. The larger section had four primary sides but was irregular in shape due to the proximity of a river. Its north wall was ca. 3,300 m in length, the east about 5,200 m, the west 2,800 m, and the south wall some 2,800 m long. The Linzi palace complex was located in the northern part of the smaller section, concentrated around one large packed-earth platform. The main streets of this section centered on the palace, including a major north-south street some 6–8 meters wide, which intersected with an east-west street 17 meters in width. There was a defensive moat outside the wall and 5 fortified gates. Two of those gates led into the larger section, which had 6 additional gates. There were workshops in both parts of Linzi, including foundries for bronze from the early Chunqiu period and for iron from the Warring States. The city also contained numerous residences for its population (Falkenhausen 2008:225–226; Wu 2001; Yang 1993:66–70, 88–91).

Many pre-imperial states had multiple capital cities, a pattern that Trigger (1999) describes as typical of "territorial states," large polities under a monarch that governed by means of hierarchical institutions. The state of Qin, which came to rule all others, exemplifies this, and it had a number of capitals over the course of its history. Yong 雍(Shaanxi) was the capital of Qin from the late seventh until the early fourth centuries BCE. Its city wall formed an irregular rectangle, approximately 3,300 m east/west and 3,200 m north/south. Archaeologists have identified a walled complex that held palace buildings, such as inner and outer court halls, and associated residences. Nearby is what they deem to have been the ancestral temple complex, with an open area where remains from 181 sacrificial burials were found, including oxen, goats, and humans. Yong does not exhibit the clear two-part division characteristic of cities like Linzi, yet its places of political power were concentrated in the southwest, while markets and associated buildings were located to the northeast. This suggests Yong followed the broader pattern of delineating elite and non-elite spheres of activity (Yang 1993:75–81).

Xianyang 咸陽 was the final capital of the state of Qin and also the imperial capital of the Qin dynasty. Xianyang was located on both banks of the River Wei 渭, near modern Xi'an. The Qin established their capital here in the fourth century BCE, and it remained their capital until the end of the Qin dynasty in 207 BCE. As Qin power and wealth expanded, Xianyang developed into the most ostentatious of the Warring States capitals. It was in use for more than 140 years, and extensive remains exist today. Xianyang is also the best understood of the Warring States capitals due to decades of archaeological excavation at the site (Shaanxisheng 2004:3–5; Wu 1998:21–22).

Archaeologists have found sections of the wall that surrounded Qin-era Xianyang and identified more than 30 medium- and large-sized buildings within the city area, all built on bases of rammed earth. Xianyang was encircled by a wall of irregular shape 426 m long on the east side, 576 on the west side, 902 m on the south, and 843 m long. Damage to the site has left just two gates identifiable, in the western and southern walls, and a moat has been identified outside the western and northern sides. The center of the site is the Xianyang Palace complex, which was oriented approximately according to the four directions, making Xianyang an example of the concentric form. The palace was constructed on top of a packed-earth platform and comprised 10 rooms surrounded by a corridor. The city remains contain other identified palaces, as well. In keeping with the pattern seen in other cities, Xianyang also contains extensive remains of workshops, including those for pottery, brick and tile, bone-working, and foundries. Archaeologists have excavated roads, including a major thoroughfare that was 54.4 m wide at its broadest, its roadbed 5–15 cm thick, and built with a cross slope to promote drainage. There was also an extensive underground sewer system in the city (Shaanxisheng 2004:9–18, 21–23, 212–217, 283–287). Xianyang was the location of the Qin central administration, and its capture by the Han founder Liu Bang's 劉邦 (r. 206/202–195 BCE) forces marked the end of the preceding dynasty.

POPULATION REGISTRATION

Scholars who trace the origins of population registration in China often look to Shang dynasty oracle bones for the earliest examples of demographic information. Ikeda On (1979) points to a precise count of enemy persons killed as sacrifices by the Shang, which he believes is evidence of registration. Ikeda also refers to Western Zhou inscriptions that name exact numbers of persons. He cites, for instance, a bronze vessel called the "Yihou Ze gui" 宜侯夨簋 with an inscription saying, "[I] award you commoners of Yi numbering six hundred and . . . six men" (transl. Li 2008:239), which Ikeda argues indicates recording of the populace. While these examples reflect the interest in counting persons, their relationship to population registration is uncertain, and there is no evidence that those rulers attempted to maintain a comprehensive record of the population. Nevertheless, the inscriptions do reflect the presence of related concepts, and that the Shang and Western Zhou were interested in these things (Sanft 2014).

Received texts from the Confucian canon refer to population registration and enumeration. The most important canonical source is the *Zhou Rituals* (*Zhou li*). Although no serious scholar would now accept the *Zhou Rituals* as a record of Western Zhou governance, as in the past, it is often cited as reflecting pre-imperial concepts of government. It describes officials like the "manager of the people" (*simin* 司民), who supposedly maintained records of the populace (*Zhou li zhu shu*, 534). Notably, *Zhou Rituals* depicts these records as having been created and maintained as an incidental part of broader tasks and not as the result of dedicated activities or officials. Indeed no canonical text depicts population registry as a regular occurrence or ongoing process (Sanft 2014).

The earliest historical references to a complete and ongoing population enumeration and registration date it to the fourth century BCE, during the Late Warring States period. According to *Shiji* (6.289), it is then that the state of Qin began to individually record all members of its population, an innovation traditionally attributed to Shang Yang (on this subject see Yuri Pines, chapter VII). Although this record is unique in transmitted sources, archaeologists have recovered paleographic examples of documents related to registration from the states of Chu as well as Qin (Sanft 2014).

Among the Chu documents on bamboo strips recovered at Baoshan 包山 (Hubei) are a few examples of governmental "ledgers" (*dian* 典) kept in the state of Chu, also during the fourth century BCE. These ledgers were used for all sorts of enumerated record-keeping, including matters ranging from equipment inventory to population records. Due to the limited source materials available, conclusions are mostly tentative. It appears that the names and places of residence of commoners and slaves were recorded, but only for men, probably to facilitate military conscription. Evidence suggests these records were made annually and stored in local-level government offices (Chen 1996:108–131; Sanft 2014).

Thanks to recent archaeological discoveries, there is a considerable amount of information available about Qin processes. In 2002 archaeologists discovered thousands of discarded Qin bureaucratic documents on wooden strips in an abandoned ancient well at Liye (Hunan), the location of a Qin prefectural government center (Yates 2012–2013). The Liye materials attest to a system that sought to record every person in the Qin state as part of a household (*hu* 戶). In the recovered examples, each strip contains the members of one household. Each individual member is identified by a set of information that included name and social rank, with information about place of residence coming before the name of the householder. The example registries record this information in a condensed format that organizes household members on each strip hierarchically, arranged in groups according to status in the family as defined by relationship to the householder. One such registry records: "Nanyang householder Jing *bugeng* (fourth rank) Huang De Wife called Qian Child: minor *shangzao* (second rank) Tai Child: minor *shangzao* [illegible] Child: minor *shangzao* Ding Child: minor girl Hu Child: minor girl Yi Child: minor girl Ping Group of five leader."[2]

Households were organized into groups of five (*wu* 伍). The members of each group had a legal obligation to report any crimes committed by the others. Records like the example attest to the existence of these groups by marking the householder as the leader of the group (Sanft 2015; Sanft 2014).

Ordinary people were required by statute to update their registration if they moved, and government officials were to check the accuracy of the information annually.

Officials summarized prefectural household data for submission to their superiors at the commandery (*jun* 郡), from which information would be submitted to the central government. Han-era population data recovered at Tianchang (Anhui) include a prefectural "record of household registries" (*hukoubu* 戶口簿), reflecting practices slightly later than those of Qin (Sanft 2014). That text begins:

> Total households: 9,169; fewer than before. Population: 40,970; fewer than before. East District: 1,783 households; 7,795 persons. [Prefectural] City District: 2,398 households; 10,819 persons. Yangchi District: 1,451 households; 6,328 persons . . . (Tianchangshi and Tianchangshi 2006:11)

Sites at Songbocun (Hubei) and in territory held by Han-era China near Pyongyang (North Korea) have produced similar Han documents, though containing more detailed information (Yuan 2011:61–66). While current publications leave the relationship of these documents to Qin practices uncertain, it is likely that local authorities during the Qin period produced the same types of reports based on household registries and other records.

OATHS AND COVENANTS

The swearing of covenants (*meng* 盟) played an important part in the political culture of pre-imperial China. Some evidence exists for ritual oaths under the Shang and Western Zhou. But it was only during the Springs and Autumns and Warring States periods, when effective central rule had broken down and competition and conflict between and

---

[2] Hunansheng 2007:203. This example is translated and discussed in Sanft 2015; cf. translations of a different example in Venture 2011:86; and Yates 2011:359–360.

within polities became the rule, that covenants increased in importance as means of political organization (Lewis 1990:45).

The *Zuozhuan* records hundreds of instances in which polities carried out ritual covenants. Covenants could also be pledged between individuals, though that was rare. The basic form of the covenant combined a sacrifice with an agreement between parties, who swore an oath (*shi* 誓) before ancestral or nature spirits. In a few cases the offering was jade, but animal offerings were usual, most often sheep. After killing, the victim's blood would be applied to the mouths of the covenanters in symbolic consumption. The agreement would be spoken aloud and a copy written out and marked with blood for inhumation with the sacrifice. The spirits were enjoined to enforce the terms of the oath, frequently by destroying the person(s) and lineage(s) of any who violated it. The most common form of covenant was between two polities, who bound themselves together or obliged them not to attack each other (Zhu 2010; Poo 2009:290–295; Lewis 1990:43–50). An extensive example of this type of covenant recorded in the *Zuozhuan* (Xiang 11) reads,

> All those who participate in this covenant agree not to hoard grain, not to monopolize profit, not to protect conspirators, not to harbor criminals, to give assistance in the event of civil war or insurrection, to have the same friends and enemies, and to support the royal house.
>
> If anyone violates these commands, may the guardians of reverence and covenants, the spirits of the great mountains and rivers, the collected heavenly spirits and spirits who receive sacrifice, the former kings and former lords, and the ancestors of the seven surnames and twelve states destroy him so that his people desert him, he loses rank and clan, and his state and family are extinguished. (transl. Lewis 1990:47–48)

Yu Wei and others have argued that the "lineage covenant" (*zongmeng* 宗盟) was a way the Zhou dynasty overlords bound and ordered their subordinate polities, including both members and non-members of their lineage. It has been suggested that the inscriptions on several Western Zhou bronze vessels may together reflect a lineage covenant, although that remains highly tentative (Yu 2012, 2008).

Archaeologists have recovered covenant texts at Houma 侯馬 (Shanxi) and Wenxian 溫縣 (Henan) that record oaths taken by individuals in the state of Jin during the Warring States period. Each example obligated an individual, conceivably on behalf of a group of relatives, to be loyal to a particular leader and to take or avoid specific actions. The texts call for the destruction of oath-breakers and the enemies named in the oath together with their respective lineages. As in the case of covenants between polities, these texts invoke a supernatural power as enforcing agent. Many scholars believe that the spirits of deceased past rulers were the enforcing agents, but it has recently been argued that a mountain spirit was the intended enforcer. These covenants linked individuals into groups beyond those of blood relationship and were thus political in nature and part of larger developments in social organization during the Warring States period

(Williams 2012–2013:248, 250, 262–269; Williams 2009:962–963; Williams 2005:63; Weld 1997; Weld 1990:142, 148).

The covenant texts follow set forms—six, by one count—and examples of each vary only in the name of the person who took the oath (Williams 2012–2013). One example reads as follows:

> [If] Chao dare to not split open his guts and heart [i.e., display true loyalty] in serving his lord, and, [if] he dare to not fully abide by *jia*'s covenant, and the decrees [given at] the Ding Temple and Ping Altar, and, [if] he, instead, dare to cause [name] and [name] to change, causing them to not guard the two temples, and, [if] he dare have the intention of returning Zhao Hu and his sons and grandsons, [and] [list of enemy names], along with [any one of] those who broke or breaks the covenant, to the lands of the Jin state, my superior, may [you] perspicaciously and tirelessly watching him, wipe out that *shi* [the covenentor and any direct male descendants]. (transl. Williams 2012–2013:251)

It is likely that the texts were formulated by the leaders and copied out in large numbers on stone obtained for that purpose. The grouping of the texts and the varieties of stone used indicate that persons of various ranks participated. The numbers involved are impressive: the texts record many thousands of names. Since each person may have represented others, the Wenxian covenants alone potentially represent a group of some 50,000 persons. There is some disagreement among scholars about specific dating and historical context, but the consensus is that the recovered covenant texts come from a time of political turbulence in Jin during the fifth century BCE (Williams 2012–2013:255, 259–261; Williams 2009:971–975, 980; Weld 1997:130–132).

TALLIES

Tallies (*fujie* 符節) were a class of objects that served as official symbols of authority and authorization over a long period in premodern China, typically in contexts of military command, diplomacy, resource control, and movement through passes and gates. The modern term *fujie* comprises two words of closely related meaning that were used more or less interchangeably in classical Chinese (Chen 1995:305). The Han dynasty lexicon *Shuowen jiezi* 說文解字 glosses both as signs of trust.[3]

The *fujie* came to be what would be called in English a "tally"—namely, something divided into pieces that could be reunited to show the reliability of one or both halves—no later than the Warring States, and it is in this form that it persisted into imperial times. In earlier periods *fu* and *jie* denoted specific objects that functioned as symbols of authority or power in themselves, without division. It has been suggested that jade tallies

---

[3] Tang 1997:621, 1,233–1,234. The original form of *jie* in this sense was 卪, but it merged with 節 in early times.

were the oldest form and derived directly from *gui* 圭, jade tablets that were used in rituals and were not divisible (Zheng 1985).

Zhou Rituals refers to tallies at a number of places, and while this text is no longer accepted as a historical record of Zhou practice, it portrays an influential early understanding of tallies and is widely cited in early texts and modern scholarship. The most important of the *Zhou Rituals* depictions of tallies come in its descriptions of the "tally handler" (*zhangjie* 掌節) and the "minor usher" (*xiaoxingren* 小行人) responsible for receiving emissaries (*Zhou li zhu shu*, 230–232, 567–568; Chen 1995). *Zhou Rituals* mentions a number of different kinds of tallies. One type, made of jade or horn, was given to those granted lands or towns as signs of their authority. *Zhou Rituals* also details tallies of various shapes that were borne by emissaries: tiger-shaped tallies (*hujie* 虎節) for mountainous territories, dragon tallies (*longjie* 龍節) for marshy places, and tallies in human shape (*renjie* 人節) for flat lands. All were made of metal, presumably bronze. *Zhou Rituals* further speaks of "pennant tallies" (*jingjie* 旌節) indicating authorization to travel roads and what it calls simply "tallies" (*fujie*) for presentation at gates and passes, both made from bamboo. The descriptions are at odds concerning a final type of tally, also bamboo. The entry concerning the tally handler mentions a "seal tally" (*xijie* 璽節) for cases when goods were involved, while that of the minor usher refers to a "tube-shaped tally" (*guanjie* 管節) for use in towns and the country. There are other references to tallies in various sections of *Zhou Rituals*, most often signaling authorization to pass a gate or pass, or travel a road (Chen 1995:306–308).

A number of examples of actual tallies are extant from the Warring States period. Chen Zhaorong (1995:312–313) divides the examples into three groups based on the content of their inscriptions: those that permit passage without paying taxes, those related to postal relay systems, and military tallies. A few examples remain obscure and fall out of this schema.

Military tallies are by far the best known. This is doubtless due to the photogenic character of the tiger tallies that constitute all examples from the Warring States and Qin periods (Chen Zhaorong 1995:311–312). Half of one Qin tiger tally was found in a southern suburb of Xi'an in 1973 and is now in a museum in Shaanxi. Made of bronze, it measures 9.5 cm long, 4.4 cm high, and 7 cm thick. This "Qin Du tiger tally" 秦杜虎符 bears the following inscription in forty graphs:

> Military tally. The right [half] is with the ruler, the left in Du. Whenever raising troops or putting on armor, using fifty soldiers or more, you must match the lord's tally and only then may you do it. When it is a matter of the signal fires, carry it out even without matching the tallies. (Transl. of Zhu 1983)

This text confirms how military tallies functioned as authorizing a commander to mobilize and command troops at the proven command of the ruler. Based on the script and comparison to other examples, this appears to be a Qin tally from the end of the Warring States period. There is still discussion about its exact dating but, based on the terminology in the inscription, it likely dates to the late fourth century BCE, making it the earliest extant example of this type (Zhu 1983; Zeng 1998; Chen 1995:326–328; Hei 1979; Hu and Li 2013).

Another Qin tally bears a nearly identical inscription, which contains the toponym Xinqi 新郪 and uses a different term for the ruler. This suggests both that it postdates the Qin Du tiger tally and that the text of this kind of inscription was standardized in Qin. There is an example military tally in tiger shape from the state of Chu, believed to come from Qi, and Wei is also known to have used them. It is, however, the identified Qin system that persisted into imperial times (Chen 1995:339–341; Li 1993; Hei 1979).

Tallies in what are identified as other animal shapes also exist. There are two bird-shaped tallies—believed to be eagles—that authorized travel through passes and fords without hindrance from officials. Based on their inscriptions' script, these are believed to come from the state of Yan. Seven examples of Chu tallies in the shape of dragons are extant, though difficulties interpreting their inscriptions make determining their function uncertain. There are also records of tallies in bear or horse form (Chen 1995:313–323, 341; Li 1998).

As already noted, *Zhou Rituals* mentions bamboo tallies, and indeed that was likely a usual material for tallies in common use for permitting and controlling the passage of persons and goods along roads, through passes and gates, and avoiding taxes. Indeed, the word *jie* 節 originally denoted a segment of bamboo. An exceptional tally cast of bronze in the shape of bamboo at the order of a Chu king and given to Qi, lord of E 鄂君 啟, in the late fourth century BCE is extant. It divides vertically into sections and permits travel in a specific area and the use of boat and cart for transportation. More importantly, it exempted its bearer from tariffs on the goods and granted access to the postal stations' resources. While this tally was certainly a special case and contained an unusual amount of information, its form suggests such tallies were ordinarily bamboo (Chen 1995:308–313; Zheng 1985:56–57).

BIBLIOGRAPHY

Allan, Sarah 2007. "Erlitou and the Formation of Chinese Civilization: Toward a New Paradigm." *Journal of Asian Studies* 66(2):461–496.

Chang, Kwang-chih 1980. *Shang Civilization*. New Haven, CT: Yale University Press. Chen Jie 陳絜

Chang, Kwang-chih 2009. "Liye 'Household Registry Strips' and Low-Level Society in the Late Warring States Period 里耶 "戶籍簡,"" 與戰國末期的基層社會." *Lishi yanjiu* 5:23–40.

Chen, Wei 陳偉 1996. *A First Examination of the Baoshan Chu Strips* 包山楚簡初探. Wuhan: Wuhan daxue chubanshe.

Chen, Zhaorong 陳昭容 1995. "Qin Tallies of the Warring States Period: With a Focus on Actual Examples 戰國至秦的符節 – 以實物資料為主." *Zhongyang yanjiuyuan lishi yuyan yanjiusuo jikan* 66(1):305–349.

Falkenhausen, Lothar von 2008. "Stages in the Development of 'Cities' in Pre-Imperial China." In *The Ancient City: New Perspectives on Urbanism in the Old and New World*. Edited by Joyce Marcus and Jeremy A. Saboff, 209–228. Santa Fe: School for Advanced Research Press.

Gao, Min 高敏 1987. "The Qin-Han Household Registry System 秦漢的戶籍制度." *Qiu suo* 1:72–81.

Gao, Min 高敏 2000. "The Qin-Han Household Registry System 從 "睡 虎地秦簡"看 秦的若 干制度." In *Shuihudi Qin jian chu tan*. Edited by , 149–188. Taipei: Wanjuanlou.

Ge, Jianxiong 葛劍雄 2002. *The History of China's Population* 中國人口史. Shanghai: Fudan daxue chubanshe.

Gou, Haiyan 勾海燕 2012. "An Examination of the Dongjun Tiger Tally 東郡虎符考釋." *Shoucangjia* 9:13–14.

Hei, Guang 黑光 1979. "The Du Tiger Tally Discovered in a Suburb of Xi'an 西安市郊發 現 秦國杜虎符." *Wenwu* 9:93–94.

Hu Juan 胡娟, and Li Yaguang 李亞光 2013. "Tiger Tallies in the Pre-Qin Period 先秦時 期的 虎符." *Lantai shijie* 4:55–56.

Keightley, David N. 1983. "The Late Shang State: When, Where, and What?" In *Origins of Chinese Civilization*. Edited by D. Keightley, 523–564. Berkeley: University of California Press.

Keightley, David N. 2012. *Working for His Majesty: Research Notes on Labor Mobilization in Late Shang China (ca. 1200–1045 BC), as Seen in the Oracle-Bone Inscriptions, with Particular Attention to Handicraft Industries, Agriculture, Warfare, Hunting, Construction, and the Shang's Legacies*. Berkeley: Institute of East Asian Studies, University of California.

Khayutina, Maria 2008. "Western 'Capitals' of the Western Zhou Dynasty: Historical Reality and Its Reflections until the Time of Sima Qian." *Oriens Extremus* 47:25–65.

Lewis, Mark Edward 1990. *Sanctioned Violence in Early China*. Albany: State University of New York Press.

Lewis, Mark Edward 2006. *The Construction of Space in Early China*. Albany: State University of New York Press.

Li, Feng 2006. *Landscape and Power in Early China: The Crisis and Fall of the Western Zhou, 1045–771 BC*. Cambridge, UK: Cambridge University Press.

Li, Jiahao 李家浩 1993. "The General Gui Tiger Tally and the Lord Pi Tiger Tally: Research on Warring States Period Tally Inscriptions, 1 貴將軍虎節與辟大夫虎 節 – 戰國符節銘文研 究之一." *Zhongguo lishi bowuguan guankan* 2:50–55.

Li, Jiahao 李家浩 1998. "An Examination of the Eagle Tally Inscription: Research on Warring States Period Tally Inscriptions, 2 傳遽鷹節銘文考釋 – 戰國符節銘文研究之." In *Haishang luncong*, vol. 2. Edited by Li Xueqin, Wu Zhongjie, and Zhu Minshen, 17–33. Shanghai: Fudan daxue chubanshe.

Li, Mingzhao 黎明釗 2009. "The Liye Qin Strips: A Consideration of the Household Registry Files 里耶秦簡: 戶籍檔案的探討." *Zhongguoshi yanjiu* 2:5–23.

Liu, Li, and Xingchan Chen 2003. *State Formation in Early China*. London: George Duckworth.

Liu, Li, and Xingchan Chen 2012. *The Archaeology of China: From the Late Paleolithic to the Early Bronze Age*. Cambridge, UK: Cambridge University Press.

Liu, Shuying 劉淑英 1995. "Pre-Qin Population Statistics and Management 先秦的人口統計 與管理." *Renkou yu jingji* 4:50–55.

Ouyang, Fenglian 歐陽鳳蓮 2009. "Conceptions of Household Registry Management in the Book of Lord Shang and the Qin State's System of Household Registry Management 商君 書" 戶籍管理思想與秦國戶籍管理制度." *Gudai wenming* 3(2):57–63.

Pankenier, David W. 2013. *Astrology and Cosmology in Early China: Conforming Earth to Heaven*. Cambridge, UK: Cambridge University Press.

Poo, Mu-chou 2009. "Ritual and Ritual Texts in Early China." In *Early Chinese Religion, Part One: Shang through Han (1250 BC–220 AD)*. Edited by J. Lagerwey and M. Kalinowski, 281–314. Leiden: Brill.

Sanft, Charles 2014. *Communication and Cooperation in Early Imperial China: Publicizing the Qin Dynasty*. Albany: State University of New York Press.

Sanft, Charles. Forthcoming. "Population Records from Liye: Ideology in Practice." In *Ideology of Power and Power of Ideology in Early China*. Edited by Yuri Pines, Paul R. Goldin, and Martin Kern. Leiden: Brill.

Shaanxisheng kaogu yanjiusuo 陝西省考古研究所 2004. *The Archaeological Report on the Qin Capital Xianyang* 秦都咸陽考古報告. Beijing: Kexue chubanshe.

Steinhardt, Nancy Shatzman 1990. *Chinese Imperial City Planning*. Honolulu: University of Hawai'i Press.

Tang, Kejing 湯可敬 1997. *Shuowen jiezi: A Modern Exegesis* 說文解字今釋. Changsha: Yuelu shushe.

Trigger, Bruce G. 1999. "Shang Political Organization: A Comparative Approach." *Journal of East Asian Archaeology* 1:43–62.

Venture, Olivier 2011. "Caractères interdits et vocabulaire officiel sous les Qin: L'apport des documents administratifs de Liye." *Études chinoises* 30:73–98.

Weld, Susan Roosevelt 1990. "Covenant in Jin's Walled Cities: The Discoveries at Houma and Wenxian." PhD dissertation, Harvard University.

Weld, Susan Roosevelt 1997. "The Covenant Texts from Houma and Wenxian." *New Sources of Chinese History: An Introduction to the Reading of Inscriptions and Manuscripts*. Edited by E. L. Shaughnessy, 125–160. Berkeley: Society for the Study of Early China.

Williams, Crispin 2005. "A Methodological Procedure for the Analysis of the Wenxian Covenant Texts." *Asiatische Studien* 59(1):61–114.

Williams, Crispin 2009. "Ten Thousand Names: Rank and Lineage Affiliation in the Wenxian Covenant Texts." *Asiatische Studien* 63(4):959–989.

Williams, Crispin 2012–2013. "Dating the Houma Covenant Texts: The Significance of Recent Findings from the Wenxian Covenant Texts." *Early China* 35–36:247–275.

Wu, Hung 2001. "Rethinking Warring States Cities: An Historical and Methodological Proposal." *Journal of East Asian Archaeology* 3(1–2):237–257.

Wu, Songdi 吳松弟 1998. *China's Ancient Capitals* 中國古代都城. Revised ed. Beijing: Shangwu yishuguan.

Xu, Hong 許宏 2000. *Archaeological Research on Pre-Qin Cities* 先秦城市考古學研究. Beijing: Yanshan chubanshe.

Yang, Kuan 楊寬 1993. *Research on the Institutions of China's Ancient Cities* 中國古代 都城制度史研究. Shanghai: Shanghai guji chubanshe.

Yates, Robin D. S. 1997. "The City-State in Ancient China." In *The Archaeology of City-States: Cross-Cultural Approaches*. Edited by D. L. Nichols and T. H. Charlton, 71–90. Washington, DC: Smithsonian Institution Press.

Yates, Robin D. S. 2012–2013. "The Qin Slips and Boards from Well No. 1, Liye, Hunan: A Brief Introduction to the Qin Qianling County Archives." *Early China* 35–36:291–329.

Yuan, Yansheng 袁延勝 2011. "An Analysis of the Han 'Household Roster' 漢牘 '戶口簿' 探析." *Ludong daxue xuebao* 28(3):61–66.

Zeng ,Weihua 曾維華 1998. "An Examination the Dating of the Casting of the Qin State Du Tiger Tally 秦國杜虎符鑄造年代考." *Xueshu yuekan* 5:79–80.

Zheng, Yakun 鄭雅坤 1985. "Discussing China's Ancient System of Tallies and Its Changes 談我國古代的符節(牌)制度及其演變." *Xibei daxue xuebao* 1:56–63.

Zhou Li 2001. "*Zhou li zhu shu* 周禮注疏." In *The Thirteen Classics with Commentaries* 十三經注疏. Edited by Ruan Yuan 阮元, 1,764–1,849. Taipei: Yiwen yinshuguan.

Zhu, Jieyuan 朱捷元 1983. "A Brief Discussion of the Qin State Du Tally 秦國杜虎符小 議." *Xibei daxue xuebao* 西北大學學報 1:53–55.

Zhu, Zengli 朱增力 2010. "An Explanation of the Term 'Meng' in the Zuozhuan 左傳" 中 的 "盟" 之釋義." *Shandong jiaoyu xueyuan xuebao* 6:53–55.

CHAPTER 29

....

THE ARMY, WARS,
AND MILITARY ARTS
DURING THE WARRING
STATES PERIOD

....

BY ALBERT GALVANY, THE UNIVERSITY
OF THE BASQUE COUNTRY UPV/EHU

ARISTOCRATIC combat, which characterized warfare in the early Springs and Autumns period, was the social elite's favorite way of competing in honor, valor, and virtue. If one gives credence to the descriptions provided by some textual sources of the period, many of them retrospective, combat took the form of clashes between noble warriors, who recognized each other as such and who, armed with costly bronze weapons, fought in their chariots after formally agreeing to the place, day, and hour of the battle (*Zuozhuan* Xiang 23:1,084). Insofar as combat was, at least ideally, a contest between the power of two equally forewarned and well-prepared adversaries, the laws of honor condemned any maneuver that sought to gain unfair advantage over the enemy or wrongly exploit his difficulties (*Zuozhuan* Huan 8:122). It should also be borne in mind that these frequent military engagements almost invariably occurred within the narrow margins delimited by the space between two or more adjoining territories. War, in these times, was principally the expression of what might be called a "neighborly" conflict, and great military expeditions seeking distant conquests were a very uncommon occurrence (*Zuozhuan* Xi 4:289). Then again, battles in this period had elements of representation or parading, a kind of theatrical dimension where, in order to show off their gallantry and bravery, the combatants exchanged greetings, gifts, challenging gestures, bluster, petulance, and insolence (Lewis 1990:15–52). According to the descriptions one finds in texts like the *Zuozhuan*, this was an age when only adult men belonging to the aristocratic class enjoyed the privilege of the legitimate use of arms. The remaining social classes (as well as children, women, the aged, those in mourning, and the infirm) were not only excluded from bearing arms but also from the consequences of wars (Granet 1994:289–312). However, in the harsh geopolitical reality of the Warring States period, wars excluded no one. One way or another, the whole population participated in military campaigns of such magnitude that the totality of society was exposed and thus made to suffer their consequences (Chiang 2005).

This radical change in the organization and ways of conceiving armed conflict in China is at least partially explained by the convergence of several factors. Here, it is important to recall that after the sixth century BCE and with the aim of dealing with incursions by nomad groups from mountainous regions, some states obliged their warriors to leave their chariots and fight the enemy as foot soldiers (Lan 1979; Kolb 1991). Thenceforth, and encouraged by the military successes of some outlying states like Wu and Yue, which had decided to form armies mainly constituted by foot soldiers taken from their rural populations, the use of infantry regiments was enforced. At the same time, several technological innovations ushered in decisive changes, notable among them being the manufacture of iron weapons (Bai Yunxiang 2005:36–39, 82–95), which were cheaper than those made from bronze, thus giving the infantry a considerable economic advantage not to mention an unrivaled power of destruction. Technical advances now drove mass-based warfare and there was an unprecedented development of devices invented both to assault fortified cities and as defensive measures. In this regard, it should also be mentioned that Mohism, the doctrine of the school of thought founded around the figure of Mozi, was one of the leading strands of the intense intellectual debate characterizing the Warring States period (see Chapters 31, 32, and 33 in this book for a discussion of the significance of Mohism). This school was famous for specialists who, in keeping with the pacifism in their ideology, offered strategies, devices, and highly elaborate mechanisms by means of which to counter attempts to lay siege to fortified constructions. In fact, among the written material brought together in the texts attributed to this school there are twenty chapters devoted to instruments and guidelines for military defense (Yates 1979)[1].

Levies imposed on the peasants and the generalized use of infantry meant large, fast-growing armies (Hsu 1965:62–68). War affected the entire social body without exception, and it therefore ceased to be the exclusive privilege of a particular class to become a universally applicable obligation. The culmination of this extended reach of warfare appears with the complete identification of the civilian (*wen* 文) with the military administration (*wu* 武), as depicted in works traditionally attributed to Guan Zhong and Shang Yang (*Shiji* 68:2,230). As a consequence of the implementation of these reforms, the distribution of populations, territorial geometry, and demography devised from the spheres of civilian institutions fused perfectly with the division and organization of troops, so that it was no longer possible to distinguish between the civilian and military domains (Gawlikowski 1987; McNeal 2012:13–39; Rand 2017:5–30). Hence, when the ruler decided to launch an attack against an enemy state he did not just send an army, which is to say, a more or less numerous mass of individuals specifically gathered

---

[1] A chapter, titled "The Army's Devices" (Jun yong 軍用), of the *Taigong Liutao* offers a detailed list of the sophisticated weapons, equipment and implements (including type and quantity) which, according to this text, are necessary both for attack and defence in any armed conflict: *Taigong Liutao* 31: 143–144.

for the occasion, but he projected against his rival the whole already-existent social structure, without any need for modification. The army was a perfect continuation of society, in such a way that military might was, inter alia, the product of the totality of powers constituted by the population as a whole (Levi 1989:99–101).

Accordingly, going into battle in this new epoch required formidable logistics and seamless bureaucratic functioning. Only a highly centralized state could generate and maintain a large-scale army that demanded a huge outlay of economic resources, an efficient recruitment system, and performing institutions. It was only possible to attain such resources if the state imposed a lasting and consistent taxation system and if it constructed between itself and its subjects a continuous administrative nexus. As Vandermeersch (1965:137–151) demonstrates, the newly acquired powers in the Warring States period of a class of traders and merchants who, thanks to their audacity, ambition, and new methods, managed to depose the aristocratic lineages also entailed an increasingly influential mentality that replaced the old, bloodline-based alliances by contractual agreements, ceremonial exchanges by diplomatic relations, and ritual customs by criteria based on calculation of benefits. In a nutshell, this was the definitive rise of instrumental rationality. Rational bureaucratic measures tended to penetrate every last corner of the army and of the state. It follows that behind this new conception of warfare lay an implacable administrative logic that enabled a thoroughgoing census of the population; control over tax collection; and an increasing exploitation of agricultural, livestock, mining, and human resources.

Mass armies necessarily required the development of arithmetical and topographical procedures for appropriately disposing of, combining, and distributing the large infantry divisions in the battlefield. Furthermore, in order to arm and protect these thousands of soldiers and to ensure the efficient transport of provisions and military equipment, large-scale resources and major investments were essential. In a passage from a text known as the *Zhanguo ce*, and included in a critique of the resort to armed forces as a way of resolving disputes among the different states, there is a detailed account of the cost of any military endeavour. This new situation of mass-based warfare necessarily entailed great losses. "Squandering and losses arising from any military outlay are the equivalent of ten annual harvests. Faced with the prospect of similar expenditure, few states are in a position to put together and participate in a military coalition." (*Zhanguo ce* 12:672). Financial solvency and an impeccable infrastructure were indispensable for the new military expeditions. At the same time, these risky economic and human investments called for backup support in the form of land and wealth. Warfare was burgeoning to become war of expansion. For all these reasons, military affairs during the Warring States period brooked no frivolity or even the slightest sign of jocularity. All the playful and sophisticated ceremonial elements that the previous aristocratic combat might once have cultivated were definitively eradicated. Games observe rules that are generally accepted by participants, and the effects of the losses or gains are also restricted to those taking part without being catastrophic for others. Nevertheless, with the new total warfare that would eventually define the Warring States period, victory meant survival while defeat meant annihilation of the whole state.

MASS-BASED WARFARE AND THE EMERGENCE
OF THE NEW MILITARY LITERATURE

The extension and the universally obligatory nature of war, with enormous armies consisting of thousands of soldiers conscripted from among the peasant population without any training or prior contact with the profession of soldiering, meant the decline of the aristocratic warrior, emblem of individual action, and bearer of archetypically male attributes such as gallantry, fearlessness, a predilection for displaying virtuosity, and so forth (Liu 1967). In war, once the realm of heroism, the dominant requirements are now submission and blind obedience. Soldiers can only obey and scrupulously carry out the array of strategic feats required of them as expressed in orders coming down to them from their commanders. Success in combat no longer depends on the individual qualities of men who go off to fight in a battle. The new peasant-soldier, stripped of the heroic, virile properties of the old aristocratic warrior, becomes a mere, easily manipulated object. Divested of everything that had made the latter a privileged and even unique being, he becomes an anonymous fragment of an organic mass bereft forevermore of his individual dimension.

The demise of the aristocratic warrior and his traditional values coincides with the emergence of the figure of the strategist or commander (Meyer 2017). The old skills of managing bronze weapons, bows and arrows, driving the chariot, and performing the whole panoply of the ritual gestures governing each step of this aristocratic conception of war and constituting a special form of know-how that is handed down from one generation to the next in the bosom of this exclusive social class, are replaced by other accomplishments, including management of economic and human resources, development of rational administrative institutions, achieving the total submission of the population, efficient organization of troops, their optimal employment on the battlefield, always-accurate assessment of the enemy's circumstances and resources, and so on (Meyer and Wilson 2003).

It is not surprising, then, that some of the earliest military treatises to which we have access are attributed to figures who are at once leaders in the political institutions, planners of major administrative reforms, and military commanders (Galvany 2014). The influence and success of Li Kui and Wu Qi in Wei and of Shang Yang in Qin testify to the rise of the strategist as a pivotal figure, not only in matters of war but also, and more generally, in the highest echelons of power and decision-making. His importance is seen, first of all, in the vast number of military projects, almost certainly undertaken during the Warring States period, that scholars have long known about or have discovered in manuscripts in recent decades. Among these sources, one must, of course, mention the treatises attributed to Sunzi, Wuzi, and Sun Bin as well as others known by the titles of *Wei Liaozi, Taigong liutao,* and *Sima Fa.* In some cases, as happens with writings of political and moral intent, the *Mengzi* for instance, the arguments and ideas in these military texts appear in the form of a dialogue with a monarch or ruler, which suggests that among the readers to which they were addressed were the ruling classes of the day, from whom the writers hoped to obtain recognition or official positions (Lewis 2005). However, the political and intellectual sway of these figures and their proposals can also be seen indirectly in sections of other major works of the period, for example the *Mozi*, the *Xunzi*, the *Guanzi*, the *Heguanzi*, the *Yizhou shu*, the *Lüshi chunqiu*, and the *Huainanzi*, which include whole chapters devoted to military matters, written from many different perspectives and revealing a considerable variety of interests ranging from technical issues (Yates 1980) to moral concerns (Lewis 2006; van Els 2013b) [2]. The latter texts, for example, the *Xunzi*, can be understood as an attempt to counter the success and ideological foundations of the strategic doctrines. Even a political proposal like that of the *Mengzi*, in which a clear moral vocation prevails, and that attributed to Han Fei in which the key concept is the importance of the normative domain, are not very far removed from the evident presence of strategic logic and they testify, directly or indirectly, to the influence of the vigorous military literature which was being produced at the time (Lee 2016; Galvany 2017)[3]. In any case, the proliferation of military writings alone is sufficient evidence of the sidelining of the aristocratic warrior in favor of an intellectualized conception of war in which the cognitive and strategic faculties of the commander, manager, and absolute master of violence were the only elements that mattered.

THE TURN TO EFFICIENCY: THE TRIUMPH OF INSTRUMENTAL REASON

In line with the seriousness which must preside over the management of these martial affairs, the military literature of ancient China explicitly highlights the irrevocable importance of war in the survival of a state. It is no coincidence that the text traditionally ascribed to Sunzi opens with a sentence that stresses this idea in no uncertain terms: "War is the most important affair of the State, the terrain of life and death, the way that leads to survival or extermination." (*Sunzi* 1:1). These words make explicit the risks and threats that are inevitably faced by anyone who decides to have recourse to the use of arms. There is no place in combat for frippery or the slightest sign of superficiality. It is understood, then, that the text attributed to Sunzi aspires to eliminate all irrational elements (which may, for example, take the form of feelings of revenge, bellicose ardour, and the ornamental excesses of ritual conduct) which once characterised the previous aristocratic skirmish. Accordingly, the use of procedures which aim to guarantee the success of these risky undertakings tends to be enforced both in the motivations determining the decision to initiate hostilities and in the conduct of the battle itself. This

[2] For a comprehensive study of the variety of military texts produced during the Warring States period, see Yates (1988) and Jie Wenchao (2007). The question of the various classifications of warfare in early China is studied in van Els (2012a).

[3] On the impact of the military writings in early Chinese intellectual history, see Li Guisheng (2008).

military text decrees that the sovereign and the strategist must stamp out all conduct governed by anger or resentment, and eradicate any lingering legacy of tradition prescribing behavior modelled on ritual patterns in order to embrace in their stead a sober functionalism infused with the idea of utility. In perfect harmony with this instrumental reasoning, the ultimate criterion of military action resides in an impassive reckoning of benefits (*li* 利). "The ruler should not deploy his troops out of anger and neither should the commander fight a battle because he is resentful. Action should be taken only if it is to his advantage and shunned if it is not. Rage may be followed by happiness, and resentment by joy, but the state that has been destroyed cannot be restored and the dead cannot be brought back to life. The enlightened ruler therefore acts prudently and the good commander is cautious. This is the way to keep the state secure and the army intact." (*Sunzi* 12:283–284).

Absolute rigor is therefore the condition for deployment of troops and the slightest sign of lack of seriousness or negligence is punishable. Such caution demands, first of all, a meticulous assessment of all the circumstances relevant to the battle (from the strength or weakness of the economy, through to topographical or weather conditions, the degree of social and political cohesion, the robustness of the administrative institutions, the authority and trustworthiness of the commanders, the discipline and psychological state of the troops) in order to be sure about whether to order a military attack or, on the contrary, to pronounce it inadvisable and thus to decide not to proceed. Hence, methods based on calculating these factors are prominent in the text credited to Sunzi. The work is vehement in insisting that the outcome of an armed conflict can (and must) be known before the clash takes place on the battlefield, and such foresight is possible by means of a series of questions concerning the circumstances of each of the combatants.

The appropriateness or otherwise of each military undertaking is therefore decided in accordance with a state of balance or imbalance that is ascertained beforehand by weighing up the results of these series of questions which are put forth in the ancestral temple: "Victory is achieved when the calculations (*suan*) carried out in the ancestral temple before the battle show a majority of factors in its favour; when the propitious factors are few, victory is not possible. He who finds auspicious results in all his calculations will be the victor, while he who only finds a few will be defeated. And what of the person who finds no factors in his favour? By means of these observations it becomes evident whether the result will be victory or defeat" (*Sunzi* 1:20). This passage plays with different meanings of the term *suan* 算. When it is a verb, it denotes the action of calculating or reckoning but, as a noun, it refers *inter alia* to the device (bamboo counting rods arranged to represent a decimal place system) used to carry out this exercise of arithmetic calculation. It is striking that the *Sunzi* should situate this accounting exercise in the ancestral temple (*miao* 廟), a place originally concerned with mantic, ritual, and sacrificial practices. After all, such arithmetical calculations could be done in other more appropriate administrative spaces equipped with more useful and relevant resources such as maps and reports. Indeed, according to a passage in the *Zuo zhuan*, the army commander received his orders in the ancestral temple (*Zuo zhuan*, Ming 2:271) while other, later, textual sources also note that, before launching the military offensive, the ruler came to this sacred place in order to hand the commander the battle axe or some other type of weapon as the symbol of his supreme authority (*Taigong Liutao* 21:114).

In the light of these passages, it would seem evident, then, that in the earlier model of warfare, which was dominated by the aristocratic elites and their values, the ancestral temple was used as the setting for certain ritual practices that were deemed important for guaranteeing the successful outcome of the bellicose undertaking. From this perspective, the *Sunzi* would be controversial in presenting a new use for this space since, rather than being the hallowed location for performing ritual practices long enshrined in aristocratic customs, it would be the setting for a mere numerical exercise seeking objective knowledge about the outcome of the battle before it took place. The *Sunzi* would then be testifying to the transformation of the temple –which had formerly been used for making sacrificial offerings or even for engaging in divinatory practices– into a space that now only welcomed methods based on rational deliberation and calculation. We now find, then, a new attempt at distancing from the earlier model of combat. In accordance with this rupture and despite the fact that it is possible to detect acceptance of a divinatory logic in a good part of the ancient military literature, the *Sunzi* and other ancient strategic texts also reveal an emphasis on rational methods and a critical stance *vis-à-vis* ritual and mantic practices (Galvany 2015). If one bears in mind the fact that the main burden of the model of mass-based warfare was shouldered by the figure of the commander and his exclusive authority, it is not surprising to find that military literature tends to view any resort to magical or divinatory practices as problematic. The commander is the only source of decisions. It is he who enjoys monopoly of the power of reason, he who is the true nucleus of the authority of command. This being the case, resort to divinatory practices would involve interference of an external element which might very well call into question or challenge this authority and shatter the unity of the troops.

The heroism of the past and other aristocratic virtues related with combat give way to a conception of warfare in which calculation, rational evaluation, and deliberation prevail. This, then, is the instrumental reasoning in which war becomes an object of knowledge that can be verbally formulated and transmitted. The mere existence of military texts and doctrines accentuates the tendency to see warfare as one more aspect of knowledge for which, when it comes to achieving an eventual victory, intellectual faculties deriving from careful study and discernment of these texts are all-important. This is an intellectual conception of war for which skills in driving a chariot and wielding bronze weapons or the bow and arrow have scant importance. What matter now are abilities shown in accurate evaluation of the situation and circumstances of combat, correctly fathoming the state of enemy forces, hatching plans, devising intelligent strategies adapted to the conditions of the adversary, and so on. The textual nature of military knowhow ushered in with the appearance of the new model of mass-based warfare clearly shows that combat tends to be conceived and settled within a mental scheme, and that the true warrior is the one who is able to decipher the key principles of warfare when reading and studying a text, and then to put them into practice on the battlefield (*Sunzi* 1:11). In the Warring States period, war necessarily revolves around the commander, the strategist, the man who is clearly able to perceive the patterns and evolution of events over and above the tumult dominating the battle, capable of bringing the highest degree of order in the greater part of his troops, and exploiting to maximum effect the available material resources, the qualities of his men, and the potential arising from the many strategic contingencies. The strategist occupies a privileged, exclusive position: in charge of organising the army and leading it to victory, he is exempt from actual fighting (*Wuzi* 8:128)[4].

THE FEMINIZATION OF COMBAT: THE EXTINCTION OF THE WARRIOR AND THE ADVENT OF DISCIPLINE

In the last period of the Warring States an anecdote was circulating and came to be included in several textual sources with some minor variations. The story concerns the famous strategist Sunzi and aims not so much to reconstruct his biography and professional career as to distil into one passage the lines which constitute the linchpin of the text that is attributed to him (Galvany 2011). Interviewed by Helü, ruler of the state of Wu, who was looking for a new commander for his armies, Sunzi was ordered to train a group of women coming from the palace. He divided the group into two squadrons led by the ruler's two favourite concubines. After he explained a simple manoeuvre, and even making two attempts to do so, the women burst out laughing and failed to obey the order. Sunzi then decided to make an example of them and ordered the execution of the two concubines. The ruler sent a messenger then begging Sunzi to spare the lives of the two women but Sunzi reminded him that, right then, it was he who incarnated military authority and, this said, went ahead and had the women decapitated. Then he repeated his instructions for the manoeuvre and the remaining women carried them out in perfect silence (*Shiji* 65:2161–2162).

The episode deals with the transformation of a group of women twice removed from the military sphere: first, because of their condition as women and, second, because the virtues and skills necessary for the court were completely alien to the requirements for the domain of war. The choice of a group of women as the centrepiece of the apologue was not only because of the need to challenge the candidate with an impossible task. Their categorical, unambiguous presence, and their subsequent conversion into disciplined soldiers expresses a radical transformation which, symbolically speaking, also occurs in the very heart of the military domain with the advent of a new conception of mass-based warfare in which everything depended on the key figure of the commander.

The execution of the ruler's two concubines silences in blood the spontaneous peals of laughter which the women had been unable to contain when they were made to comply with orders that, from their point of view, were simply laughable. Accustomed to

---

[4] For a general survey on the formation and development of early Chinese military thought, see Rand (2017), Gawlikowski (1996) and Luo Duxiu (2002a).

performing delicate dances, to moulding their svelte bodies into graceful rhythmical movements, it is more than likely that the crude, rigid physical manoeuvres that Sunzi made them perform to the beat of the commander's drum touched off an irrepressible sense of the ridiculous. After all, dance was not only expected of the palace women to give pleasure to the eyes and senses of their masters, but it was also part of the routine training of aristocratic warriors. Apart from its role in keeping them fit, generating a feeling of communion among combatants, fostering synergetic action and honing coordination in the use of arms, these male martial dances were doubtless a beautiful spectacle too. The composition and the high degree of formal exigency in the choreographic subtlety of these martial dances, along with the exquisiteness of their movements, were annulled with exemplary intent by the oafish manner in which the concubine-soldiers were forced to perform the disciplinary manoeuvre. In the scathing simplicity of the exercise that Sunzi imposes by means of extreme violence according to the anecdote, it is possible to perceive not only an attempt to subdue the original resistance of the concubines and to introduce them brusquely into military logic by eliminating the memory of the dances they had performed inside the palace but also, perhaps, a shifting of levels, this being aimed at the ruler: the aesthetic delight of the now-obsolete martial dances is replaced with the overwhelming spectacle of troops subjugated to the discipline of the new military science, now divested of their own volition, malleable and perfectly obedient.

Within this new symbolic framework, the cautionary tale of the concubine-soldiers contains one of the linchpins of this strategic conception of war that is linked with the values traditionally ascribed to the feminine realm: obedience and submission before the threat of punishment that is both swift and severe. The anecdote robustly expresses the decisive importance that discipline, or achieving a biddable and manageable regiment, now has for the final victory. The soldier, an anonymous member of a mass army, must submit to the commander's edicts, making sure that his body scrupulously performs the automatic movements that are required of him. What is demanded of him is not so much bravery as docility. This new conception of war generates mechanical, passive subservience as the ineluctable condition, not only for victory but even for being in a position to enter into contest for it. The prime objective of the art of warfare is that of extracting from every soldier obedient, docile, and useful submission thanks to the sustained, constant, analytical, and thoroughgoing application of a tenacious disciplinary technique that is aimed at wholly neutralising any resistance that these individuals might originally have harboured. Strictly speaking, the meaning of war no longer pertains to the person who wages it, to the person whose blood is spilled in the heat of combat.

But how is the effectiveness of this levelling accomplished? And what instruments are used by political and military power to ensure that this exercise of total discipline is achieved? The original answer of military science is unanimous: the crucial factor of discipline resides in human nature itself. While, in general lines, some of the main currents of classical Chinese thought contemplated the innate goodness of the human being, the more authoritarian political schemes energetically rejected this notion although without going so far as to opt for the opposite thesis. For them, human nature is neither originally good nor basically bad. Man, like any living organism, aspires only to satisfy essential needs and appetites and this is not good or bad but "natural". So, if it is possible to govern men, it is because humans belong to the realm of living beings and, as such, they are governed by the same innate drives and the same biological laws."People can be governed thanks to the fact that, as part of their innate condition, they have likes and aversions. The prince, then, must give his whole attention to these, for inclinations and aversions constitute the root of punishments and rewards. Hence, since it is in the nature of men to covet gratuities and perquisites and to detest penalty and punishment, the prince can, by means of both strands, channel the will of the people and determine their desires" (*Shangjunshuin* 9:65).

The very bedrock of the social order resides, authoritarian and military thinkers believe, in the passion-goaded nature of man, which is to say the dimension he shares with other living organisms, and not in that which makes him distinctive. The law would be nothing other than the crystallisation and transposition on to the level of the different kinds of conduct of the standard of ordering that works on the natural dimension. Once the essential mechanism of man's behaviour is discovered, it is clear how he is to be governed and controlled: it is sufficient to gain total command over his life through the ability to punish with extreme severity actions that do not comply with what is stipulated in the norms, and to give generous rewards for those that do, thereby obtaining a docile mannequin-man who is willing to obey "spontaneously".

Faced with the challenge of governing and supervising an enormous number of peasant-soldiers, political and military power found in this apparently simple system of rewards and punishments the key to achieving all its ambitions: subject to their own natural inclinations, the masses tend to be mere manipulatable, objects, unable to resist or oppose. If these strategic and authoritarian thinkers are right and human beings really do have a natural inclination to desire with all his might something that benefits him, and to avoid by every means possible anything that might adversely affect him the theory, nevertheless, apparently comes up against a major stumbling block or even contradiction in the case of warfare since, to the extent that humans are living organisms governed by natural laws, they automatically recoil from any situation in which they might lose their lives and would, therefore, put up the utmost resistance against going to fight on the battlefield. Nevertheless, the answer to the problem is to turn to the strategist's advantage what would, in principle, seem to be an obstacle. Exploiting the power of the survival instinct, these authoritarian and military thinkers managed to invert and capitalize on the situation by making fear of death their best ally. Dread at the idea of losing one's life would provide or, at least, would serve as the basis for two kinds of solutions. The first was simple, direct coercion, which is to say threats from commanders that anyone who tried to escape going into battle, who was not sufficiently bellicose, and who attempted to desert would simply face death. The death sentence was applied to everyone who failed to obey official orders and, moreover, it would be a death more certain and atrocious than that which might await soldiers on the battlefield. On this point, the theoreticians of war took their intimidation to the extreme of extending the punishment to include, with equal mercilessness, the families of soldiers accused of noncompliance (*Shangjunshu* 10:70).

Second, to the extent that troops have been previously trained and that, thanks to constant disciplinary action, they represent nothing more than raw material allowing the strategist to carry out his plans and ploys, the theory of warfare set out to extract maximum benefit from the survival instinct in order to obtain from the available man-power—independently of whether the men were courageous or cowardly—the best possible levels of performance and commitment to the struggle. By placing their men in positions from which there was no escape except for just one possible path to salvation, which was routing the enemy, the generals managed to convert all their men into killing machines ready to spill their last drop of blood on the battlefield. "Send your troops into a position from which there is no escape, where they will have to die before they retreat. If there is no other alternative but death, officers and soldiers will commit themselves to the combat with all their strength. If they fall into a trap, they no longer fear anything; if there is no escape, they will act with resolve; if they are in hostile territory, they will remain more united; and with no other solution they surrender themselves to the fight" (*Sunzi* 11:189).

Hence, once the military strategist manages to ensure that the army's power and abil-ity to fight no longer depends on the individual attributes of the soldiers comprising it but simply his own ability to position them according to some kind of stratagem, or to place them before a circumstantial situation which allows him to take advantage of their survival instinct, the submission of the soldiers is total. And along these lines, and returning for a moment to the anecdote about the concubines attributed by tradition to the biography of Sunzi, there seems to be a twofold lesson here. First and foremost, the apologue reveals that women are not destined for a military career but, in particular—and this is the important part—if given instructions by a competent general, anyone, including a woman, can become a good soldier. In some sense, war is then independent of the particular individual qualities of those who fight, at least in terms of engagement on the battlefield. The new peasant-soldier, stripped of the heroic, virile qualities of the old-style warrior, and with no chance of acting as a free agent, is turned into a mere dis-ciplined object. Hence, the decapitation of the favourite concubines of the monarch Helü and their instant replacement not only exemplifies the undeniable efficacy of ter-ror as an instrument in the service of authority but also, submerged in this disciplinary act, is an inherent logic of the interchangeability of soldiers in mass-based warfare, the setting into operation of a logic of "replacements" or, in other words, the introduction of an idea of the dispensability of human beings as an axiom of the new way of conceiving the military arts.

THE FEMINIZATION OF THE STRATEGIST: WHEN THE ROOSTER BECOMES THE HEN

As might be expected with this symbolic transformation and far-reaching changes which are starting to be introduced in the exercise of power, the military treatises of the time flow into other political and philosophical writings as part of a generalised criti-cism of values traditionally ascribed to the masculine sphere and associated with the aristocracy. From chapter 28 of the *Laozi*, which emphasises "knowing the masculine and conserving the feminine", to the *Huainanzi*, which advises the wise man to affect a passive and quiescent air so as to "take shelter in 'I do not dare' and to practice 'I am not able' while remaining in repose" (*Huainanzi* 1:72). In the *Sunzi* it is stated that troops should present themselves as being "as shy as a virgin" (*Sunzi* 11:266). Awareness began to crystallise in the Warring States period about the drawbacks of characteristically masculine patterns of action, values and principles (audacity, dash, ferocity, initiative, and verve) *vis-à-vis* the advantages to be derived from conduct enshrined in traits traditionally ascribed to the female domain (subtlety, caution, furtiveness, quietude and moderation).

The contrasts between these two guides for action are elucidated in a passage of a manuscript recovered in 1973 from the archaeological site of Mawangdui. The passage to which I refer, significantly titled "The Ways of the Hen and the Rooster" (*Cixiong jie*), is as follows: "Excess is the attribute of masculine conduct; moderation that of feminine demeanour. Benefits acquired through masculine conduct are not auspicious; however, losses occasioned by feminine behaviour eventually become recompenses. [...] Adopting a feminine stance, one does not suffer adversity even if one moves first; adhering to masculine behaviour does not bring good fortune even if one moves later. If moving before and after the rest, one does not suffer misfortune it is because of persisting with the feminine position. And, on the contrary, if moving before and after the rest one never has good fortune, this is because one persists with masculine behaviour. Anyone who prefers and resorts to masculine behaviour risks his life. [...]. He will not be able to defend his positions or succeed in any endeavour or be the victor in any combat." (*Huangdi sijing*:332–338).

In order to understand this change, one should see it from a dual perspective since the feminization of warfare works at two different levels. First, as just noted, the symbolic transformation affects the soldier himself by divesting him of his individual characteristics and inflicting upon him values that are traditionally associated with the female realm and, in particular, obedience, submission and discipline. However, it is also necessary to include the standpoint of those who direct the manoeuvres and decide the orders that are to be given to these anonymous soldiers now dispossessed of their individual features. From the perspective of the commander, this transfiguration into a being with female traits does not concern obedience or submission but, rather, conforming to a type of behaviour in which initiative is abandoned in favour of passivity, calm, and composure. It is not surprising, therefore, that a passage from the *Zhuangzi* describes the transformation of a fighting cock, emblem of masculine gallantry, bravery and ferocity, into a sort of hen after a meticulous process of training which, paradoxically, consists of eliminating all attributes which were initially associated with the rooster's condition as a fighting cock (*Zhuangzi* 19:654–655). However, just after the end of the process which transforms it into an imperturbable, passive, and serene creature, the cock acquires such an aura of power that its mere presence is sufficient to terrify its most fearsome adversaries, so much so that they withdraw from the fight. In other words, after this variety of inner mutation, the cock comes to incarnate a dissuasive ideal which, as I shall show below, is shared by a good part of the ancient military literature. The anecdote about training the fighting cock whose fighting powers reach their apogee when it turns into a sort of hen, an immobile and unyielding creature, is related with the notion which I would translate here as "vital force" (*qi* 氣). This term is prominent in ancient cosmological literature but it also has a significant part to play in the military treatises. To be specific, in the text attributed to Sunzi, one of the tasks of the commander consists precisely in managing the vital force which imbues the soldiers in the heat of battle. For the new conception of war, constructed around the figure of the strategist, the aim is to arouse, administer, and measure out these violent impulses of the soldiers from a position of command, making sure there is no trace of irrationality (Lewis 1990:222–231). From this standpoint, the steadfast fighting cock in the story included in the *Zhuangzi* would consummately incarnate this determination to eliminate from military affairs the aristocratic tradition related with the outmoded warrior who was guided by his arrogant bellicosity and, in contrast, to adopt values of stillness, serenity, and even passivity, which are associated with the symbolic field of what is deemed to be feminine.

Nevertheless, if as I have noted above the new model of armed conflict is characterised above all by an unrelenting quest for effectiveness and victory beyond any subjection to the ritual or moral order, how might we understand this transformation that ends up with appropriating and even elevating to ideal status typically feminine values that, at least in the beginning, seem to embody a position that is contrary to these goals? This paradox is not, in fact, a paradox in any more than in superficial appearance. A good part of its conceptual edifice, and also of the fundamental architecture of Chinese strategic thinking, is sustained on the intuition that the strong and the tough, represented in the symbolic realm of the masculine, are only thus in appearance. The art of war is therefore articulated around this insight and the discovery of the ferocious efficacy hidden beneath the mask of the weakness and fragility of femininity.

MALLEABILITY, FLEXIBILITY, AND ADAPTATION: THE LIE AS A RULE AND THE VICTORY OF NON-BEING

The military literature of ancient China revolved around a continuous dialectical process in which the will to know and the obligation to penetrate the circumstances of the enemy, the need to understand the foe's reality in order to prevail over him is countered by the essential condition of remaining constantly opaque oneself, concealed from any intrusive gaze. Hence, there is a great deal of insistence on the need for knowing all the factors involved in the conflict, of getting the most complete information possible about the enemy as well as the obligation of cloaking all military plans and manoeuvres in the most impenetrable secrecy. The aim is to place the adversary in a position of disadvantage in such a way that he is exposed to the strategist's gaze while the latter and all his resources remain imperceptible. Deception, then, plays an essential role in preventing the enemy from obtaining access to one's reality while also giving rise to the error or distraction that will lead to his defeat. The ruse uses disguise in order to confuse one's rival by adopting a form which, instead of revealing one's true being, acts as a mask: "War is the art of deception. Hence, when able to attack, you must seem unable; when ready to go into battle, you must act as if you are not; when you are near, you must seem far away; when far away, you must make the enemy believe you are near." (*Sunzi* 1:12–18).

Also important is the notion of the extraordinary or irregular (*qi* 奇), which is closely linked with deception. This, in concert with the concept of the regular or the straightforward (*zheng* 正), creates a key conceptual polarity in Chinese strategic thinking (Wallacker 1966). Carefully presented by means of artifice and the unexpected, appearance and reality merge to produce an illusory effect, leading the enemy into error and, by extension, defeat. Unfettered by any kind of moral consideration, the practice of war embraces deception as one of its indispensable principles. Thus, for instance, in a passage from the manuscripts unearthed at Yinqueshan and attributed to the figure of Sun Bin, we read: "deception is the means by which it is possible to trap the enemy" (*Sun Bin* 2:28); in a similar vein, a passage from another important ancient military treatise states explicitly: "It is through mendacity and traps, stratagems, and irregular procedures, lures and falsification that one can rout enemy troops and capture their general" (*Taigong Liutao* 28:130).

It is therefore natural enough that the text attributed to Sunzi should devote an entire chapter to the matter of intelligence services, spies and double agents (*Sunzi*, 13:289-301). The notion of information is of supreme importance (Sawyer 1998, 2013 and Handel 1992). One must penetrate the enemy side in order to obtain the knowledge that will ensure the correctness of one's manoeuvres since the choice and execution of military actions largely depend on one's knowledge of one's foe. This means, for example, deploying one's troops in zones in which the enemy defenses, inferior in numbers and tactics, cannot offer any meaningful resistance (*Sunzi*, 6:110). It is necessary to keep moving and continue advancing through the "empty" points, that is, the gaps in the enemy's ground (*xu* 虛) while avoiding his stronger, more consistent or "full" areas (*shi* 實). Success in battle depends on one's degree of adaptation to the adversary and this is why there is so much insistence on acquiring flexibility, understood as the ability to change at the slightest warning, to adjust instantly to changing circumstances and to avoid being encumbered by deep-rooted customs and timeworn patterns. In brief, it means the ability to combine versatility, speed, and unpredictability.

In fact, war presents a reality in constant mutation (*Sun Bin* 2:19), part of a dynamic process (von Senger 1994), requiring continuous adaptation (*yin* 因) both to the circumstances that form part of the conflict (climate, topography, and so on) and, in particular, to one's adversary. Hence, several military writers turn to the metaphor of water to give expression to this imperative of adaptation (*Sunzi* 6:124; *Wei Liaozi* 8:106). Water can never be shaped to fit a setting since the nature of its movement depends on its adaptation to the terrain over which it flows. If water can deploy this tremendous power of constantly reshaping itself, it is because it lacks a permanent form of its own. It is this absence of form or disposition (*wu xing* 無形) that endows it with continuous scope for variation and, accordingly, its constant ability to accommodate new circumstances. Taking as its basic principle the equivalence between the term used to designate a military formation and that for the external shape of things (*xing* 形), the strategic reflection of ancient China postulates the supremacy of that which lacks form, over that which has an established composition. Indeed, if it should happen that one side in a conflict leaves this ungraspable dimension to irrupt into the sphere of presences with form, into the plane of being, the other side will then be at an advantage. Its commander can now assess, gauge and, as a result, adopt the appropriate military strategies for adapting to this new circumstance and neutralising the foe. Some of the main military treatises of the time state that an army attains perfection when it is capable of showing no flank, no constant formation-form (*xing*) to which the enemy might easily adapt. Victory over a sinuous reality in perpetual metamorphosis can only be achieved by means of a superabundance of mobility thanks to an even greater power of transformation and adaptation, all of which explains the emphasis on reaching the highest possible degree of flexibility, understood as the ability to change direction at short notice, to adapt instantly to changing circumstances, and not being burdened with habits and overly ingrained patterns of behaviour; in sum, the accent is on versatility, speed, and unpredictability. All the strategic vocabulary of ancient China is connected with this principle. Like water, the army must present a continuous polymorphous plasticity, a form in constant movement or transformation so that it is impossible to stop it and thus permit any subsequent adaptation.

The metaphor of water, now as a raging torrent, is associated with the important notion of strategic potential (*shi* 勢), which must be exploited by the strategist starting from the specific formations of each moment (Ames 1983:65–107; Luo Duxiu 2004b:76–89; and Goldin 2005). The recurrent image of a build-up of water that breaks through the dike and surges out to destroy everything in its path (*Sunzi* 4:79) is a representation of the essential role military literature reserves for this idea. Moreover, water evokes, both by association and at the symbolic level, the occult potency of the female factor (*yin* 陰), whose apparent ductility, flexibility and frailty prevail by pounding against harder and more compact objects. Finally, water also refers to a cosmological plane since, as something elusive and ungraspable, it is an element which, thanks to its negative qualities (formless, colourless, flavourless, odourless), is close to the Way (*dao* 道). In this highly metaphysical rhetoric, which one finds in the *Sunzi* in particular, the army that is able to embrace the negative virtues attributed to water tends to fuse with and be confused with the principle-without-principle of the universe which, subtle and fathomless, lies beyond the rival's reach (Levi 2006). From this point of view, war as it appears in the military literature of late pre-imperial China is not just about maximum rationalisation of practical efficiency applied to a specific domain. In their plasticity of images, metaphors and terminology, the strategic texts always move on three different planes: military, political and cosmic. The great commander becomes a demiurge and the army, on being confused with the fathomless matrix of the void, having transcended the specific dimension of forms, unfolds in pure virtuality, and has access to control over forms because, like the principle-free principle ruling over the universe, it is able to withdraw from them, and remain without any permanent shape.

From economic awareness to the idea of deterrence: the art of non-war

If Chinese strategic thinking occupies a privileged niche in the history of ideas, this is due to the fact that these writings have taken on the task of thinking about war from an anti-war volition. Nevertheless, this stance does not signal any kind of pacifism but, rather, reasoning of an economic nature which could certainly be seen as a result of the tragic effects of mass warfare at the time. Military literature insists on defeating the enemy with minimum effort and outlay of resources, to the point of not engaging in any kind of combat whatsoever (*Sunzi* 3:45; *Sun Bin* 6:59). This, then, is a theory of military action in which the main principle is that of easy victory. It is a long way from a position that might be described as typically aristocratic, which entailed, first and foremost, military feats performed at the price of great sacrifice and hardship. Ideally, at least, the perfect military action is that which, so to speak, has zero energy cost (Billeter 1984:49).

This remarkable conception of war would seem to derive from evidence that the toll of all armed conflicts, even those that end up in victory, is inevitable debilitation in the long run. "Hence, the states which require five victories to conquer the world will end in disaster; those which need four will be exhausted; those which need three will be powerful; those which need two will be sovereign; and those which need only one will be proclaimed emperors. Consequently, states which have managed to conquer the world through numerous victories will be scarce, and those which have perished will be numerous" (*Wuzi* 1:7). Instead of being presented with a theory of war, one finds a theory of non-war. According to the *Sunzi* and other ancient military treatises, the ultimate aim of strategic thought would not consist so much in the complete annihilation of the adversary as in bringing him into a relationship of subjugation with no need of using violence: "The good commander vanquishes the enemy forces without going into combat, takes the enemy fortifications without assaulting them, breaks up rival states without allowing prolonged military action. In this way he can conquer the whole world yet conserve his strength; his regiments do not perish and his riches remain intact. Herein lies the method of offensive plans" (*Sunzi* 3:46–48)[5].

From this perspective, battle, understood as a direct confrontation and clash, must be avoided at any price because, even if it ends in victory, this tends to come after part of

---

[5] In the same vein, the chapter devoted to military arts included in the *Huainanzi* claims: "In the army of he who possesses the Way, chariots are not employed, the trappings of the horses are not made ready, the drums are not beaten, the standards are not unfurled, armour shows no arrow marks, and the blades of swords are not reddened with blood" (*Huainanzi* 15:1569).

one's own resources have been squandered and the booty thus conquered has also been depleted by the costs of war on the enemy side. It is therefore essential to avoid the main cause of ruin in any military endeavour: armed confrontation (Jullien 1995:34–35). In this regard, Chinese military thinking perceived with dazzling clarity the fact that every clash requires one condition in order for it to happen and this is basic equilibrium. The confrontation is not, for Chinese strategic thinking, anything but the consequence of symmetry or, at least, an insignificant difference between the warring factions because, otherwise, there would be a manifest, irreversible imbalance between the two camps, which would give rise to two possibilities. First, when the clash finally occurs, it would be an unequal fight between a strong side and a weak side which would swiftly end in favour of the former in such a way as to obviate the undesirable consequences of a drawn-out battle. The second possibility would be that, as a consequence of the dissuasive nature of the disparity between the strong and weak sides, the latter would forsake its bellicose plans and concede defeat. In both cases, confrontation, understood as a process of reciprocal wear and tear, is ruled out. As the *Sunzi* puts it, "In early times, those who were easily able to defeat the enemy were considered skilled strategists. Skillful strategists did not deserve their renown, either for farsightedness or for courage, since their victories were free of all uncertainty. This absence of uncertainty is due to the fact that they acted where victory was certain and conquered an enemy that was previously defeated." (*Sunzi* 4:74–75).

Nevertheless, in order to achieve this deterrent ideal and disarm the adversary before going to battle with him, it is necessary to extend the logic of war to other human activities, including the ostensibly peaceful ones. Politics, economics, and diplomacy become the perfect extension of war, which is no longer envisaged as confrontation or conflict but, instead, as a process of domination. It would seem logical, then, that the military text known as *Taigong liutao* should include a chapter titled "Civil Offensives" (*wenfa* 文伐)", which details up to twelve techniques of non-violent subversion by means of which it is possible, *inter alia*, to lead the enemy into error in his administrative decisions, sabotage social cohesion by inciting insurrection, bring him into disrepute in the international sphere, bribe his officials, among many other actions, so that it becomes possible to ensure his complete submission without any need for undesirable bloodshed (*Taigong Liutao* 14:88–93). Paradoxically, this "non-war" or anti-war approach actually entails an upsurge and spread of war and the permeation of strategic logic through all levels of society. In other words, the civil sphere (*wen*) now becomes part of the means and ends of the military domain (*wu*).

BIBLIOGRAPHY

Primary sources

Yang, Bojun 楊伯峻. Beijing: Zhonghua shuju. *Huainanzi, with collated explanations* 淮南子校譯 1997. Edited by Zhang Shuangdi 張雙棣. Beijing: Beijing daxue chubanshe.

*A new commentary and translation of the four classics of the Yellow Emperor*黃帝四經今註今譯 1995. Edited by Chen Guying 陳鼓應. Taibei: Taiwan shangwu.

*Pointing an Awl at the Book of Lord Shang*商君書錐指 1986. Edited by Jiang Lihong 蔣禮鴻. Beijing: Zhonghua shuju.

*Records of the historian*史記 1959. Primarily composed by Sima Qian 司馬遷. Beijing: Zhonghua shuju.

Sunzi, with the commentaries of the eleven schools and collated rearrangements十一家注孫子校理 1999. Edited by Yang Bingan 楊丙安. Beijing: Zhonghua shuju.

Sun Bin's Art of War, with collated rearrangements孫臏兵法校理 1984. Edited by Zhang Yunze 張震澤. Beijing: Zhonghua shuju.

A new commentary and translation of the *Taigong liutao* 太公六韜今註今譯 1984. Edited by Xu Peigen 徐培根. Taibei: Taiwan shangwu.

A new commentary and translation of the *Wei Liaozi*尉繚子今註今譯 1985. Edited by Liu Zhongping 劉仲平. Taibei: Taiwan shangwu.

A new commentary and translation of the *Wuzi* 子今註今譯 1985. Edited by Fu Shaojie 傅紹傑. Taibei: Taiwan shangwu.

Zhanguo ce, with brief explanations 戰國策戔證 2008. Edited by Fan Xiangyong 范祥雍. Shanghai: Shanghai guji chubanshe.

*Zhuangzi with collected explanations*莊子集釋 1968. Edited by Guo Qingfan 郭慶藩. Beijing: Zhonghua shuju.

Secondary sources

Ames, R. T. 1983. *The Art of Rulership: A Study in Ancient Chinese Political Thought*. Albany: State University of New York Press.

Ames, R. T. 1993. *Sun-tzu: The Art of Warfare*. New York: Ballantine Books.

Bai, Yunxiang 白雲翔 2005. Archaeological Research on Iron Utensils of the Pre-Qin and Han Dynasties 先秦兩漢鐵器的考古學研究. Beijing: Kexue chubanshe.

Billeter, J.-F. 1984. "Pensée chinoise et pensée occidentale: Le regard et l'acte." In *Différences, Valeurs, Hiérarchie: Textes offerts à Louis Dumont*. Edited by J. C. Galey, 25–51 Paris: Éditions de l'École des Hautes Études en Sciences Sociales.

Chiang, Chi Lu 2005. "The Scale of War in the Warring States Period." PhD dissertation, Columbia University, New York.

Galvany, A. 2011. "Philosophy, Biography, and Anecdote: On the Portrait of Sun Wu," *Philosophy East and West* 61.4:630–646.

Galvany, A. 2014. "Pouvoir souverain, discipline militaire et stratagèmes dans la Chine des Royaumes Combattants." In *Guerre et Politique*. Edited by J. Baechler and J.-V. Holeindre, 139–152. Paris: Hermann.

Galvany, A. 2015. "Signs, Clues and Traces: Anticipation in Ancient Chinese Political and Military Texts," *Early China* 38:151–193.

Galvany, A. 2017. "The Court as a Battlefield: The Art of War and the Art of Politics in the Han Feizi," *Bulletin of the School of Oriental and African Studies* 80.1:73–93.

Gawlikowski, K. 1987. "The Concept of Two fundamental Social Principles: *Wen* and *Wu* in Chinese Classical Thought." *Annali dell Instituto Universitario Orientali* 47–48:397–439.

Gawlikowski, K. 1996. "Chinese Literature on the Art of War." In *Science and Civilisation in China*, vol. 5.6. Edited by R. D. S. Yates, 10–100. Cambridge, UK: Cambridge University Press.

Goldin, P. R. 2005. "The Theme of the Primacy of the Situation in Classical Chinese Philosophy and Rhetoric." *Asia Major* 18(2):1–25.

Granet, M. 1994 [1929]. *La civilisation chinoise*. Paris: Albin Michel.

Handel, M. 1992. "Intelligence in Historical Perspective." In *Go Spy the Land: Military Intelligence in History*. Edited by K. Neilson and B. J. C. McKercher, 179–192. Westport: Praeger.

Hsü, C. Y. 1965. *Ancient China in Transition: An Analysis of Social Mobility, 722–222 B.C.* Stanford, CA: Stanford University Press.

Jie, Wenchao 解文超 2007. Research on Pre-Qin Texts on Warfare *Xianqin bingshu yanjiu* 先秦兵書研究. Shanghai: Shanghai guji chubanshe.

Jie, Wenchao 解文超 2007. *A Research on the Treatises of the Military School in the Pre-Qin era*先秦兵書研究. Shanghai: Shanghai guji chubanshe.

Jullien, F. 1995. *Le detour et l'accès. Stratégies du sens en Chine, en Grèce*. Paris: Grasset & Fasquelle.

Kolb, R. T. 1991. *Die Infanterie im alten China: Ein Beitrag zur Militärgeschichte der Vor-Zhan-Guo-Zeit*. Main am Rheim: Verlag Philipp von Zabern.

Lan, Yongwei 藍永蔚 1979. *Infantry Armies in the Springs and Autumns Period*春秋時期的步兵. Beijing: Zhonghua shuju.

Lee, Ting-mien 2016. "Benevolence-Righteousness as Strategic Terminology: Reading Mengzi's ren-yi through Strategic Manuals." *Dao: A Journal of Comparative Philosophy* 16.1:15–34.

Levi, Jean 1985. "Le tigre et le fonctionnaire: Ordre naturel et lois sociales en Chine ancienne." *Le Genre Humain* 12:151–165.

Levi, Jean 1989. *Les Fonctionnaires divins: Politique, despotisme et mystique en Chine ancienne*. Paris: Éditions du Seuil.

Levi, Jean 2006. "Morale et Trascendance dans le Sunzi." In *Théologies de la guerre*. Edited by J.-Ph. Schreiber, 119–140. Bruxelles: Éditions de l'Université de Bruxelles.

Lewis, M. E. 1990. *Sanctioned Violence in Early China*. Albany: State University of New York Press.

Lewis, M. E. 2005. "Writings on Warfare Found in Ancient Chinese Tombs." *Sino-Platonic Papers* 158:1–15.

Lewis, M. E. 2006. "The Just War Theories in Early China." In *The Ethics of War in Asian Civilizations: A Comparative Perspective*. Edited by T. Brekke, 185–200. London: Routledge.

Li Guisheng 李桂生 2008 *Masters Literature Culture and the Pre-Qin Military School*. 諸子文化與先秦兵家. Changsha: Yuelu shushe.

Liu, C. Y. 1967. *The Chinese Knight-Errant*. Chicago: Chicago University Press.

Luo, Duxiu 羅獨修. 2002a. *A Study on the Thought of the Military School in the Pre-Qin era*先秦兵家思想探源. Taibei: Zhongguo wenhua daxue chuban.

Luo, Duxiu 羅獨修 2002b.*A Study on the Strategic Power and Government in the Pre-Qin era*先秦勢治思想探微. Taibei: Zhongguo wenhua daxue chubanshe.

McNeal, R. 2012. *Conquer and Govern: Early Chinese Military Texts from the Yizhou shu*. Honolulu: Hawaii University Press.

Meyer, A., and A. Wilson 2003. "*Sunzi Bingfa* as History and Theory." In *Strategic Logic and Political Rationality*. Edited by B. A. Lee and M. I. Handel, 95–113. London: Frank Cass.

Rand, C. 1977. "The Role of Military Thought in Early Chinese Intellectual History." PhD dissertation, Harvard University, Cambridge, MA.

Rand, C. 2017. *Military Thought in Early China*. Albany: State University of New York Press.

Sawyer, R. D. 1998. *The Tao of Spycraft: Intelligence Theory and Practice in Traditional China.* San Francisco: Westview Press.

Sawyer, R. D. 2013. "Subversive Information: The Historical Thrust of Chinese Intelligence." In *Intelligence Elsewhere: Spies and Espionage outside the Anglosphere.* Edited by P. Davies and K. Gustafson, 29–48. Washington, DC: Georgetown University Press.

Vandermeersch, L. 1965. *La formation du Légisme.* Paris: École Française d'Extrême-Orient.

van Els, P. 2013a. "Righteous, Furious, or Arrogant? On Classifications of Warfare in Early Chinese Texts." In *Debating War in Chinese History.* Edited by P. Lorge, 13–40. Leiden: Brill.

van Els, P. 2013b. "How to End Wars with Words: Three Argumentative Strategies by Mozi and His Followers." *The Mozi as an Evolving Text: Different Voices in Early Chinese Thought.* Edited by C. Defoort and N. Standaert, 69–94. Leiden: Brill.

von Senger, H. 1994. "The Idea of Change as a Fundament of the Chinese Art of Cunning." *Notions et perceptions du changement en Chine.* Edited by V. Alleton and A. Volko, 21–28. Paris: Institut des Hautes Études Chinoises.

Wallacker, B. 1966. "Two Concepts of Early Chinese Military Thought." *Language* 42(2):295–299.

Yates, R. 1980. "The Mohists on Warfare: Technology, Techniques, and Justification." *Journal of the American Academy of Religion* 47(3):549–603.

Yates, R. 1988. "New Lights on Ancient Military Texts: The Development of Military Specialization." *T'oung Pao* 74(4–5):212–248.

......

CHAPTER 30

THE *SHI*, DIPLOMATS, AND URBAN EXPANSION DURING THE WARRING STATES PERIOD

......

BY ANDREW MEYER, BROOKLYN COLLEGE

THE *SHI*

......

DURING imperial times the "*shi*土" were the ruling elite, those deemed worthy to serve as the emperor's officials. It has been a common misconception to speak of the *shi* as a class in pre-Qin times. During the Warring States 戰國 (481 BCE–221 BCE), however, those identified as *shi* played such divergently various social and economic roles that together they could never have formed a group as coherent as a "class." (For an exhaustive taxonomy of the different kinds of "knights" recorded in Warring States texts, see Liu 2004:2–14.) For Han 漢 (206 BCE–220 CE) times or later, English-language scholars have frequently translated the term as "scholar officials," "literati," or "scholar gentry." These translations all reflect the meanings that gradually accrued to "*shi*" over the course of the Warring States through the early Han, thus none of them fit the usage of the term in pre-Qin times.

Hsü Cho-yun's seminal study posited that the Warring States saw a new age of social mobility, characterized chiefly by the rise of the "*shi* class" to a position of political prominence (Hsü 1965:24–52, see also Pines 2009). This impression of "the rise of the *shi*" is fostered by transmitted testimony of the period. Confucius, Mencius, Su Qin, Li Si, and many other prominent cultural and political leaders of the fifth through third centuries BCE are identified in surviving texts as *shi*. However, though there is much evidence to support Hsu's observation of increasing social mobility at this time, the sources tell a more complicated story about the figures they identify as "*shi*." The prominence and evolution of "*shi*" as a category in early Chinese discourse was not driven by the rise of a particular class but by the general restructuring of society that took place in the centuries leading up to and beyond imperial unification.

From the Shang through the Qin dynasties, Chinese society was led by a hereditary aristocracy. The social identity of these aristocrats was defined by two primary roles: warfare and sacrifice. The status of an individual noble was displayed in both these realms (Lewis 1999b:17–28; see also Li 2013:140–161). The higher the rank of an aristocrat, the more central was his position in the battle array and the more prominent his part in the sacrifices at the ancestral temples. Nobles who commanded on the battlefield and presided over the altars to their clan ancestors were acknowledged to have high titles such as *hou* 侯 (marquis) or *zi* 子 (viscount). Aristocrats who fought under the command of a higher lord and who did not preside over their own temples (but served in some adjunct capacity in the temple of their kinsmen) had no high title. The highest rank that they could claim was *shi*. Because "*shi*" thus basically designated an untitled aristocrat in pre-Qin times, the closest corresponding English translation for the term in that period is "knight." During the Western Zhou (ca. 1045 BCE–771 BCE) and Springs and Autumns (771 BCE–481 BCE) periods, an individual acknowledged to be a knight was thus not generally a powerful leader but was securely ensconced in the ranks of the aristocracy, as demonstrated by bronze inscriptions and other contemporary evidence (Chan 2004:28–49). This condition changed over the course of the Warring States period due to the fundamental restructuring of the political economy of the early Chinese world.

The lynchpin of aristocratic society during the Bronze Age had been the *guo* or "state." Every noble's place in the social hierarchy was displayed and maintained through his ongoing participation in the military and especially the religious activities of the state. Thus a knight could be distinguished from a commoner because he might have a role in the rituals at his state's ancestral temples (marking him as one the founder's descendants and the ruler's kin) or would at least publicly receive a share of the meat from its sacrificial altars.

These marks of social distinction were crucial, because even in early times significant downward mobility existed at the margins of the aristocracy. Polygamy and high birth rates caused the aristocracy to expand faster than the resources on hand to support all progeny, thus in every generation some aristocratic scions would be cast off and join the ranks of the commoners. A knight might have had cousins or even siblings who no longer ranked among the aristocracy, thus his public participation in state ceremonies was key to the maintenance of his elite status.

As competing states assaulted and annexed one another over the course of the Springs and Autumns and Warring States periods, the number of regional polities in the early Chinese world declined at a persistently accelerated rate. This process of consolidation was driven by economic, demographic, and political factors, but it had unintended social consequences. Though many of the rulers who had presided over the ancestral temples of defeated states were incorporated into the regimes of their conquerors, through loss of their ancestral cult they were reduced to the rank of knight. The population of knights thus steadily rose over this period, not because this "class" was on the ascent, but because there was a general restructuring of aristocratic society through political consolidation.

The general burgeoning of the population of knights was accompanied by a corollary change in their position in aristocratic society. As states consolidated, the number of aristocrats who exercised the genuine bona fides of a "viscount" or "marquis" dwindled. Titled aristocrats became a rarity, while the vast majority of aristocrats became knights whose relationship to the land and the state had been stripped of cultic and traditional content. With no regional temples at which he could participate, a knight's political position (to the extent that he had one) was no longer buttressed by the dynastic prerogatives of his own clan and ancestors, making him effectively an employee of the ruler (Li 2013:162–182).

This produced a general distortion of the structure of noble society, vastly widening the status gap between the upper and lower echelons of the aristocratic hierarchy. The rulers of surviving states were much wealthier and more powerful than the regional lords of the traditional Zhou order had ever been. Indeed, the rulers of the largest states eventually abandoned quaint titles like "marquis" or even "duke" (*gong* 公) in favor of the sobriquet "king" (*wang* 王) that had once been the exclusive province of the Son of Heaven.

As the position of the supreme elites became loftier, that of the vast majority of aristocrats became more tenuous. The winnowing of ancestral cult centers not only produced hordes of new knights, it depleted the social mechanisms by which knightly status had been constructed and maintained. Knightly rank became both easier to claim and less secure as a means of political purchase in aristocratic society. By the mid-fourth century BCE, texts evince that the aristocratic bona fides of those who could not claim rank higher than "knight" were in doubt.

The case of one well-attested knight of the late third and fourth centuries BCE may illustrate the problem in concrete terms. Xun Kuang 荀況 (ca. 310–ca. 217 BCE), known from the eponymous text attributed to him (the *Xunzi* 荀子 or "Master Xun") as well as other sources, is said to have been a native of Zhao (Sima Qian 1962:74:2,348; see also the reconstruction of Xun Kuang's bibliography in Knoblock 1988:3–35). His surname suggests the possibility that he was a scion of the Zhonghang 中行 clan, who had once been high ministers of the state of Jin 晉 (the state that controlled Xun Kuang's birthplace prior to its partition into the states of Zhao, Wei, and Han), and whose head had maintained his own ancestral temple as a privilege of the rank of viscount 子 (*Shi ji* 39:1,669). It is also possible, however, that Xun Kuang was of no relation to the Zhonghang but merely hailed from a locally successful family that had accrued enough wealth to support him through his education (perhaps assuming the "Xun" surname in the process by way of acquiring an air of aristocratic pedigree). Because both the court of Jin and the subsidiary fief of the Zhonghang had been annihilated by Xun Kuang's own time, leaving behind no temple complex in which Xun Kuang would have participated or where his heritage would have been commemorated, we can never be certain which of these two scenarios is closer to the truth. His contemporaries, moreover, would have been left in the same state of uncertainty as to his origins.

Because Warring States society remained, to the end, one in which birth was the ultimate arbiter of political fitness, knights like Xun Kuang (whose situation was typical of that of most knights by the late fourth century BCE) were caught in an irreducibly ambivalent position. On the one hand, their claims to a basic aristocratic pedigree were highly plausible; on the other hand, these claims were ultimately unverifiable. This ambivalence was exacerbated by the wide variability of economic circumstances in which those acknowledged as "knights" could be found. According to contemporary accounts, many knights lived in relative poverty (see, for example, *Zhuangzi* [Lau and Chen 2000d]:20/55/5–7). This perception was intensified by comparison to the extreme wealth of the kings at the top of the newly steep aristocratic hierarchy (von Falkenhausen 2006:326–399). Though some knights maintained the life of a leisured aristocrat, many (perhaps most) depended upon salaried employment as men-at-arms, engaged in commerce, or even undertook manual agricultural labor like common farmers (*Guanzi* [Lau and Chen 2001a]:9.3 [24]/72/5, 8–10).

Many texts attest to the suspicion and contempt in which knights were often held by the securely highborn aristocrats at the apex of the status ladder, who continued to monopolize political power. A typical account of an encounter between the King of Qi and Yan Chu, a poor knight, has the King's courtiers declare (in response to Yan's defense of the dignity of knights): "Now among knights the most eminent are called 'commoners,' they travel by foot and live among farmers' fields. Those below them serve as ward patrollers, gate watchmen, or village headmen. The baseness of knights truly runs deep!" (*Zhanguoce* [Lau and Chen 1992c]:136B/67/12–22).

Throughout the surviving textual record of the Warring States we find evidence of the insecurity and ambivalence of knights' social position within the aristocracy. In the *Mozi*, for example, the King of Chu is depicted as being reticent to use the words of Mo Di because they are those of a "base person" (*jian ren* 賤人) (*Mozi* [Lau and Chen 2001b]:12.1(47)/104/3–8). Some scholars have understood this to mean that Mo Di might have been born a commoner or a slave, but in the larger context of the *Mozi* and Warring States letters it is clear that this judgment is applied to Mo Di as a knight (see, for example, *Mozi* [Lau and Chen 2001b]:2.1(8)/9/11–12). By the time that passage was composed the perceived distance between knights and kings had grown so wide as to cast doubt on the fitness of their interacting with one another.

Far from showing a knightly "class" on the rise and imbued with growing confidence, the textual record evinces the persistent vulnerability of those deemed "knights" in elite society during the Warring States. Because their claims of birth no longer sufficed to establish their political fitness, secondary characteristics of noble status became increasingly important in establishing and negotiating a knight's social position. Ideal aristocrats were expected to be physically attractive, courageous, leisured, cultured, free from deformity or defilement of any kind, well-spoken and, especially, well-dressed. A knight who was perceived to be lacking in any of these areas risked being shunned by aristocratic society and thus effectively banished from the political arena.

The issue of dress illustrates the point. Few knights could afford to dress to the standards of the kings and their courtiers, thus this perceived deficit seems to have been a source of persistent and pervasive anxiety. Virtually every Masters text of the Warring States, even one so scornful of social mores as the *Zhuangzi*, contains passages defending knights against the sartorial snobbery of higher-born elites.[1] "Knights who wear cloth 布衣之士" became a stock phrase to distinguish those knights whose impoverished lifestyle made them least distinguishable from commoners.[2]

The notion of knights being on the ascent during the Warring States misconstrues aspects of the historical record. It is true that most texts we possess from the period identify strongly with knights and contain powerful rhetoric asserting knightly worth, dignity, and even superiority. But these texts clearly manifest the particular interests of a self-selecting group. Most of our surviving texts from the Warring States are the composite products of groups consisting of Masters 子 and their disciples 弟子. Young men joined such groups in order to distinguish themselves as learned and engaged, in hopes of furthering their political careers or boosting their social capital. This path was obviously most attractive to those with the least hereditary advantages. A high-born royal scion or courtier did not need to become a disciple, as his birth status gave him ample opportunity to advance. The composers and compilers of our texts were therefore almost invariably men who ranked no higher than knight, and their writings naturally cast the world in the terms most advantageous to that perspective. Thus texts as ideologically opposed to one another as the *Lun yu* and *Mozi* agree in asserting that progress will only be achieved if knights are treated more favorably and relied upon more robustly by those in power.

For all these bold pronouncements, however, the Masters texts, taken together, do not evince a coherent, secure, or empowered community. Not only do the texts' pervasive apologetics for knightly speech, dress, labor, and other perceived deficits undermine their self-confident assertions, but their attempts to police the boundaries of knightly identity also suggest a divided and embattled condition. Though the majority of Masters and disciples were knights, there is little reason to believe that the majority of individuals deemed knights were Masters or disciples. Though our surviving texts were largely produced by Master-disciple groups, they describe a wide variety of different individuals (wandering swordsmen, diviners, medical practitioners, merchants) who, though they did not identify with the producers of Masters texts, were nonetheless (and to the chagrin of the texts' authors) acknowledged to be "knights" by society at large.

---

[1] For example: *Lun yu* 4.9/7/25, 5.26/11/18–19, 6.4/12/13, 8.21/19/29,9.27/22/11; *Mencius* 2.16/13/26, 3.9/18/25, 5.4/27/16, 10.1/50/23–24, 14.6/73/27–28; *Mozi* 1.6(6)/6/23, 1.6(6)/7/1–15, 4.2(15)/26/1–3, 8.4/(32)/56/26–29, 12.1(47)/105/25–29, 12.2(48)/107/11–18, 13.1(49)/114/13; *Zhuangzi* 20/55/5–7, 28/82/14–17, 28/83/25–27, 28/85/7–8, 32/97/1–2; *Xunzi* 10/48/10–11, 27/136/1–2, 29/142/28–143/6, 31/144/27–145/5; *Lüshi chunqiu* 15.3/82/25–83/4, 15.5/86/1–8, 19.8/128/10–17, 20.2/130/18–23, 20.5/134/6–11.

[2] *Zhanguo ce* 218/112/21, 343/171/23; *Xunzi* 10/48/10; *Han Feizi* 14/26/26, 32/86/24, 36/116/6–7; *Lüshi chunqiu* 12.5/61/8, 15.3/83/14, 24.5/158/13. By the mid-third century BCE this expression was so recognizable that it was often shortened to merely "布衣." See, for example, *Lüshi chunqiu* 18.6/115/3, 19.2120/10.

Wandering swordsmen, for example, appealed to the idealized self-perception of high-born aristocrats, who continued to cherish the ideal of themselves as warriors, even though their lofty position kept them far from the battlefield. (For a general historical survey of this phenomenon see Liu 1967.) Masters texts disparage martial pursuits more generally, and those of wandering swordsmen in particular, as being beneath the proper dignity of a "true knight" (*Zhuangzi* [Lau and Chen 2000d]:30/91/1–92/16; *Mozi* [Lau and Chen 2001b]:11.3 (46)/103/15–17; *Mencius* [Lau and Chen 1995b]:2.2/8/24–25; *Xunzi* [Lau and Chen 1996]:4/13/13–17, 23/117/5–10; *Lüshi chunqiu* [Lau and Chen 2004]:11.4/56/11–13, 15.5/85/13–26). Self-confident agents would not need to deploy such defensive rhetoric. The texts' attempts to control who could be deemed a knight and how a knight's worth should be measured against that of other aristocrats demonstrate that real social leadership fell outside the circle of the texts' authors (and, by extension, those who shared their social rank).

It would be wrong to infer that all knights were impoverished, embattled, and marginalized. Ample testimony exists of knights who rose to heights of immense wealth and power. Indeed, it is precisely because the conditions of knights were in all respects so variable that it is erroneous to treat them as a coherent social class. Within the newly routinized and meritocratic framework of Warring States government, a knight such as Fan Sui 范雎 (d. 255 BCE; Fan Sui's tale features prominently in the *Zhanguo ce*, esp. Lau and Chen 1992c:72/28/26–74/33/2, 76/33/14–81/37/20, and his biography is at *Shi ji* [Sima Qian 1962]:79.2401–18) could rise to take charge of a state's civil and military policy, enjoying authority over aristocrats of ancient lineage. Such career promotions, moreover, were most often accompanied by a corollary raise in rank to marquis or viscount. These ranks evolved over the course of the Warring States, changing from hereditary entitlements held within a family line to emoluments dispensed by the state in compensation for extraordinary service.

The Warring States thus did see a profound social revolution and a new era of social mobility, but it was not driven by shifting relations between different groups within the aristocracy. Rather, it was effected by a transformation of the relationship between the state and the aristocracy. During the Bronze Age, titled nobles had expected a certain fixed measure of prestige and deference from others, even rulers, as a function of their birth, regardless of their loyalty or service to the state. The conversion of the vast majority of aristocrats into undifferentiated "knights" had nullified those entitlements, giving the state control over the prioritization of aristocratic society. During the Warring States most aristocrats enjoyed only the prestige and status that the state granted them, since only a very small minority could claim any due them by birth.

This social revolution, however, had hard limits. Though by the early third century there were only about a dozen independent states in the Zhou realm (of which only the "seven heroes"—Qin, Chu, Zhao, Wei, Han, Qi, and Yan—were genuinely autonomous strategic peers), each of those states was led by a small nexus of highborn aristocrats centered upon the ruler and his close kin. These groups were the controlling oligarchies of the Warring States, and down to the moment of imperial unification their positions of supremacy remained uncontested. The fluidity of status and power within the large field of "knightly" aristocrats never abrogated the absolute prerogative of the ruling oligarchies. That is to say, no matter how high a knight rose, he was always outranked by hereditary aristocrats to whose whims he was vulnerable. The one time that this "ceiling" was breached, when in 318 BCE Zizhi 子之, the prime minister of Yan, accepted the abdication of King Kuai 王噲 (d. 312 BCE), the event triggered a multistate invasion that quickly restored the hereditary power of the ruling clan (*Shi ji* [Sima Qian 1962]:69:2,268; Yang 571).

Thus, though meritocracy profoundly reshaped Warring States society, birth remained the final arbiter of authority throughout the era. Sources demonstrate that no matter how high he rose or what elevated rank he obtained, being born a knight remained a liability for an individual all his life. For example, in the *Zhan guo ce*, we read of Yan Sui 嚴遂, a knight who became a favored courtier in Han. There he incurred the jealousy of the state's prime minister, Han Kui 韓傀, a member of the royal clan. When Han shouted at Yan in public, Yan was forced to choose between drawing his sword (and incurring death or exile) or being shunned by his peers as a coward (*Zhanguo ce* [Lau and Chen 1992c]:385/185/18–21). This kind of vulnerability was one of the few common experiences of all knights, irrespective of position. No matter how much power or wealth they might accrue, those born knights could always be put in the position of having to defend their aristocratic bona fides from the challenges of more securely highborn nobles.

Given these conditions, it is clear why the Masters texts of the era, despite their doctrinal conflicts with one another, accorded in articulating a discourse of knightly empowerment. They celebrated figures such as hermits (*Lun yu* [Lau and Chen 2006]:5.23/11/11, 7.15/15/29–16/1; *Mencius* [Lau and Chen 1995b]:3.2/16/25–17/1, 3.9/18/24–30, 10.1/5022–25; *Xunzi* [Lau and Chen 1996]:25/121/7; *Mozi* [Lau and Chen 1995a]:2.1(8)/10/6–10), who spurned the elitism of the royal court; or assassins, who placed the high and the low on the level plane of mortality (*Lüshi chunqiu* [Lau and Chen 2004]:8.2/39//9, 12.5/61/12–17, 12.6/62/14–18, 20.1/129/11–16; *Han Feizi* [Lau and Chen 2000b]:14/26/30–27/2; *Zhanguo ce* [Lau and Chen 1992c]:343/171/18–26). Historiographically, the Masters placed their own time in a state of decline from a past era in which knights had been treated with proper dignity and insisted that the political crisis of the Warring States would not end until the problems that vexed the position and careers of knights were redressed (*Shizi* [Lau and Chen 2000c]:1.1/1/21–2/4).

These polemics bore little pragmatic fruit during the Warring States. With the Qin conquest and imperial unification, however, the tensions expressed in the Masters' social protests were exacerbated. Qin's destruction of its rivals (eliminating the ruling clans of all but one of the independent states) narrowed the scope of the titled aristocracy to an excessively narrow core. The Qin imperial elite was too steeply bifurcated to maintain the coherence of the regime, and the alienation of knights from the tight circle of the ruling oligarchy contributed significantly to the political crisis that ultimately brought the dynasty down.

With the founding of the Han under China's first commoner emperor, Liu Bang 劉邦 (256–195 BCE), the slate was wiped clean, creating the conditions for the formation of a new ruling elite. During the struggles and negotiations that ensued among the founders and early leaders of the Han over their collective identity, it was natural for them to draw upon the resources provided by the Masters texts of the Warring States, with all of their rhetorically powerful justifications for a new kind of social and political leadership. The emergent elite of the new empire thus identified themselves as *shi*, and for the rest of imperial history being recognized as such was the final and unimpeachable qualification of fitness to lead.

DIPLOMATS

In the same way that the Warring States saw a profound evolution in the status and role of knights, it likewise (and for common reasons) was marked by a sea change in the function of diplomats. Diplomacy had been a fixture of Chinese political life since the earliest recorded times, but during the Warring States the nature of diplomacy changed radically, and the frequency and magnitude of diplomatic exchange vastly intensified. By the late fourth and early third centuries BCE, some of the most influential figures in the strategic and political affairs of the Warring States distinguished themselves chiefly (in some cases virtually exclusively) in the realm of diplomacy.

The Shang dynasty had presided over a segmented, multipolar polity, thus interstate communication and negotiation had been an organic dimension of the Chinese political economy even in that early era. The Zhou founders' decision to delegate control of conquered Shang territory to their kin and close allies had amplified this dimension of political life. In the early Zhou, however, "diplomacy" was an enterprise deeply enmeshed in (and to a large degree overdetermined by) a complex and somewhat inelastic matrix of rituals and kinship protocols. Formally designated "delegations" 使 were constantly traveling between states on the occasions of marriages, births, funerals, and the observance of rites to common ancestors, and these exchanges provided opportunities for state leaders to communicate about affairs of common concern. The ceremonial conventions that prefigured these meetings, however, placed unwieldy constraints on the pursuit of discrete policy goals.

The pursuit of flexible and effective diplomacy was likewise inhibited by the structure of the early Zhou polity. Though by the early Eastern Zhou the suzerainty of the Zhou kings was largely nominal, the legitimating framework of inter-state relations required that many accommodations between regional states be conducted through (or at least sanctioned by) the Son of Heaven. That is to say, though the Zhou kings lacked real power over their vassals, the terms on which the regional states understood their relations to one another compelled them to seek the imprimatur of the royal court in many cases, depriving diplomacy of much convenience and potential for secrecy.

The intra-state power dynamics of a segmented realm also impeded fluid diplomacy in the early Zhou. Every action a regional lord undertook had to be done in deference to the quasi-sovereign prerogatives of the vassals he hoped to utilize. The networks of allegiances and subordination in which these aristocrats were embedded, moreover, were complex. Kinship and tradition could bind local grandees into conflicting ties of obligation with various peers and superiors. The power and authority at the disposal of a regional lord in service of a particular policy goal was thus highly variable and dependent on context. This blurred the line between diplomacy and domestic affairs and compelled ambitious regional lords to make a new accounting and alignment of their own forces on virtually each occasion of and in concert with negotiating a strategic enterprise with other states.

This imperative determined the form in which significant diplomatic endeavors were most frequently conducted during the early Zhou: the covenant. Large-scale punitive expeditions, intercessions to end or prevent a succession crisis, coordination of famine relief or flood control—such endeavors could not generally be undertaken through a series of bilateral negotiations but required a ritual conclave at which all the rulers involved gathered and took an oath, binding them to the policy under the auspices of a "covenant lord" (see, for example, the report of the covenant at Kuiqiu in 651 BCE at *Mengzi* [Lau and Chen 1995b]:12.7/64/28–29). This was a versatile mechanism for defusing much potential strife during the early Eastern Zhou, but it was a cumbersome system that placed severe limits on the speed and magnitude of what was achievable through diplomacy.

These conditions began to change in the fifth century BCE as the process of political consolidation that was transforming Chinese society rapidly accelerated. An early example can be seen in the career of Tian Chang 田常, the usurper who effectively assumed control of the state of Qi in a coup of 481 BCE. His murder of Duke Jian 簡公 (r. 484–481 BCE) would ordinarily have triggered a spontaneous invasion of Qi by other Zhou vassals, but with the dispatch of envoys to multiple states Tian was able to forestall such action and secure the fruits of his mutiny. We do not know the particulars of the negotiations these envoys undertook, but it seems clear why this diplomacy succeeded. The coup of 481 BCE left Tian Chang in direct control of half the arable land in Qi, giving him a broader and more secure power base than that enjoyed by any prior Eastern Zhou ruler and enabling him to offer unprecedentedly robust incentives and concessions in exchange for peace (*Zuo zhuan* [Lau and Chen 1995c]:B12.14.3/456/28–457/19).

The political revolution of the Warring States thus both facilitated and was facilitated by a tandem diplomatic revolution. As rulers consolidated control over larger and more integral realms, it became possible to achieve greater things diplomatically. At the same time, the growing scope and reach of diplomacy helped rulers consolidate control over and expand their own states.

This trend reached a watershed in the career of Marquis Hui of Wei 魏惠侯 (369–319 BCE). Hui inherited a state in crisis, having lost key territory to conquest over recent decades. From 361 to 355 he arranged a group of face-to-face summits with the rulers of other Warring States, using each occasion to broker accords that achieved states' mutual interests in the absence of armed conflict, reshaping Wei's borders in the process through a series of negotiated territorial exchanges. Hui's success demonstrated that the newly powerful throne could expedite the implementation of significant foreign policy, provided that a protocol for direct throne-to-throne negotiation could be established.

In 344 Hui assumed the title of king (becoming known thereafter as King Hui of Liang, reflecting the move of his capital to Daliang). This entailed risk, as it transgressed on the venerable prerogative of the Zhou Son of Heaven. Hui, however, was able to secure his position through diplomacy, persuading the ruler of Qi, at a summit in 334 BCE, to assume the title of king and to enter a protocol of mutual recognition of royal status between the two states. Other states soon followed suit, until by the early third century BCE all of the rulers of the major powers of the Warring States had assumed the regnal title (Yang 1955:315–322). Hui thus led Chinese ruling elites into a final, formal break with the conventions of the early Zhou, initiating a new set of parameters within which states would interact with one another as fully sovereign and autonomous peers.

This shift facilitated the emergence of a new system that maximized the potential of states to employ diplomacy to strategic ends. Rulers enjoying direct control over their own realms, and acting on their own sole authority as kings were freed to efficiently and predictably mobilize human and material resources in fulfillment of negotiated agreements. Thus swift changes in the strategic situation of the entire Chinese world could be effected through a rapid series of short bilateral negotiations.

New protocols evolved to accommodate the needs of this dynamic diplomacy. Rulers could no longer be tied to the fixed occasions and ceremonial patterns that had structured interstate communication in the early Zhou. The royal courts of the major states thus exchanged tallies (*fujie* 符節), which could be used to provide diplomatic credentials to an envoy at a moment's need. These were small bronze ornaments broken to create unique halves, each of which was retained separately at points of issuance and reception. If a knight arrived at the court of Qi bearing the matching half of a tally provided to the Qi court by the king of Zhao, the Qi king could be confident that this was an envoy fully empowered to negotiate on behalf of Zhao, and that whatever concessions or inducements he offered represented authentic commitments from Zhao's ruler. (For collected sources relating to the use of tallies, see Yang and Wu 2005:303–307.)

These new channels of direct, discrete, and swift communication from court to court made the diplomatic sphere more autonomous and significant as a dimension of state policy than it had ever been before. A well-timed diplomatic mission could halt an invading army in its tracks or reverse the tide of an ongoing campaign. The importance of this new contingency is reflected in the emergent political and military literature of the period. The *Sunzi bingfa*, for example, enjoins that a commander should first attack the foe's alliances before assaulting its cities or armies (*Sunzi* [Lau and Chen 1992a]:A3/2/22).

Diplomacy thus evolved to become a specialty of skilled practitioners, though these were not professional diplomats like those of modern nation-states. Courts did not maintain a dedicated "diplomatic corps" but issued new credentials to an envoy each time one was needed. This might be a kinsman of the ruler or a longstanding official of the state, but it did not have to be, and (if the sources are to be believed) often was not.

Any individual who could convince the ruler of the wisdom of a proposed negotiation might be given a diplomatic tally. Those who could claim some knowledge of the personnel and disposition of foreign courts obviously had greater credibility in this regard, thus a cadre of "wandering persuaders" developed who moved between the courts of the Warring States promoting various schemes of alliance and conflict.

This group developed a worldview and shared terminology distinctive and coherent enough to make its impact on the larger literature of the era. By the early third century BCE, two general conceptual models formed a joint paradigm for understanding the diplomatic field. Qin, the westernmost of the Warring States, was by that time the most powerful. Advocacy of alignment with or subordination to Qin thus came under the general rubric of *heng* 橫 (horizontal), because any line connecting Qin with one or more of its rivals would form a roughly horizontal east-west mark on a standard map. By contrast, advocacy of joint resistance to Qin was labeled *zong*縱 (vertical), because any line connecting two or more of Qin's rivals would form a vertical north-south mark. Together these terms formed a binome (*zongheng*) signifying diplomacy as a tool of statecraft more generally (Yang 1955:322–323; Lewis 1999a:632–641).

Celebrated diplomats became colorful literary figures akin to the hermits and assassins of fabled stories. An outstanding example is Su Qin 蘇秦 (d. 284 BCE), who is said to have brokered his own rise to the prime ministerial seat of six states simultaneously. His machinations purportedly stopped the advance of Qin and brought down the throne of Qi (*Shi ji* [Sima Qian 1962]:69:2,241–2,266; Nienhauser 1994:97–112). The stories in which he figures are so fantastic as to seem the stuff of legend, but the romance surrounding him as a literary icon well testifies to the mixed fascination and terror that this new arena of diplomatic manipulation inspired in the political players of the Warring States.

URBANIZATION

A growth in the size and importance of cities was another distinguishing hallmark of the Warring States. It has long been noted that urbanization followed a different path in early China than in the ancient Mediterranean or early Mesopotamia. Where in the latter regions cities tended to emerge at the nexus of trade routes, in early China urban centers were situated at locations mandated by those in political authority (Wheatley 1971).

Thus in the Bronze Age a "city" was basically a fortified compound housing the ancestral temples of the ruling family of a state. Apart from the temples, it would contain the residential palaces of the rulers, their kin, and close allies, and it might also house workshops for artisans that produced and maintained the ritual implements and weapons used by the aristocracy. All of the human and material assets housed in an urban center were deployed in support of its religious and military functions. There was thus not much in the way of urban culture or economy apart from what served the needs of the state.

This began to change in the early fifth century BCE. As the population grew and sur-plus wealth was generated through public works, new technology, and new farming methods, the volume and variety of goods moving over commercial markets burgeoned. At the same time (and partly in response to accelerating commercialization), as success-ful states conquered and annexed their neighbors, the fund of exploitable wealth avail-able to victorious state capitals expanded exponentially.

These changes made commerce ever-increasingly more central to the lives of aristo-cratic elites, not only for the comforts and luxuries the marketplace could supply but also for the importance of markets in arming and provisioning the expanding conscript armies of the era. As was the case in the realm of diplomacy, political consolidation and commercialization were linked in a mutually reinforcing cycle. The more profitable markets became, the more states expanded and consolidated to exploit them; the more states expanded and consolidated, the more favorable were the conditions for the growth and intensification of trade.

All of these changes made their mark on the development of urban centers. Though the location of settlements was continuous with the Bronze Age, the nature and evolu-tion of particular towns diverged in response to the movements of the marketplace. Those cities that through geographic good fortune or strategic ascendency became tied into robust trade networks grew and thrived. Those cities that failed to achieve purchase in the marketplace shrank or disappeared. The capitals of the most powerful states, such as Handan 邯鄲 in Zhao, Jinyang 晉陽 in Zhao, and Linzi 臨淄 in Qi, became great met-ropolitan centers. Even the capital of a lesser power, like Shangqiu 商丘, seat of the state of Song, could grow into a major city because it sat astride important trade routes.

These cities continued to be military and religious centers, but new conditions pro-duced new dimensions of urban space and life. Political consolidation made govern-ment more complex, creating the need for expanded districts within the state capital to house the residences and offices of state officials. The expansion of the commercial mar-ketplace likewise radically transformed the demographics and spatial dynamics of urban centers. New wards sprang up to house artisans producing an array of goods beyond the equipment and weapons needed by the army: dyed silks and linen, lacquer, jewelry, furniture, wine, and prepared delicacies. Merchants trading in domestically produced and imported products filled specialized bazaars and marketplaces dispersed throughout the city (Yang 1955:95–105).

The residents of these metropolises were a newly urbane group. The wealth and diver-sity of the city gave them distinct experiences and perspectives. They dressed and talked differently than their more rustic compatriots and had particular tastes and leisure pursuits that were fostered by the cosmopolitan environment in which they lived.

A speech describing Linzi, the Qi capital, attributed to Su Qin, gives some idea of the novel dynamism of this emerging urban society: "There are 70,000 households in Linzi.... Not one of her people does not play the flute, strum the zither, strike the harp, beat the drum, fight cocks, race dogs, play *liu bo* 六博 (a board game like chess), or kick a ball. On the roads of Linzi, carts rub hubcaps and men rub shoulders.... Families are rich, men are well off, their will high, their spirits soaring" (*Shi ji* [Sima Qian 1962]:69:2257; translated in Nienhauser 1994:106).

The architectural design of cities likewise manifested the influence of traditional and novel factors. The growing importance of commercial wealth led rulers toward attempts at conspicuous consumption. High towers and expansive palaces were built to impress visitors with the prosperity of the state, akin to the monumental architecture of Periclean Athens or imperial Rome. At the same time, the traditional military function of cities remained paramount in their layout and planned infrastructure. Double and triple walls were erected in an attempt to make the city unassailable, prompting the creation of a whole literature on siege-craft (see chapter 35 by Shi Jie; Wu 1999:653–675).

The Warring States was the first great era of urbanization in Chinese social life. It thus imparted a legacy that was carried over into imperial times. Cities such as Changan, Luoyang, Kaifeng, and Beijing grew upon the foundation of uniquely urban traditions and cultural patterns laid during the centuries prior to the Qin unification.

BIBLIOGRAPHY

Berkowitz, Alan J. 2000. *Patterns of Disengagement: The Practice and Portrayal of Reclusion in Early Medieval China*. Stanford, CA: Stanford University Press.

Chan, Shirley 2004. *The Confucian Shi: Official Service and the Confucian Analects*. Lampeter: Edwin Mellen Press.

Ch'ü, T'ung-tsu 瞿同祖 1972. *Han Social Structure*. Seattle: University of Washington.

Crump, J. I., trans. 1996. *Chan-kuo Ts'e: Intrigues of the Warring States* 戰國策, rev. ed. Ann Arbor: Center for Chinese Studies.

Hsu Cho-yun 許倬雲 1965. *Ancient China in Transition*. Stanford, CA: Stanford University Press.

Knoblock, John 1988. *Xunzi: A Translation and Study of the Complete Works*, vol. 1. Stanford, CA: Stanford University Press.

Lau, D. C. 劉段爵, and Chen Fangzheng 陳方正, eds. 1992a. *Concordance to Four Military Writings* 兵書四種逐字索引. The ICS Ancient Chinese Text Concordance Series. Hong Kong: Commercial Press.

Lau, D. C. 劉段爵, and Chen Fangzheng 陳方正, eds. 1992b. *Concordance to the Huainanzi* 淮南子逐字索引. The ICS Ancient Chinese Text Concordance Series. Hong Kong: Commercial Press.

Lau, D. C. 劉段爵, and Chen Fangzheng 陳方正, eds. 1992c. *Concordance to the Intrigues of the Warring States* 戰國策逐字索引. The ICS Ancient Chinese Text Concordance Series. Hong Kong: Commercial Press.

Lau, D. C. 劉段爵, and Chen Fangzheng 陳方正, eds. 1992d. *Concordance to the Record of Rites* 禮記逐字索引. The ICS Ancient Chinese Text Concordance Series. Hong Kong: Commercial Press.

Lau, D. C. 劉段爵, and Chen Fangzheng 陳方正, eds. 1994. *Concordance to the Annals of Master Yan* 晏子春秋逐字索引. The ICS Ancient Chinese Text Concordance Series. Hong Kong: Commercial Press.

Lau, D. C. 劉段爵, and Chen Fangzheng 陳方正, eds. 1995a. *Concordance to the Mao Odes* 毛詩逐字索引. The ICS Ancient Chinese Text Concordance Series. Hong Kong: Commercial Press.

Lau, D. C. 劉段爵, and Chen Fangzheng 陳方正, eds. 1995b. *Concordance to the Mengzi* 孟子逐字索引. The ICS Ancient Chinese Text Concordance Series. Hong Kong: Commercial Press.

Lau, D. C. 劉段爵, and Chen Fangzheng 陳方正, eds. 1995c. *Concordance to the Zuo Tradition of the Spring and Autumn* 春秋左傳逐字索引. The ICS Ancient Chinese Text Concordance Series. Hong Kong: Commercial Press.

Lau, D. C. 劉段爵, and Chen Fangzheng 陳方正, eds. 1996. *Concordance to the Xunzi* 荀子逐字索引. The ICS Ancient Chinese Text Concordance Series. Hong Kong: Commercial Press.

Lau, D. C. 劉段爵, and Chen Fangzheng 陳方正, eds. 2000a. *Concordance to the Elegies of Chu* 楚辭逐字索引. The ICS Ancient Chinese Text Concordance Series. Hong Kong: Commercial Press.

Lau, D. C. 劉段爵, and Chen Fangzheng 陳方正, eds. 2000b. *Concordance to the Han Feizi* 韓非子逐字索引. The ICS Ancient Chinese Text Concordance Series. Hong Kong: Commercial Press.

Lau, D. C. 劉段爵, and Chen Fangzheng 陳方正, eds. 2000c. *Concordance to the Shenzi, Shizi, and Shenzi* 申子, 尸子, 慎子逐字索引. The ICS Ancient Chinese Text Concordance Series. Hong Kong: Commercial Press.

Lau, D. C. 劉段爵, and Chen Fangzheng 陳方正, eds. 2000d. *Concordance to the Zhuangzi* 莊子逐字索引. The ICS Ancient Chinese Text Concordance Series. Hong Kong: Commercial Press.

Lau, D. C. 劉段爵, and Chen Fangzheng 陳方正, eds. 2001a. *Concordance to the Guanzi* 管子逐字索引. The ICS Ancient Chinese Text Concordance Series. Hong Kong: Commercial Press.

Lau, D. C. 劉段爵, and Chen Fangzheng 陳方正, eds. 2001b. *Concordance to the Mozi* 墨子逐字索引. The ICS Ancient Chinese Text Concordance Series. Hong Kong: Commercial Press.

Lau, D. C. 劉段爵, and Chen Fangzheng 陳方正, eds. 2004. *Concordance to the Annals of Mr. Lü* 呂氏春秋逐字索引. The ICS Ancient Chinese Text Concordance Series. Hong Kong: Commercial Press.

Lau, D. C. 劉段爵, and Chen Fangzheng 陳方正, eds. 2006. *Concordance to the Analects* 論語逐字索引. The ICS Ancient Chinese Text Concordance Series. Hong Kong: Commercial Press.

Lewis, Mark Edward 1990. *Sanctioned Violence in Early China*. Albany: State University of New York Press.

Lewis, Mark Edward 1999a. "Warring States Political History." In *The Cambridge History of Ancient China*. Edited by Michael Loewe and Edward L. Shaughnessy, 587–650. Cambridge, UK: Cambridge University Press.

Lewis, Mark Edward 1999b. *Writing and Authority in Early China*. Albany: State University of New York Press.

Li, Feng 2006. *Landscape and Power in Early China: The Crisis and Fall of the Western Zhou*. Cambridge, UK: Cambridge University Press.

Li, Feng 2008. *Bureaucracy and the State in Early China: Governing the Western Zhou*. Cambridge, UK: Cambridge University Press.

Li, Feng 2013. *Early China: A Social and Cultural History*. Cambridge, UK: Cambridge University Press, 2013.

Liu, James J. Y. 劉若愚 1967. *The Chinese Knight-Errant*. Chicago: University of Chicago Press.

Liu, Zehua 劉則華 2004. *Pre-Qin Knights and Society* 先秦士人與社會, rev. ed. Tianjin: Tianjin renmin chubanshe.

Matsui, Yoshinori 松井嘉德 2002. *State and Society in the Zhou Dynasty* 周代國制の研究. Kyūko sōsho 34. Tokyo: Kyūko Shoin.

Nienhauser, William H., Jr., ed. 1994. *The Grand Scribe's Records*, vol. 3: *The Memoirs of Pre-Han China*. Bloomington: Indiana University Press.

Pines, Yuri 2009. *Envisioning Eternal Empire: Chinese Political Thought of the Warring States*. Honolulu: University of Hawai'i Press.

Qian, Mu 錢穆 1935. *Chronology of the Pre-Qin Masters* 先秦諸子繫年. Shanghai: Shangwu chubanshe.

Sima Qian 司馬遷 1962. *Records of the Historian* 史記. Beijing: Zhonghua shuju.

Tao, Xisheng 陶希聖 1933. *Debating Knights and Wandering Bravoes* 辨士與遊俠. Shanghai: Shangwu chubanshe.

Vervoorn, Aat 1990. *Men of the Cliffs and Caves: The Development of the Chinese Eremitic Tradition to the End of the Han Dynasty*. Hong Kong: Chinese University Press.

von Falkenhausen, Lothar 2006. *Chinese Society in the Age of Confucius (1000–250 BC): The Archaeological Evidence*. Los Angeles: Cotsen University of Archaeology.

Wang, Yandong 王延棟, and Qingchang Zhang 張清常 1993. *Annotated Intrigues of the Warring States* 戰國策箋注. Tianjin: Nankai daxue chubanshe.

Wheatley, Paul 1971. *The Pivot of the Four Quarters: A Preliminary Enquiry into the Origins and Character of the Ancient Chinese City*. Chicago: Aldine.

Wu, Hung 巫鴻 1999. "The Art and Architecture of the Warring States Period." In *The Cambridge History of Ancient China*. Edited by Michael Loewe and Edward Shaughnessy, 651–744. Cambridge, UK: Cambridge University Press.

Wu, Hung 巫鴻 2001. "Rethinking Warring States Cities: An Historical and Methodological Proposal." *Journal of East Asian Archaelogy* 3(1–2):237–257.

Xu, Shen 許慎 1981. *Annotated Explications of Writing and Logographs* 說文解字注. Shanghai: Shanghai guji.

Yang, Kuan 杨宽 1955. *Warring States History* 戰國史. Shanghai: Renmin chu banshee.

Yang, Kuan 杨宽 2005. *Essential Institutions of the Warring States* 戰國會要. Shanghai: Shanghai guji chubanshe.

Yan, Buke 閻步克 1996. *Draft History of Scholar-Gentry Governance* 士大夫政治演生史稿. Beijing: Beijing Daxue chubanshe.

CHAPTER 31

··

CONFUCIUS, MENCIUS, AND THEIR DAOIST-LEGALIST CRITICS

··

BY MOSS ROBERTS, NEW YORK UNIVERSITY

THE words of Confucius and his disciples have been handed down in a text called the *Analects*, which means "gathered from before," that is, gathered from Confucius' own time (he died in 479 BC) and that of many of his disciples. The Chinese title, *Lunyu*, means either *Collected Conversations* or *Conclusions and Conversations*. The *Analects* is an informal and fragmented text that includes many voices, making it one of the most democratic philosophical works east or west. It almost invites the reader to join in. Like Proverbs in the Old Testament it is a long series of passages, nearly five hundred, not closely related but mutually relevant within the whole.

Confucius' voice often carries the main themes but does not overpower. Returning to his village as an accomplished figure, Confucius remains silent lest he overawe his old acquaintances or fail to hear all that they have to say (5.1)[1] He also connects his primary value term, *ren* (love of mankind, benevolence, humane), to reticence, implying listening receptively to others. The power of his formulations notwithstanding, he cuts a modest, almost diffident figure. Ultimately Confucius is a tragic hero, a noble failure, as attested in 14.41, which describes him as a man who knows he cannot succeed but perseveres undaunted. In the eighteenth chapter he is openly mocked for his fruitless efforts at bringing about political reform.

His world consisted of scores of small family-ruled kingdoms. It was early days in a three-centuries-long process of modernization. Major advances in agriculture, metallurgy, and weaponry were enabling the more ambitious of these rulers to expand into and often annex neighboring kingdoms or unclaimed land. This in turn led to a need for more complex political forms of government and for experts in various fields—technical,

---

[1] Legge, James, Confucius: Confucian Analects (Oxford: The Clarendon Press 1893; reprinted by Dover Books 1971). Analects passages are numbered following Legge, but translations are author's.

cultural, bureaucratic, diplomatic—capable of serving rulers of enlarged polities. Other texts, the Laozi and Mencius for example, distinguish between large and small kingdoms. The larger tended to be more advanced and more aggressive. All had need of advisers, managers, and experts.

Confucius had organized something like a graduate school of political management and took on a variety of students. Their education had two main branches, character formation and acquisition of knowledge, particularly cultural and historical, exemplified by the two works the Shi and the Shu, the Classic of Poetry and the Classic of Documents, respectively. It was Confucius' aspiration to provide the rulers of his day with well-prepared young men who would staff the newly created bureaucracies of their kingdoms and fortify hereditary rulers.

It was no longer possible for a ruler to restrict appointments to his immediate family, though he had many wives, and so he had to recruit strangers into his service. The title Confucius gave to such promising young men was *junzi*, meaning a son of a ruler. His *junzi* typically surpassed in skill and integrity the royal relatives and so were meant to supplement or if necessary supplant them, as an idealized son, so to speak. The *junzi* is the central type of the Analects, the role model par excellence of son/minister. As minister the *junzi* is subordinate and not a potential successor, a sensitive issue raised in the Mozi and the Mencius.

Confucius' voices his doubts about the prospects of his followers at the end of the opening passage: "Is it not inspiring to study and steadily master your studies? Is it not occasion to celebrate when like-minded companions come from afar? Is he not a true *junzi* who feels no resentment though the world ignores him?" This last sentence warns that appointment is uncertain and principled service could well end in dismissal from office, however promising one's studies and fellowship.

The date of compilation of the received Analects is not known but probably postdates the contents by hundreds of years. Most of the material comes from the early Warring States period, late sixth to late fifth centuries. One clue is that the word *renxing* or *xing*, meaning human nature, is not a key term; it is only used twice and not significantly. Toward the end of the fifth century, however, the term *xing* became a center of interest within the Confucian school and remained debated down to the time of Xunzi (ca. 313–238) and beyond, even to modern times. By this measure the Analects predates the advent of human nature as a dominant topic among Confucians. Notably, the term does not appear in the Laozi and has no significant role in the Mozi.

Xing became important to the Confucians, because the internal or subjective factors are major categories in their discussions of political action. Daoists and Mohists have no interest in such psychological matters, while the Mencius offers an exhaustive inquiry into the human psychological constitution. Even though the term "nature" occurs only twice in the Analects, the structure of the mind and the internalization of values are nonetheless important themes and the basis for Mencius' theories.

Confucius' intent is to build the model *junzi* through learning in order to serve the purpose of political reform and good government. Learning for Confucius has two branches, development of character and intellect. The two branches must never be separated.

To keep them together self-examination or reflection is called for. Confucius was once a magistrate, and so it is not surprising that he uses a metaphor for this process: holding a trial against one's self in one's own mind (5.26).

One of the most famous passages in the Analects speaks of virtue and intellect through metaphors of nature (6.21). "Men of knowledge are gladdened by waters; men of humanity by mountains. Men of knowledge are active; men of humanity inwardly at peace; men of knowledge are celebrated; men of humanity revered through time." This passage refers to the two branches of learning and their inseparability. Christ warned his disciples to be cunning as serpents and gentle as doves. Knowledge without a moral foundation becomes an amoral instrument; humaneness without exercise of intelligence becomes naïve and dangerously exploitable. Confucius means for the *junzi* to educate intellect and develop character, combining the moral and intellectual faculties. The two are as interdependent as mountains and streams, a cliché now of Chinese art. In the Analects passage mountains represent fundamental principles that remain stable through time, while water stands for the ever-changing flow of events in the course of time. The unchanging mountains guide and direct the course of water as principles guide events.

Continuity of civilization is an important Analects theme. Ritual and ceremonial traditions (*li*) is one means by which a culture reproduces itself. The graph shows a ritual vessel to the right of the word sacred; the vessel is a metonym for the entire ceremony in which family roles are performed and social status is presented. In 2.23 Confucius affirms his faith that if the community filially maintains its heritage (*li*) it will remain generally recognizable even a hundred generations into the future. So ritual means the total set of social forms and formalities that give a society its coherence and continuity.

Li combines with other words, such as *yue* (music), *ren* (humanity), and *yi* (honor); this suggests that it is a form requiring content. Yue (musical performance) is always in the second position. *Li-yue* is an important compound term. *Li* alone involves social and personal discipline, even repression, but music offers some relief or sublimation, an occasion when the different levels of society can share a common performance. Moreover, music reaches into the emotions and conveys the meanings of ritual and other moral concepts.

In addition to cultural heritage *li* is also a form of social interaction, mediating personal virtues so that they become socially effective. Thus in 8.3, "Courage without *Li* becomes disorder." Li controls passions through forms and thus makes human interaction workable. Here again *li*, like *zhi* (knowledge), has to combine with a virtue. In 3.3, "If a man is not humane, he has no business with Ritual or with Music." There is a functional difference among the key Analects terms. Ritual and knowledge are instrumental terms, not terms of value in and of themselves; they must combine and make operational terms of value like love of mankind (*ren*), acting rightly (*yi*, related to courage), filial devotion (xiao), and moral charisma (*de*). In 12.2 Confucius explains humaneness (*ren*) this way: "Out in the world, treat all men as honored guests; engaging their service, treat the commoners as though you were officiating at the ancestral sacrifices; do not impose on any man what is disagreeable to you; and none will resent you, in kingdom or clan." Thus we see that humaneness involves the expansion of clan ritual to include all commoners in service. Ritual is a form of governance that treats all subject to it as family members. The state is modeled from the clan. This is made clear in 1.2: "Filial devotion and fraternal respect, are these not the basis of humaneness?" The phrase from 12.5, "All men are brothers," makes the same point.

In 2.3 we find an important correlation between *li* and *de*. "Lead the people with law/governmental administration and keep order with punishments, then they will act so as to evade punishment, losing their sense of shame. Lead them with virtue (*de*) and keep order with Ritual then the people will retain their sense of shame and observe discipline as well." Here we find Confucius' doubts about the efficacy of law, the state, and any form of external coercion. Such pressure, he argues, can extinguish the inborn sense of shame that is instilled within the family. Confucius counts on the inner voice of conscience to order men's conduct. And it is the charismatic effect of the paternal role model that animates the conscience. As a magistrate Confucius had reservations about the workings of law and his ability to settle cases. He thought it was essential to eliminate litigation. The ideal he hoped to find but never did was a person who could conduct litigation against himself inside his own mind (5.12).

Finally then, we see that for Confucius there is a parallel between the kingdom and the clan. In 12.11 he states: "The ruler must rule rightly for the vassals to serve rightly; the father must behave rightly for the sons (children) to be filial." This is role model theory: those in authority set standards of conduct for their subordinates. For Confucius the linking of family and state is essential for this model to work. His adversary <u>Mozi</u> argued for the separation of family and kingdom. That Confucianism absorbed Mohism, keeping some connection between state and family, at least in common parlance, is seen in the word used today for the Chinese nation state, *guojia*.

Mozi and Mencius

Mozi created a breakthrough theory of universality by delinking *guo* and *jia*, clan and kingdom. He was working toward a concept of governance applicable anywhere. Unlike Confucius, Mozi did not think that *ren*-humanity, love of mankind based on family love, could lead to a universal political family. Instead he replaced *ren* with *jian ai* (comprehensive love), which redefined filial service: one should serve the parents of others so that others will serve yours. *Jian ai* also called for mutual respect between kingdoms and between clans to prevent warfare between them. Mozi sought for principles of government that applied everywhere in the same way, objectively, as instruments of measurement (square and compass) do, as law and institutions do.

Toward this end he redefined the concept of Heaven (tian), which he treated as a universal lawgiver rather than as a collective sky-tomb for ancestors both lineal and cultural. Mozi's Heaven enjoined *yi*, right action, on all humans. In Mozi *yi* is a stand-alone value and supersedes all other terms such as *ren* and *li* (ritual and social formalities), under Heaven's authority, an authority that supersedes all human authority, above all the king's. According to the way Mozi formulates the concepts, there is a gap not a connection between ruler and Heaven, a gap filled by ghosts who enforce Heaven's will. As an objectified and knowable entity Heaven is easily accessible to all men just as reading instruments of measurement is accessible to all. "The will of Heaven is to me like a compass to a wheelwright or a square to a carpenter."[2] In the Analects *yi* is important but linked to enlightened judgment based on occasion and context only. Mozi gives *yi* a broad definition, an independent term for what is beneficial to all men. Mencius defines *yi* as subordinate to *ren*.

Mencius' mission was to answer Mozi's critique of Confucian philosophy, to restore the validity of Confucius' main ideas by universalizing them on a new basis and thereby answering the critiques by Mozi. Above all, he tried to rescue the concept of *ren* as the essential principle of governing, bringing yi under *ren*'s aegis and thus restoring the primacy of enlightened human authority. In this way he followed Confucius, who made virtuous rule preferable to administrative (legal) authority (2.3).

The instrument that Mencius uses for this purpose is the concept of (human) nature (*xing*), the seedbed of *ren*. The Analects had little to say about *xing* nature (two minor passages); it becomes central in Mencius. In addition Mencius drew on the terms *tian* (Heaven) and *yi* (righteousness) to enhance further the concept of *ren*. Heaven appears about half a dozen times in the Analects but is treated more personally than philosophically; like *xing* it is not a major part of the Analects system of terms. Mozi has no use for a term like *xing*, since he does not acknowledge internal forces. In his system Mencius uses both *xing* and heaven to fortify *ren*, a concept that via Mencius' reconstruction has remained central to Confucian thought in the imperial period and even down to the present day. At the same time Mencius moves yi under the aegis of *ren*, thus away from the aegis of heaven.

In the Mencius sometimes *ren* dominates. Mencius called *ren* the gate and *yi* the road, suggesting direction followed by practice. Mencius advocated *ren-yi*, conventionally translated "benevolence and righteousness." He could not simply reuse the former terminology. To preserve it, Mencius had to bring it into a new framework consisting not only of nature (*xing*) and Heaven (tian) but of a third crucial term, min, the people, which worked in tandem with Heaven in legitimating rulers. Like Mozi, Mencius emphasizes the active role of the people and their connection with Heaven, citing the Great Declaration: "Heaven sees according as my people see; Heaven hears according as my people hear"[3] (the Analects lays less stress on the people and does not connect them to Heaven). A benevolent king can rule even in adversity. This explains the well-known opening of the Mencius in which Mencius rebukes the king for seeking li (gain), another

---

[2] Watson, Burton, Mo Tzu: Basic Writings (New York: Columbia Univ Press 1963, 1970) p. 92.

[3] Legge, James, The Works of Mencius, (Oxford: The Clarendon Press 1895, reprinted by Dover 1970) p. 357. This quote from the Classic of Documents (Shujing) is not in the received text but is consonant with its meaning.

primary value term in the Mozi; Mencius sternly warns the king that only *ren-yi* can save his kingdom; the pursuit of gain will only destroy the kingdom.

In this new context *ren-yi* as a compound term has an enhanced meaning, close to "civilized values." In the Analects the words are separate concepts and never occur as a pair. Mencius locates the highest authority in the mind of the benevolent king and his benevolent rule (*ren zheng*), reinforced by Heaven above and the people below. Mencius thus reestablishes the authority of Confucius and the authority of mind and nature (xin and *xing*) over the objective world in which men must act.

By making *ren* a mental factor, as Confucius had done, Mencius was reestablishing the dominance of the internal factors in maintaining social morality; like Confucius, Mencius had little use for laws or other external pressures. For Mencius conduct had to come from right motivation. In the opening to Book 6, Mencius strives to refute Gaozi, who concedes that *ren* may be internal but insists that *yi* is external. He is trying to salvage part of Mozi's position, since Mozi's philosophy makes no allowance for internal or psychological factors such as love of mankind. The rules for Mozi are external and shape human conduct from the outside, a form of what in modern times is called behaviorism; he relies on reward and punishment enforced by ghosts, a sort of ancestor corps universalized to serve all of society rather than the living lineal descendants of the elites.

For Mencius the formation of the social self depends on the development of potential virtues or subjective powers located in *xing*, literally meaning inborn in the mind. The word resembles the Latin ingenium, an inborn capacity, though generally ingenium refers to skills rather than virtues. This philosophical position depends on a special interpretation of the word *xing* (nature), which eliminates from it all biological instinct and appetite. Mencius opposes Gaozi in Book 6, who maintains that food and sex constitute nature. To this biological definition, Mencius argues that human nature is purely social, that the Confucian value system exists prefabricated in the human heart as potentials (*duan*).

Thus in Book 2.1.6 we find, "All men have a mind unwilling to be cruel to others. The great kings of yore had such a mind and thus had humane government. Were such government put into effect today, then the rule of the realm would be in the king's palm." There follows the well-known anecdote of the witness to a child falling in a well. The witness instinctively experiences shock, fright, and empathy, for which there is no external reason. The witness sought no praise, reward, or name. The response is reflexively sympathetic. The passage then proceeds to detail the four potentialities of the heart: the empathetic mind is the seed of benevolence, the mind that knows shame for wrongdoing is the seed of right action, the mind that knows to relinquish and yield place is the seed of ritual and social formality, and the mind that approves and condemns is the seed of knowledge." As the opening of the following Book 3 says: Mencius instructed the Prince of Teng about "the goodness of human nature." By using the word *ren* (human being) nature becomes universal by definition. Mencius elaborates on the Analects' idea of human development through persistent self-examining; the Analects' *junzi* points toward a universal model.

What explains Mencius delving into psychology? If *xing* is present in each and every person then the role of virtuous leadership in bringing *xing* to fulfillment is restored. Everyone knew that King Hui of Liang was about to lose power when Mencius boldly counsels him to lead only with *ren-yi* and to abandon the Mohist utilitarianism. The implication is that the people would be moved to follow him even in adversity. This echoes Confucius' point that trust in the ruler is more important than arms, even than food.

Mencius has argued that humane government stems from the humane mind of the king. Mencius tells of of a population that left their homes and farms to follow a humane ruler, rather than fall under the rule of a barbarian or a bad king. For this model to work, it is necessary for the king's thinking to be transmitted effectively. The theory of human nature serves as the critical mediating factor uniting ruler and people. The king's humanity is a more developed form of those seeds that are in the minds and hearts of every human, regardless of geographical or cultural differences. The king's virtue or moral force (*de*) is tied to heavenly authority. De's charismatic energy reaches the limits of the *tianxia*, the whole realm of kingdoms, even if his territory is as small as 100 li (half miles). Mencius names this force the *haoran zhi qi*, the transcendent spirit with which a king (or a sage) can fill the void between heaven and earth. Such a leader the people will follow anywhere; Mencius calls this the *wangdao* or way of the true king, close to the chakravartin of the Upanishads.

Human nature resonates with the humane king, like a transponder receiving an electrical signal. The *xing* is the receptor. That is how Mencius holds on to the ideal of the charismatic king and minimizes the importance of law and institutions. Institutions and law were essential to Xunzi and the Legalists, who disdained Mencius for overemphasizing the internal factors.

Why does Mencius locate these fundamentals of civilization—humanity, right conduct, observance of formalities, and knowledge—in the mind and heart of all humans? What explains this dramatic subjective turn in Confucian thought? Perhaps there is a general and also a particular way to approach this question. In general Mencius, like many philosophers, maintains an optimistic attitude to humanity and human society, and faith in human nature is at the core of such an attitude. More particularly, Mencius lived in a time when the multi-kingdom wars were in progress and the social fabric suffered great destruction. In the text itself are phrases like "leading beasts to feed on humans," and "bodies of men lying unburied in roadside ditches." Heavy flooding is also in the text as a metaphor of social disorder. It may be then that Mencius was pessimistic about his historical moment even if optimistic about mankind and the human potential for goodness and good order, and the only way to preserve those potentialities was to locate them in the safest possible place, inborn human nature. This transfer of civilized values into the human mind guarantees their invulnerability to the vicissitudes of history; they will survive the worst of times and can flower forth when such times pass and better objective conditions return. The values are thus eternal, whether or not objectively materialized in human institutions and conduct.

LAOZI

The Confucius of the *Analects* carefully limited the subjects he would address. Social and political roles and rules, human motivation, consciousness and conscience, relations of clan and kingdom—all came within his purview. At the center of his value system is the father-son relation, parallel to the ruler-minister relation. Beyond that he fell silent, refusing to speak on matters that went beyond the scope of daily life and understanding. This is why he kept his distance from religion. "Respect the gods but keep your distance from them," he advises. (Indeed, there is no Chinese word for religion except as a translation from European languages.) Laozi, to whom the *Dao De Jing* is attributed, expands dramatically the parameters of discussion by creating a vast panorama of all phenomena (*wanwu* or the ten thousand things), which are then presented as the children birthed by a universal single mother called the Dao. Commonly translated The Way, the word in Chinese has more of the sense of processes of birth and development, decay and death, visible nature and invisible time.

Powers of procreation are part of the definition of the Dao in stanza 1, "mother of the ten thousand," in its manifested (*you*, existent) aspect. In its unmanifest aspect (*wu*, negation) the Dao gestates Heaven and Earth, the framework but not the origin of all that exists. In this way Laozi delivers a well-calculated rebuke to the paternal authority so valued by Confucians and also subordinates to Dao the sacred concept of Heaven, where all ancestors dwell, turning Heaven and Earth into functions of Dao.

Laozi's formulation also demotes parental authority. After all, a single mom can hardly be expected to properly care for even a handful of children much less ten thousand of them. They'll simply have to govern themselves, and that's exactly what Laozi advocates in a number of stanzas, the withdrawal of "superior" authority so that those subject to it can develop on their own inner momentum freed of it. As stanza 57 phrases the point: "May we under-govern and/the ruled uplift themselves."[4] This is not the role-model-emulation model is dispensed with.

Laozi does not merely dispense with parental authority, he subjects it to the authority (or the energized "being") of the ten thousand. At the end of stanza 25 we find this transvaluation of the chain of being: "And the moving Way is following/the self-momentum of all becoming." The word "following" translates fa, which means law; thus the ten thousand embody a "law" (or laws) that the Dao must follow. This inverts the parent-child relation. For the first and only time in the text the terms *Dao* and *fa*, the Way and the Law, are connected. We will return to this point when we discuss the Legalist Han Feizi and his debts to Laozi.

In addition to doing away with parental authority, the Dao as Grand Creator also does away with generational continuity and its social concomitant inheritance. The Dao is a pathway and a carrier on which things move forward and backward.

---

[4] Roberts, Moss, <u>Dao De Jing: the Book of the Way (Berkeley: University of California Press 2004)</u> <u>p. 145. All quotes in the Laozi section from this version.</u>

All things find their destiny and destination in their origins, to which all return. From its womb, the Dao first casts onto the earth's surface the totality of its creation, and after each has fulfilled its self-momentum, its life force, it is drawn back into the maw of its creator, passing from existence to negation, from presence to absence (stanza 2). This cuts off the influence of the past by interdicting generational continuity and redefining time as seasonal rather than generational. No previous generation can project itself forward into its successor generation. Each generation begins anew, ab ovo, but none can influence the next cycle of creation, which comes wholly from the Dao, not from the past.

Stanza 60 says that when the ruler rules by Dao the ghosts of the dead will lose their spiritual force, unable to extend themselves in time. Thus Laozi renders obsolescent ancestral authority as well as paternal and parental authority to complete the liberation of the ten thousand, which are now subject to the law of Dao alone, which is paradoxically subject to the laws (or life energy) of the ten thousand, almost like Spinoza's bold conflation of God with Nature. In this grand scheme the human scale is reduced to a tiny proportion of the vastness of things, and man is no measure even of himself. The limits of Confucian doctrine are thus surpassed. The human is removed from the social and returned to the natural order. For Laozi the biological (maternal) principle supersedes the social.

ZHUANGZI

One mission Laozi and Confucius share is the reform of government. For Confucius reform is an ethical mission, comparable to Hegel's confidence in the evolution of the state. For Laozi reform means the reduction of human authority over nature and over other men as well. Zhuangzi, however, is not mission-oriented. One of the most memorable passages in the text is Zhuangzi's refusal to assume a high governmental position, comparing himself to a tortoise. Zhuangzi rejects the invitation brought by the king's emissary, saying "I prefer to be a tortoise wagging my tail in a mudpond than a sacred shell resting on a pillow in the palace." Here Zhuangzi takes a swipe at divination practice (for which the shell was used) that kings resorted to instead of learned advice. "Begone," he told the king's messenger.[5]

The <u>Dao De Jing</u> reduces man to no more than one of the ten thousand and urges mindfulness of his true place in nature together with respect and protection of nature, opposing its exploitation. Zhuangzi goes a step further and looks to achieve identity with nature by breaking away from his social identity. He proves to his close friend that his affinity for a swimming fish is closer than their (human-to-human) friendship.

---

[5] Watson, Burton, Chuang Tzu: Basic Writings, (New York: Columbia Univ Press 1964, 1996) p. 109, translation slightly revised by author.

He has a dream that he is a butterfly winging this way and that, which on awakening wonders if he might not now be a butterfly dreaming he is a human being. These famous anecdotes serve to erase the boundary line, so vigilantly guarded by the Confucians, between the animal and the human realms, the biological and the social, for the difference is to them the very definition of civilization.

How is that boundary line, so essential to culture and civilization, crossed? How does Zhuangzi move back and forth across it? This task is given to the mind, the imagination. For this reason it may be said that Zhuangzi is the Muse of Chinese poetry. In order to fulfill the task the mind has first to be set free of all that hems it in, all shibboleths, conventions, assumptions, duties, idees fixe. Only then can the mind performs feats of imaginative transposition.

In the chapter entitled "The Great Ancestral Teacher," Yan Hui, Confucius' favorite disciple, speaks for Zhuangzi: "I smash up my limbs and body, drive out perception and intellect, cast off form, do away with understanding, and make myself identical with the Great Thoroughfare."[6] In this passage Yan Hui is instructing Confucius in the superiority of Zhuangzi's thought, inverting the teacher-student relation, as Daoism and Confucianism are conflated under the aegis of the *Dao*, which admits no distinctions, social or conceptual. Zhuangzi in effect exchanges identities with Confucius by subverting the identity of Yan Hui, who has learned to demolish himself.

Confucian social thought revolves around self-development, that is the social self (character and identity). Yan Hui is able to host the mind of Zhuangzi as a result of an extreme demolition of the self. Once rid of all the accouterments and encumbrances that trammel it up in the world, the self can as liberated ideation enter into the identity of any other creature or human. The self-other distinction, which is at the heart of Confucian morality, is overcome.

The liberated self-as-imagination suffers no friction in its relationship with external forms. Like the ever-sharp blade of the Butcher Ding in the chapter "The Secret of Caring for Life," the mind is free to move unhindered in any direction, back and forth, like the butterfly. The butcher's knife never dulled because in cutting up oxen it never touched bone or sinew, always striking in the tiny hollows of the carcass. This is the meaning of the description of the sage that opens the second chapter, "On the Same Level with All Things": "body like a withered tree and the mind like dead ashes."[7] The sage is said to have lost his relationship of opposition (*ou*) to all things, that is, to be able freely to move into and out of all phenomena in opposition to nothing. This is how Zhuangzi took Laozi's celebration of the infinite variety of the ten thousand to a new level of intimacy with humanity. All distinctions dissolve in a philosophy that would be better described as synthesizing than polemical, one major difference between the Zhuangzi and the Dao De Jing.

---

[6] Watson, Chuang Tzu, p. 87.   [7] Watson, Chuang Tzu, p. 31.

THE *HAN FEIZI* AND THE LEGALISTS

Han Feizi and his teacher Xunzi were both deeply influenced by the innovative ideas of the two great Daoist masters. However, jn the final analysis, Xunzi was a Confucian who sought to reestablish the teachings of Confucius by subjecting them to critical integration with the approaches of the Daoists, and Mozi too.

Xunzi's purpose was to wrest the reputation of Confucius from the followers of Mencius; Xunzi was an institutionalist and a structuralist and so did not want to depend on the psychological inclination of the ruler to practice good government. However, Xunzi still attached great importance to human factors in government, to counterbalance his emphasis on building government institutions. By comparison Han Feizi was strictly anti-Confucian and used Daoist concepts to refute Confucianism. Like his teacher, Han Feizi was also an institutionalist and a structuralist, but he gave little emphasis to human factors in government, just as Laozi diminished the role of humans in the world. Han Feizi strictly applied the teachings of the Dao De Jing to his philosophy of Law, and even composed two chapters of commentary on parts of Laozi's text, indicating a close relationship of ideas. Han Feizi meant to govern not with role models but with strictly enforced rules and regulations. He saw reward and punishment as the key to effective rule.

Since he diminished the human factor in governing, it is no surprise that one target of Han Feizi's polemic is the Confucian concept of virtue (*de*), which is at the heart of role model theory. As we have seen, in Analects 2.3 law (or administration) was contrasted unfavorably with virtue: lead the people by virtue and they will retain their sense of shame and maintain discipline too. For Han Feizi there can be no maintaining of good order except by law, specifically by reward and punishment, a theory that today would be called absolute behaviorism. Thus the law, which for Confucius could exist as a court inside the mind, is now fully externalized, leaving no theory of human nature with any content other than receptivity to incentives.

For the Confucians inborn capacities and faculties inform virtue and shape virtuous conduct; to the Legalists external conditioning molds good conduct by preventing misconduct. Prohibition not self-governance is the aim of the law.

As Han Feizi states, "If the ruler depends on people doing good of themselves, then within his borders he can count less than ten instances of success. But if he sees to it that they are not allowed to do what is bad, then the whole state can be brought to a uniform level of order. . . . [Successful rulers] devote themselves not to virtue but to law."[8] Han Feizi dismisses entirely the core Confucian values *ren* and *yi*, stating: "To teach people to be benevolent and righteous is the same as saying you can make them wise and long-lived."[9] Also, "Hence the court is filled with men discoursing on the former kings and discussing benevolence and righteousness, and the government cannot escape disorder."[10]

---

[8] Watson, Burton, Han Fei Tzu: Basic Writings (New York: Columbia Univ Press 1964, 1970) p. 125.
[9] Watson, Han Fei Tzu, p. 126–127.   [10] Watson, Han Fei Tzu, p. 109.

Thus for Han Feizi the keepers of the law, the officials, are also the teachers of the people. They do not reach back in time for founding culture-heroes and study their times and their lives. Like Laozi, Han Feizi has no use for remote history. In their teaching officials must confine themselves to inculcating respect for law to ensure the compliance of the people. The idea of the people having some agency, which we find in the Analects and the Mencius, is absent in Legalist thought. The people follow the law as if it were a transcendent force like the Dao. "Keep their bellies full and their minds empty," Laozi advises. Han Feizi follows this advice in his views on governance but also on economics, since he advocates the primacy of agriculture and war. Other occupations such as commerce, crafts, and culture are denounced for complicating the main task of governing, which Han Feizi (following Laozi) wants to reduce to its simplest radical essentials—a Spartan recipe for rule.

Law for Han Feizi has two aspects: in addition to the management of the population there is the need to control officials. His principal warning is not to let any faction, group, or highly placed individual get into a position of favoritism or power sharing. The chapter "The Ruler's Way" advises the ruler to keep the inner circles with which he has to work in the dark about his true aims and intentions. He needs to know them, their interests and capabilities, in order to use them properly. It is equally important that they do not know the ruler, so that they are unable to manipulate him. This will give the ruler absolute dominance over all who serve him.

Thus in the three-centuries-long evolution of political thinking from the time of Confucius, when the state was merely a kingdom rather small in scale and scope, to the time of Xunzi and Han Fei, when the government, economy, and boundaries of the kingdoms had grown in size and complexity far beyond anything imagined at the outset, the role of ruler and minister as "father figure" and valued counselor (at times near equals) has turned into a bureaucracy under an autocracy.

It was essential for this ruler in a new age to keep what the Daoists had called an empty mind, for he was no longer a charismatic leader but an organizer and a director, like a conductor who plays no instrument but leads the orchestra. To fulfill that role the ruler may have no predispositions, prejudices, favorites. He has to keep his options as wide open as possible, and his processing of new information as neutral as possible. Only then can he manage the infinite variety of tasks that face his state. And so, two millennia ago the Chinese had created a polity that to a certain degree resembles the lineaments of the modern state.

BIBLIOGRAPHY

Chan, Alan Kam-leung, ed. 1956. *Mencius: Contexts and Interpretations.* Honolulu: University of Hawai'i Press.

Chen, Guying 陳鼓應 1984. *Laozi Commentary and Review* 老子註譯及評介. Beijing: Zhonghua shuju, Xin hua shu dian.

Goldin, Paul R., ed. 2017. *A Concise Companion to Confucius.* Oxford: John Wiley.

Han, Linhe 韩林合 2006. *Negating the Self to Wander the World: Research on the Philosophy of Zhuangzi* 虚己以游世《庄子》哲学研究. Beijing: Beijing daxue chubanshe.

Kim, Chong Chong 2016. *Zhuangzi's Critique of the Confucians: Blinded by the Human.* Albany: State University of New York Press.

Legge, James 1893, 1971. Confucius: Confucian Analects. Oxford: The Clarendon Press, reprinted by Dover <u>Books.</u>

Legge, James 1895, 1970, The Works of Mencius, (Oxford: The Clarendon Press, reprinted by Dover.

Roberts, Moss 2004. Dao De Jing: The Book of the Way. Berkeley: University of California Press.

Shi, Juehuai 施觉怀 2002. *Han Feizi Commentary* 韩非评传. Nanjing: Nanjing daxue chubanshe.

Wang, Weiwei 王威威 2012. *Research on Han Fei's Thought Taking Huang-Lao as the Foundation* 韩非思想研究: 以黄老为本. Nanjing: Nanjing daxue chubanshe.

Watson, Burton 1970, Mo Tzu: Basic Writings. New York and London: Columbia University Press.

Watson, Burton 1996. Chuang Tzu: Basic Writings. New York and London: Columbia University Press.

Watson, Burton 1970 Han Fei Tzu: Basic Writings. New York and London: Columbia University Press.

Xing, Zhaoliang 邢兆良 1993. *Critical Biography of Mozi* 墨子评传. Nanjing: Nanjing daxue chubanshe.

CHAPTER 32

···

MOZI

···

BY VINCENT S. LEUNG,
LINGNAN UNIVERSITY

IN the earliest biography of Mozi (fl. late fifth century BCE), or Master Mo, we read the
following: "It was said that Mo Di [i.e., Mozi] was a gentleman of the state of Song who
excelled in military defense and practiced moderate expenditure. Some said he was a
contemporary of Confucius; others said he may have come after Confucius."[1] And this is
the entire biography, a mere vignette buried in the pages of the massive compilation that
is the *Records of the Grand Historian* (*Shiji*) by Sima Qian (d. 86 BCE), written almost
three centuries after when Mozi was supposed to have lived. Terse and hesitant, this earliest biography of Mozi nevertheless typifies a predominant pattern in how Mozi was
remembered in ancient China. For all the interest in his ideas, his historical significance
was largely articulated on the basis of his relationship to the career of another, namely
Confucius (551–479 BCE). More specifically, Mozi was remembered as the one who cast
the first stone against Confucius and his followers. He and his followers were among the
earliest and most rancorous critics of the teachings of Confucius. This Mohist tradition,
as it developed in the fourth and third centuries BCE, clearly saw itself as a radical alternative to what it understood to be the Confucian ethical and political dogmas.[2] It was a
war of ideas that the Mohists had wanted, and it was a war that they ultimately lost. In
the centuries to come, while the idea of Confucianism generated ever more ideological
investment and institutional support, Mozi and the intellectual movement that he had
inspired were always teetering on historical oblivion. It was remembered, poorly and
sporadically for much of the past two millennia, as little more than a failed challenge to

---

[1] Sima Qian, *Shiji* 74.2,350. For an excellent recent survey of the little that we know about the life of
Mozi, see Johnston 2010:xviii–xxii; see also Knoblock and Riegel 2013:1–6.

[2] The Mohist tradition persisted and flourished after the time of Mozi in the third and fourth centuries
BCE. Very little is known about its history for certain, except that the followers eventually split into three
factions. For a summary of the reconstruction of this history, see Johnston 2010:xxii–xxv; and Knoblock
and Riegel 2013:7–13. See Graham 1985 for a provocative reconstruction of these three factions of the
Mohist tradition.

Confucius and the early Confucians. It was a road not taken in the intellectual history of ancient China.

This ancient tradition of Mohist thought, though long consigned to the dustbin of history, was never entirely forgotten thanks to the fortuitous survival of its canonical text, the *Mozi*. None of it was written by the master himself but was instead compiled by his followers, as a record of the teachings of the master, over the course of the fourth and third centuries BCE. Different versions of this repository of Mohist thought had been in circulation no later than the start of the Common Era, but it was only in the late eighteenth and nineteenth centuries that we have for the very first time critical editions that aimed at a systematic reconstruction of the original text. On the basis of these philologically sound recensions, studies of the *Mozi* and the history of Mohism at large have experienced a veritable renaissance throughout the twentieth century to today.[3] (Also see Chapter 33 by Carine Defoort and Chapter 31 by Moss Roberts in this book for additional Mozi studies). While we still know almost nothing about the life of Mozi and his followers—we still do not know his exact dates or any verifiable detail of his life, for example—we now have a much clearer view of the cherished ideals that they so fiercely advocated once upon a time in ancient China. It does not change the fact that Mohism was still the road not taken, but now, thanks to more than a century's worth of scholarship, it is at long last a road that one can choose to revisit.

In this chapter, we will do precisely just that. On the basis of the content of the *Mozi*, I will discuss the basic methodologies and core doctrines of the Mohists. To those already familiar with the text, this may seem like a quixotic or even impossible task given the text's disparate nature. It is indeed a sprawling tome with many distinct parts that were written by different individuals at different times. It has the titles for 71 chapters, but only 53 chapters have survived in the extant version. The other 18 chapters were either lost or may have never existed. And the chapters can be divided into at least 5 distinct groups. The first group is the 7 opening chapters, sometimes called the "Epitomes," short essays that offer what seems to be digests of arguments that are more elaborately laid out elsewhere in the text.[4] This is followed by the "Core Chapters" (chapters 8 to 39), the portion of the text that has garnered the most attention from scholars in the last century. It consists of 10 triads on the 10 "core" doctrines of the Mohists (of which 7 chapters are missing), and 2 chapters (with 1 missing) on the many offenses of the Confucians.[5] This is followed by the so-called "Dialectical Chapters" (chapters 40 to 46) that deal with a host of technical subjects including logic, optics, mathematics, and language. The penultimate section (chapters 46 to 50) is sometimes called the "Mohist *Analects*," records of

---

[3] For a survey of modern scholarship on the *Mozi* in mainland China, see Defoort et al. 2011. For a more comprehensive and detailed survey of twentieth-century scholarship on the history of Mohism, see Zheng 2002.

[4] The use of the term "Epitomes" follows Durrant 1975.

[5] Note that for some scholars, the convention is to use the term "Core Chapters" to refer to only chapters 8 to 37, leaving out the two chapters against the Confucians (chapters 38 and 39) as its own section. See, for example, Defoort and Standaert 2013:4.

purported dialogues between Mozi and his contemporaries. Finally, the last group (chapters 52 to 71, of which only 11 chapters are extant) is on military science. There is a basic consensus that the "Dialectical Chapters" and chapters on military science were probably the last to be written by late followers of the Mohist tradition.[6] Beyond that, there is very little agreement on the details of the textual history of the *Mozi*. It is a veritable rabbit hole of textual accretions and corruptions that has reached us over the course of more than two millennia. Many scholars have burrowed deeply into it, chasing after clues of all sorts to reconstruct its complex textual history, often with vastly different results in the end.[7]

The *Mozi* is most definitely a composite text, but yet so much of it is remarkably coherent in terms of its concerns and methods. It strikes one less as a grab bag of scattered pieces than a series of thoughtful elaborations on a common set of problematics with shared interpretative strategies. This is especially true in the case of the "Core Chapters," whose 10 triads of essays and the one polemic against the Confucians constitute the bulk of the extant version of the text. In the past few decades, scholars have convincingly demonstrated that each of the triads is comprised of chronologically distinct materials with very significant differences between them, pointing to either partisan bickering or an evolution of the Mohist tradition.[8] But yet, it is important to remember that these differences within the "Core Chapters" and the *Mozi* at large are so eminently discernible in the first place because they are articulated on a common ground of ideological concerns and interpretive methods foundational to what we now recognize as the Mohist tradition of thought. In the rest of this chapter, in contrast to this recent scholarship that emphasizes the internal differences within the *Mozi*, I will instead attempt to delineate this common ground on which the evolution of the Mohist tradition was possible in the first place.

This account of the basic elements constitutive of the Mohist tradition will be related in two parts in the rest of this chapter. The first will be on the key interpretive methods found in the *Mozi*, and the second will be on the text's core doctrines that result from the application of its methods. It will be primarily based on the "Core Chapters" of the text. I will also draw on the "Epitomes" and the "Mohist *Analects*" occasionally, but only minimal references will be made to the "Dialectical Chapters" and the ones on military science, which are the most corrupted and still most understudied portions of the *Mozi*.

[6] These are the least-studied portion of the *Mozi*. See Graham (1978) for the most thorough discussion of the "Dialectical Chapters" to date, and Yates (1980) for a discussion of the chapters on military science.

[7] For a basic summary of the textual history of the *Mozi*, see Loewe (1993) 336–341. See Watanabe 1962–1963; Brooks 2010; and Maeder 1992 for three different reconstructions of the composition of the text in the last half century. See, also, Johnston 2010:xxv–xxxiv; and Knoblock and Riegel 2013:14–25, for the history of transmission of the text in later periods.

[8] Graham (1985) argues that we can identify the three ideological factions within the Mohist tradition in the "Core Chapters." The edited volume by Defoort and Standaert, *Mozi as an Evolving Text* (2013), approaches the text as a document of the evolution of the Mohist tradition in the fourth and third century BCE, with great interpretive dividends.

ETIOLOGICAL METHOD OF THE *MOZI*

The *Mozi*, more than any other text from ancient China, is interested in articulating its own methodology. This stands in sharp contrast to other classics from this period, such as the Confucian *Analects* or the *Daodejing*, whose complex hermeneutics were never made explicit but were always just quietly embodied in their arguments. Mozi and his followers, however, are anxious for readers to know the methods with which they arrived at their positions. And for them, the reason for this epistemological transparency is simple; part of their arguments is that only by knowing and adhering to objective investigative methods can we discover truths about the world. Without methods, there will be no direction, and without direction, we will be lost in a fog of confusion. As the text argues:

> Master Mo says: When making a statement, we must first establish the standards before speaking. If we do not first establish the standards, it would be like trying to figure out the direction of sunrise and sunset with the surface of a revolving potter's wheel; even though we may still be able to recognize the difference between the two directions, we will not be able to get the correct measurements in the end.[9]

And what are these "standards"? The text continues with the following pronouncement, that for any statement we can evaluate its veracity by "three criteria":

> Therefore, when making a statement, there are three criteria [that we must follow]. What are the three criteria? They are evaluation, origin, and application. By evaluation, I mean evaluating the statement according to the affairs of great kings and former sages. By origin, I mean corroborating the statement with the sensory perceptions of the people. By application, I mean that we should implement it as a policy in the country and observe its effects on the people. These are the three criteria. (*Mozi jiangu* 37.252)

So, we are to assess a statement with exemplary precedents from the past, empirical testimonies from individuals, and its practical effectiveness among the people. Elsewhere in the *Mozi*, we will find two more iterations of these "three criteria." They are largely similar, except in one instance the second criterion, still referred to as the "origin," has nothing to do with the collective sense of the people but a "corroboration with the writings of the former kings" (*Mozi jiangu* 36.247–248). Reading through the *Mozi*, a good case can be made that it does practice what it teaches for the most part, especially within

---

[9] Sun, *Mozi jiangu*, 37.252. All references to the original text of the *Mozi* are based on this classic edition compiled by Sun Yirang (2001) in the late nineteenth century. Citations will be in-text in the rest of the chapter, with the chapter number followed by the page number. All translations are my own, unless otherwise noted. I am indebted to the excellent translations by Johnston (2010); Knoblock and Reigel (2013); and Watson (2003).

the confine of the "Core Chapters." We do see, time and time again, applications of one or more of these three criteria when proffering its own arguments or dismantling those of others. Of the three criteria, or four if we count one in the variant version, the most ubiquitous by far is the text's invocation of the past, namely the exemplary deeds and writings of the kings and sages from antiquity. On first reading of the *Mozi*, this may seem to be one of the more pedestrian aspects of the text, given how prevalent references to the past are throughout the entire ancient Chinese corpus, but upon closer examination this historicist tendency actually reveals itself to be the effect of a very specific utilization of the past, what I would call its etiological method, as I will explain later in the chapter, that informs the philosophy of the entire text.[10] Let us now turn our attention to this aspect of the *Mozi* in order to appreciate its method beyond this overt declaration of the "three criteria."

References to the past abound in the *Mozi*. Invocation of antiquity is a common gesture across the entire ancient Chinese corpus, but what actually constitutes antiquity in each text is never quite the same. This points to the fact that the past was a field of cultural capital susceptible to various appropriations and mobilizations in the contentious debates between different intellectual traditions in ancient China. In the case of the *Mozi*, among its great number of references to the past, one theme that quickly emerges is its celebration of the kings and sages from antiquity. Oftentimes, these legendary figures are unspecified, referred to simply as "sages" (*sheng*) and "kings" (*wang*) from times past (*xi, gu*). In one of the most elaborate, celebratory accounts of these unnamed kings and sages from the past, they were lauded for the civilizing progress that they had made through their inventions of the idea of shelter, agriculture, clothing, and transportation in antiquity (*Mozi jiangu* 6.125). In numerous other accounts in the *Mozi*, they were celebrated for embodying the very same cardinal virtues that the Mohist were trying to champion; in the chapter "Moderate Expenditure II" ("Jie yong zhong," *Mozi jiangu* 21), for instance, certain "enlightened kings" (*mingwang*) and "sages" (*shengren*) were said to have embraced the ideal of frugality, and for that very reason they became the effective rulers that they were (*Mozi jiangu* 21.163). Moreover, as if to reassure the readers that these laudatory remarks scattered throughout the *Mozi* are not mere platitudes, the text time and again quotes from ancient speeches and writings attributed to these kings and sages and declares repeatedly that it relies on the transmitted writings of these legendary figures.[11] So, these are not just banal celebrations of antiquity, perceptions of the past through rose-tinted glasses, but are in fact thoughtful historical assessments based on careful studies of the records of the past.

Not all past figures are celebrated, though, in the *Mozi*. These laudatory accounts of the "enlightened kings" (*mingwang*) are sometimes paired with harsh condemnations of

[10] This prevalence of historical references in the *Mozi* has attracted a fair amount of scholarly commentaries. Miranda Brown (2013) recently argues that this invention of "ancient authority" is in fact one of the most innovative attributes of the *Mozi*, in contrast to earlier scholarship that sees this backward gaze of the text as no more than a remnant of the prevalent conservative attitude toward the past in ancient China. See, for example, Graham 1978:11–12.

[11] See *Mozi jiangu* 16.111, 27.185, 27.186, 31.214, 36.250, 37.254, 47.207, and 49.431.

"violent kings" (*baowang*). While the virtues of the good kings and sages elevated humanity and gave us a civilizing order over time, the ethical deviances of the violent kings debased humanity, throwing the whole world into a despairing chaos that was only rectified when the next sage came along. These legendary villains too are often unnamed, and when the text does care to name names, they are usually a relatively small cast of characters. The "enlightened kings" or "sages" are typically a cast of four, namely the founders of the great dynasties from the past: Yu, Tang, King Wen, and King Wu; sometimes two even more ancient figures, namely Yao and Shun, would be added (*Mozi jiangu* 9.46). The "violent kings" is almost always just a cast of four characters, namely Jie, Zhou, You, and Li, whose various transgressions helped bring down the very same dynasties (i.e., Xia, Shang, and Western Zhou) that the other four good kings had created (*Mozi jiangu* 9.54–55). The text's vision of the past is vast, chronologically speaking, stretching from the beginning of civilization in great antiquity to the end of the most recent dynasty, but it is populated by only a few individuals about whom the text's judgments are anything but ambiguous.

But what is the point behind these celebrations of the kings and sages from antiquity? What useful lessons are there beyond just the fact that very good and very bad men once lived in the distant past? What does it mean to evaluate a statement about the "affairs of great kings of former ages" according to the "three criteria"? To be sure, it is not to simply replicate what the sages and kings had done; we do not need, for instance, the invention of shelter and agriculture once more. The point, rather, is to learn the methods with which they were able to come up with precisely the right measures, to cultivate the correct virtues in themselves and others, in order to restore order to the world or, better yet, to give it an even greater, more civilized order. So, it is not a matter of what these past kings and sages had done, but how they knew what needed to be done in the first place.

And for the *Mozi*, they knew what needed to be done because they all had this ability to diagnose the origins of the disorder in their own times. Nothing ever comes from nothing, and if we do live in a time of chaos and strife, anything short of a perfect order, there has to be a reason for how the disorder came into being in the first place. It follows that we must first understand the causes leading to the disorder before we would know what we can do to fix it. As the text argues, in its typically repetitive prose, "Sages who took it upon themselves to order the world must first know the origins of disorder. If they do [know the origins of disorder], they would be able to give order to the world. If they do not [know the origins of disorder], then they won't be able to give order to the world" (*Mozi jiangu* 14.99).[12] Immediately following this pronouncement, the text drives home this point with a medical analogy:

> It is like when a doctor is treating a person's illness, he must first find out the causes of the illness, and only then can he properly treat it. If he does not know the causes

---

[12] This repetitiveness is typical of the "Core Chapters" as a whole. For an excellent discussion of the literary quality of the *Mozi* and how it relates to its philosophical agenda, see Denecke 2011:128–152.

of the illness, then he will not be able to treat it. How is this any different for those who wanted to rectify disorders [in the world]? He must first find out the causes of the disorders, and only then can he rectify them. If he does not understand the causes from which the disorders first arose, then he would not be able to rectify them. Sages who took it upon themselves to give order to the world cannot fail to study the causes from which disorders first arose. (*Mozi jiangu* 14.99)

This search for the etiology of disorder is an ability that the *Mozi* ascribes to the kings and sages of the past, and it is what we must be able to do once again if we hope to put an end to the disorder in our own time. To assess the veracity of a statement, we refer to the standards of the "three criteria"; in the end, this epistemological apparatus is to be directed in the service of this crucial, urgent fundamental inquiry into the origins of disorder. The kings and sages in antiquity understood this, and therefore they cultivated virtues and created institutions that were designed to counter the harmful causes that lie at the root of the chaos in their own time. Whatever good work that they had done, the good order that they had once created had obviously fallen into disrepair and been perverted by our degeneracy over time. We have once again lapsed into chaos and must await the next sages, perhaps someone like Mozi and his followers, to perform a proper diagnosis of the ills of our time. Humanity is pathologically prone toward disorder, and in times of chaos, we must perform etiological analyses, understanding the origins of our disorder, before we can remedy it. In this latter age, however, we do have one advantage over the ancient sages and former kings—we can study the work that they had done, thanks in part to the writings that they had passed down to us, and find guidance in the virtues they had so wonderfully cultivated and the methods with which they did what they did.

This commitment to the etiological method, this faith in the utility of the search for the origins of disorder, is a defining feature of the *Mozi*. While it is not the only text from early China that shares this harrowing vision of a pathologically, chronically disorderly humanity, relieved only on occasions by the grace of a few good men who truly understand the world, it is the only tradition that is so singularly invested in this etiological method as the necessary first step in our periodic redemption. This is particularly evident in the "Core Chapters," whose pages are filled with forceful diagnoses of the ills of the world (and how we can address them, as we will discuss in the next section). This impulse for etiologies is also detectable, if only faintly, in the rest of the text. In the "Dialectical Chapters," for example, the long list of definitions for basic ethical and political categories tacitly reflects the belief that words and their meanings have been so thoroughly corrupted that they need to be properly defined once again (e.g., *Mozi jiangu* 40.285). Perversion of the meaning of words is therefore yet another probable cause of our disorderly world, awaiting the enlightened few for their rectifications. All in all, a Mohist is one who assumes the role of a "good doctor" (*liangyi*), to use the text's own expression, who patiently diagnoses what really plagues us and then prescribes the remedies that we need (*Mozi jiangu* 47.404).

CORE DOCTRINES OF THE *MOZI*

And what, according to the *Mozi*, are the remedies we need? What are its authors' diagnoses of all that is wrong with the world? To these all-important questions, the text gives not just one but a multitude of answers. They are what we now understand to be the "core doctrines" of the *Mozi*, the basic tenets of the Mohist tradition that are the results of this methodological intervention that we discussed in the previous section. Articulated mostly in the "Core Chapters," they do not seem to aggregate to a comprehensive manifesto, like interlocking pieces of a full puzzle, but rather they represent key concerns and polemics of the Mohist tradition as it developed over the course of the fourth and third centuries BCE. In the rest of this chapter I will present a brief, select overview of these core doctrines. In them, we shall see the Mohist invectives against the foolish things that we do to have unleashed this cruel chaos in the world, rueful lamentations over how we, as human beings, tend to do the very things that are inimical to our collective well-being, and earnest calls for virtuous reforms that will restore us to our orderly, flourishing existence.

Diagnoses of the ills of humanity abound in the "Core Chapters" of the *Mozi*, and they are the basis on which these core doctrines are presented and justified. Some of these diagnoses are historically specific, while others are more theoretical. Let us begin with one of the most theoretical, sweeping diagnoses in the whole text, on a key reason why we were originally mired in a brutish, hostile existence before the sages' civilizing interventions:

> In antiquity, when humanity first came into being, in a time before there were laws and governance, it was said that "people had different principles." So, with one person, there was one principle; when there were two people, there would be two different principles; when there were ten people, there would be ten different principles. When the number of people multiplied, these so-called "principles" also multiplied. So, a person always upheld his own principle while condemning those of others. In the end, they all condemned one another. At home, fathers, sons, and brothers became resentful of one another, and they grew apart because they cannot live together harmoniously. Out in the world, people harmed each other with water, fire, and poisons. Those with strength to spare did not care to work for other people; people would rather let their excess wealth rot than to share with others; and people keep their wisdom secret and refuse to teach one another. The whole world was in chaos, like that of birds and beasts. (*Mozi jiangu* 11.74–75)

So, in the beginning, there was a diversity in our individual beliefs, and even though that was naturally how we were, it was nevertheless what plunged us into an animalistic chaos where we all became indifferent or even hostile to one another. What then was the solution? The text goes on to say that having recognized this as the cause of disorder, the enlightened few saw the necessity for a government, headed by the most worthy individual and his capable subordinates, that will impose, by force if necessary, a uniform set of principles upon the entire world. Diversity of opinions, as the cause of disorder, is to be eradicated in favor of a uniformity of principles disseminated and enforced through a hierarchical structure from the head of the government to the populace (*Mozi jiangu* 11).

But what are the sources of these uniform principles that the head of the government is supposed to impose upon the world? How are we to know that they are indeed the right principles, truly beneficial to all, and not arbitrary decrees of an authoritarian regime? We know this cannot be the case because, according to the *Mozi*, the very existence of such a government depends on the approval of the moral cosmos that the text calls "Heaven" (*tian*). It is a word that enjoyed extremely wide currency across the intellectual landscape of ancient China, and in the *Mozi* it is specifically understood as the source of all moral principles in the entire cosmos. Our compliance with these righteous, invariable moral truths will lead to our flourishing, with ever more life, wealth, and order, and conversely, our violations of them will inevitably lead to deaths, poverty, and disorder. And as if Heaven is playing a cruel joke on us, none of us is born with knowledge of these moral truths inherent in the cosmos, but we must struggle mightily to discover them with proper reasoning like, for example, the aforementioned "three criteria." In other words, for the *Mozi*, moral principles are not human constructs but a fact of the cosmos, always impersonal and always true. It is up to us to either discover and abide by them or ignore and fail to live by them at our own peril. This is no easy task, of course, to try to discern "Heaven's will" (*tian zhi*), as the text calls it, but luckily not all of us have to do it. The one person with the greatest and finest understanding of Heaven should be recognized as the most worthy man of all, installed as the ruler of men who, as already discussed, will govern in accordance with these cosmically proper principles from Heaven. We, the largely ignorant masses, will in turn learn to suppress our natural inclination to proffer our own idiosyncratic "principles" and happily defer to the higher principles taught to us by our superiors. Such a government, headed by the "Son of Heaven" (*tianzi*), as the text calls him, given its absolute conformity to Heaven's will, is certain to flourish for the benefit of all. It will lead to more life, wealth, and order, the criteria that the *Mozi* sees as the measure of a good society. Likewise, a government headed by a charlatan ignorant or dismissive of the will of Heaven will inevitably lead to more deaths, poverty, and disorder, and it will be met with certain destructions sooner or later (*Mozi jiangu* 26, 27).

The ancient sages and legendary kings that the text invokes time and again, as we discussed earlier, were precisely these enlightened figures who understood Heaven and translated its principles into the world of humanity for the benefit of all. This is how they managed to emancipate us from animal savagery and enabled our civilizing progress. In this latter day, Mozi is precisely such an enlightened figure who, according to the text, "possesses Heaven's will, like a wheelwright holding a compass or a carpenter holding a square" (*Mozi jiangu* 27.187–188). With "standards and rules" that he had successfully deduced from Heaven, Mozi would have been the one to set the world right, if only the world had listened (*Mozi* 28.193–194). It was a measure of how far we had fallen that Mozi was only able to cultivate a limited following and never rose to position of sufficient prominence to implement these cosmic principles for all. Our fog of moral confusion was so immense that even the righteous voice of someone like Mozi, who truly understood Heaven, got muffled. Here, we see the logic behind the impulse among his followers to write up his teachings, so that his important discoveries of the moral principles of Heaven can be preserved for an appreciative, redeemable audience in a later age, not unlike sages and kings in antiquity who, according to the text, also committed their ideas to writing in order to properly instruct later generations (*Mozi jiangu* 16.111).

Presuming the existence of a moral cosmos ("Heaven") and conforming to its principles are two core doctrines that one finds in the "Core Chapters" of the *Mozi*. The other core doctrines are likewise presented with the conceit that they are the objective, immutable principles from Heaven. In one triad of essays, entitled "Exalt the Worthy" ("Shangxian," *Mozi jiangu* 8, 9, 10), we are told that the kings and sages of antiquity "took their standards from Heaven," and so when they made official appointments, it was always based on merit alone (*Mozi jiangu* 9.54). Worthy individuals, meaning those who understand the idea of Heaven and behave in ways that contribute to the generation of life, wealth, and order of the group, are to be rewarded, and likewise, unworthy individuals deleterious to the well-being of the group are to be punished. Government bureaucracy should be purely meritocratic, because Heaven is purely meritocratic. And this is the remedy for the prevalence of aristocratic or plutocratic privileges, at the expense of meritocracy, a cause of the world's disorder, in the governments of his time.

Another such cosmically sanctioned principle is the idea of "impartiality" (*jian'ai*), considered by many scholars to be a signature doctrine of the Mohist tradition (*Mozi jiangu* 14, 15, 16). The diagnosis in this case, for the disorder in the world, is that people "do not love each other" (*Mozi jiangu* 14.91). The remedy is what the text calls "impartiality," a radical variation of the Golden Rule where a person loves every other person in the world as much as he loves himself (*Mozi jiangu* 14.92). In other words, one achieves "impartiality" by being partial to no one, not even himself. It is, according to the text, the basis for all ethical behaviors. "If one loves another as much as he loves himself, then how can anyone in the world be unfilial? If he regards his father, older brother, and lord as himself, how is it possible not to be filial? Can anyone not be compassionate? If he regards his younger brother and subordinates like himself, how is it possible not to be compassionate?" (*Mozi jiangu* 14.92–93). The text admits that this demand to undo the hierarchy of privileges between the self and others, creating a non-distinction between the two, can be extremely challenging. But should we all achieve this, we would have created a perpetually peaceful order where there will never be any transgression of any kind between individuals, their families, and their states (*Mozi jiangu* 14.93).

This pacifist position resonates with another core doctrine, one that calls for an end to offensive warfare, which the text considers simply to be a case of mass murder (*Mozi jiangu* 17.119). This is one of the few core doctrines that are negatively defined, that is to say, they are about what we shouldn't do rather than what we should do. We also should not indulge in lavish musical performances, the text argues, despite the tremendous pleasure that they may afford us, because they do little to further the generation of life, wealth, and order (*Mozi jiangu* 32). We should also not subscribe to fatalism, the belief that our fates are more or less predetermined, which was really an invention by the violent kings in antiquity to convince their suffering people to accept their unnecessary misery (*Mozi jiangu* 36.249–250). Finally, the most withering polemic in the *Mozi* for what we should not engage in is reserved for the teachings of Confucius and the Confucians, a group that the text calls "Ru." Nothing that Confucius and his followers ever taught or did was met with the approval by the Mohists. They indulged in unnecessary rituals, whose lavishness had a corrupting effects on men, and subscribed to the idea of fatalism, which made all their followers become apathetic sloths (*Mozi jiangu* 39.263–264). They also blindly followed past traditions and failed to understand the importance of innovations (*Mozi jiangu* 39.265–267). These are just a few of the many accusations in the chapter "Against the Confucians II" ("Fei Ru xia," *Mozi* 39), the oldest polemics against the Confucius and his followers.

These negative tracts on the wastefulness of extraneous rituals and lavish musical performances are further elaborated in two triads of essays on the ethics of moderate expenditure. One of the triads, called "Moderate Expenditure" ("Jie yong," *Mozi jiangu* 20, 21), inveighs against wasteful spending of all sorts, especially among the ruling elite, and the other focuses on the virtue of moderation in funerary rites ("Jie zang," *Mozi jiangu* 25). While it recognizes the value of a proper burial, it nevertheless considers any lavishness that exceeds the basic purpose of the funerary rites, namely a sense of closure for the living and proper decomposition of the deceased, as wrongheaded. Functional arguments like these in the *Mozi* have led some recent scholars to label Mohism as an utilitarian ethics. This is of course an overt attempt to inscribe Mohism in the world history of philosophy by inviting comparison with Western utilitarianism developed by figures such as Jeremy Bentham (1748–1832) and John Stuart Mill (1806–1873).[13]

There is one more core doctrine in the *Mozi*, and it is one that may seem somewhat confounding at first. It is the text's call for a belief in the existence of ghosts and spirits (*gui*) and also in their power to actively intervene in human affairs. For a text that is supposedly appreciative of logical deductions and empirical evidence, it seems surprising that it would argue for the existence of something that is so elusive and intangible. But upon reading the chapter "Explaining Ghosts and Spirits III" ("Ming gui xia," *Mozi jiangu* 31), we see that it is not at all an intellectual lapse but is entirely consistent with the rest of the core doctrines. As we discussed earlier, in the *Mozi* Heaven consists of a set of moral principles. If we comply with them, we will be rewarded, and if we violate them, we will be punished. In this moral cosmos, therefore, ghosts and spirits are simply the agents who are always observing our actions, and reward or punish us accordingly. So, our belief in them, as this superhuman system of moral surveillance, will certainly make us behave more ethically, and for that utilitarian reason alone it is enough for the text to argue for it. It is less an ontological argument for the true existence of ghosts and spirits than a pragmatic doctrine for its supposed beneficial effects in bringing us closer to the ways of Heaven.

---

[13] See, for example, Ahern (1976) and Goldin (2001) for a critique of this heavy emphasis on the *Mozi* as a work of utilitarian ethics in recent secondary scholarship.

So, these are the core doctrines of the *Mozi*: Heaven's will, uniformity of principles, meritocracy, impartiality, moderation in expenditure, moderation in funerary rites, the existence of ghosts of spirits, anti-warfare, anti-music, anti-fatalism, and anti-Confucians. For more than two centuries, these powerful ideas from Mozi and his followers captivated large swaths of the intellectual landscape of ancient China. They were the objects of admiration or derision, and either way, they were widely disseminated ideas that cannot be ignored. But then the tradition vanished. For reasons that we still do not quite fully understand, these ideas disappeared from virtually all discussion among the political and literary elite beginning around the turn of the Common Era.[14] The tradition was lost for so long, and now it has been found again with the rediscovery of its canonical text and the flurry of scholarship on it in the last century. Heaven's will has at long last revealed itself again, as Mozi might have said, and since its moral principles are objectively true and infallible for all times and all places, they will serve us in the here and now just as well as they would have served those in ancient China, if only we are wise enough to subjugate our opinionated selves and submit to those worthy individuals who understand the dictates of Heaven.

BIBLIOGRAPHY

Ahern, Dennis M. 1976. "Is Mo Tzu a Utilitarian?" *Journal of Chinese Philosophy* 3(2):185–193.

Brooks, A. Taeko 2010. "The Mician Ethical Chapters." *Warring States Papers* 1:100–118.

Brown, Miranda 2013. "Mozi's Remaking of Ancient Authority." In *The* Mozi *as an Evolving Text: Different Voices in Early Chinese Thought*. Edited by C. Defoort and N. Standaert, 143–174. Leiden and Boston: Brill.

Defoort, Carine, Annick Gijsbers, and Ting-Mien Lee 2011. "Mo Zi Research in the People's Republic of China." *Contemporary Chinese Thought* 42(4):3–11.

Defoort, C., and N. Standaert, eds. 2013. *The* Mozi *as an Evolving Text: Different Voices in Early Chinese Thought*. Leiden and Boston: Brill.

Denecke, Wiebke 2011. *The Dynamics of Masters Literature: Early Chinese Thought from Confucius to Han Feizi*. Cambridge, MA: Harvard University Press.

Durrant, Stephen 1975. "An Examination of Textual and Grammatical Problems in Mo Tzu." PhD dissertation, Seattle: University of Washington.

Or, Why There Is More to Mohism than Utilitarian Ethics." In *How Should We Live? Comparing Ethics in Ancient China and Greco-Roman Antiquity*. Edited by R. A. H. King and Dennis Schilling, 63–91. Berlin: De Gruyter.

Graham, A. C. 1978. *Later Mohist Logic, Ethics and Science*. Hong Kong and London: Chinese University Press.

Graham, A. C. 1985. *Divisions in Early Mohism Reflected in the Core Chapters of Mo-tzu*. Singapore: Institute of East Asian Philosophies.

Johnston, Ian 2010. *Mozi: A Complete Translation*. New York: Columbia University Press.

---

[14] For Mohism under the Han dynasty (206 BCE–220 CE), the last period in which the tradition persisted before its modern rediscovery, see Nylan (2009).

Knoblock, John, and Jeffrey Riegel 2013. *Mozi: A Study and Translation of the Ethical and Political Writings*. Berkeley: Institute of East Asian Studies and the University of California Berkeley.

Loewe, Michael, ed. 1993. *Early Chinese Texts: A Bibliographical Guide*. Berkeley, CA: Society for the Study of Early China and the Institute of East Asian Studies.

Maeder, Erik W. 1992. "Some Observations on the Composition of the 'Core Chapters' of the *Mozi*." *Early China* 17:27–82.

Nylan, Michael 2009. "Kongzi and Mozi, the Classcists (Ru) and the Mohists (Mo) in Classical-Era Thinking." *Oriens-Extremus* 48:1–20.

Sima, Qian 司馬遷 1982. *Grand Archivist's Records Shiji* 史記. Beijing: Zhonghua shuju.

Sun, Yirang 孫詒讓 2001. *Mozi: Critical Exegesis* 墨子閒詁. Beijing: Zhonghua shuju.

Watanabe, Takashi 渡邊卓 1962–1963. "Periods of Composition of Various Chapters of the *Mozi* 墨子諸篇の著作年代." *Tōyō Gakuhō* 45(3):1–38 (part 1); and 45(4) (March 1963): 20–38 (part 2).

Watson, Burton, trans. 2003. *Mozi: Basic Writings*. New York: Columbia University Press.

Yates, Robin D. S. 1980. "The Mohists on Warfare: Technology, Technique, and Justification." *Journal of the American Academy of Religion* 47(3):549–603.

Zheng, Jiewen 鄭傑文 2002. *History of Mozi Scholarship in the Twentieth Century* 二十世紀墨學研究史. Beijing: Qinghua daxue chubanshe.

CHAPTER 33

··

MOHISM AND THE EVOLVING NOTION OF *JIAN AI*

··

BY CARINE DEFOORT, UNIVERSITY OF LEUVEN

MOHISM is the philosophical school (*Mojia* 墨家) or trend of thought (*Moxue* 墨學) named after Mozi 墨子 (Mo-tzu, Master Mo, Mo Di 墨翟, c. 479–381 BCE). The book *Mozi* was largely written by successive groups of followers in approximately the fourth and third centuries BCE. It was recorded in the Han dynasty as a work of 71 *pian*, only 53 of which have been transmitted (*Hanshu* 30:1738). Since the twentieth century—more specifically since Hu Shi (1891–1962)—scholars tend to divide the book into five parts. Part 1 consists of the opening chapters (chaps. 1–7, also called "epitomes"), generally considered late essays with more-or-less Mohist ideas; part 2 consists of the core chapters (chaps. 8–37, also called "essays," "triads," or "triplets"), usually seen as the original core of Mohist political and moral teaching; part 3 contains the dialectical chapters (chaps. 40–45, also called *Mobian* 墨辯 or "Mohist Dialectics"), attributed to later Mohists discussing logic, language, and science; part 4 consists of the dialogue chapters (chaps. 46–50, or "Mohist Analects") portraying the master in conversation with disciples, rulers, or rivals; and part 5 contains the defense chapters (chaps. 52–71, also called "military chapters") giving advice for the defense of a city. Chapter 39, "Fei ru," wavers between parts 2 and 4.[1]

Early Mohism or Mozi himself are usually associated with a philosophy or thought system, even though the earliest stories about Mo Di may have presented him more as a master craftsman than a teacher or philosopher (Graham 1989:33). The core idea of Mohism is often said to be *jian ai* 兼愛, variously translated as "universal love," "impartial caring," "concern for everyone," "inclusive care," and so on. This claim is not unfounded: the portrayal of Mo Di as a fervent promoter of this type of inclusive or

---

[1] Dating of the various parts and chapters is tentative: this chapter mostly follows Watanabe 1977 and Fraser 2012.

universal care is as old as the book *Mozi* itself and still constitutes the most common characterization of Mohist philosophy today. But the association of Mozi with *jian ai* is not static nor unchanging. This chapter therefore traces the major historical steps of this association. These different steps are not only a good introduction to Mohism but also to the meanders of Chinese intellectual history. This overview roughly distinguishes three steps: the pre-imperial, imperial, and post-imperial eras. Each step contains its own major portrayal of Mohism in relation to the idea of *jian ai*: First, in the Warring States period, the idea of "inclusive care" gradually comes into being along with the creation of the book *Mozi*, but the connection between Mohism and inclusive care is neither exclusive nor constant. From the mid Han dynasty onward the concept dominates Mencius's critical portrayal of Mozi as the immoral promoter of ungraded love; divergence from this view in the Tang, Ming, and Qing is exceptional and cautious. And finally in the twentieth century *jian ai* reemerges as the most valuable among the "ten Mohist theses"; its translation and philosophical interpretation become topics of contention and reflection.

The emergence of *jian ai* in the pre-imperial era

It is generally believed that the earliest promotion and defense of *jian ai* occurred in the book *Mozi*, more specifically in its core chapters. The "triads" or "triplets" are presented as ten sets of three consecutive chapters carrying the same title distinguished only by *shang* 上 (Upper), *zhong* 中 (Middle), and *xia* 下 (Lower). The idea of *jian ai* appears for the first time in what is probably the oldest triplet, namely the three "Jian ai" chapters, respectively dated around ca. 380 BCE (chapter 14, "Jian ai, shang"), 350 BCE (chapter 15, "Jian ai, zhong"), and ca. 300 BCE (chapter 16, "Jian ai, xia") (Watanabe 1977:6–8). Most scholars treat these three chapters indiscriminately as representative of one and the same central Mohist idea preached by the founder of Mohism, Mo Di. But I have argued that the ideal of inclusive care was probably not promoted at the very outset of Mohism, and that the "Jian ai" chapters attest to the gradual emergence of the ideal among the followers of Mo Di (Defoort 2013). The oldest or Upper chapter ends by stating that "this is what Master Mozi meant when he insisted that we must encourage people to care for others (*ai ren*)" (*Mozi* 14:24/22). The expression *jian ai* does not occur in this chapter, but the author—presumably one of Mozi's followers—explains what his master must have meant by his injunction to care for others: he wanted people to "care for each other" (*xiang ai*) instead of "caring for themselves" (*zi ai*). In the latter part of this chapter, the word *jian* (inclusively, universally, or impartially) makes its first appearance, but only as an adverb indicating a scope of caring that goes beyond relationships of traditional reciprocity: people should "inclusively care for each other" (*jian xiang ai*), hence also for members of other clans or states. What the author seems to have in mind is basically that one should not attack or rob others. In the second or Middle "Jian ai" chapter, the idea of *jian* is for the first time singled out as a concept (inclusiveness, universality, or impartiality) and defended against the attacks of supposed opponents. These opponents are remarkably mild, admitting that inclusiveness is indeed a good thing, their only worry being its feasibility. An important response by the Mohist authors is that in the long run inclusiveness will benefit those who apply it in their own caring, because "who cares for others will inevitably as a consequence be cared for by them; one who benefits others will inevitably as a consequence be benefited by them" (*Mozi* 15:25/24–25). Compared to the previous chapter, these authors speak of caring more actively and specifically, including the assistance to childless widowers and small orphans. The third or Lower chapter, finally, insists even further on caring for the weak, poor, vulgar, stupid, and even the dead, hence including people from whom little or no reward is to be expected. It is also in this chapter that the expression *jian ai* occurs once and for the very first time: King Wen's impartial caring for everyone is compared to the sun and the moon spreading warmth and light over the whole world (*Mozi* 16:29/1–3). Thus, in the "Jian ai" triplet—probably before the current titles were added to the text[2]—the idea of inclusive care had barely emerged.

In the slightly later "Tian zhi" (Will of Heaven) triplet, consisting of chapters 26, 27, and 28, respectively dated around 280, 260, and 240 BCE (Fraser 2012; Watanabe 1977:15–16), the idea of inclusive care takes flight. The expression *jian ai* occurs several times in the description of Heaven as a political model of caring equally for everybody without expecting anything in return. Heaven is even quoted praising the sage kings because "all those from whom I care, they also inclusively cared for; and all those whom I benefit, they also inclusively benefited. Their care for others was expansive and their benefit to others was most substantial" (*Mozi* 26:43/11–12). Even though the expression *jian ai* does not literally occur in any of the other core chapters—at least not in the Daozang version[3]—it is clear that their authors actively promote care for others, as well as the expansion of one's scope of caring beyond the limits of one's own family or state. Both *jian* and *ai* seem to become increasingly important in the *Mozi*. Even though the Dialectical chapters are difficult to reconstruct and interpret, one can tell that the authors—especially of chapter 44, "Da qu" (Choosing the greater)—were intrigued or concerned by the notions of caring (*ai*) and benefiting (*li*), their nature and limits, the difference between intentions and effects, and the combination of an inclusive concern with a division of tasks. These reflections show that the Mohist promotion of inclusive care may have been increasingly in need of polemic defense. Indeed, some Dialogue chapters—especially chapter 46, "Gengzhu"—show that Master Mo was explicitly identified with the ideal of

---

[2] Archeological finds show that Warring States manuscripts mentioned no author and seldom had titles. Dating the chapter titles is therefore tentative. They may have been invented by late Warring States or Han editors, such as Liu Xiang and Liu Xin, who are usually considered the editors of the *Mozi*, even though there is little evidence for this claim. See Defoort 2016.

[3] The Daozang edition of 1447 is the earliest currently extant edition. There is some variation in older sources with indirect evidence from *Mozi* such as *Qunshu zhiyao* 群書治要 (from 631) and *Yilin* 意林 (from 786) and in the emendations made by Qing scholars. See Defoort 2016.

inclusive care and challenged to defend it. At one instance, Wumazi characterizes Master Mo as somebody who is "able to inclusively care for all," while Wumazi finds differences in distance morally relevant (*Mozi* 46:102/24). He also points out that Mozi's caring for all does not amount to benefiting all (*Mozi* 46:100/20–21).

Despite this growing promotion of *jian ai* in the book *Mozi*, the association of Master Mo with inclusive care is not straightforward in other contemporary sources, except for the *Mengzi* 孟子. Mencius (c. 371–289 BCE) is the only early master who exclusively and consistently associates Mozi with *jian ai* and vice versa. The book contains four explicit records on Mozi or Mohists, and they are all critical of inclusive care. In one well-known fragment Mencius laments that: "The claims of Yang Zhu and Mo Di fill the world. All claims made in the world either revert to Yang or to Mo. Mr. Yang is 'for oneself,' which amounts to be without lord (無君); Mr. Mo 'cares inclusively,' which amounts to be without father (無父). To be without [= fail to respect and particularly care for] lord or father is something for birds and beasts" (*Mencius* 3B9). This negative portrayal of Mozi's ideal of inclusive care became increasingly influential from the middle of the Han dynasty onward (see section 2: portrayal of *jian ai* in the imperial period) but it had little influence before that time. In other Warring States and early Han sources, the link between Mozi and inclusive care is tenuous: on the one hand, Mozi is praised or criticized for a variety of attitudes, skills, and views, some of which identified as caring inclusively or broadly;[4] on the other hand, the idea of inclusive care is often associated with other masters or simply promoted as an uncontroversial value. Xunzi 荀子 (c. 298–238 BCE), for instance, never explicitly associates Mozi with *jian ai*, never criticizes *jian ai*, pays little attention to it, and uses it with approval. Nor does he ever challenge Mencius for identifying Mozi's thought with *jian ai* or for criticizing it. The same holds for many other Warring States and early Han sources: we find positive, unattributed, unproblematic, and uncontroversial references to *jian ai* in various sources of different affiliations, such as *Shizi*, *Lüshi chunqiu*, *Xinshu*, *Da Dai Liji*, *Wenzi*, *Chunqiu fanlu*, *Taixuanjing*, *Qianfulun*, *Simafa*, *Hanshu*, *Guanzi*, *Sui Caozi*, the Mawangdui text "Jingfa," and the Shanghai manuscript "Cao Mo zhi chen." The ideal of *jian ai* is often associated with "humaneness" (*ren*) and with "having no bias" (*wu si*), as in Gongsun Hong's advice to Emperor Wudi that "bringing about benefit and removing disaster, to care inclusively and have no bias, is what we call humaneness" (*Shiji* 58:2,616). These authors express no agreement nor disagreement with Mencius. Mencius's peculiar views on this matter were apparently unknown or overlooked during the Warring States and the early Han dynasty.[5]

---

[4] *Hanfeizi* "Wu du" (Five vermin) ascribes the promotion of *jian ai* to the Ru Mo, and *Zhuangzi* "Tian dao" (Heaven's Way) ascribes it to Confucius. Mozi is associated with *jian ai* among other ideals in some Han sources such as *Huainanzi*, "Fan lun xun" (Boundless discourses); and *Hanshu*, "Yiwenzhi" (Treatise on literature). *Zhuangzi*, "Tianxia" (The world) attributes to Mozi the ideal of *fan ai* 泛愛 (general love) and *jian li* 兼利.

[5] For more details on associations of Mozi with *jian ai* and on views about *jian ai* in these sources, see Defoort 2014.

THE MENCIAN PORTRAYAL OF *JIAN AI*
IN THE IMPERIAL PERIOD

During most of the imperial era Mozi was discussed in Mencian terms, not his own. Mencius's complaints about Yang and Mo filling the world had been couched in an apology for speaking up in favor of Confucius's ideals and in defense of humanity. "If the Ways of Yang and Mo do not stop, Confucius' Way will not be visible. This means that heterodox theories mislead the people, totally blocking the values of humaneness and righteousness. If this happens, it allows beasts to eat people, and people will end up eating each other. I worry about this." That is Mencius's only motivation to enter into debate. "One who is able to stop Yang and Mo with arguments is the follower of the Sages" (*Mencius* 3B9). This portrayal exclusively associates Mozi with inclusive care, which is identified as a failure to respect one's father, and opposed to the equally pernicious egoism of Yang Zhu; the true follower of the Sage tries everything in his power to stop the great threat posed by these heterodox persuaders. This portrayal contains all the rhetorical ingredients of a cliché vision of Mozi that was endlessly repeated in imperial sources from the middle of the Han dynasty till the end of the Qing.

Around the middle of the Han some scholars began picking up Mencius's view on Mozi and almost literally repeating it. Ying Shao (c. 140–204 CE), for instance, the author of *Fengsu tongyi*, discussed Mencius's moral worth, perseverance, and final success as follows: Mencius was once in deep trouble and believed that, since there was no sage king, lords were doing as they pleased and unemployed scholars debated all around, so that Yang Zhu and Mo Di's words were filling the world. People all turned to either Yang Zhu or Mo Di. But Yang's egoism and Mozi's extreme altruism all amounted to the failure to acknowledge either ruler or father, which is an attitude for birds and beasts. Hence, Mencius felt a strong calling to save Confucius's Way from destruction, and he spoke up in favor of the values of humaneness and righteousness and to prevent humans from becoming beasts devouring each other. For Mencius this was a holy duty, and this was the reason why King Hui of Liang, according to Ying Shao, made him minister in the state of Wei (*Fengsu tongyi* "Meng Ke"). Similar references to Mozi in Mencian terms are made by Yang Xiong (53 BCE–18 CE) in the *Fayan* "Wu zi" and Wang Chong (27–100 CE) in the *Lunheng* "Dui zuo." When giving expression to their worries and moral calling, both authors explicitly compare their own predicament with that of Mencius. Criticism of Mozi's *jian ai* thus becomes part of a specific discourse-cluster. There is no sign of interest in Mozi's thought nor of having read the book named after him: these Han scholars use Mencius's words for expressing their moral outrage toward the moral crisis of their own times, their worries about the success of heterodox views, and their pressing urge to speak up in favor of Confucius's legacy. A critique of Mozi (and Yang Zhu) is not the main issue, but the acceptable means to give shape and authority to their indignation about contemporary rivals. Mencius's rejection of inclusive care thus became a rhetorical trope that circulated relatively independently from other occasional references to Mozi in early imperial times.[6]

This Mencian (mis)representation of Mozi's thought was during most of the imperial era unhindered by any actual reading of the *Mozi*, since the book seems not to have circulated before the Song dynasty, when it was included in the (now lost) Daoist Canon. A shorter edition may have been available around the Tang but probably without the "Jian ai" triplet. That makes us wonder whether the first dissonant in this Confucian orthodoxy, a short essay titled "Reading Mozi" 讀墨子 by Han Yu 韓愈 (768–824), really resulted from his actually reading the text.[7] The great Tang scholar was the first to defend four Mohist core ideas, among which was inclusive care, by pointing out that Confucius also implicitly supported them. In his eyes the agreements between Ru and Mo by far exceeded the differences, and the disagreements were produced by later followers each trying "to sell their masters' theories" 售其師之說 (Zhou 2011:35–38). This seems a daring statement for a Ru scholar and promoter of Mencius. Han Yu's Mozi essay, however, does not contain any reference to Mencius, (let alone a challenge to his evaluation of *jian ai*), nor any sign of the Mencian portrayal. But interestingly, almost all of his references to Mozi in other writings closely follow that rhetorical cliché—except for its criticism of inclusive care—when giving vent to his frustration about the popularity of Daoist and Buddhist heterodoxies in his time, and when expressing his moral duty to block them (e.g., Zhou 2011:4–9, 176–177, 239–41, 373–376). All in all, Han Yu's "Reading Mozi" was still relatively orthodox in taking Confucius as the standard for evaluating Mozi and in refraining from explicitly challenging Mencius's view. The possible contradiction between Han Yu's praise of inclusive care in "Reading Mozi" versus his use of the Mencian rhetorical trope in other writings was resolved by taking out the kernel of this clichéd view, namely the criticism of inclusive care.

While Mencius's star kept rising and gained momentum with his promotion to the Second Sage, "Ya sheng" (亞聖), his Mozi portrayal remained dominant and his rejection of *jian ai* influential. But there was also room for some appreciation and nuances by Ru scholars such as Cheng Yi 程頤 (1033–1107), Zhu Xi 朱熹 (1130–1200), and Wang Yangming 王陽明 (1472–1529). Even if *Mozi* editions were circulating, they may not all have read it since their views on *jian ai* seem exclusively inspired by the clichéd portrayal of a heterodox idea that needs to be blocked by a courageous scholar. Allthough the earliest extant *Mozi* edition was published before Wang Yangming's lifetime (in the Daozang of 1447), it was not yet widely available; nor was Wang particularly interested. But he did not totally agree with Mencius's portrayal either: for example, in a letter of ca. 1520, he pointed out that Mencius's criticism of respectively Yang and Mo as being

---

[6] There was also some interest in the *Mobian* (chapters 40–45) and in the figure of Mozi as a Daoist god (Lou Jin 2011; Knoblock and Riegel 2013:18–21).

[7] Angus Graham speculated that Han Yu read an edition in 3 *juan* and only 13 *pian*, including the 7 opening chapters and the 2 first triplets, namely "Shang xian" and "Shang tong" (Graham 1978:68–69). Rather than be based on that partial edition, Han Yu's essay may have been inspired by the limited information on Mozi available in bibliographical chapters. He even points out that book *Mozi* is not available in his days (Zhou 2011: 176–177).

without father or lord was somewhat extreme. "Those two masters were also worthies in their age. . . . Mozi's inclusive care went too far in the practice of humaneness." And again, Wang's real target was not Mo Di nor Yang Zhu but the heterodoxies of his own days, namely Buddhism, Daoism, and sometimes also Zhu Xi (Li 1996:338–342; trans. Chan 1963:163).

One later follower of Wang Yangming and member of the unconventional Taizhou school was Li Zhi 李贄 (1527–1602). As a self-proclaimed Ru scholar, he was frustrated about the corruption, superficiality, and greed of the narrow-minded scholar-bureaucrats in his days. In his selected edition of the *Mozi, Mozi pixuan* 墨子批選, Li ridiculed the claim that inclusive care amounted to being without father: "Inclusive care means mutual care. To make people care for each other, how can we say that this harms humaneness? If you say that making people care for each other is harming humaneness, then you must make people hurt each other so that they do not harm humaneness! If others all care for my father when I care for theirs, how can you explain this as 'be without father'. If you say that making others all care for my father is to be without father, then I must make others hurt my father, and that would then count as 'being with father'! How does that differ from beasts and barbarians?" His regret that people "sell such a theory" as well as his addition that "Mr Meng was not such a person" both ultimately keep Mencius out of the wind in a way somewhat reminiscent of Han Yu (Ren and Li 2004: :6:72–73).

Praise for Mozi's *jian ai* remained very exceptional, and the inevitable clash with Mencius's portrayal was something to be avoided. One further step was the publication of restored *Mozi* editions in the late eighteenth century, by scholars such as Bi Yuan 畢沅 (1730–1797) and the editors of the Siku quanshu 四庫全書 project (1770–1780). One of their colleagues was Wang Zhong 汪中 (1745–1794) who also made a (now lost) edition and wrote a preface (in 1780) that has been preserved. His "Mozi Preface" (*Mozi xu*) was another milestone in the revival of the Mohist ideal of inclusive care: "As for inclusive care, that was Mozi's one specific idea. But what he meant by 'inclusive' was that, while being careful about the preservation of one's own state, one does not destroy the livestock of a neighboring state's population. Even those diplomats who were installed by the kings of antiquity to pay friendly visits to other lords using the ritual rules of interstate visits and condolences, did not differ from this! They [the Mohists] moreover taught inclusive care to those acting as sons in the world, making them filial to their parents. To accuse them of being without father how perverse is that!" Wang Zhong pointed out that in the Warring States period it was only natural that Ru and Mo would attack each other. "Hence Mozi slandering Confucius was like Mencius slandering (*wu* 誣) Mozi" (in Sun 2011:672). Wang clearly had the courage to attack the Second Sage and he was, in turn, vilified for it. The powerful literatus Weng Fanggang 翁方綱 (1733–1818) considered Wang Zhong's view simply infuriating. He found it shocking that "the candidate Wang Zhong brazenly wrote a preface to the *Mozi*, claiming himself that he could arrange the book, and even daring to say that Mencius's statement about 'inclusive care being without father', was slandering Mozi. This is even a crime against civilisation, and again without any doubt" (Weng 1969:619). Weng therefore called him the "Mohist

Wang Zhong" (墨者汪中), analogous to the "Mohist Yizhe" characterized by Mencius
as the promoter of ungraded love (*Mencius* 3A5). This attack probably hit Wang Zhong
hard when he was on the verge of dying at the age of 51; his only son, Wang Xisun 汪喜孫
(1786–1848), made sure that his father's comment on Mencius's "slandering" Mozi disappeared from the preface (Tian 2005:19–21). The last important statement on Mozi's *jian ai*
during the imperial era occurs in the preface (1792) of Zhang Huiyan 張惠言 (1761–1802),
who worked on four Dialectical chapters (chapters 40–43). Zhang believed that all non-
Ru Warring States trends of thought derived from either Mo Di or Yang Zhu, and that
Mencius therefore had good reasons to attack them fiercely. "Of the Masters' theories of
those days, Yang and Mo were the common ancestors. Mencius believed that if they
would stop, the learning of the Hundred Specialists would dry up and not be worth sell-
ing. . . . Therefore the book *Mencius* also attacks him [Mozi]. Alas! How could he know
that his followers would be even more fierce." Echoing Han Yu's views in "Reading
Mozi," Zhang remarks that "if in the past there had not been a Mencius, then how many
later Ru would not have practiced and loved its theories!" Mencius was right to focus on
jian ai, because this was indeed the root of Mohism and the most attractive part of his
thought. "The claims of 'inclusive care' are that one who cares for others, will also be
cared for by them; one who benefits others, will also be benefited by them. If a humane
lord makes all the people in the world use their clear eyes and sharp ears to look and lis-
ten for the sake of each other and their limbs and full strength to work and arrange for
the sake of each other, how would this differ from the way in which a Sage orders the
world?" Zhang points out that Mencius "resolutely accused him of the crime of being
without father, but this argument at the outset had no foothold. Really! If we imagine
that Mozi's book had been totally lost, how would we now have been able to see that
Mencius' arguments are stern and critical, simple and going to the heart of the matter?"
(in Sun 2011:679–680). Wavering between praise for Mencius and for Mozi, Zhang
Huiyan attributes the age-long rejection of Mohist thought to the Mencian dominance.
He is also the first scholar who puts Mohist ideas into a hierarchy and firmly locates
inclusive care at its roots. The great Mozi scholar Sun Yirang 孫詒讓 (1848–1908) only
discovered this preface in 1901 and was so pleased with it that he included it in his appen-
dix of important prefaces in the 1907 edition of his *Clarifying Commentary on the* Mozi
(*Mozi jiangu* 墨子閒詁).

THE RISE OF *JIAN AI* IN THE
POST-IMPERIAL ERA

New approaches toward Mozi thus converged around the beginning of the twentieth
century in Sun Yirang's *opus magnum*, which was a milestone in the renaissance of *Mozi*
studies, published several times between 1893 and 1907. Sun not only scrupulously
incorporated the philological work of his predecessors, he also gathered their prefaces

containing the earliest positive or at least nuanced views on Mohism, and he added his own appreciation (Defoort 2015). For the first time Mohism was discussed in terms of a set of ten core ideas, which were increasingly presented as a system of thought, in which inclusive care was often—but not always—seen as the most crucial idea: "the corner-stone of the system" (Forke 1922:82); "Mozi's core and quintessence" (Tan Jiajian, in Ren and Li 2004 :80:35); its "unifying principle of morality" (Graham 1989:41); the "center of Mohism" (Ding 1999:70); the "heart of their ethics" (Fraser 2012); and a "startling, origi-nal, and even revolutionary concept" (Watson 1963:10), generally seen in opposition to the Ru view of graded love. Only now *jian ai* regained a mainly positive aura, compara-ble to powerful Western ideas and international trends. It took a path that can roughly be traced through different fields—from religious inspiration, via political concerns, to academic debates. What follows is no more than a small selection of some dominant voices within this plethora of views on the Mohist "inclusive care." These views are, of course, intertwined with each other as they are with previous trends, and the selected voices are not only representative of one type of view on inclusive care, but they also tell a specific story of their own.

One influential voice on *jian ai* was from the Scottish Sinologist, James Legge (1815–1897). He was a Christian missionary to China but also much influenced by the orthodox Ru tradition: this combination shaped his view on Mozi's idea of *jian ai*. In his *Mencius* translation (of 1861), Legge felt obliged to include an explanatory chapter on the opin-ions of Yang Zhu and Mo Di, considering their enormous influence on Mencius. The Second Sage fought the idea of *jian ai* so effectively that after him it was generally con-sidered, "save by some eccentric thinkers, as belonging to the Limbo of Chinese vanities, among other things 'abortive, monstrous, or unkindly mixed' " (Legge 1991:117). Thus far the missionary clearly presents and supports the orthodox view. He further seems to fol-low Han Yu's "Reading Mozi" while being more critical of Mencius. He points out that the latter wrongly attributed to Mozi what was probably a later Mohist interpretation of *jian ai*, namely ungraded love: "It is to be observed that Mo himself nowhere says that his principle was that of loving all EQUALLY. His disciples drew this conclusion from him"—such as Yizhi who was quoted in the Mencius as defending the idea "as if love were to be *without difference of degree*" (Legge 1991:118, referring to *Mencius* 3A5; capitals and italics in the original). Mencius, hence, failed to confront Mozi's original idea, a mis-take that Confucius would not have made, according to Legge. "Confucius might have conceded, therefore, to Mo, that the rule of conduct which he laid down was the very best that could be propounded" (Legge 1991:120). In his remarkable agreement with Han Yu's "Reading Mozi," which is fully quoted, and in these critical remarks on the Mencian portrayal, Legge also fits well into the Mozi revival of his days previously described above (section 2: portrayal of *jian ai* in the imperial period). And this, finally, relates to his own Christian inspiration: associated with "Mo stumbled on a truth, which . . . is one of the noblest which can animate the human breast" (Legge 1991:119), namely "that we are to love our neighbour as ourselves" (Legge 1991:118). Legge particularly disliked Mencius's disdain for physical labor, which the Second Sage associatedwith Mozi. Unfortunately, Mozi's idea was inspired by expediency instead of duty, and his concern was restricted to the good government of China alone, not the love of humanity. Otherwise, "he would have done the greatest service to his countrymen, and entitle himself to a place among the sages of the world" (Legge 1991:120).

A well-known Christian who did attribute to Mozi a place among the sages of the world was Sun Yatsen (1966–1925), the founding father of the Chinese Republic: in his eyes, Mozi figured alongside such great men as the Yellow Emperor, George Washington, and Jean-Jacques Rousseau. In his sixth speech on democracy, Sun pointed out that Westerners going to China with their schools, hospitals, and charitable works did not have a monopoly on love. "In antiquity nobody spoke more of love than Mozi. The '*jian ai*' that Mozi talked about is the same as the '*bo ai*' 博愛 (broad love) of Jesus. What politics of antiquity meant by the principle of love was to 'love the people as your children'" (Ren and Li 2004 :100:1). But the first systematic and outspoken promoter of the Mohist ideal of care was Liang Qichao 梁啟超 (1873–1929). He had received Sun Yirang's *Mozi* collation when he was only 23 years old (in 1894), and he later reported that he was absolutely crazy (*kuang* 狂) about it: it had not only totally transformed his view on the Masters but also caused the entire revival of Mohism in China. Inspired by the research collected by Sun and borrowing from Japanese scholars,[8] Liang was the first to actually write books on Mohist thought. In both *Zi Mozi xueshuo* (of 1904) and *Mozi xue'an* (of 1921) there is a major stress on the idea of inclusive care—Liang even introduces the neologism *jian ai*-ism (兼愛主義). He presents Mohism as a relatively systematic thought system, makes intercultural comparisons, and reflects on the pros and cons of *jian ai*. In the book of 1904, Liang distinguishes between five types of love, the fourth being: "Equal and ungraded love reaching to the whole of mankind is the theory on love that Mozi in the Far East and Jesus in the Far West promoted." While Jesus was inspired by God, and Mozi by Heaven, "their basic theories were totally the same" (Ren and Li 2004: 26:456–457). Almost two decades later, after the experiences of World War I, Liang was disappointed by Western Europe and enthusiastic about the establishment of the Soviet Union. His regard for religion had diminished, while that for a universal non-patriotic love had increased. This further raised *jian ai* in his eyes: it no longer depended on Heaven's will but functioned as the very foundation of Mohist thought: "As for the central principles promoted by Mohism, even though there are ten of them, they in fact all come out of one fundamental idea, which is inclusive care." Liang goes on to explain how some other core ideas relate to *jian ai*, concluding "that the 'will of Heaven' and 'explaining ghosts' are the promotion of *jian ai*-ism by means of religious superstition" (Ren and Li 2004: 26:23–24). Liang thus took a crucial step in systematizing Mozi's thought and propelling *jian ai* to the foreground.

The academic habit of presenting the ten theses or dogmas as early Mohist philosophy and of identifying one of them as its core has become the norm. Scholars promoting *jian ai* as the foundation of Mohist thought outnumber those who give priority to another thesis such as "the will of Heaven" or "against aggression." The Marxist interpretations of Mohism from the 1940s onward followed this trend while adding new layers

---

[8] Liang Qichao seems to have copied from Takase Takejiro (高瀬武次郎), 杨墨哲学, 1902, which was translated by Jiang Weiqiao (蔣維喬) in the 1920s.

to the interpretation of Mozi: social background, class struggle, historical periodization, idealism versus materialism, and so on. At first view one would have expected a simple and straightforward praise by communists of the age-long underdog of the Confucian tradition, and more specifically of his urge to care for the poor and weak. Surprisingly, the reactions toward Mohism were vague and varied, complex, changing, and at best luke-warm. In a class society *jian ai* could not possibly be inclusive or universal but had to express the needs of one class. But which class did Mozi belong to? He was perhaps an artisan whose concern extended to the lower classes. He seemed too knowledgeable to be an exploited slave or peasant. But that hardly made him a good candidate for the only alternative class of the exploiting slave-owner. The fact that Mozi did not fit well in this rigid frame was also related to the then-current periodization. If Mozi was regarded a progressive activist between the stages of slavery and feudality at the end of the Springs and Autumns period, how could he then possibly have criticized feudal morality, as some Marxists had claimed on the basis of his being "without father" in Mencius's portrayal. Moreover, the generally accepted connection between inclusive care and the religious idea of a will of Heaven also shed a dark idealist shadow on *jian ai*. On top of all these con-cerns, Mohism may also have suffered, as Louie Kam points out, from the age-old disdain for equality and physical labor that even the reddest among the communist intellectuals had inherited from their literati predecessors (Kam 1986:140–149). Hence, "though his class credentials were the most acceptable of the pre-Qin philosophers, Mozi's thinking did not arouse much interest in cultural inheritance terms" (Kam 1986:136). As the Marxist interpretations faded away with the Open Up and Reform policy beginning in 1978, interpretations of Mozi's *jian ai* also became less rigid. Debates on its meaning and importance largely remained within the "ten theses" frame. They sometimes connected with Republican, pre-communist debates or with Western discussions, including the translation of the expression that I have thus far either left untranslated or rendered as "inclusive care." In the current field of early Chinese philosophy, especially Mozi studies, various views have been presented for the translation and interpretation of *jian* (univer-sal, inclusive, impartial, for everyone, and so on) and *ai* (love, care, caring, concern, and so on) separately as well as combined in a fixed expression (universal love, impartial love, impartial caring, inclusive care, concern for everyone, and so on). The following brief overview, limited to the English-speaking world, shows the explosive potential of this topic for further research. The most popular translation of *jian ai* is "universal love," for which the Protestant James Legge in 1861 indicated that he did not know how to render it in any better way (Legge 1991:101n1). Many scholars have followed him: most implicitly but some after pondering the alternatives. Scott Lowe, for instance, insisted that for Mozi, *ai* "does not admit any other translation," adding that "it is clear that 'love' is to be under-stood as something radically different from romantic sentiments the term may call to mind for English speakers" (Lowe 1992:93). Ian Johnston also believes that Legge's well-established translation captures well the universal scope and religious connotations of the Mohist ideal (Johnston 2010:xliii–xliv). Legge himself was probably more concerned with the interpretation of *jian* than of *ai*: he believed that Mencius had already, under the influence of later Mohists, misunderstood *jian ai* as indiscriminate love, namely without differences or gradations (Legge 1991:118–119). While many scholars have followed Mencius and stressed the idea of impartiality, others have pointed out that the Mohist injunction to care inclusively does not necessarily mean that people should abandon all particularistic attachments, but rather that they should not excessively or exclusively love their own kin (Robins 2012, Fraser 2016). Criticism of Legge's translation originally came from A. C. Graham, who suggested instead "Concern for Everyone," to better express the adverb *jian* (for each) and the unemotional or unromantic pledge to benefit others and save them from harm. While Confucians may have conceived of the duty to care for others as a guideline through a web of ritual obligations, Mozi took it as an abstract principle of moral obligations, according to Graham, irrespective of kin relations (Graham 1989:41–42). I have settled for "care" or "caring," thereby referring to actions (take care of) as well as feelings (care for), since I find both to be present in the Mohist argument; my own translation of *jian* has wavered, evolving throughout the *Mozi* from "inclusive" toward "impartial," as Heaven is increasingly taken as the model of *jian ai* (Defoort 2013). These views do not exhaust the current and increasing debates on the translation and interpretation of the Mohist ideal of *jian ai*. Discussion will certainly go on for some time as the *Mozi* gains importance for its philosophical interest, intercultural dimension, and its possible implications in contemporary politics. Mozi is on the rise and so is his ideal of *jian ai*, after a long, eventful history.

BIBLIOGRAPHY

Chan, Wing Tsit, transl. with notes, 1963. *Instructions for Practical Living and Other Neo-Confucian Writings by Wang Yang-Ming*. New York: Columbia University Press.

Defoort, Carine 2013. "Are Mozi's Three 'Jian Ai' Chapters about Universal Love?" In *The Mozi as an Evolving Text: Different Voices in Early Chinese Thought*. Edited by Carine Defoort and Nicolas Standaert, 35–67. Leiden: Brill.

Defoort, Carine 2014. "Do the Ten Mohist Theses Represent Mozi's Thought? Reading the Masters with a Focus on Mottos." *Bulletin of the School of Oriental and African Studies* 77(2):1–34.

Defoort, Carine 2015. "The Modern Formation of Early Mohism: Sun Yirang's *Exposing and Correcting the* Mozi," *T'oung Pao* 101-1-3, 208–238.

Defoort, Carine 2016. "The Gradual Growth of the Mohist Core Philosophy: Tracing Fixed Formulations in the *Mozi*," *Monumenta Serica* 64(1): 1–22.

Ding, Weixiang 丁为祥 1999. "The Evolution of Mohist and Views of Jian Ai墨家兼爱观 的 演变." *Shaanxi shifan daxue xuebao* 陕西师范大学学报 4:70–76.

Forke, Alfred 1922. *Mê Ti: Des Socialethikers und seiner Schüler philosophische Werke*. Berlin: Kommissionsverlag der Vereinigung wissenschaftlicher Verleger.

Fraser, Chris 2012. "Mohism." In *The Stanford Encyclopedia of Philosophy*. Edited by Edward N. Zalta, 25. Stanford: Stanford University Press. http://plato.stanford.edu/archives/fall2012/entries/mohism/

Fraser, Chris 2016. *The Philosophy of the Mòzǐ*, New York: Colombia University Press.

Graham, Angus C. 1978. *Later Mohist Logic, Ethics, and Science*. Hong Kong: Chinese University Press.

Graham, Angus C. 1989. *Disputers of the Tao: Philosophical Argument in Ancient China.* Chicago: Open Court.

Hanshu 漢書 1983. By Ban Gu 班固. Beijing: Zhonghua shuju.

Jiang, Weiqiao 蔣維喬, transl. 1922. *Yang Mo Philosophy* 楊墨哲学. Shanghai: Shangwu. (Translation of the work of Takase Takejiro 高瀬武次郎, 1902)

Johnston, Ian, transl. 2010. *The Mozi. A Complete Translation,* Hong Kong: The Chinese University Press.

Knoblock, John, and Jeffrey Riegel 2013. *Mozi: A Study and Translation of the Ethical and Political Writings.* Berkeley: University of California Press.

Legge, James 1991 [1861]. *The Chinese Classics, with a Translation, Critical and Exegetical Notes, Prolegomena, and Copious Indexes,* vol. 2: *The Works of Mencius.* Taibei: SMC.

Li, Shenglong 李生龍, ed. 1996. *New Translation of the Mozi Reader* 新譯墨子讀本. Taibei: Sanmin shuju.

Li, Zhi 李贄. *Selected Works of Mozi* 墨子批選. In *Mozi Daquan 6.* Edited by Ren Jiyu and Li Guangxing. Beijing: Beijing tushuguan chubanshe.

Lou, Jin 樓勁 2011. "The Spread of the Mo School of the Wei Jin Period and Related Issues 魏晋墨学之流传及相关问题." *Zhongguo shi yanjiu* 2:47–58.

Louie, Kam 1986. *Inheriting Tradition: Interpretations of the Classical Philosophers in Communist China, 1949–1966.* Hong Kong, Oxford, and New York: Oxford University Press.

Lowe, Scott 1992. *Mo Tzu's Religious Blueprint for a Chinese Utopia: The Will and the Way.* Lewiston, Queenston, and Lampeter: Mellen.

Mozi 墨子 2001. *Index to Mozi.* Edited by D. C. Lau. ICS Ancient Chinese Texts Concordance Series 41 墨子逐字索引. Hong Kong: Commercial Press. (For in-text citations, the chapter number is given first, followed by a colon and then the page number and line number separated by a slash.)

Ren, Jiyu 任继愈, and Li Guangxing 李广星, eds. 2004. *The Complete Collection of Mozi* 墨子大全, 100 vols. Beijing: Beijing tushuguan chubanshe.

Robins, Dan 2012. "Mohist Care." *Philosophy East West,* 62.1, 60–91.

Tan, Jiajian 谭家健. "Research on Mozi 墨子研究." In *Mozi daquan,* vol. 80. Edited by Ren Jiyu and Li Guangxing. Beijing: Beijing tushuguan chubanshe.

Tian, Hanyun 田汉云, ed. 2005. *New Edition of Wang Zhong* 新编汪中集. Yangzhou: Guangling shushe.

Shiji 史記 1985. By Sima Qian 司馬遷. Beijng: Zhonghua shuju.

Sun, Yatsen (or Sun Zhongshan 孫中山). "Nationalism 民族主義." In *Mozi daquan,* vol. 100. Edited by Ren Jiyu and Li Guangxing. Beijing: Beijing tushuguan chubanshe.

Sun, Yirang 孫詒讓 2011. *Mozi: Critical Exegesis* 墨子閒詁. Beijing: Zhonghua shuju.

Watanabe, Takashi 渡邊卓, translated by Hong Shunlong 洪順隆 1977. "The Thought of Mojia 墨家思想." In *Zhongguo sixiang zhi yanjiu,* vol. 3. Edited by Uno Seiichi 宇野精一, 1–88. Taibei: Youshi wenhua shiye gongsi.

Watson, Burton 1963. *Mo-tzu: Basic Writings.* New York: Columbia University Press.

Wang, Zhong 汪中. "The Preface of Mozi 墨子序." In *Mozi jiangu.* Edited by Sun Yirang, 669–673. Beijing: Zhonghua shuju.

Weng, Fanggan 翁方綱 1969. "The Collection of Fuchuzhai 復初齋文集," 近代中國史料 叢刊第四十三輯 *Jindai Zhongguo ziliao congkan di sishier ji,* 3 vols. 421. 書墨子 *Shu Mozi* 2. Taipei: Wenhai chubanshe.

Zhang, Huiyan 張惠言. "Explanations of the Book Mozi 書墨子經說解後." In *Mozi jiangu.* Edited by Sun Yirang, 679–681.

Zhou, Qicheng 周啓成 et al., eds. 2011. *New Translation of Mr. Chang Li's Anthology* 新譯昌黎先生文集, 2 vols. Taibei: Sanmin shuju.

CHAPTER 34

··

CHU RELIGION AND ART

··

BY JOHN S. MAJOR, INDEPENDENT SCHOLAR, AND ELIZABETH CHILDS-JOHNSON, OLD DOMINION UNIVERSITY

ALTHOUGH the origins of Chu 楚 are still unclear, by the Western Zhou period Chu entered the historical record as a polity in the mid–Han River Valley. And, although politically part of the Zhou system, Chu was criticized by the Zhou court for its aggressive expansionism. Chu enlarged its territorial hold steadily east and southward, eventually controlling all of the middle Yangzi River basin.

Cosmology played a large role in Chu intellectual life. Likewise shamanism was characteristic of Chu culture and pervades such texts as the *Chuci* 楚辭 (Elegies of Chu) and the *Shanhaijing* 山海經 (Classic of mountains and seas). The cosmological deity Taiyi (Great Undifferentiated Unity) originated in Chu and appears to have been directly related to the concept of immortality. The metamorphic, antler-bearing wooden figures (interpreted as guardians or guides for the soul) found in Chu tombs are sculptural monuments of shamanic origin.

Chu created sophisticated works in a variety of media including distinctive bronze and lacquer vessels with the earliest Sinitic narrative scenes. These often portrayed ritual subjects, such as hunting, feasting, and warfare in this world as well as in the liminal world of the afterlife. As both follower and innovator, Chu gave the Sinitic dominion a distinctive and unique artistic voice.

The early Chinese state of Chu likely organized as a polity in the middle reaches of the Han River Valley during late Shang times (thirteenth to eleventh centuries BCE), as is suggested by the abundant finds of Shang bronzes in the south where the Chu capitals were later located. Some Shang oracle-bone inscriptions refer to a polity called Jing 荆, which in later times was an alternative name for Chu. By the early Western Zhou period (mid-eleventh century BCE), the state of Chu emerges into the historical record by means of bronze inscriptions. The state occupied some portion of the Han River Valley at that time; its leaders are depicted as allies and officials of Zhou King Wen. But much of the early history of Chu remains unknown. Remains of its capital, Danyang, have not been discovered, and the location of Danyang is a subject of lively scholarly dispute (Blakeley 1999a:10–12). The ethnic identity of the ruling house of Chu is not clear. It might be the case that when Chu was brought into the political orbit of the Zhou state, sometime in the Western Zhou period, a ruling house for Chu was established by Zhou royal authority, so that at least at the highest elite level Chu was affiliated with the Zhou royal lineage. The rulers of Chu certainly participated in the Chinese linguistic community of the Western Zhou, as attested by bronze inscriptions and by accounts in the *Springs and Autumns* chronicle referring to Chu participation in multistate conferences. But it is also the case that Chu (like other large states on the periphery of the Zhou "Central States," such as Qin and Zhongshan) included diverse populations that may have been distinct from the dominant Huaxia Sinitic ethnolinguistic group.

The Chu rulers were at least somewhat distinctive in their nomenclature; the rulers referred to themselves as "kings" (*wang* 王), rather than as one or another of the Zhou titles of nobility (*gong* 公, *hou* 侯, *bo* 伯, *zi* 子, and *nan* 男); in Zhou usage the title *wang* was reserved for the Zhou ruler alone. (In the Late Springs and Autumns and Early Warring States periods rulers of some other states, such as Qin and Zheng, followed Chu's example in calling themselves *wang*.) Also, the Chu kings took as part of their name the title *xiong* 雄, a distinctive Chu term that might originally have designated a ritual specialist of some kind (Blakeley 1999b:53–54).

Chu relations with the Western Zhou court were unstable. Much of the time, Chu sent tribute to the Western Zhou court, as was expected of the rulers of territorial states; however, Western Zhou troops attacked Chu, in what were described as "punitive expeditions," in 960, 956, and 823 BCE. By the end of the Western Zhou period in 771, Chu had begun its long-term project of territorial aggrandizement southward and eastward, absorbing the territories of other states and becoming one of the great powers in the Springs and Autumns period (Blakeley 1999a:13–17). In 690, Chu established a new capital called Ying, the location was probably somewhere in Hubei. Confusingly, this may have been the first of two or more Chu capitals, all called Ying, presumably sited to remain in the central region of the Chu state as it continued its eastern expansion (Blakeley 1999a:11–13). In the course of its expansion, Chu must have incorporated additional populations of Sinitic and non-Sinitic peoples, speaking diverse languages and expressing their own cultural practices. By the beginning of the Warring States period, Chu had expanded its territory to include almost all of the greater Yangzi River Valley below the gorges but was blocked from extending its power all the way to the seacoast by the presence of two formidable coastal states, Wu and Yue. Chu was too powerful a state to be ignored by the rulers of the other territorial states, but Chu, like Qin, was not one of the "Central States" (*Zhongguo* 中國) of the Zhou system. Some northerners regarded the people of Chu as "barbarians." Mencius, of much later date and associated with Confucian institutions, famously referred to a Chu envoy as a "shrike-tongued barbarian of the south" (*Mencius* 3A4).

The Chu royal tombs have yet to be discovered, and many excavated Chu materials are both rather late in time—Warring States rather than Springs and Autumns—and from widely separated locations in the vast Chu territory. Physical factors of soil and water may have skewed the balance of organic materials in excavated tombs from the East Asian Heartland region in favor of Chu, since they contain more objects of wood, lacquer, bamboo (including texts on bamboo strips), and other organic materials (such as residues of food and medicines) than tombs from the northern plains.

Bearing in mind those caveats, it is possible to identify some important features of Chu and mainstream religion, using several types of evidence: texts in the received tradition, newly discovered texts from excavated tombs, and art works recovered from tombs. As will become clear the art, religion, and culture of Chu are founded on belief and fear of the otherworld, the unknown realm of the wilderness whether represented by deities from that realm or by metaphors of imagery of that world of metamorphosis.

It is important to recognize that, at least on the elite level, Chu religion was conservative, yet innovative retaining elements of belief and ritual that can be traced back to the Shang and Western Zhou periods. Moreover, it shared with the larger Sinitic culture characteristics that might be described as defining early Chinese religion more generally, evolved in some cases from very ancient religious beliefs and practices, and stabilized by the Warring States period (Major 1999:122–123). These essential characteristics include:

- Worship of a ruler's ancestors as necessary to the continued existence of a state, as shown by inscriptions on bronze vessels and texts on bamboo strips
- Ascription of divine ancestors to a ruling house, seen, for example, in *Shijing* 詩經 Ode 245, which asserts that the Zhou royal house was descended from the divine Hou Ji 厚稷, "Lord Millet"
- Worship of an aristocrat's ancestors as necessary to the continued existence of an aristocratic family, as seen in numerous bronze inscriptions expressing the wish that "son's sons and grandson's grandsons" would continue to cherish the vessel
- A sense of religious obligation to worship and honor ancestors, and to provide a male heir for the continuation of the family line. This obligation came to be identified especially with Confucius and his followers; it pervades later ritual works such as the *Liji* 禮記, the "Record of Rites"
- A religious obligation to provide a proper funeral for one's parents, including grave goods and other ritual elements appropriate to their hierarchical status in society, with as much lavish pomp as was financially possible and ritually permissible, as generously revealed in Hubei Chu and related tomb excavations, such as at Xingang, Leigudun, and Xiasi.
- Belief that each person has a complex soul—with both corporeal and ethereal components—often but not necessarily thought of as distinct *po* and *hun* souls, as revealed in the funerary text describing the illness and death of Shao Tuo (Cook 2006) as well as the "Zhou hun" 招魂 and "Da zhao" 大招 poems in the *Chuci* anthology (Sukhu 2017, 169–188)
- State-sponsored rites of sacrifice and propitiation to high divinities, such as the gods of the four directions and the four (or eight) winds, and the god of the soil, as depicted on the Chu Silk Manuscript and as implied by the widespread use of the stock phrase "altars of soil and grain" as a synecdoche for an aristocratic state; also

as seen by the revival by Han emperor Gaozu of imperial worship of the gods of the four directions (Queen and Major 2015:453)

- Popular belief in, and rites directed toward, deities of local mountains, rivers, old trees, and the like, as well as household deities such as the Stove God and the Door God, whether or not such rites were sanctioned by the state, as indicated by texts such as the *Mozi* 墨子

- Belief in ghosts, spirits, sprites, and minor divinities, sometimes manifested in fog, whirlwinds, and other natural phenomena, capable of causing injury or illness and requiring, according to circumstances, propitiation or exorcism, as mentioned in the medical texts from Mawangdui tomb 3 (Harper 1992)

- A requirement that religious buildings (including tombs) and the rites conducted in or about them be properly oriented in space in order to be efficaciously used. A notable example of a religious building constructed on cosmological principles was the *mingtang* 明堂, "Bright Hall," where Zhou kings and Han emperors carried out rites of worship based on the solilunar calendar (Lewis 2006:260–272).

To these widely-shared characteristics of early Chinese religion may be added some features that, on present evidence, were mainstream Chinese but were accorded special emphasis in Chu religion (Major 1999:124) and its artistic statement. Artistic works, for example, include sculptures in polychrome lacquered wood, bronze, or painted pottery. Chu imagery favored a combination of the fantastic and naturalistic, including specific wild animals such as tigers, deer, birds, snakes, and the typical mythic mainstream *long* 龍 dragons and *feng* 鳳 spirit birds, and therianthrope characters. Artistic expressions of most of these beliefs are abundant (Chang 1972).

COSMOLOGY AND CHU RELIGION

Since the Neolithic period, Sinitic cultures have emphasized orientation to the cardinal directions, and to the celestial north pole and the celestial equator, in important ritual contexts, such as the siting of buildings and graves. The well-known Lingjiatan (in present-day Anhui province) jade plaque with incised arrow-like markings pointing to the eight directions is an early example of this emphasis on orientation (Anhui 2006; see chapters 2 by Fang Xiangming; 4 by Childs-Johnson; and 6 by He Nu). Similarly well known is the Shang dynasty's emphasis on the centrality of the royal domain (*zhong* 中), with royal power projecting out into the Four Quarters (*sifang* 四方). This emphasis on orientation is found throughout the early Sinitic cultural sphere and seems to continue to have been strong and important in the southern regions that constituted the Chu realm. Chu religion was to some extent based on, and a continuation of, beliefs and practices that were widespread in the early Sinitic world. But, as noted, relatively fewer finds of material goods, particularly in wood and lacquer, have been recovered archaeologically in northern areas, while such materials are relatively abundant from Chu sites. It is clear that Chu was a major artistic innovator during the Zhou era and gave rise to many different Sinitic arts, including narrative and figure painting that was both fantastic and realistic, abstract and representational in subject (lacquers, bronzes, ceramics, bamboo); the art of calligraphy (e.g., bird script); sculptural arts (wood, ceramic, bronze); textile arts (e.g., silk, hemp); and others. Chu art was inspired and free-spirited, full of emotion and humor, constantly expressing motion while also being static and iconic. Chu shared with the Western Zhou a preference for the *feng* peacock-like bird as a key icon, yet Chu never discarded the underlying concept of the Shang metamorphic power mask or its image. Chu art included tropes common in the art of other Sinitic traditions but accorded special emphasis to deer antlers and long tongues, both of which are known in earlier guises but not to the extent favored by Chu. Again, this may be due to the numerous extant Chu works in lacquer and wood, which are rare in northern burial contexts, with the exception of Shang lacquer painted wood sculptures remaining in the royal cruciform tombs.

The artistic genius of Chu is revealed in two domestic, lacquer bowls (Figure 1). Picked out in black or red, a peacock-like *feng* bird runs in pursuit of two swimming fish (Figure 1A). Or, strings of airborne *feng* tail feathers compete with feline dragons in a fast-paced circle around a bowl's interior (Figure 1B). One is representationally realistic and the other entirely mythical. The beauty created by the Chu artisan for an elite clientele is extraordinary in its ability to create works based on both observation of the natural world and deeply held beliefs in the power of the metamorphic realm.

Chu examples of *sifang* cosmology may be represented by a lacquer box from the tomb of Zeng Hou Yi (Marquis Yi of Zeng, 433 BCE) (Figure 2). The top depicts the "White Tiger of the West" and the "Blue-Green Dragon of the East," along with the Northern Dipper and the names of the 28 Lunar Lodges 宿. Another example, dating

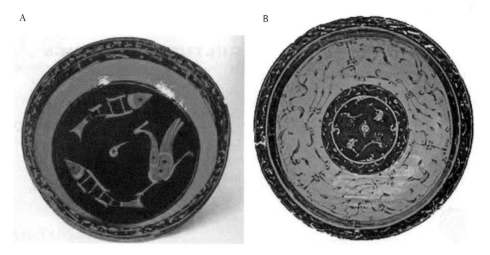

A   B

FIGURE 1 **A** Chu-influenced lacquer bowl with peacock pursuing fish. **B** Chu lacquer bowl with internal design of *feng* and *long* mythic icons. Courtesy of the Seattle Art Museum, Washington.

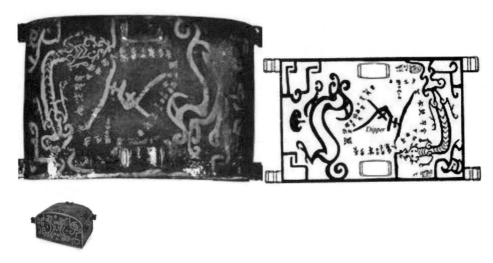

FIGURE 2 Dragon of the east and tiger of the west icons framing the Big Dipper (北斗 Beidou, center) and 28 lunar lodges (the names of which are written in a circle surrounding the Big Dipper) decorating a lacquer box, Marquis Yi of Zeng burial, Leigudun, Suizhou, Hunan. After Hunansheng Bowuguan 1980:plate 89.

from the Han dynasty, is the astronomical model known as the *shi* 式 or "cosmograph," a device having a fixed, square "earth plate" and a round, rotatable "heaven plate" engraved with an image of the Northern Dipper; this could be used to ascertain where auspicious or inauspicious cosmic influences would be felt in the human realm (Figure 3A) (Tseng 2011:47–49; Kalinowski 2012–2013). The majority of cosmographs now extant have been excavated from Han dynasty tombs in the former territory of Chu (Harper 1978–1979:1–2).[1]

Conceptually related to the cosmograph was the game-board of the game *liubo*, which portrayed the square Earth in microcosm (Figure 3C) (see e.g., Tseng 2004:169–204). The game, which involved the casting of dice to propel counters along a defined path through the board's markings, was played both as a form of gambling and as a method of divining good or ill fortune in response to some situation such as setting out on a journey. Numerous extant inscribed pictures on stone show individuals playing *liubo*; often the players are shown as winged and feathered beings, immortals playing the game as masters of fate (Figure 3D). Closely related to the *liubo* board was the Han-era TLV mirror (so-named from the distinctive markings on the reverse side of the mirror) of the Han, Xin, and Early Eastern Han periods (Figure 3B). The décor of the TLV mirror is derived from the markings on a square *liubo* board surrounded by several circular bands representing,

---

[1] Cosmographs of late Western Han, Xin, and Eastern Han dates have been found from a number of tombs in widely separated parts of China and Korea, but the oldest examples, dating to the early decades of Western Han, have been found in Chu tombs (in Hunan and Anhui). See Wang 2000:118–120; see also the numerous illustrations at http://babelstone.blogspot.com/2009/05/lost-game-of-liubo-part-1-funerary.html (accessed June 3, 2016).

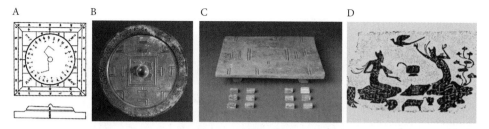

FIGURE 3 (A) Drawing of a cosmograph, Kalinowski 2012–2013. (B) "TLV" mirror with four directional animals, Han period. Courtesy of the Zacke collection, Vienna. (C) "TLV" *liubo* game board, Han period. Courtesy of the Metropolitan Museum of Art collection. (D) Rubbing of a pictorial brick showing two winged immortals playing *liubo*. After Sichuan 1955:Figure 35.

for example, the animal gods of the four directions and the great continent-surrounding ocean—in other words, square Earth set within a round Heaven, a miniature cosmos that could fit in the palm of a person's hand. Neither the game of *liubo* nor the TLV mirror was exclusive to Chu, but both seem to have enjoyed great popularity there (Tseng 2004).

The cosmological designs of these game-boards and mirror designs derive directly from the Chu interest in traditional *sifang* cosmology. These and other depictions of divine realms and supernatural beings are modest in size and scope. Compared with the monumental statues of gods found in ancient Babylon or Egypt, or the elegant marble depictions of Olympian gods of ancient Greece, the Chinese visual pantheon seems modest. (China's later tradition of monumental religious statuary was in part a product of the introduction of Buddhism and Han-period contact with the West via the Central Asian Silk Road.) Depictions of gods in pre-Buddhist China are known mainly from Chu sources; the images are identifiable as depictions of deities and probably distantly related to the metamorphic power masks (the so-called *taotie* 饕餮, an anachronistic term of Han origin) found on Shang and Zhou bronzes that represent powerful deified ancestors. One famous example is the so-called Chu Silk Manuscript, now in the Sackler Collection of the Smithsonian Institution in Washington, DC, with central texts of an astrological and cosmogonic nature and peripheral texts with brief descriptions of the auspicious and inauspicious activities associated with the 12 months (Figure 4) (Jao 1972). The month texts are accompanied by sketches of the 12 monthly gods, miniature monsters with multiple heads and other bizarre features (Hayashi 1972; Barnard 1972b, 1973; Li and Cook 1999). Similar deities are described in the *Shanhaijing*, the oldest sections of which date to the Late Warring States period (Lewis 2006:284–305). A number of scholars associate this text with southern culture (Fracasso 1993:359–361).

Many of the monthly deities of the manuscript show correspondence with similar spirit powers rendered elsewhere in Chu or post–Warring States Chu-influenced art. The deity with antlers, the deity with snakes emanating from its mouth, the multiple-headed humanoid, the deer, and the peacock-like *feng* spirit bird are familiar themes in Chu art. Features including snakes, antlers, and animals undoubtedly had various meanings in different contexts in Chu art, whether as fantastic concoctions associated with shamans or other religious personnel or simply renderings borrowed from nature and mainstream metamorphosis themes stemming ultimately from Shang and Western Zhou times.

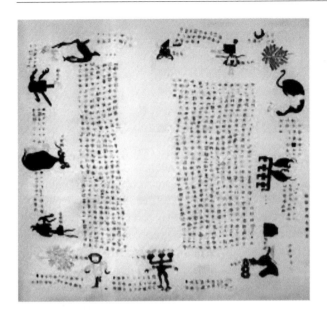
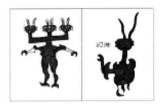

FIGURE 4 The Chu Silk Manuscript. Warring States period, ca. fourth century BCE and details of 4 images of the 12 months. Sackler Art Museum, Smithsonian Institution. After Barnard 1973.

The manuscript is a solilunar calendar, written on a rectangular piece of silk. The images of the 12 monthly gods follow the shape of the silk panel, with three god-images to each side; these evidently represent lunar months. The solar element is found in the division of the year into seasons. At each of the four corners is an image of a tree, no two of which are exactly alike. These apparently represent the directions northeast, southeast, southwest, and northwest, which in Chinese calendrical practice mark the transition from one season to the next. (In traditional Chinese calendars, the solstices and equinoxes mark the mid-points, not the beginnings, of the seasons.) The use of tree images to mark or symbolize the change of seasons seems, on present evidence, to be unique to this document.

TAIYI AND THE INTERMEDIARY REALM

An important new god appeared on the scene in Chu during the late fourth century BCE. This was Taiyi 太一, "Great Undifferentiated Unity." This new supreme deity was beginning to displace the old Shang and Zhou high gods. Taiyi figures prominently in both transmitted texts and in two newly excavated texts from the Chu culture area dating to the Warring States and Han periods. Taiyi appears to have been thought of as a celestial deity, somewhat on the order of the Shang high god Di, or the Zhou god Tian ("Sky Power," "Heaven"). Taiyi was given material form as a constellation but also was a cosmic prime mover (in this sense being an instantiation of the Dao) that initiated the process whereby primordial undifferentiation evolved into the present-day world of "ten thousand things"

(萬物 *wanwu*). Worship of Taiyi under imperial auspices was initiated by Emperor Wu of the Han and maintained by a few of his successors but was discontinued thereafter; none-theless Taiyi remained an important deity in post-Han religious Daoism.

Taiyi's role in the creation of the tangible world is emphasized in the Guodian bamboo manuscript *Taiyi sheng shui* 太一生水, "Taiyi gave birth to water" (S. Cook 2014). This previously unknown work was among the many texts found at Guodian in 1993, dated to ca. 300 BCE (Allan 2003), and is a cosmogonic text in which Taiyi gives birth to water, which then evolves through a series of "reversions" (*fan* 反) into Heaven and Earth and the whole phenomenal world.

A second Taiyi text appears on a badly damaged silk manuscript from the Western Han period Tomb 3 at Mawangdui (168 BCE) (Figure 5). The manuscript portrays seven figures, including a central figure identified by inscription as Taiyi 太一. Other figures include dragons, the war-god Chiyu 蚩尤, and other less certainly identifiable semi-humans, in a style similar to that of the Chu Silk Manuscript (Fu and Chen 1992:35). These deities are flanked with an incantatory text designed to protect a traveler about to set off on a journey—in this case, the journey of the soul to the realm of the dead. It reads, "The Incantation of the Grand One (Taiyi): "Today so-and-so is about to (travel)... draw the bow. The Great Yu goes first. Red *qi* and white *qi* dare not to turn toward me. The hundred weapons dare not harm me... is called insincere. Use the Northern Dipper as the right direction. Spit to the left and the right. Go straight, do not look back" (see Figure 5 on

FIGURE 5 Details and the silk manuscript with Taiyi flanked by other divinities and an incantation to Taiyi, Mawangdui, Tomb 3, Western Han, Hunan Provincial Museum. After *Hunan Mawangdui M3 Hanmu Chutu* and *Kaogu* 1990.10: 925–928; Fu and Chen 1992: 35.

right for enlarged detail of the inscription. (For another translation see Lai 2015:131–132). These texts show Taiyi as both a cosmogonic creator and as a deity able to use magical means to avert harm to his devotees.

In the Mawangdui version Taiyi is represented as the central figure, flanked by other divinities. He has somewhat squatting legs, extended arms, and jagged horns, perhaps abstractions of antlers. He stands above what appear to be three contorting dragons. Secondary deities also face forward with one arm raised in guardian fashion. Two wear triangular, three-pointed headdresses (horns?), the same as worn by humanoid divinities on the Leigudun lacquer coffin (see below in this section). The eyes of Chiyu glance sideways as if in warning. His head is crowned with jagged antler horns similar to those of Taiyi.

Another image of Taiyi is found on a dagger-axe blade dated to the Warring States period (Figure 6A). It is a straightforward icon, portrayed as a displayed image with metamorphic attributes. The figure faces forward with squatting legs and extended arms, gripping reptilian and dragon forms. The costume of the deity is meticulously defined: it includes an elaborate headdress as if representing sprays of curling feathers, or possibly horns, large ears framed by a pair of matching snakes, and a belt with similar serpentine extensions cinching the waist of a body covered by scales. The feet of Taiyi stand above sun and moon symbols, such as were usually represented in bird form during the Jade Age, evolving in the Shang into a pair of symbols of transformation flanking the semi-human yi 異 metamorphic power mask. Images of the sun and moon, whether portrayed as disks or as swirling birds on Liangzhu jades or Warring States silk paintings, symbolized the powerful natural forces that a shaman sought to control. Taiyi is a cosmogonic deity. The displayed disposition of Taiyi images and faces with wide open eyes replicate the Sumitomo bronze drum image of Kui, the legendary founder of the Shang and the precedent for the representation of other metamorphic images. This is an example of continuity and adaptation in mainstream Sinitic metamorphic belief. The small-scale image on the bronze bell is another example of Tai Yi related imagery (Figure 6B).

With the recent discovery of the richly decorated coffins belonging to members of Chu society in southern Henan and northern Hubei (Thorpe 2012), it becomes apparent that Taiyi and Taiyi manifestations were powerful metamorphic tropes of protection and guidance for the soul of the deceased. As established by certain terms in divinatory texts of Shang and Western Zhou date, and by the concepts of yi 異, "to spiritually transform," and wei 畏 (威), "to be spiritually awesome" (Childs-Johnson 2007), transformation after death meant facing a realm of unknown forces, an intermediary liminal space as described in the "Li Sao" that a hun spirit or soul, set adrift from its former human body, must traverse. Protective deities within this realm were either feathered or scaled, bird-like or snake-like. The massively dense décor of intertwining and transforming dragon and bird forms alongside displayed humanoids on the innermost coffin of Marquis Yi of Zeng at Leigudun (Figure 7), show clearly that spirit metamorphosis was an intrinsic feature of the afterlife.

The smothering effect of these transformational forms on the Leigudun coffin is quite different from the decoration of a Chu coffin from Baoshan. The latter is decorated with a composition of allegro abstractions of a similar theme, here the common mythic spirits of long and feng spirit birds (Figure 8), vehicles of metamorphic transportation.

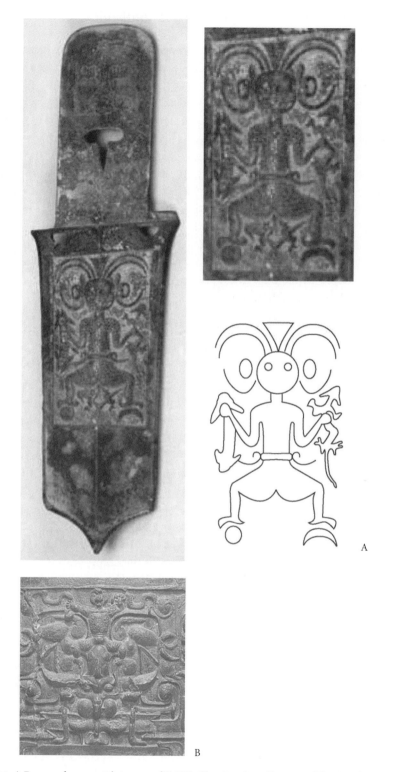

A

B

FIGURE 6 **A** Bronze dagger with image of Tai Yi, Cheqiao dam, Jingmen, Warring States Period, 4th c BCE Jingzhou Museum, Hubei. Drawing by Margaret Panoti. **B** Bronze bell depicting the *yi* spirit empowered deity riding a wild buffalo beast (as a frontal mask) and surrounded by curling feline and bird forms—the four standard metamorphic tropes of Bronze Age China. Leigudun, Hubei, last phase, Springs and Autumns Period/early Warring States, 5th c BCE. after Hubei meishu 1995.

FIGURE 7 Zeng Hou Yi (Marquis Yi of Zeng) inner lacquer burial and drawings of images on the front and back long sides. Leigudun, ca. 433 BCE. Hubei 1989:30, figure 18; 34, figure 20; 36, figure 21.

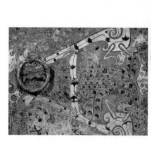

FIGURE 8 Coffin (innermost of three) from Baoshan, Hubei, fourth century BCE, entirely covered in black lacquer with detail of the 72 yellow and red depictions of interconnected snake-bodied dragons and mythical *feng* birds. It is currently on display in the Hubei Provincial Museum, Wuhan, Hubei.

Probable depictions of the deity Taiyi or similar otherworldly deities on the Mawangdui manuscript and Eastern Zhou dagger may be compared with the ghostly humanoid guardian figures (some of which hold double-bladed *ge* dagger-axes) spread across all surfaces of the inner coffin of Zeng Hou Yi (Figure 7). Those who hold poles mounted with dagger and spear or double daggers are clearly identified in their function as guardian spirits. Their repetition and variability convey a sense of the ubiquity and variety of creatures that inhabited the liminal realm the soul must cross on its journey to the afterlife. As guardian images these deities are also auspicious symbols. Their headdresses and costumes vary between bird wing and tail feathers and snakes, and simplified abstractions of body armor. Ears are framed with snakes, as is the case of the Taiyi on the Jingmen dagger (Figure 6A). The figures without weapons appear to be the same deity, in the form of ghostly phantoms replicated in the displayed frontal disposition of metamorphosis, their limbs forming static W and M shapes. Their lower body parts may disappear, melting into the background of profile birds, dragon-like snakes, and braids of snakes that also twist in thin air (Figure 7A and 7B).). Birds are similarly both iconic and in constant movement, displayed erect and perched on tail feathers. Their profile heads face defiantly in opposite directions. Otherwise profile birds of different sizes float as if amorphously suspended in a tapestry of metamorphic icons.

TAIYI IMAGERY AND HYBRIDITY

The image of Taiyi on the Mawangdui painting is unusual in being clearly labelled with the deity's name. Other images from Chu representing Taiyi are identified on the basis of typological and conceptual similarities. The image on the Zhou bronze dagger from Jingmen clearly represents a deity with cosmological power over the animal and spirit realms. The deity's association with sun and moon symbols and power over mythic and real animals, and the displayed static iconic disposition are substantiated and approximated in earlier Jade Age, Bronze Age, and later Han art (Childs-Johnson and Major, forthcoming).

A number of Chu tombs have yielded sculptural figures with distinctive hybrid attributes; these are possibly manifestations of Taiyi and definitely manifestations of the liminal world. Some are worked in lacquer or lacquered wood, others are cast in bronze and often inlaid with colorful gemstones (Figure 10). Constance Cook identifies these images, usually one per tomb, as deities that escort the deceased in the afterworld (C. Cook 2006); Lai Guolong considers them to be fertility gods (Lai 2015). Most commonly they are identified as tomb guardians (Salmony 1954; Demattè 1994). They show a range of attributes common to Chu deities: antlers, feathers, snakes, scales, tiger visages, human visages, birds, and tree forms. They may depict birds with antlers, and when preserved with inlay may be covered with the same intertwining *long* and *feng* dragon and spirit-bird concoctions that cloak the Leigudun coffin with spiritual power (Figures 8 and 9). Attributes are drawn from both natural and mythic realms. One unusual burial good is the lacquer version of a cosmological tree (tree of life) with birds (looking like antlers), evidently a guide for the soul to transcend (Figure 10D). The branches are covered by the familiar natural world featuring snakes, birds, lizards, and other animals. The hybrid animal buried in a Chu tomb at Mashan, Jiangling (Figure 10C) is created out of tree root and bamboo. The large-scale bronze bird with antlers may have served another function in the life of the deceased and then been planted next to the coffin of Zeng Hou Yi upon burial, again for reasons of guaranteeing protection and deliverance to the afterworld (Figure 10B). The most common of these hybrid deities has a sculpted tiger head(s) (Figure 10A). Birds and cosmological trees are less rare but equally potent parts of the liminal unknown (Figure 10B, D). Some hybrid spirit helpers retain multicolored remnants of red, yellow, blue, white, and black lacquer and tiny repeated images in repeated teardrop shapes.

The antlers that are such a conspicuous aspect of the decoration of these sculptures link them to shamanism, a topic that is explored further in this chapter. One symbolic feature that often appears in conjunction with antlers is a long, pendulous tongue. This too originates in Western Zhou (and to a lesser extent, Shang) metamorphic power masks but is greatly exaggerated in the Chu versions. Like antlers, the exposed tongue is found in many artistic traditions of the ancient world, not just in the Sinitic sphere (Salmony 1954, Nielsen 2005). In many Austronesian cultures exposing the tongue is a highly aggressive gesture. To that extent it may not be an exaggeration to see the pendulous tongue as a phallic symbol, conveying a message of physical potency (Major 1999). The lolling tongue of the female deities, the Gorgon and Kali images of ancient Greece and India, are also seen as threatening and devouring evil symbols.

A

Ba

Bb

Bc

FIGURE 9 A Lacquer zither and detail of the image of the metamorphic icon trope. After Hubei 1995: colorpl 57. B North end of the inner lacquer coffin of Zeng Hou Yi (Marquis Yi of Zeng) and drawings of images, primarily humanoids, with some bodies represented as decomposed ghostly apparitions; braided snakes; variations of *feng* and other profile birds, snake-like dragons; and the ubiquitous intertwining of all forms. Leigudun, ca 433 BCE. Hubei 1989:34, figure 20, figure 21, 38.

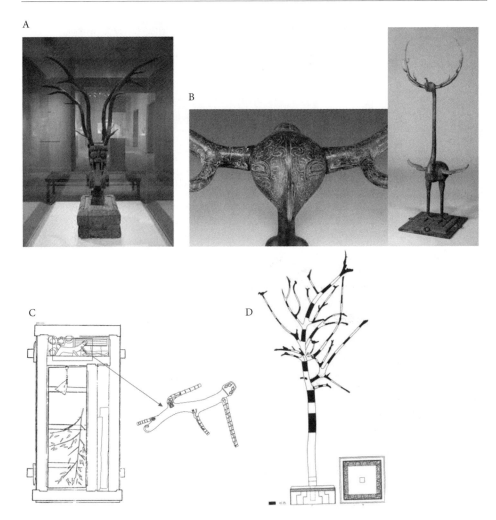

FIGURE 10 Lacquered wood and bronze versions of the single deity accompanying the deceased in Chu burials. **A** Lacquer painted wood deity, Chu attr., Zheng Gong tomb, Xinzheng, Henan, Warring States period. **B** Inlaid bronze crane deity with antlers and head detail, Leigudun Tomb No. 1, Suizhou, Hubei, ca, 433 BCE, height 1,43l.5 cm, weight 38.4 kg. Found on east side of major coffin. Collection of the Hubei Provincial Museum. **C** Ground plan of burial M1 and drawing of the burial deity made out of bamboo and wood. Mashan, Jiangling, Hubei, Warring States period. After Hubei 1985:10, figure 12; and 83, figure 68. **D** Lacquer painted "tree of life" (cosmological tree) with various birds, snakes, snails, frogs, various animals, branches (as if simulating antlers), M2, Tianxingguan, Jingzhou, Hubei, Warring States period, 4th–3rd c BCE. After Hubei 2003:pl 67.1.

THE HUNT METAPHOR FOR THE REALM
OF THE INTERMEDIARY

Another variation of metamorphism and the intermediary realm of the afterlife is the popular image of the hunt in Chu and related arts of the era (Figure 11). The hunt is a metaphor for the intermediary wilderness through which the *hun* soul must travel after death, meeting *qi*—wispy clouds, birds, tigers, anthropomorphic tigers as hunters, deer as hunters with tridents, anthropomorphic birds with spears, or humanoids with flowing hair. These are the familiar subjects of the once so-called hunting *hu* as well as exteriors of lacquer coffins or perforated lacquer screens. The subject is reminiscent of *Aesop's Fables*, known from early Greece of comparable date.

Wild animals, such as mountain sheep, wild buffalo, several species of deer, tigers, and various birds and reptiles, are prominent features of the composite metamorphic power masks that decorate ritual bronze vessels of the Shang and Western Zhou periods (Childs-Johnson 1998). Chu religious art preserves the spirit of this sacred animal art, although animal imagery in Chu art may feature a greater variety of beasts. Giant long-legged birds with outspread wings (sometimes with antlers) were made to serve as stands for large drums featured in orchestral music. Tigers, prominent in bronze art from the Shang period onward, remained important in Chu imagery, especially as directional icons or as the heads of anthropomorphic hybrids. Snakes are also known in Shang art but are especially common in Chu art, seen for example in the décor of a lacquer screen from Wangshan tomb No. 2 (Jiangling, Hubei Province) that also includes frogs and real and imaginary birds (Cook and Major 1999: colorplate 3) (Figure 12). The animals are portrayed as struggling with one another—this is the hunt of the natural world as a metaphor for survival, if not in the afterworld, in the wilderness of the living human. The juxtaposition of bird and snake is a well-known symbol of Heaven and Earth in many early Old World cultures. The same snakes wrap around the foot of the hybrid deities or are clutched in mouths of the same hybrids, as already noted.

FIGURE 11 Examples of Eastern Zhou bronze vessels decorated with Chu subject matter of the hunt within the liminal realm of the traveling *hun* soul. Drawings based on Munakata 1991.

At least two of the month gods portrayed on the Chu Silk Manuscript appear to be gnawing on a snake, as do several of the dragon-headed sprites of the Mawangdui No. 1 inner coffin. A number of semi-divine figures mentioned in the *Shanhaijing* are described as handling snakes. The prominence of snake imagery in Chu art is sometimes taken as evidence of shamanism in Chu, snakes being closely identified with shamanic regalia. The fact that snakes shed their skin periodically as they grow larger has been interpreted as a symbol of transformation or rebirth; the same can be said of antlers, which deer shed annually.

Ritual hunting was an important part of royal conduct in early China, from at least the Shang dynasty onward. Hunts were large-scale and elaborately planned and executed events involving hundreds of beaters spread out over many miles of territory, driving game to the waiting bows and spears of the king and his favored aristocrats. Hundreds of beasts, large and small, were slain; others were captured for display in the royal game park or to be victims in sacrificial rituals. Such hunts served as exercises in military training, fostered a sense of aristocratic solidarity among members of the ruling class, and demonstrated the ruler's awe-inspiring ability to control and dominate the animal realm. With the decline in royal power and authority that accompanied the fall of the Western Zhou dynasty in 771 BCE, the conduct of large-scale hunts devolved onto the rulers of the territorial states of the Eastern Zhou. This occurred all over ancient China and was by no means limited to Chu. But there is good evidence for hunting as a more widespread activity in Chu, still fairly large in scale but not necessarily limited to the Chu monarch and his entourage. This evidence consists of narrative panels cast in relief on so-called Huai-style bronze vessels produced in Chu, beginning in the late Springs and Autumns period and continuing into the Warring States period. Such narrative panels depict a variety of elite activities, including feasting, warfare, dancing, and travel by boat or chariot; depictions of hunting birds (with bows and tethered arrows) or land animals (with spears) are prominent in this kind of narrative art (Munakata 1991). This kind of hunting evidently still carried some of the intense ritual symbolism that featured in the Shang and early Zhou hunts.

It is the subject formalized on the Han-period Mawangdui inner coffin featuring supercharged clouds, racing mythic and wild animals, and humans with windblown hair (similar to the metamorphic Western Zhou humanoid icon), all engaged in either fighting with swords, spears, *ge* dagger axes, or bow and arrow or playing musical instruments (zither, *qin*, chimes) (Figure 13). The tenor is raucous. The wisps of energetic clouds depict *qi*, the basic substance of all phenomena as manifested in the "ten-thousand things." These are also metamorphic images of the supraterrestrial hunt imagined by the Chu and contemporaries during the Eastern Zhou period and continued in a more benign narrative during the Han periods. It is certain that the activities portrayed on Huai-style bronzes are more than simply the agreeable pursuits of the upper class; all of them were hedged about with religious rituals, including divination and sacrificial rites

FIGURE 12 Short lacquer wood screen featuring stylized *feng* and attacking birds, leaping stags, snakes, toads (frogs?), and other animals, Chu state, Warring States period, ca 4th–3rd c BCE. Hubei Provincial Museum, Wuhan, Hubei.

conducted at temples or altars. Bronze vessels depicting hunting were also produced in northern regions of the Sinitic heartland, but in quantity and style they are the heart and soul of Chu inspiration.

CHU: THE CREATIVE APPLICATION OF THE NEW INTERTWINING LONG AND FENG, TIGER WITH LOLLING TONGUE, AND CRANE AND LOTUS MOTIFS

It must be kept in mind that Chu was a mainstream state during the Eastern Zhou Springs and Autumns and Warring States periods. Although their tripod *ding* and *fou* bronzes may have legs that are flat on their inner sides, and *gui* bronzes may carry lotus leaf and petal lids, these are simply stylistic variations of the Zhou ritual bronze assemblage that came in sets of two to nine exactly similar vessels, although sizes may be graduated (see Figure 14) (see chapter 24 by Xiaolong Wu on Springs and Autumns). The exquisite pair of bronze *hu* with crane and perforated lotus-leaf-shaped lid discovered in a Zheng state tomb at Xinzheng, Henan was found together with the typical Chu wood-sculpted hybrid (Figure 15A) (The National History Museum 2000: colorplates 112–113 and 144–147). This pair of *hu* are defined by three Chu innovations: (1) the placement of matching flamboyant handles in the shape of tigers with reverted heads, antlers, and lolling tongues,

FIGURE 13 Outer lacquer painted wood coffin showing, amid clouds, hunting and musical entertainment in the liminal realm of the afterworld, Chu state, Mawangdui, Lady Dai M1, Changsha, Hunan. After Hunan 1973:pl X, figure 18.

juxtaposed with (2) features strikingly naturalistic including a crane that has just flown in to settle on a pool of lotuses, rendered perforated as a lid to the *hu* vessels; and (3) the dense intertwining of *long* and *feng* alongside the occasional humanoid face as a background in bas relief (Figure 15Ab). The latter type of décor, particularly the intertwined images and humanoid face, would dominate the new efflorescence of bronze working during the eighth through third centuries BCE throughout China, in both north and south areas of the kingdom.

Bronze vessels and other media took on a life of their own, stimulated by Chu inventions and the Chu love for sculpturally moving detail, both naturalistic and mythic. The pair of *hu* in the British Museum, dated ca. fifth century BCE, may be used to represent the continued interest in elaborate intertwined *feng* and *long* in addition to the occasional feature of animal or humanoid mask. The metamorphic *yi* mask on this fifth-century-BCE *hu* (see detail in Figure 15C) is typically Chu in style and inspiration, as told by the flanking snakes crowning the upper left and right of the image.

It is also significant that the Chu were responsible for adapting the innovative use of the lost wax technique, as represented by the openwork bronzes from Xiasi and Leigudun (Figure 16). The perforated mass of interlocking, writhing *long* and *feng*, and openwork bodies of the tiger with antlers serving as handles, are striking for their complexity and creativity. The same effect of the openwork motifs is copied in a lacquer

FIGURE 14 A–C Representative Chu bronze vessels and an in situ image of sets of *fou*, *ding*, and *gui*. After Hubei 1989:xia:pl 23.2; 190, figure 91 (large tripod *ding*); figure 56.1 (*fou*); pl 58.1 (*gui*).

dou from Leigudun and décor on bells in sets (Figure 17), indicating again Chu as the source for introducing such interplay and exchange between media, such as lacquer and bronze or, in other cases, silk and hemp textiles (see Figure 18).

FANTASTIC, ANIMAL, AND NATURAL IMAGERY

Here one may add that Chu culture produced works of art in various media, including bronze and lacquer, of superlative beauty and spiritual force.

Despite the relative paucity and small scale of religious imagery in early China, the people of Chu lived in a world replete with ghosts and spirits, many of which were capable of inflicting harm on humans. Many things that to modern sensibilities are simply natural phenomena of no special note, such as lightning and thunder, or dust-devils and hailstorms, were understood by Chu people [and others] as malevolent manifestations of ghosts (often ancestors angry at their living descendants for skimping on or neglecting

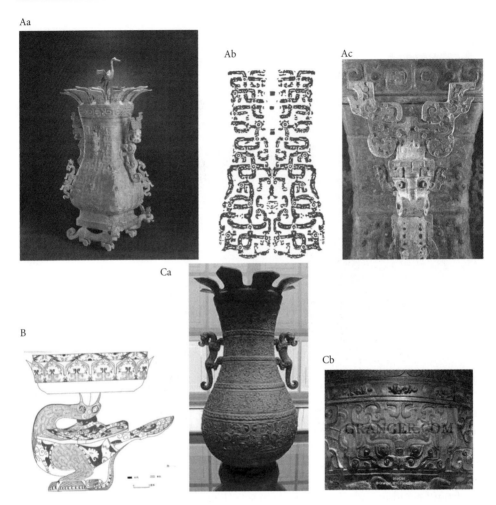

FIGURE 15 A Detail of feline dragon with antlers (ac) and rubbing of intertwined décor (ab) of Chu bronze *hu* from Zheng state tomb, Xinzheng, Henan, Springs and Autumns period, CA. sixth century BCE. After Henan 2001:colorplate 4, figures 63–64. **B** *Feng* bird with reverted neck standing on a snake and holding a lotus shaped *dou* bowl with lid. **C** Bronze hu vessel with feline tiger handles, lotus petal lid and dense raised décor of yi mask and intertwining bodies, in addition to a detail of the metamorphic yi mask. British Museum.

the proper ancestral sacrifices) or minor deities. In particular, illness was understood to be the work of such supernatural beings. A bamboo text from Baoshan describing the final illness of a Chu official named Shao Tuo, and the efforts of diviners in his service to identify and placate the ancestors or deities responsible for the illness, is a striking example of this intersection of religion and medicine (C. Cook 2006). Medical texts found in Tomb 3 at Mawangdui and similar documents unearthed elsewhere confirm the role of ghosts and spirits in causing disease, and of targeted sacrifice, exorcism, and other spiritual interventions as favored treatments for illness (Harper 1992). Again our information on these matters comes largely from both transmitted and newly discovered texts from the Chu culture area.

FIGURE 16 **A** Bronze *zun* in *pan* vessel with drawing of the *zun*, Zeng Hou Yi, Leigudun, Hubei. After Hubei 1995:colorplate 42; Hubei 1989:228, figure 127. **B** Bronze table with 14 feline dragon handles and a detail of feline with antlers, Xiasi, Xichuan, Henan. After Henan 1991:pl 49.

FIGURE 17 Chu lacquers and bells with densely raised *feng* and *long* intertwine and interchange with the metamorphic power mask. **A** Lacquer *dou* and *zhong* bell from Zeng Hou Yi tomb, Leigudun. After Hubei 1995:colorplates 65, 46. **B** Drawing of *zhong* bell from Tianxingguan, Jingzhou, M2 tomb. After Hubei 2003:73, figure 48.

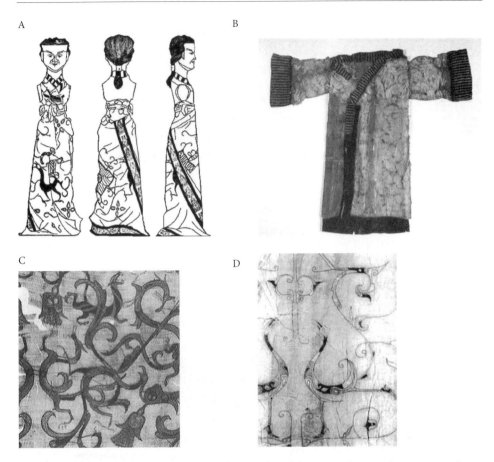

FIGURE 18 Chu textile examples from burial M1 at Mashan, Jiangling, Hubei, Warring States period, fourth to third centuries BCE. **A** Drawing of lacquer painted wood female sculpture dressed in floral and *feng* robe. **B** Yellow silk robe with paired *feng* and *long* and detail of paired *feng*, 182 cm long x 80 cm wide, sleeve width 47 cm. **C** Detail of silk robe with *feng* images. **D** Detail of silk robe with tiger, *feng*, dragon, and floral eyed peacock feathers. After Hubei 1985:81, figure 66; colorplates 22.2, 6.2, 25.3, 28.3. Currently housed in the Jingzhou Museum, Hubei.

Chu peoples contributed another form of imagery, a pictorial narrative that documents both natural observation and myth. The half-life-size recumbent deer with extensive antlers is a creation based on nature but exaggerated for a mannered effect of living grace (Figure 19BC). Lacquer was modeled into antlers which fit mortise and tenon into a wood-carved hollow body with playful teardrop shapes, the same theme which covered the body of the feline hybrid spirit illustrated in Figure 12. The other aspect of pictorial imagery invented by Chu artists is conveyed by the representation of mythic and ritual subjects, such as the Lord Archer on a traveling box (Figure 19B) from the tomb of Marquis Yi of Zeng. The ritual detail on the otherwise naturalistic lacquer duck features images of masked performers playing bells suspended on a rack (Figure 19C).

DEATH AND THE SOUL: FAR-FLIGHT

Silk *feiyi* funerary banners were draped over coffins of female and male Chu aristocrats, one featuring a profile woman with billowing robe and rippling hem with her spirit bird, the *feng* who serves as her transport guide in the afterlife (Figure 20A). The other features a profile male with starched cap and robe riding on his spirit mount and guide, a *long* chariot (Figure 20B). An umbrella overhead signifies the high class of the aristocrat. Fish and owl are included not as afterthoughts but as members of the wild world of nature, the sky and earth below. The third is a lacquer image depicting a toad-like amphibian with snakes upholding a bird, upon which stands a winged sprite of the afterworld. In the latter case the bird is clearly the vehicle for this otherworldly crouching human with bird parts of wings, tail, claws, and feathered lower body (Figure 20C).

A

B

Ca

Cb

FIGURE 19 Lacquer painted wood sculptures exhibiting naturalism, ritual, and mythic subjects, from Leigudun. **A** Hollow lacquer painted recumbent deer. **B** Hollow lacquer duck painted with scene of masked entertainers playing *zhong* bells. **C** Clothing box painted with mythical scene of Hou Yi (Archer Yi) shooting down 9 of 10 suns threatening to scorch the earth. Hubei 1995:Colorplates 69, 81–82, 66–67.

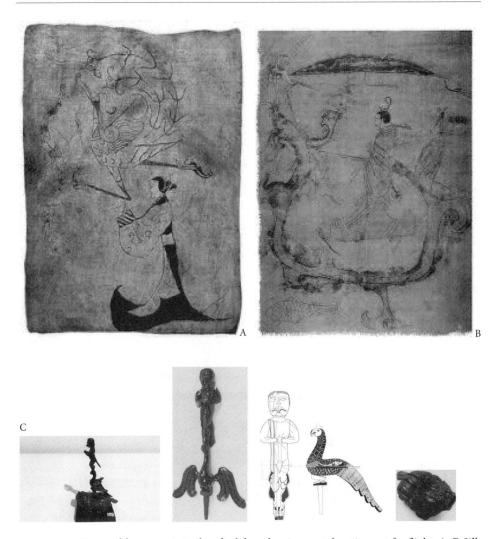

FIGURE 20 *Feng* and *long* escorts to the afterlife and an immortal setting out for flight. **A–B** Silk *feiyi* funerary silk banners from Changsha, Hunan draped over coffins of female and male Chu aristocrats. Chenjiashan, Changsha. Hunan Provincial Museum, and M365.1 from Changsha, Hunan, Hunan Provincial Museum. After Hunan 2000:colorplate 48. **C** Lacquer image of an immortal birdperson setting out in flight on a mythic *feng* grounded in a toad-like animal covered with snakes and small-scale animals. Tianxingguan, Jingzhou, Hubei. After Hubei 2003:colorplates 42–43, 46, and drawing figure 153.

A widespread belief in Warring States, Qin, and Han China, well attested from the Chu culture area but likely also found elsewhere in early China, held that living human beings were animated by two souls: the *po* 魄, an earthly or material soul, and the *hun* 魂, a tenuous and immaterial soul. The presence of both was necessary to maintain life. Death occurred when the *hun* soul left a person's physical body. The *po* soul, in that case, remained with the now-inanimate body and was buried with it; the *po* presumably enjoyed the offerings included in his or her tomb—the sacrificial animals, the retinues of clay or wooden servants, the boxes of food and cosmetics, the textiles and garments, the texts on bamboo and silk, and so on. The *po* was also the entity that received periodic sacrifice and was nourished by it. The *hun* soul, in contrast, left the body and presumably dissipated in the atmosphere, or in extraordinary cases became transformed into one of the vast number of stars or other asterisms visible in the night sky. Because death occurred with the separation of the *hun* from the body, it became customary in Chu and other southern cultures, on the occasion of someone's death, to perform a ritual known as the "summoning of the *hun*," whereby the son or other close relative would climb to the roof of the deceased's dwelling, wave clothing of the deceased, and call for the *hun* to return to the dead person's body. Two long poems in the collection of Chu poetry called the *Chuci* 楚辭 (Elegies of Chu), the "Zhao Hun" 招魂 (Summons of the soul) and the "Da Zhao" 大招 (Great summons) provide details of this ritual (Sukhu 2017:169–188). The speaker would warn the soul of the danger that lurked in the four directions and then offer a tempting account of the splendid banquet that would be offered if the soul consented to return to its body. The failure of the *hun* to return to the body of the deceased was proof that death had actually occurred and thus was the signal for funerary rites and mourning rituals to commence. The ritual of summoning the soul endured for many centuries in some cultures of southern China and Southeast Asia; for example, a simpler version of the "Zhao Hun" ritual is attested from the Hmong culture of Laos well into the twentieth century.

The quests for longevity or immortality were phenomena found throughout China and were not peculiar to Chu culture (Yü 1964–1965). One feature related to immortality did, however, resonate particularly strongly in Chu: the belief in far-flight, or the ability of the *hun* soul to leave the body at will and roam through the sky on long-distance journeys. (The phrase "far-flight" for *zhao-yao* 招搖 is Edward Schafer's. *Zhao-yao* is also the name of a star in the "handle" of the Big Dipper. See Schafer 1977:52.) This type of soul-journey is described most famously in the signature poem of the *Chuci*, "Li Sao" 離騷 (Leaving my sorrow), in which the poet-protagonist drives his flower-bedecked chariot, drawn by dragon-like steeds, through the sky on his way to a tryst with an immortal goddess (Sukhu 2017:35–60). This conception of the flight of the soul seems to have influenced the way in which immortality was perceived.. The corpse of a religious leader might be mummified or embalmed so as not to decay (and therefore perceived as not dead), a physical husk no longer needed by the adept as his *hun* has departed to live on as an immortal (Brown 2002:206–208). The silk *feiyi* 飛衣 from Warring States Chu tombs in Hubei are portraits of the deceased whose escort to the afterworld is none other than the ubiquitous *feng* or *long* mythic transports (Figure 20AB). The other dramatic image of spirit transport depicts a bird-person (whose upper body is human and lower body is bird) in lacquer, evidently already transformed in flight on the back of a *feng* spirit in turn supported at the base by an earthly spirit, a toad covered with snakes (Figure 20C). The people of ancient Chu saw themselves as surrounded by deities, ghosts, spirits, and other spiritual entities and perceived their lives as being influenced by such beings at every turn.

THE QUESTION OF SHAMANISM

Whether or not shamanism was characteristic of early China generally, and Chu in particular, is the most contentious topic in the study of early Chinese religion. Classical shamanism, as found widely in northern Eurasia, involves a highly trained person (male shaman, female shamanka) who has mastered techniques for entering a state of trance (induced by dancing, drumming, inhaling smoke, or other means) in order to make contact with, and channel the instructions of, a deity of some kind, such as a deceased ancestor or nature god. The god, speaking through the shaman, may intervene in various ways in the affairs of the social group concerned, such as giving advice or laying down prohibitions, or aid in carrying out exorcisms or treating illness. Shamans often occupied a marginal role in their society, admired and perhaps feared for their abilities but regarded suspiciously for their strangeness; they typically had spiritual power but not political power (Eliade 2004).

Some scholars, notably K. C. Chang, have argued strongly that shamanism was an important social and political (as well as religious) phenomenon in early China, and that in the Shang dynasty particularly the king was the head shaman (Chang 1983; also Hayashi 1972:134–139). Michael has emphasized the importance of shamanism in early Chinese religion (Michael 2015), while Sukhu points out that shamanism was integral to the imperial rites practiced by Emperor Wu of the Han (Sukhu 2017:3–4). E. Childs-Johnson has used Shang-period data to illustrate that metamorphism (shamanic transformation) formed the basis of Shang belief and that a type of "institutional shamanism" governed the way the king ruled, which is something quite different from the tribal shamanism of the boreal world. These views are based in part on the undoubted fact that the Shang kings consulted their ancestors, as well as various divinities, by means of oracle bones, enlisting those supernatural forces in the conduct of government. Corroborative evidence is found in well-attested Shang rituals involving masked dancing and percussive music (Childs-Johnson 1995; Childs-Johnson and Major, forthcoming). It is evident that the political role of the Shang kings did not resemble the marginal semi-outcast role of shamans in classical shamanism. There is no evidence that the Shang kings entered into a state of trance in performing bone divination or other rites.

The question then arises whether Chu especially was distinguished by a shamanistic culture, whether as a legacy from Shang or as part of the distinctive coastal-riverine culture of the northeastern coast and the Yangzi valley, different from the Sinitic culture of China's Central Plains (Major 1978). Both Paper and Sukhu reject the restrictive view of shamanism as applying only to its Siberian paradigm, showing with copious evidence that spirit-possession was a widespread and widely recognized feature of early Chinese (and Chu) religious life (Paper 1985:51–61; Sukhu 2012). They adduce terms such as *wu* 巫 (magician, shaman) and *xian* 仙 (immortal) as embracing the concept of spirit-possession. Paper draws a useful distinction between shamanism and mediumism in the Chinese context, the latter specifically implying trance and prophetic utterances in the voice of a god. Sukhu specifically sees the poet-persona of the "Li Sao" and certain other *Chuci* poems as a shaman engaged in a flight of the spirit (Sukhu 2017:25–34).

There is good evidence for altered states of consciousness on the part of the Shang rulers. Childs-Johnson has shown that the written word *yi* 異 denotes "spirit-transformation" in the language of Shang oracle bones, a concept linked to masked dance and other features of royal ritual with shamanic overtones (Childs-Johnson 2007). "Spirit-transformation" practices were part of Chu royal rituals and undoubtedly were inherited from earlier dynastic times. Based on a preponderance of evidence, we may conclude that a form of shamanism, in a broad sense of that term, was adapted to the needs of a dynastic culture originating in pre-Shang and by the Shang era was institutionalized to become an important feature of Sinitic religious life.

FIGURE 21 A Lacquer *dou* serving utensil in the shape of the mythic *feng* (peacock), Xiasi burial, Xichuan, Henan. After Henan 1990: B Lacquer cosmetic case featuring the narrative of a funeral cortege sending off a relative to the afterworld. After Alamy stock photo.

Conclusions: Nature's beauty
and the superlative art of Chu

The gift of creating works of art based on nature and myth belongs to Chu during the Zhou period and into the Han. The Chu people by the late phase of the Warring States were also responsible for creating the earliest narratives primarily by means of lacquer painting. It shouldn't be surprising that one of the earliest narratives, one encircling a

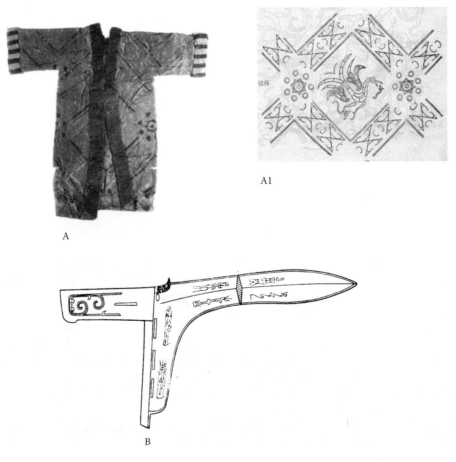

A1

A

B

FIGURE 22 **A** *Qiu Yi* Covered box with bathrobe decorated with otherworldly imagery (front, back, and drawing of robe reverse). Length 45.5 cm, width 52 cm (totally), width of sleeves 10.7 cm, width of waist 26 cm. M1 at Mashan, Jiangling, Warring States period, fourth to third centuries BCE. After Hubei 1985:Colorplate 7.1–2; 69, figure 58. **B** One of three *ge* dagger blades with Chu bird script belonging to Zeng Hou Yi. After Hubei shang 1989:267, figure 157 (top).

lacquer cosmetic case, features a cortege enacting a funeral ritual, a pictorial description that realistically narrates a story based on death (Figure 21A). Another lacquer box, made for otherworldly travel, features the tree of life (cosmological tree) and the myth of Archer Yi shooting down nine of the ten suns thereby saving the world from scorching (Figure 21B). Another gifted Chu artist turned the mythical *feng* bird into a naturalistic lacquer *dou* sculpture and utensil (Figure 21C). The bird's head turns outward 45 degrees and its upper body fills out the rest of the *dou*'s lid. Colors are imaginatively applied, ranging from orange to yellow to red, white, and black. Another innovation of the Chu artistic genius is the creation of so-called "bird script"—the addition of elegantly mannered linear bird parts to graphs, as represented on one of the large-scale *ge* dagger blades from Zeng Hou Yi's burial. The inscription translates "the *ge* and *ji* [weapon] for use by Zeng Hou Yi" 曾侯乙之 用戈 戟 (Figure 22A). The shirt called *qiu yi* (bathrobe in covered box) is another surprising feature documenting mainstream Chinese belief in the preparation of the journey into the afterlife (Figure 22B). The piece of clothing was packed in its own box (separate from the 13 layers encompassing the deceased). The design on front features abstractions of what may be constellations and the back exhibits one large-scale *feng* bird in flight with minuscule snake and dragon. The farewell gift was designed for surmounting whatever waits the *hun* soul—the almost singular concern of Chu and contemporary Sinitic art during the Eastern Zhou period.

BIBLIOGRAPHY

Allan, Sarah 2003. "The Great One, Water and the *Laozi*: New Light from Guodian." *T'oung Pao* 89:237–285.

Anhuisheng Wenwu Kaogu Yanjiusuo 安徽省文物考古研究 所. 2006. *Lingjiatan: Field Archaeology Excavation Report 1* 凌 家滩: 田野考古发掘报告之一. Beijing: Wenwu Chubanshe.

Barnard, Noel, ed. 1972a. *Early Chinese Art and Its Possible Influence in the Pacific Basin*, 3 vols. New York: Intercultural Arts Press.

Barnard, Noel, ed. 1972b. "The Ch'u Silk Manuscript and Other Archaeological Documents of Ancient China." In *Early Chinese Art and Its Possible Influence in the Pacific Basin*. Edited by Noel Barnard, 1:77–102. New York: Intercultural Arts Press.

Barnard, Noel, ed. 1973. *The Ch'u Silk Manuscript: Translation and Commentary*. Canberra: Australia National University Press.

Blakeley, Barry B. 1999a. "The Geography of Chu." In *Defining Chu: Image and Reality in Ancient China*. Edited by Constance A. Cook and John S. Major, 9–20. Honolulu: University of Hawai'i Press.

Blakeley, Barry B. 1999b. "Chu Society and State: Image Versus Reality." In *Defining Chu: Image and Reality in Ancient China*. Edited by Constance A. Cook and John S. Major, 51–66. Honolulu: University of Hawai'i Press.

Brown, Miranda 2002. "Did the Early Chinese Preserve Corpses? A Reconsideration of Elite Conceptions of Death." *Journal of East Asian Archaeology* 4:201–223.

Chang, Kuang-Chih 1972. "Major Aspects of Ch'u Archaeology." In *Early Chinese Art and Its Possible Influence in the Pacific Basin*. Edited by Noel Barnard, 1:5–52. New York: Intercultural Arts Press.

Chang, Kuang-Chih 1983. "Shamanism and Politics." In *Art, Myth, and Ritual: The Path to Political Authority in Ancient China*, 44–55. Cambridge, MA: Harvard University Press.

Childs-Johnson, Elizabeth 1995. "The Ghost Head Mask and Metamorphic Shang Imagery." *Early China* 20:79–92.

Childs-Johnson, Elizabeth 1998. "The Metamorphic Image: A Predominant Theme in the Ritual Art of Shang China." *Bulletin of the Museum of Far Eastern Antiquities* 70:5–171.

Childs-Johnson, Elizabeth 2007. *The Meaning of the Graph Yi* 異 *and Its Implications for Shang Belief and Art*. East Asia Journal monograph series. London: Saffron Books.

Childs-Johnson, Elizabeth, and John S. Major forthcoming. *Metamorphic Imagery in Early Chinese Art and Religion*.

Cook, Constance A. 2006. *Death in Ancient China: The Tale of One Man's Journey*. Leiden: Brill.

Cook, Constance A., and John S. Major, eds. 1999. *Defining Chu: Image and Reality in Ancient China*. Honolulu: University of Hawai'i Press.

Cook, Scott, trans. 2014. *The Bamboo Texts of Guodian: A Study and Complete Translation*, 2 vols. Ithaca, NY: Cornell East Asian Center.

Demattè, Paola 1994. "Antler and Tongue: New Archaeological Evidence in the Study of the Chu Tomb Guardian." *East and West* 44(2–4):353–404.

Eliade, Mircea 2004. *Shamanism: Archaic Techniques of Ecstasy*. Translated by Willard R. Trask. Originally published 1951, Princeton, NJ: Princeton University Press.

Fracasso, Riccardo 1993. "Shan hai ching." In *Early Chinese Texts: A Bibliographical Guide*. Edited by Michael Loewe, 357–367. Berkeley: Society for the Study of Early China and the Institute of East Asian Studies, University of California.

Fu Juyou 傅舉有, and Chen Songchang 陳松長 1992. *Cultural Relics from the Han Tombs at Mawangdui* 馬王堆漢墓文物. Changsha: Hunan chubanshe.

Harper, Donald J. 1978–1979. "The Han Cosmic Board (*shi* 式)." *Early China* 4:1–10.

Harper, Donald J. 1992. *Early Chinese Medical Literature: The Mawangdui Medical Transcripts*. London: Kegan Paul International.

Hayashi, Minao 林司奈夫 1972. "The Twelve Gods of the Chan-Kuo Period Silk Manuscript Excavated at Ch'ang-Sha." In *Early Chinese Art and Its Possible Influence in the Pacific Basin*. Edited by Noel Barnard, 1:123–186. New York: Intercultural Arts Press.

Henansheng Bowuguan 河南省博物馆, and Taibei guoli lishi bowuguan 台北国立 历史博物馆 2001. *Bronze Wares from the Large Tomb of Duke Zheng at Xinzheng* 新郑郑公大墓青铜器. Beijing: Daxiang chubanshe.

Henansheng Bowuguan 河南省博物馆 1990. *The Springs and Autumns Chu Burial at Xichuan Xiasi* 淅川下寺春秋楚墓. Beijing: Wenwu chubanshe.

Hubeisheng Jingzhou Diqu Bowuguan 湖北省地区博物馆 1985. *Chu Tomb M1 at Mashan, Jiangling* 江陵马山一号 楚墓. Beijing, Wenwu chubanshe.

Hubeisheng Bowuguan 湖北省博物馆 1995. *The Appreciation of the Cultural Relics of the Zeng Hou Yi Tomb* 曾侯乙墓文物珍赏. Wuhan: Hubei meishu chubanshe.

Hubeisheng Jingzhou Diqu Bowuguan 湖北省地区博物馆 2003. *Chu Burial No. 2 at Jingzhou Tianxingguan M2* 荆州天星观二号楚墓. 1991. *The Chu Burial at Baoshan* 宝山楚墓. Beijing: Wenwu chubanshe.

Hubeisheng Bowuguan 湖北省博物館, eds. 1980. *The tomb of Zeng Hou Yi in Suixian* 隨縣曾侯乙墓. Beijing: Wenwu chubanshe.

Hunansheng Bowuguan 湖南省博物館, and Zhongguo Kexue Yanjiusuo 中國科學 研究所 1973. *The Han Tomb Number 1 at Mawangdui, Changsha* 長沙馬王堆一號漢墓. Beijing: Wenwu chubanshe.

Hunansheng Bowuguan, "Taiyi on the Move," http://www.hnmuseum.com/en/zuixintuijie/taiyi-move

Hunansheng Wenwu Kaogu Yanjiu suo, Changshashi Bowuguanm Changshi WenwuKaogu Yaniusuo, Changsha Bowuguan 湖南省博物馆, 湖南省文物考古研究所, 长沙市文物 考古研究所, 长沙市博物馆 2000. *A Chu Burial from Changsha* 长沙楚墓. Beijing: Wenwu chubanshe.

Jao, Tsung-i 1972. "Some Aspects of the Calendar, Astrology, and Religion of the Ch'u People as Revealed in the Ch'u Silk Manuscript." In *Early Chinese Art and Its Possible Influence in the Pacific Basin*. Edited by Noel Barnard, 1:113–122. New York: Intercultural Arts Press.

Kalinowski, Mark 2012–2013. "The Notion of '*Shi* 式' and Some Related Terms in Qin-Han Calendrical Astrology." *Early China* 35–36:331–360.

Lai, Guolong 2015. *Excavating the Afterlife: The Archaeology of Early Chinese Religion*. Seattle and London: University of Washington Press.

Lewis, Mark Edward 2006. *The Construction of Space in Early China*. Albany: State University of New York Press.

Li Ling and Constance A. Cook 1999. "Translation of the Chu Silk Manuscript." In *Defining Chu: Image and Reality in Ancient China*. Edited by Constance A. Cook and John S. Major, 171–176. Honolulu: University of Hawai'i Press.

Major, John S. 1978. "Research Priorities in the Study of Ch'u Religion." *History of Religions* 17(3–4):226–243.

Major, John S. 1999. "Characteristics of Late Chu Religion." In *Defining Chu: Image and Reality in Ancient China*. Edited by Constance A. Cook and John S. Major, 121–143. Honolulu: University of Hawai'i Press.

Michael, Thomas 2015. "Shamanism Theory and the Early Chinese *Wu*." *Journal of the American Academy of Religion* 83(3):649–696.

Munakata, Kiyohiko 1991. *Sacred Mountains in Chinese Art*. Champaign: University of Illinois at Urbana.

Nielsen, S., et al. 2005. "The Gundestrup Cauldron: New Scientific and Technical Investigations." *Acta Archaeologica* 76:1–58.

Queen, Sarah A., and John S. Major (2010). *Luxuriant Gems of the Spring and Autumn*. New York: Columbia University Press.

Paper, Jordan 1985. *The Spirits Are Drunk: Comparative Approaches to Chinese Religion*. Albany: State University of New York Press.

Puett, Michael J. 2002. *To Become a God: Cosmology, Sacrifice, and Self-Divinization in Early China*. Cambridge, MA: Harvard University East Asian Center.

Salmony, Alfred 1954. *Antler and Tongue: An Essay on Ancient Chinese Symbolism and its Implications*. Ascona: Artibus Asiae.

Schafer, Edward H. 1977. *Pacing the Void: T'ang Approaches to the Stars*. Berkeley, Los Angeles, and London: University of California Press.

Sichuan 1955. *A Selection of Han Dynasty Images from Sichuan* 四川漢代畫象選集. Shanghai: Shanghai chubanshe gongsi.

Sukhu, Gopal 2012. *The Shaman and the Heresiarch: A New Interpretation of the Li Sao*. Albany: State University of New York Press.

Sukhu, Gopal, ed. and trans. 2017. *The Songs of Chu: An Anthology of Ancient Chinese Poetry by Qu Yuan and Others*. New York: Columbia University Press.

Tseng, Lillian Lan-ying 2004. "Representation and Appropriation: Rethinking the TLV Mirror in Han China." *Early China* 29:163–215.

Tseng, Lillian Lan-ying 2011. *Picturing Heaven in Early China*. Cambridge, MA: Harvard East Asia Center.

Thote, Alain 2012. "Chinese Coffins from the First Millennium BCE and Early Images of the Afterworld." *RES Anthropology and Aesthetics* 61–62:22–40.

Wang, Aihe 2000. *Cosmology and Political Culture in Early China*. Cambridge, UK and New York: Cambridge University Press.

Yü, Ying-shih 1964–1965. "Life and Immortality in the Mind of Han China." *Harvard Journal of Asiatic Studies* 25:80–122.

CHAPTER 35

THE ARTISTIC REVOLUTION IN THE WARRING STATES PERIOD

BY JIE SHI, BRYN MAWR COLLEGE

THE Warring States period (475–221 BCE) was one of the most creative eras in Chinese history, if not world history. New arts of all types and architectural innovations flourished and proliferated. On the macro level towns and cities grew into bustling metropolises hitherto never witnessed in China. New cities emerged in unprecedentedly large numbers across newly cultivated lands; monumental buildings grew higher than anything the Chinese had ever built, soaring from kingdom to kingdom; and cemeteries and tombs not only became larger, higher, and richer but also transformed into another center of social space. On the micro level, while traditional ritual arts including bronze and jade were invigorated by the introduction of novel types, shapes, materials, and technologies, fashionable secular objects represented by lacquers and textiles began to show increasing importance due to their greater quantity and unparalleled quality. Figurative and pictorial arts began to emerge with a new skill in representation.

CITIES AND PALACES

Hailed as "the second urbanizing revolution in Chinese history," the Warring States period witnessed a dramatic increase in the number of walled towns and cities (*cheng* 城) (Du 1992:703–712). Based on the traditional method of ramming earth in a temporary wooden frame to erect walls, Warring States artisans developed new ways to increase the structure's tenacity and its defensive capacity (Zhang 2004). Unlike earlier walls that were often stepped or sloped, by adding wooden poles the rammed-earth walls could be steeper and higher. It was during this period that different kingdoms constructed the earliest sections of the Great Wall, only later to be linked by the first emperor of Qin, Shihuangdi (r. 246–210 BCE), who finally united China (Cosmo 2006). Walled cities and towns developed rapidly. By the year 2000 archaeological excavations had brought to light more than 400 Eastern Zhou remains of walled cities or towns, many of which were constructed or used during the Warring States period (Xu 2000a:84). The actual number of such sites was most likely greater than what has thus far been discovered. A passage in *Zhanguoce* 戰國策 relates that the Qi kingdom (in present-day Shandong province), for example, boasted of some 120 walled towns (*cheng*) within an area of 1,000 square *li* (i.e., 173 square kilometers) (Crump 1979:152).

Meanwhile, cities also grew bigger, shifting from small religio-political centers as typified the Shang and Western Zhou periods into true metropolises as large as 10 to 30 square kilometers. Yan Xiadu (the Lower Capital of the Yan kingdom), the largest of all Warring States cities so far excavated, features a wall 8 kilometers long and 4–6 kilometers wide, covering an area about 40 times larger than one of the largest Shang cities in present-day Yanshi in Henan province, which measures nearly a square kilometer (Hebei 1996a:1:13).

The extended urban space within the cities was more divided and better organized. Despite their irregular shapes and orientations, in terms of structure most large cities shared a bipartite plan conventionally called *cheng-guo* 城郭. Both walled, *cheng* ("inner city") referred to the city's major area reserved mainly for kings and aristocrats, and *guo* 郭 ("outer city") denoted its accompanying area inhabited by commoners (*guoren* 國人) (Yang 1993:90; Xu 2000b:36). Meanwhile in some cities, such as Yan Xiadu (Figure 1), Lingshou of the Zhongshan kingdom, Xinzheng of the Han kingdom, and Handan of the Zhao kingdom, *cheng* and *guo* were either separated by a partition wall or totally disconnected. Among them Yan Xiadu, Lingshou, and Xinzheng have two interconnected zones (Hebei 1996a:1:11–21; Hebei 2005:10–11; Henan 1980:56–66); Handan features two disconnected adjacent zones (Duan 2009:92–109). In other places such as the Linzi of the Qi kingdom, and Anyi of the Wei kingdom, the outer *guo* either partly or entirely enclosed the inner *cheng* (Figure 2) (Zhongguo 1963:474–479). The only exception was Xianyang, the last capital of the Qin, in which no outer walls (or cities) have been found (Xu 2000c:145–151).

The spatial division of the cities coheres with functional division. In terms of social function, *cheng* remained mainly as the political, ritual, and religious center, and *guo* developed into bustling residential, manufacturing, and commercial centers (Yang 1993:88–89). More importantly, marketplaces (*shi* 市), located in both the inner and the outer cities, emerged as special trading zones managed and administrated by government (Qiu 1980). In Linzi, for example, archaeologists discovered rich remains of pottery, bone, bronze, and iron workshops in the central, northeast, and west sections of the outer city, which also included cemeteries in the northeast and in the south. The inner city, in which archaeologists excavated a group of ruined architectural foundations, embraced the palaces of the Qi royal house (see Figure 2) (Qunli 1972).

Sumptuous palaces were built in and outside of the large cities, especially the royal capitals. Compared with their predecessors in the Shang, Western Zhou, and Springs and Autumns periods, architects in this new era began to pursue not only more spacious but

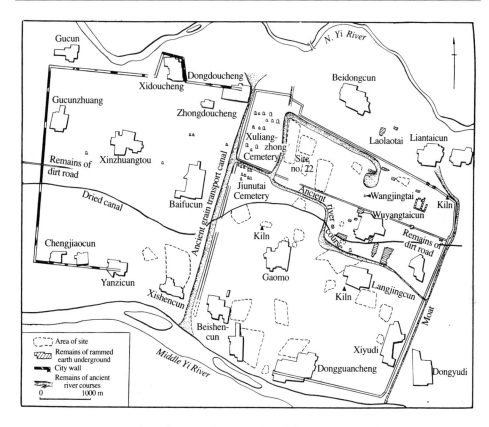

FIGURE 1   Plan of Yan Xiadu. Reproduced from Li 1985:113, figure 48.

also higher structures. For example, the modern city of Ji'nan in Hubei province, once the capital of the Chu kingdom, has yielded 40 foundations of palace buildings, of which the largest of them measures 130 by 100 meters (Guo 1998:130). Following a north-south central axis (Guo 1998:135), these royal palaces stood on raised, sometimes stepped, terraces, which significantly increased the physical stature and visibility of the structures.

Buildings based on such high earthen terraces were called *tai* 臺 in Eastern Zhou texts. The solid terraces constructed of rammed earth formed the whole structure's core foundation, around which wooden chambers and galleries were constructed (Thorp 1986:364). An important site located about 50 kilometers to the southeast of Ji'nan in present-day Qianjiang, Hubei province, has revealed what has been tentatively identified as the Palace of Splendor and Brilliance (*Zhanghua gong* 章華宮), one of the most renowned royal Chu palaces first established in 535 BCE and burned down to the ground by Qin troops in 278 BCE (Guo 1998:190–195). Within this huge palatial complex the best-preserved Fangying Terrace (*Fangying tai* 放鷹臺), No. 1, measures 130 by 90 meters in area. Surrounded by a courtyard on the east and galleries in the northwest, southwest, and east, the terrace was a three-stepped structure based on a foundation 2.5 meters high, which was purported to reach about 10 *zhang*, or 23 meters when it was intact (Figure 3) (Jingzhou 2003; Yang 2000:145–151).

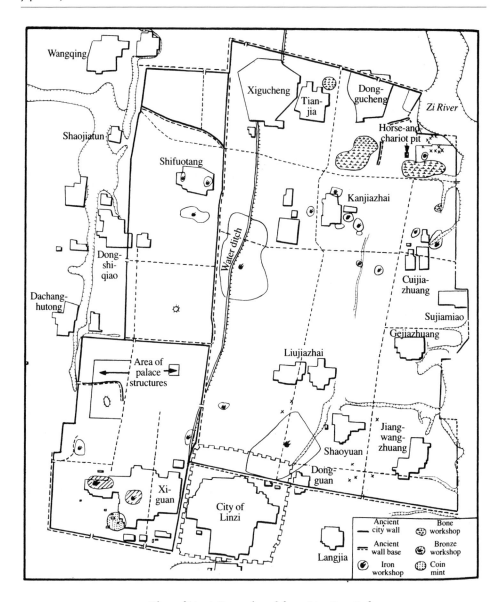

FIGURE 2 Plan of Linzi. Reproduced from Li 1985:128, figure 55.

The only partially revealed palace remains in Xianyang, the last capital of the Qin kingdom, preserve another new type of building called by Eastern Zhou authors as *guan* 觀 (literally "overlooking building") or *que* 闕 (pillar tower), which often stood in pairs at the gate of the palace (Shaanxi 2004:283–256). Measuring 130 meters wide, remains of the *guan*, in Palace Complex No. 1 in the Xianyang Palace, consisted of two parallel terraces separated by a ditch dug in between. On each of the terraces stood a central building surrounded by smaller side-chambers. Between these tall buildings a suspended

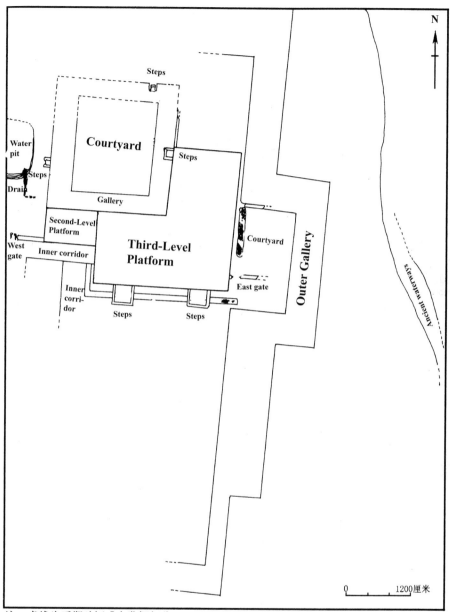

注：虚线为后期破坏或未发掘部分

FIGURE 3 Plan of the Fangying Terrace at Zhanghua Palace. Adapted from Jingzhou 2003:figure 7.

overpass crossing high above the ditch enabled people to walk from one side to the other, as if in the "air," a novel experience previously unimaginable before such high buildings were invented (Figure 4) (Yang 1987:153–168). As with *tai*, such innovative structures demonstrate interest in pursuing elevation and visibility.

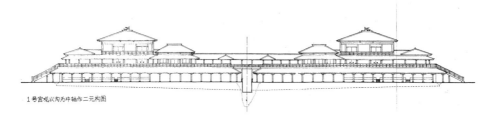

1 曡宫观以沟为中轴作二元构图

FIGURE 4 Reconstruction of Palace Complex No. 1, Xianyang. Yang 1987:156, figure 5. 17

Funerary parks and tombs

Generally speaking, Chinese tombs of the Warring States period, like their predecessors from the preceding Spring and Autumn period, still fall into the category of vertical pit graves. In a typical pit grave, the coffin was usually located in the center of a rectangular wooden burial chamber constructed at the bottom of an earthen shaft dug deep into the ground. Before the lid of the wooden casket was finally laid down to conceal all the burial contents, the burial chamber would have remained open from above, visually accessible to the funerary participants on the ground. Tomb passages, sometimes ramps and other times steps, led down to the burial chamber but almost always terminated above it. Mourners were not expected to physically enter the burial chamber, leaving the structure entirely to the deceased. This vertical configuration suggests that the deceased (or their souls) would have to follow an upward or downward direction, ascending or descending between the aboveground world and the underground "Yellow Springs" (*huangquan*黃泉), where the bodily remains were thought to reside (Poo 1998:65). However, some new developments that occurred in this period suggest a growing significance of the burial in the society.

During the Warring States period, tombs became so important that in many cities, including such great capitals as Yan Xiadu (Lower Capital of the Yan kingdom) and Linzi (of the Qi kingdom), they were included in the outer cities protected by walls (see Figures 1, 2).

Conceptually distinguished from lower-ranked cemeteries, Warring States royal cemeteries, formally called *ling* 陵 ("hills"), were collective necropolises consisting of multiple tombs belonging to a number of generations of a royal lineage. Whereas none of the royal cemeteries has been fully unearthed, a number of them were probed or partially excavated. Either walled or moated, most of the cemeteries included not only underground burials but also aboveground buildings maintained by a staff who perhaps lived near the cemeteries (Ruan 1980:786; Hebei 1996b:1:7–10). By the end of the Warring States period, these royal cemeteries, conventionally called "funerary parks" (*lingyuan* 陵園), had become so large and complex that they even rivaled cities to some contemporary eyes (Knoblock and Riegel 2000:230). Two major types of funerary parks

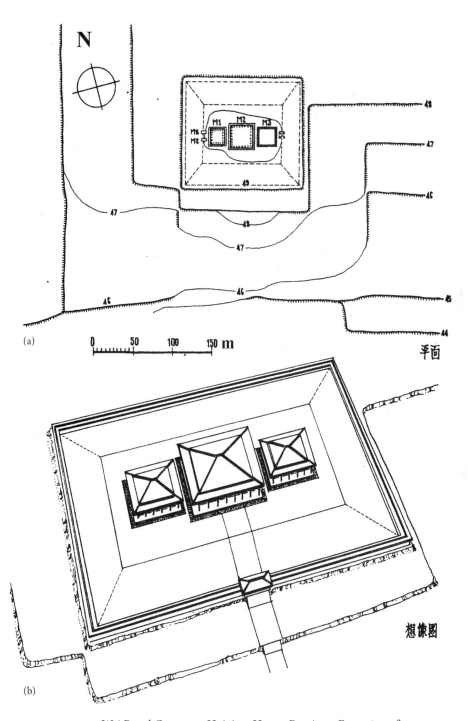

FIGURE 5 Wei Royal Cemetery, Huixian, Henan Province. Fu 1998:79, figure 14.

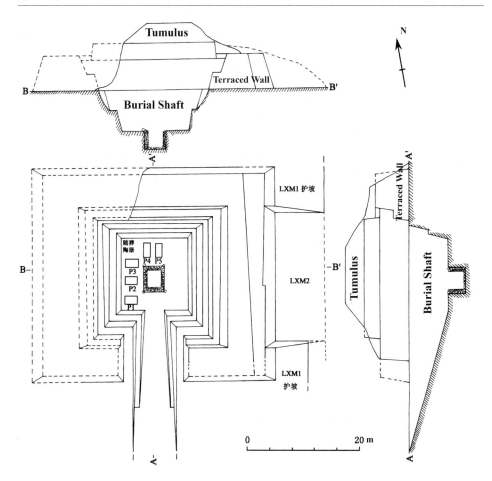

FIGURE 6 Qi Royal cemetery, Linzi, Shandong Province. Adapted from Shandong 2007:198, figure 132.

stood out: the grave surmounted by a building and the grave covered under a tumulus (mound) (Thote 2004:1:68). However, these two major types did not follow a diachronic sequence but rather largely coexisted. These are represented by two royal cemeteries respectively, one located in present-day Huixian in Henan province, and one in Linzi in Shandong province (Figures 5–6) (Zhongguo 1956; Shandong 2007). The former was characterized by a freestanding offering shrine (sometimes based on a terraced earthen foundation) surmounting the interred burial; the latter type substituted the shrine with a tall mound made of rammed earth. Although none of the offering shrines survives and their precise function remains controversial, the general ritual purpose of these free-standing structures seems indisputable (Yang 2000:68–76; Yang 1985:100–105). The sizes of tumuli were regulated by the ruling class in signifying the social status of the deceased (Hu 1994:558). The tombs with a tumulus most likely included some ground-level struc-tures, presumably for ritual purposes. Based on archaeological surveys, the tumuli type

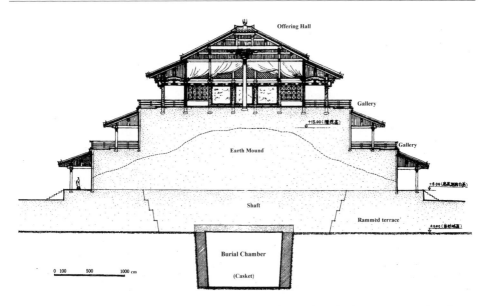

FIGURE 7 Section of King Cuo's Tomb, Pingshan, Hebei. Adapted after Yang *Gongdian kaogu tonglun*, figure 162, slightly modified.

appears to have been more numerous than the tomb type with crowning shrine (Shi 2014:Tables 1 and 2).

The aboveground structures connect directly and vertically with the underground ones in the cemetery. Large tombs of this period could be viewed as extending vertically upward from below to aboveground level. King Cuo's 譽 tomb represents perhaps the most complex vertical structure in all excavated Warring States tombs (Figure 7). This monumental tomb consisted of three levels of a three-story building (Shi 2015). The bottom level conventionally called *guoshi* 槨室, or "burial chamber," was a pit dug deep into the ground to contain a wooden casket. The interstices between the walls of the casket and the walls of the pit were filled with protective stones, a popular funerary practice to baffle tomb robbers. In the casket lay a coffin (possibly multi-layered) for the king's corpse. Upon discovery the casket had been plundered and disrupted, but archaeologists still found many funerary jades and small metal articles in the totally disintegrated casket. Most grave goods including ritual bronzes, "spirit objects" (*mingqi* 明器) (Falkenhausen 2006:302–306; Wu 2009:91–99), and various mundane objects were buried in the two side pits that flanked the burial chamber on the same level (Hebei 1996b:1:111–141, 404). After the coffin had been ensconced and the burial chamber furnished, the bottom pit and its funerary passage were interred and a middle level—an aboveground shaft—was constructed on top of the burial chamber. Approached by two ramps, one in the north and one in the south, this new shaft, in the shape of a reversed truncated pyramid, measures 30 meters wide at the top and 26.7 meters wide at the bottom with a height of nearly six meters. No burial objects were uncovered within this middle level, which perhaps played some ritual role during the funerary ceremony.

After the middle level was filled, the top level was finally constructed, featuring a free-standing offering shrine, designed to endure permanently after the funerary ceremony.

In south China burials were made differently in being characterized by richly furnished wooden caskets divided horizontally into separate compartments for grave goods. A good example is the tomb of Marquis Yi of Zeng (d. late fifth century BCE), located in present-day Suixian in Hubei province (Figure 8). Consisting of four connected rectangular wooden compartments, the entire casket formed an irregular plan reminiscent of a large household compound (Beckman 2002; Falkenhausen 2006:306–308). Two nested coffins with lavish paintings on the exterior faces contained the deceased's corpse in the east compartment, accompanied by coffins of the deceased's consorts. The largest compartment in the center was filled with various ritual bronzes, including sets of musical instruments and sacrificial vessels. Upon discovery, the bronze bells still remained suspended on the wooden stand; the vessels were displayed in working order. The north compartment yielded weapons and chariot fittings; the west compartment yielded 13 coffins for human sacrifices. It seems as if each compartment mirrored one section of the royal residence: the central compartment represented the deceased's ritual hall, the north compartment, the arsenal, the east, the living room, and the west, the place for the attendants. Small rectangular holes were made in the wall of the outer coffin as well as in

FIGURE 8 Plan and section of Marquis Yi of Zeng's Tomb, Suixian, Hubei. Hubeisheng 1989:1:9, figure 5.

FIGURE 9 Plan of Baoshan Tomb 2. Hubei 1991:1:82, figure 35.

other compartment walls, probably to make sure the souls could travel freely among these symbolic places (Hubei 1989:1:14).

In large tombs of the Chu kingdom postdating Marquis Yi's 乙 tomb, the casket chamber was still divided by walls into multiple compartments, but the overall shape of the wooden casket was regularized into a rectangular case (Thote 2000). Baoshan Tomb 2, an outstanding example belonging to a high aristocrat named Shaotuo邵佗 (d. late fourth century BCE), included a rectangular casket consisting of five compartments, among which the central one contained the coffins and the others held grave goods (Figure 9) (Hubei 1991:1:51–63; Lai 2015:75–77). The inventory of grave goods buried in the tomb suggests that these compartments were associated with symbolic meanings. For example, the "tail compartment" (*xiangwei* 廂尾) was reserved for traveling paraphernalia, and some bronze food vessels were interred in the "dining room" (*shishi* 食室) (Hubei 1991:1:369). Densely packed with almost no space between compartments, the tomb was like a "shipping container," perhaps designed to serve the deceased's posthumous journey to the afterlife (Lai 2005; Cook 2006).

BRONZE, JADE, LACQUER, AND TEXTILE

Although ornament remained as the dominant artistic presence in the Warring States period, artists developed new tools and devices to dazzle the eyes, charm viewers, and thereby exert an impact on the society.

Warring States bronzes developed an interest in dramatizing the surface of the art work with two seemingly contradictory aesthetics: sculptural and pictorial. The first refers to the artist's efforts of "opening up the surfaces of the bronzes" (Lawton 1982:21) and the second, keeping it smooth, glossy, and sometimes painted. Despite the difference, both responded against the moderate low-relief forms of ornament in the previous Late Western Zhou and Early Eastern Zhou periods. Although the traditional techniques of piece-mold casting with the extensive use of pattern blocks and inlay continued, two main technological developments—lost-wax casting and gilding—provided powerful new means for the artists to push the limits of surface decoration.

The sculptural style is exemplified by Marquis Yi's remarkable bronze vessels, among which a two-piece set of *zun* 尊 and *pan* 盘 achieved a dramatic effect with extremely ornate ornamentation that almost completely covers their bodies (Figure 10). Both the *zun* and *pan* vessels are ornamented with numerous S-shaped tiny dragons densely stacked on the rims of the vessels' upper opening, turning the latter into intricate openwork. It would have been difficult to cast such honeycomb-like parts without using the lost-wax method, which remained largely unknown to the Chinese until this period (White 1988:175–181; Hubei 1989:1:646). The traditional technique of welding was exploited to create far more intensive sculptural effects on the vessel. On the *zun* vessel, for example, a group of three-dimensional dragons, which were cast separately, are welded around the vessels' circular bases and rounded bellies; four openwork felines are evenly attached to the long neck of the vessel at the same level. The *pan* vessel is treated in a similar manner, leaving little room for even a hand to hold the object. It is thus clear that the artist's interest was not simply to decorate a ritual object but to turn the object's wall into a sculptural ensemble.

Meanwhile, another artistic impulse resulted in a glossy style that highlights the flatness and evenness of surface and became increasingly popular from circa the fourth century BCE onward. In this style the use of welding is limited and exterior ornamentation remains minimal. Consequently, the exterior of the bronze vessel is transformed into a curving picture plane, almost like a bended canvas, to bear inscriptions or two-dimensional patterns and images. For example, a *ding* tripod found in King Cuo's tomb carries a long inscription of 469 characters, indicating its important ritual role (Figure 11) (Shaughnessy 1997:104–109; Wu 2017:149–170). The vessel's exterior face is smooth and polished throughout to create a perfectly lustrous background for the commemorative words to stand out. What's more, taking advantage of (newly developed) iron tools, which are harder and stronger than bronze, artists could engrave characters directly on the vessel without relying on a mold.

To increase the luster and color on the glossy surface, many ritual bronzes bear gold, silver, copper, or turquoise inlays that filled the depressions cast on the exterior face of the vessels (Shi 1973:72). These inlays might form fluent geometric or figurative motifs (So 1995:46–54). Whereas inlay was a traditional Chinese craft traceable to the Shang dynasty, gilding, conventionally known as *jinyincuo* 金銀錯, was a completely new technique that was used to "paint" directly on the bronze vessel surface. This gold paint could be either smoothly applied or depressed, thanks to the development of chemistry and

FIGURE 10 Painted pottery ritual surrogates from Yan Xiadu. Yixian, Hebei province, third century BCE. Hebei 1996a:2:Plates 21.2, 22.1.

FIGURE 11 Zun and pan from Marquis Yi of Zeng's Tomb at Suixian, Hubei province, fifth century BCE. Wenwu 1994:5:Plates 42.

alchemy at that time (Liang 2000). Normally the artist used mercury to dissolve gold or silver foils and turn the latter into a paste, which was applied onto the wall of the vessel in a way similar to painting (Lins and Oddy 1975; Gao 2012). The gilt or inlaid patterns on the surface of the vessel became pure ornaments, reflecting the "seductive elegance of the rising lacquer and textile industries in the south" (So 1980:308). The composition of the decorative patterns also changed, as ostentatious ornamentation breaks down use of horizontal registers of earlier bronzes, now easily covering the entire vessel as one unified composition. A remarkable bronze flat *hu* in the Freer Gallery of Art, Washington, DC., demonstrates such a striking visual effect achieved by the brilliant silver inlay that forms feather-curl patterns across the vessel's exterior (Figure 12). On each oval face, the diagonal, occasionally interlacing lines are arranged in a roughly symmetrical manner along an invisible vertical central axis. The glistening silver filling the patterns sharply contrasts against the dimmer bronze in the background, dazzling the viewer's eye. Despite the technical differences, both inlay and gilding aim at achieving a smooth and lustrous surface, which invites not only viewing but also touching.

   Although it is tempting to assume a linear evolution between the two styles, namely sculptural and pictorial, archaeological data suggest that they might have developed

FIGURE 12 Inscribed bronze *ding* tripod from Cuo's Tomb at Pingshan, Hebei province, fourth century BCE. *Sekai* 2002:1:199, plate 190.

side by side. The two seemingly contradictory styles coincide in an ingenious way on one extraordinary round *hu* pot once owned by an aristocrat named Chen Zhang 陳璋 (fl. fourth century BCE). The vessel on the one hand has a smooth surface with angular geometric patterns inlaid with gold and silver, and on the other hand is cloaked on the shoulder by an openworked bronze web consisting of interlocking dragons and flowers, which creates a sculptural effect (Figure 13) (Yao 1982). A viewer might wonder about the complex purpose of such apparently superfluous ostentation: although covered by the porous cloak, the vessels' ornate exterior with precious inlays still shines through the openings. The tension and balance between the two decorative layers epitomizes the innovative spirit of Warring States artists for such a daring experiment.

A variety of mundane bronze objects also gained sudden popularity. Among them bronze mirrors, mostly circular but sometimes square, were found in their hundreds in tombs, especially in the Chu kingdom (Liu 1985). Arguably representing one of the highest achievements of ancient Chinese metallurgy, these extremely thin (0.1–0.2 cm) mirrors were cast of bronze with a high percentage of tin (20%–26%) and sometimes polished with an abrasive rich in tin, which makes the mirror look whiter and brighter (He 1999:46, 49–55; Needham and Lu 1974:238). The reverse is often lavishly decorated symmetrically with several types of abstract patterns or figurative images, sometimes even inlaid or gilt (for a typology of Eastern Zhou bronze mirrors and their ornaments, see Kong and Liu 1984:24–55). A great example, excavated from a tomb at Zhangjiashan, Hubei province in 1975 consists of two parts: the front specular side and the back decorative side, with the former tightly set in the latter (Figure 14) (Jingzhou 1984:15). To make the two sides fit, the

FIGURE 13 Wine flask (*bianhu*) with geometric decoration, third century BCE. Late Eastern Zhou dynasty, Late Warring States period. Bronze with silver inlay, height 31.3 cm, width 30.5 cm, depth 11.7 cm. China Gift of Charles Lang Freer F1915.103a–b.

back side was perhaps cast first before it was placed in a second mold to cast the frontal side (He 1999:124–125). The plain specular side is made of highly polished tin bronze, and the decorative side is cast into openwork comprising two concentric zones separated by a very slim circular groove. The wider inner disk is divided into four sectors by pairs of confronting low-relief S-shaped dragons, which gather their heads around a central lotus-shaped knob in a perfectly symmetrical composition. The narrower outer zone is a band with repeating diagonal feather-curl lines, which are symmetrically interlaced.

Other daily items, including most notably bronze lamps and belt or garment hooks, became especially fashionable in Warring States tombs (Lawton 1982:89–94). The creative design of the lamps includes, for example, modeling the stand of the lamp after a human figure riding a Bactrian camel while supporting the stem of the lamp (Figure 15) (Lai 2002). The belt or garment hook, sometimes gilt or inlaid with jade, gold, silver, or turquoise, boast ingenious designs and exquisite craftsmanship (Figure 16) (Wang 1985).

Jade (or its stone simulations) is another yet traditional type of ritual art crafted for various ritual purposes, particularly on sacrificial and funerary occasions, because of its magical transformative properties (Rawson 1995:54–55; Childs-Johnson 1998, 2001–2002). In a deposit (dated to the first half of the fifth century BCE) at Houma in the Jin state, a large

FIGURE 14 "Chenzhang" bronze *hu* from Xuyi, Jiangsu province, fourth to third centuries BCE. Height 24 cm. Nanjing Museum. *Sekai* 2002:1:204, plate 197.

group of jade blades inscribed with oaths were interred with human sacrifices (Li 1985:52–58). More frequently, jades were found in large quantities in tombs, particularly around or on the corpse within the coffin. For example, Marquis Yi's coffins alone contained more than 500 pieces (Hubei 1989:1:401). Toward the end of the third century BCE, a new category of "grave jades" (*sangyu* 喪玉), including *bi* 璧 discs (set around the head), *huang* 璜 half-rings (held in hands), mouth and nostril plugs, and others, began to develop, presumably to preserve if not to aid the deceased in the afterlife (Shi and Chen 2011:25–58; Childs-Johnson 1998).

New jade styles also developed. Warring States jade artists were armed with better iron tools, which could be used to improve designs and precision in general, as represented by drilling more evenly, straight and smoothly finished holes, or more complex and difficult compositions (Salmony 1963:113–114). One of the most popular techniques was openwork, covered with intricate non-representational patterns. A favorite motif distinctive in the period is the elegantly twisting dragon that features an S-shape with a protruding "hunchback," as exemplified by a piece from Cuo's tomb (Hebei 1996b:1:199, 2, colorplate 27.2; Childs-Johnson 2017:colorplate 14). With a fluid contour the dragon winds its pliable body, ornamented with individual cloud-scrolls, raises its back to form a soft "W" shape, and turns its head backward to approach its back (Figure 17). This

FIGURE 15 Bronze mirror from Zhangjiashan, Jiangling, Hubei province, fourth century BCE. *Zhongguo* 16:15, plate 15.

piece was found in the tomb with a group of other jade artifacts, presumably made as pendant sets stringed together by wires and suspended from a subject's waistband (Figure 18) (Hayashi 1991:141–160).

Lacquerwares, primarily serving daily life rather than ritual occasions, represented a rising art tradition that began to rival bronzes in both quality and quantity (Knight 1992). During the last two hundred years of the Warring States period, they were excavated by the thousands, mostly from Chu tombs, which stands in contrast to the fact that there were only a few hundred pieces known from all previous times (Chen 2003:299). Inscriptional evidence suggests that government workshops began mass-producing lacquerwares in the late Warring States period (Hong 2006:145, 160). Unlike bronzes or jades, lacquer is in effect a technique of surface treatment, using multiple layers of natural varnish to coat an object, mostly wooden. In the Chu area the wooden cores were carved from single pieces of wood with iron chisels, and the round shapes were turned with a lathe (Thote 2003:353). After the plain core had been fashioned, one or multiple layers of natural varnish were applied onto both the exterior and the interior faces of the object, before the artist finally added an extra layer of paint or lacquer solvent that mixes with color pigments onto the primary coating.

FIGURE 16 Bronze lamp with decoration of a camel-riding man from Wangshan Tomb 2, Wangshan, Hubei province, fourth century BCE. Height 19.2 cm. *Zhongguo* 10:Plate 83.

Some lacquerwares achieved a distinctive aesthetic by imitating bronze vessels. In Marquis Yi's tomb, one remarkable object was a *dou* 豆 vessel featuring two excessively carved handles with ornate interlacing patterns reminiscent of the honeycomb design seen in the famous bronze *zun* vessel of the same tomb (Figure 19, and also see Figure 10). What makes it different from the bronze, however, is the glossy coat of varnish and the vivid contrast between red patterns and the black ground, which turn this vessel into a symphony of light and color no traditional bronzes could emulate.

Another innovation in art was represented by textiles, including not only traditional plain tabby weaves (*juan* 絹), crossed-warped gauze weaves (*luo* 羅), and monochrome damasks (*qi* 綺), but also polychrome brocades (*jin* 錦), an invention of this period (Kuhn 1995; Kuhn 2004:1:307). The earliest archaeological example of brocades found in Changsha dates from the Early Warring States period (Zhu 1992:77), when artists developed a technique of alternating two or three warp threads of different colors, interlaced with wefts to form polychrome patterns, whose complexity and richness surpassed anything produced earlier. Unlike textiles made in the Springs and Autumns period, which bear only simple lozenges or other geometric motifs, the increased stitch density of brocades, which at Mashan Tomb 1 reached up to a remarkable level of 156 warp ends to

FIGURE 17 Bronze garment hook with jade inlay from Guweicun, third century BCE. Gu ed, *Zhongguo yuqi quanji* 3:131, figure 202.

FIGURE 18 Jade pendant with dragon motif. Reproduced from *Sekai*:216, plate 229.

52 weft picks per centimeter (Hubei 1985:38; Peng 1995:26), enabled weavers to introduce figurative motifs such as dragons, phoenixes, unicorns, and human figures never seen before (Figure 20) (Hubei 1985:56–71; Kuhn 1995:84–85). Superb brocade samples were further enriched by embroideries, which in the bamboo inventory slips of Baoshan

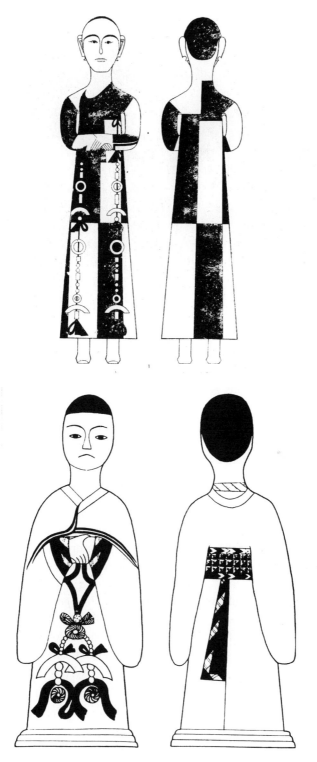

FIGURE 19 Painted wooden figurines with jade pendants from Yidi Tomb 6 at Jiangling, Hubei province, and Xinyang Tomb 2 at Xinyang, Henan province. *Wenwu* 1989.4:48, figure 35; Henan 1986:115, figure 79.

FIGURE 20 Lacquer *dou zun* from Marquis Yi of the Zeng's Tomb. *Wenwu* 1994.5: Plate 85.

Tomb 2 are called *xiu* 繡 (Hubei 1991:1:370). The value of such colorful embroideries is beyond doubt. As luxurious goods, they were exported as far as the Altai region in Mongolia (Robinson 1990:53).

PICTORIAL AND FIGURATIVE ART

One of the most significant artistic innovations during the Warring States period was the development of narrative elements in Chinese pictorial art. Just a humble beginning of a centuries-long art tradition, these early pictures were not yet independent paintings but affiliated with the surface of decorated bronzes, lacquerwares, or funerary banners.

Pictorial bronzes, especially water containers including *pan, yi* 匜, *jian* 鑒, and *hu* 壺 popular from the late Springs and Autumns period to the mid–Warring States, pioneered a new art of representing events or scenes in two-dimensional compositions (Falkenhausen 2008a:82). Spreading across present-day Hebei, Shanxi, Shandong, Sichuan, Henan, Hunan, and Jiangsu, over 50 of them have been discovered (Weber 1968; Xu 2002). These pictures were made in two major manners: one by incising or punctuating images on hammered sheet metal and the other by filling inlays in pre-cast depressions. Although the exact origin of such vessels remains inconclusive, many scholars speculate that this new style might have had its roots beyond the center of Chinese civilization, either in the

Eurasian Steppes or in the east coastal region of Wu-Yue in present-day Jiangsu and Zhejiang provinces (Weber 1968; He 1995; Thote 2008).

As an example of the latter type, a remarkable *hu* vessel excavated from Baihuatan in Chengdu, Sichuan province, bears lavish decorations on the exterior face (Figure 21) (Sichuan 1976). The composition extends horizontally around the vessel's surface in three parallel registers, one around the neck, one above the belly, and one below the belly. The topmost register consists of scenes of shooting arrows and mulberry-picking; the middle register represents hunting, bells and chimes striking, and ritual performing; the bottom register, land and naval battling (Fong 1988–1989). The pictures show no interest in distinguishing individuality but comprise collective scenes with groups of generic sketchy human figures all executed in profile (Keightley 1990:2–6; Falkenhausen 2008a:83–84). Although the spatial and temporal relationships between adjacent registers remain undefined, a narrative vitality impresses behind the unsymmetrical compositions of the scenes, the absence of centralized formality, and the interaction among figures. Even though the overall decoration still remains dominantly ornamental, the new narrative quality differentiates it from earlier Chinese art, which is content with isolated patterns or motifs (Jacobson 1984).

Similar simple narrative elements also survive on painted lacquerwares found in southern tombs. Representations of fantastic or shamanic scenes appear on a lacquer case from Marquis Yi's tomb and on another fragmentary zither found in a Chu tomb in present-day Xinyang, Henan province (Figure 22) (Henan 1986:25–31). Unlike the expressive renditions that capture the wild, uncontainable power of

FIGURE 21 Embroidered Brocade from Mashan Tomb 1. Zhongguo zhixiu 2004:2:9.

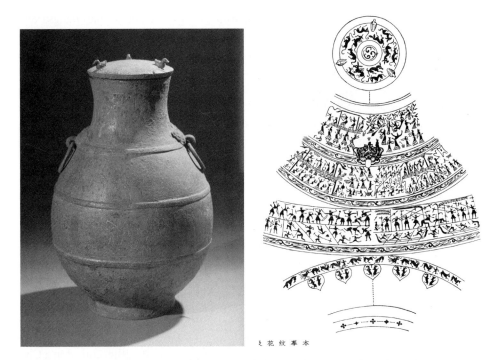

之花纹摹本

FIGURE 22 Bronze *hu* with inlaid pictorial motifs from Baihuatan in Chengdu, Sichuan province. Late fourth century BCE. *Wenwu* 1976.3:Plate 2.

the supernatural in these works, a sense of order, regularity, and even rhythm is conveyed on another painted lacquer case from Baoshan Tomb 2 that represents an outdoor episode in the aristocratic life (Figure 23) (Hubei 1991:1:144–146). Despite the stylistic difference, both painted objects share a similar interest with the Baihuatan *hu* vessel in bearing narrative compositions of generic figures rendered in full side view.

Unlike the bronzes and lacquerwares, silk banners found in late Warring States tombs carry arguably the earliest Chinese figure paintings. Placed on top of the coffin, these banners were probably idealized images of the tomb occupants on their way to heaven (Sōfukawa 1979:114–118). One example from Zidanku portrays a gentleman standing on the back of a dragon roaming against the wind (Figure 24) (Hunan 2000:1:428). Shown in full profile, the gentleman's clearly defined face and calm expression suggest certain degrees of individuality or even personality. Although the entire picture is predominantly flat and silhouette, the drapery folds on the figure's left sleeve, inflated by blowing air, convincingly express volume and roundness, which has not been found in previous Chinese paintings.

Another fresh motif is associated with the so-called "Animal Style." The animals found in the Zhongshan royal cemetery reflect the impact of the arts in the Eurasian steppes and West Asia (Bagley 2006). The marriage between Western motifs and Chinese elements gave birth to a new figurative art in China, which emphasizes motion

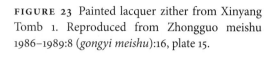

FIGURE 23 Painted lacquer zither from Xinyang Tomb 1. Reproduced from Zhongguo meishu 1986–1989:8 (*gongyi meishu*):16, plate 15.

FIGURE 24 Painted toiletry case from Baoshan Tomb 2, Baoshan, Hubei province. Reproduced from Zhongguo qiqi 1993:2:69, plate 63.

and realistic depiction of the body. For example, a group of bronze animal statuettes from the east and west side pits in Cuo's tomb represent fantastic winged felines, perhaps originally used as mat weights (Figure 25) (Hebei 1996b:1:139–143). Originating in western Asia, the motif of winged animals, identified as either chimeras or griffins, must have been introduced into China via Central Asia and the Eurasian steppes about this time.

FIGURE 25 Bronze winged animal from Cuo's Tomb. Reproduced from Zhongguo kaogu 1994:6:49.

These exotic animals inlaid with gold or silver are covered with ornamental patterns of Chinese flavor: the motifs of feather-curls or cloud-scrolls (So 1980:310–311). A sculptural decoration on a bronze stand of a disintegrated wooden object from Cuo's tomb portrays a prowling tiger crushing a paralyzed deer with teeth and claws (Figure 26). The tiger's powerful grip on the deer's leg in a gesture of tearing it off shows a thrilling moment of body dismemberment.

Such an animal-attacking motif in Zhongshan represents perhaps one of the most exotic and mind-refreshing concepts to the Chinese audience. Similar animal depictions were prosperous during the fourth to third centuries BCE in the present-day Ordos, Inner Mongolia, on the Chinese northern frontiers (Tian and Guo 1985; Bunker 1997; Rawson and Bunker 1990). Although it remains a question whether this border region was under Xiongnu or Chinese control, interactions between Chinese and nomadic arts are evident on the Ordos bronzes (So and Bunker 1995:53–75). For example, in a bronze belt-buckle from the Ordos (Figure 27), the exaggerated inversion of the deer's body captures the fatal moment when the prey is just being taken down by its predator. Such an intense emphasis on motion and time, absent from any earlier Chinese art works, must have refreshed the Chinese eyes with their vigor, which was quickly to be assimilated by artists of the following Qin and Han empires (Rostovcev 1929:78–112). Despite their obvious nomadic inspiration, many of these Ordos bronzes, as the Chinese inscriptions and ornamentation suggest, were products of state workshops in China (Bunker 1997:51–52).

FIGURE 26 Bronze base decorated with animal attack motif from Cuo's Tomb. Zhongguo kaogu 1994:6:Plate 43.

FIGURE 27 Bronze plaque decorated with animal attack motif from Ordos, third century BCE. Zhongguo qingtongqi 15:77, plate 105.

CONCLUSION

The profound change in art might have been closely related to the dynamic social and historical context in the Warring States period, which witnessed "the creation of the major political institutions that define early imperial China" (Lewis 1999:587). In this sense, the artistic revolution was coincident with, if not dependent upon, the social revolution during this period.

The fast development of towns and cities coincided with a rapid social transformation. With the wide application of iron tools and sophisticated irrigation works, agricultural productivity soared and the population exploded. As the competition for lands and human resources heated among kingdoms, it became urgent for each kingdom to protect its towns and people with stronger, higher, and steeper walls. To accommodate growing sectors of the society, the cities were divided into multiple zones such as the inner city and outer city.

In terms of architecture, the lavish terrace and tower structures represent not only the increasing wealth and power of the regional lords, who began to officially claim the title of "king" (*wang*) and embraced a sumptuous lifestyle, but also the enhanced royal power and the centralized political system (Falkenhausen 2008b:225). From one perspective, these high buildings granted their inhabitants greater visual access, which reflects their greater power; from another perspective, these soaring buildings must have generated awe in the passers-by, who might have been impressed by the might of their builders.

As the consciousness of posthumous afterlife grew, tombs became as important as collective ancestral temples in the contemporary ritual life. Xunzi (313–238 BCE) remarked that funeral and sacrifice were parallel to each other, because they both represented "the institutions of the kingship" (Knoblock 1994:101). Marked by monumental tumuli or ritual structures, sumptuous tombs figured not only as secular monuments extolling the tomb occupants' power and wealth but also as sacred sites where an abundant afterlife was guaranteed.

The gradually waning importance of traditional ritual art, essentially derived from temples, echoed the changing social structure. By the mid-fifth century BCE, the already shrinking power of the Zhou royal house had become a shadow of its former grandeur. On the ruins of the Zhou social structure emerged a new meritocratic system, which supplemented and to some extent replaced the previous hereditary system. Although the early faith in clan or lineage entitlements still existed among old aristocrats, those who earned their nobilities or official titles with personal merits would have reasonably appreciated their own secular accomplishments more than they did ancestral virtue, which was embodied by traditional ritual objects. Consequently, various mundane objects, such as lamps and garment hooks, were invented or introduced as new means of celebrating secular achievements and personal life (Powers 2006).

The changing content of bronze inscriptions also reflected this social change. Such mundane information as the object's production date, its dimensions and weight, and the name of the artist/artisan or the manufacturing director responsible for the making, replaced traditional commemorative inscriptions that frequented Western Zhou and early Eastern Zhou ritual bronzes. These inscriptions attest to the establishment of a new bureaucratic agency, conventionally called "Workshop Offices" (*gongguan* 工官), in the kingdoms to supervise the production and to monitor the quality (Dong 2002). It seems to suggest that these earthly authorities rather than the ancestor became the assumed "reader" of these objects.

The increasing popularity of "spirit objects" not only reflected the rising role of tombs in the society but also registered the change of religious notions and practice. Although the concept of a separate world of the dead had not fully developed by this time (Poo 1998:62–66), Chinese people began to use tombs to simulate a posthumous "living" place or to prepare a journey toward it. This resulted in the increasing quantity and quality of "spirit objects."

The transforming figurative and emerging pictorial art might have been a result of cultural interaction between China and her neighboring civilizations, particularly those in the west. The expanding territories of Chinese kingdoms and the eastward expansion of the nomadic tribes (Scythians or the like) during the fourth and third centuries BCE brought forth a dynamic cross-cultural interaction with unprecedented extensiveness and intensiveness. (The best example is perhaps King Wuling of the Zhao, who adopted nomadic costumes and lifestyle [e.g., shooting on horseback] to defend the rising threat of the nomads; see Sima 1959:43:1806.) As the nomadic powers pressed on the northern frontiers of Chinese kingdoms, steppe art also made its way into the Chinese heartland with a new manner of representing realistic animals acting in real space, which became an integral part of new forms of representational art in early imperial China.

BIBLIOGRAPHY

Bagley, Robert 2006. "Ornament, Representation, and Imaginary Animals in Bronze Age China." *Arts Asiatiques* 61:17–29.

Beckman, Joy 2002. "Minister Zhao's Grave: Staging an Eastern Zhou Burial." *Orientations* 34(5):22–26.

Bunker, Emma C. 1997. *Ancient Bronzes of the Eastern Eurasian Steppes from the Arthur M. Sackler Collection.* New York: Arthur M. Sackler Foundation.

Chen, Zhenyu 陳振裕 2003. *Research on Chu Culture and Lacquer* 楚文化與漆器研究. Beijing: Kexue chubanshe.

Childs-Johnson, Elizabeth 1998. "Jade as Material and Epoch." In *China, 5000 Years: Innovation and Transformation in the Arts.* Edited by Brinker Helmut et al. 55–68. New York: Harry N Abrams.

Childs-Johnson, Elizabeth 2001–2002. *Enduring Art of Jade Age China: Chinese Jades of the Late Neolithic through Han Periods,* 2 vols. New York: Throckmorton Fine Art.

Childs-Johnson, Elizabeth 2017. "Jade Dragons and Dragon Origins." In *Mythical Beasts: The Power of the Dragon.* Catalog, 9–18. New York: Throckmorton Fine Art.

Cook, Constance 2006. *Death in Ancient China: The Tale of One Man's Journey.* Leiden: Brill.

Cosmo, Nicola Di 2006. "The Origins of the Great Wall." *The Silk Road* 4(1):14–19.

Crump, J. I., transl. 1979. *Chan-kuo Ts'e*, 2nd ed. San Francisco: Chinese Materials Center.

Dong, Shan 董珊 2002. "Warring States Titles and Officialdom Administration 戰國題銘與工官制度." PhD dissertation, Peking University (Beijing).

Duan, Hongzhen 段宏振 2009. *Research on the Zhao Capital at Handan* 趙都邯鄲城研究. Beijing: Wenwu chubanshe.

Falkenhausen, Lothar von 2006. *Chinese Society in the Age of Confucius (1000–250 BC): The Archaeological Evidence.* Los Angeles: Cotsen Institute of Archaeology, UCLA.

Falkenhausen, Lothar von 2008a. "Action and Image in Early Chinese Art." *Cahiers d'Extrême-Asie* 17:51–91.

Falkenhausen, Lothar von 2008b. "Stages in the Development of 'Cities' in Pre-Imperial China." In *The Ancient City: New Perspectives on Urbanism in the Old and New World.* Edited by Joyce Marcus and Jeremy A. Sabloff, 209–228. Santa Fe, NM: School for Advanced Research Resident Scholar Series.

Fong, Mary 1988–1989. "The Origin of Chinese Pictorial Representation of the Human Figure." *Artibus Asiae* 49(1–2):5–38.

Fu, Xinian 傅熹年 1998. *Fu Xinian jianzhushi lunwenji* 傅熹年建築史論文集. Beijing: Wenwu chubanshe.

Gao, Xisheng 高西省 2012. "A Preliminary Discussion on the Gilt Objects and Related Issues. 戰國時期鎏金器及其相關問題初論." *Zhongguo guojia bowuguan guankan* 中國國家博物館館刊 (4):43–55.

Gu, Fang 古方 2005. *The Complete Set of Excavated Chinese Jades* 中國出土玉器全集, 15 vols. Beijing: Kexue chubanshe.

Guo, Dewei 郭德維 1998. *Research on the Restoration of the Chu Capital at Jinan* 楚都紀南城復原研究. Beijing: Wenwu chubanshe.

Hayashi, Minao 林巳奈夫 1991. *Research on Chinese Jade* 中國古玉の研究. Tokyo: Yoshikawa Kōbunkan.

He, Tangkun 何堂坤 1999. *Research on the Art of the Bronze Mirror in Ancient China* 中國古代銅鏡的技術研究. Beijing: Zijincheng chubanshe.

He, Xilin 賀西林 1995. "Research on Eastern Zhou Bronzes with Engraved Imagery 東周線刻畫像銅器研究." *Meishu yanjiu* 美術研究 1995(1):37–42.

Hebeisheng wenwu yanjiusuo 河北省文物研究所 1996a. *The Lower Capital of Yan* 燕下都, 2 vols. Beijing: Wenwu chubanshe.

Hebeisheng wenwu yanjiusuo 河北省文物研究所 1996b. *Cuo's Burial: The Burial of the King of Zhongshan from the Warring States* 𰀉墓--戰國中山國國王之墓, 2 vols. Beijing: Wenwu chubanshe.

Hebeisheng wenwu yanjiusuo 河北省文物研究所 2005. *The City of Lingshou of the Zhongshan State from the Warring States Period: Excavation Report of 1975–1993* 戰國中山國靈壽城: 1975–1993 年發掘報告. Beijing: Wenwu chubanshe.

Henansheng bowuguan Xinzheng gongzuozhan 河南省博物館新鄭工作站 1980. "Probing and Tentative Excavation of the Ancient City of the Zheng and Han States in Xinzheng, Henan 河南新鄭鄭韓故城的鑽探和試掘." *Wenwu ziliao congkan* 文物資料叢刊 3:55–66.

Henansheng wenwu yanjiusuo 河南省文物研究所 1986. *The Chu Burial at Xinyang* 信陽楚墓. Beijing: Wenwu chubanshe.

Hong, Shi 洪石 2006. *Study of Warring States, Qin, and Han Lacquers* 戰國秦漢漆器研究. Beijing: Wenwu chubanshe.

Hu, Fangping 胡方平 1994. "The Birth and Popularity of Tumuli in China 中國封土墓的產生和流行." *Kaogu* 考古 1994(6):556–558.

Hubeisheng Bowuguan 1989. *The Tomb of Marquis Yi of the Zeng State* 曾侯乙墓, 2 vols. Beijing: Wenwu chubanshe.

Hubeisheng Jingzhou Diqu Bowuguan 1985. *Mashan Tomb No. 1 at Jiangling* 江陵馬山一號楚墓. Beijing: Wenwu chubanshe.

Hubeisheng Jingsha Tielu Kaogudui 湖北省荊沙铁路考古队 1991. *The Chu Burial at Baoshan* 包山楚墓, 2 vols. Beijing: Wenwu chubanshe.

Hunansheng Bowuguan 湖南省博物館 2000. *Chu Burials at Changsha* 長沙楚墓, 2 vols. Beijing: Wenwu chubanshe.

Jacobson, Esther 1984. "The Structure of Narrative in Early Chinese Pictorial Vessels." *Representations* 8:61–83.

Jingzhou Diqu Bowuguan 荊州地區博物館 1984. "Preliminary Report on Opening the Chu Burial M201 at Zhangjiashan, Jiangling 江陵張家山201號楚墓清理簡報." *Jianghan kaogu* 江漢考古 2:13–16.

Jingzhoushi. Jingzhoushi Bowuguan 荊州市博物館, and Qianjiang shi bowuguan 潛江市博物館 2003. "Preliminary Report on the Excavation of Foundation No. 1 of the Chu Palace Site at Fangyingtai, Longwan, Qianjiang, Hubei 湖北潛江龍灣放鷹臺一號楚宮基阯發掘簡報." *Jianghan kaogu* 3:3–15.

Keightley, David 1990. "Ancient Chinese Art: Contexts, Constraints and Pleasures." *Asian Art* 3(2):2–6.

Knight, Michael John 1992. "Bronze to Lacquer: Changes in Preferred Media in the Arts of the Kingdom of Chu." PhD dissertation, Columbia University, New York.

Knoblock, John 1994. *Xunzi: A Translation and Study of the Complete Works.* Stanford, CA: Stanford University Press.

Knoblock, John, and Jeffrey Riegel 2000. *The Annals of Lü Buwei: A Complete Translation and Study.* Stanford, CA: Stanford University Press.

Kong, Xiangxing 孔祥星, and Liu Yiman 劉一曼 1984. *Ancient Chinese Bronze Mirrors* 中國古代銅鏡. Beijing: Wenwu chubanshe.

Kuhn, Dieter 1995. "Silk Weaving in Ancient China: From Geometric Figures to Patterns of Pictorial Likeness." *Chinese Science* 12:77–114.

Kuhn, Dieter 2004. "Textiles in the Chu Kingdom of the Warring States Period." In *New Perspectives on China's Past*, vol. 1. Edited by Yang Xiaoneng, 305–315. New Haven, CT: Yale University Press.

Lai, Guolong 2002. "Lighting the Way in the Afterlife: Bronze Lamps in Warring States Tombs." *Orientations* 34(4):20–28.

Lai, Guolong 2005. "Death and the Otherworldly Journey in Early China as Seen through Tomb Texts, Travel Paraphernalia, and Road Rituals." *Asia Major* 18(1):1–44.

Lai, Guolong 2015. *Excavating the Afterlife: The Archaeology of Early Chinese Religion.* Seattle, WA: University of Washington Press.

Lawton, Thomas 1982. *Chinese Art of the Warring States Period: Change and Continuity, 480–222 B.C.* Washington, DC: Smithsonian Institution Press.

Lewis, Mark Edward 1999. "Warring States Political History." In *The Cambridge History of Ancient China: From the Origins of Civilization to 221 B.C.* Edited by Edward Shaughnessy, 587–649. Cambridge, UK: Cambridge University Press.

Li Xueqin 1985. *Eastern Zhou and Qin Civilizations.* Translated by K. C. Chang. New Haven, CT: Yale University Press.

Liang, Shutai 梁書臺 2000. "Questions on Inlaid Gold and Silver 錯金銀質疑." *Wenwu chunqiu* 文物春秋 2000(4):71–72.

Lins, P. A., and W. A. Oddy 1975. "The Origins of Mercury Gilding." *Journal of Archaeological Science* 4:365–373.

Liu, Yiman 劉一曼 1985. "On the Regional Divisions of Warring States Bronze Mirrors 試論戰國銅鏡的分區." *Kaogu* 11:1,008–1,014.

Needham, Joseph, and Gwei-djen Lu 1974. *Spagyrical Discovery and Invention: Magisteries of Gold and Immortality, Science and Civilisation in China.* Vol. 5, pt. 2. Cambridge, UK: Cambridge University Press.

Peng, Hao 彭浩 1995. *Textiles and Clothing of Chu People* 楚人的紡織與服飾. Wuhan: Hubei jiaoyu chubanshe.

Poo, Mu-chou 1998. *In Search of Personal Welfare: A View of Ancient Chinese Religion.* Albany: State University of New York Press.

Powers, Martin 2006. *Pattern and Person: Ornament, Society, and Self in Classical China.* Cambridge, MA: Harvard University Asia Center.

Qiu, Xigui 裘錫圭 1980. "On the Character 'Shi' in Warring States Documents 戰國文字中的市." *Kaogu xuebao* 考古學報 3:285–296.

Qunli 群力 1972. "Summary of the Exploration of the Ancient City of the Qi Kingdom at Linchu 臨淄齊國古城勘探紀要." *Wenwu* 文物 5:45–54.

Rawson, Jessica 1995. *Chinese Jade from the Neolithic to the Qing.* London: British Museum.

Rawson, Jessica, and Emma Bunker 1990. *Ancient Chinese and Ordos Bronzes.* Hong Kong: Oriental Ceramics Society of Hong Kong.

Robinson, K. S. 1990. "The Textiles from Pazyryk: A Study in the Transfer and Transformation of Artistic Motifs." *Expedition* 32(1):49–61.

Rostovcev, Mihail Ivanovič 1929. *The Animal Style in South Russia and China.* Princeton, NJ: Princeton University Press.

Ruan, Yuan 阮元 1980. *The Thirteen Classics with Annotations and Commentary* 十三經註疏. Beijing: Zhonghua shuju.

Salmony, Alfred 1963. *Chinese Jade: Through the Wei Dynasty.* New York: Ronald Press.

Sima, Qian 司馬遷 1959. *Records of the Historian* 史記. Beijing: Zhonghua shuju.

Shaanxisheng Kaogu Yanjiusuo 陝西省考古研究所 2004. *Archaeological Report on the Qin Capital at Xianyang* 秦都咸陽考古報告. Beijing: Kexue chubanshe.

Shandongsheng Wenwu Kaogu Yanjiusuo 山東省文物考古研究所 2007. *Qi Burials at Linzi* 臨淄齊墓. Beijing: Wenwu chubanshe.

Shaughnessy, Edward 1997. *New Sources of Early Chinese History: An Introduction to the Reading of Inscriptions and Manuscripts.* Berkeley: Society for the study of Early China and the Institute of East Asian Studies, University of California, Berkeley.

Shi, Rongchuan, and Chen Jie 石榮傳 陳傑 2011. "Archaeological Research on Mortuary Jade and Its Regulations in Western and Eastern Zhou 兩周葬玉及葬玉制度之考古學研究." *Zhongyuan wenwu* 5:25–58.

Shi, Jie 2014. "Incorporating All for One: The First Emperor's Tomb Mound." *Early China* 37:359–391.

Shi, Jie 2015. "The Hidden Level in Space and Time: The Vertical Shaft in the Royal Tombs of the Zhongshan Kingdom in Late Eastern Zhou (475–221 BCE) China." *Material Religion: The Journal of Objects, Art, and Belief* 11(1):76–103.

Shi Shuqing 史樹青 1973. "Art of Gold Inlays in Ancient China 我國古代的金錯工藝." *Wenwu* 6:66–72.

Shōgakkan 小学館 1997–2002. *The Complete Collection of World Art: The East, Sekai bijutsu daizenshū, Tōyō hen* 世界美術大全集. 東洋編. Tōkyō: Shōgakkan.

Sichuansheng Bowuguan 四川省博物館 1976. "Excavation Report on Tomb No. 10 from the Site in Baihuatan Middle School in Chengdu 成都百花潭中學十號墓發掘簡報." *Wenwu* 3:40–46.

So, Jenny 1980. "The Inlaid Bronzes of the Warring States Period." In *The Great Bronze Age of China*. Edited by Wen Fong, 303–320. New York: Metropolitan Museum of Art.

So, Jenny 1995. *Eastern Zhou Ritual Bronzes from the Arthur M. Sackler Collections*. Washington, DC: Arthur M. Sackler Foundation.

So, Jenny, and Emma Bunker 1995. *Traders and Raiders on China's Northern Frontier*. New York: Diane Publishing.

Sōfukawa, Hirōshi 曽布川寛 1979. "Mt. Kunlun and Ascension for Immortality" 崑崙山と昇僊." *Tōhō gakuhō* 51:83–185.

Thorp, Robert 1986. "Architectural Principles in Early Imperial China: Structural Problems and Their Solution." *Art Bulletin* 68(3):360–378.

Thote, Alain 2000. "Continuities and Discontinuities: Chu Burials during the Eastern Zhou Period." In *Exploring China's Past: New Discoveries and Studies in Archaeology and Art*. Edited by R. Whitfield and Wang Tao, 189–204. London: Saffron International Series in Chinese Archaeology and Art.

Thote, Alain 2003. "Lacquer Craftsmanship in the Qin and Chu Kingdoms: Two Contrasting Traditions (Late 4th to Late 3rd Century B.C.)." *Journal of East Asian Art* 5:337–374.

Thote, Alain 2004. "Burial Practices as Seen in Rulers' Tombs of the Eastern Zhou Period: Patterns and Regional Traditions." In *Religion and Chinese Society: A Centennial Conference of the École française d'Extrême-Orient*, 2 vols. Edited by John Lagerway, 65–107. Paris: École Française d'Extrême-Orient.

Thote, Alain 2008. "Image d'un Royaume Disparu." *Cahiers d'Extrême-Asie* 17:93–123.

Tian, Guanjin 田廣金, and Guo Suxin 郭素新 1985. *The Ordos Style of Bronzes* 鄂爾多斯式青銅器. Beijing: Wenwu chubanshe.

Wang Renxiang 王仁湘 1985. "Introduction to the Belt Buckle 帶鉤概論." *Kaogu xuebao* 3:267–312.

Weber, Charles 1968. *Chinese Pictorial Bronze Vessels of the Late Chou Period*. Ascona: Artibus Asiae.

White, J. C. 1988. "Early East Asian Metallurgy: The Southern Tradition." In *The Beginning of the Use of Metals and Alloys: Papers from the Second International Conference on the Beginning of the Use of Metals and Alloys, Zhengzhou, China, 21–26 October 1986*. Edited by R. Maddin, 175–181. Cambridge, MA and London: MIT Press.

Wu, Hung 2009. *Art of the Yellow Springs: Understanding Chinese Tombs*. London: Reaktion Books.

Wu, Xiaolong 2017. *Material Culture, Power, and Identity in Ancient China*. Cambridge, UK: Cambridge University Press.

Xu, Hong 許宏 2000a. *An Archaeological Study of Pre-Qin Cities* 先秦城市考古學研究. Beijing: Yanshan chubanshe.

Xu, Pingfang 徐萍芳 2000b. "Several Questions Concerning the Archaeology of Ancient Cities in China 關於中國古代城市考古的幾個問題." *Wenhua de kuizeng: Hanxue yanjiu guoji huiyi lunwenji (kaoguxue juan)* 文化的饋贈——漢學研究國際會議論文集 (考古學卷). Edited by Beijing daxue Zhongguo chuantong wenhua yanjiu zhongxin, 33–40. Beijing: Beijing daxue chubanshe.

Xu, Weimin 許衛民 2000c. *Study of the Qin Capitals* 秦都城研究. Xi'an: Shaanxi remin jiaoyu chubanshe.

Xu, Yahui 許雅惠 2002. "Eastern Zhou Bronze Imagery and Engraved Motifs 東周的圖像紋銅器與線刻畫像銅器." *Gugong xueshu jikan* 故宮學術季刊 20(2):63–108.

Yang, Hongxun 楊鴻勳 1976. "Preliminary Study of the Restoration of Palace Remains No. 1 of the Xianyang Palace of the Qin 秦咸陽宮第一號遺阯複原問題的初步探討." *Wenwu* 11:31–41.

Yang, Hongxun 楊鴻勳 1987. *Collected Essays on Architectural Archaeology* 建築考古學論文集. Beijing: Wenwu chubanshe.

Yang, Hongxun 楊鴻勳 2000. *A General Discussion of Palace Architecture* 宮殿考古通論. Beijing: Zijincheng chubanshe.

Yang, Kuan 杨寬 1993. *Research on the History of Ancient Chinese Capitals* 中國古代都城制度史研究. Shanghai: Shanghai guji chubanshe.

Yang, Kuan 杨寬 1985. *Research on the History of the Ancient Chinese Mausoleum System* 中國古代陵寢制度史研究. Shanghai: Shanghai guji chubanshe.

Yao, Qian 姚遷 1982. "Caches of Chu and Han Cultural Relics from Nanyao, Xuyu, in Jiangsu 江蘇盱眙南窯莊楚漢文物窖藏." *Wenwu* 11:5–12.

Zhang, Yushi 張玉石 2004. "Research on the Techniques of Ramming Earthen Walls in Ancient China 中國古代版築技術研究." *Zhongyuan wenwu* 中原文物 4:68–70.

Zhongguo Kaogu 1994. *Beauties of Archaeological Cultural Relics* 中國考古文物之美, 6 vols. Beijing: Wenwu chubanshe.

Zhongguo Kexueyuan Kaogu Yanjiusuo 中國科學院考古研究所 1956. *Huixian Excavation Report* 輝縣發掘報告. Beijing: Kexue chubanshe.

Zhongguo Kexueyuan Kaogu Yanjiusuo Shanxi Gongzuodui 中國科學院考古研究所山西工作隊 1963. "Investigation of Yu's Royal Capital in Xiaxian, Shanxi 山西夏縣禹王城調查." *Kaogu* 9:474–479.

Zhongguo Meishu Quanji Bianji Weiyuanhui 中國美術全集編輯委員會 1986–1989. *The Complete Set of Chinese Art: Volume on Craft Art* 中國美術全集工藝美術編. Beijing: Wenwu chubanshe.

Zhongguo Qiqi Quanji Bianjibu 中國漆器全集編輯部 1993–1997. *The Complete Set of Chinese Lacquer Art* 中國漆器全集, 6 vols. Fuzhou: Fujian meishu chubanshe.

Zhongguo Qingtongqi Quanji Bianji Weiyuanhui 中國青銅器全集編輯委員會 1996–1998. *The Complete Set of Chinese Bronzes* 中國青銅器全集, 16 vols. Beijing: Wenwu chubanshe.

Zhongguo Zhixiu Fushi Quanji Bianji Weiyuanhui 中國織繡服飾全集編輯委員會 2004. *The Complete Set of Chinese Weaving and Embroidery* 中國織繡服飾全集, 6 vols. Tianjin: Tianjin meishu chubanshe.

Zhu, Xinyu 朱新予 1992. *The History of Silk in China* 中國絲綢史. Beijing: Fangzhi gongye chubanshe.

INDEX

....

Note: Tables and figures are indicated by an italic "*t*" and "*f*" following the page number.

Z
Z.
Zh
Zh

a
a
be
br
b
c
i